THE BOOK
OF THE STATES

1956-1957

VOLUME XI

THE COUNCIL OF STATE GOVERNMENTS

CHICAGO, ILLINOIS

Library of Congress Catalog Card Number: 35–11433

PRINTED IN THE UNITED STATES OF AMERICA

Price (with 1957 Supplement) $10

THE BOOK
OF THE STATES

FOREWORD

The Book of the States is designed to provide an authoritative source of information on the structures, working methods, financing and functional activities of the state governments, together with listings of state officials and members of the legislatures. It deals with the three branches of state government—executive, legislative, and judicial —and with the major areas of public service performed by the states. It also reports on the work of the Council of State Governments, the Commissions on Interstate Cooperation and other agencies concerned with intergovernmental problems.

The *Book*, of which this is Volume XI, is published biennially, and emphasis is given to developments of the two years preceding publication. It is issued at the beginning of even-numbered years, which permits presentation of significant data resulting from the legislative sessions of the immediately preceding, odd-numbered years, in which most of the legislatures hold regular sessions. Coverage in the current volume extends to a late period in 1955. A *Supplement* will be published early in 1957 listing elective officials as of that time and bringing the present rosters of legislators up to date.

Thus *The Book of the States* and its *Supplement* offer comprehensive information on the work of state governments and convenient directories of the men and women, both elected and appointed, who comprise them.

The Council of State Governments wishes to acknowledge the invaluable help of many state officials and members of the legislative service agencies who have furnished for the 1956–57 volume information on a wide variety of subjects. Contributions from individual authors are acknowledged separately in the *Book*.

Frank Bane
Executive Director
The Council of State Governments

Chicago, Illinois
December, 1955

985

THE BOOK OF THE STATES

IS PUBLISHED BIENNIALLY BY THE
COUNCIL OF STATE GOVERNMENTS AT
1313 EAST SIXTIETH STREET
CHICAGO 37, ILLINOIS

FRANK SMOTHERS, *Editor*

M. CLAIR COTTERILL, *Assistant Editor*

CONTENTS

Section I. INTERGOVERNMENTAL RELATIONS

1. INTERSTATE RELATIONS

2. STATE-FEDERAL RELATIONS

3. STATE-LOCAL RELATIONS

Section II. CONSTITUTIONS AND ELECTIONS

1. CONSTITUTIONS

2. ELECTIONS

vii

Section III. LEGISLATURES AND LEGISLATION

1. LEGISLATIVE ORGANIZATION AND SERVICES

2. LEGISLATION

Section IV. ADMINISTRATIVE ORGANIZATION

1. ADMINISTRATION

2. PERSONNEL SYSTEMS

Section V. THE JUDICIARY

1. JUDICIAL ADMINISTRATION AND PROCEDURE

Section VI. FINANCE

1. REVENUE, EXPENDITURE AND DEBT

2. TAXATION

Section VII. MAJOR STATE SERVICES

1. EDUCATION

Section VIII. DIRECTORY OF THE STATES, COMMONWEALTHS AND TERRITORIES

1. STATE AND TERRITORIAL PAGES

2. ROSTERS OF STATE OFFICIALS

Section I
INTERGOVERNMENTAL RELATIONS

1. Interstate Relations
2. State-Federal Relations
3. State-Local Relations

1

Interstate Relations

THE COUNCIL OF STATE GOVERNMENTS

1. ORGANIZATION

THE Council of State Governments is a joint governmental agency established by the states, supported by the states, for service to the states. The Council acts as:

1. A medium for improving legislative, administrative and judicial practices within the states.

2. An agency for securing full cooperation among the states in solving interstate problems, both regional and national.

3. A means of facilitating and improving federal-state relations.

In brief, the Council exists to serve governmental progress in the individual states, among the states working together, and by the states in their relations with the federal government.

The Council is composed of Commissions or Committees on Interstate Cooperation, established in all forty-eight states as official entities of the state governments. A typical Commission consists of ten members of the legislature and five administrative officials. Legislation which created the Commissions provides:

"The Council of State Governments is hereby declared to be a joint governmental agency of this state and of the other states which cooperate through it."

The Commissions work for cooperative governmental action on numerous fronts. They are the bases on which the Council is founded. (Memberships of the Commissions in the individual states are listed among the contents of pages 448–500.)

The states themselves govern and control the Council. Its policies are determined by a Board of Managers, comprising forty-eight delegate members representing the forty-eight states, eighteen ex-officio members, and ten members at large.

Each state selects its own delegate member. Ex-officio Managers are the nine members of the Executive Committee of the Governors' Conference; the presiding heads of seven other state organizations representing executive, legislative and judicial branches of government; the Honorary President of the Council; and its Executive Director. To provide continuity of membership, the Board itself elects ten Managers at Large who serve five-year, staggered terms.

The Board meets annually and at special call to consider Council policy. It has an Executive Committee which works with the Executive Director for solution of numerous problems. The Executive Committee comprises the President of the Council, who is a Governor; the First Vice-President, who is a legislator and who also serves as Chairman of the Board of Managers; two additional Vice-Presidents; the Auditor, who is a state fiscal officer; the Honorary President of the Council; and the Executive Director.

The Executive Committee appoints the Executive Director, subject to the Board's approval. He selects all members of the Council staff, and they operate under his direction and supervision.

Along with its responsibility to all the state governments in all their branches,

3

the Council is the secretariat for a number of groups composed of separate categories of officials or representing different functions. It is the secretariat for America's 7,500 state legislators, organized through the American Legislators' Association; the Governors' Conference; the Conference of Chief Justices; the National Association of Attorneys General; the National Association of State Budget Officers; the National Legislative Conference; the National Association of State Purchasing Officials; and The Parole and Probation Compact Administrators Association. The Council has a cooperative arrangement with the National Conference of Commissioners on Uniform State Laws and works closely with other organizations serving state government.

Because of its activities for many state associations and its day-to-day work with individual state officials and legislators, the Council is in a position to bring to the service of each a wide understanding of the problems of all.

The Council has its central office in Chicago, eastern and western regional offices in New York and San Francisco, and another office in Washington, D. C. Regional representatives, working from the central and regional offices, cooperate closely with state legislators and officials in their areas. The Washington office is charged specifically with responsibility for "facilitating and improving federal-state relations" and for keeping the states currently informed of activities of the federal government which interest the states.

2. ACTIVITIES

As the responsibilities of modern government grow, the states increasingly are working together—for progress in their own internal affairs, for solution of problems that cross state lines, and for improved federal-state relations.

The Council of State Governments, as the agency of all the states, contributes to the realization of these goals by:

Conducting major research projects—making the results of these projects available to the states and to many interested agencies.

Maintaining an inquiry-and-information service available to state agencies, officials and legislators.

Serving as a clearinghouse through which the states exchange their own information.

Holding national and regional meetings—ranging from a biennial General Assembly of the States to frequent working panels or conferences on particular questions—in which state officials and legislators survey common problems.

Acting as secretariat for a number of interstate organizations.

The Council's publications, in addition to special research reports on individual subjects, include the biennial reference work *The Book of the States* and a monthly magazine of state affairs, *State Government.*

SERVICE FOR INTRASTATE PROGRESS

Most of the work of every state government necessarily is concentrated on its internal affairs. But this does not mean working in isolation. Almost every home task of every state has its counterparts in other states. Through meetings, publications, and informal communication aided by the Council of State Governments, the experience of all states in these matters is shared.

If, for example, a given state is considering introduction of a new governmental technique, or adoption of a new public service, or improvement of an old one, it can obtain information through the Council as to action of other states on similar problems, and the results. It can judge from such shared experience what practices have worked best elsewhere. Individual states repeatedly obtain such information from the Council or at its meetings.

Certain intrastate problems, moreover, are perennial for all states or assume special significance for all at certain times. The Council undertakes special studies of such subjects, often at the specific direction of the Governors' Conference.

Thus, the Council in recent years has made extensive studies in the fields of public school and higher education, mental health programs, problems of the aging, highway safety and motor truck regulation, occupational licensing, state governmental reorganization, legislative processes and procedures, state judicial systems, and state-local relations. On each of these and other subjects the Council has published reports for official and public use, ranging from brochures to such major volumes as *The Forty-eight State School Systems, Higher Education in the Forty-eight States, The Mental Health Programs of the Forty-eight States, Training and Research in State Mental Health Programs, The States and Their Older Citizens,* and *Highway Safety—Motor Truck Regulation.* In some instances studies are conducted by research specialists under Council supervision; in others by members of the Council's staff; in still others by special Council committees assisted by staff members.

Such fact-finding and study among the states have contributed to steady progress in the organization, procedures and public services of state governments.

SERVICE FOR INTERSTATE ACTION

Numerous problems that confront government call for interstate action. The states are adding new programs to meet these needs while improving projects already in existence. Much of the Council's work is directed to the service of the states in this broad field.

Functional areas of interstate agencies and agreements include higher education, civil defense, disaster relief, river problems, forest fire prevention, coastal fisheries, oil conservation, regional institutions for care of the handicapped, and problems of crime control, probation and parole. Some of the agencies and organizations comprise a large number of states, some two or more states that adjoin each other. Many have been created through interstate compact, others through less formal arrangements. The Council of State Governments and the Commissions on Interstate Cooperation have assisted in studies and conferences that led to the establishment of many of them. The Council and the Commissions continue to aid them in fulfilling their functions.

In addition, the Council serves the states continuously in a variety of com-

mon tasks not performed by separate interstate agencies. For many years the states have worked successfully through the Council to prevent or eliminate interstate trade barriers. They are working through it for concerted action on highway problems. The Council, as noted, cooperates with the National Conference of Commissioners on Uniform State Laws, which sponsors legislation in various fields. In recent years, the Council's Drafting Committee, in consultation with other groups, has prepared and sponsored a series of suggested legislative acts dealing with subjects on which uniform or similar state laws might serve the public interest. Many of these now are on the statute books.

SERVICE IN FEDERAL-STATE RELATIONS

In war and peace, federal-state cooperation has been increasing through the last decade. The Council of State Governments is a principal channel through which this has been fostered and through which specific federal-state programs have been devised, then put into effect.

During World War II the Council cooperated with the United States government and the governments of the states in setting up our nation-wide system of civilian defense. Similar cooperation led to state programs for selective service, rationing, conservation and salvage, soldier-sailor voting, motor transport regulation and other related matters.

Since the war the Council has continued to act for federal-state cooperation through numerous means, including its studies of federal grants-in-aid, overlapping taxes and other intergovernmental problems, followed by conferences with federal officials and members of Congress on these subjects. An extensive study by the Council in 1948, requested by the National Commission on Organization of the Executive Branch of the Government, served as a basis for that commission's recommendations on federal-state relations. In 1950 and thereafter the Council again assisted in preparing a nation-wide program of civil defense.

With the Governors' Conference, the Council long urged establishment by Congress of a commission to study and report upon the functions, roles and financing of government in America at all levels—federal, state and local—with the objective of improvement for each and sound cooperation among all. At the request of the President of the United States, Congress created such a body in 1953, the Commission on Intergovernmental Relations, and the Commission made its report in 1955. The Council of State Governments cooperated closely with it in its extensive studies.

The Council issues at frequent intervals the *Washington Legislative Bulletin*, to inform state officials and legislators of actions in the nation's capitol with particular bearing on state activities.

The strength of our federal, democratic system requires self-reliance and strength at each level of government—state, local, national. It also requires cooperation among all levels. The Council works for the effective operation of both those principles.

SERVICE TO THE PUBLIC

All of the Council's activities are directed to the public service. It was created by the states to assist them for that over-all purpose. The Council contributes directly, moreover, particularly through its publications, to citizen information on state governmental affairs; thus it stimulates interest in them. Its reference works, its monthly journal and its special studies are used in public libraries, schools and universities throughout the nation. Citizens concerned with special civic problems—education, mental health, needs of the aging, highway traffic, public taxation, governmental structure and many other subjects—study these materials.

OFFICES OF
THE COUNCIL OF STATE GOVERNMENTS

Central Office
1313 East Sixtieth Street, Chicago 37, Illinois

Eastern Regional Office
522 Fifth Avenue, New York 36, New York

Western Regional Office
582 Market Street, San Francisco 4, California

Washington Office
1737 K Street, N.W., Washington 6, D.C.

THE BOARD OF MANAGERS OF THE COUNCIL OF STATE GOVERNMENTS

Membership, December, 1955

EXECUTIVE COMMITTEE: 1955-56

President
HON. ARTHUR B. LANGLIE
Governor of Washington

First Vice President and
Chairman of the Board of
Managers
SENATOR ROBERT A. AINSWORTH,
JR.
Member of Legislature
Louisiana

Second Vice President
(Vacancy)

Third Vice President
HON. CHARLES TOM HENDERSON
Assistant Attorney General
Florida

Auditor
HON. MAURICE F. WILLIAMS
Administrative Assistant to the Governor
Maine

Honorary President
HENRY W. TOLL
Colorado

FRANK BANE
Executive Director, Council of
State Governments

STATE DELEGATE MEMBERS

Alabama
(Vacancy)

Arizona
HON. HARRY S. RUPPELIUS
Speaker, House of Representatives

Arkansas
SENATOR TOM ALLEN
*Member of General Assembly and
Chairman, Legislative Council*

California
SENATOR JAMES J. McBRIDE
Member of Legislature

Colorado
SENATOR DONALD G. BROTZ-
MAN
Member of General Assembly

Connecticut
(Vacancy)

Delaware
HON. CLAYTON M. HOFF
*Chairman, Commission on
Interstate Cooperation*

Florida
HON. CHARLES TOM
HENDERSON
*Assistant Attorney General and
Chairman, Commission on
Interstate Cooperation*

Georgia
HON. JOHN E. SHEFFIELD, JR.
*Member of General Assembly and
Chairman, Commission on
Interstate Cooperation*

Idaho
HON. GEORGE L. BLICK
Member of Legislature

Illinois
HON. BERNICE T. VAN DER
VRIES
*Member of General Assembly and
Chairman, Commission on
Intergovernmental Cooperation*

Indiana
SENATOR JOHN W. VAN NESS
Member of General Assembly

Iowa
(Vacancy)

Kansas
HON. JOHN McCUISH
*Lieutenant Governor and
Chairman, Commission on
Interstate Cooperation*

Kentucky
(Vacancy)

Louisiana
HON. ALLISON R. KOLB
State Auditor

Maine
SENATOR WILLIAM R. COLE
*Member of Legislature and
Chairman, Commission on
Interstate Cooperation*

Maryland
HON. BLANCHARD RANDALL,
JR.
*Secretary of State and
Chairman, Commission on
Interstate Cooperation*

Massachusetts
SENATOR RICHARD H. LEE
*Member of General Court and
Chairman, Commission on
Interstate Cooperation*

Michigan
SENATOR HARRY F. HITTLE
Member of Legislature

Minnesota
SENATOR VAL IMM
Member of Legislature

Mississippi
SENATOR STANTON A. HALL
Member of Legislature

Missouri
SENATOR JOHN W. NOBLE
Member of General Assembly

Montana
(Vacancy)

Nebraska
SENATOR EARL J. LEE
Member of Legislature

Nevada
HON. J. E. SPRINGMEYER
Legislative Counsel

New Hampshire
HON. LOUIS C. WYMAN
*Attorney General and
Chairman, Commission on
Interstate Cooperation*

New Jersey
HON. JOSEPH E. McLEAN
*Commissioner, Department of
Conservation and Chairman,
Commission on Interstate
Cooperation*

New Mexico
HON. JACK E. HOLMES
*Director, Legislative Council
Service*

New York
HON. ELISHA T. BARRETT
*Member of Legislature and
Chairman, Joint Legislative
Committee on Interstate
Cooperation*

North Carolina
HON. J. V. WHITFIELD
*Chairman, Commission on
Interstate Cooperation*

North Dakota
HON. RALPH BEEDE
*Member of Legislative Assembly
and Chairman, Legislative
Research Committee*

Ohio
HON. ROBERT MOULTON
*Chairman, Public Utilities
Commission and Chairman,
Commission on Interstate
Cooperation*

Oklahoma
HON. RALPH HUDSON
State Librarian

Oregon
HON. CHAS. H. HELTZEL
*Public Utilities Commissioner
and Chairman, Commission on
Interstate Cooperation*

Pennsylvania
SENATOR JOHN H. DENT
*Member of General Assembly and
Chairman, Commission on
Interstate Cooperation*

Commonwealth of Puerto Rico
HON. ROBERTO SANCHEZ-
VILELLA
Secretary of State

Rhode Island
SENATOR RAYMOND A.
MCCABE
*Member of General Assembly and
Chairman, Commission on
Interstate Cooperation*

South Carolina
SENATOR EDGAR A. BROWN
*Member of General Assembly and
Chairman, Commission on
Interstate Cooperation*

South Dakota
HON. PHIL SAUNDERS
*Attorney General and
Chairman, Commission on
Interstate Cooperation*

Tennessee
HON. HAROLD V. MILLER
*Executive Director, Tennessee
State Planning Commission and
Chairman, Commission on
Intergovernmental Cooperation*

Texas
HON. TOM REAVLEY
Secretary of State

Utah
SENATOR C. TAYLOR BURTON
*President of Senate and
Chairman, Legislative Council*

Vermont
SENATOR CARLETON G. HOWE
*Member of General Assembly and
Chairman, Commission on
Interstate Cooperation*

Virginia
(Vacancy)

Washington
HON. JOHN L. O'BRIEN
*Speaker of the House and
Chairman, Legislative Council*

West Virginia
HON. CARL M. FRASURE
*Chairman, Commission on
Interstate Cooperation*

Wisconsin
SENATOR ARTHUR L. PADRUTT
Member of Legislature

Wyoming
HON. EVERETT T. COPEN-
HAVER
*Secretary of State and
Chairman, Commission on
Intergovernmental Cooperation*

EX-OFFICIO MEMBERS

Executive Committee, Governors' Conference
HON. ARTHUR B. LANGLIE, Washington
HON. NORMAN BRUNSDALE, North Dakota
HON. FRANK G. CLEMENT, Tennessee
HON. LEROY COLLINS, Florida
HON. EDWIN C. JOHNSON, Colorado
HON. WALTER J. KOHLER, Wisconsin
HON. ROBERT B. MEYNER, New Jersey
HON. MILWARD L. SIMPSON, Wyoming
HON. G. MENNEN WILLIAMS, Michigan
Chairman, Conference of Chief Justices:
HON. WILLIAM H. DUCKWORTH, Georgia
President, National Association of Attorneys General:
HON. JOHN BEN SHEPPERD, Texas
President, National Association of State Budget Officers:
HON. MAURICE F. WILLIAMS, Maine

President, Parole and Probation Compact Administrators' Association:
HON L. B. STEPHENS, Alabama

President, National Association of State Purchasing Officials:
HON. C. L. MAGNUSON, Connecticut

President, National Legislative Conference:
SENATOR ROBERT A. AINSWORTH, JR., Louisiana

President, National Conference of Commissioners on Uniform State Laws:
HON. BARTON H. KUHNS, Nebraska

Honorary President of the Council of State Governments:
HENRY W. TOLL

Executive Director of the Council of State Governments:
FRANK BANE

MANAGERS-AT-LARGE

HON. EDMUND G. BROWN
Attorney General of California

HON. JOHN E. BURTON
*Vice President, Cornell University,
New York*

HON. THOMAS E. DEWEY
Former Governor of New York

HON. ARTHUR Y. LLOYD
Former Director, Kentucky Legislative Research Commission

HON. J. MAYNARD MAGRUDER
Former Member, House of Delegates, Virginia

HON. OKEY L. PATTESON
Former Governor of West Virginia

HON. ALLAN SHIVERS
Governor of Texas

HON. GORDON M. TIFFANY
Former Attorney General of New Hampshire

HON. BERNICE T. VAN DER VRIES
Member of House of Representatives, Illinois

HON. ROSCOE R. WALCUTT
Probate Judge and Former Member of Senate, Ohio

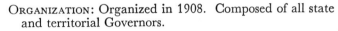

INTERSTATE ORGANIZATIONS AFFILIATED
WITH THE COUNCIL OF STATE GOVERNMENTS

THE GOVERNORS' CONFERENCE

ORGANIZATION: Organized in 1908. Composed of all state and territorial Governors.

PURPOSE: The Governors' Conference is an organization for improving state government, working on those problems that require interstate cooperation and facilitating federal-state relations with respect to cooperative governmental problems.

ARTHUR B. LANGLIE

OFFICERS: Members of the Executive Committee for 1955–56:
ARTHUR B. LANGLIE, Governor of Washington, *Chairman*
NORMAN BRUNSDALE, Governor of North Dakota
FRANK G. CLEMENT, Governor of Tennessee
LEROY COLLINS, Governor of Florida
EDWIN C. JOHNSON, Governor of Colorado
WALTER J. KOHLER, Governor of Wisconsin
ROBERT B. MEYNER, Governor of New Jersey
MILWARD L. SIMPSON, Governor of Wyoming
G. MENNEN WILLIAMS, Governor of Michigan

SECRETARY-TREASURER: FRANK BANE, Executive Director of the Council of State Governments.

ANNUAL MEETINGS: August 9–12, 1955, at Chicago, Illinois. The 1954 Annual Meeting was held July 11–14 at Lake George, Bolton Landing, New York.

PUBLICATIONS: *Proceedings of the Governors' Conference* (annual).

ACTIVITIES: Since May 13, 1908, when its first session was called at the White House by President Theodore Roosevelt, the Governors' Conference has been a strong and constructive force for the improvement of state government, the development of effective methods of interstate cooperation, and the furtherance of the ideals and purposes of the Union of the States. The Conference participates in the program and activities of the Council of State Governments, including its General Assembly and other national and regional conferences, and serves as a clearinghouse for information on administrative subjects and problems in the field of government. The Conference makes use of the informational facilities of the Council of State Governments and calls upon it for various research studies and reports on major state problems. The Executive Committee of the Conference serves on the Board of Managers of the Council. Individually, the members of the Governors' Conference further cooperate with the Council through their administrative appointees to the state Commissions on Interstate Cooperation.

THE CONFERENCE OF CHIEF JUSTICES

ORGANIZATION: Organized in 1949. Composed of the Chief Justices of State Supreme Courts.

PURPOSE: To provide for the exchange of ideas and information on the operation of the judiciary in the states, and for consultation between their highest courts concerning improvement of the administration of justice.

OFFICERS: Members of the Executive Council for 1955–56:
WILLIAM H. DUCKWORTH, Georgia, *Chairman*
STANLEY E. QUA, Massachusetts, *Vice-Chairman*
FREDERICK W. BRUNE, Maryland
ROGER L. DELL, Minnesota
FRANK R. KENISON, New Hampshire
HARVEY McGEHEE, Mississippi
CHARLES M. MERRILL, Nevada

WILLIAM H. DUCKWORTH

SECRETARIAT: The Council of State Governments.

ANNUAL MEETING OF 1955: August 17–20 at Philadelphia, Pennsylvania.

ACTIVITIES: The Conference provides a forum for the exchange of experience, views and suggestions to improve the organization and procedures of state courts. Special committees study and report on procedural practices. The secretariat undertakes such research as the Conference requests.

The Chairman of the Conference is a member of the Board of Managers of the Council of State Governments.

THE NATIONAL ASSOCIATION OF ATTORNEYS GENERAL

ORGANIZATION: Organized in 1907. Composed of all state and territorial Attorneys General and the Attorney General of the United States.

PURPOSE: To provide clearinghouse facilities and machinery for cooperation among the chief legal executives of the states and territories.

OFFICERS: Members of the Executive Committee for 1955–56:
JOHN BEN SHEPPERD, Texas, *President*
LOUIS C. WYMAN, New Hampshire, *Vice-President*
J. LINDSAY ALMOND, JR., Virginia
LATHAM CASTLE, Illinois
JOHN M. PATTERSON, Alabama
GROVER C. RICHMAN, JR., New Jersey
RICHARD H. ROBINSON, New Mexico
GRAYDON W. SMITH, Idaho
ROBERT T. STAFFORD, Vermont
VERNON W. THOMSON, Wisconsin

JOHN BEN SHEPPERD

SECRETARIAT: The Council of State Governments.

ANNUAL MEETING OF 1955: September 11–14, Bretton Woods, New Hampshire.

PUBLICATIONS: *Proceedings of the Conference of the National Association of Attorneys General* (annual); *Digest of Opinions*, with digests of opinions of state Attorneys General which are of widespread interest, issued weekly. The complete text of any opinion digested is furnished on request; from time to time the *Digest* includes opinions in full on important topics. An annual index facilitates use of the material for research.

ACTIVITIES: The secretariat performs research services and makes available information of general interest to members of the Association. The secretariat also serves as a clearinghouse for opinions of the Attorneys General to facilitate uniformity in the interpretation of state laws.

The President of the Association is a member of the Board of Managers of the Council of State Governments.

THE NATIONAL ASSOCIATION OF STATE BUDGET OFFICERS

MAURICE F. WILLIAMS

ORGANIZATION: Organized in 1945. Composed of all state and territorial budget officers, their assistants and deputies.

PURPOSE: To provide machinery for cooperation among state budget officers, to foster the more effective exercise of the function of budget administration, and to attain greater efficiency in state administration.

OFFICERS: Members of the Executive Committee for 1955–56:
MAURICE F. WILLIAMS, Maine, *President*
LAVERNE J. YOUNG, Oregon, *Vice-President*
E. C. GIESSEL, Wisconsin
FRANK M. LANDERS, Michigan
D. S. COLTRANE, North Carolina
T. H. MUGFORD, California
HARRY G. SMITH, Florida

SECRETARIAT: The Council of State Governments.

ANNUAL MEETING OF 1955: September 12–15, Miami Beach, Florida.

PUBLICATIONS: Résumés of annual meetings and reports of interest to state budget officers.

ACTIVITIES: The secretariat performs research services and makes available information of general interest to the Association's members. From time to time surveys are made of existing practices and procedures in all of the states. The Executive Committee is responsible for liaison and cooperation with any federal agency whenever federal-state problems arise.

The President of the Association is a member of the Board of Managers of the Council of State Governments.

THE NATIONAL LEGISLATIVE CONFERENCE

ROBERT A. AINSWORTH, JR.

ORGANIZATION: Organized in 1948. Composed of legislators who are officers of legislative service agencies; legislative librarians, reference and research officials, fiscal officers, statutory and code revisors, drafting officials; legislative chief clerks and secretaries; and others designated by the Conference.

PURPOSE: To cooperate for more effective service to the legislatures and to aid in improving legislative procedures.

OFFICERS: Members of the Executive Committee for 1955–56:
ROBERT A. AINSWORTH, JR., Louisiana, *President*
VERNON A. McGEE, Texas, *Vice-President*
MRS. ZYLPHA ZELL BURNS, Oregon
JOHN H. DENT, Pennsylvania
FRANK H. EDWARDS, Georgia
RALPH N. Kleps, California
HERMAN C. LOEFFLER, Massachusetts
C. EMERSON MURRY, North Dakota
WILLIAM R. NELSON, Missouri
EARL SACHSE, Wisconsin

SECRETARIAT: The Council of State Governments.

ANNUAL MEETING OF 1955: October 16–19, Miami Beach, Florida.

PUBLICATIONS: Studies and reports of interest to legislative reference agencies, officials and librarians; and *The Legislative Research Checklist*.

ACTIVITIES: The secretariat performs research services and makes available information of interest to the members. Legislative procedures in the states are surveyed from time to time.

The President of the Conference is a member of the Board of Managers of the Council of State Governments.

THE NATIONAL ASSOCIATION OF STATE PURCHASING OFFICIALS

C. L. MAGNUSON

ORGANIZATION: Organized in 1947. Composed of all state and territorial purchasing officials, their assistants and deputies.

PURPOSE: To promote cooperation for the more efficient exercise of state purchasing and for greater efficiency in administration.

OFFICERS: Members of the Executive Committee for 1955–56:
C. L. MAGNUSON, Connecticut, *President*
J. B. KING, Alabama, *Vice-President*
J. STANLEY BIEN, Michigan
CHARLES A. BYRLEY, Kentucky
WILLIAM E. CLARKSON, Indiana
KENNETH S. EASTON, Nevada
P. T. PETERSON, Minnesota

SECRETARIAT: The Council of State Governments.

ANNUAL MEETING OF 1955: October 25–28 at Louisville, Kentucky.

PUBLICATIONS: Résumés of meetings and special reports of interest to purchasing officials.

ACTIVITIES: The secretariat performs research services and makes available information of general interest to the members. It publishes reports on practice in inspection and analysis of state purchases and the organization and operation of purchasing agencies.

The President of the Association is a member of the Board of Managers of the Council of State Governments.

THE PAROLE AND PROBATION COMPACT ADMINISTRATORS' ASSOCIATION

L. B. STEPHENS

ORGANIZATION: Organized in 1945. Composed of administrators of the Interstate Compact for the Supervision of Parolees and Probationers, their assistants and deputies.

PURPOSE: To promote cooperation and the exchange of information among administrators of the Compact, for its effective implementation.

OFFICERS: Members of the Executive Committee for 1955–56:
L. B. STEPHENS, Alabama, *President*
HERMAN P. FAILS, Idaho, *Vice-President*
FRANCIS R. BRIDGES, JR., Florida, *Treasurer*
CHARLES P. CHEW, Virginia
EDWARD C. CUPIT, Nevada
QUENTIN L. FERM, Wisconsin
CAMPBELL LEFLORE, Oklahoma
LEE B. MAILLER, New York
HUGH P. O'BRIEN, Indiana

SECRETARIAT: The Council of State Governments.

ANNUAL MEETING OF 1955: September 25–26, Des Moines, Iowa.

PUBLICATIONS: Reports of meetings and topical reports of interest to members.

ACTIVITIES: The secretariat performs research services and makes available information of general interest to the members.

The President of the Association is a member of the Board of Managers of the Council of State Governments.

THE NATIONAL CONFERENCE OF COMMISSIONERS ON UNIFORM STATE LAWS

BARTON H. KUHNS

ORGANIZATION: Organized in 1892. Composed of from one to five commissioners from each state, appointed by their respective Governors.

PURPOSE: To promote uniformity in state laws on subjects where uniformity is deemed desirable and practicable, and to draft model laws for the states where such statutes are believed to be useful.

OFFICERS: For 1955–56:
BARTON H. KUHNS, Nebraska, *President*
HICKS EPTON, Oklahoma, *Vice-President*
TOM MARTIN DAVIS, Texas, *Treasurer*
WILLOUGHBY A. COLBY, New Hampshire, *Secretary*
EXECUTIVE COMMITTEE:
JAMES C. DEZENDORF, Oregon, *Chairman*
WALTER P. ARMSTRONG, JR., Tennessee
HAROLD C. HAVIGHURST, Illinois
WILLIAM A. MCKENZIE, Ohio
GEORGE R. RICHTER, JR., California
Ex-Officio Members:
JOE C. BARRETT, Arkansas
HARRY H. LUGG, Connecticut
WILLIAM A. SCHNADER, Pennsylvania

ANNUAL MEETING OF 1955: August 15–19 at Philadelphia, Pennsylvania.

PUBLICATIONS: *Handbook of the National Conference of Commissioners on Uniform State Laws* (annual).

ACTIVITIES: A committee of the Conference receives suggestions as to possible topics for uniform and model legislation and approves those deemed practicable. Bills are drafted by committees of the Conference; after due consideration by the Conference and approval by the commissioners of at least twenty states, and by the American Bar Association, the laws are released for presentation to the legislatures.

Copies of the *Handbook*, committee reports, proposed drafts and approved drafts may be obtained from the Executive Secretary, Frances D. Jones, 1155 East Sixtieth Street, Chicago 37, Illinois.

The Council of State Governments, with which the Conference has a cooperative agreement, has interested the various commissions on interstate cooperation in the uniform law program. The President of the Conference is a member of the Board of Managers of the Council of State Governments.

INTERSTATE COMPACTS*

SEVERAL years ago this biennial survey could aspire to present at least a modest amount of detail concerning each development in the compact field during the preceding two years. The large number of compacts recently consummated or now in various stages of negotiation and enactment makes this difficult to attain in a summary article. Consequently, these pages concentrate on selected aspects of recent compact developments. The authors invite the reader's attention to the appended table, which lists new compacts that in each instance have been enacted by the number of states required to put them into effect.

SOCIAL SERVICES AND CORRECTION

Perhaps the outstanding development of the past two years has been the increasing application of the interstate compact to the field of state services, particularly in the welfare, correctional and educational fields. The New England Higher Education Compact, highly significant for interstate cooperation in the provision of educational opportunities, is an application, in another part of the country, of arrangements embodied in the Southern and Western Regional Education compacts, previously treated in these reports. The Interstate Compact on Juveniles and the proposed South Central Interstate Corrections Compact present less familiar and, in a sense, pioneering ventures.

For some time it had seemed anomalous that adult parolees and probationers should be able to receive out-of-state supervision in those cases where it would assist in their rehabilitation, while similar benefits were not available to juvenile offenders. The situation has been even more unfortunate than might appear to the casual observer,

because restrictions placed on the juvenile parolee or probationer often affect the movements and mode of living of his family unit, as well as that of the juvenile himself, in a way that is not necessary when the offender is an adult, able to establish his own place of abode as circumstances may require. The adult parole and probation compact is only available to persons who have been convicted of crime. Consequently, the special nonconvict status for juvenile offenders, although inspired by humane and praiseworthy considerations, has, until now, barred them from the benefits of out-of-state supervision and the improved opportunities for rehabilitation frequently made possible by it.

From time to time other interstate juvenile problems also have received some recognition. In some instances these may be even more serious than the absence of interjurisdictional parole and probation. Notably, there has been a need to develop regular legal machinery for the expeditious return of children who simply run away from home and who are found in another state. Also, it has been thought that some types of problem juveniles might benefit from treatment in specialized institutions. But the provision of such facilities has lagged because of heavy financial burdens involved in their establishment and maintenance. Finally, procedures for returning juvenile escapees from institutional confinement have been uncertain, because juvenile delinquency is technically not a crime. As a result, the constitutional remedy of extradition is not available.

The new Interstate Compact on Juveniles provides means for handling all four of the situations discussed above. Its parole and probation provisions parallel those of the adult compact. The escapee return provisions accomplish the same result as extradition, but in simplified fashion. Procedures for the return of runaways emphasize and authorize voluntary, informal methods of return in all those cases where

---

*Prepared by FREDERICK L. ZIMMERMANN and MITCHELL WENDELL, members of the faculties of Hunter College and American International College, respectively, and authors of *The Interstate Compact Since 1925.*

the factual situation permits, but also provide for compulsory process where necessary. The problem of institutional treatment of juveniles is handled through enabling provisions. One of the compact articles provides for supplementary agreements with regard to joint or cooperative use of institutions for juveniles. A number of specific standards for the making and the contents of such agreements are spelled out, but the actual negotiation and entry into force of any arrangements for joint or cooperative institutions are left to administrative determination in the various states, in accordance with specific needs.

The Interstate Compact on Juveniles was the result of a painstaking drafting process during most of 1954. The final draft was approved at an interstate conference in New York City on January 20 and 21, 1955. This was after most of the state legislatures had begun their sessions. Nevertheless, at the conclusion of the 1955 sessions eleven states and Hawaii had enacted the compact.

Since the juvenile compact does not call for the exercise of any powers which impinge on the constitutional province of the national government, it does not require consent of Congress to become effective as among the states which so far have enacted it. Nevertheless, legislation for such consent is before Congress. The principal reason for this is that the compact envisages participation by the territories and possessions, the Commonwealth of Puerto Rico, and the District of Columbia. Hawaii, as noted, already has enacted it. Congressional consent probably will be necessary to include these jurisdictions. To date, the only other instance in which a territory has become a party to a compact is that of Alaska's recent ratification of the Western Education Compact.

The proposed South Central Interstate Corrections Compact was developed later than the Interstate Compact on Juveniles. Accordingly, the final draft could not be considered extensively by state administrators and legislators before the close of the 1955 sessions. Tennessee enacted it, and there are indications that it will receive serious consideration in sessions elsewhere during 1956 and 1957. Possible participants are all the states from Georgia and

Florida on the southeast to Kansas and Missouri on the northwest.

The compact provides for the cooperative use of institutions for women prisoners. Because of the small number of such prisoners in many individual states, the per capita cost of providing satisfactory facilities for them has proven to be extremely high. Consequently, consolidation of facilities on a regional basis is thought to offer great opportunities for improved treatment of women prisoners. For obvious geographic reasons, it is not contemplated that all the states from Florida to Kansas should use the same institutions. Instead, the compact contemplates development of subgroups of adjacent or neighboring states for use of particular facilities, located conveniently for their common purposes. Cooperative use of a specific facility would result from the conclusion of contracts among the states immediately concerned. These contracts are authorized by the compact, which provides for their minimum contents and contains detailed provisions for protection of the prisoners' constitutional rights.

The South Central Interstate Corrections Compact is not the first institutional compact in the corrections field. The Out-of-State Incarceration Amendment to the Interstate Compact for the Supervision of Parolees and Probationers is similar in many respects. However, that amendment is limited to use for incarceration of such parole and probation violators as may have been supervised under the parent compact, and only if out-of-state incarceration is determined to be more appropriate than return to the sending state. The South Central Compact thus promises to be more extensive in its application.

COMPACTS AND PRIVATE LAW

Some forty years ago, the late Dean John H. Wigmore of the Northwestern University Law School proposed the use of interstate compacts to permit states to join with foreign nations in developing uniform commercial law. Little came of this suggestion and, until recently, little or no thought was given to possible compacts dealing with any phase of private law, despite the fact that there are many jurisdictional problems in this field that might be handled through formal interstate agreement. In 1954, however, New York enacted an interpleader compact. Its basic purpose is to permit the holder of a debt or property claimed by two or more other persons to obtain jurisdiction over all such parties so that complete and final settlement of the dispute may be had in a single proceeding. This remedy of interpleader long has been available in individual jurisdictions, and, subject to certain limitations, in the federal courts, but not on an interjurisdictional basis. An additional point of note is that the new compact, subject to special safeguards, is open to participation by foreign nations as well as by jurisdictions within the United States. In 1955 Maine enacted the interpleader compact. At present Congressional consent has not been sought, and the compact is not yet in force.

WATER COMPACTS

Compacts for allocation of the waters of interstate streams continue to be negotiated and enacted. Their basic purposes and many of their provisions are similar except insofar as their precise wording may vary to embody language dealing with the specific needs of individual areas. However, the recent Sabine River Compact between Texas and Louisiana and the proposed Bear River Compact among Idaho, Utah and Wyoming are unusual in that each of them provides for a degree of administrative adjudication of water rights by the interstate compact agency.

In other fields of water use, the Great Lakes Compact was enacted by the necessary number of states in 1955. It creates a Great Lakes Commission to study and investigate problems relating to water resources in the Great Lakes Basin and to make recommendations to member states and the federal government. Five states—Illinois, Indiana, Michigan, Minnesota and Wisconsin—so far have enacted it. Membership is open to the three other Great Lakes states and to the provinces of Ontario and Quebec. Congressional consent has been requested.

There have been additional developments concerning major proposals for the Missouri, Columbia and Delaware basins, discussed in previous editions. A 1954 decree of the United States Supreme Court, allocating additional Delaware River water to New York City, would seem to obviate the realization, in its original form, of the plan of the Interstate Commission on the Delaware River Basin on the issues involved. But there has been growing belief that the court decree provided only a temporary and partial answer to the problem. A recently enacted amendment of the old Pennsylvania-New Jersey compact of 1783 allows construction of reservoirs at Wallpack Bend and Yardley and would permit the construction of an important segment of the plan of the Interstate Commission on the Delaware River Basin.

During 1954 a Columbia River Compact was formulated by the Columbia Interstate Compact Commission. The agreement would establish an interstate commission to function in the major fields of multiple resource development and would provide formulas for allocation of water and hydroelectric energy. The compact was ratified by Idaho, Nevada and Utah but was not acted upon in the four other basin states. All seven states have reconstituted their negotiating commissions, and a revised proposal may be presented to the legislative sessions of 1957.

The Missouri proposal for establishing a basin agency by interstate agreement has encountered opposing interests, both governmental and private, and has not been ratified. Legislation granting Congressional consent for formal negotiation of the compact has twice been passed by the United States Senate, but has not been passed by the House of Representatives. Such Congressional action assumes special significance in the case of the Missouri proposal because it is contemplated that the United States government would be an actual party to the compact if adopted.

REFERENCE SOURCES
ON INTERSTATE COMPACTS

FREDERICK L. ZIMMERMANN and MITCHELL WENDELL, *The Interstate Compact Since 1925*, published by The Council of State Governments, Chicago, 1951.

FELIX FRANKFURTER and JAMES M. LANDIS, "The Compact Clause of the Constitution," *Yale Law Journal*, vol. 34, May, 1925.

Colorado Water Conservation Board, *Interstate Compacts—A Compilation of Articles from Various Sources*, Denver, 1946.

NEW COMPACTS RATIFIED BY THE STATES 1954–55*

NAME	SUBJECT	STATE RATIFICATION	CONSENT OF CONGRESS	CITATION
Sabine River Compact	Allocation of waters of Sabine River, establishes an interstate administrative agency.	Texas, 1953 Louisiana, 1953	1954	68 Stat. 690
Breaks Interstate Park Compact	Agreement to create, develop and operate an interstate park and establish the Breaks Interstate Park Commission.	Kentucky, 1954 Virginia, 1954	1954	68 Stat. 571
Southeastern Interstate Forest Fire Protection Compact	Mutual aid in forest fire protection and control.	1953: Georgia; 1954: Kentucky, Mississippi, South Carolina; 1955: Alabama, Florida, North Carolina, Tennessee, West Virginia	1954	68 Stat. 563
Middle Atlantic Forest Fire Protection Compact	Mutual aid in forest fire protection and control.	Pennsylvania, 1953 Delaware, 1955 New Jersey, 1955	In process	
Amendment to Delaware River Compact of 1783	To permit construction of certain dams on Delaware River.	New Jersey, 1953 Pennsylvania, 1955	In process	
New England Regional Education Compact	Cooperation in the operation of programs of higher education.	1954: Massachusetts; 1955: Maine, New Hampshire, Vermont, Connecticut	1954	68 Stat. 962
Great Lakes Compact	Establishes interstate commission to plan and recommend measures for the development of water resources of the Great Lakes.	1955: Illinois, Indiana, Michigan, Minnesota, Wisconsin	In process	
Interstate Compact on Juveniles	Provide interstate cooperation in a broad area affecting juveniles.	1955: California, Maine, Massachusetts, Missouri, New Hampshire, New Jersey, New York, Tennessee, Utah, Washington, Wisconsin, Hawaii	In process	

*This table does not include in its listing any compact on which the minimum number of states required by the compact have not acted.

RECORD OF RATIFICATION OF EXISTING COMPACTS IN WHICH ADDITIONAL STATES
HAVE JOINED IN 1954–55*

NAME	SUBJECT	STATE RATIFICATION	CONSENT OF CONGRESS	CITATION
Civil Defense†	Mutual aid in civil defense and related matters	(a) Model Interstate Civil Defense Compact 1951: Conn., Del., Maine, Mass., Mont., N. H., N. J., N. Y., Pa., R. I., Tex.; 1952: Ariz., Calif., Colo., Idaho, Kans., Nev., N. Mex., Okla., Ore., S. Dak., Wash., Wyo.; 1953: Ala., Ohio, Nebr., W. Va.; 1955: Ark., Ind., Ky., Md., Utah, Va., Dist. of Columbia, Virgin Islands and Puerto Rico. (b) Other Civil Defense Compacts 1952: Fla., Ga., S. Car., Tenn. and Vt.	1951	64 Stat. 1245
Interstate Oil Compact	Conservation of oil and gas by prevention of physical waste	Ala., Ark., Colo., Fla., Ill., Ind , Kans., Ky., La., Mich., Miss., Mont., Nebr., N. Mex., N. Y., N. Dak., Ohio, Okla., Pa., Tenn., Tex., W. Va.; 1955: Nev., S. Dak., Wyo. — (Alaska, Ariz., Ga. and Wash. are associate members).	1955 extended to 1959	P.L. 185 84th Cong. 1st Sess.
New England Pollution Compact	Established New England Interstate Water Pollution Control Commission	Connecticut, 1947 Massachusetts, 1947 Rhode Island, 1947 New York, 1949 Vermont, 1951 New Hampshire, 1951 Maine, 1955	1947	61 Stat. 682
Western Regional Education Compact	Provides for establishment, financing and operation of programs of higher education at existing institutions or in new ones	Colorado, 1951 Montana, 1951 New Mexico, 1951 Oregon, 1951 Utah, 1951 Arizona, 1952 Idaho, 1953 Wyoming, 1953 Alaska, 1955 California, 1955 Washington, 1955	1953	67 Stat. 490
South Central Interstate Forest Fire Protection Compact	Mutual aid in forest fire prevention and control	Arkansas, 1953 Oklahoma, 1953 Louisiana, 1954 Mississippi, 1954 Texas, 1955	1954	68 Stat. 783

*This is a continuation of earlier tables carried biennially in *The Book of the States*. See 1954–55 edition for last preceding lists.

†A more detailed table of interstate civil defense compactual arrangements can be secured from The Federal Civil Defense Administration, Washington, D. C.

THE INTERSTATE COMMISSION ON THE DELAWARE RIVER BASIN*

O N June 7, 1954 the Supreme Court of the United States issued an order granting the petition of the City of New York (referred to in the last edition of *The Book of the States*, 1954–55) asking for the right to increase the amount of water it may take from the Delaware River Basin from 440 million gallons daily (as authorized in 1931) to 800 million gallons a day. The same order imposed upon New York City, in compensation for the authorized diversion, the obligation to release sufficient water from its reservoirs in the Delaware River watershed during periods of dry weather to maintain certain stipulated minimum flows in the river where it leaves the State of New York.

The same Supreme Court decree gave the State of New Jersey the right to divert 100 million gallons of water a day out of the Delaware River without any obligation to make compensating dry weather releases.

The decree also gives recognition to a proposed agreement between Pennsylvania and New Jersey repealing a provision in a compact ratified by these states in 1783 that prohibits construction of dams across the Delaware River. Under the terms of the proposed agreement, Pennsylvania would have the right to build a storage dam and a diversion dam in the Delaware River between the two states. New Jersey enacted a statute embodying this agreement in December, 1953. The act required Pennsylvania's concurrence by July 1, 1955. The Pennsylvania law was approved by the Governor the day before this deadline.

The Supreme Court decree apparently is completely acceptable to New York. It enables the city independently to meet its water supply requirements for many years in the foreseeable future. But, by the same token, it probably removes any further interest on the part of the city in the four-state water conservation program proposed by the Interstate Commission on the Delaware River Basin (Incodel).

By contrast, northeastern New Jersey and the greater Philadelphia area, comprising southeastern Pennsylvania, southwestern New Jersey and eastern Delaware, all have a stake in the utilization of the waters of the Delaware which the 1954 Supreme Court decree leaves largely unanswered and unsolved.

At the present time (July, 1955) these problems are receiving careful and serious consideration from the states of Pennsylvania and New Jersey under the administrations of Governors George M. Leader and Robert B. Meyner. Both of these chief executives took office after the institution of the case that was decided by the Supreme Court in 1954. The new administrations are directing their efforts toward a new look at the Delaware River Basin water resources problems in the light of the Supreme Court decree, with the view of finding a solution that will be mutually acceptable and beneficial to all affected governmental entities. Incodel is furnishing every possible assistance and service in this endeavor.

Other activities in which Incodel is concurrently engaged include the completion of its basin-wide stream pollution abatement program; acceleration of progress in the protection and conservation of soil and forest resources; promotion of small watershed organizations; enhancement of the recreational potentialities of the Delaware Valley; and participation in development of a sound national water policy.

OFFICERS OF THE COMMISSION, 1955

FRANCIS A. PITKIN, Director, Bureau of Community Development, Pennsylvania, *Chairman*

JOSEPH E. McLEAN, Commissioner, New Jersey Department of Conservation and Economic Development, *Vice-Chairman*

ELISHA T. BARRETT, Assemblyman, State of New York, *Vice-Chairman*

RAYMOND B. PHILLIPS, former Senator, State of Delaware, *Vice-Chairman*

JAMES H. ALLEN, *Executive Secretary*

COMMISSION HEADQUARTERS

Suburban Station Building, Philadelphia 3, Pennsylvania

---

*Prepared by JAMES H. ALLEN, Executive Secretary, Interstate Commission on the Delaware River Basin.

THE INTERSTATE COMMISSION ON THE POTOMAC RIVER BASIN*

WITHOUT losing sight of the importance of pollution control, the Interstate Commission on the Potomac River Basin has devoted an increasing amount of its attention to the affairs of the Potomac Valley Conservancy District, created by the same compact that created the commission.

Pollution reports by the commission have been widely distributed and have received much attention in the newspapers and on radio and television. Probably as a direct result of this publicity, a number of organizations whose aims and objectives are in harmony with those of the commission have sought affiliation with it in order to increase their effectiveness. The commission is amending its by-laws to make such affiliation possible.

New citizen groups have organized, both in the upper part of the river basin and in the metropolitan area, and are jealously watching developments which might increase pollution in the river.

Partly as a result of publicity, and partly because of other circumstances, important corrective waste treatment works are being built.

The state water pollution control authorities from the basin states are supplying to the commission detailed information concerning the waste treatment facilities now in operation in their states, and listing those still needed. This information is being used to complete a comprehensive plan for dealing with pollution in the Potomac River Basin.

An agreement which required ten years for its development has been signed between the Washington Suburban Sanitary Commission and the District of Columbia. Sewers under construction will convey all the sewage from the Metropolitan Area on the Maryland side to the Blue Plains Sewage Treatment Plant, now undergoing extensive modernization which is to be completed by 1960.

On the Virginia side, Arlington County has completed a primary plant. A large portion of the sewage from Fairfax County and all of Alexandria's sewage will receive complete treatment in a plant being built by the Alexandria Sanitation Authority.

Private industries throughout the basin continue their cooperation with the commission.

The increasing demand for clean water is giving the commission's work increased urgency and importance. To deal with competition that has arisen among agriculture, industry and the municipalities for use of the available water supply, changes will be needed in state laws governing water rights. To assist in this the commission provided a forum in which the various aspects of the problem were discussed. Nationally known speakers presented papers on the subject at the spring meeting at Winchester, Virginia, in May, 1955.

A sampling program, facilitated by the assistance of many industries in the basin, continues to accumulate valuable information on the condition of the river.

Publications of the commission during the last biennium have included "A Clean River for the Nation's Capital," "Report on Water Pollution in the Washington Metropolitan Area, Section 2 and Section 3," "Second and Third Industrial Waste Forums," "Upper Potomac Basin Industrial Waste Investigation," "Conservation Measures for the Potomac Valley Conservancy District," "Parks and Forests in the Potomac River Basin," "Summary of the Work of the Water Committee" and "Summary of the Work of the Land Committee."

---

*Prepared by LAWRENCE M. FISHER, Acting Director, Interstate Commission on the Potomac River Basin.

OFFICERS OF THE COMMISSION, 1955

GEORGE F. HAZELWOOD, *Chairman*

JOHN I. ROGERS, *Vice-Chairman*

OLIVER GASCH, *General Counsel*

DANIEL L. SECKINGER, M.D., *Treasurer*

LAWRENCE M. FISHER, *Acting Director*

COMMISSION HEADQUARTERS

203 Transportation Building, Washington 6, D.C.

OHIO RIVER VALLEY SANITATION COMMISSION*

THE most significant index of progress by the eight states that comprise the Ohio River Valley Water Sanitation Commission is that sewage-treatment facilities, in terms of population served, are being installed at a rate four times faster than they were in a similar period prior to establishment of the commission, on June 30, 1948. During the past year, the percentage increase of population served by treatment works was as great as that secured during the entire eight years prior to the signing of the interstate sanitation compact.

Sewage-disposal facilities to treat the wastes from more than four million people are now in operation in the Ohio Valley. New facilities under construction or approved for construction will treat the sewage from another 3,400,000 people. These accomplishments in the 155,000 square-mile area of Illinois, Indiana, Kentucky, New York, Ohio, Pennsylvania, Virginia and West Virginia—constituting the interstate drainage district—reveal the impetus that has been given for municipal sewage-treatment works.

Forty-five per cent of the population now is served by sewage treatment facilities. Another 12 per cent has treatment plants under construction, and 24 per cent has plans approved for construction. Sewered population in the district is 9,600,000. This is the tangible evidence of the manner in which the eight compact states are cooperating on a regional pollution control program.

One of the commission's major accomplishments during 1954 was the completion of engineering studies, public hearings and the promulgation of requirements for sewage discharges in the entire 981 miles of the Ohio River. The regulations are set forth in seven standards, each applying to a different section of the river.

Meantime, quantity of flow and quality variations of water in the Ohio River continue to receive special study by the commission.

---

*Prepared by EDWARD J. CLEARY, Executive Director and Chief Engineer, Ohio River Valley Water Sanitation Commission.

The river is being monitored twice weekly at ten sampling stations. The data, furnished by managers of municipal and industrial water supply systems, is providing a constant check on pollution conditions and is aiding the commission in determining the need for additional remedial measures.

The situation with regard to industrial-waste control is revealed from reports from the signatory states. They show that of the 1,424 industries discharging directly into streams of the district 508—or 36 per cent—are rated as adequate; 487—or 34 per cent—provide some form of control, but more will be required; 40 new installations are under construction; and 132 new facilities are in the planning stage.

In addition, reduction of pollution loads from thousands of industries is being accomplished through discharge into municipal sewer systems where treatment plants have been built. For example, there are some 1,800 industries in the City of Cincinnati, the wastes from which will be treated along with domestic sewage.

Adoption in April, 1955, of an industrial-waste control policy by the signatory states represents one of the commission's most complex and satisfying accomplishments during the past year. The policy was formulated following two years of study by the commission and its 150-member industry-action committees. Having achieved unanimity of approach, the commission is now in a position to expedite industrial-waste control in the same orderly and effective fashion by which municipal sewage-treatment requirements were established on the Ohio River.

The policy provides that requirements for the modification or restriction of industrial-waste discharges will be designed to safeguard and maintain water uses that will serve the public interest in the most beneficial and reasonable manner. Certain basic restrictions, applying to every industrial-waste discharge, are stipulated. The restrictions spell out a statutory provision in the Ohio River Valley interstate compact that all waters are to be "free from unsightly or malodorous nuisances due to floating solids or sludge deposits."

Determinations with regard to additional control measures will be based on studies now under way involving separate investigations of each industrial plant and the stretch of stream on which it is located. Data for these studies is being furnished by the appropriate state pollution-abatement agencies represented on the commission.

OFFICERS OF THE COMMISSION, 1955–56

EARL DEVENDORF, *Chairman*
KENNETH M. LLOYD, *Vice-Chairman*
F. H. WARING, *Secretary*
ROBERT K. HORTON, *Treasurer*
EDWARD J. CLEARY, *Executive Director and Chief Engineer*

COMMISSION HEADQUARTERS
414 Walnut Street, Cincinnati 2, Ohio

UPPER COLORADO RIVER COMMISSION*

THE Upper Colorado River Commission is an interstate organization created under the authority of the Upper Colorado River Basin Compact. The compact was executed in 1948 by the states of Arizona, Colorado, New Mexico, Utah and Wyoming, ratified by their respective legislatures, and consented to by Congress. The commission is composed of one commissioner representing the United States and one each from Colorado, New Mexico, Utah and Wyoming.

The commission has the power, among other things, to construct, operate and maintain water gauging stations; to make estimates forecasting run-off of the Colorado River and its tributaries; to engage in cooperative water supply studies; to collect, analyze and report data pertaining to stream flows, storage, diversions and use of the waters of the Colorado River System; to make findings as to the quantity of water of the Upper Colorado River System used each year in the Upper Colorado River Basin and in each of its states. It also has power to make findings as to the quantity delivered at Lee Ferry, Arizona, during each water year; as to necessity for and the extent of curtailment of use required, if any, in order that the flow at Lee Ferry shall not be depleted below compact requirements; as to the quantity of reservoir losses and as to the share thereof chargeable to each state. It is authorized to make findings of fact in the event of the occurrence of extraordinary drought or serious accident to the irrigation system in the Upper Basin, whereby delivery of water in order to fulfill treaty obligations to Mexico becomes difficult. Findings under that

heading must be reported to the Governors of each of the Upper Basin states, the President of the United States, the United States Section of the International Boundary and Water Commission and other appropriate federal and state agencies and officials, so that water allotted to Mexico may be reduced in accordance with the terms of the treaty.

In making findings as to the consumption of water in the Upper Basin the commission follows the inflow-outflow method, as required by the Upper Colorado River Basin Compact. Investigations now are being made in this field.

The commission works closely with state and federal agencies, both executive and legislative, in formulation of state and national water resources policies; in the collection, refinement and analysis of hydrological data; and in the promotion of water resource development programs.

One of the commission's major purposes is to "secure the expeditious agricultural and industrial development of the Upper Basin." In this respect, while Congress was in session during 1954 and 1955, it maintained temporary offices in Washington, D. C. and actively sponsored legislation to authorize construction of the initial phase of the Colorado River Storage Project and participating projects, which constitute parts of a comprehensive basin-wide development of the water resources of Colorado, New Mexico, Utah and Wyoming.

OFFICERS OF THE COMMISSION, 1955

ROBERT J. NEWELL, *Commissioner for the United States and Chairman*
GEORGE D. CLYDE, *Vice-Chairman*
IVAL V. GOSLIN, *Engineer-Secretary*
BARNEY L. WHATLEY, *Treasurer*
RICHARD F. COUNLEY, *Assistant Treasurer*

COMMISSION HEADQUARTERS
520 Rood Avenue, Grand Junction, Colorado

*Prepared by IVAL V. GOSLIN, Engineer-Secretary, Upper Colorado River Commission, June 1, 1955.

INTERSTATE SANITATION COMMISSION*

NOTABLE progress has been achieved in the three phases of the pollution abatement program of the Interstate Sanitation Commission in the New York Metropolitan area of the States of New York, New Jersey and Connecticut. Phase 1 of its program, encompassing the removal of all raw sewage discharges from the recreational waters under the commission's control (covering an estimated total of 1,500 miles of shoreline), has been 99 per cent completed. Phase 2, to rid all non-recreational waters of untreated sewage, is 73 per cent completed. The last phase—to free all of the waters from the discharge of inadequately treated sewage—is 89 per cent completed.

The third phase of the commission program will be increasingly difficult to achieve in future, inasmuch as it is expected that plants presently considered adequate by commission standards will become inadequate, due to obsolescence, increasing population, and accompanying sewage flow. It has been the commission's experience that in this area treatment plants are designed for a twenty-year period so far as capacity is concerned. Thirty of the 138 plants in the district are over 20 years old.

Some concept of the commission's considerable cumulative achievements as regards pollution abatement can be indicated by noting the amount of solid material removed from the water ways since the commission has been in existence. Total sludge removed amounts to approximately 50 million cubic yards of wet solids, which is considerable even when compared to the estimated 15 million cubic yards dredged annually from New York Harbor.

During 1954–55 five sewage treatment plants were completed to bring the total of treatment plants under the commission's jurisdiction to 138. The total of approximately $11 million in capital investment represented by these five treatment plants raises the total capital investment in pollution abatement projects under the jurisdiction of the commission to more than $200 million. Although this is a considerable in-

vestment, it is dwarfed in some instances by investments in the existing sewers themselves. In Nassau County, for instance, approximately $100 million is invested in sewers, and a considerably larger sum is indicated for the near future.

The commission continues its plant investigation program, designed to gather data as to whether the specific provisions of the Tri-State Compact, under which the commission operates, are being met by the sewage treatment plants discharging into the district waters. Inspections at given plants are proceeding at approximately the same frequency as previously—despite the fact that neither the field inspection staff nor the laboratory and engineering staffs have increased, while other work, including surveys, has grown considerably.

Major surveys were conducted during the past two years on the Upper Hudson River, the Upper East River, in Upper New York Bay and on the Raritan River. The Upper New York Bay survey, conducted in conjunction with the United States Army Corps of Engineers, New York District Office, is unique in many respects. Approximately 3,500 samples, collected over a period of three years, provide the basic data for this survey. No comparable study of its size has been conducted in the United States. Information of basic value has been disclosed as a result.

Further progress has been made against pollution from small boats. Contract studies were initiated by the commission with New York University in 1953. These included field surveys of small boat pollution and laboratory studies for the treatment of such wastes. The potential seriousness of small boat pollution was recognized by Connecticut in the passage of legislation which forbade the deposit or discharge of waste material of any kind from a water-borne craft without effective treatment.

OFFICERS OF THE COMMISSION, 1955

WILLIAM C. COPE, *Chairman*
DANIEL F. B. HICKEY, *Vice-Chairman*
HUGH W. ROBERTSON, *Vice-Chairman*
JEREMIAH D. MAGUIRE, *Treasurer*
SETH G. HESS, *Executive Secretary*
EDITH G. KNIGHT, *Assistant Secretary*

COMMISSION HEADQUARTERS
110 William Street, New York 38, N.Y.

---

*Prepared by ALEX N. DIACHISHIN, Assistant Chief Engineer, Interstate Sanitation Commission.

NEW ENGLAND INTERSTATE
WATER POLLUTION CONTROL COMMISSION*

THE New England Interstate Water Pollution Control Commission was created in 1947 when the states of Connecticut, Massachusetts and Rhode Island entered into a compact for the control of pollution of interstate waters, with approval by an act of Congress. Eligible for membership were the New England states and New York, the latter because of waters in that state common with those in the New England area. New York became a signatory to the compact in 1949, followed by Vermont and New Hampshire in 1951. Ratification of the compact by the 1955 Maine legislature completes the commission's membership.

The commission is composed of five representatives from each of the signatory states, appointed in the manner and for terms provided by the ratification legislation of the states. In general there is representation from the state health department, the state water pollution control agency, municipal interests, industry, recreational interests and fisheries and conservation. The technical phase of the work is under the direction of a Technical Advisory Board, composed of the directors of the state water pollution control agencies.

The compact is based on cooperation by the states to restore and preserve the water resources of an area which is virtually a network of interstate streams. In order to secure a balanced use of its waters to meet the various degrees of water quality necessary for domestic, industrial and recreational uses, the compact is built around a classification of waters according to highest use. Under the compact's terms each state prepares and submits to the commission for approval proposed classifications of its interstate waters. Upon approval by the commission, the states are pledged to secure action by municipalities and industries in the installation of treatment works necessary to meet the classification. Thus enforcement powers are retained by the individual states, and the commission acts as an agency of the states in coordinating a mutually agreed plan to improve and control the waters for their most beneficial uses.

Several of the interstate rivers in the area have been classified in accordance with the water quality standards adopted by the commission. These include large sections of two major river basins, the Thames and the Connecticut. In various stages of completion by the states are many proposed classifications for presentation to the commission for approval.

To assist industry in the control and treatment of its various wastes, the commission since 1949 has sponsored industrial waste research, particularly in connection with textile wastes, which constitute one of the most serious pollution problems. Reports on these studies, conducted for the commission at Wesleyan University in Connecticut and the University of Rhode Island, have been published for distribution to industry and have received commendation for their contributions to the science of waste disposal and treatment.

Actual construction of waste treatment works is probably the best index of the success of the pollution control program. Since 1949 construction of sewage works costing over $106 million has been completed or started in the compact area. These include forty-one new sewage treatment plants serving a total population of more than two million and treating large quantities of industrial wastes. The long-range construction program has been advanced immeasurably by the adoption of stream classifications which provide definite plans of action for promotion and support by all interests concerned.

OFFICERS OF THE COMMISSION, 1955

WALTER J. SHEA, Rhode Island, *Chairman*
WILLIAM S. WISE, Connecticut, *Vice-Chairman*
JOHN F. CASEY, Massachusetts, *Treasurer*
JOSEPH C. KNOX, *Secretary*

COMMISSION HEADQUARTERS
73 Tremont Street, Boston 8, Massachusetts

---

*Prepared by JOSEPH C. KNOX, Secretary, New England Interstate Water Pollution Control Commission.

ATLANTIC STATES MARINE FISHERIES COMMISSION*

THE Atlantic States Marine Fisheries Commission was organized in 1942 under an interstate compact assented to by Congress. The compact embraces fifteen signatory states, each with three commissioners—its administrator of fisheries, a legislator appointed by the Commission on Interstate Cooperation, and a citizen appointed by the Governor. The commission functions through special committees and four sections, all reporting to the full commission. Each section is composed of states having a common interest in a part of the coast: *North Atlantic*—Maine, New Hampshire, Massachusetts, Rhode Island, Connecticut; *Middle Atlantic*—New York, New Jersey, Pennsylvania and Delaware; *Chesapeake Bay*—Maryland and Virginia; *South Atlantic*—North Carolina, South Carolina, Georgia and Florida.

In earlier years the commission emphasized the need for uniform fishery laws. It later discovered that differences in physical and biological conditions require differing regulations in different areas. Emphasis subsequently has been on increasing scientific research at state and federal levels so that fishery policy may be based on adequate data. The accumulation of scientific knowledge about marine fisheries, compared with like efforts in agriculture, is a slow and costly process, but already important results are apparent.

Research is paying cash dividends. Increasing the required mesh size of nets in the Georges Bank haddock fishery has permitted escapement of small unmarketable fish, while catching larger fish, with resultant increase in poundage and profits. Benefits from saving younger stock will not be realized until next year and may require further time for full proof. Yearly catch predictions for Georges Bank haddock and for shad in the Hudson and Connecticut rivers are proving astonishingly accurate, and permit maximum take consistent with preservation of brood stock. This, in turn, requires flexibility in administration rather than inflexible laws as to seasons, minimum sizes, etc.

*Prepared by WAYNE D. HEYDECKER, Secretary-Treasurer, Atlantic States Marine Fisheries Commission.

The trend is toward granting fishery departments wider discretion in such matters. This approach was accepted in principle by the Middle Atlantic Section in 1954 with respect to anadromous fisheries in the Delaware River. It would require legislation by New Jersey and Pennsylvania to grant to their fishery departments such discretionary powers as already exist in New York.

The clean up of the Delaware River under the leadership of the Interstate Commission on the Delaware River Basin has progressed so far that resumption of the shad run in that river may be expected shortly. Thus it is important that the states concerned be able to act quickly in concert as occasion may require.

The Atlantic States Cooperative Striped Bass Program is gathering momentum. Massachusetts, New York, Maryland, South Carolina and Florida are operating projects with the help of federal aid funds. Connecticut has just secured a scientist for its project. Rhode Island, New Jersey, Delaware, Virginia and North Carolina are cooperating, using state funds only, but hope to secure federal aid for specific projects. Identification of stocks and the extent of migratory pattern have been clarified by racial studies conducted by the federal coordinator. The survival and development of a practically land-locked stock of striped bass in the Santee River drainage system of South Carolina has aroused much interest and speculation as to future possibilities in other areas.

The Shad Project is approaching the end of its five-year study, but the South Atlantic Section has requested its continuance for two years to complete studies in southern rivers. Federal and state scientists have produced some excellent reports and predictions, which have been distributed to commissioners and laboratories along the coast.

With the cooperation of the Holyoke Water Power Company and the Fish and Wildlife Service, during the spring spawning run of 1955, it was reported that over 5,000 mature shad were successfully lifted over the Holyoke Dam in the Connecticut River. Thus, after 107 years of absence, shad again swam upstream to their an-cestral spawning grounds, between Holyoke and Turners Falls. This new fish passage device is the only one in the Atlantic Coast that has successfully passed large numbers of shad upstream, so it may have signifi-cance for other areas. New techniques developed by the project are now available for better management of this important but depleted fishery.

This incomplete summary reveals the commission's method of operation. It acts as a forum and a clearinghouse for the states. It makes recommendations to them and to Congress, and cooperates with its sister commissions on the Gulf and Pacific coasts. It is an agency for coordinating the marine fishery work of its fifteen mem-ber states with each other and with the Fish and Wildlife Service to achieve maxi-mum yield from the fisheries of the Atlantic coast.

OFFICERS OF THE COMMISSION, 1955

CHARLES M. LANKFORD, JR., Exmore, Virginia, *Chairman*

J. BERDAN MILLER, St. Mary's, Georgia, *Vice-Chairman*

WAYNE D. HEYDECKER, Mount Vernon, New York, *Secretary-Treasurer*

COMMISSION HEADQUARTERS
22 West First Street, Mount Vernon, New York

PACIFIC MARINE FISHERIES COMMISSION*

THE Pacific Marine Fisheries Commis-sion was created in 1947 when the states of Washington, Oregon and California entered into a compact with the consent of Congress for the purpose of co-ordinating the research and management of the marine fisheries of mutual concern to them.

The commission has no regulatory pow-ers but develops concurrent action and recommends enactment of the necessary research programs and management regula-tions to the member states. With the states themselves rests the authority for the management of their own fisheries; their acceptance of the commission's recommen-dations is a voluntary action executed through prescribed procedures established by each state.

The major interests of the commission continue to be centered on the ocean salm-on, sablefish, albacore tuna, and bottom fishes taken by the trawl fishery. Through current research, quantitative measures are being developed to determine the con-tribution to the ocean fisheries of chinook and silver salmon produced by various rivers along the coast. This information is essential in considering further improve-ment in the management of the ocean troll fishery for salmon.

The results of research on sablefish in-

dicate that the sablefish population along the Pacific Coast consists of several more or less separate stocks. It is evident, also, that the more desirable larger sablefish have become increasingly scarce off Wash-ington and Oregon, while the stocks off California seem to be maintaining them-selves. With the objective of protecting the young sablefish, and possibly reducing the fishing intensity on the stocks off Washing-ton and Oregon, the commission has rec-ommended that a minimum size limit of three pounds dressed head-off or a cor-responding length measurement be estab-lished in Oregon and Washington. This recommendation is under consideration by the two states.

A previous recommendation by the com-mission, for a minimum mesh size of $4\frac{1}{2}$ inches for otter trawl nets—with exceptions for certain specialized fisheries—has now been effected. This, it is anticipated, will provide additional protection to the young sablefish as well as the young of various other bottom fish species which are taken by the trawl fishery.

The Pacific Marine Fisheries Commis-sion has been requested and has accepted the responsibility of coordinating the Amer-ican albacore research of the central and eastern North Pacific. Advising on such coordination is an Albacore Steering Com-mittee consisting of representatives from various fisheries research agencies. Study is being directed toward determining the factors of the oceanic environment which

*Prepared by JOHN T. GHARRETT, Research Coordinator, Pacific Marine Fisheries Com-mission.

govern the distribution of the albacore in the ocean.

The benefits of the commission are proving to be many. Through the commission, the fisheries biologists of the three states are brought together to coordinate their research. In addition, the voluntary cooperation of the Alaska Department of Fisheries, Fisheries Research Board of Canada and the United States Fish and Wildlife Service has resulted in an integration of marine fisheries research on a coastwide basis. Through the commission, the various fisheries administrators meet to discuss their problems and develop coordinated management programs. And the commission brings the fisheries industry men to the conference table, where their problems and those of the administrators and scientists are carefully reviewed, resulting in a better understanding of all phases of the problems of fisheries management.

OFFICERS OF THE COMMISSION, 1955

RICHARD S. CROKER, California, *Chairman*
ROBERT J. SCHOETTLER, Washington, *Vice-Chairman*
ROBERT L. JONES, Oregon, *Secretary*
H. F. LINSE, Oregon, *Treasurer*

COMMISSION HEADQUARTERS
340 State Office Building, 1400 S. W. Fifth Avenue, Portland 1, Oregon

GULF STATES MARINE FISHERIES COMMISSION*

THE Gulf States Marine Fisheries Commission, created in 1949, has as its primary objective the proper utilization of the fisheries common to the territorial waters of the states of Alabama, Florida (Gulf waters), Louisiana, Mississippi and Texas. In pursuance of this objective the commission is authorized to recommend to the proper state officials the enactment of laws or the institution of regulations designed to establish improved fishery management practices. Knowledge of life histories, habits and environmental conditions, among other data, are important to the preparation of fishery recommendations of this character. Information resulting from both state and federal programs is disseminated to the member states by the commission.

During the period covered by this report (May, 1953–May, 1955) the Gulf states have been very active in numerous categories of fisheries work. Primary attention has been given by Alabama to shrimp and oyster fisheries. Florida has conducted research on the shrimp, oyster, mullet, blue crab, scallop, red snapper and red tide. Shrimp and oyster research programs have progressed in Louisiana, and a sectional study of Lake Pontchartrain instituted. Shrimp and oysters have been subjects of investigation in Mississippi. Shrimp, speckled trout, redfish, drum and oysters are the principal species to which research has been directed in Texas. Other research work involving the fisheries include bottom studies, oyster reef development and rehabilitation, gear development, and fish cultural stations.

During this period the commission arranged a meeting of state, federal, and university scientists for the purpose of developing a research program that would provide scientific data considered necessary to a better understanding of the important shrimp fisheries of the Gulf states. The commission requested the Department of the Interior to initiate such a program through the Fish and Wildlife Service. Such investigations are now under way, having been made possible under the terms of Public Law 466, 83rd Congress.

Other Fish and Wildlife Service programs, made possible under the terms of the Saltonstall-Kennedy Act—which legislation the commission actively supported in Washington—include biological and technological research on the oyster, technological research on menhaden, investigation of organisms causing mortality among fishes; economic survey of the shrimp fishery, gear development, improved statistical coverage, and marketing studies. Much of this research has been contracted to universities of the Gulf area.

Fish and Wildlife Service programs not requiring special allotments have progressed during the period. These include

---

*Prepared by W. DUDLEY GUNN, Secretary-Treasurer, Gulf States Marine Fisheries Commission.

oyster predator life history and control studies; a general survey of the Gulf of Mexico related to the classification of fish eggs, larvae and juveniles, chemistry of sea water, and red tide investigations; explorations for and locating of new shrimp grounds in the 200–250 fathom range, and the catching of tuna in commercially important quantities.

In the aggregate, the fisheries of the Gulf of Mexico continue to show a year-to-year increased production and value. It appears that with the continued expansion of many of the fisheries now in production, and with prospects exceedingly promising for the development of new fisheries, the curve is likely to continue upward. It is the aim of the commission, and agencies associated both directly and indirectly with the compact on which it is based, to develop scientific knowledge required of the expanding fisheries of the Gulf.

OFFICERS OF THE COMMISSION, 1955–56

WILLIAM J. HENDRY, *Chairman*
DONALD G. BOLLINGER, *Vice-Chairman*
W. DUDLEY GUNN, *Secretary-Treasurer*

COMMISSION HEADQUARTERS

Audubon Building, 931 Canal Street, New Orleans 16, Louisiana

NORTHEASTERN FOREST FIRE PROTECTION COMMISSION*

THE mission of the Northeastern Forest Fire Protection Commission, as mandated by Congress in 1949, is the promotion of improved forest fire prevention and control in New York, New England and adjacent provinces in Canada, by providing mutual aid in times of forest fire disaster and by establishment of uniform standards and methods of forest fire protection and suppression.

Now in its sixth year of operation as the pioneer agency of its kind, the commission has not only made substantial progress in its own area but has been able to render some assistance to sister states in the Middle Atlantic, Southern and South Central regions in connection with the establishment of similar forest fire control agencies.

For some time subsequent to its organization in July, 1950, the commission made haste slowly. That its approach to its problems, as finally worked out, has been worth while and businesslike is attested by the enthusiasm and continued cooperation of all concerned. In addition, the several compacting states report a marked increase in the efficiency of their normal fire control operations which they ascribe to the work of the commission. Activities which have contributed most to this feeling are the commission's formulation of a regional fire plan, its teacher training program and the publication of reference manuals.

The regional fire plan establishes procedures for the action to be taken, respectively, in times of fire disaster and normal fire hazard, by the several states and the commission's executive office. The latter acts as dispatcher when mutual aid is required. The plan also requires that a Board of Review be held after every mutual aid operation.

The purpose of the teacher training program is to train selected fire personnel to conduct in-state training on a uniform basis in their own states. Seven such training sessions have been held with an average attendance of sixty-five. Forty of those attending have been teacher trainees, the balance comprising the training team, outside speakers, United States Forest Service personnel, and observers from outside states and adjacent Canadian provinces. Two of the sessions were field exercises.

The commission believes that the in-state training of fire control employees and other interested groups in its uniform methods of fire control will return big dividends, and that the commission's future may well depend upon the extent to which the several compacting states continue their in-state training.

As a natural corollary to the training program, the commission has compiled, published and distributed reference manuals on radio procedure and fire control organization. The radio booklet relates to

*Prepared by ARTHUR S. HOPKINS, Executive Secretary, Northeastern Forest Fire Protection Commission.

the manner of using radio to convey the desired fire message in the clearest way and shortest time. All fire rangers, observers and other fire control officers in the member states have received copies.

The manual on fire control organization is a digest of the teacher training material presented at three winter meetings. It is sponsored jointly by Region 7 of the United States Forest Service and the commission, and consists of 260 pages. Copies have been supplied in quantity to the region and all compacting states. Single copies also were sent to all state foresters in the United States, all regional offices of the United States Forest Service, all forestry colleges and a number of interested individuals and organizations.

A recent forward step has been the decision by the Technical Committee to publish at least three additional reference manuals on other forest fire fighting fundamentals, as rapidly as they are covered at the teacher training meetings.

To the commission the future looks bright. Its area of work is enlarging, and despite its lack of "power to enforce," it expects a continuation of the congenial cooperation which so far has marked all its endeavors.

OFFICERS OF THE COMMISSION, 1955

W. FOSTER SCHREEDER, State Forester of Connecticut, *Chairman*
WILLIAM M. FOSS, Director of Lands and Forests, New York, *Vice-Chairman*
ARTHUR S. HOPKINS, *Executive Secretary*

COMMISSION HEADQUARTERS

Patlen Building, Chatham, New York

PALISADES INTERSTATE PARK COMMISSION*

IN 1900, the Commissioners of the Palisades Interstate Park, predecessor of the present Palisades Interstate Park Commission, was formed by joint, cooperative action of New Jersey and New York.

The original board of commissioners was authorized to preserve and maintain the natural beauty of the Palisades, which was threatened by quarries in the process of demolishing them. Later the commission's authority was extended into New York State as far north as Newburgh and westerly to the Ramapo Mountains.

In 1937, a compact between New York and New Jersey, approved by Congress, provided for creation of the Palisades Interstate Park Commission as a joint, corporate, municipal instrumentality of the two states, with appropriate rights, powers, duties, and immunities; for the transfer to the commission of certain functions, jurisdiction, rights, powers and duties, together with the properties of the bodies politic created in 1900; and for continuance of the Palisades Interstate Park for public use and enjoyment.

There are ten commissioners, five appointed by the Governor and confirmed by the Senate of each state. All commissioners serve without pay. The term is five years or until a successor is appointed and has qualified.

Since its creation in 1900, the commission has acquired additional areas in New York and New Jersey, and it now exercises jurisdiction over a chain of eleven parks in both states. They are the Palisades in New Jersey, including the world famous Palisades of the Hudson River, comprising approximately 1,900 acres, and ten parks in New York State. There are approximately 50,000 acres of the Palisades Interstate Park in New York, which, when combined with the acreage in New Jersey, brings the total of the park in both states to approximately 52,000 acres.

Along with acquisition of park lands, the commission adopted a policy of providing a maximum of recreational facilities for the public. Facilities for picnicking, fishing, boating, camping, horseback riding, hiking, swimming, soft ball, and other field games are available. In winter, there are skiing facilities for the novice and the more advanced skiers, competitive day and night ski jumps on a 50-meter hill, and skating.

Two major public recreation areas have been completed in the Bear Mountain–Harriman section of the park—New Sebago Beach and the Anthony Wayne development. The latter is adjacent to the Palisades Interstate Parkway, about three

*Prepared by A. K. MORGAN, General Manager, Palisades Interstate Park Commission.

miles west of Bear Mountain. The two new facilities can accommodate 20,000 people at one time. Plans for additional recreational areas have been completed, and construction will go forward as soon as appropriations are available.

The Palisades Interstate Parkway is a dual, scenic drive, which extends from the George Washington Bridge north along the crest of the Palisades, then northwest across Rockland County and enters the Harriman section of the Palisades Interstate Park in the vicinity of the present Tiorati Brook Road. It continues in a northerly direction through a narrow valley, with mountains on either side, until it reaches the Anthony Wayne area in the heart of the Harriman section. Here it divides, one branch extending east to the Bear Mountain Bridge Circle—the other west to Central Valley and New York Route 17.

The New Jersey section of the Parkway, eleven miles in length, has been completed. In New York thirteen miles have been finished, and the remaining eighteen will be completed by 1958.

OFFICERS OF THE COMMISSION, 1955

GEORGE W. PERKINS, *President*
ALBERT R. JUBE, *Vice-President*
LAURANCE S. ROCKEFELLER, *Secretary*
CATESBY L. JONES, *Treasurer*
A. K. MORGAN, *General Manager*

COMMISSION HEADQUARTERS

Administration Building, Bear Mountain, New York

THE INTERSTATE OIL COMPACT COMMISSION*

THE Interstate Oil Compact Commission has continued its growth during 1954 and 1955. Enabling legislation has been passed in the states of Arizona, Nevada, South Dakota, and Wyoming, and these states are now full members of the commission. Arizona and Nevada formerly were associate members and with the discovery of oil became eligible for full membership.

The commission is now composed of twenty-six member states, and four associate member states. Two provinces of Canada and two countries of South America send official observers.

During 1954, construction of a new, modern building was completed for the commission's headquarters offices. The money and ground for this building were provided by the State of Oklahoma; the building was deeded to the commission for so long as it is used for the commission's purposes.

In 1955 a number of states either passed new oil and gas conservation legislation or amended their laws to improve their present conservation measures.

All of the member states have again signed the Interstate Compact to Conserve Oil and Gas for another four-year extension, from September 1, 1955, to September 1, 1959. Bills are now pending in Congress for its consent to such extension, and unanimous approval already has been given by the Senate.

Committee Activities: The standing committees of the commission have continued studies of matters affecting oil and gas conservation and have continued to keep the commission advised on them.

All of the oil producing states now have state secondary recovery committees working in cooperation with the Secondary Recovery Division of the commission in securing and publishing information on improved oil recovery in each state.

The Legal Committee has continued its study of oil and gas conservation laws and related court decisions.

The Engineering Committee is revising its 1941 report on engineering principles in the production of oil.

Experts in the individual fields regularly appear before all of the committees to assist in their studies of conservation.

Educational Activities: The commission is continuing its educational program in oil and gas conservation. Several pamphlets on the subject are published each year.

Well over a half-million copies of two pamphlets published in 1954 have been distributed. One, "Oil for Today and for Tomorrow," has been listed in teachers' guides as an aid in geology and engineering courses, and is being used in a large number of schools and universities.

*Prepared by LAWRENCE R. ALLEY, Assistant Executive Secretary, Interstate Oil Compact Commission.

"Oil and Gas Production," published by the commission, is being used as a text in several schools on oil and gas law.

A film produced by the commission several years ago is still being shown extensively throughout the nation. It is used both by schools and industry to illustrate the advantages of oil and gas conservation.

The library in the headquarters office has been enlarged, and plans are pending to attempt to secure listings of all books and pamphlets on oil and gas conservation and their locations, to be of further service to students and others interested in conservation.

The staff of the headquarters office is available to any state, whether or not a member of the commission, to render any service possible, and it is always eager to assist in any way.

OFFICERS OF THE COMMISSION, 1955

GOVERNOR WILLIAM G. STRATTON of Illinois, *Chairman*

MAURICE ACERS, Texas, *First Vice-Chairman*

JOHN R. MARCHI, Montana, *Second Vice-Chairman*

EARL FOSTER, *Executive Secretary*

COMMISSION HEADQUARTERS
900 Northeast 23rd Street, Oklahoma City 5, Oklahoma

PORT OF NEW YORK AUTHORITY*

THE Port of New York Authority is a self-supporting corporate agency of the states of New Jersey and New York. Operating without burden to the taxpayer, it was created in 1921 by treaty between the two states to deal with the planning and development of terminal and transportation facilities and to improve and protect the commerce of the Port District.

The Authority's Lincoln and Holland tunnels and George Washington Bridge spanning the Hudson River, and its Bayonne and Goethals bridges and Outerbridge Crossing connecting Staten Island and New Jersey, join the states into one vast industrial, residential and recreational area.

The bi-state agency's marine terminal facilities are Port Newark and the Hoboken-Port Authority Piers in New Jersey and the Port Authority Grain Terminal and Columbia Street Pier at Gowanus Bay, Brooklyn. It also operates La Guardia Airport and New York International Airport in New York City and Newark Airport and Teterboro Airport in New Jersey. Its inland terminals include the Port Authority Building at 111 Eighth Avenue, Manhattan, housing the Union Railroad Freight Terminal; the New York Union Motor Truck Terminal; the Newark Union Motor Truck Terminal, largest in the world; and the world's largest bus terminal, the Port Authority Bus Terminal in Manhattan.

To September 30, 1955 the Authority

has issued bonds for financing and refunding purposes totaling $910,301,000, of which $303,555,000 are outstanding. Its investment in its seventeen facilities totals more than $530 million.

Charged by statute with the protection of port commerce, the Authority appears before such regulatory bodies as the Interstate Commerce Commission, the Civil Aeronautics Board and the Federal Maritime Board. It maintains trade promotion offices in New York, Chicago, Cleveland, Washington and Rio de Janeiro, Brazil.

New York International, La Guardia and Newark airports are operated by the Authority under long-term leaseholds from the cities of New York and Newark, respectively. Since assuming responsibility for them, as well as Teterboro Airport, the agency had spent or committed about $108 million by the end of 1954 on improvements at its regional airports.

In February, 1955, the Port Authority announced plans for a $60 million passenger terminal development at New York International Airport, a "Terminal City" of ten terminal buildings capable of accommodating 140 aircraft at one time. Construction of the development, within a 655-acre central landscaped oval, was to begin in the fall of 1955, and the first buildings, an International Arrival Building and two Airline Wing Buildings, will be completed early in 1957.

At Port Newark, also under lease from the City of Newark, the Authority had spent or committed by the end of 1954 over

*Prepared by LEE K. JAFFE, Director of Public Relations, Port of New York Authority.

$20 million on new and rehabilitated facilities.

In 1952, the Port Authority leased the government-owned Hoboken Piers for a fifty-year term under an agreement with the City of Hoboken and the United States Maritime Administration. The Authority in 1954 leased the Hoboken facility to the American Export Lines, Inc., for fifteen years. The terminal is being improved at a cost of $17 million to include by the end of 1956 two new piers of the most modern design.

Two miles of Brooklyn's choice waterfront, one of the most important port areas in the world, will be rebuilt by the Port Authority in the greatest marine terminal development program ever undertaken in the New York-New Jersey Harbor. The improvement program, announced in September, 1955, is made possible by the bi-state agency's purchase of the properties of the New York Dock Company which extend south of the Brooklyn Bridge.

The existing piers, ranging in age from 36 to 65 years, handle a fourth of the port's general cargo. They comprise a third of the deep-water general cargo piers in Brooklyn and an eighth of such facilities in the entire port.

Ground was broken in Manhattan in 1952 for a $100 million Third Tube of the Lincoln Tunnel. When completed in 1957, it will increase by 50 per cent the annual capacity and will double the peak-hour capacity of the Lincoln Tunnel in the preponderant direction of traffic.

Early in 1955 a $400 million program of bridge and arterial construction over the next five years was recommended in a Joint Report on Arterial Facilities in the New Jersey-New York metropolitan area by the Port of New York Authority and the Triborough Bridge and Tunnel Authority. The report also recommends that extensive connecting highways be constructed beyond the immediate approaches to the proposed bridge projects.

The Port Authority Commissioners, six from each state, are appointed by the Governors of New Jersey and New York. They serve without pay for overlapping terms of six years.

OFFICERS OF THE AUTHORITY, 1955

DONALD V. LOWE, Commissioner from New Jersey, *Chairman*
HOWARD S. CULLMAN, Commissioner from New York, *Honorary Chairman*
BAYARD F. POPE, Commissioner from New York, *Vice-Chairman*
EUGENE F. MORAN, *Executive Director*

COMMISSION HEADQUARTERS

111 Eighth Avenue at 15th Street, New York 11, New York

DELAWARE RIVER PORT AUTHORITY*

THE Delaware River Port Authority is the public corporate instrumentality of the Commonwealth of Pennsylvania and the State of New Jersey, created by a compact that was approved by Congress in 1952. The Authority succeeded the old Delaware River Joint Commission, which operated and maintained the Delaware River Bridge between Philadelphia and Camden—now renamed the Benjamin Franklin Bridge.

The area over which the Authority has jurisdiction is defined in the compact as all the territory within the counties of Delaware and Philadelphia, in Pennsylvania, and all within the counties of Atlantic, Burlington, Camden, Cape May, Cumberland, Gloucester, Ocean and Salem in New

*Prepared by WILLIAM A. GAFFNEY, Public Relations Aide, Delaware River Port Authority.

Jersey. The district includes the ports of Philadelphia, Chester and Marcus Hook, Pennsylvania, and Camden, Gloucester and Paulsboro, New Jersey.

Although only three years old, the Authority is well-advanced in construction of a new vehicular suspension bridge between Packer Avenue, South Philadelphia, and Gloucester City, New Jersey, to be called the Walt Whitman Bridge. Work was begun in August, 1953. When completed in mid-1957, this structure, costing $90 million will provide another link between the two states in an area familiarly known as the Delaware Valley, which has had marked industrial growth in recent years. The new span also will provide a measure of relief for patrons of the existing bridge, which in 1954 carried almost 31 million vehicles. This count was exceeded only by the Triborough and George Washington bridges in New York.

Another development of major importance to the Delaware Valley was the Authority's recent application to the Pennsylvania legislature for permission to build another river crossing, to replace the outmoded and overly congested Tacony-Palmyra Bridge in the northeast section of Philadelphia. This crossing has become a hindrance to motor vehicle traffic and is proving detrimental to further development of the Delaware River port, since it has a draw that must be opened and closed for ship passages, which are increasing. The Authority plans to erect a seven-lane, high-level bridge that will end the present delays to motorists and sea-going shipping. The costs will range between $25 million and $60 million, according to the length of the approaches. As in the case of the Walt Whitman Bridge, no appropriation for the replacement for Tacony-Palmyra is requested of either Pennsylvania or New Jersey, the financing of both being the responsibility of the Port Authority; the credit of neither state is involved.

Early in 1956, the Authority will have the results of an extensive survey that is now being made for it by an engineering firm concerning a Southern New Jersey Mass Transportation System. The survey, authorized in August, 1954, will cost a maximum of $325,000 and will cover a 2,000-square mile area. The Authority now owns a high-speed rail transit line running across the Benjamin Franklin Bridge from central Philadelphia to central Camden.

Charged by statute with development and improvement of the Delaware River as a highway of commerce, the Authority's Port Development Department maintains offices in New York, Pittsburgh and Chicago which provide information on the facilities of the Port of Philadelphia to potential customers. It also has a traffic bureau which provides protection for port interests in litigation involving rates, rebates or other matters. Its statistical and research departments compile information of many types for the convenience of public and civic agencies and individuals.

The Port Authority consists of sixteen commissioners, eight from Pennsylvania and eight from New Jersey, who serve without compensation. Six of the eight Pennsylvania commissioners are appointed by the Governor with the advice and consent of the Senate for terms of five years; the remaining two, the Auditor General and State Treasurer, are ex-officio. The New Jersey commissioners are appointed by the Governor with the advice and consent of the Senate for terms of five years.

OFFICERS OF THE AUTHORITY, 1955

WELDON B. HEYBURN, Pennsylvania, *Chairman*
J. WILLIAM MARKEIM, New Jersey, *Vice-Chairman*
JOSEPH K. COSTELLO, *Executive Director*

AUTHORITY HEADQUARTERS
Administration Building, Bridge Plaza, Camden, 2, N. J.

DELAWARE RIVER JOINT TOLL BRIDGE COMMISSION*

DELAWARE River Joint Toll Bridge Commission was established in December, 1934, by legislation enacted by the Commonwealth of Pennsylvania and the State of New Jersey, approved by Congress on August 30, 1935. Its territorial jurisdiction, as defined by supplemental agreements between the two states, extends along the Pennsylvania and New Jersey banks of the Delaware River from the New York-New Jersey state boundary, on the north, to the Philadelphia-Bucks County boundary line and its extension across the

river to New Jersey, on the south.

The commission fulfills a dual function.

First, as successor to the "Joint Commission for the Elimination of Toll Bridges over the Delaware River between Pennsylvania and New Jersey," it operated and maintained for the states sixteen bridges that its predecessor had purchased from private owners and had freed of tolls. Funds for the operation and maintenance of fourteen of these free bridges (two subsequently having been declared unsafe and closed to all traffic) are provided by the two states in equal amounts, after approval of the budget by the fiscal officers of New Jersey.

*Prepared by ALEXANDER R. MILLER, Chairman, Delaware River Joint Toll Bridge Commission.

Second, in accordance with its legislative mandate, the commission plans, finances, constructs and collects tolls for such additional bridge crossings and approaches as it may deem essential to the public welfare. The commission in no manner pledges the faith or credit of either of the states; the toll projects are self-supporting. The commission has issued bonds totaling $29,500,000 for construction of toll bridges and auxiliary facilities. As of December 31, 1954, the value of outstanding bonds amounted to $28,924,000.

In the planning, designing, locating and construction of its toll bridges, the commission has collaborated closely and constantly with the highway departments of both states. The decisions for the locations of the facilities were made after exhaustive surveys, which were studied by all interested departments of the state and national governments, and after the highway departments had determined that construction of new feeder roads was in the public interest.

By the construction and operation of five toll bridges and the operation and maintenance of fourteen free bridges, the commission has made an important contribution in developing transportation, commerce, recreation and industry within its territory. Although there are no immediate plans for additional river crossings, the commission is constantly studying plans for future development.

In 1952 the commission completed the rebuilding and improvement of the Pennsylvania approach to the Easton-Phillips-burg Toll Bridge, originally opened to traffic on January 17, 1938. The improvement made possible the more expeditious and safe movement of vehicular traffic through the U. S. Route 22 section of the heavily industrialized Lehigh Valley.

The Trenton-Morrisville Toll Bridge, opened to traffic on December 1, 1952, was the second structure built by the commission. Connecting the Trenton Freeway and the Morrisville By-Pass on U. S. Route 1, it provides a route for through traffic that avoids the narrow, heavily congested city streets of both communities, thereby reducing traveling time to a minimum and increasing safety.

The commission's building program was completed in December, 1953, with the opening of the Portland-Columbia, Delaware Water Gap and Milford-Montague toll bridges. For the first time, the recreational areas of northern New Jersey and northeastern Pennsylvania were linked by high-speed facilities capable of carrying modern passenger and commercial vehicles.

The commission is composed of ten commissioners. New Jersey appoints five, each of whom serves for a term of three years. Pennsylvania appoints two for indefinite terms, and Pennsylvania's Secretary of Highways, Treasurer and Auditor General are ex-officio members.

OFFICERS OF THE COMMISSION, 1955
ALEXANDER R. MILLER, Pennsylvania, *Chairman*
LESLIE BROWN, New Jersey, *Vice-Chairman*

COMMISSION HEADQUARTERS
Administration Building, Morrisville, Pa.

PROBATION AND PAROLE COMPACT*

STATE PROBATION and parole officers long have recognized that rehabilitation of persons convicted of crime frequently can be facilitated by transfer of a parolee or probationer to a jurisdiction where conditions for successful readjustment are more favorable. Formerly, without a binding interstate agreement, thousands of such persons lived outside the state of their offense, free from enforceable supervision.

The Interstate Compact for the Supervision of Parolees and Probationers was de-

*See page 13 for a description of the Parole and Probation Compact Administrators' Association.

veloped to answer this need, and every state is now signatory. It supplies essential protection to the public by providing legal means and administrative machinery for maintaining supervision of transferred offenders under the terms and conditions of the compact.

As an administrative arrangement among the states, the compact serves many practical purposes. It serves the negative function of facilitating capture of criminals who have violated the terms of their freedom. It performs the positive one of encouraging rehabilitation by permitting transfer to a receptive environment. The compact calls for interstate cooperation along a wide front in the fields of probation and parole. It provides a simple method of granting and controlling interstate transfers of probationers and parolees.

The instrument continues to meet without difficulty all court tests of its validity. During the last two years the Supreme Courts of Louisiana and Mississippi upheld the compact, bringing to seven the total of favorable decisions in state courts of last resort. Favorable decisions also were handed down in the lower courts of Florida, Idaho, New York and North Carolina. No new cases have arisen in the federal courts, but earlier federal decisions have been favorable, and the United States Supreme Court has always refused to review such compact cases as have been brought before it.

The so-called "out-of-state incarceration" amendment to the compact now has been ratified by four states—Connecticut, Idaho, New Jersey and Utah. Rules, regulations and model forms have been developed to implement this amendment, under which it is possible to avoid expensive returns of violators by having them incarcerated in the receiving state, which acts as agent for the sending state. This amendment is operative only among those states which have specifically ratified it.

Although Congress has not yet taken definitive action to permit it, there is reason to believe that the fairly near future may see participation in the compact by the United States territories and possessions and the District of Columbia. The compact administrators have gone on record as favoring such an extension.

Relationships between the compact administrators and federal agencies continue to improve. The United States Parole Board has revised its rules regarding parole to state detainers, and the Attorney General of the United States has appointed two representatives to serve as advisory members of the compact administrators' association.

During 1954–55, the administrators changed the name of the organization to the Parole and Probation Compact Administrators' Association, revised the official forms used under the compact, and contributed toward the Council of State Governments' publication of a 1955 edition of the *Handbook on Interstate Crime Control*. The administrators recommended for state adoption an act permitting deputization of out-of-state agents for the return of violators. The act provides the statutory authority needed in some states for participation in the association's money-saving "cooperative return plan," which eliminates duplications in long distance trips by permitting agents of one state to return violators for another.

The association was one of the groups instrumental in the development of the Interstate Compact on Juveniles, promulgated in 1955. This compact permits interstate supervision of delinquent juveniles, and provides for the return of escapees, absconders and non-delinquent runaways. It also authorizes the making of supplementary agreements for the institutionalization of special types of juveniles, such as psychotics and defective delinquents. As of June, 1955, the juvenile compact had been adopted by California, Maine, Missouri, New Hampshire, New Jersey, New York, Tennessee, Utah, Washington and Wisconsin.

THE SOUTHERN REGIONAL EDUCATION BOARD*

THE Southern Regional Education Board during 1954–55 improved its research services, achieved major results under several Memoranda of Agreement, strengthened its relations with the constituent legislatures, and maintained the well known contract-for-services pro-

gram. It reorganized its staff to accommodate these developments, allowing for units devoted to university studies and to the encouragement of interstate arrangements to expand mental health training and research. At its 1955 meeting the board favored an amendment to the Southern Regional Education Compact to increase board membership to five from each constituent state and welcomed Delaware as the fifteenth participant, pending approval

*Prepared by REDDING S. SUGG, JR., Publications Associate, Southern Regional Education Board.

by the legislatures of the states already participating.

Most notable achievements under Memoranda of Agreement were the Southern Regional Program of Graduate Education in Nursing, the cooperative graduate summer sessions in statistics, and the Southeastern Interlibrary Research Facility. Following several years of studies and conferences, the board and six universities obtained grants from two foundations to help start master's programs in nursing and provide graduate fellowships at the cooperating schools, and to finance a "regional seminar" conducted by the board in which the several programs are coordinated. In statistics, three universities joined the board in offering a series of graduate summer sessions, held in rotation on the campuses of the universities, for which internationally distinguished faculties are assembled. Two such sessions have been held, and a third is scheduled for the summer of 1956. The interlibrary facility is designed to promote cooperative use and development of research materials at six Georgia-Florida universities, which may be joined by others.

The scope of the board's work in the academic fields may be suggested by reference to its publications. Generally speaking, these are surveys of needs and resources leading to recommendations as to the region's requirements for new schools and programs, for expansion of existing ones, and related questions. During the biennium the board published materials relating to graduate work in city planning, forestry, marine sciences, veterinary medicine, political science, recreation, special education and architecture.

Since 1953 the board has conducted a number of large-scale studies and surveys in addition to those concerning particular academic fields. One has produced college and university enrollment projections for each of the states in the compact; the data are periodically revised and distributed as an aid to states and institutions in planning their programs of higher education. Another resulted in the first comprehensive, classified listing of graduate doctoral programs offered by southern universities, a document which will also be revised periodically.

The most extensive of the board's studies

was requested by the 1953 Southern Governors' Conference in line with recommendations prepared by the Council of State Governments—for interstate cooperation to overcome deficiencies in mental health training and research which hamper state mental health programs. Each of the sixteen states of the Southern Governors' Conference surveyed its needs and resources, chiefly with respect to training and research in psychiatry, clinical psychology, psychiatric nursing and psychiatric social work. The results were brought to a regional conference at which specific recommendations for interstate projects were derived. At its 1954 meeting the board recommended, and the Southern Governors' Conference subsequently agreed, that the Southern Regional Council on Mental Health Training and Research be formed. This group, whose work will be supported by special appropriations from the participating states, advises the board staff on implementation of the survey recommendations.

Annually since 1952 the board has held the Legislative Work Conference on Southern Regional Education, to which the Governors of the participating states appoint delegations of key legislators. They review the entire regional education activity and, on the basis of committee work, express their views and recommendations to the board. At the request of the fourth Legislative Work Conference, the board established a permanent Legislative Advisory Council, with membership to include two legislators from each state in the compact.

Meanwhile, three classes of "regional students" were graduated under the contracts in medicine, veterinary medicine, dentistry and social work. A total of about 700 degrees have been granted. For 1955–56, about 1,042 students are enrolled at eighteen schools of the region under the contracts; about $1,364,550 will be paid by the students' home states to the receiving institutions, where the students are treated as residents.

The 1955 Southern Governors' Conference placed the board in a new field and in a somewhat different role when it requested it to make the necessary preliminary studies and hold a regional conference on the industrial potentials of nuclear energy in the South. As suggested by the Governors, this conference is expected to include leaders from education, industry, state governments, and the Atomic Energy Commission.

OFFICERS OF THE BOARD, 1955–56

LeRoy Collins, Governor of Florida, *Chairman*

State Representative GEORGE PAYNE COSSAR, Charleston, Mississippi, *Vice-Chairman*
M. T. HARRINGTON, Chancellor, A. and M. College of Texas System, *Secretary-Treasurer*

JOHN E. IVEY, JR., *Director*

BOARD HEADQUARTERS

881 Peachtree Street, N. E., Atlanta, Georgia

WESTERN INTERSTATE COMMISSION
FOR HIGHER EDUCATION*

CALIFORNIA, Washington and Alaska ratified the Western Interstate Compact for Higher Education during their 1955 legislative sessions, to make a total of ten western states and one territory cooperating for higher efficiency in higher education. The compact was formulated by the Western Governors' Conference in 1949, and became effective in 1951 when ratified by five states—Colorado, Montana, New Mexico, Oregon, and Utah. Subsequently Arizona, Idaho, and Wyoming ratified the compact.

The compact is designed to encourage efficient use of existing graduate, technical and professional facilities in the West. It is entirely permissive, allowing states to work out mutually advantageous interstate arrangements for the education of students in these high cost fields.

The task of the Western Interstate Commission for Higher Education, created under the compact, and of its staff, is two-fold: to undertake studies of needs for professional and graduate educational facilities in the region, reporting its findings to the Western Governors' Conference and to the legislatures of the compacting states and territories, and recommending uniform legislation dealing with problems of higher education in the region; and to negotiate and administer interstate arrangements for regional educational services.

The compact directs that first priority be given to the health sciences. Two surveys already are under way: one of dental manpower needs and training facilities, financed jointly by the commission, the Kellogg Foundation and the United States Public

Health Service; and one of mental health training and research needs and resources, financed by a grant from the Public Health Service (The National Institute of Mental Health). Both of these studies are guided by representative advisory committees.

Cooperative programs in medicine, dentistry and veterinary medicine permit states without professional schools to send their residents to professional schools in other compact states. The "sending state" pays a fixed sum for each student ($2,000 in medicine, $1,600 in dentistry and $1,200 in veterinary medicine) to the receiving institution, buying space in a "school away from home" and sharing in the support of expensive professional facilities. More than one hundred students crossed state boundaries during 1954–55 to attend professional schools elsewhere in the West under this program. State legislatures have expanded the program in each year since its inception.

The commission is made up of three members from each state, appointed by the Governor for staggered four year terms. At least one Commissioner from each state or territory must be an active educator in the field of higher education. The commission meets annually and elects a Chairman and Vice-Chairman. An Executive Committee, composed of one Commissioner from each state, provides direction and guidance to the staff, which is headed by an Executive Director.

Programs of interstate cooperation are not imposed "from outside" but grow out of the felt needs of the West, as expressed by those with responsibility for training and research at the graduate level. The commission seeks constantly to enlist the participation of the leaders of western higher education. The objective is not studies *per se*

---

*Prepared by HAROLD L. ENARSON, Executive Director, Western Interstate Commission for Higher Education.

but practical solutions to educational problems of mutual concern in the western states.

OFFICERS OF THE COMMISSION, 1955

FRANK McPHAIL, M.D., Director, Great Falls Clinic, Montana, *Chairman*

WARD DARLEY, M.D., President, University of Colorado, *Vice-Chairman*

HAROLD L. ENARSON, *Executive Director*

COMMISSION HEADQUARTERS

328 Norlin Library, Univ. of Colorado, Boulder

2

State-Federal Relations

RECENT DEVELOPMENTS IN STATE-FEDERAL RELATIONS

GOVERNMENT responsibilities have grown immeasurably during twenty-five years of rising population, economic growth and international difficulties. Currently, a long accretion of changes in the size, age distribution and needs of our population are compounding demands on governments. The growing dimensions of highway, urban, school and other problems all reflect complexity and change in society. In consequence, concern is focused as rarely before on the roles, relationships and efficiency of the several levels of the federal system.

The following pages review state-federal relations during approximately the last two years.

Table 1 on page 49 shows federal grants-in-aid totals by state for selected years in the last decade. Federal grant expenditures by major categories and the percentage of each category to the whole for the fiscal years 1952 and 1954 are shown in the following table. Reductions in most categories are more than counterbalanced by increases in federal aid for public welfare and highway purposes.

THE COMMISSION ON INTERGOVERNMENTAL RELATIONS

In June, 1955, the Commission on Intergovernmental Relations, established by the 83rd Congress, first session, completed the first official reappraisal of the relations between the national government and the states and their political subdivisions. In addition to its report, the commission pub-

FEDERAL GRANTS-IN-AID, FISCAL YEARS 1952 AND 1954
(In millions of dollars)

	Expenditures		Percentage to total	
	1952	*1954*	*1952*	*1954*
Public Welfare...	1,149	1,426	49.3	53.4
Education.......	293	277	12.6	10.4
Highways........	413	542	17.7	20.3
Health and Hospitals..........	114	88	4.9	3.3
Employment Security Administration.......	187	198	8.0	7.5
Other..........	174	137	7.5	5.1
Total......	2,329	2,668	100.0	100.0

Source: Bureau of the Census, *Compendium of State Government Finances in 1954*, Table 1.

lished a series of task force studies of significant areas of intergovernmental activity, particularly those involving grants-in-aid. This summary touches upon many of its findings and recommendations.

Given the many and increasing pressures for government activity, the commission noted the responsibility of all citizens and levels of government for maintaining a healthy, balanced federalism. Its report warned that nonuse of state and local initiative, as well as overuse of national authority in serving legitimate needs, can be harmful to the federal system.

Viewing a permanent division of public responsibilities between the states and the national government as inconsistent with the need for a flexible dynamic federalism, the commission observed:

The National Government and the States should be regarded not as competitors for authority but as two levels of government cooperating with or complementing each other in meeting the growing demands on both.

The commission offered the following general guide to allocate governmental responsibilities:

Leave to private initiative all the functions that citizens can perform privately; use the level of government closest to the community for all public functions it can handle; utilize cooperative intergovernmental arrangements where appropriate to attain economical performance and popular approval; reserve National action for residual participation where State and local governments are not fully adequate, and for the continuing responsibilities that only the National Government can undertake.

National Government

With the limits of national action increasingly a subject for legislative determination, the commission noted great need for restraint on the part of the national government in entering new fields or fields traditionally within the powers of the states and localities. Controls and other arrangements in interlevel programs affecting the initiative and autonomy of the smaller governmental units, the report asserted, should be reduced to a minimum, and efforts calculated to improve their role increased. It recommended creation of a new staff agency attached to the Executive Office of the President for continuous study and recommendations concerning the condition and efficiency of intergovernmental relations.

The commission suggested that national action is indicated:

(a) When the National Government is the only agency that can summon the resources needed for an activity. . . .
(b) When the activity cannot be handled within the geographic and jurisdictional limits of smaller governmental units, including those that could be created by compact. . . .
(c) When the activity requires a nation-wide uniformity of policy that cannot be achieved by interstate action. . . .
(d) When the State through action or inaction does injury to the people of other states. . . .
(e) When States fail to respect or to protect basic political and civil rights that apply throughout the United States.

Where federal action is indicated, either for services or regulation, the commission preferred, in general, joint action to national action alone. Concerning the field of regulation it suggested—subject to circumstances:

First, the fact that the National Government has not legislated on a given matter in a field of concurrent power should not bar State action.
Second, National laws should be so framed that they will not be construed to preempt any field against State action unless this intent is stated.
Third, exercise of National power on any subject should not bar State action on the same subject unless there is positive inconsistency.
Fourth, when a National minimum standard is imposed in a field where uniformity is not imperative, the right of States to set more rigorous standards should be carefully preserved.
Fifth, statutes should provide flexible scope for administrative cessions of jurisdiction where the objectives of the laws at the two levels are substantially in accord. State legislation need not be identical with the National legislation.

State Government

The commission believed that the success of the federal system rests heavily on the performance of the states. It found proof of state vitality in the fact that more than two-thirds of the costs of domestic government—in recent years an increasing share—is borne by states and their political subdivisions. In its view, however, this trend, as well as the need, form and degree of national participation, will be affected by the extent to which state and local governments develop and exercise their capacities.

The commission believed that most states would profit from basic revision of their constitutions. Many states, it added, could improve their system of representation, act to improve the efficiency of the legislature and reorganize to provide Governors with more adequate authority. It urged the development and greater use of techniques of interstate cooperation; fewer and stronger political subdivisions; more home rule; more extensive use of counties; and search for solutions to urgent metropolitan problems. It strongly recommended a broad-based and intensive effort in each state to examine and determine its own capacity to discharge greater governmental responsibility.

Fiscal Problems in the Federal System

The commission noted the need for larger revenues if state and local governments were to bear an increasing share of public responsibility. Although the national government could assist the states by moderating its own tax needs and by measures to strengthen and stimulate the economy, the commission's emphasis was on state self-help. It urged an easing of constitutional and statutory taxing and borrowing powers of state and local governments, a reappraisal of state fiscal policies, and review of tax sources and rates to determine possible avenues of additional revenue.

The commission considered complete elimination of overlapping taxes neither feasible nor desirable, but it would improve tax coordination to ease the impact of overlapping and, as federal taxes are lowered, would consider the reduction of overlapping. Other recommendations include a broad system of federal payments in lieu of property taxes to state and local governments and continued exemption of the interest on state and local bonds from federal taxes. The commission rejected subventions to equalize tax sources of the states but approved of equalizing factors in grant-in-aid formulas.

Grants-in-Aid

Grants were regarded by it as useful devices to begin or expand services considered primary responsibilities of state and local governments, to transfer activities from the federal to other levels and to compensate local governments for unusual burdens induced by federal operations. It observed that the grant device could be used to conserve state responsibility and it endorsed the use of conditional grants. "A grant," it declared,

. . . should be made only for a clearly indicated and presently important national objective. . . , should be employed only when it is found to be the most suitable form of national participation . . . and should be carefully designed to achieve its specified objective. . . .

The report recognized weaknesses in the grant system and recommended improvements. It noted that grants made two years in advance facilitated the state budgetary process. While rejecting block grants, it suggested as alternatives prescribing minimums for each program within broad functional areas—the balance to be expended within the area as the state

determines. The commission also observed that plans, audits and records required of the states for purposes of supervision may be so comprehensive as to lead to the undesirable result of transferring decision-making authority from the state to the federal agency.

Selected recommendations of the commission on individual programs are summarized below.

Agriculture

The commission favored greater use of state research facilities through grants or national-state contracts, consolidation of research grants to state experiment stations, and permission to use Morrill Act money for research. It recommended that apportionment of funds for agricultural extension and research give greater weight to factors of need, per capita farm income, farm population and the relative dependence of the state on agriculture. Matching formulas would be placed on a sliding scale based on state fiscal capacity. The commission also suggested increases in state and county contributions for extension activities. It would require that state legislation and state budgetary practice and procedure be followed in channeling agricultural grants to state agencies and land grant institutions.

The commission would place the soil conservation technical assistance program on a grant basis in any state submitting a plan and a pledge of financial support for an improved and extended program. It would place agricultural conservation payments on a matching-grant footing and, until then, would implement existing legislation which provides for state administration of payments. The commission recommended a determination of interlevel responsibility for agricultural inspection and grading.

Civil Aviation

The report recommended that airport planning in the current program be based on regional rather than state need, supported an inquiry into possible need for larger federal airport grants, and asked for clarification of intent regarding the distribution of grants between small and large airports. Broader participation by state and local officials in developing grant programs and airport plans also was suggested.

Civil Defense and Urban Vulnerability

The commission recommended allocating primary responsibility for Civil Defense to the national government, with states and local officials responsible for day-to-day planning and for adapting national policies to local conditions. It would increase national financial contributions to help defray the costs of training, administration and planning in states and critical target areas; authorize direct civil defense relationships between the national government and critical urban target areas; and encourage state and local participation in national planning to reduce urban vulnerability.

Education

Believing that the states and localities possess the necessary capacities, the commission urged vigorous and prompt action by them to fulfill their responsibility for general education. However, on a show of need together with a proven insufficiency of taxable resources in one or more states, it held that the national government would be justified in providing appropriate, temporary assistance in financing construction of school facilities—with safeguards against national interference in education programs.

It recommended that states act to extend the school-lunch program; approved commodity donations for as long as the national government holds surplus food stocks; and urged the gradual elimination of cash grants, to be replaced by state, local and family funds. It favored limiting grants for vocational education to categories, old or new, with clear and special national interest—other grants gradually to be eliminated.

Employment Security

Recommended changes affecting employment security include simplification of federal administrative controls on state employment security agencies, replacement of national by state fiscal controls where adequate to assure proper expenditures of federal funds, federal consultations with a broad range of interested state officials before changes are adopted that affect state programs, and provisions requiring that state requests and estimates concerning federal grants flow through established state executive and budgetary channels. The commission also suggested creation of a hearing board to advise the Secretary of Labor prior to decisions in conformity and compliance cases; national legislation extending coverage to employers of one or more persons; and periodic recommendations to the states concerning minimum standards for the amount and duration of benefits, eligibility and disqualification.

Highways

In supporting an expanded highway program, the commission recommended that grant increases reflect national responsibility for highways of major importance to security and civil defense and assure a balanced highway improvement program designed to serve a growing economy. It favored financing of the larger federal program on substantially a pay-as-you-go basis, primarily through increased motor fuel taxes, and opposed the use of federal funds for toll roads. Reduction in federal supervision incident to grant programs was recommended, as well as repeal of legislation requiring states to dedicate portions of specific taxes for highways.

Housing and Urban Renewal

The commission asserted that initiation and administration of public housing and related activities are responsibilities of states and local governments. Accordingly, it urged state guidance (as well as enabling legislation) and local action in developing and adopting effective over-all area plans; building codes, zoning laws and related regulations; and coordinated neighborhood conservation efforts. Where private and local public resources are inadequate, it urged considerably increased state activity to satisfy housing requirements—including the lending of financial and other assistance to localities.

It approved current federal assistance to state and local governments for slum clearance and urban renewal, metropolitan area planning and low-rent public housing, but recommended that national technical and financial assistance be administered on a state basis wherever comprehensive state legislation for public housing and slum clearance provides significant state financial participation. The commission urged states and local subdivisions to consider unifying community services through metropolitan planning authorities, financed and assisted by the states where localities are unable to meet their own planning needs. It also recommended that planning for slum clearance and public housing, at all levels of government, consider the problem of urban decentralization for defense.

Natural Disaster Relief

The commission would require that a state obligate itself and such political subdivisions as it chooses for a share of cash expenditure for disaster relief as a qualification for receiving federal assistance. Such state and local qualifying obligation would be at least "one-fiftieth of 1 per cent of the 3-year average of the total income payments of the people in the state during the most recent years reported"—the state alone to supply at least one-fourth of the full amount needed. Any state which had expended at least the qualifying amount within the previous twelve months would automatically be eligible for federal aid.

Natural Resources and Conservation

The commission recommended creation of a permanent advisory Board of Coordination and Review to deal with intrafederal and federal-state natural resources policy. It suggested that a comparable group or existing state agency be charged with similar responsibilities, including cooperation with federal agencies in planning, building and operating natural resource projects. One goal of these groups would be a balanced division of responsibility for activities in multipurpose, basinwide water resource development. The report suggested that capital costs of such projects be shared between states concerned and the national government according to benefits received, ability to pay and other factors.

Other recommendations would require federal agencies to give full consideration to views of state and local agencies before approving any federal water development projects; afford states an opportunity for greater initiative and responsibility in multipurpose, basin-wide development of water resources; and observe local inland water laws as broad general policy. The commission supported elimination of earmarking of certain state revenues as a condition of federal grants for restoration and management of wildlife resources, and would apply funds appropriated under reforestation provisions of the Clarke-McNary Act to cooperative forest management.

Also suggested were improvement and vigorous enforcement of state water pollution laws; federal technical and financial assistance as a stimulus to state and interstate pollution control agencies; and a study of the possible merits of federal financial assistance in temporary cooperative programs for construction of pollution abatement facilities.

Public Health

The commission recommended that special (categorical) health grants to states should taper off as goals are achieved, should foster adoption of improved disease-control measures, and should encourage demonstration of new public health methods. It suggested that general health grant programs strive for a national pattern of minimal standards of public health practices, operations and administration—such standards to be developed jointly by all levels of government with the advice of non-governmental groups.

All health grants, it held, should be allocated according to a uniform formula based on need factors; should provide for matching requirements varying with fiscal capacity; and should permit flexible administration—including, within limitations, the transfer of funds from one program to another.

As additional federal funds are made available, the commission would decentralize health research, where practical, to qualified state and non-public institutions.

Vocational Rehabilitation

The report recommended minimum levels of vocational rehabilitation services for all states as an added goal of the grant program. It suggested that states be permitted to assign the program to any agency administering a related operation, with the director of the rehabilitation program directly responsible to the head of the agency. It also suggested an advisory council for each state vocational rehabilitation agency.

Welfare

To equalize burdens the commission recommended new formulas for grants in support of all public assistance programs. In all cases the maximums in state expenditures in which the national government would participate would be expressed in terms of an average of all payments in each program, rather than in terms of payments to individuals. Matching requirements would vary according to state fiscal capacity.

In the case of old-age assistance, the commission believed it would be reasonable if states with the highest and lowest per capita income were required to support two-thirds and one-fourth respectively of allowable expenditures. As total expenditures for old-age assistance decrease, the commission would favor reductions in national contributions by an approximately equivalent amount.

Finally, the report of the Commission on Intergovernmental Relations suggested that the aid-to-dependent-children program be extended to needy children receiving foster care.

Civil Defense

Developments of the last two years affecting specific spheres of state-federal relations have covered a wide range, as indicated in the following pages on civil defense, social security, education, highways and other subjects.

Civil defense has been an area in which primary operating responsibilities have been lodged in state and local governments.

All except two states have the authority to complete civil defense compacts with other states for mutual aid and operations; thirty-eight have completed such compacts with one or more other states. State and local expenditures for civil defense in fiscal 1954 were $45 million, of which $8 million represented federal funds. Federal appropriations for fiscal 1954 and 1955 were $45 and $46 million respectively, of which $9 and $13 million were available for grants to the states and localities. Legislation to make state and local civil defense units eligible for donations of certain federal surplus property has passed the House and is pending in the Senate.

Social Security

For State and Local Employees

Social Security Act amendments of 1954 permit Old-Age and Survivors Insurance coverage for state and local employees previously ineligible by reason of membership in public retirement systems. Such employees, about 80 per cent of the total number, now can be covered, provided a majority in any public retirement system approves.

Arrangements extending coverage to the members of one or more public retirement systems have been completed in Alabama, Arizona, Kentucky, Maine, New Hampshire, Texas and Virginia. Arrangements to assure coverage for state and local employees who were made eligible by the 1950 amendments have been completed by forty-four states.

Employment Security

An act of the 83rd Congress earmarks federal employment tax collections for use in the employment security program. Tax collections in excess of state and federal administrative expenses will be used to build a $200 million reserve for loans to states for meeting unemployment compensation claims. Collections above those necessary to maintain the reserve will be returned to the states.

The 83rd Congress also made employers of four or more subject to the federal unemployment tax. It extended coverage to most federal employees under conditions set by the state in which they last worked —the federal government to reimburse the states for the costs. The act authorizes the states to extend experience-rating tax reductions to new and newly covered employers after one year of coverage, instead of three years as previously.

Vocational Rehabilitation

The 83rd Congress provided the basis of support for a greatly increased state program of vocational rehabilitation. A system of allotments to the states, rising from $30 million for fiscal 1955 to $65 million in fiscal 1958, replaced the open-end method of grant assistance. States, however, must expand their programs greatly to secure the maximum allotments. In August, 1955, a resolution of the Governor's Conference pledged support for an expanded vocational rehabilitation program.

Public Assistance

Temporary increases in the matching formulas, first provided in 1952 for payments to the states on behalf of the four public assistance programs, were extended to September 30, 1956 by the 83rd Congress. Extensions in Old-Age and Survivors Insurance coverage and increased benefits provided by 1954 amendments, as well as provision for an expanded vocational rehabilitation program, were expected ultimately to ease the state burden of old-age assistance.

HEALTH

The 84th Congress established a grant program to states requesting assistance in providing children and expectant mothers an opportunity for polio innoculations. The act requires states to submit plans, listing the procedures for making vaccinations available; stipulates that means tests shall not be applied; and permits the United States Surgeon-General to establish a scale of priorities for the several categories of eligibles. Amounts sufficient to buy vaccine for a third of unvaccinated eligibles, adjusted for variations in per capita income plus an additional 20 per cent for administration costs or the purchase of more vaccine, will be available to each state until February, 1956.

The 84th Congress authorized $1,250,000 in grants over three years for an integrated study covering all phases of the mental health problem. The study is to be directed by a non-governmental group or groups consisting of leaders in the mental health field. The Governors' Conference in August, 1955 endorsed a full scale national survey and report on mental illness.

A bill approved by the Senate and pending in the House would provide a new matching grant program of up to $30 million for each of the next three years. The funds would be used by qualified, nonprofit public or private institutions to construct facilities and purchase equipment for research concerning the major crippling and killing diseases.

The 83rd Congress amended the Hospital Construction and Survey Act (Hill-Burton) to cover public or other non-profit rehabilitation centers, nursing homes and hospitals for the chronically ill as well as diagnostic and treatment centers. Sixty million dollars was authorized for the new program for each fiscal year through 1957.

EDUCATION

Programs of assistance for constructing and operating schools in areas affected by federal activities, first provided by the 81st Congress, were liberalized and extended to June 30, 1956. The 83rd Congress also provided for the support of conferences to study educational needs, resources and problems in the separate states. The White House Conference on Education in November, 1955, was to consider and report on pressing problems in the field. Meantime, proposals for federal aid for expanded school construction were pending in Congress as it adjourned in 1955.

HOUSING

The Housing Act of 1954 authorized 35,000 new, low rent housing units for fiscal 1955 in connection with projects for slum clearance, urban redevelopment and urban renewal—a new category embracing rehabilitation and conservation. Full participation by local agencies required enactment of, or amendments to, existing state legislation. The 1955 act authorizes 45,000 new public housing unit starts for fiscal 1956 and establishes a loan fund for urban renewal programs—$200 million to be available for each of the fiscal years 1956 and 1957, with an additional $100 million to be made available at the direction of the President. It also permits loans for basic public works to states and localities otherwise unable to obtain reasonable financing rates. Small communities seeking to construct water, sewage and gas facilities will receive priority. Other provisions liberalize loan provisions for college housing and extend to September, 1956 the program to supply housing for military personnel in areas where reasonable rentals are unavailable.

HIGHWAYS

The Federal-Aid Highway Act of 1954 authorized expenditures of $700 million for each of the fiscal years 1956 and 1957, of which 45 per cent is allocated to the primary rural system, 30 per cent to the secondary and 25 per cent to the primary urban system. Each state can shift allotments for one aid system to others, provided no system gains or loses more than 10 per cent. An additional $175 million was authorized for each fiscal year for the national system of interstate highways.

The act directed the Secretary of Commerce to make a comprehensive study of highway financing and the cost of completing all highway systems. Done in cooperation with highway departments of the states, the resulting "needs" study ("Needs of the Highway Systems, 1955–84," House Document No. 120, 84th Congress, first session) supplied much basic data for studies and recommendations subsequently submitted to the President by a Special Committee on Highways of the Governors' Conference, the President's Advisory Committee on a National Highway Program (Clay Committee) and the Commission on Intergovernmental Relations.

The Senate in the 84th Congress, first session, approved authorizations of $900 million for the primary, secondary and urban systems in each of five years beginning with fiscal 1957. An additional $7.75 billion was approved for the interstate system during the same period. Like the Senate, the House Committee on Public Works rejected "administration" bills patterned on recommendations of the Clay Committee. The House committee reported a bill providing $725 million for the primary, secondary and urban systems in fiscal 1957 to be increased by at least $25 million annually through 1968. For the interstate system it would provide $24 billion over a twelve-year period. The bill included increases in excise taxes on fuels, larger tubes and tires and trucks, buses and trailers. All

measures failed, largely because of differences concerning methods of financing the programs.

The reports and the proposed legislation suggest substantial agreement for an expanded highway program, particularly on the interstate system. Other widely accepted views concerning the interstate network appeared to include major federal financing responsibility; use of undesignated portions of that system for urban radial and circumferential routes—in part to satisfy civil defense evacuation needs; and the use of limited-access features wherever traffic warrants. All major bills considered assume continuing state and local responsibility for actual construction, operation, maintenance and policing, as well as a large part of the financing of federal-aid highways.

WATER RESOURCES

Public Law 566, 83rd Congress, provides a basis for a federal-state-local cooperative program to conserve, develop, use and dispose of water on minor watersheds and sub-watersheds for purposes of flood prevention and agricultural phases of water management. The act offers technical and financial assistance to state and local organizations in developing integrated small watershed programs and works of improvement planned in them.

Public Law 130, 84th Congress, and H.R. 5881, still pending, also encourage greater state and local initiative, participation and responsibility for small water resource project development. The former authorizes loans to irrigation districts or other public agencies for financing major portions of the construction of distribution systems in authorized reclamation projects. The latter would extend loans and other assistance similar to those provided by Public Law 130 to the forty-eight states for a broader range of water management purposes.

The 83rd Congress created a St. Lawrence Seaway Development Corporation to construct, operate and maintain deep water navigation in United States territory in coordination with its Canadian counterpart. H.R. 660, approved in the House and before the Senate, would modify existing projects to provide controlling depths not less than 27 feet for connecting channels of the Great Lakes above Lake Erie.

S. 890, approved by the Senate and pending in the House, would strengthen the existing federal water pollution control program and place it on a permanent footing. Changes would increase technical assistance to the states; provide $2 million annually in grants to defray part of the cost of developing and administering the water pollution control programs of state and interstate agencies; and authorize grants to individuals and non-federal groups for research and training, as well as widen and intensify federal research activities. Federal enforcement procedure to secure abatement of interstate pollution would be modified, principally in permitting federal court action with prior consent of the state receiving polluted waters or, as under existing law, the consent of the state in which pollution originates.

OTHER DEVELOPMENTS

Public Law 159, 84th Congress, provides technical services and financial assistance to state, local and other groups for air pollution research programs. The 84th Congress also authorized airport development grants of $42.5 million for fiscal 1956 and $63 million in each of the subsequent three years. Apportionment among the states is based on population and territory.

A measure to limit the abuse of writ of habeas corpus in lower federal courts by prisoners convicted in state courts has been reported by a House committee. It has the support and approval of the Conference of Chief Justices, the National Association of Attorneys General, the Judicial Conference of the United States, and the Department of Justice. The bill would provide that any writ of habeas corpus entertained by a federal court must involve a substantial constitutional question not determined or raised previously in the state court proceeding for lack of proper opportunity, and, further, "which cannot thereafter be raised and determined in the state court by an order or judgment subject to review by the Supreme Court of the United States on writ of certiorari."

For federal consent action bearing on interstate compacts, see pages 18–19.

TABLE 1

FEDERAL GRANTS-IN-AID, BY STATE

(In thousands of dollars)

State	1944	1946	1948	1950	1952	1953	1954
Alabama............	$ 14,614	$ 12,546	$ 32,448	$ 44,296	$ 53,943	$ 56,398	$ 55,065
Arizona.............	6,885	5,542	13,389	17,000	19,413	20,516	21,060
Arkansas...........	11,542	9,062	29,752	41,684	38,159	43,058	39,227
California..........	96,801	86,166	154,064	227,313	232,465	293,774	309,272
Colorado...........	16,939	13,328	26,483	38,652	38,902	42,378	47,344
Connecticut.........	7,115	7,690	14,970	21,604	20,853	19,585	18,702
Delaware...........	2,275	1,694	3,176	4,621	4,896	5,481	4,661
Florida.............	19,285	16,069	36,064	47,539	53,877	50,136	53,946
Georgia............	19,994	17,788	38,543	59,989	67,271	72,534	73,598
Idaho..............	7,369	4,148	10,382	13,497	14,728	16,095	17,008
Illinois.............	56,502	46,512	79,312	104,086	105,500	115,228	113,910
Indiana............	24,072	17,368	34,904	47,444	41,774	47,112	45,775
Iowa...............	18,378	14,120	32,432	44,443	41,745	44,813	46,544
Kansas............	14,106	9,701	30,625	39,550	40,185	42,182	42,177
Kentucky...........	13,375	11,110	29,120	43,042	45,182	51,832	53,962
Louisiana...........	16,229	21,709	29,369	84,081	89,897	89,769	89,256
Maine..............	6,562	5,422	9,863	14,595	14,351	15,065	15,630
Maryland...........	12,833	7,383	15,246	21,834	20,585	21,337	21,515
Massachusetts......	27,365	26,390	43,454	61,152	61,646	71,752	77,277
Michigan...........	42,113	34,840	70,194	89,232	88,762	98,102	88,643
Minnesota..........	21,712	18,765	41,114	49,082	47,026	57,747	53,625
Mississippi.........	9,610	8,868	28,891	39,326	40,557	53,642	49,600
Missouri...........	27,499	26,768	59,117	85,492	87,714	99,165	111,776
Montana...........	5,806	5,483	12,520	17,931	17,352	20,822	19,081
Nebraska...........	9,448	9,352	19,091	23,112	22,724	24,111	21,294
Nevada.............	3,660	2,221	5,352	7,258	6,784	9,402	8,824
New Hampshire......	3,665	2,882	6,145	7,257	7,929	8,109	9,122
New Jersey.........	14,028	12,817	27,913	35,995	31,320	39,178	40,825
New Mexico.........	6,581	6,207	13,883	18,938	23,665	23,565	26,541
New York...........	53,952	50,912	97,969	134,319	152,491	166,136	179,766
North Carolina......	16,983	16,594	38,581	55,227	55,285	55,706	61,616
North Dakota.......	6,370	5,412	9,085	13,616	13,857	16,775	14,948
Ohio...............	47,755	36,415	61,892	85,394	87,744	92,000	107,101
Oklahoma..........	27,312	29,004	54,383	70,282	67,899	71,487	67,612
Oregon.............	13,958	10,589	22,324	26,612	30,328	33,613	35,988
Pennsylvania........	47,358	42,566	83,490	102,302	101,492	102,549	113,204
Rhode Island........	3,694	3,398	6,682	9,312	12,847	12,857	11,032
South Carolina......	12,460	11,027	24,110	32,871	32,915	35,391	39,155
South Dakota.......	5,512	4,379	11,055	14,771	15,923	19,999	18,690
Tennessee...........	16,515	15,167	39,340	58,495	48,100	60,923	61,809
Texas..............	52,206	44,263	102,151	133,225	132,391	138,010	147,511
Utah...............	11,338	6,392	13,143	15,408	17,001	21,409	21,549
Vermont............	1,919	2,092	4,962	6,187	5,728	7,738	7,855
Virginia............	11,230	8,876	22,689	25,834	29,270	32,701	36,769
Washington.........	27,408	24,650	43,310	49,579	55,342	54,521	62,394
West Virginia........	10,197	8,472	19,023	27,817	27,349	37,266	31,254
Wisconsin...........	19,034	15,440	32,636	50,918	45,629	52,650	57,496
Wyoming...........	4,688	4,018	8,065	12,841	17,953	15,412	16,597
Total—all states.	$926,252	$801,617	$1,642,706	$2,275,055	$2,328,749	$2,570,031	$2,667,606

Source: Bureau of the Census, *Revised Summary of State Government Finances: 1942–1950* and *Compendium of State Government Finances* (1952, 1953 and 1954).

TABLE 2

THE RELATIONSHIP OF
FEDERAL GRANTS-IN-AID TO STATE GENERAL EXPENDITURES,
TOTAL INCOME PAYMENTS, AND POPULATION, BY STATE

State	Federal grants-in-aid, fiscal year 1954(a) (thousands)	General expenditures, fiscal year 1954(b) (thousands)	Grants as per cent of expenditures	Total income payments, calendar year 1953(c) (millions)	Grants as per cent of income payments	Estimated population 7–1–53(d) (thousands)	Per capita grants
Alabama	$ 55,065	$ 253,876	21.7	$ 3,248	1.69	3,082	$17.87
Arizona	21,060	112,472	18.7	1,370	1.54	905	23.27
Arkansas	39,227	148,652	26.4	1,793	2.19	1,845	21.26
California	309,272	1,737,541	17.8	24,856	1.24	12,087	25.58
Colorado	47,344	187,234	25.3	2,367	2.00	1,456	32.52
Connecticut	18,702	191,930	9.7	4,744	.39	2,186	8.56
Delaware	4,661	60,668	7.7	825	.56	353	13.20
Florida	53,946	327,335	16.5	4,586	1.18	3,268	16.51
Georgia	73,598	339,996	21.6	4,245	1.73	3,567	20.63
Idaho	17,008	69,349	24.5	851	2.00	598	28.44
Illinois	113,910	649,395	17.5	18,800	.61	9,093	12.53
Indiana	45,775	393,842	11.6	7,584	.60	4,186	10.94
Iowa	46,544	259,663	17.9	3,954	1.18	2,587	17.99
Kansas	42,177	199,838	21.1	3,110	1.36	2,005	21.04
Kentucky	53,962	216,722	24.9	3,460	1.56	2,934	18.39
Louisiana	89,256	429,868	20.8	3,602	2.48	2,817	31.68
Maine	15,630	90,133	17.3	1,251	1.25	889	17.58
Maryland	21,515	254,296	8.5	4,719	.46	2,571	8.37
Massachusetts	77,277	523,495	14.8	8,880	.87	4,886	15.82
Michigan	88,643	791,849	11.2	13,723	.65	6,851	12.94
Minnesota	53,625	327,474	16.4	4,724	1.14	3,052	17.57
Mississippi	49,600	187,080	26.5	1,821	2.72	2,153	23.04
Missouri	111,776	325,849	34.3	6,768	1.65	4,056	27.56
Montana	19,081	74,999	25.4	1,037	1.84	618	30.88
Nebraska	21,294	98,615	21.6	2,065	1.03	1,358	15.68
Nevada	8,824	31,600	27.9	448	1.97	199	44.34
New Hampshire	9,122	50,314	18.1	854	1.07	527	17.31
New Jersey	40,825	397,007	10.3	10,771	.38	5,191	7.86
New Mexico	26,541	114,922	23.1	1,021	2.60	756	35.11
New York	179,766	1,512,227	11.9	32,871	.55	15,257	11.78
North Carolina	61,616	391,645	15.7	4,599	1.34	4,228	14.57
North Dakota	14,948	85,511	17.5	804	1.86	598	25.00
Ohio	107,101	714,018	15.0	16,840	.64	8,482	12.63
Oklahoma	67,612	301,123	22.4	2,986	2.26	2,220	30.46
Oregon	35,988	227,523	15.8	2,762	1.30	1,630	22.08
Pennsylvania	113,204	875,690	12.9	19,419	.58	10,675	10.60
Rhode Island	11,032	69,719	15.8	1,429	.77	831	13.28
South Carolina	39,155	256,832	15.2	2,403	1.63	2,199	17.81
South Dakota	18,690	70,826	26.4	895	2.09	645	28.98
Tennessee	61,809	275,212	22.5	3,948	1.57	3,280	18.84
Texas	147,511	667,611	22.1	12,279	1.20	8,397	17.57
Utah	21,549	90,135	23.9	1,108	1.94	750	28.73
Vermont	7,855	40,153	19.6	528	1.49	373	21.06
Virginia	36,769	294,086	12.5	4,829	.76	3,568	10.31
Washington	62,394	408,220	15.3	4,663	1.34	2,520	24.76
West Virginia	31,254	252,579	12.4	2,435	1.28	1,927	16.22
Wisconsin	57,496	357,791	16.1	6,023	.95	3,545	16.22
Wyoming	16,597	50,213	33.1	505	3.29	317	52.36
Total—all states	**$2,667,606**	**$15,787,128**	**16.9(e)**	**$268,803**	**.99(e)**	**157,522**	**$16.93(e)**

Source: Bureau of the Census, *Compendium of State Government Finances in 1954; Current Population Reports, Population Estimates,* Series P-25, No. 89, January 25, 1954. Percentages and per capita amounts are derived.

(a) Aid received from the federal government as fiscal aid or as reimbursement for performance of general government service, either for direct expenditure by the state or for distribution to local government. Excludes any amounts received for sale of property, commodities and utility services.

(b) All state expenditure other than liquor store and insurance trust expenditure.
(c) The income received from all sources during the calendar year by the residents of each state.
(d) Estimated total population excluding armed forces overseas.
(e) Average, all states.

3

State-Local Relations

STATE-LOCAL RELATIONS IN 1954–1955*

Two movements, at cross purposes with each other but both directed to the improvement of state and local government, continued to gain momentum during the biennium 1954–55. State legislative actions to meet the familiar demands for a greater degree of local self-government from the political subdivisions were about equally balanced by other actions extending the scope of state supervision and control of local affairs through requirements that local governments provide and maintain at least minimum standards of service for their citizens. A third important development was increased attention directed at intergovernmental relations at the state-local level.

COMMISSION ON INTERGOVERNMENTAL RELATIONS

Demands for a reappraisal of the federal system in the United States resulted in the establishment of the Commission on Intergovernmental Relations in 1953 to conduct an intensive study of national-state-local relationships. The Commission's report, transmitted to the President in June, 1955, was a monumental study of existing relationships, and it included positive recommendations to guide their future development.

The Commission recognized that the success of the federal system depended in large measure upon the performance of the states, since these units have the primary

*Prepared by GEORGE S. BLAIR, Educational Associate, Institute of Local and State Government, University of Pennsylvania.

responsibility for all government below the national level. State and local governments bear directly more than two-thirds of the growing fiscal burdens of domestic government, and their activities have experienced a faster growth than have the non-defense activities of the national government. Concerning state-local relations, the Commission was guided by a three-point philosophy in recommending a division of civic responsibility. First, it held, all functions that citizens can handle privately should be left to private initiative; second, governmental functions should be performed by the level of government closest to the community which can perform the function adequately; third, cooperative intergovernmental arrangements should be utilized, where appropriate, to attain economical performance and popular approval.

Although there is growing knowledge and understanding of the means available to strengthen state and local governments, the Commission emphasized an existing paradox: too many local governments, and not enough local government; this, it pointed out, bars an easy solution to the problem of state-local relations. The Commission placed the constitutional responsibility for the future development of local government in the states. It emphasized their responsibility to create local units of government that are effective for providing governmental services, and it supported a system of local government that achieves the traditional American goal of extensive citizen participation in the affairs of government.

In its guidelines for action, the Commission urged a fundamental review and revision of state constitutions to make sure that these documents provide for vigorous and responsible government rather than forbid it. Stronger and more effective government would result, the Commission believes, from more state leadership in some areas, more local home rule, fewer and stronger local governments, better utilization of counties, and the development of solutions for the crucial problems of metropolitan areas.

Growing interest in intergovernmental relations was also evidenced by the creation of various commissions on state-local relations, patterned more or less after the national Commission. Official study committees or commissions were created by legislative action in Oregon and West Virginia, and a legislative committee in Idaho will study state-local fiscal relationships in that state. The Connecticut Commission to Investigate the Relationship between the State and its Subdivisions, created in 1953, submitted its report in 1955, and the legislature in that state enacted positive legislation concerning five of the commission's eighteen proposals.

BROADENING HOME RULE

Progress on the road to greater home rule resulted during the biennium from continued and expanded use of constitutional home rule, flexible optional charter systems, and liberal legislative grants of municipal powers.

In the 1954 elections, voters in three states approved home rule amendments to their constitutions. A Georgia amendment authorized the legislature to provide by general law for the self-government of municipalities and to delegate its power to the advancement of that end. A Kansas amendment was permissive, looking toward increasing home rule in larger cities and toward some relief for the state legislature from its heavy load of local legislation. The amendment authorized the legislature to designate "urban areas" in counties and to enact laws giving such counties or areas power of local government and consolidation of local government. A Maryland amendment conferred the general powers of home rule on towns and cities

other than Baltimore, which already had such powers. This grant included the power to amend charters on matters relating to incorporation, organization, and government, without action by the legislature.

Constitutional home rule was also a major topic in legislative sessions of 1955. A special legislative session in Connecticut initiated a constitutional amendment which, if approved by the voters, will require legislative bills to be of general character, thus giving more local home rule. Similar movements were unsuccessful in four states. But home rule was strengthened in West Virginia by adoption of legislation permitting cities with special legislative charters to adopt home rule charters, and in Maryland by legislation implementing the home rule amendment adopted last year.

During the biennium, legislatures continued to act and receive requests for action in granting home rule charters to specific counties or municipalities. The voters of Baltimore County, Maryland, will be given the opportunity in November, 1956, to approve or reject a county charter prepared by a group of citizens elected in 1954. The charter would provide for an elected county executive, a county council of seven, and a county administrative officer appointed by the county executive, to administer the affairs of the executive establishment and the county solicitor. Voters in Dade County, Florida, will also decide in November, 1956, on the acceptability of a home rule charter for their county, which would create a metropolitan government for Miami and Dade County. This charter evolved from a study supervised by the University of Miami's Department of Government in 1954–55. The Pennsylvania General Assembly received in 1955 the report of the Metropolitan Study Commission of Allegheny County, appointed in 1953. The report recommended a home rule charter for the county, assigning to a new county government the various functions now performed by the municipalities. Voters in the City of Albany and Dougherty County, Georgia, defeated a proposal for city-county merger in November, 1954.

A new concept or theory of home rule has been evolving in Texas in recent years, with state courts upholding the position that powers available to the state legislature are, generally, available to the cities also. Under this doctrine, Texas cities and counties have the important initial power to act, subject only to veto by a general state law. Local governments have more freedom to take care of their own problems under this concept, and yet the state is not hampered in its control over municipalities where necessary in the interests of the state as a whole. The position of the Texas courts lends support to the basic approach recommended by the American Municipal Association in its *Model Constitutional Provisions for Municipal Home Rule*, published in September, 1953.

Other actions during the biennium included that of a growing number of cities taking advantage of opportunities granted them in states providing optional charter plans. In New Jersey, some thirty cities have taken some action under the optional municipal charter act passed in 1950. Enabling legislation to permit optional forms of county and/or city government was considered in a number of states, including Illinois, Oklahoma and Pennsylvania. The Home Rule Association of Massachusetts was organized to prepare home rule bills for the 1956 session of the legislature. In a number of states legislative acts and constitutional amendments were passed lengthening the terms of county officers, abolishing some county offices, raising salaries, and accomplishing other related results.

An important movement affecting the administrative organization of large cities spread to New York and Chicago during the biennium with the creation of a mayor's administrative officer, to supervise the administration of all or most city departments, boards and commissions. Luther Gulick was appointed the first city administrator of New York City and the Chicago City Council created the position of city administrator by ordinance. The addition of these two cities brought to eight the total of cities over 500,000 population with the city administrator plan.

The continued growth of and interest in home rule in 1954–55 seemed to stem in part from an increasing recognition that home rule not only strengthens local government but is a means of strengthening state government as well. When local matters can be handled by local action, state legislatures are freed to concentrate on matters of state-wide concern. This point was a central theme of a discussion of the model home rule proposals of the National Municipal League and the American Municipal Association at the annual meeting of the former in 1954 at Kansas City.

METROPOLITAN AREAS

Spectacular changes in population patterns and increasing citizen demands for governmental services have made modern metropolitan areas pose some of the most intricate aspects of state-local relations. Under the definitions of the U. S. Census Bureau, there were 172 standard metropolitan areas in 1955, each of which included a central city of 50,000 or more population and an urban fringe. A majority of the nation's population now lives in metropolitan areas, with the fringe area populations increasing at a much faster rate than the populations of the center cities.

The need for studies to provide a basis for state action to assist in dealing with problems of these areas was recognized increasingly during the past two years. The Governors' Conference in 1955 directed the Council of State Governments to make a study of the problems of metropolitan area government and to formulate recommendations for changes in local government organization in these areas, including desirable changes in state legislation. A second major study was being undertaken by the Government Affairs Foundation in New York City. It began with a thorough analysis of the needs for research in the field of metropolitan areas, an exploration of techniques to facilitate the conduct of research on a coordinated nation-wide basis, and an outline of certain research projects to be carried out. A third indication of interest was the establishment of an inter-disciplinary Center for Metropolitan Studies at Northwestern University.

In addition, the research efforts of individuals and small groups in the field of metropolitan problems continued to grow rapidly in number. Citizen groups displayed an active interest in metropolitan government as study commissions were created in cities throughout the United States. Typical study groups were those of Seattle, Boston, Toledo, Detroit, Flint (Michigan), and Hartford (Connecticut), all of which have been especially active during 1954–55.

A significant trend of the past few years has been the growing recognition of the county as a logical instrumentality of metropolitan government in many areas. Two outstanding examples of urban counties assuming responsibility for provision of governmental services are Los Angeles County, California, and Erie County, New York. In Louisville, Kentucky, it is expected that the 1956 legislature will be asked to create a metropolitan government for Louisville and Jefferson County, by making the boundaries of the two units coterminous, and a similar request regarding Portland and Multnomah County is expected to be submitted to the Oregon legislature in 1956.

There were a number of city-county arrangements during the biennium for joint provision of specific services. Voters of St. Louis and St. Louis County, Missouri, approved the creation of the Metropolitan St. Louis Sewer District in 1954, to replace numerous small operations in the area. This was the first successful attempt to join the areas in the performance of a governmental function since their separation in 1876. Voters in the same jurisdictions, in January, 1955, rejected a proposal to create a Metropolitan Transit District.

Legislative action in two states enabled counties to create urban districts outside incorporated areas to provide needed urban services. A California act prescribed a complete procedure for establishing county service areas; proceedings may be initiated by the County Board of Supervisors or by petition of 10 per cent of the registered voters of the area to be served. Under a North Carolina act, the first urban service districts established were fire districts, but the permissive law enables such districts to perform a wide variety of municipal functions.

In 1955, the Connecticut legislature enacted legislation permitting towns, cities, and boroughs to establish metropolitan districts, to provide certain municipal functions more economically and equitably. Legislation less broad in scope was passed in Arizona in 1955, permitting municipalities and counties to enter into agreements with school districts and other municipalities for the construction, development, maintenance and operation of recreational facilities. Voters in New York were to decide the fate of a proposed constitutional amendment in November, 1955, which would permit cities to contract debt for sewage disposal or drainage purposes in excess of their own needs so that adjoining municipalities could use the facilities.

A unique approach to the problems of providing adequate and economical services in urban areas was incorporated in two bills introduced in the 1955 session of the Pennsylvania General Assembly. One bill would permit the creation of joint service districts by small municipalities, for the joint provision of services to citizens. The joint service district would be governed by a board composed of members of the governing bodies of the participating municipalities.

The second bill would permit establishment of regional service districts by counties or parts of counties. These districts would be governed by a board of three representatives from each participating county, with two elected by the citizens of the county and one appointed by or from the county governing body. Again, this board would be directly responsible to the people and would have an official tie-in with the existing governmental body. The devices of establishing "weighted votes" and required "extra majorities" were permissive aspects of the proposed legislation, to give more democratic controls to the municipalities or counties participating in the districts.

FISCAL RELATIONS

Increasing public demands for more and better local governmental services of all types in recent years have necessitated legislation to permit a greater variety of local taxes to meet revenue needs. They also have resulted in increased payments of state aid to local governments. These two trends continued through the last biennium. State aid to local governments is discussed in the article that begins on page 57, but the rapidly growing adoption of non-property taxes by municipalities merits emphasis here.

Since the close of World War II, twenty-four states have expanded the taxing powers of all or a selected group of their municipalities. Municipalities have used this taxing power by adopting taxes on income, retail sales, admissions, alcoholic beverages, tobacco, gasoline, motor vehicles, private utilities, gross receipts, business licenses, hotel room rentals and other sources. These non-property tax levies by local governments do not imply a lesser use of the property tax, but rather the growing inadequacy of it alone to produce the needed revenues. It appears that both non-property taxes and state-aid dollars have become basic elements of contemporary and future local government finance in the United States.

During the biennium constitutional amendments were approved in a few states, and legislation was enacted in most states, to give local governments some relief from pressing financial problems. A 1954 amendment in Maine gave municipalities, regardless of size, the power to increase indebtedness from 5 per cent to 7.5 per cent of their last regular valuations. The bonded indebtedness of school districts was increased by amendments in 1954 from 5 to 10 per cent of assessed valuation in South Dakota, and from 6 to 10 per cent in Wyoming for purposes of erecting or enlarging school buildings; county school boards in Georgia may increase the 15-mill school tax to 20 mills under a referendum procedure established by a 1954 amendment. In 1955 Oklahoma increased the taxing power for school support. Legislation permitting municipal sales taxes was extended to all cities in Mississippi, enacted for all cities in Illinois, and for all cities over 75,000 in New Mexico. In California, 1955 legislation extended to counties the right to levy sales and use taxes. Illinois granted municipalities the power to levy two new taxes —a local retailer's occupation tax and a tax not to exceed 5 per cent on the gross receipts of utilities. A constitutional amendment permitting increases in local taxation will be submitted to West Virginia voters in 1956.

UNITS OF GOVERNMENT

The only significant change in the number of governmental units during the period under review was a sharp decrease in the number of independent school districts. Consolidation and reorganization of school districts continued throughout the United States, bringing a reduction from 67,346 districts in 1952, as recorded by the Census Bureau, to 59,631 in 1954,[1] a decline of 11 per cent. The greatest reduction in these two years occurred in Missouri, a drop of 35 per cent to 3,204 districts in 1954 from 4,891 in 1952.

CONCLUSION

This brief summary has by no means covered all of the many developments in state-local relations of the past two years. Developments in major problem areas have been pointed out, however, to indicate the direction these relations are taking in selected areas. There are many unsolved problems—as regards home rule, metropolitan areas, fiscal relations, and units of government. Yet as a whole optimism is justified concerning these aspects because of the increased attention devoted to them and the ingenuity of states in advancing solutions for them, in whole or in part.

For the future, it appears likely that additional states will establish commissions, patterned somewhat after the national Commission on Intergovernmental Relations, to study state-local relations. A cooperative pattern of state-local relations for provision of services has been established, and a greater degree of cooperation is emerging in state-local fiscal relations. Intergovernmental cooperation among more local governmental units has become possible under permissive legislation, as at least a partial solution to many problems of supplying adequate and economical services to citizens.

Governmental and fiscal problems of metropolitan areas can be expected to continue as major concerns of both state and local governments. Short-term palliatives for various aspects of intergovernmental relations

[1] A slightly different basis of figuring set the 1954–55 estimated total at 60,416. (See table on page 255, in the chapter on "State Public School Systems.")

continue to be required. But there is evidence of increasing search for long-range solutions that can be worked out to the mutual satisfaction of both levels of government.

REFERENCE WORKS

COMMISSION ON INTERGOVERNMENTAL RELATIONS, *A Report to the President for Transmittal to the Congress*, Washington, 1955.

WILLIAM ANDERSON and EDWARD W. WEIDNER, *State and Local Government in the United States*, New York, 1951.

WILLIAM ANDERSON and EDWARD W. WEIDNER, eds., *Intergovernmental Relations in the United States* (as observed in Minnesota), a series, Minneapolis, 1950—.

COMMITTEE ON STATE-LOCAL RELATIONS, Council of State Governments, *State-Local Relations*, Chicago, 1946.

J. CASS PHILLIPS, *State and Local Government in America*, New York, 1954.

PRESSLY S. SIKES and JOHN E. STONER, *Bates and Field's State Government*, 4th ed., New York, 1954.

ALLEN B. GOSNELL and LYNWOOD M. HOLLAND, *State and Local Government in the United States*, New York, 1951.

CLYDE F. SNIDER, *American State and Local Government*, New York, 1950.

W. BROOKE GRAVES, *American State Government*, 4th ed., Boston, 1953.

AUSTIN F. MACDONALD, *State and Local Government in the United States*, New York, 1955.

CLAUDIUS O. JOHNSON, *State and Local Government*, New York, 1950.

LANE W. LANCASTER, *Government in Rural America*, 2nd ed., New York, 1952.

STATE AID TO LOCAL GOVERNMENTS IN 1954*

I N fiscal 1954, the forty-eight state governments made payments to local governments totaling more than $5½ billion, or about as much as the total of all state government spending—both direct and intergovernmental—twelve years earlier. As shown by the chart on page 58, intergovernmental expenditure rose somewhat more rapidly than did state general revenue between 1942 and 1950, and has kept pace with general revenue since 1950.

Payments to local governments amounted to 30.4 per cent of all state expenditure in fiscal 1954, or 36.0 per cent of state general expenditure—i.e., excluding liquor store and insurance trust amounts.

NATURE OF STATE INTERGOVERNMENTAL EXPENDITURE

Although they include minor amounts of reimbursements for general government services locally performed, state payments to local governments primarily represent fiscal aid—including not only payments in the form of grants-in-aid but also local shares of taxes imposed and collected by the states, and amounts of federal aid received by the states and distributed to local governments. Accordingly, the following discussion uses the phrase "state aid" interchangeably with the slightly broader concept involving all state intergovernmental expenditure.

State governments may "aid" local governments in various ways other than by actual payment of money to them. Such aid, however, is not directly considered here. Thus, the definition stated above excludes the following:

1. Non-fiscal assistance by a state to local governments in the form of advisory or other services or aid in kind (e.g., free provision of commodities, textbooks, etc., or loan of equipment).

*Adapted from Bureau of the Census, *State Payments to Local Governments in 1952* and *Compendium of State Government Finances in 1954.*

2. Assumption by a state of direct operating responsibility for functions traditionally performed by local governments (e.g., direct maintenance by the State of North Carolina of a basic nine-month public school term and, in several states, provision of local streets and highways or of general relief).

3. Joint state-local activities involving state expenditure of the state's share of costs directly for goods, services or public assistance payments rather than in the form of payments to local governments.

4. Contribution by a state to trust funds it administers for the financing of retirement benefits to local government employees.

5. Shares of state-imposed taxes which are collected and retained by local governments.

The items above do not constitute state aid as here considered because no funds actually pass between a state and its local governments.

CLASSIFICATION OF STATE AID

By Type of Receiving Government

Five major types of local government are to be distinguished. These are:

1. Counties.

2. Cities, which include all incorporated places having powers of general government, thus including units known locally as villages, boroughs and towns (except in New England states and in New York and Wisconsin) as well as "cities."

3. Townships, which include units locally called "towns" in the New England states and in New York and Wisconsin.

4. School districts, which include only those units of school administration that have status as independent units of local government rather than as administrative segments of state, county, city or township governments.

5. Special districts, which include districts and authorities established for the performance of a single function or a desig-

nated combination of specific functions, and which have status as independent units of government rather than as administrative segments of state, county, city or township governments.

Certain state aids are distributed in such a manner that information is not available as to amounts going to particular types of governments. The Census Bureau reports $419 million of state aid in 1954 not allocable by type of receiving government.

School districts received a major fraction of all other state intergovernmental payments—$2,438 million. Additional amounts of state aid for school purposes, of course, were distributed to those county, city and township governments which operate public schools.

Ascertainable amounts of state payments to local units other than school districts amounted to $1,649 million for counties, $1,036 million for cities, $115 million for townships, and $21 million for special districts.

Individual state figures by type of receiving government appear in Table 4.

By Function

Most state payments to local governments are made available for certain specified functions and activities, although a little over one-tenth—$600 million in 1954 —represented aid for general local government support.

By far the largest segment of state aid is for local education purposes—$2,934 million in 1954, more than one-half of all state intergovernmental expenditure. Nearly one-fifth, or $1,004 million, was distributed for public welfare, and $871 million for local highways and streets. State fiscal aid for health and hospitals amounted to $126 million, and all other specified functions and purposes together accounted for $124 million.

Intergovernmental expenditure of individual states, by major function, is shown in Table 2.

By Source of Funds

There is widespread interest in sources for financing of state aid. However, no summary classification by source is attempted here, because of technical difficulties and the fact that data so presented might easily be misinterpreted.

Some items lend themselves readily to direct classification by source—e.g., a specific share of a state tax which is passed on to local governments, either directly as collected or after payment into a fund which is devoted solely to state aid. At the other extreme, of course, are grants payable from a state "general fund" fed by numerous revenue sources. An intermediate situation involves aid payable from a special fund which in turn is fed by two or more earmarked revenue sources. Aid

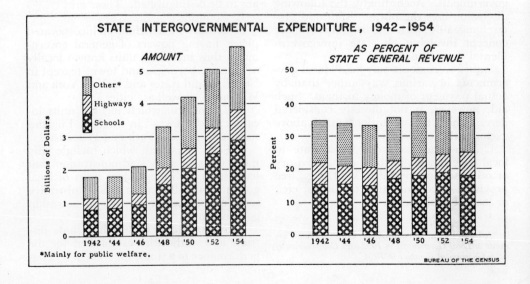

STATE INTERGOVERNMENTAL EXPENDITURE, 1942–1954

*Mainly for public welfare.

BUREAU OF THE CENSUS

amounts so payable are sometimes directly or indirectly determined by the amounts flowing into the fund, rather than—as is commonly true of "general fund" grants—by specific-amount appropriations. However, such resources lose their exact source identity when deposited to the fund.

There are, thus, serious technical obstacles to a valid statistical classification of aid amounts by source, other than one ending with a large category comprising "multiple source" items. Even more important, figures so classified would be subject to possible misinterpretation by tending to exaggerate interstate differences. For example, they would suggest a major difference, rather than only one of fund structure and accounting method, as between State A, where sales tax revenue is paid into a general fund from which various grants to local government are payable, and State B, where similar amounts of aid are payable directly from sales tax revenue as received or deposited into a special fund.

Such exaggeration of interstate differences could be avoided only by some procedure for statistical allocation of aid amounts paid from multiple sources, which in turn would involve questionable assumptions in many instances.

State Aid Formulas

Particular programs of state aid to local governments involve various means by which (a) the total amount available for a particular fiscal year or biennium is established; and (b) the shares payable to various individual governments are determined.

Setting of Total Amount

The amount of some items of state aid is set by a specific appropriation of such a nature that a particular total sum named will be distributed without diminution or modification.

At the other extreme are aid items whose total amount is not explicitly determined, or even limited, in advance. One example of this type is the distribution of a specified share of some particular state revenue source, with the actual current amount of aid determined by the yield of that source. Another example is the "open-end" authorization of whatever amount is needed to meet the requirements of a particular distributive formula.

Between the absolutely fixed and the completely indeterminate types of aid provisions are numerous gradations and combinations of methods. Thus, a specified share of some revenue source may be authorized for aid, but with the total sum for the current period limited also by a specific-amount appropriation. Again, a definite amount may be appropriated as a maximum, subject to reduction by the operation of a distributive formula or by administrative action.

Basis of Distribution

The bases for determining individual governments' shares of a particular grant or shared tax are also extremely varied.

The term "shared tax" has sometimes been applied strictly to specified portions of state taxes distributed back to local governments of origin without restriction as to use. On the other hand, some aid thus distributed on a source basis is limited to particular functions or purposes.

More generally, aid for the support of specific local government functions is distributed with reference to some measure of local need or activity (e.g., for education—school-age population, enrollment or attendance, or actual local expenditure; for highways—miles of roads, number of vehicles, or particular local requirements; for public welfare programs—actual or estimated local expenditures).

A broad measure of need finds expression in formulas based on local population and applied to the distribution of money for general local government support.

For many aid programs using a measure of local need, some standard of local financial effort or ability also is applied, aiming at a degree of "equalization" as between relatively poor and more prosperous local units. A contrasting principle is applied where a "floor" is provided in terms of a minimum amount of aid payable to each local governmental unit involved. Finally, some aid programs provide an identical amount to all local units of a particular type.

Interstate Comparisons

Tables 2 to 4 afford a basis for comparing amounts of aid to local governments provided by individual states. It is important that such comparisons take adequate account of the aid concept employed and of the great variations which exist in the pattern of state-local responsibility for particular governmental functions throughout the nation. Thus, State A directly provides public schools, local highways or public assistance; State B grants to its local governments funds for local performance of these functions under state supervision.

The total cost to each state may be similar although involving a different form of state expenditure.

Hasty conclusions and interpretations therefore must be avoided in this area. Interstate comparisons can be made only with caution and, usually, some qualification.

Conclusions can be drawn only by considering the whole area of state-local relations and the economic, historical and political factors affecting them.

TABLE 1

SUMMARY OF STATE INTERGOVERNMENTAL PAYMENTS TO LOCAL GOVERNMENTS: 1942–1954*

| | | | Amounts in millions | | | | Total state payments to local governments | |
| | | | | For specified purposes | | | | As per cent of total general revenue of state governments |
Fiscal year	Total	Purpose unspecified	Total	Schools	Highways	All other (a)	Per capita	
1942	$1,780	$224	$1,556	$ 790	$344	$ 422	$13.45	34.7
1944	1,842	274	1,568	861	298	409	13.81	33.7
1946	2,092	357	1,735	953	339	443	15.90	33.3
1948	3,283	428	2,855	1,554	507	794	23.02	35.5
1950	4,217	482	3,735	2,054	610	1,071	28.52	37.4
1951	4,678	513	4,165	2,248	667	1,250	31.64	37.7
1952	5,044	510	4,534	2,525	734	1,275	33.06	37.6
1953	5,384	592	4,971	2,740	803	1,248	34.75	37.1
1954	5,679	600	5,079	2,934	871	1,273	36.06	37.1

*Source: U. S. Bureau of the Census, Compendium of State Government Finances in 1954; similar annual Compendium reports for 1951 through 1953; and Revised Summary of State Government Finances, 1942–1950.
(a) Principally public welfare.

TABLE 2
STATE INTERGOVERNMENTAL EXPENDITURE IN TOTAL AND FOR SELECTED FUNCTIONS, BY STATE: 1954*
(In thousands of dollars)

State	Total	Function not specified	Public safety	Public welfare Total (a)	Old-age assistance	Aid to dependent children	Education	Highways	Health and hospitals	Housing and community redevelopment	Other, combined and unallocable
All states....	$5,678,533	$600,027	$7,755	$1,003,572	$569,158	$223,313	$2,933,960	$871,346	$125,933	$11,468	$124,472
Alabama........	104,737	4,732	367	....	....	....	70,829	24,703	3,282	......	824
Arizona.........	33,702	13,297	....	....	....	....	14,918	4,681	74	......	732
Arkansas........	43,825	4,751	....	....	....	....	31,457	7,286	41	......	290
California......	925,903	43,622	1,778	297,188	214,583	68,433	419,665	96,591	13,773	......	53,286
Colorado.......	91,701	59	35	60,765	50,912	5,058	16,068	12,995	767	......	1,012
Connecticut.....	26,203	4,065	157	2,504	....	....	17,627	1,697	33	......	120
Delaware........	13,485	....	....	1,278	....	639	11,668	234	....	......	305
Florida.........	104,044	4,313	....	....	....	....	81,302	12,774	1,525	......	4,130
Georgia.........	109,630	....	147	2,693	....	....	83,654	16,359	6,777	......	....
Idaho...........	15,876	1,563	....	....	....	....	8,183	6,107	6	......	17
Illinois..........	175,850	....	....	24,015	....	....	76,716	70,592	3,271	......	1,256
Indiana.........	136,099	3,394	66	25,587	18,058	7,021	68,270	37,110	1,275	......	397
Iowa............	87,127	27,578	....	108	....	....	26,119	31,730	1,155	......	437
Kansas..........	80,551	8,736	....	33,146	20,761	3,853	24,833	12,523	1,299	......	14
Kentucky.......	44,387	441	184	....	....	....	35,721	2,377	3,064	......	2,600
Louisiana.......	128,075	34,217	....	....	....	....	81,342	8,322	2,066	......	2,128
Maine..........	12,355	323	....	588	....	....	7,310	4,030	3	......	101
Maryland.......	95,646	21,110	....	15,920	5,049	5,887	33,447	22,065	343	......	2,761
Massachusetts...	212,887	56,637	127	102,816	73,394	14,977	29,781	6,481	863	3,149	13,033
Michigan........	370,139	63,867	554	6,146	....	....	194,431	89,487	13,996	......	1,658
Minnesota......	133,051	8,632	....	39,415	30,614	7,390	69,188	13,902	850	......	1,064
Mississippi.....	61,584	7,683	....	....	....	....	34,147	17,598	1,347	......	809
Missouri........	64,855	4,295	241	....	....	....	55,353	1,969	1,921	......	1,076
Montana........	13,253	....	23	108	....	....	12,187	....	34	......	901
Nebraska........	34,135	500	....	15,856	11,331	2,709	4,699	12,326	301	......	453
Nevada..........	6,929	124	....	....	....	....	4,893	1,484	163	......	265
New Hampshire.	3,681	1,829	....	....	....	....	1,285	103	206	......	258
New Jersey.....	68,280	1,158	....	17,349	12,922	....	29,190	14,928	4,712	......	943
New Mexico.....	39,194	862	38	....	....	....	36,087	1,869	....	......	338
New York.......	704,840	90,495	1,078	219,182	78,799	66,916	315,742	42,427	24,036	7,291	4,589
North Carolina..	61,144	6,941	....	31,984	16,669	11,258	11,604	5,244	4,631	......	740
North Dakota...	15,083	354	....	198	....	....	9,433	4,623	....	......	475
Ohio............	287,788	46,268	95	42,163	....	13,121	101,831	91,485	4,238	......	1,708
Oklahoma.......	84,796	....	....	....	....	....	53,257	29,062	844	......	1,633
Oregon..........	57,974	2,423	47	850	100	....	35,473	18,617	10	......	554
Pennsylvania....	233,383	5,973	455	....	....	....	188,302	27,855	167	1,028	9,603
Rhode Island....	13,041	6,369	....	2,477	....	....	3,853	142	200	......	....
South Carolina..	114,918	6,914	....	....	....	....	99,384	5,960	2,036	......	624
South Dakota...	7,038	624	....	214	....	....	4,478	1,297	37	......	388
Tennessee.......	102,023	9,286	....	....	....	....	66,480	22,882	2,961	......	414
Texas...........	204,186	....	....	....	....	....	187,518	11,973	3,476	......	1,219
Utah...........	26,029	1,000	1	....	....	....	21,704	2,527	255	......	542
Vermont........	9,143	4	....	96	....	....	5,457	3,524	....	......	62
Virginia.........	100,735	11,843	2,133	15,982	5,558	5,854	64,561	5,234	379	......	603
Washington.....	143,180	8,510	....	....	....	....	92,992	22,006	12,759	......	6,913
West Virginia...	54,570	....	....	1,608	....	....	52,220	....	512	......	230
Wisconsin.......	203,190	82,495	229	39,817	28,105	9,677	30,045	42,069	5,991	......	2,544
Wyoming........	18,288	2,740	....	3,519	2,303	520	9,256	2,096	254	......	423

*Source: U. S. Bureau of the Census, *Compendium of State Government Finances in 1954.* Note explanation on pages 59, 60 on "Interstate Comparisons," which points out that great variations exist from state to state as to state-local responsibility for various functions. Thus, lack of an entry for a particular function for a given state in this table does not indicate lack of state expenditure for this function.

(a) Includes amounts for public welfare categories not shown separately.

Table 3

PER CAPITA AMOUNTS OF STATE INTERGOVERNMENTAL EXPENDITURE AND RELATION TO STATE GENERAL REVENUE, BY STATE: 1954*

State	Per capita state intergovernmental expenditure						Per cent intergovernmental expenditure is of state general revenue					
		Function not specified	Specified functions					Function not specified	Specified functions			
	Total		Education	Highways	Public welfare	Other	Total		Education	Highways	Public welfare	Other
Total.........	$36.06	$3.81	$18.63	$5.53	$6.37	$1.71	37.1	3.9	19.2	5.7	6.6	1.8
Alabama........	33.63	1.52	22.75	7.93	.....	1.44	43.0	1.9	29.1	10.1	.....	1.8
Arizona........	36.24	14.30	16.04	5.03	.....	.87	29.5	11.6	13.1	4.1	.....	.7
Arkansas.......	22.96	2.49	16.48	3.82	.....	.17	28.3	3.1	20.3	4.7	.....	.2
California......	75.96	3.58	34.43	7.92	24.38	5.65	55.6	2.6	25.2	5.8	17.9	4.1
Colorado.......	64.90	.04	11.37	9.20	43.00	1.28	50.0	(a)	8.8	7.1	33.1	1.0
Connecticut....	12.12	1.88	8.15	.78	1.16	.14	12.7	2.0	8.5	.8	1.2	.1
Delaware.......	37.67	.....	32.59	.65	3.57	.85	22.1	.....	19.1	.4	2.1	.5
Florida........	31.03	1.29	24.25	3.81	.....	1.69	30.4	1.3	23.8	3.7	.....	1.7
Georgia........	30.58	.....	23.33	4.56	.75	1.93	33.9	.....	25.9	5.1	.8	2.1
Idaho..........	26.33	2.59	13.57	10.13	.....	.04	24.5	2.4	12.6	9.4	.....	(a)
Illinois........	19.53	.....	8.52	7.84	2.67	.50	25.3	.....	11.1	10.2	3.5	.7
Indiana........	32.91	.82	16.51	8.97	6.19	.42	36.2	.9	18.1	9.9	6.8	.5
Iowa...........	33.45	10.59	10.03	12.18	.04	.61	32.5	10.3	9.8	11.8	(a)	.6
Kansas.........	40.16	4.35	12.38	6.24	16.52	.65	40.2	4.4	12.4	6.3	16.6	.7
Kentucky.......	14.97	.15	12.05	.80	.....	1.97	21.6	.2	17.3	1.2	.....	2.8
Louisiana......	44.41	11.86	28.20	2.89	.....	1.45	28.3	7.6	18.0	1.8	.....	.9
Maine..........	13.52	.35	8.00	4.41	.64	.11	14.8	.4	8.8	4.8	.7	.1
Maryland.......	37.64	8.31	13.16	8.68	6.27	1.22	41.6	9.2	14.6	9.6	6.9	1.4
Massachusetts...	43.45	11.56	6.08	1.32	20.98	3.50	47.6	12.7	6.7	1.4	23.0	3.8
Michigan.......	54.02	9.32	28.38	13.06	.90	2.37	47.2	8.1	24.8	11.4	.8	2.1
Minnesota......	43.58	2.83	22.66	4.55	12.91	.63	37.7	2.4	19.6	3.9	11.2	.5
Mississippi.....	28.21	3.52	15.64	8.06	.....	.99	33.3	4.2	18.5	9.5	.....	1.2
Missouri.......	15.83	1.05	13.51	.48	.....	.79	18.5	1.2	15.8	.6	.....	.9
Montana.......	21.58	.....	19.85	.....	.18	1.56	18.4	.....	16.9	.....	.1	1.3

Nebraska	25.34	.37	3.49	9.15	11.77	.56	32.1	.5	4.4	11.6	14.9	.7
Nevada	33.64	.60	23.75	7.20	. . .	2.08	21.5	.4	15.2	4.6	. . .	1.3
New Hampshire	6.98	3.47	2.44	.20	. . .	.88	8.0	4.0	2.8	.2	. . .	1.0
New Jersey	13.28	.23	5.68	2.90	3.37	1.10	21.9	.4	9.4	4.8	5.6	1.8
New Mexico	51.71	1.14	47.61	2.47	14.39	.50	29.5	.6	27.1	1.4	. . .	.3
New York	46.27	5.94	20.73	2.79	7.63	2.43	50.6	6.5	22.7	3.0	15.7	2.7
North Carolina	14.58	1.66	2.77	1.25	. . .	1.28	15.7	1.8	3.0	1.3	8.2	1.4
North Dakota	24.29	.57	15.19	7.44	.32	.76	16.8	.4	10.5	5.2	.2	.5
Ohio	34.39	5.53	12.17	10.93	5.04	.72	40.1	6.5	14.2	12.8	5.9	.8
Oklahoma	37.67	. . .	23.66	12.91	. . .	1.10	28.1	. . .	17.6	9.6	. . .	.8
Oregon	36.19	1.51	22.14	11.62	.53	.38	31.1	1.3	19.0	10.0	.5	.3
Pennsylvania	21.90	.56	17.67	2.61	. . .	1.06	28.7	.7	23.2	3.4	. . .	1.4
Rhode Island	15.96	7.80	4.72	.17	3.03	.24	18.0	8.8	5.3	.2	3.4	.3
South Carolina	52.35	3.15	45.28	2.72	. . .	1.21	53.1	3.2	45.9	2.8	. . .	1.2
South Dakota	10.71	.95	6.82	1.97	.33	.65	9.7	.9	6.2	1.8	.3	.6
Tennessee	30.65	2.79	19.97	6.87	. . .	1.01	36.9	3.4	24.0	8.3	. . .	1.2
Texas	24.61	1.36	22.60	1.44	. . .	.57	28.1	1.2	25.8	1.6	. . .	.6
Utah	35.46	.01	29.57	3.44	. . .	1.09	30.1	(a)	25.1	2.9	. . .	.9
Vermont	24.25	. . .	14.47	9.35	.25	.16	24.1	. . .	14.4	9.3	.3	.2
Virginia	28.40	3.34	18.20	1.48	4.51	.88	36.8	4.3	23.6	1.9	5.8	1.1
Washington	57.78	3.43	37.53	8.88	.83	7.94	38.2	2.3	24.8	5.9	. . .	5.2
West Virginia	28.17	. . .	26.96	. . .	. . .	.38	32.2	. . .	30.8	. . .	.9	.4
Wisconsin	57.76	23.45	8.54	11.96	11.32	2.49	57.0	23.2	8.4	11.8	11.2	2.5
Wyoming	59.76	8.95	30.25	6.85	11.50	2.21	32.7	4.9	16.6	3.8	6.3	1.2

63

*Source: U. S. Bureau of the Census. Per capita amounts are based on estimated population, July 1, 1953, excluding armed forces overseas. Note explanation on pages 59, 60 on "Interstate Comparisons," which points out that great variations exist from state to state as to state-local responsibility for various functions. (a) Less than 1/20 of 1 per cent.

TABLE 4
STATE INTERGOVERNMENTAL EXPENDITURE, BY TYPE OF RECEIVING GOVERNMENT AND BY STATE: 1954*
(In thousands of dollars)

State	Total	Counties	Cities	School districts	Townships and New England "towns"	Special districts	Combined and unallocable
All states.............	$5,678,533	$1,649,805	$1,036,612	$2,437,834	$114,508	$ 20,673	$419,101
Alabama....................	104,737	30,760	2,970	70,829	......	......	178
Arizona....................	33,702	14,483	4,301	14,918	......	......	.....
Arkansas..................	43,825	8,826	3,287	31,369	......	......	343
California.................	925,903	412,024	98,346	412,449	......	3,029	55
Colorado..................	91,701	56,358	19,275	16,068	......	......	.....
Connecticut...............	26,203	1,657	8,983	.....	15,563	......	.....
Delaware..................	13,485	1,517	4,628	7,340	......	......	.....
Florida....................	104,044	21,887	297	81,302	......	558	.....
Georgia...................	109,630	24,694	1,352	83,584	......	......	.....
Idaho.....................	15,876	7,246	447	8,183	......	......	.....
Illinois...................	175,850	36,147	31,433	75,559	9,663	1,514	21,534
Indiana...................	136,099	53,232	14,557	68,270	40	......	.....
Iowa......................	87,127	26,960	8,083	26,119	......	305	25,660
Kansas....................	80,551	49,100	6,511	23,075	1,627	70	168
Kentucky..................	44,387	6,987	1,352	35,661	......	......	387
Louisiana.................	128,075	8,554	16,688	81,068	......	380	21,385
Maine.....................	12,355	135	......	......	65	......	12,155(a)
Maryland..................	95,646	51,822	43,624	......	......	......	200
Massachusetts.............	212,887	22	206	......	......	12,256	200,403(a)
Michigan..................	370,139	67,049	71,614	195,190	19,019	287	16,980
Minnesota.................	133,051	56,180	4,845(b)	69,188(b)	999	66	1,773
Mississippi................	61,584	52,267	958	8,329	......	......	30
Missouri..................	64,855	4,229	2,847	54,815	......	......	2,964
Montana..................	13,253	790	263	12,187	......	13	.....
Nebraska..................	34,135	27,960	1,476	4,699	......	......	.....
Nevada....................	6,929	1,954	82	4,893	......	......	.....
New Hampshire.............	3,681	......	813	949	1,583	......	336
New Jersey................	68,280	29,872	8,950(c)	......	18(c)	596	28,844(d)
New Mexico................	39,194	2,461	646	36,087	......	......	.....
New York..................	704,840	111,395	410,897	160,369	21,683	431	65
North Carolina............	61,144	40,625	8,982	......	......	......	11,537(e)
North Dakota.............	15,083	5,126	539	9,418	......	......	.....
Ohio......................	287,788	90,654	46,630	101,669	10,090	......	38,745
Oklahoma.................	84,796	26,263	5,276	53,257	......	......	.....
Oregon....................	57,974	16,361	6,140	35,473	......	......	.....
Pennsylvania..............	233,383	11,906	20,417	188,201	11,547	1,028	284
Rhode Island..............	13,041	......	9,186	......	3,855	......	.....
South Carolina............	114,918	12,795	2,546	99,541	......	......	36
South Dakota.............	7,038	1,898	513	4,478	30	......	119
Tennessee.................	102,023	69,404	32,236	......	......	......	383
Texas.....................	204,186	16,860	1,894	185,298	......	12	122
Utah......................	26,029	2,234	1,856	21,704	......	......	235
Vermont..................	9,143	......	617	480	8,046	......	.....
Virginia..................	100,735	65,672	33,273	......	......	......	1,790
Washington................	143,180	31,947	17,512	92,992	......	115	614
West Virginia.............	54,570	1,846	491	52,220	......	13	.....
Wisconsin.................	203,190	84,035	77,389	1,347	10,680	......	29,739(f)
Wyoming..................	18,288	5,611	1,384	9,256	......	......	2,037

*Source: U. S. Bureau of the Census, *Compendium of State Government Finances in 1954.*
(a) Paid to cities and towns.
(b) School aid paid to St. Paul, which operates its own school system, is included under school districts.
(c) Unsegregable amount for townships is included under cities.

(d) To cities and townships operating school systems, and to independent school districts.
(e) To cities and counties.
(f) To cities operating school systems and to independent school districts.

Section II
CONSTITUTIONS AND ELECTIONS

1. Constitutions
2. Elections

1

Constitutions

STATE CONSTITUTIONS AND CONSTITUTIONAL REVISION—JULY, 1953 TO JULY, 1955*

CONSTITUTIONAL developments in the biennium 1953–1955 are not simple to evaluate. Since no general revisions occurred, one might conclude that no real progress was made. Such a conclusion, however, is not accurate.

Although no state held a convention for general revision, the subject was under consideration in many states. The normal grist of individual amendments to state constitutions were submitted and voted upon in various states, and some of them dealt with basic questions that are normally reserved for consideration during a general revision.

Significant also was the fact that proposals for general revision came more frequently from Governors, leading legislators and other top level officials, whereas in the past they came chiefly from civic and reform organizations and professors of government. Good published materials on problems of constitutional revision, meantime, have become somewhat more abundant.

GENERAL DEVELOPMENTS

Writers on state government have long called attention to the contrast between the original state constitutions and the more modern ones as regards length. It has been noted that the original constitutions were brief and concise, limited to basic and essential matters, whereas recent ones tend to much greater length, due to the inclusion of increasing amounts of statutory matter. In 1954 Professor Alfred De Grazia constructed a chart which confirmed graphically that over the years constitutions very definitely have grown longer;[1] he writes:

... almost from the beginning the length of constitutions began to increase, at first slightly in the period before 1840, then markedly up to 1890, and finally the period from 1900 to the present has given us some rather fantastic examples of lengthy constitutions.

He points out that many old constitutions, once fairly brief, have since been amended a number of times and have assumed large proportions for that reason. But, he continues:

Since 1910 the several state constitutions that have been adopted show no clear pattern. If one takes the last three, for example, one finds them less long than the preceding two. Even then, these last three constitutions vary from about sixty pages to about twenty-five pages in length.

One would be rash, on the basis of these figures, to predict that the next generation of state constitution making in the United States will reveal either an increase from the lengthy constitutions of the recent past or a decrease in size as men realize the impossibility of putting down everything in the basic document of the state.

For years, also, writers have pointed out that many provisions in existing constitutions are so restrictive that the states are unable to do numerous things their gov-

*Prepared by W. BROOKE GRAVES, Chief, Government Division, Legislative Reference Service, Library of Congress.

[1]Alfred De Grazia, "State Constitutions—Are They Growing Longer?" *State Government*, April, 1954, pp. 82–83.

ernments and the people want done. Emphasis on this fundamental now comes from a new source. The Commission on Intergovernmental Relations, which reported in 1955, stresses the fact that if state and local governments are to assume greater responsibilities under the federal system, they must be capable of performing these functions well. The need for modernizing constitutions is particularly underlined. The report says:[2]

Early in its study, the Commission was confronted with the fact that many state constitutions restrict the scope, effectiveness, and adaptability of state and local action. These self-imposed constitutional limitations make it difficult for many states to perform all of the services their citizens require, and consequently have frequently been the underlying cause of state and municipal pleas for federal assistance. . . .

The Commission finds a very real and pressing need for the states to improve their constitutions. A number of states recently have taken energetic action to rewrite outmoded charters. In these states this action has been regarded as a first step in the program to achieve the flexibility required to meet the modern needs of their citizens.

Increasing emphasis on constitutional revision on the part of Governors and legislative bodies has been noted. In each round of messages to the legislatures, one now finds a number of recommendations for constitutional revision. Some of them are repeated in successive sessions by individual Governors, or by a Governor of one political party driving home a position taken by a predecessor of the other party. Meantime, support for revision by important citizen groups continues.

PROPOSALS AND ACTION ON GENERAL REVISION

Recent examples of proposals for general constitutional revision, and of resulting action, include the following among others:

Connecticut. At a special election on July 26, 1955, Connecticut's voters approved an amendment that will facilitate future amendment of the state's constitution. Heretofore approval of an amendment required that a majority of those "present"

at an election vote in favor of it. Many voters ignored such proposals when on the ballot in general elections. The 1955 amendment, approved by a majority of almost five to one at the special election, provides that only a majority of those who vote on the question itself is required for approval of an amendment.

Florida. Extensive activity on the part of the State Bar Association and organized citizen groups long has sought to bring a constitutional convention and general revision of the state's constitution. Early in 1955 the Governor appointed a Citizens Committee to draft proposals for constitutional revision and present them to the legislature. On April 5 he recommended to the legislature establishment of a commission to study revision. A commission of thirty-seven members resulted in June. It is to report to the 1957 session of the legislature, making recommendations for revision, article by article; if approved by a three-fifths vote in each house, these recommendations may then be passed upon by the voters at the 1958 general election.[3] Latest development in a state-wide campaign of education is the publication of a ninety-two page critique of the present constitution.[4]

Illinois. Illinois facilitated future amendments of its constitution in 1950 by adopting the Gateway Amendment to it.[5] The Illinois General Assembly in 1953 submitted three constitutional amendments, all three of which were approved by the voters at the 1954 general election. One was relatively minor, authorizing the sale or lease of certain canals or waterways owned by the state upon such terms as the General Assembly might prescribe by law. The second provides that after 1958, the term of the State Treasurer shall be increased from two years to four. The third,

---

[2]Commission on Intergovernmental Relations, *A Report to the President for Transmittal to the Congress,* pp. 37-38 (Washington, June, 1955).

[3]Manning J. Dauer, "Florida Moves to Change Basic Law," *National Municipal Review,* July, 1955, pp. 365-366.

[4]Manning J. Dauer, and William C. Havard, "The Florida Constitution of 1885—A Critique" (Public Administration Clearing Service, University of Florida, 1955), reprinted from the *University of Florida Law Review,* Spring 1955.

[5]See *The Book of the States, 1954-1955,* p. 66. Current data supplied by Professor Neil F. Garvey, Division of University Extension, University of Illinois.

and most notable, provided a means of breaking the deadlock existing for more than half a century between Cook County and "down-state" over the question of apportionment. The legislature in 1955, in accordance with the amendment, re-apportioned the state, for the first time since 1901. Provision is made in the amendment for means of effecting apportionments in the future, should the General Assembly fail to act in 1963 or at the expiration of any ten-year interval thereafter.

The General Assembly in 1955 passed one amendment to be submitted to the voters at the general election in 1956. It represents another attempt to amend the revenue article in such a way as to permit the legislature to classify property for purposes of taxation, subject to certain enumerated restrictions. The amendment would also revise and simplify other provisions dealing with the levy of miscellaneous types of taxes.

Kentucky. A new Constitutional Review Commission was created by the Kentucky General Assembly in 1953, to report in 1954.[6] The General Assembly in its 1954 session did not accept the commission's recommendations in proposing amendments to the constitution. It did, however, submit two amendments of its own for consideration at the 1955 general election.

Louisiana. Prospects for a constitutional convention in Louisiana have increased. Publication of the very extensive State Law Institute's *Projet of a Constitution for Louisiana, with Notes and Studies* now has been completed. The State Bar Association and the State League of Women Voters continue to help keep the question before the public.

Minnesota. Endorsements of a proposal for a constitutional convention in Minnesota have been made by the Governor and his predecessor. The State League of Women Voters has been studying the problem and preparing pertinent materials for publication. Because several attempts at revision in recent years had failed, at least in part because of the absence of a requirement that proposed changes be submitted to direct vote of the people, the legislature

passed for submission at the general election in 1952 a safeguarding amendment specifically providing for a popular referendum on any provision approved by a convention. This proposal received 656,-000 votes as compared with 424,000 against, but it then failed of adoption because in Minnesota a constitutional amendment requires a majority of all votes cast in a general election. The 1953 legislature acted to resubmit the question for vote in the general election of 1954. This time, 638,818 citizens voted for, 266,434 against.[7]

A bill to submit to the electorate a proposal for a convention was introduced early in the 1955 session. Hearings were held, and in the Senate the bill was reported favorably. The Governor described it as "a measure of extreme importance to the cause of good government in Minnesota."[8] After extensive discussion and debate, it failed to obtain the necessary two-thirds majority in each house.

New Hampshire. Constitutional conventions are no rarity in New Hampshire; since amendments may be proposed only by a convention, conventions have been held with considerable regularity at seven-year intervals during the last several decades. In a referendum in November, 1954, the voters favored the calling of a convention, and on the recommendation of the Governor the General Court in 1955 provided for one to be held in May, 1956. It appropriated $75,000 for its use. As in the case of practically all previous conventions, delegates are to be elected in the various towns and cities on town meeting day—the second Tuesday in March, 1956. The President of the 1948 convention believes that three measures are almost sure to be considered by the 1956 convention: (1) to reduce the size of the General Court from some 400 members to perhaps 250; (2) to authorize the General Court to levy graduated taxes, at present prohibited by judicial interpretation of the existing constitution; (3) to authorize the General Court to propose amendment to the state constitution.[9]

(*Continued on page 76*)

---

[6]Constitutional Review Commission, *Report* (Frankfort, 1954).

[7]*Minneapolis Star*, November 16, 1954.
[8]*Minneapolis Tribune*, February 17, 1955.
[9]Information furnished by Professor Robert B. Dishman, Department of Government, University of New Hampshire.

STATE CONSTITUTIONS AND CONSTITUTIONAL CONVENTIONS
As of July, 1955

State	Number of conventions(a)	Effective date of present constitution	Estimated length (number of words)	Number of amendments adopted	Amendment procedure Proposal by legislature	Amendment procedure Ratification by electorate
Alabama	6	1901	39,899	110	3/5 members elected	Majority vote on amendment
Arizona	1	1912	15,369	36	Majority members each house	Majority vote on amendment
Arkansas	6	1874	21,500	42(c)	Majority members each house(d)	Majority vote on amendment
California	..	1879	72,000	372(c)	2/3 members elected	Majority vote on amendment
Colorado	1	1876	23,095	56(c)	2/3 members elected(e)	Majority vote on amendment
Connecticut	2	1818	6,741	48	Majority of House Representatives; next Assembly, 2/3 each house	Majority of voters in town meeting
Delaware	5	1897(f)	13,409	21	2/3 members elected, 2 successive sess.	None
Florida	5	1887	30,000	102	3/5 members elected	Majority vote on amendment
Georgia	12	1945(g)	25,000	18(h)	2/3 members elected	Majority vote on amendment
Idaho	1	1890	13,492	53	2/3 of all members	Majority vote on amendment
Illinois	5	1870	13,838	8	2/3 members elected(i)	Majority voting at next election of members of General Assembly or 2/3 vote on amendment
Indiana	2	1851	7,816	18	Majority members elected, 2 successive sess.(j)	Majority vote on amendment(j)
Iowa		1857	7,997	19	Majority members elected, 2 successive sess.	Majority vote on amendment
Kansas	4	1861	8,052	42(c)	2/3 members elected(d)	Majority vote on amendment

(a) For dates of conventions and action taken at each, see *The Book of the States, 1941-1942*, pp. 48–55, and subsequent volumes. Constitutional conventions for the purpose of proposing amendments were held in New Hampshire in 1930, 1938, 1941 and 1948; a constitutional convention will assemble on the third Tuesday of May, 1956. A single amendment to Virginia's constitution was effected by a convention on May 2, 1945.

(b) In the states which make no provision for revision or amendment by constitutional convention, it appears that such conventions have been held permissible as an inherent right of the people acting through elected representatives.

(c) In some states where a single amendment amends more than one section of the constitution it may or may not be counted as more than a single amendment.

(d) No more than three amendments may be submitted at a time.

(e) Legislature may not propose amendments to more than six articles at the same session.

(f) Although it is the usual practice to submit revisions of constitutions to the voters for their approval, this footnote indicates those instances in which this practice was not followed,

e.g., constitutions promulgated or adopted by the state convention.

(g) A single amendment adopted at election August 7, 1945, created the constitution of 1945.

(h) This figure does not include amendments of a local nature, such amendments not becoming a part of the constitution unless they receive both a majority of those voting in the state as a whole and also a majority of those voting in the particular subdivision or subdivisions affected. Local amendments to the constitution of 1877 were continued in effect though not incorporated in the constitution of 1945.

(i) Amendments to no more than three articles may be submitted by same legislative session and the same article may not be amended more often than once in four years.

(j) No new amendments may be submitted while an amendment is awaiting its second legislative action or action of the electors. The Supreme Court has ruled (*In re Todd*, 208 Ind. 168) that if more votes are cast for than against an amendment submitted to the voters, it is ratified even though the total vote cast in favor of the amendment is less than a majority of the total number of votes cast at the election at which the amendment was voted on.

STATE CONSTITUTIONS AND CONSTITUTIONAL CONVENTIONS
As of July, 1955—Continued

Amendment procedure by initiative		Procedure for calling a convention(b)		Popular ratification (convention proposals)	State
Size of petition	Referendum vote	Vote in legislature	Referendum vote		
....	....	Majority members elected	Majority voting at election	No provision	......Alabama
15% of total voters for Governor at last election	Majority vote on amendment	Majority vote	Majority vote on question	Majority vote on proposals	.......Arizona
10% of legal voters for Governor at last election including 5% in each of 15 counties	Majority vote on amendment	....	....	....	.......Arkansas
8% of total voters for Governor at last general election	Majority vote on amendment	2/3 members elected	Majority vote on question	Majority vote cast at special election	......California
8% of legal voters for Secretary of State at last general election	Majority vote on amendment	2/3 members elected	Majority vote on question	Majority vote at election which may be special election	.......Colorado
....	....	....	....	....	....Connecticut
....	....	2/3 members elected	Majority vote on question	No provision	.......Delaware
....	....	2/3 all members	Majority vote on question	No provision	........Florida
....	....	2/3 all members	No referendum	Majority vote on proposals in state as a whole and majority vote of local electors in subdivision affected	........Georgia
As legislature provided	Majority voting at general election	2/3 members elected	Majority of electors voting in next general election	"Adopted by people"	.........Idaho
....	....	2/3 each house	Majority voting at next gen. election	Majority vote at special election	........Illinois
....	....	....	....	....	........Indiana
....	....	Question mandatory every 10 years beginning 1870; leg. may provide for submission of question	Majority voting on the question	No provision	...........Iowa
....	....	2/3 members elected	Majority voting at next gen. election	No provision	........Kansas

(k) No more than two amendments may be submitted at a time; no amendment may be resubmitted within five years.

(l) Proposal must be introduced within first thirty days of session.

(m) A rearrangement of the constitution was made by inserting amendments at appropriate places; the original constitution, as amended and rearranged, is still in force. In Maine (1954) and Vermont (1913) the rearrangement was accomplished by the Supreme Court of the state.

(n) One of these was not a convention, but a special constitutional commission appointed by the Governor, under authority of an act of the legislature.

(o) Legislature is empowered to fix a smaller percentage. The percentage actually prescribed in Missouri is 5.

(p) Proposals must be devoid of party designations.

(q) Minimum vote on amendment, 35 per cent total cast.

(r) Rejected amendments may not be considered again until after three years. Minimum vote necessary, 35 per cent of total vote cast.

(s) In New Jersey rejected amendments may not be considered again until the third general election thereafter (in Pennsylvania may not be submitted again for five years).

(t) Amendments dealing with franchise and elections must be proposed by a ¾ vote of legislature and ratified by ¾ vote of electorate, and ⅔ vote in each county.

(u) In spite of the constitutional convention of 1938, the New York Constitution has been considered as the constitution of 1894, as amended.

(v) The North Carolina convention of 1876 used the constitution of 1868 as a basis but made numerous amendments to it. The present constitution has been considered both as the constitution of 1868 and 1876. The North Carolina amendments or constitution were ratified in November, 1876, and took effect on January 1, 1877.

(w) The legislature, by two-thirds vote, may require a special election on amendments. Any initiative or referendum measure rejected by the voters cannot be presented again for three years, unless by vote of 25 per cent or more of the legal voters.

(x) Convention may not be held oftener than once in six years.

(y) Since 1910, amendments may be submitted only at 10-year intervals.

(z) Revised Organic Act July 22, 1954.

(aa) Effective upon Hawaiian statehood.

(ab) Majority vote must constitute 35% of total vote cast at general election, or of registered voters at special election.

(ac) Excludes amendments made by legislature and those adopted by electorate but never in effect because of court decisions.

STATE CONSTITUTIONS AND CONSTITUTIONAL CONVENTIONS
As of July, 1955—Continued

State	Number of conven- tions(a)	Effective date of present consti- tution	Esti- mated length (number of words)	Number of amend- ments adopted	Amendment procedure Proposal by legislature	Ratification by electorate
Kentucky.........	6	1891(f)	21,500	16	3/5 members elected(k)	Majority vote on amendment
Louisiana.........	10	1921(f)	201,423	326	2/3 members elected(l)	Majority vote on amendment
Maine..............	1	1820(m)	10,302	77	2/3 both houses	Majority vote on amendment
Maryland.........	4	1867	23,300	79(c)	3/5 members elected	Majority vote on amendment
Massachusetts.....	5	1780	28,760	81	Majority members elected, 2 successive sess.	Majority vote on amendment
Michigan..........	5(n)	1909	15,290	59	2/3 members elected	Majority vote on amendment
Minnesota........	1	1858	15,465	80	Majority both houses	Majority voting at election
Mississippi........	7	1890(f)	15,302	32	2/3 each house, on each of 3 separate days	Majority vote cast
Missouri..........	6	1945	30,000	4	Majority members elected	Majority vote on amendment
Montana..........	1	1889	17,409	23(c)	2/3 members elected(d)	Majority vote on amendment
Nebraska.........	4	1875	16,555	69	3/5 members elected(p)	Majority vote on amendment(q)
Nevada...........	2	1864	16,657	56(c)	Majority members elected 2 successive sess.	Majority vote on amendment
New Hampshire....	14(a)	1784	10,900	94	....	....
New Jersey.........	4	1948	12,500	None	3/5 all members of each house; or majority all members of each house for 2 successive sess.	Majority voting at election(s)
New Mexico.......	1	1912	15,150	36(c)	Majority members elected	Majority vote on amendment(t)
New York..........	8	1894(u)	19,036	127	Majority members elected, 2 successive sess.(u)	Majority vote on amendment
North Carolina.....	6	1876(v)	8,861	28	3/5 each house	Majority voting at election
North Dakota......	1	1889	17,797	64	Majority members elected	Majority vote on amendment
Ohio..............	4	1851	15,417	72	3/5 members elected	Majority vote on amendment
Oklahoma.........	1	1907	35,360	37(ac)	Majority members elected	Majority voting at election(w)

STATE CONSTITUTIONS AND CONSTITUTIONAL CONVENTIONS
As of July, 1955—Continued

Amendment procedure by initiative		Procedure for calling a convention(b)		Popular ratification (convention proposals)	State
Size of petition	Referendum vote	Vote in legislature	Referendum vote		
....	....	Majority members elected, 2 successive sessions	Majority vote on question at least 1/4 qualified voters at last election	No provision	......Kentucky
....	....	No constitutional provision; practice is proposal by legislature, approved by referendum vote	No constitutional provision; practice is proposal by legislature, approved by referendum vote	....	......Louisiana
....	....	2/3 both houses	....	No provision	.........Maine
....	....	Question mandatory every 20 years beginning 1930	Majority voting at election	Majority vote on proposals	......Maryland
Not less than such number of voters equal to 3% of entire vote cast for Governor in preceding biennial State election	30% of total voters at election and majority vote on amendment	No constitutional provision; but legislature has submitted question of calling convention to people under its general powers	Majority voting on question	....	..Massachusetts
10% legal voters for Governor at last election	Majority vote on amendment	Question mandatory every 16 years beginning 1926	Majority voting at election	Majority vote on proposals	......Michigan
....	....	2/3 members elected	Majority voting at election	3/5 voting on question	......Minnesota
....	....	....	....	....	......Mississippi
Not more than 8% legal voters at last election of justice of Sup. Ct. in each of at least 2/3 Cong. dist.(o)	Majority vote on amendment	Question mandatory every 20 years	Majority vote on question	Majority vote on proposals	........Missouri
....	....	2/3 members elected	Majority vote on question	Majority vote at elections	......Montana
10% voters for Governor at last election; electors including 5% of each of 2/5 of counties	Majority vote on amendment(r)	3/5 members elected	Majority voting at election	Majority vote on proposals	......Nebraska
Constitution of Nevada cannot be amended by use of the initiative		2/3 members elected	Majority voters at election	No provision	.........Nevada
....	....	Question mandatory every 7 yrs.	Maj. vot. in town meetings	2/3 vot. in ann. town meetings	New Hampshire
....	....	....	....	....	.....New Jersey
....	....	2/3 members elected	Majority vote on question	"Ratified by people"	....New Mexico
....	....	Maj. of legislature. Question mandatory every 20 years beginning in 1957	Majority vote on question	Majority vote on proposals	......New York
....	....	2/3 members elected	Majority voting at election	No provision	.North Carolina
20,000 of electors	Majority vote on amendment	....	....	....	...North Dakota
10% of electors for Gov. last elec. incl. 5% in each of 1/2 of the counties	Majority vote on amendment	2/3 members elected. Question mandatory every 20 yrs. beginning 1932	Majority vote on question	Majority vote on proposals	...........Ohio
15% legal voters in last gen. State elec. for office receiving highest votes(w)	Majority voting at election	Majority vote of legislature. Question mandatory every 20 years beginning 1907	Majority vote on question	Majority vote on proposals	......Oklahoma

STATE CONSTITUTIONS AND CONSTITUTIONAL CONVENTIONS
As of July, 1955—Concluded

State	Number of conventions(a)	Effective date of present constitution	Estimated length (number of words)	Number of amendments adopted	Amendment procedure	
					Proposal by legislature	Ratification by electorate
Oregon............	2	1859	18,100	94(c)	Majority members elected	Majority vote on amendment
Pennsylvania......	5(n)	1874	15,092	54	Majority members elected, 2 successive legislatures	Majority vote on amendment(s)
Rhode Island......	7	1843	6,650	33	Majority members elected, 2 successive sess.	3/5 voters on amendment
South Carolina....	7	1895(f)	30,063	220	2/3 members elected	Maj. vote on amendment; ratification by majority next Gen. Assem.
South Dakota......	1	1889	24,545	60	Majority members elected	Majority vote on amendment
Tennessee.........	4	1870	9,460		Majority members elected; 2/3 members elected succeeding sess.	Majority of vote cast for Governor
Texas..............	5	1876	39,000	121	2/3 members elected	Majority vote on amendment
Utah..............	1	1896	13,261	29	2/3 members elected	Majority vote on amendment
Vermont..........	11	1793(f, m)	5,759	40	2/3 vote Senate, majority House; majority members elected succeeding sess.(y)	Majority freemen voting on amendment
Virginia...........	9(n)	1902(f)	23,101	87	Majority members elected, 2 successive sess.	Majority vote on amendment
Washington........	1	1889	14,650	28	2/3 members elected	Majority vote on amendment
West Virginia......	2	1872	14,928	27	2/3 members elected	Majority vote on amendment
Wisconsin.........	1	1848	10,517	59	Majority members elected, 2 successive sess.	Majority vote on amendment
Wyoming..........	1	1890	14,603	13	2/3 of all members	Majority of electors at next general election
Alaska.............	Constitutional Convention to frame a constitution for Alaskan Statehood convened November 8, 1955				....	....
Guam.............	..	1950(z)	6,500	1	....	....
Hawaii............	1	(aa)	11,412	..	2/3 both houses	Majority vote on amendment(ab)
Puerto Rico........	1	1952	8,500	2	2/3 both houses	Majority of electors voting thereon
Virgin Islands......	..	1954(z)	8,500	None	Amendment procedure would be by Congress of United States	

STATE CONSTITUTIONS AND CONSTITUTIONAL CONVENTIONS
As of July, 1955—Concluded

Amendment procedure by initiative		Procedure for calling a convention(b)		Popular ratification (convention proposals)	State
Size of petition	Referendum vote	Vote in legislature	Referendum vote		
Not more than 10% legal voters in last election for justice of Sup. Ct.(o)	Majority vote on amendment	Majority of Legislature	Majority vote on question	No provision	.........Oregon
....	....	....	....	....	...Pennsylvania
....	....	Majority votes of legislature	Majority votes on question	According to terms of act calling convention	..Rhode Island
....	....	2/3 members elected	Majority voting at election	No provision	..South Carolina
....	....	2/3 members elected	Majority voting at election	No provision	..South Dakota
....	....	Majority members elected(x)	Majority voting on question	Majority voting on question	.....Tennessee
....	....	....	....	....	...........Texas
....	....	2/3 members elected	Majority voting at next general election	Majority vote at next general election	..........Utah
....	....	....	....	....	.......Vermont
....	....	Majority members elected	Majority vote on question	No provision	......Virginia(a)
....	....	2/3 members elected	Majority voting at election	"Adopted by people"	....Washington
....	....	Majority members elected	Maj. vot. at elec. which can be a spec. elec.	"Ratified by voters"	...West Virginia
....	....	Majority of Legislature	Majority vote on question	No provision	......Wisconsin
....	....	2/3 members elected	Majority voting at next general election	"Adopted by people"	.......Wyoming
....	....	....	....	....	.........Alaska
....	....	....	....	....	...........Guam
....	....	Question mandatory every 10 years	Majority voting at election(ab)	Majority vote on proposals(ab)	.........Hawaii
....	....	2/3 members elected	Majority electors voting thereon	Majority electors voting thereon	....Puerto Rico
....	....	....	....	....	..Virgin Islands

Oregon. A constitutional study committee was authorized in Oregon by the 1953 legislative session; it consisted of nine persons appointed by the Governor outside the legislature, including two from each congressional district and one at large; the President of the Senate and three Senators appointed by him, the Speaker of the House and three Representatives appointed by him.

This study committee reported in January, 1955 that Oregon's was the "twelfth oldest, fifteenth longest, and eighth most amended of state constitutions," and made two specific recommendations: (1) that a constitutional convention be held in July, 1959; (2) that a preparatory commission be created to conduct research into what a new constitution should contain and to lay the results before the convention. At about the same time the Governor stated that he shared "the opinion of the majority of the committee—that a constitutional convention should be called, because it is through that means alone that needed reform in the fundamental document will be accomplished."[10]

The fact that the commission was divided, presenting both a majority and a minority report, contributed to the failure of its recommendations to win adoption in the 1955 legislative session. The bill was read in the Senate a first and second time, and referred to a committee where it remained until the end of the legislative session.[11]

Pennsylvania. A proposal to call a constitutional convention failed of adoption at the 1953 general election in Pennsylvania, although supported, as previously, by both major parties. Philadelphia and Pittsburgh favored revision but their majorities for it were overcome by adverse votes in other parts of the state. This was the fifth defeat in a state-wide referendum on the proposition since 1891, the last having occurred in 1935.

Rhode Island. Under authority of legislative action in 1954, Rhode Island voters on June 9, 1955, elected delegates to the state's third limited constitutional convention. The legislature had proposed that the constitution be amended to increase legislative compensation, provide life tenure for higher court judges, and provide for redevelopment of blighted urban areas. The convention held a ten-hour session on June 20 and adopted the three proposals. These were submitted to the electorate in a special election on July 20. The redevelopment amendment was adopted, the other two defeated.

Tennessee. The 1954–55 edition of *The Book of the States* reported (p. 67) on the Tennessee Constitutional Convention of 1953 and summarized eight proposals for change it approved for submission to the voters. All of these proposals—the first changes to be made in a constitution adopted in 1870—were approved at the general election of 1953. Increased public interest in the constitution, some observers believe, is even more important than the content of the amendments adopted, important as they were.[12]

Alaska. Earlier issues of *The Book of the States* have reported on constitutional revision in Hawaii and Puerto Rico. Now the Alaska legislature has authorized a constitutional convention, to be composed of fifty-five delegates elected in September, 1955, from twenty-two pre-established election districts. It was provided that the convention was to meet at the University of Alaska, College, Alaska, from November 8, 1955. Although the delegates were to draft the new constitution, preparatory staff work was done by a firm of professional consultants. The resulting document is to be submitted to the people; terms of

---

[10]Governor's and Legislative Constitutional Committee, *Constitutional Revision, Report of . . .* (Salem, January, 1955); see also "Governors Speak up for Constitutional Revision," a note in *National Municipal Review*, March, 1955, pp. 145–146.

[11]Information furnished by Professor Waldo Schumacher, Department of Political Science, University of Oregon.

[12]See Prentice Cooper, President of the Convention, "November's Constitutional Election," *Tennessee Planner*, October, 1953, pp. 67–72; H. L. Trewhit, "Tennessee Amends Her Constitution," *State Government*, June, 1954, pp. 119–122, 128; Martha Ragland, "Constitutional Climate Improves in Tennessee," *National Municipal Review*, April, 1955, pp. 202–203; unsigned, "Our 1870 Constitution Gets Its First Amendments," *Tennessee Planner*, December, 1953, pp. 118–120.

the submission will be laid down in an enabling act to be passed upon by Congress.

Constitutional amendments were adopted in more than half of the states during the biennium. They dealt with a wide range of subjects. To ascertain the general characteristics of such amendments the author recently examined a sample of some 200 proposals for constitutional change submitted during the 1953–55 biennium. Several points stood out. First, the voters approved a much larger number of amendments than they rejected. Secondly, the amendments submitted and adopted tended to center upon major problems in state government. A number were essentially local or minor in character, but most of them dealt with one or another of about a dozen topics: the governorship, the legislature, the courts, suffrage and elections, education, highways, taxation, debt, personnel administration, public officers, and veterans. For example:

In Colorado, Ohio and Tennessee, amendments increased the terms of Governor from two to four years; New York assured that the Governor and Lieutenant Governor shall be of the same political party; Tennessee authorized the item veto for appropriation bills; Florida, New Mexico and Tennessee extended the time available to the Governor for disposing of bills following adjournment of the legislature. In three states—Illinois, Ohio and Texas —amendments lengthened the terms of certain other officials from two years to four.

Georgia, Kansas, Louisiana and West Virginia established annual legislative sessions. Amendments in eight states provided for increased legislative compensation. Illinois, as noted above, provided for the state's first legislative reapportionment in more than half a century. A reapportionment amendment also was adopted in Arizona.

Amendments in four states—Georgia, Louisiana, Maryland and Tennessee— provide for greater home rule for cities and/or counties. Affecting metropolitan areas, Kansas authorized the legislature to designate "urban areas" and to enact special laws giving them appropriate powers of local government and consolidation; Tennessee adopted an amendment making city-county consolidation possible.

Those are examples only—from a sample of 200 proposals that included by no means all the propositions offered to the voters. Some amendments on lines indicated above were defeated at the polls. A few other amendments adopted tended to restrict rather than advance governmental powers or flexibility. But the sample showed that, by and large, the amendments submitted and adopted were important— many of them in line with proposals advanced by recognized authorities on state government for years; and that, as a rule, the voters were not loath to amend their constitutions when well-planned proposals were set before them.

To significant materials listed in previous editions of *The Book of the States*, four new entries have been added. Professor Burdine has rendered a highly useful service in his brief commentary on sources relating to state constitutions, the work of constitutional conventions, and state constitutional development, to which is appended a list of all published debates relating to state constitutional conventions. The five volumes of the *Projet of a Constitution for the State of Louisiana* contain a vast amount of information on the subject, including in Vol. I, Part II the series of approximately fifty special studies, grouped under a dozen major headings. A comparable series of special studies prepared for the Governor's Committee on Preparatory Research for the New Jersey Constitutional Convention, slightly shorter than the Louisiana collection, appears in Vol. II of the *Convention Proceedings*. Finally, Professor Sturm, in his *Methods of State Constitutional Reform*, has given us a highly useful analysis of the methods of operation, and of the advantages and disadvantages of the constitutional convention, the amending procedure, and the initiative as means of constitutional change.

SELECTED RECENT REFERENCES ON
STATE CONSTITUTIONS AND REVISION

RICHARD N. BAISDEN. *Charter for New Jersey: the New Jersey Constitutional Convention of 1947* (State Department of Education, Trenton, 1952).

J. ALTON BURDINE. "Basic Materials for the Study of State Constitutions and State Constitutional Development," *American Political Science Review*, December, 1954, pp. 1140–1152.

WILLIAM N. ETHRIDGE, JR., *Modernizing Mississippi's Constitution* (Bureau of Public Administration, University of Mississippi, 1950).

MARTIN L. FAUST. *Five Years Under the New Missouri Constitution* (Missouri Public Expenditure Survey, Jefferson City, 1950).

Hawaii. Legislative Reference Bureau, University of Hawaii, *Manual on State Constitutional Provisions* (Honolulu, 1950).

JOHN P. KEITH. *Methods of Constitutional Revision* (Bureau of Municipal Research, University of Texas, 1949).

Louisiana. State Law Institute, *Projet of a Constitution for the State of Louisiana, with Notes and Studies*, 4 Parts, 5 Vols. (Baton Rouge, 1954).

National Municipal League. Committee on State Government, *Model State Constitution, with Explanatory Articles*, Fifth Ed. (New York, 1948).

New Jersey. State of New Jersey, *Constitutional Convention of 1947, Held at Rutgers University, New Brunswick, New Jersey*, 5 Vols.

New York. New York State Constitutional Convention Committee, *Report*: Vol. III, *Constitutions of the States and of the United States* (Albany, 1938).

Oklahoma. Legislative Council, *Constitutional Convention Series* (Oklahoma City, 1948).

VERNON A. O'ROURKE and D. W. CAMPBELL. *Constitution Making in a Democracy* (Johns Hopkins Press, 1943). Analysis of the New York Convention of 1938.

ALBERT L. STURM. *Methods of State Constitutional Reform* (University of Michigan Press, 1954).

————. *The Need for Constitutional Revision in West Virginia* (Bureau for Government Research, West Virginia University, 1950).

RAYMOND UHL and others. *Constitutional Conventions: Organization, Powers, Functions and Procedures* (Bureau of Public Administration, University of South Carolina, 1951).

2

Elections

ELECTION LEGISLATION, 1953–55*

ELECTION legislation in 1953–55 resulted chiefly in changes in absentee voting, a gain in the number of presidential short-ballot states, extension of the use of voting machines, referenda on lowering of the voting age, and, in Connecticut, adoption of a direct primary. Connecticut thus became the forty-eighth state in use of the primary. Many changes occurred in the deadline for registration and for application for absentee ballots.

ABSENTEE VOTING

In November, 1954, Maryland, which had absentee voting for armed service personnel, adopted a constitutional amendment (referendum provided in Laws, 1953, Ch. 480) to authorize the legislature to enact a general absent voter law for all qualified voters in the state. Such legislation has been drafted and will be acted upon at the next session of the General Assembly. The New York legislature submitted a constitutional amendment in 1955, and the voters approved, to liberalize the absentee voter privilege by adding disability as a cause for absence. And New York (Laws, 1955, Ch. 789) changed the final date for application for ballots by absent voters from the tenth to the seventh day before the election.

Connecticut amended its absentee voting law (1955, Act No. 505): to reduce the

period for applying for absentee ballot from four to two months before the election; to eliminate the "agent" in securing absentee ballot forms and to require that if the application is brought to the municipal clerk by anyone other than the applicant, the clerk must mail the form to the absent voter; to allow only one absentee ballot set to be issued to a voter; to provide for manual counting of all absentee ballots at each polling place; and to provide that absentee voting forms shall be preserved for six months after the election.

Some changes were made in the application for absentee ballot in Arizona (Laws, 1953, Ch. 98): for the voter's age there is the statement "more than twenty-one years of age"; confinement in a hospital is added as cause of absence. Arizona now requires that absentee ballots be prepared for special as well as regular elections.

Colorado in 1955 prohibited solicitation of absentee ballots in elections. Georgia (Acts, 1955, No. 105) allowed ordinary mail for the absentee ballot rather than requiring registered mail. Kentucky (Acts, 1955, Ch. 208) extended the right to civilians necessarily absent from the state, whereas previously it had been only for those absent from the city or county. Louisiana (Acts, 1954, No. 557) allowed registration by persons in the armed forces and their spouses, and re-enacted its absentee military ballot law (Act No. 68). Michigan (1953 Acts, No. 12) granted the absent voting privilege to persons who "on account of the tenets of religion cannot attend the

---

*Prepared by SPENCER D. ALBRIGHT, University of Richmond, Virginia. At the time of writing, the session laws for 1955 were not yet available from a majority of the states. The summary is therefore incomplete for that year.

polls on the day of election or primary election." In 1954 (Acts, No. 116) Michigan rewrote its election code, in Rhode Island the absent voting law was revised to permit social workers with military and naval forces, and wives of armed service personnel, to vote without re-registering, and to facilitate voting by shut-ins.

Virginia in 1954 amended her absent voting law (Laws, 1954, Ch. 511): the clerk's office must forward to the election officials the lists of absent voters, to be available for public inspection; the voter must sign a sworn statement that he has complied with the election laws; he may appear at the polls on election day and have his ballot marked "voided at request of voter," and then he may see that his name is removed from the list of absent voters and he may proceed to "vote in the same manner as any other voter."

Presidential Short Ballot

West Virginia has adopted and Ohio has restored the presidential short ballot. States which do not at present have this ballot plan are scattered; they include one state in New England and one on the West Coast, six states in the South, five in the Great Plains, and five in the Rocky Mountain area. Most of the states which do not omit presidential electoral names from the ballot are of less than average population, and hence of less than the average number of presidential electors. In the 1954 election Wisconsin voters approved a measure to permit a vote for presidential electors by persons residing in the state less than one year.

Ballot Forms, Write-ins, Vacancies

New York (Laws, 1954, Ch. 380) provides a single vote for Governor and Lieutenant Governor through linking of the party candidates on the ballot, thus eliminating the possibility of filling the offices by a Governor from one party and a Lieutenant Governor from another. In 1955 Idaho restored the circle at the top of the party column to allow a straight ticket vote; this had been removed some years earlier. Montana (Laws, 1953, Ch. 72) has changed the ballot pattern from columns for different sets of offices to a consecutive arrangement—to include all printed matter, equally apportioned among three columns. In Texas (Laws, 1955, Ch. 34) it is provided that "The name of no candidate shall appear more than once on the official ballot, except as a candidate for two or more offices permitted . . . to be held by the same person."

Arizona enacted a law to require of a write-in candidate as many votes as the number of signatures required for nominating petitions. North Carolina, through a constitutional amendment adopted in 1954, provided that positions filled by appointment shall not have "short term" elections for the period between the November election and the first of January, except for United States Senators. (State legislation cannot alter provisions of the United States Constitution relating to the appointment and election of Senators. Vacancies among Representatives in Congress must be filled by elections, since there is no provision for appointment to this office.) Colorado (March 4, 1955) provided that no person shall be elected to fill a vacancy when the unexpired term is less than ninety days; the appointee shall serve out the term.

Primaries

Connecticut adopted her primary law, noted at the outset of this summary, in 1955, replacing a nominating system based on conventions and caucuses. In 1954 Montana provided for presidential preferential primaries, and Nevada in 1955 repealed its 1953 presidential primary law. Nebraska (Laws, 1953, Ch. 106) and New Mexico (Laws, 1955, Ch. 218) abolished pre-primary conventions. New York (Laws, 1955, Ch. 791) provided for the holding of one primary only in 1956, to be on Tuesday, June 5th, thereby eliminating both the spring and the fall primaries.

Voting Machines

In 1955 Connecticut adopted a number of acts relating to the voting machine: to prescribe the order of nominees if a party is entitled to two or more candidates, and to increase the hours authorized for instruction in the use of voting machines. In Maryland the use of voting machines was made mandatory for the 1956 primaries. Through an extensive law on the subject,

Mississippi has joined the states authorizing the voting machine (Acts, 1954, Ch. 360). In New Mexico the legislature authorized the State Canvassing Board to purchase voting machines for counties that cannot afford them. North Dakota (Laws, 1953, Ch. 159) authorized cities to use voting machines and to divide the cost of machines between a city and a county.

SUFFRAGE

In 1953 Tennessee, in amending its constitution for the first time since its adoption in 1870, removed the poll tax as a requirement for voting. In 1954 Alabama adopted an amendment to exempt blind or deaf persons from paying a poll tax.

Maine, through an amendment to its constitution approved in 1954, gave Indians the right to vote on an equal status with other citizens.

Proposals to lower the voting age have been introduced in many legislatures. In recent years the voters have been inclined to reject such liberalizing of suffrage requirements when presented in the form of constitutional amendments, Kentucky's voters, however, in November, 1955, approved a constitutional amendment to lower the voting age to 18. South Dakota rejected an amendment to lower the voting age in 1954. Indiana (Laws, 1953, Ch. 292) had such a proposal for a constitutional amendment, relating to voting at 19, but the plan was rejected in the 1955 session.

MISCELLANEOUS

Arizona (Laws, 1954, Ch. 13) provides that the United States flag is to be displayed in or near every polling place on election day. Connecticut provides that in addition to the United States flag (1955, Act No. 2) the state flag is permitted on the wall inside each polling place.

In South Dakota (Laws, 1955, Ch. 58) a recount board is provided, to consist of a county judge and two persons appointed by him; if the county judge is disqualified, then the circuit judge shall act. Counting procedure has received attention in North Carolina (Laws, 1955, Ch. 891), with the provision that all ballots marked as straight party votes shall be piled together and counted accordingly, and "all split-voted ballots" shall be counted separately. This plan speeds the count, and often has been used in many states, regardless of formal language to count the ballots in order. North Carolina (Laws, 1955, Ch. 767) allows the purchase and use of ballot boxes into which only unfolded ballots may be deposited, and removes a previous provision requiring folding of ballots.

Provisions for annual sessions of legislatures, although not a change in elections, are bound to affect future candidacies for election to the legislature. Georgia, Kansas, Louisiana and West Virginia provided for annual sessions through constitutional amendments adopted in 1954.

REFERENCE WORKS ON BALLOTS AND ELECTION SYSTEMS

SPENCER D. ALBRIGHT, *The American Ballot*, American Council on Public Affairs, Washington, D.C., 1942. HUGH A. BONE, *American Politics and the Party System* (2nd ed.), New York, 1955. J. B. JOHNSON and J. J. LEWIS, *Registration for Voting in the United States*, Chicago, 1946. V. O. KEY, *Politics, Parties, and Pressure Groups* (3rd ed.), New York, 1952. G. F. MILLER, *Absent Voters and Suffrage Laws*, Washington, D.C., 1948.

LIMITATIONS ON CAMPAIGN EXPENDITURES IN THE STATES

State	Filing of statements required					Sources of contributions restricted	Contributions by corporations prohibited	Contributions by labor unions prohibited	Restrictions on character of expenditures	Total expenditures by candidate limited	Amount spent in behalf of candidate limited
	Campaign receipts by parties	Campaign receipts by candidates	Campaign disbursements by parties	Campaign disbursements by candidates	Required time for filing statements						
Alabama	Yes	Yes	Yes	Yes	Between 15 and 10 days before and within 15 days after elections	Yes	Yes	No	Yes	Yes	No
Arizona	Yes	Yes	Yes	Yes	Receipts before, expenditures after election	Yes	Yes	No	No	No	....
Arkansas	No	No	No	Yes	Corrupt practice pledge before, candidate expenses after election	No	....	....	No	Yes	No
California	No	Yes	No	Yes	After election	No	No	No	Yes	No	No
Colorado	Yes	No	Yes	Yes	After election	No	No	No	No	No	No
Connecticut	Yes	Yes	Yes	Yes	After election	Yes	Yes	No	Yes	Yes	No (if spent by independent political committee)
Delaware	No	No	No	No		No	No	No	No	No	No
Florida	No	No	No	Yes	Before and after election	Yes	Yes	No	Yes	No	No
Georgia	No	Yes(a)	No	Yes(a)	Within 20 days after election	....	....	No	....	Yes	....
Idaho	No	No	No	Yes	After election	Yes	No	No	....	Yes	Yes
Illinois	No	No	No	No	After election	No	No	No	Yes	No	No
Indiana	Yes	Yes	Yes	Yes	Within 30 days after election	Yes	Yes	Yes	Yes	Yes	Yes
Iowa	Yes	Yes	Yes	Yes	After election	Yes	No	No	No	Yes	No
Kansas	Yes	Yes	Yes	Yes	After election	Yes	Yes	No	Yes	Yes	Yes
Kentucky	No(b)	Yes	No(b)	Yes	15 days before and 30 days after election	Yes	Yes	No	Yes	Yes	No
Louisiana	No	No	No	No	None	Yes(c)	Yes	No	No	No	No
Maine	Yes	Yes	Yes	Yes	Within 15 days after election	No	No	No	Yes	No	No
Maryland	Yes	Yes	Yes	Yes	After election	Yes	Yes	No	No	Yes	Yes
Massachusetts	Yes	Yes	Yes	Yes	After election	Yes	Yes	No	Yes	Yes	No (if spent by political committee)
Michigan	Yes	Yes	Yes	Yes	After election but before certification to office	Yes	Yes	No	Yes	Yes	Yes
Minnesota	Yes	Yes	Yes	Yes	Before and after election	Yes	Yes	No	Yes	Yes	Yes
Mississippi	No(d)	Yes(d)	No(d)	Yes(d)	Contribution statements filed 1st and 15th each month of campaign	Yes	No	No	No	Yes	Yes
Missouri	Yes	No	Yes	Yes	After election	Yes	Yes	No	No	Yes	Yes
Montana	Yes	Yes	Yes	Yes	After election	No	No	Only if union is a corporation	No	Yes	Yes
Nebraska	Yes	No	Yes	Yes	After election	Yes	Yes	No	Yes	No	No
Nevada	No	No	No	No		No	No	No	No	No	No
New Hampshire	Yes	Yes	Yes	Yes	1st statement Wednesday (6 days) before; 2nd, second Friday (10 days) after election	Yes	Yes	Yes	Yes	Yes	Yes

State						Date of filing statements	By insurance corporations				
New Jersey	Yes	Yes	Yes	Yes	Yes	Friday or Saturday before and 20 days after election	No	No	Yes	Yes	No
New Mexico	Yes	Yes	Yes	Yes	No(e)	Candidates, within 10 days after election; parties, within 30 days after election	No	No	No	Yes	No
New York	Yes	Yes	Yes (in general elections)	Yes	Yes	Before and after elections	Yes	No	No	Yes	Yes
North Carolina	Yes	Yes		Yes	Yes	Before and after elections	Yes	No	No	No	No
North Dakota	No	No	No	Yes	Yes	After elections	Yes	No	Yes	Yes	Yes
Ohio	Yes	Yes	Yes	Yes	Yes	By 4:00 p.m. 10th day after election	Yes	No	Yes	Yes	No
Oklahoma	No	Yes	No	Yes	No	10 days after election	No	No	No	No	Yes
Oregon	Yes	Yes	Yes	Yes	Yes(f)	15 days after election	(f)	(f)	Yes	Yes	Yes
Pennsylvania	Yes	Yes	Yes	Yes	Yes	Within 30 days after each primary and general election	Yes	Yes	Yes	No	No
Rhode Island	No corrupt practices act(g)					Before elections	..	..	..	..	..
South Carolina	No	No	No	Yes	No		Yes	No	Yes	No	Yes
South Dakota	Yes	Yes	Yes	Yes	Yes	Within 30 days after elections	Yes	No	Yes	Yes	Yes
Tennessee	No	No	Yes (by campaign chairman)	Yes	No	Candidate's statement 5 to 10 days before convention or election; manager's within 30 days after	No	No	No	No	Yes
Texas	No	Yes	No	Yes	Yes	Before and after elections	Yes	Yes	Yes	No	Yes
Utah	Yes	Yes	Yes	Yes	Yes	2nd Sat. after 1st disbursement; 2nd Sat. each calendar month thereafter; Sat. preceding any primary or election	Yes	No	Yes	Yes	No (if spent by other than committee)
Vermont	No	No	No	Yes	..	Within 10 days after primary	..	..	Yes	..	No
Virginia	..	..	....	Yes	..	Within 30 days after election, caucus, convention or primary election	..	..	Yes	Yes	....
Washington	No	Yes	No	Yes	No	After primary only	No	No	No	No	No
West Virginia	Yes	Yes	Yes	Yes	Yes	Before and after elections	Yes	No	Yes	Yes	Yes
Wisconsin	Yes	Yes	Yes	Yes	Yes	By 5 p.m. on Tues. preceding election; Sat. following election or primary	Yes	Yes	Yes	Yes	Yes
Wyoming	Yes	Yes	Yes	Yes	Yes	Within 20 days after election	Yes	No	Yes	Yes	Yes
Alaska	No	No	No	No	No	None	..	No	No	No	No
Guam	Yes	Yes	Yes	Yes	No	Within 15 days after election	..	No	..	..	....
Hawaii	No	No	Yes(h)	Yes	No	Within 20 days after election	No	No	Yes	No	No
Puerto Rico	No	No	No	No	No	No	No	No	No	No	No
Virgin Islands	No parties					....	No	No	No	No	No

(a) And agents.
(b) Campaign committee manager must file.
(c) Certain state employees prohibited from making political contributions.
(d) Primaries only, does not apply for elections.
(e) Political parties cannot contribute in primaries.
(f) Certain corporations only—O.R.S. 260.280.
(g) Only restrictions are those imposed by federal statutes.
(h) By agent or committee acting for or on behalf of any candidate.

QUALIFICATIONS FOR VOTING

State	Minimum age	U. S. citizen	Residence in — State	Residence in — County	Residence in — District	Property	Literacy test	Poll tax(a)
Alabama	21	★	2 yrs.	1 yr.	3 mo.	....	....	(b)
Arizona	21	★	1 yr.	30 da.	30 da.	....	★	....
Arkansas	21	★	12 mo.	6 mo.	1 mo.	....	....	★
California	21	(f)	1 yr.	90 da.	54 da.	....	★	....
Colorado	21	★	1 yr.	90 da.	15 da. (g)	....	....	....
Connecticut	21	(i)	1 yr.	......	6 mo.	....	★	....
Delaware	21	★	1 yr.	3 mo.	30 da.	....	★	....
Florida	21	★	1 yr.	6 mo.	......	....	....	....
Georgia	18	★	1 yr.	6 mo.(e)	......	....	(j)	....
Idaho	21	★	6 mo.	30 da.	......	....	....	....
Illinois	21	★	1 yr.	90 da.	30 da.	....	....	....
Indiana	21	★	6 mo.	60 da.(l)	30 da.	....	....	....
Iowa	21	★	6 mo.	60 da.	10 da.	....	....	....
Kansas	21	★	6 mo.	30 da.(l)	30 da.	....	....	....
Kentucky	18	★	1 yr.	6 mo.	60 da.	....	....	....
Louisiana	21	★	2 yrs.	1 yr.	3 mo.(m)	....	(n)	....
Maine	21	★	6 mo.	3 mo.	3 mo.	....	★	....
Maryland	21	★	1 yr.	6 mo.	6 mo.	....	....	....
Massachusetts	21	★	1 yr.	......	6 mo.(o)	....	★	....
Michigan	21	★	6 mo.	......	30 da.	(p)	....	....
Minnesota	21	(f)	6 mo.	......	30 da.	....	....	....
Mississippi	21	★	2 yrs.	......	1 yr.(q)	....	★	(r)
Missouri	21	★	1 yr.	60 da.	60 da.	....	....	....
Montana	21	★	1 yr.	30 da.	......	(p)	....	....
Nebraska	21	★	6 mo.	40 da.	10 da.	....	....	....
Nevada	21	★	6 mo.	30 da.	10 da.	(p)	....	....
New Hampshire	21	★	6 mo.	......	6 mo.	....	★	....
New Jersey	21	★	1 yr.	5 mo.	......	....	....	....
New Mexico	21	★	12 mo.	90 da.	30 da.	(p)	....	....
New York	21	(f)	1 yr.	4 mo.	30 da.	....	(t)	....
North Carolina	21	★	1 yr.	......	4 mo.	....	★	....
North Dakota	21	★	1 yr.	90 da.	30 da.	....	....	....
Ohio	21	★	1 yr.	40 da.	40 da.	....	....	....
Oklahoma	21	★	1 yr.	6 mo.	30 da.	....	....	....
Oregon	21	★	6 mo.	......	30 da.	....	★	....
Pennsylvania	21	★	1 yr. (w)	......	2 mo.	....	....	....
Rhode Island	21	★	1 yr.	......	6 mo.	....	....	....
South Carolina	21	★	2 yrs.(q)	1 yr.	4 mo.	(x)	(x)	....
South Dakota	21	★	1 yr.	90 da.	30 da.	....	....	....
Tennessee	21	★	12 mo.	6 mo.	......	....	....	....
Texas	21	★	1 yr.	6 mo.	6 mo.	(p)	....	(r)
Utah	21	(f)	1 yr.	4 mo.	60 da.	(p)	....	....
Vermont	21	★	1 yr.	......	3 mo. (l)	....	....	....
Virginia	21	★	1 yr.	6 mo.	30 da.	....	★	(z)
Washington	21	★	1 yr.	90 da.	30 da.	....	★	....
West Virginia	21	★	1 yr.	60 da.	......	....	....	....
Wisconsin	21	★	1 yr.	......	10 da.	....	....	....
Wyoming	21	★	1 yr.	60 da.	10 da.	....	★	....
Alaska	21	★	12 mo.	......	30 da.(ac)	....	★	....
Guam	21	★	2 yrs.	......	......	....	....	....
Hawaii	21	★	1 yr.	......	3 mo.	....	(ae)	....
Puerto Rico	21	★	1 yr.	......	1 yr.	....	....	....
Virgin Islands	21	★	1 yr.	......	......	....	★	....

(a) Poll or head taxes are levied in many other states. Those listed here, however, provide that payment of the poll tax is a prerequisite for voting.
(b) Must pay all poll taxes owed for the two years next preceding election at which person offers to vote. Persons who have honorably served in the military service of the United States while the United States is engaged in hostilities, whether war is declared or not, are exempt from payment of poll taxes.
(c) Registration is permanent unless removed for cause.
(d) Conditioned upon voting and continued residence.
(e) Except for irrigation district elections.
(f) Must have been citizen ninety days.

(g) City or town, thirty days.
(h) All except certain minor elections.
(i) Must have been citizen five years.
(j) Under 1949 act, all voters must re-register and pass literacy test. Those failing test may qualify by answering 10 of 30 oral questions prescribed by law.
(k) For all state and federal elections.
(l) Township.
(m) Municipality, four months.
(n) Literacy test required but exception allowed if person can pass certain specified requirements.
(o) In city or town.
(p) For vote on bond issues or special assessments only.

QUALIFICATIONS FOR VOTING—Continued

Registration							
Type					Coverage		
Permanent		Periodic			All elections	Some elections	*State*
All areas	Some areas	All areas	Some areas	Frequency			
(c)					★		Alabama
(d)					(e)		Arizona
							Arkansas
★					★		California
★						(h)	Colorado
★					★		Connecticut
★					★		Delaware
★					★		Florida
★(t)					★		Georgia
★					★		Idaho
★						(k)	Illinois
★						(h)	Indiana
	★		★	4 years		(h)	Iowa
	★		★		★		Kansas
★					★		Kentucky
	★		★	4 years	★		Louisiana
★					★		Maine
	★		★		★		Maryland
★					★		Massachusetts
★					★		Michigan
(c)	★		★		★		Minnesota
						(s)	Mississippi
	★		★	4 years	★		Missouri
★						(h)	Montana
	★		★	6 years		(h)	Nebraska
★					★		Nevada
★					★		New Hampshire
★					★		New Jersey
★					★		New Mexico
	★		★	Annual		★	New York
★					★		North Carolina
	★		★			★	North Dakota
	★		★		★		Ohio
(v)					★(u)		Oklahoma
★					★		Oregon
★					★		Pennsylvania
★					★		Rhode Island
		★		Decennial	★		South Carolina
★					★		South Dakota
★					★		Tennessee
(y)	(y)	(y)	(y)	Annual			Texas
★						(h)	Utah
★						★	Vermont
(aa)					★		Virginia
(d)					(e)		Washington
★					(ab)		West Virginia
	★		★		★		Wisconsin
		★		Every gen. elec.		★	Wyoming
★					(ad)		Alaska
(d)					★		Guam
(af)					★		Hawaii
★					★		Puerto Rico
							Virgin Islands

(q) Ministers of the Gospel and teachers in public schools may vote after six months' residence.
(r) Assessed upon citizens 21 to 60 years of age except those specifically exempted.
(s) Registration is for all elections of state and county, but voter must be registered in municipality also to vote in municipal elections.
(t) A person who became entitled to vote after January 1, 1922, must be able except for physical disability, to read and write English.
(u) Except school district elections.
(v) Re-register in two years if not voting within that time.
(w) Six months if previously an elector or native of U. S.
(x) Ownership of property is an alternative to literacy.
(y) Constitution provides for registration in cities over 10,000, but no system exists. Poll tax receipts determine eligibility of voters aged 21 to 60 years; exemption certificates for those over 60 in cities over 10,000, and certain others.
(z) Must owe no past due taxes.
(aa) Except in some cities.
(ab) All elections except special elections.
(ac) Precinct.
(ad) Municipal election.
(ae) English or Hawaiian language.
(af) Name subject to removal from registration list after failure to vote in a general election.

GENERAL ELECTIONS IN 1956

State	Date of general elections in 1956	State officers to be elected	State legislators percentage Senate	State legislators percentage House	United States Congress Senate	United States Congress House	Other elections for state officers
Alabama	Nov. 6	2 Members of Supreme Court, President of Public Service Commission	None	None	Yes	Yes	No
Arizona	Nov. 6	Governor, Attorney General, Secretary of State, 1 Judge of Supreme Court, Treasurer, Auditor, Superintendent of Public Instruction	100	100	Yes	Yes	No
Arkansas	Nov. 6	Governor, Lt. Governor, Attorney General, Secretary of State, Chief Justice of Supreme Court, 1 Judge of Supreme Court, Treasurer, Auditor, Land Commissioner	50	100	Yes	Yes	No
California	Nov. 6	None	50	100	Yes	Yes	No
Colorado	Nov. 6	Governor, Lt. Governor, Attorney General, Secretary of State, 2 Judges of Supreme Court, Treasurer, Auditor, 2 Regents of University of Colorado	51	100	Yes	Yes	No
Connecticut	Nov. 6	None	100	100	Yes	Yes	No
Delaware	Nov. 6	Governor, Lt. Governor, Treasurer, Auditor, Insurance Commissioner	41	100	No	Yes	No
Florida	Nov. 2	Governor, Attorney General, Secretary of State, 4 Justices of Supreme Court, Treasurer, Comptroller, Commissioner of Agriculture, 3 Railroad and Public Utilities Commissioners, Superintendent of Public Instruction	50	100	Yes	Yes	No
Georgia	Nov. 6	Chief Justice of Supreme Court, Presiding Justice of Supreme Court, 2 Judges of Court of Appeals	100	100	Yes	Yes	No
Idaho	Nov. 6	None	100	100	Yes	Yes	No
Illinois	Nov. 6	Governor, Lt. Governor, Attorney General, Secretary of State, Treasurer, Auditor, Clerk of Supreme Court	100	100	Yes	Yes	No
Indiana	Nov. 6	Governor, Lt. Governor, Attorney General, Secretary of State, 3 Judges of Supreme Court, Treasurer, Auditor, 2 Judges of Appellate Court, Reporter of Supreme and Appellate Courts, Superintendent of Public Instruction	50	100	Yes	Yes	No
Iowa	Nov. 6	Governor, Lt. Governor, Attorney General, Secretary of State, Treasurer, Auditor, Secretary of Agriculture, 1 Commerce Commissioner	50	100	Yes	Yes	No
Kansas	Nov. 6	Governor, Lt. Governor, Attorney General, Secretary of State, Treasurer, Auditor, 3 Justices of Supreme Court, Superintendent of Public Instruction, Commissioner of Insurance, State Printer	100	100	Yes	Yes	No
Kentucky	Nov. 6	1 Justice of Court of Appeals	None	None	Yes	Yes	No
Louisiana	April 17	Governor, Lt. Governor, Attorney General, Secretary of State, Treasurer, Auditor, Commissioner of Agriculture and Immigration, Registrar of State Land Office, Superintendent of Public Education	100	100	No	No	Nov. (a)
Maine	Sept. 10	Governor	100	100	No	Yes	No
Maryland	Nov. 5	None	None	None	Yes	Yes	No
Massachusetts	Nov. 6	Governor, Lt. Governor, Attorney General, Secretary of Commonwealth, Treasurer-Receiver General, Auditor	100	100	No	Yes	No
Michigan	Nov. 6	Governor, Lt. Governor, Attorney General, Secretary of State, Treasurer, Auditor General	100	100	No	Yes	No
Minnesota	Nov. 6	Governor, Lt. Governor, Attorney General, Secretary of State, Treasurer, 2 Justices of Supreme Court, 1 member of Railroad and Warehouse Commission	None	100	No	Yes	No

GENERAL ELECTIONS IN 1956—Continued

State	Date of general elections in 1956	State officers to be elected	State legislators percentage		United States Congress		Other elections for state officers
			Senate	*House*	*Senate*	*House*	
Mississippi.........	Nov. 6	None	None	None	No	Yes	No
Missouri...........	Nov. 6	Governor, Lt. Governor, Attorney General, Secretary of State, Treasurer, Auditor	50	50	Yes	Yes	No
Montana..........	Nov. 6	Governor, Attorney General, Secretary of State, Treasurer, Auditor, 2 Justices of Supreme Court, Clerk of Supreme Court, 1 member of Railway and Public Service Commission, Superintendent of Public Instruction	50	100	No	Yes	No
Nebraska..........	Nov. 6	Governor, Lt. Governor, Attorney General, Secretary of State, Treasurer, Auditor, 1 Railway Commissioner, 2 members of State Board of Education	100(b)		No	Yes	No
Nevada............	Nov. 6	1 Justice of Supreme Court, 1 Regent of University of Nevada	47	100	Yes	Yes	No
New Hampshire.....	Nov. 6	Governor, Members of Executive Council	100	100	Yes	Yes	No
New Jersey.........	Nov. 6	None	None	None	No	Yes	No
New Mexico........	Nov. 6	Governor, Lt. Governor, Attorney General, Secretary of State, Treasurer, Auditor, 1 Justice of Supreme Court, Commissioner of Public Lands, 1 Corporation Commissioner, Superintendent of Public Instruction	100	100	No	Yes	No
New York..........	Nov. 6	None	100	100	Yes	Yes	No
North Carolina......	Nov. 6	Governor, Lt. Governor, Attorney General, Secretary of State, some Justices of Supreme Court, Treasurer, Auditor, Commissioner of Agriculture, Commissioner of Insurance, Commissioner of Labor, Superintendent of Public Instruction	100	100	Yes	Yes	No
North Dakota.......	Nov. 6	Governor, Attorney General, Secretary of State, Treasurer, Auditor, Commissioner of Agriculture and Labor, Commissioner of Insurance, 1 Public Service Commissioner, Tax Commissioner, Superintendent of Public Instruction, 1 Judge of Supreme Court	50	100	Yes	Yes	No
Ohio...............	Nov. 6	Governor, Attorney General, Secretary of State, Treasurer, Auditor	100	100	Yes	Yes	No
Oklahoma..........	Nov. 6	3 Judges of Supreme Court, 1 Judge of Criminal Court of Appeals, 1 Corporation Commissioner	50	100	Yes	Yes	No
Oregon............	Nov. 6	Attorney General, Secretary of State, Treasurer, 4 Justices of Supreme Court	50	100	Yes	Yes	No
Pennsylvania.......	Nov. 6	Treasurer, Auditor General, 1 Judge of Supreme Court	50	100	Yes	Yes	No
Rhode Island.......	Nov. 6	Governor, Lt. Governor, Attorney General, Secretary of State, General Treasurer	100	100	No	Yes	No
South Carolina.....	Nov. 13	None	50	100	Yes	Yes	No
South Dakota.......	Nov. 6	Governor, Lt. Governor, Attorney General, Secretary of State, Treasurer, Auditor, Commissioner of School and Public Lands, 1 member of Public Utilities Commission, Superintendent of Public Instruction, 1 Judge of Supreme Court	100	100	Yes	Yes	No
Tennessee..........	Nov. 6	1 Member of Public Service Commission	100	100	No	Yes	No
Texas..............	Nov. 6	Governor, Lt. Governor, Attorney General, Treasurer, Comptroller of Public Accounts, Commissioner of General Land Office, Commissioner of Agriculture, 1 member of Railroad Commission, 3 Justices of Supreme Court, 1 Judge of Court of Criminal Appeals	50	100	No	Yes	No

GENERAL ELECTIONS IN 1956—Concluded

State	Date of general elections in 1956	State officers to be elected	State legislators percentage		United States Congress		Other elections for state officers
			Senate	House	Senate	House	
Utah..............	Nov. 6	Governor, Attorney General, Secretary of State, Treasurer, Auditor, 1 Justice of Supreme Court	52	100	Yes	Yes	No
Vermont...........	Nov. 6	Governor, Lt. Governor, Attorney General, Secretary of State, Treasurer, Auditor	100	100	Yes	Yes	No
Virginia...........	Nov. 6	None	None	None	No	Yes	No
Washington........	Nov. 6	Governor, Lt. Governor, Attorney General, Secretary of State, Justices of Supreme Court, Treasurer, Auditor, Insurance Commissioner, Commissioner of Public Lands, Superintendent of Public Instruction	50	100	Yes	Yes	No
West Virginia......	Nov. 6	Governor, Attorney General, Secretary of State, Treasurer, Auditor, Commissioner of Agriculture, Superintendent of Schools	50	100	No	Yes	No
Wisconsin.........	Nov. 6	Governor, Lt. Governor, Attorney General, Secretary of State, Treasurer	50	100	Yes	Yes	April (c)
Wyoming..........	Nov. 6	None	100	100	No	Yes	No
Alaska.............	Oct. 9	Attorney General, Highway Engineer	50	100	No	Yes(d)	No
Guam.............	Nov. 14	None	100(b)		No	No	No
Hawaii............	Nov. 6	None	53	100	No	Yes(d)	No
Puerto Rico........	Nov. 6	Governor	100	100	No	Yes(d)	No
Virgin Islands......	Nov. 6	None	100(b)		No	No	No

(a) State officers elected in November are members of Board of Education, members of Public Service Commission and Justices of Supreme Court. Senators and Representatives to United States Congress are also to be elected at that time.
(b) Unicameral legislature.

(c) Justice of Supreme Court to be elected.
(d) Alaska and Hawaii each elect a Delegate to the United States Congress. Puerto Rico elects a Resident Commissioner who sits in the House of Representatives.

PRIMARY ELECTIONS IN THE STATES

State	Date of primary—1956	Date of run-off primary 1956	Voters recive ballots of		Nomination of candidates*	Date of Presidential primary
			All parties participating	One party		
Alabama	May 1	May 29	...	Yes	CP(a)	No
Arizona	Sept. 11	No	...	Yes	P	No
Arkansas	July 31 (b)	Aug. 14	...	Yes	CP	No
California	None	No	...	Yes	P	June 5
Colorado	Sept. 11	No	...	Yes	P	No
Connecticut	Sept. 5(c)	No	...	Yes	X	No
Delaware	Aug. 18	No	...	Yes	CP	No
Florida	May 8	May 29	...	Yes	P	May 29
Georgia	(d)	(d)	...	Yes	CP(a)	No
Idaho	Aug. 14	No	Yes	...	P	No
Illinois	April 10	No	...	Yes	P	April 10
Indiana	None	No	...	Yes	C	May 8
Iowa	June 4	No	...	Yes	X	No
Kansas	Aug. 7	No	...	Yes	CP(e)	No
Kentucky	Aug. 4	No	...	Yes	P	No
Louisiana	Jan. 17	Feb. 21	...	Yes	P	No
Maine	June 18	No	...	Yes	P	No
Maryland	None	No	...	Yes	X	May 7
Massachusetts	Sept. 18	No	...	Yes	P(f)	April 24
Michigan	Aug. 7	No	Yes	...	CP	No
Minnesota	Sept. 11	No	Yes	...	P	Mar. 20
Mississippi	Aug. 28	Sept. 18(g)	...	Yes	P	No
Missouri	Aug. 7	No	...	Yes	P	No
Montana	June 5	No	Yes	...	P	June 5
Nebraska	May 15	No	...	Yes	P	May 15
Nevada	Sept. 4	No	...	Yes	P	No
New Hampshire	Sept. 11	No	...	Yes	P	Mar. 13
New Jersey	April 17	No	...	Yes	P	No
New Mexico	May 8	No	...	Yes	P	No
New York	None	No	...	Yes	C	June 5
North Carolina	May 26	June 23 (g)	...	Yes	P	No
North Dakota	June 26	No	...	Yes	P	No
Ohio	May 8	No	...	Yes	P	May 8
Oklahoma	July 3	July 24	...	Yes	P	No
Oregon	May 18	No	...	Yes	P	May 18
Pennsylvania	April 24	No	...	Yes	P	April 24
Rhode Island	Not Set	No	Yes	...	P	No
South Carolina	June 12	June 26	Yes	...	P	No
South Dakota	June 5	No	...	Yes	CP	June 5
Tennessee	Aug. 2	No	...	Yes	CP	No
Texas	July 28 (h)	Aug. 25 (g)	...	Yes	CP(a)	No
Utah	Sept. 4	No	...	Yes	C	No
Vermont	Sept. 11	No	...	Yes	P	No
Virginia	None	No	...	Yes	CP	No
Washington	Sept. 11	No	Yes	...	P	No
West Virginia	May 8	No	...	Yes	P	No
Wisconsin	Sept. 11	No	Yes	...	P	April 3
Wyoming	None	No	...	Yes	P	No
Alaska	April 24	No	Yes	...	P	April 24
Hawaii	Oct. 6	No	Yes	...	P	No

*Abbreviations: P—direct primary; C—convention; CP—some candidates in direct primary, some in convention; X—combination of direct primary and convention; NA—information not available.
(a) Usually Democratic party nominates in primary and Republican party in convention.
(b) Preferential primary.

(c) Incumbent party; Sept. 7 for other parties.
(d) Date set by party authority.
(e) Nominations may also be by nomination papers.
(f) Except "minority" parties which select candidates for general election by convention.
(g) Run-off primary if necessary.
(h) Democratic only.

VOTING STATISTICS: SELECTED DATA ON PERSONS REGISTERED AND VOTING BY STATE

State	Registered Number	Registered Year	Voting for Governor Year	Voting for Governor General election	Voting for Governor Primary (a) election
Alabama	(b)	....	1954	333,089	594,381
Arizona	307,545	1954	1954	243,970	289,487
Arkansas	532,162(c)	1953	1954	335,125	324,599
California	5,885,237	1954	1954	4,030,368	3,042,677
Colorado	737,027	1954	1954	489,540	188,564
Connecticut	1,185,234	1952	1950	878,735	(d)
Delaware	NA	....	1952	170,749	NA
Florida	1,093,735	1954	1954	357,621	694,521
Georgia	1,273,793(e)	1954	1954	391,626	646,235
Idaho	330,000(e)	1952	1954	228,685	129,223
Illinois	(b)	....	1952	4,415,864	1,984,755
Indiana	2,424,469	1952	1952	1,931,869	(d)
Iowa	(b)	....	1954	848,591	320,984
Kansas	(b)	....	1954	622,633	331,976
Kentucky	(b)	....	1951	634,359	410,859
Louisiana	1,056,511	1952	1952	123,681	785,045
Maine	480,658	1954	1954	248,971	114,273
Maryland	1,092,730	1954	1954	700,484	406,732
Massachusetts	2,523,414	1954	1954	1,942,071	604,795
Michigan	(b)	....	1954	2,187,027	426,680
Minnesota	(b)	....	1954	1,151,417	579,439
Mississippi	(b)	....	1951	43,422	407,774
Missouri	(b)	....	1952	1,870,999	962,371
Montana	304,053	1952	1952	146,252	263,792
Nebraska	(b)	....	1954	414,841	225,667
Nevada	108,373	1954	1954	78,462	36,705(g)
New Hampshire	327,329	1954	1954	194,631	88,704
New Jersey	2,744,165	1952	1949	1,414,527	704,869
New Mexico	361,919	1954	1954	193,956	90,526
New York	6,214,366	1954	1954	5,241,177	(d)
North Carolina	(b)	....	1952	1,179,635	564,505
North Dakota	(b)	....	1954	193,501	159,367
Ohio	2,914,355	1954	1954	2,597,790	739,093
Oklahoma	(b)	....	1954	609,194	577,919
Oregon	819,539	1954	1954	566,701	325,833
Pennsylvania	5,154,734	1954	1954	3,720,457	1,537,099
Rhode Island	447,249	1952	1952	409,689	....
South Carolina	567,467	1950	1950	50,642	336,329
South Dakota	330,000(e)	1954	1954	236,255	133,679
Tennessee	(b)	....	1954	706,830(f)	322,591
Texas	(b)	....	1954	620,558	1,350,757
Utah	(b)	....	1952	327,704	153,513
Vermont	201,000	1952	1952	150,862	73,253
Virginia	827,835	1955	1953	412,457	....
Washington	1,392,594	1952	1952	1,078,497	703,359
West Virginia	1,176,428	1952	1952	882,527	572,026
Wisconsin	(b)	....	1954	1,158,666	557,741
Wyoming	(b)	....	1950	96,959	65,911

NA—Figures not available.
(a) Includes figures only for initial primary elections—not run-off primaries.
(b) Registration not required or no central records maintained.
(c) For 1954 primary election; 1954 registration for general election, 561,007.

(d) Candidates for Governor nominated at party conventions.
(e) Estimate.
(f) Democratic primary only; no gubernatorial candidate in Republican primary.
(h) No Republican primary as only one candidate filed.

Section III

LEGISLATURES AND LEGISLATION

1. Legislative Organization
   and Services
2. Legislation

1

Legislative Organization and Services

STRUCTURE AND PROCEDURES

THE citizens of the states through their constitutions have vested the supreme law-making power in their legislatures. They have provided for the popular election at frequent intervals of those who comprise the legislative bodies. Except in Nebraska they have established two-house legislatures in each state.

Beyond these common elements, a very wide variety of constitutional provisions, statutory requirements, rules and precedents govern the workings of the state legislatures. Together these determine the many details of legislative structure, organization and procedure, the purpose of which is to enable the legislatures to carry out their responsibilities in an orderly and effective manner.

SIZES AND TERMS

In size the American state legislatures range from a total of forty-three members in the unicameral Nebraska legislature to 423 in New Hampshire. The smallest bicameral legislature is that of Delaware, with fifty-two members. (See page 100.) State Senates vary in membership from seventeen in Delaware and Nevada to sixty-seven in Minnesota. The lower houses differ even more widely—from thirty-five members in Delaware and less than sixty each in Idaho, Nevada, New Mexico and Wyoming up to 399 in New Hampshire, 279 in Connecticut and 246 in Vermont.

In all states legislative terms are either of two or four years. State Senators in thirty-two states serve for four years; in sixteen

states (including Nebraska) they serve for two. Shorter terms are the rule for members of lower houses. In forty-three states House members serve for two-year terms; only in the states of Alabama, Louisiana, Maryland and Mississippi do they have four-year terms.

Legislatures in a quarter of the states in 1952–53 considered measures to lengthen legislative terms. Only in Ohio and California did these proposals get as far as popular vote, and in both cases they were defeated. Again in 1954–55, ten states considered measures to lengthen terms, but only in Ohio has a measure been sent to the people for vote. The vote, to be held November, 1956, will decide whether Ohio Senate terms will be increased from two to four years.

SESSIONS

As indicated in the table on "Legislative Sessions," fourteen state and three territorial legislatures meet annually—a significant change since 1943, when only four state legislatures had annual sessions. The remaining thirty-four states hold biennial regular sessions, all but three (Kentucky, Mississippi and Virginia) in the odd-numbered years.

The trend toward annual sessions is continuing. Sixteen state legislatures in 1954–55 considered the matter. In four states—Georgia, Kansas, Louisiana and West Virginia—the voters in 1954 adopted constitutional amendments providing for annual sessions. The legislatures of Con-

93

necticut and Nevada in 1955 approved annual session amendments. If re-enacted in 1957, both then go to the voters. Missouri voters in 1956 will pass on an annual session amendment.

Restrictions on length of the regular session exist in thirty-two states and take a variety of forms, both direct and indirect. Sixty calendar days is the most common limitation. Where they exist, most limits on session length are expressly provided in the constitution. In nine states, however, the length is limited indirectly, through cessation of legislative pay after a specified period of time. In the case of special sessions, twenty-seven states have no limits on length. Several states utilize the device of the "split session" or "recess session" to enable legislators to study pending proposals in greater leisure, to review executive vetoes, or for other purposes. These states include Alabama, California, Florida, New Jersey and Wisconsin. The Massachusetts legislature is empowered to use this device but in practice does not.

The Missouri annual session amendment, referred to above, would provide fifteen-day veto-review sessions, three months after adjournment. This innovation would be in addition to the budget session in the even-numbered year, and an increase in length of the odd-year session from five to six months.

COMPENSATION

There is general agreement that compensation of state legislators has been and in most states continues to be too low, and it has been recommended increasingly that annual salaries rather than daily pay plans be employed. In both respects there have been extensive changes in recent years. In 1943 less than half of the states employed the salary plan; at present, thirty-two states use it. The present range of legislative salaries in these thirty-two states is from $200 in New Hampshire to $12,000 in California and $15,000 in New York, per biennium. The median salary, per biennium, is in the $2,400–$2,750 range.

Eighteen states employ a daily pay plan for legislators, two of them—Colorado and Oklahoma—using a combination of daily pay and biennial salary. The amounts paid under daily pay plans vary greatly—from $5.00 in Kansas, North Dakota and Rhode Island up to $30 in Louisiana. For these eighteen states, the median daily pay is $12.

As indicated in an accompanying table, legislators in a number of states receive appreciable expense allowances in addition to their salaries or daily pay. In fifteen states, this allowance is payable in the form of a per diem during the session; in six other states there are lump-sum allowances. In Louisiana, $150 a month is paid when the legislature is not in session. Travel allowances in some form are paid legislators in all states except North Carolina, and a constitutional amendment, for voter action in 1956, would provide travel and per diem expenses in that state. In some states—Alabama, Arizona, Kansas, North Dakota and Pennsylvania—the expense allowance amounts to more than the daily pay or salary.

Thirty-two states and Hawaii in 1954–55 took action affecting legislative compensation. Basic pay rates were increased during the biennium in sixteen states: by statutory action in ten (Colorado, Indiana, Maine, Michigan, Minnesota, Montana, New Jersey, New York, Ohio and Vermont); by constitutional amendments approved in six (California, Florida, New Mexico, Tennessee, Texas and West Virginia). Expense and travel allowances were increased during the biennium in twelve states and Hawaii.

COMMITTEES

Much of the work of the legislative sessions is done by standing committees. For a number of years it has been felt widely that most legislative bodies have too many committees to permit efficient conduct of committee work. The results include conflicts of committee meetings, inadequate advance notice and publicity of hearings, and the assignment of individual legislators to more committees than they can serve effectively. There have been numerous instances of consolidation of standing committees in recent years. The trend is toward fewer committees and fewer committee assignments for individual legislators. A recent survey by the Council of State Governments revealed that reductions in committees between 1946 and 1955 have lowered the median number of House standing committees from 39 to 25 and of Senate committees from 31 to 22, during that ten year period. The following table illustrates these decreases.

Number of Standing Committees	House		Senate(a)		Joint	
	1946	1955	1946	1955	1946 (b)	1955 (c)
10 or under..	0	4	0	5	23	24
11–20.......	2	11	8	17	0	0
21–30.......	9	13	15	15	0	1
31–40.......	15	6	13	10	2	2
41–50.......	12	8	9	1	1	0
51–60.......	7	3	2	0	0	0
61–70.......	2	2	1	0	0	0

(a) Nebraska is included only under "Senate" in this section.

(b) Excludes 20 states reporting no joint standing committees.

(c) Excludes 21 states reporting no joint standing committees.

The number of House standing committees (excluding states where the major share of referral work is done by joint committees) ranges from 8 in South Carolina and 13 in Maryland up to 59 in Arkansas, 63 in Georgia and 64 in Missouri. Senate standing committees (again excluding states which rely chiefly on joint committees) range from 7 in New Mexico, 9 in Wisconsin and 14 in Maryland and Rhode Island, up to 39 in Iowa and Texas and 46 in Mississippi. In several states, notably in New England, joint standing committees carry on all or a major share of referral work. These include Connecticut with 32 joint committees, Massachusetts with 31, and Maine with 23.

RULES

The rules of legislative bodies, ordinarily adopted at the beginning of each session, are the basis for the orderly discharge of business. They govern all phases of legislative procedure; they are the means by which the legislature is enabled to handle its large volume of work expeditiously while at the same time safeguarding the rights of legislative minorities. For these reasons students of the legislative process have suggested that arrangements be made for regular review and modernizing of the rules. According to a recent survey by the Council of State Governments, fourteen states have made arrangements of this sort—Arkansas, California, Florida, Idaho, Iowa, Michigan, Minnesota, Nebraska, New Jersey, North Dakota, Pennsylvania, South Dakota, Vermont and Virginia.

MECHANICAL DEVICES

The use of mechanical and other technological devices to expedite and improve the work of legislatures has increased in recent years. The electric roll call machine, in particular, has been a means of conserving much valuable legislative time. Between 1917 (when the first such machine was installed in the Wisconsin Assembly) and 1943, a total of thirteen machines was installed in eleven states. Since that time, an additional fifteen machines have been installed, and new installations currently are authorized for the Connecticut, Georgia and Kansas Houses. Installations in the Kentucky House and Tennessee Senate are under consideration.

Use of radio and television broadcasting in conjunction with state legislative sessions and committee hearings still appears to be in the experimental stage. A sizeable number of states have used those techniques, particularly on special occasions, such as opening sessions and addresses by the Governors to joint sessions. Systematic coverage, however, has been confined to a few states.

ORIENTATION CONFERENCES

Of increasing popularity in recent years have been orientation conferences for legislators—organized opportunities, either before the session or early in it, to enable legislators to become acquainted with each other and with parliamentary rules and procedures, to obtain guidance as to sources of information and assistance, and in the conferences held in some states to become more familiar with the problems and operations of the state government. Sixteen states conduct such conferences in advance of the legislative session—Arizona, Arkansas, Florida, Indiana, Kentucky, Louisiana, Maryland, Nebraska, New Jersey, New Mexico, Oklahoma, Tennessee, Utah, Washington, Wisconsin and Wyoming. In fourteen other states, orientation conferences for legislators are held after the session has opened. Not included in these totals are informal discussions in California and West Virginia and the political party conferences in Pennsylvania and Rhode Island. Legislative leaders, clerks and service agencies frequently participate in orientation conferences. In some states, state university and law school faculty play an active part. In most states, these conferences were initiated within the past decade, although a few—in Arkansas, Massachusetts and South Carolina—antedate the 1940's.

APPORTIONMENT

Apportionment is one of the major problems of state government. As indicated on pages 112 to 116, provisions relating to it appear in the constitution of every state. In two states, however—Delaware and Maryland — no constitutional provision relates to subsequent reapportionment.

In the great majority of states, the legislature is the agency designated by the constitution to reapportion. In most cases the legislatures enjoy this power exclusively. Six states, however, have provided alternative procedures in the event the legislature does not act: California (by a Reapportionment Commission which includes five state officials, ex officio); Illinois (by a bipartisan commission appointed by the Governor); Michigan (by the State Board of Canvassers, who may reapportion the House only); Oregon (by the Secretary of State); South Dakota (by a board of five state officials, ex officio); and Texas (by the Legislative Redistricting Board, which includes five state officials, ex officio). Illinois was added to this group of states by a constitutional amendment approved by the electorate in November, 1954.

Another group of four states has placed the reapportioning power in non-legislative hands. Arizona, which makes no provision for Senate reapportionment, places responsibility for redistricting the House in the County Boards of Supervisors. Arkansas redistricts through a Board of Apportionment (Governor, Secretary of State and Attorney General). Missouri's House is reapportioned by the Secretary of State and local governing bodies, the Senate by a commission appointed by the Governor. And Ohio redistricts by action of the Governor, Auditor and Secretary of State.

As indicated in the table on apportionment, all ten states employing non-legislative boards in conjunction with reapportionment actually have reapportioned since 1950. Among the thirty-eight states which do not employ this method, fifteen states have had their most recent reapportionments in the 1950's, ten in the 1940's, four in the 1930's, three in the 1920's, four in the period from 1900 to 1920, and two prior to 1900.

OFFICIAL NAMES OF LEGISLATIVE BODIES AND CAPITOL BUILDINGS

State	*Both bodies*	*Senate*	*House*	*Capitol building*
Alabama, State of..............	Legislature	Senate	House of Representatives	State Capitol
Arizona, State of..............	Legislature	Senate	House of Representatives	State House(a)
Arkansas, State of.............	General Assembly	Senate	House of Representatives	State Capitol
California, State of.............	Legislature	Senate	Assembly(b)	State Capitol
Colorado, State of..............	General Assembly	Senate	House of Representatives	State Capitol
Connecticut, State of..........	General Assembly	Senate	House of Representatives	State Capitol
Delaware, State of.............	General Assembly	Senate	House of Representatives	Legislative Hall
Florida, State of...............	Legislature	Senate	House of Representatives	State Capitol
Georgia, State of...............	General Assembly	Senate	House of Representatives	State Capitol
Idaho, State of................	Legislature	Senate	House of Representatives	State Capitol
Illinois, State of...............	General Assembly	Senate	House of Representatives	State Capitol
Indiana, State of...............	General Assembly	Senate	House of Representatives	(c)
Iowa, State of.................	General Assembly	Senate	House of Representatives	State Capitol
Kansas, State of...............	Legislature	Senate	House of Representatives	State House(a)
Kentucky, Commonwealth of...	General Assembly	Senate	House of Representatives	State Capitol
Louisiana, State of.............	Legislature	Senate	House of Representatives	State Capitol
Maine, State of................	Legislature	Senate	House of Representatives	State House
Maryland, State of.............	General Assembly	Senate	House of Delegates	State House
Massachusetts, Commonwealth of....................	General Court	Senate	House of Representatives	State House
Michigan, State of.............	Legislature	Senate	House of Representatives	State Capitol
Minnesota, State of............	Legislature	Senate	House of Representatives	State Capitol
Mississippi, State of............	Legislature	Senate	House of Representatives	State Capitol
Missouri, State of..............	General Assembly	Senate	House of Representatives	State Capitol
Montana, State of..............	Legislative Assembly	Senate	House of Representatives	State Capitol
Nebraska, State of	Legislature	Unicameral		State Capitol
Nevada, State of...............	Legislature	Senate	Assembly	State Capitol
New Hampshire, State of.......	General Court	Senate	House of Representatives	State House
New Jersey, State of............	Legislature	Senate	General Assembly	State House
New Mexico, State of...........	Legislature	Senate	House of Representatives	State Capitol
New York, State of.............	Legislature	Senate	Assembly	State Capitol
North Carolina, State of........	General Assembly	Senate	House of Representatives	State Capitol
North Dakota, State of.........	Legislative Assembly	Senate	House of Representatives	State Capitol
Ohio, State of.................	General Assembly	Senate	House of Representatives	State House(a)
Oklahoma, State of............	Legislature	Senate	House of Representatives	State Capitol
Oregon, State of...............	Legislative Assembly	Senate	House of Representatives	State Capitol
Pennsylvania, Commonwealth of....................	General Assembly	Senate	House of Representatives	State Capitol
Rhode Island and Providence Plantations, State of........	General Assembly	Senate	House of Representatives	State House
South Carolina, State of.......	General Assembly	Senate	House of Representatives	State House
South Dakota, State of.........	Legislature	Senate	House of Representatives	State Capitol
Tennessee, State of.............	General Assembly	Senate	House of Representatives	State Capitol
Texas, State of.................	Legislature	Senate	House of Representatives	State Capitol(a)
Utah, State of.................	Legislature	Senate	House of Representatives	State Capitol
Vermont, State of.............	General Assembly	Senate	House of Representatives	State House
Virginia, Commonwealth of.....	General Assembly	Senate	House of Delegates	State Capitol
Washington, State of...........	Legislature	Senate	House of Representatives	Legislative Building
West Virginia, State of.........	Legislature	Senate	House of Delegates	State Capitol
Wisconsin, State of.............	Legislature	Senate	Assembly	State Capitol
Wyoming, State of.............	Legislature	Senate	House of Representatives	State Capitol
Alaska, Territory of............	Legislature	Senate	House of Representatives	Federal & Territorial Bldg.
Guam.......................	Legislature	Unicameral		Congress Building
Hawaii, Territory of............	Territorial Legislature	Senate	House of Representatives	Iolani Palace
Puerto Rico, Commonwealth of .	Legislative Assembly	Senate	House of Representatives	Capitol
Virgin Islands, Territory of......	Legislature	Unicameral		Municipal Bldg.

(a) Unofficial.
(b) Constitutional amendment to be voted on in 1956 proposes changing the name of the lower house to "House of Representatives."

(c) No official name. Both "State House" and "State Capitol" used.

LEGISLATIVE SESSIONS

State	Years in which sessions are held	Sessions convene Month	Sessions convene Day	Limitations on length of sessions Regular	Limitations on length of sessions Special	Length of last regular session (a)	Special sessions Legislature may call	Special sessions Legislature may determine subject
Alabama	Odd	May	1st Tues. (b)	36 L	36 L	36 L	No	2/3 vote those present
Arizona	Annual	Jan.	2nd Mon.	60 C(c)	20 C(c)	84 C	Petition 2/3 members	Yes
Arkansas	Odd	Jan.	2nd Mon.	120 C	15 C(d)	60 C	No	(d)
California	Annual (e)	Mar.	Odd-Mon. after Jan. 1	120 C	None	120 C	No	No
Colorado	Annual (e)	Jan.	Wed. after 1st Mon.	120 C(c)	None	92 C	No	No
Connecticut	Odd	Jan.	Wed. after 1st Mon.	150 C(f)	None	145 C	Yes	Yes
Delaware	Odd	Jan.	1st Tues.	None	30(c)	(z)	No	Yes
Florida	Odd	Apr.	Tues. after 1st Mon.	60 C(g)	20 C(h)	60 C	No	2/3 vote
Georgia	Annual	Jan.	2nd Mon.	40 C	(i)	40 C	Petition 3/5 members (j)	Yes
Idaho	Odd	Jan.	Mon. after Jan. 1	60 C(c)	20 C	60 C	No	No
Illinois	Odd	Jan.	Wed. after 1st Mon.	None (k)	40 C	175 C	No	No
Indiana	Odd	Jan.	Thurs. after 1st Mon.	61 C		61 C	No	Yes
Iowa	Odd	Jan.	2nd Mon.	None (l)	None	115 C	No	Yes
Kansas	Annual (e)	Jan.	Odd-2nd Tues.	60 L(c)	30 L(c)	86 C	No	Yes
Kentucky	Even	Jan.	Tues. after 1st Mon.	60 L	None	60 L	No	No
Louisiana	Annual (e)	May / May	Even-2nd Mon. / Odd-2nd Mon.	60 C / 30 C	30 C	60 C	Petition 2/3 members	No (m)
Maine	Odd	Jan.	1st Wed.	None	None	70 L	No	Yes
Maryland	Annual(e)	Jan.	Odd-1st Wed. / Even-1st Wed.	90 C / 30 C	30 C	90 C	Yes	Yes
Massachusetts	Annual	Feb.	1st Wed.	None	None	255 C	Yes	Yes
Michigan	Annual	Jan.	2nd Wed.	None	None	185 C	No	No
Minnesota	Odd	Jan.	Tues. after 1st Mon.	90 L	None	H-79 L / S-78 L	No	Yes
Mississippi	Even	Jan.	Tues. after 1st Mon.	None	None	122 C	No	No
Missouri	Odd(n)	Jan.	Wed. after Jan. 1	150 C(f,n)	60 C(c)	147 C	No	No
Montana	Odd	Jan.	1st Mon.	60 C	60 C(c)	60 C	No	No
Nebraska	Odd	Jan.	1st Tues.	None	None	114 C	Petition 2/3 members	No
Nevada	Odd	Jan.	3rd Mon.	60 C	20 C	60 C	No	No
New Hampshire	Odd	Jan.	1st Wed.	None	15 C(c)	213 C	Yes	Yes
New Jersey	Annual	Jan.	2nd Tues.	None	None	(z)	(o)	Yes

State	Year	Month	Day convened					
New Mexico	Odd	Jan.	2nd Tues.	60 C	30 C(p)	60 C		Yes (p)	Yes (p)
New York	Annual	Jan.	Wed. after 1st Mon.	None	None	88 C		No	No
North Carolina	Odd	Jan.(q)	Wed. after 1st Mon.	90 C(c)	25 C(c)	142 C		No	Yes
North Dakota	Odd	Jan.	Tues. after 1st Mon.	60 L	None	60 C		No	Yes
Ohio	Odd	Jan.	1st Mon.	None	None	103 L		No	No
Oklahoma	Odd	Jan.	Tues, after 1st Mon.	None	None	81 L		No	No(r)
Oregon	Odd	Jan.	2nd Mon.	None	None	115 C		No	No
Pennsylvania	Odd(s)	Jan.	1st Tues.	None	None	(z)		No	No
Rhode Island	Annual	Jan.	1st Tues.	60 L(c)	None	65 L		No	Yes
South Carolina	Annual	Jan.	2nd Tues.	None	None	137 C		No	Yes
South Dakota	Odd	Jan.	Tues, after 1st Mon.	60 C	None	60 C		No	Yes
Tennessee	Odd	Jan.	1st Mon.	75 C(c)	20 C(c)	75 C		No	No
Texas	Odd	Jan.	2nd Tues.	120 C(c)	30 C	148 C		No	No
Utah	Odd	Jan.	2nd Mon.	60 C	30 C	60 C		No	No
Vermont	Odd	Jan.	Wed. after 1st Mon.	None	None	158 L	Petition 2/3 members	Yes
Virginia	Even	Jan.	2nd Wed.	60 C(c,t)	30 C(c,t)	60 C		No	Yes
Washington	Odd	Jan.	2nd Mon.	60 C	None	60 C		No	Yes
West Virginia	Annual (e)	Jan.	Odd-2nd Wed.	60 C(u)	None	62 C	Petition 2/3 members	No
			Even-2nd Wed.	30 C(u)	None			
Wisconsin	Odd	Jan.	2nd Wed.	None	None	(z)		No	No
Wyoming	Odd	Jan.	2nd Tues.	40 C	None	40 C		No	Yes
Alaska	Odd	Jan.	4th Mon.	60 C(v)	30 C	60 C		No	No
Guam	Annual	Jan.	2nd Mon.	60 C(v)	14 C	60 C		No	No
Hawaii	Odd	Feb.	3rd Wed.	60 L(w)	None	60 L(x)		Yes	Yes
Puerto Rico	Annual	Jan.	2nd Mon.	111 C(f,aa)	20 C	142 L		No	No
Virgin Islands	Annual	Apr.	2nd Mon.	60	15(y)	60		No	No

Abbreviations: L—Legislative days; C—Calendar days;

(a) 1955 session, except for Kentucky, Louisiana, Mississippi and Virginia, where last general session was held in 1954.

(b) Legislature meets quadrennially on second Tuesday in January after election for general session.

(c) Indirect restriction on session length. Legislators' pay ceases but session may continue.

(d) Governor may convene General Assembly for specified purpose. After specific business is transacted, a 2/3 vote of members of both houses may extend sessions up to 15 days.

(e) Alternate year budget sessions are held, all except the Louisiana session meeting in the even-numbered years.

(f) Approximate length of session. Connecticut session must adjourn by first Wednesday after first Monday in June, Missouri by May 31, and Puerto Rico by April 30.

(g) Length of session may be extended by 30 days, but not beyond Sept. 1, by 2/3 vote of both houses.

(h) Proposed constitutional amendment referred for vote in 1956 would permit the legislature to call 30-day special session by 2/3 vote of the legislature in a poll conducted by the Secretary of State.

(i) Seventy-day session limit except for impeachment proceedings if Governor calls session; 30-day limit if legislature convenes itself.

(j) Thirty-day limit.

(k) By custom, legislature adjourns by July 1, since all bills passed after that day are not effective until July 1 of following year.

(l) Custom and pay limit session to 100 calendar days.

(m) Unless legislature petitions for session.

(n) Proposed constitutional amendment referred for vote in 1956 would provide for annual sessions, odd-year sessions to be six months long, even-year budgetary sessions to be two months long, and, in addition, a 15-day session to be scheduled three months after each session for consideration of vetoes.

(o) Petition by majority members of each house to Governor, who then "shall" call special session.

(p) Limitation does not apply if impeachment trial is pending or in process. Legislature may call 30-day "extraordinary" session if Governor refuses to call session when requested by 3/4 of legislature.

(q) Proposed constitutional amendment referred for vote in 1956 would change convening date to first Wednesday after first Monday in February.

(r) Governor may convene Senate alone in special session.

(s) Legislature in 1953 adopted a proposal calling for annual sessions with even-year budgetary sessions which, if re-enacted in 1955, will be submitted for vote as a proposed constitutional amendment.

(t) May be extended up to 30 days by 2/3 vote of each house, but without pay.

(u) Must be extended by Governor until general appropriation passed; may be extended by 2/3 vote of legislature.

(v) Organic Act specifies legislature may meet for 60 days during each year, statutes specify legislature shall meet for 30 days twice each year.

(w) Governor may extend session up to 30 days, with no additional legislative pay.

(x) Sixtieth legislative day lasted from April 29 to May 27.

(y) No special session may continue longer than 15 calendar days and the aggregate for the year may not exceed 30.

(z) 1955 legislature was in session when table was compiled.

(aa) Session may be extended by adoption of joint resolution.

THE BOOK OF THE STATES
THE LEGISLATORS
Numbers, Terms, and Party Affiliations
As of 1955

State	Senate Democrats	Republicans	Other	Vacancies	Constitutional total	Term	House Democrats	Republicans	Other	Vacancies	Constitutional total	Term	Constitutional total of legislators
Alabama	35	..	..	..	35	4	106	...	..	...	106	4	141
Arizona	26	2	..	..	28	2	60	20	..	...	80	2	108
Arkansas	34	..	..	1	35	4	97	2	1(a)	...	100	2	135
California	16	23	..	1	40	4	32	44	..	4	80	2	120
Colorado	15	20	..	..	35	4	28	36	..	1	65	2	100
Connecticut	19	16	..	1	36	2	92	184	3(a)	1	280	2	316
Delaware	12	5	..	..	17	4	27	8	..	...	35	2	52
Florida	37	1	..	..	38(b)	4	89	6	..	...	95(b)	2	133(b)
Georgia	53	1	..	..	54	2	202	3	..	...	205	2	259
Idaho	20	24	..	..	44	2	23	36	..	...	59	2	103
Illinois	19	31	..	1	51(c)	4	74	78	..	1	153(c)	2	204(c)
Indiana	14	32	..	4	50	4	37	62	..	1	100	2	150
Iowa	6	43	..	1	50	4	19	89	..	...	108	2	158
Kansas	5	33	..	2	40	4	36	89	..	...	125	2	165
Kentucky	30	8	..	..	38	4	77	23	..	...	100	2	138
Louisiana	39	..	..	..	39	4	100	...	..	1	101	4	140
Maine	6	27	..	..	33	2	32	116	..	3	151	2	184
Maryland	18	11	..	..	29	4	98	25	..	...	123	4	152
Massachusetts	19	21	..	..	40	2	127	113	..	...	240	2	280
Michigan	11	23	..	..	34	2	51	58	1(a)	...	110	2	144
Minnesota	Nonpartisan election			..	67	4	Nonpartisan election			...	131	2	198
Mississippi	49	..	..	..	49	4	140	..	..	...	140	4	189
Missouri	19	15	..	..	34	4	97	60	..	...	157	2	191
Montana	23	33	..	..	56	4	49	45	..	...	94	2	150
Nebraska	Nonpartisan election. Unicameral legislature, 2 year term.												43
Nevada	4	12	..	1	17	4	30	17	..	...	47	2	64
New Hampshire	6	18	..	..	24	2	134	259	..	6	399	2	423
New Jersey	7	14	..	..	21	4	20	40	..	...	60	2	81
New Mexico	23	9	..	..	32	4	52	3	..	...	55(d)	2	87(d)
New York	24	34	..	..	58	2	60	90	..	...	150	2	208
North Carolina	47	1	..	2	50	2	110	9	..	1	120	2	170
North Dakota	4	45	..	..	49	4	2	111	..	3	116	2	165
Ohio	12	20	..	1	33	2(e)	45	87	..	4	136	2	169
Oklahoma	39	5	..	..	44	4	101	19	..	1	121	2	165
Oregon	6	24	..	..	30	4	25	35	..	...	60	2	90
Pennsylvania	23	27	..	..	50	4	112	97	..	1	210	2	260
Rhode Island	22	22	..	..	44	2	67	33	..	...	100	2	144
South Carolina	46	..	..	..	46	4	124	...	..	...	124	2	170
South Dakota	6	29	..	..	35	2	18	57	..	...	75	2	110
Tennessee	28	4	1(a)	..	33	2	79	19	..	1	99	2	132
Texas	30	...	..	1	31	4	146	...	..	4	150	2	181
Utah	7	16	..	..	23(f)	4	27	33	..	...	60(f)	2	83(f)
Vermont	7	22	1(a)	..	30	2	24	217	2(a)	3	246	2	276
Virginia	37	3	..	..	40	4	94	6	..	...	100	2	140
Washington	22	23	..	1	46	4	50	49	..	...	99	2	145
West Virginia	23	9	..	..	32	4	75	24	..	1	100	2	132
Wisconsin	8	23	..	2	33	4	36	62	..	2	100	2	133
Wyoming	8	19	..	..	27	4	24	32	..	...	56	2	83
Alaska	11	4	..	1	16	4	21	3	...	...	24	2	40
Guam	..	..	21(g)	..	21	2	...Unicameral...						21
Hawaii	8	7	..	..	15	4	22	8	..	...	30	2	45
Puerto Rico	25(h)	3	4(i)	..	32	4	47(h)	7	10(i)	1	65	4	97
Virgin Islands	1	1	9(j)	..	11	2	...Unicameral...						11

(a) Independent.
(b) Proposed constitutional amendment to be voted on in November, 1956, would fix size of Senate at 67 and House at 135, a total legislature of 202.
(c) 1955 reapportionment fixed size of Senate at 58 and House at 177, a total legislature of 235.
(d) Size of House increased from 55 to 66 by constitutional amendment approved September 20, 1955. Total size of legislature will be 98.

(e) Constitutional amendment to be voted in November, 1956, proposed four-year Senatorial terms.
(f) 1955 reapportionment fixed size of Senate at 25 and House at 64, a total legislature of 89.
(g) Popular Party, 18; Independent, 3.
(h) Popular Democratic Party.
(i) Independentist.
(j) Unity, 4; Independent, 5.

LEGISLATIVE PROCEDURE: STANDING COMMITTEES AND HEARINGS

State	House committees appointed by speaker	Senate committees appointed by	No. of standing committees at most recent regular session			Range in size of committees			Hearings open to public*
			House	Senate	Joint	House	Senate	Joint	
Alabama..........	★	President	15	30	0	7–15	2–21	....	Dis.
Arizona..........	★ *	President	19	28	0	15	5–11	....	Dis.
Arkansas.........	★	President	59	21	1	3–29	5–12	12	Dis.
California........	★	Comm. on Rules	25	22	1	4–28	5–13	....	Yes
Colorado.........	★	Resolution	16	20	1	5–19	4–20	6	Dis.
Connecticut......	★	Pres. pro tem	0	0	32	....	....	NA	Yes
Delaware.........	★	Pres. pro tem	26	26	0	NA	NA	....	Dis.
Florida...........	★	Pres.	56	38	1	6–27	7–13	6	Yes (a)
Georgia..........	★	Pres	63	38	0	5–60	5–28	....	Dis.
Idaho............	★	Pres.	21	20	3	3–11	5–11	9	Dis.
Illinois..........	★	Comm. on Comms.	22	24	0	5–42	3–24	....	Yes
Indiana..........	★	President	41	38	2	4–17	5–11	8–12	Dis.
Iowa.............	★	President	37	39	2	7–51	1–28	6	Dis.
Kansas...........	★	President	43	30	1	3–23	5–13	12	Dis.
Kentucky.........	Committee on Committees	Comm. on Comms.	43	38	0	10–48	6–29	....	Dis.
Louisiana.........	★	President	16	15	0	16–20	6–17	....	Dis.
Maine............	★	President	8	3	23	4–23	4–12	7–12	Yes
Maryland.........	★	President	13	14	2	5–32	5–14	6–10	Yes
Massachusetts.....	★	President	6	4	31	2–15	3–7	15	Yes
Michigan.........	★	Comm. on Comms.	47	19	0	5–15	5–7	....	Dis.
Minnesota........	★	Comm. on Comms.	41	32	3	9–29	9–23	6–18	Yes.
Mississippi........	★	Lt. Governor	47	46	5	5–29	3–26	5–13	Dis.
Missouri..........	★	Pres. pro tem	64	25	1	6–45	5–13	14	Dis.
Montana..........	★	Special comm. (b)	36	36	0	3–15	3–13	....	Dis.
Nebraska.........	(c)	Comm. on Comms.	(c)	17	(c)	(c)	1–9	(c)	Yes
Nevada...........	★	President	27	20	0	5–11	3–5	....	Dis.
New Hampshire....	★	President	24	18	1	3–21	3–7	8	Yes
New Jersey........	★	President	16	16	4	7	5–7	12	Dis.
New Mexico.......	★(d)	Comm. on Comms.	24(e)	7	0	7–17	5–12	....	Dis.
New York.........	★	Pres. pro tem	36	28	0	15–20	6–25	....	Dis.
North Carolina....	★	President	46	28	0	8–62	6–26	....	Yes
North Dakota.....	★	Comm. on Comms.	20	20	0	3–21	3–15	....	Dis.
Ohio.............	★	Pres. pro tem	22	20	1	5–23	7–9	8	Yes
Oklahoma........	★(f)	Pres. pro tem (g)	33	32	0	3–30	3–28	....	Yes
Oregon..........	★	Pres.	22	20	1	5–11	5–9	NA	Yes
Pennsylvania......	★	Pres. pro tem	34	22	0	9–20	9–24	....	Dis.
Rhode Island.....	★	Named in rules	15	14	6	8–18	5–10	8–9	Dis.
South Carolina....	★	Elected (h)	8	33	3	5–27	6–19	6–15	Dis.
South Dakota.....	★	President	51	27	0	3–15	3–15	....	Dis.
Tennessee........	★	Speaker	17	17	0	16–30	7–16	....	Dis.
Texas............	★	President	43	39	0	5–21	3–21	....	Dis.
Utah............	★	President	15	15	1	14–17	4–7	28	Yes
Vermont..........	★	Special comm.	18	18	3(i)	5–15	3–6	6–56	Yes
Virginia..........	★	Elected	34	21	3	NA	NA	NA	Dis.(j)
Washington.......	★	President	28	26	0	7–33	3–23	....	Dis.
West Virginia.....	★	President	25	29	3	10–25	3–18	5	Dis.
Wisconsin........	★	Comm. on Comms.	23	9	2	3–11	3–10	5–14	Yes
Wyoming.........	★	President	21	19	1	4–10	2–7	12	Dis.
Alaska...........	(k)	(k)	12	16	2	5	NA	NA	Dis.
Guam...........	(c)	Comm. on Rules	(c)	7	(c)	(c)	NA	(c)	Yes
Hawaii..........	★	President (l)	19	14	0	6–13	2–7	....	Dis.
Puerto Rico.......	★	President	16	16	0	7–23	5–17	7–16	Dis.
Virgin Islands......	(c)	Elected	(c)	3	(c)	(c)	NA	(c)	Dis.

* Abbreviation: Dis.—Discretionary; NA—Information not available.
(a) Senate committees sometimes meet in executive session.
(b) Confirmation by Senate.
(c) Unicameral legislature.
(d) Standing Committee on Committees advises him.
(e) House had 24 committees at 1955 session and reduced number to 16 at end of session.
(f) Confirmation by House.

(g) Senate elects Senate standing committees.
(h) Special committees are appointed.
(i) Corresponding committees of each house usually meet jointly.
(j) Final vote by a House committee must be in open session.
(k) Nominated by Committee on Committees and elected by House and Senate respectively.
(l) Except four select committees made up of Senators from each of the four islands.

LEGISLATIVE PROCEDURE: BILL INTRODUCTION AND REFERENCE

State	Time limits on introduction of bills	Exceptions to limitations — By indicated vote of appropriate house	Exceptions — For committee bills	Exceptions — Revenue and appropriation bills	Exceptions — At request of Governor	Exceptions — Other	Pre-session bill drafting service provided	Pre-session bill filing permitted	Bills referred to committee by — House	Bills referred to committee by — Senate	Committee must report all bills
Alabama	No limitations	⅔					Yes (a)	No	Speaker	President	No
Arizona	Senate—50th day						Yes (a)	No	Speaker	President	No
Arkansas	None last 3 days						Yes	No	Speaker	President	Yes
California	Regular—Constitutional Recess (b); Budget Session—No limitations	¾ (b)					Yes (a)	No	Speaker	Rules Comm.	Yes (c)
Colorado	Set at last week						Yes (a)	No	Speaker	President	Yes (c)
Connecticut	Fixed at session						Yes (a)	Yes	Speaker	P.O.	No
Delaware	....						Yes (a)	No	Speaker	President	No
Florida	No limitations						Yes	No	Speaker	President	Yes
Georgia	No limitations						Yes	Yes	Speaker	President	No
Idaho	30th day						No	No	Speaker	President	Yes
Illinois	Minor limitations (d)						Yes (a)	No	Speaker	Bills Comm.	No
Indiana	Senate—33rd day; House—30th day	Majority					Yes	No	Speaker	President	No
Iowa	....						No	No	Speaker	President	No
Kansas	No limitations						Yes (a)	No	Speaker	President	No
Kentucky	No limitations						Yes (a)	No	Comm. on Comms.	Comm. on Comms.	No
Louisiana	Regular—21st day; Budget session—10th day	⅔ elected				Const. Amendments, 30 days	Yes	Yes	Speaker (e)	President (e)	No
Maine	Fixed at session	Unanimous					Yes (a)	(f)	Joint Committee (g)	(g)	No
Maryland	Regular—80th day; Budget session—20th day	⅔					Yes (a)	No	Speaker	President	No
Massachusetts	Must be introduced one month before session	⅘ present and voting			X	Bills in reports due after convening	Yes (a)	Required (h)	Clerk (i)	President	Yes
Michigan	63rd day		X				Yes (a)	Yes (j)	Speaker	President	No
Minnesota	59th day				X		Yes	Yes (j)	Speaker	President	No
Mississippi	None last 3 days (k)			X	X		Yes	No	Speaker	President	Yes
Missouri	60th day	Majority			X		Yes (a)	No	Speaker	President	Yes
Montana	Senate—30th day; House—40th day	⅔		X			No	No	Speaker	President	Yes
Nebraska	20th day	⅔ elected					Yes (l)	Yes (m)	Members (n)	Reference Comm.	No
Nevada	Senate—No limitations; House—40th day	⅔		X			Yes	No	Members	President	Yes
New Hampshire	3rd Thursday	⅔					Yes (l)	Yes	Speaker	President	Yes
New Jersey	6th week		(o)				Yes (a)	No	Speaker	President	No
New Mexico	45th day		X (p)				Yes (a)	No	Speaker	President	No
New York	Fixed at Session						Yes (m)	Yes	Speaker	President pro tem	No

	Deadline for introduction of bills								
North Carolina	Senate—56th day, local bills; 65th, department bills (q)	…	…	…	Yes (a)	No	Speaker	President	Yes
North Dakota	25th day	…	…	…	Yes	(s)	Speaker	President	Yes
Ohio	Senate—No limitations	…	45th day(r)	…	Yes (a)	No	Reference Comm.	Majority Leader	No
Oklahoma	No limitations (k)	…	40th day	…	Yes	No	Speaker	President	No
Oregon	…	…	…	…	Yes (a)	No	P.O.	P.O.	No
Pennsylvania	Senate—No limitations / House—May 25 (q)	…	X	…	Yes (a)	No	Speaker	P.O.	No
Rhode Island	42nd day	…	…	One day notice, title and explanation read	Yes (a)	No	Speaker	President	No
South Carolina	No limitations	…	…	…	Yes (a)	No	P.O.	P.O.	No
South Dakota	None last 3 days	…	…	…	Yes	No	Speaker	President	No
Tennessee	60th day	4/5 members	…	…	Yes	No	Speaker	Speaker	No (t)
Texas	30th day	Unanimous	X	…	Yes (u)	No	Speaker	President	No
Utah	…	…	…	…	No (v)	No	Speaker	President	Yes
Vermont	5th week (w)	…	…	…	Yes (a)	Yes (m)	Speaker	President	No
Virginia	40th day	2/3 elected	…	…	Yes (a)	No	Speaker	President	No
Washington	50th day	2/3 present and voting (x)	X	…	Yes (a)	No	Speaker	President	No
West Virginia	…	…	…	…	Yes (y)	Yes (m)	Speaker	President	No
Wisconsin	38th day (w)	…	52nd day	No limits for Legislative Council or for committees	Yes (a)	(f)	Speaker	P.O.	Yes
Wyoming	20th day	Unanimous	…	…	No	No	Speaker	President	Yes
Alaska	45th day	2/3 vote	55th day	…	Yes	No	Speaker	President	No
Guam	No limitations	…	…	…	Yes	No	(n)	Comm. on Rules	No
Hawaii	60th day	…	X	…	Yes	No	Speaker	President	Yes
Puerto Rico	No limitations	Majority	…	…	Yes	No	President	Comm. of the Whole	No
Virgin Islands	No limitations	…	…	…	No	Yes	(n)	…	…

P. O.—Presiding Officer.
(a) Continuous service.
(b) No bills may be introduced after the constitutional recess which must be held not less than 30 days after convening of session, except that each member may introduce two bills at general session.
(c) In practice, those not acted upon are reported back last day of session without recommendation.
(d) Some minor time limits are set at each session by rule but commonly are waived. Bills may be introduced any Tuesday or by standing committees.
(e) No limitation of author.
(f) No official arrangement for pre-session filing, assignment of bill number, etc., but to a limited extent bills are filed in advance of session.
(g) Composed of President of Senate, Speaker of House, one Senate member, and two House members.
(h) Bills must be introduced in December one month in advance of session.
(i) Subject to approval of presiding officer.
(j) Pre-session filing permitted at second session of biennium, not at first session.

(k) No appropriation or revenue bills may be passed during last five days; in Oklahoma no revenue bills.
(l) Established month prior to session.
(m) Permitted if engaged in to limited extent.
(n) Unicameral legislature.
(o) Only those reported by Committee on Rules.
(p) Only bills approved by Committee on Introduction of Bills.
(q) Date is established at each session. Date given is limit set at 1955 session.
(r) Only bills approved by Delayed Bills Committee.
(s) Bills processed by Legislative Research Committee and Budget Board printed in advance of session.
(t) Bills may be forced out by majority vote after seven days in committee.
(u) Theoretically, but not as matter of practice.
(v) Legislative Council has authority to assist.
(w) Except for bills delivered to draftsmen by that time.
(x) House only.
(y) Permission must be granted by concurrent resolution setting out title of bill.

LEGISLATIVE PROCEDURE: PRINTING OF BILLS

State	House All	House Some	House Man-datory	House Op-tional	Senate All	Senate Some	Senate Man-datory	Senate Op-tional	Upon intro-duction	Upon assign-ment to com-mittee	After com-mittee ap-proval	After sec-ond read-ing	Upon pas-sage by legis-lature	Amend-ments printed
Alabama	..	(a)	..	X	..	(a)	..	X	(b)	(b)	(b)	(b)	(b)	No
Arizona	X	..	(c)	..	X	..	(d)	..	..	X	..	..	..	No
Arkansas	X	..	X	..	X	..	X	..	X	..	..	..	..	Yes
California	X	..	(e)	..	X	..	(e)	..	X(e)	..	..	..	..	Yes
Colorado	..	X	..	X	..	X	..	X	..	..	(f)	..	..	(g)
Connecticut	X	..	(d)	..	X	..	(d)	..	X	..	..	..	..	Yes
Delaware	X(h)	..	X	..	X(h)	..	X	..	X	..	..	..	..	Yes(h)
Florida	..	(i)	..	X	..	(i)	..	X	..	(i)	(i)	..	..	(j)
Georgia	..	(k)	X	..	..	(l)	X	..	(m)	..	(n)	X	..	Yes(m)
Idaho	X	..	X	..	X	..	X	..	..	..	X	..	..	Yes
Illinois	X	..	X	..	X	..	X	..	X	..	..	..	..	Yes(o)
Indiana	..	(p)	X	..	..	(p)	X	..	..	..	X	(q)	..	(r)
Iowa	X	..	X	..	X	..	X	..	X	..	..	..	..	(s)
Kansas	X	..	X	..	X	..	X	..	X	..	..	..	..	Yes(t)
Kentucky	X	..	X	..	X	..	X	..	X	..	..	..	..	No
Louisiana	X	..	X	..	X	..	X	..	X	..	..	..	..	(u)
Maine	(v)	..	..	..	(v)	..	..	..	(w)	..	..	..	..	(x)
Maryland	X	..	X	..	X	..	X	..	X	X	..	..	..	(j)
Massachusetts	X	..	X	..	X	..	X	..	X	..	..	..	..	(j)
Michigan	X	..	X	..	X	..	X	..	X	..	..	..	..	(j)
Minnesota	..	(p)	X(p)	..	..	(p)	X(p)	..	..	..	(p)	..	..	(x)
Mississippi	X	..	X	..	X	..	X	..	X	..	..	..	..	(x)
Missouri	X	..	X	..	X	..	X	..	X	..	..	..	..	(j)
Montana	..	(p)	X	..	..	(p)	X	..	..	..	(p)	..	..	Yes
Nebraska	Unicameral				X	..	X	..	..	..	X	..	..	Yes
Nevada	(y)	..	X	..	(y)	..	X	..	X	..	..	..	..	Yes(d)
New Hampshire	X	..	(d)	..	X	..	(d)	..	..	X(z)	..	X(z)	..	(j)
New Jersey	X	..	X	..	X	..	X	..	X	..	..	..	..	Yes
New Mexico	X	..	X	..	X	..	X	..	X	..	..	..	..	No
New York	X	..	X	..	X	..	X	..	..	..	(aa)	..	..	Yes
North Carolina	..	X	..	X	..	X	..	X	X	..	..	..	..	No
North Dakota	X	..	X	..	X	..	X	..	X	..	..	..	..	(ab)
Ohio	..	X	..	X	..	X	..	X	(n)	..	(f,m)	..	..	(j)
Oklahoma	..	(p)	X	..	..	(p)	X	..	X	..	X	..	..	(j)
Oregon	X	..	X	..	X	..	X	..	X	..	..	..	..	Yes
Pennsylvania	X	..	X	..	X	..	X	..	..	..	X	(ac)	..	Yes
Rhode Island	..	X	..	X	..	X	..	X	(b)	(b)	(b)	(b)	(b)	No
South Carolina	X	..	X	..	X	..	X	..	(ad)	..	X	..	X	Yes
South Dakota	X	..	X	..	X	..	X	..	X	..	..	..	..	(j)
Tennessee	(h, ae)	..	X	..	(h, ae)	..	X	..	X	..	..	..	..	No(af)
Texas	X	..	(l)	..	X	..	(l)	..	..	..	X	..	..	(j)
Utah	X	..	(d)	..	X	..	(d)	..	X	..	..	..	..	(j)
Vermont	X	..	X	..	X	..	X	..	X	..	..	..	..	(j)
Virginia	X	..	X	..	X	..	X	..	(v)	..	..	..	..	(s)
Washington	X	..	X	..	X	..	X	..	..	X	..	..	..	(s)
West Virginia	X	..	X	..	X	..	X	..	..	..	..	X	..	(ag)
Wisconsin	X	..	X	..	X	..	X	..	X(ah)	..	..	..	..	Yes
Wyoming	X	..	X	..	X	..	X	..	..	..	..	..	..	Yes
Alaska	X	..	..	..	X	..	..	..	X	..	..	..	..	Yes
Guam	Unicameral				X	..	..	..	X	X	..	..	..	Yes
Hawaii	X	..	..	..	X	..	..	..	X	..	..	..	..	Yes(ai)
Puerto Rico	X	..	..	..	X	..	X	..	X	..	X	..	..	Yes
Virgin Islands	Unicameral				..	..	..	..	X	..	X	..	X	Yes

(a) Unusually important or controversial bills and appropriation bills. Any bill may be ordered printed by either house, a standing committee of either house, or the chairman of a standing committee.
(b) At any stage.
(c) If no objection by Committee on Printing.
(d) Unless otherwise ordered.
(e) Mandatory before passage; optional on introduction.
(f) After Referral Committee orders bill to be printed.
(g) Only if adopted. Either on second or third reading or as recommended by Conference Committee.
(h) Duplicated by means other than printing.
(i) General House bills printed at 1955 session. Senate bills printed or otherwise duplicated by order of President.
(j) In the journals.
(k) All general public bills as introduced.
(l) Bills and resolutions favorably reported by committee.
(m) In the House.
(n) In the Senate.
(o) When adopted on second reading.
(p) All bills that have committee approval. (In Minnesota, a bill may be ordered printed by a majority vote in either house. In Montana, one-third vote in House and majority vote in Senate may order a bill printed at any time.)
(q) If amended.
(r) Committee and second reading amendments are incorporated in printed bill.
(s) If extensively amended, bill is usually reprinted.
(t) Bill reprinted with committee amendments in heavy type.
(u) Senate amendments are printed in journal; in House if amended in committee only amendments is ever printed; in practice floor amendments are printed in journal.
(v) Usually.
(w) Committee on Reference of Bills generally directs the printing of pending legislation prior to referral to committee.
(x) Optional.
(y) If time and circumstances permit.
(z) After second reading, which is by title only, bills are referred to committee and then printed.
(aa) All bills, if reported with amendments and in the Senate, are reprinted immediately, unless amendment restores bill to an earlier printed form.
(ab) Reprinted on colored paper if amended in house of origin. Other amendments printed in journals.
(ac) Reprinted; also bills are reprinted as amended.
(ad) All bills not referred to committees.
(ae) All public bills must be reproduced; local bills are not.
(af) Amendments to major bills may be mimeographed.
(ag) Upon motion.
(ah) 1949 law authorizes the printing of bills between sessions, but no distribution until session convenes.
(ai) With redrafts of bills, if time and circumstances permit,

LEGISLATIVE PROCEDURE: OFFICIAL RECORD

	Journal			
State	*Published daily*	*Shows rulings of chair*	*Shows all votes*	*Checked by*
Alabama..............	Yes(a)	No	No	House—Rules Committee; Senate—Committee on Revision of Journal
Arizona..............	No	No	Yes	House—Chief Clerk; Senate—Secretary
Arkansas.............	No	Yes	Yes	Journal committee
California............	Yes	Not consistently	Yes	House—Chief Clerk; Senate—Secretary
Colorado.............	Yes	Yes	Yes	House—Clerk; Senate—Secretary
Connecticut..........	Yes	Yes	Yes	Clerks
Delaware.............	(a, b)	Yes	Yes	House—Clerk; Senate—Secretary
Florida..............	Yes	Yes	Yes(c)	House—Chief Clerk; Senate—Secretary
Georgia..............	No	Yes	No	Committees on Journals
Idaho................	Yes	Senate—Partially	Yes	House—Chief Clerk; Senate—Secretary
Illinois..............	Yes	Partially	No	House—Speaker; Senate—President
Indiana..............	No	No	Yes	House—Assistant Clerk; Senate—Assistant Secretary
Iowa.................	Yes	Yes	No	House—Chief Clerk; Senate—Secretary
Kansas...............	Yes	No	Yes	Journal Committees of each house
Kentucky.............	(d)	Yes	Yes	Chief Clerk and Assistant Clerk
Louisiana............	Yes	Yes	Yes	Journal Clerk
Maine................	(e)	Yes(f)	Yes(f)	House—Clerk; Senate—Secretary
Maryland.............	Yes	Yes	Yes	Journal Clerk; Legislative Reference Dept.
Massachusetts........	Yes	Yes	Yes	Clerks
Michigan.............	Yes	Yes	Final passage	House—Clerk; Senate—Secretary
Minnesota............	Yes	No	No	House—Chief Clerk; Senate—Secretary
Mississippi...........	Yes(a)	Yes	Yes	House—Clerk; Senate—Secretary
Missouri.............	Yes	Yes	Yes	House—Clerk; Senate—Secretary
Montana.............	No	Yes	Yes	Journal committee
Nebraska.............	Yes	No	Final reading(g)	Journal Clerk
Nevada..............	Yes	Yes	Yes	Assembly—Chief Clerk; Senate—Secretary
New Hampshire.......	Yes	Yes	Yes	House—Journal committee; Senate—Clerk
New Jersey...........	No	No	Yes	Assembly—Clerk; Senate—Secretary
New Mexico..........	No	Yes	Yes	House—Chief Clerk; Senate—Chairman of Judiciary Committee
New York............	Yes	Yes	Yes	Journal Clerk
North Carolina.......	(a)	No	No	Journal committee
North Dakota........	Yes	Yes	Yes	Committee
Ohio.................	Yes	Yes	Yes	Journal Clerk
Oklahoma............	Yes	Partially	Yes	Journal Clerk
Oregon..............	No(b)	Yes	Yes	Chief Clerks
Pennsylvania.........	Yes	Yes	Yes	Journal Clerks
Rhode Island.........	Yes	Yes	Yes	House—Recording Clerk; Senate—Secretary of State(h)
South Carolina.......	Yes	Yes	Yes	Clerks
South Dakota........	Yes	Yes	Yes	Legislative committee
Tennessee............	(a)	Yes	Yes	Clerks
Texas................	Yes	Yes	Yes	Journal Clerks
Utah.................	Yes	Yes	Yes	Committee on Revision and Enrolling
Vermont.............	Yes	Yes	Yes	Clerk
Virginia.............	Yes	....	Yes	Clerk and Journal Clerk
Washington..........	No	Yes	Yes	House—Chief Clerk; Senate—Secretary
West Virginia........	Yes	Yes	Third reading	Clerks and Journal Clerks
Wisconsin............	Yes	Yes	Yes	Journal Clerks
Wyoming.............	No	Yes	Yes	Chief Clerks
Alaska...............	Yes	Yes	Yes	Committees on Engrossment and Enrollment
Guam................	Yes	Yes	Yes	Executive Secretary
Hawaii...............	Yes(a)	Yes	Yes	Clerks
Puerto Rico..........	Yes	No	(Bills) Yes	Secretary of each House
Virgin Islands........	(a)	....	Yes	Executive Secretary of Legislature

(a) Daily journal prepared; printed after close of session.
(b) Daily calendars.
(c) On bills and joint resolutions; in other cases, a show of five hands is required.
(d) Constitution provides for daily publication, but this is not done.
(e) Advance daily journal printed.
(f) In completed journal which is not printed.
(g) Others at request of one member.
(h) Secretary of State is *ex officio* Secretary of the Senate.

LEGISLATIVE PROCEDURE: HOUSE AND SENATE ACTION

State	Readings			Roll call on final passage; mandatory on request of		Electric roll call device	Majority of members required to pass bill (a)
	Number	On separate days	In full	Senate members	House members		
Alabama	3	Yes	3rd	1/10 present	1/10 present	House	Present & voting
Arizona	3	Yes	1st(b), 2nd(b), 3rd	2	2	No	Elected
Arkansas	3	Yes (b)	1st, 3rd	5	5	House	Membership
California	3	Yes (b)	3rd	3	3	Assembly	Elected
Colorado	3	(c)	2nd (d), 3rd (d)	1	1	No	Elected
Connecticut	3	(e)	2nd, 3rd	1/5 present	1/5 present	No	Present & voting (f)
Delaware	3	(c)	1st, 3rd (g)	All bills, joint and concurrent resolutions		No	Elected
Florida	3	Yes	(h)	5	5	House	Present
Georgia	3	3	3rd (i)	5	15	(j)	Elected
Idaho	3	Yes (b)	3rd	3	3	No	Present
Illinois	3	Yes (b)	1st, 2nd, 3rd	2	5	House	Elected
Indiana	3	Yes (b)	1st(b), 2nd(b), 3rd	2	2	Both houses	Elected
Iowa	3	(k)	1st, 2nd, 3rd (l)	1	1	House	Elected
Kansas	3	Yes (b)	3rd	5	25	(j)	Elected
Kentucky	3	Yes (m)	1st, 2nd(m), 3rd(m)	2	2	No	2/5 elected & maj. voting
Louisiana	3	Yes	1st	All bills and resolutions		Both houses	Elected
Maine	(n)	Yes (b)	1st (b), 2nd (b)	1/5 present	1/5 present	No	Present & voting (f)
Maryland	3	Yes	....	1	5	House	Elected
Massachusetts	3	Yes (o)	....	1/5 present	30	No	Present & voting (f)
Michigan	3	(c)	3rd (d)	1/5 present	1/5 present	House	Elected
Minnesota	3	Yes (b)	1st, 3rd	1	15	Both houses	Elected
Mississippi	3	Yes (b)	3rd	1/10 present	1/10 present	House	Present & voting (f)
Missouri	3	Yes	....	5	5	House	Elected
Montana	3	....	3rd (1)	2	10	No	Present
Nebraska	2	(p)	1st, 3rd	1	....	Yes (Unicameral)	Elected
Nevada	3	Yes (b)	3rd	All bills and joint resolutions		No	Elected
New Hampshire	3	(c)	....	1	1	No	(q)
New Jersey	3	Yes (r)	....	1/5 present	1/5 present	House	Membership
New Mexico	3	(s)	3rd	1	1	No	Present
New York	3	(t)	....	1	1	No	Elected
North Carolina	3	Yes (b)	1st, 2nd, 3rd	1/5	1/5	No	Present & voting (f)
North Dakota	2	Yes	2nd	1/6 present	1/6 present	Both houses	Elected (u)
Ohio	3	Yes (v)	3rd	All bills	All bills	House	Elected
Oklahoma	3	Yes	3rd	Maj. elected	Maj. elected	No	Elected
Oregon	3	Yes (b)	3rd (w)	All bills and joint resolutions		No	Elected
Pennsylvania	3	Yes	1st, 2nd, 3rd	All bills	All bills	No	Elected
Rhode Island	2(d)	Yes (d)	2nd	1/5 present	1/5 present	No	Present & voting
South Carolina	3	Yes	2nd	5	10	No	Present & voting (f)
South Dakota	2	Yes	1st, 2nd (1)	1/6	1/6	No	Elected
Tennessee	3	Yes (x)	3rd	3	5	House	Membership
Texas	3	Yes	1st, 2nd, 3rd (l)	3	3	House	Present & voting (f)
Utah	3	Yes (b)	3rd	Majority	Majority	No	Elected
Vermont	3	....	2nd	1	5	No	Present & voting (f,y)
Virginia	3(z)	Yes (z)	....	1/5 present	1/5 present	Both houses	2/5 elected & maj. voting
Washington	3	Yes(aa)	House—2nd, 3rd Senate—3rd	1/6 present	1/6 present	House	Elected
West Virginia	3	Yes(aa)	Yes	1/10	1/10	House	Present & voting
Wisconsin	3	(ab)	....	1/6 present	1/6 present	House	Present & voting (f)
Wyoming	3	Yes (l)	1st, 2nd, 3rd (l)	1	1	No	Elected
Alaska	3	Yes	2nd	3	1/5 present	No	Membership
Guam	3	(o)	1st	3	....	No	Elected
Hawaii	3	Yes	1st, 2nd (ac), 3rd	All bills (ad)	All bills (ad)	No	Membership
Puerto Rico	2	Yes	2nd	All bills	All bills	No	Elected
Virgin Islands	...	....	....	...	...	No	Present

(a) Special constitutional provisions requiring special majorities for the passage of emergency legislation or appropriation or revenue measures not included.
(b) Except by two-thirds vote.
(c) Second and third readings only on separate days.
(d) Except by unanimous consent.
(e) Bills or joint resolutions originating with a committee may receive second reading same day.
(f) House rules or custom determine procedure.
(g) Third reading often by title or partial reading.
(h) Except by two-thirds vote whereby a bill may be read the first time, the second time (by title only or in full), and the third time (which must be in full) all on the same day.
(i) First and second readings of local and private bills by title only unless ordered engrossed.
(j) Roll call equipment to be installed in House for 1956 session.
(k) Senate: May not have second and third readings same day without suspending rules except last day. House: Second and third readings same day by two-thirds vote.
(l) Requirements often waived.
(m) Second and third readings may be dispensed with by vote of majority of elected members.
(n) Senate: Two readings of all bills and resolves. House: Three readings of all bills, two of all resolves.
(o) Except under suspension of rules, then all readings in one day.
(p) Second reading abolished. Rules often suspended and referred to committee same day as first reading.
(q) House: A majority of the members is a quorum for doing business, but when less than two-thirds of elected members are present, the assent of two-thirds of those members is necessary to render acts and proceedings valid. Senate: Not less than thirteen senators shall make a quorum for doing business; and when less than sixteen are present, the assent of ten is necessary to render their acts and proceedings valid.
(r) Bill may receive second and third reading on same day when three-fourths of membership agree.
(s) No more than two readings same day.
(t) Assembly: May receive second and third readings same day by special provision of Rules Committee or by unanimous consent. Senate: Bills receive first and second readings upon introduction before committee reference.
(u) Two-thirds vote required for amendment or repeal of initiated or referred measures.
(v) Except by three-fourths vote.
(w) On final passage in House the rule provides for reading in full unless requirement is suspended by two-thirds vote.
(x) Passed each time read.
(y) Quorum for state tax is two-thirds.
(z) Except a bill codifying the law or where emergency declared and a four-fifths vote.
(aa) Except two readings permitted on same day by four-fifths vote.
(ab) Senate: No two readings on same day. Assembly: Second and third readings on separate days.
(ac) If printed, second reading by title only.
(ad) For final passage of bills. Otherwise, in Senate, on request of one-fifth members present.

LEGISLATIVE PROCEDURE: EXECUTIVE VETO

State	Days after which bill becomes law (before adjournment) unless vetoed (Sundays excepted)	Fate of bill —after adjournment— Days after which bill is law unless vetoed (Sundays excepted)	Days after which bill dies unless signed (Sundays excepted)	Item veto on appropriation bills	Votes required in House and Senate to pass bills or items over veto(a)	Constitution prohibits Governor from vetoing — Initiated measures	Referred measures
Alabama	6	..	10	★	Majority elected	(b)	(b)
Arizona	5	10	..	★	Two-thirds elected(c)	★	★
Arkansas	5	20(d)	..	★	Majority elected	★	★
California	10	..	30	★	Two-thirds elected	★	★
Colorado	10(d)	30(d)	..	★	Two-thirds elected	★	★
Connecticut	5(e)	15(d)	..	★	Majority present	(b)	(b)
Delaware	10	..	30(d)	★	Three-fifths elected	(b)	(b)
Florida	5	20(d)	..	★	Two-thirds present	(b)	(b)
Georgia (f)	30	..	(g)	★	Two-thirds elected	(h)	..
Idaho	5	10	..	★	Two-thirds present	..	..
Illinois	10	10	..	★	Two-thirds elected	(b)	(b)
Indiana	3	5(d,i)	..	..	Majority elected	(b)	(b)
Iowa	3	(j)	30	..	Two-thirds elected	..	..
Kansas	3	(k)	..	★	Two-thirds elected	(b)	(b)
Kentucky	10	10	..	★	Majority elected	..	..
Louisiana	10(d,l)	20(d)	..	★	Two-thirds elected	(b)	(b)
Maine	5	(m)	..	..	Two-thirds present	(n)	★
Maryland (o)	6	..	6(p)	★	Three-fifths elected	(b)	(b)
Massachusetts	5(e)	..	(q)	★	Two-thirds present	★	★
Michigan	10	..	5	★	Two-thirds elected	★	★
Minnesota	3	..	3	★	Two-thirds elected	(b)	(b)
Mississippi	5	(m)	..	★	Two-thirds elected	(b)	(b)
Missouri	(r)	..	..	★	Two-thirds elected	★	★
Montana	5	..	15(d,s)	★	Two-thirds present	★	★
Nebraska	5	5	..	★(t)	Three-fifths elected	★	★
Nevada	5	10	..	..	Two-thirds elected	★	★
New Hampshire	5	..	(g)	..	Two-thirds elected	(b)	(b)
New Jersey	10(u)	45	..	★	Two-thirds elected	(b)	(b)
New Mexico	3	(g)	20(s)	★	Two-thirds present	(h)	..
New York	10	..	30(d)	★	Two-thirds elected	..	..
North Carolina	(v)	(v)	(v)	(v)	....	(b)	(b)
North Dakota	3	15(d)	..	★	Two-thirds elected	★	★
Ohio	10	10	..	★	Three-fifths elected	★	★
Oklahoma	5	..	15	★	Two-thirds elected	★	★
Oregon	5	20	..	★(w)	Two-thirds present	..	..
Pennsylvania	10(d)	30(d)	..	★	Two-thirds elected	(b)	(b)
Rhode Island	6	10(d)	..	..	Three-fifths present	(b)	(b)
South Carolina	3	(m)	..	★	Two-thirds elected	(b)	(b)
South Dakota	3	10(d)	..	★	Two-thirds present	★	★
Tennessee	5	10	..	★(x)	Majority elected	(h)	..
Texas	10	20(j)	..	★	Two-thirds present	(b)	(b)
Utah	5	10	..	★	Two-thirds elected	★	★
Vermont	5	..	(g)	★	Two-thirds present	(b)	(b)
Virginia	5	..	10(j)	★	Two-thirds present(y)	(b)	(b)
Washington	5	10	..	★(z)	Two-thirds elected	★	★
West Virginia	5(aa)	5(d)	..	..	Majority elected	(b)	(b)
Wisconsin	6(l)	..	6(l)	★	Two-thirds present	(b)	(b)
Wyoming	3	15(d)	..	★	Two-thirds elected	(b)	(b)
Alaska	3	..	3	★	Two-thirds elected	..	..
Guam	10	..	30(g)	★	Two-thirds elected	(b)	(b)
Hawaii	10	..	10(p)	★	Two-thirds elected	(b)	(b)
Puerto Rico	10	..	30(ab)	★	Two-thirds elected	..	..
Virgin Islands	10	..	30	★	Two-thirds elected	..	..

(a) Bill returned to house of origin with objections, except in Georgia, where Governor need not state objections, and in Kansas, where all bills are returned to House.
(b) No provision for initiative or referendum in state.
(c) Three-fourths in case of an emergency measure.
(d) Sundays not excepted unless last day is Sunday.
(e) Sundays and legal holidays excepted.
(f) New constitution, passed by General Assembly, withholds right to veto constitutional amendments.
(g) Unsigned bills do not become laws after adjournment.
(h) No provision for initiative in state.
(i) Bill becomes law if not filed with objections with Secretary of State within five days after adjournment.
(j) Sundays not excepted.
(k) In practice, the legislature closes consideration of bills three days before adjournment *sine die.*
(l) Governor has 10 days (in Wisconsin 6 days) from time bill was presented to him in which to approve or disapprove.
(m) Bill becomes law if not returned within 2 days (Maine and Mississippi 3) after reconvening.
(n) Constitution provides that Governor may veto initiated measures and if legislature sustains veto, measure is referred to vote of people at next general election.
(o) 1950 constitutional amendment requires any bill vetoed after adjournment, or dying because of pocket veto after adjournment, to be returned to the legislature when it next convenes, for a vote on overriding the veto.

(p) Within 6 days (in Hawaii 10 days) after presentation to the Governor, regardless of how long after adjournment.
(q) Within 5 days of receipt by Governor. In practice General Court not prorogued until Governor has acted on all bills.
(r) If Governor does not return bill in 15 days, a joint resolution is necessary for bill to become law.
(s) Governor must file bills with Secretary of State.
(t) Governor may not veto items in budget submitted by himself after it has passed legislature with three-fifths vote.
(u) If house of origin is in temporary adjournment on 10th day, becomes law on day house of origin reconvenes unless returned by Governor on that day. Governor has power of veto after repassage of bills in amended form with condition bill must be approved in 10 days or pocket veto.
(v) No veto; bill becomes law 30 days after adjournment of session unless otherwise expressly directed.
(w) Also may veto items in new bills declaring an emergency.
(x) Governor may reduce or eliminate items but must give written notice of item veto either 3 days before adjournment or one day after bill is presented for signature.
(y) Including majority elected.
(z) May veto items in any bill containing items or sections.
(aa) Budget (appropriation) bill not submitted to Governor after passage.
(ab) Sundays are not excepted.

1954 AND 1955 SESSIONS, INTRODUCTIONS AND ENACTMENTS
(As of December, 1955)

State	Regular Sessions Convened	Adjourned*	No. of introductions	No. of enactments	Extra Sessions Convened	Adjourned*	No. of introductions	No. of enactments
Alabama	May 3, 1955	Sept. 2, 1955	1,611	579	Jan. 25, 1955 Mar. 4, 1955 Apr. 13, 1955	Feb. 24, 1955 Apr. 8, 1955 July 21, 1955(a)	135 160 48	70 80 4
Arizona	Jan. 11, 1954 Jan. 10, 1955	Apr. 10, 1954 Apr. 3, 1955	585 563	160 159	Oct. 24, 1955 Nov. 28, 1955	Nov. 28, 1955 (c)	NA (c)	NA (c)
Arkansas	Jan. 10, 1955	Mar. 10, 1955	1,099	429				
California	Mar. 1, 1954 Jan. 3, 1955	Mar. 30, 1954 June 8, 1955(b)	33 5,841	10 1,966	Mar. 1, 1954	Apr. 1, 1954	162	67
Colorado	Jan. 6, 1954 Jan. 5, 1955	Feb. 13, 1954 Apr. 6, 1955	122 807	62 326	Mar. 17, 1954	Mar. 23, 1954	9	4
Connecticut	Jan. 5, 1955	June 8, 1955	3,535	1,270	June 22, 1955 Nov. 21, 1955	June 24, 1955 (c)	NA (c)	NA (c)
Delaware	Jan. 4, 1955	(c, d)	(c)	(c)	Aug. 30, 1954	Aug. 30, 1954	NA	NA
Florida	Apr. 5, 1955	June 3, 1955	3,379	1,801	June 6, 1955	(c, e)	(c)	(c)
Georgia	Jan. 10, 1955	Feb. 18, 1955	981	440	June 6, 1955	June 17, 1955	49	18
Idaho	Jan. 3, 1955	Mar. 5, 1955	571	285				
Illinois	Jan. 5, 1955	June 30, 1955	2,158	973				
Indiana	Jan. 6, 1955	Mar. 7, 1955	1,016	363				
Iowa	Jan. 10, 1955	Apr. 29, 1955	1,080	321				
Kansas	Jan. 11, 1955	Apr. 6, 1955	879	447				
Kentucky	Jan. 5, 1954	Mar. 19, 1954	949	318				
Louisiana	May 10, 1954 May 9, 1955	July 8, 1954 June 7, 1955	1,658 321	767 142	Jan. 3, 1955	Jan. 14, 1955	NA	NA
Maine	Jan. 5, 1955	May 21, 1955	1,877	883	Sept. 21, 1954	Sept. 23, 1954	50	31
Maryland	Feb. 3, 1954 Jan. 5, 1955	Mar. 4, 1954 Apr. 4, 1955	384 1,492	79 725(f)				
Massachusetts	Jan. 6, 1954 Jan. 5, 1955	June 11, 1954 Sept. 16, 1955	3,412 3,697	813 933	Sept. 7, 1954	Sept. 8, 1954	7	3
Michigan	Jan. 13, 1954 Jan. 12, 1955	May 14, 1954 July 15, 1955(g)	744 914	217 283	Aug. 18, 1954 Nov. 1, 1955	Aug. 19, 1954 (c)	6 (c)	3 (c)
Minnesota	Jan. 4, 1955	April 21, 1955	3,507	892(h)	Apr. 26, 1955	Apr. 26, 1955	12	6
Mississippi	Jan. 5, 1954	May 6, 1954	1,855	670	Sept. 7, 1954 Jan. 11, 1955	Sept. 30, 1954 Apr. 7, 1955	199 481	123 276
Missouri	Jan. 5, 1955	May 31, 1955	943	291	Feb. 23, 1954	Apr. 23, 1954	38	13
Montana	Jan. 3, 1955	Mar. 5, 1955	634	279				
Nebraska	Jan. 4, 1955	June 17, 1955	559	354				
Nevada	Jan. 17, 1955	Mar. 25, 1955	912	553(i)	Jan. 5, 1954	Jan. 9, 1954	26	24
New Hampshire	Jan. 5, 1955	Aug. 5, 1955	752	460	Apr. 6, 1954	Apr. 9, 1954	7	3

State	Convened	Adjourned*			Convened	Adjourned*		
New Jersey	Jan. 12, 1954 Jan. 11, 1955	Jan. 10, 1955 (c, j)	940 (c)	320 (c)	Sept. 17, 1954	Sept. 17, 1954	NA	NA
New Mexico	Jan. 11, 1955	Mar. 12, 1955	860	377	Sept. 26, 1955	Oct. 6, 1955	NA	NA
New York	Jan. 6, 1954 Jan. 5, 1955	Apr. 19, 1954 Apr. 2, 1955	6,121 6,677	NA NA	June 10, 1954	June 10, 1954	9	6
North Carolina	Jan. 5, 1955	May 25, 1955	1,997	1,426				
North Dakota	Jan. 4, 1955	Mar. 11, 1955	612	355				
Ohio	Jan. 3, 1955	July 13, 1955(k)	1,355	331	Jan. 11, 1954	Jan. 15, 1954	2	2
Oklahoma	Jan. 4, 1955	May 28, 1955(l)	1,033	436				
Oregon	Jan. 10, 1955	May 4, 1955	1,432	856				
Pennsylvania	Jan. 4, 1955	(c, m)	(c)	(c)				
Rhode Island	Jan. 5, 1954 Jan. 4, 1955	Apr. 23, 1954 Apr. 30, 1955	957 1,121	433 519				
South Carolina	Jan. 12, 1954 Jan. 11, 1955	Apr. 2, 1954 May 27, 1955	863 1,204	418 604				
South Dakota	Jan. 4, 1955	Mar. 4, 1955	815	442				
Tennessee	Jan. 3, 1955	Mar. 18, 1955	2,291	947				
Texas	Jan. 11, 1955	June 7, 1955	1,431	530(n)	Mar. 15, 1954	Apr. 13, 1954	211	58
Utah	Jan. 10, 1955	Mar. 10, 1955	577	212	Apr. 23, 1955	Apr. 23, 1955	4	4
Vermont	Jan. 5, 1955	June 11, 1955	571	351(n)				
Virginia	Jan. 13, 1954	Mar. 31, 1954	NA	NA				
Washington	Jan. 10, 1955	Mar. 10, 1955	1,387	430	Mar. 11, 1955	Mar. 24, 1955	64	21
West Virginia	Jan. 12, 1955	Mar. 14, 1955	931	210	May 9, 1955	May 13, 1955	16	2
Wisconsin	Jan. 12, 1955	Oct. 21, 1955(o)	1503	NA				
Wyoming	Jan. 11, 1955	Feb. 19, 1955	437	267				
Alaska	Jan. 24, 1955	Mar. 25, 1955	493	259	Jan. 28, 1955	Apr. 7, 1955	22	19
Guam	Jan. 11, 1954 June 14, 1954 Jan. 10, 1955 June 13, 1955	Feb. 9, 1954(p) July 13, 1954(p) Feb. 8, 1955(p) July 12, 1955(p)	NA NA	188 148	Feb. 15, 1954 July 26, 1954	Feb. 17, 1954 July 28, 1954	NA NA	NA NA
Hawaii	Feb. 16, 1955	May 27, 1955	2,963	545				
Puerto Rico	Jan. 11, 1954 Jan. 10, 1955	May 31, 1954 May 31, 1955	NA NA	217 234	July 19, 1954 Sept. 7, 1954 Sept. 27, 1954 Aug. 8, 1955 Oct. 24, 1955 Nov. 21, 1955	July 24, 1954 Sept. 25, 1954 Aug. 27, 1955 Nov. 11, 1955 Dec. 10, 1955	1 28 12 18 NA NA	
Virgin Islands	NA	NA	NA	NA	NA	NA	NA	NA

*Actual adjournment dates are listed regardless of constitutional limitation.

NA: Information not available.

(a) Recessed April 22–July 21.
(b) Recessed January 21–February 28.
(c) 1955 legislature still in session when table was compiled.
(d) Recessed August 11–September 26.
(e) Special reapportionment session recessed August 10–September 26 and September 29–June 4, 1956.
(f) The legislature at the 1956 session will consider sixty 1955 bills vetoed by the Governor.
(g) Recessed June 4–July 14.
(h) Excluding resolutions not requiring Governor's signature.
(i) The legislature at the 1957 session will consider three 1955 acts vetoed by the Governor.

(j) Recessed January 31–March 7; April 4–April 25; June 9–August 8; August 29–September 12; and September 23–December 5.
(k) Recessed June 23–July 12.
(l) Recessed March 31–April 6.
(m) Recessed May 11–May 23; June 29–July 11; House recessed August 5–August 29; Senate recessed August 9–August 29; both houses recessed September 3–September 12.
(n) Figures do not include resolutions.
(o) Recessed June 24–October 3.
(p) Legislature meets for two 30-day periods of each year, the first convening the second Monday in January, the second convening the second Monday in June.

SALARIES AND COMPENSATION OF LEGISLATORS

State	Regular Session — Daily Pay Plan — Amount per day	Regular Session — Daily Pay Plan — Limit on no. of days of pay	Regular Session — Salary Plan — Amount of salary calculated for biennium	Special Session — Amount of pay per day	Special Session — Limit on no. of days of pay	Basic salary is fixed by	Date basic salary established	Travel Allowance — Amount per mile	Travel Allowance — Number of trips during session	Additional expense allowances during session
Alabama	$10	36 L(a)		$10	36 L	Const.	1946	10c	One round trip	$20 per day (a)
Arizona	8	60 C(b)		8	20 C	Const.	1932	20c	One way	$17 per day (c)
Arkansas			$ 1,200	6	15 C	Const.	1946	5c	One round trip	None
California			12,000(b)			Const.	1954	5c(d)		$14 per day; extra allowances for committee members (d)
Colorado	20(e)	120 C	3,600(b,e)	20(e)	None	Stat.	1953	(f)	One round trip	None
Connecticut			600			Stat.	1946	10c		None
Delaware			2,000			Stat.	1949	10c	Unlimited mileage	None
Florida			2,400			Const.	1954	7½c	Eight round trips	$15 per day
Georgia	10	40 C(b)		10	70 C (g)	Const.	1945	10c	One round trip	$5 per day
Idaho	10	60 C		10	20 C	Const.	1946	10c	One round trip	Additional $5 a day for maximum of 60 days for committee members
Illinois			10,000			Stat.	1951	10c	Round trip per week	$50 for postage and stationery
Indiana			3,600(h)			Stat.	1955	6c	Round trip per week	$10 per day (i)
Iowa		90(b,j)	2,000	20	None	Stat.	1949	5c	One round trip	None
Kansas	5			5	30 L	Const. & Stat.	1949	15c	One round trip	$7 per day
Kentucky	25			25	None	Stat.	1950	15c	One round trip	$10 per day; $50 in lieu of stationery
Louisiana	30(1)	90 C(b,j)		30	30 C	Stat.	1952	10c	Eight round trips and four round trips during budget session	$150 per month while legislature not in session(l)
Maine			1,250(h)	10	None	Stat.	1955	5c	Round trip per week	Small allowance for postage, telephone, etc.
Maryland			3,600(b)	(n)		Const.	1946	20c(m)		$800 per biennium
Massachusetts			9,000(b)		None	Stat.	1951	7c(o)	Each day (o)	$800 per biennium; weekly expense allowance according to distance from capitol (o)
Michigan			8,000(b)			Stat.	1954	10c	Round trip per month	$2,000 per biennium; plus allowance for postage, telephone and telegraph
Minnesota			4,800(h)	25(h)	None	Stat.	1955	15c	One round trip	House, $1,100; Senate $1,200 at 1955 session (p)
Mississippi			2,000	15		Stat.	1946	10c	One round trip (q)	None
Missouri			3,000		60 C	Const.(r)	1945	10c(r)	One round trip (r)	$10 per day
Montana	20(h)	60 C		20(h)	60 C	Stat.	1955	7c	One round trip	None
Nebraska			1,744			Const. & Stat.	1934	6c	One round trip	$100 postage allowance
Nevada	15	60 C		15	20 C	Stat.	1945	7½c (t)	Daily commuting (s)	$10 per day (s); $60 for postage, etc.
New Hampshire			200	3	15 C	Const. & Stat.		(t)	Rate-distance ratio (t)	None
New Jersey			10,000(b)			Const. & Stat.	1954		State railroad pass	None
New Mexico	20	60 C		20	30 C	Const. & Stat.	1953	10c	One round trip	Stationery, postage, telephone and telegraph allowance
New York			15,000(b)			Const. & Stat.	1954	(f)	Round trip per week	$1,000 expense allowance at 1955 annual session.
North Carolina	15	90 C(u)		15	25 C	Const.	1950	None (u)		None (u)
North Dakota	5(v)	60 L		5(v)	None	Const.	1889	10c	One round trip	$10 per day

L—Legislative Days; C—Calendar Days

State				Salary	Basis	Year	Mileage	Travel allowance	Additional allowances
Ohio	15	75 L(w)		10,000(h)	Stat.	1955	10c	Round trip per week	Postage and stationery
Oklahoma			15	3,950(w)	Const.	1948	10c	One round trip	Postage, stationery, telephone and telegraph allowance and shipping legislative supplies
Oregon			(z)	1,200(x)	Const.	1950	10c		Postage, stationery and shipping legislative supplies
Pennsylvania			(z)	3,000(y)	Stat.	1937(y)	5c	Round trip per week	$3,600 per biennium
Rhode Island	5	60 L(b)	5		Const.	1900	8c		None
South Carolina			(z)	2,000(b)	Stat.	1947	7c	Round trip per week	None
South Dakota	10		10	1,050	Stat.	1953	5c	One round trip	None
Tennessee	10	75 C	20 C		Stat.		16c	One round trip	$5 per day
Texas	25	120 C	30 C		Const.	1954	10c	One round trip	Small expense allowance determined at session
Utah			25	1,000	Const. & Stat.	1951	10c	One round trip	$5 per day
Vermont				1,600(aa)	Stat.	1955	20c	One round trip	Stationery
Virginia			(z)	1,080	Stat.	1948	7c	One round trip	None
Washington			10	2,400	Stat.	1949	10c	One round trip	$15 per day
West Virginia				3,000(b)	Const.	1954	10c	One round trip	None
Wisconsin	12		12	4,800	Stat.	1949	(ab)	Rate-distance ratio (ab)	$100 monthly expense allowance (ac)
Wyoming		40 C	None		Stat.	1941	8c	One round trip	$6 per day
Alaska	15	60 C	30 C		Organic Act, Amend. & Stat.	1942; 1949	15c		$20 per day
Guam	15	60 C(b)	15		Organic Act	1950	None		None
Hawaii			(z)	1,000	Organic Act, Amend. & Stat.	1931; 1949	20c	One round trip	$10 per day for members from Oahu; $20 for legislators from outer islands
Puerto Rico				6,000(b)	Stat.	1953	15c	Round trip per week (ad)	$15 per day; $200 for telephone; $100 for postage; $100 for stationery
Virgin Islands				1,200(b)	Stat.		(f)	Eight round trips	$10 per day

111

(a) In practice the legislature meets for 18 weeks. Legislators receive $210 a week in combined daily salary and expense allowance, a total of $3,780 for each regular biennial session.
(b) Annual sessions.
(c) For regular and special sessions.
(d) 10c a mile for committee meetings and $15 a day for maximum of 60 days for interim committee meetings.
(e) Legislators receive $50 a month during biennium plus $2,400 per biennium, paid at rate of $20 a day during regular and special sessions with remainder paid as a lump sum. Salary applied to all House members and Senators elected in 1955 and will become effective for holdover Senators or their successors in 1957.
(f) Actual and necessary expenses.
(g) 70-day limit on special sessions called by Governor; 30-day limit on sessions convened by legislature except for impeachment proceedings.
(h) Salary shown is new salary which becomes effective at 1957 session.
(i) Determined at each session. Figure represents amount at latest session.
(j) 90 days biennial total: 60-day regular session, 30-day budget session.
(k) Legislators are paid for Sundays and holidays during session, consequently compensation period usually is 72 to 74 days.
(l) Determined at each session.
(m) In terms of fixed amount for each legislator.
(n) Determined at each session.
(o) Within 40-mile radius, $10 per week expense allowance plus 7c a mile daily, to amount to not less than $4.50 a week; outside 40-mile radius, $38.50 per week living expenses plus 7c a mile for one round trip per week.
(p) Effective 1957, per diem at rate paid to state officials will replace lump sum expense allowance.
(q) Plus one extra round trip each 7 days at 6c a mile.

(r) Proposed constitutional amendment to be voted on in November, 1956, and effective upon adoption, would remove constitutional limitations on salary and permit legislature to determine salary in future. It also carries provisions for weekly round trips at mileage rate allowed state officials.
(s) 7½c a mile for daily commuting or $10 per day if living in capital.
(t) 15c per mile for first 45 miles, 8c for next 25 miles, 6c over 95 miles.
(u) Proposed constitutional amendment to be voted on in November, 1956, and effective upon adoption, would increase the period for which legislators may be paid from 90 to 120 days and would establish expense allowance of $8 and travel at 7c a mile.
(v) Proposed constitutional amendment to be voted on June, 1956, and effective for 1957 if adopted, would increase daily pay from $5 to $10.
(w) Legislators receive $15 for first 75 legislative days, including intervening non-legislative days, for regular or special sessions, otherwise $100 a month.
(x) Proposed constitutional amendment to be voted November, 1956, and effective upon proclamation of the Governor, if adopted, would increase legislative salaries from $1,200 to $2,400 a biennium.
(y) 1955 statute makes provision for $3,000 annual salary in the event annual sessions are adopted.
(z) Fixed amount for special sessions: Pennsylvania, $500, or $750 if longer than one month; South Carolina, $1,000; Virginia, $540; Hawaii, $500.
(aa) Weekly salary of $70 adopted effective May 10, 1955; previous rate of $1,250 per session, was in effect from January of the session to that date. The salary for the 1955 session totalled $1,600.
(ab) 10c a mile for one round trip; thereafter, 7c a mile for first 2,000 miles per month, 6c a mile for each additional mile.
(ac) For legislators filing affidavit regarding necessity of establishing temporary residence at capital during regular or special sessions.
(ad) Minimum $10.

APPORTIONMENT OF LEGISLATURES
As of November, 1955

State	Citation: art. & sec. of const.	Basis of apportionment — Senate	Basis of apportionment — House	Frequency of required reapportionment — Required every 10 years*	Frequency of required reapportionment — Other schedules for reapportioning	Apportioning agency	Dates of last two apportionments	
Alabama............	IV, 50; IX, 197–203	Population, except no county more than one member.	Population, but each county at least one member.	X	.....	Legislature.	1901	1880
Arizona.............	IV, 2, 1 (1)	Districts specifically established by constitution.	Votes cast for Governor at last preceding general election, but not less than if computed on basis of election of 1930.	..	After every gubernatorial election (every 2 years).	No provision for Senate; redistricting for House by County Boards of Supervisors.	H-1954	1952
Arkansas...........	VIII, 1–5	Population.	Each county at least one member; remaining members distributed among more populous counties according to population.	X	.....	Board of Apportionment (Governor, Secretary of State, and Attorney General). Subject to revision by State Supreme Court.	1951	1941
California..........	IV, 6	Population, exclusive of persons ineligible to naturalization. No county, or city and county, to have more than one member; no more than three counties in any district.	Population, exclusive of persons ineligible to naturalization.	X	.....	Legislature or, if it fails, a Reapportionment Commission (Lieutenant Governor, Controller, Attorney General, Secretary of State, and Superintendent of Public Instruction). In either case, subject to a referendum.	1951	1941
Colorado...........	V, 45–47	Population.	Population.	X	.....	General Assembly.	1953	1933
Connecticut........	III, 3, 4	Population, but each county at least one member.	Two members from each town having over 5,000 population; others, same number as in 1874.	Senate	.....	General Assembly for Senate, no provision for House.	H-1876	S-1941
Delaware...........	II, 2	Districts specifically established by constitution.	Districts specifically established by constitution.	..	.....	No provision.	1897	....
Florida.............	VII, 3, 4	Population, but no county more than one member.	3 to each of 5 largest counties, 2 to each of next 18, 1 each to others.	X(a)	.....	Legislature.	1945(a)	1935

Georgia............	III, 2; (Par. i), 3 (Par. ii)	Population, but no county more than one member.	Population, i.e., 3 to each of 8 largest counties, 2 to each of next 30, 1 each to others.	X	.....	General Assembly "may" change Senatorial districts. Shall change House apportionment at first session after each U.S. census.	1950	1940
Idaho............	III, 2, 4, 5; XIX, 1, 2	One member from each county.	Total House not to exceed 3 times Senate. Each county entitled to at least one representative, apportioned as provided by law.	X	.....	Legislature.	1951	1941
Illinois............	IV, 6, 7, 8	Fixed districts based on area.	Population.	House	Senate is fixed.	General Assembly, or, if it fails, a reapportionment commission appointed by the Governor.	1955	1901
Indiana............	IV, 4, 5, 6	Male inhabitants over 21 years of age.	Male inhabitants over 21 years of age.	..	Every 6 years.	General Assembly.	1921	1915
Iowa............	III, 34, 35	Population, but no county more than one member.	One to each county, and one additional to each of the nine most populous counties.	X	.....	General Assembly.	H-1927 S-1911	1921 1906
Kansas............	II, 2; X, 1-3	Population.	Population, but each county at least one.	..	Every 5 years.	Legislature.	H-1945 S-1947	....
Kentucky............	Sec. 33	Population.	Population, but no more than two counties to be joined in a district.	X	.....	General Assembly.	1942	1918
Louisiana............	III, 2-6	Population.	Population, but each parish and each ward of New Orleans at least one member.	X	.....	Legislature.	1921	1902
Maine............	IV, Pt. I, 2, 3; IV, Pt. II, 1	Population, exclusive of aliens and Indians not taxed. No county less than one nor more than five.	Population, exclusive of aliens. No town more than seven members, unless a consolidated town.	X	.....	Legislature.	H-1955 S-1951	1941(b) 1941
Maryland............	III, 2, 5	One from each county and from each of six districts constituting Baltimore city.	Population, but minimum of two and maximum of six per county. Each of Baltimore districts as many members as largest county.	..	No requirements.	Membership frozen for House; no provision for Senate.	1943	....
Massachusetts........	Amdt. LXXXI	Legal voters.	Legal voters.	X	.....	General Court.	H-1947 S-1948	1939 1939
Michigan............	V, 2-4	Districts specifically prescribed by constitution.	Population.(c)	House	Senate is fixed.	Legislature or, if it fails, State Board of Canvassers (Secretary of State, Treasurer, Commissioner of State Land Office) apportions House. Senate is fixed.	H-1953	1943
Minnesota............	IV, 2, 23, 24	Population, exclusive of nontaxable Indians.	Population, exclusive of nontaxable Indians.	X	And after each state census.	Legislature "shall have power."	1913	1897

113

APPORTIONMENT OF LEGISLATURES—Continued

As of November, 1955

State	Citation: art. & sec. of const.	Basis of apportionment — Senate	Basis of apportionment — House	Frequency of required reapportionment — Required every 10 years*	Frequency of required reapportionment — Other schedules for reapportioning	Apportioning agency	Dates of last two apportionments	
Mississippi	XIII, 254–256	Prescribed by constitution.	Prescribed by constitution, each county at least one. Counties grouped into three divisions, each division to have at least 44 members.	X	.....	Legislature "may."	1916	1904
Missouri	III, 2–11	Population.	Population, but each county at least one member.	X	.....	House: Secretary of State apportions among counties; county courts apportion within counties. Senate: by commission appointed by Governor.	1951	1946
Montana	V, 4; VI, 2–6	One member from each county.	Population.	..	No requirements.	Legislative Assembly.	1943	1939
Nebraska	III, 5	Unicameral legislature—population excluding aliens.		..	From time to time.	Legislature "may."	1935	1920
Nevada	I, 13; XVII, 6	One member for each county.	Population.	X	.....	Legislature.	1951	1947
New Hampshire	Pt. II, 9, 11, 26	Direct taxes paid.	Population.(d)	House	Senate—from time to time.	General Court.	H-1951 S-1915	1943 1877
New Jersey	IV, ii, 1; IV, iii, 1	One member from each county.	Population, but at least one member from each county.	X	.....	Legislature.	1941	1931
New Mexico	IV, (3)	One member from each county.	At least one member for each county and additional representatives for more populous counties.	X	.....	Legislature.	1955	1949
New York	III, 3–5	Population, excluding aliens. No county more than ⅓ membership, nor more than ½ membership to two adjoining counties.	Population, excluding aliens. Each county (except Hamilton) at least one member.	X	.....	Legislature. Subject to review by courts.	1954	1944
North Carolina	II, 4–6	Population, excluding aliens and Indians not taxed.	Population, excluding aliens and Indians not taxed, but each county at least one member.	X	.....	General Assembly.	1941	1921
North Dakota	II, 26, 29, 32, 35	Population.	Population.	X	Or after each state census.	Legislative Assembly.	1931	1921

114

State	Constitution	Basis (one house)	Basis (other house)		Frequency	Responsible body		
Ohio	XI, 1-11	Population.	Population, but each county at least one member.	X(e)	Each biennium(e)	Governor, Auditor, and Secretary of State, or any two of them.	1953	1951
Oklahoma	V, 9-16	Population.	Population, but no county to have more than seven members.(j)	X	.....	Legislature.	1951	1941
Oregon	IV, 6, 7	Population.	Population.	X	.....	Legislative Assembly, or failing that, Secretary of State. Reapportionment subject to Supreme Court review.	1954	1911
Pennsylvania	II, 16-18	Population, but no city or county to have more than ⅙ of membership.	Population, but each county at least one member.	X	.....	General Assembly.	1953	1921
Rhode Island	XIII; Amdt. XIX	Qualified voters, but minimum of 1 and maximum of 6 per city or town.	Population, but at least one member from each town or city, and no town or city more than ¼ of total, i.e., 25.	House	Senate—after each presidential election.	General Assembly "may."	1940	1936
South Carolina	III; 1-8	One member from each county.	Population, but at least one member from each county.	X	.....	General Assembly.	1952	1942
South Dakota	III, 5	Population.	Population.	X	.....	Legislature, or failing that, Governor, Superintendent of Public Instruction, Presiding Judge of Supreme Court, Attorney General, and Secretary of State.	1951	1947
Tennessee	II, 4-6	Qualified voters.	Qualified voters.	X	.....	General Assembly.	1945(f)	1903
Texas	III, 25-26a, 28	Qualified electors, but no county more than one member.	Population, but no county more than 7 representatives unless population greater than 700,000, then 1 additional representative for each 100,000.	X	.....	Legislature or, if it fails, Legislative Redistricting Board (Lieutenant Governor, Speaker of House, Attorney General, Comptroller of Public Accounts, and Commissioner of General Land Office).	1951	1921
Utah	IX, 2, 4	Population.	Population. Each county at least one member, with additional representatives on a population ratio.	X	.....	Legislature.	1955	1931
Vermont	II, 13, 18, 37	Population, but each county at least one member.	One member from each inhabited town.	Senate	Senate—or after each state census.	Legislature apportions Senate; no provision for House.	1793(g)	....
Virginia	IV, 43	Population.	Population.	X	.....	General Assembly.	1952	1942

115

APPORTIONMENT OF LEGISLATURES—Continued
As of November, 1955

State	Citation: art & sec. of const.	Basis of apportionment — Senate	Basis of apportionment — House	Required every 10 years*	Other schedules for reapportionment	Apportioning agency	Dates of last two apportionments	
Washington	II, 3, 6; XXII, 1, 2	Population, excluding Indians not taxed and soldiers, sailors and officers of U. S. Army and Navy in active service.	Population, excluding Indians not taxed and soldiers, sailors and officers of U. S. Army and Navy in active service.	X	....	Legislature, or by initiative.	1931	1909
West Virginia	VI, 4–10, 50	Population, but no two members from any county, unless one county constitutes a district.	Population, but each county at least one member.	X	....	Legislature.	1950	1940
Wisconsin	IV, 3–5	Population and area.	Population.	X	....	Legislature.	1951	1921
Wyoming	III, 3; III, 2–4	Population, but each county at least one member.	Population, but each county at least one member.	X	....	Legislature.	1931	1921
Alaska	Organic Act: 37 Stat. 512, 4	Four members from each judicial district.	Population, excluding military and families.	House	....	U. S. Director of Census.	1953	1945
Guam	Organic Act: 1950 (2d) Sec. 512	Legislature elected at large.		..	....	....	....	....
Hawaii	Organic Act: Sec. 55	Population.(h)	Population.(h)	..	....	Territorial Legislature.	1900(i)	....
Puerto Rico	III, 3, 7	Two senators for each of eight senatorial districts, and eleven at large.	One representative for each of 40 representative districts and eleven at large.	X(k)	....	Board composed of Chief Justices and two additional members representing different political parties, appointed by Governor with Senate consent.	1917	1952
Virgin Islands	Organic Act	....	....	..	....	....	....	....

*Every ten years, or after each federal census.
H—House; S—Senate.
(a) Extraordinary reapportionment session convened June 6, 1955, and in September recessed to June 4, 1956. Legislature may not adjourn until reapportionment is effected.
(b) 1941 action duplicated 1931 apportionment.
(c) Any county with a moiety of ratio of population is entitled to separate representation.
(d) Amendment adopted in November, 1942, sets the membership of the House of Representatives at not more than 400 and not less than 375. It requires, for each representative additional to the first, twice the number of inhabitants required for the first, with the provision that a town or ward which is not entitled to a representative all of the time may send one a proportionate part of the time, and at least once in every 10 years.

(e) Constitution requires reapportionment every 10 years and also sets up a ratio and apportionment procedure so that reapportionment is actually accomplished in each biennial period for the succeeding session. This is mandatory, and the legislature has no power to take action in the matter.
(f) Not a basic reapportionment; two counties moved from one district to another.
(g) Apportionment plan for House is provided in the constitution with provisions for reapportionment. House apportionment thus dates from adoption of constitution in 1793.
(h) Citizens of the Territory (U.S. citizens residing one year in Territory of Hawaii).
(i) Date Hawaii became a territory.
(j) In practice no county has less than one member.
(k) Beginning in 1960.

LEGISLATIVE SERVICE AGENCIES

A MAJOR legislative development since 1900 has been the creation and expansion of various types of permanent staff agencies to provide state legislators with needed assistance. This development has been occasioned primarily by the increasing number and complexity of the problems arising for legislative consideration and by the rapidly mounting costs of state government.

Major areas of assistance to legislators which have taken institutional form in recent years include:

1. Reference and research assistance on any subject of legislation;
2. Drafting of legislation;
3. Statutory, code and law revision;
4. Advance study of important subjects expected to come before future legislative sessions;
5. Development of recommendations for legislative action;
6. Continuous review of state revenues and expenditures and pre-session review of the budget;
7. Post-audit of state fiscal operations.

The oldest of the permanent service agencies are the legislative reference libraries, now established in more than forty states.

Some or all of the following services are provided by legislative reference agencies in the various states: factual research information; spot research and counseling; preparation of legislative manuals and state directories, indexes and digests of legislative material, up-to-date reports on the content and status of pending legislation, and legislative newsletters; assistance in drafting bills; and statutory revision. In 1901 Wisconsin established the first integrated agency to provide most of these services for its legislators, following development during the previous decade of specialized legislative reference divisions within the state libraries of New York and Massachusetts. The success of the Wisconsin reference library led more than half of the states, by 1917, to create legislative reference facilities.

These reference agencies vary in organizational structure as well as in specific services. A majority are sections of the state library, state law library, or department of library and archives. This method of organization is most common when the bureau does little or no bill drafting. In several states where drafting is a major activity—notably in Alabama, Delaware, Florida, Illinois, Indiana, Maryland, Michigan, Ohio, Pennsylvania and Virginia—the bureau is independent of the library.

The technical nature of bill-drafting and statutory revision services has led to the creation, in more than a third of the states, of specialized agencies with primary responsibility for carrying out one or both of these activities. Among them are the Legislative Counsels in California, Massachusetts and Oregon; the Legislative Commissioner in Connecticut; statutory or code revisors in Colorado, Florida, Kansas, Minnesota, Mississippi, Nebraska, Nevada, North Carolina, Rhode Island, Washington and Wisconsin; code commissions in South Dakota, Tennessee and Virginia; and the Legislative Bill Drafting Commission in New York. In several other states the functions are part of the services legislative councils perform.

As now practiced in most states, code and statutory revision consists primarily of form revision or modified substantive revision, i.e., the systematic classification and compilation of statute law; elimination of obsolete, outmoded, or unconstitutional parts; and, to some extent, the rectification of conflicts and inconsistencies. In recent years an increasing number of states have authorized revision along these lines on a continuous basis.

Extensive revision in the substance of the law, involving major changes in policy, is carried on systematically by only a few state agencies at present—notably by the New York Law Revision Commission, created in 1934; to some extent by the New Jersey Law Revision and Legislative Services Commission; the General Statutes Commission in North Carolina; the quasi-public State Law Institute in Louisiana; and the California Law Revision Commission, created in 1953.

The most significant development in the legislative service agency field during the past twenty years has been expansion of the legislative council idea. More than two-thirds of the states have established agencies of this nature, following creation of the Kansas Legislative Council in 1933. Essentially, legislative councils are permanent joint legislative committees which meet periodically between sessions and consider problems expected to confront the next session of the legislature. In most instances, councils are composed exclusively of legislators. They range in size from five members (in South Carolina) to 165 (in Oklahoma), with fifteen members a median. If the three councils which include all members of the legislature (those of Nebraska, Oklahoma and South Dakota) are omitted, the median is fourteen.

The councils have the services of continuing research staffs with their accumulated resources. Thus equipped, they can develop comprehensive, impartial analyses of public issues and make these analyses available to all legislators for study and use. Most councils—or research committees, as they are called in many states—may undertake studies on their own initiative; many councils formulate legislative programs based on their interim research.

Ten of the thirty-four jurisdictions with council or council-type agencies in operation established them during the first decade of the council movement. Since 1943 an additional twenty-four legislatures have activated similar agencies, as shown in Table 2. In only one instance, that of the Michigan Legislative Council, has a law creating a council been repealed outright. One council statute, that of Rhode Island, has never been activated. One council act was ruled unconstitutional by a state supreme court, that creating the Montana Legislative Council in 1953.

Legislative councils, staffed with competent research assistants, meet two long-felt needs: they provide machinery for effective and continuing legislative participation in forming policy; and means by which legislatures can obtain a sound factual basis for deliberations and decisions.

In addition, many councils perform a highly valuable educational function for the general public, through means including open hearings on important issues and distribution of council research reports.

Most of the legislative council laws adopted since 1943 provide in one way or another for coordinating the legislative council and legislative reference functions and activities. The laws in Alabama, Alaska, Arizona, Arkansas, Florida, Kentucky, Louisiana, Missouri, Nebraska, Nevada, New Mexico, North Dakota, South Carolina, Tennessee and Utah provide for such combination of functions.

Integration was a major objective in Ohio when the legislature in 1953 combined most legislative services as responsibilities of the new Legislative Service Commission, in New Jersey in 1954 when the Law Revision and Legislative Services Commission was established, and in Kentucky in 1954 when numerous functions were consolidated in the Legislative Research Commission and new functions assigned to it.

An important development since the early forties has been the creation in several states of specialized staff facilities under legislative supervision to provide continuous review of state revenues and expenditures and pre-session analysis of the budget. Since the California Legislature in 1941 created its Joint Legislative Budget Committee, with a staff headed by a legislative auditor, the legislatures of more than one-third of the states, as indicated in Table 1, have established comparable facilities for continuing fiscal investigation and budgetary review.

This fiscal function has been assigned to the legislative council, a committee of the council, or the staff serving the council in ten states: Arizona, Arkansas, Kansas, Maryland, Minnesota, Nebraska, Nevada, New Jersey, Ohio and Oklahoma. In contrast, Illinois, Massachusetts, New Hampshire, Texas, Washington and Wyoming, all of which have legislative councils or council-type agencies, have lodged fiscal review authority in separate legislative budget commissions, committees, or boards.

In the related field of legislative post-auditing, significant developments have been taking place. By the close of 1955, seventeen states, Alaska and Puerto Rico, had created such facilities. Three agencies —those in California, Florida and Alaska —were established in 1955. A bill to create one in West Virginia in that year was vetoed. Two of these agencies are among the oldest legislative services in the country—the Connecticut Auditors of Public Accounts, founded in 1702, and the Tennessee Department of Audit which dates from 1835.

DEVELOPMENTS OF 1954–55

During the 1954–55 biennium, interest in legislative service agencies was unabated. The period was marked by various reorganizations of agencies, intensification of services, and addition of new services by older agencies.

Creation of the legislative post-audit agencies in California, Florida and Alaska is mentioned above.

In the field of permanent legislative research facilities, the legislative council area, Massachusetts created a new agency in 1954; its six-member Legislative Research Council receives staff assistance from the Legislative Research Bureau, created by the same act.

Developments in New Jersey covered many aspects of legislative organization and services. A joint interim legislative committee recommended extensive changes to the 1954 session, after a two-year study. In line with its recommendations, numerous procedural and organizational changes were made to streamline legislative operation. A multi-service Law Revision and Legislative Services Commission was created, to provide research, drafting, revision and related services. It replaces the older Law Revision and Bill Drafting Commission. An office of Legislative Budget and Finance Director was established to provide fiscal analysis and budgetary review services. The state library's reference services also were expanded.

During the closing days of Iowa's 1955 session the legislature created a Legislative Research Bureau, designed to provide the legislature and legislative committees with factual reports and analyses on important problems. The statute creates a committee to hire a director and set salaries for the staff, but in other respects the act appears not to have been designed as a legislative council proposal. There are indications as this is written that the new agency may develop along the lines of the legislative research committee.

Other action during the biennium includes creation in South Carolina of a Committee on Statutory Laws, with statutory revision responsibilities. In Puerto Rico a Legislative Reference Service with broad responsibilities was activated in 1954. The Alaska legislature in 1955 created a Department of Library Service, one of the activities of which is expected to be legislative reference assistance. In North Dakota, the legislature in 1955 provided funds for the Legislative Research Committee to undertake a continuous program of statutory revision. New Hampshire's Legislative Council, created in 1951, was staffed for the first time in 1955.

The trendt oward consolidation of services continued, as reflected by the New Jersey developments. Even more notably, Kentucky's legislature in 1954 abolished the independent Statute Revision Commission and gave the Legislative Research Commission its duties of statutory revision, bill drafting and publication of administrative regulations. The commission also was granted extensive responsibilities of a legislative "housekeeping" nature.

Of interest to legislative service agencies were several opinions of courts and Attorneys General in 1954 and 1955. In Montana the State Supreme Court by a divided opinion held the 1953 legislative council act unconstitutional on numerous grounds (*State ex rel. Mitchell* vs. *Holmes,* 274 P. 2d 611). An opinion by the Attorney General of Arizona in 1955 (Opinion 55-105) upheld the constitutionality of the legislative council in that state. Earlier rulings in Alaska, Arkansas, Maryland, Michigan, Oklahoma and Washington have upheld the constitutionality of such agencies. In mid-1955, in an opinion of the Attorney General of Missouri, all of the twenty-one special interim committees created by the 1955 legislative session were held to be unconstitutional.

LEGISLATIVE COUNCILS AND COUNCIL-TYPE AGENCIES

State	Agency	Year created	1955–57 Appropriations for council and research service	Number of Members				Term No. of years
				Total	Senators	Representatives	Ex-officio and others	
Alabama	Legislative Council(a)	1945	$ 53,700(b)	12	4	6	2(c)	2
Arizona	Legislative Council	1953	150,000	12	5	5	2(c)	2
Arkansas	Legislative Council	1947	81,200	21	6	12	3(f)	2(g)
Colorado	Legislative Council	1953	42,000(i,j)	13	5	6	2(c)	2(k)
Connecticut	Legislative Council	1937	78,952	18	4	8	6(l)	2(g)
Florida	Legislative Council(a)	1949	200,000	18	8	8	2(c)	(n)
Illinois	Legislative Council	1937	107,520	22	10	10	2(c)	2(r)
Indiana	Legis. Advisory Commn. (a)	1945	(t)	8	3	3	2(c)	2
Kansas	Legislative Council	1933	94,963(j,v)	27	10	15	2(c)	2
Kentucky	Legis. Research Commn.	1936(y)	256,625(z,aa)	7	(ab)	(ab)	7(ab)	(ab)
Louisiana	Legislative Council	1952	160,000(aa)	18	8	8	2(c)	2
Maine	Legis. Research Comm.	1939	112,432(ad)	16	7	7	2(c)	2
Maryland	Legislative Council	1939	80,000	20	6	6	8(ae)	2(g)
Massachusetts	Legis. Research Council(a)	1954	88,422(j,af)	6	2	4	..	1
Minnesota	Legis. Research Comm.	1947(y)	115,000	18	9	9	..	2(ah)
Missouri	Comm. on Legis. Research	1943	300,000(aj)	20	10	10	..	(ak)
Nebraska	Legislative Council	1937	72,500	43(al)	43(am)	(am)	..	(al)
Nevada	Legislative Commission (a)	1945	111,431(ao)	8	4	4	..	(ap)
New Hampshire	Legislative Council	1951	24,500	15	3	9	3(aq)	2(ar)
New Jersey	Law Revision & Legis. Services Commission	1954	67,120	8	4	4	..	(ak)
New Mexico	Legislative Council(a)	1951	90,570(as)	13	5	6	2(c)	(at)
North Dakota	Legis. Research Comm.	1945	85,700(au)	11	5	6	..	2(g)
Ohio	Legis. Service Commn.	1943(y)	400,000	14	6	6	2(aw)	2(g)
Oklahoma	State Legis. Council	1939(y)	100,000	165(al)	44	121	..	(al)
Pennsylvania	Joint St. Govt. Commn.	1937	(ba)	26	12	12	2(aw)	2(g)
South Carolina	Legislative Council	1949	80,100(j)	5	(bb)	(bb)	5(bb)	(bb)
South Dakota	Legis. Research Council	1951	75,500(bd)	110(al)	35	75	..	(al)
Tennessee	Legis. Council Comm.	1953	110,000(bf)	15	5	8	2(c)	2(bg)
Texas	Legislative Council	1949	153,380	17	5	10	2(c)	(bi)
Utah	Legislative Council	1947	50,000	13	4	4	5(bj)	2
Virginia	Advisory Legis. Council	1936	44,000(aa)	11	4	7	..	2(g)
Washington	State Legis. Council	1947	127,000(bk)	21	9	10	2(aw)	2(k)
Wisconsin	Joint Legis. Council	1947	90,000	15	5	8	2(aw)	2
Wyoming	Legis. Interim Comm.	1943(y)	60,000	12	6	6	..	2(bm)
Alaska	Legislative Council	1953	67,356	8	3	3	2(c)	2

* Excluding ex-officio members.

(a) The research staff arm for the agency in certain states by statute is given a different name, as follows: Alabama, Legislative Reference Service; Florida, Legislative Reference Bureau; Indiana, Legislative Bureau; Massachusetts, Legislative Research Bureau; Nevada, Legislative Counsel Bureau; New Mexico, Legislative Council Service.

(b) Includes $6,200 for Legislative Council and $47,500 for Legislative Reference Service.

(c) President of Senate and Speaker of House are named ex-officio members in statute.

(d) Elected by legislature.

(e) Appointees representative of all sections of the state.

(f) Ex-officio members include President Pro Tem of Senate, Speaker of House and one legislator named by the Governor to represent him on the Council.

(g) Members appointed to serve until next regular session or until successors selected.

(h) Members chosen by Congressional District Caucus of Senators and Representatives respectively.

(i) Includes $2,000 for special Council committees.

(j) Fiscal year 1955–1956.

(k) Members serve until appointment of successor or termination of term of office in the legislature.

(l) President Pro Tem of Senate, Speaker of House, Majority and Minority Leaders of Senate and House are named ex-officio members in statute.

(m) Senate and House members of each political party elect Council members. The President Pro Tem of Senate and Speaker of House appoint the Senate and House membership in the event that the legislature fails to elect the members.

(n) Members serve at pleasure of House and Senate respectively.

(o) Vacancies are filled by remaining Council members.

(p) Chairman and Vice-chairman are elected by Council membership, one representing each house. Customarily chairmanship rotates between House and Senate.

(q) Annual meeting in January, all others on call.

(r) Term is for two years except that a Senator appointed at the beginning of a new term serves for four years.

(s) Approval of the Executive Committee is required in the appointment of Senate members.

(t) No appropriated amount available to Legislative Advisory Commission; members receive per diem and other expenses in unlimited amount. Research and staff services are provided the Commission by the Legislative Bureau, which received an appropriation of $118,720 for the biennium.

(u) Indiana, President of Senate named Chairman; Kansas, Maryland, Texas, President of Senate named Chairman, Speaker of House, Vice-Chairman; Kentucky, Governor named Chairman but may designate Lieutenant Governor to act as Chairman; Oklahoma, Chairmanship alternates each session between President Pro Tem of Senate and Speaker of House.

(v) Includes $30,000 for special studies; does not include unexpended balances.

(w) Appointment of members subject to approval by respective houses.

(x) Plus $7.00 per day.

(y) Kentucky, Legislative Research Commission in 1948 replaced Legislative Council created in 1936; Minnesota, Legislative Research Committee established as a temporary commission in 1947 became permanent in 1951; Ohio, Legislative Service Commission in 1953 replaced Program Commission created in 1943; Oklahoma, Legislative Council was created in 1939 but not activated until 1947; Wyoming, Legislative Interim Committee, re-created each session since 1943, was made permanent in 1949.

(z) Includes $76,875 for statute revision.

(aa) 1954–1956 biennium.

(ab) Legislative Research Commission composed ex-officio of Governor, President Pro Tem of Senate, Speaker of House, Majority and Minority Floor Leaders of House and Senate. Members serve for term of office.

(ac) At least three regular meetings each year are required.

(ad) Includes cost of printing session laws and $25,000 for special study.

(ae) Members named ex-officio are President of Senate, Chairman of Senate Finance Committee, Chairman of Senate Judicial Proceedings Committee, Minority Floor Leader of Senate, Speaker of House, Chairman of House Ways and Means.

LEGISLATIVE COUNCILS AND COUNCIL-TYPE AGENCIES—Continued

General legislative membership*		Statute requires representation of		Officers		Meetings required		Compensation		
Appointed by presiding officers	Other methods of selection	Political parties	Congressional districts	Ex officio	Elected by membership	At least quarterly	Only on call	Per diem	Expenses	
	(d)				★	★		$..	★	Alabama
★			(e)		★	★		15	Travel	Arizona
	(h)		(h)		★		★	15	Travel	Arkansas
★		★			★	★			★	Colorado
(m)	(m)	★			★	★		20	★	Connecticut
★(o)		★	★		★(p)		(q)		★	Florida
★(s)		★			★	★			★	Illinois
★		★		★(u)			★	15	★	Indiana
★(w)		★	★	★(u)		★		5	Travel(x)	Kansas
				★(u)			★(ac)	25	Travel	Kentucky
★			★		★			20	Travel	Louisiana
★					★	★		10	★	Maine
★(w)		★	(e)	★(u)		★		20	Travel	Maryland
★		★			(ag)		★		★	Massachusetts
(ai)	(ai)		★(ai)		★	★			★	Minnesota
★		★			★	★			★	Missouri
	(d)	★			★		(an)		★	Nebraska
★		★	(e)		★		★		Travel	Nevada
★					★				★	New Hampshire
★		★			★				★	New Jersey
★		★			★		★	15	Travel	New Mexico
★(av)		★			★	★		10	★	North Dakota
★(ax)		★			★	★			★	Ohio
(ay)			(ay)	★(u)		(az)	★(az)	6	Travel	Oklahoma
★					★		★	15	Travel	Pennsylvania
					★		(bc)	10		South Carolina
	(ay)				(be)	★		10	★	South Dakota
★		★	(bh)		★	★		10	★	Tennessee
★			★	★(u)		★			★	Texas
★		★			★	★			★	Utah
★					★	★		10	★	Virginia
★(w)		★	★		★	★		15	Travel	Washington
(bl)			★		★	★			★	Wisconsin
★		★			★	★		12	★	Wyoming
★		★	★(bn)		★		★(bo)	20	Travel	Alaska

Committee, Chairman of House Judiciary Committee, and Minority Floor Leader of House.

(af) Includes $1,000 for Legislative Research Council and $87,422 for Legislative Research Bureau. The Bureau's appropriation includes unexpended balance from previous fiscal year.

(ag) Chairman appointed by President of Senate, Vice-Chairman by Speaker of House.

(ah) Members are appointed during or after legislative session and serve until convening of next regular session.

(ai) House members appointed by Speaker, one from each congressional district; Senate members chosen by caucus of Senators, one from each congressional district.

(aj) Includes $50,000 for printing supplements to Revised Statutes.

(ak) Members serve for term of office as member of the legislature.

(al) All members of legislature are members of Council and serve for period of their term in the legislature.

(am) Unicameral legislature.

(an) Full Council is required to meet at least once each biennium and may meet at other times on call of Chairman.

(ao) Includes $25,000 for special study.

(ap) Members serve until successors elected and qualified.

(aq) Governor appoints three citizen members of which two are of majority and one of minority party.

(ar) Members are appointed prior to adjournment and serve until their successors are appointed and organized.

(as) Includes $4,000 for special study.

(at) House members appointed for term of two years, Senate members for four-year term.

(au) Includes $20,700 for statutory revision program and $15,000 for special studies.

(av) House members chosen by Speaker of House as other committees are chosen, from list of nine recommended by each political faction and equally divided between factions. Senate members chosen similarly by Lieutenant Governor.

(aw) President Pro Tem of Senate and Speaker of House are named ex-officio members in statute.

(ax) House members appointed by Speaker of House, Senate members by President Pro Tem of Senate.

(ay) All legislators are Council members; executive committee in Oklahoma is appointed by presiding officers and is representative of congressional districts; South Dakota executive board is elected by legislature.

(az) Executive committee meets quarterly; full Council meets on call.

(ba) Appropriation bill not enacted when table was compiled. Governor's budget contains $425,000 for Commission.

(bb) President of Senate, Speaker of House, Chairman of House and Senate Judiciary Committees and Secretary of State comprise ex-officio membership and serve for term of office.

(bc) Three regular meetings required each year between sessions. During sessions Council meets on call of Chairman or majority of members.

(bd) Includes $15,500 for special studies.

(be) Chairman chosen by Executive Board of Council.

(bf) Plus additional funds as needed for school program study.

(bg) Members appointed within sixty days after convening of session for terms ending with their terms of office or when their successors are appointed.

(bh) Each of the three grand divisions of the state must have representation on the Council.

(bi) Members appointed during or after the legislative session and serve until convening of the next regular session or termination of membership in legislature.

(bj) Three public members, one appointed by Governor, one appointed by Speaker of House, and one appointed by President of Senate. President of Senate and Speaker of House are named in statute, but may choose to appoint substitutes to serve in their stead.

(bk) Council does not receive direct appropriation. This is amount budgeted out of total legislative expense appropriation item.

(bl) Assembly members appointed by Speaker; Senate members appointed by Committee on Committees as other committees are chosen.

(bm) Members appointed during session and serve until January 1 prior to convening of next regular session.

(bn) One Senator and one Representative from each of four Judicial Divisions.

(bo) Three meetings per biennium required by law; other meetings on call of Chairman or upon written petition of two members.

TABLE 1
PERMANENT LEGISLATIVE SERVICE AGENCIES

State	Date agency established	Service agency and staff head	Reference library facilities	Bill drafting for legislature	Statutory revision	Prepares bill and law summaries	Recommends substantive legislative program	Prepares research reports	Spot research and counseling for legislators	Continuous study of state revenues and expenditures	Budgetary review and analysis	Legislative post audit
Alabama	1945	Legislative Council Charles M. Cooper, Secretary	★	—	—	—	★	—	—	—	—	—
	1945	Legislative Reference Service Charles M. Cooper, Director	★	★	★	★	—	★	★	—	—	—
	1907(a)	Dept. of Archives and History Peter A. Brannon, Director	★	—	—	—	—	—	—	—	—	—
	1947	Legislative Committee on Public Accounts	—	—	—	—	—	—	—	—	—	★
	1947	Dept. of Examiners of Public Accounts Ralph P. Eagerton, Chief Examiner	—	—	—	—	—	—	—	—	—	★
Arizona	1953	Legislative Council Jules M. Klagge, Director	★	★	—	★	★	★	★	★	—	—
	1937	Dept. of Library and Archives Mulford Winsor, Director	★	—	—	—	—	—	—	—	—	—
	1950	Post Auditor Wilson R. Bland, Post Auditor	—	—	—	—	—	—	—	—	—	★
Arkansas	1947	Legislative Council Marcus Halbrook, Director	★	★	★	★	★	★	★	★	★(b)	—
	1953	Joint-Auditing Committee	—	—	—	—	—	—	★	—	—	★
	1953	Division of Legislative Audit Orvel M. Johnson, Legislative Auditor	—	—	—	—	—	—	★	—	—	★
California	1913	Legislative Counsel Bureau Ralph N. Kleps, Legislative Counsel	—	★	—	★	—	★	★	★	—	—
	1904(a)	Administrative-Legislative Reference Service (State Library) Carma R. Zimmerman, State Librarian Melvin Oathout, Reference Librarian	★	—	—	—	—	—	★	—	—	—
	1941	Joint Legislative Budget Committee A. Alan Post, Legislative Auditor	—	—	—	—	—	★	—	—	★	—
	1953	Law Revision Commission John R. McDonough, Jr., Exec. Secy.	—	—	★	—	★	—	—	—	—	—
	1955	Joint Legislative Audit Committee	—	—	—	—	—	—	—	—	—	★
	1955	Legislative Audit Bureau Auditor General (To be appointed)	—	—	—	—	—	—	—	—	—	★
Colorado	1953	Legislative Council Shelby F. Harper, Director	★	—	—	—	★	★	★	★	—	—
	1927	Legislative Reference Office (Department of Law) Clair T. Sippel, Secretary	—	★	—	★	—	—	★	—	—	—
	1951	Committee on Statute Revision Charles M. Rose, Rev. of Statutes	—	—	★	—	—	—	—	—	—	—

122

State	Year	Agency / Official
Connecticut.....	1937	*Legislative Council* — Harry H. Lugg, Director
	1907	*Legislative Reference Department* *(State Library)* — James Brewster, State Librarian; Muriel A. Naylor, Chief
	1947	*Legislative Research Department* — Robert A. Wall, Legis. Commissr.
	1902	*Auditors of Public Accounts* — Joseph B. Downes, Auditor; Raymond J. Longley, Auditor
Delaware......	1945	*Legislative Reference Bureau* — Andrew D. Christie, Exec. Director
Florida.........	1949	*Legislative Council*
	1949	*Legislative Reference Bureau* — S. Sherman Weiss, Director
	1939	*Statutory Revision & Bill-Drafting Depts.* *(Office of Attorney General)* — Charles T. Henderson, Director
	1955	*Legislative Auditing Committee* — Senator Verle A. Pope, Chairman
Georgia........	1914(a)	*State Library* — Jane Oliver, State Librarian
	1951	*Bill Drafting Unit* *(Office of Attorney General)* — Atty. Gen. Eugene Cook, Director; Frank H. Edwards, Deputy Dir.
	1923	*Department of Audits and Accounts* — B. E. Thrasher, Jr., State Auditor
Idaho..........	1947	*Legislative Counsel* (inoperative)
Illinois.........	1937	*Legislative Council*
	1913	*Legislative Reference Bureau* — Jack F. Isakoff, Dir. of Research; Jerome Finkle, Executive Secretary
	1937	*Budgetary Commission* — Senator Everett R. Peters, Chmn.
Indiana........	1945	*Legislative Advisory Commission* — Samuel T. Lesh, Secretary
	1907	*Legislative Bureau* — Samuel T. Lesh, Director
Iowa..........	1955	*Legislative Research Bureau* — Director (to be appointed)
	1939	*Legislative Reference Bureau* *(State Law Library)* — Geraldine Dunham, Act. Law Libn.
	1951	*Budget & Financial Control Committee* — Rep. Henry H. Stevens, Chairman
Kansas........	1933	*Legislative Council* — Frederic H. Guild, Research Dir.
	1947	*Legislative Budget Committee* *(of the Legislative Council)*
	1909(a)	*State Library* — Louise McNeal, State Librarian
	1929	*Revisor of Statutes* — Franklin Corrick, Revisor
Kentucky.......	1936(c)	*Legislative Research Commission* — Arthur Y. Lloyd, Director; James A. Tyler, Revisor of Statutes

123

TABLE I
PERMANENT LEGISLATIVE SERVICE AGENCIES—Continued

State	Date agency established	Service agency and staff head	Reference library facilities	Bill drafting for legislature	Statutory revision	Prepares bill and law summaries	Recommends substantive legislative program	Prepares research reports	Spot research and counseling for legislators	Continuous study of state revenues and expenditures	Budgetary review and analysis	Legislative post audit
Louisiana......	1952	*Legislative Council* Emmett Asseff, Exec. Director	—	★	—	★	—	★	★	—	—	—
	1946(a)	*State Library* Essae M. Culver, State Librarian	★	—	—	—	—	—	—	—	—	—
	1938	*State Law Institute* J. Denson Smith, Director	—	—	★	—	—	—	—	—	—	—
Maine..........	1939	*Legislative Research Committee* Samuel H. Slosberg, Dir. of Legislative Research	—	★	★	★	—	★	★	—	—	—
	....	*Legislative Reference Section* *(State Library)* Marion B. Stubbs, State Librarian Edith L. Hary, Law and Legislative Reference Librarian	★	—	—	★	—	—	★	—	—	—
	1907	*Department of Audit* Fred M. Berry, State Auditor	—	—	—	—	—	—	—	—	—	★
Maryland.......	1939	*Legislative Council* Carl N. Everstine, Secretary and Director of Research	—	—	—	—	★	—	★	—	—	—
	1916(d)	*Department of Legislative Reference* Carl N. Everstine, Director	★	★	—	★	—	★	★	—	—	—
	1947	*State Fiscal Research Bureau* *(Dept. of Legislative Reference)* John S. Shriver, Director	—	—	—	—	—	★	★	★	★	—
	....	*State Library* Nelson J. Molter, Director	★	—	—	—	—	—	—	—	—	—
Massachusetts...	1954	*Legislative Research Council*	—	—	—	—	—	★	★	—	—	—
	1954	*Legislative Research Bureau* Herman C. Loeffler, Director	—	—	—	—	—	★	★	—	—	—
	1908(a)	*Legislative Reference Division* *(State Library)* Dennis A. Dooley, Librarian Vacancy—Legislative Reference Assistant	★	★	★	★	—	—	—	—	—	—
	....	*Counsel to Senate and Counsel to House of Representatives* Thomas R. Bateman, Senate Counsel Frederick B. Willis, House Counsel	—	★	—	—	—	—	★	—	—	—
	1946(e)	*House Ways and Means Committee* Charles E. Shepard, Legislative Budget Director	—	—	—	—	—	—	—	—	—	—
Michigan........	1941	*Legislative Service Bureau* Eugene F. Sharkoff, Director	★	★	—	★	—	★	★	★	★	—
	1947	*Committee on Audit and Appropriations* C. J. McNeill, Legis. Comptroller	—	—	—	—	—	★	—	★	★	—

State	Year	Agency / Official
Minnesota......	1947(f)	*Legislative Research Committee*
		Louis C. Dorweiler, Jr., Director of Research
	....	*State Law Library*
		Margaret S. Andrews, State Libn.
	1939	*Revisor of Statutes*
		William B. Henderson, Revisor
		Duncan L. Kennedy, Asst. Revisor
Mississippi......	....	*State Library*
		Julia Baylis Starnes, State Librarian
	1944	*Revisor of Statutes (Dept. of Justice)*
		Lester C. Franklin, Jr., Revisor of Statutes and Asst. Atty. Gen.
Missouri........	1943	*Committee on Legislative Research*
		William R. Nelson, Dir. of Research
		Edward D. Summers, Rev. of Statutes
Montana........	1921(a)	*Legislative Reference Bureau (State Law Library)*
		Adeline J. Clarke, Librarian
Nebraska........	1937	*Legislative Council*
		Jack W. Rodgers, Dir. of Research
	1945	*Revisor of Statutes*
		Walter D. James, Revisor and Reporter of the Supreme Court
Nevada..........	1945	*Legislative Commission*
	1945	*Legislative Counsel Bureau*
		J. E. Springmeyer, Legis. Counsel
	1949	*Legislative Auditor (of the Legislative Counsel Bureau)*
		A. N. Jacobson, Legislative Auditor
	1951	*Statute Revision Commission*
		Russell W. McDonald, Director
	....	*Law and Legislative Reference Section (State Library)*
		Constance C. Collins, State Libn.
New Hampshire.	1951	*Legislative Council*
		Mrs. Mary B. Parsons, Res. Analyst
	1913(a)	*Legislative Service (State Library)*
		Mildred P. McKay, Librarian
		Philip Hazelton, Legislative Reference Librarian
	1947	*Legislative Budget Assistant*
		Remick Laighton
New Jersey......	1954	*Law Revision and Legislative Services Commission*
		Charles DeF. Besore, Executive Director and Chief Counsel
		John W. Ockford, Counsel to the Legislature
	1954	*Legislative Budget and Finance Director* (to be appointed)
	1945	*Bureau of Law and Legislative Reference (Division of the State Library, Archives and History, Dept. of Education)*
		Roger H. McDonough, Director, Division of the State Library, Archives and History
		Margaret E. Coonan, Head, Bureau of Law and Legis. Reference
	1933	*Department of State Audit*
		Frank Durand, State Auditor

125

TABLE I

PERMANENT LEGISLATIVE SERVICE AGENCIES—Continued

State	Date agency established	Service agency and staff head	Reference library facilities	Bill drafting for legislature	Statutory revision	Prepares bill and law summaries	Recommends substantive legislative program	Prepares research reports	Spot research and counseling for legislators	Continuous study of state revenues and expenditures	Budgetary review and analysis	Legislative post audit
New Mexico.....	1951	*Legislative Council Service*	★	★	★	★	—	★	★	—	—	—
	1951	Jack E. Holmes, Director										
New York.......	....	*Legis. Reference Library (State Library)*	★	—	—	★	—	★	★	—	—	—
		Charles F. Gosnell, State Librarian										
		William P. Leonard, Legislative Reference Librarian										
	....	*Legislative Bill Drafting Commission*	—	★	—	—	—	—	★	—	—	—
		Theodore E. Bopp, Commissioner										
		J. Daniel Fink, Commissioner										
	1944	*Law Revision Commission*	—	—	★	★	★	—	—	—	—	—
		John W. MacDonald, Exec. Secy.										
North Carolina..	1945	*General Statutes Commission (Department of Justice)*	—	—	★	★	—	—	—	—	—	—
		Vacancy (g), Secretary										
	1939	*Division of Legislative Drafting & Codification of Statutes (Department of Justice)*	—	★	★	—	—	—	—	—	—	—
		Vacancy (g), Director										
	1947	*Revisor of Statutes (Department of Justice)*	—	★	★	★	—	—	—	—	—	—
		Vacancy (g), Revisor										
North Dakota...	1945	*Legislative Research Committee*	★	★	★	★	★	★	★	—	★	—
		C. Emerson Murry, Director										
		William J. Daner, Revisor of Statutes										
Ohio..........	1953	*Legislative Service Commission*	★	★	★	★	★	★	★	★	★	—
		John A. Skipton, Director										
	1910	*Legislative Reference Bureau*	★	★	—	—	—	—	★	—	—	—
		Arthur A. Schwartz, Director										
Oklahoma.......	1939(f)	*State Legislative Council*	—	—	★	★	★	★	★	★	★	—
		Jack A. Rhodes, Director										
	1951	*Legislative Audit Committee (of the Legislative Council)*	—	—	—	—	—	—	—	—	—	★
		Paul S. Cooke, Legislative Auditor										
	1917(h)	*Legislative Reference Division (State Library)*	★	—	★	★	—	—	★	—	—	—
		Ralph Hudson, State Librarian										
Oregon.........	1953	*Legislative Counsel Committee*	—	—	★	★	★	★	★	—	—	—
		Sam R. Haley, Legislative Counsel										
	1913(a)	*State Library*	★	—	—	—	—	—	★	—	—	—
		Eleanor S. Stephens, State Libn.										
		Josephine Baumgartner, Legislative Reference Librarian										
Pennsylvania....	1937	*Joint State Government Commission*	★	—	★	—	★	★	★	—	—	—
		Guy W. Davis, Director										
	1909	*Legislative Reference Bureau*	★	★	—	—	—	—	★	—	—	—
		S. Edward Hannestad, Director										

State	Year	Agency / Office												
Rhode Island....	1907(a)	*Legis. Reference Bureau (State Library)*	★	—	★	—	★	—	★	—	—	—	★
		Grace M. Sherwood, State Librarian											
		Mabel G. Johnson, Legis. Reference Librarian											
	....	*Assistant in Charge of Law Revision (Office of Secretary of State)*	—	★	★	—	★	★	★	—	—	—	—
		Maurice W. Hendel, Assistant in Charge of Law Revision											
	1939	*Finance Committee of House of Representatives*	—	—	—	—	—	—	—	—	—	—	—
		Rep. John J. Wrenn, Chairman											
South Carolina..	1939	*Legislative Council (inoperative)*	★	★	★	★	★	★	★	—	—	—	—
	1949	*Legislative Council*	★	—	—	—	—	★	—	—	—	—	—
		L. G. Merritt, Director											
	1954	*Committee on Statutory Laws*	—	★	—	—	★	—	★	—	—	—	★
		L. G. Merritt, Secretary and Code Commissioner											
South Dakota...	1951	*Legislative Research Council*	★	—	★	★	★	★	★	—	—	—	—
		Loren M. Carlson, Director of Legislative Research											
	1951	*Revisor of Statutes*	—	★	—	—	—	—	—	—	—	—	★
		Leo D. Heck, Revisor and Supreme Court Reporter											
	1943	*Department of Audits and Accounts*	★	—	★	—	★	—	★	—	—	—	—
		John C. Penne, Comptroller											
Tennessee.......	1953	*Legislative Council*	★	★	★	★	★	★	★	—	★	—	★
		Thomas A. Johnson, Exec. Dir.											
	....	*State Library and Archives*	★	—	—	—	★	—	★	—	—	—	—
		Dan Robison, State Librarian and Archivist											
	1953	*Code Commission*	—	★	—	—	—	—	—	—	—	—	—
		Justice A. B. Neil, Chairman											
	1835	*Department of Audit*	—	—	★	—	★	★	★	—	—	—	★
		William Snodgrass, Comptroller of Treasury											
Texas..........	1949	*Legislative Council*	—	★(i)	—	—	★	★	★	—	—	—	—
		Read Granberry, Exec. Dir.											
	1909	*Legislative Reference Division (State Library)*	★	★(i)	—	—	★	★	★	—	—	—	—
		Doris H. Connerly, Legislative Reference Librarian											
	1949	*Legislative Budget Board*	—	—	—	—	—	★	★	★	★	★(b)	—
		Vernon A. McGee, Budget Director											
	1943	*Legislative Audit Committee*	—	—	—	—	—	★	★	★	★	★	★
		C. H. Cavness, State Auditor											
Utah..........	1947	*Legislative Council*	—	—	—	★	★	★	★	—	—	—	—
		Lewis H. Lloyd, Director											
Vermont.......	1931(a)	*Legislative Reference Bureau (State Library)*	★	★	★	★	★	★	★	—	—	—	—
		Lawrence J. Turgeon, State Librarian											
		Hazel Chisholm, Assistant Librarian											
Virginia........	1936	*Advisory Legislative Council*	★	★	★	★	★	★	—	—	—	—	—
		John B. Boatwright, Jr., Secretary											
	1914	*Division of Statutory Research and Drafting*	—	—	★	★	—	★	★	—	—	—	★★
		John B. Boatwright, Jr., Director											
	1948	*Code Commission*	—	★	—	—	—	—	—	—	—	—	—
		John B. Boatwright, Jr., Secretary											
	1928	*Auditing Committee*	—	—	—	—	—	—	—	—	—	—	—
	1928	*Auditor of Public Accounts*	—	—	—	—	—	—	—	—	—	—	—
		J. Gordon Bennett, Auditor											

127

TABLE I

PERMANENT LEGISLATIVE SERVICE AGENCIES—Concluded

State	Date agency established	Service agency and staff head	Reference library facilities	Bill drafting for legislature	Statutory revision	Prepares bill and law summaries	Recommends substantive legislative program	Prepares research reports	Spot research and counseling for legislators	Continuous study of state revenues and expenditures	Budgetary review and analysis	Legislative post audit
Washington......	1947	State Legislative Council / Donald C. Sampson, Executive Sec.	—	—	—	—	★	★	★	—	—	—
	....	State Library / Maryan E. Reynolds, State Librarian	★	—	—	—	—	—	★	—	—	—
	1951	Legislative Budget Committee / Paul W. Ellis, Legislative Auditor	—	—	—	—	—	—	—	★	★	—
	1951	Statute Law Committee / Richard O. White, Revisor	—	★	★	★	—	★	—	—	—	—
West Virginia...	1947	Joint Committee on Government and Finance (j)	—	—	—	—	—	★	★	—	—	—
	1953	Legislative Auditor (of the Joint Committee on Government and Finance) / C. H. Koontz, Legislative Auditor	—	—	—	—	—	—	—	★	★	—
Wisconsin.......	1947	Joint Legislative Council / Earl Sachse, Executive Secretary	—	★	—	—	★	★	★	—	—	—
	1901	Legislative Reference Library / M. G. Toepel, Chief	★	—	—	—	—	—	—	—	—	—
	1909	Revisor of Statutes / James J. Burke, Revisor	—	—	★	—	—	—	—	—	—	—
Wyoming........	1949(f)	Legislative Interim Committee / E. L. Newton, Executive Secretary	—	—	—	—	—	★	★	★	★	—
	....	State Library / May Gillies, State Librarian	★	—	—	—	—	—	—	—	—	—
	1953	Permanent Legislative Ways and Means Committee / A. H. Michelsen, Exec. Secretary	—	—	—	—	—	—	★	—	—	—
Alaska..........	1953	Legislative Council / Jack F. McKay, Executive Director	★	★	—	—	★	★	★	—	—	—
	1955	Legislative Audit Committee	—	—	—	—	—	—	—	—	—	★★
	1955	Division of Legislative Audit / Legislative Auditor (to be appointed)	—	—	—	—	—	—	—	—	—	
Guam...........	....	Legislative Aide and Liaison Officer / Juan M. Tuncap, Legislative Aide	★	★	—	★	—	★	—	—	—	—
Hawaii..........	1950	Legislative Counsel to the Legislature / John A. Bohn, Legislative Counsel	—	★	★(k)	★	—	—	★	—	—	—
	1943	Legislative Reference Bureau / Robert M. Kamins, Director	★	★	—	★	—	★	★	—	—	—
Puerto Rico.....	1954	Legislative Reference Service / Carlos V. Davila, Director	★	★	—	★	—	★	★	—	—	—
	....	Office of Legislative Services	—	★	—	—	—	★	★	—	—	—
	1950	Commission for the Codification of the Laws / Sec. of Justice José Trías-Monge, Chairman	—	—	★	—	—	—	—	—	—	—
	1952	Office of Controller / Rafael de J. Cordero, Controller	—	—	—	—	—	—	—	—	—	★
	1947	Legislative Counsel (inoperative)	—	—	—	—	—	—	—	—	—	—

(a) Year legislative reference services **first** provided within existing library agency.
(b) Also responsible for preparing a state budget.
(c) Legislative Council originally created in 1936; replaced by present Legislative Research Commission in 1948. Statute Revision Commission, organized in 1938, was consolidated with Research Commission in 1954.
(d) Established as a department of the government of the City of Baltimore in 1907; in 1916 functions were expanded to include service to the state legislature.
(e) Year full-time research staff was organized.
(f) Minnesota: established on a temporary basis in 1947 and made permanent in 1951; Oklahoma: created in 1939 but not activated until 1947; Wyoming: established on a temporary basis in 1943 and made permanent in 1949.
(g) Revisor of Statutes is ex officio Secretary of the General Statutes Commission and head of the Division of Legislative Drafting and Codification of Statutes.
(h) Services established in 1917; division formalized by statute in 1949.
(i) Bulk of bill drafting is done by Attorney General's office as a courtesy to the legislature. Legislative Council and Legislative Reference Librarian also do some general drafting.
(j) Carries on interim research program in conjunction with Commission on Interstate Cooperation.
(k) Is serving presently as secretariat for special Compilation Commission.

2

Legislation

TRENDS IN STATE LEGISLATION, 1954–1955

LEGISLATURES of fourteen states met in regular session in 1954 and of forty-five in 1955. In addition, more than half of the states had special legislative sessions in one or the other of the two years.

Elsewhere in this volume sections on individual fields of state action include treatment of important legislation in various categories. This chapter summarizes overall trends during the biennium.

The prevailing trend has been one of expansion of services and facilities, backed by record budgets and, in 1955, more tax legislation than in any other year since World War II.

Accounting for the expansion have been, above all, the rise in population and an accumulated backlog of public needs. Basic factors have included rising public school enrollments, coupled with shortages of teachers and of adequate buildings; needs for construction and for faculty at state institutions of higher education; the obsolescence of thousands of miles of highways; the necessity of making highway travel safer; the requirements of mental hospitals and mental hygiene.

Not only is the population rising. Increasing percentages of children and of older people in the total population, the mobility of the population, and numerous social changes that have accompanied continuing industrialization and the shift of people from rural to metropolitan areas, all have brought increased demands for governmental services. All had their effects on the legislative sessions of 1954–55.

FINANCE

The expansion of services and facilities required substantial increases in appropriations. Record budgets were the norm in both years, which continued the trend of all the post-war years. As reported by the Bureau of the Census, total general expenditures of the states had risen from $5.2 billion in 1946 to $15.8 billion in 1954, and higher totals are being registered now. In two states appropriations of 1955 far exceeded $1 billion—in California a total of $1,529 million and in New York $1,259 million.

For the revenue needed to meet the bills the states still were able to depend to a considerable extent on the automatic increases from existing taxes that come with growth of the population and the economy. But the tempo of automatic increase in revenue that accompanied the Korean war starting in 1950 had tapered off. Previous surpluses in state treasuries were depleted or greatly reduced. A number of states were able to avoid major tax legislation in the biennium, but increased taxes were enacted by a substantial majority of the legislatures.

Most of the increases were voted in the major legislative year of 1955. Rises in special excise taxes and in motor vehicle fees were the most common; some fifteen states raised gasoline taxes in 1955; about a dozen increased their cigarette taxes, and Missouri adopted a cigarette tax for the first time. But there was much activity in the income and general sales tax fields also; some twenty legislatures in 1955 adopted measures to increase revenue from one or the other of those sources— in most cases by raising rates; in some by broadening the tax base or adopting income tax withholding; in one, Nevada, by adopting the sales tax for the first time. The growth of income tax withholding was marked during the biennium—the states providing for it increasing from three to ten. Arizona, Colorado and Kentucky enacted it in 1954, and Alabama, Idaho, Maryland and Montana in 1955. (See "Recent Trends in State Taxation," page 228.)

GOVERNMENTAL ORGANIZATION

With the growth of state government, proposals designed to improve organization and facilities in its three branches— legislative, executive and judicial—continued, and a number of important measures for these objectives were enacted during the biennium.

Action of 1954 included substantial reduction by the Louisiana legislature of the number of House and Senate standing committees; establishment by Maryland of a central office for a number of the state's licensing boards; abolition by the New Jersey legislature of its long-standing "secret caucus" system, for which it substituted an entirely new committee structure; and adoption in New York of a code of fair procedure for legislative and executive investigating bodies, with a series of safeguards for witnesses, as well as a code of ethics to divorce private interests from public duties of state officials and legislators.

Among measures of 1955 affecting the legislatures were a series of enactments in Connecticut to reform legislative practices of a century's standing that had led to log jams and confusion; and action by the Illinois legislature to reapportion the state for legislative seats, in accordance with a constitutional amendment of 1954. Bearing on the executive departments, legislation included, for example, substitution by Arkansas of a single State Medical Board for three separate boards; authorization for extension of the merit system in Florida; provision of a Director of Administration

in Idaho; and establishment of an appointive Pardon Board, replacing a board of elective officials, in Montana. The Pennsylvania legislature authorized the Governor to initiate and put into effect governmental reorganization plans at the bureau level, subject only to legislative veto. Among enactments on the judiciary, Florida established a uniform retirement system for Supreme Court Justices and Circuit Court Judges; Nebraska likewise created a retirement system for the Supreme and District Courts; and New York set up a nine-member Judicial Conference to provide more efficient administration of the state courts.

Increases of salary were not as numerous as in the previous biennium, but a number of sessions provided for them in one or more of the three branches of government. Several legislatures that had not previously done so authorized coverage under Old-Age and Survivors' Insurance for state employees, or authorized integration of OASI and state retirement plans.

(See "Legislative Organization and Services," pages 93 to 128; "State Administrative Organization," page 149; and "Judicial Administration and Procedure," page 193.)

STATE SERVICES

A large majority of the legislatures during the biennium increased state aid for public schools, many of them by very large amounts. Thus they maintained the trend of years. State money continued to be voted primarily for operating expenses, above all instruction. At the same time legislatures paid increasing attention to the pressing problem of school construction needs. Several took important steps to relieve building shortages, either by increasing the fiscal ability of communities to finance construction or by direct provision of state funds. Likewise, several legislatures during this two-year period gave further impetus to the movement for school district reorganization and consolidation, which over the country has led to replacement of uneconomical, poorly staffed and inadequately equipped small schools with modern community establishments. As a result of state and local legislative and administrative measures, the number of school districts had been cut from 127,244 in 1933 to about 60,000 in 1955.

The legislatures generally again increased appropriations for state institutions of higher education. And the movement for providing better opportunities for advanced education through joint arrangements under interstate compacts—in which the Southern Regional Education Board has pioneered successfully—gained further momentum. The Western Interstate Compact for Higher Education was ratified in 1955 by California, Washington and Alaska —raising the member jurisdictions to ten states and one territory; the newly developed New England Higher Education Compact was ratified by Massachusetts in 1954 and by Connecticut, Maine, New Hampshire and Vermont in 1955.

(See "State Public School Systems," page 245, and "The States and Higher Education," page 258.)

The sessions of 1954–55 provided for a broad, nation-wide advance in highway building, backed by the widespread increases in gasoline and other motor fuel taxes and in motor vehicle fees. Increased appropriations and bond issues promised that the current, unprecedented rate of road building would be stepped up markedly. Along with the basic, free-road systems, the toll road movement continued to grow; during the last two years five states created toll road authorities, and a sixth authorized turnpike construction by an existing agency. Among the western states legislatures assisted in a program for reciprocal handling of fixed-fee taxation of heavy interstate vehicles. Legislation across the nation, meantime, included numerous enactments to increase highway safety.

(See "Highway Systems and Motor Vehicle Regulation," page 273, and "Highway Safety Regulation," page 285.)

Affecting public health and welfare, measures for mental treatment and mental health again were prominent. The bulk of the funds voted were for mental hospitals. At the same time several legislatures made special provisions for mental health research and for training of mental health personnel. Enactments in several states assured development of mental hygiene clinics. New facilities for treatment of al-

coholism, or studies of it, were provided in a number of states. In another outstanding public health area, legislatures of states where statutory action was needed adopted measures in 1955 to facilitate the nation-wide program of polio vaccination through the state health departments. During the biennium, moreover, there was widespread legislation to combat tuberculosis. State concern over problems of the aging has increased notably in recent years as the problems themselves have grown, due to the increased numbers of older people and the complex of modern social conditions that affect them. This concern was reflected in a series of enactments creating state commissions, committees or other agencies to assist in study of the problem, or for action to improve the status of the aging, or both. Numerous measures were passed for the purpose of increasing protection for children and combatting juvenile delinquency.

(See entries on "Health and Welfare," pages 296 to 346.)

During the biennium the legislatures adopted more water legislation than in any corresponding period for many years. Several set up new agencies to plan and administer water resource programs. Numerous legislatures initiated studies of water resources and of water rights and use. At least twenty voted measures to permit and encourage action in small watershed development—generally in line with the Watershed Protection and Flood Prevention Act adopted by Congress in 1954 to promote a joint federal-state-local program. And various legislatures acted to strengthen water pollution control programs in their states.

(See "Water Resources," page 373.)

In labor legislation, some thirty-five legislatures in the two-year period improved benefits under the workmen's compensation laws; three adopted minimum-wage laws for the first time; two approved fair employment practice acts; four adopted legislation to aid older workers, and several strengthened their procedures for industrial mediation. More than a third of the legislatures adopted laws on standards of employment for women. These included three acts prohibiting employers from discriminating on the basis of sex as regards pay—enactments that raised to six-teen the number of states with such equal-pay statutes.

(See entries in "Labor and Industrial Relations," pages 404 to 433.)

The legislative sessions brought much significant legislation in other fields, in-cluding corrections, crime control, state regulatory activities, and important aspects of conservation and management of natur-al resources in addition to the measures on water noted above. Separate articles, indi-cated in the index, deal with these areas as well as those for which legislative trends are summarized here.

INTERSTATE ACTION

The legislatures in 1954 and 1955 adopted many acts to further interstate co-operation, through interstate compacts and other means. In addition to the ratifications of the interstate compacts in the West and New England for increasing higher educa-tional opportunities, important develop-ments and extensions in the compact field included action on the Interstate Compact on Juveniles; the South Central Interstate Corrections Compact, for cooperative use of institutions for women prisoners; various water compacts, including the new Great Lakes Compact, which created a commis-sion to investigate problems of water re-sources and recommend action in the Great Lakes Basin; and compacts for co-operative protection against forest fires. Enactments of uniform state laws were fre-quent, and of measures suggested by the Drafting Committee of State Officials to deal with common state problems. Much legislation within individual states, more-over, was aided by prior cooperative studies on behalf of groups of states or all the states.

(See "Interstate Compacts," page 15; "Uniform State Laws," page 137; "Sug-gested State Legislation," page 143.)

DIRECT LEGISLATION, 1953–54

NUMEROUS proposals received the direct approval of the voters in state-wide elections in 1953 and 1954, as amendments to state constitutions or as measures submitted under referendum procedures. During the two years the voters passed upon such proposals in a large majority of the states. Measures adopted included provisions affecting elections, constitutional rights, the organization and administration of government, and individual state services. In most cases the adoptions were in the form of constitutional amendments.

The following summary of enactments is by no means all inclusive but indicates the nature of many measures that held wide interest.

ELECTIONS, CONSTITUTIONAL RIGHTS

Action affecting elections included a constitutional amendment by the people of Tennessee—one of a series of eight amendments proposed by a constitutional convention which they approved in 1953—eliminating the poll tax. Alabama's voters adopted two amendments reducing the scope of the poll tax. Late in 1953 they approved one reducing its cumulative feature—permitting persons to vote on payment of two years' back poll taxes, a maximum of $3.00 as compared with a previous maximum of $36. In 1954 they exempted blind or deaf persons from paying poll taxes.

The people of Maine in 1954, by constitutional amendment, placed all Indians on an equal footing with other citizens as regards the right to vote. Previously, Indians living off reservations and paying normal taxes could vote; those living on reservations, and thus tax exempt, could not. Maryland voters in the same year approved an amendment permitting the legislature to extend to other citizens of the state absentee voting privileges hitherto restricted to members of the armed forces. A North Carolina amendment of 1954 reduced precinct requirements for voting registration from four months to sixty days. Wisconsin voters in 1954 approved an act of the 1953 legislature permitting persons who have resided in the state less than a year to vote for Presidential and Vice Presidential electors.

Montana's voters in 1954 provided for Presidential preference primaries. A New York amendment, adopted in 1953, provides for joint election of the Governor and Lieutenant Governor, so that a single vote is cast for both offices.

In action affecting constitutional rights outside the field of elections, New Mexico in 1953 removed a constitutional prohibition of the sale of liquor to Indians; California's voters in 1954 extended to resident foreigners who are eligible for United States citizenship the same privileges relating to property ownership that native-born citizens have; and a Texas amendment gave women the right and duty of jury service. Washington, in the same year, amended its constitution to permit corporations whose majority stock is owned by aliens to own land in the state; the previous prohibition, it was explained, had discouraged certain American corporations from investing capital and providing new payrolls.

ADMINISTRATION, EXECUTIVE BRANCH

Measures bearing on administration or organization of the executive branch of state government included the following in 1953:

New Mexico's voters increased from six to twenty days the period after adjournment of the legislature during which the Governor may approve bills presented him during the last three days of the session. A New York amendment authorized the legislature to increase the Governor's salary from $25,000 to $50,000 and that of the Lieutenant Governor from $10,000 to $20,000. The people of Tennessee, in two of their eight amendments that year, increased the Governor's term from two year to four, without right of immediate

133

succession, and, in changing the Governor's veto powers, authorized him to reduce or veto items in appropriation bills.

Enactments in 1954 included establishment in California of a Department of Alcoholic Control to administer liquor licensing laws, in place of the State Board of Equalization; and a Colorado amendment vesting in the Public Utilities Commission exclusive jurisdiction over the regulation of the facilities, services and rates of all public utilities except those municipally owned. An Illinois amendment increased the term of State Treasurer from two years to four, the Treasurer remaining ineligible to succeed himself. Maryland's voters raised the Governor's salary from $4,500 to $15,000 a year and authorized the General Assembly to fix the salary of the Secretary of State. North Carolina voted to vest the power of parole in the State Board of Paroles instead of the Governor —the Governor retaining the power to commute sentences and grant pardons. In Ohio an amendment increased the terms of Governor, Lieutenant Governor, Attorney General, Secretary of State and Treasurer to four years, effective with the 1958 election; under the amendment the Governor's tenure is limited to two successive four-year terms. The Texas electorate adopted an amendment permitting the legislature to fix the salaries of the Governor and other state constitutional officers, provided that the salaries are not less than those provided in the constitution of January 1, 1953.

LEGISLATURES

Voters in four states provided through constitutional amendments in 1954 for annual sessions of their legislatures. In Georgia they called for annual sessions not to exceed forty days, in contrast to the former seventy-day biennial sessions. Kansas adopted annual sessions of which those in even-numbered years are to be budget sessions, limited to thirty days. Louisiana, likewise, voted for annual sessions including a budget session limited to thirty days; in her case the budget session is in odd-numbered years. And in West Virginia the voters provided for annual sessions with those in the even-numbered years to be on budget matters.

A reapportionment amendment adopted in Arizona in 1953 increased the Senate from a total of nineteen members to two from each county—a total of twenty-eight; changed the basis for apportionment for the House of Representatives; and limited membership of the latter to eighty. In Illinois a constitutional amendment of 1954 required the General Assembly to redistrict the state for legislative seats and provided the basis for redistricting. (The legislature reapportioned the state accordingly in 1955.) Oregon's voters in 1954 adopted an amendment authorizing the legislature to divide counties having more than one State Senator or Representative into subdistricts for election of Senators and Representatives.

In 1953 New Mexico's voters approved an amendment raising legislators' per diem pay from $10 to not more than $20; one of the Tennessee amendments of that year increased legislative compensation from $4.00 to $10 a day, with an additional $5.00 a day for expenses, and authorized future change by legislative action rather than constitutional amendment. In the following year a California amendment raised legislators' salaries from $300 to $500 a month; one in Texas fixed legislative pay at $25 a day, not to exceed 120 days in any session, as compared with previous compensation of $10 a day up to 120 days and $5.00 a day thereafter; and a West Virginia amendment increased legislators' salaries from $500 a year to $1,500. In South Carolina, subject to legislative approval, the voters eliminated a constitutional limit of five cents a mile for travel expense of legislators.

Other measures affecting legislatures included a Tennessee amendment in 1953 placing restrictions on special, local and private acts that may be passed by the General Assembly; and a Louisiana amendment of 1954 requiring the Governor to notify each member of the legislature, in writing, five days in advance of the proclamation of special sessions, except in cases of epidemic, enemy attack or public catastrophe.

JUDICIARY

A New Mexico constitutional amendment of 1953 provided for the fixing of salaries of Supreme and District Court Judges by law rather than in the constitution as previously. New York's voters in the same year approved two amendments to help relieve court congestion, including authorization of temporary assignments of General Sessions Judges in New York City to the State Supreme Court. In 1954 Louisiana voters provided by constitutional amendment that candidates for election as District Judges must be members in good standing of the Louisiana Bar Association; and that when new judgeships are created by the legislature the offices shall be filled by special election called by the Governor. A Maryland amendment of 1954 provided for six new County Judges and clarified the rights of the General Assembly to increase the number of County Judges by statute. In another 1954 amendment North Carolina voters authorized return to the bench of retired Supreme Court Justices in emergencies.

LOCALITIES

Tennessee's voters in 1953—besides restricting special, local and private acts that may be passed by the legislature as noted above—adopted an optional home rule amendment and provisions to make consolidations of city and county functions possible. A New York amendment of the same year authorized municipalities to join together in developing water supplies. Georgia in 1954 adopted a constitutional amendment authorizing the General Assembly to provide by delegation of its powers for self-government of municipalities.

A Kansas amendment of 1954 authorized the legislature to designate "urban areas" in counties and to enact laws giving designated counties or urban areas powers of local government and consolidation of local government. Eliminating a former distinction between municipalities of different size, Maine voters in the same year adopted an amendment permitting all municipalities, regardless of size, to increase their indebtedness from 5 per cent to 7.5 per cent of their last regular valuations. A 1954 Maryland amendment conferred home rule on municipal corporations.

FUNCTIONAL AREAS

Education. Kentucky's voters in 1953 adopted an amendment which facilitated movement toward a foundation program by eliminating a requirement that state school-aid funds be distributed on a pupil-census basis whether or not the school-age children are in school. An Ohio amendment of 1953 authorized creation of a State Board of Education with power to appoint a Superintendent of Public Instruction.

In California the voters in 1954 approved a $100 million bond issue to provide loans and grants to school districts for such purposes as school site acquisition and improvement, school building and equipment. In Georgia one amendment was voted to permit the General Assembly to provide for grants of state, county or municipal funds to citizens of the state for educational purposes, in discharge of all obligation of the state to provide adequate education. Another Georgia amendment provided a referendum procedure by which county school boards may increase the existing 15-mill school tax limit up to 20 mills, thus making greater support for local education possible. Rhode Island's electorate approved a $3.5 million bond issue to relocate the Rhode Island College of Education. In South Dakota a 1954 amendment increased the limit on bonded indebtedness for school districts from 5 to 10 per cent on the assessed valuation of taxable property. Similarly, a Wyoming amendment of the same year increased the over-all debt limit of school districts, for the purpose of erecting or enlarging school buildings, from 6 to 10 per cent on assessed value of the taxable property.

Highways. Ohio's voters in 1953 by constitutional amendment authorized the state to borrow up to $500 million for highway purposes. Colorado voters in 1954 approved a referred measure authorizing revenue anticipation warrants not exceeding $35 million for highway construction. Texas in the same year adopted a constitutional amendment prohibiting the legislature from lending the credit of the state or granting use of state funds for toll roads. A 1954 Wyoming amendment dedicated all gasoline and other road user taxes to construction and maintenance of streets and highways, costs of highway administration and enforcement of state traffic laws.

Welfare and Health. Georgia in 1954 adopted an amendment authorizing the legislature to permit cities, towns or housing authorities to undertake slum clearance and redevelopment as a government function for public purposes. Voters in New York approved a proposition in 1954 authorizing a bond issue up to $350 million for mental hospitals and other mental hygiene facilities, and another proposition for a $200 million bond issue for slum clearance and public housing. Rhode Island voters, also in 1954, approved a bond issue of $3 million for expansion of welfare institutions.

OTHER ACTION

Voters in several states adopted measures affecting veterans or their kin. In 1953 New Jersey voted a constitutional amendment extending certain tax exemptions to widows of all war veterans, and New Mexico extended an existing $2,000 veterans' property tax exemption to apply to veterans of the Korean conflict and those who serve in any period when the armed forces are engaged in conflict under orders of the President. This exemption is applicable also to widows of veterans. In 1954 California's electorate approved a $175 million bond issue to assist war veterans of that state in acquiring farms and homes. In Louisiana the voters adopted a constitutional amendment providing for bonuses ranging from $50 to $250, depending upon the service area, to

veterans of the Korean conflict and to certain of their relatives, and $1,000 for certain survivors of veterans who died of service-connected injury or disease.

Nebraska adopted two amendments in 1954 relative to taxation. One permits the legislature to prescribe standards and methods for determining the value of real or other tangible property at uniform and proportionate values. The other provided that if the legislature should adopt a general sales or income tax, or combination of the two, the state would be prohibited from levying a property tax for state purposes. A third Nebraska amendment required that general management of all lands and funds set apart for educational purposes be vested in a five-member Board of Educational Lands and Funds appointed by the Governor, with qualifications, terms and compensation set by the legislature. A South Dakota amendment of 1954 authorized pooling of income from state lands owned by the various state institutions and redistribution of the income in a ratio based on that of the acreage owned by the individual institutions.

Idaho's voters adopted an initiative measure in 1954 regulating dredge mining. Its provisions include prohibition of dredging without a permit and a requirement that dredge-mining ground be smoothed over and water courses replaced for fish, wildlife and recreation.

A South Carolina amendment, voted in 1954 and ratified by the legislature in 1955, eliminated an anti-dueling provision from the state oath of office.

(See also "State Constitutions and Constitutional Revision," page 67.)

UNIFORM STATE LAWS*

THE National Conference of Commissioners on Uniform State Laws for the past two years has adhered to its objectives, namely, the promotion of uniformity in state laws on all subjects where uniformity is deemed desirable and practicable, the drafting of model acts on suitable subjects, and the promotion of uniformity of judicial decisions throughout the United States. A review of this period will demonstrate the accomplishments of the National Conference.

At the 1953 meeting of the conference in Boston, Massachusetts, final approval was given to the Uniform Rules of Evidence, and these rules are now available for adoption by the states. The conference considers the rules as one of its most important and far-reaching work products. Dealing largely with procedural rather than substantive law, they are so drafted that they may be put in force as rules of court in those jurisdictions where the court possesses unquestioned rule-making power. Under the leadership of Chief Justice Arthur T. Vanderbilt the Supreme Court of New Jersey named a committee to study the rules and make recommendations to it. The committee report has been filed, and it recommends adoption of the Uniform Rules almost in toto.

The conference undertook drafting in the evidence field at the request of the American Law Institute. The Model Code of Evidence prepared by that body was not acceptable to the bar, and hence it never was adopted in any state. At the Institute's request, the conference undertook to revise the draft in such a way as to retain the basic provisions but to eliminate the objectionable features that had made it unacceptable. The conference believes this objective has been accomplished.

In addition to the rules of evidence, the conference completed in 1953 the Uniform

Adoption Act and certain desirable amendments to the Uniform Ancillary Administration of Estates and Simultaneous Death Acts.

The 1954 Annual Meeting of the Conference, held in Chicago, was a very productive session. Five Uniform Acts and one Model Act were approved at the meeting and are now available to the states for adoption: Uniform Supervision of Charitable Trusts Act, Uniform Aircraft Responsibility Act, Uniform Civil Liability for Support Act, Uniform Disposition of Unclaimed Property Act, Uniform Preservation of Private Business Records Act, Model Post-Mortem Examination Act.

With the increase in the number of aircraft owned and operated by private owners, it became obvious that there should be available to the states language of an act designed to accomplish a basic purpose similar to that embodied in the Automobile Financial Responsibility Acts now on the statute books in most of the states. It is believed that the draft approved by the conference after some three years of study and research will accomplish that result.

One of the most popular acts ever drafted by the conference was the Uniform Reciprocal Enforcement of Support Act. It now has been adopted in all forty-eight states. It had become apparent, however, that there was great lack of uniformity dealing with the civil liability for support and that the Reciprocal Enforcement Act did not provide the maximum remedy. A Civil Liability for Support Act therefore was drafted to fill this need.

Disposition of unclaimed property and preservation of private business records long have been subjects under study by the conference. As a result acts in these fields were approved at the 1954 meeting.

The bench and bar generally have long recognized that the County Coroner system, as in practical use throughout the

(Continued on page 142)

---

*Prepared by JOE C. BARRETT, President, National Conference of Commissioners on Uniform State Laws.

RECORD OF PASSAGE OF UNIFORM AND MODEL ACTS*
As of September 1, 1955

State	UNIFORM ACTS	Negotiable Instruments (1896)	Warehouse Receipts (1906)	Sales (1906)	Bills of Lading (1909)	Stock Transfer (1909)	Desertion and Non-Support (1910)	Partnership (1914)	Limited Partnership (1916)	Fraudulent Conveyances (1918)	Proof of Statutes (1920)	Foreign Depositions (1920)	Declaratory Judgments (1922)	Fiduciaries (1922)	Federal Tax Lien Registration (1926)	Reciprocal Transfer Tax (1928)	Veterans' Guardianship (1928)	Principal and Income (1931)	To Secure Attendance of Out-of-State Witnesses (1931)	Narcotic Drug (1932)	Trust Receipts (1933)	Transfer of Dependents (1935)	Vendor and Purchaser Risk (1935)
Alabama		★	★	★	★	★	★							★	★			★	★		★	★	
Arizona		★	★	★	★	★		★	★	★	★	★		★	★		★	★	★	★	★	★	
Arkansas		★	★	★	★		★	★	★	★	★		★	★	★	★		★	★	★	★	★	
California		★	★	★	★	★	★	★	★	★		★			★	★	★	★		★	★	★	★
Colorado		★	★	★		★		★	★			★		★	★			★	★	★	★	★	
Connecticut		★	★	★	★	★		★	★			★	★					★	★	★	★	★	★
Delaware		★	★	★	★	★		★	★		★	★		★				★	★	★	★	★	
Florida		★	★			★		★		★			★				★	★		★	★	★	
Georgia		★	★					★												★	★		
Idaho		★	★	★	★	★		★	★								★	★		★	★		
Illinois		★	★	★	★	★		★	★	★						★	★	★		★	★		
Indiana		★	★		★	★		★												★	★		
Iowa		★	★	★	★	★		★				★		★			★	★		★	★		
Kansas		★	★	★	★	★	★		★			★		★			★	★	★	★	★		
Kentucky		★	★		★	★		★						★			★	★		★	★		
Louisiana		★	★		★	★							★	★		★				★	★		★
Maine		★	★	★	★	★		★	★	★		★	★	★		★	★	★	★	★	★		
Maryland		★	★	★	★	★		★	★	★	★	★	★	★		★	★	★	★	★	★		
Massachusetts		★	★	★	★	★	★	★	★	★		★	★		★	★		★	★	★	★		
Michigan		★	★	★	★	★		★				★	★		★			★	★		★		★
Minnesota		★	★	★	★	★		★	★									★	★	★	★		
Mississippi		★	★			★	★										★		★	★	★		
Missouri		★	★		★	★		★	★						★	★			★	★	★		
Montana		★	★		★			★	★	★					★			★	☆	★		
Nebraska		★	★	★		★		★	★	★		★	★			★		★	★	★	★		
Nevada		★	★	★	★	★	★	★	★	★	★	★	★		★		★	★	★	★	★		
New Hampshire		★	★	★	★	★		★	★	★		★	★	★		★		★	★	★	★		
New Jersey		★	★	★	★		★	★				★	★				★		★	★		
New Mexico		★	★		★	★							★	★			★	★	★	★		
New York		★	★		★	★		★	★	★				★	★	★		★	★	★	★	★
North Carolina		★	★		★	★		★				★			★		★	★	★	★		
North Dakota		★	★					★				★	★		★			★	☆	★	★	
Ohio		★	★	★	★	★		★				★							★		★		
Oklahoma		★	★	★	★	★		★	★			★			★			★	★	☆	★		
Oregon		★	★	★	★	★		★	★	★		★	★					★		☆	★	★
Pennsylvania		★	★	★	★	★	★	★	★	★	★	★	★	★	★	★		★		★	★	★
Rhode Island		★	★	★	★	★														★		
South Carolina		★	★		★		★		★				★		★				★		
South Dakota		★	★		★	★	★	★	★	★		★	★	★	★		★	★	★	★	★	★
Tennessee		★	★		★			★				★	★	★	★		★	★	★	★		
Texas		★	★		★	★		★	★	★			★				★	★	★	★		
Utah		★	★	★	★	★	★	★	★			★	★	★		★	★	★	★	★		
Vermont		★	★	★	★	★	★	★	★						★		★	☆	★		
Virginia		★	★			★		★								★	★	★	★		
Washington		★	★	★		★	★	★	★	★		★				★	★	☆	★		
West Virginia		★	★		★	★		★	★	★	★				★	★	★	★	★		
Wisconsin		★	★	★	★	★	★	★	★	★		★				★	★	★	★		
Wyoming		★	★		★	★		★	★			★	★	★				★	★	★		★
District of Columbia		★	★	★	★	★		★	★	★		★	★					★	★		
Alaska		★	★	★	★		★	★	★		★		★	★		★		☆	★	★	
Hawaii		★	★	★		★	★		★		★		★	★		★		★	★		★
Puerto Rico		★	★												★			★		
Total		52	52	37	33	51	21	36	38	20	30	14	39	24	25	20	42	19	46	48	34	9	7

*Prepared by the National Conference of Commissioners of Uniform State Laws.
♦ These states have adopted the Council of State Governments' form of Support of Dependents Act which is similar to the Conference Act.
☆ As Amended.

RECORD OF PASSAGE OF UNIFORM AND MODEL ACTS—Continued

As of September 1, 1955

State	Criminal Extradition (1936)	Business Records as Evidence (1936)	Judicial Notice of Foreign Law (1936)	Official Reports as Evidence (1936)	Trustees' Accounting (1936)	Trusts (1937)	Property (1938)	Unauthorized Insurers (1938)	Common Trust Fund (1938)	Absentees' Property (1939)	Acknowledgment (1939)	Participation by Secured Creditors in Insolvent Estates (1939)	Joint Tortfeasors (1939)	Insurers Liquidation (1939)	Statute of Limitations (1939)	Pistol (1940)	Simultaneous Death (1940)	Vital Statistics (1942)	Interstate Arbitration of Death Taxes (1944)	Interstate Compromise of Death Taxes (1944)	Powers of Foreign Representatives (1944)	Reverter of Realty (1944)	Criminal Statistics (1946)
Alabama	★	★							★					★			★	★					
Arizona	★	★							★		★						★						
Arkansas	★							★	★		★		★				★						
California	★	★							★								★		★	★			★
Colorado	★								★		★			★			★		★	★			
Connecticut	★	★	★														★		★	★			
Delaware	★	★	★						★		★			★			★						
Florida	★	★	★						★								★						
Georgia	★	★												★			★						
Idaho	★	★		★							★	★					★	★					
Illinois	★	★	★								★	★		★			★		★				
Indiana	★	★										★					★						
Iowa	★	★				★			★		★						★						
Kansas			★		★				★		★						★						
Kentucky			★											★			★		★				
Louisiana						★			★								★						
Maine	★	★							★				★	★			★		★	★			
Maryland	★	★						★	☆		★		★	★			★		★	★			
Massachusetts	★								★		★		★	★			★						
Michigan	★								★		★		★	★			★						
Minnesota	★	★							★					★			★	★	★				
Mississippi	★	★	★						★		★						★	★					
Missouri	★	★	★	★					★		★						★	★					
Nebraska	★	★	★		★	★	★		★		★						★						
Nevada	★	★	★						★	★	★						★						
New Hampshire	★	★							★	★						★	★				★		
New Jersey	★		★									★		★			★				★		
New Mexico	★	★			★	★		★	★		★		★	★			★						
New York	★	★	★			★			★	★		★		★	★		★						
North Carolina	★	★	★		★					★	★			★			★						
North Dakota		★	★	★							★					★	★						
Ohio	★	★	★	★					★								★						
Oklahoma	★	★	★						☆		★			★			★	★					
Oregon	★	★	★								★						★	★					
Pennsylvania	★	★	★								★						★	★	★	★			
Rhode Island	★	★	★					★					★	★			★						
South Carolina	★	★	★					★	★								★						
South Dakota	★	★	★					★	★	★	★	★	★	★			★						
Tennessee	★								☆	★							★		★	★	★		
Texas	★	★			★		★		★								★						
Utah	★		★			★			★	★							★						
Vermont	★	★							★		★						★		★	★			
Virginia	★	★															★						
Washington		★	★						★		★			★			★						
West Virginia	★	★	★						☆		★						★						
Wisconsin	★	★	★						★	★	★	★					★						
Wyoming	★	★	★	★						★							★	★					
District of Columbia									★								★	★					
Alaska	★	★	★						★		★		★				★	★					
Hawaii																							
Puerto Rico																							
Total	42	25	28	6	3	7	1	8	30	3	26	5	11	16	0	2	43	13	11	3	0	0	1

RECORD OF PASSAGE OF UNIFORM AND MODEL ACTS—Continued
As of September 1, 1955

State	*Divorce Recognition (1947)*	*Enforcement of Foreign Judgments (1948)*	*Ancillary Administration of Estates (1949)*	*Photographic Copies as Evidence (1949)*	*Marriage License Application (1950)*	*Prenatal Blood Test (1950)*	*Probate of Foreign Wills (1950)*	*Reciprocal Enforcement of Support (1950)*	*Commercial Code (1951)*	*Blood Tests to Determine Paternity (1952)*	*Single Publication (1952)*	*Rules of Criminal Procedure (1952)*	*Rules of Evidence (1953)*	*Adoption (1953)*	*Aircraft Financial Responsibility (1954)*	*Civil Liability for Support (1954)*	*Disposition of Unclaimed Property (1954)*	*Preservation of Private Business Records (1954)*	*Supervision of Trustees for Charitable Purposes (1954)*	*Arbitration (1955)*	*Contribution Among Tortfeasors (1955)*	*Motor Vehicle Certificate of Title and Anti-Theft (1955)*	*Post-Conviction Procedure (1955)*
Alabama				★				☆			★												
Arizona								☆		★													
Arkansas		★		★				☆		★													
California	★			★				☆		★	★						★		★				
Colorado								★															
Connecticut								☆															
Delaware								♦															
Florida				★				☆															
Georgia				★				☆															
Idaho				★				☆			★												
Illinois		★						☆															
Indiana								☆															
Iowa				★				♦															
Kansas				★				☆															
Kentucky				★				☆															
Louisiana	★							★															
Maine								☆								★							
Maryland				★				☆															
Massachusetts								☆															
Michigan								☆		★						★							
Minnesota				★				★															
Mississippi								☆															
Missouri		★						☆															
Montana				★				★															
Nebraska	★	★		★				★															
Nevada				★				☆															
New Hampshire	★			★				☆		★					★	★			★				
New Jersey				★				☆															
New Mexico				★				☆					★										
New York				★				♦															
North Carolina				★				☆															
North Dakota	★			★				☆					★										
Ohio								☆															
Oklahoma				★				☆															
Oregon		★						☆		★	★												
Pennsylvania				★				☆	★		★												
Rhode Island	★							☆															
South Carolina	★							☆															
South Dakota				★				☆															
Tennessee								☆															
Texas								☆										★					
Utah								★		★													
Vermont				★				☆															
Virginia				★				☆															
Washington	★	★		★				★											★				
West Virginia	★	★						★															
Wisconsin	★	★	★	★			★	☆															
Wyoming		★		★				☆															
District of Columbia				★																			
Alaska				★				☆															
Hawaii				★				☆															
Puerto Rico								★															
Total	9	8	1	32	0	0	1	48	1	5	6	0	0	0	2	4	1	1	1	0	0	0	0

RECORD OF PASSAGE OF UNIFORM AND MODEL ACTS—Concluded
As of September 1, 1955

MODEL ACTS

State	Interparty Agreement (1925)	Joint Obligations (1925)	Written Obligations (1925)	Business Corporation (1928)	Composite Reports as Evidence (1936)	Expert Testimony (1937)	Estates (1938)	Execution of Wills (1940)	Power of Sale Mortgage Foreclosure (1940)	Resale Price Control (1940)	Act to Provide for the Appointment of Commissioners (1944)	Cy-Pres (1944)	State Administrative Procedure (1944)	War Service Validation (1944)	Rule Against Perpetuities (1944)	Court Administrator (1948)	Small Estates (1951)	Anti-Gambling (1952)	Crime Investigating Commission (1952)	Department of Justice (1952)	Perjury (1952)	Police Council (1952)	State Witness Immunity (1952)	Post-Mortem Examinations (1954)
Alabama											★													
Arizona											★										★			
Arkansas											★													
California															★									
Colorado																								
Connecticut																								
Delaware																								
Florida																								
Georgia																								
Idaho				★																				
Illinois																					★		★	
Indiana																					★			
Iowa																								
Kansas											★													
Kentucky				★							★													
Louisiana				★																				
Maine																								
Maryland	★											★												
Massachusetts																								
Michigan														★										
Minnesota																								
Mississippi											★													
Missouri													★											
Montana											★													
Nebraska					★						★													
Nevada																								
New Hampshire	★	★									★													
New Jersey											★													
New Mexico																								
New York																								
North Carolina		★																						
North Dakota																								
Ohio																								
Oklahoma						★							★											
Oregon													★											
Pennsylvania	★		★																					
Rhode Island																								
South Carolina																								
South Dakota					★	★																		
Tennessee					★			★								★								
Texas											★													★
Utah	★	★	★								★													
Vermont																								
Virginia												★						★						
Washington				★																				
West Virginia				★																				
Wisconsin															★									
Wyoming		★																						
District of Columbia																								
Alaska																								
Hawaii		★																						
Puerto Rico																								
Total	4	5	2	5	3	2	0	1	0	0	12	2	3	1	2	1	0	1	0	0	3	0	1	1

United States, was ineffective for the detection of crime. Drafting designed to cure at least some of the defects of this system was recommended by the American Medical Association as well as by various groups concerned with the detection of crime and punishment of the offender. The Model Post-Mortem Examinations Act is a result of this recommendation. In preparing the act the conference worked closely with committees from peace officers' organizations and American Medical Association.

The Uniform Supervision of Charitable Trusts Act was designed to provide a means by which appropriate state officers would be furnished information about the creation of such trusts and means by which to compel their execution in the interest of the beneficiaries. It was found that in some states there were literally thousands of dormant charitable trusts which apparently had been forgotten by the beneficiaries or the trustees. There is great deficiency in existing law through failure to provide means by which proper administration of those trusts can be compelled. The subject matter was first brought to the attention of the conference by the National Association of Attorneys General, with which the conference worked closely in preparation of the act. It is felt that the act will serve a real need in many of the older and more populous states.

Thus the conference has not been idle. It proposes to continue its activities to improve the administration of justice and to promote greater uniformity in the law. It continues to work closely with the Council of State Governments and provides a substantial part of the Council's drafting committee. The Council has been quite effective in promoting adoption of uniform and model acts drafted by the conference. The splendid working arrangement between the two bodies is a source of great satisfaction to the conference officers.

SUGGESTED STATE LEGISLATION—1955 PROGRAM

THE Drafting Committee of the Council of State Governments has been in existence since 1940. It was created to develop emergency defense legislation for suggested enactment by the states at that time. During World War II the committee prepared suggested state legislation to facilitate state-federal cooperation in the war effort. Since then there has been a transition to more normal continuing problems, and the committee has developed draft proposals in a great variety of fields. From its inception, it has worked closely with the National Conference of Commissioners on Uniform State Laws.

The Drafting Committee is composed of state legislators, members of Commissions on Interstate Cooperation, Uniform Law Commissioners and other state officials. Sidney Clifford of Rhode Island has served as chairman since 1949. The staff of the Council of State Governments acts as secretariat; advisory and technical services are provided by the United States Department of Justice and many other agencies and organizations.

The program of suggested state legislation prepared by the Drafting Committee each year is widely distributed among the states, and individual items are selected in the states for introduction and enactment. The program prepared for the 1955 legislative sessions included about sixty separate proposals, in such widely varying areas as regulation of charitable fund raising, civil defense, proof of wills, voting laws, flammable fabrics and hypnotic drugs. This article summarizes certain items of major interest, and the accompanying table presents a general listing, by categories, of the bills and recommendations carried in the committee's report for 1955.[1]

ELECTIONS

A series of proposals on election laws was presented in the 1955 program. These

[1]For details see *Suggested State Legislation: Program for 1955*, The Council of State Governments.

included recommendations for amendment of state laws to facilitate absentee voting by members of the armed forces; suggested legislation to prevent loss of voting residence in national elections, by providing for temporary retention of the right to vote after having left the state to reside elsewhere; general recommendations for improvement of absentee voting laws; and a statement regarding model state laws on election administration, registration and direct primaries.

HIGHWAYS

An act was suggested under which a person suspected of driving while intoxicated must either submit to a chemical test to determine whether he was under the influence of alcohol or face revocation of his driver license. Language also was suggested to provide for interstate notice of traffic violations, so that appropriate action may be taken by the home state against violators. Other recommendations dealt with the immediate taking of land under eminent domain for highway construction purposes and with respect to controlled-access highways.

HEALTH, WELFARE AND SAFETY

In this field the 1955 program included proposals dealing with regulation of hypnotic and somnifacient drugs; care and treatment of narcotic addicts; protection against the sale of dangerously flammable fabrics; protection, especially of children, against dangerous excavations and abandoned iceboxes; care, treatment and commitment of the mentally ill; and rehabilitation services for the physically handicapped.

STATE AND LOCAL GOVERNMENT

The Drafting Committee developed important amendments to its earlier enabling act for coverage of state and local employees under the federal social security program. In accordance with action by

Congress, provision was made for the integration of public retirement systems with Old-Age and Survivors Insurance. Previously, federal social security coverage was denied if the worker was already covered by a public retirement system. A suggested act was presented to permit the loan of state employees to other governmental units, within and without the United States, with full protection of the employee's rights. Recommendations were made concerning investment of state funds and development of proper administrative machinery in that connection. A statement was included relating to model acts to strengthen local fiscal management in such fundamental respects as budgeting, borrowing and tax collections.

AGRICULTURE AND FORESTRY

One suggested act has the purpose of providing appropriate measures to control forest insects and diseases on state and private lands. The act authorizes surveys to detect infestations, procedures for establishing control zones and applying control measures, and means for apportioning costs. Acts were carried to improve conditions related to migrant farm labor, including registration of crew leaders and farm labor contractors, and to amend state health laws so that sanitary codes will apply to farm labor camps. Recommendations also were made for improvement of laws for control of agricultural pests and animal diseases.

UNIFORM LAWS

In recent years it has been the practice of the Drafting Committee to present in its reports the full texts of uniform acts newly promulgated by the National Conference of Commissioners on Uniform State Laws. In this way state legislatures and state administrative officials are made aware as soon as possible of new and important proposals for uniform state action. In the 1955 report six such uniform measures were carried—covering supervision of charitable trustees, disposition of unclaimed property, civil liability for support, preservation of private business records, aircraft financial responsibility and post-mortem examinations.

OTHER PROPOSALS

Among other proposals in the report for 1955 were a series of acts to regulate charitable fund-raising organizations so as to prevent racketeering; an act to permit proof of wills out of court, simplifying probate when there is no contest of the will; several measures to strengthen and activate civil defense programs; and an act to protect radio and television stations from libel suits arising out of statements made by political speakers over whom the stations have no control.

Also included were a proposed interstate compact on interpleader; provision for co-operative returns of parole and probation violators in order to save duplicate trips by state corrections officials; an act prohibiting "bait advertising" by unscrupulous dealers who have no intention of selling the goods advertised at the indicated price; and an act providing penalties against persons who refuse to give up a party-line telephone in case of emergency.

PROPOSALS OF THE DRAFTING COMMITTEE
PROGRAM FOR 1955

(Titles are in abbreviated form)

NATIONAL DEFENSE

1. Compensation Benefits for Civil Defense Workers
2. Illumination Control
3. Tuition Charges for Military Personnel
4. Absentee Voting by Servicemen
5. Model State Civil Defense Act*
6. Emergency Civil Defense Funds*
7. Civil Defense Loyalty Oath*
8. State Code of Military Justice*
9. Use of Phrase "Armed Forces"*

HEALTH AND WELFARE

1. Regulation of Charity Rackets
2. Social Security Coverage Enabling Act
3. Determination of Disability
4. Migratory Farm Labor (three acts on health and welfare regulation)
5. Care and Treatment of Mentally Ill*
6. Hospitalization and Commitment of the Mentally Ill*
7. Rehabilitation of the Handicapped*
8. State Unemployment Benefits*

SAFETY

1. Regulation of Flammable Fabrics
2. Dangerous Excavations and Abandoned Articles (three acts)
3. Fireworks Regulation
4. Emergency Use of Telephones

LEGAL AFFAIRS

1. Proof of Wills Out of Court
2. Broadcasters' Liability Immunity
3. Interstate Compact on Interpleader
4. Registration of Trademarks

HIGHWAYS AND MOTOR VEHICLES

1. Driver Intoxication Tests
2. Interstate Notice of Driving Violations
3. Taking Highway Rights of Way*
4. Controlled Access Highways*

NARCOTICS AND CRIME CONTROL

1. Hypnotic and Somnifacient Drugs
2. Care and Treatment of Narcotic Addicts
3. Cooperative Returns of Parole and Probation Violators
4. Standard Probation and Parole Act*

CONSERVATION

1. Control of Forest Insects and Diseases
2. Watershed Legislation and Programs*
3. Plant Disease and Pest Control*
4. Animal Disease Control*

MISCELLANEOUS

1. Payroll Savings Plans
2. Governmental Leaves of Absence
3. Loss of Voting Residence in National Elections
4. Absentee Voting in General
5. Bait Advertising
6. State and Regional Planning*
7. Slum Clearance and Urban Renewal*
8. Commission on Intergovernmental Relations*
9. Weights and Measures Laws*
10. Election Administration*
11. Investment of State Funds*
12. Local Fiscal Enabling Acts*
13. Exchange Teacher Programs*

UNIFORM ACTS†

1. Supervision of Trustees for Charitable Purposes
2. Disposition of Unclaimed Property
3. Civil Liability for Support
4. Preservation of Private Business Records
5. Aircraft Financial Responsibility
6. Post-Mortem Examinations

---

*Indicates descriptive statements only, no suggested legislation carried.
†As promulgated by the National Conference of Commissioners on Uniform State Laws.

DRAFTING COMMITTEE OF STATE OFFICIALS OF
THE COUNCIL OF STATE GOVERNMENTS,
1955–56

SIDNEY CLIFFORD, *Chairman*
Commissioner on Uniform State Laws (Rhode Island)

HARRINGTON ADAMS (Pennsylvania)
Deputy Attorney General

MILTON ALPERT (New York)
Deputy Attorney General

ELISHA T. BARRETT (New York)
Joint Legislative Committee on
   Interstate Cooperation

JOHN B. BOATWRIGHT, JR. (Virginia)
Commissioner on Uniform State Laws

JAMES M. BULLARD (Oklahoma)
Member, House of Representatives

LOWRY N. COE (District of Columbia)
Commissioner on Uniform State Laws

WILLOUGHBY A. COLBY (New Hampshire)
Commissioner on Uniform State Laws

DAYTON COUNTRYMAN (Iowa)
Attorney General

SENATOR DONALD P. DUNKLEE (Colorado)
Commission on Interstate Cooperation

MRS. MARJORIE D. FARMER (Connecticut)
Commission on Interstate Cooperation

CARL M. FRASURE (West Virginia)
Commission on Interstate Cooperation

FRED GULICK (Kansas)
Commission on Interstate Cooperation

S. EDWARD HANNESTAD (Pennsylvania)
Commissioner on Uniform State Laws

CHARLES TOM HENDERSON (Florida)
Assistant Attorney General

ROGER HOWELL (Maryland)
Commissioner on Uniform State Laws

W. O. HUGHES (Indiana)
Member, House of Representatives

THOMAS M. KAVANAUGH (Michigan)
Attorney General

SENATOR EARL J. LEE (Nebraska)
Commission on Interstate Cooperation

SAM M. LEVINE (Arkansas)
Member, House of Representatives

ARTHUR Y. LLOYD (Kentucky)
Commissioner on Uniform State Laws

SENATOR OTTIS E. LOCK (Texas)
Commission on Interstate Cooperation

LLOYD W. LOWREY (California)
Commission on Interstate Cooperation

DALE MacIVER
Assistant Attorney General

MRS. MARIE F. MAEBERT (New Jersey)
Member of the General Assembly

E. J. McCAFFREY (Illinois)
Legislative Reference Bureau

ROBERT L. MOULTON (Ohio)
Commission on Interstate Cooperation

C. EMERSON MURRY (North Dakota)
Legislative Research Committee

ARNOLD OLSEN (Montana)
Attorney General

EDWARD L. SCHWARTZ (Massachusetts)
Commissioner on Uniform State Laws

R. JASPER SMITH (Missouri)
Commissioner on Uniform State Laws

HENRY P. THOMAS (Virginia)
Commissioner on Uniform State Laws

VERNON W. THOMSON (Wisconsin)
Attorney General

SENATOR CHARLES E. TOOKE, JR.
   (Louisiana)
Commission on Interstate Cooperation

MISS INEZ WATSON (South Carolina)
Clerk, House of Representatives

WILLIAM WINTER (Mississippi)
Commission on Interstate Cooperation

Section IV

ADMINISTRATIVE ORGANIZATION

1. Administration
2. Personnel Systems

1

Administration

STATE ADMINISTRATIVE ORGANIZATION, 1954–55

S TUDY by official bodies of state governmental administrative organization continued in 1954 and 1955, and several states adopted important changes affecting administrative departments or agencies. Some of these were based upon recommendations of earlier reorganization study committees. In the main, state governmental structure did not undergo major alteration, nor did essentially new trends emerge. Numerous state leaders, however, including Governors in messages to their legislatures, insistently called for measures to strengthen administrative structures, through legislation or constitutional amendment or both.

Thus, although wholesale change as envisioned in some of the reorganization movements of a few years ago was not emerging, steady efforts continued to improve the machinery available for the conduct of state government.

The following pages summarize, first, examples of committee recommendations made and, secondly, reorganization action taken during the biennium.

REORGANIZATION STUDIES

Special reorganization study committees in Missouri, North Carolina and South Dakota submitted final reports during 1954–55. Missouri's State Reorganization Commission made 112 recommendations, the majority of which concerned internal organization and procedures of state agencies. Included were proposals for strengthening the Division of

Budget and Comptroller, for improvements in purchasing procedures, for establishment of a records management center and for changes in personnel policies.

The North Carolina Commission on Reorganization of State Government submitted a series of eight reports dealing with various subjects, including finance and fiscal control, personnel management and the office of Governor. The commission recommended some transfer of functions among the state's various fiscal agencies, and changes in the organization and powers of the personnel department and related agencies. It proposed that the Governor be relieved of some of his responsibilities for appointing minor officials as well as some ex-officio duties, and that he be provided a larger personal staff and increased office space.

The South Dakota Little Hoover Committee recommended several major changes in administrative organization. It proposed that the terms of the Governor, Lieutenant Governor and other constitutional executive officers be increased from two to four years, and further suggested that consideration be given to increasing legislators' terms from two to four years. Both of these proposals would require constitutional amendments. The committee recommended another constitutional amendment to abolish the office of Superintendent of Public Instruction and establish a State Department of Education with a Commissioner appointed by a State Board of Education, which would be appointed by the

Governor. In additional areas, the committee recommended establishment of departments of commerce, natural resources, military affairs and revenue, and proposed the creation of a Division of Administration within the Department of Finance to have responsibility for various central administrative services. It recommended that the state's institutions of higher education be integrated into a South Dakota State University System.

The Committee on State Government Organization in Washington was reactivated in 1954 to give further consideration to some of the recommendations it previously had made to the legislature. On the basis of its review, the committee again recommended establishment of an Office of Administration with responsibility for fiscal management, purchasing and property management. It renewed its recommendation for a central personnel agency and a new and broadened personnel management program. Finally, the committee again proposed the establishment of a Department of Natural Resources to include functions now performed by several state agencies. On the basis of a new study, the same committee recommended establishment of a Department of Taxation and a Board of Tax Appeals to exercise functions now vested in the State Tax Commission.

Legislatures in at least eight states in 1955 took action to begin or continue studies of the organization and operation of the executive branch of their governments. Colorado and North Carolina continued their studies of reorganization. Maine established an interim commission to study its state government and authorized the Governor to employ a consulting firm to make necessary surveys. Maryland set up a joint legislative-public commission to study the programs, organization and finance of state agencies. The Montana legislature established a reorganization commission. In New York the legislature continued its Commission on Coordination of State Activities and also created a Joint Legislative Committee on Government Operations. Oklahoma set up an interim commission to study the duties and functions of all state boards, commissions, institutions and authorities. And in Utah the

legislature directed the Legislative Council to investigate the administrative organization of boards and commissions and to study possible consolidation of governmental functions.

REORGANIZATION ACTION

The Pennsylvania legislature in 1955 passed an important act granting the Governor power to reorganize state agencies at the bureau level. Under the new law, the Governor may initiate reorganization proposals and submit his plans to both houses of the legislature. If neither house votes to disapprove a proposal within thirty days, it automatically takes effect. The Pennsylvania legislation is similar to acts of the federal government and of New Hampshire and Puerto Rico in giving the Chief Executive power to put reorganization plans into effect, subject only to a legislative veto.

Several states altered significantly the organization of their fiscal agencies. These are covered in the article on "Finance Management," (page 156) but should be mentioned here because of their effect on the over-all administration of government in the states concerned. Pennsylvania's legislature in 1954 created the Office of Secretary of Administration, which is responsible for budgeting, accounting and personnel services for all departments under the jurisdiction of the Governor. The office also supervises the activities of comptrollers in these departments. In addition, the act directs the office to make studies of management methods and to evaluate existing programs of agencies with a view to improving their procedures. Under terms of a 1955 enactment in Idaho, the Budget Director of the state will serve as Director of Administration. In New Mexico the Office of State Budget Director has been placed in the Office of the Comptroller.

In North Carolina, where the Governor is designated as the chief budget officer, a new law, based on a recommendation of the reorganization committee, provides that the Assistant Budget Director shall serve at the Governor's pleasure rather than for a fixed term. The law also gives the Assistant Budget Director responsibility for pre-audit functions and frees both the State Auditor and the State Treasurer from executive budgetary controls. Also acting in accordance with recommendations of its Little Hoover Committee, the South Dakota legislature established a Department of Revenue, including divisions of taxation and licensing, and gave the Finance Department some general administrative responsibilities for the work of other state agencies. New legislation in Alaska created a Department of Finance with divisions of budgeting, accounting and purchasing.

At least two states made significant changes in their personnel agencies. Again, these are described in more detail in the article which follows, on "Personnel." Florida established a State Personnel Board, with the Governor as Chairman; the board may bring under its jurisdiction the employees of various state departments. The Illinois legislature adopted a new personnel code which includes provision for establishment of a Personnel Department; the Director of the Department is to be appointed by the Governor.

Important developments affecting educational organization occurred in three states. North Carolina's legislature created a nine-member State Board of Education, with responsibility for coordinating the fiscal affairs of the various state institutions of higher education. South Dakota accepted a part of the recommendations of its Little Hoover Committee in this field by authorizing the appointment of an Executive Director for the Board of Regents. In North Dakota the legislature established a Board of Education to supervise the state's elementary and secondary schools.

In actions affecting natural resources, Nevada created a State Board of Forestry and Fire Control, and New Mexico a State Forest Conservation Commission. Kansas provided for a State Park Resources Board which has authority to issue revenue bonds and to operate facilities in the state parks.

Several states during the past two years made changes in the organization of important operating departments. By constitutional amendment California created a Department of Alcoholic Beverage Control and transferred to it functions formerly exercised by the Board of Equalization. Minnesota's legislature passed a general reorganization act making numerous transfers of functions among agencies, changing the names of some departments, and creating a Department of Commerce.

Other developments included creation of a Department of Commerce and Development in Idaho; establishment of a State Pardon Board, replacing an ex-officio board, in Montana; and creation of a Parole Board, as a separate agency from the Prison Commission, in New Mexico. The New Mexico legislature also authorized the Governor to merge the departments of Health and Welfare and, subject to vote by the electorate, approved the merging of the Corporation Commission and Public Service Commission. Oregon established a Motor Vehicle Department, to which it transferred functions formerly exercised by the Secretary of State with respect to laws on gasoline taxes, motor vehicle registration, licensing fees and drivers' licenses. Rhode Island replaced the Division of Public Utilities, which was part of the Department of Business Regulation, with an independent Administrator of Public Utilities.

The South Dakota legislature made several changes in accordance with recommendations of its reorganization committee. It established a Department of Military Affairs, to be headed by the Adjutant General; reconstituted the Board of Charities and Corrections as the Department of Probation and Parole; authorized the appointment of an Executive Director for Charitable and Penal Institutions; and provided for increased authority for the head of the Department of Highways.

At least six states—Kansas, Minnesota, North Carolina, Oregon, Rhode Island and South Dakota—established new administrative agencies with responsibilities affecting water. In general, the new agencies are charged with the duty of studying the water resources in their respective states, of making plans for the most effective use of existing resources, and of administering at least some legislation governing the rights to use water. Creation of these new agencies, along with other state legislative actions affecting water resources in 1955 reflects the concern of many states about the management of their water resources. (See the article on "Water Resources," page 373.)

State governments are continuing to

make considerable use of public authorities as a means of financing and operating various activities. Toll road and other types of highway authorities are especially common. The Virginia legislature in 1954 created two highway authorities. During the same year Rhode Island approved the establishment of one highway authority and one bridge authority. In 1955 Alabama, Idaho and Iowa each established toll road authorities. The Georgia legislature created a Rural Roads Authority, empowered to issue revenue bonds and to use the proceeds for construction of free roads in rural areas; bonds will be retired through payments made by the Georgia Highway Department to the Authority. Georgia also established a Farm Market Authority. New Hampshire created a State Industrial Park Authority, Maryland set up the Baltimore City Civic Authority, and Washington created a general State Building Authority. In contrast to these actions, two states, Georgia and Nebraska, repealed legislation for toll road authorities.

Actions affecting gubernatorial terms or succession took place in three states during the biennium. Ohio voters in November, 1954, approved an amendment to the constitution providing a four-year term for Governor and other officials of the executive branch. The Arkansas electorate at the same time rejected a similar proposed amendment. In Idaho the legislature in 1955 approved for submission to the voters a proposed amendment which if adopted will permit the Governor to succeed himself.

TABLE 1
APPOINTING POWER OF THE GOVERNOR

	Sec. of State	Treasurer	Auditor (b)	Attorney General	Tax Commissr.	Finance (a)	Budget Officer	Comptroller (c)	Education	Agriculture	Labor	Health	Welfare	Insurance	Highways	Conservation
Alabama	E	E	E	E	G	G	O	O	E	E	G	B	B	G	G	G
Arizona	E	E	E	E	E	GS	O	O	E	G	GS	G	GS	E	GS	G
Arkansas	E	E	E	E	GS	O	DG	G	B	O	GS	BG	G	GS	B	GS
California	E	E	L(v)	E	E	G	O	E	E	G	G	G	GS	GS	G	G
Colorado	E	E	E	E	CS	O	CS	CS	B	CS	CS	CS	CS	CS	CS	CS
Connecticut	E	E	L	E	GE	GE	GS	E(d)	B	GE	GE	GE	GE	GE	GE	O
Delaware	GS	E	E	E	GS	O	B(e)	B(e)	B	B	B	B	E	·B	B	
Florida	E	E	GS	E	E(f)	O	G	E(f)	E	E	G	GS	G	E	G	
Georgia	E	E	L	E	GS	O	G(g)	E	E	E	E	GS	GS	E	L	O
Idaho	E	E	E(d)	E	GS	O	G	E(d)	B	G	GS	G	G	G	GS	G
Illinois	E	E	E	E	GS	O	O	E	GS	GS	GS	GS	GS	GS	G	GS
Indiana	E	E	E(d)	E	G	O	G	O	E	E	G	G	G	G	G	G
Iowa	E	E	E	E	GS	GS	O	G	B	E	GS	GS	GS	GS	GS	GS
Kansas	E	E	E	E	GS	G	DG	DG	B	B	GS	GS	B	E	G	O
Kentucky	E	E	E	E	G	G	DG	DG	E	E	G	B	G	G	G	G
Louisiana	E	E	E	E	GS	G	O(h)	O	E	E	GS	GS	B(j)	(i)	B(j)	GS
Maine	L	L	L	L	(k)	GC	O	(k)	B	L	GC	GC	GC	GC	GC	GC
Maryland	GS	E	G	E	O	O	G	E	B	GS	GS	G	G	G	G	G
Massachusetts	E	E	E	E	GC	GC	O	O	B	GC	GC	GC	GC	GC	GC	GC
Michigan	E	E	E	E	G	G	O	E	B	GS	GS	GS	GS	GS	E	GS
Minnesota	E	E	E(d)	E	GS	GS	GS	O	E	GS	GS	B	GS	GS	GS	GS
Mississippi	E	E	E	E	GS	O	G(e)	G(e)	E	E	O	GS	GS	E	E	GS
Missouri	E	E	E	E	GS	GS	GS	GS	B	GS	GS	GS	GS	GS	GS	B
Montana	E	E	E	E	G	G	O	O	E	GS	GS	G	E	G	G	G
Nebraska	E	E	E(d)	E	GS(l)	O	(l)	E(d)	B	GS	GS	B	GS	GS	GS	O
Nevada	E	E	O	E	G	O	G	E	E	G	G	G	G	G	E	G
New Hampshire	L	L	O	GC	SC	GC	O	O	B	GC	GC	B	B	GC	GC	O
New Jersey	GS	GS	L	GS	GS	GS	O	O	GS	BG	GS	GS	GS	GS	GS	GS
New Mexico	E	E	E	E	G	O	G	G	E	O	GS	GS	GS	E	GS	G
New York	GS	GS	O	E	GS	O	G	E	B	GS	GS	B	GS	GS	GS	GS
North Carolina	E	E	E	E	G	O	G	(m)	E	E	E	GS	G	E	GS	GS
North Dakota	E	E	E(d)	E	E	O	B	E(d)	E	E(n)	E(n)	G	B	E	G	O
Ohio	E	E	E	E	GS	GS	O	O	B	GS	GS	GS	GS	GS	GS	GS
Oklahoma	E	E	E	E	GS	G	O	O	E	(o)	E	(o)	(o)	E	(o)	(o)
Oregon	E(p)	E	E(p)	E	G	G	G	O	E	G	E	GS	G	G	GS	GS
Pennsylvania	GS	E(u)	E	GS	GS	GS	O	G	E(u)	GS	GS	GS	GS	GS	GS	GS
Rhode Island	E	E	O	E	DG	GS	DG	DG	BG	GS	GS	GS	GS	DG	GS	GS
South Carolina	E	E	B(q)	E	GS	B(q)	O	E	E	E	GS	G	B	L	B	B
South Dakota	E	E	E	E	GS	GS	O	L	E	GS	E(w)	GC	G	GS	G	G
Tennessee	L	L	O	SC	G	O	G	L	G	G	G	G	G	G	G	G
Texas	GS	E	L	E	(r)	O	G(s)	E	B	E	GS	B	B	GS	B	O
Utah	E	E	E	E	GS	GS	O	O	B	GS	GS	GS	GS	GS	GS	GS
Vermont	E	E	E(d)	E	GS	O	G	E(d)	B	GS	GS	GS	GS	GS	GS	GS
Virginia	GSH	GSH	L	E	GSH	O	G	GSH	GSH	GSH	GS	G	GSH	B(t)	GSH	GSH
Washington	E	E	E(d)	E	GS	O	GS	E(d)	E	GS	GS	GS	E	GS	GS	GS
West Virginia	E	E	E	E	GS	O	GS	O	E	GS	GS	GS	GS	GS	GS	GS
Wisconsin	E	E	GS	E	GS	GS	O	O	E	B	B	GS	B	B	GS	B
Wyoming	E	E	E(d)	GS	GS	O	G	E(d)	E	G	GS	GS	GS	GS	GS	GS

Legend: E—Elected. G—Appointed by Governor alone. GS—Appointed by Governor and approved by Senate. O—Office or equivalent does not exist. [See footnote (a) below.] B—Appointed by appropriate departmental board. GE—Appointed by Governor and approved by either House. L—Chosen by Legislature. GC—Appointed by Governor and Council. SC—Appointed by Judges of Supreme Court. DG—Director with approval of the Governor. GSH—Appointed by Governor and approved by both Houses of the Legislature. BG—Appointed by appropriate departmental board with approval of Governor. CS—Civil service appointment by competitive examination.

(a) The term finance refers to a department, variously designated a finance, revenue, administration, treasury, or executive department, in which fiscal and related operations have been grouped together. The department is ordinarily distinguished by the inclusion of a division of the budget and a division of accounts and control. In a few cases, either budget preparation or accounting control may be performed by another agency; yet the department is included under finance because the department head is the chief fiscal advisor of the Governor. Where it is indicated that a state has a finance department and it includes divisions of taxation, budget, or accounting, the columns with these headings will be marked with an "O" to indicate that there are no separate agencies for these functions.

(b) The auditor does not have post-audit functions in every state. See table on page 167.

(c) See table on page 167 for performance of pre-audit functions.

(d) Audit and accounting control are responsibilities of the same person.

(e) Budget preparation and accounting control are the responsibilities of the same person.

(f) The Comptroller collects most of Florida's taxes.

(g) Governor ex-officio budget officer assisted by auditor.

(h) Governor is Director of Budget; Assistant Director appointed by Governor.

(i) Secretary of State is ex-officio Insurance Commissioner.

(j) Board of eight appointed by Governor from recommendations. Governor is ex-officio member of board.

(k) Appointed by Commissioner of Finance; approved by Governor and Council.

(l) The office of Tax Commissioner is responsible for budget preparation as well as revenue collection.

(m) Appointed by Auditor.

(n) There is a combined Department of Agriculture and Labor in North Dakota headed by a single elective official.

(o) Governor appoints board with consent of Senate, board appoints Executive Director except in Agriculture where board elects a member as President.

(p) Secretary of State is ex-officio auditor.

(q) State Auditor, appointed by Budget and Control Board, is head of Finance Division.

(r) The Tax Commission in Texas is an ex-officio body which fixes the tax rate. The Comptroller is Tax Administrator.

(s) Legislative Budget Board separate. In Texas this agency and Governor's budget officer work in the same budget field.

(t) Appointed by State Corporation Commission.

(u) Treasurer also serves as comptroller.

(v) Auditor General is appointed by Joint Legislative Audit Committee; authority of Auditor General confined to examining and reporting.

(w) Attorney General serves ex-officio as Industrial Commissioner.

TABLE 2

CONSTITUTIONAL AND STATUTORY ELECTIVE ADMINISTRATIVE OFFICIALS

State	Governor	Lt. Governor	Secretary of State	Attorney General	Treasurer	Auditor	Controller	Education	Agriculture	Labor	Insurance	Mines	Land	University Regents	Board of Education	Public Utilities Commission	Executive Council	Miscellaneous	Total Agencies	Total Officials
Alabama	C	C	C	C	C	C		C	C(a)			C				S3		Tax Commission—S3	9	11
Arizona	C	C	C	C	C	C		C					C			C3			9	13
Arkansas	C		C	C	C	C	C	C					C						7	7
California	C	C	C	C	C		C	C	C	C	C			C6	C5			Board of Equalization—C4(b)	8	17
Colorado	C	C		C	C	C													6	6
Connecticut	C	C	C	C	C														7	7
Delaware	C	C		C	C	C		C								S3		Collector of Oyster Revenue—S	8	10
Florida	C		C	C	C		C	C	C	C	C	S				C5			11	15
Georgia	C	C	C	C	C	SL	C	C	C					S9					7	7
Idaho	C	C	C	C	C	C		C	C										8	16
Illinois	C	C	C	S	C	C			C						C11				7	7
Indiana	C	C	C	C	C	C		C												
Iowa	C	C	C	C	C	C		S(c)	S				C(e)				CL7		7	8
Kansas	C	C	C	C	C	C		C	C(d)				C			C3		Printer—C	9	9
Kentucky	C	C	C	C	C	C	C	C	C(f)	C	S	S				C3(g)			11	11
Louisiana	C	C	C	C	C	C		C	SL										11	23
Maine			CL	CL	CL	SL			SL										7	13
Maryland				CL	CL		C	C									C8		4	4
Massachusetts	C	C	C	C	C	C		C					S	C8	C3(h)			Highway Commissioner—S	7	14
Michigan	C	C	C	C	C	C		C					S					Board of Agriculture—C6	12	26
Minnesota	C	C	C	C	C	C		C				S				S3		Tax Collector—S	7	13
Mississippi	C	C	C	C	C	C		C	S(i)							S3		Highway Commission—S3	13	17

154

Table of state elective offices (rotated). Rows are states; unlabeled symbol columns (C, S, L, CL, SL, etc.) precede office-specific columns and two numeric columns at right.

State											Office	No.	No.
Missouri	C	C	C	C				:C			......	6	6
Montana	C	C	C	C				:	:S3	C3	......	8	10
Nebraska	C	C	C	C				C	C6	:	Surveyor General—C(j)	9	21
Nevada	C	C	C	:	S	:(j)		C5	S5(k)	:	Printer—S, Fish & Game Commission—S17	13	37
New Hampshire	C	CL	CL	:	:	:	:	:	:	:	......	4	8
New Jersey	:	:	CL	:	:	:	C5	:	:	:	......	2	2
New Mexico	C	C	C	C	C	:	C	:	:	C	Corporation Commission—C3	9	11
New York	:C	:C	:C	:C	:C	:C	CL13	:C	:	:	Board of Public Welfare—CL7	5	13
North Carolina	C	C	C	C	C	:	CL 100	:	:	:	......	12	117
North Dakota	C	C	C	C(l)	C	:	:	C3	:	C	Tax Commissioner—C	11	13
Ohio	C	C	:C	:C	:C	:	:	:	:	:	Commissioner of Charities & Corrections—C; Examiner & Inspector—C	7	29
Oklahoma	C	C	C	:	:C	:C	CL23	C3	:	:		13	15
Oregon	:C	C	C	S	S	:	:	:	:	:	Secy. of Internal Affairs—C	6	6
Pennsylvania	C	C	C	:	:C	:	:	:	:	:		5	5
Rhode Island	:CC	C	C	:	:	:	:	:	:	:		5	5
South Carolina	C	CL	SL	:C	:S	SL	CL7	:	:	:	Adjutant & Inspector General—C; Librarian—SL; Bd. of Public Welfare—SL7; Employment Security Commission—SL3	14	28
South Dakota	C	SL	CL	C	C	:	S3	:	:	:	......	10	12
Tennessee	CL	CL	:	:	:	:	S3	:	:	:	......	6	8
Texas	C	:CC	C	C	S	C	S21	C3(g)	:	:	......	9	31
Utah	C	C	C	:	:	:	C9	:	:	:	......	6	14
Vermont	C	:CC	C	S	S	:	:	:	:	:	......	6	6
Virginia	:CL	C	C	:	:	:	CL3	:	:	:	......	5	7
Washington	C	C	C	:C	:S	C	S12(m)	S	:	:	......	10	21
West Virginia	C	C	C	:S	:S	S	S	S	:	:	......	12	12
Wisconsin	:C	C	C	:C	:C	:	:	:	:	:	......	6	6
Wyoming	C	C	C	:C	:C	C(n)	:	:	:	:	......	5	5

Source: U. S. Department, Commerce, Bureau of the Census, *Elective Offices of State and County Governments* (Washington: Government Printing Office, 1946); modified in accordance with the most recent information available to Council of State Governments.

Symbols: C—Constitutional. L—Elected by Legislature. S—Statutory. Numbers indicate number of officials.

(a) Commissioner of Agriculture and Industries.
(b) Plus Controller, ex officio.
(c) After January, 1955, Superintendent will be appointed by new 9-member State Board of Education.
(d) Commissioner of Agriculture, Labor and Statistics.
(e) Secretary of State.
(f) Commissioner of Agriculture and Immigration.
(g) Railroad Commission.
(h) Plus 1 ex officio.
(i) Commissioner of Agriculture and Commerce.
(j) Surveyor General is ex officio State Land Register.
(k) Plus 2 ex officio.
(l) Commissioner of Agriculture and Labor.
(m) Elected by local school board members in convention, plus 1 ex officio.
(n) Secretary of State, Treasurer and Attorney General constitute a Board of Commissioners for the sale of school and university lands and investment of funds therefrom.

FINANCE MANAGEMENT*

CONTINUED expansion of state revenues and expenditures, resulting from the rapidly increasing population, marked the period 1953–55. Pressing programs in highways, education and mental health heightened the burden on the resources of the states and forced them to re-examine revenue structures for new sources of funds. At the same time, the states continued to seek economies in administration.

This article briefly reviews the major changes and developments that have occurred in the area of finance management, with particular reference to general reorganization, auditing, budget and revenue administration. It is based primarily upon replies to questionnaires received from forty-six states and four territories.

REORGANIZATION

The biennium 1953–55 covered a tapering-off in the drive for administrative reorganization which developed after the work of the original Hoover Commission in the late 1940's. By early 1953 more than thirty states had undertaken, with varying degrees of enthusiasm, to review and reorganize their administrative structures. Few of them adopted changes as basic as recommended by their "little Hoover" committees. A substantial number, however, achieved significant advances, chiefly in the form of centralization of management functions in departments of administration. These usually covered accounting, budgeting, purchasing, personnel and property management. Their over-all effect was a general strengthening of the role of the governor as Chief Executive.

As indicated, this movement was less widespread in the past biennium, but

*Prepared by FRANK M. LANDERS, Director, Budget Division, Michigan Department of Administration, and President, National Association of State Budget Officers, with the assistance of HENRY PRATT, Budget Division Internee (Dartmouth College).

there were important developments. Colorado, in 1955, set up a "Hoover commission" type of study group consisting of twelve members—four each from the House and Senate and four from private life. The commission was directed to study and suggest, by December 1, 1956, a method of reorganizing the executive branch. Idaho's legislature amended its budget law to provide that the Budget Director would also be Director of Administration, with such duties as might be prescribed by law and as designated by the Governor. Montana's 1955 legislature created a "little Hoover" commission to consider government reorganization, with particular attention to the state's tax structure. South Dakota expanded its finance department to include administration and directed it "to investigate centralization of office equipment and services."

One of the major developments in this area of reorganization was in Pennsylvania where, in 1955, the office of the Governor was thoroughly overhauled. Briefly, the office is divided into two major groups of activities. One of these, headed by the Secretary to the Governor, assists the Chief Executive in the performance of his "political and ceremonial responsibilities." The other, under the Secretary of Administration, covers budget (including procurement), accounting, management methods, personnel, program evaluation and comptrollers (in agencies under the Governor's jurisdiction).

Alaska, under a general reorganization act of 1955, created a department of finance and placed under it the responsibility for budget, accounts and purchases.

POST AUDIT

The period under review encompassed a flowering of the movement to separate the post-audit function from administrative control and place it under the legislative branch. This development may be attributed to a variety of factors. In some instances, it was the logical outgrowth of the drive for centralization of operating responsibility under the general manager (the Governor) with the after-the-fact audit reporting directly to the board of directors (the legislature). In others, the move was simply a reaction from the strengthening of the Governor's position and, along with the creation of legislative budget units, may be said to reflect the traditional legislative concern over the powers of the executive.

California established a Legislative Audit Bureau to which it transferred the post-audit function from the Department of Finance. The functions of the Legislative Auditor were not affected by this change. As staff for the joint Legislative Budget Committee, his office is concerned with budget analysis and fiscal control in connection with proposed appropriations, including the Budget Act. Florida created a Joint Legislative Auditing Committee of six members, three from each house. The committee reviews the work of the State Auditing Department. The Governor appoints the State Auditor, from a list of three names submitted by the committee. The Auditor designates one of his staff to serve as secretary to the committee and as liaison between the two.

Minnesota created the office of Legislative Post Audit, headed by a director whose appointment, compensation and duties are to be defined by the 1957 legislature. Presently, the Post Auditor is appointed by the Governor and confirmed by the Senate. In Mississippi and New Hampshire the post-audit function was transferred from the Department of Administration to the office of the Legislative Budget Assistant. The North Carolina legislature moved the pre audit from the Auditor's office to the Budget Bureau and, vice versa, a partial post-audit operation from the latter to the former. Tennessee established a State Finance Advisory Committee consisting of the Governor, the Budget Director, the Comptroller and the Commissioner of Finance and Taxation. The committee meets monthly and attempts to coordinate state financial actions.

West Virginia's legislature passed a bill that would have taken the post-audit function from the Tax Commissioner's office and placed it under the Legislative Auditor. This measure was vetoed by the Governor. Alaska, as part of its general reorganization act of 1955, created the office of Legislative Post Audit and made it responsible for all territorial auditing.

BUDGET

Developments in state budget administration continued along familiar paths, but at a somewhat slower rate. Generally, the changes reflected a continuing desire to extend and improve the executive budget system. The trend toward annual sessions of state legislative bodies was maintained during this period. Six states— California, Colorado, Kansas, Louisiana, Maryland and West Virginia—now hold off-year sessions limited to budget and fiscal matters.

Of the units reporting, Connecticut, Maryland and The Commonwealth of Puerto Rico have made significant progress toward program or performance budgeting. In Connecticut, the legislature authorized replacement of the old object-expenditure budget with a program-type budget which will go into effect July 1, 1956. Maryland continued in development of its performance budget, adopted several years earlier. Puerto Rico is also making strides in that direction; all agencies in the commonwealth have been divided into budgetary units, and the Governor's budget has been established on a functional classification rather than on an organizational unit basis. Several states have used other methods to strengthen the Governor's hand in the budget area.

In Arizona, the legislature appropriated $15,000 for the budget division of the Governor's office. "Purpose of the appropriation is to make available funds with which the Governor will be enabled to review budget requests by the various departments of the state government before such requests are submitted to the legislature." Arkansas, which previously relied on the Legislative Council as the budget-making authority, as part of its general accounting law (1955) vested the budget job in the State Comptroller in behalf of the Governor. As spelled out in the statute, the Arkansas budget is to be a detailed "line-item" type, including the listing of the name and salary of each employee.

Idaho moved the date for submitting budget requests up to August 15 and, at the same time, set up a six-man Legislative Budget Committee to attend budget hearings and formulate recommendations to the Governor and the legislature. Maine moved from lump sum toward the object code classification. Budgets and appropriations are now to be broken into (1) personal services, (2) capital expenditures and (3) all other. This, it is hoped, will (1) "keep expenditures more in line with the program presented and approved by the legislature," (2) "bring about better planning and budgeting," and (3) "result in a savings to the taxpayer." Ohio established a capital improvement planning division in its Finance Department, with the hope that it will produce efficiency and economy in future building programs.

New Jersey established a Legislative Budget and Finance Director as a counterpart of the Budget Director. In New Mexico, the legislature placed on the statutes the duties to be performed by the Budget Director, and the Budget Director has proceeded to establish a system of monthly audits of state agencies. In New York the executive budget has been expanded and the initial step taken to include a five-year projection of cash expenditures. At the request of the Governor of Wyoming, where the Governor is the Budget Officer, the office of Assistant Budget Officer was established April 1, 1955. This position was formerly held by the Governor's Executive Secretary.

REVENUE ADMINISTRATION

As indicated earlier, the major concern of the states in respect to revenues has been to find additional sources. The number of formal study commissions dropped off considerably in this period. Probably because of the great emphasis on the search for new revenue, fewer efforts were directed toward revamping or reorganizing the administrative machinery. Among the developments reported along this line were the following:

Massachusetts, in October, 1953, changed the top control of its Department of Corporations and Taxation. That agency, which had been under the direction of a single administrator is now headed by a Commissioner and two Associate Commissioners. The Commissioner has assumed responsibility for administration and has assigned one Associate to tax collection and the other to supervision of local taxes. Since the reorganization it is reported that: (1) the responsibility of the Commissioner is less absolute; (2) tax regulations are being more completely formulated and distributed; and (3) the process of recording and analyzing tax returns has been mechanized.

Kentucky cut its field offices from eight to five, all of which are located in metropolitan areas. By doing so it achieved some savings without seriously affecting services to taxpayers. New Mexico reorganized its Tax Commission to provide three full-time Commissioners in order to undertake state-wide reassessment and equalization.

Oregon likewise reorganized its three-man Tax Commission into three functional divisions, each headed by a Commissioner. The administrative services division provides general services, including research and legal counsel; the income division engages in the direct revenue collection activities; and the valuation division undertakes the work related to property assessment. The report of a legislative interim committee which had recommended movement toward centralization of revenue-collecting in a single agency was shelved by the 1955 Oregon legislature. At the same time, the legislature did remove the motor vehicle department from the office of the secretary of state and set it up as a separate agency under the Governor.

South Dakota set up a Department of Revenue, built largely upon the former taxation division of the finance department. Idaho, Indiana and Kansas created formal study commissions to review the whole problem of taxes and administration.

OTHER DEVELOPMENTS

Formal efforts to develop more effective organization patterns and methods of operating were reported in three states. California established a division of organization and cost control in its Department of Finance. The division is to "provide consultation and coordination to the departments and agencies . . . with respect to organization planning and the development and application of controls over manpower and costs . . . and to conduct research . . . in the field of management." Connecticut established a management analysis section of its budget division and staffed it with seven full-time employees. The section, upon request of the Governor, the Commissioner of Finance and Control, the Budget Director or an agency, is available to undertake management and operational studies. It has already completed several such studies. Pennsylvania, as noted earlier, has established a Bureau of Management Methods as part of its reorganization of the executive office. This unit will operate in six managerial fields: (1) work simplification, (2) forms analyses and design, (3) organizational analysis, (4) developing of operating procedures, (5) records management and (6) review of operating methods.

Arkansas and Illinois have revamped their accounting systems and procedures. As indicated above, Arkansas enacted a complete and new accounting procedures law. Subsequently, the Comptroller has issued regulations further outlining and explaining the new system and its operation. The Illinois Department of Finance has substantially strengthened its central accounting division functions during the past two years by comprehensive pre audit of expenditures and encumbrances for all state agencies under the Governor's jurisdiction.

Finally, there have been developments of interest in reporting. Indiana, with a "budget-in-brief," reported the broad outlines of the budget to be presented a month later to the legislature. New York changed its budget presentation to clarify the financial picture by showing the total income and expenditures rather than the operations of the general fund alone, as had been the custom in the past. Virginia's budget division, rather uniquely, is producing a film on the state's health activities in cooperation with the Department of Education, and it expects to cover similarly most of the major functions of the state government.

STATE BUDGETARY PRACTICES

State	Budget-making authority	Official or agency preparing budget	Date estimates must be submitted by dept. or agencies	Date submitted to Legislature	Power of Legislature to change budget	Power of item veto by Governor	Fiscal year begins
ALABAMA	Governor	Division of the Budget in Department of Finance	Feb. 1 or before, preceding each regular session	By the 5th day regular business session	Unlimited	Yes	Oct. 1
ARIZONA	Governor	Auditor	Sept. 1 each year	No date set	Unlimited	Yes	July 1
ARKANSAS	Legislative Council	Legislative Council	Nov. 1 even years	Date of convening session	Unlimited	Yes	July 1
CALIFORNIA	Governor	Budget Division, under Director of Finance	Small agencies, Sept. 15 Larger agencies, Oct. 1	January in odd years, March in even years	Limited: Constitution makes continuous appropriations, notably state support of public schools	Yes	July 1
COLORADO	Governor	Budget section of Division of Accounts and Control under State Controller who is civil service employee	Oct. 1 or before	10th day of session	Unlimited	Yes	July 1
CONNECTICUT	Governor	Director of Budget	Sept. 1 or before	1st session day after Feb. 14	Unlimited	Yes	July 1
DELAWARE	Governor	Budget Commission	Sept. 15 even years	By 5th day of session	Unlimited	Yes	July 1
FLORIDA	Budget Commission: Governor as chairman and budget officer, and six elected officers: Secretary of State, Comptroller, Treasurer, Attorney General, Commissioner of Agriculture, Superintendent of Public Instruction	Budget Director, appointed by Governor	Nov. 15 in even years, before meeting of Legislature in April in odd years	1st day of session	Unlimited	Yes	July 1
GEORGIA	Governor	Head of each state agency	Governor sets a date before meeting of General Assembly	By 15th day of session	Unlimited	Yes	July 1
IDAHO	Governor	Director of Budget and 6-man Budget Committee	Aug. 15 before Jan. session	Not later than 5th day of session	Unlimited	No	July 1
ILLINOIS	Governor	Director of Finance	Nov. 1 in even years	April 1 in odd years	Unlimited	Yes	July 1
INDIANA	Budget Committee: Two Senators of opposite parties, two Representatives of opposite parties, and Director of Budget, all appointed by Governor	Director of Budget	Sept. 1 in even years	Feb. 10 or before in odd years	Unlimited	No	July 1
IOWA	Governor	Comptroller	Sept. 1	Feb. 1 or before	Unlimited	No	July 1

State		Budget agency	Date prepared	Submission to legislature	Legislative power	Item veto	Fiscal year begins
KANSAS	Governor	Budget Division of Department of Administration	Oct. 1 of year before session	Within 3 weeks after convening of regular session (odd years); within 2 days after convening of budget session (even years)	Unlimited	Yes	July 1
KENTUCKY	Governor	Division of Budget, Department of Finance	Oct. 1	3rd Mon. after convening of regular session or before	Unlimited	Yes	July 1
LOUISIANA	Governor	Budget Director	Jan. 15 before annual session 2nd Mon. in May	20th day of regular session or before	Unlimited	Yes	July 1
MAINE	Governor	Commissioner of Finance and Administration	Oct. 1 of even years	End of 2nd week of session or before	Unlimited	No	July 1
MARYLAND	Governor	Director of Department of Budget and Procurement	Sept. 1	20th day of session in odd years; 1st Wed. in Feb. in even years; (30th day for new Governor)*	Limited: Legislature may decrease but not increase except for own operating budget	No	July 1
MASSACHUSETTS	Governor	Budget Commissioner	Sept. 15	Between 1st and 4th Wed. in Jan.	Unlimited	Yes	July 1
MICHIGAN	Governor	Budget Division of Department of Administration	Set by administrative action	10th day of session	Unlimited	Yes	July 1
MINNESOTA	Governor	Commissioner of Administration	Oct. 1 or before, preceding convening of Legislature	Within 3 weeks after inauguration of Governor	Unlimited	Yes	July 1
MISSISSIPPI	Governor	Budget Commission: Governor as *ex-officio* Chairman, and Chairman House Ways and Means Committee, Chairman House Appropriations Committee, Chairman Senate Finance Committee, and President pro tem of Senate	Oct. 15 preceding convening of Legislature	Opening day of session	Unlimited	Yes	July 1, 1954 Appropriation on biennial basis
MISSOURI	Governor	Division of Budget and Comptroller	Oct. 1	Jan. at beginning of biennial session	Unlimited	Yes	July 1
MONTANA	Controller	Each Department submits individual budget	Sept. 1 of year before session	1st day of session (1st Mon. in Jan., odd years)	Limited	Yes	July 1
NEBRASKA	Governor	Tax Commissioner	Sept. 15 in even years	15th day of regular session	Limited: Three-fifths vote required to increase Governor's recommendations; majority vote required to reject or decrease such items	No	July 1
NEVADA	Governor and Budget Director	Budget Director	Oct. 1	10th day of session or before	Unlimited	No	July 1
NEW HAMPSHIRE	Governor	Comptroller	Oct. 1 in even years	Feb. 15 in odd years	Unlimited	No	July 1

*A proposed amendment eliminating this provision is to be voted upon in November, 1956.

161

STATE BUDGETARY PRACTICES—Continued

State	Budget-making authority	Official or agency preparing budget	Date estimates must be submitted by dept. or agencies	Date submitted to Legislature	Power of Legislature to change budget	Power of item veto by Governor	Fiscal year begins
NEW JERSEY	Governor	Director of Division of Budget and Accounting of Department of the Treasury	Sept. 15	Feb. 1	Unlimited	Yes	July 1
NEW MEXICO	Governor	Budget Director	Nov. 15	On or before 25th day of session	Unlimited	Yes	July 1
NEW YORK	Governor	Division of Budget	Sept. 15	Feb. 1	Limited: Cannot change form. Line item budget cannot be changed to lump sum budget	Yes	April 1
NORTH CAROLINA	Governor	Advisory Budget Commission: Chairman of Appropriations and Finance Committees and two members appointed by Governor	Sept. 1 preceding session	1st week of session	Unlimited	No	July 1
NORTH DAKOTA	State Budget Board: Governor, Attorney General, Auditor, Chairman of Appropriations Committees of House and Senate	Budget Director	No date set: about Aug. 1	Beginning of session	Unlimited	Yes	July 1
OHIO	Governor	Director of Finance	Nov. 1	1st week in Feb. in odd years	Unlimited	Yes	July 1
OKLAHOMA	Governor	Budget Director	No date set	1st day of session	Unlimited	Yes, in general appropriation act only	July 1
OREGON	Governor	Budget Division, Department of Finance and Administration	Sept. 1 of even year preceding legislative year	Dec. 20 of even year preceding legislative year	Limited: Appropriations set by constitutional amendment cannot be altered	Yes, constitutional	July 1 in odd years
PENNSYLVANIA	Governor	Budget Secretary	Nov. 1 of even years	As Governor desires	Unlimited	Yes	June 1
RHODE ISLAND	Governor	Budget Officer	Oct. 1	24th day of session	Limited: If increases or additions cannot be covered by revenue estimates or surplus, additional financing must be enacted as part of same legislation	No	July 1
SOUTH CAROLINA	State Budget and Control Board; Governor as chairman; Treasurer, Comptroller General, Chairman Senate Finance Committee, Chairman House Ways and Means Committee	Finance Division of State Budget and Control Board	Nov. 1 or discretion of Board	2nd Tues. in Jan.	Unlimited	Yes, in appropriations bill	July 1

State	Budget authority	Budget agency	Date budget submitted	Date appropriation acts	Budget type	Balanced	Fiscal year begins
SOUTH DAKOTA	Governor	Division of Purchasing and Printing in Department of Finance	Oct. 15	By 5th day of session	Unlimited	Yes	July 1
TENNESSEE	Governor	Director of the Budget	Dec. 1 or before of even years	Jan. 14 or before unless change in Governor; then Mar. 1 or before	Unlimited	Yes	July 1
TEXAS	Governor	Executive Budget Officer, Executive Department	Aug. 15 of even years	5th day of session or before	Unlimited	Yes	Sept. 1
UTAH	Governor	Finance Commission	No date set	10 days after conv. of session or before	Unlimited	Yes	July 1
VERMONT	Governor	Governor-elect; Treasurer, Auditor of Accounts	Oct. 1, biennially	3rd Tues. of regular biennial session or before	Unlimited	No	July 1
VIRGINIA	Governor	Governor appoints a Director of Division of Budget, and other assistants	Sept. 15 in odd years	2nd Wed. in Jan. in even years	Unlimited	Yes	July 1
WASHINGTON	Governor	Director of Budget	1st Mon. in Sept.	5th day after conv. of sess. or before	Unlimited	Yes	July 1
WEST VIRGINIA	Board of Public Works: Governor as chairman; Secretary of State, Auditor, Attorney General, Treasurer, Superintendent of Schools and Commissioner of Agriculture	Director of Budget	Oct. 15 or before, of year preceding annual session	10 days after conv. of sess. or before	Limited: May not increase items of budget bill except appropriations for Legislature and Judiciary	No	July 1
WISCONSIN	Governor	Director Department of Budgets and Accounts	Oct. 20 in even years	Feb. 1 in odd years or before	Unlimited	Yes	July 1
WYOMING	Governor	Assistant Budget Officer	Oct. 1 preceding session in Jan.	Within 5 days after beginning of session	Unlimited	Yes	July 1
ALASKA	Budget Director	Budget Director, Department of Finance	Between Sept. 1 and Nov. 1 of even years	5th working day of session	Unlimited	Yes	July 1
GUAM	Governor	Director, Budget Management	Nov. 1 preceding session in Jan.	1st week in Jan.	Unlimited	Yes	July 1
HAWAII	Governor	Bureau of Budget. Governor appoints a Director	Oct. 15 or before, preceding each biennial session	3rd Wed. in Feb. in odd years, 20 days in advance to members of legislature	Unlimited	Yes	July 1 (biennium) in odd years
PUERTO RICO	Governor	Director, Bureau of the Budget	Date set by Budget Director	2nd Mon. in Jan.	Unlimited	Yes	July 1
VIRGIN ISLANDS	Governor	Commissioner of Insular Affairs	90 days before end of fiscal year	Upon convening	Limited	Yes	July 1

163

ANNUAL SALARIES OF STATE ADMINISTRATIVE OFFICIALS*
Maximum or current figures, as of August, 1955

State	Governor	Executive Secretary to the Governor	Attorney General	Lieutenant Governor	Secretary of State	Auditor	Treasurer
Alabama...............	$12,000	$ 8,500	$10,000	$ 12(a)	$ 6,000	$ 6,000	$ 6,000
Arizona...............	15,000	6,300	10,000	None	7,200	8,400	6,600
Arkansas.............	10,000	7,500	6,000	2,500	5,000	5,000	5,000
California.............	40,000(b)	15,000	23,000	17,500(b)	17,500(b)	18,000(b)	17,500(b)
Colorado.............	17,500	7,000	9,000	3,600	8,000	8,000	8,000
Connecticut...........	15,000	11,400	12,500	5,000	8,000	12,000	8,000
Delaware.............	12,000	6,000	12,000	12(a)	8,000	6,000	6,000
Florida...............	20,000	10,500	15,000	None	15,000	10,000	15,000
Georgia...............	12,000(c)	7,500(c)	7,500(c)	2,000(c)	7,500(c)	10,000(c)	7,500(c)
Idaho................	10,000(d)	5,400(e)	7,500	20(a)	6,500	6,500	6,500
Illinois...............	25,000	......	16,000	12,500	16,000	16,000	16,000
Indiana...............	15,000	11,000	11,500	11,500(f)	11,500	11,500	11,500
Iowa.................	12,500	5,670	8,500	4,000	7,500	7,000	7,000
Kansas...............	15,000	10,000	8,500	2,400(a)	7,500	7,500	7,500
Kentucky.............	15,000	10,000	11,000	6,000(g)	9,000	9,000	9,000
Louisiana............	18,000	......	12,500	7,500	16,800(h)	10,000	10,000
Maine................	10,000	8,684(e)	8,000	None	8,000	8,000	6,000
Maryland.............	15,000	11,183	12,000	None	10,000	9,000	2,500
Massachusetts........	20,000	12,000	15,000	8,000	9,000	9,000	9,000
Michigan.............	22,500	11,000	12,500	8,500(i)	12,500	12,500	12,500
Minnesota............	15,000	8,500	13,000	9,600(j)	11,000	11,000	11,000
Mississippi...........	15,000	7,500(k)	10,000	1,500	8,250	8,250	8,250
Missouri.............	25,000(l)	7,200	15,000(l)	12,000(l)	15,000(l)	7,500	15,000(l)
Montana.............	12,500	7,500	7,500	12(a)	7,500	5,000	5,000
Nebraska.............	11,000	7,500	6,500	1,744	6,500	6,500	6,500
Nevada...............	15,000(m)	7,200	8,400	17(n)	8,000	7,764	8,000
New Hampshire........	12,000	10,000	9,810	None	8,080	F. 10,350	8,050
New Jersey............	30,000	15,000	20,000	None	13,000	10,000	18,000
New Mexico...........	15,000	12,000	10,000	35(a)	8,400	8,400	8,400
New York.............	50,000	18,500	25,000	20,000	17,000	C. 25,000	12,000
North Carolina........	15,000(o)	9,504	12,080	2,100(p)	10,000	10,000	10,000
North Dakota.........	9,000	6,000	7,500	1,000	5,000	5,000	5,000
Ohio.................	25,000(l)	8,500	15,000(l)	6,000	15,000(l)	15,000(l)	15,000(l)
Oklahoma.............	15,000(q)	6,000	12,000	3,600	6,000	6,000	7,200
Oregon...............	15,000(r)	8,000	11,000	None	11,000	(s)	11,000
Pennsylvania..........	25,000	15,000(e)	15,000	15,000	15,000	15,000	15,000
Rhode Island..........	15,000	7,150	11,000	5,000	9,000	9,174	9,000
South Carolina........	15,000(t)	7,350	10,000	1,000(u)	10,000	9,000	10,000
South Dakota.........	12,000	6,000	7,500	2,100	6,000	6,000	6,000
Tennessee.............	12,000(t)	10,000	12,000	750(v)	10,000	C. 10,000	10,000
Texas................	25,000(t)	10,000	20,000	25(w)	15,000	15,000	17,500
Utah.................	10,000	7,200	7,500	None	7,200	6,000	6,000
Vermont..............	11,500	6,000	7,500	2,500	7,500	7,500	7,500
Virginia..............	17,500	9,000	12,500	1,260	6,500	9,500	9,500
Washington...........	15,000	8,500(e)	10,000	6,000	8,500	8,500	8,500
West Virginia.........	12,500	7,800(e)	7,500	None	7,250	7,250	7,250
Wisconsin............	18,000(l)	......	15,000(l)	10,000	10,000(l)	12,500	10,000
Wyoming.............	12,000	6,000	7,500	None	8,400	8,400	8,400
Alaska...............	15,000	12,000	14,500	14,850(x)		10,000	10,000
Guam................	13,125(y)	......	9,880(z)	15,525(z)		7,800(z)	7,800(z)
Hawaii...............	16,000	10,827	12,500	15,336		11,250	11,000
Puerto Rico...........	10,600(aa)	11,000	14,000(ab)	None(ac)	14,000	16,000(ad)	14,000(ae)
Virgin Islands.........	15,000	7,040	12,000(af)	None	10,500	None	11,000

*For specific titles, see "Administrative Officials Classified by Functions."

B—Budget Officer; F—Finance Officer; C—Comptroller or Controller; R—Revenue Officer; T—Taxation Officer.

(a) Per diem. Delaware, Idaho and Montana, per diem served. Alabama, plus $10 and Kansas, plus $6, per diem during legislative sessions.

(b) Effective on expiration of present term.

(c) Minimum; Acts 1953 provided a minimum salary for elected officials with an automatic increase of $800 for each four years of service until fixed maximum is reached. Minimum for Governor, $12,000; maximum $16,000. Other elected officials, minimum $7,500; maximum $11,500.

(d) Plus residence.

(e) Idaho and Maine, Administrative Assistant; Pennsylvania, Secretary to the Governor; Washington, Assistant to Governor; West Virginia, Executive Assistant.

(f) Plus $1,200 as President of Senate and $5 per legislative day.

(g) Same compensation as Governor when serving as Governor, plus per diem during sessions of General Assembly.

(h) $8,000 as Secretary of State; $4,000 as Chairman of Insurance Commission; $4,800 as custodian of voting machines.

(i) Salary $4,000; expense account $1,000; member of State Administrative Board, $3,500.

(j) Per term (2 years), plus $50 per day for special sessions; effective 1957.

(k) For Executive Counsel; Executive Assistant, $6,000.

(l) Effective January, 1957.

(m) Plus mansion fund of $7,200.

(n) Per diem while presiding in the Senate; plus $15 per diem while acting as Governor.

(o) Plus $4,000 travel expense allowance.

(p) Plus $700 as President of Senate and $1,000 expense allowance.

(q) Plus maintenance; in Oklahoma, plus $9,000 maintenance.

(r) Plus $400 per month for expenses.

ANNUAL SALARIES OF STATE ADMINISTRATIVE OFFICIALS*—Continued
Maximum or current figures, as of August, 1955

State	Chief Budget Officer	Revenue and/or Taxation	Public Instruction	Adjutant General	Agriculture	Chief Health Officer	Highways
Alabama	$ 7,200	$ 10,000	$ 10,000	$ 7,500	$ 8,400	$10,000	$ 10,000
Arizona	(ag)	8,400(ah)	9,600	6,000	300(ah)	8,400	15(ai)
Arkansas	C. 8,500	R. 7,500	8,400	7,200	9,500(aj)	12,500(ak)	15,000
California	B. 15,000	15,600	18,000(b)	(al)	15,500	17,500	16,200
Colorado	8,894	8,500	12,000	7,500	9,264	12,660	11,400
Connecticut	B. 10,200	11,400	15,000	16,200	10,000	15,000	12,000
Delaware	7,500	T. 8,000	10,000	6,000	4,000	7,250	12,500
Florida	B. 12,500	C. 15,000	15,000	9,500	15,000	15,000	12,500
Georgia	......	10,000	7,500(c)	9,234	7,500(c)	7,500(c)	7,500(c)
Idaho	B. 5,400	T. 6,500	6,500	5,500	5,500	9,600	12,000
Illinois	F. 12,000	R. 12,000	12,000	10,000	12,000	12,000 1,000–1,500(am)	10,000
Indiana	11,000	11,000	11,500	10,000	......	17,850(an)	10,000
Iowa	B.&C. 9,000	T. 6,500	10,000	7,500	7,500	8,400	4,500
Kansas	9,924	R. 7,500	8,000	6,000	8,500	15,000	9,500
Kentucky	B. 12,000	R. 12,000	10,000	10,000	9,000	12,000	12,000
Louisiana	B. 10,000	14,000(ao)	12,500	12,900	10,000	12,000	17,500
Maine	11,232	8,788	10,000	8,000	8,000	10,000	12,000
Maryland	17,500	C. 12,000	17,500	6,000	......	15,000	15,000
Massachusetts	B. 10,000	T. 15,000	11,000	11,916	9,000	12,500	(ap)
Michigan	B. 12,500	12,000(aq)	12,500	11,652(ar)	12,000	18,000	12,500
Minnesota	B. 11,300	T. 11,300	11,300	(as)	11,300	11,300	11,300
Mississippi	B. 7,500	9,350	8,250	7,500	8,250	9,350	6,600
Missouri	B.&C. 7,000	R. 12,000	12,000	7,000	10,000	7,500	15,000
Montana	C. 7,000	7,000	6,000	9,734(at)	7,000	12,000	10,000
Nebraska	7,500		9,000	6,600	7,000	11,500	12,000
Nevada	7,200	15,000	9,000	1,600(au)	7,200	10,956	10,000
New Hampshire	C. 10,350	T. 8,625	10,350	8,625	8,625	10,350	10,350(ap)
New Jersey	C. 16,000	T. 13,000	18,000	16,000(av)	18,000	18,000	18,000
New Mexico	C. 11,200	R. 11,400 / T. 10,000	9,000	10,000	......	12,500	13,400
New York	18,500	18,500	22,500	14,250	17,000	18,500	......
North Carolina	13,398	13,200	10,000	8,910	10,000	14,500	15,000
North Dakota	B. 6,000	T. 6,000	5,400	5,000	5,000(aw)	10,000	9,600
Ohio	F. 12,000	T. 10,000(b)	10,000(b)	11,915	10,000	12,000	12,000
Oklahoma	B. 10,000	T. 12,000	12,000	7,200	7,200	12,000	15,000
Oregon	F. 11,500	T. 9,500(ah)	11,000	8,000	9,500	13,000	15,000
Pennsylvania	B. 12,108(ax)	15,000	15,000	15,000	15,000	15,000	15,000
Rhode Island	B. 11,242	T. 11,242	8,500	7,280	9,500	8,000	10,164
South Carolina	Auditor 9,000	8,775	10,000	10,000	10,000	11,000	15,600
South Dakota	B. 6,500	T. 6,500	6,000	4,800	6,000	10,080	11,000
Tennessee	B. 10,000	T. 10,000	10,000	10,000	10,000	12,000	10,000
Texas	(ay)	17,500	18,500	10,000	15,000	16,000	17,500
Utah	F. 6,000	T. 6,000	8,000	7,500	6,000	11,500	6,000
Vermont	Governor	T. 7,500	7,500	7,500	7,500	8,996	7,500
Virginia	B. 9,500	11,500	12,500	8,500	9,500	13,000	13,500
Washington	B. 10,000	T. 11,000(ah)	8,500	9,918	10,000	12,000	15,000
West Virginia	B. 8,000	T. 8,000	7,250	7,000	7,250	10,000	9,000
Wisconsin	B. 12,500	T. 12,500	15,000	10,858	11,500	12,500	12,000
Wyoming	Governor	7,000(az)	8,400	6,000	6,200	10,400	10,800
Alaska	B. 9,000	T. 11,500	14,500	9,000	9,000	14,500	11,000
Guam	8,580(z)	F. 8,190(z)	8,580(z)	......	7,800(z)	7,800(z)	(ap)
Hawaii	B. 12,500	T. 11,000	12,000	15,543	11,000	12,500	(ba)
Puerto Rico	B. 12,000	T. 14,000(ae)	14,000	8,500	14,000	14,000	14,000(ap)
Virgin Islands	F. 11,000	T. 5,600	11,000	None	11,000	11,000	11,000(ap)

(s) Secretary of State is Auditor.
(t) Plus $1,500 as President of Senate.
(u) Plus $1,500 for supplies and expenses.
(v) Plus $1,500 as President of Senate.
(w) Per diem, not to exceed 120 days, during regular session; $25 per day for called sessions; same as Governor when serving as Governor.
(x) Official title is Territorial Secretary.
(y) Statutory, Organic Act of Guam.
(z) Plus territorial post differential where applicable.
(aa) $20,000 effective with next office holder.
(ab) Official title is Secretary of Justice.
(ac) Secretary of State succeeds Governor in his absence. In case of permanent vacancy, Secretary holds office for rest of term.
(ad) Post-audit by Controller, who is an officer of legislative branch. Pre-audit function performed by Secretary of Treasury.
(ae) Official title is Secretary of Treasury; also responsible for collection of revenues.

(af) Virgin Islands do not have an Attorney General; the corresponding officer is the United States Attorney. Salary set by U. S. Attorney General.
(ag) Vested in Governor and State Auditor.
(ah) For each of three members.
(ai) Per diem for each of five members to 100 days, plus travel.
(aj) $7,234 state, $2,266 federal.
(ak) $6,500 state, $6,000 federal.
(al) Pay and allowances of Major General of U. S. Army.
(am) Per month.
(an) Plus $2,500 in lieu of maintenance.
(ao) $12,000 as Collector of Revenue; $2,000 as head of Automobile Title Division.
(ap) Public Works includes Highways.
(aq) Plus $2,000 as chairman of Tax Commission.
(ar) Quarters and subsistence, $2,628.
(as) Pay and allowances of rank held.
(at) Paid from federal funds.

ANNUAL SALARIES OF STATE ADMINISTRATIVE OFFICIALS*—Continued
Maximum or current figures, as of August, 1955

State	Insurance	Labor	Mines and Minerals	Personnel	Public Safety	Public Works and Buildings	Purchasing	Welfare
Alabama	$7,500	$ 7,500	$ 7,200	$ 7,500	$ 10,000	$ 12,000	$ 7,200	$ 10,000
Arizona	8,400(ah)	8,400(ah)	6,000	......	......	......	......	8,400
Arkansas	7,500	6,000	7,500	......	6,000(bb)	......	7,500	7,500
California	15,500	15,000(bc)	12,000	15,000	......	18,000	13,800	14,500
Colorado	8,156	7,500(ah)	7,000	7,500(ah)	6,038	7,114	8,500	8,900
Connecticut	10,200	11,400	....	12,000	12,680	12,000	12,180	11,400
Delaware	6,000	2,500	....	....	....	....	....	5,750
Florida	(ba)	12,000	....	....	9,000	10,000	....	8,000
Georgia	7,500(c)	7,500(c)	7,800	9,060	6,000	5,000	7,500	7,000
Idaho	5,500	5,500	6,500	....	4,400	5,500	5,500	7,200
Illinois	12,000	12,000	12,000	12,000	12,000	12,000	10,000	12,000
Indiana	9,500	9,000	....	7,800	10,000	11,000	....	10,000
Iowa	7,000	4,600	4,200	5,220	6,500	8,000	4,500	5,000
Kansas	7,500	6,500	....	9,924	....	....	9,924	12,000
Kentucky	10,000	10,000	10,000	12,000	10,000	10,000	12,000	10,000
Louisiana	4,000(h)	10,000	10,000	12,600	9,000	14,400	8,100	11,160
Maine	8,000	7,000	3,900	7,592	6,916	6,344	6,604	(bd)
Maryland	10,000	7,500	8,062	12,700	8,500(bb)	12,000	(be)	14,000
Massachusetts	12,000	10,000	....	10,000	10,000	15,000	10,000	10,000
Michigan	10,500	8,500	......	15,597	13,500	....	13,530	15,597
Minnesota	9,200	8,375	9,200	11,300	7,920(bb)	......	8,112	11,300(bf)
Mississippi	8,250	......	5,750	....	7,000	....	....	8,000
Missouri	10,000	7,500(ah)	4,500	7,500	9,000(bb)	7,500	6,000	10,000
Montana	(bg)	5,000	....	......	6,000	....	(bh)	7,800
Nebraska	6,500	7,000(bi)	....	....	6,600	....	5,000	5,340
Nevada	9,000	7,200	8,000	7,404	6,744	....	7,068	8,148
New Hampshire	8,625	7,475	....	8,050	......	10,350(ap)	8,050	10,350
New Jersey	18,000	18,000	....	18,000(bj)	....	....	13,000	18,000(bk)
New Mexico	10,000	7,500	7,800	....	8,250	....	10,200	10,200(bl)
New York	18,500	18,500	....	14,056(bj)	15,400	19,500	17,000	18,500
North Carolina	10,000	10,000	....	9,900	....	8,000	10,098	8,910
North Dakota	5,000	5,000(aw)	4,800	......	6,000	......	3,840	9,600
Ohio	9,000	10,000	7,920	......	10,000	10,000(b)	11,760	12,000
Oklahoma	6,000	6,000	5,400	....	10,000	7,500	5,400	12,000
Oregon	8,000	9,500	9,000	(bj)	....	....	7,200	9,500
Pennsylvania	15,000	15,000	15,000	......	15,000	15,000		15,000
Rhode Island	8,151	9,500	....	9,174	....	(bm)	9,620	7,500(q)
South Carolina	7,500	7,500	....	....	....	....	7,800	8,100
South Dakota	6,000	....	3,600	....	....	6,000	....	6,000
Tennessee	10,000	10,000	5,340	10,000	10,000	6,780	10,000	10,000
Texas	15,000	8,400	17,500	....	17,500	12,000	12,000	7,500(au)
Utah	6,000	6,000	6,000	6,000	6,000	6,000	6,000	6,000
Vermont	7,500	7,500	....	7,500	7,500	....	7,500	7,500
Virginia	9,500	9,000	5,936	8,500	9,500	8,040	8,040	10,000
Washington	8,500	12,000	8,016	9,552	10,000(bb)	10,000(bn)	8,376(bo)	12,000
West Virginia	7,000	7,000	7,000	....	7,000	....	7,000	7,000
Wisconsin	10,000	11,500	....	11,000	....	11,000	11,000	14,000
Wyoming	6,200	5,400	6,200	(bp)	6,000	....	(bp)	6,780
Alaska	10,000	10,000	11,000	7,560	10,000	(ap)	(bh)	11,000
Guam	....	7,800(z)	....	7,800(z)	7,800(z)	7,800(z)	7,488(z)	....
Hawaii	(ba)	10,080	....	10,600	....	12,000	(ba)	10,500
Puerto Rico	8,500	14,000	(bq)	10,800	10,800(bb)	14,000(ap)	7,200	9,000
Virgin Islands	.....	(br)	....	7,500	11,000	11,000	7,500	11,000

(au) State's share to be supplemented by federal funds.
(av) Chief of Staff, Department of Defense.
(aw) Commissioner of Labor serves as Commissioner of Agriculture, with a total salary of $5,000.
(ax) Budget Secretary.
(ay) Salary set by Governor.
(az) $4,000 as member of Public Service Commission; $3,000 as member of Board of Equalization.
(ba) Highways Engineer is Public Works Superintendent; Budget Director is Purchasing Executive; Treasurer is Insurance Commissioner.
(bb) State Police. In Minnesota, Missouri and Nevada, State Highway Patrol. In Washington, State Patrol.
(bc) Director of Industrial Relations.
(bd) Health and Welfare.
(be) Budget and Procurement.

(bf) Commissioner of Public Welfare is also Superintendent of Public Institutions.
(bg) Auditor is also Insurance Commissioner.
(bh) Controller is also Purchasing Agent.
(bi) $3,000 state funds; $4,000 federal funds.
(bj) Administrator of Civil Service.
(bk) Department of Institutions and Agencies.
(bl) Subject to increase during fiscal 1955-56.
(bm) Chief, Division of Public Buildings, $7,293; Director of Public Works, $12,500.
(bn) Director of Dept. of General Administration.
(bo) Purchasing Div., Dept. of General Administration.
(bp) Combined Secretary of Board of Supplies and Secretary of Board of Charities and Reform handles Personnel and Purchasing.
(bq) Mining Commission responsible for mines and minerals registration.
(br) Dept. of Labor includes Agriculture.

STATE OFFICERS OR DEPARTMENTS IN CHARGE OF PRE AUDIT and POST AUDIT
(As of July, 1955)

	Pre Audit	Post Audit
Alabama	Comptroller (a)	Auditor (b) / Chief Examiner (c)
Arizona	Auditor (b)	Post Auditor (d)
Arkansas	Comptroller (e) and Auditor (b)	Legislative Audit Div.
California	Controller (b)	Auditor General (o) / Director of Finance (e)
Colorado	Controller (f)	Auditor (b)
Connecticut	Comptroller (b)	Auditors (i)
Delaware	Auditor (b)	Budget Commission (h)
Florida	Comptroller (b)	Auditor (g)
Georgia	Auditor (i)	Auditor (i)
Idaho	Auditor (b)	Auditor (b)
Illinois	Director of Finance (e) / Auditor (b)	Auditor (b)
Indiana	Auditor (b)	State Examiner (e)
Iowa	Comptroller (e)	Auditor (b)
Kansas	Controller in the Department of Administration (l)	Director of Post Audits (k)
Kentucky	Controller (a)	Auditor (b)
Louisiana	At Agency Level	Auditor (b)
Maine	Controller (a)	Auditor (i)
Maryland	Comptroller (b)	Auditor (e)
Massachusetts	Comptroller (e)	Auditor (b)
Michigan	Controller (e)	Auditor (b)
Minnesota	Auditor (b)	Public Examiner (e)
Mississippi	Auditor (b)	Auditor (b)
Missouri	Comptroller (e)	Auditor (b)
Montana	Board of Examiners (b) / Controller (e) / Auditor (b)	Controller (e) / State Examiner (e) / Auditor (b)
Nebraska	Auditor (b) / Tax Commissioner (e)	Auditor (b) / Tax Commissioner (e)
Nevada	Budget Officer (e) / Comptroller (b)	Legislative Auditor (j)
New Hampshire	Director of Accounts (m)	Legislative Budget Assistant
New Jersey	Director of the Division of Budget and Accounting (e)	Auditor (i)
New Mexico	Auditor (b)	Comptroller (e)
New York	Comptroller (b)	Comptroller (b)
North Carolina	Assistant Budget Director (e)	Auditor (b)
North Dakota	Auditor (b)	State Examiner (e) / Board of Audits (b)
Ohio	Auditor (b) / Director of Finance (e)	Auditor (b)
Oklahoma	State Budget Officer	State Examiner and Inspector (b)
Oregon	Director of Finance and Administration (e) / Secretary of State (b)	Auditor (b) / Secretary of State (b)
Pennsylvania	Auditor General (b)	Auditor General (b)
Rhode Island	Director, Department of Administration (e)	Finance Committee of General Assembly
South Carolina	Comptroller (b)	Auditor (n)
South Dakota	Auditor (b) / Comptroller (i)	Comptroller (i)
Tennessee	Director of Accounts (e)	Comptroller (i)
Texas	Comptroller (b)	Auditor (o)
Utah	Department of Finance	Auditor (b)
Vermont	Auditor (b)	Auditor (b)
Virginia	Comptroller (e)	Auditor (i)
Washington	Director of the Budget (e) / Auditor (b)	Auditor (b)
West Virginia	Auditor (b) / Director of the Budget (e)	Tax Commissioner (e)
Wisconsin	Director of Budget and Accounts (e)	Auditor (e)
Wyoming	Auditor (b)	State Examiner (e)
Alaska	Controller (p)	Legislative Auditor (o)
Hawaii	Auditor (e)	Auditor (e)
Puerto Rico	Secretary of the Treasury (e)	Controller (q)
Virgin Islands	Commissioner of Insular Affairs	Govt. Controller

(a) Appointed by Commissioner of Finance; in Alabama appointed by Director of Finance from Civil Service Register.
(b) Elected.
(c) Appointed by Legislative Committee on Public Accounts, with consent of Senate.
(d) Appointed by Speaker of House and President of Senate, with consent of Legislature.
(e) Appointed by Governor.
(f) Position subject to Civil Service.
(g) Appointed by Governor from list of three names recommended by Legislative Audit Committee.
(h) Three members elected; two members appointed by Governor.
(i) Appointed by Legislature.
(j) Appointed by Legislative Counsel Bureau.
(k) Appointed by State Auditor.
(l) Appointed by Executive Director of Department of Administration from Civil Service Register.
(m) Appointed by the Comptroller subject to approval of Governor.
(n) Appointed by State Budget and Control Board; heads Finance Division of this Board.
(o) Appointed by Legislative Audit Committee; in Texas and Alaska, with consent of Senate.
(p) Appointed by Director of Finance.
(q) Appointed by the Governor with the advice and consent of the majority of the total members of each house

RECENT DEVELOPMENTS IN STATE PURCHASING*

FOR several years there has been a continuing trend in state government to place the purchasing function in an integrated unit, often a division of an over-all administrative and fiscal department. Usually the executive head of such a department is appointed by the Governor, with the consent of the Senate, and serves at the Governor's pleasure. In an increasing number of states, the other personnel of the department, including the purchasing agent, consist entirely of civil service career employees whose duties are concerned strictly with technical matters.

The consolidation of previously separate agencies into a single integrated governmental unit has brought cooperation and coordination into many areas formerly affected by jurisdictional disputes, duplicated effort, and lack of full exchange of mutually beneficial information.

In twenty-four states, the Commonwealth of Puerto Rico and the Virgin Islands the purchasing division is now operating under the integrated plan indicated, or a system closely akin to it. Study groups in some of the remaining states continue to support this system of governmental management.

SPECIFICATIONS AND STANDARDS

Many perplexing problems confront state purchasing divisions. Chief among them perhaps is the need for specifications. This is readily understandable because the purchasing divisions procure the supplies and materials for many widely diversified state agencies: for example, tuberculosis sanatoria, mental hospitals, training schools, colleges, penal and reformatory institutions, highway and conservation departments, all with their highly specialized programs. The number of different commodities required run into many thousands. Under those cir-

cumstances accurate and up-to-date specifications are essential.

The general public, moreover, is becoming increasingly conscious of how its tax money is being spent. It insists that governmental buyers be on the alert to expend the tax dollar wisely and efficiently. Good purchasing involves more than seeking the lowest price. It is measured in end costs, and these start with the specification.

The National Association of State Purchasing Officials, organized in 1947, has been concerned with specifications for years, and has been particularly active in this regard during the past year.

A poll of the thirty-six states represented at the annual meeting of the Association in November, 1954, revealed that only thirteen had a standards engineer on their staffs—a total that now probably has risen to fifteen or sixteen. From the standards engineers a committee was selected to work with the Executive Committee of the Association in developing a plan to make the most effective use of existing specifications and add others most urgently needed by state purchasing officials.

The Specifications Committee believes that almost all present federal specifications are adequate, but that each should be studied individually to determine whether it can best be used in its present form or a slightly modified one. The committee, accordingly, is making a thorough study of federal specifications for use by the various state purchasing departments.

Purchasing offices in various states, especially those employing standards engineers, have volunteered to assist in this study. Each office participating in the project is listing the federal specifications in which it is interested. The committee has assigned to individual states groups of federal specifications for their study and evaluation, in cooperation with manufacturers, suppliers and distributors whose products are sold on a nation-wide basis. A complete report of the study on each specification, when com-

*Prepared by J. STANLEY BIEN, Director, Purchasing Division, Michigan Department of Administration, and President of the National Association of State Purchasing Officials.

pleted, will be forwarded to the committee for further study and for determination whether the specification is to be recommended for state use.

Efforts are being made to standardize specifications, insofar as possible, for use on a nation-wide basis. The first attempt along this line will be for meat and meat products. In March, 1955, a marketing specialist of the U. S. Department of Agriculture met with the Executive and Specifications Committees of the National Association of State Purchasing Officials to learn firsthand of problems encountered by states using the grading and inspection service of the Department of Agriculture, and to discuss some of the difficulties experienced by its inspectors in performing this service. He reported that thirty-one states are now using the service. All of the states have their own specifications, which vary in minor respects. This, in the large packing and shipping areas, requires each inspector to become familiar with each set of specifications. As it is also necessary to stamp each shipment of meat with an identification stamp of the state to which it is consigned, the extra work involved seemed excessive to the department. It was agreed at the joint meeting that the Department of Agriculture would prepare pilot specifications and submit them to the states for further study. The Specifications Committee believes that if specifications on meat are adopted on a nation-wide basis it can hasten the standardization of specifications on a large scale.

Basically there are two classes of standards:

(1) Those which deal with things—their size, shape, color, physical and chemical properties and performance characteristics. (2) Those which deal with operating rules, accounting practices and personnel procedures; these are known as managerial standards. Obviously the governmental purchasing director is very much concerned with both. One function of a standard or specification is to identify a commodity so that the requisitioning agency, the buyer, and the vendor are all talking about the same thing. Otherwise they are apt to become involved in many complications.

Agreement to utilize standard specifications lowers costs by making mass production possible. For example, a few years ago a vendor received within a short interval four fairly large orders for men's work shoes. One order was from the purchasing division of a large city in the Great Lakes area, another from the county in which the city was located, the other two from the purchasing departments of two nearby states. All four orders were accompanied by specifications which called for shoes of comparative types and value, but which had slight differences that necessitated changes in the manufacturing process. Hence mass production of the entire quantity was impossible, and the shoes cost the agencies more than would have been the case had the specifications been identical. This is typical of thousands of cases in which costs could be lowered materially by use of standardized specifications.

Most of the states have standardized to a large degree many of the specifications used within their own domains, particularly those for purchasing for institutions of the same type. It is becoming more and more evident that governmental agencies of different levels, such as municipalities, counties, states and possibly the federal government, could gain by cooperating insofar as possible in standardized specifications on a nation-wide basis. In cases where, due to climatic or other conditions, specifications identical to those suitable in other regions are impractical, regional specifications are an alternative.

ASSOCIATION REPORTS

The National Association of State Purchasing Officials likewise is continuing its "Price Comparison Reports." These consist of lists of various commodities on which states are interested in learning the prices paid by other states. The reports have become popular as a means of preventing, to a degree at least, overcharging by suppliers.

The Association now is preparing a new edition of its report of 1947, "Purchasing by the States," to bring up to date its information on the organization and operation of centralized state purchasing agencies. Similarly, the Association has greatly expanded its *Newsletter*, as a medium for exchange of ideas and information among purchasing officials.

One problem which from time to time causes concern among state purchasing divisions arises from proposed legislation for granting a percentage preference to in-state bidders. Purchasing officials readily agree that, all things being equal, purchase of commodities grown or produced within the state is to be preferred. Beyond that point, however, there is considerable difference of opinion. A number of states have statutes which permit a fixed percentage preference on purchases for goods grown, produced or manufactured within the state. In some states with preference provisions, these are optional with the purchasing director, in others mandatory. Generally, the purchasing directors themselves do not favor preference policies. In 1949 a report of the National Association of State Purchasing Officials summarized: "Preference should be given to state bidders or on state produced commodities only when there is no sacrifice or loss to the state in price or quality." A resolution adopted at the annual meeting in 1954 concluded: "The National Associa-tion of State Purchasing Officials desires to re-affirm its unalterable opposition to the practice of allowing preferential treatment to any firm or individual doing business with a state."

STATE MANUALS

During the period covered by this report, Connecticut published an inspection manual. It outlines in detail the methods used by the state in performing this important function. California published a pamphlet titled, "Selling to the State of California," for presentation to those interested in doing business with the state. This is an excellent, well illustrated treatise fully explaining the manner in which the state takes bids and the things the vendor should and should not do. Following an established custom, copies of both publications were sent to all of the states. They undoubtedly will be used to advantage by many of the states as patterns for similar publications.

2

Personnel Systems

DEVELOPMENTS IN STATE PERSONNEL SYSTEMS*

RECENT developments in state personnel management reflect a continuing desire to find new ways to meet the growing and changing needs of state government. Some of these changes are inaugurated by state legislatures, but equally important improvements are developed on the initiative of elective and career officials. This summary records some of the more important developments in 1954 and 1955.

PERSONNEL STUDY COMMISSIONS

Special personnel study commissions which have been appointed in many states in recent years exemplify the interest of the states in improving personnel administration. During 1955 study groups in Colorado, New Jersey, Illinois, Minnesota and Florida made their reports.

PERSONNEL ACT AMENDMENTS

California. A California amendment of 1955 removes from the Civil Service Law the provision that when the State Personnel Board is considering an appeal by an employee from disciplinary action "it shall be a presumption that the statement of the causes (for the action) is true."

Minnesota. The Minnesota method of appointing the State Personnel Director has been changed under an amendment adopted in 1955. The Civil Service Commission will still make the appointment from among a list of from three to five

*Prepared by the CIVIL SERVICE ASSEMBLY OF THE UNITED STATES AND CANADA.

names, submitted to it by a special examining committee. But the appointment will be for a term of six years; formerly they were without fixed term. The Director may be reappointed by the commission, with Senatorial reconfirmation.

New York. An amendment of 1955 to the New York personnel act provides that a permanent competitive-class employee against whom disciplinary charges are made shall be entitled to a hearing, and that the burden of proving incompetency or misconduct shall be on the person making the charges. Formerly, if the Civil Service Commission found that an employee had been improperly dismissed, it could modify the determination of the appointing officer to permit the employee's transfer to another agency or place his name on a preferred employment list, but the commission had no authority to direct his reinstatement. Now the Civil Service Commission is granted power to reverse a determination of the appointing officer and, if a transfer cannot be arranged, to direct the employee's reinstatement to his former position.

ORGANIZATION OF PERSONNEL SYSTEMS

Florida. An "Act to Create a Merit System of Personnel Administration," adopted in Florida in 1955, provides the basis for what may eventually become a state-wide system. The act gives statutory foundation for the existing Merit System Council, which had been established on the basis of a mutual agreement between the state departments participating in the grant-in-aid programs now administered by the Federal Department of Health, Education, and Welfare. The new law authorizes the Governor to extend the jurisdiction of the Merit System Council to any departments or agencies under his control. Other state agencies, headed by elective officers, may be included under the merit system's jurisdiction through action of these officers, subject to approval by the State Personnel Board.

The State Personnel Board is a new statutory body, created by the act. It consists of the Governor as Chairman, the Secretary of State, the Comptroller, the Commissioner of Agriculture, the Attorney General, the Superintendent of Public Instruction and the Treasurer. These are the constitutional, elective officers. The Personnel Board appoints the Merit System Council, adopts and amends rules to carry out the purpose of the act and performs "such other duties as may be elsewhere specified in the Act, or, if not prohibited, as in the judgment of such Board are deemed necessary to effectuate the provisions hereof." Thus the board has general supervision of the merit system program but is not charged with responsibility for day-to-day operation.

Responsibility for detailed administration is vested, as at present, in the staff of the Merit System Council. The council consists of five members, appointed for overlapping terms of four years each. Its members must "be in sympathy with the application of merit principles to public employment" and cannot be active in partisan politics. The council will act as a hearing board to consider employee appeals. Its decisions on such administrative matters as acceptance or rejection of job applications will be final. Council decisions on disciplinary actions, however, will be subject to review and final action by the State Personnel Board.

Illinois. The provisions of a Personnel Code enacted in Illinois in 1955 will completely revamp the administrative structure of personnel management in this state when they become effective July 1, 1957. The code creates a Personnel Department of cabinet rank, headed by a Personnel Director appointed by the Governor and confirmed by the Senate. The person chosen must have had practical working experience in personnel administration and must not have been active in any political party during the two years preceding appointment. Assisting him will be a bi-partisan Advisory Board of nine members and a Civil Service Commission of three. The Advisory Board will (a) submit names to the Governor for consideration in filling vacancies on the Civil Service Commission; (b) advise the Governor, the Personnel Director and the commission on problems concerning personnel administration; and (c) foster the interest of institutions of learning and of industrial, civic, professional and employee organizations in the improvement of personnel standards in the state service.

The three members of the Civil Service Commission are to be persons "in sympathy with the application of merit principles to public employment." The commission will (a) approve or disapprove civil service rules and amendments to them; (b) approve or disapprove the position classification plan and its amendments; (c) hear appeals of employees who do not accept the allocation of their positions under the classification plan; (d) submit a pay plan and amendments to the Governor; and (e) act as an appeals board for employees covered by the merit provisions of the act.

The Personnel Code has a number of noteworthy features. It creates three separate "areas of jurisdiction" for the Personnel Department. Jurisdiction A concerns the classification and compensation of positions in the state service. Jurisdiction B concerns those positions in the service to which appointments are made on the basis of "merit and fitness." Jurisdiction C concerns conditions of employment. Control of positions may be assigned to the Personnel Department for any or all of those purposes. Thus, a position may be under the Personnel Department for purposes of classification, pay administration and working conditions (such as sick leave, vacation and hours of work) but not for purposes of competitive recruitment and protection against dismissal.

Initially, the new Personnel Code applies only to departments under the Governor. However, jurisdictions may be extended to other departments on request of the appropriate officials and approval of the Governor and the Civil Service Commission. Nonacademic employees of the state colleges and universities will continue under the jurisdiction of the University Civil Service System of Illinois, and Highway Police under the State Police Merit Board. Functions of the present Merit System Council, which serves downstate county departments of welfare, will be transferred to the new Personnel Department.

In addition to the Personnel Code, legislation prohibiting political activities was enacted in Illinois. It applies to all employees "whose employment or tenure is subject to recognized merit principles of public employment"; thirteen specific political activities are prohibited.

SIGNIFICANT CHANGES IN PERSONNEL PRACTICES

One of the major areas of progress in personnel administration has been an increasing recognition that the ultimate goal is to assist operating departments to carry out their primary functions. Significant developments which reflect this concern include the following:

Continuous Examinations. Personnel administration of the states of Illinois, Maryland and Vermont report that they have speeded up their programs of "continuous examinations." Under these programs applicants for employment can be examined and referred to departmental appointing authorities with a minimum of delay.

Promotion Programs. In California, Michigan and Wisconsin, officials of the operating departments are being given a greater part to play in selection of employees for promotion. This is being accomplished through use of "promotional potential ratings." The ratings emphasize preparation for advancement to higher positions rather than proficiency in the employee's present position, measured by the normal "service" or "performance rating."

"Generalist" Personnel Administration. Ten states now have organized their personnel agencies along "generalist" lines, with one personnel agency staff member dealing with operating officials on all or most personnel matters. This type of administrative organization permits personnel actions to be handled more speedily and results in a closer understanding of operating-agency problems by personnel agency staff members.[1]

Personnel Councils. New York and Oregon report that in 1955 they established "personnel councils" to give departmental personnel officers an opportunity to participate in the policy-decision discussions of the central personnel agencies. Oregon also has set up a Personnel Advisory Committee, comprising the heads of the major departments, which meets regularly with the State Personnel Director. Similar groups are in existence in a few other states.

Suggestion Programs. "Suggestion systems"—to encourage employee initiative in proposing means of improving state services—now have been established in at least five states. Oregon and Wisconsin inaugurated theirs in 1955. In New Jersey the limit on awards for individual ideas was raised from $500 to $1,000. California and New York programs, in operation for a number of years, have demonstrated that suggestion systems can make important contributions to the development of better and more efficient ways to conduct the public business.

Certification Methods. Three states have broadened the choice of appointing authorities in selecting employees from eligible lists or employment rosters. Illinois is the first state to adopt the much discussed proposal that candidates for appointment be certified to appointing authorities on the basis of broad categories of competence. The new Personnel Code provides that, with the approval of the Civil Service Commission in each instance, the Personnel Director may certify eligibles on the basis of the following ratings: Superior, Excellent, Well-qualified and Qualified. When these ratings are used they will replace certification of the three highest ranking persons on the list.

Rhode Island also has modified the
(*Continued on page 178*)

---

[1]For an extensive discussion of this type of personnel program see "Personnel Generalist: Experience and Advice," by Lyman H. Cozad and Kenneth O. Warner, *Public Personnel Review*, July, 1955, pp. 131–38.

THE BOOK OF THE STATES
STATE PERSONNEL AGENCIES
Coverage, Organization and Selected Policies

State	Coverage (a)	Number of employees covered	Board members No.	Board members How appt.	Board members Term (years)	Work week for office workers Hrs.	Work week for office workers Sat.	Overtime pay Office workers Comp. time off	Overtime pay Office workers Str. time	Overtime pay Office workers Time and ½
Alabama										
State Personnel Bd......	General	9,678	3	G(b)	6	40	none	X	..	..
Merit System Council...	Local	459	3	G	4	40	(c)	X	..	..
Arizona										
Merit System Council...	Grant-in-aid	850	3	G(d)	6	39	(c)	X	..	..
Merit System Council...	State Police	...	..	..	..	40	....	..	..	..
Arkansas										
Merit System Council...	Grant-in-aid	...	3	G(d)	3	40	none	X	..	..
California										
State Personnel Bd......	General	...	5	G(b)	10	40	none	..	X	..
Colorado										
Civil Service Commn....	General	6,500	3	G	6	37½	none	X	..	..
Merit System Council...	Local	750	3	G	3	40	....	X	..	..
Connecticut										
State Personnel Dept....	General	16,426	none	..	..	35	none	(h)		
Delaware										
Merit System Council...	Grant-in-aid	397	3	A	3	40	none	..	..	X
Florida										
Merit System Council...	Grant-in-aid	3,000	5	GC	4	40	....	X	..	..
Georgia										
Merit System for Pers. Admn..........	General	10,600	3	G(b)	7	37½	(c)	X	..	..
Idaho										
Personnel Council.......	Pub. Asst.	160	3	G	3	40	none		no plan	
Merit System Council...	Grant-in-aid	725	3	G	6	40	none	X	..	..
Illinois										
Civil Service Commn....	General	22,327	3	G(b)	6	40	(c)	X	..	..
Merit System Council...	Local	1,000	3	G(b)	6	37½	(c)	X	..	..
State Police Merit Bd....	State Police	600	3	G(b)	6	40	(c)	..	..	..
Univ. Civil Serv. System.	Nonacademic	6,000	5	(j)	(k)	40	none	X	..	..
Indiana										
State Personnel Bureau..	Grant-in-aid(l)	9,000	4	G	4	38½	none	X	..	..
Iowa										
Merit System Council...	Grant-in-aid	2,000	3	G(d)	6	40	none	X	..	..
Kansas										
Personnel Div., Dept. of Admin.......	General	18,000	3	G(b)	4	42	(c)	X	..	..
Kentucky										
Personnel Council.......	Grant-in-aid(l)	1,517	5	G	4	37½	none	X	..	..
Merit System Advisory Counc.......	Health Dept.	1,150	5	A	3	37½	none	X	..	..
Div. of Personnel.......	General	11,000	3	G	..	37½	none	X	..	..
Fish & Wildlife Commn..	Fish & Wildl.	...	..	..	..	....	....	X	..	..
Police Personnel Bd.....	State Police	...	..	..	..	40	none	X	..	..
Louisiana										
Dept. of Civil Serv......	General	26,000	5	G(m)	6	40	....	X	..	..
Maine										
Dept. of Personnel......	General	6,000	5	(n)	..	40	none	X	..	..
Maryland										
Commnr. of Personnel...	General	15,820	1	G	6	35½	....	(h)		
Massachusetts										
Div. of Civil Service....	General	30,000	5	G(o)	5	37½	none	X	..	..
Michigan										
Civil Service Commn....	General	25,042	4	G	8	40	none	(h)		
Minnesota										
Dept. of Civil Service....	General	14,000	3	G(b)	6	40	....	varies		
County Welfare Merit Sys.	Local	...	..	..	..	....	....	..	..	..
Mississippi										
Merit Sys., Empl. Sec. Commn..........	Empl. Sec.	415	3	G	4	40	none	(h)		
Merit System Council...	Health	812	3	A	3	40	(c)	X	..	..
Merit System Council...	Pub. Welf.	740	3	A	3	40	none	..	..	..
Merit System Council...	Crippled Child. Serv.	...	..	..	..	..	..	..	..	..
Missouri										
Div. of Personnel.......	Grant-in-aid(l)	7,500	3	G(b)	3	40	none	X	..	..
Merit System..........	Crippled Child. Serv.	36	3	C	3	40	none	X	..	..

*Prepared by the Civil Service Assembly of the United States and Canada.

Abbreviations: G—Governor; A—Agencies; GC—Governor and cabinet; Comp.—compensatory.

(a) The pattern of personnel agency coverage varies widely from state to state. Where coverage is shown as "General," most employees in the state agencies are covered by the program. Seldom, however, is coverage complete. "Grant-in-aid" indi-cates that the program covers employees engaged in activities covered by the grant-in-aid programs administered by the U.S. Department of Health, Education and Welfare. "Local" indi-cates that the program covers only local government employees administering grant-in-aid programs. Other entries indicate that the program covers the activities designated, e.g., state police, public welfare, health, employment security.

(b) With confirmation of legislature.
(c) Skeleton force working half day

STATE PERSONNEL AGENCIES (Continued)

Coverage, Organization and Selected Policies

Comp. time off	Str. time	Time and ½	After 1 yr.	Cumulative	No.	Cumulative	Paid holidays	Hospitalization	Medical or surgical	Group life	State
											Alabama
..	X	..	12	24	12	60	13	X	X	X	State Personnel Bd.
..	..	..	12	24	12	60	13	X	X	X	Merit System Council
											Arizona
X	..	..	varies		varies		11(e)	X	X	..	Merit System Council
..	..	..	15	30	15	60	11	..	..	..	Merit System Council
											Arkansas
..	..	..	24	30	18	90	..	..	..	..	Merit System Council
											California
..	X	..	15(f)	30	12	no lim.	11(e)	X	X	X(g)	State Personnel Bd.
											Colorado
X	..	..	15	30	15	60	11(e)	X	X	X(g)	Civil Service Commn.
..	..	..	15	30	15	60	..	..	..	..	Merit System Council
											Connecticut
(h)			15	none	15	90	11	X	X	X(i)	State Personnel Dept.
											Delaware
..	..	..	varies		15	90	10(e)	..	..	..	Merit System Council
											Florida
..	..	..	18	60	13½	90	..	..	..	..	Merit System Council
											Georgia
..	X	..	15	30	15	no lim.	11	X	..	X	Merit System for Pers. Admn.
											Idaho
	no plan		12	24	12	18	8	..	..	..	Personnel Council
..	..	..	14	24	15	30	8	X	X	X	Merit System Council
											Illinois
X	..	..	12	..	12	...	11(e)	..	..	..	Civil Service Commn.
..	..	..	12	24	12	24	11(e)	..	..	..	Merit System Council
..	..	..	12	..	15	30	10	..	..	..	State Police Merit Bd.
..	..	X	10(f)	..	12	no lim.	6	..	..	..	Univ. Civil Serv. System
											Indiana
X	..	..	12	no lim.	12	no lim.	11(e)	X	X	..	State Personnel Bureau
											Iowa
..	..	..	5(f)	..	30	90	6	X	X	X	Merit System Council
											Kansas
..	X	..	18	..	12	90	6	..	..	..	Personnel Div., Dept. of Admin.
											Kentucky
X	..	..	12	24	12	60	13	..	..	..	Personnel Council
X	..	..	12	24	12	60	13	X	X	..	Merit System Advisory Council
..	X	..	12	24	12	60	13	X	X	..	Div. of Personnel
..	..	..	..	..	..	..	..	..	..	..	Fish & Wildlife Commn.
X	..	..	12	24	12	60	13	X	X	..	Police Personnel Bd.
											Louisiana
X	..	..	15	60	15	no lim.	8	X	X(i)	..	Dept. of Civil Service
											Maine
..	..	..	12(f)	24	12	90	9	..	..	X	Dept. of Personnel
											Maryland
(h)			15	30	30	100	13(e)	X	X	X	Commnr. of Personnel
											Massachusetts
X	..	..	10(f)	20	15	no. lim.	11½	X	X	X	Div. of Civil Service
											Michigan
(h)			13(f)	30	13	no lim.	9	X	X	X	Civil Service Commn.
											Minnesota
	varies		12(f)	24	12	100	11	X	X	X	Dept. of Civil Service
..	..	..	..	..	..	...	..	..	..	..	County Welfare Merit Sys.
											Mississippi
..	..	..	24	75	12	60	10	X	X	..	Merit Sys., Empl. Sec. Comn.
X	..	..	12	no lim.	12	no lim.	10	X	X	..	Merit System Council
..	..	..	14	28	60	none	10	X	X	X(i)	Merit System Council
..	..	..	..	..	..	...	..	..	..	..	Merit System Council
											Missouri
X	..	..	15	30	15	75	11	..	..	..	Div. of Personnel
..	..	..	15	30	15	45	4	X	..	..	Merit System

(d) Appointed from names submitted by covered agencies.
(e) Plus election days.
(f) Additional vacation after a number of years, usually ten.
(g) Available through employees' association.
(h) Method optional.
(i) State pays all or part of premium.
(j) Trustees of colleges and universities from among their own membership.

(k) No fixed term.
(l) Plus some additional coverage.
(m) From names submitted by panel of university presidents.
(n) Governor appoints three members for four years each, employees elect one member for two years; these four members choose a fifth member.
(o) With confirmation of Governor's council.
(p) Elected by General Assembly.

STATE PERSONNEL AGENCIES (Continued)
Coverage, Organization and Selected Policies

State	Coverage (a)	Number of employees covered	No.	How appt.	Term (years)	Hrs.	Sat.	Comp. time off	Str. time	Time and ½
Montana										
Joint Merit System.....	Grant-in-aid	625	3	G	6	38	....	X	..	..
Nebraska										
Merit System Council...	Grant-in-aid	941	3	G(b)	3	44	½	X	..	..
Nevada										
Dept. of Personnel......	General	1,800	5	G	4	40	....	X	..	..
New Hampshire										
Div. of Personnel.......	General	4,215	3	G	3	37½	none	X	..	..
New Jersey										
Civil Service Commission	General	23,000	5	G(b)	5	35	none		(h)	
New Mexico										
Merit System Council...	Grant-in-aid	855	3	A	3	38¾	none	X	..	..
New York										
Dept. of Civil Service....	General	75,865	3	G(b)	6	37½	(c)	X	..	..
North Carolina										
State Personnel Dept....	General	25,000	5	G	4	40	none	X	..	..
Merit System Council...	Grant-in-aid	3,600	5	G	6	40	none	X	..	..
North Dakota										
Merit System Council...	Grant-in-aid	503	5	G(d)	5	40	....	..	..	..
Ohio										
Civil Service Commn....	General	45,000	2	G	4	40	(c)	X	..	..
Oklahoma										
State Personnel Board...	Grant-in-aid	1,967	3	G	3	42	(c)	X	..	..
Oregon										
Civil Service Commn....	General	14,500	3	G	3	40	none	X	..	..
Merit System Council...	Local	300	3	G	3	40	(c)	X	..	..
Pennsylvania										
Civil Service Commn....	Grant-in-aid	14,073	3	G	6	37½	none	X	..	..
Rhode Island										
Div. of Personnel Admin.	General	5,976	none	..	..	35	none		(h)	
South Carolina										
Merit System Council...	Emply. Sec.	500	3	A	5	40	none		(h)	
Merit System Council...	Pub. Welf.	600	7	(p)	4	39	(c)	..	X	..
Merit System Council...	Health	...	..	..	..	..	....	..	..	..
South Dakota										
Merit System Council...	Grant-in-aid(l)	500	3	G	3	44	½	no plan		
Civil Service Commn....	State Police	...	..	..	..	....	....	..	..	..
Tennessee										
Dept. of Personnel......	General	14,000	3	G	6	38¾	none	X	..	..
Texas										
Merit System Council...	Grant-in-aid	3,300	3	G	(k)	40	none	X	..	..
Merit System Council...	Health	...	..	..	..	....	....	..	..	..
Utah										
Merit System Council...	Grant-in-aid(l)	890	3	G	6	38	(c)	X	..	..
Vermont										
Personnel Board........	General	2,885	3	G	6	37½	none		(h)	
Virginia										
State Personnel Dept....	General	21,000	none	..	..	40	none	X	..	..
Merit System Council...	Grant-in-aid	2,300	3	A	6	40	none	X	..	..
Washington										
State Personnel Board...	Grant-in-aid(l)	6,300	3	G	6	40	none	X	..	..
West Virginia										
Merit System Council...	Grant-in-aid	1,560	3	G(b)	3	37½	(c)	X	..	..
Wisconsin										
Bureau of Personnel.....	General	14,598	3	G(b)	6	40	none	X	..	..
Wyoming										
Joint Merit System.....	Grant-in-aid	250	3	G(d)	3	38	(c)	..	..	..
Alaska.................										
Merit System Council...	Grant-in-aid	309	3	G	6	37½	none	X	..	..
Guam										
Dept. of Labor & Personnel............	General	1,800	3	G	..	....	....	..	..	..
Hawaii										
Dept. of Civil Service...	General	5,152	5	G(b)	5	40	(c)	X	..	..
Puerto Rico										
Office of Personnel......	General	34,000	3	G(b)	4	37½	none	X	..	..
Virgin Islands										
Div. of Personnel.......	General	1,100	3	G	2	40	none	varies		

STATE PERSONNEL AGENCIES (Continued)

Coverage, Organization and Selected Policies

Overtime pay — Labor & trades			Paid vacation (days)		Sick leave (days)		Paid holidays	Group insurance			State
Comp. time off	Str. time	Time and ½	After 1 yr.	Cumulative	No.	Cumulative		Hospitalization	Medical or surgical	Group life	
..	..	..	15	30	12	60	10(e)	..	..	..	**Montana** Joint Merit System
..	..	..	12	..	12	60	11	X	X	..	**Nebraska** Merit System Council
..	X	..	15(f)	30	15	30	8	X	X	..	**Nevada** Dept. of Personnel
..	X	..	15	30	15	90	11	..	..	..	**New Hampshire** Div. of Personnel
	(h)		12(f)	..	15	no lim.	12	X	X	X(i)	**New Jersey** Civil Service Commission
..	..	..	15	24	12	36	10	X	X	X(i)	**New Mexico** Merit System Council
..	X	..	20	20	12	150	10(e)	X	X	X(g)	**New York** Dept. of Civil Service
	(h)		15	30	10	no lim.	9	..	..	..	**North Carolina** State Personnel Dept.
..	..	..	15	30	10	no lim.	8	..	..	..	Merit System Council
..	..	..	..	..	..	..	11	..	..	..	**North Dakota** Merit System Council
..	X	..	12(f)	..	15	90	10	X	X	..	**Ohio** Civil Service Comm.
..	..	..	15	22½	15	45	9	X	X	X	**Oklahoma** State Personnel Board
X	..	..	10(f)	24	12	90	9	X	X	X	**Oregon** Civil Service Comm.
X	..	..	10(f)	25	12	90	9	..	..	..	Merit System Council
X	..	..	15	none	15	none	12(e)	..	..	..	**Pennsylvania** Civil Service Comm.
	(h)		13(f)	26	18	90	11(e)	..	..	X(i)	**Rhode Island** Div. of Personnel Admin.
..	..	..	18	45	15	90	12(e)	..	..	..	**South Carolina** Merit System Council
..	..	..	18	26	15	26	11(e)	..	..	..	Merit System Council
..	..	..	..	..	..	..	..	..	..	..	Merit System Council
	no plan		15(f)	30	15	30	9(e)	X	X	..	**South Dakota** Merit System Council
..	..	..	..	..	..	..	..	..	..	..	Civil Service Commn.
X	..	..	12	24	12	120	14(e)	X	X	X	**Tennessee** Dept. of Personnel
..	..	..	10	20	18	36	17	X	X	X	**Texas** Merit System Council
..	..	..	..	..	..	..	..	..	..	..	Merit System Council
X	..	..	12	..	12	..	12	X	X	..	**Utah** Merit System Council
	(h)		12(f)	25	12(f)	no lim.	12	X	X	X(i)	**Vermont** Personnel Board
..	X	..	12(f)	24	15	90	8(e)	..	..	..	**Virginia** State Personnel Dept.
X	..	..	12(f)	24	15	90	8(e)	..	..	..	Merit System Council
..	X	..	12(f)	25	12	60	9(e)	..	..	..	**Washington** State Personnel Board
..	..	..	15	30	18	60	11(e)	X	X	X	**West Virginia** Merit System Council
X	..	..	15	..	12	60	10(e)	X	X	..	**Wisconsin** Bureau of Personnel
..	..	..	varies		..	..	10(e)	..	..	..	**Wyoming** Joint Merit System
..	..	..	30	60	15	60	11(c)	X	X(i)	..	**Alaska** Merit System Council
..	..	..	..	..	..	..	..	..	..	..	**Guam** Dept. of Labor & Personnel
X	..	..	21	75	21	54	11(e)	..	..	..	**Hawaii** Dept. of Civil Service
X	..	..	30	60	18	90	18(e)	X	X	X(i)	**Puerto Rico** Office of Personnel
	varies		26	60	15	90	11	..	..	..	**Virgin Islands** Div. of Personnel

"rule of three" to provide that at least six names shall be certified to fill a vacancy when the employment list contains that many names. However, an appointing authority must accept any certification which contains at least three names. In Minnesota appointing authorities will still receive the names of the three highest persons on the list, plus all other applicants who have a score within three points of the highest ranking person certified. All of these changes will give responsible departmental officials greater leeway in appointing the applicant who best fits the requirements of the immediate vacancy.

Survey of Selected Personnel Practices

Such are some of the highlights of recent personnel developments. Additional information on current practices and policies of state personnel agencies is presented in the accompanying table. The data were obtained in a special survey made by the Civil Service Assembly in the summer of 1955.

General Reference Works On State Merit Systems

William E. Mosher, J. Donald Kingsley, and O. Glenn Stahl, *Public Personnel Administration* (3rd ed.), Harper and Brothers, New York, 1950. Civil Service Assembly of the United States and Canada, *Public Personnel Review* (a quarterly journal); *Position Classification in the Public Service; Employee Training in the Public Service; Public Relations of Public Personnel Agencies; Employee Relations in the Public Service; Recruiting Applicants for the Public Service; Oral Tests in Public Personnel Selection; Placement and Probation in the Public Service.* 1313 E. 60th Street, Chicago 37, Illinois.

STATE EMPLOYMENT IN 1954 AND 1955*

STATE GOVERNMENT payrolls amounted to $319 million per month in January, 1955. This compares with $275 million a year earlier and with $136 million in January, 1947.

During 1954, state employment reached a new high, exceeding 1.2 million for the first time. The total ranged closely about this level during the twelve months that ended in January, 1955, except for the summer months which were marked by the usual seasonal drop in educational employees. Even in midsummer of 1954, however, the level of state employment was above 1 million.

As indicated by the chart below and in Table 1, state employment rose rapidly after World War II and then more gradually, while state payroll expenditure has climbed at an even more consistent and rapid rate during recent years. January-to-January changes in state employment and payrolls since 1947 have been as shown in the following table in column two.

*Adapted from U. S. Bureau of the Census, *Public Employment in January, 1955* and *State Distribution of Public Employment in 1954.*

| Year | Per cent change | |
	Number of employees	Monthly payrolls
1954–1955........	6.5	8.9
1953–1954........	1.8	6.7
1952–1953........	4.3	9.1
1951–1952........	2.2	14.8
1950–1951........	2.1	5.3
1949–1950........	6.6	11.5
1948–1949........	6.4	13.7
1947–1948........	6.5	20.3

Figures available for nonschool personnel of state governments back to 1940 show that their total number dropped off from a 1940–41 level of about 530,000 to a wartime low for January of less than 450,000 in 1944 and 1945. The postwar increase rapidly cancelled out this drop, and by January, 1955 state nonschool employees numbered 843,000, or 59 per cent more than before World War II.

Of the total number of persons on state government payrolls in January, 1955, 1,027,000 were employed on a full-time basis and 180,000 were part-time employees. All but 7,000 of the rise of 94,000 in state employment during the twenty-

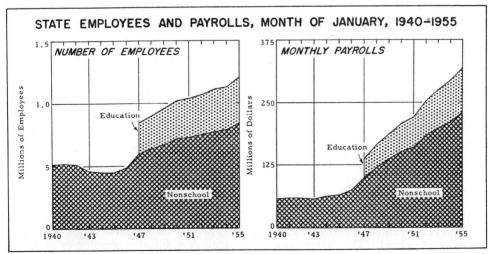

STATE EMPLOYEES AND PAYROLLS, MONTH OF JANUARY, 1940–1955

four month interval from January, 1953, to January, 1955, involved full-time personnel.

FUNCTIONAL DISTRIBUTION OF STATE PAYROLLS

More state personnel and payrolls are required for education than for any other function. As indicated in Table 2, the 359,000 state educational employees include 287,000 working for institutions of higher education, 50,000 directly engaged with public elementary and secondary schools, and 23,000 others—mainly employees of central state educational agencies and offices. Altogether this function involves about three-tenths of all personnel and payrolls of state governments.

Hospitals and highways are close together as the next ranking functions in terms of state employment, and together they account for another one-third of the total. Next, as employing functions, come natural resources activities, general control, administration of employment security, and public welfare.

A functional distribution of the employment and payrolls of individual state governments appears in Tables 5 and 6. Some of the interstate differences evident there result from differing degrees of delegation of responsibility to local governments for particular functions.

THE STATES' SHARE OF PUBLIC EMPLOYMENT

State governments accounted for almost 17 per cent of the 7,232,000 persons on public payrolls—federal, state and local—in October, 1954. The states have about 50 per cent as many employees as the federal government and about one-third as many as all local governments combined. Of total public payrolls amounting to $2,088,000 for the month of October, 1954, the states accounted for 15 per cent.

The states' share of public employment differs widely as among various governmental functions. National defense and the postal service are federal functions, involving more than one-fifth of all public employment at that level. At the other extreme, local schools, police and fire protection, and local recreation and public utility services primarily involve local government personnel. The states account,

however, for most employment of public institutions of higher education and for a sizeable fraction of all governmental employees engaged in highway, public welfare, health and hospital, and natural resources activities. These facts are reflected in Table 2, relating to employment and payrolls of state and local governments, and in the following summary distribution of civilian public personnel of all governmental levels as of October, 1954:

Function	Number of employees (in thousands)			
	Total	Federal (civilian)	State	Local
National defense.....	1,157	1,157	(a)	.....
Postal service........	504	504	.....	.....
Education...........	2,059	9	359	1,691
Highways...........	482	4	199	278
Health and hospitals..	662	166	244	252
Police..............	281	22	23	236
Local fire protection..	174	.....	.....	174
Natural resources.....	279	158	92	29
General control......	508	111	68	329
All other............	1,126	242	213	672
Total............	7,232	2,373	1,198	3,661

(a) Minor numbers for state National Guard included in "All other."

Differences between states in the pattern for assignment of functional responsibilities as between the state and local governments also result in considerable geographic variation in the fraction of all state and local employment accounted for by the state governments.

Nationally, local government personnel outnumbers the personnel of the states by a ratio of three to one, and in some areas the ratio is over four to one. In North Carolina and Delaware, however, persons on state payrolls outnumber local employees—mainly reflecting direct state payment of local school staffs—and employees of some other state governments also comprise a considerably larger-than-average fraction of the state-local total.

AVERAGE MONTHLY EARNINGS

Average monthly earnings of full-time state government employees in October, 1954 amounted to $292. This compares with $287 in October, 1953 and with $271 in October, 1952.

There is considerable range in average earnings of full-time employees as among various individual states. As indicated in Table 4, the average earnings in October, 1954 ranged from over $300 per month for twelve state governments down to less than $240 per month for ten others.

EMPLOYMENT BY INDIVIDUAL STATES

Practically one-half of all payrolls and employees of the forty-eight state governments are accounted for by eight states. These, in descending order of number of employees, are New York, California, North Carolina, Pennsylvania, Ohio, Illinois, Texas and Michigan.

The relatively high volume of state employment in North Carolina reflects state operation of local public schools there, in lieu of local operation as is commonly the case elsewhere.

As this example suggests, care must be exercised in comparing employment and payroll data for individual state governments, which differ considerably in the scope and intensity of functions they perform. These differences arise from economic, geographic and traditional factors that influence the total scale of public services and the allocation of responsibility as between the states and their respective local governments, particularly in such fields as schools, highways, public welfare, and health and hospitals.

It will be noted from the summary state-by-state figures in Table 3 that a relatively high level of state government employment often is associated with a relatively low level of employment by local governments. The Bureau of the Census report, *State Distribution of Public Employment in 1954*, provides additional data in this regard by showing employment and payrolls for both state and local governments, by state-area, in terms of various functions.

TABLE 1
SUMMARY OF STATE EMPLOYMENT: 1940–1955

| Month and year | Number of employees (in thousands) | | | | | | Monthly payroll (in millions) | | | | | |
| | Total | | | Full-time | | | Total | | | Full-time | | |
	All	School	Non-school	All	School	Non-school	All	School	Non-school	All	School	Non-school
1955:												
January.........	1,207	364	843	1,027	245	781	$318.8	$89.2	$229.6	$301.1	$80.3	$220.7
1954:												
December.......	1,196	362	834	1,019	245	774	316.6	88.2	228.4	299.0	79.9	219.2
November.......	1,205	366	839	1,023	246	778	317.2	89.8	227.4	298.5	79.6	218.8
October.........	1,198	359	839	1,015	239	776	314.6	87.3	227.3	296.1	77.7	218.5
September.......	1,166	322	844	999	220	779	305.0	78.6	226.4	286.8	69.9	217.0
August.........	1,098	249	849	960	177	783	293.2	65.1	228.1	275.0	57.3	217.7
July...........	1,089	253	837	954	181	773	290.0	66.4	223.6	271.6	58.0	213.6
June...........	1,138	308	830	973	209	765	296.1	76.2	220.0	277.8	67.5	210.3
May...........	1,164	348	816	989	234	754	303.4	86.0	217.3	284.0	76.8	207.2
April...........	1,154	351	804	975	233	742	295.0	85.7	209.3	281.8	76.2	205.6
March.........	1,156	355	801	974	233	741	299.9	85.0	215.0	282.0	75.7	206.3
February.......	1,150	353	797	971	233	738	296.4	84.7	211.6	278.5	75.5	203.0
January.........	1,133	346	786	959	232	726	292.8	82.2	210.6	275.5	73.8	201.7
January, prior years:												
1953...........	1,113	341	773	940	233	707	274.5	77.0	197.6	257.4	69.4	188.0
1952...........	1,067	315	752	906	215	691	251.6	68.4	183.2	234.6	61.2	173.3
1951...........	1,044	312	732	NA	NA	NA	219.1	61.2	157.9	NA	NA	NA
1950...........	1,023	306	717	NA	NA	NA	208.1	58.1	150.0	NA	NA	NA
1949...........	960	288	672	NA	NA	NA	186.6	51.6	135.0	NA	NA	NA
1948...........	902	267	635	NA	NA	NA	164.1	45.4	118.7	NA	NA	NA
1947...........	847	246	601	NA	NA	NA	136.4	36.5	99.9	NA	NA	NA
1946...........	NA	NA	488	NA	NA	NA	NA	NA	76.2	NA	NA	NA
1945...........	NA	NA	445	NA	NA	NA	NA	NA	64.3	NA	NA	NA
1944...........	NA	NA	451	NA	NA	NA	NA	NA	62.4	NA	NA	NA
1943...........	NA	NA	464	NA	NA	NA	NA	NA	57.4	NA	NA	NA
1942...........	NA	NA	512	NA	NA	NA	NA	NA	58.4	NA	NA	NA
1941...........	NA	NA	517	NA	NA	NA	NA	NA	58.5	NA	NA	NA
1940...........	NA	NA	513	NA	NA	NA	NA	NA	57.3	NA	NA	NA

"NA" indicates data not available.

TABLE 2
EMPLOYMENT AND PAYROLLS' OF STATE AND LOCAL GOVERNMENTS, BY FUNCTION: OCTOBER, 1954

| Function | Number of employees (in thousands) | | | October payrolls (in millions) | | |
	Total	State	Local	Total	State	Local
Total all functions..........................	4,859	1,198	3,661	$1,318.3	$314.6	$1,003.6
Education, total..........................	2,050	359	1,691	600.1	87.3	512.8
Public schools........................	1,720	50	1,670	521.2	14.0	507.2
Institutions of higher education..........	307	287	21	72.6	67.0	5.6
Other................................	23	23	....	6.3	6.3	....
Highways................................	478	199	278	118.9	53.6	65.3
Public welfare............................	100	42	59	25.6	11.2	14.4
Health..................................	73	27	46	19.5	7.6	11.9
Hospitals................................	423	217	206	95.6	50.9	44.7
Police...................................	259	23	236	79.3	7.3	72.0
Local fire protection......................	174	....	174	41.4	....	41.4
Natural resources........................	121	92	29	30.0	23.7	6.3
Sanitation...............................	114	....	114	31.5	....	31.5
Local parks and recreation................	68	....	68	16.8	....	16.8
Housing and community redevelopment.....	26	....	26	7.6	....	7.6
Employment security administration........	46	46	....	14.1	14.1	....
State liquor stores........................	14	14	....	3.8	3.8	....
Local utilities, total......................	233	....	233	75.3	....	75.3
Water supply..........................	101	....	101	27.2	....	27.2
Electric light and power................	48	....	48	16.6	....	16.6
Transit...............................	79	....	79	30.4	....	30.4
Gas supply............................	4	....	4	1.2	....	1.2
General control...........................	397	68	329	86.7	21.5	65.2
All other................................	284	112	172	72.4	34.0	38.4

TABLE 3
NUMBER OF STATE AND LOCAL EMPLOYEES: OCTOBER, 1954

State	Number of employees				Number per 10,000 population (a)		
	State		Local		Full-time equivalent		
	Total	Full-time equivalent	Total	Full-time equivalent	State and local	State	Local
United States..............	1,197,861	1,071,474	3,661,265	3,237,051	267.3	66.5	200.8
Alabama......................	20,284	17,529	57,611	54,057	229.4	56.2	173.2
Arizona......................	8,060	7,014	20,727	19,182	263.8	70.6	193.2
Arkansas.....................	12,933	10,699	31,385	27,462	199.8	56.0	143.8
California....................	89,130	81,641	349,642	319,359	319.4	65.0	254.4
Colorado.....................	13,704	11,310	37,835	33,201	305.7	77.7	228.0
Connecticut..................	NA	NA	45,026	39,632	NA	NA	178.6
Delaware.....................	6,149	5,715	5,328	4,759	285.4	155.7	129.7
Florida.......................	26,032	24,823	83,894	80,270	298.2	70.4	227.8
Georgia......................	20,584	19,423	69,096	64,975	230.6	53.1	177.5
Idaho........................	7,106	5,742	14,037	11,461	279.7	93.4	186.3
Illinois.......................	47,594	41,277	203,694	177,314	238.5	45.0	193.5
Indiana.......................	30,050	25,569	90,675	78,179	246.5	60.7	185.8
Iowa.........................	23,201	19,596	67,410	56,837	289.7	74.3	215.4
Kansas.......................	18,372	15,684	50,863	42,699	289.6	77.8	211.8
Kentucky.....................	18,297	16,589	48,029	43,306	200.0	55.4	144.6
Louisiana....................	34,354	31,556	57,794	54,224	293.4	107.9	185.5
Maine........................	9,371	8,587	21,555	15,400	257.9	92.3	165.6
Maryland	18,732	17,925	50,919	47,835	252.7	68.9	183.8
Massachusetts................	36,264	35,353	131,257	115,162	303.8	71.4	232.4
Michigan.....................	44,495	39,991	176,837	151,239	272.3	56.9	215.4
Minnesota....................	27,185	22,916	87,358	70,127	299.8	73.9	225.9
Mississippi...................	15,890	14,241	41,153	36,980	232.4	64.6	167.8
Missouri......................	23,188	19,720	85,663	74,985	228.0	47.5	180.5
Montana......................	7,121	5,994	15,127	12,991	302.3	95.4	206.9
Nebraska.....................	12,869	10,971	38,738	32,250	316.4	80.3	236.1
Nevada.......................	1,966	1,746	6,247	5,633	338.5	80.1	258.4
New Hampshire...............	6,554	5,414	14,505	9,001	271.0	101.8	169.2
New Jersey...................	27,251	25,447	122,176	108,367	254.9	48.5	206.4
New Mexico...................	9,673	7,922	15,180	14,155	282.7	101.4	181.3
New York.....................	96,217	94,346	443,858	408,142	325.6	61.1	264.5
North Carolina...............	80,275	75,237	28,628	24,639	235.0	177.0	58.0
North Dakota.................	5,730	4,783	19,175	13,250	283.5	75.2	208.3
Ohio.........................	48,186	41,503	206,429	174,222	252.2	48.5	203.7
Oklahoma....................	24,104	19,530	52,572	45,949	288.7	86.1	202.6
Oregon.......................	18,684	16,282	38,250	33,407	303.2	99.3	203.9
Pennsylvania.................	73,805	65,734	186,383	164,337	213.4	61.0	152.4
Rhode Island.................	8,083	7,618	14,753	13,334	254.3	92.5	161.8
South Carolina...............	16,098	15,071	42,685	39,286	242.9	67.3	175.6
South Dakota.................	6,178	5,377	19,130	14,113	292.2	80.6	211.6
Tennessee....................	19,398	16,692	67,790	61,909	233.8	49.6	184.2
Texas........................	47,371	40,538	182,861	171,177	250.0	47.9	202.1
Utah.........................	8,873	6,950	19,731	15,497	296.5	91.8	204.7
Vermont......................	4,860	4,110	8,142	5,761	256.4	106.8	149.6
Virginia......................	33,372	30,736	62,737	57,532	246.0	85.7	160.3
Washington...................	24,939	20,622	69,254	59,155	314.1	81.2	232.9
West Virginia.................	18,489	15,472	32,111	29,619	231.6	79.5	152.1
Wisconsin....................	23,714	18,815	95,780	75,437	263.4	52.6	210.8
Wyoming.....................	3,476	2,977	8,935	7,631	340.0	95.4	244.6

"NA" indicates data not available.
(a) Computation based on estimated population in continental United States as of July 1, 1954.

THE BOOK OF THE STATES

TABLE 4

STATE AND LOCAL GOVERNMENT PAYROLLS, BY STATE: OCTOBER, 1954

State	Total payroll for October					Computed average October earnings		
	Amount (in thousands)			Per cent of state-local total		Full-time employees		
	Total	State	Local	State	Local	State and local	State	Local
United States	$1,318,259.9	$314,641.3	$1,003,618.6	23.9	76.1	$306	$292	$310
Alabama........	16,531.7	4,284.2	12,247.5	25.9	74.1	231	244	227
Arizona.........	8,190.1	2,010.3	6,179.8	24.5	75.5	313	289	322
Arkansas........	8,422.0	2,562.7	5,859.3	30.4	69.6	221	239	214
California.......	151,723.2	30,884.7	120,838.5	20.4	79.6	378	377	378
Colorado........	12,528.4	3,321.9	9,206.5	26.5	73.5	282	294	278
Connecticut......	NA	NA	13,614.8	NA	NA	NA	NA	344
Delaware........	3,127.9	1,596.1	1,531.8	51.0	49.0	299	280	321
Florida..........	27,955.1	6,288.4	21,666.7	22.5	77.5	266	253	270
Georgia.........	18,944.1	4,611.2	14,332.9	24.3	75.7	224	237	221
Idaho...........	4,686.0	1,591.6	3,094.4	34.0	66.0	273	278	271
Illinois.........	77,575.5	12,974.2	64,601.3	16.7	83.3	352	298	365
Indiana.........	31,714.5	7,417.5	24,297.0	23.4	76.6	306	285	312
Iowa............	20,253.3	5,222.0	15,031.3	25.8	74.2	265	264	265
Kansas..........	15,713.8	4,211.2	11,502.6	26.8	73.2	269	267	270
Kentucky........	14,429.6	3,920.5	10,509.1	27.2	72.8	241	235	243
Louisiana........	21,903.2	7,187.4	14,715.8	32.8	67.2	256	227	272
Maine...........	5,859.2	2,257.3	3,601.9	38.5	61.5	246	264	235
Maryland........	19,775.6	5,194.9	14,580.7	26.3	73.7	301	289	305
Massachusetts....	44,944.4	10,430.2	34,514.2	23.2	76.8	299	295	300
Michigan........	71,412.5	14,459.1	56,953.4	20.2	79.8	373	360	376
Minnesota........	29,178.4	7,276.0	21,902.4	24.9	75.1	312	308	313
Mississippi.......	10,482.5	3,156.7	7,325.8	30.1	69.9	205	221	199
Missouri..........	24,422.7	4,970.6	19,452.1	20.4	79.6	257	247	260
Montana.........	5,939.0	1,901.8	4,037.2	32.0	68.0	314	317	312
Nebraska.........	11,117.8	2,643.0	8,474.8	23.8	76.2	258	241	263
Nevada..........	2,387.4	646.1	1,741.3	27.1	72.9	323	369	309
New Hampshire...	3,860.6	1,495.7	2,364.9	38.7	61.3	268	276	263
New Jersey.......	44,850.8	8,157.6	36,693.2	18.2	81.8	335	320	339
New Mexico.......	6,513.6	2,214.5	4,299.1	34.0	66.0	295	277	304
New York........	172,878.2	31,372.2	141,506.0	18.1	81.9	344	332	347
North Carolina...	26,931.6	21,377.8	5,553.8	79.4	20.6	270	285	226
North Dakota.....	4,875.7	1,441.7	3,434.0	29.6	70.4	271	301	260
Ohio............	65,976.6	12,375.9	53,600.7	18.8	81.2	306	296	308
Oklahoma........	16,397.3	4,654.9	11,742.4	28.4	71.6	251	238	256
Oregon..........	16,250.1	5,195.8	11,054.3	32.0	68.0	327	318	331
Pennsylvania.....	70,613.8	19,040.9	51,572.9	27.0	73.0	308	287	314
Rhode Island.....	5,987.1	1,999.4	3,987.7	33.4	66.6	286	262	300
South Carolina...	11,774.0	3,504.6	8,269.4	29.8	70.2	216	232	211
South Dakota....	4,924.2	1,455.8	3,468.4	29.6	70.4	251	264	247
Tennessee........	18,702.7	3,870.4	14,832.3	20.7	79.3	238	232	240
Texas............	59,206.4	11,954.8	47,251.6	20.2	79.8	279	294	276
Utah............	6,391.7	2,074.2	4,317.5	32.5	67.5	285	298	280
Vermont.........	2,515.8	1,103.8	1,412.0	43.9	56.1	256	268	247
Virginia.........	22,106.7	7,339.4	14,767.3	33.2	66.8	250	238	257
Washington......	26,343.8	6,925.8	19,418.0	26.3	73.7	330	333	329
West Virginia.....	11,783.8	3,633.9	8,149.9	30.8	69.2	261	234	276
Wisconsin........	30,760.2	6,243.4	24,516.8	20.3	79.7	325	327	325
Wyoming.........	3,008.1	937.1	2,071.0	31.2	68.8	284	314	272

"NA" indicates data not available.

TABLE 5
FUNCTIONAL DISTRIBUTION OF STATE EMPLOYEES, BY STATE:
OCTOBER, 1954

State	Total, all functions	Education	High-ways	Health and hospitals	Police	Public welfare	Natural resources	State liquor stores	General control	All other
United States..	1,197,861	359,265	199,415	243,595	23,107	41,621	91,987	14,051	67,629	157,191
Alabama.........	20,284	6,578	3,215	2,790	592	966	2,530	631	433	2,549
Arizona..........	8,060	3,144	1,609	856	143	277	688	...	585	758
Arkansas.........	12,933	4,534	2,436	2,418	231	500	1,107	...	881	826
California........	89,130	27,047	9,727	12,642	2,485	1,603	9,999	...	7,797	17,830
Colorado.........	13,704	5,790	1,420	2,327	256	191	1,249	...	1,275	1,196
Connecticut.......	NA	NA	NA	NA	NA	NA	NA	NA	NA	NA
Delaware.........	6,149	2,272	965	1,230	175	154	442	...	573	338
Florida...........	26,032	8,045	5,160	4,430	510	1,210	3,158	...	1,014	2,505
Georgia..........	20,584	6,044	4,977	3,448	455	204	2,313	...	1,376	1,767
Idaho............	7,106	2,429	1,507	701	153	168	1,090	223	334	501
Illinois...........	47,594	12,322	6,425	12,241	936	2,673	1,381	...	3,748	7,868
Indiana..........	30,050	11,134	3,778	7,137	702	591	1,771	...	1,771	3,166
Iowa.............	23,201	8,747	2,328	5,426	279	1,347	1,538	842	876	1,818
Kansas...........	18,372	7,607	3,019	3,425	148	400	1,092	...	1,034	1,647
Kentucky.........	18,297	4,216	5,932	2,052	437	794	1,554	...	626	2,686
Louisiana.........	34,354	9,294	5,113	9,937	450	1,913	3,198	...	1,853	2,596
Maine............	9,371	1,537	2,969	1,472	195	312	1,128	290	701	767
Maryland.........	18,732	4,154	3,138	5,920	425	47	1,030	...	1,278	2,740
Massachusetts.....	36,264	2,773	7,277	12,471	535	1,171	994	...	3,071	7,972
Michigan.........	44,954	16,135	3,066	11,175	990	1,817	2,697	846	2,710	5,059
Minnesota........	27,185	10,719	4,003	5,470	290	397	2,502	...	1,375	2,429
Mississippi........	15,890	4,248	2,774	3,113	331	726	3,073	...	318	1,307
Missouri..........	23,188	5,444	4,833	4,511	531	1,692	1,543	...	1,220	3,414
Montana..........	7,121	2,071	1,445	765	122	341	1,143	299	402	533
Nebraska.........	12,869	4,070	2,143	2,335	250	92	1,372	...	751	1,856
Nevada...........	1,966	426	723	136	40	53	194	...	155	239
New Hampshire....	6,554	1,585	1,641	1,288	80	207	526	236	358	633
New Jersey........	27,251	4,525	3,864	6,594	916	1,057	1,809	...	2,952	5,534
New Mexico.......	9,673	3,228	1,750	776	117	835	1,289	...	691	987
New York.........	96,217	9,834	13,085	33,860	1,315	1,657	4,702	...	3,837	27,927
North Carolina....	80,275	56,129	9,425	5,686	663	108	2,843	...	1,442	3,979
North Dakota.....	5,730	2,130	821	919	47	102	606	...	272	833
Ohio..............	48,186	13,039	7,821	13,081	947	2,138	1,994	1,943	2,018	5,205
Oklahoma.........	24,104	9,674	2,665	4,552	512	1,124	2,675	...	1,196	1,706
Oregon...........	18,684	4,417	3,096	2,345	446	909	2,632	507	2,379	1,953
Pennsylvania......	73,805	9,857	16,913	18,470	2,115	3,615	2,852	4,822	5,875	9,286
Rhode Island......	8,083	1,198	987	2,081	186	669	541	...	640	1,781
South Carolina....	16,098	3,963	4,040	2,540	368	639	2,351	...	747	1,450
South Dakota.....	6,178	2,260	1,250	852	105	242	521	...	118	830
Tennessee.........	19,398	5,245	4,249	3,005	513	1,068	2,627	...	807	1,884
Texas.............	47,371	17,069	11,614	6,542	580	1,842	3,313	...	1,185	5,226
Utah..............	8,873	4,436	1,020	550	165	236	878	196	299	1,093
Vermont..........	4,860	1,394	1,039	550	180	121	461	102	541	472
Virginia..........	33,372	7,728	10,705	6,990	707	220	2,556	1,343	707	2,416
Washington.......	24,939	9,021	3,430	2,855	560	1,579	2,543	968	1,528	2,455
West Virginia.....	18,489	5,545	5,172	2,240	286	651	1,788	783	796	1,228
Wisconsin........	23,714	11,073	1,075	2,983	89	1,990	2,270	...	1,275	2,959
Wyoming.........	3,476	1,140	833	375	42	176	454	20	115	321

"NA" indicates data not available.

TABLE 6

TABLE 6
FUNCTIONAL DISTRIBUTION OF STATE PAYROLLS, BY STATE: OCTOBER, 1954

(In thousands of dollars)

State	Total, all functions	Education	Highways	Health and hospitals	Police	Public welfare	Natural resources	State liquor stores	General control	All other
United States...	$314,641.3	$87,302.8	$53,621.5	$58,466.1	$7,274.4	$11,158.6	$23,656.2	$3,755.6	$21,474.5	$47,931.6
Alabama.........	4,284.2	1,194.1	699.7	477.4	168.3	238.3	514.3	155.5	161.1	675.5
Arizona.........	2,010.3	573.4	522.3	184.8	50.5	78.9	182.5	....	187.9	230.0
Arkansas........	2,562.7	712.2	536.2	537.7	62.0	95.6	187.4	....	205.8	225.8
California.......	30,884.7	8,394.5	4,001.5	3,901.2	887.5	496.4	3,811.7	....	2,855.8	6,536.1
Colorado........	3,321.9	1,135.2	484.6	571.6	86.1	52.9	312.9	....	327.4	351.2
Connecticut.....	NA	NA	NA	NA	NA	NA	NA	NA	NA	NA
Delaware........	1,596.1	711.1	254.4	238.3	53.9	35.8	78.4	....	149.1	75.1
Florida..........	6,288.4	1,925.6	1,146.6	1,003.5	138.5	229.1	804.6	....	378.1	662.4
Georgia.........	4,611.2	1,374.5	1,044.8	728.5	98.3	59.9	469.2	....	363.7	472.3
Idaho...........	1,591.6	420.6	445.3	147.7	44.7	47.7	232.0	34.4	97.4	121.8
Illinois..........	12,974.2	3,198.9	1,893.9	2,928.8	301.5	773.5	366.3	....	1,208.8	2,302.5
Indiana.........	7,417.5	2,863.6	993.1	1,521.6	203.7	128.4	484.2	....	451.2	771.7
Iowa............	5,222.0	2,045.0	624.8	1,030.0	76.6	253.9	372.1	176.9	212.9	429.8
Kansas..........	4,211.2	1,631.4	822.1	682.2	47.7	99.1	250.1	....	267.0	411.6
Kentucky.......	3,920.5	931.0	1,068.7	448.7	113.8	174.7	279.6	....	196.5	707.5
Louisiana.......	7,187.4	1,685.6	1,096.3	1,645.2	126.0	575.5	762.0	....	525.5	771.3
Maine...........	2,257.3	315.6	651.4	376.6	59.2	78.6	286.8	72.5	206.4	210.2
Maryland........	5,194.9	1,205.2	889.4	1,434.8	112.0	17.9	315.0	....	396.3	824.3
Massachusetts....	10,430.2	712.6	1,911.0	3,265.6	180.1	329.5	324.7	....	1,058.4	2,648.3
Michigan........	14,459.1	5,158.0	1,195.5	3,184.9	356.8	595.1	940.9	284.4	998.2	1,745.3
Minnesota.......	7,276.0	2,732.7	1,087.2	1,409.6	95.3	100.9	716.8	....	365.3	768.2
Mississippi......	3,156.7	799.3	543.9	453.0	86.4	179.1	627.5	....	122.7	344.8
Missouri........	4,970.6	958.8	1,234.6	772.3	157.6	345.5	375.9	....	373.7	752.2
Montana........	1,901.8	453.5	541.4	185.9	36.5	86.6	292.3	73.3	96.4	135.9
Nebraska........	2,643.0	679.1	542.6	478.7	88.5	24.7	371.3	....	201.6	256.5
Nevada.........	646.1	122.5	243.6	37.1	15.7	16.2	61.3	....	72.4	77.3
New Hampshire..	1,495.7	304.4	341.2	314.3	28.4	53.7	110.7	65.8	110.4	166.8
New Jersey......	8,157.6	1,215.7	1,261.1	1,757.0	315.4	347.9	460.3	....	1,010.6	1,789.6
New Mexico.....	2,214.5	680.7	444.5	157.3	40.1	208.6	226.2	....	202.9	254.2
New York.......	31,372.2	3,339.9	3,910.7	10,382.7	416.3	559.8	1,198.3	....	1,693.0	9,871.5
North Carolina...	21,377.8	15,508.5	2,334.1	1,104.2	201.0	33.3	720.4	....	466.8	1,009.5
North Dakota.....	1,441.7	500.9	262.6	194.2	14.6	24.8	144.2	....	76.0	224.4
Ohio............	12,375.9	2,739.5	2,357.5	3,173.8	320.5	568.6	545.1	494.7	690.1	1,486.1
Oklahoma........	4,654.9	1,558.2	638.1	804.3	161.5	279.2	471.0	....	280.9	461.7
Oregon..........	5,195.8	1,115.6	1,054.9	584.9	158.6	245.1	665.5	141.8	666.9	562.5
Pennsylvania.....	19,040.9	2,289.4	4,067.0	4,279.5	687.6	1,039.5	738.5	1,337.5	1,807.9	2,794.0
Rhode Island.....	1,999.4	311.7	242.7	429.6	64.6	166.1	126.5	....	210.0	448.2
South Carolina...	3,504.6	874.6	750.9	509.4	96.7	159.4	540.6	....	199.4	373.6
South Dakota....	1,455.8	482.9	375.7	139.0	27.8	62.7	137.7	....	29.5	200.5
Tennessee.......	3,870.4	1,055.4	849.6	556.5	137.3	250.2	407.0	....	192.5	421.9
Texas...........	11,954.8	3,673.5	3,640.0	1,420.9	178.5	447.3	754.6	....	358.3	1,481.7
Utah............	2,074.2	946.7	332.1	140.9	45.1	66.0	150.1	32.8	71.8	288.7
Vermont.........	1,103.8	252.0	266.8	134.7	54.5	33.2	122.9	27.0	81.1	131.6
Virginia.........	7,339.4	1,693.6	2,124.0	1,447.7	218.9	56.9	596.9	384.3	199.9	617.2
Washington......	6,925.8	2,142.6	1,214.0	680.0	186.3	466.4	766.1	258.0	456.1	756.3
West Virginia.....	3,633.9	828.0	1,143.9	389.8	73.5	141.0	316.8	210.6	231.2	299.1
Wisconsin........	6,243.4	2,592.5	371.6	729.0	29.2	572.0	626.9	....	418.0	904.2
Wyoming........	937.1	271.7	268.4	74.2	16.2	43.6	131.9	6.1	37.6	87.4

"NA" indicates data not available.

PUBLIC EMPLOYEE RETIREMENT SYSTEMS AND FEDERAL SOCIAL SECURITY*

THE 1954 amendments to the Social Security Act, effective September 1, 1954, established permissive coverage under its old-age and survivors provisions to about 3.5 million state and local government employees who were members of retirement systems.

The 1950 social security amendments had extended eligibility to state and local government employees who were not members of retirement systems, but continued the exclusion of employees who were in positions covered by an existing system on the date their group was brought under social security. The 1954 legislation extended coverage to the latter group under certain prescribed conditions, with the exception of policemen and firemen who are members of retirement funds.

Thus public agencies desiring to coordinate their retirement systems with federal social security may do so. This can be accomplished through certain legislative procedures and upon the affirmative approval of at least a majority of the active members of the retirement system (pensioners excluded). Action on social security coverage is optional, first with the state legislature; then with the local legislative body if the retirement plan was originally established by local ordinance; and lastly with the members of the retirement system, who must approve any change in their status which involves social security coverage.

The states are granted the privilege of entering into a voluntary agreement with the federal government for the extension of social security coverage to members of existing retirement systems if the Governor of the state certifies to the Secretary of Health, Education, and Welfare that the following conditions have been met:

(a) A referendum by secret ballot was held on the question of whether service in positions covered by such retirement system should be excluded from or included under an agreement with the federal government;

(b) An opportunity to vote in such referendum was given and was limited to eligible employees;

(c) Not less than ninety days' notice of such referendum was granted to all such employees;

(d) The referendum was conducted under the supervision of the Governor or an agency or individual designated by him; and

(e) A majority of the eligible employees voted in favor of social security coverage under the federal-state agreement.

The law contains a statement of policy on the part of Congress, as follows:

"It is hereby declared to be the policy of the Congress in enacting the succeeding paragraphs of this subsection that the protection afforded employees in positions covered by a retirement system on the date an agreement under this section is made applicable to service performed in such positions, or receiving periodic benefits under such retirement system at such time, will not be impaired as a result of making the agreement so applicable or as a result of legislative enactment in anticipation thereof."

Because the 1950 amendments did not permit extension of social security coverage to members of retirement systems, the only method by which it could be obtained for them was through dissolving their retirement systems. This was done by several states and local governments. Most of these units reinstated their local retirement systems on a reduced basis after the extension of social security coverage. This method was rather involved and gave rise to a number of important legal and technical problems. The 1954 amendments specifically prohibit a dissolution of a retirement system for the express purpose of providing social security coverage, without the approval of members of the retirement system under a referendum plan.

*Prepared by A. A. WEINBERG, Actuary, Chairman, Committee on Public Employee Retirement Administration, Municipal Finance Officers Association.

CONTRASTING OBJECTIVES

The primary objective of social security is to provide a measure of protection for aged persons and the dependents of workers. Its motivations are social and humanitarian. The basic formula of social security provides disproportionately higher benefits in relation to earnings for those employees who are at the lower wage levels, and disproportionately lower benefits for employees in the higher wage brackets. In addition, the service-qualifying conditions for maximum benefits are so low that there is no difference in the final amount of benefit between a fully insured worker with five years of coverage and an employee who has had thirty years of coverage. The objective is a measure of adequate subsistence to the aged and to survivors. Salary and service factors are of secondary importance.

A public employees' retirement plan, on the other hand, although concerned with financial security after retirement, has other primary aims. It seeks, first, to induce the entry of competent people into public administration; and, through a formula which relates the measure of benefits directly to length of service, age and salary—thus providing increasingly greater benefits to those who continue in service—it provides an incentive for staying in government employment. Finally, by providing an annuity reasonably related to the average of final earnings (which are in almost all cases at the highest level of the entire period of service) it encourages the retirement of the superannuated employee. Through this orderly system of retirement, the plan affords an opportunity for the systematic promotion of younger employees in salary and rank.

The entire philosophy of the governmental retirement plans is geared to these personnel objectives. In contrast, federal social security is wholly unconcerned with those aims, since the federal government is not in the relationship of employer to the vast percentage of employees under or eligible for social security. Thus, at the very outset, the marked distinction between objectives shows that federal social security and local retirement plans do not operate in areas of mutual concern and that the function of each may be justified separately.

IMPACT OF SOCIAL SECURITY

Federal social security continues its profound impact upon local retirement plans for public employees. In several jurisdictions, social security has superseded local retirement coverage to a full or partial extent. In a number of states, coordination of social security with state and local plans has already been effected, and the movement in this direction is growing rapidly.

The public employee's attitude in respect to social security is characterized largely by uncertainty. On the one hand, the benefits for short term service, survivorship benefits, the current lesser rates of contribution and the factor of preservation of service credit upon change in employment attract many employees. On the other hand, the more generous retirement annuity under state and local plans, disability benefit provisions, and the privilege of a refund of contributions upon termination of service, are equally attractive. Since the 1954 amendments to the Social Security Act permit coordination of social security with public employees' retirement plans, in a manner that enables employees to share in the advantages of both, it would appear that this should be uniformly acceptable to them. However, there is fear in some quarters that coordination would lead to the repeal of the state and local plans; for that reason the uncertainty continues.

Social security will continue to have a profound effect upon the whole subject of employee protection under public employee plans. Its philosophy is now deeply ingrained in the national consciousness. With its continuous expansion of coverage, an increasing number of public employees will earn credits under social security which they will not want to relinquish. Moreover, if the trend for liberalization of social security benefits continues, the remaining opposition among public employees may be expected to abate. These and related factors make it important that there be a continuing appraisal of the action and interaction of the national and state-and-local plans, and a constructive and enlightened consideration of their respective functions. The problem becomes one of balance and adjustment, to the end that the legitimate objectives of both the national and the state-local plans are fostered and preserved.

GROWTH OF COVERAGE

The first step in obtaining social security coverage under the 1954 amendments for members of a retirement system is an amendment to the state social security enabling law eliminating the exemption of members of public retirement systems from social security coverage. The second step is formulation of a plan in the form of a legislative act providing for social security coverage and a downward adjustment, if one is to be made, of benefits and contributions under the public retirement system. The third step is a referendum, in which the members of the retirement system vote on the proposed plan of coverage. If a majority vote affirmatively, a fourth step is necessary before social security coverage can become fully operative—the signing of an agreement with the Secretary of Health, Education, and Welfare with respect to coverage of the particular group of members.

When the 1954 social security amendments became effective, ten states already had approved social security coverage for members of certain retirement systems—Alabama, Arizona, Delaware, Iowa, Mississippi, Oregon, South Dakota, Utah, Virginia and Wyoming. All of these states except South Dakota provided for additional benefits under an adjusted public retirement system as a supplement to social security. In 1955, the South Dakota legislature authorized local school districts to provide supplementary retirement benefits, in their discretion.

Of the remaining thirty-eight states, twenty-two have enacted legislation to permit extension of social security coverage to members of public retirement systems. All told, thirty-eight legislatures have authorized coverage of general state personnel or categories of personnel under OASI, and twenty-two states now have such coverage. Four states—Indiana, Kansas, Michigan and South Carolina—held referendums in 1955 for certain retirement systems in which coverage was approved. Several of the remaining states are in process of holding similar referendums, and the matter continues under consideration in others of the states.

STATE RETIREMENT COVERAGE

State	State has own retirement program (a)		State has O.A.S.I. coverage		Legislation has been adopted authorizing O.A.S.I. coverage in future (b)	Legislation authorizes local governments to arrange O.A.S.I. coverage for employees	
	For general state personnel	For some categories only	For general state personnel	For some categories only		Mandatory	Permissive
Alabama	★	...	★	...	....	....	★
Arizona	★	...	★	...	....	....	★
Arkansas	...	★	...	★	....	....	★
California	★	...	(c)	...	★	....	★
Colorado	★	...	...	★	....	....	★
Connecticut	★	...	...	...	....	....	★
Delaware	★	...	★	...	....	....	★
Florida	★	...	...	...	★	....	★
Georgia	★	...	...	...	....	....	★
Idaho	...	...	★	...	....	★	....
Illinois	★	...	...	...	★	....	★
Indiana	★	...	...	...	★	....	★
Iowa	★	...	★	...	....	....	....
Kansas	...	★	★	...	....	★(d)	★(e)
Kentucky	...	...	★	...	....	....	....
Louisiana	★	...	...	...	★	....	★
Maine	★	...	...	...	....	....	★
Maryland	★	...	...	...	★	....	★
Massachusetts	★	...	...	...	....	....	★
Michigan	★	...	...	...	★	....	★
Minnesota	★	...	...	...	....	....	....
Mississippi	★	...	★	...	....	....	★
Missouri	...	★	★	...	....	....	★
Montana	★	...	...	...	★	★	....
Nebraska	...	...	★	...	....	....	★
Nevada	★	...	...	★(f)	....	....	★(f)
New Hampshire	★	...	...	★	★	....	★
New Jersey	★	...	★	...	....	....	★
New Mexico	★	...	...	...	★	....	★
New York	★	...	...	★(f)	....	....	★
North Carolina	★	...	...	...	★	....	★
North Dakota	★	...	...	...	★	....	★
Ohio	★	...	...	...	....	....	....
Oklahoma	...	...	...	...	....	....	★
Oregon	★	...	★	...	....	....	★
Pennsylvania	★	...	...	...	....	....	★
Rhode Island	★	...	...	...	★	....	★
South Carolina	★	...	...	...	....	....	★
South Dakota	...	★	★	...	....	....	★
Tennessee	★	...	...	...	....	....	★
Texas	★	...	★	...	....	....	★
Utah	...	★	★	...	....	....	★
Vermont	★	...	...	...	★	....	★
Virginia	★	...	★	...	....	....	★
Washington	★	...	...	...	★	....	....
West Virginia	...	★	★	...	....	....	★
Wisconsin	★	...	★	...	....	....	★
Wyoming	★	...	★	...	....	★	....

(a) One or more separate systems may be involved.
(b) In each case the legislation applies to general state personnel.
(c) Referendum pending.

(d) On counties only.
(e) For local taxing districts other than counties.
(f) Applies only to those employees not covered by the state's program.

Section V

THE JUDICIARY

1. Judicial Administration and Procedure

1

Judicial Administration and Procedure

STATE JUDICIAL SYSTEMS

THERE has been an unmistakable forward movement in achieving greater integration, efficiency and responsibility in state court systems during the last two years through reorganization. This has developed by vesting greater authority in the Supreme Court and its Chief Justice, and through establishment of well staffed offices of administrative services, along with judicial conferences or councils. The importance of the trend was emphasized in the report of the Committee on the Administration of the State Judicial System, submitted to the Conference of Chief Justices in 1954. The committee set forth the following recommendations:

1. The office of the Chief Justice of the court of last resort of each state should be a permanent one, and the Chief Justice should be responsible for the administration of the state judicial system. He should be empowered to assign and reassign judges to expedite court business, establish an administrative office, require reports from judges on the status of their dockets, be responsible for preparing financial budgets for the courts, and publish reports on the work of the courts.

2. Each state should adopt an act similar to the Model Act to Provide for an Administrator of the State Courts, as approved by the Conference of Commissioners on Uniform State Laws, to provide for a court administrator to assist the Chief Justice in carrying out his administrative responsibilities.

3. Provision should be made in each state for the holding of regular meetings of state judicial conferences with membership composed of judges, legislative leaders, law officers, deans of law schools, representatives of state and city bar associations, and laymen. The conference should meet at least once a year to discuss judicial administration and procedure.

Provision also should be made for a smaller body, a representative judicial council, to study the judicial administration in the state and to assist in formulating and activating programs to improve the state's judicial system.

4. The granting of rule making power to the courts of the state is essential to the effective and efficient administration of justice and should be adopted by every state. The process of rule making should be a continuous one and basic to the work of the judicial councils and conferences.

Through these recommendations, the Committee stated: "We may achieve a system of procedure and practice adapted to the needs of justice and the subsequent rights of litigants."

COURT REORGANIZATION

A significant number of states considered and adopted proposals in the biennium for comprehensive reorganizations of their state court systems to simplify and speed up the administration of justice.

An extensive study and hearings in New York resulted in the report of that state's Temporary Commission on Courts, published in 1955. The commission found that the New York court system was overly complex and confusing. Costs of litigation and appeal were excessively high. Court calendars were too congested, and court facilities often inadequate. The report especially cited a need for comprehensive administrative organization in the courts of the state. The commission's major proposal was to establish a Judicial Conference to serve as a policy making body in setting court standards. This was enacted into law. A second report by the commission's Subcommittee on Court Organization proposed a unified court system, consisting of five state-wide courts to displace the present complex system. Other changes would involve the operation of the entire court system under a state-wide budget, and a plan to require all judges and magistrates in the new system to be lawyers.

In Delaware a constitutional amendment was passed giving the Supreme Court administrative and supervisory power over all courts in the state. Under the amendment, the Superior Court or Court of Chancery can request the assignment of a state judge, including the justices of the Supreme Court, to help lighten congested dockets.

The Florida legislature submitted a constitutional amendment to the judicial article for vote by the electorate in November, 1956. It would create an intermediate appellate court, to lighten the overload of cases in the Supreme Court, and would give the Supreme Court supervision of rules of practice and procedure as well as machinery for removing judges for disability. Mandatory retirement of all judges on reaching the age of 70 would be provided.

In Minnesota the legislature submitted a consitutional amendment to the judicial article for approval by the people at a general election in November, 1956. Under the amendment, justice courts would be abolished and the criminal jurisdiction transferred to District Courts. Two additional Supreme Court Judges would be authorized, and District Judges could be assigned to act as Judges of the Supreme Court. The terms of all judges would be fixed at six years, and the legislature would be empowered to make provision for their retirement.

The Wisconsin legislature also proposed an amendment designed to effect a thorough revision of the court system. To become effective this amendment must be approved again by the 1957 legislature, and then by the electorate. It would vest all judicial power in the Supreme Court, Circuit Courts, and justice courts, with branches of the Circuit Court taking over the work now done by the lower courts. The Judicial Council, which recommended the amendment, is to prepare a detailed court organization bill for the 1957 legislature.

ADMINISTRATIVE OFFICES

An important milestone for improving the administration of justice was passed in Chicago on August 14, 1954, with the first meeting of state court administrators. Administrators attended from Colorado, Connecticut, Louisiana, Maryland, Michigan, New Jersey, Oregon, Rhode Island, Virginia and the District of Columbia. The group met again in 1955 and formally organized as the Conference of Court Administrators, dedicated to the improvement of the administration of the courts.

Many observers have characterized the growth and extension of the administrative office as one of the most significant developments of the last decade affecting the courts. A number of new offices of court administrator have been created in the last two years.

In New York the new Judicial Conference Act provides for establishment of an Office of State Administrator, on the nomination of the Chairman of the Judicial Conference, to assist the conference in the performance of its duties.

The Ohio legislature provided for an Administrative Assistant to the Supreme Court with the duty of examining court dockets and making recommendations for judicial assignments.

Following a year's study, the Maryland legislature created an administrative office of the courts. Its Director is appointed by the Chief Judge of the Court of Appeals and is empowered to examine dockets, determine the need for assistance of any court, make recommendations concerning the assignment of judges, collect and compile statistical data, prepare budget estimates for the judicial system, and recommend improvements for it.

The Iowa legislature established the position of Court Statistician in the office of the Clerk of the Supreme Court, with the duty to collect and compile statistical data, make reports on court business, and offer recommendations concerning assignment of judges and improvement of court organization.

Bills to establish similar offices were introduced in Indiana and Texas, among other states, but failed of enactment.

JUDICIAL COUNCILS AND JUDICIAL CONFERENCES

Largely as a result of the discussions at annual meetings of the Conference of Chief Justices, there has been a considerable expansion in the formation and use of judicial councils and conferences.

For example, Michigan's legislature in 1955 repealed a 1929 law under which a judicial council was established, transferred its functions of collecting and compiling statistics to the newly created office of Court Administrator, and provided for creation of a state-wide judicial conference, to be called by the Court Administrator.

In Tennessee an act of 1955 provided for a biennial conference of all judges of courts of record whose salaries are paid by the state.

The previously noted New York act set up a Judicial Conference, to be composed of nine judges—the Chief Judge of the Court of Appeals, the presiding Justice of each Appellate Division, and one Justice of the Supreme Court for each judicial district. The conference will be concerned with the organization, procedures and rules of court, and with court administration, judicial assignments and preservation of records.

In 1955 Delaware's legislature created a Council on the Administration of Justice, which is to make a continuous study of administration in the state courts, collect statistical information on their work and make any recommendations it deems advisable respecting the administration of justice. The Governor named five non-lawyers to serve with ten ex-officio members, all jurists, attorneys or legislators, on the council.

Legislation in Oregon provided for establishment of a Judicial Council consisting of the Justices of the Supreme Court and the judges of other courts. It is charged with making a continuous survey of the organization, procedures and methods of administration of the various courts of the state.

In 1954 the Governor of Maine, acting under the authority of a 1935 statute, appointed a twelve member Judicial Council, directed to study all phases of the state's judicial system, including the field of criminal indictments.

At the 1955 meeting of the Conference of Chief Justices an entire session was devoted to state judicial conferences. Papers on the work and operation of judicial conferences in Maryland, Virginia and Nevada emphasized their importance in improving the administration of justice. The Conference previously had called for establishment of judicial conferences in all states.

SELECTION AND TENURE

The states have continued to give attention to means of selecting judges with high qualifications in learning, courage and judicial temperament. Few basic changes in the selection process or in judicial tenure were adopted, but a number were considered.

The Idaho legislature, in 1955, required candidates for District and Supreme Court Justices, in elections where two candidates are to be elected, to declare which judge the candidate desires to succeed in office. The effect of the law is to require any candidate seeking office to make a declaration as to which office he is seeking. Thus he cannot "run against the field."

In Michigan a proposed constitutional amendment was adopted in 1955 which changes the mechanics of non-partisan judicial selection. It provides that elections of judicial officers shall be prescribed by law and shall remain non-partisan.

In a number of states various modifications of non-partisan plans for selection were proposed in the biennium but not adopted. The Florida legislature rejected the Missouri Plan of selection sponsored by the Judicial Council in 1955. Other states in which proposals for the Missouri Plan, or modifications of it, were defeated included Illinois, Kansas, New Mexico, Oklahoma and Wisconsin. However, in Missouri, a proposed constitutional amendment to replace the non-partisan system of selecting Appellate Court Judges was defeated and the existing system continued.

COMPENSATION AND RETIREMENT

More than half of the legislatures meeting in the last two years enacted legislation increasing salaries of state court judges. This growing emphasis on adequate compensation is based on the assumption that, although salary alone does not secure the most qualified candidates, it is an essential element and often the deciding factor—other things being equal—in attracting to judicial office capable lawyers who otherwise might hesitate to give up successful practices. Twenty-five states and one territory raised salaries of their appellate judges: Arkansas, California, Connecticut, Florida, Georgia, Illinois, Indiana, Iowa, Kansas, Maine, Maryland, Massachusetts, Mississippi, Montana, Nebraska, Nevada, New Mexico, Ohio, Oregon, South Dakota, Tennessee, Texas, Utah, West Virginia, Wisconsin and Hawaii.

These increases raised the median salary of Supreme Court Justices to $14,400, which is $1,400 more than the median two years ago, and $2,400 more than in 1951.

Almost half the states and one territory raised the salaries of judges of trial courts of general jurisdiction. These included California, Colorado, Connecticut, Illinois, Indiana, Iowa, Kansas, Maine, Massachusetts, Maryland, Michigan, Minnesota, Montana, Nebraska, Nevada, New Mexico, Oregon, South Dakota, Tennessee, Utah, Virginia, Wisconsin and Hawaii. The median salary for trial courts is now approximately $11,000—about 22 per cent above the 1951 median of $9,000.

An interesting development in this field was a California act of 1955 establishing a formula for fixing salaries of judges of appellate courts and trial courts of record. The new formula relates trial court salaries to those of appellate courts and recognizes distinctions in size of population, workloads, number of judges and financial condition of the various counties. The salary of the Chief Justice of the Supreme Court is the controlling factor; under the formula all other judges receive the salary of the Chief Justice less a specified amount for each of three classes based on population

of Superior and Municipal Courts. Thus in future only one bill has to be enacted by the legislature to increase or decrease judges' salaries.

In the area of retirement notable legislation was enacted in 1954 and 1955. The Virginia legislature provided for compulsory retirement at 75, with permissive retirement at 65 after twelve years' service, and with possible recall for 90-day periods to assist in the expeditious disposition of court business.

In Delaware a judicial pension law was enacted, providing for a contribution pension plan. Each judge who elects to accept the benefits of the act must contribute 5 per cent a year of the first $7,500 of his salary; he thereby becomes eligible for retirement at 65 or after twenty-four years of service, whichever date is earlier.

Florida amended its retirement system for Supreme and Circuit Court Judges; it allows eligibility for retirement at age 60 after ten years' service, or after twenty years' service without regard to age. Tennessee provided for retirement due to disability at two-thirds of last salary.

Maryland increased its judicial pensions and also, for the first time, provided a pension for widows of judges. Oregon provided for payment of widows' pensions from the judges' retirement fund in the case of judges who die after more than six years of judicial service. Colorado and South Carolina also provided for widows' pensions.

A retirement act adopted in Nebraska provides for mandatory retirement of District and Supreme Court Judges at 70. A retirement fund will be built up by contributions from judges' salaries and a percentage of court costs, the legislature appropriating any additional money needed. A special board is to administer the fund.

In Wisconsin a constitutional amendment to provide for mandatory retirement of Supreme and Circuit Court Judges at age 70 was ratified by the voters in April, 1955. The amendment also provides for temporary recall of retired judges when necessary to relieve court congestion.

PRACTICE AND PROCEDURE

Proposals for lodging the rule-making power in the court and suggestions for improving procedures have been studied and advanced in the biennium. In general, they aim at minimizing decisions based on technicalities and at developing a simpler, more expeditious system of administering justice.

In California the legislature amended the Code of Civil Procedures to authorize the Judicial Council to promulgate rules concerning the time, manner and nature of all pre-trial conferences in civil cases tried in Superior and Municipal Courts. The Wisconsin Legislative Council has received a report from its Criminal Court Advisory Committee recommending a revised criminal code. In Illinois the legislature enacted a new Civil Practice Act and adopted the rules promulgated by the Supreme Court. Revised rules of appellate practice issued by the Alabama Supreme Court went into effect in 1955.

In New York a new advisory committee of six legal experts was appointed to advise the Temporary Commission on the Courts as to methods of simplifying the state's complicated system of practice and procedure. Developing a final draft of new rules and procedures is expected to require several years. The Supreme Court of North Dakota held hearings on proposed new rules of civil procedure for the District Courts of that state, and the rules were expected to go into effect shortly.

In Florida new rules of the Supreme Court, patterned after those of the United States Court of Appeals for the Fourth Circuit Court, went into effect on March 15, 1955. Among many changes are provisions for the manner of preparation of records on appeal and for the form and content of briefs.

In several states, including Montana, North Carolina, Tennessee, Texas and Vermont, proposals to vest the Supreme Court with rule-making power failed to pass.

The Conference of Chief Justices, meantime, maintained intensive interest in problems arising from the possible abuse of the writ of habeas corpus in federal courts as a means of reviewing the actions of state courts in criminal cases. A committee of the Conference, working in close cooperation with a similar committee of the National Association of Attorneys General and of the Judicial Conference of the United States, developed an amendment to the United States Code to help solve the problem. The proposed legislation was approved unanimously in 1955 by the House Judiciary Committee in Congress, by the three organizations mentioned above, and by the Section of Judicial Administration of the American Bar Association and the United States Department of Justice. Under the proposal an application for writ of habeas corpus on behalf of a person imprisoned under the judgment of a state court may be entertained by a federal court or judge only if it presents a substantial federal constitutional question, and then only if it meets all three of the following conditions:

1. The question must be one which was not theretofore raised and determined in a state court proceeding.

2. The prisoner did not have a fair and adequate opportunity theretofore to raise and have the question determined.

3. The question must be one which cannot thereafter be raised and determined in the state court, subject to review by the Supreme Court of the United States.

The Conference of Chief Justices authorized its Chairman to appoint a special committee to work directly with Congress to expedite this legislation. The Conference believed it would go far toward elimination of abuses and at the same time amply protect the constitutional rights of prisoners held pursuant to state court judgments.

JUDICIAL STUDIES

In a number of states special studies of the judicial system were undertaken.

The Alabama legislature created a Judiciary Advisory Council and a Commission for Judicial Reform to make a joint study of the practice and procedure of the courts of the state.

In Vermont the legislature authorized the Governor to appoint a commission to make a complete review of the justice, municipal and probate court systems of the state, with a view to reorganizing the court structure. The commission is to report to the Governor and legislature by November, 1956.

The Governor of Massachusetts appointed a commission to survey the state's entire judicial system, including organization of the District Courts and problems of congestion in the Superior Courts.

In Maine the Governor requested the State Judicial Council to submit recommendations to the 1957 legislature on court reorganization.

A new Council on the Administration of Justice, created by the Delaware legislature, is to make a continuing study of the administration of justice there. It is asked to recommend to the Governor, the legislature, the courts or the bar such changes in the law or in rules of organization and operation of the courts as it considers desirable for improving the administration of justice.

TABLE 1

CLASSIFICATION OF COURTS AND TERMS OF JUDGES

| | Appellate Courts | | Major Trial Courts | | | | | Courts of Limited Jurisdiction | | | | |
| | Court of Last Resort | Intermediate Appellate Court | Chancery Court | Circuit Court | District Court | Superior Court | Other Trial Courts | Probate Court | County Court | Municipal Court | Justice, Magistrate or Police Court | Other Courts |
State												
Alabama	6	6	....	6	....	....	....	6	....	....	4	....
Arizona	6	....	....	....	....	4	....	....	....	....	4	....
Arkansas	8	....	6	4	....	....	....	....	2	4	2	2(a)
California	12	12	....	....	....	6	....	....	....	6	6	....
Colorado	10	....	....	....	6	....	....	....	4	....	2	....
Connecticut	8	....	....	....	....	8	....	4	....	4	4	4(a), 6(b)
Delaware	12	....	12	....	....	12	....	....	....	....	4	4-12(a)
Florida	6	....	....	6	....	....	4-6(c)	4	4	2-4	4	4(b)
Georgia	6	6	....	....	....	4	....	4	....	1-4	4	6(b)
Idaho	6	....	....	....	4	....	....	2	....	....	2	....
Illinois	9	3	....	6	....	6	6(d)	4	4	6	4	4(b)
Indiana	6	4	....	6	....	4	4(e)	4	....	4	4	4(b)
Iowa	6	....	....	....	4	4	....	....	....	4	2	....
Kansas	6	....	....	....	4	....	....	2	2	2	2	....
Kentucky	8	....	....	6	....	....	....	....	4	....	4	....
Louisiana	14	12	....	....	6(f)	....	....	....	....	4-6	4	6-8(b)
Maine	7	....	....	....	....	7	....	4	....	4	....	....
Maryland	15	....	....	15	....	....	15(g)	4	....	8(h)	2	....
Massachusetts	Life	....	....	....	Life	Life	....	Life	....	....	3	Life(i)
Michigan	8	....	....	6	....	6	6(j)	4	....	6	4	6(a)
Minnesota	6	....	....	....	6	....	....	4	....	4	2	....
Mississippi	8	....	4	4	....	....	....	....	4	....	4	....
Missouri	12	12	....	6	....	....	4(a)	4	....	....	4	4(k)
Montana	6	....	....	....	4	....	....	....	....	2	2	....
Nebraska	6	....	....	....	4	....	....	....	4	4	2	6(l)
Nevada	6	....	....	....	4	....	....	....	....	4	2	....
New Hampshire	To age 70	....	....	....	....	To age 70	....	To age 70	....	To age 70	5	....
New Jersey	7 with reappointment for life	7 with reappointment for life	....	....	....	7 with reappointment for life	5(m)	5	....	3	....	2(n), 5(b,o)
New Mexico	8	....	....	....	6	....	....	2	....	....	2	4(p)
New York	14	5	....	....	....	....	6(m),14(q)	6	2-4	....	4	....
North Carolina	8	....	....	....	....	8	....	....	2-4	2	2-6	2(b)
North Dakota	10	....	....	....	6	....	....	....	4	....	2	....
Ohio	6	6	....	....	....	....	6(a)	6	....	6	4	6(b)
Oklahoma	6	....	....	....	4	4	....	....	2	....	2	4(a), 6(b)
Oregon	6	....	....	6	....	....	....	....	6	....	6	....
Pennsylvania	21	10	....	....	....	....	10(a)	10	10	10	5	....
Rhode Island	Life	....	....	....	....	Life	....	....	....	....	....	3(r), 10(b)
South Carolina	10	....	....	4	....	....	....	4	4	....	2	....
South Dakota	6	....	....	4	....	....	....	....	2	4	2	....
Tennessee	8	8	8	8	....	....	8(e)	....	4	....	6	....
Texas	6	6	....	....	4	....	....	....	4	....	4	....
Utah	10	....	....	....	6	....	....	....	....	6	4	4(b)
Vermont	2	....	....	....	....	....	2(m)	2	....	2	2	....
Virginia	12	....	....	8	....	....	8(s)	....	....	....	4	4-6(b)
Washington	6	....	....	....	4	....	....	....	....	....	4	....
West Virginia	12	....	....	8	....	....	....	....	6	....	4	....
Wisconsin	10	....	....	6	....	....	....	....	6	2-6	2	4-6(b),6(t)
Wyoming	8	....	....	....	6	....	....	....	....	....	2	....
Hawaii	4	....	....	....	4	....	....	....	....	....	....	2(r)
Puerto Rico	To age 70	....	....	....	....	12	....	....	....	....	4	8(r)

(a) Courts of common pleas.
(b) Juvenile courts.
(c) Courts of record.
(d) City courts.
(e) Criminal courts.
(f) Judges in New Orleans serve 12 years.
(g) Supreme Bench of Baltimore.
(h) People's Court of Baltimore.
(i) Land Court of Massachusetts.
(j) Recorder's Court of Detroit.
(k) St. Louis Court of Criminal Corrections.

(l) Workmen's Compensation courts; Court of Industrial Relations.
(m) County courts.
(n) County traffic courts.
(o) Criminal judicial district courts.
(p) Small claims court.
(q) Supreme Court and Court of General Sessions.
(r) District courts.
(s) Corporation and hustings courts.
(t) Statutory courts: superior, district, civil, and small claims.

TABLE 2

FINAL SELECTION OF JUDGES OF ALL STATE COURTS

Alabama.........	All elected on partisan ballot except that some juvenile court judges are appointed. Of these appointments, some are made by the Governor, some by the legislature and some by county commissions.
Arizona.........	Supreme and superior court judges elected on non-partisan ballot; justices of the peace elected on partisan ballot; police magistrates appointed by city councils.
Arkansas.......	All elected on partisan ballot.
California.......	Supreme Court and district courts of appeals judges appointed initially by Governor with approval of Commission on Qualifications. Runs for reelection on record. All others elected on non-partisan ballot.
Colorado........	All elected on partisan ballot except in some cities police magistrates and municipal judges are appointed.
Connecticut.....	All selected by legislature from nominations submitted by Governor except that probate judges and justices of the peace are elected on partisan ballot.
Delaware.......	All appointed by Governor with consent of the Senate.
Florida..........	All elected on partisan ballot.
Georgia..........	All elected on partisan ballot except county and some city court judges are appointed by the Governor with the consent of the Senate.
Idaho...........	Supreme Court and district court judges are elected on non-partisan ballot; all others on partisan ballot.
Illinois..........	All elected on partisan ballot except that appellate court judges are appointed by the Supreme Court from those serving on circuit and superior courts.
Indiana..........	All elected on partisan ballot except that judge of Municipal Court is appointed by Governor.
Iowa.............	All elected on partisan ballot.
Kansas..........	All elected on partisan ballot.
Kentucky.......	All elected on partisan ballot.
Louisiana.......	All elected on partisan ballot except that some judges of municipal courts are appointed by city councils.
Maine..........	All appointed by Governor with consent of Executive Council except that probate judges are elected on partisan ballot.
Maryland.......	All elected on non-partisan ballot except that trial justices are appointed by Governor. People's Court judges appointed by Governor initially but run on record for reelection.
Massachusetts...	All appointed by Governor with consent of the Council.
Michigan.......	All elected on non-partisan ballot.
Minnesota.......	All elected on non-partisan ballot.
Mississippi.......	All elected on partisan ballot.
Missouri.........	Judges of Supreme Court, appellate courts, circuit and probate courts in St. Louis and Kansas City and St. Louis Court of Criminal Corrections appointed initially by Governor from nominations submitted by special commissions. Run on record for reelection. All other judges elected on partisan ballot.
Montana........	All elected on non-partisan ballot except that some judges of police courts are appointed by city councils or commissioners.
Nebraska.......	All elected on non-partisan ballot except justices of the peace are on a partisan ballot; judges of Workmen's Compensation Court and Court of Industrial Relations are appointed by the Governor.
Nevada..........	All elected on non-partisan ballot.
New Hampshire..	All appointed by Governor with confirmation of the Council.
New Jersey.......	All appointed by Governor with consent of Senate except that surrogates are elected, and Magistrates of Municipal Courts serving one municipality only are appointed by governing bodies.
New Mexico......	All elected on partisan ballot.
New York........	All elected on partisan ballot except that Governor appoints judges of Court of Claims and designates members of appellate division of Supreme Court, and mayor of New York appoints judges of some local courts.
North Carolina...	All elected on partisan ballot except that a few county court judges are appointed by Governor or county commissioners, some magistrates are appointed by Governor or General Assembly and juvenile court judges are appointed by county commissioners or city boards.
North Dakota....	All elected on non-partisan ballot.
Ohio.............	All elected on non-partisan ballot.
Oklahoma.......	All elected on partisan ballot, except judge of Tulsa County Juvenile Court who is appointed from a list submitted by a committee of lawyers and laymen.
Oregon..........	All elected on non-partisan ballot.
Pennsylvania....	All elected on partisan ballot.
Rhode Island.....	Supreme Court justices elected by legislature. Superior and district court judges and justices of the peace appointed by Governor with consent of Senate and probate judges appointed by city or town councils.
South Carolina...	Supreme Court and circuit court judges elected by legislature. City judges, magistrates and some county judges appointed by Governor. Probate judges and some county judges elected on partisan ballot.
South Dakota....	All elected on non-partisan ballot.
Tennessee.......	All elected on non-partisan ballot.
Texas...........	All elected on partisan ballot.
Utah............	All elected on non-partisan ballot except that juvenile court judges are appointed by Governor with consent of Department of Welfare and town justices appointed by town trustees.
Vermont........	Supreme Court and county court presiding judges elected by legislature. Municipal judges appointed by Governor. Assistant judges of county courts and probate judges elected on partisan ballot.
Virginia.........	Supreme Court and circuit and corporation court judges elected by legislature. Trial justices in counties and juvenile or domestic relations court judges appointed by circuit or corporation courts. Some civil and police justices elected on partisan ballot; some civil justices elected by legislature, and some police justices elected by city councils.
Washington......	All elected on non-partisan ballot.
West Virginia....	All elected on partisan ballot.
Wisconsin.......	All elected on non-partisan ballot.
Wyoming........	Supreme Court justices and district court judges elected on a non-partisan basis and other judges on a partisan basis.
Hawaii...........	Supreme Court justices and circuit court judges appointed by the President of the United States with consent of the Senate. District court judges appointed by Chief Justice of the Territory.
Puerto Rico......	All appointed by the Governor with consent of the Senate.

TABLE 3
QUALIFICATIONS OF JUDGES OF STATE APPELLATE COURTS AND TRIAL COURTS OF GENERAL JURISDICTION*

State	U.S. citizenship		Years of minimum residence				Minimum age		Learned in the law		Years of legal experience		Other	
			In state		In district									
	A.	T.	A.	T.	A.	T.	A.	T.	A.	T.	A.	T.	A.	T.
Alabama........	★	★	5	5	....	★	25	25	★	★	....	....	....	....
Arizona.........	...	★	5	2	....	★	30	25	★	★	5	2	....	....
Arkansas.......	★	★	2	2	....	....	30	28	★	★	8	6	....	★(a)
California.......	★	★	5	5	....	★	21	21	....	★	5	5	....	....
Colorado........	★	★	2	2	....	★	30	30	★	★	★	....	....	....
Connecticut....							No legal qualifications							
Delaware.......	★	★	....	....	....	....	....	....	★	★	....	....	....	....
Florida.........	...	...	....	....	....	★	25	25	★	★	★	★	....	★(b, c)
Georgia.........	★	★	3	3	....	....	30	30	....	★	7	7	....	....
Idaho...........	★	★	2	2	....	★	....	30	★	★	★	....	★(c)	....
Illinois.........	★	★	5	5	★	★	30	25	....	....	....	....	....	....
Indiana.........	★	...	....	....	★	★	21	....	....	....	★	★	★(d)	★(d)
Iowa............	...	...	....	....	....	★	21	21	....	★	★	★	....	....
Kansas.........	★	★	★	....	....	....	30	...	....	★	4	★	....	....
Kentucky.......	★	★	5	2	★	★	35	35	★	★	8	8	★(b, c)	★(b, c)
Louisiana.......	★	★	2	2	2	2	35	....	★	★	10(e)	5	★(b, c)	★(b, c)
Maine..........	...	...	...	...	....	....	30	30	★	★	....	....	★(f)	★(f)
Maryland.......	★	★	5	5	★	★	30	30	★	★	....	★	....	★(a)
Massachusetts..							No legal qualifications							
Michigan.......	...	...	...	...	....	....	....	....	....	....	....	....	....	....
Minnesota......	...	...	...	...	....	★	....	21	★	★	★	★	....	★(c)
Mississippi.....	...	...	5	5	....	....	30	26	★	★	★	5	....	★(c)
Missouri........	★	★	10	4	....	★	30	30	★	★	....	★	....	★(c)
Montana.......	★	★	2	1	....	★	30	25	★	★	....	★	....	....
Nebraska.......	★	★	3	3	★	★	30	30	....	★	....	★	....	★(b)
Nevada.........	...	...	2	2	....	★	25	25	★	★	....	★	....	★(c)
New Hampshire.							No legal qualifications							
New Jersey.....	★	★	★	10	....	....	21	21	★	★	10	10	★(a,b)	★(a, b)
New Mexico.....	★	★	3	3	....	★	30	30	★	★	★	3	....	....
New York.......	★	★	★	....	....	★	21	21	★	★	....	★	....	....
North Carolina..	★	★	1	1	★	....	21	21	....	....	....	....	★(g)	★(g)
North Dakota...	★	★	3	2	....	★	30	25	....	★	★	....	....	....
Ohio...........	...	★	★	....	....	★	....	....	★	....	6	6	....	....
Oklahoma......	★	★	2	2	....	★	30	25	★	★	★	4	....	....
Oregon.........	★	★	3	3	....	★	21	....	★	★	★	★	....	....
Pennsylvania....	★	★	1	1	....	....	21	21	★	★(h)	....	....	....	....
Rhode Island...	★	★	2	2	....	....	21	21	....	....	....	....	....	....
South Carolina..	★	★	5	5	...	★	26	26	....	★	5	5	....	....
South Dakota...	★	★	2	1	★	★	30	25	★	★	....	....	....	....
Tennessee......	...	...	5	5	....	★	35	30	★	....	....	....	....	....
Texas...........	★	★	★	★	....	★	35	....	....	....	10	4	....	....
Utah...........	...	...	5	3	....	★	30	25	★	★	★	★	....	....
Vermont........	★	★	★	★	....	•...	....	....	....	....	★	★	....	....
Virginia........	★	...	....	....	....	★	21	....	....	....	5	5	....	....
Washington.....	★	★	1	1	....	....	21	21	★	★	★	★	....	....
West Virginia...	...	...	5	5	....	....	30	30	....	....	....	....	....	....
Wisconsin......	★	★	1	1	....	★	25	25	....	....	....	....	★(c)	★(c)
Wyoming.......	★	★	3	2	....	....	30	28	★	★	9	★	....	....
Hawaii..........	★	★	1	1	....	....	....	....	....	....	10	....	....	....
Puerto Rico.....	★	....	5	....	....	....	....	25	....	....	10	....	....	★

*Explanation of symbols:
  A. Judges of courts of last resort and intermediate appellate courts.
  T. Judges of trial courts of general jurisdiction.
  ★ Indicates requirement exists.
(a) Good character.
(b) Member of Bar.
(c) Qualified voter.
(d) Admitted to practice at the bar of the Supreme Court of Indiana or having acted as judicial officer of the state or any municipality therein.
(e) Supreme Court, 10; courts of appeal, 6.
(f) Sobriety of manner.
(g) Belief in God.
(h) Except associate judges.

TABLE 4
COMPENSATION OF JUDGES OF STATE APPELLATE COURTS AND TRIAL COURTS OF GENERAL JURISDICTION*

State	Appellate Courts		Major trial courts				
	Court of Last Resort	Inter-mediate Appel-late Court	Chan-cery Court	Circuit Court	District Court	Superior Court	Other Trial Courts
Alabama............	$12,000	$11,500	....	$8,500–12,000	....	....	....
Arizona............	12,500	....	....	....	....	$10,000	....
Arkansas...........	9,000	....	$7,200	7,200	....	....	....
California.........	23,000 (a)	21,500 (b)	....	....	....	15,000–18,000	....
Colorado...........	12,000	....	....	....	$9,000	....	....
Connecticut........	19,000 (a)	....	....	....	....	18,500	....
Delaware...........	17,000 (a)	(b)	15,000 (b)	....	....	15,000 (b)	....
Florida.............	15,000	....	....	10,000–16,000	....	....	$3,600–12,000 (c)
Georgia............	14,000	10,400	....	....	....	6,000–12,000	....
Idaho..............	8,500	....	....	....	7,500	....	....
Illinois.............	24,000	15,000–22,000	....	15,000–22,000	....	19,500	3,125–8,125 (e)
Indiana............	15,000	15,000	....	6,600–13,500	....	7,800–10,500	9,600–10,500 (f)
Iowa...............	12,000	....	....	....	10,000	5,000	....
Kansas.............	12,000 (a)	....	....	....	8,000	....	....
Kentucky..........	12,000	....	....	7,500–8,400	....	....	....
Louisiana..........	18,000	15,000 (g)	....	....	10,000–16,000	....	....
Maine..............	12,000 (a)	....	....	....	....	11,500	....
Maryland..........	19,000 (a)	....	....	13,000	....	....	17,500 (h)
Massachusetts.....	22,000 (a)	(b)	....	....	2,500–12,000	19,000 (b)	....
Michigan..........	18,500	....	....	12,000–21,500	....	11,000	16,500 (i)
Minnesota.........	13,500 (a)	....	....	....	10,200–11,700	....	....
Mississippi........	12,500 (a)	....	7,500	7,500	....	....	....
Missouri...........	17,500	16,000	....	11,000–14,000	....	....	8,000 (j)
Montana...........	11,000	....	....	....	9,000	....	....
Nebraska..........	12,000	....	....	....	10,000	....	....
Nevada............	16,500	....	....	....	15,000	....	....
New Hampshire....	12,000	....	....	....	....	12,000	....
New Jersey........	24,000 (a)	20,000	....	....	....	20,000	7,500–16,000 (k)
New Mexico.......	15,000	....	....	....	12,500	....	....
New York..........	35,500 (a)	25,000 (l)	....	....	....	....	{ 24,000–30,000 (m) { 2,500–28,000 (k)
North Carolina.....	16,000 (a)	....	....	....	....	13,500	....
North Dakota......	10,000	....	....	....	8,000	....	....
Ohio...............	18,000 (a)	17,000	....	....	....	....	5,300–13,000 (j)
Oklahoma..........	12,500	....	....	....	7,200–12,400	7,200–10,000	7,200–10,000 (j)
Oregon.............	13,500	....	....	11,000	....	....	....
Pennsylvania	25,000 (a)	23,000 (b)	....	....	....	....	11,000–18,000 (j)
Rhode Island......	17,000 (a)	....	....	....	....	15,000 (b)	....
South Carolina.....	12,500 (a)	....	....	12,500	....	....	....
South Dakota......	10,000	....	....	8,000	....	....	....
Tennessee..........	12,000 (a)	10,000	10,000	7,500	....	....	7,500 (f)
Texas..............	17,500	12,000	....	....	9,000 (n)	....	....
Utah...............	10,000	....	....	....	8,000	....	....
Vermont...........	10,000 (a)	(b)	....	....	....	....	9,500 (b, k)
Virginia...........	12,750 (a)	....	....	9,250	....	....	9,250 (o)
Washington........	15,000	....	....	....	....	12,000	....
West Virginia......	17,500	....	....	9,000–11,000	....	....	....
Wisconsin..........	14,000 (a)	....	....	9,000–16,000	....	....	....
Wyoming...........	11,000	....	....	....	9,500	....	....
Guam..............	....	....	....	....	13,125	....	(d)
Hawaii.............	17,000 (a)	....	....	15,000	....	....	....
Puerto Rico........	16,000 (a)	....	....	....	....	8,600–11,600 (p)	....

*Compensation shown according to most recent legislation, even though laws have not taken effect as yet. General expense allowances or payments in lieu of expense allowances included in compensation figures.

(a) These jurisdictions pay additional amounts to the chief justices of the courts of last resort. These additional sums are: $480 in Georgia; $500 in Delaware, North Carolina, Pennsylvania, Vermont, Virginia, Wisconsin, Hawaii and Puerto Rico; $1,000 in California, Connecticut, Kansas, Maine, Maryland, Massachusetts, Minnesota, Mississippi, New Jersey, Rhode Island and South Carolina; $1,500 in Tennessee; $2,000 in Ohio; $2,500 in New York.

(b) Presiding judges of these courts receive an additional $500 in California, Delaware, Pennsylvania and Vermont; $1,000 in Massachusetts and Rhode Island.

(c) Courts of record.

(d) Chief judge of Island Court, $9,360; the Island judge, $7,800.

(e) City courts.

(f) Criminal courts.

(g) Appellate judges in New Orleans receive additional pay from the city. Total salary, $17,250.

(h) Supreme Bench of Baltimore.

(i) Recorder's Court of Detroit.

(j) Courts of common pleas.

(k) County courts.

(l) Associate judges of the Appellate Division in New York City receive $30,000. Presiding judges in the city receive $31,500 and elsewhere in the state $25,500.

(m) Supreme Court.

(n) From state. Additional amounts paid by counties; in some instances up to $15,000.

(o) Corporation or hustings courts.

(p) Salary depends upon length of service with $600 increment for each two years of service.

TABLE 5

COMPENSATION OF JUDGES OF STATE COURTS OF LIMITED JURISDICTION

State	Probate Court	County Court	Municipal Court	Justice, Magistrate, or Police Court	Other Courts
Alabama	Fees	....	....	Fees	....
Arizona	....	....	....	$3,300–6,000	....
Arkansas	....	$1,800–5,000	$600– 5,000	Fees	....
California	....	....	13,500–16,500	....	....
Colorado	....	480– 9,500	up to $5,600	Fees	$9,000 (a)
Connecticut	Fees	....	varies	....	13,000 (a),15,500 (b)
Delaware	....	....	....	....	{ 5,000 (b) 3,500–12,000 (c) up to $7,500 (d) 240–10,490 (a)
Florida	Fees	1,800 & fees	....	....	....
Georgia	Fees	....	....	Fees	1,000–10,000 (a)
Idaho	$1,500– 4,300	....	....	Fees	....
Illinois	4,200–19,500	4,200–19,500	10,000 (e)	Fees	....
Indiana	6,600–13,500	....	10,500	....	10,500 (a)
Iowa	....	....	4,875– 5,750	1,200	....
Kansas	1,600 minimum	....	....	up to $6,300	....
Kentucky	....	up to $7,200	....	....	....
Louisiana	....	....	3,000–13,700	....	12,000–15,000 (f)
Maine	1,500– 6,500	....	300– 4,500	....	....
Maryland	$6–$21 day	....	8,500	650–3,000	....
Massachusetts	4,000–14,500	....	15,000 (q)	....	19,000 (g),9,500 (a)
Michigan	3,000–17,500	....	4,500–10,000	Fees	12,500 (b)
Minnesota	2,400–10,000	....	500–12,000	Fees	....
Mississippi	....	3,600– 6,000	....	Fees	....
Missouri	15,000	....	....	2,400–5,000	10,000 (h)
Montana	....	....	300 & fees	600–3,000	....
Nebraska	....	1,800–10,400	8,000	up to $2,400	6,000 (i)
Nevada	....	....	....	75–300	....
New Hampshire	2,500– 3,800	....	150–4,600	Fees or per diem	....
New Jersey	3,500–10,000	....	100–7,400	....	7,500–16,000 (a)
New Mexico	500– 2,400	....	....	Fees	6,000 (d)
New York	3,500–21,000	....	....	....	17,000 (j)
North Carolina	....	....	....	Fees	....
North Dakota	....	2,700– 6,000	....	....	....
Ohio	5,300–13,000	....	2,000–10,500	Fees	1,500 (a)
Oklahoma	....	3,200–10,000	....	Fees	7,200–10,000 (b)
Oregon	....	1,500– 8,000	....	....	....
Pennsylvania	14,000–18,500	14,000–18,500	14,000	Fees–$7,500	20,000 (k)
Rhode Island	200– 5,000	....	....	Fees	4,680–9,490
South Carolina	....	6,000	....	500–3,000	....
South Dakota	....	1,900– 6,300	1,200– 8,000	Fees	....
Tennessee	....	....	....	Fees	....
Texas	....	up to $15,000	....	1,500–10,000	....
Utah	....	....	2,400–6,500	Fees	3,800–4,320 (a)
Vermont	900– 2,400	....	925–2,450	....	....
Virginia	....	....	....	....	1,500–10,500 (l)
Washington	....	....	....	600–5,400	....
West Virginia	....	300– 4,200	....	Fees	....
Wisconsin	....	2,412–13,500	Fees–$14,000	Fees	4,800–12,000 (m)
Wyoming	....	....	....	up to $2,100	....
Guam	....	....	....	6,552	....
Hawaii	....	....	....	....	2,100–8,280 (n)
Puerto Rico	....	....	....	1,200–2,100 (o)	5,100–6,600 (p)

(a) Juvenile courts; in Colorado, juvenile and superior courts.
(b) Courts of common pleas.
(c) Family courts and Municipal Court.
(d) Small claims courts.
(e) Chief Justice of Municipal Court of Chicago receives $15,000.
(f) Caddo Juvenile $12,500; Orleans Juvenile $12,000; East Baton Rouge Family $15,000.
(g) Land Court of Massachusetts.
(h) St. Louis Court of Criminal Corrections.
(i) Workmen's Compensation Court. Court of Industrial Re-

lations is only in session subject to call and judges are paid $50 per day on a per diem basis.
(j) New York Court of Claims.
(k) Dauphin County, Commonwealth Court.
(l) Trial justices and juvenile and domestic relations courts.
(m) Superior, district, civil, children's and small claims courts.
(n) District Courts.
(o) Salary of justices of the peace depends upon length of service with $300 increment for each four years of service.
(p) Salary of district court judges depends upon length of service with $300 increment for each two years of service.
(q) Boston Municipal Court.

TABLE 6

RETIREMENT AND PENSION PROVISIONS FOR JUDGES OF STATE APPELLATE COURTS AND TRIAL COURTS OF GENERAL JURISDICTION

State	*Minimum age*	*Years minimum service*	*Amount of annuity*	*Amount of judges' contribution*	*Judges to whom applicable*
Alabama	70	15	$6,000 (a)	none	Supreme
	70	15	4,000 (a)	none	Appeals
	65(b)	15	4,000 (a)	none	Circuit
	Any age	25	4,000 (a)	none	Circuit
Arizona	65	20 (c)	⅔ pay	5%	Supreme, superior
Arkansas	70	10	½ pay	1½–3% (d)	Supreme
	65	15	½ pay	(d)	Supreme, circuit, chancery
	70	20	½ pay	(d)	Circuit, chancery
	Any age	24	½ pay	(d)	Circuit, chancery
California	70	10	½ pay (e)	2½%	Supreme, appeals, superior
	65	20	½ pay (e)	2½%	Supreme, appeals, superior
Colorado	65	10	$3,000– 5,000(f)	none	Supreme
	65	20	4,000	none	Supreme
	65	30	5,000	none	Supreme
	65	10	⅖ pay (g)	5%	District
	65	16	½ pay (g)	5%	District
Connecticut	70	No minimum	⅔ pay	none	Supreme, superior
Delaware	65	12	$3,600 (Min.)	5% (Max. $375)	....
Florida	Any age	20	Full pay	2% (h)	Supreme
	60	10	⅔ pay	2%	Circuit
	Any age	20	⅔ pay	2% (h)	Supreme, circuit
Georgia	70	10	⅔ pay	none	Supreme, appeals
	65	20	⅔ pay	none	Supreme
	65	20	⅔ pay	....	Superior
Idaho	70	10	½ pay	3%	Supreme, district
Illinois	60	12 (c)	¼ pay (i)	5% (j)	Supreme, appellate, circuit, superior
	60	18	½ pay	5% (j)	Supreme, appellate, circuit, superior
Indiana	65	12 (k)	up to $4,000 (l)	5% (m)	Supreme, appellate, circuit, superior
Iowa	67	6	up to ⅔ of last salary (n)	3%	Supreme, district
Kansas	65	10	3⅓% of pay for each year of service	4%	Supreme, district
Kentucky	Any age	8	$5,000 (o)	none	Court of appeals
	60	10	$3,500 (p)	2%	Circuit
Louisiana	80(q)	20	Full pay	none	Supreme, appeals, district
	70	15	⅔ pay	none	Supreme, appeals, district
	65	20	⅔ pay	none	Supreme, appeals, district
	Any age	23	⅔ pay	none	Supreme, appeals, district
Maine	70 (r)	7	¾ pay	none	Supreme
	70 (r)	7	¾ pay	none	Superior
Maryland	60	No minimum	up to $9,000 (s)	none	Court of appeals, circuit, Supreme Bench of Baltimore
Massachusetts	70	10	¾ pay	none	Supreme, superior, district
Michigan	70 (r)	12	$7,500	5% (Max. $750)	Supreme
	70 (r)	12	4,500	5% (Max. 450)	Circuit, superior, recorders
	65	18	4,500	5% (Max. 450)	Circuit, superior, recorders
	Any age	30	4,500	5% (Max. 450)	Circuit, superior, recorders
Minnesota	70	12 (c)	½ pay (t)	none	Supreme
	70 (r)	15 (c)	½ pay	none	District
Mississippi	65	15	(u)	1.65%	Supreme, chancery, circuit
Missouri	75	No minimum	⅓ pay (o)	none	Supreme, appellate, circuit
	65	12	⅓ pay (o)	none	Supreme, appellate, circuit
Montana	....	....	(u)	....	Supreme, district
Nebraska	65(v)	10	3⅓% of pay for each year of service	4%	Supreme, district
Nevada	70	20	⅔ pay	none	Supreme, district
	65	16	⅓ pay	none	Supreme, district
New Hampshire	65	No minimum	up to ½ pay (u)	up to 7.24% (w)	Supreme, superior
New Jersey	70	10	¾ pay	none	Supreme, superior
New Mexico	64	10	$6,000	6%	Supreme, district
	60	18	6,000	6%	Supreme, district
New York	60	No minimum	up to ½ pay (u)	....	Court of appeals, supreme, county
North Carolina	80	No minimum	⅔ pay (o)	none	Supreme
	65	12 (c)	⅔ pay (o)	none	Supreme
	65	15 (c)	⅔ pay (o)	none	Superior
	Any age	24	⅔ pay (o)	none	Supreme, superior
North Dakota	70	18 (x)	½ pay	5%	Supreme, district

TABLE 6—Continued

RETIREMENT AND PENSION PROVISIONS FOR JUDGES OF STATE APPELLATE COURTS AND TRIAL COURTS OF GENERAL JURISDICTION

State	Minimum age	Years minimum service	Amount of annuity	Amount of judges' contribution	Judges to whom applicable
Ohio	60	5	(y)	6%	Supreme, appeals, common pleas
	55	30	(y)	6%	Supreme, appeals, common pleas
	Any age	36	(y)	6%	Supreme, appeals, common pleas
Oklahoma			Social Security		Supreme, district, superior, common pleas, county
Oregon	70	12 (c)	½ pay	5% of salary	Supreme, circuit
	65(z)	16	½ pay	5% of salary	Supreme, circuit
Pennsylvania	Any age	25 (c)	½ pay	varies (aa)	Supreme, superior, common pleas
Rhode Island	70	15	¾ pay	none	Supreme, superior
	Any age	25	¾ pay	none	Supreme, superior
South Carolina	72	10 (c)	$7,200	none	Supreme, circuit
	70	15	7,200	none	Supreme, circuit
	65	20	7,200	none	Supreme, circuit
	Any age	25	7,200	none	Supreme, circuit
South Dakota	65	15 (c)	½ pay	3%	Supreme, circuit
Tennessee	70	20 (c)	Full pay	8%	Supreme, appeals, circuit
	65	24	Full pay	8%	Supreme, appeals, circuit
	60	30	Full pay	8%	Supreme, appeals, circuit
Texas	65	10	½ pay	5%	Supreme, appeals, district
	Any age	24	½ pay	5%	Supreme, appeals, district
Utah		Social Security			Supreme, district
Vermont	65	No minimum (c)	up to ½ pay (ac)	up to 10.21% (v)	Supreme, superior
Virginia	65(al)	12	¾ pay	up to 3% (v)	Supreme
			¾ pay	up to 3% (v)	Circuit, corporation
			(u)	up to 3% (v)	Circuit, corporation
Washington	70	10 (c)	½ pay	6½%	Supreme, superior
	Any age	18	½ pay	6½%	Supreme, superior
West Virginia	65	16	up to ½ pay (ad)	4%	Supreme, circuit
	73	8	½ pay	4%	Supreme, circuit
Wisconsin	70(r,v)	No minimum	up to ½ pay (u, v)	7%	Supreme, circuit
Wyoming	65	18	40% of salary (e)	none	Supreme, district
Hawaii	....	16 (ae)	$10,000 (ae)	....	Supreme
Puerto Rico	60	10 (aj)	(am)	none	Supreme, superior, district

(a) Because the Alabama Constitution prohibits the payment of pensions, retired judges serve as supernumerary judges and are subject to call to assist judges in the state.
(b) 60 if permanently and totally disabled.
(c) Disabled judges in these states may retire on pensions at any age if they have completed the following number of years of service: Pennsylvania, 5; Oregon, 6; South Carolina, 7; North Carolina, 8: Arizona, Florida, South Dakota, Tennessee and Washington, 10; Illinois, Minnesota (Supreme), and Vermont, 12; Minnesota (District), 15.
(d) 1½ per cent the first 4 years; next 6 years, 2 per cent; next 5 years, 2½ per cent; thereafter, 3 per cent.
(e) Pension is ½ of salary (40% in Wyoming) being paid to sitting justices. Amount of pension changes with changes in salary.
(f) Justices may come under Public Employees Retirement System in lieu of above pension.
(g) Based on average salary during last 10 years of service.
(h) Except Supreme Court justices who have not served as circuit judges.
(i) Plus 25/72 of 1 per cent for each month in excess of 12 years' service, with a maximum of 50 per cent of pay.
(j) Full cent during the first 18 years (plus 1¼ per cent if married); nothing thereafter.
(k) Judges must contribute to pension system for 16 years. Can retire after 12 years by paying up for remaining 4 years.
(l) Pension is 50 per cent of average salary received from state but not more than $4,000.
(m) 5 per cent of salary paid by state.
(n) 2 per cent of pay for each year of service, up to 40 per cent of last salary.
(o) Retired judges may be called to serve as commissioners of the Court of Appeals in Kentucky; as referees or commissioners in Missouri; and as emergency judges in North Carolina.
(p) Plus $150 per year for each year (not exceeding 20) of service in excess of 10 years.
(q) Disabled judges retired at ⅔ pay when certified by majority of Supreme Court.
(r) Failure of judges in Maine, Michigan, Minnesota or Wisconsin to retire at the ages shown causes them to lose all pension benefits.
(s) $450 for each year of service; judges of Court of Appeals allowed $100 additional for each year of service.
(t) Plus 2½ per cent of annual salary for each year (not exceeding 10) of service in excess of 12 years.

(u) Mississippi, Montana, New Hampshire, New York, Virginia, Wisconsin. Based on length of service.
(v) Also under social security. Retirement optional at 65, compulsory at 70.
(w) Depending on age upon taking office: New Hampshire, 5.48 per cent, at age 35, to 7.24 per cent, at 64 or older; Vermont, at 35, 5.86 per cent, at 40, 6.14 per cent, at 50, 7.04 per cent, at 60, 10.21 per cent; Virginia, under 40, 2 per cent, to 55, 2½ per cent, over 55, 3 per cent.
(x) A judge in North Dakota who leaves the bench after 18 years of service but has not reached 70, upon application for retirement, shall be entitled to retirement pay upon reaching 70 years of age, provided that during the interim he will contribute to the pension fund 5 per cent of the salary he was receiving when he retired.
(y) Based on age and length of service.
(z) Judges under 60 when defeated for reelection and having served for an aggregate of 18 years, may begin to receive a pension at 65.
(aa) Depending on age, from 5.08 per cent of salary at age 20 to 8.33 per cent at age 59 or over.
(ab) Incumbents who were under former state retirement system will also receive benefits from this fund to bring total pension to a maximum of $100 per month.
(ac) Judges receive 1/70 of pay for each year of service, up to ½ average salary for last 5 years.
(ad) 4 per cent for each year of service, up to ½ pay.
(ae) Can retire after ten years service at a lower pension.
(af) No minimum age or years of service required for pension if retirement is for reasons of disability.
(ag) With the Government of the Commonwealth, including ten years as a Supreme Court justice.
(ah) May include up to ten years as a Superior Court judge.
(ai) In the judicial branch of the government.
(aj) No minimum age required for pension if retirement is for reason of disability.
(ak) Average salary means the average of salaries earned during last 5 years of creditable service.
(al) Compulsory retirement at 75.
(am) 25% average salary plus 25/72 of 1% of said average salary for each month of creditable service in excess of 10 years. Creditable service includes services rendered as judge or to the Government of Puerto Rico in any capacity if last 8 years of service were as judge.

TABLE 7
STATE COURTS OF LAST RESORT

	Name of court*	Number of Justices	Justices chosen at large	Justices chosen by dist.	Chief Justice — Method of selection†	Chief Justice — Term†
Alabama	S.C.	7	★	..	Popular election	6 yrs.
Arizona	S.C.	5	★	..	Justice with shortest time to serve	Remainder of term as Justice
Arkansas	S.C.	7	★	..	Popular election	8 yrs.
California	S.C.	7	★	..	Appointed by Governor	Remainder of term as Justice
Colorado	S.C.	7	★	..	Appointed by Court-rotation	Remainder of term as Justice
Connecticut	S.C.E.	5	★	..	Nominated by Gov. Apptd. by Gen. Assembly	Remainder of term as Justice
Delaware	S.C.	3	★	..	Appointed by Governor. Confirmed by Senate	12 yrs.
Florida	S.C.	7	★	..	Appointed by Court-rotation	2 yrs.
Georgia	S.C.	7	★	..	Appointed by Court	Remainder of term as Justice
Idaho	S.C.	5	★	..	Justice with shortest time to serve	Remainder of term as Justice
Illinois	S.C.	7	..	★	Appointed by Court-rotation	1 yr.
Indiana	S.C.	5	..	★	Appointed by Court-rotation	6 mos.
Iowa	S.C.	9	★	..	Appointed by Court-rotation	6 mos.
Kansas	S.C.	7	★	..	Seniority of service	Remainder of term as Justice
Kentucky	C.A.	7(a)	..	★	Seniority of service-rotation	1 yr.
Louisiana	S.C.	7	..	★	Seniority of service	Remainder of term as Justice
Maine	S.J.C.	6(b)	★	..	Appointed by Governor	7 yrs.
Maryland	C.A.	5	..	★	Selected by Governor from Justices	Remainder of term as Justice
Massachusetts	S.J.C.	7	★	..	Appointed by Governor	Life
Michigan	S.C.	8	★	..	Appointed by Court-rotation	1 yr.
Minnesota	S.C.	7	★	..	Popular election	6 yrs.
Mississippi	S.C.	6	..	★	Seniority of service	Remainder of term as Justice
Missouri	S.C.	7(a)	★	..	Appointed by Court-rotation	4 yrs.
Montana	S.C.	5	★	..	Popular election	6 yrs.
Nebraska	S.C.	7	..	★(c)	Popular election	6 yrs.
Nevada	S.C.	3	★	..	Seniority of service-rotation	2 yrs.
New Hampshire	S.C.	5	★	..	Appointed by Governor and Council	To age 70
New Jersey	S.C.	7	★	..	Appointed by Governor with consent of Senate	7 yrs. with re-appointment for life
New Mexico	S.C.	5	★	..	Justice with shortest term to serve	Remainder of term as Justice
New York	C.A.	7	★	..	Popular election	14 yrs.
North Carolina	S.C.	7	★	..	Popular election	8 yrs.
North Dakota	S.C.	5	★	..	Justice with shortest term to serve	2 yrs.
Ohio	S.C.	7	★	..	Popular election	6 yrs.
Oklahoma	S.C.(d)	9	★(f)	★(f)	Appointed by Court	2 yrs.
Oregon	S.C.	7	★	..	Majority vote of members of Supreme Court	2 yrs.
Pennsylvania	S.C.	7	★	..	Justice with shortest time to serve	Remainder of term as Justice
Rhode Island	S.C.	5	★	..	Elected by Legislature	Life
South Carolina	S.C.	5	★	..	Elected by General Assembly	10 yrs.
South Dakota	S.C.	5	..	★	Appointed by Court-rotation	1 yr.
Tennessee	S.C.	5	★(e)	..	Appointed by Court	Pleasure of Court
Texas	S.C.(d)	9	★	..	Popular election	6 yrs.
Utah	S.C.	5	★	..	Justice with shortest time to serve	Remainder of term as Justice
Vermont	S.C.	5	★	..	Elected by General Assembly	2 yrs.
Virginia	S.C.A.	7	★	..	Seniority of service	Remainder of term as Justice
Washington	S.C.	9	★	..	Appointed by Court-rotation	2 yrs.
West Virginia	S.C.A.	5	★	..	Appointed by Court-rotation	1 yr.
Wisconsin	S.C.	7	★	..	Seniority of service	Remainder of term as Justice
Wyoming	S.C.	3	★	..	Justice with shortest time to serve	Remainder of term as Justice
Puerto Rico	S.C.	7	(g)	(g)	Appointed by Governor with consent of Senate.	To age 70

*Explanation of symbols:
S.C. Supreme Court.
S.C.E. Supreme Court of Errors.
C.A. Court of Appeals.
S.J.C. Supreme Judicial Court.
S.C.A. Supreme Court of Appeals.

†Method of selection and term as Chief Justice rather than term as Justice on the Court.

(a) In addition, there are 4 commissioners assisting the Court in Kentucky and 6 in Missouri.

(b) In addition, there is 1 "active retired" Justice.

(c) Chief Justice is elected at large.

(d) There is a separate 3-judge Court of Criminal Appeals which is the court of last resort in criminal cases.

(e) Justices are chosen at large (each voter may vote for 5) but not more than two may reside in any one of the three geographical regions of the state.

(f) Nominated by district, elected at large.

(g) Justices are appointed by Governor with advice and consent of Senate.

Section VI

FINANCE

1. Revenue, Expenditure and Debt
2. Taxation

1

Revenue, Expenditure and Debt

STATE FINANCES IN 1954*

REVENUE of state governments from all sources totaled $18,834 million in the fiscal year 1954.[1] This was 4.8 per cent more than in fiscal 1953, and 174 per cent more than in 1942. These totals include gross sales revenue of liquor stores operated by sixteen states and contributions and investment earnings of social insurance systems administered by state governments. General revenue alone—i.e., excluding liquor store and insurance trust amounts—totaled $15,299 million in 1954, up 5.4 per cent from 1953.

State government borrowing in 1954 amounted to $2,239 million, so that the grand total of borrowing and revenue from all sources amounted to $21,073 million, or $133.82 per capita.

State spending for all purposes in fiscal 1954 was $18,686 million, as against $16,850 million in 1953 and $5,343 million in 1942. Insurance trust expenditure rose 48.1 per cent from 1953 to 1954 and liquor store spending increased 6.0 per cent. General expenditure alone—i.e., excluding liquor store and social insurance amounts—totaled $15,787 million in 1954, or 7.6 per cent more than in 1953. The 1942 to-

tal of state general expenditure was $4,549 million.

Debt redemption during fiscal 1954 amounted to $497 million, so that the total of debt redemption and expenditure for all purposes was $19,184 million, or $121.83 per capita.

State debt outstanding rose to a new high of $9,600 million at the end of fiscal 1954, as compared with $7,824 million a year earlier, $2,353 million in 1946, and $3,257 million at the end of fiscal 1942.

National totals of state finances for the period 1942 through 1954 are presented in Table 1 and summarized in Figure 1, following. Major 1954 income and outgo totals for individual states appear in Table 2.

GENERAL REVENUE

Taxes supplied $11,089 million or almost three-fourths of all state general revenue in 1954. State tax yields rose 5.1 per cent from the previous year's amount. Intergovernmental revenue from the federal government supplied $2,668 million in 1954, slightly more than in 1953. Intergovernmental revenue from local governments amounted to $215 million. Charges and miscellaneous general revenue amounted to $1,328 million, 10.8 per cent more than in the preceding year.

Altogether, general and selective sales and gross receipts taxes yielded $6,573 million, or nearly three-fifths of the total collected from all state tax sources.

Table 2 provides summary 1954 figures on general revenue of each state. Later and more detailed data on taxes appear in

*Adapted from Bureau of the Census, *Compendium of State Government Finances in 1954* and *Revised Summary of State Government Finances 1942–1950*.
[1]Data contained in the Census Bureau's annual series on "State Finances" are for state fiscal years that end on June 30, except for four states with earlier closing dates (in the same calendar year—May 31 for Pennsylvania and March 31 for New York; in the previous calendar year—September 30 for Alabama and August 31 for Texas).

the section on "State Tax Collection in 1955," beginning on page 231.

GENERAL EXPENDITURE

Education accounts for a considerably larger fraction of state general expenditure than any other function. In 1954, the states spent $4,656 million for this purpose, 6.3 per cent more than in 1953 and 294 per cent more than in 1942. Of the 1954 total, $2,934 million was in the form of fiscal aid to local governments for support of public schools, as against $790 million in 1942. Expenditures for state institutions of higher education totaled $1,324 million in 1954, including $243 million for operation of commercial activities, such as dormitories and dining halls. State revenue from charges for these activities amounted to $262 million.

State expenditure for highways in 1954 amounted to $4,126 million, or 15.1 per cent more than in the previous year. About two-thirds of the total was spent for construction and maintenance of regular highway facilities, $871 million was transferred to local governments for highway purposes, and $477 million was spent for state toll roads and bridges.

Public welfare cost, including $1,004 million in fiscal aid to local governments, totaled $2,552 million. The related 1942 total was $913 million. Health and hospital spending amounted to $1,402 million

in 1954. Some increase occurred from 1953 to 1954 in state spending for most of the other general government functions. Figures on general expenditure of each state appear in Table 5.

EXPENDITURE BY CHARACTER AND OBJECT

Current operation spending, which accounts for almost one-third of total state expenditure, amounted to $5,886 million in 1954, or 6.2 per cent more than in 1953. Capital outlay, mainly for contract construction, was up 17.5 per cent, to total $3,347 million. Insurance benefits and repayments rose 48.1 per cent to $2,096 million. Expenditure for assistance and subsidies declined slightly to $1,486 million. Interest payments on debt were up 18.9 per cent to $193 million. Together, these various kinds of direct state expenditure totaled $13,008 million in 1954, as against $11,467 million in 1953, and $3,563 million in 1942.

Intergovernmental expenditure, comprising primarily fiscal aid but also including reimbursements to local governments for services, amounted to $5,679 million in 1954. This compares with $5,384 million in 1953 and $1,780 million in 1942.

Total state spending for personal services was $3,491 million, or about one-fifth of all state expenditure in 1954. Personal service costs are mainly for "current operation,"

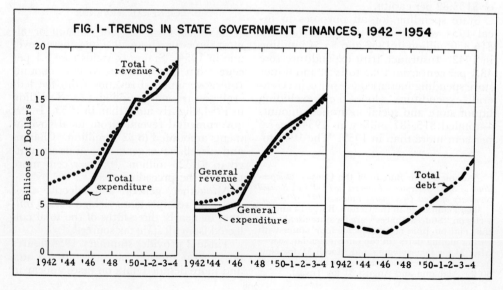

FIG. I – TRENDS IN STATE GOVERNMENT FINANCES, 1942 – 1954

but include also some amounts for force account construction.

Table 4 provides individual-state figures for these character and object classes of state spending. Additional data on state intergovernmental expenditure appear in the section "State Aid to Local Governments in 1954."

INSURANCE TRUST FINANCES

Every state operates a system of unemployment insurance and one or more public employee retirement systems. Most states also administer workmen's compensation systems, and a few have other social insurance systems. Transactions of these various systems—exclusive of administrative costs (treated as general expenditure) and state contributions (which are classified as intragovernmental transactions)—are reported as insurance trust revenue and insurance trust expenditure in Tables 1 and 2.

State unemployment compensation systems received revenue of $1,466 million in 1954 and made benefit payments of $1,504 million. State-administered employee-retirement systems had revenue of $757 million in 1954 and expenditure of $355 million. The smaller amounts involved for workmen's compensation and scattered other systems brought total insurance trust revenue to $2,560 million and insurance trust expenditure to $2,096 million.

INDEBTEDNESS, BORROWING AND DEBT REDEMPTION

Of the $9,600 million of state debt outstanding at the end of fiscal 1954, all except $283 million was of long-term nature. In addition to $5,770 million of long-term obligations backed by the states' full faith and credit, $3,547 million of nonguaranteed debt was outstanding. Net long-term state debt—allowing for debt offsets of $1,440 million—amounted to $7,877 million.

Half of the $2,239 million total of state borrowing in fiscal 1954 was accounted for by four states—Indiana, New Jersey, New York and Pennsylvania. However, at least minor amounts of borrowing were reported for all except six of the remaining states. The $497 million devoted to redemption of debt in 1954 includes some amount for every state. Debt statistics for individual states appear in Table 6, and data as to borrowing and debt redemption are in Table 2.

CASH AND SECURITY HOLDINGS

Cash and security holdings of the forty-eight states amounted to $25,536 million at the end of fiscal 1954. Of this total, $8,362 million represented unemployment fund balances in the United States Treasury, $6,559 million was for other insurance trust reserves, and $1,440 million was held as debt offsets; the holdings of all other funds and accounts amounted to $9,175 million.

INDIVIDUAL STATE COMPARISONS

Caution must be used in attempting to draw conclusions from direct comparison of financial amounts for individual state governments. The states vary widely in the scope and intensity of their responsibilities. Such variations reflect differences in state and local traditions as to the extent and character of public services; in economic ability to support such services; and in the patterns for distribution of responsibility, as between the state and local levels, for performing and financing particular governmental functions. Some state governments directly administer certain activities which elsewhere are undertaken by local governments, with or without state fiscal aid. The fraction which state government amounts make up of total state and local finances therefore differs materially from one state area to another.

TABLE 1

NATIONAL TOTALS OF STATE GOVERNMENT FINANCE: 1942–1954*

Item	Amounts in millions								Per cent change		Per cent distri-bution 1954	Per capita	
	1954	1953	1952	1950	1948	1946	1944	1942	1953–1954	1942–1954	1954	1954	1942
Revenue and borrowing	$21,073	$19,330	$17,962	$15,331	$12,736	$8,652	$7,721	$7,040	9.0	199.3		$133.82	$53.19
Borrowing	2,239	1,351	1,147	1,428	910	77	26	170	65.7	1,220.0		14.22	1.28
Revenue, total	18,834	17,797	16,815	13,903	11,826	8,576	7,695	6,870	4.8	174.1	100.0	119.60	51.91
General revenue	15,299	14,511	13,429	11,262	9,257	6,283	5,465	5,132	5.4	198.1		97.16	38.77
Taxes, total (a)	11,089	10,552	9,857	7,930	6,743	4,937	4,071	3,903	5.1	184.1	72.5	70.42	29.49
Intergovernmental revenue	2,882	2,761	2,485	2,423	1,740	864	981	858	4.4	236.1	18.8	18.31	6.48
From Federal Government	2,668	2,570	2,329	2,275	1,643	802	926	802	3.8	232.7	17.4	16.94	6.06
Public welfare	1,426	1,328	1,149	1,107	731	432	415	369	7.3	286.0	9.3	9.05	2.79
Education	277	306	293	345	320	99	215	137	-9.4	102.6	1.8	1.76	1.03
Highways	542	511	413	438	303	66	144	169	6.2	220.0	3.5	3.44	1.28
Employment security administration	198	194	187	168	152	63	36	57	2.0	245.2	1.3	1.25	.43
Other	225	231	288	217	137	140	116	69	-2.6	226.8	1.5	1.43	.52
From local governments	215	191	156	148	97	63	55	56	12.4	284.2	1.4	1.36	.42
Charges and miscellaneous general revenue	1,328	1,198	1,087	909	774	482	413	370	10.8	258.4	8.7	8.43	2.80
Liquor stores revenue	974	967	924	810	857	798	528	373	0.8	161.7		6.19	2.82
Insurance trust revenue	2,560	2,501	2,462	1,831	1,711	1,494	1,702	1,366	2.4	87.4	100.0	16.26	10.32
Employee retirement	757	634	579	425	296	193	142	115	19.3	557.3	29.6	4.81	.87
Unemployment compensation	1,466	1,551	1,597	1,176	1,203	1,162	1,405	1,134	-5.5	29.3	57.3	9.31	8.57
Other	337	316	287	229	212	140	154	117	6.6	189.3	13.1	2.14	.88
Debt outstanding at end of fiscal year, total	9,600	7,824	6,874	5,285	3,676	2,353	2,776	3,257	22.7	194.8	100.0	60.96	24.61
Long-term	9,317	7,504	6,640	5,168	3,568	2,328	2,768	3,096	24.1	200.9	97.1	59.17	23.39
Full faith and credit	5,770	5,158	4,926	4,209	3,070	1,970	2,281	2,641	11.9	118.5	60.1	36.64	19.95
Nonguaranteed	3,547	2,347	1,714	958	499	358	486	455	51.1	679.6	36.9	22.52	3.44
Short-term	283	320	235	118	108	25	8	161	-11.5	75.9	2.9	1.80	1.22
Net long-term	7,877	6,296	5,620	4,246	2,911	1,727	2,112	2,563	25.1	207.3	82.1	50.02	19.37
Full faith and credit only	4,481	4,069	3,984	3,379	2,440	1,381	1,710	2,123	10.1	111.1	46.7	28.46	16.04
Expenditure and debt redemption	19,184	17,254	16,329	15,373	11,382	7,296	5,400	5,746	11.2	233.9		121.83	43.41
Debt redemption	497	404	495	291	202	231	240	403	23.1	23.5		3.16	3.04
Expenditure, total	18,686	16,850	15,834	15,082	11,181	7,066	5,161	5,343	10.9	249.7		118.67	40.37
General expenditure	15,787	14,677	13,697	12,250	9,469	5,245	4,508	4,549	7.6	247.0	100.0	100.26	34.37
Public safety	451	414	378	328	249	162	149	146	8.8	208.8	2.9	2.86	1.10
Public welfare	2,552	2,514	2,386	2,358	1,610	1,056	945	913	1.5	179.5	16.2	16.20	6.90
Old age assistance	1,474	1,484	1,400	1,396	988	709	647	509	-0.7	189.9	9.3	9.36	3.84
Aid to dependent children	518	520	506	480	306	153	121	134	-0.4	287.1	3.3	3.29	1.01
Other (including all public welfare administration)	559	510	479	481	315	195	177	270	9.6	106.9	3.6	3.55	2.04
Education	4,656	4,382	4,026	3,413	2,636	1,471	1,350	1,182	6.3	294.1	29.5	29.57	8.93
State institutions of higher education	1,324	1,277	1,180	1,107	895	397	380	296	3.7	346.9	8.4	8.41	2.24
Intergovernmental expenditure	2,934	2,740	2,525	2,054	1,554	953	861	790	7.1	271.4	18.6	18.63	5.97
Other	398	365	321	251	186	121	109	95	9.2	318.3	2.5	2.53	.72
Highways	4,126	3,584	3,290	2,668	2,016	952	838	1,134	15.1	263.9	26.1	26.20	8.56
Regular state highway facilities	2,777	2,587	2,266	1,953	1,476	606	534	771	7.4	260.0	17.6	17.64	5.83
State toll highway facilities	477	194	290	105	34	7	6	19	146.1	(b)	3.0	3.03	.14
Intergovernmental expenditure	871	803	734	610	507	339	298	344	8.5	153.6	5.5	5.53	2.60
Health and hospitals	1,402	1,313	1,258	1,042	700	447	347	311	6.7	351.0	8.9	8.90	2.35
State hospitals and institutions for handicapped	1,089	1,014	968	788	533	308	253	235	7.5	362.7	6.9	6.92	1.78
Other	312	299	290	254	167	139	94	75	4.3	314.5	2.0	1.98	.57

212

Expenditure (continued)

	1	2	3	4	5	6	7	8	9	10	11	12	13
Natural resources	572	543	548	477	346	209	165	160	5.3	256.4	3.6	3.63	1.21
Employment security administration	190	187	177	172	150	60	35	59	1.6	221.0	1.2	1.21	.45
General control	426	406	368	322	270	195	164	166	4.8	156.3	2.7	2.70	1.25
Miscellaneous and unallocable	1,414	1,335	1,267	1,470	1,493	692	515	479	6.0	195.1	9.0	8.99	3.62
Veterans' services	103	114	143	462	633	54	1	1	-9.9	(b)	0.7	.65	....
State aid for unspecified purposes	600	592	510	482	428	357	274	224	1.3	167.5	3.8	3.81	1.69
Interest	193	162	144	109	86	84	101	122	18.9	58.0	1.2	1.23	.92
Other (includes intergovernmental aid for specified purposes not elsewhere classified)	519	467	470	417	345	196	138	132	11.1	291.9	3.3	3.29	1.00
Liquor stores expenditure	803	757	723	654	691	663	426	288	6.0	178.5		5.10	2.18
Insurance trust expenditure	2,096	1,416	1,413	2,177	1,020	1,158	226	505	48.1	314.9	100.0	13.31	3.82
Employee retirement	355	292	247	163	123	92	71	65	21.9	443.5	17.0	2.26	.49
Unemployment compensation	1,504	908	971	1,845	756	965	65	369	65.5	307.6	71.7	9.55	2.79
Other	237	216	195	169	141	102	90	71	9.7	234.8	11.3	1.50	.54
Total expenditure by character and object	18,686	16,850	15,834	15,082	11,180	7,066	5,161	5,343	10.9	249.7	100.0	118.67	40.37
Direct expenditure	13,008	11,467	10,790	10,864	7,897	4,974	3,319	3,563	13.4	265.1	69.6	82.61	26.92
Current operation	5,886	5,540	5,173	4,450	3,837	2,701	2,134	1,827	6.2	222.1	31.5	37.38	13.81
Capital outlay	3,347	2,847	2,658	2,237	1,456	368	330	642	17.5	421.7	17.9	21.25	4.85
Construction	2,831	2,472	2,323	1,966	1,268	292	288	NA	14.5	....	15.2	17.98	.....
Purchase of land and existing structures	342	218	178	131	71	33	15	NA	57.3	....	1.8	2.17	.....
Equipment	173	157	158	141	117	42	27	NA	10.0	....	0.9	1.10	.....
Assistance and subsidies	1,486	1,501	1,402	1,891	1,499	663	527	466	-1.0	218.7	8.0	9.44	3.52
Interest on debt	193	162	144	109	86	84	101	122	18.9	58.0	1.0	1.23	.92
Insurance benefits and repayments	2,096	1,416	1,413	2,177	1,020	1,158	226	505	48.1	314.9	11.2	13.31	3.82
Intergovernmental expenditure	5,679	5,384	5,044	4,217	3,283	2,092	1,842	1,780	5.5	218.9	30.4	36.06	13.45
Cash and security holdings at end of fiscal year	25,536	23,663	21,492	NA	NA	NA	NA	NA	7.9	NA	100.0	162.17	NA
Unemployment fund balance in U.S. Treasury	8,362	7,757	7,757	NA	NA	NA	NA	NA	-0.6	NA	32.7	53.10	NA
Cash and deposits	3,887	3,558	3,558	NA	NA	NA	NA	NA	6.8	NA	15.2	24.68	NA
Securities	13,287	11,609	10,177	NA	NA	NA	NA	NA	14.5	NA	52.0	84.38	NA
Total by purpose:													
Insurance trust	14,921	14,153	12,810	NA	NA	NA	NA	NA	5.4	NA	58.4	94.76	NA
Debt offsets	1,440	1,208	1,019	NA	NA	NA	NA	NA	19.2	NA	5.6	9.14	NA
Other	9,175	8,302	7,662	NA	NA	NA	NA	NA	10.5	NA	35.9	58.27	NA

EXHIBIT DATA

	1	2	3	4	5	6	7	8	9	10	11	12	13
Estimated population, July 1 of preceding calendar year (thousands) (c)	157,465	154,931	152,572	147,858	142,558	131,605	133,345	132,357	.....	19.0	.....	.....	.....
Income payments to resident individuals during preceding calendar year (in millions of dollars) (d)	$268,803	$254,338	$241,248	$195,322	$183,984	$155,928	$140,687	$91,438	.....	194.0	.....	$1,707.07	$690.84

*Source: Bureau of the Census, Compendium of State Government Finances in 1954 and Revised Summary of State Government Finances: 1942–1950.
NOTE: Because of rounding, detail does not always add to total. Per capita and per cent figures are computed on the basis of amounts rounded to the nearest thousand. "NA" signifies data not available.

(a) For detail, see Table 1 of section on "State Tax Collections in 1955," page 234.
(b) Not computed.
(c) Figures relate to total population excluding armed forces overseas.
(d) Source: Department of Commerce, Survey of Current Business.

TABLE 2

SUMMARY FINANCIAL AGGREGATES, BY STATE: 1954*

(In thousands of dollars)

State	Revenue and borrowing	Expenditure and debt redemption	Borrowing	Debt redemption	Revenue	Expenditure	General revenue	General expenditure	Liquor stores revenue	Liquor stores expenditure	Insurance trust revenue	Insurance trust expenditure
All states	$21,072,711	$19,183,726	$2,239,182	$497,346	$18,833,529	$18,686,380	$15,299,284	$15,787,128	$974,186	$802,926	$2,550,059	$2,096,326
Alabama	309,703	300,414	3,405	3,918	306,298	296,496	243,530	253,876	41,219	30,998	21,549	11,622
Arizona	135,775	123,192	400	181	135,375	123,011	114,238	112,472	......	......	21,137	10,539
Arkansas	168,196	164,714	3,745	6,440	164,451	158,274	154,783	148,652	......	......	9,668	9,622
California	2,130,565	1,991,059	128,000	23,952	2,002,565	1,967,107	1,664,506	1,737,541	......	......	338,059	229,566
Colorado	204,357	200,832	6,808	2,942	197,549	197,890	183,440	187,234	......	......	14,109	10,656
Connecticut	382,763	234,835	135,886	15,228	246,877	219,607	207,098	191,930	......	......	39,779	27,677
Delaware	84,222	70,050	21,138	6,654	63,084	63,396	61,077	60,668	......	......	2,007	2,728
Florida	373,492	343,872	7,107	1,211	366,385	342,661	341,713	327,335	......	......	24,672	15,326
Georgia	478,138	363,915	125,612	2,958	352,526	360,957	323,508	339,996	11,410	9,010	29,018	20,961
Idaho	84,928	84,912	......	55	84,928	84,857	64,831	69,349	......	......	8,687	6,498
Illinois	801,271	793,003	2,050	28,849	799,221	764,154	694,168	649,395	......	......	105,053	114,759
Indiana	707,881	450,400	293,642	861	414,239	449,539	376,348	393,842	......	......	37,891	55,697
Iowa	327,070	325,352	925	2,377	326,145	322,975	267,786	259,663	37,512	29,278	20,847	34,034
Kansas	215,489	213,566	1,800	1,068	213,689	212,498	200,219	199,838	......	......	13,470	12,660
Kentucky	240,733	248,740	9,761	836	230,972	247,904	205,916	216,722	......	......	25,056	31,182
Louisiana	502,060	464,907	19,398	15,694	482,662	449,213	452,676	429,868	......	......	29,986	19,345
Maine	171,209	119,007	55,776	2,208	115,433	116,799	83,227	90,133	20,590	15,640	11,616	11,026
Maryland	300,388	296,029	46,750	14,267	253,638	281,762	229,723	254,296	......	......	23,915	27,466
Massachusetts	663,305	629,858	103,267	30,158	560,038	599,700	447,076	523,495	......	......	112,962	76,205
Michigan	1,177,756	1,048,031	118,227	19,944	1,059,529	1,028,087	784,137	791,849	160,304	127,075	115,088	109,163
Minnesota	386,359	375,219	4,670	22,337	381,689	352,882	353,193	327,474	......	......	28,496	25,408
Mississippi	193,536	203,578	760	6,319	192,776	197,259	184,672	187,080	......	......	8,104	10,179
Missouri	375,306	359,013	......	4,296	375,306	354,717	349,631	325,849	......	......	25,675	28,868
Montana	101,066	97,618	390	1,551	100,676	96,067	72,135	74,999	17,163	14,107	11,378	6,961

Nebraska	111,532	104,222	35	296	111,497	103,926	106,408	98,615	.....	.....	5,089	5,311
Nevada	41,725	38,651	635	101	41,090	38,550	32,196	31,600	.....	.....	8,894	6,950
New Hampshire	90,666	79,336	16,350	5,362	74,316	73,974	46,174	50,314	18,355	14,670	9,787	8,990
New Jersey	736,204	545,694	270,000	23,910	466,204	521,784	312,151	397,007	.....	.....	154,053	124,777
New Mexico	143,082	123,353	4,117	3,770	138,965	119,583	133,000	114,922	.....	.....	5,965	4,661
New York	2,236,310	1,913,719	312,265	99,668	1,924,045	1,814,051	1,392,829	1,512,227	.....	.....	531,216	301,824
North Carolina	477,392	439,340	45,250	10,857	432,142	428,483	388,885	391,645	.....	.....	43,257	36,838
North Dakota	96,154	94,974	.....	4,474	96,154	90,500	89,696	85,511	.....	.....	6,458	4,989
Ohio	1,098,663	1,051,966	8,740	13,860	1,089,923	1,038,106	717,257	714,018	182,101	165,565	190,565	158,523
Oklahoma	318,467	320,621	1,474	6,007	316,993	314,614	302,225	301,123	.....	.....	14,768	13,491
Oregon	320,017	302,810	53,625	4,609	266,392	298,201	186,398	227,523	43,109	30,305	36,885	40,373
Pennsylvania	1,470,011	1,307,782	272,965	48,422	1,197,046	1,259,360	812,463	875,690	216,560	187,844	168,023	195,826
Rhode Island	104,865	100,716	5,600	2,625	99,265	98,085	72,556	69,719	.....	.....	26,709	28,366
South Carolina	276,933	285,785	39,450	12,692	237,483	273,093	216,566	256,832	.....	.....	20,917	16,261
South Dakota	73,646	76,941	.....	4,882	73,646	72,059	72,265	70,826	.....	.....	1,381	1,233
Tennessee	326,484	316,150	20,500	9,770	305,984	306,380	276,721	275,212	.....	.....	29,263	31,168
Texas	796,237	691,470	21,470	4,180	774,767	687,290	726,906	667,611	.....	.....	47,861	19,679
Utah	109,749	112,452	1,800	162	107,949	112,290	86,397	90,135	13,197	10,003	8,355	12,152
Vermont	50,378	51,137	1,584	646	48,794	50,491	38,000	40,153	7,084	7,429	3,710	2,909
Virginia	389,690	395,738	.....	2,128	389,690	393,610	274,040	294,086	100,771	83,230	14,879	16,294
Washington	539,312	526,384	29,080	11,864	510,232	514,520	374,971	408,220	60,424	42,150	74,837	64,150
West Virginia	279,958	333,867	44,491	11,801	235,467	322,066	169,489	252,579	37,221	29,126	28,757	40,361
Wisconsin	402,080	407,471	234	809	401,846	406,662	356,173	357,791	.....	.....	45,673	48,871
Wyoming	67,588	61,037	.....	147	67,588	60,890	55,887	50,213	7,166	6,496	4,535	4,181

*Source: Bureau of the Census, Compendium of State Government Finances in 1954.

TABLE 3

STATE GENERAL REVENUE, BY SOURCE AND BY STATE: 1954

(In thousands of dollars, except per capita)

| State | Total general revenue | | Taxes | | | | | | | | Inter-governmental revenue | Charges and miscellaneous general revenue |
| | Amount | Per capita | Total(a) | Sales and gross receipts | | | Licenses | | Individual income | Corporation income | | |
				Total(a)	General	Motor fuels	Total	Motor vehicle				
All states	$15,299,284	$97.16	$11,088,934	$6,573,030	$2,539,776	$2,218,097	$1,706,726	$1,030,715	$1,004,448(b)	$771,527(b)	$2,882,484	$1,327,866
Alabama	243,530	78.20	159,890	119,512	60,689	42,837	12,247	3,495	15,207(b)	1,036(b)	60,432	23,208
Arizona	114,238	122.84	77,926	49,146	24,913	15,538	7,474	5,020	5,098	5,032	21,892	14,420
Arkansas	154,783	81.08	105,737	74,170	29,094	29,399	14,904	9,945	3,933	8,114	39,860	9,186
California	1,664,506	136.55	1,242,401	793,686	463,733	230,508	120,547	85,977	96,254	125,841	321,714	100,391
Colorado	183,440	129.82	113,043	69,302	33,855	27,048	14,065	8,273	12,867	6,153	49,324	21,073
Connecticut	207,098	95.79	165,302	111,118	53,773	24,362	19,126	10,206	.....	25,337	20,901	20,895
Delaware	61,077	170.61	41,985	11,548	.....	5,756	10,902	2,679	10,945	.....	5,196	13,896
Florida	341,713	101.91	267,766	203,545	65,889	74,673	51,607	31,236	.....	.....	56,898	17,049
Georgia	323,508	90.24	224,666	185,647	102,676	57,332	11,119	6,906	13,053	13,121	77,404	21,438
Idaho	64,831	107.51	37,593	17,598	.....	12,173	9,209	5,388	5,218	2,908	18,905	8,333
Illinois	694,168	77.10	545,844	447,827	208,557	116,288	85,491	70,844	.....	.....	120,781	27,543
Indiana	376,348	90.99	285,928	226,726	139,174	53,389	39,796	29,415	.....	.....	48,713	41,707
Iowa	267,786	102.80	187,972	118,995	61,825	41,004	40,551	36,059	20,881	2,258	58,189	21,625
Kansas	200,219	99.81	140,050	92,702	46,680	31,410	21,291	16,273	11,537	3,550	45,252	14,917
Kentucky	205,916	69.45	138,128	78,121	.....	46,206	15,620	9,110	20,493	8,343	54,195	13,593
Louisiana	452,676	156.96	294,710	172,763	63,459	45,278	23,743	9,062	17,028(b)	(b)	97,148	60,818
Maine	83,227	91.06	56,403	41,915	13,777	15,515	11,703	6,653	.....	.....	18,639	8,185
Maryland	229,723	90.41	181,304	103,577	32,797	38,085	23,836	17,973	28,654	13,961	24,332	24,087
Massachusetts	447,076	91.24	328,446	125,911	.....	53,743	89,237	14,023	71,539	26,066(c)	98,289	20,341
Michigan	784,137	114.44	616,365	433,430	288,658	88,913	115,501	56,002	.....	.....	94,956	72,816
Minnesota	353,193	115.69	246,467	93,939	.....	42,649	36,558	28,706	50,917	14,505	57,645	49,081
Mississippi	184,672	84.60	119,881	86,747	35,567	35,281	8,715	3,771	5,297	10,940	51,487	13,304
Missouri	349,631	85.36	224,370	145,398	92,201	37,921	40,382	28,371	26,126(b)	(b)	113,416	11,845
Montana	72,135	117.48	39,351	20,002	.....	13,326	5,818	2,379	4,923	1,812	20,710	12,074

216

Nebraska	106,408	79.00	65,190	37,527		28,295	7,064	3,372			27,412	13,806
Nevada	32,196	156.29	17,848	10,514		6,388	4,355	2,602			9,380	4,968
New Hampshire	46,174	87.62	29,134	16,456		7,606	7,240	4,626	1,291		11,321	5,719
New Jersey	312,151	60.72	204,863	116,025		44,357	73,182	47,144			62,401	44,887
New Mexico	133,000	175.46	74,049	50,746	27,259	16,779	9,616	6,310	2,237	1,052	26,851	32,100
New York	1,392,829	91.43	1,134,307	365,776		110,740	158,340	105,135	351,067	204,449	185,850	72,672
North Carolina	388,885	92.75	294,771	164,905	55,507	75,853	42,651	22,499	38,832	37,907	64,757	29,357
North Dakota	89,696	144.44	43,597	27,695	12,770	7,561	8,640	6,793	2,612	940	17,316	28,783
Ohio	717,257	85.70	545,533	413,463	188,293	117,971	98,080	71,118			115,358	56,366
Oklahoma	302,225	134.26	203,644	119,383	43,493	46,560	32,555	25,252	9,411	7,844	68,307	30,274
Oregon	186,398	116.35	126,634	36,413		30,631	29,751	22,074	41,523	14,811	42,493	17,271
Pennsylvania	812,463	76.24	616,941	292,970	37,012	132,836	148,773	56,707		121,797	131,206	64,316
Rhode Island	72,556	88.81	57,004	40,454	13,649	7,988	7,254	4,915		7,095	11,503	4,049
South Carolina	216,566	98.66	157,019	115,647	45,662	39,495	11,105	5,633	12,504	14,305	41,352	18,195
South Dakota	72,265	109.99	38,771	30,509	12,145	10,661	6,763	4,617		148	20,990	12,504
Tennessee	276,721	83.12	194,685	138,345	53,073	56,072	32,012	14,378	3,446	16,266	69,713	12,323
Texas	726,906	87.60	470,340	216,520		109,839	66,269	40,448			153,383	103,183
Utah	86,397	117.71	56,707	34,760	17,985	12,703	5,862	3,803	5,658	3,982	21,851	7,839
Vermont	38,000	100.80	27,112	11,910		5,601	6,204	4,856	5,412	2,142	9,202	1,686
Virginia	274,040	77.26	196,038	85,976		56,724	32,067	16,467	39,282	21,958	38,171	39,831
Washington	374,971	151.32	273,899	222,780	140,046	47,966	25,700	14,112			65,036	36,036
West Virginia	169,489	87.50	128,204	108,588	66,798	20,460	16,815	12,533			31,791	9,494
Wisconsin	356,173	101.24	261,271	73,706		38,544	40,921	33,562	71,203	47,854	63,706	31,196
Wyoming	55,887	182.64	29,845	18,637	8,767	7,833	6,065	3,993			16,856	9,186

Source: Bureau of the Census, Compendium of State Government Finances in 1954.
(a) Includes amounts for categories not shown separately.
(b) Combined corporation and individual income taxes for three states—Alabama, Louisiana, and Missouri—are included with individual income taxes. Amount shown as corporation
(c) tax for Alabama represents taxes on financial institutions only. Amounts for corporation excises and surtaxes, measured in part by net income and in part by corporate excess, are included with license taxes.

217

Table 4
SUMMARY OF EXPENDITURE BY CHARACTER AND OBJECT AND BY STATE: 1954

(In thousands of dollars)

State	Total	Current operation	Capital outlay Total capital outlay	Construction Total construction	Construction Contract construction only	Purchase of land and existing structures	Equipment	Assistance and subsidies	Interest	Insurance benefits and repayments	Intergovernmental expenditure	Exhibit: Total personal services
All states	$18,686,380	$5,885,900	$3,346,711	$2,831,370	$2,558,879	$342,454	$172,887	$1,485,869(a)	$193,041	$2,096,326	$5,678,533	$3,491,130
Alabama	296,496	103,258	39,709	34,956	32,805	510	4,243	34,966	2,204	11,622	104,737	48,550
Arizona	123,011	37,280	26,009	23,916	23,134	286	1,807	15,333	148	10,539	33,702	20,915
Arkansas	158,274	50,787	22,865	21,119	20,586	209	1,537	27,337	3,838	9,622	43,825	28,455
California	1,967,107	463,360	331,702	224,729	197,642	86,164	20,809	2,184	14,392	229,566	925,903	353,878
Colorado	197,890	56,583	37,865	32,517	25,223	2,646	2,702	609	476	10,656	91,701	39,556
Connecticut	219,607	101,721	39,402	29,889	26,359	6,179	3,334	20,847	3,757	27,677	26,203	64,854
Delaware	63,396	24,761	17,067	15,536	13,965	903	628	2,399	2,956	2,728	13,485	16,691
Florida	342,661	106,051	63,416	55,302	50,602	4,754	3,360	51,465	2,359	15,326	104,044	67,139
Georgia	360,957	84,803	83,238	77,417	66,205	550	5,271	59,050	3,275	20,961	109,630	57,590
Idaho	84,857	35,011	18,145	15,459	13,533	1,397	1,289	9,304	23	6,498	15,876	17,876
Illinois	764,154	243,150	131,040	108,276	98,273	14,480	8,284	91,888	7,467	114,759	175,850	157,638
Indiana	449,539	127,703	61,448	50,186	46,973	7,181	4,081	63,251	5,341	55,697	136,099	83,702
Iowa	322,975	116,035	45,795	40,943	39,787	2,559	2,293	39,529	455	34,034	87,127	58,797
Kansas	212,498	72,538	46,250	40,041	38,362	3,067	3,142	346	153	12,660	80,551	49,577
Kentucky	247,904	73,450	60,240	49,855	40,745	8,260	2,125	38,367	278	31,182	44,387	48,491
Louisiana	449,213	125,294	70,821	63,453	56,429	707	6,661	99,261	6,417	19,345	128,075	76,691
Maine	116,799	56,683	21,352	20,042	16,210	569	741	12,613	2,770	11,026	12,355	25,049
Maryland	281,762	89,400	63,153	55,522	48,084	5,264	2,367	1,418	4,679	27,466	95,646	56,065
Massachusetts	599,700	161,919	114,155	100,853	89,999	9,441	3,861	27,088	7,446	76,205	212,887	118,814
Michigan	1,028,087	355,206	109,968	87,016	82,284	17,817	5,135	77,041	6,570	109,163	370,139	164,046
Minnesota	352,882	124,271	65,852	56,133	50,415	5,414	4,305	2,194	2,106	25,408	133,051	81,298
Mississippi	197,259	55,634	39,601	35,755	32,583	1,397	2,449	28,056	2,205	10,179	61,584	34,720
Missouri	354,717	92,830	58,802	53,233	50,204	2,962	2,607	108,752	610	28,868	64,855	55,180
Montana	96,067	43,765	19,112	16,774	14,867	1,094	1,244	11,872	1,104	6,961	13,253	19,350

Nebraska............	103,926	45,736	18,181	15,797	14,731	843	1,541	487	76	5,311	34,135	30,274
Nevada.............	38,550	14,303	8,328	7,912	7,684	266	150	1,999	41	6,950	6,929	7,334
New Hampshire.....	73,974	41,485	13,356	11,198	8,492	1,520	638	5,990	472	8,990	3,681	18,442
New Jersey.........	521,784	129,834	174,999	145,851	140,303	24,751	4,397	9,897	13,997	124,777	68,280	97,446
New Mexico........	119,583	39,170	23,142	21,032	18,544	821	1,289	12,727	689	4,661	39,194	24,285
New York..........	1,814,051	446,984	328,378	302,804	283,953	18,090	7,484	6,292	25,733	301,824	704,840	328,435
North Carolina.....	428,483	252,105	67,261	55,439	43,717	5,046	6,776	4,603	6,532	36,838	61,144	195,486
North Dakota......	90,500	43,804	17,914	16,371	15,630	190	1,353	7,991	719	4,989	15,083	16,224
Ohio...............	1,038,106	363,965	150,733	117,104	104,199	28,033	5,596	63,556	13,541	158,523	287,788	134,839
Oklahoma..........	314,614	86,963	41,412	36,285	35,942	1,541	3,586	84,987	2,965	13,491	84,796	54,704
Oregon............	298,201	115,045	54,905	45,288	40,690	6,451	3,166	27,431	2,473	40,373	57,974	61,745
Pennsylvania.......	1,259,360	474,053	223,453	195,433	170,340	18,563	9,457	110,727	21,918	195,826	233,383	214,067
Rhode Island.......	98,085	33,166	10,740	10,093	9,278	325	322	11,416	1,356	28,366	13,041	22,782
South Carolina.....	273,093	67,512	46,618	40,271	34,369	1,668	4,679	24,697	3,087	16,261	114,918	41,142
South Dakota.......	72,059	29,375	25,115	23,232	20,992	930	953	8,977	321	1,233	7,038	15,464
Tennessee..........	306,380	65,949	57,608	54,709	50,577	349	2,550	47,385	2,247	31,168	102,023	43,258
Texas..............	687,290	181,843	162,932	129,241	117,763	25,688	8,003	116,862	1,788	19,679	204,186	123,444
Utah...............	112,290	41,702	19,113	17,134	15,635	598	1,381	13,258	36	12,152	26,029	24,154
Vermont...........	50,491	24,924	7,541	7,080	6,239	193	268	5,916	58	2,909	9,143	10,192
Virginia............	393,610	206,190	67,816	55,748	42,632	7,964	4,104	1,644	931	16,294	100,735	82,431
Washington........	514,520	168,559	68,297	58,308	51,567	5,273	4,716	63,986	6,348	64,150	143,180	77,222
West Virginia......	322,066	92,085	100,501	88,911	87,106	8,846	2,744	28,155	6,394	40,361	54,570	41,573
Wisconsin..........	406,662	97,166	55,681	52,833	50,244	570	2,278	1,547	207	48,871	203,190	70,345
Wyoming...........	60,890	22,489	15,680	14,374	12,983	125	1,181	169	83	4,181	18,288	10,920

Source: Bureau of the Census, Compendium of State Government Finances in 1954.
(a)Includes bonus payments to veterans, amounting to $88,785 thousand.

219

TABLE 5

STATE GENERAL EXPENDITURE IN TOTAL AND FOR SELECTED FUNCTIONS, BY STATE: 1954

State	Amount in thousands					Per capita				
	Total general expenditure	Public welfare	Education	Highways	Health and hospitals	Total general expenditure	Public welfare	Education	Highways	Health and hospitals
All states	$15,787,128	$2,551,548	$4,656,253	$4,125,627	$1,401,544	$100.26	$16.20	$29.57	$26.20	$ 8.90
Alabama............	253,876	37,838	98,048	62,833	13,868	81.53	12.15	31.49	20.18	4.45
Arizona............	112,472	16,507	27,693	28,655	5,598	120.94	17.75	29.78	30.81	6.02
Arkansas...........	148,652	29,037	48,644	34,434	11,664	77.87	15.21	25.48	18.04	6.11
California..........	1,737,541	304,786	614,722	358,953	106,736	142.54	25.00	50.43	29.45	8.76
Colorado...........	187,234	61,706	43,373	46,906	13,556	132.51	43.67	30.70	33.20	9.59
Connecticut........	191,930	31,646	41,353	44,696	34,140	88.77	14.64	19.13	20.67	15.79
Delaware...........	60,668	3,616	29,186	12,658	5,611	169.46	10.10	81.53	35.36	15.67
Florida.............	327,335	53,857	114,466	81,076	23,680	97.62	16.06	34.14	24.18	7.06
Georgia............	339,996	64,226	142,621	66,848	28,380	94.84	17.92	39.78	18.65	7.92
Idaho..............	69,349	9,923	15,433	26,169	4,701	115.01	16.46	25.59	43.40	7.80
Illinois.............	649,395	140,533	150,838	191,820	67,330	72.13	15.61	16.75	21.31	7.48
Indiana.............	393,842	28,738	127,414	98,240	30,436	95.22	6.95	30.81	23.75	7.36
Iowa...............	259,663	43,105	64,306	80,307	19,046	99.68	16.55	24.69	30.83	7.31
Kansas.............	199,838	35,563	52,592	63,188	16,670	99.62	17.73	26.22	31.50	8.31
Kentucky...........	216,722	41,826	51,325	75,832	13,954	73.09	14.11	17.31	25.58	4.71
Louisiana	429,868	109,007	120,035	76,045	30,096	149.05	37.80	41.62	26.37	10.44
Maine..............	90,133	15,279	15,008	33,696	7,760	98.61	16.72	16.42	36.87	8.49
Maryland...........	254,296	16,191	57,739	79,920	33,774	100.08	6.37	22.72	31.45	13.29
Massachusetts......	523,495	113,479	43,712	110,203	65,998	106.84	23.16	8.92	22.49	13.47
Michigan...........	791,849	87,493	289,812	184,095	84,776	115.56	12.77	42.30	26.87	12.37
Minnesota..........	327,474	42,965	115,582	84,385	31,109	107.26	14.07	37.86	27.64	10.19
Mississippi.........	187,080	30,765	56,483	56,248	11,724	85.70	14.09	25.87	25.77	5.37
Missouri............	325,849	113,699	77,404	69,328	18,996	79.55	27.76	18.90	16.93	4.64
Montana...........	74,999	12,935	22,527	20,844	4,331	122.15	21.07	36.69	33.95	7.05
Nebraska...........	98,615	16,973	24,144	32,921	9,853	73.21	12.60	17.92	24.44	7.31
Nevada.............	31,600	2,384	7,018	12,624	1,182	153.40	11.57	34.07	61.28	5.74
New Hampshire.....	50,314	7,721	7,240	17,145	6,038	95.47	14.65	13.74	32.53	11.46
New Jersey.........	397,007	29,304	57,135	163,053	63,159	77.22	5.70	11.11	31.72	12.29
New Mexico........	114,922	15,683	50,208	28,125	4,846	151.61	20.69	66.24	37.10	6.39
New York..........	1,512,227	224,144	381,752	339,121	215,278	99.27	14.71	25.06	22.26	14.13
North Carolina.....	391,645	35,474	171,020	99,662	30,416	93.40	8.46	40.79	23.77	7.25
North Dakota.......	85,511	9,195	19,947	22,767	4,577	137.70	14.81	32.12	36.66	7.37
Ohio...............	714,018	116,158	159,622	248,733	52,666	85.32	13.88	19.07	29.72	6.29
Oklahoma..........	301,123	89,696	89,072	75,574	15,716	133.77	39.84	39.57	33.57	6.98
Oregon.............	227,523	33,118	58,329	77,351	13,999	142.02	20.67	36.41	48.28	8.74
Pennsylvania.......	875,690	103,182	272,732	255,444	96,105	82.18	9.68	25.59	23.97	9.02
Rhode Island.......	69,719	16,574	10,428	11,561	8,615	85.34	20.29	12.76	14.15	10.54
South Carolina......	256,832	26,921	126,954	43,739	18,188	117.01	12.26	57.84	19.93	8.29
South Dakota.......	70,826	10,281	13,214	29,468	3,988	107.80	15.65	20.11	44.85	6.07
Tennessee..........	275,212	51,574	91,334	76,119	16,398	82.67	15.49	27.44	22.87	4.93
Texas..............	667,611	122,412	262,056	166,272	39,516	80.45	14.75	31.58	20.04	4.76
Utah...............	90,135	14,286	37,618	22,148	3,921	122.80	19.46	51.25	30.17	5.34
Vermont............	40,153	5,853	7,967	14,453	4,259	106.51	15.53	21.13	38.34	11.30
Virginia............	294,086	17,096	102,274	89,265	30,174	82.91	4.82	28.83	25.17	8.51
Washington.........	408,220	79,567	133,267	91,755	39,159	164.74	32.11	53.78	37.03	15.80
West Virginia	252,579	31,717	68,664	115,833	9,988	130.40	16.37	35.45	59.80	5.16
Wisconsin..........	357,791	43,672	69,292	86,986	27,164	101.70	12.41	19.70	24.73	7.72
Wyoming...........	50,213	3,843	14,650	18,129	2,405	164.09	12.56	47.88	59.25	7.86

Source: Bureau of the Census, *Compendium of State Government Finances in 1954.*

TABLE 6
STATE DEBT OUTSTANDING AND LONG-TERM DEBT
ISSUED AND RETIRED, BY STATE: 1954
(In thousands of dollars, except per capita)

	Debt outstanding at end of fiscal year								
	Total		Long-term			Short term	Net long-term		
State	Amount	Per capita	Total	Full faith and credit	Non-guaranteed		Total Amount	Per capita	Full faith and credit
All states	$9,599,664	$ 60.96	$9,316,652	$5,769,981	$3,546,671	$ 283,012	$7,876,700	$ 50.02	$4,480,795
Alabama...........	72,741	23.36	72,716	60,020	12,696	25	56,400	18.11	45,168
Arizona...........	2,998	3.22	2,998	304	2,694	....	2,407	2.59	252
Arkansas..........	123,261	64.57	123,261	111,637	11,624	....	109,097	57.15	98,060
California..........	794,557	65.18	794,557	704,437	90,120	....	361,533	29.66	304,321
Colorado..........	20,870	14.77	18,874	....	18,874	1,996	17,992	12.73	....
Connecticut.......	385,531	178.32	211,831	211,831	....	173,700	199,353	92.21	199,353
Delaware..........	125,035	349.26	125,035	76,791	48,244	....	123,834	345.91	76,791
Florida............	77,663	23.16	77,663	....	77,663	....	69,842	20.83	....
Georgia...........	192,960	53.82	192,960	38	192,922	....	179,480	50.06	....
Idaho	1,163	1.93	1,163	....	1,163	....	1,010	1.67	....
Illinois...........	332,264	36.91	332,264	307,851	24,413	....	297,400	33.03	273,750
Indiana...........	316,906	76.62	316,906	....	316,906	....	309,698	74.88	....
Iowa..............	29,205	11.21	29,205	26,250	2,955	....	29,192	11.21	26,237
Kansas............	5,295	2.64	5,295	1,250	4,045	....	3,945	1.97	....
Kentucky..........	19,123	6.45	19,123	....	19,123	....	18,724	6.32	....
Louisiana..........	216,167	74.95	216,167	196,454	19,713	....	202,148	70.09	184,787
Maine.............	118,004	129.11	118,004	39,457	78,547	....	117,772	128.85	39,373
Maryland..........	266,865	105.02	266,865	137,075	129,790	....	196,710	77.41	79,989
Massachusetts.....	495,983	101.22	462,632	426,505	36,127	33,351	456,921	93.25	422,150
Michigan..........	455,438	66.47	455,438	203,938	251,500	....	441,663	64.46	195,274
Minnesota.........	95,835	31.39	95,835	94,708	1,127	....	93,747	30.71	92,746
Mississippi.........	75,702	34.68	75,625	....	75,625	77	73,565	33.70	....
Missouri...........	15,064	3.68	15,064	10,500	4,564	....	10,310	2.52	6,492
Montana...........	45,429	73.99	45,429	4,800	40,629	....	32,218	52.47	3,315
Nebraska..........	3,228	2.40	3,228	....	3,228	....	3,149	2.34	....
Nevada............	1,429	6.94	1,429	1,429	....	....	1,368	6.64	1,368
New Hampshire.....	41,930	79.56	41,930	40,890	1,040	....	40,914	77.64	39,874
New Jersey.........	677,680	131.82	677,680	270,956	406,724	....	659,884	128.36	261,430
New Mexico........	28,236	37.25	28,236	15,433	12,803	....	26,793	35.35	14,188
New York..........	1,176,299	77.22	1,161,299	1,132,123	29,176	15,000	666,412	43.75	639,728
North Carolina......	298,601	71.21	298,601	297,887	714	....	237,554	56.65	237,037
North Dakota.......	26,355	42.44	25,605	23,920	1,685	750	5,631	9.07	4,030
Ohio..............	473,205	56.54	473,205	135,813	337,392	....	466,483	55.74	129,258
Oklahoma..........	124,376	55.25	124,376	33,163	91,213	....	114,411	50.83	26,463
Oregon............	183,848	114.76	183,848	183,731	117	....	125,544	78.37	125,544
Pennsylvania........	1,178,184	110.57	1,178,184	415,291	762,893	....	1,156,576	108.54	405,599
Rhode Island.......	58,342	71.41	58,342	58,342	....	....	52,023	63.68	52,023
South Carolina.....	169,676	77.30	169,376	121,197	48,179	300	154,333	70.31	108,937
South Dakota.......	9,164	13.95	9,164	8,934	230	....	1,498	2.28	1,360
Tennessee..........	122,082	36.67	122,082	119,521	2,561	....	112,502	33.79	110,146
Texas..............	110,433	13.31	110,433	73,782	36,651	....	107,384	12.94	72,915
Utah..............	3,154	4.30	3,154	170	2,984	....	2,867	3.91	....
Vermont...........	5,288	14.03	5,288	5,288	....	....	5,288	14.03	5,288
Virginia............	33,389	9.41	33,389	11,229	22,160	....	27,146	7.65	7,100
Washington........	293,440	118.42	235,627	55,072	180,555	57,813	220,050	88.80	51,245
West Virginia.......	288,569	148.98	288,569	151,964	136,605	....	275,272	142.11	139,204
Wisconsin..........	4,844	1.38	4,844	....	4,844	....	4,844	1.38	....
Wyoming..........	3,853	12.59	3,853	....	3,853	....	3,813	12.46	....

Source: Bureau of the Census, *Compendium of State Government Finances in 1954.*

2

Taxation

RECENT TRENDS IN STATE TAXATION*

THE heaviest volume of tax legislation in any year since the end of the war has emerged from the 1955 legislative sessions. At mid-year[1] it appeared that higher taxes would have been imposed in at least two-thirds of the forty-six states in which sessions were held during 1955.

The many new revenue measures reflected the impact of population growth on spending for virtually every state function. Governors' messages to legislatures consistently recommended higher appropriations to meet expanded requirements for schools, highways, state institutions and general government. With tax collections apparently tapering off from the sustained postwar upswing, and surpluses generally depleted, legislatures were asked to search their tax systems for additional sources of revenue.

Across the nation as a whole, the measures adopted encompassed every major tax category and assumed a great variety of forms. In many states the accelerated output of tax legislation did not meet fully the additional revenue requirements suggested in proposed budgets. In these states, the revenue programs enacted usually represented a compromise between the original budget recommendations and the reluctance of legislatures to add to existing tax burdens. In mid-1955, however, the extent to which further revenues might be needed

in certain states to finance the approved level of appropriations remained in question.

The spurt in business activity which began at the end of 1954 provided the impetus for a rise in revenues, in most states substantially above estimates for fiscal 1955. Because revenue estimates for the budget periods beginning in 1955 were based, generally, on the assumption that the economy would remain more or less stable, a continued expansion in business activity might again result in unanticipated revenues for the states. At the outset of the 1956 fiscal year, the adequacy of state tax provisions seemed to rest on whether the rise in state revenues, if it continued, would be sufficient to offset the increased demand for state services which appeared an inevitable consequence of population projections.

Enactments involving new tax sources were infrequent in 1955, but many more states than in recent years turned to broad-based sales and income taxes for additional revenues. In the five-year span 1950–54, there were four new sales tax adoptions but only nine instances of states raising the rate of an existing levy on income or sales. In 1955 almost half of the states took action to increase tax collections from one or another of these sources, mainly by raising rates but also by broadening the tax base and adopting methods of accelerated collection.

Equally significant in 1955 was adoption of "tax packages," a series of increases in

*Prepared by LEON ROTHENBERG, Research Director, Federation of Tax Administrators.

[1]Several legislatures were still considering major proposals at that time.

taxes of a more selected nature. Problems in highway financing resulted in motor fuel tax raises in one-third of the states. More than one-fourth of the states enacted tobacco tax revenue legislation. Rate raises in alcoholic beverage, severance and corporation franchise taxes were prominent in the list of enactments.

Local taxing capacity also was a matter of concern for state legislatures in 1955. Several passed enabling acts authorizing cities to adopt new nonproperty taxes. Perhaps most noteworthy in this field, however, was a considerable amount of legislation to strengthen the administration of the property tax, still the principal source of local revenue. Underlying this action was the frequently expressed view of state executives and legislators that local governments could and should assume greater responsibility for financing education through more effective property assessment procedures. Legislation in 1955 included provisions for state-wide property revaluation, the extension of state tax agencies' supervisory authority over the local assessment process, state equalization of local assessments, and reorganization of the local assessment structure.

In 1954, although tax legislation was more extensive than usual in legislative "off" years, there was little suggestion of the large volume that would be enacted in the next year. Income taxes were raised by the District of Columbia and by Maryland, which allowed a 15 per cent credit to expire, and were lowered on earned income by Massachusetts on a one-year basis. Three states, Arizona, Colorado and Kentucky, adopted income tax withholding. Motor fuel tax rates were raised by New Jersey and the District of Columbia, and cigarette taxes by the District of Columbia, Kentucky and Utah. Higher rates on alcoholic beverages were imposed by the District of Columbia, Kentucky, Maryland and Texas. Corporation franchise taxes were raised in New Jersey and Texas, and parimutuel taxes in Kentucky, New Jersey and New York.

Principal tax changes enacted in 1955 are summarized below, with certain of the changes of 1954. Unless otherwise indicated, the measures reported were enacted in 1955.

INCOME TAXES

Eleven states raised rates on individuals or corporations or both. Five increased both personal and corporate income tax rates, three raised them only for individuals, and three increased them on corporations only. Idaho replaced a 15 per cent credit for both individuals and corporations with a 7.5 per cent surtax for tax years 1955 and 1956. Mississippi added a 14 per cent surtax for a fifteen-month period ending June 30, 1956, unless the level of revenues permits an earlier reduction. Minnesota imposed a 5 per cent surtax on individuals and raised corporation tax rates 1 per cent for the 1955 and 1956 tax years. Iowa raised its personal income tax bracket rates by one-fifteenth and its corporate income tax rate from 2 to 3 per cent. In Vermont, rates for personal income tax brackets were raised by a range of ½ per cent to 2 per cent, while the corporation tax was increased from 4 to 5 per cent. The higher rates are effective beginning with 1955, but the old ones may be restored if the state has more than $1.5 million in unappropriated surplus on June 30, 1956.

The three states providing for higher individual income taxes without changing the corporation income tax rate were Oregon, which imposed a 45 per cent individual income tax surtax; Wisconsin, which added a 20 per cent surtax to its individual income tax; and New York, which allowed a 10 per cent tax credit to expire. New York raised its unincorporated business tax by allowing it to revert from a temporary 3 per cent rate to the normal 4 per cent. The three states boosting corporation tax rates while leaving personal income tax rates unchanged were Maryland, 4 to 4.5 per cent, South Carolina, 4.5 per cent to 5 per cent and Utah, 3 to 4 per cent.

Colorado extended for another year a 20 per cent credit currently allowed both individual and corporate income tax payers. Georgia reduced its corporate tax rate from 5.5 to 4 per cent and lowered the tax on individual incomes in excess of $20,000 from 7 to 6 per cent, but provided for higher collections by removing the federal income tax deduction. Connecticut and Rhode Island extended temporary corporate income tax increases. Massachusetts allowed a one-year 25 per cent earned income tax reduction adopted in 1954 to lapse. Virginia, which had granted tax credits to both individuals and corporations in every year since 1951 on the basis of an automatic tax reduction law, in 1954 raised the revenue requirements on which the credit was contingent. As a result no credit was given in 1955.

Personal exemptions were revised in several states. Notably, as revenue raising measures, they were reduced by Oregon from $600 to $500 for each taxpayer, his spouse and each dependent. Oregon provided an additional flexible "hardship" exemption which, for single individuals, will be the amount by which $1,000 exceeds adjusted gross income and, for married persons, the amount by which $1,500 exceeds adjusted gross income.

In 1954 and 1955, the number of states with income tax withholding laws was increased from three to ten. Delaware, Oregon and Vermont already were imposing withholding requirements at the outset of 1954. Arizona, Colorado and Kentucky added such provisions in 1954. In 1955, Idaho, Maryland and Montana imposed them effective July 1, 1955, and Alabama effective January 1, 1956. Withholding tax statutes are characterized by several significant differences which are reflected in the most recent adoptions. Colorado and Idaho withhold on the basis of a fraction of the amount withheld by the federal government: 4 per cent in Colorado, 10 per cent in Idaho. Kentucky and Maryland base their withholding on tables designed to approximate the taxpayer's annual liability. Arizona permits withholding at either 1/2 per cent of gross wages or by the use of a withholding table. In Alabama withholding may be computed either by imposing a range of graduated rates on taxable income or through a withholding table. Montana's withholding rate is 1 per cent of gross wages after deducting amounts for personal exemptions. Alabama, Kentucky, Maryland and Montana require taxpayers with specified levels of income not subject to withholding to file declarations of estimated tax. Oregon raised its withholding rate from 1 to 2 per cent.

New Mexico and Utah, the only two states that had been allowing taxpayers the option of reporting income taxes on a basis other than that prescribed in their basic income tax statutes, repealed the optional provisions. New Mexico in 1953 had allowed individuals with gross incomes under $10,000 to pay taxes at the rate of 4 per cent of taxes due the federal government. Utah in 1953 had replaced a similar measure with one giving taxpayers the option of applying state rates to their federal net income after deduction of federal credits and federal taxes paid or accrued. The 1955 repealing acts of both New Mexico and Utah were ascribed to administrative difficulties and taxpayer inequities resulting from inclusion of two distinct methods of computation under a single statute.

A number of states took further steps to bring their income tax laws into line with federal law. Notably, Iowa in 1955 and Kentucky in 1954 adopted provisions defining "net income" by specific reference to the federal internal revenue code. California revised its income tax law extensively to conform with the 1954 federal internal revenue amendments. Many states moved the income tax payment date forward one month, in line with action taken by the federal government.

SALES TAXES

A 2 per cent sales and use tax imposed by Nevada on July 1, 1955, made it the thirty-third state in this field. In addition, six states raised existing sales tax rates. Washington increased its rate from 3 to 3 1/3 per cent; Illinois and Iowa, for a two-year period, from 2 to 2.5 per cent; and Mississippi, South Dakota and Tennessee raised their rates from 2 to 3 per cent. The South Dakota increase was one of a series of measures imposed to finance a Korean veterans' bonus and will expire when sufficient funds have been accumulated to pay it.

In addition, Michigan, which imposes a business receipts tax—a levy which has been termed a "value-added" tax and has characteristics of both a gross receipts tax and an income tax—raised rates from 1 to 1.5 mills on public utilities and from 4 to 6.5 mills on other taxpayers. Washington and West Virginia revised their business and occupation taxes upward. Connecticut extended for two more years a temporary 1 per cent increase in its sales tax rate. Illinois adopted a use tax to complement its retailers' occupation tax.

Iowa extended its sales tax to cigarettes and beer, and South Dakota, to cigarettes and alcoholic beverages, while Tennessee removed an exemption that had been allowed alcoholic beverage sales. Mississippi deleted from its sales tax deductibles the proceeds from state taxes on beer and tobacco and federal gasoline taxes. North Carolina, South Carolina and Tennessee made rentals from transient lodgings subject to sales tax. Tennessee also added charges for parking services to taxables under its act. North Carolina modified and South Carolina repealed provisions limiting the tax on a single transaction.

MOTOR FUEL TAXES

Gasoline tax rates were raised by sixteen legislatures in 1955, the increases ranging from $^2/_{10}$ to 2 cents per gallon. Increases of $\frac{1}{2}$ cent were enacted in Vermont, 5 to 5.5 cents per gallon; Nevada, 5.5 to 6 cents; and Georgia, 6 to 6.5 cents. One cent increases were adopted by Texas, 4 to 5 cents per gallon; Iowa, North Dakota, Pennsylvania and West Virginia, 5 to 6 cents; and Alabama, Maine and Montana, 6 to 7 cents per gallon. Michigan raised its motor fuel tax rate from 4.5 to 6 cents per gallon, and Connecticut and Wisconsin from 4 to 6 cents. The New York legislature submitted a proposal to the voters which, if approved, will raise the gasoline tax rate from 4 to 6 cents per gallon effective January 1, 1956. In addition, Tennessee increased its petroleum inspection fees from $\frac{1}{2}$ cent to $^7/_{10}$ cent per gallon. California, Kansas, Nebraska, North Dakota, Oklahoma and Pennsylvania extended or made permanent temporary rate raises that had been scheduled for expiration.

States raising gasoline tax rates usually provided for similar increases in special fuel tax rates. Exceptions were Michigan, which eliminated its differential tax on diesel fuel by raising the tax on all motor fuel up to the 6 cents per gallon diesel tax rate, and Texas, which raised the tax on diesel fuel $\frac{1}{2}$ cent per gallon and on other motor fuels a full cent, narrowing the difference between the two to 1.5 cents

per gallon. In contrast, Montana increased the rate on diesel 3 cents per gallon, compared with a 1 cent increase on other motor fuels. Kansas added 2 cents per gallon to its special fuels tax while leaving its rate on other fuels unchanged, and New York, if its voters approve, will raise the diesel tax rate from 6 to 9 cents per gallon while boosting the gas tax rate from 4 to 6 cents.

A number of states shifted the collection of special fuel taxes from the user to the seller. Montana, New Mexico and Tennessee placed responsibility for collection on the seller delivering the fuel in the supply tank of the motor vehicle. North Dakota provided for collection on a much broader basis, requiring the seller to collect taxes when delivering special fuel to any user except when placed in a fuel tank connected with a heating appliance. The North Dakota law will necessitate payment of refunds for non-highway use. Under a new act, North Carolina, which also had collected its special fuel tax on a user-report basis, will require collection by suppliers.

Gasoline use-tax statutes were adopted by Georgia, Kansas, North Carolina and Tennessee in 1955, and by Kentucky in 1954, to curb tax avoidance by commercial operators who previously had used the highways of these states but had filled their supply tanks in adjoining states taxing motor fuel at lower rates.

TOBACCO TAXES

New cigarette taxes were adopted by Missouri, at 2 cents per pack, and by Oregon, at 3 cents, but both required submission to the voters in order to become effective—Missouri's to be voted on in October, 1955,[2] and Oregon's at the next state-wide election. Eleven states increased rates. One of them, Georgia, raised rates twice in the course of a regular and special session; first by increasing the tax on king-size cigarettes to 4 cents per pack (1 cent higher than the tax on regular cigarettes) and then by increasing the rate on both types of cigarettes to 5 cents. South Dakota raised its rate from 3 to $3\frac{1}{4}$ cents per pack. The other rate raising states adopted 1 cent per pack increases—from 3 to 4 cents

[2] Missouri's voters approved the measure on October 4.

in Alabama, Idaho, and Wisconsin; from 4 to 5 cents in Maine, Mississippi, New Mexico, Pennsylvania, Texas and Washington. Ohio voters in November, 1955, were to consider a proposed 1 cent increase in the cigarette tax rate, the proceeds to be used to finance a capital improvement program. Minnesota, which taxes cigarettes at 4 cents per pack, added a tax on other tobacco products of 15 per cent of the wholesale price. Mississippi, which raised its cigarette tax rate, reduced its tax on cigars from 1 cent on each 5 cents of selling price to a maximum of $14 per 1,000 units selling at more than 20 cents per unit retail.

Alcoholic Beverage Taxes

Rates were raised on each class of alcoholic beverage; distilled spirits, wine, and beer. Alabama and Idaho added taxes to the price of distilled spirits sold in their state-operated stores. Alabama also imposed added taxes on wine and beer. California increased its rates on proof strength liquor from 80 cents to $1.50 per gallon and raised taxes on champagne and sparkling wines. In Georgia state warehouse charges on liquor were raised by executive order $1.25 per gallon, and by legislation taxes on beer and most types of wine were doubled. South Carolina for a one-year period, while suspending various license taxes, raised the rates of two additional taxes imposed on liquor on a per case basis and raised the tax on beer permanently from 30 cents to 37.5 cents per gallon. South Dakota increased the rate on non-intoxicating beer and wine from $1.75 to $2.00 per barrel. Texas raised its beer tax from $2.00 to $4.30 per barrel. North Carolina raised its tax on liquor from 8.5 to 10 per cent of retail price and provided for additional taxes on beer and wine. Maine imposed an additional tax on wines.

One state, Arkansas, lowered distilled spirits taxes by repealing in March a temporary additional tax of 1/4 cent per pint and 1/2 cent per fifth which had been scheduled to expire in 1957.

Motor Carrier Taxes

Four states took action with respect to truck mileage taxes. Idaho, which in 1953 had repealed a weight mileage tax adopted

in 1951, reimposed such a tax in 1955. Kansas and New Mexico replaced mileage taxes with a set of registration fees graduated according to the gross weights of vehicles. Colorado's legislature, which in 1954 replaced a ton-mile tax based on cargo weight with a gross ton-mile tax, revised this latter levy in 1955. The levy had called for a 1.5 mills tax per gross ton mile; the new Colorado law, which became effective April 1, taxes empty weight at .8 mill per ton mile and cargo weight at 2 mills per ton mile.

Other significant legislation in this field included California's extension to 1960 of higher license and weight fees enacted in 1953, which had been scheduled for expiration in 1955; and increases in truck fees in Georgia, Michigan, Montana, Nevada, North Dakota and Tennessee.

Property Taxes

State-wide property revaluations were ordered in 1955 by Arkansas, Idaho, Maryland, Oregon, Washington and West Virginia. In each instance the revaluations were to be made by local assessors, with some supervision by the state. In Arkansas, the State Public Service Commission is to supply guidance to county assessors. In Idaho the State Tax Commission will step in and make the revaluations in counties which have not complied by 1961. Maryland's Tax Commission has been given authority to enforce annual reassessment in every county. Oregon required county appraisers, subject to state civil service certification, to appraise real property at least once every six years. In Washington the State Tax Commission received power to compel assessors by court action to reassess all property quadrenially in accordance with established statutory standards. In West Virginia, the State Tax Commissioner was required to make an annual state-wide appraisal of property values.

Nebraska, Nevada and Oregon enacted legislation extending the state tax agency's supervisory authority over the local assessment process, either through promulgation of rules and regulations or by imposing assessment ratio requirements. In Washington, the legislature declared public schools a state function and provided for state equalization of district assessments. A

1955 West Virginia law made school aid to counties contingent upon the ratio of their assessments to property values as determined by the State Tax Commissioner. In Indiana, assessment ratios, to be computed at least once every fourth year, will be used in determining school aid distributions. On the basis of existing powers, the California Board of Equalization initiated a program to equalize county assessments.

Two other states sought to improve assessment administration by strengthening local assessment structure. Kansas provided for a county assessor system on an appointive or elective basis, dependent on the will of the voters. South Dakota gave the county voters the option of accepting a county assessor or a county supervisor of local assessors.

Local Taxing Powers

While some states were enacting legislation to expand the property tax base, additional states were extending local taxing powers in other fields. Authorization to impose sales taxes was given to cities in Illinois and New Mexico and to counties in California. In California, where more than 170 cities already were taxing sales, cities continued to have priority in levying the tax through a tax credit device. In each state, provision was made for collection of the local levies along with the state sales tax by the state taxing agency. The action taken by these states raises to four the number of states with coordinated state and local sales taxes. Mississippi has had such a law on its books since 1950.

Miscellaneous

Corporation franchise taxes based on capital stock or capital used in the state were raised by Alabama, Idaho, Maine, Mississippi and Texas. Severance tax rates were raised in Minnesota on iron ore, in Mississippi on oil and gas and in South Dakota on mineral products. Utah imposed a new oil and gas conservation tax. Mississippi, which previously taxed chain theaters at 3 per cent and other theaters at 2 per cent, made the 3 per cent rate applicable to all movie admissions. Two additional states—Mississippi in 1954 and West Virginia in 1955—adopted laws authorizing other states to sue in their courts for taxes owed. Ohio and West Virginia raised pari-mutuel rates, and Nevada increased its tax on gambling proceeds.

TABLE 1

RANGE OF STATE INDIVIDUAL INCOME TAX RATES

As of July 1, 1955*

State / Individual income	Tax rate (per cent)	State / Individual income	Tax rate (per cent)
Alabama		**Missouri**	
$0 to $1,000	1.5	$0 to $1,000	1(f)
Over $5,000	5	Over $9,000	4(f)
Arizona		**Montana**	
$0 to $1,000	1	$0 to $2,000	1
Over $7,000	4.5	Over $6,000	4
Arkansas		**New Hampshire**	
$0 to $3,000	1	Income from intangibles	Average property tax rates(g)
Over $25,000	5	**New Mexico**	
California		$0 to $10,000	1
$0 to $5,000	1	Over $100,000	4
Over $25,000	6	**New York**	
Colorado(a)		$0 to $1,000	2
$0 to $1,000	1	Over $9,000	7
Over $11,000	10	Net capital gains	One-half regular rates
Surtax on income from intangibles in excess of $600	2	Unincorporated businesses	3
Delaware		**North Carolina**	
$0 to $3,000	1	$0 to $2,000	3
Over $100,000	6	Over $10,000	7
Georgia		**North Dakota**	
$0 to $1,000	1	$0 to $3,000	1
Over $20,000	6	Over $15,000	11
Idaho		**Oklahoma**	
$0 to $1,000	1.6125(b)	$0 to $1,500	1
Over $5,000	8.6(b)	Over $7,500	6
Iowa		**Oregon**	
$0 to $1,000	0.8	$0 to $500	2.9(h)
Over $5,000	4	Over $8,000	11.6(h)
Kansas		**South Carolina**	
$0 to $2,000	1	$0 to $2,000	2
Over $7,000	4	Over $6,000	5
Kentucky		**Tennessee**	
$0 to $3,000	2	Dividends and interest	6
Over $8,000	6	Dividends from corporations of whose property at least 75 per cent is assessable for property tax	4
Louisiana		**Utah**	
$0 to $10,000	2	$0 to $1,000	1
$10,001 to $50,000	4	Over $4,000	5
Over $50,000	6	**Vermont**	
Maryland		$0 to $1,000	2
Investment income	5	Over $5,000	7.5
Other income	2	**Virginia**	
Massachusetts		$0 to $3,000	2
Earned income, professional income	3.075(c)	$3,000 to $5,000	3
Annuities	1.845(c)	Over $5,000	5
Capital gains	7.38(c)	**Wisconsin**	
Interest and dividends	7.38(c)	$0 to $1,000	1.2
Minnesota		Over $14,000	10.7
$0 to $1,000	1.1(d)	**District of Columbia**	
Over $20,000	11(d)	$0 to $5,000	2.5
Mississippi		Over $15,000	4
$0 to $4,000	1.14(e)		
Over $25,000	6.84(e)		

*Prepared by the Federation of Tax Administrators.
(a) A credit of 20 per cent of the net tax due is allowed for tax year 1955.
(b) Includes a surtax of 7½ per cent imposed for the tax years 1955 and 1956.
(c) For calendar year 1955, rates given include additional taxes of 1 per cent on earned income and professional income and 3 per cent on capital gains, plus an additional tax of 23 per cent of the regular tax on all income categories.
(d) Includes a surtax of 5 per cent imposed for the tax years

1955 and 1956 plus a second temporary 5 per cent surtax for veterans' bonus purposes.
(e) Includes a surtax of 14 per cent imposed effective April 1, 1955 to June 30, 1956, subject to an earlier reduction if state revenues are sufficient.
(f) Deductions: $0 to $9,000—$5 to $90; over $9,000—$135.
(g) Effective 1956, the rate will be 4.25 per cent.
(h) Includes a surtax of 45 per cent imposed for tax years ending after August 3, 1955.

TABLE 2

RANGE OF STATE CORPORATE INCOME TAX RATES
As of July 1, 1955*

State	Corporate income	Tax rate (per cent)	State	Corporate income	Tax rate (per cent)
Alabama			**Mississippi**		
	Net income, in excess of credits......	3		$0 to $4,000......................	1.14(i)
	Financial corporations..............	6		Over $25,000....................	6.84(i)
Arizona			**Missouri**		
	Business corporations:			Business corporations..............	2
	$0 to $1,000..................	1		Banks and trust companies.........	7
	Over $6,000..................	5	**Montana**............................		3
	Banks........................	5	**New Mexico**........................		2
Arkansas			**New York**		
	$0 to $3,000....................	1		Business corporations..............	5.5(j)
	Over $25,000....................	5		National banks...................	4.5
California				State banks and financial corporations	4.5
	Business and public utility corporations...........................	4	**North Carolina**.....................		6
	National and state banks and financial corporations...................	4–8(a)	**North Dakota**		
	Corporations not taxed as above.....	4		Business corporations:	
Colorado				$0 to $3,000..................	3
	Business corporations..............	5(b)		Over $15,000..................	6
	Banks and financial corporations in lieu of other taxes................	6		Banks and trust companies..........	4
Connecticut			**Oklahoma**...........................		4
	Business corporations, banks and financial corporations.............	3.75(c)	**Oregon**.............................		8(k)
Georgia.............................		4	**Pennsylvania**.......................		5
Idaho			**Rhode Island**		
	Business corporations and banks:			Business corporations..............	5(l)
	$0 to $1,000..................	1.6125(d)		Banks...........................	4
	Over $5,000..................	8.6(d)	**South Carolina**		
Iowa...............................		3(e)		Business corporations..............	5
Kansas.............................		2		Banks...........................	4.5
Kentucky...........................		4.5	**South Dakota**		
Louisiana..........................		4		Banks............................	3
Maryland..........................		4.5	**Tennessee**..........................		3.75
Massachusetts			**Utah**		
	Business corporations..............	6.765 (f)		National banks....................	4
	Banks, trust companies............. Not to exceed 8			Business corporations and state banks	4(m)
	Utility corporations...............	4	**Vermont**...........................		5
Minnesota			**Virginia**............................		4
	Net income above exemption of $500.	7.3(g)	**Wisconsin**		
	National and state banks..........	8.4(h)		$0 to $1,000.....................	2
				Over $6,000.....................	7
			District of Columbia.................		5

*Prepared by the Federation of Tax Administrators.

(a) Rate adjusted annually with maximum of 8 per cent, minimum of 4 per cent, but never less than $25 for financial corporations.

(b) A credit of 20 per cent of the net tax due is allowed for the tax year 1955.

(c) Effective for the tax years 1955 and 1956 when tax paid shall not be less than $20, or 1.9 mills per $1.00 of capital less stock holdings.

(d) Includes surtax of 7.5 per cent imposed for tax years 1955 and 1956.

(e) Increased from 2 to 3 per cent for the tax years 1955 and 1956.

(f) Effective rate in 1955 is 6.765 per cent, comprising the following: permanent tax, 2½ per cent; temporary additional excise of 3 per cent; temporary surtax of 20 per cent of taxes assessed; additional surtax for old-age pensions, 3 per cent of taxes assessed.

(g) Includes an additional 1 per cent tax for the tax years

1955 and 1956 and a 5 per cent temporary veterans' bonus surtax imposed on the basic 6 per cent rate.

(h) Includes a 5 per cent temporary veterans' bonus surtax; trust companies not doing a banking business are taxed at 6 per cent of gross earnings in lieu of ad valorem taxes on capital stock and personal property.

(i) Includes a 14 per cent surtax effective April 1, 1955 to June 30, 1956, subject to an earlier reduction if state revenues are sufficient.

(j) Or $25 or 1 mill per $1.00 of capital if either is greater than the tax computed on net income.

(k) Mercantile, manufacturing and business corporations are allowed an offset for personal property taxes paid, up to 50 per cent of income tax.

(l) Or 40 cents per $100 of corporate excess is collected if greater than the tax computed on net income.

(m) State banks and corporations pay 4 per cent of net income or 1/20 per cent of value of tangible property, whichever is greater, but not less than $10.

TABLE 3

STATE EXCISE TAX RATES
As of July 1, 1955*

State	State sales and gross receipts (per cent)	Cigarettes (cents per pack)	Gasoline (cents per gallon)	Distilled spirits(a) (per gallon)	State	State sales and gross receipts (per cent)	Cigarettes (cents per pack)	Gasoline (cents per gallon)	Distilled spirits (per gallon)
Alabama	3	4	7	....	Nebraska		3	6	1.20
Arizona	2(b)	2	5	$1.20	Nevada	2	3	6(l)	.80
Arkansas	2	6	6.5	2.50(c)	New Hampshire	..	3	5	....
California	3	..	6(d)	1.50	New Jersey	..	3	4	1.50
Colorado	2	..	6	1.60	New Mexico	2(m)	5	6	1.30
Connecticut	3	3	6	1.00	New York	..	3	4(n)	1.50
Delaware	..	3	5	1.15	North Carolina	3(o)	..	7	....
Florida	3	5(e)	7	2.17-4.34	North Dakota	2	6	6	2.50
Georgia	3	5	6.5	1.00 (f)	Ohio	3	2(p)	5	....
Idaho	..	4	6	....	Oklahoma	2	5	6.5	....
Illinois	2.5	3	5	1.00	Oregon	..	..(q)	6	....
Indiana	¼-1(g)	3	4	2.08	Pennsylvania	1(r)	4(s)	5(t)	....
Iowa	2.5(h)	3	6	....	Rhode Island	2	3	4	1.50
Kansas	2	3	5	1.00	South Carolina	3	3	7	2.72
Kentucky	..	3	7	1.28	South Dakota	..	3(u)	5	.75
Louisiana	2	8	7	1.58	Tennessee	3	5	7	2.00
Maine	2	5	7	....	Texas	..	4(v)	4(w)	1.41
Maryland	2	..	6	1.50	Utah	2	4	5	....
Massachusetts	..	5	5	2.25	Vermont	..	4	5.5	....
Michigan	3	3	6	....	Virginia	..	..	6	....
Minnesota	..	4	5	2.75(i)	Washington	3⅓	5	6.5	....
Mississippi	3(j)	5	7	....	West Virginia	2	4	6	....
Missouri	2	..(k)	3	.80	Wisconsin	..	4	6	2.00
Montana	..	4	7	....	Wyoming	2	2	5	....
					D. of C.	2	2	6	1.00

*Prepared by the Federation of Tax Administrators.

(a) Two states, Mississippi and Oklahoma, prohibit the sale of liquors of alcoholic content above 3.2 per cent and 4 per cent, respectively. Sixteen states have liquor monopoly systems (Alabama, Idaho, Iowa, Maine, Michigan, Montana, New Hampshire, Ohio, Oregon, Pennsylvania, Utah, Vermont, Virginia, Washington, West Virginia and Wyoming). Some of the monopoly states impose taxes, generally expressed in terms of a percentage of retail price. Vermont, however, levies a tax of $2.80 per gallon. North Carolina has county-operated stores in counties which vote in favor of their operation, and the state imposes a tax of 10 per cent of retail price.

(b) This rate is for retailers. Also gross income tax rates varying from ¼ per cent for manufactures to 1 per cent for extractive industries and 2 per cent for rentals.

(c) In addition, manufacturers pay a tax of 10 cents per case of liquor, and wholesalers a tax of 20 cents per case. A special excise of 3 per cent is imposed on the retail receipts from sale of liquor.

(d) A 6 cents per gallon tax is in effect through December 31, 1959, after which the rate is reduced to 5.5 cents per gallon.

(e) Municipalities may impose a like tax at the same rate, with full credit given in such instances for the state tax.

(f) In addition, a state warehouse charge of $2.25 per gallon is imposed.

(g) Wholesale, ¼ per cent; retail, ½ per cent; income from personal services, 1 per cent.

(h) Motor vehicles, trailers and motor vehicle equipment are taxed at 2 per cent.

(i) Includes a 10 per cent veterans' bonus surtax effective through December 31, 1958.

(j) Wholesalers, ⅛ per cent; sales of automobiles, trucks and truck-tractors, 2 per cent; farm tractors sold to farmers, 1 per cent.

(k) If the voters approve a 1955 legislative act on October 4, 1955, a 2 cents per pack tax is to go into effect on January 1, 1956.

(l) Includes a 1 cent per gallon additional tax, optional with individual counties but approved by all.

(m) Wholesalers, ⅛ per cent.

(n) Tax to be raised to 6 cents per gallon on January 1, 1956, if approved by the voters.

(o) Wholesale merchants, 1/10 per cent. Sales of motor vehicles and airplanes are taxed at 1 per cent, with a maximum tax of $80 per vehicle.

(p) Rate to be increased to 3 cents per pack, if voters approve at November, 1955, election.

(q) At the next state-wide election, a 3-cents-per-pack tax enacted by the legislature in 1955 will be submitted to the voters.

(r) Expired August 31, 1955.

(s) Increased to 5 cents per pack October 1, 1955.

(t) Increased to 6 cents per gallon September 13, 1955.

(u) One per cent of the tax enacted in 1955 to finance a Korean war veterans' bonus will expire when requirements are met.

(v) Increased to 5 cents per pack on September 6, 1955.

(w) Increased to 5 cents per gallon on September 6, 1955.

STATE TAX COLLECTIONS IN 1955*

STATE tax collections in the 1955 fiscal year[1] totaled $11.6 billion. This amount was up 4.5 per cent from the $11.1 billion collected in 1954 and was three times the 1942 amount of $3.9 billion.

The 1954–1955 rise of $0.5 billion was almost as large as that of the preceding year. Although these annual increases were substantially less than those of the three previous years, they were about equal to the average annual increase of the eight-year period 1942–1950. The chart (page 232) shows trends in state tax revenue since 1942.

Tax figures discussed here are net of refunds paid, but include amounts of state-imposed taxes collected or received by the state and subsequently distributed to local governments. Locally collected and retained tax amounts are not included. The 1955 figures are preliminary.

Statistics on state revenue in 1955 from nontax sources have not been compiled at this writing. In fiscal 1954, the states received $7.7 billion from such sources, including $2.7 billion from the federal government and $2.6 billion from insurance trust sources. About three-fifths of all state insurance trust revenue in 1954 represented "contributions" collected for unemployment compensation. Such contributions were classified as tax revenue in Census reports for several years prior to 1951. However, in Census reports for 1951 and subsequent years, tax revenue figures (including prior year amounts) are exclusive of such unemployment compensation contributions.

This article relates to revenue from state taxes only. In 1954, tax revenue of local governments amounted to $11.0 billion[2], or about the same total as taxes collected by the states in fiscal 1954.

MAJOR TAX SOURCES

Most major tax categories shared in the 1954–1955 net rise in state tax yields. The largest amount of increase was provided by sales taxes on motor fuel—up $135 million, or 6.1 per cent. General sales and gross receipts taxes were up $97 million, or 3.8 per cent.

General sales and gross receipts taxes continued as the largest single source of state tax revenue, providing $2.6 billion. This category accounted for more than one-fifth of total state tax yields in 1955, even though such taxes were in effect in only thirty-two states.

The next ranking source was the sales tax on motor fuel, which produced $2,353 million. Alcoholic beverage sales taxes produced $471 million in 1955 as compared with $463 million in 1954 and $465 million in 1953. For the second successive year, tobacco sales tax revenues declined slightly, providing $459 million in fiscal 1955. Altogether, general and selective sales and gross receipts taxes yielded $6,864 million, or nearly three-fifths of the total collected from all state tax sources.

Corporation and individual income taxes together rose slightly from $1,776 million in 1954 to $1,821 million in 1955. The yield of individual income taxes (imposed by thirty-one states) was up 7.9 per cent, to reach a new high of $1,084 million. This figure includes corporation tax amounts for three states which reported combined income tax figures in both 1954 and 1955, and an additional small amount for one state, as indicated by footnote (a), Table 2.

*Adapted from U. S. Bureau of the Census, *State Tax Collections in 1955* (August, 1955).

[1]Data contained in the Bureau of the Census annual series on "State Finances" are for state fiscal years that end on June 30, except for four states with earlier closing dates (two in the spring and two between the preceding August and December), as shown in Table 5.

[2]U. S. Bureau of the Census, *Summary of Governmental Finances in 1954* (September, 1955). Fiscal 1954 figures on local government taxes and other revenue, expenditure and debt are presented in that publication.

Corporation net income taxes amounted to $737 million, or 4.5 per cent less than the 1954 amount.

Motor vehicle and motor vehicle operators' license taxes provided $1,184 million in 1955, up $86 million or 7.9 per cent from the 1954 level. Motor vehicle licenses include truck mileage and weight taxes and other motor carrier taxes except those measured by gross receipts, net income, or assessed valuation.

State property taxes totaled $412 million in 1955, or 5.6 per cent more than in 1954. This source, of course, has been almost entirely relinquished to local governments by most states. State property levies are generally at only nominal rates or apply to limited types of property, such as intangibles, motor vehicles or particular classes of utility property.

Increases appear also for selective sales and gross receipts taxes on public utilities (up 7.9 per cent to $283 million), and on insurance companies (up 4.9 per cent to $370 million) and for license taxes on corporations in general (up 6.1 per cent to $266 million). Death and gift taxes were up slightly, to reach $249 million. Severance taxes declined from $312 million in 1954 to $303 million in 1955.

INDIVIDUAL STATE COMPARISONS

Forty-one states reported higher total tax yields in 1955 than in 1954. The collections of twenty-three states rose by less than 5 per cent, fourteen states reported gains of 5 to 10 per cent, two states show increases of 10 to 15 per cent, and two states show a rise of more than 15 per cent—Kentucky (17.4 per cent) and New Jersey (16.2 per cent). The greatest amounts of increase are shown for California (up $92 million or 7.4 per cent) and New York (up $66 million or 5.8 per cent).

Tax revenue of Indiana dropped 11.2 per cent from the 1954 level, reflecting expiration of various taxes which had been enacted to finance bonus payments to veterans. New Hampshire reported a decrease of 5.4 per cent, and decreases of less than 5 per cent appear for five states.

California collected $1,334 million in state taxes and New York $1,200 million in fiscal 1955, far more than the next ranking states: Michigan ($646 million), Pennsylvania ($629 million), Ohio ($584 million) and Illinois ($552 million).

Per capita amounts of state tax revenue in 1955 ranged from about $116 in the State of Washington down to $45 in New

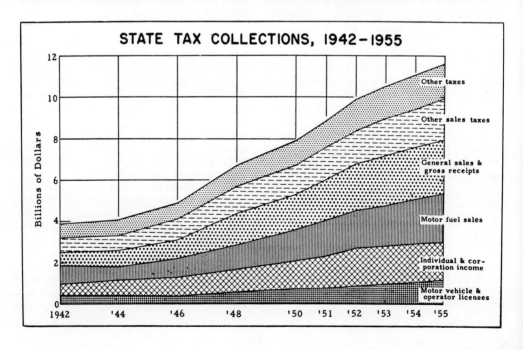

Jersey. The forty-eight-state average equaled $72.

Caution must be used in attempting comparisons of tax figures for individual state governments. The states vary greatly as to the scope and intensity of public services, in economic resources, and in the pattern for distribution of responsibility, as between the state and local levels, for performing and financing particular functions.

Some states directly administer certain activities which elsewhere are undertaken by local governments, with or without state fiscal aid. In particular, it should be noted that the proportion of state-local tax revenue which is contributed by state-imposed taxes differs markedly from one state area to another. Percentage figures illustrating this variation, in terms of 1953 tax revenue data, are presented in Table 5.

TABLE 1

STATE TAX COLLECTIONS, BY TYPE OF TAX: 1942–1955*

Tax source	1955 (Prelim.)	1954	1953	1952	1951	1950	1942	From 1954 to 1955	From 1953 to 1954	Per cent distribution 1955	Per capita (b) 1955
Total collections	$11,584	$11,089	$10,552	$9,857	$8,933	$7,930	$3,903	4.5	5.1	100.0	$72.25
Sales and gross receipts	6,864	6,573	6,209	5,730	5,268	4,670	2,218	4.4	5.9	59.3	42.81
General sales or gross receipts	2,637	2,540	2,433	2,229	2,000	1,670	632	3.8	4.4	22.8	16.44
Motor fuels	2,353	2,218	2,019	1,870	1,710	1,544	940	6.1	9.9	20.3	14.68
Alcoholic beverages	471	463	465	442	469	420	257	1.9	—0.6	4.1	2.94
Tobacco products	459	464	469	449	430	414	130	—1.1	—1.1	4.0	2.86
Insurance	370	353	320	284	254	241	113	4.9	10.3	3.2	2.31
Public utilities	283	263	249	228	199	185	100	7.7	5.5	2.4	1.76
Other	291	273	255	228	206	195	45	6.5	7.4	2.5	1.82
License	1,823	1,707	1,630	1,476	1,359	1,228	708	6.8	4.7	15.7	11.37
Motor vehicles and operators	1,184	1,098	1,012	924	840	755	431	7.9	8.4	10.2	7.39
Corporations in general	266	251	266	226	211	176	93	6.1	—5.7	2.3	1.66
Alcoholic beverages	79	79	79	77	77	77	56	—0.5	—0.4	0.7	.49
Hunting and fishing	83	78	77	70	63	60	24	5.2	2.4	0.7	.51
Other	212	201	196	178	168	160	104	5.4	2.3	1.8	1.32
Income	1,821	1,776	1,779	1,751	1,492	1,310	518	2.5	—0.2	15.7	11.36
Individual income (c)	1,084	1,004	969	913	805	724	249	7.9	3.7	9.4	6.76
Corporation net income (c)	737	772	810	838	687	586	269	—4.5	—4.8	6.4	4.60
Property	412	391	365	370	346	307	264	5.6	7.0	3.6	2.57
Death and gift	249	247	222	211	196	168	110	0.8	11.3	2.2	1.55
Severance	303	312	286	272	222	211	62	—3.0	8.9	2.6	1.89
Other	112	83	61	47	50	36	23	33.8	37.3	1.0	.70

Amount in millions / Per cent change(a) / Per cent distribution

*Source: U.S. Bureau of the Census, *State Tax Collections in 1955.*
NOTE: Because of rounding, detail does not always add to total. Per capita and per cent figures are computed on the basis of amounts rounded to the nearest thousand.
(a) Changes are increases unless preceded by a minus sign (—), which denotes a decrease.

(b) Based on provisional estimates of population on July 1, 1954. (See Table 5.)
(c) Individual income tax figures include corporation net income tax amounts for from one to four states in each fiscal year shown. (See also footnote a, Table 2.)

TABLE 2

STATE TAX COLLECTIONS, BY MAJOR SOURCE AND BY STATE: 1955*

(In thousands of dollars)

State	Total	Sales and gross receipts (Table 3)	Licenses (Table 4)	Individual income	Corporation net income	Property	Death and gift	Severance	Poll	Document and stock transfer	Other
Number of states using tax	48	48	48	31	33	45	47	25	9	13	10
Total	$11,583,536	$6,863,844	$1,823,048	$1,083,905(a)	$736,906(a)	$412,442	$249,051	$302,637	$8,469	$72,387	$30,847
Alabama	163,205	119,433	14,093	16,458(a)	1,098(a)	9,681	285	965	549	605	
Arizona	80,313	52,605	7,760	5,300	5,235	9,217	196				38
Arkansas	107,486	75,754	15,240	4,640	7,469	288	158	3,937			
California	1,334,391	846,552	129,579	106,557	133,412	86,820	30,303	1,168			
Colorado	129,218	74,630	17,143	18,092	5,677	8,127	3,427	2,122			
Connecticut	173,497	118,504	21,496		23,190	12	10,295				
Delaware	40,820	12,319	12,212	12,551		1,823(b)	1,915				
Florida	293,783	222,254	55,829			7,747	2,221	53		5,623	56
Georgia	235,572	195,351	12,385	15,112	11,574	507	643				
Idaho	38,032	18,364	8,922	5,385	2,678	2,199	402	82			
Illinois	551,823	447,137	89,058			563	15,065				
Indiana	254,004	192,122	41,661			14,980	4,034	308	899		
Iowa	197,850	125,952	42,880	21,900	2,284	133	4,701				
Kansas	144,523	99,023	21,436	12,865	3,777	5,811	1,338	273			
Kentucky	162,189	85,842	15,876	33,233	10,591	12,632	3,224	208		583	
Louisiana	303,497	176,762	27,257	19,129(a)	(a)	11,162	2,264	66,923			
Maine	58,902	43,424	12,621			1,069	1,785				
Maryland	199,181	116,460	23,860	32,225	14,639	7,895	4,070		3	32	
Massachusetts	334,412	131,498	87,824(c)	77,075	22,344(c)	169	14,460			1,042	
Michigan	645,877	450,099	119,642		(a)	34,969	10,492	699			29,976(d)
Minnesota	245,391	95,902	39,107	54,356	16,238	15,723	4,828	19,040		197	
Mississippi	125,041	90,501	10,188	3,977	10,360	3,149	333	6,533			
Missouri	225,780	147,176	39,218	27,382(a)	(a)	8,038	3,966				
Montana	41,581	21,134	6,259	5,308	1,573	4,336	1,389	1,582			

Nebraska	68,649	40,740	6,319	......	......	20,561	227	......	......	......
Nevada	20,396	12,773	4,311	......	......	3,058	1,144	134	802	120
New Hampshire	27,554	14,642	7,289	1,426	......	1,712	......	14	1,327	......
New Jersey	238,081	136,257	86,160	......	......	2,869	12,795	......	......	......
New Mexico	80,210	52,432	11,393	3,707(a)	(a)	5,534	535	6,527	40,923	82
New York	1,200,204	384,762	169,513	367,466	207,215	2,329	27,996	......	......	......
North Carolina	307,411	174,524	44,991	40,053	34,957	6,847	5,978	......	......	61
North Dakota	45,935	28,425	9,366	2,695	997	3,500	195	757	......	......
Ohio	584,189	437,631	111,790	......	......	29,043	5,725	28,999	......	......
Oklahoma	210,434	124,964	34,533	10,437	8,147	1(e)	3,353	741	......	......
Oregon	129,828	37,859	30,835	42,795	14,027	19	3,552	......	......	......
Pennsylvania	628,956	323,083	154,737	......	97,911	2,194	33,382	......	17,649	......
Rhode Island	58,614	42,297	8,010	......	6,227	......	2,080	......	......	......
South Carolina	156,861	118,081	11,538	12,327	11,941	1,246	731	......	997	......
South Dakota	40,423	31,874	7,069	......	173	117	508	682	1,100	385
Tennessee	204,761	144,502	37,579	3,646	14,390	15(e)	3,144	......	......	......
Texas	489,030	217,835	76,395	......	......	27,463	6,241	158,781	2,085	230
Utah	54,964	36,894	6,676	6,456	2,415	259	504	1,760	485	......
Vermont	27,153	12,164	6,648	5,398	1,594	350	514	......	1,634	......
Virginia	205,765	90,141	33,912	42,216	20,916	10,263	3,745	201	......	46
Washington	293,483	241,600	26,040	......	......	20,037	5,091	......	715	......
West Virginia	126,509	105,052	18,522	......	......	340	1,910	148	......	......
Wisconsin	266,971	78,296	41,883	73,738	43,857	21,296	7,685	......	......	68
Wyoming	30,787	18,218	5,993	......	......	6,339	222	......	......	15

*Source: U. S. Bureau of the Census, State Tax Collections in 1955.
(a) Combined corporation and individual income taxes for four states—Alabama, Louisiana, Missouri and New Mexico—are tabulated with individual income taxes. Amount shown as corporation tax for Alabama represents only tax on financial institutions.
(b) Tax for State Board Unit Schools.
(c) Amount for licenses includes $49,120 thousand corporation taxes measured in part by net income.
(d) Tax on adjusted business receipts.
(e) Back taxes only; not counted with "Number of states using tax" at top of column.

TABLE 3

SALES AND GROSS RECEIPTS TAX COLLECTIONS, BY STATE: 1955*

(In thousands of dollars)

State	Total	General sales or gross receipts	Selective sales and gross receipts								
			Total	Motor fuels	Alcoholic beverages	Tobacco products	Insurance	Public utilities	Pari-mutuels	Amusements	Other
Number of states using tax	48	32	48	48	48	41	48	36	24	32	30
Total	$6,863,844	$2,636,552	$4,227,292	$2,353,388	$471,220	$458,583	$370,106	$282,819	$191,933	$12,678	$86,565
Alabama	119,433	58,862	60,571	44,590	1,377	7,479	4,235	2,372	....	29	489
Arizona	52,605	27,225	25,380	16,494	2,585	2,203	1,406	1,718	974	....	....
Arkansas	75,754	30,154	45,600	30,332	5,251	6,440	2,680	....	884	13	....
California	846,552	490,992	355,560	250,025	19,790	....	38,501	15,354	23,422	130	8,338(a)
Colorado	74,630	36,982	37,648	28,707	4,113	....	3,061	6,873	1,757	8	2
Connecticut	118,504	59,377	59,127	25,803	6,145	8,494	9,153	24	....	4	2,655(b)
Delaware	12,319	....	12,319	6,108	1,440	1,504	1,184	....	1,949	110	....
Florida	222,254	74,027	148,227	81,661	30,888	4,724	6,394	4,110	19,662	783	5
Georgia	195,351	107,044	88,307	60,497	11,395	9,698	6,087	....	....	....	630
Idaho	18,364	....	18,364	12,920	794	1,698	1,638	804	....	9	501
Illinois	447,137	205,532	241,605	117,306	23,362	30,261	20,925	33,952	15,208	591	....
Indiana	192,122	102,797	89,325	55,800	12,712	13,306(c)	7,475	....	....	32	....
Iowa	125,952	65,666	60,286	44,223	3,214	7,020	5,441	....	....	....	388
Kansas	99,023	50,506	48,517	33,039	5,103	5,231	4,864	280	....	....	....
Kentucky	85,842	....	85,842	48,054	10,805	7,968	4,657	3,935	1,823	1,678	7,192(d)
Louisiana	176,762	64,811	111,951	45,534	17,155	19,594	6,627	18,122	1,858	78	2,983(e)
Maine	43,424	14,475	28,949	16,596	2,084	4,819	1,830	2,926	694	....	9,548(d)
Maryland	116,460	....	81,567	40,892	6,938	27,692	6,068	10,452	7,205	464	6,543(f)
Massachusetts	131,498	....	131,498	55,681	22,358	....	8,404	....	10,799	21	....
Michigan	450,099	301,161	148,938	94,055	7,369	25,467	15,141	....	6,881	25	....
Minnesota	95,902	....	95,902	45,061	14,429	11,294	6,676	18,167	....	6	269
Mississippi	90,501	37,870	52,631	36,882	4,103	6,888	3,028	....	....	411	1,319
Missouri	147,176	92,384	54,792	39,031	5,765	....	9,810	101	....	....	85
Montana	21,134	....	21,134	14,407	1,756	2,761	1,376	800	....	34	....

236

Nebraska	40,740	.....	.....	31,313	2,821	3,883	2,671	6	.....	.....	46
Nevada	12,773	.....	.....	6,996	837	1,090	494	14	.....	.....	3,342
New Hampshire	14,642	.....	.....	8,055	1,016	2,957	1,408	1,206	.....	.....	.....
New Jersey	136,257	.....	.....	63,084	17,528	19,201	13,871	22,563	.....	.....	10
New Mexico	52,432	27,778	24,654	17,613	1,667	2,604	1,500	917	75	9	269
New York	384,762	.....	.....	119,023	49,230	58,141	49,232	50,049	57,033	2,054	.....
North Carolina	174,524	58,355	116,169	80,351	11,143	2,909	7,985	16,439	.....	.....	251
North Dakota	28,425	13,055	15,370	8,202	2,814	1,144	3	3	.....	.....	298
Ohio	437,631	201,070	236,561	126,480	33,768	19,956	21,377	29,045	5,935	.....	6,291(d)
Oklahoma	124,964	46,249	78,715	47,911	6,056	10,739	7,280	438	275	.....	115
Oregon	37,859	.....	.....	31,924	1,209	3,496	840	.....	.....	.....	26
Pennsylvania	323,083	62,501	260,582	137,559	44,706	43,087	22,099	13,081	.....	.....	24
Rhode Island	42,297	13,951	28,346	8,745	2,258	3,166	1,963	3,416	7,952	.....	846(b)
South Carolina	118,081	46,649	71,432	40,575	12,069	5,655	3,604	4,119	78	.....	5,122(g)
South Dakota	31,874	12,762	19,112	11,106	2,611	1,682	1,349	3	.....	.....	2,283(h)
Tennessee	144,502	55,096	89,406	59,270	7,763	13,614	6,428	1,574	311	.....	446
Texas	217,835	.....	.....	112,978	17,185	34,239	20,975	9,802	.....	303	22,353(i)
Utah	36,894	18,846	18,048	13,243	770	1,781	1,553	107	.....	.....	594
Vermont	12,164	.....	.....	5,765	2,787	1,731	864	1,016	.....	(j)	1
Virginia	90,141	.....	.....	60,064	7,569	8,001	14,495	.....	.....	12	.....
Washington	241,600	153,648	87,952	50,673	8,776	10,643	5,212	9,908	896	1,844	6,331(k)
West Virginia	105,052	63,117	41,935	20,911	3,251	6,096	3,121	.....	2,225	.....	394
Wisconsin	78,296	.....	.....	40,372	11,919	10,448	7,022	8,134	.....	.....	.....
Wyoming	18,218	8,717	9,501	7,477	536	690	796	2	.....	.....	.....

*Source: U. S. Bureau of the Census, State Tax Collections in 1955.
(a) Agricultural marketing taxes.
(b) Tax on gross income of unincorporated businesses.
(c) Includes related license taxes.
(d) Tax on motor vehicles.
(e) Includes $1,739 thousand on lubricating oil and $1,018 thousand on soft drinks.
(f) Tax on meals.
(g) Tax on soft drinks.
(h) Includes $1,887 thousand tax on motor vehicles.
(i) Includes (in thousands): $16,161 on motor vehicles, $1,810 on cement, $1,692 on radios, $1,067 on carbon black, and $1,006 on oil and gas well servicing.
(j) Less than $500.
(k) Comprises $3,442 thousand on motor vehicles and $2,889 thousand on soft drinks.

TABLE 4

LICENSE TAX COLLECTIONS, BY STATE: 1955*

(In thousands of dollars)

State	Total	Motor vehicles	Motor vehicle operators	Corporations in general	Public utilities	Alcoholic beverages	Chain stores	Amusements	Occupations and businesses, n.e.c.†	Hunting and fishing	Other
Number of states using tax	48	48	48	48	28	48	16	34	48	48	28
Total	$1,823,048	$1,110,701	$73,370	$266,201	$18,343	$78,687	$4,963	$4,496	$180,081	$82,522	$3,684
Alabama	14,093	3,319	1,954	3,798	338	130	100	...	3,707	747	...
Arizona	7,760	5,073	386	455	...	214	...	...	717	915	...
Arkansas	15,240	10,468	712	495	138	406	...	80	1,562	1,379	...
California	129,579	93,157	5,841	705	342	9,214	...	...	13,919	6,174	227
Colorado	17,143	10,403	656	363	59	769	190	15	1,593	3,092	3
Connecticut	21,496	10,835	4,717	511	...	3,085	...	119	1,567	525	137
Delaware	12,212	2,945	316	6,821	256	272	151	7	1,323	82	39
Florida	55,829	34,919	1,884	1,091	84	1,377	364	10	14,558	1,542	...
Georgia	12,385	7,677	110	1,414	...	238	...	...	2,453	493	...
Idaho	8,922	5,372	193	238	...	419	...	4	1,256	1,364	76
Illinois	89,058	72,504	3,272	4,280	...	1,263	...	500	4,906	2,333	...
Indiana	41,661	32,033(a)	(a)	369	830	3,926	594(b)	13	2,758	1,136	2
Iowa	42,880	38,314	1,276	284	20	73	33	...	1,300	1,198	382
Kansas	21,436	17,215	156	677	169	208	...	45	2,184	743	39
Kentucky	15,876	9,444	843	950	...	807	182	129	2,084	1,516	103
Louisiana	27,257	9,701	2,428	7,583	...	932	...	12	5,463	956	...
Maine	12,621	7,157	772	206	...	488	...	25	2,464	1,423	86
Maryland	23,860	18,992	439	571	...	110	...	258	2,801	684	5
Massachusetts	87,824	14,967	5,258	49,986(c)	6,364	417	...	281	9,559	992	...
Michigan	119,642	60,172	2,338	41,404	144	5,008	458	14	4,138	5,956	10
Minnesota	39,107	30,414	611	140	21	94	...	8	4,233	3,586	...
Mississippi	10,188	4,119	974	1,829	390	73	92	...	1,984	727	1
Missouri	39,218	27,495	1,101	3,993	272	1,495	...	28	2,412	2,421	...
Montana	6,259	2,500	550	81	...	980	160	...	800	1,150	38

Nebraska	6,319	3,952	77	233	...	161	...	21	1,136	739	...
Nevada	4,311	2,343	91	310	...	17	...	463	277	664	146
New Hampshire	7,289	4,952	517	136	...	234	...	...	520	929	1
New Jersey	86,160	48,267	7,668	22,161	1,198	869	...	...	4,364	1,542	91
New Mexico	11,393	6,857	490	663	961	78	...	9	1,042	1,293	...
New York	169,513	112,935	6,981	2,434	4,462	24,048	...	485	14,117	3,845	206
North Carolina	44,991	24,046	944	6,299	46	86	197	527	11,422	1,424	...
North Dakota	9,366	6,989	55	23	551	165	...	53	1,092	438	...
Ohio	111,790	84,326	1,435	11,778	294	7,481	...	99	3,314	3,040	23
Oklahoma	34,533	27,297	1,823	2,534	1	279	...	291	1,025	1,283	...
Oregon	30,835	22,838	707	527	...	591	...	419	2,780	2,678	295
Pennsylvania	154,737	62,971	6,033	60,758	7	7,826	...	17	11,100	5,125	900(d)
Rhode Island	8,010	5,214	1,148	130	...	62	313	26	1,327	103	...
South Carolina	11,538	5,981	831	402	...	782	51	305	2,081	843	...
South Dakota	7,069	4,930	5	38	...	157	171	...	694	1,189	5
Tennessee	37,579	20,422	598	5,767	110	273	1,790	100	9,046	1,092	...
Texas	76,395	44,141	3,121	20,868	...	1,357	...	10	3,507	1,601	...
Utah	6,676	4,330	94	106	3	2	...	...	458	1,609	74
Vermont	6,648	5,083	414	19	14	165	...	54	366	526	7
Virginia	33,912	18,002	423	887	...	235	...	67	12,564	1,538	196
Washington	26,040	13,587	2,171	567	962	1,265	117	...	3,479	3,445	564
West Virginia	18,522	14,129	310	926	250	475	...	...	1,290	1,010	15
Wisconsin	41,883	34,150	556	267	57	69	...	2	3,096	3,673	13
Wyoming	5,993	3,764	91	124	...	12	...	...	243	1,759	...

*Source: U. S. Bureau of the Census, State Tax Collections in 1955.
†N.e.c. signifies not elsewhere classified.
(a) Amount for motor vehicles includes operators' licenses.
(b) Includes license tax on single stores.
(c) Includes $49,120 thousand, corporation excise taxes and surtaxes, measured in part by net income and in part by corporate excess.
(d) Dog licenses.

TABLE 5

FISCAL YEAR, POPULATION, AND INCOME PAYMENTS, BY STATE*

State	Date of close of fiscal year	Total population excluding armed forces overseas		Income payments to individuals(b)				State taxes as per cent of state and local taxes, 1953(c)
		July 1, 1954 (estimated)(a)	April 1, 1950 (enumerated)	1953		1952		
				Amount (millions)	Per capita	Amount (millions)	Per capita	
Total(d)	....	160,334,000	149,895,183	$268,803	$1,707	$254,338	$1,642	50.5
Alabama	Sept. 30, 1954	3,121,000	3,061,743	3,248	1,043	3,087	999	69.2
Arizona	June 30, 1955	993,000	749,587	1,370	1,473	1,308	1,503	61.8
Arkansas	June 30, 1955	1,910,000	1,909,511	1,793	939	1,785	967	71.8
California	June 30, 1955	12,554,000	10,586,223	24,856	2,039	23,257	1,978	52.5
Colorado	June 30, 1955	1,456,000	1,325,089	2,367	1,675	2,315	1,630	50.3
Connecticut	June 30, 1955	2,219,000	2,007,280	4,744	2,194	4,393	2,071	46.2
Delaware	June 30, 1955	367,000	318,085	825	2,304	768	2,207	72.0
Florida	June 30, 1955	3,524,000	2,771,305	4,586	1,368	4,137	1,335	57.2
Georgia	June 30, 1955	3,660,000	3,444,578	4,245	1,184	3,997	1,139	64.6
Idaho	June 30, 1955	615,000	588,637	851	1,411	874	1,484	47.9
Illinois	June 30, 1955	9,165,000	8,712,176	18,800	2,088	17,771	1,988	42.2
Indiana	June 30, 1955	4,209,000	3,934,224	7,584	1,834	6,986	1,668	52.4
Iowa	June 30, 1955	2,638,000	2,621,073	3,954	1,518	4,094	1,573	43.8
Kansas	June 30, 1955	2,016,000	1,905,299	3,110	1,550	3,211	1,629	47.5
Kentucky	June 30, 1955	2,995,000	2,944,806	3,460	1,167	3,316	1,125	59.5
Louisiana	June 30, 1955	2,924,000	2,683,516	3,602	1,249	3,397	1,230	75.9
Maine	June 30, 1955	930,000	913,774	1,251	1,369	1,207	1,358	48.8
Maryland	June 30, 1955	2,602,000	2,343,001	4,719	1,857	4,454	1,754	53.7
Massachusetts	June 30, 1955	4,954,000	4,690,514	8,880	1,812	8,421	1,772	40.4
Michigan	June 30, 1955	7,024,000	6,371,766	13,723	2,003	12,206	1,830	58.1
Minnesota	June 30, 1955	3,103,000	2,982,483	4,724	1,547	4,524	1,502	49.3
Mississippi	June 30, 1955	2,204,000	2,178,914	1,821	834	1,781	826	64.0
Missouri	June 30, 1955	4,154,000	3,954,653	6,768	1,652	6,406	1,610	49.4
Montana	June 30, 1955	628,000	591,024	1,037	1,689	1,009	1,690	45.4

Nebraska	June 30, 1955	1,366,000	1,325,510	2,065	1,533	2,132	1,584	36.8
Nevada	June 30, 1955	218,000	160,083	448	2,175	412	2,227	47.6
New Hampshire	June 30, 1955	532,000	533,242	854	1,620	824	1,555	38.6
New Jersey	June 30, 1955	5,250,000	4,835,329	10,771	2,095	10,041	1,975	25.9
New Mexico	June 30, 1955	781,000	681,187	1,021	1,347	975	1,327	78.9
New York	March 31, 1955	15,433,000	14,830,192	32,871	2,158	31,097	2,062	39.2
North Carolina	June 30, 1955	4,250,000	4,061,929	4,599	1,097	4,404	1,058	72.3
North Dakota	June 30, 1955	636,000	619,636	804	1,295	750	1,244	51.7
Ohio	June 30, 1955	8,554,000	7,946,627	16,840	2,012	15,443	1,872	50.4
Oklahoma	June 30, 1955	2,268,000	2,233,351	2,986	1,327	2,880	1,293	69.5
Oregon	June 30, 1955	1,639,000	1,521,341	2,762	1,724	2,746	1,712	53.9
Pennsylvania	May 31, 1955	10,779,000	10,498,012	19,419	1,822	18,310	1,734	49.4
Rhode Island	June 30, 1955	824,000	791,896	1,429	1,749	1,362	1,661	53.0
South Carolina	June 30, 1955	2,238,000	2,117,027	2,403	1,095	2,365	1,088	73.9
South Dakota	June 30, 1955	667,000	652,740	895	1,362	811	1,229	39.4
Tennessee	June 30, 1955	3,362,000	3,291,718	3,948	1,186	3,658	1,127	64.6
Texas	Aug. 31, 1954	8,468,000	7,711,194	12,279	1,480	11,916	1,457	52.1
Utah	June 30, 1955	757,000	688,862	1,108	1,510	1,075	1,459	52.6
Vermont	June 30, 1955	385,000	377,747	528	1,401	500	1,362	53.9
Virginia	June 30, 1955	3,588,000	3,318,680	4,829	1,361	4,693	1,338	59.8
Washington	June 30, 1955	2,540,000	2,378,963	4,663	1,882	4,458	1,810	68.7
West Virginia	June 30, 1955	1,947,000	2,005,552	2,435	1,257	2,414	1,233	71.5
Wisconsin	June 30, 1955	3,578,000	3,434,575	6,023	1,712	5,861	1,676	46.0
Wyoming	June 30, 1955	312,000	290,529	505	1,650	507	1,657	57.6

*Source: U.S. Bureau of the Census, State Tax Collections in 1955.
(a) These provisional estimates will be revised to take account of data as to recent internal migration.
(b) U.S. Department of Commerce, Survey of Current Business, August, 1954. Estimated income payments are for calendar years. Figures herein for six states (Maine, Maryland, New Hampshire, New Jersey, New York and Virginia) are adjusted to a "residence basis," as described in footnote 2, Table 5, on page 16 of the cited source.
(c) Bureau of the Census, State and Local Government Revenue in 1953, Table 7.
(d) Does not include data for the District of Columbia.

TABLE 6

STATE TAX COLLECTIONS, BY STATE: 1942–1955*

(In thousands of dollars)

State	Amount (in millions)					Per cent change (a)		1955 amount per capita (b)
	1955 (prelim.)	1954	1953	1952	1942	1954 to 1955	1953 to 1954	
Total..........................	$11,584	$11,089	$10,552	$9,857	$3,903	4.5	5.1	$72.25
Alabama......................	163	160	159	132	52	2.1	0.6	52.29
Arizona......................	80	78	75	70	24	3.1	4.5	80.88
Arkansas.....................	107	106	102	100	41	1.7	3.2	56.28
California....................	1,334	1,242	1,142	1,065	336	7.4	8.8	106.29
Colorado.....................	129	113	111	106	39	14.3	1.4	88.75
Connecticut..................	173	165	138	132	58	5.0	19.5	78.19
Delaware	41	42	26	24	11	−2.8	64.2	111.23
Florida.......................	294	268	252	229	60	9.7	6.1	83.37
Georgia......................	236	225	218	228	59	4.9	3.0	64.36
Idaho........................	38	38	39	38	13	1.2	−3.0	61.84
Illinois......................	552	546	514	455	230	1.1	6.1	60.21
Indiana......................	254	286	284	259	97	−11.2	0.6	60.35
Iowa.........................	198	188	169	168	71	5.3	11.0	75.00
Kansas.......................	145	140	137	133	45	3.2	2.0	71.69
Kentucky....................	162	138	138	129	53	17.4	0.2	54.15
Louisiana....................	303	295	287	283	81	3.0	2.6	103.80
Maine........................	59	56	57	56	23	4.4	−0.5	63.34
Maryland....................	199	181	165	153	48	9.9	9.6	76.55
Massachusetts...............	334	328	322	315	124	1.8	2.1	67.50
Michigan.....................	646	616	582	503	184	4.8	5.8	91.95
Minnesota....................	245	246	228	233	92	−0.4	8.3	79.08
Mississippi...................	125	120	112	110	42	4.3	6.6	56.73
Missouri.....................	226	224	207	185	84	0.6	8.3	54.35
Montana.....................	42	39	37	37	14	5.7	5.2	66.21
Nebraska.....................	69	65	61	56	24	5.3	7.5	50.26
Nevada......................	20	18	17	14	5	14.3	6.2	93.56
New Hampshire..............	28	29	27	25	13	−5.4	8.0	51.79
New Jersey...................	238	205	189	178	102	16.2	8.4	45.35
New Mexico..................	80	74	70	65	18	8.3	5.2	102.70
New York....................	1,200	1,134	1,120	1,024	484	5.8	1.3	77.77
North Carolina...............	307	295	288	278	99	4.3	2.4	72.33
North Dakota................	46	44	44	45	19	5.4	−2.0	72.22
Ohio.........................	584	546	492	451	229	7.1	11.0	68.29
Oklahoma....................	210	204	196	188	73	3.3	3.8	92.78
Oregon......................	130	127	130	128	36	2.5	−2.4	79.21
Pennsylvania.................	629	617	595	540	290	1.9	3.7	58.35
Rhode Island.................	59	57	56	53	17	2.8	1.5	71.13
South Carolina...............	157	157	159	147	45	−0.1	−1.6	70.09
South Dakota................	40	39	36	39	15	4.3	7.5	60.60
Tennessee....................	205	195	185	179	54	5.2	5.0	60.90
Texas........................	489	470	447	414	135	4.0	5.1	57.75
Utah.........................	55	57	50	54	21	−3.1	13.9	72.61
Vermont.....................	27	27	28	28	11	0.2	−1.8	70.53
Virginia......................	206	196	189	167	66	5.0	3.9	57.35
Washington..................	293	274	266	249	90	7.2	3.1	115.54
West Virginia................	127	128	124	123	57	−1.3	3.4	64.98
Wisconsin....................	267	261	253	244	111	2.2	3.3	74.61
Wyoming.....................	31	30	27	24	7	3.2	8.7	98.68

*Source: U. S. Bureau of the Census, *State Tax Collections in 1955.*
NOTE: Because of rounding, detail does not always add to total. Per capita and per cent figures are computed on the basis of amounts rounded to the nearest thousand.

(a) Changes are increases unless preceded by a minus sign (—), which denotes a decrease.
(b) Based on provisional estimates of population on July 1, 1954. (See Table 5.)

Section VII

MAJOR STATE SERVICES

1. Education
2. Highways, Highway Safety and Aviation
3. Health and Welfare
4. Defense and Public Protection
5. Corrections
6. Planning and Development
7. Natural Resources
8. Labor and Industrial Relations
9. State Regulatory Activities

1

Education

STATE PUBLIC SCHOOL SYSTEMS*

MORE than thirty million pupils were enrolled in public schools in the United States in 1955, and the number was increasing at the rate of more than a million children a year. The total number of teachers had passed the million mark, but was not increasing rapidly enough to maintain a stable ratio between pupils and teachers. Rising enrollments and shortages of qualified teachers brought results that in many communities included shortened school days, overcrowded classrooms, employment of inadequately qualified teachers, and laxity in enforcement of compulsory attendance laws. The Bureau of the Census estimated in 1953 that more than four and a half million children of school age were not attending school at all, and the National Education Association has estimated that in 1954–55, 700,000 pupils were attending half-day sessions.

This disparity between enrollments and teacher supply presented no temporary emergency to state school systems. Concern has been growing that the teacher shortage may remain a permanent problem as long as industry and other employers continue their heavy demands on the limited resources of highly trained manpower available. The technical competencies developed by teachers have found a ready market in industry and governmental services other than teaching. Teachers' salaries, although they continue to rise, have not been effectively competitive

*Text and tables prepared by HENRY THOMAS JAMES, Assistant Director of the Midwest Administration Center, The University of Chicago.

with those offered in many of the alternate markets.

The impression thus has grown among students of the problem that it may be impossible to increase the supply of teachers to the level generally considered necessary to maintain the present staff arrangements. It has been suggested that re-examination of these arrangements may be necessary to see if the demand for teachers can be reduced to a level more in line with anticipated supply. Suggestions advanced by educators in this connection have included shortening the period of education—by introduction of double sessions, extension of the school year to a three quarter system and staggering of enrollments; or by reorganization of the curriculum, eliminating one or more grade levels—kindergarten, seventh or eighth grade or both, or one year of the secondary school program. Experimenting with larger groupings for instruction also has been suggested, on the theory that the generally accepted ratio of twenty-five or thirty pupils per teacher is not necessarily the best arrangement for all kinds of learning situations. Likewise educators have discussed the desirability of developing a corp of technicians who would supplement the services of master teachers and would allow the professional staff to concentrate their efforts on activities requiring the high level of skill which is in short supply. This would leave custodial and routine clerical functions to the technical assistants, who could be drawn from the less highly trained and more plentiful part of the labor force.

On the other hand, one of the aspects of the teacher shortage is that schools best able to experiment successfully with innovations to make better use of available trained manpower frequently are the ones least likely to do so, because they are least pressed by the shortage. School districts with the largest financial resources are accumulating the best of the available supply by getting to the source of supply first, with the largest offer.

The states and the school districts, similarly, have faced increasing problems in shortages of school plant for the rising enrollments, and in the obsolescence of many school structures. (See section on "Capital Expenditures" following.)

The most hopeful aspect of these and related problems at the midpoint of a most difficult decade in school administration was the amount of public interest and attention that was focussed on educational problems. State conferences on education, culminating in the White House Conference late in 1955, reflected this national interest.

District Organization

Both state and local responsibility for education have long been recognized. The effectiveness with which a state can discharge its responsibility is related to the degree to which it is able to develop school districts of a size and population that permit efficient operation. Striking progress made in reduction of school districts in recent years is shown in Table 5. In 1933 there were 127,244 school districts in the nation.

A study by the Council of State Governments in 1947–48 showed 99,713 school districts. By 1955 estimates of the National Education Association indicated that this number had been reduced to 60,416.

The sharpest reductions usually have occurred in the central states, where the rural one-teacher elementary districts that developed a century ago to fit the needs of those times have been yielding to the twelve-grade districts. Illinois, with 11,061 school districts in 1946–47, has made the largest reduction by eliminating almost 9,000 districts since then. Missouri shows a reduction of 4,437 districts in the eight-

year period, and Minnesota eliminated 3,418. More than 2,000 districts each were eliminated by Kansas, Mississippi, New York, Texas and Wisconsin.

The usual goal of school district reorganization is simple: that all territory within the state shall be included in districts operating at least twelve grades of education and capable of operating in accordance with accepted standards at a reasonable cost. Considerations that have prompted the unprecedented record of reorganizations of recent years have included:

1. A state school system, it has been recognized increasingly, must deal with a manageable number of local units if its financial participation in the costs of the local programs is to insure maintenance of minimum educational standards. Most of the southern states and several in the West have achieved a manageable administrative structure by organizing school districts on a county basis. Northern and central states appear to be approaching a similar objective by creating larger districts on a community basis, without reference to other existing political subdivisions.

2. Local administrative units that are too small sacrifice quality of educational program or economic efficiency or both.

3. Sparsity of population in large areas of many states continue to force districts to operate at less than maximum efficiency if children are to receive an education of acceptable quality without undue inconvenience to them or their parents; but the advantages of larger tax bases and increased administrative efficiency can and are being achieved in many states by creation of larger administrative districts, which continue to maintain small attendance units in areas where sparsity of population does not permit convenient grouping into larger units.

Reorganization methods have varied widely among the states. In some states outright reorganization of all districts has been accomplished by legislative action. In others legislation to encourage and permit reorganization has been enacted.

The most effective state programs appear to have had certain elements in common: (1) encouragement through legislative policy statements and active and effective leadership by the Governor and the chief state school officer; (2) creation of local committees to study the local situation, usually on a county basis, to make recommendations and to hold public hearings so that the recommendations are understood and widely disseminated; (3) action by the legislature to remove legal and financial blocks to sound reorganization, and mandatory legislation when local interests are contrary to the best interest of the state, as in the case of the non-operating school districts.

A recent development in improving district structure in the Midwest has been vigorous action by several states to eliminate non-operating school districts. Such districts served for many years as a sign that the district structure was in need of remodeling. More than 11,000 districts which operate no schools were found in a recent United States Office of Education survey, most of them in the Midwest. Illinois abolished almost 2,000 of them in 1951.

Wisconsin acted to eliminate almost 1,000 in 1953, and in 1955 Michigan took action which will abolish about 850 closed districts. In each instance the territory in the districts involved was required to be attached to a district that did operate a school, and two years' grace was allowed by the legislatures to permit an orderly rearrangement of district lines. In all three instances the action was taken primarily on the grounds that the power to tax is a power guarded jealously by the states and by the people; that it is extended to local units of government for the performance of specified services of government; and that when a unit of government ceases to perform the function for which it was created, the taxing power should be withdrawn, the unit abolished, and the territory involved attached to a unit which does provide the service. In all three states this decisive action was taken by the legislatures with virtually unanimous votes.

THE INTERMEDIATE UNIT

The traditional functions of the county superintendent of schools have been changing in many states as the number of local districts has declined and as local districts have increased in self-sufficiency. A number of states, including California, Michigan and Wisconsin, have been conducting extensive studies in an attempt to identify the place of the county superintendent in the emerging pattern of school district organization. A consensus appears to have been forming that his services would continue to be needed in most states, but that the nature of his duties was changing— from traditional supervisory and administrative functions to functions of service to local school districts and of leadership in formulating broad educational policy on matters affecting more than one local school district. A trend has been noted toward creation of elective county boards of education, which in turn appoint professionally qualified county superintendents, and away from popular election of county superintendents of schools.

THE STATE SCHOOL OFFICE

In 1947 thirty-nine states had state boards of education, of which only three selected members by popular election. By 1955 forty-four states had established state boards, of which eight selected members by popular election. In 1947 thirty-one states selected the chief state school officer by popular election; in only ten was he appointed by a state board of education. By 1954 the number of elective state superintendents had decreased to twenty-six, and state boards of education were making the selection in eighteen states. (See Table 7.)

Apparently, therefore, the trend is toward placing responsibility for broad policy decisions affecting the state educational program in a policy-making board, representative of the people and directly responsible to them, and to securing execution of those policies through a chief administrative officer selected on the basis of his professional qualifications for the office.

SCHOOL FINANCE

A steady decline in the percentage of public school revenues derived from property taxes continues. Estimates by the United States Office of Education show this to have been uninterrupted for the past quarter of a century. Yet property taxes continue to account for more than half of the revenue.

PER CENT OF PUBLIC SCHOOL REVENUES
FROM PROPERTY TAXATION
1930–1954

Year	Per cent
1930	84.4
1940	69.0
1950	55.4
1953–54	54.2

Source: Adapted from Arvid Burke, *Financing Public Schools in the United States*, p. 118. 1953–54 data from *Public School Finance Programs of the United States*, U.S. Office of Education, 1955, p. 17. (See Table 2.)

Increasing streams of state collected revenues, derived principally from income and sales taxes, have made possible this substantial shift in the school support pattern. The rather general abandonment of state taxes on property, meantime, and the declining dependence of schools on this revenue source, have contributed materially to continuing deterioration of the property tax structure in many jurisdictions. Competitive underassessment, controlled in some measure through state supervision of assessments in certain of the states, has even been encouraged, inadvertently, by some of the state school support formulas. Seven states have found it necessary to develop a special index of taxpaying ability as the basis for distributing state school funds, because assessed valuations were totally unsatisfactory for this purpose. Twenty-three states use state equalized valuations or adjusted state ratios for this purpose, and only fifteen distribute state funds on the basis of locally determined valuations. In 1955 West Virginia adopted a law which threatens a district with loss of state aid for schools if it fails to raise assessed values within a prescribed period.

Underassessment of property creates problems not only for schools but for local units of government in general, and these at times have been unmanageable when coupled with restrictive levy and debt limitations.

Despite the steady decline in the percentage of revenue for school support that comes from the property tax, the *amount* of school revenues from this source has been steadily increasing. The property tax continues to be a crucial item for support of schools in most states.

DISTRIBUTION OF STATE FUNDS

Formulas for distributing state funds to school districts are complex. The United States Office of Education found in a study in 1955 that the number of separate funds or distribution procedures totaled 382 for the nation and averaged about eight per state. The Office of Education has classified all distributions into two categories, flat grants and equalizing grants. The flat grants are usually made on some per pupil or per teacher basis; equalizing grants are usually in terms of a state minimum standard of educational program and a measure of local taxpaying ability.

Despite the complexity of many state distribution programs, it is possible to identify general characteristics, present or evolving, that are common to most of them:

1. A minimum educational program which the state guarantees to every district. This usually is called the basic or foundation program.

2. A minimum local tax effort which must be made before a district is eligible to receive state funds.

3. A flat grant to most or all local districts, usually on a per pupil or per teacher basis.

4. Equalizing grants to provide the local district with the funds needed to pay the difference between costs of the minimum foundation program and the amount produced by the prescribed local tax effort.

Variations on this basic pattern account for most of the wide differences among the states in the percentage of local costs paid from state revenue. The level of state contributions is controlled by the level of unit cost set for the foundation program and the level prescribed for the local tax effort. Table 2 shows the per cent of costs paid by the states in 1953–54, ranging from a low of 6.3 per cent to a high of 85.6 per cent, with a mean percentage of 41.4 per cent computed for the nation. Caution needs to be observed, however, in interpreting these percentages or in comparing them without close examination into the individual patterns of state support for other services of government and into shared tax programs, which often have important influences on revenue sources available for school support.

CAPITAL EXPENDITURES

Rapidly rising enrollments are generating enormous pressures for school plant expansion. These pressures have been creating severe problems for local school districts, above all when complicated by underassessment of property and restrictive constitutional or statutory limitations on district indebtedness. Evidence that the states and districts are taking extraordinary action to meet the problem is found in an estimated 60,000 classrooms built in 1955, and in total expenditures for capital outlay estimated in excess of $2 billion in that year.

The most direct attack on the problem, that of forcing assessments up to adequate levels, appears to be unusual, but certain states are proceeding to do so, and means of improving assessments are under close study in others. West Virginia's act of 1955, noted above, is one example of action to raise assessments, and New York has been very successful with state equalization of assessments.

Three other approaches to solutions at the state level can be identified as follows:

1. State grants-in-aid to local school districts to be used for building purposes. By 1954 twenty-three states had incorporated some provision for assistance to local districts for school building costs, either as part of the basic foundation support program or by special provisions. The grants varied widely in amount.

2. Easing of debt limitations. In Wisconsin, for instance, the state constitution was amended in 1955 to change the debt limitation from a percentage of the local assessed valuation to the same percentage of the state equalized valuation, which increases the borrowing power of Wisconsin school districts, on the average, by about 40 per cent. New York's limitation, also, is on state equalized valuation. Idaho, South Carolina, South Dakota and Wyoming have eased debt limitations in recent years, and Kansas and New Jersey have provided methods of gaining permission to exceed present bonding limits.

3. Creation of school building authorities, not bound by constitutional or statutory limitations on debt. Four states had such authorities by the end of 1954. School building authorities moved sharply into focus in 1955 with a proposal at the federal level to use this corporate device as a means of channeling federal aid to local districts for school construction. The school building authority is not an innovation but an adaptation of a device long used by states and local municipalities to finance such diverse services as highways, housing, ports, sewage disposal, drainage, irrigation and power development. Reports of experience in states which have made extensive use of school building authorities indicate much success in meeting construction problems. On the other hand, court decisions and other legal opinions would appear to bar the use of school building authorities in a number of states.

EXTENSION UPWARD

There is growing evidence of a developing trend for extension of the twelve-grade common school system to include the thirteenth and fourteenth years. The United States Office of Education in a recent study notes the tendency to make the majority of newly established junior and community colleges an upward extension of the common school system. The following table, from that study, indicates that as of July, 1954, twenty-seven states had authorized establishment of junior or community college districts, and that in twenty-four of these states the colleges were in operation. In most instances the states have found it necessary to set certain requirements to prevent districts of inadequate population and taxable wealth from undertaking the task; usually, however, provisions have been included to permit school districts which may be too small individually to do so on a cooperative basis.

The Office of Education sees this trend as part of a continuing effort to round out the state school systems to meet the needs of all the people. Its study in 1954 showed 252 public junior and community colleges in operation, of which 226 came under the jurisdiction of the state board of education or the chief state school officer or both. California had the largest number, fifty-nine, followed by Texas with thirty-one, Iowa with sixteen, and Kansas, Michigan and Mississippi, each with fourteen.

The trend in individual states will be determined by many factors. One of the most important undoubtedly is the degree to which existing institutions of higher learning are able to serve the growing demand for a terminal program of education beyond the secondary school but short of the traditional four-year college program.

LEGISLATIVE AUTHORIZATION FOR PUBLIC JUNIOR AND COMMUNITY COLLEGES AS OF JULY, 1954(a)

States authorizing junior and community colleges by general legislation		States specifically authorizing each junior college by special legislation	States having no junior college legislation
Arizona	Mississippi	Arkansas	Alabama
California	Missouri	Georgia	Connecticut
Colorado	Montana	Maryland	Delaware
Florida	Nebraska	North Carolina	Indiana
Idaho	New Jersey	Utah	Maine
Illinois	New York		Nevada
Iowa	North Dakota		New Hampshire
Kansas	Oklahoma		New Mexico
Kentucky	Oregon (b)		Ohio
Louisiana (b)	Pennsylvania		Rhode Island
Massachusetts	South Carolina(b)		South Dakota
Michigan	Texas		Tennessee
Minnesota	Washington		Vermont
	Wyoming		Virginia
			West Virginia
			Wisconsin
Total	27	5	16

(a) U.S. Department of Health, Education, and Welfare, Office of Education, *The State and Education,* Misc. No. 23. Washington, D.C.: U.S. Government Printing Office, 1955. Table 21, p. 35.

(b) No public junior or community colleges were operated in these states under the existing legislation at the time of the survey.

TABLE 1

ESTIMATED PUPIL ENROLLMENT, PUBLIC ELEMENTARY AND SECONDARY SCHOOLS*

State	1953–54 Total enrolled	1954–55 Enrollment		
		Elementary	Secondary	Total
Alabama	686,021	448,970	254,677	703,647
Arizona	188,100	158,000	39,500	197,500
Arkansas	421,674	271,000	155,000	426,000
California	2,097,299	1,778,400	483,400	2,261,800
Colorado	266,534	224,000	68,000	292,000
Connecticut	340,373	231,000	126,000	357,000
Delaware	56,340	35,372	22,549	57,921
Florida	648,609	444,000	252,000	696,000
Georgia	862,761	663,800(a)	221,200(a)	885,000 (a)
Idaho	136,376	103,176	35,883	139,059
Illinois	1,398,990	1,132,400	357,600	1,490,000
Indiana	755,353(a)	569,400(a)	210,600(a)	780,000 (a)
Iowa	525,300	411,000	130,000	541,000
Kansas	361,735	285,225	92,822	378,047
Kentucky	593,218	494,534	115,968	610,502
Louisiana	552,441	460,000	115,000	575,000
Maine	170,000(a)	134,940(a)	38,060(a)	173,000 (a)
Maryland	427,475	289,037	164,763	454,800
Massachusetts	672,000	472,000	226,000	698,000
Michigan	1,254,466	879,000	445,500	1,324,500
Minnesota	559,134	368,945	210,357	579,302
Mississippi	540,157	451,000	91,000	542,000
Missouri	710,000	575,000	157,000	732,000
Montana	112,779	89,614	29,028	118,642
Nebraska	245,000	195,000	60,000	255,000
Nevada	39,215	33,289	8,898	42,187
New Hampshire	80,272	59,290	24,443(b)	83,733
New Jersey	807,000	670,000	169,000	839,000
New Mexico	173,268	149,207	38,273	187,480
New York	2,315,900	1,556,000	860,000	2,416,000
North Carolina	965,742	798,417	219,650	1,018,067
North Dakota	118,307(a)	93,555(a)	27,945(a)	121,500 (a)
Ohio	1,419,449	1,031,827	469,580	1,501,407
Oklahoma	522,970	410,000	125,000	535,000
Oregon	312,564	249,287	78,611	327,898
Pennsylvania	1,749,634	1,171,868	637,000	1,808,868
Rhode Island	108,500	75,710	37,290	113,000
South Carolina	539,437	410,698	142,791	553,489
South Dakota	128,439	101,000	31,000	132,000
Tennessee	716,295	599,643	140,657	740,300
Texas	1,591,534	1,313,733	351,096	1,664,829
Utah	183,164	119,799	72,033	191,832
Vermont	67,905	52,500	18,057	70,557
Virginia	695,277	540,000(a)	180,000(a)	720,000 (a)
Washington	458,123	372,431	112,368	484,799
West Virginia	451,991	298,000	159,000	457,000
Wisconsin	554,000	401,000	160,000	561,000
Wyoming	68,271	54,000(a)	16,000(a)	70,000 (a)
District of Columbia	102,810	66,103	38,388	104,491
Total	28,752,132	21,792,170	8,218,987	30,011,157

*Research Division, National Education Association, "Advance Estimates of Public Elementary and Secondary Schools for the School Year 1954–55" as revised February, 1955. Table 10, p. 21.

(a) Estimated by National Education Association Research Division.
(b) Includes grades 7 and 8 of junior high schools.

TABLE 2

ESTIMATED PUBLIC SCHOOL REVENUES, BY SOURCE, 1953–54

State	Total revenues (a)	Per cent of revenue by source (b)			Per cent derived (d) from property tax
		Federal	State	Local (c)	
Alabama	$95,689,617	3.3	75.5	21.2	25.4
Arizona	54,622,871	9.1	27.1	63.8	66.6
Arkansas	57,736,312	6.1	52.5	41.4	41.5
California	787,773,438	2.0	52.7	45.3	45.8
Colorado	87,167,546	9.8	17.1	73.1	77.2
Connecticut	91,375,000	1.5	26.8	71.7	70.1
Delaware	17,944,806	1.3	85.6	13.1	13.3
Florida	160,415,729	4.0	50.7	45.3	43.5
Georgia	137,223,460	2.3	74.7	23.0	23.6
Idaho	32,205,260	3.5	25.0	71.5	71.3
Illinois	430,975,689	0.8	20.3	78.9	79.5
Indiana	213,870,345	1.3	33.2	65.5	50.2
Iowa	178,868,000	1.4	11.0	87.6	87.4
Kansas	112,658,654	3.5	21.4	75.1	76.5
Kentucky	84,517,900	4.7	42.4	52.9	54.4
Louisiana	134,588,230	3.6	66.1	30.3	29.5
Maine	34,931,939	3.1	25.8	71.1	69.5
Maryland	126,989,728	8.9	31.2	59.9	65.4
Massachusetts	189,531,520	1.3	24.9	73.8	73.2
Michigan	365,239,193	0.8	53.9	45.3	41.4
Minnesota	249,993,157	0.8	29.5	69.7	68.7
Mississippi	53,630,595	6.1	51.7	42.2	29.5
Missouri	162,392,795	2.4	31.5	66.1	55.0
Montana	42,210,625	3.8	27.0	69.2	70.4
Nebraska	57,416,463	4.1	6.3	89.6	95.0
Nevada	12,934,513	18.1	39.4	42.5	64.9
New Hampshire	21,461,115	3.6	8.7	87.7	89.6
New Jersey	257,246,606	1.0	16.6	82.4	82.4
New Mexico	41,430,218	1.6	84.2	14.2	14.9
New York	756,156,000	0.8	41.2	58.0	55.1
North Carolina	227,701,531	1.9	79.9	18.2	15.2
North Dakota	28,000,000	1.6	29.6	68.8	69.2
Ohio	376,352,400	0.9	32.2	66.9	66.5
Oklahoma	111,046,452	3.8	32.3	63.9	44.4
Oregon	111,725,004	1.9	29.9	68.2	69.5
Pennsylvania	503,949,837	0.7	43.4	55.9	43.5
Rhode Island	29,638,700	6.5	16.6	76.9	82.2
South Carolina	108,500,000	7.8	64.6	27.6	29.0
South Dakota	35,239,592	3.4	11.6	85.0	83.1
Tennessee	106,455,133	3.1	65.0	31.9	27.9
Texas	376,156,569	4.9	56.9	38.2	45.1
Utah	48,699,808	4.9	42.2	52.9	60.8
Vermont	17,493,839	2.5	28.5	69.0	59.0
Virginia	109,617,245	6.6	43.3	50.1	51.2
Washington	163,795,989	5.6	63.4	31.0	28.6
West Virginia	86,272,279	2.0	64.1	33.9	34.6
Wisconsin	170,512,692	2.2	19.3	78.5	80.3
Wyoming	20,001,900	18.0	36.5	45.5	81.1
Continental United States(e)	**$7,712,738,267**	2.6	41.4	56.0	54.2

(a) U.S. Department of Health, Education, and Welfare, Office of Education. *Public School Finance Programs of the United States.* Washington, 1955. Table 4, p. 13.

(b) *Ibid.,* Table 5, p. 14.

(c) County and local, shown separately in the original table have been combined here, since in most of the states where the county levy is an important item, the county unit is the local unit of school administration.

(d) *Op. cit.,* Table 7, p. 17.

(e) Summary figures include data for District of Columbia, but these are not shown separately here.

TABLE 3

ESTIMATED PUBLIC SCHOOL EXPENDITURES, 1954–55*

State	Total current expense (in thousands)	Current expense per pupil in ADA (a)	Total capital outlay (in thousands)	Per cent of total revenue from state 1954–55
Alabama	$100,000	$164.00	$ 7,700	73.7
Arizona	47,000	280.00	15,000	27.0
Arkansas	45,100	125.00	13,500	49.8
California	770,000	341.00	320,000	48.8
Colorado	77,400	293.98	28,000	17.1
Connecticut	94,500	318.00	34,500	17.4
Delaware	18,200	335.00	6,000	85.0
Florida	134,308	230.00	63,000	51.7
Georgia	120,000	160.00	30,000	73.3
Idaho	28,811	227.57	9,500	24.5
Illinois	390,000	305.00	150,000	10.9
Indiana	179,000(b)	255.00(b)	22,000(b)	38.4(b)
Iowa	142,000	285.00	48,000(b)	9.5
Kansas	90,518	265.00	6,615	19.7
Kentucky	78,550	150.00	9,000	41.1
Louisiana	128,000	247.00	40,000	67.7
Maine	32,000(b)	205.00(b)	4,000(b)	17.2(b)
Maryland	110,028	242.00(c)	45,888	34.6
Massachusetts	175,000	251.00(c)	40,000	16.0
Michigan	320,000	266.66	145,000	60.7
Minnesota	168,449	320.00	84,031	39.2
Mississippi	59,243	131.00	3,500	56.2
Missouri	148,000	242.00	30,000	32.4
Montana	37,000	309.00(c)	10,000	23.7
Nebraska	61,000	250.00	10,000	4.4
Nevada	10,508	276.00	6,000	42.0
New Hampshire	20,901	253.00(c)	2,990	4.1
New Jersey	253,000	349.00	49,000	18.0
New Mexico	44,254	280.00(b)	7,589	81.9
New York	760,000	360.00	275,000	37.0
North Carolina	153,265	168.00	27,500	72.2
North Dakota	31,000(b)	260.00(b)	6,000(b)	23.8(b)
Ohio	340,000	250.00(c)	130,000	34.4
Oklahoma	98,091	225.00	25,000	30.5
Oregon	97,700	340.00	40,000	29.6
Pennsylvania	469,800	298.86	200,000	33.1
Rhode Island	33,000	315.00	2,800	11.4
South Carolina	81,500	176.00	55,000	74.4
South Dakota	32,000	275.00	5,000	12.2
Tennessee	99,630	151.00	28,500	59.1
Texas	365,570	253.27	85,000	54.4
Utah	40,500	230.00	14,000	38.1
Vermont	15,000	240.00	4,000	26.1
Virginia	120,000	185.00	50,000	32.1
Washington	133,797	304.00	43,000	53.4
West Virginia	75,173	178.00	22,000	62.3
Wisconsin	143,000	291.00	40,000	19.5
Wyoming	22,000(b)	380.00(b)	2,500(b)	34.1(b)
District of Columbia	26,500	285.00	4,000	0.0
United States	$7,020,296	$261.68	$2,300,113	37.9

*Research Division, National Education Association, *Advance Estimates of Public Elementary and Secondary Schools for the School Year 1954–55* as revised February, 1955. Table 9-B, p. 20.
(a) Current expense per pupil in Average Daily Attendance.

(b) Estimated by N.E.A. Research Division.
(c) Current expense per pupil in Average Daily Membership. Some states have only ADM figures available. ADA and ADM are roughly comparable, though ADM tends to run slightly higher than ADA, and thus yield slightly lower costs per pupil.

THE BOOK OF THE STATES

TABLE 4

ESTIMATED AVERAGE SALARIES OF TEACHERS IN PUBLIC ELEMENTARY AND SECONDARY SCHOOLS*

State	Instructional staff (a)		Classroom teachers, 1954–55	
	1953–54	1954–55	Elementary school	Secondary school
Alabama	$2,500	$2,625	$2,330	$2,950
Arizona	4,110	4,200	4,000	4,600
Arkansas	2,256	2,260	2,000(b)	2,400(b)
California	4,753	5,050	4,650	5,400
Colorado	3,457	3,600	3,400	3,900
Connecticut	4,197	4,400	4,050	4,550
Delaware	4,290	4,395	4,039	4,401
Florida	3,772	3,800	3,650(b)	3,850(b)
Georgia	2,850	3,000	2,675	3,250
Idaho	3,479	3,497	3,224	3,771
Illinois	4,300	4,500	4,250	4,600
Indiana	4,025(b)	4,185(b)	3,900(b)	4,350(b)
Iowa	3,050	3,260	2,800	3,801
Kansas	3,311	3,460	3,065	3,790
Kentucky	2,475	2,625	2,300(b)	2,900(b)
Louisiana	3,472	4,100	3,725(b)	4,100(b)
Maine	2,700(b)	2,850(b)	2,575(b)	3,275(b)
Maryland	4,153	4,275	4,015(b)	4,315(b)
Massachusetts	4,025	4,125	3,800	4,300
Michigan	4,200	4,400	4,100	4,625
Minnesota	3,479	3,600	3,100	4,100
Mississippi	1,864	2,200	1,880	2,400
Missouri	3,197	3,320	3,060	3,700
Montana	3,531	3,610	3,350	4,055
Nebraska	2,900(b)	3,000(b)	2,600(b)	3,700(b)
Nevada	3,861	4,165	3,977	4,367
New Hampshire	3,276	3,425	3,175	3,650
New Jersey	4,230	4,470	4,200	4,775
New Mexico	4,150	4,436	4,280	4,420
New York	4,725	5,050	4,700	5,375
North Carolina	3,310	3,329	3,240(b)	3,215(b)
North Dakota	2,750(b)	2,850(b)	2,600(b)	3,350(b)
Ohio	3,975	4,100	3,800	4,250
Oklahoma	3,436	3,511	3,325	3,625
Oregon	4,134	4,300	4,000	4,320
Pennsylvania	3,951	4,141	3,850	4,180
Rhode Island	3,900	4,100	3,900	4,200
South Carolina	2,890	2,975	2,700	3,200
South Dakota	2,850	2,950	2,700	3,400
Tennessee	2,793	2,800	2,525	3,200
Texas	3,720	3,975	3,740	4,050
Utah	3,687	4,041	3,790	4,076
Vermont	2,922	2,975	2,690	3,350
Virginia	3,045	3,250	3,000	3,370
Washington	4,331	4,400	4,195	4,585
West Virginia	3,040	3,060	2,750	3,280
Wisconsin	3,711	3,840	3,425	4,290
Wyoming	3,500(b)	3,575(b)	3,300(b)	3,875(b)
Continental United States	**$3,741**	**$3,932**	**$3,615**	**$4,194**

*Research Division, National Education Association, *Advance Estimates of Public Elementary and Secondary Schools for the School Year 1954–55* as revised February, 1955. Table 6, p. 16.

(a) Includes principals, supervisors and classroom teachers.
(b) NEA Research Division estimate.

TABLE 5

ESTIMATED CHANGES IN NUMBER OF SCHOOL DISTRICTS, 1946–55

State	Number of school districts 1947–48 (a)	Estimated number of school districts 1954–55 (b)	Decrease from 1947 to 1955	Per cent decrease 1947 to 1955
Alabama	108	115	−7	−6.5
Arizona	325	295	30	9.2
Arkansas	1,589	423	1,166	73.4
California	2,349	1,900	449	19.1
Colorado	1,794	1,106	688	38.4
Connecticut	174	174	0	0.
Delaware	126	105	21	16.7
Florida	67	67	0	0.
Georgia	189	203	−14	−7.4
Idaho	648	180	468	72.2
Illinois	11,061(c)	2,100	8,961	81.0
Indiana	1,191	1,065(d)	126	10.6
Iowa	4,709(c)	4,450	259	5.5
Kansas	5,643	3,265	2,378	42.1
Kentucky	246	224	22	8.9
Louisiana	67	67	0	0.
Maine	493	492(d)	1	.2
Maryland	24	24	0	0.
Massachusetts	351	348	3	.8
Michigan	5,434(c)	4,270	1,164	21.4
Minnesota	7,518	4,100	3,418	45.5
Mississippi	4,211	1,300	2,911	69.1
Missouri	8,422	3,985	4,437	52.7
Montana	1,152	1,145	7	.6
Nebraska	6,864	5,900	964	14.0
Nevada	222	170	52	23.4
New Hampshire	239	230	9	3.8
New Jersey	561	559	2	.4
New Mexico	497	99	398	80.5
New York	4,609	2,250	2,359	51.2
North Carolina	172	174	−2	−1.2
North Dakota	2,271	1,950(d)	321	14.1
Ohio	1,539	1,337	202	13.1
Oklahoma	2,669	1,802	867	32.5
Oregon	1,363	788	575	42.1
Pennsylvania	2,540	2,463	77	3.0
Rhode Island	39	39	0	0.
South Carolina	1,680	103	577	34.3
South Dakota	3,409	3,374	35	1.0
Tennessee	150	152	−2	−1.3
Texas	4,832	1,950	2,882	59.6
Utah	40	40	0	0.
Vermont	268	265	3	1.1
Virginia	125	129	−4	−3.2
Washington	584	527	57	9.8
West Virginia	55	55	0	0.
Wisconsin	6,385(c)	4,358	2,027	31.7
Wyoming	354	298	56	15.8
District of Columbia	1	1	1	0.
Continental United States	99,713	60,416	39,297	39.4

(a) The Council of State Governments *The Forty-Eight State School Systems, 1949.* Table 18, p. 192.
(b) Research Division, National Education Association *Advance Estimates of Public Elementary and Secondary Schools for* the School Year 1954–55 as revised February, 1955. Table 1, p. 11.
(c) 1946–47 data.
(d) Estimated by NEA Research Division.

TABLE 6

ESTIMATED NUMBER OF INSTRUCTIONAL STAFF AND ESTIMATED NUMBER OF TEMPORARY (EMERGENCY) TEACHERS, 1954–55*

State	Total instructional staff 1954–55	Temporary (emergency) teachers 1954–55	
		Number employed	Per cent employed in rural areas
Alabama	27,110	3,000	80
Arizona	7,375	35	100
Arkansas	13,898	6,000	50
California	84,900	7,000	70
Colorado	12,456	600	98
Connecticut	14,675	875	5
Delaware	2,515	65	75
Florida	24,375	3,739	40
Georgia	29,391	750	90
Idaho	5,439	1,250	78(a)
Illinois	55,750	550	90
Indiana	27,800(a)	550(a)	75(a)
Iowa	23,774	450(a)	65(a)
Kansas	19,871	0	..
Kentucky	20,084	2,400	97
Louisiana	20,380	1,000	80
Maine	6,975(a)	500(a)	80(a)
Maryland	16,894	3,317	45(a)
Massachusetts	27,965	400	25
Michigan	46,800	7,200	50
Minnesota	24,710	400	30
Mississippi	16,360	400	90
Missouri	26,131	7,000	36
Montana	5,722	600	89
Nebraska	12,630	1,200	35
Nevada	1,823	4	50
New Hampshire	3,418	261	63
New Jersey	33,675	3,000	42
New Mexico	7,361	2	100
New York	94,000	4,200	65
North Carolina	34,172	2,400	80
North Dakota	7,150(a)	500(a)	90(a)
Ohio	52,045	2,785	75
Oklahoma	19,115	0	..
Oregon	13,486	1,503	65
Pennsylvania	69,002	1,600	55(a)
Rhode Island	4,600	75	50
South Carolina	18,785	234	90
South Dakota	7,713	1,100	91
Tennessee	25,463	1,200	93
Texas	57,611	2,600	50
Utah	6,360	1,005	28
Vermont	2,680	550	40
Virginia	26,600(a)	2,800	95
Washington	19,140	1,500	25(a)
West Virginia	16,390	1,400	85
Wisconsin	24,933	2,000	55
Wyoming	3,200(a)	230	90
District of Columbia	3,859	450	0
Continental United States	1,126,561	80,680	60

*Research Division, National Education Association, *Advance Estimates of Public Elementary and Secondary Schools for the School Year 1954–55* as revised February, 1955. Tables 3 and 4, pages 13 and 14.

(a) Estimated by N.E.A. Research Division.

TABLE 7

STATE BOARDS OF EDUCATION AND CHIEF SCHOOL OFFICERS FOR THE COMMON SCHOOL SYSTEMS, 1947(a)–1954(b)

State	Chief method of selecting state board						Method of selecting chief state school officer					
	Elected by people		Appointed by Governor		Other		Elected by people		Appointed by state board		Appointed by Governor	
	1947	1954	1947	1954	1947	1954	1947	1954	1947	1954	1947	1954
Alabama			★	★			★	★				
Arizona					★	★	★	★				
Arkansas			★	★					★	★		
California			★	★			★	★				
Colorado		★			★		★			★		
Connecticut			★	★					★	★		
Delaware			★	★					★	★		
Florida					★	★	★	★				
Georgia			★	★			★	★				
Idaho			★	★			★	★				
Illinois	No state board						★	★				
Indiana			★	★			★	★				
Iowa(c)		★					★			★		
Kansas			★	★			★	★				
Kentucky			★	★			★	★				
Louisiana	★	★					★	★				
Maine(c)				★						★	★	
Maryland			★	★					★	★		
Massachusetts			★	★					★	★		
Michigan(d)	★						★	★				
Minnesota			★	★					★	★		
Mississippi					★	★	★	★				
Missouri			★	★					★	★		
Montana			★	★			★	★				
Nebraska(c)		★					★			★		
Nevada	★	★					★	★				
New Hampshire			★	★					★	★		
New Jersey			★	★							★	★
New Mexico			★	★			★	★				
New York					★	★			★	★		
North Carolina			★	★			★	★				
North Dakota	No state board						★	★				
Ohio(c)		★					★			★		
Oklahoma			★	★			★	★				
Oregon			★	★				★			★	
Pennsylvania			★	★							★	★
Rhode Island(c)				★						★	★	
South Carolina			★	★			★	★				
South Dakota(c)				★			★	★				
Tennessee			★	★							★	★
Texas		★	★				★			★		
Utah		★			★		★			★		
Vermont			★	★					★	★		
Virginia			★	★							★	★
Washington					★	★	★	★				
West Virginia			★	★			★	★				
Wisconsin	No state board						★	★				
Wyoming					★	★	★	★				
Total	3	8	28	30	8	6	31	26	10	18	7	4

(a) Adapted from The Council of State Governments *The Forty-Eight State School Systems*, 1949. Tables 11 and 12, pp. 185 and 186.

(b) Adapted from U.S. Department of Health, Education, and Welfare, Office of Education, *The State and Education*, 1955. Table C, p. 166.

(c) No state board in 1947.

(d) No state board in 1955.

THE STATES AND HIGHER EDUCATION*

URING 1955 it is expected that for the first time in history each of the states will have made an appraisal and projection of its program in public education. The appraisals were undertaken as part of a state-wide examination of all levels of education, in preparation for the White House Conference scheduled by the President for late November. Congress has assisted the states in this undertaking by appropriating $700,000 for distribution among them, according to their respective populations.

The rising tide of students that has overrun our elementary school facilities and that threatens to inundate our high schools is expected to hit the public and private colleges of the nation with tremendous force about 1960. Most of the states are developing comprehensive plans for taking care of an increasing college and university population which is expected by 1965 to double the current enrollment of some 2.5 million students.

Action programs are under way in nearly all states to reduce and if possible wipe out the existing backlog of need for classrooms, laboratories, land, utilities and other capital facilities required for offering modern programs of higher education. Altogether, this backlog is estimated at $6 billion. The states are spending approximately $600 million a year toward eliminating it. If the capital facilities backlog were worked off over a ten-year period, and if the additional facilities required for estimated current growth during that period were put in place, the expenditure would average $1¼ billion per year. Approximately two-thirds of this burden would fall on the taxpayer of the states. The difficulty of the states in assuming so large a capital expenditure burden for higher education is increased by the fact that current expenditures for higher educa-

*Prepared by ERNEST V. HOLLIS, Chief of College Administration, U. S. Office of Education, Department of Health, Education, and Welfare.

tion, $2.5 billion in 1954, may be expected by 1965 to exceed $5 billion annually. That these public and private investments in higher education nevertheless are within the financial capacity of our citizens, as taxpayers and philanthropists, is indicated by the fact that the 1954 current expenditure of $2.5 billion for higher education was less than 1 per cent of the individual and family income of the nation for that year.

STATE-WIDE SURVEYS OF HIGHER EDUCATION

Most states did not wait on the outcome of the White House Conference as the basis for projecting their programs of higher education. As this is written in mid-1955 they have already completed, have in process, or are initiating systematic studies of the status of their colleges and universities. They are estimating future quantitative needs for higher education in terms of population growth, and future qualitative needs in terms of projected agricultural, industrial, commercial and cultural developments.

Privately controlled colleges and universities are being invited to participate in these studies and are being encouraged to indicate the character and amount of the future work-load they want to undertake. As measured by enrollment, privately controlled institutions currently carry slightly more than two-fifths of the higher education work-load of the nation, the proportion in the several states varying from none in Nevada and Wyoming to three-fourths in several Middle Atlantic and New England states.

A significant number of the state-wide surveys have been and are being done under the auspices of legislative councils, which legislatures increasingly use to conduct studies in their several areas of responsibility. Among the states in which comprehensive studies have been initiated recently are Arizona, California, Florida,

258

Louisiana, Maryland, Mississippi, Nevada, North Carolina, South Dakota, Tennessee, Texas, West Virginia and Wisconsin. These studies have compiled data and have produced analyses and findings in justification of recommendations concerning (a) higher education programs, (b) institutional and state-wide coordination, (c) interstate cooperation, (d) capital and current financing, (e) enrollment and degrees. Those headings will be used below in reporting some developments of 1955, and the last two will be used in presenting for the nation as a whole certain statistics gathered by the Office of Education, Department of Health, Education, and Welfare on current higher education finances, enrollment, and degrees awarded.

HIGHER EDUCATION PROGRAMS

Legislators, Governors and university trustees who have a state-wide responsibility for higher education have generally specified that one of the objectives of state-wide surveys and studies should be to produce feasible recommendations for reducing wasteful duplication and unnecessary overlapping of educational programs at the several institutions. They have been nearly as much interested in having recommendations concerning new or modified programs that are needed to produce the professional and technical manpower on which the economic and cultural development of the state depends.

In one state, for example, wasteful duplication had proceeded to the point of each tax supported institution except the woman's college having a school of engineering. An examination of where the engineering graduates were employed showed that not more than 20 per cent worked in the state that paid the bill for their preparation. Another state had three full-fledged colleges of agriculture where the economy could have been served by the land-grant college. One state in which adequate support of one medical school presented difficulty was providing funds at two such institutions, and still other states found that they had unnecessary duplication in the professional aspects of agriculture, home economics, the fine arts, and business and public administration.

In the face of such duplication, survey reports of higher education in these states indicate a significant number of fields, important to the economy of the state, in which the colleges and universities do not prepare any professional and technical manpower. Even though it is established that in professional fields—such as medicine, engineering and agriculture—there is a need for six semi-professional and technical employees for each fully trained professional person, most of the states did not have an appreciable amount of facilities for training the semi-professionals and technicians. Survey recommendations, and the actions of states and their political subdivisions in creating junior and community colleges and technical institutes, indicate that the next wave of expansion in higher education may be in these areas. In addition, one or more of the established degree-granting institutions in each of the states have added some of the most needed programs leading to less than the bachelor's degree.

The state-wide studies of higher education also show that in some states the inclination has been to fill in the gaps in their programs by offering extremely costly professional programs that are beyond their means and that might be secured more economically through regional interchange arrangements. The most frequently recurring instances include the establishment of medical schools, dental schools, law schools, veterinary schools and schools of forestry. More subtle instances of this tendency may be found in graduate school programs where governing boards fail to restrict research and training for the doctorate to fields in which the state's economy needs additional personnel and for which adequate staff and facilities have been provided.

INSTITUTIONAL AND STATE-WIDE COORDINATION

Governing boards and those who support colleges and universities are increasingly concerned to know that these institutions are efficiently and economically managed. The mandate from the legislatures or other public bodies that initiate state-wide surveys of higher education nearly always calls for a study of internal organization, a study of space utilization, a study of class size, and a review of business management practices. The day is rapidly passing when the administrative officers of a college or university can secure additional capital or current funds from a legislature or from philanthropic sources without showing with some specificity the effectiveness of the enterprise as it is then being conducted.

Legislatures more and more decline to deal directly or through committees with the increasing complexities of college institutional organization, management and programming. Instead, with increasing intensity, state governments are seeking ways to coordinate state institutions of higher education so as to assure the effective utilization of available resources. Various coordinating mechanisms have been developed over the years, including: (1) the informal, voluntary inter-institutional council, composed of officials of higher educational institutions or of boards that govern them; (2) the multi-institution board, which directly governs two or more separate institutions; and (3) the formally established central coordinating board, created for the purpose of coordinating programs and activities carried on by institutions which operate under the immediate supervision of their respective direct governing boards.

Voluntary, informal councils are found in almost all the states. Most of them are state-wide in scope, their memberships including representatives of all institutions receiving state support. Their internal structures vary widely; most of them meet infrequently; and none maintains a separate, full-time staff. The scope of their activities generally is quite limited, and the degree of actual coordination they achieve is difficult to assess.

Two-thirds of all state institutions of higher education are governed by boards which have more than one institution each under their jurisdiction. Thirty-six states group institutions in this manner. Thirteen of them—Arizona, Florida, Georgia, Iowa, Kansas, Mississippi, Montana, New Jersey, New York, North Dakota, Oregon, Rhode Island and South Dakota—have single boards that govern all state institutions of higher education. These boards

perform both the coordinating and governing functions with respect to state institutions of higher education.

During the last few years a new type of board—the central state coordinating board—has been established in three states, Oklahoma, New Mexico and North Carolina. The Oklahoma State Regents for Higher Education, established by constitutional amendment in 1941 as a state-wide coordinating agency, possess broad authority over all state institutions of higher education; they do not, however, directly operate any of the institutions. The North Carolina State Board of Higher Education, established by the legislature in 1955, has powers and duties similar to the Oklahoma Regents. The New Mexico Board of Educational Finance, established by statute in 1951, exercises no powers of direct supervision but has authority to review and coordinate budget requests of the several institutions and to recommend appropriate action to the Governor and the legislature.

Coordinating machinery necessarily varies from one political jurisdiction to another in order to serve individual state needs. There is, however, an important trend toward closer coordination of the programs and activities of state institutions of higher education. Legislative councils and special interim committees in several states are studying the existing organizational structures in an effort to find ways of achieving more effective over-all coordination. In other states central budget and educational agencies are attempting to develop yardsticks that may be used in determining institutional needs and to devise formulas on which a legislature may base appropriations for the support of higher education.

INTERSTATE COOPERATION

Since World War II interstate cooperation in higher education has developed rapidly. Regional programs are operating in the South and West, and one is being initiated in New England.

Expanding programs and soaring costs ordinarily mean that only heavily populated, relatively wealthy states can hope to provide complete selections of undergraduate, graduate and professional programs. Most states in less heavily populated regions, such as the South and the West, have neither adequate resources nor sufficient student demand to justify the maintenance of a full catalog of programs on all academic levels. Recognizing the seriousness of the problem in the South, the Southern Governors' Conference in 1948 officially endorsed a plan for regional cooperation in higher education which operates as the Southern Regional Education Board. (See article on page 36.) Under the plan the fourteen southern states, by interstate compact, pooled their established facilities in order that institutions within each state might better serve the entire region.

First applied in the fields of medicine, dentistry and veterinary medicine—all of them high-cost fields—the program provides that a state without educational facilities in these fields may pay the cost of educating its students at established public and private colleges and universities in other states of the region. The idea has since been extended to forestry, social work and other professional areas, and other forms of interstate cooperation in graduate study and research have been developed. Through the plan specialized programs in established institutions, both public and private, may be strengthened significantly, and the needs of the states within the region may be better and more economically met.

In 1950 the West, under the leadership of the Western Governors' Conference, undertook a similar program of regional cooperation in higher education. It operates as the Western Interstate Commission for Higher Education. (See article on page 38.) Ten states and Alaska cooperate in the western compact. The states are Arizona, California, Colorado, Idaho, Montana, New Mexico, Oregon, Utah, Washington and Wyoming. Nevada is eligible for membership but has not yet ratified the compact. Here, as in the South, the plan envisions more effective utilization of established institutions in meeting the needs of the entire region.

CAPITAL AND CURRENT FINANCING

Space does not permit an elaboration of the capital funds statement made in the third paragraph of this article. The *Biennial Survey of Education*, Section 2, Chapter 4, *Statistics of Higher Education, 1951–52*, published by the United States Office of Education, provides a detailed analysis of receipts and expenditures for plant funds and related capital projects. Table 2 accompanying this summary presents in historical perspective a picture of current expenditures for higher education from 1932 through 1952. In it may be seen the changing pattern of expenditures, by major categories, in the several types of institutions. Table 3 shows by types of institutions the major sources from which institutions of higher education derived their current income in 1951–52.[1]

Over the past three or four decades taxes (state, federal and local) and student fees have been the primary sources of revenues for public and private institutions of higher education. All other sources, including income from endowment and gifts, rank as a poor third in producing income. It is interesting to note that since 1950 privately controlled institutions, while relying primarily on student fees, have received more income from gifts and grants than from endowments.

Despite the annually increasing dollar value of state appropriations to publicly controlled institutions of higher education, the states in 1952 did not contribute as large a portion of the educational and general fund as they did in 1918. The states remained the primary source, but their contribution in 1918 was 60 per cent and in 1952 51.5 per cent of the educational and general income of publicly controlled institutions. The state appropriation in 1952 for all institutions, $611 million, was barely 4 per cent of total state expenditures for government. During the past three decades total state expenditures have multiplied seventeen times, those for higher education eleven times. This is in contrast to expenditures for elementary and secondary education, which in the same span have multiplied seventeen times, and those for public welfare, which have multiplied fifty times.

[1]For figures on current income from 1918 to 1950 for higher education derived from the major sources, see Table 4, pp. 258–59, 1954–55 edition, *The Book of the States*.

ENROLLMENT AND DEGREES

The volume, character and distribution of college enrollment is basic in any examination of the nation's higher educational enterprise. For ready reference Table 1 presents a brief but comprehensive picture, by states, of enrollment in public and private institutions of higher education for the autumns of 1953 and 1954. Enrollments in the fall of 1954, totalling almost 2.5 million, represented an 11 per cent increase over 1953. Advance estimates in September, 1955, indicated a total college and university enrollment of more than 2.7 million in the autumn of that year.

Those interested in detailed facts on students, faculties, and degrees may consult the *Biennial Survey of Education* (cited above), Section 1, Chapter 4, *Statistics of Higher Education*. Projections of college enrollment indicating that the student body will approximate 5 million between the years 1965 and 1970 are contained in *The Impending Tidal Wave of Students*, published by the American Association of Collegiate Registrars and Admissions Officers.

TABLE 1

TOTAL ENROLLMENT AND FIRST-TIME STUDENTS IN INSTITUTIONS OF HIGHER EDUCATION, PUBLIC AND PRIVATE, BY STATE:

Fall, 1954 and Fall, 1953 *

State	Total enrollment			First-time students		
	1954	1953	Per cent change	1954	1953	Per cent change
Aggregate U.S.	2,499,750	2,250,701	+11.1	642,420	571,533	+12.4
Continental U.S.	2,477,847	2,231,054	+11.1	636,208	565,969	+12.4
Alabama	33,963	28,609	+18.7	9,323	7,764	+20.1
Arizona	15,687	13,575	+15.6	4,411	4,375	+ 0.8
Arkansas	17,975	16,274	+10.5	5,557	4,983	+11.5
California	277,016	233,932	+18.4	80,378	71,247	+12.8
Colorado	28,884	25,867	+11.7	8,124	6,941	+17.0
Connecticut	35,416	32,699	+ 8.3	8,040	7,381	+ 8.9
Delaware	5,119	4,603	+11.2	867	837	+ 3.6
Florida	39,693	35,778	+10.9	10,395	9,595	+ 8.3
Georgia	39,402	34,001	+15.9	11,881	9,439	+25.9
Idaho	7,953	7,041	+13.0	3,081	2,861	+ 7.7
Illinois	139,582	128,039	+ 9.0	31,759	28,125	+12.9
Indiana	67,866	59,459	+14.1	17,109	15,309	+11.8
Iowa	40,602	36,392	+11.6	12,230	10,406	+17.5
Kansas	34,130	30,554	+11.7	11,255	10,226	+10.1
Kentucky	30,907	26,653	+16.0	8,366	6,710	+24.7
Louisiana	39,758	36,674	+ 8.4	10,348	9,451	+ 9.5
Maine	8,446	7,168	+17.8	2,510	2,363	+ 6.2
Maryland	36,925	32,978	+12.0	7,860	6,565	+19.7
Massachusetts	97,655	92,869	+ 5.2	27,142	21,552	+25.9
Michigan	107,074	99,132	+ 8.0	24,632	22,535	+ 9.3
Minnesota	54,711	41,898	+30.6(a)	12,780	11,619	+10.0
Mississippi	24,113	20,185	+19.5	7,027	6,686	+ 5.1
Missouri	58,229	53,669	+ 8.5	15,553	13,705	+13.5
Montana	7,834	7,098	+10.4	2,713	2,472	+ 9.7
Nebraska	22,375	19,417	+15.2	5,978	5,531	+ 8.1
Nevada	1,763	1,321	+33.5	418	435	− 3.9
New Hampshire	8,665	8,206	+ 5.6	2,642	2,440	+ 8.3
New Jersey	51,577	45,571	+13.2	11,098	9,684	+14.6
New Mexico	10,027	8,742	+14.7	2,534	2,189	+15.8
New York	291,610	286,168	+ 1.9	55,278	50,440	+ 9.6
North Carolina	46,870	42,840	+ 9.4	14,922	13,731	+ 8.7
North Dakota	7,815	7,238	+ 8.0	2,995	2,889	+ 3.7
Ohio	121,404	113,168	+ 7.3	30,158	27,963	+ 7.8
Oklahoma	44,791	36,436	+22.9	11,985	11,417	+ 5.0
Oregon	26,485	22,685	+16.8	7,903	6,137	+28.8
Pennsylvania	139,050	131,943	+ 5.4	32,796	28,155	+16.5
Rhode Island	12,496	10,858	+15.1	3,526	2,984	+18.2
South Carolina	26,177	21,617	+21.1	6,227	6,124	+ 1.7
South Dakota	9,306	7,548	+23.3	3,331	2,628	+26.8
Tennessee	40,219	36,710	+ 9.6	11,694	10,502	+11.4
Texas	138,850	123,052	+12.8	38,677	34,706	+11.4
Utah	23,369	21,080	+10.9	7,151	6,063	+17.9
Vermont	7,037	6,866	+ 2.5	2,165	2,177	− 0.6
Virginia	40,007	32,137	+24.5	10,358	10,231	+ 1.2
Washington	41,881	37,757	+10.9	11,837	10,846	+ 9.1
West Virginia	20,453	17,730	+15.4	5,929	5,400	+ 9.8
Wisconsin	50,399	45,283	+11.3	14,528	12,589	+15.4
Wyoming	4,330	3,442	+25.8	1,342	989	+35.7
District of Columbia	34,068	30,290	+12.5	5,524	4,594	+20.2
Service academies	7,883	7,802	+ 1.0	1,871	1,978	− 5.4
Outlying parts	21,903	19,647	+11.5	6,212	5,564	+11.6
Alaska	409	304	+34.5	145	122	+18.9
Canal Zone	262	369	−29.0	199	201	− 1.0
Guam	219	260	−15.8	101	59	+71.2
Hawaii	5,364	4,619	+16.1	1,348	1,193	+13.0
Puerto Rico	15,649	14,095	+11.0	4,419	3,989	+10.8

*Source: *Fall Enrollment in Higher Educational Institutions,* 1954, Office of Education, U.S. Department of Health, Education, and Welfare, Washington, 1955.

(a) This figure is not comparable with the percentage change in other states in that the 1953 fall enrollment figure for Minnesota was underreported by the colleges by approximately 7,000 (consisting of college-grade extension students).

TABLE 2

EXPENDITURE DATA BY MAJOR CLASSES FOR ALL INSTITUTIONS OF HIGHER EDUCATION, BY TYPE OF CONTROL, FOR SELECTED YEARS 1932 TO 1952*

(In thousands of dollars)†

	Number inst'ns reporting	Educational and general (a)	Rate of change (%)	Auxiliary enterprises (b)	Rate of change (%)	Other noneducational (c)	Rate of change (%)	Total current (d)	Rate of change (%)	Capital outlay (e)	Rate of change (%)
All Institutions											
1932	1,356	$ 418,624	(f)	$ 90,897	(f)	$24,993	(f)	$ 534,514	(f)	$ 98,290	(f)
1934	1,326	368,280	−12.04	77,766	−14.44	20,938	−16.22	466,984	−12.63	29,503	−69.98
1936	1,539	416,849	13.20	95,152	22.35	24,154	15.35	536,156	14.81	47,369	60.55
1938	1,586	475,191	13.99	115,620	21.51	23,574	−2.40	614,385	14.59	70,465	48.75
1940	1,607	517,043	8.80	123,473	6.79	26,782	13.65	667,299	8.61	80,260	13.90
1942	1,626	567,519	9.76	136,617	10.64	26,644	−.51	730,780	9.51	46,696	−41.81
1944(g)	1,563	656,802	15.73	199,344	45.91	20,928	−21.45	877,074	20.01	27,427	−41.26
1946	1,767(h)	819,169	24.72	242,028	21.41	26,067	24.59	1,087,264	23.96	71,317	160.02
1948	1,787	1,377,919	68.20	434,040	79.33	52,687	102.12	1,864,647	71.49	306,371	329.59
1950	1,868	1,692,858	22.85	471,973	8.73	62,816	19.22	2,227,647	19.46	416,745	36.02
1952	1,827	1,907,056	12.65	473,077	0.23	72,127	14.82	2,452,259	10.08	403,231	−3.24
Publicly Controlled Institutions											
1932	499	$203,855	(f)	$ 33,621	(f)	$ 3,426	(f)	$ 240,903	(f)	$ 39,423	(f)
1934	484	175,024	−14.14	28,158	−16.24	3,061	−10.65	206,243	−14.38	11,440	−70.98
1936	565	205,350	17.32	37,773	34.14	4,690	53.21	247,814	20.15	32,095	180.55
1938	586	238,906	16.34	47,933	26.89	3,543	−24.45	290,382	17.17	40,926	27.51
1940	592	264,434	10.68	51,567	7.58	5,023	41.77	321,025	10.58	59,706	45.88
1942	603	295,574	11.77	61,060	18.40	4,904	−2.36	361,537	12.61	25,447	−57.37
1944(g)	582	319,888	8.22	93,767	53.56	4,519	−7.85	418,174	15.66	15,205	−40.24
1946	623(h)	391,933	22.52	119,314	27.24	6,263	38.59	517,510	23.75	32,316	112.53

Publicly Controlled Institutions (Cont'd)

Year											
1948	629	699,312	78.42	216,747	81.66	17,110	173.19	933,169	80.31	183,196	465.38
1950	665	884,468	26.47	231,085	6.61	19,960	16.65	1,135,514	21.68	275,985	50.65
1952	636	1,038,673	17.43	227,271	-1.65	20,455	2.48	1,286,498	13.29	260,172	-5.73

Privately Controlled Institutions

Year											
1932	857	$214,769	(f)	$ 57,276	(f)	$21,567	(f)	$ 293,611	(f)	$ 58,867	(f)
1934	842	193,256	-10.01	49,608	-13.38	17,877	-17.10	260,741	-11.19	18,063	-69.31
1936	974	211,499	9.43	57,379	15.66	19,464	8.87	288,342	10.59	15,274	-15.44
1938	1,000	236,285	11.71	67,687	17.96	20,031	2.91	324,003	12.36	29,539	93.39
1940	1,015	252,609	6.90	71,906	6.23	21,759	8.62	346,274	6.87	20,554	-30.41
1942	1,023	271,945	7.65	75,557	5.07	21,740	-.08	369,243	6.63	21,249	3.38
1944(g)	981	336,914	23.89	105,577	39.73	16,409	-24.52	458,900	24.28	12,222	-42.48
1946	1,144(h)	427,235	26.80	122,714	16.23	19,804	20.68	569,754	24.15	39,000	187.74
1948	1,158	678,606	58.83	217,293	77.07	35,577	79.64	931,476	63.48	123,175	215.83
1950	1,203	808,390	19.12	240,888	10.85	42,855	20.45	1,092,133	17.24	140,760	14.27
1952	1,191	868,384	7.42	245,806	2.04	51,671	20.57	1,165,861	6.75	143,059	1.63

Source: Figures through 1950 are from *Higher Education in the Forty-Eight States*, The Council of State Governments, 1952; 1952 data are from *Biennial Survey of Education*, Department of Health, Education, and Welfare: 1955.

*The data in this table are for the continental United States only and do not include the United States Service Schools.

†Totals presented do not always represent exact totals since each entry was independently rounded.

(a) Educational and general expenditures include expenditures for administrative and general expense, resident instruction, organized research (separately budgeted), libraries, physical plant operation and maintenance, extension, and organized activities related to instruction.

(b) Auxiliary enterprises include expenditures for the following purposes primarily: dormitories and dining halls, student unions, bookstores, and in some institutions, university presses, and athletics.

(c) Other noneducational expenditures include expenditures for the following purposes primarily: fellowships, scholarships, and interest on debt (not payment on principal).

(d) This expenditure category includes educational and general expenditures, auxiliary enterprises, and other noneducational expenditures.

(e) Capital outlay includes expenditures for the following purposes primarily: increase in the physical property of the institution such as purchase, construction and remodeling of buildings (does not include maintenance), purchase of new land, and equipment.

(f) Data comparable to those of preceding year not available.

(g) The data for 1944 include expenditures for federal contract courses (preparation for specific wartime tasks) to the extent that these expenditures were not segregated by the reporting institutions from the outlay shown for this year under one or more of the four major expenditure classes. However, some institutions did report their expenditures of such federal funds separately, and the totals (not included in any data shown for 1944) were: public institutions $66,828,251, private institutions $30,215,635, and all institutions $97,043,886.

(h) Data include estimates for those schools not reporting—public, 156; private, 144; all, 400.

TABLE 3

CURRENT INCOME OF INSTITUTIONS OF HIGHER EDUCATION BY SOURCES, IN CONTINENTAL UNITED STATES: 1951–52

Data on all Institutions and Selected Categories of Institutions*

(In thousands of dollars. Detail does not necessarily add to total due to rounding)

Item	All institutions Amount	Per cent of Educational and general income	Per cent of Total current income	Publicly controlled institutions Amount	Per cent of Educational and general income	Per cent of Total current income	Privately controlled institutions Amount	Per cent of Educational and general income	Per cent of Total current income
I. All Institutions:									
Educational and general income:									
Student fees	$ 446,591	22.1	17.4	$ 116,201	10.4	8.4	$ 330,390	36.6	27.8
Federal government:									
Veterans' tuition and fees	146,900	7.3	5.7	57,647	5.2	4.2	89,253	9.9	7.5
Other current purposes(a)	304,111	15.0	11.9	163,323	14.6	11.9	140,787	15.6	11.9
State governments	611,302	30.2	23.9	575,656	51.5	41.9	35,646	3.9	3.0
Local governments	72,013	3.6	2.8	70,617	6.3	5.1	1,396	.2	.1
Endowment earnings	112,859	5.6	4.4	12,089	1.1	.9	100,771	11.2	8.5
Private benefactions	149,826	7.4	5.8	26,233	2.3	1.9	123,593	13.7	10.4
Organized activities related to instructional departments	136,442	6.8	5.3	79,097	7.1	5.8	57,344	6.3	4.8
Other sources	40,835	2.0	1.6	16,765	1.5	1.2	24,070	2.7	2.0
Total educational and general income	2,020,878(a)	100.0	78.8	1,117,628	100.0	81.3	903,251	100.0	76.0
Auxiliary enterprises	509,545		19.9	245,580		17.9	263,966		22.2
For scholarships, fellowships, prizes	20,635		.8	6,376		.5	14,260		1.2
Other current income	11,392		.4	5,720		.4	5,672		.5
Total current income	2,562,451		100.0	1,375,303		100.0	1,187,148		100.0
II. Universities:									
Educational and general income:									
Student fees	216,766	17.7	14.6	71,950	9.7	7.9	144,816	30.3	24.9
Federal government:									
Veterans' tuition and fees	79,902	6.5	5.4	34,160	4.6	3.8	45,742	9.6	7.9
Other current purposes	216,039	17.7	14.5	126,425	17.0	13.9	89,614	18.7	15.4
State governments	408,703	33.4	27.4	375,325	50.3	41.3	33,378	7.0	5.7
Local governments	27,254	2.2	1.8	26,357	3.5	2.9	897	.2	.2
Endowment earnings	66,671	5.4	4.5	9,751	1.3	1.1	56,920	11.9	9.8
Private benefactions	77,948	6.4	5.2	24,964	3.3	2.7	52,984	11.1	9.1
Organized activities related to instructional departments	102,643	8.4	6.9	64,911	8.7	7.1	37,732	7.9	6.5
Other sources	27,959	2.3	1.9	11,730	1.6	1.3	16,229	3.4	2.8
Total educational and general income	1,223,886	100.0	82.2	745,573	100.0	82.0	478,312	100.0	82.4
Auxiliary enterprises	246,562		16.6	153,932		16.9	92,630		16.0
For scholarships, fellowships, prizes	11,851		.8	4,747		.5	7,104		1.2
Other current income	7,205		.5	4,761		.5	2,444		.4
Total current income	1,489,503		100.0	909,012		100.0	580,491		100.0

Note: the three numeric groups for each section (column headings for this table appear on the preceding page). Within each group the columns are: Amount, percent of total educational and general income, and percent of total current income.

III. Liberal Arts Colleges:

Item	Amount	%	%	Amount	%	%	Amount	%	%
Educational and general income:									
Student fees	145,485	42.4	28.5	13,671	12.9	9.9	131,814	55.6	35.3
Federal government:									
Veterans' tuition and fees	29,333	8.6	5.7	7,078	6.7	5.1	22,255	9.4	6.0
Other current purposes	8,945	2.6	1.7	6,967	6.6	5.1	1,978	.8	.5
State governments	68,161	19.9	13.3	67,500	63.8	48.9	661	.3	.2
Local governments	3,072	.9	.6	3,004	2.8	2.2	68	(b)	(b)
Endowment earnings	27,997	8.2	5.5	592	.6	.4	27,405	11.6	7.3
Private benefactions	43,756	12.8	8.6	536	.5	.4	43,220	18.2	11.6
Organized activities related to instructional departments	8,376	2.4	1.6	4,313	4.1	3.1	4,063	1.7	1.1
Other sources	7,759	2.3	1.5	2,101	2.0	1.5	5,659	2.4	1.5
Total educational and general income	**342,884**	**100.0**	**67.1**	**105,762**	**100.0**	**76.7**	**237,122**	**100.0**	**63.5**
Auxiliary enterprises	160,111	.....	31.3	31,270	.....	22.7	128,841	.....	34.5
For scholarships, fellowships, prizes	5,815	.....	1.1	438	.....	.3	5,377	.....	1.4
Other current income	2,367	.....	.5	472	.....	.3	1,895	.....	.5
Total current income	**511,177**	.....	**100.0**	**137,942**	.....	**100.0**	**373,235**	.....	**100.0**

IV. Teachers Colleges:

Item	Amount	%	%	Amount	%	%	Amount	%	%
Educational and general income:									
Student fees	18,739	15.7	11.8	15,887	14.0	10.6	2,852	48.6	36.2
Federal government:									
Veterans' tuition and fees	7,945	6.7	5.0	7,111	6.3	4.7	834	14.2	10.6
Other current purposes	2,241	1.9	1.4	2,206	1.9	1.5	35	.6	.4
State governments	80,731	67.6	51.0	80,730	71.1	53.7	1	(b)	(b)
Local governments	4,825	4.0	3.0	4,825	4.2	3.2	.....	.....	.....
Endowment earnings	465	.4	.3	169	.1	.1	297	5.1	3.8
Private benefactions	1,539	1.3	1.0	75	.1	.1	1,463	25.0	18.6
Organized activities related to instructional departments	1,749	1.5	1.1	1,509	1.3	1.0	241	4.1	3.1
Other sources	1,210	1.0	.8	1,069	.9	.7	141	2.4	1.8
Total educational and general income	**119,444**	**100.0**	**75.4**	**113,580**	**100.0**	**75.5**	**5,863**	**100.0**	**74.4**
Auxiliary enterprises	38,262	.....	24.2	36,332	.....	24.1	1,930	.....	24.5
For scholarships, fellowships, prizes	488	.....	.3	424	.....	.3	64	.....	.8
Other current income	140	.....	.1	119	.....	.1	22	.....	.3
Total current income	**158,334**	.....	**100.0**	**150,456**	.....	**100.0**	**7,878**	.....	**100.0**

V. Junior Colleges: (c)

Item	Amount	%	%	Amount	%	%	Amount	%	%
Educational and general income:									
Student fees	23,169	21.7	17.1	7,132	9.1	8.2	16,038	57.0	33.3
Federal government:									
Veterans' tuition and fees	10,043	9.4	7.4	6,420	8.2	7.4	3,623	12.9	7.5
Other current purposes	743	.7	.5	727	.9	.8	16	.1	(b)
State governments	25,307	23.7	18.7	25,062	31.9	28.7	245	.9	.5
Local governments	36,277	34.0	26.8	35,912	45.6	41.1	365	1.3	.8
Endowment earnings	2,259	2.1	1.7	1,222	1.6	1.4	1,037	3.7	2.2
Private benefactions	5,783	5.4	4.3	14	(b)	(b)	5,769	20.5	12.0
Organized activities related to instructional departments	1,272	1.2	.9	924	1.2	1.1	348	1.2	.7
Other sources	1,949	1.8	1.4	1,267	1.6	1.5	682	2.4	1.4
Total educational and general income	**106,802**	**100.0**	**78.8**	**78,681**	**100.0**	**90.2**	**28,122**	**100.0**	**58.4**
Auxiliary enterprises	27,734	.....	20.5	8,162	.....	9.3	19,572	.....	40.7
For scholarships, fellowships, prizes	560	.....	.4	372	.....	.4	188	.....	.4
Other current income	312	.....	.2	90	.....	.1	222	.....	.5
Total current income	**135,409**	.....	**100.0**	**87,305**	.....	**100.0**	**48,104**	.....	**100.0**

*Adapted from *Biennial Survey of Education*, Section 2, Chapter 4, *Statistics of Higher Education*, U. S. Department of Health, Education, and Welfare, 1955.

The data for "All Institutions" at the top of the table include income of certain categories of institutions (technological schools, theological schools and other professional schools) for which separate figures are not presented in the table.

"Current income," throughout the table, refers to amounts available for immediate or recurring needs and does not include income for plant.

"Educational and general income" comprises income available for instruction, research, extension and public services, and general expenses.

"Auxiliary enterprises" comprise enterprises operated primarily for service to students and intended to be self-supporting: residence and dining hall accommodations, bookstores, intercollegiate athletics, concert courses, etc.

(a) Includes $13.7 million received by the five United States Service Academies.

(b) Less than 0.05 per cent.

(c) Includes community colleges, normal schools, technical institutes, and other non-degree-granting institutions operating on the undergraduate or adult education level.

LIBRARY SERVICES AND LEGISLATION*

T HE NATION'S need for an educated citizenry affects all types of libraries and library legislation. Increased support by the states in extending educational opportunities is shown by recent activities of state libraries, in cooperation with state library associations, and by the record of the 1954–55 legislatures.

The role of the state library has been studied during the past two years by both the American Library Association and the National Association of State Libraries. The A.L.A. reviewed the functions of state libraries in connection with the preparation of revised standards for public library service. A general statement of the role of the state library was issued in 1955 by the National Association of State Libraries. The goals set forth by it reflect the experience and trends in development of state libraries over approximately fifty years. The statement declares:

"The state library is the focal point of statewide library service. It has the dual function: (1) to serve all branches, agencies, commissions, departments and officers of its government and (2) to serve the state as a whole. Its functions further include developing legislation affecting libraries, promoting library development in the state, improving library standards, and fostering a climate of acceptance and understanding of libraries and the value of library service."

The statement outlines the recognized functions of an integrated state library agency as follows:

1. *General Library Services*—including statistics, publications, reference, research and loans.

2. *Library Extension Service*—including traveling libraries and advice and aid in establishing local libraries.

3. *Archives and History.*

4. *Legislative Reference Services.*

5. *Law Library.*

6. *Government Publications*—maintaining for

use state, federal and local collections.

7. *Special Library Services*—e.g., to the blind, to correctional and other specialized state institutions and the recruiting, certification and placement of library personnel.

Librarians expected the statement to serve increasingly as a guide for the improvement and extension of state services.

The following summary of 1954–55 legislation and related activities is based on reports from state library agencies that include among their legal responsibilities the two functions of general library service and library extension service.

STUDIES AFFECTING LIBRARY SERVICE

At least nine states are currently engaged or in the last two years have been engaged in fact-gathering as a prerequisite to legislative action affecting libraries. On the request of the Legislative Council, the Alabama Legislative Reference Service in 1954 made a study of state library organization. Its report, *A Study of State Library Systems*, briefly describes the legal responsibilities of the four agencies comprising the Alabama state library system and reviews the organizational patterns in other states. The Nevada Legislative Council conducted a survey of library service in that state. In South Dakota the Legislative Research Council recommended legislation to abolish the State Library Commission and transfer its function to a proposed Department of Education; this legislation did not pass. In California and Wisconsin, house resolutions were voted providing for study of library conditions, including in Wisconsin a special examination of the organization and performance of the Free Library Commission. In Ohio, the Legislative Research Commission has listed as one of its next major projects a study of the financing of public libraries. The Governors of Massachusetts and New Jersey have appointed special commissions: in Massachusetts an Administrative Commission to study the financial needs of

*Prepared by S. JANICE KEE, Executive Secretary, Public Libraries Division, American Library Association.

public libraries, and in New Jersey an eleven-member Commission to Study Libraries. A private organization, the Texas Research League, is conducting a study of library conditions in that state.

ADMINISTRATIVE CHANGES

The Kentucky legislature in 1954 abolished the Department of Library and Archives, which included three agencies: the Legislative Law Library, the Historical Society and the Library Extension Division. A new State Law Library was created, and the Historical Society and Library Extension Division became independent agencies of government. A merger, however, will take place on July 1, 1956. The Kentucky legislature also established a new State Library consisting of the present State Library and the Library Commission. An eight-member Governing Board will include six appointees by the Governor and two ex-officio members.

In Iowa and Oregon ex-officio members of state library boards were eliminated by the legislatures in favor of all-lay-member boards, with five members in Iowa and seven in Oregon. A newly constituted State Library Board in Ohio was approved, five members to be appointed by the State Board of Education. In Missouri a change in the law establishes a commission to govern the State Library, to include four members appointed by the Governor. In Nevada the responsibility for providing law books for use of the legislators was shifted from the State Library to the Legislative Council.

Several amendments and new laws affect the administration of local libraries. The Tennessee legislature authorized the counties comprising a state regional library system to form a regional library board for the purpose of administering, under contract with the State Library and Archives Commission, the services of a regional library service center. This is a permissive act. In Mississippi the law governing regional library boards was changed to provide for as many members of a board as the number of counties represented in the region, if more than five are represented.

An amendment to the county library law in Florida eliminates the necessity for appointment of a library board if the county commissioners wish to enter into a contract for library service. In Missouri an act of the 1955 legislature limits city library trustees to three terms.

FINANCIAL SUPPORT OF LIBRARIES[1]

Thirty-four legislatures approved increases in over-all budgets for state library services. Kentucky's Library Extension Division received the highest percentage increase. Others reporting substantial increases were Colorado, Connecticut, Michigan, Nevada, Tennessee and Washington.

State Grants-in-aid. Twenty states reported appropriations for grants-in-aid to establish and strengthen local library service, and six reported increases. In Connecticut, payments to local libraries were increased from $100 to $500 annually, and in Washington a grants program was restored after having been dropped by the 1953 legislature. Laws establishing eligibility for state grants were changed in Maine and Missouri; in both states formulas increasing local support were adopted.

Local Financial Support. Several other measures were enacted which affect the financial support of local libraries. An increased cigarette tax in New Mexico will benefit library service to juveniles. In North Dakota each school board was required to spend no less than $25 each year for library books for one-room schools. A raise was approved in the maximum permissible tax rate for libraries in Indiana. Tax millage levies were regulated for selected city libraries in Minnesota and Kansas and for county libraries in Kansas. In Nevada a bill was passed to raise the maximum support of county libraries.

LARGER UNITS OF LIBRARY SERVICE

A current and important project of the American Library Association is the revision of existing suggested standards for public library service. This new guide to evaluation of libraries, as it relates to library structure and government, will emphasize the necessity of libraries working together, sharing their services and materials, in order to meet the full needs of

---

[1]See table, page 272.

their users. Thus the cooperative approach is the basic recommendation.

Among acts of the 1955 legislatures were amendments and laws relating to county, multi-county and district libraries. In Idaho enabling legislation for creation of public library districts was enacted; a tax not to exceed two mills may be levied in the districts, and contractual services were authorized. The Oklahoma legislature approved a new multi-county law which permits counties and cities within them to join in a cooperative library effort based on contracts. Oregon also adopted enabling legislation providing for multi-county library systems by contract.

In Missouri a new "regional" library provision in the county library law allows for full cooperation, including interstate, between localities in offering library service by contract, under a unified governing board; up to ten counties may cooperate under this law. Further Missouri amendments made more difficult the establishment and dissolution of county libraries, changed the fiscal year to be the calendar year and extended bonding power. The Michigan legislature authorized a district library which may include two or more governmental units of any kind.

Connecticut and Michigan provided for extension of state library service to regional areas. A branch of the State Library in the Upper Peninsula of Michigan was authorized; and in Connecticut a supplementary library service center for public and school libraries, under the administration of the State Bureau of Library Services, was provided for a designated county area. In both states appropriations were made to implement the new laws.

New Services

Legislatures in a number of states established new state library services. Authorized in New Jersey was a Deposit and Exchange Unit within the Public and School Library Services Bureau. In New York various state departments and commissions are required by a new law to deliver 200 copies of printed publications to the State Library for distribution to other libraries. A revolving fund was established in Oregon to launch a microfilm service from the State Archivist to state agencies,

municipal corporations, districts and political subdivisions, which will pay a fee for the service. The state librarian in Nevada was authorized to collect fees for photostatic services. The State of Washington for the first time provided for library service to the blind by making an appropriation to reimburse the Seattle Public Library for its work with the blind and for making contracts with other libraries for such service.

Maine will operate a second bookmobile, approved by the 1955 legislature. The State Library Commission in Washington was permitted to assume the expenditures of the State Board for the Certification of Librarians.

Personnel

In California the State Librarian's salary was raised from $10,000 to $11,000 a year, and a general state-wide pay raise of 5 per cent affected all state-employed librarians. Legislation relating to state retirement plans and social security, affecting librarians, was passed in Indiana, Maine, Michigan, Montana, New Mexico, Ohio and South Carolina. A new position of field worker in the Library Extension Commission was authorized in Montana. The Public Library Service Division of Alabama and the State Library of Nevada will be able to add two or three new staff members each, and New Jersey's Division of State Library will have six new positions. The New Hampshire legislature passed a law preventing summary dismissal of library employees without formal charges and a hearing before library trustees.

The New York legislature approved an amendment to certification regulations affecting librarians. Candidates for positions who have served in very responsible administrative positions may be certified without examination. Reciprocity was provided with other states meeting the New York standards.

Library Buildings

In 1954 the Louisiana legislature included $2 million for a state library building in a capital improvements bond issue. In addition to other construction projects, the 1955 Washington legislature authorized construction of a state library building and furnishings, to cost $1,250,000.

The Texas legislature revised laws relating to county libraries so that counties may acquire land, issue bonds and levy taxes for library buildings. Laws in Missouri and Washington were amended to permit county libraries to incur indebtedness for building purposes. In Kansas municipalities were authorized to levy taxes within stated limitations for remodeling or constructing library buildings.

APPROPRIATIONS FOR THE STATE LIBRARY AGENCIES THAT INCLUDE PUBLIC LIBRARY EXTENSION SERVICE AS ONE FUNCTION*

State	Name of agency and functions	Date	Appropriation for agency	Appropriation for grants-in-aid to public libraries
Alabama	Public Library Service Division, Department of Archives and History (2)	1955–56	$230,000	none
Arizona	Department of Library and Archives (3) (4) (5) (7)	1955–56	57,272(a)	none
Arkansas	Arkansas Library Commission (1) (2) (12) (14)	1953–55	307,700	$80,000(b)
California	State Library, Department of Education (1) (2) (3) (4) (5) (6) (7) (8) (11) (14) (15)	1955–56	576,221	none
Colorado	State Library, Dept. of Ed. (1) (2) (3) in part	1955–56	66,241.10	none
Connecticut	Bureau of Library Services, Department of Education (1) in part (2) (9) (12) (14)† (15)	1955–56	80,657.50	100,000(d)
Delaware	Library Commission for the State (1) (2)	1955–57	59,190	10,000(d)
Florida	Florida State Library (1) (2) (3) (14)†	1955–57	110,889	none
Georgia	Div. of Instructional Materials and Library Service, Dept. of Education (1) (2) (10) (12) (14) (15)	1955–56	963,420(c)	none
Idaho	State Traveling Library (1) (2)	1955–57	29,500	none
Illinois	State Library (1) (2) (3) in part (11) (14) (15)	1955–57	1,211,300	none
Indiana	State Library (1) (2) (3) (6) (7) (8) (10) (14) (15)	1955–57	629,030	none
Iowa	State Traveling Library (1) (2) (14)	1955–57	123,640	none
Kansas	State Library and Traveling Libraries Commission (1) (2) (4) (5) (14)	1955–56	157,218	none
Kentucky	Library Extension Division (1) (2) (10) (14)†	1954–56	322,300	100,000(d)
Louisiana	State Library (1) (2) (4) (10)	1955–56	267,000(e)	none
Maine	State Library (1) (2) (3) in part (4) (5)	1955–57	259,527	26,800(b)
Maryland	Div. of Lib. Extension, Dept. of Ed. (1) (2) (11) (12)	1954–55	100,868.50	269,185(d)
Massachusetts	Division of Library Extension, Department of Education (1) (2) (10) (11) (12)	1954–55	114,610(e)	none
Michigan	State Library and State Board for Libraries (1)	1955–56	523,437(e,f)	305,000
Minnesota	Library Div., Dept. of Ed. (1) (2) (12) (14)	1955–57	34,795.57	none
Mississippi	Library Commission (1) (2) (14)	1954–56	191,175	54,000(b)
Missouri	State Library (1) (2) (11) (12) (14) (15)	1955–57	783,400	500,000(b)
Montana	State Library Extension Commission (1) (2) (14)	1955–56	21,507	none
Nebraska	Public Library Commission (1) (2) (8) (14)†	1955–57	129,814.16	none
Nevada	State Library (1) (2) (4) (5) (14)†	1955–57	130,439	none
New Hampshire	State Library (1) (2) (3) in part (4) (5) (14)	1955–57	272,773.46(g)	3,000(b)
New Jersey	Division of the State Library, Archives and History, Department of Education (1) (2) (3) (4) (5) (12)	1955–56	279,363.11	none
New Mexico	State Library Commission (1) (2) (10) (12) (14)	1955–57	218,300	40,000(b)
New York	Library Extension Division, State Library, Department of Education (2) (8) (10) (11) (14)	1955–56	921,545	2,350,000(d)
North Carolina	Library Commission (2) (10) (14)†	1955–57	82,700	833,402(d)
North Dakota	State Library Commission (1) (2) (14)†	1955–57	90,000	none
Ohio	State Library, Department of Education (1) (2)	1955–57	534,612	320,000(b)
Oklahoma	State Library (1) (2) (3) in part (4) (5) (7) (8) (10) (14)	1955–57	281,000	none
Oregon	State Library (1) (2) (3) (4) (12) (14)†	1955–57	525,143	none
Pennsylvania	Library Extension Division, State Library, Department of Public Instruction (1) (2) (5)	1953–55	456,500	206,000(d)
Rhode Island	State Library (1) (2) (3) (4) (5) (13)	1954–55	89,000	20,000(b)
South Carolina	State Library Board (1) (2) (14)	1954–55	101,638	66,000(b)
South Dakota	Free Library Commission (1) (2) (4) (12) (14)	1955–57	110,000	none
Tennessee	State Library and Archives (2) (3) (15)	1955–57	950,000(e)	none
Texas	State Library (1) (2) (3) (4) (5) (8) (14)	1955–57	337,004	none
Utah	Library Administrative Agency, Department of Public Instruction (2) statistics only	1954–55	none	none
Vermont	Free Public Library Commission (1) (2) (12) (14)	1955–57	282,072(e)	1,000(b)
Virginia	State Library (1) (2) (3) (10) (14)	1955–56	473,175	95,000(b)
Washington	State Library (1) (2) (3) in part (4) (10) (14)	1955–57	329,133	62,000(b)
West Virginia	Library Commission (1) (2)	1955–56	72,320	none
Wisconsin	Free Library Commission (1) (2) (4) (10) (11) (14) (15)	1955–57	346,210	none
Wyoming	State Library (1) (2) (4) (5)	1955–57	67,000	none

*Prepared by the American Library Association.
The functions of state library agencies reported are:
(1) General library service, including reference.
(2) Library Extension, including traveling libraries and/or establishing public libraries.
(3) Archives and History.
(4) Legislative reference.
(5) Law Library.
(6) Government publications.
(7) Genealogy.
(8) Service to the blind.
(9) Special Education library.
(10) Works with legal certification of public librarians.
(11) Service to correctional institutions.
(12) Special service to schools.
(13) Operates book pool for Armed Forces.
(14) Publications.
(14)† Mimeographed Newsletter.
(15) Placement service.
(a) Does not provide funds for extension services.
(b) Grants-in-aid are included in the agency appropriation.
(c) Includes funds for books and locally employed librarians. Administrative costs are borne by Department of Education.
(d) Grants-in-aid are not included in agency appropriation.
(e) Includes funds for state supported county (or parish) and regional library demonstrations or centers.
(f) Includes grant for establishment of a Branch of the State library in The Upper Peninsula.
(g) Does not include building maintenance, janitor, etc.

2

Highways, Highway Safety, Aviation

HIGHWAY SYSTEMS AND MOTOR VEHICLE REGULATION

ALTHOUGH responsibility for the highways of America is spread among all levels of government, states and localities share most of the burden. For some years states have paid for more than three-fifths of the combined costs of constructing, maintaining and policing all roads. Local governments have accounted for about two-thirds of the remaining expenditures.

Approximately a fifth of all roads and highways are eligible for federal construction grants on a state-matching basis. Construction on aided highways is a state responsibility, and this has normally been under joint state-federal supervision. In place of joint supervision, legislation adopted by Congress in 1954 permits states to certify that aided secondary road projects have been completed according to state standards previously approved by the federal government.

Local governments are responsible for the construction and maintenance of most urban and rural roads—usually from their own funds. Some states provide considerable assistance for local roads. Also, many important road arteries serving urban areas are becoming objects of federal aid or are being absorbed by state road networks.

State revenues for all highway purposes approached $3,448 million in 1954. The total for 1955 is expected to reach $3,600 million, twice the level of 1948 and 20 per cent over the figure for 1952. Preliminary estimates for 1954 and the forecast for 1955 place local highway revenues at $1,329 million and $1,394 million. Corresponding figures for federal highway contributions are $675 million and $771 million.

Bond issues to finance state road construction have increased more rapidly. There were $6,250 million in state highway obligations outstanding at the close of 1954, more than double the 1952 total. A rise to $7,200 million is expected by the end of 1955. Total road bond proceeds in 1954 were $2,800 million, about $2,400 million of this from state issues—mostly for toll roads. Forecasts suggested that bond issues for 1955 would total $1,600 million—including something under $1,200 million from state issues.

State expenditures for highways and streets were $4,138 million in 1954 and were expected to reach $4,796 million in 1955. Of these sums, $155 million and $169 million, respectively, represent debt retirement. Highways are second to education in demands on state funds. Moreover, road expenditures account for a growing share of state disbursements. In 1951 roads accounted for 22.9 per cent of state general expenditures. That percentage has increased in each succeeding year, up to 26.1 per cent in 1954.

Total highway disbursements by all levels of government were estimated at $6,776 million in 1954. They were expected to reach $7,552 million in 1955—fully twice the corresponding figure for 1948.

HIGHWAY NEEDS

Road needs are increasing in the face of vastly increased construction expenditures

273

for a variety of reasons. Highway use reached an estimated 560 billion vehicle miles in 1954, an increase of 85 per cent over the rate prevailing in 1946. By 1965 it is expected to rise to 800 billion vehicle miles. Moreover, rising costs have reduced the purchasing power of highway dollars. The price of a given composite of work and material necessary to construct an identical unit of highway has more than doubled since 1940. Expressed in 1940 price levels, 1954 expenditures for road construction were 23 per cent higher than in 1940 and only 11 per cent higher than in 1938, the year of our greatest previous highway construction. Finally, modern traffic volumes, weights and speeds require advanced road standards involving much higher construction costs. Many roads of recent construction still in good repair are already inadequate for current traffic.

A recent study conducted by the Secretary of Commerce indicates that a ten-year program to bring all roads up to an adequate level would cost $101 billion for construction at 1954 prices. During the same period $19.4 billion would be needed for maintenance. The interstate network—about 40,000 miles of roads connecting our major population centers—accounts for about a fourth of over-all construction needs.

HIGHWAY CONSTRUCTION AND MAINTENANCE

In 1953 the states expended $1,837 million in building 41,744 miles of road along state-administered highways. These totals include work on federally aided projects but exclude toll-road construction. Estimates of comparable efforts for 1954 show that $2,133 million was spent in constructing 41,982 miles of road on state-controlled highways.

Federally aided projects were completed on 21,136 miles of highway during 1953 at a total cost of $1,078 million. Of this amount $519 million were state funds. In 1954 an estimated 20,548 miles were constructed on aided projects at a cost of $1,146 million, of which $555 million comprised state funds.

Construction contracts awarded offer another yardstick of road building efforts. During 1953 states let contracts on more than 14,200 projects for 49,000 miles of

highway at a cost of $2,316 million. In 1954 contracts were made for 16,000 projects to build 56,660 miles of road at a cost of $2,324 million.

Capital outlay for roads by all levels of government amounted to $3.2 billion in 1953, $4 billion in 1954, and was expected to reach $4.6 billion in 1955.

The maintenance of road systems is the responsibility of the states and localities. State expenses for this purpose amounted to $626 million in 1953 and $651 million in 1954, and were expected to reach $664 million in 1955. Disbursements by local governments for road maintenance were $1,095 million in 1953, $1,142 million in 1954, and may reach $1,184 million in 1955.

HIGHWAY FINANCE

The choice between bond issues and taxation for road funds, the proper balance among motor-fuel taxes and license and registration fees as sources of highway revenue, and the right variation in tax treatment of the several classes of motor vehicles are traditional problems of highway finance. Others of major importance include the role of the federal government in financing road construction, and the toll road as an alternative method of financing expressways.

The Highway Act of 1954 authorized $875 million in federal highway aid for each of the fiscal years 1956 and 1957—an increase of $300 million annually over grant levels for the two preceding fiscal years. Half of the added funds are intended for the interstate system—an increase from $25 million to $175 million for each fiscal year. In another departure, basic federal-state matching requirements were reduced from 50-50 to 60-40 for the interstate system. This shift in emphasis appeared likely to sharpen in subsequent federal legislation. All congressional proposals considered or pending would provide for greatly increased construction on the interstate system, with federal funds financing much the larger share of the costs.

The 1954 act enables each state to divert federal construction funds from one to another of the federally-aided systems provided no one system within the states loses or gains more than 10 per cent of its original allotment.

Thirty-eight of the forty-six states whose legislatures met during 1955 had acted by November 1 to increase funds available for highways. Prior to these changes, the average gasoline tax was 5.42 cents per gallon —an increase of 21.1 per cent since 1945. Increases raising the average gasoline tax to 5.75 cents per gallon were expected to yield an additional $175 million annually at current consumption levels.

Three states raised the rate by one-half cent per gallon: Georgia from 6 to 6.5; Nevada from 5.5 to 6; and Vermont from 5 to 5.5.

One-cent increases were enacted by eight states: Texas from 4 to 5 cents per gallon; Iowa, North Dakota, Pennsylvania and West Virginia from 5 to 6 cents; and Alabama, Maine and Montana from 6 to 7 cents. Michigan raised the rate from 4.5 to 6 cents and Connecticut and Wisconsin from 4 to 6 cents a gallon. Tennessee raised its petroleum inspection fee from .5 to .7 cents per gallon. Temporary rate increases about to expire were extended or made permanent in California, Kansas, Nebraska, North Dakota, Oklahoma and Pennsylvania.

States raising gasoline-tax rates usually provided for equivalent increases in diesel and other special fuels levies. However, Texas provided for an increase from 4.5 to 5 cents per gallon for liquefied gas and from 6 to 6.5 cents for diesel fuel. Michigan left its diesel fuel rate unchanged, thereby eliminating the differential between gasoline and diesel fuel rates. Montana, on the other hand, raised special fuels tax rates from 6 to 9 cents per gallon while raising the gasoline rate from 6 to 7 cents. Kansas increased its special fuels tax from 5 to 7 cents per gallon and left other fuel rates unchanged.

A large number of states enacted various changes in mileage, registration, license and related vehicle user taxes. Colorado replaced a gross ton-mile tax in effect since January, 1955 with a tax of 2 mills per ton-mile of cargo and .8 mills per ton-mile on unladen vehicle weight. Kansas and New Mexico repealed mileage taxes on trucks and substituted higher schedules of registration fees. Idaho reinstated a ton-mile tax repealed two years ago and increased truck registration fees from $55 to $100. It also increased auto license fees from $5 to a sliding scale of $7.50 to $17.50.

Nevada raised the basic fee for motor carriers more than 10 per cent. It also imposed a basic registration fee on interstate operators and gave fleet operators the option of paying a mileage tax on all power-unit mileage traveled in the state. The rate varies down from 2.5 cents per mile for the first 75,000 miles to 1 cent for each mile in excess of 2 million. Montana raised gross vehicle-weight taxes on vehicles over 12 tons when laden from a range of $95–$320 to one of $100–$435.

Minnesota enacted a 5 per cent increase in motor vehicle-license fees and North Dakota increased both license and tonnage fees. Georgia doubled the sliding scale for auto license fees, increased truck tax charges by 10 per cent, and provided for an annual assessment of $1.00 on each driver's license. Arizona raised motor vehicle-registration fees.

New authorizations for state road bond issues, mostly for free roads, reached $1 billion by August 1. The following are among the more extensive. Georgia and Alabama provided for issues of $100 million and $50 million for rural road construction programs. Michigan made provision for issues of $230 million over a three-year period to finance the construction of limited access freeways.

Through the Western Interstate Committee on Highway Policy Problems of the Council of State Governments, the eleven western states have developed a program for handling taxation of heavy interstate vehicles by prorating annual fixed fee type taxes (registration, license, or weight fees, etc.) on the basis of mileage. Under the plan, each state collects the taxes which are automatically related to the number of miles traveled (such as motor vehicle excises, mileage or gross receipts levies) on all operations within the state; these taxes are not waived. The fixed fee type taxes, however, may be prorated for fleet operators. The amount the operator pays each state depends on the relationship of fleet mileage in that state to total fleet mileage. Administrative officials in nine of the eleven western states now possess statutory authority for prorating annual fixed fee type taxes. These states now are developing a single interstate agreement to put the plan into effect on a uniform basis throughout the region.

TOLL ROADS

Limited access, high speed facilities, among the most urgent of road construction needs, require exceptionally large capital outlays. Available revenues frequently are inadequate to support any considerable expressway construction. Consequently, a growing number of these facilities are being supplied by states on a toll-road basis. Usually, for this purpose, special agencies or authorities are empowered to issue revenue bonds, construct road facilities with the proceeds, and charge tolls to redeem bond issues and defray operating costs. However, in Colorado, Connecticut and New Hampshire the state highway departments have been provided with the necessary authority to construct and operate specific toll-road facilities.

In November, 1952, 627 miles of toll roads, constructed at a cost of $580 million, were in service in seven states. By 1955, 1,239 miles of toll facilities, representing an investment of $1,552 million, were operating in nine states—Colorado, Maine, New Hampshire, New Jersey, New York, Ohio, Oklahoma, Pennsylvania and West Virginia. All except Colorado and West Virginia were constructing new links. Toll road construction was also under way in Connecticut, Indiana, Kansas, Kentucky and Massachusetts. All told, an additional 1,382 miles of toll roads were under construction at an estimated cost of $2,303 million in twelve states. Finally, 5,569 miles of toll facilities, expected to cost $6 billion, were either authorized or projected in twenty-one states.

In the last two years Alabama, Idaho, Iowa, Rhode Island and Virginia created authorities to construct toll roads; Maryland authorized the State Road Commission to issue revenue bonds and to construct and operate a toll expressway. Georgia, on the other hand, abolished an inactive authority previously authorized to construct 290 miles of toll road.

MOTOR VEHICLE REGULATIONS

Regulations concerning the types, sizes and weights of motor vehicles, primarily a responsibility of the states, seek to permit the optimum in highway use consistent with the structural limitations and safety requirements of the several road systems. Appropriate and duly enforced standards substantially reduce the costs of maintaining roads and tend to eliminate driving hazards. During the last two years a number of states have made changes in statutes covering the subject.

Alabama replaced a gross vehicle-weight formula with a new table based on axle spacing; a new weight maximum of 64,000 pounds replaces the former limit of 56,000 pounds. Enactments in Arkansas and Mississippi retain an 18,000-pound single axle maximum, limit gross loads to 56,000 pounds, and raise the upper limits on tandem axles to 32,000 and 28,650 pounds respectively. The Arkansas enactment, a substitute for another declared unconstitutional, allows loads in excess of the statutory limit upon special permission. A similar enactment in California allows a 25 per cent overload in certain logging operations for distances under 75 miles.

Idaho raised weight maximums from 72,000 to 76,800 pounds and provided a special scale of limits varying from 37,800 to 79,000 for vehicles engaged in particular hauling operations. Maryland retained the 40,000 pound maximum for a combination of tandem axles but raised the limit for any one tandem axle to 22,400 pounds. New Mexico provided for an increase in the single axle weight maximum from 18,000 to 21,600 pounds. The law also permits weights above the prescribed 32,000 pounds for those tandem axles four or more feet apart up to a maximum weight of 34,320 pounds as the distances between axles increase.

North Dakota enacted a formula whereby maximum weights are determined by multiplying 750 by the sum of the distance between axles plus 40. Allowing for six feet of overhang on the largest legal vehicle, the maximum weight permitted would be 59,250 pounds. Pennsylvania raised the single axle limit to 22,400 pounds, placed a 36,000 pound limit on tandem axles, and raised weight limits for single-axle trailer combinations to 50,000 pounds and for tandem-axle trailer combinations to 60,000 pounds. Vermont increased the weight maximum from 50,000 to 60,000 pounds for certain vehicle combinations, and the State of Washington increased the weight limit for a two-axle trailer from 32,000 to 36,000 pounds.

Alabama, North Dakota and Texas increased maximum permissible lengths of trucks from 45 to 50 feet. Illinois raised its previous maximum of 43 feet to 50. Arkansas increased the maximum allowable height from 13 to 13.5 feet. The latter standard was also put in force in Washington and New Mexico.

States which have adopted new schedules of penalties, or which have otherwise provided for improved vehicle law enforcement during the last two years, include Arkansas, Colorado, Illinois, Indiana, Maryland, New Jersey, North Dakota, Ohio and Wisconsin.

TABLE 1
EXISTING MILEAGE OF STATE-ADMINISTERED ROADS AND STREETS—SUMMARY 1954*

State	Rural Roads — State primary system	State secondary system	County roads under state control	Total	Municipal extensions of state systems (a)	Total existing mileage, state systems	Other state roads (b)	Total state-administered roads and streets
Alabama......	7,026	......	4,217	11,243	875	12,118	.....	12,118
Arizona........	3,871	......	......	3,871	104	3,975	3	3,978
Arkansas......	9,437	......	......	9,437	591	10,028	57	10,085
California.....	12,537	......	......	12,537	1,230	13,767	.....	13,767
Colorado......	7,599	......	......	7,599	342	7,941	17	7,958
Connecticut....	2,394	......	......	2,394	585	2,979	238	3,217
Delaware......	460	1,228	2,095	3,783	165	3,948	.....	3,948
Florida........	8,705	2,266	......	10,971	1,299	12,270	28	12,298
Georgia........	13,498	......	......	13,498	1,608	15,106	28	15,134
Idaho.........	4,529	......	......	4,529	212	4,741	5	4,746
Illinois........	10,464	......	......	10,464	1,823	12,287	.....	12,287
Indiana........	9,753	......	......	9,753	904	10,657	.....	10,657
Iowa..........	8,662	......	......	8,662	1,050	9,712	118	9,830
Kansas........	9,469	......	......	9,469	520	9,989	.....	9,989
Kentucky......	16,905	......	......	16,905	716	17,621	.....	17,621
Louisiana......	2,209	11,847(c)	......	14,056	980	15,036	.....	15,036
Maine..........	2,921	7,676(d)	......	10,597	474	11,071	128	11,199
Maryland	4,559	......	......	4,559	244	4,803	.....	4,803
Massachusetts..	1,639	......	......	1,639	510(a)	2,149	141	2,290
Michigan......	8,317	......	......	8,317	1,038	9,355	.....	9,355
Minnesota......	10,309	......	......	10,309	1,512	11,821	1,256	13,077
Mississippi.....	7,443	......	......	7,443	550	7,993	.....	7,993
Missouri.......	7,914	13,532	......	21,446	1,059	22,505	.....	22,505
Montana.......	5,548	3,630	......	9,178	211	9,389	19(e)	9,408
Nebraska.......	9,457	3,402	......	12,859	414	9,871	33	9,904
Nevada........	2,132	......	325(f)	2,457	76	5,935	.....	5,935
New Hampshire.	1,485	2,160	......	3,645	286	3,931	15	3,946
New Jersey.....	1,248	......	......	1,248	551	1,799	724	2,523
New Mexico....	10,851	......	......	10,851	439	11,290	3	11,293
New York......	12,072	......	......	12,072	892(a)	12,964	922	13,886
North Carolina.	10,882	......	55,514	66,396	2,514	68,910	45	68,955
North Dakota...	6,369	......	......	6,369	247	6,606	18	6,624
Ohio..........	16,002	......	......	16,002	2,415	18,417	.....	18,417
Oklahoma......	9,907	......	......	9,907	525	10,432	88	10,520
Oregon........	4,499	2,396	......	6,895	393	7,288	803	8,091
Pennsylvania...	12,830	25,311	......	38,141	3,041	41,182	3,693	44,875
Rhode Island...	608	......	......	608	268	876	64	940
South Carolina.	8,140	13,850	......	21,990	2,238	24,228	131	24,359
South Dakota..	6,470	......	......	6,470	223	6,693	63	6,756
Tennessee......	7,529	......	......	7,529	673	8,202	351	8,553
Texas..........	44,976	......	......	44,976	2,568	47,544	.....	47,544
Utah..........	4,805	......	......	4,805	592	5,397	.....	5,397
Vermont.......	1,791	......	......	1,791	165	1,956	67	2,023
Virginia........	7,690	......	40,237	47,927	1,307	49,234	12	49,246
Washington....	3,832	2,084	......	5,916	460	6,376	143	6,519
Wext Virginia...	4,472	......	26,252	30,724	575	32,299	410	31,709
Wisconsin......	10,023	......	......	10,023	1,286	11,309	84	11,393
Wyoming......	4,835	......	......	4,835	121	4,956	.....	4,956
Total.......	379,063	89,382	128,640	597,095	40,871	637,956	9,707	647,663

* Prepared by the Bureau of Public Roads, U. S. Department of Commerce. Compiled for end of calendar year from reports of state authorities.

(a) May include mileage that is not designated by law as part of the state system but which constitutes the municipal portion of a state route entering a city or town. Massachusetts and New York do not have jurisdiction over all trans-city connections of state highways. The mileage given here is limited chiefly to that portion of the state system that is coincident with federal-aid mileage in urban areas of 5,000 or more population.

(b) Includes mileage of state park, forest, institutional, toll and other roads under state control.
(c) Includes 6,604 miles designated as farm-to-market system, all of which are surfaced.
(d) State-aid system.
(e) State-aid mileage which was formerly shown with state secondary system.
(f) Mileage maintained by the state without being added to the existing state highways system.

TABLE 2

MILEAGE OF DESIGNATED FEDERAL-AID HIGHWAY SYSTEMS, BY STATE

As of June 30, 1955*

State or other jurisdiction	Federal-aid primary highway system									Federal-aid secondary highway system
	National system of interstate highways(a)			Other			Total			
	Total	Rural	Urban	Total	Rural	Urban	Total	Rural	Urban	
Alabama...............	904	790	114	4,273	4,007	266	5,177	4,797	380	13,488
Arizona...............	1,181	1,148	33	1,314	1,278	36	2,495	2,426	69	3,394
Arkansas..............	528	467	61	2,962	2,844	118	3,490	3,311	179	13,428
California.............	1,899	1,680	219	5,203	4,482	721	7,102	6,162	940	9,724
Colorado..............	661	628	33	3,414	3,343	71	4,075	3,971	104	3,777
Connecticut............	267	158	109	826	646	180	1,093	804	289	1,112
Delaware..............	26	23	3	510	467	43	536	490	46	1,283
Florida................	1,136	993	143	3,191	2,911	280	4,327	3,904	423	10,727
Georgia...............	1,104	996	108	6,318	6,047	271	7,422	7,043	379	12,853
Idaho.................	655	635	20	2,453	2,419	34	3,108	3,054	54	4,194
Illinois................	1,548	1,283	265	8,897	8,034	863	10,445	9,317	1,128	10,276
Indiana...............	1,068	884	184	3,741	3,354	387	4,809	4,238	571	15,683
Iowa..................	697	632	65	9,040	8,670	370	9,737	9,302	435	33,072
Kansas................	728	677	51	6,904	6,675	229	7,632	7,352	280	22,639
Kentucky..............	656	590	66	3,180	3,054	126	3,836	3,644	192	15,171
Louisiana..............	606	507	99	2,047	1,903	144	2,653	2,410	243	5,630
Maine.................	299	272	27	1,322	1,260	62	1,621	1,532	89	2,260
Maryland..............	270	204	66	1,730	1,507	223	2,000	1,711	289	5,758
Massachusetts..........	347	206	141	1,703	1,078	625	2,050	1,284	766	2,216
Michigan..............	985	849	136	5,540	5,170	370	6,525	6,019	506	20,772
Minnesota.............	856	750	106	6,775	6,327	448	7,631	7,077	554	19,580
Mississippi............	684	608	76	4,434	4,302	132	5,118	4,910	208	9,085
Missouri...............	1,075	996	79	7,172	6,992	180	8,247	7,988	259	17,883
Montana...............	1,237	1,209	28	4,653	4,614	39	5,890	5,823	67	3,723
Nebraska..............	477	455	22	4,877	4,764	113	5,354	5,219	135	12,336
Nevada................	540	529	11	1,658	1,640	18	2,198	2,169	29	2,316
New Hampshire........	213	183	30	987	901	86	1,200	1,084	116	1,474
New Jersey............	204	102	102	1,526	1,010	516	1,730	1,112	618	1,948
New Mexico...........	1,013	968	45	2,902	2,820	82	3,915	3,788	127	4,992
New York.............	1,041	740	301	9,645	8,010	1,635	10,686	8,750	1,936	19,316
North Carolina........	714	627	87	6,220	5,932	288	6,934	6,559	375	24,153
North Dakota..........	517	496	21	2,772	2,740	32	3,289	3,236	53	11,629
Ohio..................	1,231	996	235	6,375	5,566	809	7,606	6,562	1,044	16,720
Oklahoma.............	809	747	62	6,563	6,369	194	7,372	7,116	256	11,164
Oregon................	729	668	61	3,248	3,169	79	3,977	3,837	140	5,084
Pennsylvania...........	1,364	1,068	296	5,753	4,923	830	7,117	5,991	1,126	13,270
Rhode Island..........	47	21	26	423	220	203	470	241	229	376
South Carolina........	749	694	55	3,982	3,776	206	4,731	4,470	261	11,458
South Dakota..........	520	503	17	3,829	3,767	62	4,349	4,270	79	12,337
Tennessee..............	1,038	958	80	4,384	4,174	210	5,422	5,132	290	9,359
Texas.................	2,770	2,487	283	13,277	12,530	747	16,047	15,017	1,030	27,927
Utah..................	716	659	57	1,482	1,426	56	2,198	2,085	113	3,077
Vermont...............	343	309	34	906	876	30	1,249	1,185	64	1,787
Virginia...............	908	796	112	3,745	3,523	222	4,653	4,319	334	17,407
Washington............	593	507	86	3,026	2,924	102	3,619	3,431	188	8,415
West Virginia..........	221	179	42	2,120	2,010	110	2,341	2,189	152	11,070
Wisconsin..............	472	427	45	5,520	5,125	395	5,992	5,552	440	18,555
Wyoming..............	1,019	991	28	2,445	2,431	14	3,464	3,422	42	2,059
District of Columbia.....	17	......	17	107	....	107	124	....	124	81
Hawaii................	......	......	.....	538	506	32	538	506	32	593
Puerto Rico............	......	......	.....	554	435	119	554	435	119	1,045
Total...............	37,682	33,295	4,387	196,466	182,951	13,515	234,148	216,246	17,902	507,676

* Prepared by the Bureau of Public Roads, U.S. Department of Commerce.
(a) Present traveled way.

TABLE 3

RECEIPTS FOR STATE-ADMINISTERED HIGHWAYS—1954*(a)

(In thousands of dollars)

State	Receipts from current state imposts (b) — Highway-user revenue: Motor-fuel taxes	Motor-vehicle and carrier taxes	Total	Road, bridge, and ferry tolls	Appropriations from general funds	Other state imposts (c)	Total	Federal funds: Bureau of public roads	Other agencies	Transfers from local governments: From counties, etc.	From cities	Other receipts — Issue of bonds notes, etc.: For construction, etc.	For debt service, including refunding	Miscellaneous receipts	Total	Total receipts
Alabama	15,312	4,124	19,436	—	—	415	19,851	14,139	—	27	—	—	—	164	14,330	34,181
Arizona	10,771	6,259	17,030	—	—	—	17,030	5,204	30	—	—	—	—	40	5,274	22,304
Arkansas	23,027	9,342	32,369	—	—	—	32,369	10,213	—	—	—	—	—	229	10,442	42,811
California	164,599	96,460	261,059	11,335	—	—	272,394	27,058	162	2,793	499	—	—	3,436	33,948	306,342
Colorado	18,248	5,118	23,366	455	—	—	23,821	8,780	—	1,032	—	2,389	—	250	12,451	36,272
Connecticut	20,474	9,110	29,584	4,530	—	—	34,114	2,793	—	17	—	92,713	8,475	1,569	105,567	139,681
Delaware	4,380	2,347	6,727	6,662	—	—	13,389	2,988	—	—	—	8,045	15	293	11,341	24,730
Florida	62,556	3,612	66,168	2,564	—	—	68,732	9,572	—	236	69	6,249	82	400	16,608	85,340
Georgia	31,691	3,412	35,103	—	—	—	35,103	11,231	354	14	111	26,911	690	354	39,665	74,768
Idaho	8,666	3,284	11,950	—	—	—	11,950	7,303	753	—	—	—	—	36	8,092	20,054
Illinois	39,000	60,488	99,488	36	—	—	99,524	21,835	—	2,667	1,995	—	—	758	27,255	126,779
Indiana	30,594	15,044	45,638	—	—	—	45,638	10,013	—	107	—	237,851	36,149	2,778	286,898	332,536
Iowa	20,667	16,826	37,493	—	409	4,621	42,523	10,108	—	151	—	—	—	255	10,514	53,037
Kansas	22,423	12,882	35,305	—	—	—	35,305	10,128	—	—	216	139,490	16,385	318	166,537	201,842
Kentucky	42,554	12,252	54,806	399	—	—	55,205	9,718	—	20	—	39,002	3,750	535	53,025	108,230
Louisiana	36,431	8,442	44,873	—	12,056	2,256	59,185	8,865	1,481	3,233	—	70,128	11,750	587	96,044	155,229
Maine	14,587	6,567	21,154	1,867	—	—	23,021	4,198	—	1,638	190	—	—	1,524	7,550	30,571
Maryland	19,636	16,245	35,881	7,575	—	—	43,456	4,153	—	688	336	167,473	36,390	703	209,743	253,199
Massachusetts	42,013	10,034	52,047	1,766	—	—	53,813	12,469	—	—	—	299,621	4,515	1,369	317,974	371,787
Michigan	41,294	25,310	66,604	2,986	3,182	—	72,772	11,898	—	696	25	88,805	17,623	2,181	121,228	194,000
Minnesota	29,036	29,596	58,632	—	—	—	58,632	10,386	—	—	—	—	—	219	10,605	69,237
Mississippi	21,697	996	22,693	742	683	44	24,162	7,928	350	408	4	13,017	9	10	21,726	45,888
Missouri	36,903	25,563	62,466	103	—	773	63,342	17,502	873	388	—	1,715	24	387	20,889	84,231
Montana	13,674	2,889	16,563	—	—	—	16,563	10,364	413	37	137	—	—	141	11,092	27,655
Nebraska	16,413	4,276	20,689	—	—	—	20,689	7,420	14	72	918	—	—	15	8,439	29,128
Nevada	4,643	2,445	7,088	—	—	—	7,088	5,447	—	6	13	—	—	—	5,466	12,554
New Hampshire	7,087	4,997	12,084	1,156	—	—	13,240	2,378	3	180	388	9,500	36	77	12,562	25,802
New Jersey	26,991	24,194	51,185	25,210	—	—	76,395	9,592	—	—	—	170,626	11,467	5,741	197,426	273,821
New Mexico	16,064	4,299	20,363	—	—	—	20,363	9,104	21	51	—	—	—	155	9,334	29,697
New York	77,105	67,061	144,366	51,884	—	—	196,250	38,819	—	32	1,262	377,193	15,269	7,398	439,973	636,223
North Carolina	71,528	24,528	96,056	—	—	—	96,056	12,824	—	—	495	—	—	722	14,041	110,097
North Dakota	6,397	3,826	10,223	—	16	66	10,305	5,341	78	116	153	—	—	6	5,694	15,999

Ohio	79,087	22,638	101,725	448	6,101	—	108,274	30,380	—	300	2,993	30,000	288	5,538	69,499	177,773
Oklahoma	27,716	9,510	37,226	2,211	—	—	39,437	9,931	—	64	39	—	—	232	10,163	49,600
Oregon	20,889	14,154	35,043	235	—	—	35,278	8,929	—	—	—	—	—	798	9,844	45,122
Pennsylvania	111,374	55,102	166,476	30,148	—	62	196,686	30,797	14	4,590	—	227,164	21,452	8,145	292,148	488,834
Rhode Island	3,962	2,660	6,622	234	—	—	6,856	2,201	—	—	—	7,000	74	137	9,412	16,268
South Carolina	34,116	5,780	39,896	52	—	1,618	39,948	7,048	7	—	147	100	—	332	7,634	47,582
South Dakota	9,535	4,488	14,023	—	1,347	—	16,988	5,006	1,042	—	—	—	—	—	6,048	23,036
Tennessee	22,920	11,305	34,225	—	—	—	34,225	8,754	—	500	—	—	4	169	9,427	43,652
Texas	78,655	57,473	136,128	—	—	—	136,128	22,381	1,009	260	912	—	—	1,109	25,671	161,799
Utah	12,377	1,024	13,401	—	—	—	13,401	5,158	787	283	—	—	—	6	5,951	19,352
Vermont	3,162	3,146	6,308	—	1,535	—	7,843	2,376	—	82	—	—	—	—	2,659	10,502
Virginia	54,160	17,344	71,504	6,560	—	—	78,064	12,265	—	—	3,200	76,275	16,999	949	109,770	187,834
Washington	26,247	14,365	40,612	6,852	—	—	47,464	8,202	776	760	317	2,590	24	861	13,530	60,994
West Virginia	20,791	15,530	36,321	634	713	327	37,995	6,017	—	—	—	37,074	3,826	663	47,580	85,575
Wisconsin	20,644	17,354	37,998	—	—	—	37,998	9,679	—	5	1,162	340	—	303	11,489	49,487
Wyoming	4,612	3,239	7,851	—	—	—	7,851	5,141	2,775	—	—	—	—	366	8,282	16,133
Total	1,526,708	777,140	2,303,848	166,644	26,042	10,194	2,506,728	514,036	10,942	21,453	15,584	2,131,271	205,296	52,258	2,950,840	5,457,568

* Prepared by the Bureau of Public Roads, U.S. Department of Commerce.

(a) Includes receipts of state toll road authorities.

(b) For this analysis, gross non-highway allocations of highway-user revenues are offset, in the following amounts, against appropriations for state-administered highways out of state general funds: Calif. **$2,486,000**, Conn. **$1,000,000**, Ill. $288,000, Ind. $500,000 (to Indiana Toll Bridge Commission), Iowa **$1,530,000**, La. **$1,318,000**, Mich. $520,000, Miss. $996,000, Mont. $733,000, Nebr. $1,068,000, N. Mex. $615,000, Okla. $1,068,000, S. D. $153,000, Tenn.

$2,252,000, Texas $15,000,000, Wash. $858,000, W. Va. $190,000.

(c) Ala., lubricating oil tax; Idaho, tax on contracts; Iowa, sales and use tax; La., oil royalties $682,000, lubricating oil tax $1,574,000; Miss., tax on butane gas not used in motor vehicles; Mo. and N. Dak. use (sales) tax on motor vehicles purchased out of state; Pa., tax on aviation fuel $29,000, gross receipts tax $33,000; S. Dak., petroleum inspection fees (non-highway use) $29,000, use (sales) tax on motor vehicles $1,589,000; W. Va., capitation tax.

TABLE 4

DISBURSEMENTS FOR STATE-ADMINISTERED HIGHWAYS—1954*(a)
(In thousands of dollars)

State	Capital outlay for roads and bridges (b)					Maintenance (b)					Administration, engineering miscellaneous (e)	State highway police and safety	Bond interest	Subtotal, current expenditures	Bond retirement (f)	Total disbursements
	Primary state highways (rural)	Secondary roads under state control (c)	Municipal extensions of state systems	Other state roads (d)	Total (e)	Primary state highways (rural)	Secondary roads under state control (c)	Municipal extensions of state systems	Other state roads (d)	Total (e)						
Alabama	24,871	990(c)	5,868	—	31,729	6,320	1,161(c)	1,106	—	8,587	1,324	2,662	965	45,267	2,163	47,430
Arizona	14,674	—	1,428	—	16,102	3,969	—	104	—	4,073	1,583	1,157	—	22,915	—	22,915
Arkansas	22,771	—	891	—	23,662	8,380	—	—	—	8,380	1,247	830	3,489	37,608	5,628	43,236
California	139,492	—	105,724	—	245,216	21,389	—	4,901	—	26,290	14,692	18,942	3,802	308,942	4,100	313,042
Colorado	13,574	5,681	3,787	—	23,042	3,859	2,005	151	—	6,015	2,570	1,561	239	33,427	2,084	35,511
Connecticut	6,324	—	19,797	—	26,121	9,982	—	1,500	78	11,560	3,004	838	3,024	44,547	1,012	45,559
Delaware	6,342	2,361(c)	970	—	9,673	3,070	(c)	—	—	3,070	1,279	921	2,327	17,270	6,146	23,416
Florida	32,774	18,470	17,674	421	69,339	11,835	1,148	368	5	13,356	5,158	3,501	2,216	93,570	2,767	96,337
Georgia	37,645	—	4,061	—	41,706	9,027	—	—	—	9,027	1,774	2,507	367	55,381	600	55,981
Idaho	12,237	5,235	52	—	17,524	4,851	—	—	—	4,851	1,397	459	—	24,231	—	24,231
Illinois	72,495	—	24,720(c)	171	97,386	17,647	—	3,106	—	20,753	7,768	4,583	1,581	132,071	6,571	138,642
Indiana	31,863	—	8,213	13,601	53,677	12,577	—	1,095	4	13,676	3,130	2,360	7,663	80,506	—	80,506
Iowa	24,517	—	7,453	—	31,970	8,088	—	1,091	—	9,179	1,627	1,608	—	44,384	—	44,384
Kansas	27,081	—	2,535	1,609	31,225	10,741	—	418	—	11,159	3,696	1,034	185	47,299	1,000	48,299
Kentucky	47,707	—	4,109	—	51,816	14,772	—	565	—	15,337	4,311	3,374	973	75,811	80	75,891
Louisiana	18,481	20,683	6,293	—	45,457	7,389	6,719	—	—	14,108	6,025	2,141	3,388	71,119	6,329	77,448
Maine	9,838	5,781	4,502	15,433	35,554	5,326	4,742	133	354	10,555	2,290	989	3,754	53,142	2,007	55,149
Maryland	49,536	—	7,267	—	56,803	6,918	—	—	—	6,918	867	3,299	3,092	70,979	47,398	118,377
Massachusetts	52,080	—	37,001	13,071	102,152	14,465	—	262	3,085	17,812	6,009	2,185	7,352	135,510	12,412	147,922
Michigan	53,266	—	39,291	185	92,742	20,952	—	2,954	—	23,906	4,573	4,197	6,600	132,018	605	132,623
Minnesota	37,071	—	7,660	—	44,731	11,852	—	2,025	—	13,877	883	1,749	—	61,240	—	61,240
Mississippi	24,751	—	1,456	77	26,284	5,720	—	—	—	5,720	2,147	1,561	2,161	37,873	2,638	40,511
Missouri	28,732	11,652	20,315	—	60,699	7,762	7,566	383	—	15,711	3,896	2,500	948	83,754	4,400	88,154
Montana	10,225	6,443	522	4	17,194	5,720	—	14	29	5,763	1,412	903	224	25,496	7,042	32,538

State	1	2	3	4	5	6	7	8	9	10	11	12	13	14	15	16	17
Nebraska	14,950	—	1,526	—	16,476	7,784	—	—	—	7,784	1,286	1,237	—	26,783	—	26,783	—
Nevada	5,766	2,254	246	—	8,266	1,484	780	140	—	2,404	1,381	313	—	12,364	—	12,364	—
New Hampshire	4,029	1,987	1,232	6,160	13,408	3,174	2,762	—	156	6,092	1,615	535	374	22,024	1,485	23,509	—
New Jersey	12,578	—	25,187	153,963	191,728	7,772	—	4,420	4,577	16,769	4,240	5,764	22,712	241,213	1,514	242,727	—
New Mexico	19,050	—	2,906	—	21,956	6,308	—	—	4,605	6,308	1,324	660	271	30,519	1,875	32,394	—
New York	58,664	—	82,109	300,908	441,681	30,398	—	14,347	—	49,350	5,928	4,355	22,434	523,748	20,002	543,750	—
North Carolina	35,751	24,972(c)	3,600	82	64,405	7,977	18,376(c)	2,389	—	28,742	6,376	3,766	4,102	107,391	11,550	118,941	—
North Dakota	10,150	—	474	—	10,624	3,746	—	—	—	3,746	830	421	—	15,621	—	15,621	—
Ohio	73,826	—	—	156,000	229,826	26,512	—	—	100	26,612	5,970	5,929	10,688	279,025	—	279,025	—
Oklahoma	26,650	—	2,491	—	29,141	10,721	—	—	—	10,721	2,015	2,974	1,343	46,194	—	46,194	—
Oregon	33,728	2,771	3,527	89	40,115	8,216	2,789	501	31	11,537	4,767	2,073	1,261	59,753	4,275	64,028	—
Pennsylvania	89,898	34,307	55,315	38,248	217,768	16,437	14,083	4,127	4,729	39,376	14,717	7,153	16,399	295,413	16,342	311,755	—
Rhode Island	4,164	—	1,186	—	5,350	2,002	7,044	1,276	—	3,278	1,253	454	313	10,648	322	10,970	—
South Carolina	4,713	12,874	5,680	475	23,742	4,438	—	1,092	—	12,574	2,327	1,538	1,045	41,226	10,102	51,328	—
South Dakota	15,493	—	612	—	16,105	7,160	—	—	—	7,160	921	344	—	24,530	—	24,530	—
Tennessee	19,539	—	6,514	45	26,098	7,204	—	512	—	7,716	2,913	2,252	952	39,931	4,503	44,434	—
Texas	117,429	—	12,664	—	130,093	29,725	3,214	—	—	32,939	6,872	4,641	786	175,331	3,291	178,622	—
Utah	10,330	—	1,264	766	12,360	4,047	—	—	—	4,047	724	751	—	17,932	—	17,932	—
Vermont	4,663	—	474	31	5,168	4,346	—	—	—	4,346	724	354	21	10,613	294	10,907	—
Virginia	25,840	12,548(c)	9,425	—	47,813	13,804	15,039(c)	3,038	—	31,881	8,029	5,207	1,305	94,235	16,510	110,745	—
Washington	27,634	7,118	11,416	157	46,325	11,166	2,429	839	21	14,455	3,743	3,149	2,392	70,064	2,948	73,012	—
West Virginia	12,524	1,728(c)	3,650	49,729	67,631	14,772	9,994(c)	—	569	25,335	1,950	1,042	6,775	102,733	8,146	110,879	—
Wisconsin	25,777	—	7,125	545	33,447	10,947	—	395	67	11,409	2,509	607	—	47,972	456	48,428	—
Wyoming	10,292	—	940	—	11,232	3,464	—	37	—	3,501	289	388	—	15,410	—	15,410	—
Total	1,461,785	177,855	571,152	751,770	2,962,562	476,215	96,637	56,503	18,410	647,765	165,415	121,768	147,523	4,045,033	218,597	4,263,630	—

* Prepared by the Bureau of Public Roads, U.S. Department of Commerce.

(a) Includes disbursements of state toll road authorities.

(b) Segregation of expenditures by system on which expended is incomplete in a few states. Where expenditures by system are not segregated, the total is given under the heading "primary state highways (rural)."

(c) County roads are under control in Alabama (four counties), Delaware, North Carolina, Virginia (all but two counties), and West Virginia. Maintenance expenditures by Delaware are not segregated from primary state highway expenditures.

(d) Includes toll facilities, parkways and roads in forests, institutions, parks and reservations.

(e) The classification of administration, engineering, and miscellaneous expenditures is not uniform for all states because of indeterminate amounts charged to construction and maintenance. For this analysis, undistributed equipment expenditures are included with construction and maintenance expenditures on a pro rata basis.

(f) Includes refunding as follows: Maryland, Chesapeake Bay Bridge Revenue bonds, $34,037,000; Virginia, State Toll Bridge and Ferry Revenue bonds, $15,197,000.

TABLE 5

APPORTIONMENT OF FEDERAL-AID HIGHWAY FUNDS
Authorized for the Fiscal Year 1956*

State	*Sums apportioned for—*				
	Primary highway system ($315,000,000)	*Secondary or feeder roads* ($210,000,000)	*Urban highways* ($175,000,000)	*Interstate system* ($175,000,000)	*Total* ($875,000,000)
Alabama	$6,738,800	$5,221,937	$2,266,452	$3,536,466	$17,763,655
Arizona	4,723,075	3,216,555	672,891	1,967,160	10,579,681
Arkansas	5,257,058	4,207,659	967,757	2,500,144	12,932,618
California	14,495,550	7,463,481	15,378,016	9,770,990	47,108,037
Colorado	5,682,364	3,795,562	1,437,773	2,303,899	13,219,598
Connecticut	2,047,610	1,031,625	3,350,400	1,656,627	8,086,262
Delaware	1,547,437	1,031,625	354,790	1,074,610	4,008,462
Florida	5,130,153	3,353,655	3,102,050	2,930,809	14,516,667
Georgia	7,815,446	5,968,900	2,521,183	4,043,968	20,349,497
Idaho	3,892,551	2,737,969	332,940	1,734,315	8,697,775
Illinois	12,165,819	6,625,129	12,098,383	8,105,625	38,994,956
Indiana	7,496,268	5,167,153	4,138,722	4,219,185	21,021,328
Iowa	7,626,317	5,581,064	2,053,788	3,545,901	18,807,070
Kansas	7,663,996	5,365,736	1,625,973	3,169,963	17,825,668
Kentucky	5,820,681	4,832,404	1,796,525	3,216,870	15,666,480
Louisiana	4,920,796	3,561,657	2,535,907	2,824,725	13,843,085
Maine	2,649,624	1,896,107	723,013	1,387,518	6,656,262
Maryland	2,776,160	1,696,909	2,936,043	2,041,509	9,450,621
Massachusetts	4,011,085	1,489,563	7,200,476	3,655,217	16,356,341
Michigan	9,800,544	5,980,275	8,051,625	6,180,407	30,012,851
Minnesota	8,190,042	5,781,659	2,817,034	3,899,163	20,687,898
Mississippi	5,645,528	4,702,659	957,795	2,754,064	14,060,046
Missouri	9,204,910	6,228,008	4,260,427	4,707,609	24,400,954
Montana	6,342,359	4,362,904	407,361	2,419,110	13,531,734
Nebraska	6,157,523	4,366,021	1,014,628	2,436,110	13,974,282
Nevada	4,077,521	2,725,122	131,752	1,785,146	8,719,541
New Hampshire	1,547,437	1,031,625	512,324	1,074,610	4,165,996
New Jersey	4,083,014	1,373,973	7,572,939	3,753,573	16,783,499
New Mexico	5,133,654	3,526,748	567,747	2,081,652	11,309,801
New York	14,843,409	5,948,112	23,123,251	12,160,327	56,075,099
North Carolina	7,825,095	6,684,414	2,223,008	4,380,315	21,112,832
North Dakota	4,581,331	3,326,558	292,522	1,926,290	10,126,701
Ohio	11,011,801	6,698,563	10,010,967	7,369,446	35,090,777
Oklahoma	6,757,731	4,838,876	1,890,029	3,094,245	16,580,881
Oregon	5,398,620	3,772,987	1,387,166	2,330,696	12,889,469
Pennsylvania	12,394,224	7,375,924	13,096,579	9,134,669	42,001,396
Rhode Island	1,547,437	1,031,625	1,236,688	1,074,610	4,890,360
South Carolina	4,252,157	3,520,756	1,190,023	2,331,532	11,294,468
South Dakota	4,932,082	3,522,524	336,008	2,024,381	10,814,995
Tennessee	6,843,362	5,333,724	2,501,615	3,689,779	18,368,480
Texas	20,484,493	13,716,335	8,287,665	9,889,608	52,378,101
Utah	3,630,545	2,401,759	733,035	1,661,565	8,426,904
Vermont	1,547,437	1,031,625	269,364	1,074,610	3,923,036
Virginia	5,997,988	4,661,747	2,697,681	3,468,488	16,825,904
Washington	5,220,265	3,487,400	2,610,298	2,744,023	14,061,986
West Virginia	3,443,635	2,997,967	1,125,885	2,045,557	9,613,044
Wisconsin	7,460,276	5,205,165	3,387,619	3,939,418	19,992,478
Wyoming	3,938,080	2,668,860	188,100	1,746,386	8,541,426
District of Columbia	1,547,437	1,031,625	1,494,531	1,074,610	5,148,203
Hawaii	1,547,437	1,031,625	581,732	....	3,160,794
Puerto Rico	1,639,336	1,713,145	1,487,020	....	4,839,501

*Prepared by the Bureau of Public Roads, U.S. Department of Commerce.

HIGHWAY SAFETY REGULATION

DESPITE increasing attention by all levels of government, private organizations and the public at large, highway safety continues to be among the nation's most important problems. Traffic accidents in the United States during the five years 1950–54 took 182,600 lives and caused 6.5 million personal injuries, many of which were permanently or totally disabling. The more easily calculated economic costs—medical bills, property damage, lost earnings and overhead insurance expenses—reached an estimated $19 billion for the same period. The human costs are incalculable.

The rising spiral of annual casualties was reversed during 1954 for the first time in five years, only to resume an upward course in the first seven months of 1955. Traffic deaths and injuries during 1954—36,300 killed and 1,250,000 injured—were 2,000 and 100,000 respectively below the 1953 totals. Thirty-two states reported reductions in highway fatalities. However, by August, 1955, 19,840 traffic deaths had been reported, about 700 above the total for the first seven months of 1954.

On the other hand, traffic fatalities have not kept pace with the increase in highway use—an indication of progress in the field. The ratio of deaths per 100 million miles of vehicle travel decreased from 9.8 in 1946 to 6.4 in 1954. The rates in the several states varied between 2.8 and 11.5 in 1953 and 2.6 and 10.5 in 1954.

When casualties are considered in relation to population, the movement of traffic death rates is less encouraging. Although the 1954 rate of 22.3 highway fatalities per 100,000 population was 1.6 below the 1946 rate and 2 less than the 1952 rate, it was 1 above the rate for 1949.

Expected increases in vehicular use promise to compound traffic safety problems. If traffic fatalities are even to be held at the current high levels, the ratio of deaths to vehicle miles traveled, it is indicated, must drop by more than half by 1975.

Progress in highway safety requires advances in a variety of related fields. The President's Conference on Highway Safety in 1946 developed an Action Program of tested methods of prevention. Revised in 1949, this program outlines practical steps for states and localities in the fields of accident records, laws and ordinances, education, enforcement, engineering, motor vehicle administration, public information and organized public support. In 1954 a White House Conference on Highway Safety met to renew interest and develop wider citizen support for the Action Program.

Many experts believe improved driving habits to be the best hope for reducing the accident toll. Perhaps the most promising single development in the driver improvement program is the training offered by a growing number of high schools. Almost a third of American high schools provide a complete course of driver training and driving practice to one of every four eligible students. Driving record studies suggest that youths given a full course of training in high schools have about half as many accidents as those without the training.

Among recent state developments, Utah's State Board of Education adopted driver education standards for its high schools. Florida made provisions for a program of driver education in secondary schools, and Maine established a system of state financial and technical assistance for such training. High school students who have completed driving courses qualify for lower insurance rates in thirty-nine states and the District of Columbia.

The states have made considerable recent progress in the field of driver controls, particularly in licensing and in safety responsibility standards. Improvements in licensing regulations, the quality of examiner training, examination procedures, and provisions for suspending and revoking licenses all assure that fewer of the unfit are accorded the privileges of the road. Some fifteen states now use some form of the point system, one yardstick for taking the reckless and irresponsible driver off the road. Within the last biennium Wisconsin, South Carolina and Minnesota established point systems by statute, and Oklahoma put one in operation by administrative regulation.

After a concerted campaign involving significant revisions or new enactments in at least twenty-five states during the last several years, the safety responsibility laws of forty-four states and the District of Columbia are now considered adequate by most traffic authorities. There has been less success in securing wide adoption of motor vehicle inspection laws. A total of fourteen states and the District of Columbia provide for regular examination of motor vehicles. Recent accessions to the list have been counterbalanced by states repealing inspection requirements.

Better law enforcement, a major goal of the White House Conference Action Program, is being realized, but authorities in the field emphasize that much more remains to be done. Shortages of trained manpower, especially of accident investigators and patrol officers, persist. In the last two years, however, at least fifteen states have increased substantially the size or the enforcement authority of state highway patrols.

There has been a notable increase in the use of radar to apprehend speeders and of chemical tests to determine intoxication. First licensed in 1950, radar is now in use in all states. Laws regarding chemical tests were on the books of fourteen states in 1951, and tests were being used in twenty-seven states. In 1955 such laws had been adopted in nineteen states and chemical tests were in use in forty-five. During the last biennium Georgia, Delaware, Kentucky, Idaho, Wyoming and New York enacted legislation concerning the admissibility in evidence or the use of chemical tests.

There has been considerable improvement, meantime, in traffic court procedures, but a need for much further upgrading was recognized. The use of a uniform non-fix ticket is growing; traffic violation bureaus are increasing in number and quality; and more traffic judges are requiring court appearances by persons involved in serious violations.

Among the major causes of the high accident toll are engineering deficiencies of obsolete roads. Experts have testified that the application of modern design principles on the 40,000 mile interstate system alone would save 3,500 lives each year. A study of rural and urban state highways in Connecticut suggests that an up-to-date system would reduce accidents by 43 per cent. In Illinois widening the pavement from 18 to 22 and 24 feet reduced accidents between intersections by 39 per cent. Despite the costliness of road construction, the states are making much progress in eliminating deficiencies. Greater state authorizations for expressways and toll roads are only the most spectacular evidence of progress.

One of the purposes of the White House Safety Conference is to secure better and more uniform state vehicle laws and safety regulations. The Uniform Vehicle Code, first developed in 1925, has served as a guide for improving state motor vehicle laws and their administration. In 1954 the code was revised and consolidated into a single act of twelve chapters by the National Committee on Uniform Traffic Laws and Ordinances, an arm of the White House Conference. Conformity with the substance of the code is widely regarded as one measure of legislative progress in the field and of work remaining to be done.

Twelve states have adopted the substance of the code with regard to centralized administrative authority and the power to administer and enforce vehicle and highway use laws. Thirty-four states have incorporated key recommendations regarding the content of driver examinations, mandatory revocations for major traffic offenses, and discretionary authority to suspend licenses for cause. Thirty-two have adopted regulations comparable to the code covering accidents and accident reports—especially valuable for analyses leading to elimination of particular road hazards. Thirty-five states have adopted the recommended rules of the road, a matter in which uniformity is particularly important for reducing accidents. Fourteen states have adopted the code suggestions concerning periodic inspections of motor vehicles, and vehicle equipment regulations in thirty-three states are substantially similar to those embodied in the code.

States which have succeeded in obtaining recognition of highway safety problems as well as wide public support for highway safety measures have usually joined forces with private groups in intensive and continuous publicity efforts. Many have held and are holding state-wide conferences comparable to the White House Conference at the national level.

Public support, properly developed and organized, is invaluable in securing adequate safety legislation and an effective safety program. The Public Officials Advisory Group to the 1954 White House Conference recommended:

That public officials and public support organizations join forces in developing a planned action program to reduce highway accidents in every jurisdiction.

That public support be utilized to insure continuity and high performance in the developed program.

An increasing number of states are providing for integration or close coordination of the activities of departments and/or bureaus with functions related to the problem of highway safety. More states, likewise, are developing effective programs of cooperation with civic groups and other public support organizations. Almost all have provided the nucleus for administering an effective joint program. Forty-three states have official safety advisory commissions or coordinating committees—nine of them created by statute and thirty-four by appointment of the Governor. In the five remaining states this function has been assigned to a special department or employee, or is under committee study.

TABLE 1

STATE MOTOR-VEHICLE REGISTRATIONS—1954*

Compiled for Calendar Year from Reports of State Authorities (a)

	Motor vehicles								
	Automobiles			Buses			Trucks		
State	Private and commercial (including taxicabs)	Publicly owned (b)	Total	Private and commercial	Publicly owned (b)	Total	Private and commercial (c)	Publicly owned (b)	Total
Alabama.............	718,339(d)	2,509	720,848	2,071	3,847	5,918	181,276(d)	7,356	188,632
Arizona.............	288,565	2,288	290,853	837	650	1,487	82,120	5,244	87,364
Arkansas............	366,363	682	367,045	784	2,745	3,529	170,838	3,607	174,445
California...........	4,857,095	22,115	4,879,210	7,177	5,197	12,374	762,614	44,644	807,258
Colorado...........	521,654	1,997	523,651	1,508	1,185	2,693	148,119	7,862	155,981
Connecticut........	759,178	3,017	762,195	3,034	181	3,215	97,161	4,685	101,846
Delaware...........	110,105	788	110,893	470	32	502	27,438	893	28,331
Florida.............	1,180,756	3,468	1,184,224	2,078	2,071	4,149	207,304	12,020	219,324
Georgia............	892,794	1,598	894,392	3,646	2,841	6,487	224,430	8,219	232,649
Idaho..............	224,671	795	225,466	389(e)	560	949	84,178(e)	4,230	88,408
Illinois.............	2,687,784	5,854	2,693,638	5,917	4,578	10,495	370,190	13,469	383,659
Indiana............	1,387,805	3,389	1,391,194	5,822	1,161	6,983	276,651	7,602	284,253
Iowa...............	924,066	2,260	926,326	1,190	3,314	4,504	205,562	7,148	212,710
Kansas.............	756,024	3,064	759,088	794	1,178	1,972	232,060	8,482	240,542
Kentucky...........	749,516	1,984	751,500	2,937	1,805	4,742	195,176	6,178	201,354
Louisiana..........	681,485	3,168	684,653	4,156	865	5,021	178,547	5,579	184,126
Maine..............	236,901	1,004	237,905	1,266	381	1,647	63,458(f)	2,992	66,450
Maryland...........	738,359	3,083	741,442	4,668	385	5,053	121,072	3,438	124,510
Massachusetts......	1,289,320	4,891	1,294,211	5,458	90	5,548	169,215	10,915	180,130
Michigan...........	2,478,726	6,643	2,485,369	7,042	3,997	11,039	334,395	16,942	351,337
Minnesota..........	1,065,716	2,517	1,068,233	4,352	2,486	6,838	223,956	7,464	231,420
Mississippi.........	402,820	620	403,440	3,069	2,878	5,947	169,721	5,422	175,143
Missouri............	1,137,469	2,245	1,139,714	3,921	1,875	5,796	281,138	7,230	288,368
Montana...........	212,479	1,215	213,694	824	332	1,156	94,645	4,834	99,479
Nebraska...........	484,295	1,253	485,548	913	536	1,449	144,957	5,036	149,993
Nevada.............	86,722	714	87,436	232	164	396	25,209	2,141	27,350
New Hampshire....	162,568	1,106	163,674	865	61	926	33,988	3,379	37,367
New Jersey.........	1,677,717	5,967	1,683,684	7,218	337	7,555	224,428	12,410	236,838
New Mexico........	225,563	1,473	227,036	1,904	158	2,062	76,425	3,994	80,419
New York..........	3,879,564	14,416	3,893,980	11,517	7,062	18,579	453,559	26,757	480,316
North Carolina.....	1,027,881	3,782	1,031,663	2,453	10,373	12,826	247,403	12,360	259,763
North Dakota......	202,589	664	203,253	126	190	316	93,839	2,277	96,116
Ohio...............	2,884,319	7,025	2,891,344	5,360	8,306	13,666	378,681	16,795	395,476
Oklahoma..........	707,099	2,503	709,602	1,456	4,915	6,371	240,112	7,338	247,450
Oregon.............	675,060(g)	8,371	683,431	1,321	1,791	3,112	72,254(g)	6,052	78,306
Pennsylvania.......	3,010,900	10,681	3,021,581	12,011	1,008	13,019	495,866	23,515	519,381
Rhode Island.......	256,467	1,041	257,508	910	82	992	34,234	1,338	35,572
South Carolina.....	578,644	2,291	580,935	1,587	4,301	5,888	125,493	7,390	132,883
South Dakota......	228,624	746	229,370	285	405	690	81,403	3,173	84,576
Tennessee..........	886,552	3,891	890,443	1,943	2,453	4,396	212,881	10,465	223,346
Texas...............	2,739,261	7,519	2,746,780	4,603	11,684	16,287	714,363	29,169	743,532
Utah...............	242,947	1,223	244,170	434	539	973	58,142	3,361	61,503
Vermont............	115,510(g)	330	115,840	297	111	408	14,125(g)	914	15,039
Virginia............	936,265	4,743	941,008	3,081	2,935	6,016	198,046	8,043	206,089
Washington........	875,423	5,972	881,395	1,051	2,623	3,674	184,771	15,318	200,089
West Virginia......	393,997(h)	2,104	396,101	980	1,790	2,770	110,392(h)	4,146	114,538
Wisconsin..........	1,092,466	2,594	1,095,060	3,331	1,542	4,873	222,759	14,079	236,838
Wyoming...........	114,925	791	115,716	701	325	1,026	49,111	2,634	51,745
Dist. of Columbia...	170,561	2,567(j)	173,128	2,014	18	2,032	18,005	2,398	20,403
Total.............	48,323,909	174,961	48,498,870	140,003	108,343	248,346	9,411,710	430,937	9,842,647

Table 1—Continued

STATE MOTOR VEHICLE REGISTRATIONS—1954*

Compiled for Calendar Year from Reports of State Authorities (a)

Motor vehicles						Motorcycles		State
All motor vehicles			Comparison of total motor-vehicle registrations, 1953-1954			Private and commercial	Publicly owned (b)	
Private and commercial	Publicly owned (b)	Total	Total 1953 registrations	Increase or decrease, 1954	Percentage change			
901,686	13,712	915,398	859,710	55,688	6.5	6,148	170	Alabama
371,522	8,182	379,704	359,199	20,505	5.7	3,509	107	Arizona
537,985	7,034	545,019	528,814	16,205	3.1	2,209	1	Arkansas
5,626,886	71,956	5,698,842	5,504,413	194,429	3.5	49,684	2,559	California
671,281	11,044	682,325	648,641	33,684	5.2	4,398	43	Colorado
859,373	7,883	867,256	828,392	38,864	4.7	3,885	125	Connecticut
138,013	1,713	139,726	133,970	5,756	4.3	575	118	Delaware
1,390,138	17,559	1,407,697	1,300,592	107,105	8.2	16,333	472	Florida
1,120,870	12,658	1,133,528	1,081,403	52,125	4.8	7,118	274	Georgia
309,238	5,585	314,823	304,062	10,761	3.5	1,981	32	Idaho
3,063,891	23,901	3,087,792	2,958,824	128,968	4.4	22,265	610	Illinois
1,670,278	12,152	1,682,430	1,610,751	71,679	4.5	17,355	274	Indiana
1,130,818	12,722	1,143,540	1,125,551	17,989	1.6	9,153	95	Iowa
988,878	12,724	1,001,602	957,077	44,525	4.7	8,391	12,724	Kansas
947,629	9,967	957,596	907,484	50,112	5.5	5,487	...	Kentucky
864,188	9,612	873,800	816,113	57,687	7.1	5,045	147	Louisiana
301,625	4,377	306,002	296,563	9,439	3.2	1,478	15	Maine
864,099	6,906	871,005	819,897	51,108	6.2	4,781	60	Maryland
1,463,993	15,896	1,479,889	1,421,799	58,090	4.1	4,457	...	Massachusetts
2,820,163	27,582	2,847,745	2,783,122	64,623	2.3	18,677	360	Michigan
1,294,024	12,467	1,306,491	1,273,122	33,369	2.6	9,716	60	Minnesota
575,610	8,920	584,530	556,725	27,805	5.0	2,282	8	Mississippi
1,422,528	11,350	1,433,878	1,385,938	47,940	3.5	6,965	32	Missouri
307,948	6,381	314,329	302,302	12,027	4.0	1,154	...	Montana
630,165	6,825	636,990	631,796	5,194	0.8	4,012	60	Nebraska
112,163	3,019	115,182	106,645	8,537	8.0	1,310	30	Nevada
197,421	4,546	201,967	192,228	9,739	5.1	1,542	...	New Hampshire
1,909,363	18,714	1,928,077	1,836,914	91,163	5.0	8,937	578	New Jersey
303,892	5,625	309,517	303,096	6,421	2.1	3,435	8	New Mexico
4,344,640	48,235	4,392,875	4,176,495	216,380	5.2	18,651	1,095	New York
1,277,737	26,515	1,304,252	1,257,004	47,248	3.8	7,730	249	North Carolina
296,554	3,131	299,685	292,703	6,982	2.4	902	27	North Dakota
3,268,360	32,126	3,300,486	3,166,741	133,745	4.2	25,346	435	Ohio
948,667	14,756	963,423	928,551	34,872	3.8	8,303	...	Oklahoma
748,635	16,214	764,849	744,952	19,897	2.7	5,521	6	Oregon
3,518,777	35,204	3,553,981	3,419,942	134,039	3.9	22,745	572	Pennsylvania
291,611	2,461	294,072	280,710	13,362	4.8	1,627	110	Rhode Island
705,724	13,982	719,706	716,329	3,377	0.5	4,917	90	South Carolina
310,312	4,324	314,636	307,550	7,086	2.3	1,555	25	South Dakota
1,101,376	16,809	1,118,185	1,047,002	71,183	6.8	5,775	9	Tennessee
3,458,227	48,372	3,506,599	3,359,446	147,153	4.4	27,506	667	Texas
301,523	5,123	306,646	292,521	14,125	4.8	1,333	47	Utah
129,932	1,355	131,287	128,636	2,651	2.1	772	...	Vermont
1,137,392	15,721	1,153,113	1,090,721	62,392	5.7	9,639	208	Virginia
1,061,245	23,913	1,085,158	1,051,517	33,641	3.2	6,402	359	Washington
505,369	8,040	513,409	516,867	−3,458	−0.7	2,855	31	West Virginia
1,318,556	18,215	1,336,771	1,302,345 (i)	34,426	2.6	8,914	369	Wisconsin
164,737	3,750	168,487	163,154	5,333	3.3	846	14	Wyoming
190,580	4,983	195,563	192,362	3,201	1.7	406	194	Dist. of Columbia
57,875,622	714,241	58,589,863	56,270,691	2,319,172	4.1	394,027	23,469	Total

*Prepared by the Bureau of Public Roads, U.S. Department of Commerce.

(a) Data reported by the states were supplemented in some instances by information from other sources in order to present registrations as uniformly as possible. Where the registration year is not more than one month removed from the calendar year, registration-year data are given. Where the registration year is more than one month removed, registrations are given for the calendar year.

(b) Includes federal, state, county, and municipal vehicles. Vehicles owned by the military services are not included.

(c) The following farm trucks, registered at a nominal fee and restricted to use in the vicinity of the owner's farm, are not included in this table: Connecticut, 5,354; New Hampshire, 3,917; New Jersey, 8,993; New York, 12,242; and Rhode Island, 2,178.

(d) In Alabama a pickup truck that is a person's sole means of transportation is registered at the passenger car rate. An estimated number of pickup trucks has been deducted from reported passenger car registrations and added to truck registrations.

(e) Privately owned school buses are included with trucks.

(f) Commercial full trailers are included with trucks.

(g) In Oregon, trucks with gross weights of 6,000 pounds or less, and in Vermont, trucks under 1,500 pounds capacity, are not segregated from automobiles. In most states for which truck weight data are available, similar light trucks comprise half or more of all trucks registered.

(h) Station wagons previously registered as trucks were registered with automobiles in 1954.

(i) Revised.

(j) Includes 1,635 automobiles of the Diplomatic Corps.

TABLE 2

MOTOR VEHICLE LAWS*

As of September, 1955

State	New license plates can be used on	Driving license Required	Driving license Minimum age	Period of stay(a)	Border restriction	Safety responsibility law	Safety inspection	Certificate of title required
Alabama	Oct. 1	★	16	Reciprocal	..	(g)	(d)	..
Arizona	Dec. 1	★	18	(f)	★	(g)	..	..
Arkansas	Jan. 1	★	16(h)	30 days	..	(g)	..	★
California	Jan. 2	★	16(h)	(s)	★	(g)	..	★
Colorado	Jan. 1	★	16	Reciprocal	..	(g)	★	★
Connecticut	Feb. 15	★	16	Reciprocal	..	(g)	Spot	..
Delaware	(k)	★	16	Reciprocal	..	(g)	★	★
Florida	Jan. 1	★	16(h)	Reciprocal	..	(g)	..	★
Georgia	Jan. 1	★	16(h)	30 days	..	(g)	..	..
Idaho	Dec. 1	★	16(h)	Reciprocal	..	(g)	..	★
Illinois	(e)	★	16	Reciprocal	..	(g)	(d)	★
Indiana	Jan. 3	★	16	60 days	..	(g)	..	★
Iowa	Dec. 1	★	16(h)	Reciprocal(l)	..	(g)	(d)	★
Kansas	Jan. 1	★	16(h)	Reciprocal	..	(c)	..	★
Kentucky	Dec. 29	★	16	Reciprocal	..	(g)	..	★
Louisiana	Dec. 1	★	15	Reciprocal	..	(g)	(m)	★
Maine	Dec. 25	★	15	Reciprocal	..	(g)	★	..
Maryland	Mar. 1	★	16	Reciprocal	..	(g)	★	★
Massachusetts	Jan. 1	★	16	Reciprocal(p)	..	(q)	★	..
Michigan	Dec. 1	★	16(h)	90 days	..	(g)	..	★
Minnesota	Nov. 1	★	15	Reciprocal(l)	..	(g)	(d)	..
Mississippi	Nov. 1	★	17(h)	(j)	..	(g)	★	..
Missouri	(e)	★	16	Reciprocal	..	(g)	..	★
Montana	Jan. 1	★	15	30 days(r)	..	(g)	(d)	★
Nebraska	Jan. 1	★	15½(h)	Reciprocal	..	(g)	..	★
Nevada	(e)	★	16(h)	No limit	..	(g)	..	★
New Hampshire	Mar. 1	★	16(h)	Reciprocal	..	(g)	★	★
New Jersey	Mar. 1	★	17	Reciprocal	..	(g)	★	★
New Mexico	Dec. 15	★	14	90 days	..	(t)	★	★
New York	Jan. 1	★	18(h)	Reciprocal	..	(g)	..	..
North Carolina	Jan. 1	★	16	Reciprocal	..	(t)	★	★
North Dakota	Nov. 1	★	16(h)	90 days	..	(g)	..	★
Ohio	Mar. 1	★	16(h)	Reciprocal	..	(g)	..	★
Oklahoma	Dec. 11	★	16(h)	60 days	..	(g)	..	★
Oregon	(e)	★	16(h)	Reciprocal	..	(g)	..	★
Pennsylvania	Mar. 15	★	18(h)	Reciprocal	..	(g)	★	★
Rhode Island	Mar. 1	★	16	Reciprocal	..	(g)	..	..
South Carolina	Sept. 15	★	14	90 days	..	(g)	..	..
South Dakota	Jan. 1	★	15	60 days	..	(g)	..	★
Tennessee	Mar. 1	★	16(h)	30 days	..	(g)	(d)	★
Texas	Feb. 1	★	16(h)	Reciprocal(u)	..	(g)	(d)	★
Utah	Dec. 15	★	16	Reciprocal	..	(g)	(d)	★
Vermont	Mar. 1	★	18(h)	Reciprocal	..	(g)	★	..
Virginia	Mar. 15	★	15	60	..	(g)	★	★
Washington	Jan. 1	★	16	Reciprocal	..	(g)	★	★
West Virginia	June 1	★	16	90 days	..	(g)	★	★
Wisconsin	(e)	★	16(h)	Reciprocal	..	(g)	..	★
Wyoming	Dec. 1	★	15	90 days	(v)	(g)	..	★
Dist. of Columbia	Mar. 1	★	16	Reciprocal	..	(g)	★	★

*Prepared by the American Automobile Association, Washington, D.C.

(a) Applies to nonresidents. The term "reciprocal" means that the state will extend to a nonresident the identical privileges granted by his home state to nonresident motorists. In most states persons who intend to reside permanently must buy new plates and secure new driving license at once, or within a limited period. Employment or placing children in public school is considered intention to reside permanently.
(c) Old-type law, effective when motorist convicted or has failed to satisfy a judgment.
(d) Certain or all cities may provide for compulsory inspection.
(e) When issued.
(f) Until expiration of home state plates or establishment of residence. Visitors must obtain permit after 10 days.
(g) New-type security law, effective when accident happens.

(h) Special junior permit.
(i) Registration after 30 days.
(j) Visitors: until expiration of home registration; residents: reciprocal.
(k) Three months before current registration expires.
(l) Visitors must register within a specified time.
(m) Provides for compulsory instruction in some parishes.
(n) According to reciprocal agreements with various states
(o) Highway patrol authorized to establish checking stations.
(p) Permit showing compliance with state compulsory liability insurance law must be obtained after 30 days.
(q) State has compulsory insurance.
(r) For recreational travel. Extension for same period when requested. Stickers issued.
(s) Full period for which vehicle is licensed in owner's home state or establishment of residence.
(t) Has future-proof law.

AVIATION AMONG THE STATES*

AERONAUTICAL engineers and manufacturers are predicting revolutionary steps in aviation progress during the next twenty years. These include speed ranges exceeding 10,000 miles per hour; ability to operate at altitudes up to fifty miles; extensive use of guided missiles for both military and commercial purposes; the Vertical Take-off and Landing (VTOL) principle applied to all types of airplanes; more powerful chemical fuels; and nuclear power; aircraft guided entirely by electronic and mechanical devices, with the pilot retained only to monitor and compensate these devices.

When these prophesies become realities, we will be flying around the world in three hours. Nuclear power will make it possible for aircraft to continue in flight for indefinite periods. VTOL applied to small aircraft will make it possible for the private owner to take off and land in his back yard or on the garage roof, and rocket-powered, remote controlled, pilotless aircraft may be used to deliver mail and cargo internationally.

The above prophesies may appear unrealistic, but during the past ten years aircraft speeds and operating altitudes have increased at fantastic rates. World War II fighters that had to be pushed to hit 450 miles per hour and altitudes over 30,000 feet have given way to slim jets that in level flight exceed the speed of sound and maneuver faultlessly at altitudes over 50,000 feet. Research aircraft have already flown two and a half times the speed of sound, 1,650 m.p.h., at altitudes of 90,000 feet—seventeen miles.

Airliners a decade ago cruised at top speeds of around 200 m.p.h.; today's luxury liners cruise at more than 350 m.p.h. and at altitudes over 28,000 feet in pressurized comfort. Faster and more comfortable planes are on the production lines

*Prepared by A. B. McMullen, Executive Secretary, National Association of State Aviation Officials.

to meet the demands and acceptance of air travel. New jet transports will have cruising speeds almost double the speeds of today's piston engine airliners.

In 1945 the scheduled airlines flew 3.9 billion passenger miles. In 1954 this traffic totalled 20.4 billion miles. Ten years ago approximately 7.1 million persons flew the airlines. In 1954 passenger traffic climbed to over 35 million, and equalled 70 per cent of the number of passengers, excluding commuters, carried by the railroads.

The following tabulation indicates the growing public use of the United States domestic and foreign scheduled air carriers for the transportation of passengers, air mail and air freight and express.

	1946	1950	1954
	in thousands		
Number of passengers	13,255	19,099	35,184
U. S. Mail—ton miles	39,094	68,197	116,809
Freight—ton miles...	14,822	174,649	229,197
Express—ton miles..	38,878	37,280	41,166

Today private planes fly more miles and hours than do the commercial airlines, and the fleet of utility planes engaged in industry and agriculture far outnumber the scheduled airline fleet. Approximately 21,500 aircraft are now used continuously in business activities.

In 1954, 460 million pounds and 109 million gallons of chemicals were sprayed on approximately 38 million acres of land by aircraft throughout the United States, thus increasing yield and reducing production costs of farm and grove products. In addition, approximately two million acres of various types of crops were seeded by aircraft.

The lives of all citizens are increasingly affected by the growing services supplied by the aviation industry and the destructive striking power of military air forces. To assure maximum benefits from the services offered by aviation and minimum loss from aerial attack in case it should occur, states and local communities have a direct and growing responsibility.

AIRPORT DEVELOPMENT PROGRAMS

Thirty states have adopted legislation requiring state approval of Federal Aid Airport Program projects, and twenty-one states require FAAP funds to be channeled through their state aviation agencies. During the past twenty-five years seventeen states have appropriated or otherwise made available $128,298,078 (excluding appropriations made in 1955) for airport development. In the last two years, nevertheless, various persons, including members of Congress, have expressed the opinion that the individual states have not assumed their share of the responsibility in planning, developing and financing an adequate system of airports. Preparation of long range airport plans and programs requires close cooperation and coordination at local, state and national levels. Integrated in the over-all plan, it is commonly agreed, must be:

1. The large terminal airports in the interstate airways system, most of which now require modernization to provide facilities to accommodate the growing number of planes, passengers and cargo shipments; and lengthening of runways for the jet transports soon to be placed in operation.

2. The airports that are required for local air service carriers and for the charter- or air-taxi operators who supplement and feed the trunk route airlines.

3. The additional airports needed for corporation and business aircraft, and for the farmer and rancher and other types of aircraft owners whose flights are not confined to designated airways, but who fly wherever they wish to go provided airport facilities are available.

4. The heliports and landing areas needed to accommodate the helicopter, which is rapidly being adapted to commuter-type airline service and for many uses by private owners; and to accommodate the convertiplane of the future, which may bring air transportation to the back yard or roof top of many citizens.

During the early months of 1955 the National Association of State Aviation Officials, the American Association of Airport Executives and the Airport Operators Council, jointly, conducted a nation-wide, state-by-state study to determine the extent of currently needed airport development and the estimated amount of funds required. This study developed the following conclusions:

FUNDS REQUIRED AND PURPOSES

Terminals..........	$174,866,945
Landing areas.......	195,870,327
Land...............	47,455,806
Miscellaneous.......	50,160,389
Total..........	$468,353,467

The survey indicated that of the total, $222,768,195 would be needed during fiscal 1956, and $147,383,276 in fiscal 1957; and that states and political subdivisions currently had available $173,133,309 to match federal funds.

FEDERAL AID AIRPORT PROGRAM

Although the Federal Airport Act, adopted in 1946, as amended, provided for a twelve-year program and annual appropriations within a total authorization of $500 million, no funds were appropriated for fiscal 1954. However, Congress appropriated $22 million for fiscal 1955 and $20 million for 1956.

The Department of Commerce did not request an appropriation for fiscal 1954. It established criteria for airport eligibility that limited federal assistance to projects at airports at which there were a minimum of thirty based aircraft, or from which 3,000 passengers were enplaned per year, or a combination of the two factors. This largely limited federal aid to the larger and more active airports.

Congress, however, subsequently took a different stand. During its closing days, the 84th Congress, 1st session, adopted legislation amending the Federal Airport Act and directing the Secretary of Commerce to prepare, and thereafter, at least three months prior to the close of each fiscal year, to revise, a national plan for the development of public airports in the United States and territories—such plan to include all types of airport development eligible for federal aid. And it specified that projects should not be limited to any classes or categories of public airports. The legislation also authorized, for obligation in the several states, the sum of $40 million (in addition to $20 million previously appropriated) for fiscal 1956 and $60 million for each of the fiscal years 1957, 1958 and

1959. In addition, sums of $2.5 million for fiscal 1956 and $3 million for each of the fiscal years 1957, 1958 and 1959 were authorized for Alaska, Hawaii, Puerto Rico and the Virgin Islands.

This legislation (P.L. 211) permits, for the first time, development of long range plans and programs for airport development by interested federal agencies and the states and local communities. The funds thus authorized annually are substantially larger than any previous federal appropriations; on the other hand they are considerably less than the amounts believed necessary by aviation officials generally for airport development and improvement in the next four years.

The table on page 295 indicates the status of the Federal Aid Airport Program as of June 30, 1955.

AGRICULTURAL AVIATION

Use of aircraft for agricultural purposes includes such activities as spraying of insecticides, weed killers, defoliation chemicals; spraying towns for pests, chasing birds from rice fields, baiting grasshoppers, anti-frost agitation, forest fire control, seeding, livestock feeding, inspection and survey, etc. During the past two years many states have actively promoted use of aircraft for agricultural purposes by regularly sponsoring aerial demonstrations of dusting, spraying and seeding. Through the demonstrations many persons—farmers, ranchers, fruit growers, insecticide manufacturers and distributors, county farm agents and others—could learn the proper methods and equipment to use for these purposes.

During 1953 and 1954, the Illinois Department of Aeronautics assisted in promoting sixty-five soil conservation airlifts in which more than 9,500 persons were given demonstration flights. In Missouri, the Agricultural Extension Service and the Aviation Bureau initiated a cooperative program to promote and advise on aerial application of chemicals to crops; in addition two aerial applicator short courses were held.

AIR SEARCH AND RESCUE

Organization and direction of air search and rescue operations continue to be a major responsibility of most state aeronautics agencies. During the past two years the Wyoming Rescue Service flew more than 900 hours on missions to locate aircraft, lost hunters and fishermen, to drop food to persons isolated by extreme weather conditions, and for forest fire surveillance. In 1954 plans were completed in Pennsylvania for a unique type of search and rescue program; it employs the services of full-time personnel and aircraft and equipment of the State Aeronautics Commission, State Police and Air National Guard. Oregon has a state air search and rescue organization made up of eighteen volunteer groups, each of which is supervised and directed by a leader appointed by the Board of Aeronautics; in the past two years it has conducted thirty searches for missing persons or aircraft.

SAFETY

The rapid advance of both the aviation and television broadcasting industries, and the increased construction of broadcasting and receiving antenna towers between 500 and 2,000 feet high, have focused increasing attention on safety problems associated with the joint use of the airspace by these industries. The increasing height of television broadcasting and receiving towers has greatly increased the aircraft-tower collision hazard, as these skeleton structures are extremely difficult to see under many visibility conditions. Industry representatives and government agencies have been studying this problem constantly and have been holding joint meetings during the past two years in an attempt to work out equitable solutions. Relatively little thus far has been accomplished, as there is no federal control over the erection of tall structures, other than that the Federal Communications Commission can refuse to issue or renew broadcasting permits and thereby prevent construction of broadcasting towers. However, the FCC has no control over receiving antenna towers.

As a result, several states have enacted legislation designed to give state aviation commissions some control over the location and height of towers and other structures which would constitute a hazard to air navigation, and to require their adequate marking and lighting.

Navigational Aids

Following the lead of Minnesota, where the first state-owned and operated Terminal Visual Omni Range (TVOR), Very High Frequency (VHF) radio beacon was installed in 1953, South Dakota allocated sufficient funds to install three TVOR's in fiscal 1956. Nebraska installed three Omni ranges in 1954 and plans to install six additional ranges during the fiscal years 1956 and 1957. Nebraska's program includes a total of fourteen ranges.

Minnesota, in cooperation with municipalities, now operates seven TVOR ranges, and the 1955 legislature appropriated funds for the purchase of six additional ones. New Hampshire plans to install two TVOR's during fiscal 1956.

These Omni ranges, installed by the states to supplement the navigational aids installed by the federal government along established airways, provide weather and flight information where previously it was impossible for a pilot to receive information of any kind by radio. When Minnesota's ranges are completed an aircraft flying 1,000 feet or more above the ground will be able to maintain radio contact with at least one station, and possibly two stations, at all times. This service makes it possible for a pilot of aircraft equipped with directional receiver to fly directly to any point in the state, although it may not be served by a radio navigational aid. Omni ranges should contribute tremendously to the safety of air travel, both during normal visual flight conditions, and particularly during marginal or "instrument" weather.

FEDERAL AID AIRPORT PROGRAM*
Status as of June 30, 1955

| State | Federal-Aid Airport Program, 1947–1955 Inclusive (All funds given in thousands) | | | | |
	Sponsor funds	Federal funds	Total funds	Airports	Projects
Alabama.................	$ 2,247	$ 2,250	$ 4,497	19	39
Arizona.................	2,940	3,805	6,745	15	68
Arkansas................	2,279	2,226	4,505	26	58
California...............	23,892	16,935	40,827	71	181
Colorado................	4,143	3,572	7,715	21	56
Connecticut.............	1,426	1,436	2,862	7	16
Delaware................	142	146	288	1	6
Florida..................	7,815	6,754	14,569	19	48
Georgia.................	4,989	5,106	10,095	25	60
Idaho...................	1,415	1,761	3,176	37	92
Illinois..................	16,791	15,486	32,277	24	57
Indiana.................	4,654	4,353	9,007	16	42
Iowa....................	4,507	4,351	8,858	32	80
Kansas..................	2,771	2,658	5,429	41	73
Kentucky................	3,198	3,107	6,305	15	41
Louisiana...............	4,356	4,365	8,721	20	53
Maine...................	1,118	1,122	2,240	13	24
Maryland................	3,054	3,046	6,100	7	20
Massachusetts...........	5,842	5,061	10,903	17	43
Michigan................	8,475	7,759	16,234	42	94
Minnesota...............	5,337	5,280	10,617	48	93
Mississippi..............	1,160	1,146	2,306	23	50
Missouri................	6,744	6,678	13,422	37	68
Montana................	1,199	1,440	2,639	34	88
Nebraska................	2,901	2,851	5,752	55	99
Nevada..................	1,051	1,714	2,765	12	25
New Hampshire..........	250	249	499	9	16
New Jersey..............	6,085	5,689	11,774	7	16
New Mexico.............	1,261	1,518	2,779	18	37
New York...............	15,569	14,211	29,780	22	67
North Carolina..........	2,557	2,621	5,178	17	39
North Dakota...........	1,050	1,060	2,110	30	60
Ohio....................	6,869	6,346	13,215	19	47
Oklahoma...............	3,380	3,451	6,831	39	77
Oregon..................	2,405	3,051	5,456	22	62
Pennsylvania............	12,646	11,346	23,992	27	65
Rhode Island............	1,360	1,252	2,612	1	4
South Carolina..........	1,128	1,168	2,296	10	22
South Dakota...........	1,326	1,518	2,844	35	62
Tennessee...............	4,238	4,251	8,489	24	60
Texas...................	14,549	14,027	28,576	71	131
Utah....................	1,667	2,677	4,344	24	39
Vermont................	521	517	1,038	6	11
Virginia.................	3,022	3,047	6,069	9	24
Washington..............	4,918	4,179	9,097	30	60
West Virginia...........	2,920	2,889	5,809	7	25
Wisconsin...............	6,127	5,268	11,395	39	60
Wyoming................	656	845	1,501	18	37
U. S. Totals............	$218,950	$205,588	$424,538	1,161	2,595
Alaska..................	692	2,009	2,701	35	37
Hawaii..................	1,999	1,990	3,989	8	16
Puerto Rico.............	2,756	2,781	5,537	1	8
Virgin Islands...........	198	260	458	2	8
Territorial Totals........	5,645	7,040	12,685	46	69
Grand Totals...........	$224,595	$212,628	$437,223	1,207	2,664

*Prepared by The National Association of State Aviation Officials.

3

Health and Welfare

STATE HEALTH PROGRAMS*

GENERALLY, favorable health conditions continued to prevail throughout the United States during the period 1953–54. While the incidence of most communicable diseases notifiable in 1954 showed decreases from the cases reported for 1953, psittacosis and infectious hepatitis, in which there is considerable public health interest, increased during the year. A decrease occurred in the incidence of poliomyelitis in 1954, and significant reductions were noted in reported cases of smallpox and malaria.

The estimated annual death rate for 1954 was 9.2 per 1,000 of population, the seventh consecutive year in which the rate was below ten. Each year since the end of World War II has seen an increase in the birth rate. This upward movement continued in 1953 and 1954, with registered births in these years numbering 3,902,120 and 4,021,000 (estimated) respectively. At the same time, the infant mortality rate reached a new low in 1954, when the rate was 26.6 deaths under one year per 1,000 live births. Since 1936, when the rate was 57.1, the infant mortality rate has decreased annually almost without interruption.

The success in preventing needless deaths is also shown in the rapid drop of the maternal mortality rate from 56.8 per 10,000 live births in 1936 to 5.3 in 1954.

With the increasing control over infectious and respiratory diseases, there has been a rise in the rates for causes of death most often associated with middle and advanced age. The death rate for malignant neoplasms was 147.0 per 100,000 population in 1954, and the rate for diseases of the cardiovascular system was 480.2, the highest ever recorded for these two groups of chronic diseases. Together, these accounted for more than two-thirds of all the deaths during 1954, compared with less than one-fifth of all the deaths during 1900. The chief factor in the increase in rates for these causes has been the gradual aging of the population.

STATE HEALTH DEPARTMENTS

Functions

The state health department is the agency officially charged with protecting and improving the public health. In carrying out its responsibility, the department exercises regulatory control over certain facilities such as water supplies and sewage disposal systems; collects and analyzes vital records and other health statistics; provides specialized training for professional health workers; disseminates health information for the public; demonstrates new methods and techniques for the control of disease and the promotion of health; operates diagnostic laboratories; provides technical and financial assistance to local health agencies; and furnishes direct services in areas where no organized local health services are available, or where state provi-

*Prepared by the Public Health Service and the Children's Bureau of the U.S. Department of Health, Education, and Welfare.

sion of highly specialized services is more feasible economically. The administration of state-wide hospital construction programs, the operation of institutions for the treatment of tuberculosis and mental disorders, and the licensure for health reasons of individuals and establishments are health services which in some states are performed by health departments, but in many instances by other agencies of state government.

Staffing

Many professional disciplines work together in planning and carrying out state public health programs: physicians, nurses, dentists, engineers, sanitarians, and laboratory workers—to name only the more numerous groups. Shortage of trained professional and technical personnel has been a perennial problem in public health. From 1952 to 1954 the population of the United States increased by over 3.5 per cent; in the same period the number of state and local public health workers increased by 1 per cent—to a total of 54,255 in January, 1954. The inability of public health department staffs to keep pace, numerically, with the growth in the population to be served can be attributed to a number of factors. Some of these are: relatively low government salaries for professional personnel; a nation-wide shortage of physicians, engineers, nurses and others; and decreases, in some states, in total funds available for public health. Also, a recent study indicates a considerable decrease in training activities in the last three years. In 1951 state health authorities provided financial assistance to 813 persons for training of four months or more; in 1954, only 494 persons received such training aid.

Funds

In the fiscal year 1954, state and territorial health departments and other agencies administering programs for mental health, hospital construction, and crippled children services expended $308 million for public health services in the forty-eight states, the District of Columbia, Alaska, Hawaii, Puerto Rico and the Virgin Islands. This total does not include amounts expended for construction and for operation of general hospitals and tuberculosis sanatoria.

Public health services are cooperatively supported by federal, state and local governments, which jointly finance both the basic framework of the country's public health system and the provision of special services directed toward particular diseases or selected population groups. The proportion of this total program which is financed by state and local governments has been constantly increasing for several years. In the last two years, the state and local share of total expenditures has increased from 77 per cent in 1952 to 84 per cent in 1954. These figures, however, are averages, and as such tend to obscure the fact that there are wide variations in the relative financial abilities of the states to support public health services. For example, nine states look to federal sources for support of 30 per cent or more of their total public health programs.

STATE HEALTH PROGRAMS

Tuberculosis Control

The tuberculosis death rate for the United States has fallen 75 per cent in the past decade. However, the decline in prevalence has not kept pace with the decline in deaths. In 1954, 79,000 new cases were reported. In some states the need for beds for tuberculous patients is acute, although nationally the number of occupied beds has decreased 6.7 per cent. A large proportion of tuberculous persons receive treatment outside hospitals, thus placing new responsibilities on health departments. Drug therapy and surgical techniques reduce the death rate; but until an immunizing agent is developed, new cases will continue to occur, thus requiring health departments to maintain their control programs.

Venereal Disease Control

Venereal disease control operations in fiscal 1955 were directed toward holding in check, as far as possible, increases of reported syphilis and gonorrhea which were noted in all except five states during the year. Programs were oriented in particular to migrant groups from high prevalence areas and to the teen-agers and young adults who are responsible for more than half of the infectious venereal disease caseload.

Principal casefinding devices were interview-investigation, mass-screening among selected groups in known high prevalence areas, and accelerated gonorrhea casefinding, called "Speed-zone Epidemiology." Penicillin continued to be the drug of choice in therapy for both syphilis and gonorrhea.

Cancer Control

At present one or more official agencies in every state conducts some cancer control activities. State health departments and university medical schools are the outstanding official agencies in this field. These agencies work closely with state chapters of the American Cancer Society and state medical societies. State health departments provide varying amounts of direct case finding and diagnostic services and supply financial assistance to other official or voluntary agencies. University medical schools operate most of the state hospitals and clinics accepting cancer patients. However, in a few states, other agencies operate cancer hospitals or chronic disease or general hospitals accepting cancer patients. Cancer-teaching programs in almost all of the nation's medical and dental schools have been strengthened.

Large-scale studies have indicated, particularly with reference to the uterine cervix, that application of cytological techniques offers an efficient and valuable screening technique for the early detection of cancer. Efforts to stimulate the widespread use of this diagnostic aid will continue.

Heart Disease Control

Throughout the country and on a steadily growing scale, state health departments are meeting the challenge of cardiovascular disease—chiefly by developing programs in four major control areas: prevention, community services, education and research.

Prevention programs today are limited mainly to the prevention of rheumatic heart disease through the use of penicillin or sulfadiazine to forestall recurrent attacks of rheumatic fever.

A wide variety of community services, such as diagnostic clinics, casefinding, nutrition, nursing and social services, are furnished to alleviate suffering and disability and to prevent premature deaths in persons with heart disease.

Educational programs are aimed at both professional and lay groups to increase the skills of all those concerned with cardiac patients and to broaden public awareness and understanding of cardiovascular disease, the nation's leading health problem.

Research is being conducted by some states to develop, refine and evaluate heart disease control activities now under way.

Chronic Disease Control

The aging population of the United States creates new health problems and multiplies old ones. Diabetes and other chronic diseases which are most frequently found among older people are therefore receiving increased attention from agencies of state government. All of the states are at present engaged, in varying degrees, in chronic disease control programs. Sixteen state health agencies operated diabetes control programs in 1953–54. Home care and physical rehabilitation programs have been adopted by a number of states in efforts to relieve shortages of hospital beds and to return disabled patients to active and productive life. (See pages 331–337 for further material on state programs for the aging.)

Mental Health

The years 1953 and 1954 constituted a period of mounting public concern over mental health as a major health problem. This was evidenced by regional surveys of needs and resources, and recommendations for appropriate action to increase knowledge, personnel and services in community and institutional settings in every region of the country. This regional action was carried out by interstate organizations composed of Governors, legislators, representatives of mental health professions and mental health programs, and citizen-interest groups.

More attention was given to joint planning of comprehensive state and local mental health programs, responsibility for which rests with different agencies, both public and private, carrying on such activities as those concerned with public education, new approaches to institutional and out-patient care, professional training, surveys, research and evaluation.

Noteworthy progress was made in such areas as chemotherapy for psychiatric patients, alcoholism, drug addiction, mental retardation, juvenile delinquency, rehabilitation and aftercare, school mental health, aging and residential treatment of disturbed children. (A separate report on state mental health programs begins on page 307.)

Dental Public Health

Forty-seven states have formally endorsed the fluoridation of public water supplies as a measure for reducing tooth decay. This public health measure, which prevents as many as two-thirds of the cavities in children, has been adopted by 1,080 communities in forty-four states. More than 20.6 million people now drink fluoridated water. In addition, some 4.5 million people in 1,600 communities drink water naturally containing 0.7 parts or more of fluoride per million parts of water.

Seventeen state health departments are cooperating with the Public Health Service in conducting studies on the use of fluorides in reducing tooth decay and on methods of removing excessive amounts of fluoride from water supplies. Of the seventeen cooperating states, eight are engaged in studies on fluoridation, six on topical fluoride applications and four on defluoridation.

Today, forty-seven state health departments conduct programs for improving dental health; five years ago, forty-two included improvement of dental health as one of their programs.

Maternal and Child Health Services

The decrease in maternal and infant mortality in the United States as a whole during the last ten years has enabled the health departments to expand their maternal and child health programs. Preventive health services for mothers and children include such units and facilities as maternity clinics for prenatal care; well-child clinics for health supervision of infants and preschool children; health services for school children, including supervision by physicians, dentists, public health nurses, nutritionists; dental hygiene and prophylaxis dental care; nutrition education; advice to hospitals on maternity and newborn services; licensing and inspection of maternity homes; provision of incubators and hospital care for premature infants. The states, which vary considerably in these programs, also provide postgraduate training for professional personnel engaged in them.

In addition to the preventive services a feature in some states is medical care, particularly medical and hospital care for premature infants. A few states provide medical and hospital care for mothers with complications of pregnancy. Principal recent developments have been an increase in demonstration programs for care of the prematurely born infant, increase in programs for postgraduate training of personnel, emphasis on the emotional growth of infants and children, and development of good parent-child relationships.

Increasing attention is being given to means of reducing the annual total of fetal and neonatal deaths.

Services for Crippled Children

Services for crippled children are administered by the state health department in thirty-three states and territories, by the state welfare department in eight states, by a combined state health and welfare department in two states, by a crippled children's commission in four states, by the state department of education in three states and by the state medical school in three states.

State services for crippled children include a broad concept of medical care. This does not stop at surgical treatment but combines treatment of both the physical handicap and unfavorable social and psychological influences, which together determine the degree and duration of disability. Agencies provide medical, surgical, corrective and other services for the care of children who are crippled or suffering from conditions that may lead to crippling. The definition of crippling is decided by each state, either by statute or administratively. At present all state programs include children under twenty-one years of age who have a handicap of an orthopedic nature or who require plastic surgery. Other conditions included in some of the programs are services for children who are hard of hearing, children who have epilepsy, children who have rheumatic fever, and children who can be benefited by cardiac surgery.

Environmental Health

Milk and food sanitation. The model ordinance for restaurant sanitation recommended by the Public Health Service has now been adopted by 1,040 local jurisdictions in forty-two of the states and territories, and it serves as the basis of state regulations in thirty states, one territory and the District of Columbia. All shellfish-producing states and many inland states are participating in the cooperative State-Public Health Service-Industry program for certification of oysters, clams and mussels. As of June 30, 1955, the *Milk Ordinance and Code* recommended by the Public Health Service had been adopted by 1,594 municipalities and 419 counties located in thirty-eight states and one territory. Thirty-two states and the District of Columbia are cooperating in the joint State-Public Health Service-Interstate Milk Shipper Certification Program.

Hygiene of housing. In 1952, the American Public Health Association adopted a proposed housing ordinance. This has served as the basis for more than a dozen new municipal housing ordinances. These ordinances, adopted locally, represent the community intent to assure adequate minimum standards of health, sanitation and safety through a comprehensive system of codes and ordinances.

Home accident prevention. The annual toll of 28,000 deaths and more than 4 million disabling non-fatal injuries caused by accidents in the home has encouraged the study and development of effective preventive measures.. Data from a survey of home accidents made in 1951 to 1953 are being applied in the field through demonstration projects financed by the W. K. Kellogg Foundation. These twelve programs—four in local health departments (San Jose, California; Mansfield, Ohio; Cambridge, Massachusetts; and Kalamazoo, Michigan), and eight in state health

departments (California, Georgia, Kansas, Kentucky, Maryland, Massachusetts, North Carolina and Oregon)—are providing a rich source of valuable experience. Continued program development, in cooperation with safety organizations, shows promise toward the control of a major portion of this, the ninth leading cause of death—home accidents.

Municipal and rural sanitation. An additional six states recently have adopted legislation requiring the heat treatment of garbage prior to feeding it to swine. This brings the total of the states having such legislation or regulations to forty-six. State activities relative to provision of technical assistance to county and municipal governments in planning and operation of refuse collection and disposal systems have continued to increase.

Water supply and water pollution control. Increased interest in water resource development, given added impetus by serious and widespread drought conditions during 1953 and 1954, has led more than twenty states to initiate studies of their water resources and water use laws.

Continued pollution abatement progress by the states is reflected by municipal sewage treatment plant construction amounting to $191 million (615 projects) in 1953, and $228 million (716 projects) in 1954. Several additional states adopted improved water pollution control legislation in the 1953–54 period, and about two-thirds of the states now have an effective legislative base for carrying on their pollution control programs.

Continued improvement in interstate cooperation and coordination of pollution abatement work is being achieved through the mechanism of interstate compact organizations and regional pollution control councils. Working together through these interstate organizations, the states are developing and adopting uniform water quality objectives for various water uses, and uniform design and treatment standards for the respective areas.

Occupational Health

State and local industrial health agencies are currently focusing their attention upon determination and prevention of possible harmful effects resulting from the rapid technological changes now occurring in American industry. The effects of long-term exposure to small amounts of toxic substances are receiving increased attention. Problems of the physical environment, including studies of factors such as noise, illumination, heat and radiation are being investigated.

Increasing efforts are being made to expand the availability of employee health services in industry, particularly in smaller plants. At present employee absence due to sickness is estimated at 400 million man-days per year. Of 49 million gainfully employed, non-agricultural workers, an estimated 35 million do not have basic preventive industrial medical services. It is now estimated that there is, on the average, only one industrial nurse employed in industry for every four thousand workers.

In 1955 there were 375 professional persons on official industrial hygiene staffs in forty states, the District of Columbia, Hawaii, Puerto Rico and twenty local health departments. Ten of these units have staffs of at least ten persons and they account for 45 per cent of the total personnel. Fourteen are one-man units. Eight of the less heavily industrialized states have no programs.

The trend for increased legislative provision for compensation for occupational diseases has continued. At present, compensation coverage for all occupational diseases is provided by twenty-six states, Alaska, the District of Columbia and Hawaii; an additional twenty states and Puerto Rico have provided coverage for at least some occupational diseases.

Hospital and Medical Facility Planning and Construction

In the nation as a whole there are now 1,100,000 acceptable hospital beds, according to state plan inventories as of January 1, 1955. This total is 43,000 more than was recorded in 1953. Major emphasis has been placed by the state agencies, under the Federal Hospital Survey and Construction Act (P.L. 725, 79th Congress, as amended), on assistance to general hospital projects.

To date more than 2,500 hospitals, public health centers and related health facility projects have been approved. More than

1,900 of these are completed, opened and rendering service; 500 are under construction; the remainder are in planning and drawing board stages. The total cost of more than $2 billion for these projects is being met by $1⅓ billion in state and local funds and $671 million in federal aid. In 1954 the states operated 550 hospitals with more than 710,000 beds, to which more than 728,000 patients were admitted. The overwhelming bulk of these beds—90 per cent—are for nervous and mental patients. The total number of beds in hospitals operated by state governments has increased 28,000 in the past two years.

The hospital survey and construction program has had considerable impact in beginning to reduce differences in unmet need for beds. Although the unmet need for general hospital beds has been reduced by one-fourth and the need for beds for tuberculous patients by one-half, the net deficit of beds for mental and chronic patients has continued to increase. Amendments to the program in 1954 authorized appropriations for grants to the states to survey their needs and develop state construction programs, and it further authorized funds for assistance in paying part of the cost of construction of four types of facilities: hospitals for the chronically ill and impaired, nursing homes, diagnostic or treatment centers, and rehabilitation facilities. Thus the expanded program will attempt to meet more adequately the needs for facilities for the care of the long term patient as well as for rehabilitation, and will emphasize the preventive aspects of a total health program through care of the ambulatory patient.

Recent Developments

During the spring and summer of 1954 the National Foundation for Infantile Paralysis conducted an extensive field trial of the newly developed Salk poliomyelitis vaccine. The trial was undertaken in cooperation with state and local health departments in forty-four states. Following the announcement of the vaccine's effectiveness, as demonstrated in the 1954 field trials, the Foundation announced plans for providing vaccine free to all children in the first and second grades, plus all who had

(*Concluded on page 306*)

TABLE 1

AMOUNTS EXPENDED FOR PUBLIC HEALTH SERVICES, STATE BY STATE, FISCAL YEAR 1954*(a)

State	Total funds expended	State funds	Local funds	Private agencies' funds	Federal funds — Total federal funds	Public Health Service	Children's Bureau	Other(b) federal funds
Totals................	$308,122,575	$141,719,246	$113,220,410	$3,948,640	$49,234,279	$25,661,081	$23,307,256	$265,942
Alabama................	4,831,062	1,606,960	1,673,103	25,763	1,525,236	683,125	842,111	......
Arizona................	1,135,880	213,537	602,110	13,682	306,551	184,175	122,376	......
Arkansas................	2,532,283	962,568	576,021	17,390	976,304	444,584	531,720	......
California................	31,862,253	12,869,397	16,799,467	28,870	2,164,519	1,302,225	803,895	58,399
Colorado................	2,138,292	474,427	1,093,307	34,236	536,322	234,107	302,215	......
Connecticut................	3,571,843	2,018,692	1,017,092	....	536,059	244,844	291,215	......
Delaware................	755,320	529,914	....	9,817	225,406	70,902	154,504	......
Florida................	8,469,955	4,988,648	2,340,487	....	1,131,003	698,888	432,115	......
Georgia................	9,424,518	4,577,909	3,234,864	18,409	1,593,336	810,015	783,321	......
Idaho................	950,767	418,869	203,035	15,702	313,161	136,029	164,284	12,848
Illinois................	14,535,500	5,911,169	6,844,058	38,185	1,742,088	1,060,645	681,443	......
Indiana................	4,111,989	1,747,240	1,427,956	80,815	855,978	457,081	398,897	......
Iowa................	2,478,804	1,321,944	258,888	195,106	702,866	317,059	385,807	......
Kansas................	2,508,382	938,166	972,047	37,137	561,032	270,449	290,583	......
Kentucky................	7,813,692	2,298,954	4,108,114	85,966	1,320,658	589,791	730,867	......
Louisiana................	5,521,839	2,365,242	1,828,519	56,458	1,271,620	655,813	610,807	5,000
Maine................	1,474,707	1,105,944	16,644	....	352,119	149,400	202,719	......
Maryland................	8,192,159	3,118,955	3,840,461	225,135	1,007,608	397,937	609,671	......
Massachusetts................	7,210,271	3,985,519	2,043,886	96,670	1,084,196	563,519	507,794	12,883
Michigan................	12,824,042	4,541,555	6,730,020	120,209	1,432,258	744,106	688,152	......
Minnesota................	4,393,401	2,115,999	1,452,813	24,738	799,851	357,189	442,662	......
Mississippi................	4,104,145	1,637,591	1,158,366	....	1,308,188	675,623	632,565	......
Missouri................	5,841,091	1,689,024	2,924,938	147,780	1,079,349	583,095	496,254	......
Montana................	929,653	344,778	215,290	26,370	343,215	127,882	215,333	......
Nebraska................	1,457,481	438,504	628,331	21,847	368,799	176,638	192,161	......
Nevada................	459,378	169,642	61,821	5,705	222,210	70,053	143,132	9,025
New Hampshire................	876,700	641,091	....	2,480	232,541	80,247	152,294	......
New Jersey................	3,414,925	2,218,716	227,525	54,670	914,014	562,669	351,345	......

303

New Mexico	1,537,421	629,248	510,001	15,000	383,172	173,937	209,235	......
New York	41,801,678	23,922,117	15,007,791	412,798	2,458,972	1,622,991	835,981	......
North Carolina	7,863,087	2,409,031	3,662,730	15,282	1,776,044	811,331	959,713	5,000
North Dakota	1,026,196	284,596	374,094	39,856	327,650	141,178	174,591	11,881
Ohio	13,251,789	2,619,187	8,123,216	827,602	1,681,784	952,897	728,887	......
Oklahoma	3,605,347	1,735,779	962,969	31,351	875,248	398,851	412,592	63,805
Oregon	3,210,261	1,094,898	1,667,603	30,526	417,234	193,779	223,455	......
Pennsylvania	17,317,969	12,574,424	1,898,327	600,925	2,244,293	1,301,190	943,103	......
Rhode Island	1,063,181	747,918	......	......	315,263	104,952	210,311	......
South Carolina	4,220,212	2,168,343	857,660	62,255	1,194,209	626,717	567,492	......
South Dakota	730,696	276,399	104,538	70,553	287,504	123,990	163,514	......
Tennessee	5,615,454	2,360,727	1,743,150	......	1,441,024	711,018	730,006	......
Texas	11,165,908	4,262,351	4,642,699	......	2,260,858	1,218,237	1,042,621	......
Utah	1,458,821	571,781	463,501	42,387	381,152	136,668	244,484	......
Vermont	893,972	661,784	......	8,483	223,705	90,609	133,096	......
Virginia	8,286,170	3,472,036	3,468,020	139,326	1,206,788	578,468	628,320	......
Washington	5,637,371	1,638,340	3,238,065	138,079	622,887	295,565	315,312	12,010
West Virginia	2,655,848	1,161,947	743,136	22,526	728,239	343,733	384,506	......
Wisconsin	5,457,788	1,874,735	2,792,011	1,592	789,450	353,260	436,190	......
Wyoming	463,841	151,235	88,657	23,486	200,463	72,647	127,816	......
Dist. of Columbia	3,757,878	3,216,940	......	......	540,938	249,400	291,538	......
Alaska	1,351,372	283,976	35,218	33,920	998,258	711,343	228,276	58,639
Hawaii	3,335,833	1,893,142	......	49,553	1,393,138	1,113,638	279,500	......
Puerto Rico	7,831,213	6,456,270	......	......	1,374,943	648,805	726,138	......
Virgin Islands	762,937	500	557,861	......	204,576	37,787	150,337	16,452

*Source: Reported to the Public Health Service and to the Children's Bureau by State Health Departments and other state agencies administering mental hygiene programs, industrial waste studies, hospital construction programs, and crippled children's services.

(a) Includes 1954 obligations unliquidated as of June 30, 1954. Excludes amounts identified as general hospital care and operation of tuberculosis sanatoria.
(b) Funds made available to states for health purposes by other federal agencies.

TABLE 2

STATUS OF HOSPITAL CONSTRUCTION PROGRAMS*

As Reported on June 30, 1955

State	Cost of construction		All types		General and allied(b) special hospitals		Tuberculosis hospitals		Mental hospitals		Public health centers(c) (projects)	Other health facilities (projects)
	Total costs (in thousands)	Per cent of total cost from federal funds	Projects(a)	Beds	Projects	Beds	Projects	Beds	Projects	Beds		
Totals..........	$2,056,114	32.6	2,514	118,814	1,872	100,900	63	6,748	93	11,166	468	18
Alabama.........	46,586	53.1	61	2,816	41	2,369	2	302	2	145	15	1
Arizona.........	12,155	30.5	16	884	15	820	1	64	..	..	..	..
Arkansas........	37,182	46.0	34	2,658	28	2,158	..	..	..6	500	..	..
California.......	90,307	25.2	87	4,628	69	4,268	..2	360	..	..	16	..
Colorado........	20,259	25.7	19	960	16	960	..	..	..	..	3	..
Connecticut.....	33,054	13.2	25	1,142	23	1,142	..	..	..	..	2	..
Delaware........	5,188	27.0	5	411	3	101	1	76	1	234	..	..
Florida.........	45,131	34.0	61	3,519	42	2,529	2	850	2	140	14	1
Georgia.........	63,278	40.0	160	3,764	77	3,764	2	..	..	..	81	..
Idaho...........	11,085	22.9	21	816	18	766	1	50	..	..	2	..
Illinois.........	73,530	30.3	54	3,782	49	3,577	1	100	1	105	2	1
Indiana.........	43,524	37.4	43	2,201	38	1,982	2	50	2	169	1	..
Iowa...........	38,038	30.6	52	2,429	51	2,244	..	..	1	185	..	..
Kansas..........	30,893	29.3	40	1,763	39	1,699	..	..	1	64	..	..
Kentucky........	42,574	51.1	91	3,033	49	2,272	7	64	3	697	31	1
Louisiana.......	57,632	34.2	84	3,301	34	2,375	1	102	6	824	43	..
Maine..........	9,797	48.5	14	575	13	575	..	..	1	..	..	..
Maryland........	31,224	24.3	37	1,619	24	1,559	1	60	..	..	11	1
Massachusetts....	78,873	19.3	66	3,101	61	3,065	1	36	..	..	3	1
Michigan........	65,803	30.6	62	3,201	57	2,923	2	150	1	128	2	..
Minnesota.......	47,553	30.7	48	2,138	45	2,078	..	..	1	60	2	..
Mississippi......	38,583	52.9	92	3,192	53	2,778	1	154	1	260	37	..
Missouri........	43,998	38.9	33	2,375	29	2,206	1	69	1	100	2	..
Montana........	6,284	28.2	20	495	20	495	..	..	..	..	..	..

Nebraska	16,904	33.6	41	935	40	845	...	...	1	90	...	...
Nevada	3,151	39.6	10	317	7	237	...	...	3	80	...	...
New Hampshire	10,377	29.3	10	447	10	447	...	...	...	...	1	...
New Jersey	55,104	24.0	32	3,387	25	2,392	...	...	6	995	...	...
New Mexico	12,125	33.3	17	852	17	852	...	...	...	...	...	...
New York	127,002	22.9	91	5,751	88	5,751	...	...	...	...	3	...
North Carolina	78,056	34.7	191	5,457	125	4,770	2	100	6	587	58	...
North Dakota	6,310	33.4	18	524	17	320	...	...	1	204	...	...
Ohio	103,819	25.5	73	5,843	66	5,436	4	407	...	1,615	3	3
Oklahoma	37,845	41.2	87	3,696	53	1,834	5	247	14	130	12	1
Oregon	22,097	25.7	31	1,548	27	1,418	...	...	2	...	1	...
Pennsylvania	118,521	33.5	80	5,235	80	5,235	...	...	...	...	...	...
Rhode Island	11,570	23.4	12	552	11	402	...	...	1	150	...	...
South Carolina	35,815	47.5	113	2,486	30	1,739	8	457	10	290	65	1
South Dakota	9,083	30.1	21	549	20	549	...	...	...	...	...	2
Tennessee	62,268	37.0	71	3,568	43	2,406	4	526	4	636	18	...
Texas	137,931	31.6	124	9,400	108	7,509	7	1,341	1	550	7	1
Utah	9,170	40.4	16	360	12	298	...	...	2	62	1	1
Vermont	6,896	31.4	8	373	7	373	...	...	...	...	...	1
Virginia	51,452	38.1	61	2,719	38	2,719	...	...	...	...	23	...
Washington	42,627	17.4	37	1,478	32	1,478	...	...	...	...	5	...
West Virginia	30,786	38.8	27	1,787	13	1,048	3	275	8	464	2	1
Wisconsin	38,285	37.0	54	2,202	52	1,962	...	...	1	240	...	1
Wyoming	4,259	32.5	10	347	10	347	...	...	...	...	...	...
Dist. of Columbia	7,890	22.3	7	202	7	202	...	...	...	...	...	...
Alaska	4,020	32.9	7	130	7	130	...	...	...	...	...	...
Hawaii	6,886	31.3	6	504	4	396	1	108	...	...	1	...
Puerto Rico	33,304	56.5	32	3,362	27	1,100	1	800	3	1,462	1	1
Virgin Islands	30	60.0	2	.....	2	.....	...	...	...	...	...	...

*Source: Hospital Construction Under the Hospital and Medical Facilities Survey and Construction Program, Analysis of Projects Approved for Federal Aid, Department of Health, Education, and Welfare, Public Health Service, Division of Hospital and Medical Facilities, June 30, 1955.

(a) Of the total, 1,905 of the projects, constructed at a cost of $1,389,504,000, were in operation; 503 projects, costing $568,165,000 were under construction; and 106, to cost $98,445,000, had been initially approved.

(b) Includes 79 combined hospitals and health centers.

(c) Includes 127 auxiliary health centers which are largely concentrated in Georgia and South Carolina.

participated in the field trials. This program, too, was being conducted through state and local health departments and the schools. Plans for vaccination programs for other children were being made by a number of states by July, 1955. State health departments were also playing a key role in the voluntary distribution plan which was developed to assure that the vaccine would be distributed equitably during the period of short supply.

In fiscal year 1955 key officials of state health departments, medical societies and civil defense organizations met with Public Health Service personnel in a series of regional conferences. The purpose of these conferences was to determine state needs for improvement of their public health civil defense programs and the actions that should be taken to fill those needs. Thirty-three states had written public health civil defense plans at the time of the conferences. Most of these plans were limited to consideration of needs for casualty care and did not cover public health aspects of the new mass evacuation concept or the problems of radioactive fall-out. It is anticipated that one of the results of the regional civil defense conferences will be the revision of many of the plans in the light of current civil defense concepts. Lack of funds for support of full time civil defense staff will continue to be a deterrent in development of adequate public health civil defense programs in most of the states.

Over the years, state health programs have reflected health problems identified within the state. As these problems changed in character or in degree, program emphasis also shifted. A population group that is attracting growing interest and concern today comprises the migratory agricultural workers and their dependents. As problems of special population groups are identified, states are developing services to meet them.

PROGRESS IN MENTAL HEALTH 1954-1955

PROBABLY the most important recent development in the field of mental health has been an expanding awareness that only a heavy investment in improved treatment, research and training can stem the mounting costs of caring for the mentally ill.

With more than half a million patients in state mental hospitals, and the number rising at a rate of 10,000 a year, the states are spending approximately $560 million annually for maintaining and operating their hospitals alone. The problem is further complicated by the fact that people are living longer and therefore are more susceptible to mental deterioration. Of every three patients admitted to mental hospitals in 1953, one was 60 years of age or over. In the last fifty years, while the total population 65 and over tripled, the number 65 and over in state hospitals multiplied nine times.

Added to these complicating factors are the mental health needs of approximately 134,000 mentally deficient persons in institutions and the even larger number outside of institutions; the great numbers who suffer from alcoholism; the delinquents, both juvenile and adult; and the expanding number of prisoners committed to penal institutions.

Thus state leaders in mental health work have felt increasingly in the last two years that unless the states emphasized treatment, training and research to an unprecedented degree, they could look forward to housing progressively growing numbers of patients, to misery on the part of patients, to much higher building costs, and to sharply rising burdens on taxpayers.

THE GOVERNORS' CONFERENCE

As a consequence, beginning in 1949, each of the Governors' Conferences has been concerned with this crucial health problem. At the direction of the Governors, the Council of State Governments conducted two comprehensive studies of the care and treatment of the mentally ill in the states. The first report, published in 1950, emphasized the overcrowding of buildings, the need for more adequate facilities and the urgency of more intensive treatment programs. The second, published in 1953, stressed the inadequacy of the funds for research in mental health, the shortage of qualified personnel, and the needs for training. Both reports presented extensive factual findings and specific recommendations for meeting the problems.

Following completion of these studies, the Governors adopted a resolution to hold a National Governors' Conference on Mental Health. That Conference met in Detroit, Michigan, in February, 1954. For the first time, Governors, legislators, mental health and other state officials, and leaders of all the mental health professions gathered together in one place, to discuss means of attacking the great social problem of mental illness. Representatives of forty-six states and Puerto Rico attended.

The Governors present adopted a Ten Point Program which subsequently has become a guide for mental health action in many states. The program called for increased appropriations to secure additional mental health personnel. It urged special appropriations to be used for training and research. And it recommended support from legislatures to raise the level of teaching and supervision in institutions in order to attract and retain the best personnel.

The Governors' Conference as a whole, moreover, felt that specific steps should be taken on a cooperative basis among the states. It therefore directed the Council of State Governments to establish an Interstate Clearing House on Mental Health, for exchange of mental health information and to aid the states in organizing effective programs of interstate cooperation in this field.

The Council established the Clearing House in 1954, and it has undertaken the following four general functions:

(1) It disseminates information to all states in the areas of care, treatment and

prevention. It compiles and analyzes such information and attempts to make the experience of all of the states available to each.

(2) It makes arrangements with mental health organizations and outstanding professional leaders to provide technical and professional service on a consultative basis to any state desiring such service in developing, expanding and perfecting its mental health programs.

(3) It undertakes to formulate model legislation in the mental health field and to assist in interstate arrangements for supervision of and psychiatric service to recently released hospital patients.

(4) It has developed interstate cooperative agreements and arrangements to pool existing facilities for concerted, regional attacks on problems of mental illness.

REGIONAL DEVELOPMENTS

One of the most promising recent movements has been the initiation and growth of regional cooperation by states in the field of mental health. This type of cooperation, developed largely in the last two years, has permitted groups of states to pool their mental health resources. Thus each participating state can receive the maximum benefits of a total area, rather than relying only on its own facilities.

The regional program farthest advanced to date in this field is that of the Southern Regional Education Board, undertaken at the request of the Southern Governors' Conference in 1954. The Governor of each southern state, from Delaware to Texas, appointed a state mental health training and research committee, made up of state officials, professionals from all fields, legislators and others. These committees appraised their resources, listed their needs and made recommendations for improving their situations. As a result, a Southern Regional Council on Mental Health Training and Research was established in 1955. It has appropriations of $8,000 per year from each of eight states thus far, and the support of the National Institute of Mental Health.

A survey of mental health training and research was undertaken in the Midwest in 1954, highlighted by a Midwest Governors' Conference on Mental Health in Chicago on November 30. It was a regional duplicate of the National Governors' Conference on Mental Health, and it adopted a series of resolutions to implement the earlier Ten Point Program. One of the major points stressed was that an additional 10 per cent of total state funds for mental health should be appropriated for training and research. A continuing Midwest Governors' Committee on Mental Health was formed in 1955 to strengthen regional cooperation in the area.

States in the far West also have moved for cooperation in mental health. At a meeting in March, 1955, of Governors' representatives in San Francisco, the Western Interstate Commission for Higher Education was requested to undertake an appraisal of training and research resources in the West, and of preventive efforts. The Governors of the eleven western states have appointed official committees representing government, the professions and the public, to conduct the survey, which has been aided by a grant of $61,000 from the National Institute of Mental Health. It is expected that its report will present both factual findings and new ideas for a more effective attack on mental health problems in the West.

The northeastern states have developed a continuing regional conference in line with the recommendations of the Ten Point Program. In October, 1954, a well-established conference of state mental health authorities in that area decided to enlarge its purposes and membership and altered its name to the Northeast State Governments Conference on Mental Health. Participation was expanded to include Governors' representatives, legislators, budget officers and other state administrators—who now have a means for fruitful exchange of ideas and experience. Meeting in Burlington, Vermont, in September, 1955, the Northeast Conference adopted a resolution proposing, for all states, an interstate compact to deal with the problem of non-resident mental patients. The compact provides that a person needing hospitalization because of mental illness or mental deficiency will receive care and treatment regardless of his legal residence and may be transferred to a hospital in another state solely on the basis of clinical considerations. It also permits cooperative interstate arrangements for after-care of

MAJOR STATE SERVICES 309

convalescing patients and for development of joint facilities. The compact was introduced in the legislatures of a number of states in 1955 and passed in Connecticut.

MENTAL HOSPITALS

The attempt in the last two years to secure personnel needed to staff institutions and clinics has reached record proportions as measured by funds provided. In a survey of appropriations for maintenance and operation of mental hospitals, the Council of State Governments found that thirty-eight of forty-two states from which replies were received had increased their appropriations in 1955, and primarily to obtain needed additional personnel. Probably no objective is rated higher today than that of attracting and retaining, with adequate salaries and incentives, more persons in the mental health fields.

Increases in state appropriations averaged around 10 per cent and ranged up to 45 per cent. Among states which raised appropriations for maintenance and operation of mental hospitals by roughly 25 per cent or more were Connecticut, Indiana, Missouri, Nevada, Ohio, Tennessee, Washington and Wyoming. At least twelve additional states increased their budgets by from 10 to 25 per cent; these included Arizona, Colorado, Florida, Illinois, Iowa, Maine, Montana, Nebraska, New Mexico, North Carolina, North Dakota, and Utah.

In Indiana, for example, appropriations for operation of the state hospitals and schools were increased by 40 per cent for 1955–57, as compared with 1953–55. And the amount allocated for salaries at these institutions went up by an even greater figure—49.3 per cent. From June, 1953 to June, 1955, the number of physicians in Indiana state hospitals rose from 56 to 90; psychologists from 23 to 40; social workers from 20 to 59; nurses from 91 to 168.

Connecticut increased its appropriation from $27 million in 1953–55 to $33.6 million for 1955–57. Per patient cost per day went up from $3.96 in 1954 to an estimated $4.20 in 1955, and estimates for 1956 and 1957 are $4.87 and $4.97 respectively. These increases are prompted primarily by a desire to improve staffing ratios generally and to staff new buildings which will be completed in the present biennium.

Missouri's appropriation in 1955 for maintenance and operation of its five mental hospitals was increased from $19.5 million in the last biennium to $25.7 million, the largest item of increase being for personal services. Nevada raised its appropriation in 1955 by 27 per cent over the previous biennium, the increase to be used to meet higher operating and maintenance costs, and to provide better nursing care and more adequate salaries. In Washington the legislature increased mental hospital operating appropriations by approximately 31 per cent for the 1955–57 biennium; major purposes of the increase are to pay salaries of additional staff for new buildings and expanded programs, as well as to carry through a forty-hour week and meet new salary schedules following a reclassification. In Wyoming, appropriations for operating mental hospitals were increased 34 per cent; largely to secure additional psychiatrists, psychologists and registered nurses for the State Hospital.

Considerable sums were made available both from regular appropriations and special bond issues to improve and rehabilitate existing buildings and to construct new institutions. Thus California appropriated over $14 million for a new neuropsychiatric institute and new buildings at hospitals. In Massachusetts, the capital outlay appropriation in 1954 was $19 million and amounted to $8.9 million in 1955. A bond issue of $150 million for capital improvements was approved in Ohio in a November, 1955, general referendum, half of the proceeds earmarked for institutions in the Department of Mental Hygiene and Correction. Many other building programs were approved in other states.

MENTALLY DEFICIENT

The states in the last two years have been giving unprecedented attention to mental deficiency. Of thirty-four states from which the Council of State Governments received information in its survey, all except two increased appropriations for care and treatment of their mentally deficient. The average increase was close to 20 per cent. Increases of 40 per cent or more were provided in Florida, Indiana, Missouri, Montana and Tennessee; of 30 per cent or more in Connecticut, Maine, Washington and

Hawaii; of more than 20 per cent in Iowa, Ohio and Virginia.

Modern concepts, meantime, have been advanced for developing the potentials of the mentally deficient. The Arkansas legislature in 1955, for example, created the Arkansas Children's Colony for training and education of the mentally retarded. In Illinois the legislature appropriated $150,000 from the Mental Health Fund to provide halfway-houses for pre-release training of mentally deficient patients from its two state schools. In South Dakota, for the first time, a special appropriation of $50,000 was enacted for education of mentally handicapped children, to be administered by the Department of Public Instruction. In Tennessee the legislature appropriated $230,000 for a special training program for severely mentally retarded children, to be administered by the Department of Education; the money will be used to help counties provide approved instructional and training facilities and services for children who are not educable but trainable. The Texas legislature enacted a Mentally Retarded Persons Act which requires diagnosis and examination before admission and is designed to prevent mentally retarded patients from being misplaced in state mental hospitals.

Bond issues and appropriations for construction of facilities for the mentally deficient were numerous during the biennium.

MENTAL HEALTH SERVICES

Mental Health clinics have been established and extended in many states during the same period. State hospitals likewise have expanded their outpatient services. The concern for community mental health services is based on the assumption that through them it may be possible to contribute to mental health generally, to prevent unnecessary admissions to hospitals, and to increase the number of persons who can be discharged from mental hospitals.

Several states, including Arizona, Idaho, Missouri and Nevada, provided funds for community mental health services for the first time during the 1955 legislative sessions. In certain states, including Florida, Illinois, Indiana, North Carolina and Washington, appropriations for such services have been doubled or tripled, and in

others raised materially. Use of the state hospital for outpatient clinic services has expanded in many states.

Several states, including Indiana, Kentucky, Michigan, New York and Ohio, expanded their family care programs, to relieve overcrowding in state hospitals by placing as many patients as possible in suitable homes in the community.

The extent to which travelling clinics are being used is growing. For example, the Missouri legislature in 1955 appropriated $480,000 for establishment and operation of six travelling clinics to examine, diagnose and treat mentally ill persons on an outpatient basis. The travelling clinic consists of one psychiatrist, one psychiatric social worker, and such other persons as may be necessary. Similar action has been taken recently in Maine, Nebraska, Nevada, South Dakota and other states.

The largest single stride to date in this general area of mental health, however, was the adoption in 1954 of the New York Community Mental Health Services Act. It established a permanent system of state aid to local units of government for the support of community mental health services. The act provided for state matching of local expenditures, on a fifty-fifty basis, up to a maximum of $1.00 per capita of the local population. This may result in an expenditure of as much as $15 million a year in state funds. Provisions of the act fix responsibility for the community's mental health program in a single governmental agency, the local mental health board.

Other states which provide matching funds for local mental health purposes include Alabama, Connecticut, Illinois and Massachusetts.

TRAINING AND RESEARCH

Training and research were stressed by legislatures in 1955 as never before. Although it was impossible to secure valid comparative figures of total appropriations for training and research, the survey by the Council of State Governments in 1955 indicated that the availability of such funds had approximately doubled over 1953.

An interesting development was a trend to use of funds from patient fees — paid either by the patient or his responsible relatives—for research and training purposes. In some instances, as in Illinois, the fees are put into a special mental health fund. In Illinois this fund had accumulated by 1955 approximately $12 million for training and research purposes. Of this amount, $2.2 million was allocated for training programs during 1955–57, and almost $4 million for biological and social research. In addition, the state legislature appropriated $8 million from the fund to build a psychiatric research institute. Also in 1955 the Illinois legislature established a ten-member Psychiatric Training and Research Authority to train psychiatric personnel and to advance knowledge through research.

Ohio's legislature in 1955 authorized operation of a special Bureau of Research and Training in the Division of Mental Hygiene, with an appropriation of approximately $10 million, to secure and train professional personnel in an effort to intensify treatment, research and preventive measures. Three new institutes of training and research were created.

A number of other states initiated special councils to direct training and research programs. For example, in Delaware a State Board on Mental Health was set up to supervise a program of research and training. The Florida legislature provided $250,000 for a new council for research and training in psychiatry, clinical psychology, psychiatric social work and psychiatric nursing.

The Connecticut legislature allocated approximately $215,000 for the 1955–57 biennium for training and research. Of this amount, $42,000 will finance the work of a new Coordinator of Research and Training within the Department of Mental Health; the remaining sum will cover expenses for training at the Connecticut Postgraduate Seminar in Psychiatry and Neurology as well as for employment of consultants in various specialties.

In Kansas training programs in the state mental institutions were authorized to receive allocations from the Mental Hospital Training Fund, for which the legislature appropriated $750,000 in 1955. Research projects in institutions also may receive allocations from this fund. Directors of Research and Education have been employed at two state hospitals, and a number of research projects are under way. Others are being considered.

In Nebraska the Psychiatric Institute serves as the core of its mental health training program. Appropriations for 1955–56 approximated $1 million for the Institute, which now offers training in psychiatry, clinical psychology, social services and allied fields. The legislature earmarked $60,000 for research. A state-wide program of basic and applied psychiatric investigation is being organized by a full-time Director of Research, who also serves as Associate Director for the Institute and Professor of Psychiatry at the University of Nebraska Medical School.

New Jersey established a Bureau of Research in Psychiatry and Neurology, with an appropriation of $50,000 a year. The Louisiana legislature appropriated $100,000 for research in mental illness and established a Committee on Research and Therapy to integrate research projects in mental hospitals.

Many states are setting aside sizeable sums for research in the application of new tranquillizing drugs, which have achieved remarkable results in opening therapeutic programs for patients previously considered hopeless. In Kentucky the Governor allotted $100,000 to supplement the drug budgets for the purchase of chlorpromazine and reserpine. In Louisiana, approximately $500,000 was appropriated for drug therapy. Other states that are concentrating research in this area include California, Illinois, Indiana, Michigan and New York.

LEGISLATIVE DEVELOPMENTS

The mental health codes of the various states have received careful scrutiny and analysis in the last two years to assure more adequate legal and medical protection for patients. States that have adopted legislation to modernize their codes in this period include Florida, Indiana, Massachusetts, Minnesota, Missouri, Nevada, New York, North Carolina, Ohio, Oklahoma, Oregon, South Dakota, Texas and Virginia. The Texas legislature in 1955 adopted a constitutional amendment prohibiting mandatory jury trials in the commitment of mental patients. In Arkansas a 1955 statute provides for day care of patients.

Several state legislatures enacted provisions for reorganization of certain activities. In Connecticut the responsibility for licensing mental hospitals and boarding and convalescent homes for mental patients was transferred from the Health Department to the Department of Mental Health. The Bureau of Mental Hygiene also was transferred from the Health Department to the Department of Mental Health as a Division of Community Services. In Delaware the Commission for the Feebleminded was dissolved in 1955, and the operation of the Delaware Colony was placed under the State Psychiatrist. A major reorganization was undertaken in Idaho in 1955; following a report of a Legislative Interim Committee, a Board of Health was created and all mental health facilities placed under it.

The Washington legislature in 1955 set up a new Department of Institutions responsible for mental health, adult correction, veterans' homes and services for children and youth. In Nebraska greater coordination was effected by vesting the Director of the Psychiatric Institute with the functions of Director of Mental Health for the Board of Control. The Tennessee legislature placed boarding homes and schools for the mentally deficient under the integrated Department of Mental Health. In New York an amendment to the mental hygiene law in 1955 broadened the powers of the Commissioner of Mental Hygiene to include the areas of research, education, prevention and rehabilitation in the field of mental health.

STUDY COMMISSIONS

Legislatures in many states in 1955 appointed legislative or other committees and commissions to study problems concerned with various aspects of mental health. The legislatures of California, Florida, Illinois, Kansas, Maryland, Massachusetts, Minnesota, North Dakota, Washington and Wyoming requested studies of the care and treatment of the mentally ill, with particular emphasis on the effects of tranquillizing drugs. Those of Arkansas, Illinois, Minnesota and Tennessee called for investigations of alcoholism. Care and facilities for the mentally retarded are being studied in Massachusetts, Nebraska and New York. Surveys of sex crime are being made in New Jersey, Oregon and Tennessee. Massachusetts is continuing a study of the advisability of making psychiatric services available to the district courts.

SOCIAL SECURITY IN THE STATES*

WITH the signing of the Social Security Amendments of 1954 on September 1, 1954, major liberalizations in the Old-Age and Survivors Insurance program were enacted, as well as two provisions affecting the public assistance programs. The amendments to the insurance program were reflected in the operations of both programs during the fiscal year that ended June, 1955.

In 1955 no major amendments to the Social Security Act were passed.

Old-Age and Survivors Insurance

COVERAGE

At the end of 1953 the Old-Age and Survivors Insurance program covered about eight out of ten of the nation's jobs. Under the 1954 amendments about nine out of ten gainfully employed persons will be able to build survivor and retirement protection under the program. Under the 1954 law, coverage was extended to virtually all the gainfully employed (including the self-employed). Still excluded are self-employed lawyers, physicians, dentists and members of several other medically related professions. Other major groups still outside the program are members of the Armed Forces (except for service in specified periods), most federal civilian employees, and policemen and firemen covered by a state or local government retirement system.

EMPLOYEES OF STATE AND LOCAL GOVERNMENTS

Most employees of state and local governments (except policemen and firemen covered by a state or local retirement plan) may be covered under Old-Age and Survivors Insurance if the state enters into an agreement with the Secretary of Health, Education, and Welfare for this purpose.

*Prepared by The Social Security Administration, U. S. Department of Health, Education, and Welfare.

Under the agreement, the state consents to make the necessary reports and to pay the employer's share of the federal insurance contribution.

The old law excluded from coverage under such an agreement employees in positions covered by a state or local retirement system (other than Wisconsin's) on the date the agreement was made applicable to the coverage groups to which they belonged. The 1954 law permits a state to bring members of a state or local system under its coverage agreement if a referendum by secret written ballot is held among the system's members and a majority of those eligible to vote cast their vote for coverage.

A state may cover without a referendum employees who are in positions covered by a retirement system but are not eligible for membership and, before January 1, 1958, employees not currently under a retirement system who could not have been covered when their coverage group was brought in because they had then been under a retirement system.

A state may hold a referendum among all the members of a retirement system or it may treat any political subdivision or any combination of political subdivisions as having a separate retirement system. Each public institution of higher learning may also be considered as having a separate retirement system.

Special provision is made for covering under an agreement, at the option of the state, civilian employees of state national guard units and certain inspectors of agricultural products. The 1954 law also provided specially for coverage of certain educational institution employees in Utah and retroactive coverage of members of the Arizona Teachers' Retirement System.

In general, employees made eligible for coverage by the 1954 amendments could not be covered before January 1, 1955. Coverage may be made retroactive to the beginning of 1955 for employees coming under the state agreement at any time in 1955, 1956 or 1957. This provision avoids penalizing employees in those states in which legislative action cannot be completed until 1957.

As of June, 1955, forty-four states, three territories and thirteen interstate instrumentalities had completed coverage agreements. It is estimated that at the end of the fiscal year 1955 about 1,210,000, or 29 per cent of the eligible employees, were covered under these agreements. About 395,000 of these employees were also covered by a state or local retirement system. The majority had this dual coverage as a result of the dissolution of a previous retirement system and its reinstatement after Old-Age and Survivors Insurance coverage was secured; some had no previous protection but were brought under a new retirement system after they were covered under Old-Age and Survivors insurance; the remainder were covered under the referendum provision of the 1954 amendments. By the end of September, 1955, two additional states and one interstate instrumentality had completed agreements, and the members of two more state retirement systems had been covered under the referendum provisions.

Benefit Amounts

Benefit levels were raised significantly by the 1954 amendments, both for those already on the rolls and for those qualifying thereafter. For retired workers on the rolls in September, 1954, monthly payments ranged from $30 to $98.50, compared with $25 to $85 under the old law; the average increase was about $6.00. Other types of benefits increased proportionately. For persons coming on the rolls in the future higher benefits will result from use of the 1954 formula, the higher earnings base under the new law, and the new provisions for dropping out years of lowest earnings or periods of prolonged total disability in computing average monthly earnings.

The amount payable to persons entitled to monthly benefits is based on the individual's average covered earnings over whichever of several periods specified in the law yields the largest benefit amount.

Under the 1954 amendments, nearly all persons coming on the rolls may drop from the computation of their average earnings up to four years of low or no earnings (those with twenty covered quarters may drop five years). Persons already on the rolls who have six quarters of coverage after June, 1953 may have their benefits recomputed to take advantage of the dropout provision. (By the end of August, 1955, almost one-sixth of the old-age beneficiaries receiving benefits were eligible for the dropout.)

The amendments also provide that individuals meeting specified conditions relating to covered employment may have periods of prolonged total disability disregarded in determining their insured status and in computing their average earnings. Persons already on the rolls who meet the requirements and apply before July, 1957 may have their benefits recomputed to eliminate such periods of disability and receive any increases in their benefit amounts retroactively to July, 1955. (In that month an estimated 15,000 old-age beneficiaries received increases from disability freeze recomputations.)

After the adoption of the 1954 amendments the Bureau of Old-Age and Survivors Insurance and the states began working together to develop agreements under which a state agency would make the determinations of disability for the purposes of this provision. At the end of September, 1955, all jurisdictions except the Virgin Islands had designated agencies to make these determinations. In most of the states the vocational rehabilitation agency is the designated agency; in a few the public welfare department, either alone or with the rehabilitation agency, makes the determination. By the end of September, 1955 the Commissioner of Social Security had approved agreements with fifty-two of the agencies designated, representing forty-eight jurisdictions; forty-nine of the agencies were already making disability determinations under these agreements. By August 31, 1955, a freeze period had been established for about 25,000 applicants.

The 1954 amendments provide a benefit formula that applies to most benefit computations after August, 1954. The benefit amount under the present formula is 55 per cent of the first $110 of the "average monthly wage" plus 20 per cent of the next $240. Persons on the rolls in August, 1954 had their benefits increased by use of a conversion table in the law. Those coming on the rolls later who are not eligible to use the new formula have their benefits computed by means of the 1939 or 1952 formula used with the conversion table.

Under the 1954 law the minimum benefit payable to a retired worker (or to a sole survivor beneficiary) is $30. The benefits payable to a family cannot exceed $200.

All dependents' and survivor benefits are a fixed proportion of the worker's benefit. Within the family maximum, a wife, dependent aged husband, or child receives one-half the retired worker's primary insurance amount; a widow, dependent aged widower, or dependent aged parent, if eligible, receives three-fourths of the primary amount; surviving children each receive one-half and an additional fourth is divided among them.

To acquire "fully insured" status and qualify for retirement benefits and survivor protection for his family, a worker must have received covered wages of as much as $50 or have been credited with covered self-employment income of as much as $100 in at least six calendar quarters and in as many as half the number of calendar quarters elapsed between December, 1950 (or later attainment of age 21) and the quarter in which he reaches age 65 or dies. Under the 1954 amendments in specified circumstances, periods of prolonged total disability may be omitted from the elapsed quarters. When a worker has forty covered quarters he is fully insured for life. Quarters of coverage may be earned at any time after 1936.

Under the present law, a worker who does not meet these requirements will nevertheless be fully insured if all quarters after 1954 and up to July 1, 1956, or up to the quarter of death or attainment of age 65, if later, are covered quarters (a minimum of six quarters after 1954 is required).

The 1954 amendments also provided that a worker who died uninsured after 1939 and before September 1, 1950, but who had at least six quarters of coverage, is deemed to have died fully insured and his eligible survivors may qualify for benefits.

A worker is "currently insured" and his family may qualify for survivor benefits if he has six quarters of coverage in the period consisting of the quarter in which he died or became entitled to old-age benefits and the twelve quarters immediately preceding that quarter.

As a step to protect the insurance status of veterans of military service since World War II, the 1952 amendments provided wage credits of $160 for each month of service from July 25, 1947, through December 31, 1953. Legislation in 1953 extended the effective period to July 1, 1955. In the only legislation amending the Social Security Act in 1955, the effective period was extended to March 31, 1956.

FINANCING O.A.S.I.

Under the 1954 amendments, the maximum amount of taxable earnings is $4,200 a year. For the period 1937–50 it was $3,000 a year and for the years 1951–53 it was $3,600. The tax schedule in the present law provides for a rate of 2 per cent each for employer and employee through 1959; for 1960–64 the rates are 2.5 per cent each; for 1965–69, 3 per cent each; for 1970–74, 3.5 per cent; in 1975 and thereafter, 4 per cent each. The rate of contribution for the self-employed is 1.5 times employee rate.

Public Assistance

Two provisions of the 1954 amendments related to the public assistance programs. One extended through September 30, 1956, the provisions in the 1952 law, scheduled to expire September 30, 1954, that increased the rate of federal participation in all the special types of public assistance. A second amendment extended from June 30, 1955, to June 30, 1957, a provision that permits, during the specified period, approval of certain state plans for aid to the blind although such plans do not meet the requirements in the act regarding earned-income exemptions under that program.

EFFECT OF 1954 AMENDMENTS

The increase in Old-Age and Survivors Insurance benefits provided by the 1954 amendments had an almost immediate effect on public assistance caseloads and expenditures. In October most states started making initial adjustments in assistance payments to recipients who had been getting O.A.S.I. benefits; some states started in September. With few exceptions, reviews of the remaining cases were completed in November and December. For 86 per cent of the old-age assistance cases reviewed, the increases in Old-Age and Survivors Insurance benefits did not eliminate their need for aid but did result in a reduction in their assistance payments. Only 2 per cent of the cases were closed, and for the rest of the cases no reduction was made. In aid to dependent children more than seven out of ten of the cases reviewed had their payments reduced, almost a fourth of the cases had no reduction in payment, and about 3 per cent were closed.

Another liberalization of the O.A.S.I. program made by the 1954 amendments affected the assistance programs to a limited extent—the provision making benefits payable to survivors of insured workers who died after 1939 and before September, 1950 and who had at least six quarters of coverage though they were not fully insured under the act at that time.

Perhaps the change in the Old-Age and Survivors Insurance program most significant in its effect on public assistance is the extension of coverage to about 10 million additional persons. The largest of the newly covered groups is made up of farm operators and additional farm workers. A large proportion of the O.A.A. recipients come from agricultural groups. With coverage for the first time almost universal, the number of needy aged who are dependent on public assistance is expected to diminish. Eventually, most of the retired aged will be receiving O.A.S.I. benefits, and only those beneficiaries who have high medical care costs or other special needs that cannot be met by their benefits or other resources will need old-age assistance.

CONCURRENT RECEIPT OF ASSISTANCE PAYMENTS AND O.A.S.I. BENEFITS

With liberalizations in the Old-Age and Survivors Insurance program in 1950, 1952 and 1954, the proportion of the aged population receiving insurance benefits has increased continuously. The rate was 177 per 1,000 persons aged 65 and over in September, 1950, and in February, 1955 it was 394 per 1,000. The number of old-age assistance recipients declined from 226 per 1,000 in the aged population in September, 1950 to 179 per 1,000 in February, 1955.

In September, 1950 about 13 per cent of the aged O.A.S.I. beneficiaries were also receiving old-age assistance; by February, 1955 less than 9 per cent of aged beneficiaries were getting both types of payments. Since the number with both types

Aged persons and families with children receiving both OASI benefits and assistance payments, 1948-55

| Month and year | Aged persons receiving both OASI and OAA | | | Families with children receiving both OASI and ADC | | |
| | | Per cent of— | | | Per cent of— | |
	Number	Aged OASI beneficiaries	OAA recipients	Number	OASI beneficiary families with children	ADC families
June, 1948	146,000	10.0	6.1	21,600	6.7	4.8
September, 1950	276,200	12.6	9.8	32,300	8.3	4.9
August, 1951	376,500	11.9	13.8	30,700	6.7	5.0
February, 1952	406,000	12.0	15.1	30,000	6.1	5.0
February, 1953	426,500	10.7	16.3	30,600	5.7	5.3
February, 1954	463,000	9.7	18.0	31,900[a]	5.4	5.9
February, 1955	488,800	8.7	19.2	32,100	4.9	5.2

Source: *Social Security Bulletin*, September, 1955.
[a]Data on ADC-OASI families are for November, 1953; OASI families for February, 1954.

1010

of payments has been rising at a time when old-age assistance caseloads have been declining, these individuals represent an increasing proportion of the total on the old-age assistance rolls.

Differences among the states in the relative number of aged persons receiving both types of payments reflect differences in the proportion of aged O.A.S.I. beneficiaries among the aged population and in assistance standards and levels.

Because few families receiving aid to dependent children are potentially eligible for O.A.S.I. benefits, liberalization of the insurance program does not tend to reduce the size of the caseload in aid to dependent children to the extent that it does for old-age assistance. In September, 1950 families with children, receiving payments under both programs, represented a little less than 5 per cent of the families getting aid to dependent children; in February, 1955 the proportion was only slightly higher (5.2 per cent). In aid to dependent children, as in old-age assistance, the number of Old-Age and Survivors Insurance beneficiary families getting assistance declined as the total number of O.A.S.I. beneficiaries increased. In September, 1950, 8 per cent of the O.A.S.I. beneficiary families with children were on the aid to dependent children rolls; by February, 1955 the proportion had dropped to 4.9 per cent.

O.A.S.I. Benefits and P.A. Payments

Monthly benefits paid under Old-Age and Survivors Insurance in the fiscal year 1955 amounted to $4,233 million, and lump-sum death payments totaled $100 million. In the twelve-month period since August, 1954—the last month for which benefits were paid at the old rate—the number of benefits in current-payment status went up more than 1.1 million. In August, 1955, 7.7 million persons were receiving monthly benefits at a monthly rate of $395 million—38 per cent more than the rate before the increase in the 1954 amendments became effective.

Payments to recipients of assistance—including vendor payments for medical care—in the fiscal year 1955 totaled $2,712,334,000. Of this, $2,426,703,000 went for recipients in the four categories

financed with state and federal funds jointly. In addition, general assistance, financed without federal participation, paid out $285,631,000 to needy persons not included in the four categories. The federal share in categorical assistance was 55.8 per cent for old-age assistance; 57.4 per cent for aid to dependent children; 49.4 per cent for aid to the blind. Thirty-nine states, the District of Columbia, Hawaii, Puerto Rico and the Virgin Islands received federal funds for aid to the permanently and totally disabled during the fiscal year 1955, and the federal share in the payments made under these plans was 50.4 per cent.

In August, 1955, 2,554,663 individuals were receiving old-age assistance; 2,199,223 persons, including 607,856 adult relatives, were getting aid to dependent children; 104,164 were recipients of aid to the blind; and 240,396 were receiving aid to the permanently and totally disabled.

Expenditures for Social Security and Related Programs

In the fiscal year ended June, 1954, expenditures from federal, state and local funds for social security and related programs totaled $18,117 million. This total may be considered under the following four headings:

1. For the group of social insurance and related programs, federal funds constituted about 70 per cent of the $10,746 million expended. The largest item in this category is the $3,364 million paid under the Old-Age and Survivors Insurance program.

2. For the programs classified as public aid, state and local funds met 49.3 per cent of the $2,775 million expended.

3. Nearly 71 per cent of the $3,617 million spent for health and medical services came from state and local funds.

4. State and local funds accounted for 72 per cent of the expenditures for other welfare services.

Of the total spent for all programs, about 60 per cent came from federal funds.

Administration of the Social Security Program

The basic programs and administrative programs of the Social Security Administration were not changed by the 1954 amendments to the Social Security Act. The Bureau of Public Assistance administers the federal aspects of the special types of public assistance. The other bureaus in the administration are the Bureau of Old-Age and Survivors Insurance, the Children's Bureau, and the Bureau of Federal Credit Unions. The federal aspects of the unemployment insurance program under the Social Security Act are the responsibility of the Bureau of Employment Security in the Department of Labor.

Information on the operation of the programs for which the Social Security Administration has direct responsibility and on related programs are reported monthly in the *Social Security Bulletin* and its *Annual Statistical Supplement* as well as in annual reports to Congress.

In the fiscal year ended June, 1955, the fifty-three jurisdictions included in the grant-in-aid programs under the Social Security Act received $1,667 million in federal funds.

The Aged

Estimates by the Bureau of the Census indicate that there were 13.9 million persons aged 65 and over in the continental United States in December, 1954. The distribution, by type, of the money income of the aged shows the growth in importance of public income maintenance programs for this group of the population. There were about 3.9 million who were receiving income from employment, about 6.6 million from social insurance and related programs (5.3 million of them under old-age and survivors insurance), and 2.6 million from public assistance. Some of them had income from more than one of these sources. Between the end of 1951 and the end of 1954, the number with no income from employment (either as earners or as wives of earners) or from a public income-maintenance program dropped from 2.7 million to 2.0 million.

The number of old-age assistance recipients in the continental United States has declined about 250,000 between December, 1950 and December, 1954, while the aged population has increased almost 1.5 million. The program is still of great importance, however, for many of the aged—especially widows. In a 1953 study of old-age assistance recipients, for 40 per cent of those with no spouse (or one not getting old-age assistance) their total cash income, including assistance payments, was less than $55 a month. Even for those in this group who were getting an old-age and survivors insurance benefit as well as old-age assistance, more than 16 per cent had less than $55 in cash income.

TABLE 1

EXPENDITURES FOR CIVILIAN SOCIAL SECURITY AND RELATED PUBLIC PROGRAMS, BY SOURCE OF FUNDS AND BY PROGRAM, FISCAL YEARS 1952–53 AND 1953–54*(a)

(In millions; data corrected to Aug. 10, 1955)

Program	1953–54			1952–53		
	Total	Federal	State and local	Total	Federal	State and local
Total	$18,117.4	$10,286.1	$7,831.3	$16,271.8	$9,426.9	$6,844.9
Social insurance and related programs	10,745.6	7,554.2	3,191.3	9,052.9	6,666.8	2,386.2
Old-age and survivors insurance	3,364.2	3,364.2	......	2,716.9	2,716.9	......
Railroad retirement	518.1	518.1	......	466.5	466.5	......
Public employee retirement systems(b)	1,251.8	736.8	515.0	1,124.9	664.9	460.0
Employment security(c)	1,798.0	209.1	1,588.8	1,117.4	204.5	912.9
Railroad unemployment insurance	100.4	100.4	......	57.8	57.8	......
Railroad temporary disability insurance	45.8	45.8	......	45.4	45.4	......
State temporary disability insurance, total(d)	211.7	......	211.7	197.9	......	197.9
Hospitalization and medical benefits(e)	17.6	......	17.6	14.9		14.9
Veterans' programs(f)	2,534.1	2,534.1	......	2,467.2	2,467.2	......
Workmen's compensation, total	921.5	45.7	875.8(g)	858.9	43.6	815.4(g)
Hospitalization and medical benefits(e)	290.0	6.3	283.7	270.0	6.0	264.0
Public aid	2,774.7	1,406.7	1,368.0	2,725.9	1,358.8	1,367.1
Special types of public assistance, total(h)	2,517.2	1,406.7	1,110.5	2,476.6	1,358.8	1,117.8
Vendor payments for medical care(e,i)	120.7	......	......	103.3	......	......
General assistance, total	257.5	......	257.5	249.3	......	249.3
Vendor payments for medical care(e,i)	54.7	......	......	51.3	......	......
Health and medical services(j)	3,616.9	1,053.0	2,563.9	3,474.3	1,079.1	2,395.2
Hospital and medical care(k)	2,222.3	756.4	1,465.9	2,029.4	716.3	1,313.2
Veterans	687.9	687.9	......	647.4	647.4	......
Other	1,534.4	68.5	1,465.9	1,382.0	68.8	1,313.2
Hospital construction(l)	410.3	148.3	262.0	510.4	201.4	309.0
Veterans	52.2	52.2	......	90.0	90.0	......
Other	358.1	96.1	262.0	420.4	111.4	309.0
Maternal and child health services(m)	90.0	24.0	66.0	39.8	26.9	13.0
Other community and related health services(n)	894.3	124.3	770.0(o)	894.6	134.6	760.0
Other welfare services	980.3	272.2	708.1	1,018.7	322.2	696.4
Vocational rehabilitation, total	34.9	21.8	13.1	34.6	22.9	11.6
Medical rehabilitation(e)	8.7	4.3	4.3	8.9	4.4	4.4
Veterans' programs(p)	250.9	148.1	102.8	311.2	197.1	114.1
Institutional and other care(q)	423.0	13.0	410.0	412.4	12.4	400.0
School lunch(r)	145.1	82.1	63.0	139.1	82.0	57.2
Child welfare	126.4	7.2	119.2(s)	121.4	7.7	113.6(s)

*Prepared by The Social Security Administration, U. S. Department of Health, Education, and Welfare. *Source:* Data taken or estimated from Treasury reports, federal budgets, and available reports of federal, state, and local administrative agencies.

(a) Data represent reported or estimated expenditures from public funds (general and special) and trust accounts and other expenditures under public law; exclude transfers to such accounts and loans, and include administrative expenditures unless otherwise noted. Fiscal years ended June 30 for federal government, most states, and some localities (and for estimates of state and local governments supplied by federal administrative agencies); for other states and localities fiscal years cover various 12-month periods ended within the specified year.

(b) Excludes refunds of employee contributions to those leaving service. Includes retirement pay of military personnel. Data for administrative expenses not available for all programs.

(c) Represents unemployment insurance and employment service programs.

(d) Represents cash benefits and hospitalization and medical benefits, including those paid under private plans, in the 4 states with programs. Includes state costs of administering state plans and of supervising private plans; data on administrative expenditures of private plans underwritten by private insurance carriers or self-insured not available.

(e) Included in total shown directly above; excludes administrative expenditures, not separately available but included for whole program in preceding line.

(f) Represents pensions, annuities, burial awards, readjustment allowances, and estimated administrative expenditures for these payments; excludes expenditures from the government life insurance fund.

(g) Represents payments by private insurance carriers, state funds, and self-insurers of benefits payable under state law and estimated costs of state administration.

(h) Old-age assistance, aid to the blind, aid to dependent children, and aid to the permanently and totally disabled.

(i) Represents payments made directly to suppliers of medical care and services on behalf of assistance recipients; excludes expenditures for medical care made by recipients. For 1953–54, estimated expenditures from public assistance funds for medical care of recipients (including vendor payments) totaled $280 million—$225 million for recipients of special types of assistance and $55 million for general assistance recipients. Data on source of funds for these payments not available.

(j) Excludes all medical expenditures (health services and research) of the Military Establishment and the Atomic Energy Commission; health services provided in connection with primary and secondary public education; hospital and medical payments and services included under workmen's compensation, state temporary disability insurance, and vocational rehabilitation, and vendor payments for medical care included in public aid programs, all shown elsewhere in the table; international health activities; and expenditures for medical services and research subordinate to the performance of other functions such as those of the Department of Agriculture and the Civil Aeronautics Authority.

(k) Includes hospital and outpatient care in public institutions and expenditures for maintenance of existing facilities. Excludes expenditures for domiciliary care by the Veterans Administration included under veterans' welfare services below and institutions for chronic care (other than mental and tuberculosis) included under institutional and other care below.

(l) Federal expenditures include cost of hospital planning and surveys, new construction, and major repairs; state and local expenditures represent new construction only.

(m) Federal expenditures are for maternal and child health services, services for crippled children, and estimated federal administrative costs for these programs. Beginning 1953–54, state and local expenditures represent estimated total costs attributable to these programs. In 1952–53 state and local expenditures represent required matching of federal grants for the two programs. Estimated expenditures above the matching requirements and state-local administrative expenditures for 1952–53 are included under state and local expenditures for other community and related health services.

(n) Federal expenditures represent those made by the National Institutes of Health and other units of the U. S. Public Health Service for community health programs, medical research, and training in special public health fields, and by the Food and Drug Administration; state and local expenditures represent estimated community health and sanitation operating expenditures of public agencies, including those for medical research and public health training but excluding those made in connection with schools and public welfare, and those classified as hospital and medical care. For 1953–54 excludes all expenditures under maternal and child health and crippled children's services; for 1952–53 excludes only the required matching expenditures for the two programs.

(o) Data for 1953–54 not comparable with 1952–53. See footnote (m).

(p) Federal expenditures are for Veterans Administration programs for vocational rehabilitation, automobiles and other conveyances for disabled veterans, housing for paraplegic veterans, domiciliary care, beneficiaries' travel, counseling, and loan guarantees. State and local expenditures represent state expenditures for bonus payments and services for veterans; local data not available.

(q) Federal expenditures are for education of the blind and the deaf, the U. S. Soldiers' Home, and the U. S. Naval Home, and federal funds for state soldiers' homes. State and local expenditures represent estimated costs of care in welfare institutions, institutions for the handicapped and for long-term chronic care (other than mental and tuberculosis hospitals), and other public welfare expenditures; local data not fully available, so estimates may be understated.

(r) Nongovernmental funds are also available for this program from private organizations and payments by parents; for 1952–53 they totaled $322 million; for 1953–54, $355 million.

(s) Estimated data for 1952–53 and 1953–54 based on studies made in 1953 and 1954, respectively (42 states reporting). Includes expenditures for care of children in foster homes and institutions.

TABLE 2

FEDERAL GRANTS TO STATES UNDER THE SOCIAL SECURITY ACT: CHECKS ISSUED BY THE TREASURY DEPARTMENT IN FISCAL YEARS 1953–54 AND 1954–55*

(In thousands)

State	Total, fiscal year 1953–54	Fiscal year 1954–55									
		Total	Per capita(a)	Old-age assistance	Aid to the permanently and totally disabled(c)	Aid to dependent children	Aid to the blind	Employment security(d)	Maternal and child health services	Services for crippled children	Child welfare services
Total..........	$1,667,029.7	$1,644,683.1	$10.12(b)	$920,357.8	$82,225.7	$387,599.6	$36,415.9	$188,827.2	$11,919.3	$10,613.1	$6,724.4
Alabama........	30,665.7	33,029.0	10.58	18,334.3	2,988.9	7,512.8	477.7	2,707.5	441.3	344.3	222.2
Arizona........	11,071.7	11,253.8	11.33	5,559.5	....	3,551.1	306.1	1,681.7	87.9	....	67.5
Arkansas.......	22,652.4	24,470.9	12.81	15,686.1	1,280.6	4,333.6	654.5	1,872.3	222.3	261.6	160.0
California......	191,680.5	181,344.8	14.45	112,727.4	....	42,825.6	5,367.5	19,312.4	563.5	376.8	171.6
Colorado.......	28,298.2	28,728.6	19.73	20,038.5	2,180.7	4,522.3	132.8	1,486.0	188.8	99.1	80.3
Connecticut....	13,371.4	14,715.8	6.63	7,000.1	742.7	3,486.2	129.6	2,968.0	130.3	191.2	67.8
Delaware.......	2,064.5	2,009.0	5.47	547.2	75.2	694.0	90.7	404.4	86.6	70.4	40.5
Florida........	42,140.7	38,325.6	10.88	23,402.9	....	10,406.5	1,032.1	2,895.3	263.0	191.3	134.6
Georgia........	47,222.6	49,206.9	13.44	31,981.8	3,024.7	9,460.7	1,196.8	2,581.5	357.2	392.5	211.7
Idaho..........	6,945.3	6,302.4	10.25	3,304.7	346.4	1,397.9	77.3	976.6	91.3	78.7	29.6
Illinois........	69,470.1	69,623.1	7.60	39,161.8	2,673.8	16,844.5	1,562.1	8,529.5	327.7	349.8	174.0
Indiana........	24,353.6	23,391.0	5.56	12,586.5	....	6,378.6	716.8	3,234.4	228.1	145.0	92.5
Iowa..........	23,878.2	23,186.7	8.79	15,966.4	1,343.8	4,686.5	604.1	1,430.2	192.4	206.3	100.9
Kansas........	21,871.8	20,485.1	10.16	13,921.0	....	3,253.9	265.8	1,343.8	124.3	121.9	110.6
Kentucky......	34,278.2	32,245.3	10.77	17,177.3	....	11,010.0	935.1	2,233.8	309.1	355.0	224.9
Louisiana......	68,429.0	67,626.5	23.13	48,006.0	4,389.3	11,319.3	754.5	2,414.3	308.3	266.1	168.7
Maine.........	9,921.0	9,263.4	9.96	4,756.2	....	3,074.2	225.8	956.3	92.6	89.0	69.3
Maryland......	13,723.4	14,340.0	5.51	3,733.8	1,669.8	5,037.5	178.3	3,030.1	325.0	264.8	100.7
Massachusetts..	58,174.8	62,845.7	12.69	38,769.4	4,545.4	10,220.6	699.8	7,985.1	371.7	168.6	85.1
Michigan......	57,388.3	55,075.2	7.84	28,944.6	894.3	14,224.0	732.6	9,373.3	336.3	298.0	222.0
Minnesota.....	28,822.8	28,931.4	9.32	19,321.5	239.3	5,525.2	517.8	2,746.1	227.2	201.1	153.2
Mississippi....	24,986.1	26,956.9	12.23	18,215.4	753.0	4,246.7	1,037.4	1,866.2	319.0	314.7	204.6
Missouri.......	82,124.8	77,011.1	18.54	52,717.9	5,868.9	13,285.4	1,389.2	3,099.4	241.4	240.4	168.5
Montana.......	7,927.3	7,148.0	11.38	3,583.1	624.4	1,597.0	194.3	907.9	84.3	104.5	52.5

Nebraska	10,867.9	10,046.7	7.35	6,780.8	.....	4,898.7	297.3	829.8	93.6	97.7	48.7
Nevada	1,900.9	1,929.2	8.85	1,112.8	.....	26.4	47.9	573.5	73.1	59.7	35.7
New Hampshire	4,824.7	4,720.9	8.87	2,430.1	96.8	768.7	107.6	1,115.2	68.4	67.8	48.3
New Jersey	20,639.0	24,772.9	4.72	8,206.7	1,331.1	3,959.5	372.5	10,489.5	169.2	162.4	82.0
New Mexico	11,440.6	11,277.8	14.44	4,467.0	636.3	4,729.0	163.8	1,000.0	119.8	90.8	71.2
New York	133,256.7	135,790.0	8.80	42,882.4	18,078.7	44,518.7	2,067.0	27,247.6	445.2	333.7	216.8
North Carolina	36,344.5	35,914.8	8.45	14,796.1	3,368.6	11,312.8	1,746.4	3,375.3	518.3	472.0	325.3
North Dakota	5,272.5	5,492.6	8.64	3,116.6	351.3	1,132.4	47.7	604.0	85.7	88.8	66.1
Ohio	68,654.8	63,353.8	7.41	38,952.4	3,022.5	10,540.5	1,448.4	8,450.7	379.3	326.4	233.6
Oklahoma	52,860.8	52,806.5	23.28	37,626.2	2,111.0	9,509.8	836.1	2,199.2	161.5	226.6	136.0
Oregon	15,706.7	14,923.4	9.11	7,824.7	1,349.6	3,071.8	149.3	2,253.6	106.7	95.3	72.2
Pennsylvania	70,975.6	68,854.5	6.39	20,466.8	5,011.7	22,794.0	3,563.5	15,775.5	501.9	454.3	286.6
Rhode Island	7,420.5	8,530.8	10.35	3,387.6	631.9	2,591.5	82.9	1,618.5	88.0	91.0	39.3
South Carolina	21,607.1	21,977.3	9.82	12,596.5	2,197.4	3,882.9	565.1	2,008.6	258.6	279.5	188.7
South Dakota	6,843.1	6,954.3	10.43	3,987.5	260.6	1,957.5	76.6	435.0	86.6	79.2	71.3
Tennessee	38,959.1	38,933.7	11.58	20,780.8	548.5	12,930.4	1,143.1	2,698.8	341.7	272.4	218.1
Texas	96,410.8	98,072.5	11.58	73,601.4	734.2	13,347.0	2,388.2	7,472.0	528.2	404.6	331.0
Utah	8,429.1	8,478.5	11.20	3,738.7	.....	2,299.0	94.6	1,343.1	126.5	83.4	59.1
Vermont	4,140.5	4,266.5	11.08	2,481.1	171.5	754.2	61.4	612.0	71.1	64.0	51.1
Virginia	15,125.8	13,849.9	3.86	4,416.4	1,409.0	5,092.0	455.7	1,658.1	311.7	293.1	214.0
Washington	41,193.7	36,220.1	14.26	23,227.7	2,268.5	6,286.2	331.4	3,695.9	170.8	127.2	112.5
West Virginia	23,673.0	23,289.6	11.96	6,590.7	2,169.1	12,017.1	353.6	1,564.8	205.2	219.0	170.1
Wisconsin	28,606.7	25,600.2	7.15	15,565.2	469.2	5,764.3	469.8	2,698.2	218.4	244.0	171.2
Wyoming	2,998.0	2,943.2	9.43	1,630.5	189.9	410.5	28.3	517.9	70.1	66.8	29.3
District of Columbia	4,660.6	5,340.8	6.20	1,191.1	938.4	1,964.3	104.6	819.7	152.4	141.4	28.9
Alaska	2,301.1	2,384.4	.....	687.3	.....	839.8	25.2	570.1	91.2	142.4	28.8
Hawaii	4,338.5	4,449.6	.....	670.8	498.8	2,388.4	46.2	527.6	144.9	128.7	44.2
Puerto Rico	5,831.6	5,613.2	.....	1,539.2	724.3	1,841.1	57.5	604.6	341.7	303.8	200.8
Virgin Islands	293.4	378.9	.....	109.6	15.9	58.8	5.3	23.1	70.2	65.7	30.2

*Prepared by the Social Security Administration, U. S. Department of Health, Education, and Welfare. Source: Unpublished data of administrative agencies.

(a) Based on population data from the Bureau of the Census (Series P-25, No. 108), which exclude Armed Forces stationed overseas.

(b) Represents continental United States only.

(c) States for which no grant is shown either had no approved plan or state plan was approved too late to receive grant during this period.

(d) Excludes grants made to state employment security agencies as agents for the United States for the payment of unemployment compensation to veterans under the Veterans' Readjustment Assistance Act of 1952, operating costs of the District of Columbia Employment Center, and a small payment to Railroad Retirement Board for informational services to states.

TABLE 3

BENEFICIARIES AND BENEFITS UNDER SOCIAL INSURANCE AND RELATED PROGRAMS BY RISK AND PROGRAM, 1940–54*(a)

(Corrected to July 19, 1955)

Risk and program	1940	1947	1948	1949	1950	1951	1952	1953	1954
	Amount of benefits (in thousands)								
Total	$1,540,259	$5,392,333	$5,276,305	$6,555,410	$6,303,787	$6,835,351	$7,736,321	$8,947,630	$11,164,418
Old-age retirement	326,472	887,602	1,034,475	1,226,609	1,402,849	2,189,344	2,574,046	3,300,153	3,947,377
Old-age and survivors insurance (b)	17,150	287,554	352,022	437,420	651,409	1,321,061	1,539,327	2,175,311	2,697,982
Railroad retirement	83,342	138,517	150,148	168,915	176,925	187,085	267,343	281,656	324,910
Federal civil-service	49,069	81,877	101,426	123,717	135,267	152,428	175,616	209,327	233,105
Other federal contributory (c)	714	1,802	1,987	2,140	2,440	2,790	3,200	3,575	4,568
Federal noncontributory (d)	53,427	148,567	174,671	229,686	149,222	190,630	191,340	201,000	222,716
State and local government retirement (e)	103,900	175,000	190,000	203,000	230,000	273,000	310,000	343,000	385,000
Veterans' program (f)	19,770	54,285	64,221	61,731	57,586	62,350	87,220	86,284	79,096
Survivorship:	198,271	698,169	777,481	877,845	988,510	1,294,851	1,484,576	1,735,997	1,918,766
Monthly benefits:	161,515	619,194	695,678	794,566	901,817	1,178,742	1,353,558	1,569,655	1,744,484
Old-age and survivors insurance	6,371	149,179	171,837	196,586	276,945	506,803	591,504	743,536	879,952
Railroad retirement	1,448	19,283	36,011	39,257	43,884	49,527	74,085	83,319	93,201
Federal civil-service		217	918	4,317	8,409	14,014	19,986	27,325	32,530
State and local government retirement (e)	16,000	22,000	23,000	25,000	26,000	29,000	30,000	32,000	35,000
Veterans' program	32,000	46,000	50,000	52,000	55,000	60,000	65,000	70,000	75,000
Workmen's compensation (g)	105,696	382,515	413,912	477,406	491,579	519,398	572,983	613,475	628,801
Lump-sum payments:	36,756	78,975	81,803	83,279	86,693	116,109	131,018	166,342	174,282
Old-age and survivors insurance	11,833	29,460	32,315	33,158	32,740	57,337	63,298	87,451	92,229
Railroad retirement	2,497	6,114	8,914	11,480	12,722	12,716	13,745	18,409	16,330
Federal civil-service	5,810	13,732	10,869	7,864	8,147	7,755	8,364	8,850	8,957
Other federal contributory	156	399	347	350	375	416	469	514	573
State and local government retirement (e)	12,500	16,000	17,000	18,000	20,000	25,000	30,000	35,000	40,000
Veterans' program (f)	3,960	13,270	12,358	12,427	12,709	12,885	15,142	16,118	16,193
Disability	480,855	2,020,454	2,132,318	2,179,887	2,444,545	2,488,294	2,634,130	2,860,877	3,006,655
Workmen's compensation (g)	129,000	280,000	309,000	331,000	362,000	417,000	462,000	500,000	525,000
Veterans' program (f)	298,081	1,621,744	1,646,961	1,630,484	1,674,622	1,585,588	1,635,005	1,754,153	1,842,284
Railroad retirement	30,824	38,536	58,494	71,978	77,315	81,647	93,857	92,456	103,989
Federal civil-service	12,950	24,782	31,428	35,256	40,520	44,101	49,504	59,973	65,025
Federal noncontributory (d)	(d)	(d)	(d)	(d)	148,730	157,815	161,410	188,000	191,051
State and local government retirement (e)	10,000	18,000	20,000	22,000	24,000	28,000	30,000	35,000	40,000
State temporary disability insurance (h)		26,024	35,592	59,066	89,259	147,846	167,665	186,145	190,133
Railroad temporary disability insurance		11,368	30,843	30,103	28,099	26,297	34,689	45,150	49,173
Unemployment	534,661	1,587,934	1,248,433	2,227,510	1,466,217	862,752	1,043,557	1,050,603	2,291,620
State unemployment insurance	518,700	776,165	793,265	1,737,279	1,373,426	840,411	998,237	962,221	2,026,866
Railroad unemployment insurance (i)	15,961	39,401	28,599	103,596	59,804	20,217	41,793	46,684	157,088
Veterans' unemployment allowances (i)		772,368	426,569	386,635	32,987	2,124	3,527	41,698	107,666
Self-employment allowances to veterans (i)		198,174	83,598	43,559	1,666	110	12	(i)	(i)

Beneficiaries (in thousands) (j)

Old-age retirement:									
Old-age and survivors insurance (b)	77.2	1,068.1	1,294.9	1,574.6	1,918.1	2,756.8	3,187.3	3,888.7	4,589.6
Railroad retirement	102.0	147.1	156.0	164.3	174.8	182.0	268.6	288.5	307.7
Federal civil-service	47.4	80.1	90.6	101.5	111.0	120.4	128.3	138.5	151.6
Other federal contributory (c)	.6	1.4	1.5	1.9	2.0	2.0	2.1	2.2	2.4
Federal noncontributory (d)	32.8	66.9	76.3	105.7	71.3	87.1	87.8	90.9	95.6
State and local government retirement (e)	113.0	180.0	190.0	200.0	213.0	239.0	250.0	270.0	292.0
Veterans' program (f)	29.2	61.6	59.8	57.4	53.5	57.3	78.4	71.8	65.7
Survivorship (monthly benefits):									
Old-age and survivors insurance	35.7	767.4	872.4	983.9	1,093.9	1,286.8	1,484.6	1,687.5	1,891.9
Railroad retirement	3.0	40.5	101.6	121.8	136.3	146.8	150.6	157.0	167.2
Federal civil-service		.4	2.0	9.4	18.3	30.2	40.0	50.4	60.2
State and local government retirement (e)	25.0	35.0	36.0	38.0	40.0	42.0	44.0	46.0	48.0
Veterans' program	323.2	901.5	950.0	971.2	991.7	1,011.2	1,044.2	1,086.0	1,122.2
Workmen's compensation	(k)	(k)	(k)	(k)	(k)	(k)	(k)	(k)	(k)
Disability:									
Workmen's compensation	(k)	(k)	(k)	(k)	(k)	(k)	(k)	(k)	(k)
Veterans' program (f)	580.9	2,283.7	2,252.0	2,260.0	2,301.8	2,319.1	2,343.9	2,437.0	2,735.9
Railroad retirement (f)	39.3	51.2	63.0	70.0	76.0	79.1	80.3	81.9	84.9
Federal civil-service	15.5	31.6	35.8	39.7	43.0	45.8	48.4	52.1	56.6
Federal noncontributory (d)	(d)	(d)	(d)	(d)	56.0	61.1	68.1	78.1	81.4
State and local government retirement (e)	14.3	25.0	27.0	29.0	32.0	35.0	38.0	42.0	45.0
State temporary disability insurance (h)		23.0	24.2	28.0	54.1	71.3	75.0	83.3	81.6
Railroad temporary disability insurance (l)		23.6	33.2	33.6	31.2	28.9	31.5	33.2	31.5
Unemployment:									
State unemployment insurance (m)	982.4	852.4	821.1	1,666.1	1,305.0	796.9	873.6	812.1	1,614.9
Railroad unemployment insurance (l)	41.5	52.6	38.2	120.4	76.8	29.0	42.6	40.2	110.4
Veterans' unemployment allowances (i)		760.6	434.9	387.5	32.1	2.8	15.1	33.5	89.3
Self-employment allowances to veterans (i)		181.3	78.6	40.4	1.5	1.0	.1	(i)	(i)

*Prepared by the Social Security Administration, U. S. Department of Health, Education, and Welfare. *Source:* Based on reports of administrative agencies.

(a) Partly estimated. Data for state and local government and for federal civil-service and other contributory retirement plans exclude refunds of employee contributions.

(b) Includes benefits paid to aged wives, to dependent husbands (first payable Sept., 1950), and to children of retired-worker beneficiaries; for aged wives and dependent husbands receiving benefits in 1954, the average number was 960,575; for children of retired-worker beneficiaries, 99,172; payments to these groups were $332,458,000 and $20,206,000 respectively.

(c) Includes small but unknown number and amount of disability and survivor beneficiaries and benefits.

(d) Beginning 1950, identifiable disability benefits and beneficiaries shown separately. In earlier years old-age retirement data include significant amount of disability payments. Small number and amount of survivor payments included with old-age retirement (unknown for earlier years and estimated at less than $1,000,000 and slightly more than 1,000 beneficiaries for 1954).

(e) For fiscal year, usually ending June 30. Data for 1953 and 1954, preliminary. Under survivorship, number represents families.

(f) Under Veterans' Administration. Old-age retirement data are for veterans of the Spanish-American War, the Boxer Rebellion, and the Philippine Insurrection; from Oct., 1951, include all service pensions. Disability data include pensions and compensation, and subsistence payments to disabled veterans undergoing training. Lump-sum payments are for burial of deceased veterans.

(g) Small but unknown amount of lump-sum death payments included with monthly survivor payments. Disability benefits exclude payments for medical care. Data for 1953 and 1954, preliminary.

(h) Benefits first payable in Rhode Island, Apr., 1943; in California, Dec., 1946; in New Jersey, Jan., 1949; and in New York, July, 1950. Includes maternity data for Rhode Island. Excludes hospital benefits in California and hospital, surgical, and medical care benefits paid under approved plans in New York. Number represents average weekly number of beneficiaries; excludes private-plan beneficiaries in California and New Jersey.

(i) For unemployment allowances (under the Servicemen's Readjustment Act beginning Sept., 1944 and under the Veterans' Readjustment Assistance Act beginning Oct., 1952), average weekly number. For self-employment allowances under the Servicemen's Readjustment Act beginning Nov., 1944, average monthly number. For 1953 and 1954, a small number and amount of self-employment allowances included with unemployment allowances and not shown separately.

(j) Average monthly number, except as otherwise noted.

(k) Not available.

(l) Average number of beneficiaries during 14-day registration period.

(m) Average weekly number.

TABLE 4

AID TO DEPENDENT CHILDREN: SELECTED DATA ON RECIPIENTS, PAYMENTS AND FINANCING*

(Includes vendor payments for medical care and cases receiving only such payments)

State	Number of recipients, June, 1955				Average payment per family, June, 1955	Maximum permitted in state, September, 1954				Expenditures for assistance and administration, calendar year 1954 (in thousands)	Source of funds expended for assistance and administration, calendar year 1954; percentage from	
	Families	Total (a)	Children Total	Children Per 1,000 children in population (b)		Adult	First child	Each additional child (c)	Family		Federal funds	State and local funds
Total	620,349	2,239,477	1,691,733	29	$86.78	…	…	…	…	$650,600	57.0	43.0
Alabama	18,238	70,428	54,159	43	43.78	…	$30(d)	$21(d)	$114	9,165	77.2	22.8
Arizona	4,588	17,593	13,294	33	94.64	…	66	24	173	4,916	67.8	32.2
Arkansas	8,992	33,946	26,204	36	55.49	$6	27	18-15-12-9	105(e)	4,971	78.2	21.8
California	56,066	188,483	143,966	35	126.07	…	111(f)	51-45-39-33-27-21-15-9-6(f)	387(f)	87,912	45.6	54.4
Colorado	5,914	22,209	17,014	33	107.68	…	…	…	…	7,726	56.6	43.4
Connecticut	5,210	16,915	12,547	18	136.69	…	…	…	…	7,531	42.7	57.3
Delaware	1,114	4,301	3,289	26	86.44	…	75	12-12-12-10	150	962	66.9	33.1
Florida	21,153	74,620	56,779	46	54.67	…	30	21	81	13,831	76.8	23.2
Georgia	14,635	53,098	40,555	28	75.15	21	30	21	114	12,619	70.4	29.6
Idaho	1,898	6,793	4,989	21	127.50	…	…	…	…	2,914	47.8	52.2
Illinois	20,936	80,494	60,864	21	132.82	…	…	…	…	33,121	50.0	50.0
Indiana	8,769	30,719	22,771	15	90.51	…	60(d, g)	21(d)	…	9,216	62.8	37.2
Iowa	6,577	23,911	17,891	20	115.90	…	…	…	…	9,198	49.7	50.3
Kansas	4,452	16,038	12,298	18	110.68	…	30	…	…	5,948	51.4	48.6
Kentucky	18,929	67,924	50,691	45	63.33	30	…	21	190(d, h)	14,269	74.1	25.1
Louisiana	18,378	70,931	53,888	45	65.17	…	55(i)	8-10-9-16(i)	104(i)	15,310	73.2	26.8
Maine	4,420	15,341	11,086	35	81.79	…	60(j)	21(j)	207(j)	4,412	67.8	32.2
Maryland	6,375	25,838	20,016	22	96.09	…	…	…	175(d)	7,309	62.5	37.5
Massachusetts	13,061	43,606	32,194	21	127.13	…	…	…	…	20,287	44.7	55.3
Michigan	20,464	69,837	50,729	20	111.77	(k)	95(k)	15-14-10-10-6-12(k)	…	25,498	52.1	47.9
Minnesota	7,959	27,015	20,741	19	120.39	…	15	10-5	…	11,100	47.9	52.1
Mississippi	13,500	50,879	39,243	43	22.99	…	30	21	50	5,325	76.2	23.8
Missouri	22,109	77,615	57,623	43	67.86	(l)	…	…	…	17,644	71.9	28.1
Montana	2,103	7,434	5,595	24	105.97	…	…	…	…	2,897	55.2	44.8

State	(1)	(2)	(3)	(4)	(5)	(6)	85	15-15-15-10	(9)	(10)	(11)	(12)
Nebraska	2,551	9,208	6,875	15	94.40	...	85	...	...	2,976	61.2	38.8
Nevada (m)	13	47	34	(n)	(o)	...	...	...	...	12	...	100.0
New Hampshire	1,085	4,002	3,010	18	129.37	...	...	...	...	1,737	47.4	52.6
New Jersey	6,009	20,134	15,266	9	118.37	...	...	...	...	7,888	48.4	51.6
New Mexico	6,112	22,350	17,018	49	68.93	...	75.50(p)	10.50(p)	165 plus 50 cents per child (p)	6,378	70.5	29.5
New York	54,287	195,078	142,665	31	136.58	...	...	...	...	91,396	46.1	53.9
North Carolina	19,756	74,944	57,211	34	62.47	30	30	21	...	14,159	75.9	24.1
North Dakota	1,497	5,500	4,213	18	115.16	...	...	...	...	2,137	51.1	48.9
Ohio	15,725	59,324	45,012	15	94.05	...	...	...	...	16,812	61.4	38.6
Oklahoma	15,720	51,967	40,044	51	76.99	...	...	...	197	14,153	67.8	32.2
Oregon	3,895	13,796	10,420	18	119.71	...	...	...	...	5,755	48.1	51.9
Pennsylvania	29,886	113,475	85,794	25	104.24	...	...	...	...	37,801	56.0	44.0
Rhode Island	3,506	11,945	8,763	35	110.45	...	...	...	...	4,574	50.4	49.6
South Carolina	8,287	32,150	25,034	27	47.57	...	24	15	99	4,695	77.2	22.8
South Dakota	2,851	9,390	7,184	29	82.57	...	65	25-18-18-21	...	2,954	64.5	35.5
Tennessee	21,175	75,933	56,644	45	59.93	24	24	15	129	18,192	73.0	27.0
Texas	23,631	92,684	69,359	21	56.39	(r)	46(q)	17(q)	96	15,905	78.0	22.0
Utah	3,089	10,841	8,043	25	111.40	...	(r)	(r)	209(r)	4,468	50.6	49.4
Vermont	1,132	3,923	2,955	22	78.81	...	30	21	...	1,036	68.8	31.2
Virginia	8,844	34,279	26,481	20	65.26	30	...	...	...	7,344	71.9	28.1
Washington	9,070	30,863	22,627	26	119.48	30	...	...	275(s)	11,760	53.3	46.7
West Virginia	18,605	70,462	54,743	73	73.15	...	...	21	165	17,334	70.5	29.5
Wisconsin	8,173	28,416	20,966	17	136.74	...	...	...	...	12,850	43.4	56.6
Wyoming	566	2,033	1,541	13	109.13	...	...	...	165	742	53.6	46.4
District of Columbia	2,123	8,758	6,785	27	107.24	...	...	...	200(t)	3,141	60.4	39.6
Alaska	1,231	4,260	3,134	51	89.83	...	60	30	30	1,070	66.8	33.2
Hawaii	3,346	12,810	10,149	53	93.09	...	...	...	...	3,811	59.5	40.5
Puerto Rico	42,143	144,181	110,717	94	10.38	...	...	...	...	5,372	40.0	60.0
Virgin Islands	201	756	620	56	35.26	...	...	...	...	68	49.3	50.7

*Prepared by the Social Security Administration, U.S. Department of Health, Education, and Welfare. All data subject to revision.

(a) Includes as recipients the children and 1 parent or other adult relative in families in which the requirements of at least 1 such adult were considered in determining the amount of assistance.

(b) Based on population estimated by the Social Security Administration as of July, 1955.

(c) Amount for each additional child same as last figure shown unless family maximum specified.

(d) May be exceeded for medical care or other special needs.

(e) $99 maximum for family with no eligible adult included.

(f) Counties may supplement if needs exceed state maximums.

(g) $50 maximum for first child when no eligible adult included.

(h) Or the federal maximum, whichever is larger.

(i) Payment may exceed maximum up to $125 for special needs; no maximum on vendor payment.

(j) In addition, higher maximums apply to assistance plus other income.

(k) Maximum $10 higher per case if both parents are included in assistance unit and eligibility is based on incapacity. In Wayne County, maximum per case $70 higher.

(l) If payment to children plus other income is less than 55 per cent of family need, an additional payment for adult sufficient to meet 55 per cent of need, or $30, whichever is less, is provided.

(m) Program administered without federal participation.

(n) Not computed; number of children too small.

(o) Not computed; base too small.

(p) Maximums shown are for usual maximum plus 50 cents per child for payment into a pooled fund for medical care.

(q) $30 for first child and $21 up to family maximum for successive children if no eligible adult included.

(r) Maximums expressed in terms of number of persons in assistance unit from 1 to 8 or more as follows: $68, $115, $136, $154, $171.50, $189, $207, $209. Payment may exceed maximums for hardship cases; higher maximums specified for medicine, restaurant meals, nursing home care, and board and room.

(s) May be exceeded to prevent undue hardship.

(t) May be exceeded for contingent items.

TABLE 5

OLD-AGE AND SURVIVORS INSURANCE*

Estimated number and amount of monthly benefits in current-payment status as of June 30, 1955, amount of monthly benefit payments (old-age, supplementary, and survivor), and number and amount of lump-sum death payments, fiscal year 1954–55, by region and state.

(In thousands)

Beneficiary's state of residence	Benefits in current-payment status, June 30, 1955		Amount of benefits paid in fiscal year 1954-55					Number of lump-sum death payments, fiscal year 1954–55(c)
	Number	Monthly amount	Total	Monthly benefits (a)			Lump-sum death payments(b)	
				Old-age	Supplementary	Survivor		
Total..........	7,563.5	$384,025	$4,333,148	$2,802,967	$428,847	$1,000,795	$100,539	546.8
Region I.............	631.1	34,180	385,721	261,361	38,445	77,774	8,141	42.8
Connecticut.......	129.4	7,424	83,422	55,706	8,490	17,292	1,934	9.7
Maine............	63.8	3,072	34,727	23,771	3,386	6,862	708	3.9
Massachusetts....	321.9	17,670	199,730	135,424	19,874	40,309	4,123	21.6
New Hampshire...	39.2	1,980	22,359	15,464	2,147	4,310	438	2.5
Rhode Island.....	54.6	2,960	33,459	22,903	3,307	6,508	741	3.9
Vermont..........	22.1	1,074	12,024	8,093	1,241	2,493	197	1.2
Region II............	1,776.0	96,717	1,092,640	717,890	109,308	239,477	25,965	135.2
Delaware..........	17.4	908	10,290	6,633	994	2,380	283	1.5
New Jersey........	290.9	16,319	184,118	119,926	18,830	40,986	4,376	22.2
New York........	850.5	46,176	521,563	350,706	50,215	107,947	12,695	66.5
Pennsylvania......	617.3	33,313	376,669	240,625	39,269	88,164	8,611	45.0
Region III...........	633.7	28,321	320,711	189,060	29,574	94,092	7,985	45.5
Dist. of Columbia.	28.5	1,428	16,229	10,751	1,201	3,797	480	2.9
Kentucky.........	119.9	5,231	59,223	34,946	5,816	17,050	1,411	7.6
Maryland.........	104.8	5,290	60,077	37,098	5,387	15,880	1,712	9.3
North Carolina....	125.6	5,142	58,440	31,856	5,007	20,081	1,496	9.1
Puerto Rico......	24.5	724	7,478	5,036	676	1,634	132	.9
Virgin Islands.....	.3	11	106	80	7	19	(d)	(e)
Virginia..........	125.5	5,588	63,411	37,092	5,746	18,847	1,726	10.2
West Virginia.....	104.6	4,909	55,747	32,201	5,734	16,784	1,028	5.5
Region IV...........	649.8	28,284	318,713	192,520	30,233	88,508	7,452	45.3
Alabama..........	109.7	4,464	50,705	28,230	4,638	16,619	1,218	7.4
Florida...........	196.8	9,991	110,775	76,613	12,164	20,001	1,997	11.3
Georgia..........	112.2	4,549	51,906	28,520	4,271	17,559	1,556	9.7
Mississippi........	54.9	2,080	23,450	13,499	2,053	7,328	570	3.7
South Carolina....	64.7	2,541	29,107	14,929	2,319	11,001	858	5.3
Tennessee.........	111.5	4,659	52,770	30,729	4,788	16,000	1,253	7.9
Region V.............	1,636.4	87,432	985,587	634,414	102,705	225,135	23,333	123.1
Illinois...........	456.5	24,665	278,588	182,069	27,198	62,216	7,105	36.9
Indiana...........	218.5	11,043	124,193	80,253	13,191	28,010	2,739	15.0
Michigan.........	328.2	18,035	203,390	127,906	21,498	49,204	4,782	24.8
Ohio.............	449.3	24,100	272,105	173,466	29,077	63,201	6,361	33.8
Wisconsin.........	183.9	9,589	107,311	70,720	11,741	22,504	2,346	12.6
Region VI	612.5	29,748	333,696	222,951	35,079	68,156	7,510	41.9
Iowa.............	114.0	5,460	61,022	41,144	6,744	11,857	1,277	7.3
Kansas...........	83.4	3,938	44,199	29,129	4,822	9,226	1,022	5.8
Minnesota........	134.9	6,792	76,173	51,154	7,932	15,452	1,635	8.7
Missouri..........	192.8	9,535	107,437	71,517	10,785	22,517	2,618	14.6
Nebraska.........	52.2	2,464	27,456	18,565	3,011	5,330	550	3.2
North Dakota.....	14.7	639	7,165	4,653	710	1,629	173	1.0
South Dakota.....	20.3	919	10,244	6,789	1,075	2,145	235	1.3
Region VII	508.7	22,067	249,759	147,076	23,108	73,066	6,509	38.1
Arkansas..........	66.4	2,689	30,235	19,059	2,985	7,507	684	4.2
Louisiana.........	86.6	3,687	42,118	23,830	3,537	13,564	1,187	7.1
New Mexico.......	19.8	804	9,089	4,930	759	3,165	235	1.5
Oklahoma.........	82.4	3,686	41,586	25,913	4,109	10,582	982	5.5
Texas.............	253.5	11,202	126,731	73,344	11,718	38,248	3,421	19.8
Region VIII	152.7	7,381	82,957	53,194	8,172	19,830	1,761	9.8
Colorado..........	62.2	3,035	34,183	22,390	3,426	7,608	759	4.2
Idaho.............	25.1	1,162	12,994	8,484	1,289	2,992	229	1.4
Montana..........	26.8	1,304	14,626	9,626	1,284	3,417	309	1.7
Utah.............	28.3	1,369	15,416	8,953	1,658	4,469	336	1.8
Wyoming.........	10.4	511	5,728	3,741	515	1,344	128	.7
Region IX	918.2	47,637	536,739	366,110	49,674	109,335	11,620	63.7
Alaska...........	3.8	172	2,085	1,400	85	537	63	.3
Arizona..........	33.9	1,630	18,346	11,103	1,648	5,178	417	2.3
California........	616.4	32,181	362,502	247,112	33,265	73,926	8,199	44.9
Hawaii...........	16.9	772	8,886	5,724	667	2,369	126	.7
Nevada...........	7.7	392	4,442	2,934	283	1,081	144	.9
Oregon...........	96.6	4,987	55,938	39,181	5,465	10,236	1,056	5.8
Washington.......	142.9	7,503	84,540	58,656	8,261	16,008	1,615	8.8
Foreign..............	44.5	2,257	26,625	18,391	2,549	5,422	263	1.4

*Prepared by the Social Security Administration, U. S. Department of Health, Education, and Welfare.

(a) Distribution by state and type of benefit estimated. Supplementary benefits are paid to aged wives, wives under age 65 with child beneficiaries in their care, dependent aged husbands, and children of old-age beneficiaries. Survivor benefits are paid to the following survivors of deceased insured workers: aged widows, dependent aged widowers, children, widowed mothers or divorced wives with child beneficiaries in their care, or dependent aged parents.

(b) Distribution by state based on 10-per cent sample.

(c) Distribution by state based on 10-per cent sample; exceeds number of deceased workers with respect to whose wage records lump-sum death payments were paid.

(d) Less than $500.

(e) Less than 50.

TABLE 6
OLD-AGE ASSISTANCE: SELECTED DATA ON RECIPIENTS, PAYMENTS AND FINANCING*
(Includes vendor payments for medical care and recipients receiving only such payments)

State	Recipients, June, 1955 Total number	Number per 1,000 population aged 65 and over(a)	Average payment per recipient, June, 1955	Maximum payment permitted in state, September, 1954	Expenditures for assistance and administration, calendar year 1954 (in thousands)	Federal funds	State and local funds
Total(b)	2,548,593	179	$52.30	...	$1,685,404	55.8	44.2
Alabama	70,466	328	35.44	$55(c)	23,976	73.6	26.4
Arizona	13,773	246	55.87	70(d)	9,578	58.2	41.8
Arkansas	54,695	329	33.77	55(e)	21,334	71.7	28.3
California	269,190	261	67.05	80	237,235	48.0	52.0
Colorado(b)	52,458	361	85.10	95	51,513	39.5	60.5
Connecticut	16,826	76	85.01	...	17,510	40.7	59.3
Delaware	1,627	54	39.92	50	863	67.3	32.7
Florida	69,248	234	46.31	60	39,056	64.2	35.8
Georgia	98,384	395	37.81	55	45,683	69.0	31.0
Idaho	8,764	169	54.83	...	6,120	56.3	43.7
Illinois	95,315	106	61.93	87(f,g)	73,027	54.8	45.2
Indiana	36,750	92	48.51	55(c)	23,353	57.4	42.6
Iowa	41,412	145	57.59	...	31,202	55.0	45.0
Kansas	34,151	160	65.85	...	28,287	50.0	50.0
Kentucky	55,572	230	35.38	55	24,352	70.5	29.5
Louisiana	120,134	586	50.97	55(h)	77,180	63.1	36.9
Maine	12,566	132	46.38	55	7,573	65.2	34.8
Maryland	10,542	58	45.20	175	6,160	61.7	38.3
Massachusetts	89,127	163	77.31	...	88,428	43.3	56.7
Michigan	74,906	132	55.70	70(i)	53,272	56.1	43.9
Minnesota	51,707	168	66.38	60(c)	42,245	47.6	52.4
Mississippi	70,724	453	27.90	30	23,172	75.6	24.4
Missouri	132,983	294	49.59	55	82,417	64.5	35.5
Montana	9,018	145	57.93	...	7,031	54.7	45.3
Nebraska	17,815	120	50.30	65	11,873	60.6	39.4
Nevada	2,629	175	57.46	63	1,944	57.7	42.3
New Hampshire	6,288	108	59.03	72(c,g)	5,017	52.5	47.5
New Jersey	20,330	42	68.53	...	17,897	48.2	51.8
New Mexico	10,212	255	31.90	62(g,j)	7,144	62.9	37.1
New York	101,634	68	79.07	...	107,401	42.6	57.4
North Carolina	51,780	201	31.74	55	19,939	73.1	26.9
North Dakota	8,252	156	62.83	...	6,466	50.1	49.9
Ohio	101,366	123	58.23	65(k)	75,189	55.0	45.0
Oklahoma	95,216	449	61.48	125	67,762	55.8	44.2
Oregon	19,528	121	64.96	...	16,779	48.7	51.3
Pennsylvania	56,773	56	45.73	...	37,175	59.7	40.3
Rhode Island	8,116	103	59.44	...	6,251	52.2	47.8
South Carolina	43,247	335	32.50	55	17,631	71.7	28.3
South Dakota	10,768	174	44.79	55	6,408	65.6	34.4
Tennessee	65,810	260	34.78	50	30,058	70.1	29.9
Texas	223,043	357	39.10	55	106,748	69.4	30.6
Utah	9,443	185	59.56	68(c,l)	7,131	54.3	45.7
Vermont	6,858	176	44.64	55	3,824	66.1	33.9
Virginia	17,211	71	30.14	...	6,782	71.3	28.7
Washington	58,864	238	61.61	275	48,173	50.3	49.7
West Virginia	24,242	171	27.69	55	9,937	73.0	27.0
Wisconsin	43,095	122	63.47	75	35,091	48.7	51.3
Wyoming	3,991	174	58.70	75	3,064	54.5	45.5
District of Columbia	3,076	45	53.69	200(m)	2,017	57.8	42.2
Alaska	1,699	333	63.78	90	1,320	51.8	48.2
Hawaii	1,802	73	48.24	...	1,038	62.8	37.2
Puerto Rico	44,478	507	7.86	...	4,632	41.4	58.6
Virgin Islands	689	328	18.56	...	146	49.9	50.1

*Prepared by the Social Security Administration, U. S. Department of Health, Education, and Welfare. All data subject to revision.

(a) Based on population estimated by the Social Security Administration as of July, 1955.

(b) Except for recipient rate includes 4,097 recipients under age 65 in Colorado and payments to these recipients without federal participation.

(c) May be exceeded for medical care or other special needs.

(d) $60 maximum for recipient living with self-supporting relatives.

(e) $75 maximum for recipients in approved nursing homes.

(f) May be exceeded to provide vendor payments for medical care for cases receiving only such payments.

(g) Maximum shown is for usual maximum plus a specified amount for payment into pooled fund for medical care as follows: Illinois, $74 plus $13; New Hampshire, $60 plus $12; New Mexico, $60 plus $2.00.

(h) $52 for each of 2 or more in household. $95 maximum to provide nursing care or special medical care. Maximums may be exceeded to provide vendor payment for medical care.

(i) $80 if hospitalized or receiving care in an approved convalescent home. In Wayne County, unlimited supplementation is allowed.

(j) $37 maximum for eligible spouse. $84 maximum if needs of a person essential to well-being of recipient are included. $65 maximum to provide boarding home care.

(k) $200 maximum for calendar year for medical, dental, hospital, and optometrical care.

(l) Less per recipient when 2 or more recipients in family.

(m) May be exceeded for contingent items.

Table 7

AID TO THE BLIND: SELECTED DATA ON RECIPIENTS, PAYMENTS AND FINANCING*

(Includes vendor payments for medical care and recipients receiving only such payments)

State	Number of recipients, June, 1955	Average payment per recipient, June, 1955	Maximum payment permitted in state, September, 1954	Expenditures for assistance and administration, calendar year 1954 (in thousands)	Source of funds expended for assistance and administration, calendar year 1954, percentage from	
					Federal funds	State and local funds
Total (a)	103,906	$57.41	...	$73,260	49.5	50.5
Alabama	1,617	35.32	$55 (b)	553	74.4	25.6
Arizona	749	63.89	80	555	54.8	45.2
Arkansas	2,002	40.51	55 (c)	933	68.2	31.8
California (a)	12,655	84.50	90	13,339	39.3	60.7
Colorado	316	66.87	...	292	48.7	51.3
Connecticut	329	90.20	...	352	37.7	62.3
Delaware	213	62.54	85	187	53.6	46.4
Florida	2,845	49.04	55	1,786	64.7	35.3
Georgia	3,382	42.97	55	1,735	66.7	33.3
Idaho	189	61.30	...	149	53.0	47.0
Illinois	3,557	68.59	84 (d, e)	3,019	52.1	47.9
Indiana	1,792	58.59	95 (b)	1,297	52.8	47.2
Iowa	1,431	73.47	...	1,294	46.0	54.0
Kansas	631	73.28	...	554	47.1	52.9
Kentucky	2,949	37.11	55	1,263	69.5	30.5
Louisiana	2,048	49.79	95 (b)	1,279	58.5	41.5
Maine	543	50.44	55	347	64.2	35.8
Maryland	478	51.85	175	304	59.0	41.0
Massachusetts	1,792	93.81	...	1,976	37.8	62.2
Michigan	1,801	63.49	70 (f)	1,361	52.9	47.1
Minnesota	1,248	128.12	...	1,204	42.8	57.2
Mississippi	3,590	34.55	40	1,389	71.1	28.9
Missouri (a)	4,120	55.00	55	2,708	48.7	51.3
Montana	446	64.89	...	389	51.1	48.9
Nebraska	742	58.07	70	531	56.2	43.8
Nevada	110	75.10	...	91	46.9	53.1
New Hampshire	272	63.67	69 (b, e)	225	50.4	49.6
New Jersey	869	69.31	...	772	48.7	51.3
New Mexico	388	35.38	55 (e, g)	264	64.3	35.7
New York	4,366	88.03	...	5,147	40.4	59.6
North Carolina	4,897	40.71	55	2,578	66.3	33.7
North Dakota	118	65.92	...	85	53.9	46.1
Ohio	3,738	56.91	65	2,728	56.7	43.3
Oklahoma	2,034	73.70	125	1,746	49.8	50.2
Oregon	346	73.40	...	336	45.0	55.0
Pennsylvania (a)	16,496	50.90	50 (h)	10,538	34.7	65.3
Rhode Island	177	72.82	...	170	45.8	54.2
South Carolina	1,747	38.02	55	818	68.5	31.5
South Dakota	202	43.99	55	116	65.8	34.2
Tennessee	3,297	41.40	50	1,634	67.5	32.5
Texas	6,501	44.22	55	3,490	68.3	31.7
Utah	226	67.19	68 (b, i)	180	51.7	48.3
Vermont	162	48.96	55	99	64.9	35.1
Virginia	1,308	36.17	...	630	67.5	32.5
Washington (a)	771	78.35	275	776	42.7	57.3
West Virginia	1,184	32.13	55	527	69.7	30.3
Wisconsin	1,139	68.03	75	994	48.2	51.8
Wyoming	67	65.48	75	56	52.1	47.9
District of Columbia	256	59.34	200 (j)	181	56.7	43.3
Alaska	67	63.57	100	43	55.5	44.5
Hawaii	117	55.68	...	74	57.5	42.5
Puerto Rico	1,552	7.80	...	157	39.5	60.5
Virgin Islands	34	(k)	...	8	49.8	50.2

*Prepared by the Social Security Administration, U. S. Department of Health, Education, and Welfare. All data subject to revision.

(a) Data include recipients and payments made without federal participation. The number of recipients included are as follows: California, 403; Washington, 4; Missouri, 652; and Pennsylvania, 7,715.

(b) May be exceeded for medical care or other special needs.

(c) $75 maximum for recipients in approved nursing homes.

(d) May be exceeded to provide vendor payments for medical care for cases receiving only such payments.

(e) Maximum shown is for usual maximum plus a specified amount for payment into pooled fund as follows: Illinois, $74 plus $10; New Hampshire, $60 plus $9.00; New Mexico, $52 plus $3.00.

(f) $80 maximum for recipients in hospitals or convalescent homes. In Wayne County, unlimited supplementation is allowed.

(g) $70 maximum if needs of a person essential to well-being of recipient are included. $65 maximum to provide boarding-home care.

(h) May be exceeded in two counties to provide medical care.

(i) Less per recipient when 2 or more recipients in family.

(j) May be exceeded for contingent items.

(k) Not computed; base too small.

TABLE 8

AID TO THE PERMANENTLY AND TOTALLY DISABLED: SELECTED DATA ON RECIPIENTS, PAYMENTS AND FINANCING*

(Includes vendor payments for medical care and recipients receiving only such payments)

State	Recipients, June, 1955		Average payment per recipient, June, 1955	Maximum payment permitted in state, September, 1954	Expenditures for assistance and administration, calendar year 1954 (in thousands)	Source of funds expended for assistance and administration, calendar year 1954, percentage from	
	Total number	Number per 1,000 population aged 18-64 (a)				Federal funds	State and local funds
Total............	236,840	3.3	$54.93	...	$153,201	50.8	49.2
Alabama.............	10,148	6.1	35.85	$55(b)	3,222	73.9	26.1
Arkansas............	4,913	4.9	31.08	35	1,350	71.9	28.1
Colorado............	4,957	6.3	57.09	85	3,443	55.2	44.8
Connecticut.........	1,923	1.4	107.13	...	1,719	34.8	65.2
Delaware............	258	1.2	52.15	...	102	56.5	43.5
Georgia.............	9,106	4.7	42.07	55	4,065	66.3	33.7
Idaho...............	854	2.6	61.09	...	660	53.1	46.9
Illinois.............	6,047	1.1	81.66	109(c,d)	5,605	44.8	55.2
Kansas..............	3,437	3.1	68.22	...	2,716	47.3	52.7
Louisiana...........	12,805	8.0	42.57	44(b,e)	7,002	62.7	37.3
Maine..............	103	.2	48.70	...	.....	.....	.....
Maryland...........	4,453	2.9	53.47	175	2,833	57.5	42.5
Massachusetts.......	10,349	3.6	100.35	...	11,771	36.3	63.7
Michigan...........	2,297	.6	71.85	70(f)	1,707	47.1	52.9
Minnesota..........	698	.4	54.82	60	260	58.7	41.3
Mississippi.........	2,979	2.6	24.60	25	905	75.7	24.3
Missouri............	14,154	5.9	51.91	55	9,463	63.7	36.3
Montana............	1,450	4.3	63.65	...	1,144	51.7	48.3
New Hampshire......	234	.8	73.24	80(b,d)	172	45.8	54.2
New Jersey.........	3,301	1.0	80.36	...	2,757	43.4	56.6
New Mexico.........	1,685	4.2	31.21	53.50(d,g)	1,038	64.7	35.3
New York...........	41,116	4.3	83.32	...	42,941	40.8	59.2
North Carolina......	11,321	4.9	37.70	55	4,387	68.9	31.1
North Dakota.......	880	2.5	68.28	...	725	45.4	54.6
Ohio...............	8,343	1.7	49.82	55	4,816	63.1	36.9
Oklahoma...........	5,870	4.7	58.70	125	3,160	59.6	40.4
Oregon.............	3,301	3.5	74.90	...	2,725	43.9	56.1
Pennsylvania........	13,043	2.0	53.45	...	9,209	49.8	50.2
Rhode Island........	1,483	3.2	75.83	...	1,129	45.9	54.1
South Carolina......	7,817	6.8	31.73	35	2,946	71.5	28.5
South Dakota.......	689	1.9	46.33	55	350	64.4	35.6
Tennessee...........	1,471	.8	39.89	50	659	65.5	34.5
Utah...............	1,794	4.5	64.75	68(b,h)	1,370	51.7	48.3
Vermont............	447	2.1	49.70	55	223	64.3	35.7
Virginia............	4,679	2.4	38.86	...	2,291	65.1	34.9
Washington.........	5,389	3.9	72.72	275	5,075	46.3	53.7
West Virginia.......	8,510	7.9	31.25	55	3,210	69.8	30.2
Wisconsin...........	1,133	.6	90.06	80	1,252	37.6	62.4
Wyoming............	460	2.7	60.42	75	335	55.1	44.9
District of Columbia..	2,205	4.3	60.52	200(i)	1,489	55.0	45.0
Hawaii.............	1,330	4.9	63.64	...	902	51.1	48.9
Puerto Rico.........	19,304	20.1	8.61	...	2,056	39.9	60.1
Virgin Islands.......	104	10.5	19.27	...	19	50.0	50.0

*Prepared by the Social Security Administration, U. S. Department of Health, Education, and Welfare. All data subject to revision.

(a) Based on population estimated by the Social Security Administration as of July, 1955.

(b) May be exceeded for medical care or other special needs.

(c) May be exceeded to provide vendor payments for medical care for cases receiving only such payments.

(d) Maximum shown is for usual maximum plus a specified amount for payment into pooled fund as follows: Illinois, $74 plus $35; New Hampshire, $60 plus $20; New Mexico, $52 plus $1.50.

(e) Maximum for one recipient; $24 to $60 according to composition of and other assistance grants in household.

(f) $80 maximum for recipients in hospitals or convalescent homes. In Wayne County unlimited supplementation is allowed.

(g) $67 maximum if needs of a person essential to well-being of recipient are included. $65 maximum to provide boarding-home care.

(h) Less per recipient when 2 or more recipients in family.

(i) May be exceeded for contingent items.

TABLE 9

GENERAL ASSISTANCE: SELECTED DATA ON RECIPIENTS, PAYMENTS AND FINANCING*

(Except for expenditures for assistance and administration, excludes vendor payments for medical care and recipients receiving only such payments)

State	Number of recipients, June, 1955			Average payment per case, June, 1955	Expenditures for assistance and administration, calendar year 1954 (in thousands)
	Cases	Persons			
		Total	Number per 1,000 persons under 65 years of age (a)		
Total..............	310,000(b)	...	4.9	$53.78(b)	$298,611(c)
Alabama..............	150	165	.1	23.94	54
Arizona..............	1,713	2,695	2.7	43.25	994
Arkansas..............	758	1,713	1.0	15.43	366
California..............	30,374	51,637	4.4	51.46	25,771
Colorado..............	1,406	3,479	2.6	38.77	3,390
Connecticut............	3,056	(d)	...	57.04	4,126(e)
Delaware..............	1,163	(d)	...	47.66	765
Florida (f)..............	5,600	(d)	...	.....	1,053(e)
Georgia..............	2,356	4,734	1.4	22.30	673
Idaho	80(g)	116(g)	.2(g)	45.89(g)	1,012
Illinois..............	35,896	82,500	9.8	68.11	38,906
Indiana..............	11,236(h)	30,569(h)	7.8(h)	33.76(h)	5,710
Iowa..............	3,495	7,160	3.0	31.39	4,187
Kansas..............	1,934	4,425	2.5	53.97	2,036
Kentucky..............	2,764	6,738	2.5	29.47	1,014(e)
Louisiana..............	7,531	8,217	2.9	39.29	4,011
Maine..............	3,178	8,196	9.9	43.76	3,466
Maryland..............	2,109	3,368	1.4	53.48	1,814
Massachusetts..........	12,538	26,066	5.9	55.44	11,793
Michigan..............	16,382	42,172	6.3	64.11	26,908
Minnesota.............	6,560	15,802	5.6	56.46	8,166
Mississippi............	971	1,313	.6	12.69	137(e)
Missouri.............	6,297	11,232	3.0	39.93	2,702
Montana..............	784	1,783	3.1	24.38	2,521
Nebraska..............	1,347	3,073	2.5	41.89	2,448
Nevada..............	329	616	2.9	34.23	815(e)
New Hampshire........	998	2,839	6.0	46.59	758(e)
New Jersey............	7,979(h)	20,560(h)	4.2(h)	77.21(h)	8,994
New Mexico............	428	536	.7	26.59	458
New York..............	29,369(i)	86,847(i)	6.1(i)	78.06(i)	36,460
North Carolina.........	2,011	4,689	1.2	20.41	2,629
North Dakota..........	405	1,502	2.6	42.06	558
Ohio..................	29,387	75,689	9.5	51.07	30,587
Oklahoma..............	4,800(f)	(d)	...	.....	895(e)
Oregon..............	2,827	8,011	5.3	49.26	6,557
Pennsylvania...........	27,111	68,553	6.9	68.94	20,230
Rhode Island...........	3,700	8,280	11.5	67.12	4,050
South Carolina.........	2,016	2,921	1.4	22.73	850
South Dakota..........	1,264	2,207	3.7	32.68	1,338
Tennessee..............	2,312	5,117	1.6	15.67	435(e)
Texas (f)..............	8,500	(d)	...	.....	2,241(e)
Utah..................	1,503	2,666	3.7	61.94	1,463
Vermont (f)............	1,200	(d)	...	.....	635(e)
Virginia..............	2,394	(d)	...	35.86	1,391
Washington............	9,957	15,787	7.0	59.86	9,020
West Virginia..........	2,209	4,069	2.2	28.83	2,114
Wisconsin..............	7,570	20,450	6.2	68.37	9,602
Wyoming..............	231	735	2.6	45.44	629
District of Columbia....	543	567	.7	61.90	501
Alaska................	148	273	1.5	50.87	277
Hawaii................	2,179	3,973	8.5	57.55	888
Puerto Rico...........	933	933	.4	15.43	188
Virgin Islands.........	87	89	4.3	18.79	27

*Prepared by the Social Security Administration, U. S. Department of Health, Education, and Welfare. All data subject to revision.

(a) Based on population estimated by the Social Security Administration as of July, 1955.

(b) Partly estimated; does not represent sum of state figures because total excludes for Indiana and New Jersey an estimated number of cases receiving medical care, hospitalization, and burial only.

(c) Excludes data on administration for 10 states. See footnote (e).

(d) Data not available.

(e) Represents assistance payments only; data on administration not available.

(f) Estimated.

(g) Excludes assistance in kind and, for a few counties, cash payments.

(h) Includes an unknown number of recipients of medical care, hospitalization, and burial only and payments for these services.

(i) Includes recipients of medical care only.

STATE PROGRAMS FOR THE AGING

IN RECENT YEARS public awareness has grown of the special needs and problems of the aged. Older persons comprise a large and increasing proportion of the population, and economic and social changes have altered their position. These facts have posed problems for state and local governments in all sections of the country.

The changed status of older people is in large degree the result of a shift from a rural, agricultural society to an urban, industrial one. Their rate of increase is twice that of the population as a whole, while the proportion of men over 65 who have jobs is constantly decreasing, having fallen from 68 per cent in 1890 to 42 per cent in 1950.

Maintaining an adequate income is one of the major concerns for the aged. Others include, prominently, their home life, the opportunities open to them for community activity, personal initiative and independence, and the kinds of care and services available to them when needed. Another major concern, always, is health, both physical and mental. Although persons over 65 do not have appreciably more cases of acute illness than younger persons, their illnesses tend to be of longer duration. Moreover, approximately a fourth of the patients in state mental hospitals are 65 and over, despite the fact that people in this age group are only slightly more than 8 per cent of the nation's population.

STATE GROUPS CONCERNED WITH THE AGING

In the postwar period, Connecticut, New York and North Carolina were among the first states to form special groups concerned with the aged. The Connecticut legislature in 1945 authorized the establishment of a Commission on the Care and Treatment of the Chronically Ill, Aged and Infirm. In addition to studying those problems and making recommendations on them, the commission is responsible for acquiring and operating needed facilities and for carrying on a grant-in-aid program to municipal hospitals. The 1947 session of the New York legislature established a Joint Legislative Committee on Problems of the Aging which has been continued since then. In addition to fact finding and recommending of legislation, the committee has carried on a program of public information work, has encouraged local programs, and has engaged in certain planning activities with state department personnel, local officials and private agencies. Another of the pioneer groups was the North Carolina Commission for the Study of Problems of Care of the Aged and Intellectually or Physically Handicapped, which the legislature established in 1949.

In 1950, at the request of the President, the United States Federal Security Agency sponsored the first National Conference on Aging. The conference served to focus interest on the special needs of the aged and to stimulate the formation of state groups. In September, 1952, a national Conference of State Commissions on Aging was held, with federal agencies participating. By that time state groups were active in fifteen states. By 1955, such groups—including interim committees that had completed their assignments—had been established in half of the states, some by legislative action and some by Governors.

Although they have varied considerably in scope, a function common to all has been fact-finding, and most of the commissions and committees have submitted formal recommendations for legislative and and administrative action.

The earlier groups usually were special interim study commissions appointed for limited periods, usually a biennium. Interim commissions were established in 1949 by North Carolina; in 1951 by Michigan, Massachusetts; Minnesota, Rhode Island and West Virginia; in 1953 by Connecticut, Maine, Oregon and Vermont; in

1954 by New Jersey; and in 1955 by Colorado and Illinois.

In some states the regular interim legislative study groups of the legislative council type, rather than special commissions, made studies and recommendations. Such assignments were undertaken in 1951 by the Wisconsin Legislative Council and the Pennsylvania Joint State Government Commission; in 1953 by the legislative councils in Kansas, New Hampshire and Ohio. In several states conferences called by their Governors made recommendations based on preconference study and the deliberations held. In California a 1950 Governor's Conference on the Care and Treatment of Senile Patients was followed the next year by a Conference on Problems of the Aging. In the same year a Governor's conference was held in North Carolina and in the following year in New Mexico. In 1954 a conference met in Colorado to consider that state's problems relating to the aging, and in 1955 there was a Governor's conference in Washington.

A more recent trend has been the establishment of continuing advisory, coordinating and study groups, with active programs for meeting the needs of the aged in addition to study and research. These groups carry on public information operations and planning programs, coordinate existing programs, and aid and cooperate in establishment of programs by localities. Such units were active from 1950 to 1953 in Florida and Illinois. In Washington the Governor's Council for Aging Population has functioned since 1952, and in Colorado an advisory committee on this subject to the State Department of Public Health has been active since 1953. In 1955 the California, Indiana and Michigan legislatures authorized creation of advisory commissions on the aging.

Another current development is the formation of interdepartmental committees in state governments to help plan and coordinate departmental programs, and in some cases to conduct broader programs. In the latter category are the California Interdepartmental Coordinating Committee on Aging, created in 1952, and similar committees authorized in Massachusetts and New York in 1954 and 1955 respectively. Meantime, the Governor of New York has appointed a Special Assistant on Problems of the Aging, who is also Chairman of the interdepartmental committee.

REPORT TO THE GOVERNORS' CONFERENCE

In addition to the action taken by the states individually, the Governors' Conference at its annual meeting in July, 1954, requested the Council of State Governments to undertake a study that would assess the existing situation and assist in intelligent planning for the future. The resulting report, *The States and Their Older Citizens*, was submitted to the Conference in 1955. This report presents extensive factual data in text, tables and charts on basic factors in the problem of aging, summarizes the kinds of action the states are now taking, and suggests a Bill of Objectives and a Program of Action for consideration by them.

Among its recommendations the report urges elimination of arbitrary age limits for employment; establishment of programs of rehabilitation and vocational training for aging persons; facilities for counseling older people and for early detection and follow-up of diseases; better screening of patients before admission to mental hospitals; establishment of medical home-care programs; state grants to localities for construction of medically supervised nursing homes; and special provision for medical care under the old-age assistance program. Emphasis is given to means of enabling older people to keep up or resume their participation in community affairs—for example, in community centers where they can join in interesting and productive activities.

Looking to the future, the report stresses the need for increased gerontological research and application of its results in public education and professional training. The study suggests that states establish administrative units including a qualified special assistant to the Governor, and special department personnel, to work with the aging. Interdepartmental committees are proposed as a means of increasing state coordination of resources and planning. Another suggestion is appointment of an advisory council, representative of all groups interested in the problems of aging, to work with the state authorities.

State Programs for the Aged

While the studies have proceeded, changes have been taking place in state programs for the aging. The reports of study groups have helped administrative agencies to revise and develop their relevant activities.

State activities for the aging range from old-age assistance and direct state services, such as those involved in state mental institutions, to measures aimed at encouraging and improving local programs through financial aid, consultation, professional advice and assistance in maintenance of standards. The public-welfare agencies have developed the most extensive special programs. Certain of these, such as old-age assistance, go back many years. Today, however, the shift is toward Old-Age and Survivors Insurance as the main public program to provide financial support for the aged. And the increased general interest in meeting their many needs has been reflected in social services not directly related to Old-Age Assistance. In a few state departments of public welfare, a consultant on services to the aging has been provided, in order to coordinate and encourage these services. In Illinois, for example, there is a Consultant on Aging to the Illinois Public Aid Commission, and in North Carolina a Supervisor of Services to the Aged. In some cases a similar position has been established by county or city welfare departments.

In about half the states—where public assistance is locally administered—most of the existing social services are offered by local agencies, the state participating by sharing in assistance grants and administrative expenses and by providing technical assistance. In the other states—in which the public assistance programs are state-administered, through district or county offices—state personnel may participate directly in offering social services for the aged. At least for the more populous areas, the states themselves may provide such services as those of "homemakers" and housekeepers, special counselors, visitors, group activity and recreation consultants, foster and nursing home programs, and day centers. In New York, state funds are available to aid in operating day centers, and in Cook County, Illinois, an experimental plan for recruiting, training and supervising volunteer "friendly visitors" has been inaugurated. In most states, aged recipients of public assistance receive counseling at least to the extent of the casework involved in establishing and maintaining their eligibility. In some states the casework includes arranging for suitable private or public living accommodations, for securing homemakers or housekeepers, for medical care and for means of securing employment.

Health, Rehabilitation, Employment

An important part of a state welfare department's total program is the maintenance of the health and, whenever possible, the employability of their clients. An important recent trend has been provision of medical care through so-called "vendor payments"—direct purchase by the agency of medical services for individuals. This may include an organized home care program, providing for visits by a medical team consisting of a doctor, a nurse, a caseworker and a therapist, and the services of a homemaker or housekeeper. In Illinois, the Public Aid Commission is embarking on pilot rehabilitation projects in two counties; the aim is to equip older people for self help, as well as employment when possible. In Minnesota, the State Department of Public Welfare will provide an occupational therapist in a consultant capacity to help establish local programs. In some states, public welfare agencies offer employment counseling and placement services for older welfare recipients, supplementing the regular state employment-service facilities. Frequently, the social services made available by the states in connection with the assistance program are supplemented by local public-welfare agencies.

In several states, the state employment services carry on periodical programs to encourage the hiring of older persons. In 1954 the Massachusetts legislature provided for a Division on the Employment of the Aging in the Department of Labor to maintain a continuing program of counseling and job placement for the aged, to encourage their employment, to develop rehabilitation and training facilities for them, and to facilitate expansion of the work of aged people at home and in sheltered workshops. In New York the state employment offices have added job counselors and interviewers to give special counsel and placement service to persons over 45 years of age. An amendment to the State Fair Employment Practices Act in Massachusetts has made it an unfair practice to discriminate in hiring because of age.

Institutions, Hospitals, Homes

Most of the aging persons in state institutions are in state mental hospitals. Some states, however, have developed special facilities for their older citizens who are unable to care for themselves and yet do not need hospitalization. The problem is especially acute as regards non-psychotic seniles. New emphasis has been placed on rehabilitation within state institutions to make it possible for patients and residents to care for themselves and to return to their own or foster homes.

In Connecticut the State Commission on the Care of the Chronically Ill, Aged and Infirm has developed a program of special hospital geriatric unit facilities for rehabilitation of aged patients who do not require prolonged treatment either in a mental or general hospital. Four state hospitals take patients from areas where local facilities are not adequate, and grants-in-aid assist local public and non-profit hospitals in developing such facilities. Massachusetts has established a state research hospital to study chronic diseases and the care of elderly people, and has authorized establishment of a state hospital for the care of older persons. Rhode Island is completing a new geriatric hospital designed especially for older persons and for treatment of their mental ills. In Washington, senile patients are being removed from state mental hospitals, to be cared for in their own or foster or nursing homes, at state expense if they do not have sufficient resources. New Mexico and Wyoming both operate state homes for the aged. Several other states have built geriatric wings or buildings at mental hospitals.

All of the states license some of the institutions that provide care for the aged, and the current emphasis is on raising the level of care. In Georgia, Illinois, Kansas, Minnesota, New York, North Carolina and Washington, among other states, the state departments of health or welfare, frequently in cooperation with the state university extension services, have held institutes and special courses for the operators and staffs of institutional homes for the aged. Demonstration programs for such operators are offered by a number of state and local agencies throughout the country. In many states special bulletins, reports and manuals are issued to licensed institutions that care for aged persons.

State health departments customarily have had special divisions to deal with chronic diseases, tuberculosis, cancer or heart disease. Recently some departments have established special divisions or positions to serve the aging. Thus the Indiana Department of Health has a Division of Chronic Disease and Gerontology, and the Kansas Department of Health a Division of Geriatrics. In Colorado and Connecticut a public-health physician in geriatric medicine is assigned to the respective health departments. Recent legislation in Massachusetts provides that the Department of Public Health, with the cooperation of local agencies, should establish and maintain clinics for the aging.

The states are beginning to make special provisions concerning housing for the aged —a field in which various municipal public housing authorities previously have been active. One important recent development is a requirement in New York that a certain portion of all state-aided or state-constructed housing be set aside for older persons. In Massachusetts, state aid is available to local housing authorities for the construction of low-cost housing for the aged; a set of mandatory and suggested standards for such housing has been developed.

Education and Research

Programs of adult education have long been offered in the public school systems and in extension courses of state colleges and universities. Increased emphasis now is going to courses especially suited to older adults. Some state departments of education have consultants in programs for the aging, and a number make financial aid available to local school districts to conduct programs for them. An example is Louisiana's year-round, community center school program.

State universities have been particularly active in developing programs focused on problems of aging. Several state institutions of learning, as well as other universities, offer courses on aging, both for professional workers and other students; some have separate departments or divisions devoted to the subject. The University of Kansas School of Medicine, for example, has a department of geriatric medicine; the Universities of Iowa and Florida have Institutes of Gerontology; and the University of Michigan's Institute on Human Adjustment maintains a division of gerontology. Special research on aging is being carried out at state universities in departments of anatomy, biology, psychology, education, sociology and others, and the universities have sponsored numerous conferences on aging in many states.

Thus the problem of aging, in its many aspects, has become a major area of state governmental inquiry and study. Increasingly it is becoming a major area of state governmental action as well.

State	Name of agency	Type of group (a)	Years in existence (b)	Authorization	Membership (c)	Appointed by	Paid staff	Appropriation
California.........	Interdepartmental Coordinating Comm. on Aging	Interdept.	1952—	Executive	10 Admin. 4 Legis. 5-21 Other	Governor	Yes	$13,500 (d)
	Citizens Advisory Comm. on Aging	Advisory, Coord., Study	1955—	Legislative Act		Governor	*	$10,600 (e)
Colorado.........	Advisory Comm. on Chronic Illness, Aging and Rehabilitation of the Dept. of Pub. Health	Advisory, Coord., Study	1953—	Administrative	1 Legis. 4 Admin. 18 Other	Director of Health	Yes	$43,860 (f)
	Commission on the Aged	Study	1955—	Executive Order	3 Legis. 2 Admin. 6 Other	Governor	*	*
Connecticut.........	Commn. on Care and Treatment of Chronically Ill, Aged and Infirm	Admin.	1945—	Legislative Act	2 Admin. 5 Private	Ex officio Governor	Yes	$1,347,648 (g)
	Commn. on Potentials of the Aging	Study	1953—54	Legislative Act	12 Private	Governor	Yes	$20,000
Florida.........	Citizens Comm. on Retirement in Florida	Advisory, Coord., Study	1950—53	Executive Proclamation	15 Private	Governor	Yes	†
Illinois.........	Committee on Aging	Advisory, Coord., Study	1950—53	Executive	1 Legis. 5 Admin. 11 Other	Governor	Yes	†
	Commn. on Aging and Aged	Study	1955—	Legislative Act	10 Legis. 5 Other	Legislature Governor	*	$15,000
Indiana.........	Commn. on Aging and Aged	Advisory, Coord., Study	1955—	Legislative Act	16 Private	Governor	*	None
Kansas.........	Legislative Council	Council Study	1953—54	Legislative Resolution	Lieut. Gov. 27 Legis.	Ex officio Legislature	Yes	†
Maine.........	Commn. on Aging	Study	1953—54 1955—	Legislative Act	2 Legis. 1 Admin. 4 Private	Governor	No	$1,200 (53–55) $2,500 (55–57)
Massachusetts......	Subcommittee on Problems of Aging of the Special Commn. on Pub. Welfare Laws	Study	1951—	Legislative Resolve	1 Legis. 1 Private	Legislature	Yes	†
	Council for the Aging	Interdept.	1954—	Legislative Act	5 Admin.	Ex officio	Yes	$7,500 (h)
Michigan.........	Governor's Commn. to Study Problems of Aging	Study	1951—52	Executive	4 Private	Governor	No	$5,000
	Legislative Advisory Council on Problems of Aging	Advisory, Coord., Study	1955—	Legislative Act	36 Private 8 Private	Governor Legislature	Yes	*
Minnesota.........	Commission on Aging	Study	1951—53	Legislative Act	10 Legis. 15 Other	Legislature	No	$7,000
	Governor's Advisory Commn. on Problems of Aging	Study	1953—	Executive Order	4 Legis. 5 Admin. 5 Private	Governor	No	*
New Hampshire.....	Subcommittee on Problems of Aging of the Legislative Council	Council Study	1953—54	Legislative Committee	8 Legis.	Council	Yes	†
New Jersey.........	Old Age Study Commn.	Study	1954—	Legislative Act	4 Legis. 3 Private	Legislature Governor	*	*
New Mexico.........	Citizens Advisory Comm. on Problems of Needy Aged Citizens of N. M.	Advisory, Coord., Study	1952—	Legislative Act	4 Legis. 5 Admin. 6 Private	Governor	No	†

State	Title	Type[a]	Dates[b]	Established	Composition[c]	Reports to	Report	Appropriation
New York	Joint Legislative Comm. on Problems of Aging	Legis. Study	1947—	Legislative Resolution	15 Legis.	Legislature	Yes	$25,000 (i)
	Special Assist. to the Governor on Problems of Aging	Special Asst.	1955—	Executive Order	1 Admin.	Governor	Yes	*
	Interdepartmental Comm. on Problems of Aging	Interdept.	1955—	Executive Order	9 Admin.	Governor	Yes	*
	Citizens Advisory Comm. on Problems of Aging	Advisory, Coord., Study	1955—	Executive Order	45 Private	Governor	*	*
North Carolina	Commn. for Study of Problems of Care of Aged and Intellectually or Physically Handicapped	Study	1949—51	Legislative Act	3 Admin. / 4 Other / 25 Members	Governor	*	†
Ohio	Special Comm, on Aging	Study	1951—52	Executive	9 Legis.	Governor	*	*
	Comm. to Study and Investigate Needs and Problems of Aged People in Ohio, Ohio Legislative Service	Council	1953—55	Legislative Resolution		Commission	Yes	†
Oregon	The Governor's Comm. to Study Problems of Aged	Study	1953—54	Executive	2 Legis. / 1 Admin. / 8 Other	Governor	No	†
Pennsylvania	Subcommittee on Needs and Problems of Aged and Aging of the Joint State Government Comm.	Council Study	1951—53	Legislative Resolution	14 Legis.	Commission	Yes	†
Rhode Island	The Governor's Commn. to Study Problems of Aged	Study	1951—53	Legislative Resolution	4 Admin. / 2 Legis. / 19 Other	Governor	Yes	$10,000
Vermont	Committee on Aging	Advisory, Coord., Study	1953—	Executive, Legislative Resolution (j)	4 Admin. / 10 Other	Governor	Yes	$17,000 (Gov.'s fund)
	The Commn. on Chronically Ill and Aged	Study	1953—54	Legislative Resolution	3 Legis. / 2 Private	Legislature Governor	No	$5,000 plus $3,000 private
Washington	Governor's Council for Aging Population	Advisory, Coord., Study	1952—	Executive	2 Legis. / 25 Other	Governor	Yes (k)	†
West Virginia	Governor's Temporary Comm. in W. Va. for Studying Problems of Elderly People	Study	1951—52	Executive Order	4 Private	Governor	No	None
Wisconsin	Advisory Comm. on Problems of Aged of the Legislative Council	Council Study	1951—52	Statutory	6 Legis. / 3 Private	Legislative Council	Yes	$15,000

Sources: Preliminary copy of table, "States and the Aged," from the 1955 Report of the New York State Joint Legislative Committee on Problems of the Aging; Committee on Aging and Geriatrics, U.S. Department of Health, Education, and Welfare, *Official State Groups in Aging*, 1954; the state reports as cited in the bibliography, pp. 167–76.

* Indicates no data available.

† Indicates no specific appropriation. Funds included in another general appropriation, as to a legislative council or provided by other agencies.

(a) Types of groups are identified as follows: Interdept.—Interdepartmental Committee; Advisory, Coord., Study—Study, coordinating, and study group (the Florida committee was dissolved and the Illinois committee was replaced by an Advisory Committee to the Public Aid Commission); Admin.—Operating administrative agency; Study—Legislative mixed interim study commission or Governor's interim study commission; Council Study—Legislative council-type agency which undertook a broad study; Legis. Study—a legislative committee (no public members); Special Asst.—Special Assistant to the Governor.

(b) Or years elapsed between date of assignment and submission of report in the case of legislative councils.

(c) Shows actual members appointed, when possible, identified as state administrative (Admin.) or legislative (Legis.) officials, or private citizens. "Other" is used when local officials were included or when complete information was not available.

(d) Annual total available, each department represented sharing in cost.

(e) Appropriation for fiscal 1955–56.

(f) W.K. Kellogg Foundation three-year grant to the State Department of Public Health.

(g) Direct state appropriation for current operating expenses, grants-in-aid, and other programs by biennium 1955–57.

(h) For fiscal 1954–55.

(i) Annual appropriation.

(j) Initially established by executive order, later recognized by legislative resolution.

(k) Paid by Department of Public Assistance.

PUBLIC CHILD-WELFARE SERVICES*

PUBLIC child-welfare services as they exist today are largely a development of the present century. They are deeply rooted, however, in the humanitarian traditions of this country which bespeak the conviction that the well-being of children is a primary concern of society.

The field of child welfare is served by both private and governmental agencies. In many respects they both provide the same types of service, but the private agencies are free to be selective and to specialize and set their own limits, while the public agencies, both state and local, are obligated to provide services according to statutory requirements. Because of growth of population and changing social conditions, it has been necessary for the public agencies in recent years to expand their coverage. They have done so, but often the expansion has not kept pace with the population growth. Because the services generally available do not equal the demand for them, the growth of public agencies does not displace the voluntary ones.

SCOPE OF SERVICES

The field of child welfare is not precisely definable. It includes a wide range of services, agencies, professional specialties and sponsoring bodies. Frequently the elements of a given service reach into such fields as education, health, law and psychology. There are also varying interpretations as to the extent to which such functions, for example, as corrections, juvenile and domestic relations courts, police, and recreation are properly classified as "child-welfare services." Under any definition, however, child-welfare services seek to promote the wholesome growth and development of children and to prevent and relieve situations which jeopardize their well-being. The primary objective, therefore,

*Prepared by HAROLD HAGEN, Child Welfare Consultant, American Public Welfare Association.

is to preserve and maintain normal family living for as many children as possible, and where this is not possible, to provide the best substitute care, designed to meet the needs of each individual child.

One of the central features in child-welfare services is the use of the methods and techniques of social casework, which, through a professional knowledge of human personality and behavior, takes into account the special circumstances of each individual and attempts to bring to bear the resources that are needed, or that are available, to serve each person's individual requirements. This is usually a time-consuming process, not only because it deals with people as individuals, but also because it often involves continuing relationships with each individual, and with other agencies and professions.

STATE RESPONSIBILITY

Public child-welfare services are usually a function of state and local government. The patterns of organization and administration vary considerably, but for most programs there is either centralized administration or supervision by a state agency, with direct services to individuals provided by agencies of county or (less frequently) municipal governments. In either case the state agency ordinarily has responsibility for policy formulation, for specialized technical and professional services and for the administration and allocation of federal and state funds.

State and local child-welfare services are most commonly administered in combination with other public-welfare services. The usual administering body at the state level is a division of child welfare in the state welfare department. In some states the department, through the division of child welfare or otherwise, also administers correctional and other specialized children's institutions and services.

The federal government, primarily through the Children's Bureau, conducts studies and gathers information; it provides counsel on broad lines of development and professional and technical consultation to states; in addition it allocates federal funds to states to assist them in strengthening and developing their services, especially in rural areas and areas of special need. Although states are not required to match these funds, the aggregate expenditures of states for child welfare greatly exceed the amount of federal assistance.

The Social Security Act authorizes the annual appropriation of $10 million for federal grants, but Congress has never appropriated more than $7,228,900, which is the current level. These funds are allocated on the basis of the rural child population of each state.

FUNCTIONS AND PROBLEMS

One of the important aspects of child welfare is extending care and protection to children who are deprived of the care and support of their natural parents. Contrary to a widespread impression, such children are seldom orphans and rarely full orphans. Moreover, with the advent of income maintenance programs, notably Aid to Dependent Children and Old-Age and Survivors Insurance, poverty alone is no longer a basis for the separation of children from their parents. Instead, the parental backgrounds of these children are marked by such circumstances as illness, incompetence, desertion, divorce, illegitimacy and institutionalization. Even more than orphans, children from those backgrounds often have had long experiences of family discord and instability. In addition, their legal status is frequently so complicated that they may never be free for adoption, even though they might benefit thereby. Numbered also among these are children with handicaps, and children of mixed or minority racial backgrounds, who are difficult if not impossible to place in either foster family or adoptive homes.

As a result of well established findings that institutional care as a way of life is damaging at best, the long-term trend is to place more children for care in foster family homes. Recognition has grown that institutions can more properly be used for short-term study and observation and for highly specialized and skilled professional treatment and care.

Many state welfare authorities believe that perhaps the most critically inadequate services for children today are those which could relieve situations of family discord and behavior problems of children at a point sufficiently early to prevent later tragedies. State attention to these problems has risen markedly, but welfare agencies commonly are lacking in staff or other resources to reach beyond the crises which are the end results of untreated problems.

Placement of children for adoption, and the licensing and setting of standards for placement agencies, are another important public child-welfare function. Year after year more states are enacting legislation to eliminate the adoptive placement of children by unauthorized third party intermediaries, including the commercial or so-called "black market" operators. Such laws usually limit the authority of natural parents to dispose of their children and of adopting parents to receive children except through licensed agencies. The heightened demand in recent years for adoptive children has resulted in an estimated ten-to-one ratio of applicants to available children. Widespread public interest and pressures are associated with the adoptive placement of children. But for many children the adoption process is still fraught with many hazards because of incomplete services and lack of sufficient legal safeguards.

Other current problems of primary concern include juvenile delinquency, serious personality disturbances and mental retardation.

Child welfare agencies everywhere are concerned with the apparent rise, both in extent and severity, of juvenile delinquency. Efforts to combat it include a closer coordination of existing services, initiating and strengthening of services to fill existing gaps, and research and experimentation to discover more effective methods of prevention and treatment.

Children suffering from severe emotional disturbances and psychoses require special care and they need highly skilled treatment. The number of children involved is not great as compared with the total child population. But children thus afflicted constitute a social dilemma because available treatment resources are few in comparison with the needs. As a consequence disturbed children often are kept in jails, correctional institutions and adult mental hospitals, none of which is equipped to provide the services needed. In recent years a number of state welfare departments, state hospitals, legislators and officials, recognizing these problems, have been seeking means of improving the situation. In certain states promising pilot programs and new facilities have resulted. However, treatment facilities for these children are costly, and they require highly skilled professional staff which today is not available on a scale commensurate with the demand.

Renewed efforts are being made to help mentally retarded children to attain their maximum capacities for leading useful and satisfying lives. Through the cooperation of parents, communities and state and local agencies, programs for education and training, both in institutions and in family homes, are achieving encouraging results.

Services of public child-welfare agencies also include help for unmarried parents and their children; working with courts and training schools in cases of neglect, dependency and delinquency; working jointly with other agencies and institutions, such as crippled children's services, mental hospitals and specialized children's institutions.

Youth Authorities

In recent years a few states have established agencies known as youth authorities, which have their primary focus on juvenile delinquents and youthful offenders. No two authorities are alike, but a common characteristic is that they receive commitments from the courts and conduct studies and make diagnostic determinations as to the treatment and disposition required by each case. This is in contrast to the more general plan in other states, under which courts make such determinations themselves. Youth authorities usually administer their own screening and classification services and treatment facilities, including training schools and parole services. Other activities, such as preventive programs and financial grants to local agencies, are carried on by youth authorities in some states. Administrative structures vary. Usually an authority is either an independent agency or a unit of the state welfare department.

Personnel and Training

Recognition has grown of the necessity for all child-welfare services to be carried out through staff personnel who are professionally qualified by training and experience. More positions are being established which require these qualifications, and competition for securing well trained staff has become increasingly keen among the states and the localities. In contrast to this heightened demand, however, the supply of professionally qualified persons in the field is not increasing. Expanded public training programs are among the recommendations frequently advanced for solution of the problem.

THE LEGAL STATUS OF WOMEN*

THE favorable position of women under law in the United States today reflects their substantial contribution to the social and economic life of the nation. Legal discriminations against women which still remain on the statute books are due in large measure to the fact that in the United States law generally follows practice and social custom. Concrete remedial action is taken only when the need for legislative reform is brought to public attention.

PUBLIC OFFICE

Women's increasing participation in public life is evidenced by their number in elective and appointive office. In 1955 more women were serving in federal and state posts than at any previous time. The 84th Congress has seventeen women members—sixteen in the House of Representatives and one in the Senate. This represents a gain of three over the 83rd session, and makes a total of sixty women who have been elected or appointed to Congress since 1916, when the first woman representative was elected, from Montana. In state legislatures of 1955 there were 308 women members, five more than in 1954.

The 560,000 women in the federal government service represent a fourth of the entire civilian personnel. About 2,000 of these women are in policy-making and high administrative positions. A total of eighty-five women—the largest number in any federal administration—have been appointed to important positions in the various federal agencies and commissions since 1953. Women are making great strides in the foreign service. There are two women ambassadors—to Italy and Switzerland, more than sixty women career foreign service officers and about 2,000 women serving in clerical capacities throughout the world.

Women are well represented in state posts. Thirty-seven hold important elective positions, and approximately 6,000 are in high-level appointive jobs. In addition about 18,000 women are county officials and 10,000 are in municipal government, including fifty mayors of small towns. The judiciary is another field of public service in which women are making impressive progress. There are 150 women judges in federal, state, domestic and juvenile, and county and municipal courts.

JURY SERVICE

By July, 1955, women were eligible for jury service in all except four states, Alabama, Mississippi, South Carolina and West Virginia. In one of the four, West Virginia, the 1955 legislature adopted a resolution providing for a referendum on jury service for women in November, 1956.

There are two types of jury service laws for women: compulsory laws, which require them to serve on the same terms as men, subject to reasonable grounds for exemption or release by the court; and voluntary or optional laws, which permit women to be excused from service solely on the basis of sex.

The following tabulation lists states, territories and commonwealths by type of law and year of enactment:

Compulsory laws

Arizona	1945	Montana	1939
California	1917	Nebraska	1943
Canal Zone	1949	New Jersey	1917
Colorado	1945	New Mexico	1951
Connecticut	1937	North Carolina	1947
Delaware	1935	Ohio	1923
Hawaii	1952	Oklahoma	1952
Illinois	1939	Oregon	1921
Indiana	1920	Pennsylvania	1921
Iowa	1920	South Dakota	1947
Maine	1921	Texas	1954
Maryland	1947(a)	Vermont	1943
Michigan	1918	Wyoming	1949

(a) Baltimore and nineteen counties (as of July, 1955) permit women to serve on juries; the remaining four counties, at their own request, are exempt from the state jury law.

*Prepared by ALICE K. LEOPOLD, Assistant to the Secretary of Labor for Women's Affairs, Women's Bureau, U. S. Department of Labor.

Voluntary laws

Alaska	1923	Nevada	1920
Arkansas	1921	New Hampshire	1947
District of		New York	1937
Columbia	1927	North Dakota	1921
Florida	1949	Puerto Rico	1952
Georgia	1953	Rhode Island	1927
Idaho	1943	Tennessee	1951
Kansas	1913	Utah	1898
Kentucky	1920	Virgin Islands	1945
Louisiana	1924	Virginia	1950
Massachusetts	1949	Washington	1911
Minnesota	1921	Wisconsin	1921
Missouri	1945		

MARRIAGE AND DIVORCE LAWS

The common-law age of consent to marriage—12 for females and 14 for males—is still in effect in a few states. But the most prevalent statutory minimum ages are 18 for males and 16 for females with parental consent, and without parental consent, 21 for males and 18 for females. (See table on page 346.)

The grounds for divorce in the various states are usually the same for men and women, with the exception of non-support which is allowed to the wife in twenty-one states. Of other grounds for divorce the most common under state law are mental or physical cruelty; desertion or abandonment; voluntary separation; impotency; habitual use of alcohol or drugs; insanity; and conviction of felony. (See table on page 344.)

ALIMONY AND MAINTENANCE

All states permit the court to grant alimony and maintenance to a wife for her support and that of her minor children, even though the divorce may be granted to the husband.

A few states require the court to consider the size of a wife's personal estate before granting her a maintenance allowance, prohibiting such a grant if her estate is sufficient for her own support. Alimony is barred in some states where the husband has procured a divorce on the ground of adultery. Fifteen states—California, Illinois, Iowa, Massachusetts, Michigan, Nebraska, New Hampshire, North Carolina, North Dakota, Ohio, Oklahoma, Rhode Island, Utah, Vermont and West Virginia—by law permit the court to grant alimony to a husband within certain limitations. Divorce laws may also provide for restora-

tion of the wife's prior name, attorney's fees and court costs, property settlement and care and custody of children.

By the end of 1954 all except ten states and the District of Columbia had laws requiring a premarital physical examination for both male and female applicants for a marriage license. One state, Texas, limits the examination requirement to males only. The most recent laws are those of Arkansas (1953) and Louisiana (1954). The latter superseded an earlier, non-compulsory law, applicable to males. The scope of the required tests varies. Usually it covers venereal diseases, but in a few states it also covers other types of disease. (See table on page 346.)

FAMILY SUPPORT

Uniform reciprocal enforcement of support legislation is now in effect in all states, territories and commonwealths with the exception of the District of Columbia. The last two states to enact such legislation were Mississippi in 1954 and Nevada in 1955. In addition, many states have enacted strengthening amendments to their legislation since 1952.

The husband and father is primarily responsible for family support of his wife and minor children; if he is dead or incapable the responsibility falls on the wife and mother. In the eight states having community-property laws, the common estate of the husband and wife is liable for family support, but this does not relieve the husband of his responsibility as head of the family.

PARENT AND CHILD

All states except six—Alabama, Georgia, Louisiana, New Mexico, North Carolina, Texas—(as of January 1, 1953) recognize the parents as joint natural guardians of their minor children during the marriage.

There is no legislation in any state which bars the mother from acting as guardian of her minor children if the father is unfit or incapable. On the death of one parent, the other automatically becomes the natural guardian. Children of marriages dissolved by divorce or separation in effect become wards of the court, which is empowered by law in all jurisdictions to make orders respecting their custody and maintenance. The interests and welfare of the child are the controlling factors in such court determination.

CONTRACTS AND PROPERTY RIGHTS

The few remaining legal discriminations against married women in their contractual and property rights are gradually disappearing. This has been achieved primarily through the efforts of women's organizations in the various states. These groups, through study and action programs, have stimulated interest in legislation designed to insure married women a more equitable position under the law.

State legislation of special value to women in the field of contract and property, enacted in the two-year period from 1952 through 1954 may be indicative of a current trend. It includes laws raising the value of the homestead exempt from seizure for debt; restrictions on the assignment of wages by a husband or wife to a third person without the consent of the other spouse; laws liberalizing provisions for maintenance of the family during administration of the estate of a deceased husband or wife as well as increasing the value of estates which can be summarily administered.

A summary of the most important types of legislation affecting married women's contracts and property rights is available in the 1954–1955 edition of *The Book of the States*, pp. 321–22.

DIVORCE LAWS AS OF 1954*

State	Length of residence required before filing suit	Adultery	Cruelty	Desertion	Alcoholism	Impotency	Felony conviction	Neglect to provide	Insanity	Pregnancy at marriage	Bigamy	Separation	Imprisonment	Indignities	Drug addict / Fraudulent contract
Alabama	(a)	★	★	★	★	★	★	★	★(b)	★	··	··	★(c)	★	★ ··
Arizona	1 year	★	★	★	★	★	★	★	··	★	··	★(b)	··	★	★ ··
Arkansas	60 days(h)	★	★	★	★	★	★	★	★·	··	★	★(b)	··	★	·· ··
California	1 year	★	★	★	★	··	★	★	★(b)	··	··	··	··	··	·· ··
Colorado	1 year	★	★	★	★	★	★	★	★(b)	··	··	··	··	··	★ ··
Connecticut	3 years	★	★	★	★	··	··	··	★(b)	··	★	··	★	··	★ ★
Delaware	2 years (h)	★	★	★	★	★	··	··	★(b)	★	★	··	★(i)	··	·· ··
Florida	90 days	★	★	★	★	★	··	··	★	··	★	··	··	★(k)	·· ··
Georgia	6 months	★	★	★	★	★	★(m)	··	(n,b)	★	··	··	(m)	··	★ ··
Idaho	6 weeks	★	★	★	★	★	★	★	★(b)	··	★(b)	··	··	··	·· ··
Illinois	1 year(o)	★	★	★	★	★	★	··	··	··	★	··	··	··	·· ··
Indiana	1 year	★	★	★	★	★	★	··	★(b)	··	··	··	··	··	·· ··
Iowa	1 year	★	★	★	★	★	★	··	★	··	··	··	··	··	·· ··
Kansas	1 year(r)	★	★	★	★	★	★	★	★(b)	★	··	★(b)	··	··	★ ··
Kentucky	1 year	★	★	★	★	★	★	★	··	··	··	★(b)	★(i)	··	★ ··
Louisiana	(u)	★	★	★	★	··	★	··	··	··	··	··	★(i)	··	·· ··
Maine	6 months	★	★	★	★	★	★(x)	★	★	··	··	··	··	··	★ ··
Maryland	1 year(w)	★	··	★	··	★	★(x)	··	★(b)	★	★	★(b)	··	··	·· ··
Massachusetts	5 years(y)	★	★	★	★	★	★	★	··	··	··	··	★	★(b)	★ ··
Michigan	1 year(z)	★	★(aa)	★	★	★	··	★(aa)	··	··	··	··	★	··	·· ··
Minnesota	1 year	★	★	★	★	★	··	··	★(b)	··	★	··	★(i)	★	·· ··
Mississippi	1 year	★	★	★	★	★	★	··	★(b)	★	★	··	··	★	·· ··
Missouri	1 year	★	★	★	★	★	★	··	··	★	··	··	··	··	★ ··
Montana	1 year	★	★	★	★	··	★	★	★(b)	··	··	··	··	··	·· ··
Nebraska	2 years(ae)	★	★	★	★	★	★	··	★(b)	··	··	··	★(b)	··	·· ··
Nevada	6 weeks	★	★	★	★	★	★	★	★(i)	··	··	★(b)	··	··	·· ··
New Hampshire	1 year(ag)	★	★	★	★	★	★	★	··	··	··	★	★(az)	··	·· ··
New Jersey	2 years	★	★	★	··	··	··	··	··	··	··	··	··	··	·· ··
New Mexico	1 year(ai)	★	★	★	★	★	★	★	★(b)	★	··	··	★	··	·· ··
New York	(aj)	★	··	··	··	··	··	··	··	··	··	··	··	··	·· ··
North Carolina	6 months	★	··	★	··	★	··	··	★(al)	★	··	★(i)	··	··	·· ··
North Dakota	1 year(r)	★	★	★	★	★	★	★	★(b)	(ba)	(ba)	··	··	··	★ (ba)
Ohio	1 year	★	★	★	★	★	★	★	··	★	··	··	★	··	★
Oklahoma	1 year	★	★	★	★	★	★	★	★(an)	★	··	··	··	··	★
Oregon	1 year	★	★	★	··	★	★	··	★(b)	··	··	··	··	★	★
Pennsylvania	1 year	★	★	★	··	★	★	··	··	··	★	··	··	★	★
Rhode Island	2 years	★	★	★	★	★	★	★	··	··	··	★(al)	··	★	··
South Carolina	1 year	★	★	★	★	··	··	··	··	··	··	··	··	★	··
South Dakota	1 year(ao)	★	★	★	★	★	★	★	★(b)	··	★	★	··	··	··
Tennessee	2 years	★	★	★	★	★	★	··	··	★	★	··	··	★	··
Texas	1 year	★	★	★	··	★	★(aq)	··	★(b)	··	··	★(al)	··	··	··
Utah	90 days	★	★	★	★	★	★	★	★(b)	··	··	★(b)	··	··	··
Vermont	6 months(w)	★	··	★	··	··	★	★	★(b)	··	··	★(b)	★	··	··
Virginia	1 year	★	··	★	··	★	★	··	··	··	··	★	··	··	··
Washington	1 year	★	★	★	★	★	★	★	★(i)	··	··	★(b)	★	★	★
West Virginia	2 years(ae)	★	★	★	★	★	★	··	★	··	··	★(b)	★	··	★
Wisconsin	2 years	★	★	★	★(ah)	★	★(b)	★	··	★(i)	★	★(b)	★	··	··
Wyoming	60 days	★	★	★	★	★	★	★	★(i)	··	··	★(i)	★	··	··
Alaska	2 years	★	★	★	★	★	★	★	★(b)	··	··	··	★	··	··
Dist. of Columbia	2 years(au)	★	★(bb)	★	··	··	★	··	··	··	··	★(b)	··	··	··
Hawaii	2 years	★	★	★	★	··	★	★	★(h)	··	··	★(g)	··	★	··
Puerto Rico	1 year	★	★	★	★	★	★	··	★(g)	··	··	★(b)	··	★	··
Virgin Islands	6 weeks	★	★	★	★	★	★	··	··	··	··	··	··	··	··

*Prepared by the Women's Bureau, U. S. Department of Labor.

(a) No specific period of residence required except when ground is abandonment or defendant is a nonresident, in which cases plaintiff must prove one year's residence; wife seeking divorce on non-support must prove 2 year's residence and spouses must have been separated during that time.

(b) Three years.

(c) Two years' imprisonment, sentence for 7 years or longer.

(d) Alabama and North Carolina, crime against nature; Alaska, Virgin Islands, incompatibility; Mississippi, insanity at time of marriage; Missouri, Wyoming, husband a vagrant; Rhode Island, other gross misbehavior or wickedness; Vermont, intolerable severity.

(e) Court may forbid remarriage.

(f) Wife's absence out of state 10 years.

(g) Seven years.

(h) Action for divorce based on adultery or bigamy may be commenced at time cause of action arose, when either party was bona fide resident of state and has continued to be so until commencement of action.

(i) Two years.

(j) Female under 16, male under 18, complaining party under age of consent at time of marriage not confirmed after reaching such age.

(k) Habitual violent, and ungovernable temper.

(l) Defendant obtained divorce from complainant in other state.

(m) Felony conviction must comprehend sentence for 2 years to penitentiary.

(n) Insanity at time of marriage.

(o) Six months if offense committed in state.

(p) Where obtained by default of notice on publication only.

(q) Period can be shortened if approval of court is obtained.

(r) Five years if on insanity grounds and insane spouse is inmate of out-of-state institution.

(s) Joining a religious sect disbelieving in marriage.

(t) Unchaste behavior of wife after marriage.

(u) One year in cases of separation of 2 or more years; no statutory requirement for other grounds but separation decree from bed and board prerequisite, except for adultery or felony conviction.

(v) Absence of reconciliation for 1 year after judgment of separation, or public defamation, or fugitive from justice.

(w) Insanity 2 years.

(x) Plus sentence of at least 3 years, 18 months of which has been served.

(y) Three years if both parties were state residents at time of marriage.

(z) No residence requirement if marriage solemnized in state and party applying for divorce has resided therein since marriage.

DIVORCE LAWS OF 1954*—Continued

Felony before marriage	Violence	Absence	Infamous crime	Loathsome disease	Relationship within prohibited degrees	Other grounds	Plaintiff	Defendant	State
..	★	..	..	..	..	(d)	60 days if no appeal	60 days if no appeal(e)	........Alabama
★	★	..	..	..	..	..	1 year	1 year	.........Arizona
..	..	..	★	..	..	..	30 days	30 days	........Arkansas
..	..	..	..	..	..	..	1 year	1 year	.......California
..	..	..	..	..	..	..	6 months	6 months	........Colorado
..	..	★(g)	★	..	..	..	Immediately	Immediately	....Connecticut
..	..	..	..	..	..	(j)	1 year	1 year	........Delaware
..	..	..	..	..	★	(l)	Immediately	Immediately	..........Florida
..	★	..	..	..	..	★	Fixed by court	Fixed by court	.......Georgia
..	..	..	..	..	..	..	6 months	6 months	...........Idaho
..	★	..	★	★	..	..	Immediately	Immediately	.........Illinois
..	..	..	★	..	..	..	2 years (p)	Immediately	.........Indiana
..	..	..	..	..	..	..	1 year (q)	1 year (q)	............Iowa
..	..	..	..	..	..	..	6 months	6 months	...........Kansas
..	★	..	..	★	..	(s,t)	Immediately	Immediately	........Kentucky
..	★	..	★	..	..	(v)	Wife, 10 mos.	Wife, 10 mos. (ad)	.......Louisiana
..	★	..	..	..	..	..	Immediately	Immediately	...........Maine
..	..	..	..	..	..	..	Immediately	Immediately	........Maryland
..	..	..	..	..	..	..	6 months	2 years	....Massachusetts
..	★(aa)	..	..	..	..	(ab)	6 months if children under 17 (ac)	6 months if children under 17 (ac)	.........Michigan
..	..	..	..	..	..	..	6 months	6 months	........Minnesota
..	..	..	..	..	★	(n)	Immediately	Immediately (ad)	......Mississippi
★	..	..	★	..	..	(d)	Immediately	Immediately	.........Missouri
..	★	..	..	..	..	..	Immediately	Immediately	.........Montana
..	..	..	..	..	..	..	6 months	6 months	........Nebraska
..	..	..	..	..	..	..	Immediately	Immediately	..........Nevada
..	..	★(f)	..	..	..	(s,af)	Immediately	Immediately	..New Hampshire
..	..	..	..	..	..	..	3 months	3 months	......New Jersey
..	..	..	..	..	..	..	Immediately	Immediately	.....New Mexico
..	..	..	..	..	..	(ak)	Immediately	3 years—consent of court	.......New York
..	..	..	..	..	..	(d)	Immediately	Immediately	...North Carolina
..	..	..	..	..	..	..	Immediately (aa)	Immediately (aa)	.....North Dakota
..	..	★(az)	..	..	..	(l)	Immediately	Immediately	............Ohio
..	..	..	..	..	..	..	6 months	6 months	........Oklahoma
..	..	..	..	..	..	..	6 months	6 months	..........Oregon
..	..	..	..	..	★	..	Immediately	Immediately (ad)	....Pennsylvania
..	..	★	..	..	..	(d)	6 months	6 months	.....Rhode Island
..	..	..	..	..	..	..	....	....	...South Carolina
..	..	..	..	..	..	..	Immediately	Immediately (ad)	....South Dakota
..	★	★(i)	★	..	..	(ap)	Immediately	Immediately (ad)	........Tennessee
..	..	..	..	..	..	..	Immediately; Cruelty, 1 year	Immediately; Cruelty, 1 year	.............Texas
..	..	..	..	..	..	..	6 months	6 months	.............Utah
..	..	★(g)	..	..	..	(d)	6 months	2 years (r)	.........Vermont
..	..	..	★	..	..	(ar,as)	4 months	4 months (ad)	..........Virginia
..	..	..	..	..	..	..	Immediately	Immediately	......Washington
..	..	..	..	..	..	..	60 days	60 days (ad,at)	....West Virginia
..	★	..	..	..	..	..	1 year	1 year	.......Wisconsin
★	..	..	★	..	..	(d)	Immediately	Immediately	.........Wyoming
..	..	..	..	..	..	(d)	Immediately	Immediately	..........Alaska
..	..	..	..	..	..	..	6 months	6 months	Dist. of Columbia
..	..	..	..	★	..	..	Immediately (av)	Immediately (av)	...........Hawaii
..	..	..	..	..	..	(aw)	Immediately (ax)	Immediately (ax)	......Puerto Rico
..	..	..	..	..	..	(d)	(ay)	(ay)	....Virgin Islands

(aa) In the court's discretion.

(ab) At court's discretion to resident of state whose spouse has obtained divorce in another state.

(ac) At court's discretion time may be shortened in case of unusual hardship or compelling necessity. For defendant court may prohibit remarriage within specified time not exceeding 2 years.

(ad) One divorced for adultery may not marry the paramour.

(ae) One year where the cause of divorce arose within state.

(af) When a wife of any alien or citizen of another state, living separate, has resided in the state, 3 years together, husband having left U.S. to become a foreign citizen and during that period has not come into state to claim marital rights or provide for wife.

(ag) Three years on grounds of desertion.

(ah) Husband habitual one year, wife given to intoxication.

(ai) Time spent on military reservation shall count as residence.

(aj) Parties residents when offense committed; married in state; plaintiff resident when offense committed and action commenced; offense committed in state and injured party resident when action commenced.

(ak) The so-called Enoch Arden law provides for annulment of marriage upon showing that the other party has been absent for 5 successive years and that diligent search reveals no evidence that such other party is living.

(al) Five years.

(an) Incurable insanity, the insane person having been an inmate of a state or private institution 5 years.

(ao) Divorce suits may be commenced any time if married in state and residents then until action; action may be commenced after 6 months residence if cause of action arose in state.

(ap) Refusal of wife to live with husband in the state and absenting herself 2 years.

(aq) If imprisonment follows.

(ar) Wife a prostitute; 2 years a fugitive from justice under indictment.

(as) Designated crimes against nature.

(at) Court may keep defendant from remarrying for a year.

(au) Residence of 1 year is required where the cause of divorce occurred in the District.

(av) May be limited at court's discretion not to exceed 1 month.

(aw) Attempt to corrupt sons or prostitute daughters; proposal of husband to prostitute wife; grave injury.

(ax) Man immediately, woman after 301 days.

(ay) Neither plaintiff nor defendant may remarry with a third party until action has been heard and determined on appeal, and if no appeal be taken, until expiration of 30-day period allowed by law to take appeal.

(az) One year.

(ba) May be grounds for annulment.

(bb) Legal separation for cruelty which can be enlarged into an absolute divorce after 2 years.

THE BOOK OF THE STATES

MARRIAGE LAWS*

As of 1954

State	Age of consent to marriage (a) — Male	Female	Age below which parental consent is required — Male	Female	Common law marriages recognized	Prohibit marriage of those with transmissible disease in infectious stage	Physical examination and blood test for male and female — Date of enactment	(b)	Scope of laboratory test	Waiting period — Before issuance of license	After issuance of license
Alabama	17	14	21	18	★	......	(c)	30 da.	(d)	......	......
Arizona	18	16	21	18				30 da.	(d)	......	
Arkansas	18	16	21	18			1953	30 da.	(g)	3 da.	
California	(e)	(e)	21	18	(f)		1939	30 da.	(g)	......	
Colorado	(e)	(e)	21	18	★		1939	30 da.	(j)	......	
Connecticut	16	16	21	21			1935	40 da.	(g)	5 da.	......
Delaware	18	16	21	18		★					(h)
District of Columbia	18	16	21	18	★					4 da.	......
Florida	18	16	21(i)	21(i)	★		1945	30 da.	(g)	3 da.	......
Georgia	17	14	..	18	★					5 da.	......
Idaho	15	15	18	18	★		1943	30 da.	(j)	......	
Illinois	18	16	21	18			1939	15 da.	(d)	......	
Indiana	18	16	21	18			1939	30 da.	(g)	......	
Iowa	16	14	21	18	★		1941	20 da.	(g)	......	
Kansas	(e)	(e)	21	18	★		1947	30 da.	(j)	3 da.	
Kentucky	16	14	21	21			1940	15 da.	(g)	3 da.	
Louisiana	18	16	21	21			1954(k)	7 da.	(d)	......	72 hrs.
Maine	(e)	(e)	21	18	★	★	1941	30 da.	(g)	5 da.	
Maryland	18	16	21	18						2 da.	
Massachusetts	18	16	21	18			1943	30 da.	(g)	5 da.	
Michigan	18	16	..	18	★		1939	30 da.	(d)	5 da.	
Minnesota	18	16	21	18	(l)					5 da.	
Mississippi	(e)	(e)	21	18	★		1943	30 da.	(g)	5 da.	
Missouri	15	15	21	18	(m)			15 da.	(g)	3 da.	
Montana	18	16	21	21	★		1947	20 da.	(g)	......	
Nebraska	18	16	21	21		★	1943	30 da.	(g)	......	
Nevada	18	16	21	18							
New Hampshire	20	18	20	18			1937	30 da.	(g)	5 da.	
New Jersey	(e)	(e)	21	18	(n)	★	1938	30 da.	(g)	3 da.	
New Mexico	18	16	21	18			1938(o)	30 da.	(g)	3 da.	24 hrs.
New York	16	14	21	18			1941	30 da.	(d, p)	2 da.(q)	
North Carolina	16	16	18	18			1941	30 da.	(g, r)		
North Dakota	18	15	21	18			1939	30 da.			
Ohio	18	16	21	21	★		1941	30 da.	(g)	5 da.	
Oklahoma	18	15	21	18	★	★(s)	1945	30 da.	(g)	......	
Oregon	18	15	21	18			(t)	30 da.	(j, u)	3 da.	
Pennsylvania	16	16	21	21	★		1939	30 da.	(g)	3 da.	
Rhode Island	18	16	21	18	★		1938	40 da.	(p, v)	5 da.	
South Carolina	18	14	18	18	★					1 da.	
South Dakota	18	15	21	21	★		1939	20 da.	(g)	......	
Tennessee	16	16	..	..			1939	30 da.	(d)	3 da.	
Texas	16	14	21	18	★		(w)	15 da.	(d)	......	
Utah	16	14	21	18		★	1941	30 da.	(j)	......	
Vermont	16	14	21	18		★	1941	30 da.	(g)	......	5 da.
Virginia	18	16	21	21			1940	30 da.	(g)	......	
Washington	(e)	(e)	21	18	★					3 da.	
West Virginia	18	16	21	21			1939	30 da.	(g)	3 da.	
Wisconsin	18	15	21	18			1939	15 da.	(g)	5 da.	
Wyoming	18	16	21	21	★		1943	30 da.	(d)	......	

*Prepared by the Women's Bureau, U. S. Department of Labor.

(a) With parental consent.
(b) Time allowed between date of examination and issuance of license.
(c) In 1919 law adopted applying to male only; laboratory test authorized but not required. Amendments in 1947 and 1949 rewrote law and apply to both male and female applicants.
(d) Venereal diseases.
(e) Common-law age of consent to marriage in absence of statutory requirement 14 for males and 12 for females. California requires court approval where female is under 16 and male under 18.
(f) Valid if consummated prior to 1895.
(g) Syphilis.
(h) 24 hours, residents; 96 hours, nonresidents.
(i) Parental consent not required of previously married minor.
(j) Syphilis and other venereal diseases.

(k) In 1924 law adopted applying to male only; laboratory test authorized but not required.
(l) Valid if contracted on or before April 26, 1941.
(m) Valid if contracted prior to March 31, 1921.
(n) Valid if contracted prior to November 30, 1939.
(o) Amended in 1939.
(p) Tuberculosis in infectious stage.
(q) In one county if both applicants are nonresidents.
(r) Pulmonary tuberculosis in advanced stages or with any contagious venereal disease.
(s) Person infected with venereal disease who marries any other person guilty of a felony and upon conviction may be punished by penitentiary confinement from 1 to 5 years.
(t) Amended in 1953.
(u) Free from epilepsy, feeblemindedness, mental illness or chronic alcoholism.
(v) Syphilis and gonorrhea.
(w) In 1929 law adopted applying to male only; no provision as to laboratory test.

4

Defense and Public Protection

CIVIL DEFENSE IN THE STATES*

LEGISLATION

HISTORICALLY, it may be said that the initial experience with civil defense in the United States occurred in World War I. At the national level the Secretary of War, in his capacity as Chairman of the Council of National Defense, had the responsibility for developing a program concerned with civilian protection. The states and their local governments established defense councils which reached a total number of 120,000 before the end of the war. The functions of these councils covered the direction of a broad range of programs including such matters as the conservation of scarce materials and activities to raise morale.

In a more limited sense, civil defense is now defined as embracing "the non-military measures undertaken to reduce the effects of attack and to rehabilitate the people and their communities in the period immediately following attack." In these terms, the current civil defense programs trace their roots in large part to the experiences of World War II. The national government established an Office of Civilian Defense in 1941 which functioned until mid-1945. During the same period many of the states likewise set up civil defense agencies.

Experience with civil defense entered a new phase beginning with the outbreak of hostilities in Korea in 1950. Under the

threat of open and large-scale war, the Federal Civil Defense Act of 1950 was enacted, and in January, 1951, the Federal Civil Defense Administration was established. With the completion of the legislative sessions of 1953, every state had enacted a basic civil defense law, as had Alaska, Guam, Hawaii, Puerto Rico and the Virgin Islands. The majority of the state civil defense laws follow the lines of the Model Civil Defense Act, which was developed by the Council of State Governments and the National Security Resources Board.

A number of state civil defense laws were made effective for limited periods. As a result, some states were involved in extending the terms of their acts during the legislative sessions from 1953 through 1955. Among states extending the duration of their acts were Connecticut, Massachusetts, New York, Rhode Island, Vermont and West Virginia. In Ohio the civil defense laws were recodified in a new and separate chapter. In Michigan the legislature provided for the establishment of a Civil Defense Council and, subject to legislative control, authorized the Governor to proclaim an emergency after an enemy attack.

Other legislative activity included an amendment to the civil defense act in Maryland to increase the authority of the Governor and provide for state cooperation with federal and local civil defense plans under his direction. Indiana adopted a law relieving any firm whose premises are used as an air-raid shelter from civil liability

*Prepared by VINCENT J. BROWNE, Federal Civil Defense Administration.

for injury or death of persons on the premises during an emergency.

In view of the fact that many state directors reported the recruitment of civil defense volunteers to be adversely affected by the absence of workmen's compensation, a number of states took legislative action in this area during the period 1953–55. Among them were Maine, New Hampshire, New York, Washington and Wisconsin. By mid-1955 nine states had provided compulsory compensation, six had authorized their political subdivisions to provide compensation at their own option and expense, and six had provided compulsory compensation for some workers and elective coverage for others. A total of twelve states made compensation available only for mobile support personnel. Fifteen made no provision for compensation.

A trend continued among state legislatures to authorize civil defense forces to operate in the face of natural disasters as well as in event of enemy attack. By mid-1955 forty-one legislatures had provided this authority. The hurricanes and floods of 1954 and 1955, particularly along the eastern coast, created stern tests for the civil defense organizations in the affected states. The tremendous damage suffered by New England in 1955 gave impetus to proposals that states should establish emergency funds to be set aside for use in the event of great natural diaster.

INTERSTATE CIVIL DEFENSE COMPACTS

Use of interstate compacts to provide for mutual assistance among the states continued to receive very broad support. By September, 1955, all states except two had provided statutory authority for interstate civil defense and disaster compacts. Thirty-eight of these states had placed the Model Compact into effect. Five states had compacts in effect with one or more variations from the Model Compact, and eight states with authority to make compacts had not yet filed one with Congress.

The development of more powerful nuclear weapons and the dissemination of information concerning hazards from "fall-out" stimulated more state activity in working out supplementary agreements. This was particularly true with respect to planning in the areas of evacuation and dis-

persal. Arizona and Nevada, for example, worked out plans to care for evacuees from Southern California. Utah and Oregon were well along in the establishment of plans for providing mass care resources. There were other types of supplemental agreements; for example, Connecticut and New York in 1954 signed an agreement regarding water transportation, and one on public information was signed by Massachusetts and New York.

FINANCING CIVIL DEFENSE

In view of the Federal Civil Defense Administration's discontinuance of its tabulation of appropriations by state and local governments, there was no systematic method of compiling this information after the 1953–54 fiscal year. However, for the three most recent years for which information was available, the following totals were reached concerning the availability of state funds for civil defense:

	1952 Fiscal year	1953 Fiscal year	1954 Fiscal year
For matching federal grants.....	$30,571,000	$ 9,050,591	$1,820,623
Administrative and other expenses...	9,666,907	9,807,659	6,295,581
Totals...	$40,237,907	$18,858,250	$8,116,204

In addition to the figures indicated above, many states had provided emergency funds whose uses were restricted in a variety of ways. These totaled approximately $100 million. A typical example of the restrictions imposed upon them was the frequent stipulation that they could be used only in the event of hostile action or an actual attack upon the United States. Under such conditions, the funds were not available for pre-attack purposes. The figures cited above likewise do not include a New York appropriation of $25 million for shelters, which could be spent only if matched by a grant of equal amount from the federal government. The federal government has not provided grants for this purpose.

The figures shown above for fiscal 1954 are probably somewhat incomplete, although not greatly so. The most striking fact in the three-year comparison is the marked reduction of state funds available for matching federal grants. This trend developed in large part as a result of the more extensive use of local funds to match federal grants. In addition, however, the decrease in state appropriations was prompted by the cessation of hostilities in Korea, as well as the fact that Congress did not appropriate the amounts for civil defense requested by the executive branch. Moreover, there was considerable disagreement at the state and local level with the provision of the Federal Civil Defense Act of 1950 that civil defense is primarily the responsibility of the states and their political subdivisions.

Appropriation by Congress of $68,670,000 for civil defense for fiscal 1956 represented a considerable increase over the appropriations for the three preceding years. These were $43,000,000 in 1953, $46,525,000 in 1954, and $49,325,000 in 1955. Included in the 1956 amount were $12,125,000 for operations, $12,400,000 for federal grants, $32,650,000 for supplies and equipment, $10,000,000 for evacuation surveys and research and $1,500,000 for the civil defense functions of other federal agencies. It was expected that, among other effects, this appropriation would help to reverse the trend of decreasing state appropriations.

The federal grant-in-aid program continued to have very large significance in the development of civil defense activities. Under this program more than $100 million—half federal and half state and local—had been expended by June 30, 1955. The Federal Civil Defense Administration in its 1954 annual report pointed out that the following benefits were being derived from the grant program:

1. The encouragement of civil defense preparedness in the states and municipalities by providing funds, on a matching basis, for approvable projects.

2. The maintenance of a balance among the programs by setting aside funds for priority programs.

3. Assistance to states in obtaining a maximum of preparedness in persons trained as well as items of civil defense equipment.

4. The improvement of standards of equipment best able to do the job. Through standardization of civil defense materials, facilities, and equipment, mutual aid and mobile support plans are more effectively implemented.

5. Practical cooperation between the federal government and the states in matters pertaining to civil defense.

6. Assistance to communities which normally could not afford needed programs.

7. The maintenance of good public relations between the citizens and their federal government in matters pertaining to civil defense, by helping them initiate their own programs.

8. Better knowledge of preparedness in the states through analysis of partially and wholly completed civil defense projects.

The federal funds available for matching purposes continued to be allocated among the states on the basis of population distribution. In qualifying for grants, states are required to match the federal grants on a fifty-fifty basis, either from their own funds or from local funds. In the case of Alaska, however, the matching ratio is 70 per cent federal and 30 per cent territorial funds.

The civil defense programs eligible for federal grants during fiscal year 1956 included the following: attack warning, communications, engineering, evacuation studies, health, special weapons defense, public civil defense education and information, rescue service, training and welfare service. Thus the list of eligible programs no longer includes fire services, but welfare services and evacuation studies are recent additions.

OTHER AREAS OF ACTIVITY

As a rule the areas of the country most interested in civil defense have tended to be those which contain large industrial centers and concentrations of population. However, release of public information concerning the danger of "fall-out" resulting from explosion of newly developed weapons, and the White House Conferences of Governors, have stimulated all states to participate in the development of the national civil defense program.

Emphasis continues to be placed upon the attack warning and communications system. This area of the civil defense program has remained high in priority in view of the absence of guarantee of any real warning time, and the fact that even under the best of conditions at present the coastal cities could not expect more than an hour's notice of enemy attack, while inland cities could not expect a notice of more than one to three hours. The Federal Civil Defense

Administration reported that in mid-1955 the warning systems in cities in the target areas provided about 77 per cent of the protection which these areas required.

The state civil defense agencies continued their close operation with the Air Force in the operation of the Ground Observer Corps in the thirty-two states and the District of Columbia which comprise the "Skywatch" area. By the end of 1954, 8,060 of the required 10,366 observation posts had been organized. In the states making up the "stand-by" area, 5,145 of the 6,099 required observation posts had been organized. In all of these states the problem of recruiting and holding the interest of volunteer watchers remained one of serious proportions.

Progress was made in a number of states in the preparation of operational plans which would enable the states, in an attack situation, to take action along lines carefully drawn up in advance. These plans when fully completed include provisions for civil defense education and information, warning and communications, evacuation and dispersal, and such services as health, emergency welfare, engineering, rescue, fire, police and supply. From the nationwide view, progress in the development of plans having more than a paper significance appeared to be slow. Inadequate funds and insufficient staff at both state and local levels prevented effective planning in many jurisdictions.

However, there was a very marked increase in the number and kinds of test exercises throughout the country. These served a number of purposes, such as keeping the people informed and aware of the civil defense problem, stimulating operational planning, and providing a means of testing the effectiveness of civil defense programs.

RECOMMENDATIONS OF THE COMMISSION ON INTERGOVERNMENTAL RELATIONS

The report of the Commission on Intergovernmental Relations, made to the President for transmittal to Congress in June, 1955, contained significant conclusions and recommendations with respect to civil defense and natural disaster relief. One of the commission's conclusions was to the effect that it is unsound to place so large a measure of the responsibility for civil defense upon the states and local governments. The commission held that "The States and local governments have been made primarily responsible for a function over which they are denied, by the realities of the problem, any significant degree of real policy foundation and technical leadership, and for which they are therefore unwilling to bear the preponderant financial burden." The report recommended, therefore, that Congress amend the Federal Civil Defense Act of 1950 in the following manner:

(a) to reallocate responsibility for civil defense from a primary State and local responsibility to a responsibility of the National Government, with States and localities retaining an important supporting role;

(b) to provide that the National Government will be responsible for over-all planning and direction of the civil defense effort, development of civil defense policies and technical doctrine, and stimulation of interstate cooperation; and that States and localities will be responsible for day-to-day planning operations and the adaptation of National policies and doctrines to local situations.

The commission also recommended a change in the financing of civil defense. It held that the federal government should be solely responsible for the purchase of all special purpose equipment, such as radiological monitoring equipment, for the costs of training selected state and local civil defense personnel at national training schools, and for the accumulation of federal medical and engineering stockpiles. The report further recommended that under certain conditions the federal government should assist the states and the critical target areas in defraying the costs of personnel whose duties were solely of a civil defense nature. Another recommendation concerned the authorization of direct administrative relations between the federal government and critical target cities, and the commission urged that states and local governments be called upon to join with the federal government in planning a program to reduce the vulnerability of cities.

Although the commission's proposals sought to increase the federal government's responsibility for civil defense, its report underscored the principle that disaster relief is primarily a state and local responsibility, and that the role of the federal government is to supplement their resources when there is actual need for additional assistance. It suggested that the states were not bearing an adequate share of disaster relief costs.

Under Public Law 875, 81st Congress, the federal government may grant funds to the states and local governments for the purposes of "performing on public or private lands protective and other work essential for the preservation of life and property, clearing debris and wreckage, making emergency repairs to the temporary replacements of public facilities of local governments damaged or destroyed in such major disaster, providing temporary housing or other emergency shelter. . . ." The report of the commission's subcommittee that dealt with this subject took the position that, although local governments affected by disasters frequently taxed their resources to the extreme in their rehabilitative efforts, many of the states restricted their assistance to aid-in-kind, extending little financial assistance. Some of these states have constitutional restrictions which prevent borrowing or transfer of funds for disaster relief purposes.

The commission made suggestions intended to stimulate states to engage in more planning for disaster relief, and to make more state funds available for the same purposes as those of the federal grants under Public Law 875. In the words of the report:

The Commission recommends that Congress amend Public Law 875 so that Federal financial assistance for disaster relief will be extended to any State or to its local governments only after the State has qualified for aid by passing a law or through other action which obligates it and such local governments as the law designates to pay a proportionate share of disaster relief expenditures from State or State and local funds . . .

Specifically, the commission recommended that before federal funds are made available in a disaster situation the state and its local governments "shall provide for and agree to spend or obligate for relief in case of a disaster or disasters within any twelve-month period an amount equal to at least one-fiftieth of 1 per cent of the three-year average of the total income payments of the people in the State during the most recent years reported." It was further recommended that after a state qualified for assistance there would be a matching ratio which would vary among the states in accordance with their per capita incomes. The percentage of federal financial assistance would range from 75 per cent for the states with the lowest per capita incomes to 33⅓ per cent for those with the highest. To provide for disaster situations of extraordinary magnitude, it was recommended that the President should be able to waive the requirements of a fixed formula.

The commission pointed out that its recommendations pertained only to cash payments of the federal government. The numerous types of aid-in-kind provided by the federal government would not be affected.

THE ARMY AND AIR NATIONAL GUARD
OF THE UNITED STATES*

Historically, constitutionally and in fact, the Army National Guard and the Air National Guard constitute the first-line elements of the Reserve Forces of the Army and the Air Force. Both the Army National Guard and the Air National Guard enjoy the distinction of being embodied as a whole in the "Ready Reserve" status defined in the Armed Forces Reserve Act of 1952. Congress, further, has stated several times in legislative enactments that it is essential that the strength and organization of both elements of the National Guard, as an integral part of the first-line defenses of the nation, be at all times maintained and assured.

Thus, even at a time when a comprehensive "National Reserve Plan" was being debated in Congress as fiscal year 1955 drew to a close, the Army National Guard and the Air National Guard were taking unprecedented strides for the defense of the United States.

Virtually all of the National Guard units, Army and Air, which had participated in Korean War service, had been returned to the control of the parent states. As has been the case after every war, they had to start almost from scratch in their reorganization.

By June 30, 1955, there were 5,198 federally recognized units of company, battery or detachment size in the Army National Guard, which comprised 34,665 officers and warrant officers and 323,576 enlisted men—an increase of more than 93,000 in two years.

Paralleling this growth was that of the Air National Guard, which had been almost in its entirety in active federal service during the Korean War. It had rebuilt into 572 units with a strength of 6,698 officers and 54,608 enlisted men.

Significant was the fact that all 419,547

*Prepared by the National Guard Association of the United States, in cooperation with the National Guard Bureau, departments of the Army and the Air Force.

officers and men, Army and Air, were contained in organized units—as distinct from individuals carried in a "pool"—which were functioning organizations and capable of quick expansion and service in case of mobilization.

In line with the policy of achieving the greatest possible combat-readiness, National Guard unit commanders were exercising ever-increasing care in the selection of qualified applicants for enlistment, with the result that the rate of rejections by the National Guard Bureau, Departments of the Army and Air Force, was dropping year by year. For fiscal year 1955, the Bureau's rejection rate for Army National Guard enlistments was 1 per cent and for the Air National Guard, 1.62 per cent.

Probably the most significant development within the past few years has been the increasing reliance by the Army and the Air Force upon the National Guard for prompt reinforcement, even during the period of technical peace. This has been evidenced especially in the field of defense against possible sneak aerial attack.

Within the Army's field, forty-nine National Guard antiaircraft artillery batteries had taken over fixed sites in eight defended critical "target areas," in what is known as the "AAA on-site program," worked out among the Army, Air Force and National Guard agencies involved in aerial defense of the nation. Each site is manned around the clock by a small detachment of full-time personnel employed in civilian status, but who must be members of the National Guard unit assigned to the site. These men provide guard and equipment maintenance service for the sites and the intricate AAA equipment; in the event of an "alert," they would ready the equipment for action pending arrival of the battery personnel, much as the paid drivers relate to other members of a volunteer fire department.

In the phased development of this program the first step is the transfer of specific sites from active Army organizations, which formerly manned them on a completely operational basis, to the designated National Guard units. The second is the occupation of the sites in a training status. The third is placement of the unit in "operational" status when it has met certain criteria, including personnel strength and achievement of definite training standards.

In recognition of the emphasis placed on the "AAA on-site program" and the special nature of the specially-designated AAA units' mission, every effort is made to recruit personnel from the areas adjacent to the sites; and special, higher-age limits have been placed on initial enlistments in the type of units involved in the program than for other units which, in time of war, could be expected to undergo more rigorous field operations.

Complementing this program within the Air National Guard is its Air Defense Augmentation Plan. This involves certain units at seventeen strategic locations maintaining two jet fighter aircraft and five combat-capable aircrews on "runway alert" seven days a week. The personnel are rotated for short periods of active duty —a day or several days at a stretch—taking this time away from their regular jobs or what would have been their days off.

Tied in closely with the operational set-up of the various Air Divisions of the regular Air Force Air Defense Command, this operation has involved establishment of special communications links, "alert shacks" at the various Air National Guard bases, "scramble pads," administrative procedures, and close liaison.

Actual intercepts of suspect aircraft have been performed almost from the first hour the program took effect on August 15, 1954. Each unit involved has averaged more than 100 aircraft-hours per month. Well over 750 "scrambles" have been accomplished, with an average of two intercepts per "scramble"—many of which could not have been accomplished by the active Air Force units available to Air Defense Command. The seventeen squadrons involved have logged 16,505 flying hours, 5,962 scrambles, and 13,390 intercepts, with only 34 aircraft, 85 pilots and 170 airmen augmenting the special Air Technical Detachments.

Apart from the actual operational value of the program in "beefing-up" the air defense of the country, aircrew training for the part-time fliers and aircraft crews has been invaluable. The *esprit de corps* of these units has reached a level exceeded only by units under actual combat conditions.

The nature and type of military organizations never are static, but change constantly to keep pace with technical, tactical and strategic considerations. This holds true within the National Guard as well as within the active forces, as the latters' needs for mobilization back-up change.

Thus, within the Army National Guard, the Troop Basis has been undergoing major revision, marked especially by revived emphasis on armor. Within the year, three of the National Guard's infantry divisions were converted to armored divisions, with one more to be redesignated within another year. When the conversions have been completed, the original post-World War II Troop Basis will have shifted from two armored and twenty-five infantry divisions to six armored and twenty-one infantry divisions. Similarly, many of the Guard's separate Infantry Regimental Combat Teams (Infantry Regiment, Field Artillery Battalion and Engineer Combat Company) at the close of fiscal year 1955 either had been or were slated for conversion to Armored Cavalry, Tank, Field Artillery and Engineer units.

Comparable conversion had taken place within the Air National Guard at the start of fiscal 1956. Within the Air Guard's twenty-seven wings, fighter-bomber units had been dropped as such, marking a reorganization into twenty-three fighter-interceptor wings, two tactical bombardment wings, and two tactical reconnaissance wings. These changes reflected the definite mission assigned to the Air National Guard of backing-up the air defense of the continental United States, Alaska, Hawaii and Puerto Rico in the initial stages of a possible war. Programmed for the near future was inclusion within the Air National Guard, for the first time, of personnel- and cargo-carrying units.

Paralleling the Army's development of its own aviation program to meet its specialized needs—a development stemming from the use of light aircraft for artillery fire control, reconnaissance and liaison service in World War II—was the growth of what is known as "Army Aviation" within the Army National Guard, and, significantly, the introduction of helicopters into the equipment tables of many ground units. The Army Guard's 810 pilots on flying status had flown 89,425 hours in the 84 helicopters and 561 fixed-wing craft in the year ending June 30, 1955.

The National Guard, Army and Air, was taking new steps in the field of training. Of major importance in many Air National Guard squadrons was inauguration of a program, in cooperation with the active Air Force, of requiring enlistees to agree to take eleven weeks of initial training at active Air Force bases before returning to their home-town units. Within fiscal 1955, 3,789 men had undergone such training.

At the start of fiscal 1956, the Army National Guard instituted a comparable program. The Army established a quota of 1,000 National Guard recruits monthly to receive eight weeks' basic training at selected Army camps alongside regular Army enlistees and draftees. In the first month of the plan's operation, the quota was over-subscribed by about 40 per cent, and the Army quickly agreed to accommodate approximately 400 more men than it had anticipated handling within that month.

A significant point involved was that, essentially, both the Army and Air basic training policies were purely voluntary; no law compels any man to enlist in the National Guard, and, once enlisted, no law compels him to take such extended active duty for training in peacetime as thousands already have taken of their own free will. The effect already felt and potentially to be felt, in terms not only of the individual's but the entire National Guard's state of training and readiness for combat, is immeasurable.

The law prescribes at least forty-eight armory or air base drills and fifteen days of field training, annually. In recent years, additional week-end drills for weapons firing and field exercises, and special staff training assemblies, have been authorized. Over and above that, the officers and thousands of key noncommissioned officers give countless hours of what otherwise would be their leisure time—and in many cases time from their jobs—to the administration and training of their units.

Additionally, nearly 10,000 officers and men, Army and Air, attended active Army and Air Force schools during fiscal year 1955, for courses lasting from a matter of weeks to several months. Such schooling embraces such subjects as flight training, observer training, and technical or tactical training. The total included 3,438 officers and 3,210 enlisted men of the Army National Guard, and 1,074 officers and 1,962 airmen of the Air Guard.

More than 45,000 individuals enrolled for home study extension courses in tactical and technical subjects to enhance their professional knowledge and qualify for promotion. Of these, 13,882 were officers and 24,953 enlisted men of the Army National Guard, and 6,590, commissioned and enlisted, from the Air Guard.

In a further effort to develop the highest degree of qualification for commission, five states—California, Connecticut, Massachusetts, New York and South Carolina—were operating their own State Officer Candidate Schools in coordination with Army agencies. Some other states required enlisted aspirants for commissions to attend either the regular Officer Candidate Schools—operated by the active Army primarily for its own personnel but with special provisions for National Guard attendance—or a special Officer Candidate School established by the Army at several bases for the particular purpose of giving a modified summer-time course for Guardsmen, qualifying graduates for commissions.

Of incalculable value to the National Guard and to national defense were the thousands of personnel employed full-time as civilians but required to be members of National Guard units, to handle the heavy administrative and equipment maintenance loads of their units, Army and Air. More than 24,000 officers and men were working at such jobs, to maintain personnel, supply and training records and every conceivable type of equipment from mess kits to fantastically expensive and intricate artillery pieces, tanks, aircraft and radar equipment. They did their work at every level from company to division headquarters; at state maintenance shops and in "concentration sites" where the bulk of a state's heavy materiel is stored for field training use. An aggregate payroll of more than $92 million annually thus was being invested in the proper safeguarding and maintenance of materiel worth billions of dollars.

After a slow start from the inauguration in 1950 of a cooperative federal-state armory construction program beset by legal and administrative complications, hundreds of National Guard units were getting adequate, modern armories as replacement for makeshift quarters adapted from jail cells, elevator shafts and often ramshackle sheds, garages and warehouses. Through fiscal year 1955, 249 armories had been completed at a cost of $17,689,589 in federal funds, plus many millions more represented by direct state appropriations or donations of land by municipalities or others; an additional 239 armories were under contract, costing $20,319,694 in federal funds alone.

Additionally, forty-two state mainte-nance shops, for the pooled maintenance and repair of all classes of equipment, had been completed at a cost of $2,820,997 in federal funds, with thirty-three more under contract to cost $2,337,224; seven concentration sites for heavy equipment had been completed, costing $473,198, with four under contract for another $126,671. On June 30, 1955, sixty state maintenance shops and 102 concentration sites were in operation.

The Air National Guard was operating from eighty-seven flying installations and sixty-five non-flying installations, to be increased to ninety-four flying and sixty-nine non-flying installations by the end of fiscal 1956.

The over-all effect of the giant strides taken, especially in the past several years, spurred by the incidence of the Korean War, has been to place the National Guard, Army and Air, in a state of readiness probably never matched before in time of peace. It has brought public recognition on the part of high officials in the military departments that the National Guard is the "Number One Reserve" of both the Army and the Air Force.

STATE FIRE PROTECTION*

STATE responsibility for fire prevention and control involves fire hazard legislation, state-wide building codes, acts creating the office of state fire marshal and establishing his duties and authority, arson laws, laws which form the basis for city ordinances on fire protection and prevention, and laws authorizing formation and operation of fire departments in cities, towns and other governmental districts. The civil defense acts of various states also charge the state fire marshal or other state agency with fire functions.

(For information on state action against forest fires see "State Forestry Administration," page 393; and "Northeastern Forest Fire Protection Commission," page 29.)

State fire officials operate in thirty-eight states, Hawaii and Puerto Rico. With few exceptions, they are known as State Fire Marshals, although their duties and activities vary somewhat. New York has a State Director of Safety, whose office has certain functions usually associated with fire marshals. All state fire marshals have in common the function of investigating suspicious fires and detecting arson. Almost all states now define arson in terms of the Model Arson Law developed by the state fire marshals through the National Fire Protection Association. Inspecting buildings for fire hazards and issuing corrective orders is another function common to nearly all marshals.[1]

In twenty states and Hawaii, the office of state fire marshal is organized within the department of insurance. In four states it is in the state police and in four others in a department of public safety. There are six states in which the office constitutes a separate department. In Montana and West Virginia it is part of the office of Auditor, in Ohio in the Department of Commerce. The Office of New York's Director of Safety is in the Executive Department.

*Prepared by Horatio Bond, Chief Engineer, National Fire Protection Association.

"FIRE PREVENTION" LAWS

State laws, usually the state fire marshal's law, define certain powers of local units of government in fire matters. The state fire official usually can give supervision to local administration of prevention laws or codes. In a few cases he provides technical services — laboratory testing, analyses, technical training, etc.—which small municipalities cannot provide. The municipal fire chief usually is made a deputy state fire marshal.

The term "fire prevention laws" is used, in a limited sense, to mean laws dealing with various flammable liquids, gases, chemicals and explosives which are outside the scope of "building" laws. State laws attempt to cover a considerable range of fire hazards.

There is more uniformity in treatment of these hazards than might be supposed, as most states follow recommendations prepared by such bodies as the National Fire Protection Association. Twenty-seven states now ban the unrestricted sale of fireworks.

BUILDING LAWS

A number of states have building laws or regulations which apply state-wide.

[1]See *Handbook of Fire Protection*, Eleventh Edition, 1954, published by National Fire Protection Association, 60 Batterymarch St., Boston 10, Massachusetts. Chapter IV, pages 64–92 inclusive, describes the various state offices and officers with fire protection responsibilities and includes a detailed tabulation of state fire legislation. The kind of information available in this tabulation can be demonstrated by taking one subject on which most states have laws and regulations. For example, in twenty-two states the fire marshal's office enforces requirements relating to the use of liquefied petroleum gas. In six states that particular subject is handled by a state industrial or labor department, and in twelve others by various departments. This subject also illustrates the considerable uniformity of state fire regulations, since practically all state requirements on LP-gas follow the National Fire Protection Association *Standards for Liquefied Petroleum Gases*, NFPA No. 58.

These regulations cover egress in new and existing buildings, fire safety features of construction, fire extinguishing equipment, special provisions in motion picture projection, outdoor places of assembly, and garages. Most state building laws exempt small residences, farm buildings and factories. State labor laws on exits or fire escape laws often are made to apply to industrial plants. Multiple family residences, in more populous states such as New Jersey, New York and Pennsylvania, are covered by tenement house acts. A few states have hotel laws, and state law provisions applying to theaters and places of assembly are usual. The largest properties often are not covered by any law, state or municipal. These include lumber yards, storage warehouses, large mercantile buildings, industrial plants, piers and wharves. Even where there is a code of building laws, the technical problems involved in regulating these large properties usually are beyond the capacities of building officials. Where provisions of a state law or municipal building code may forbid erection of a large structure, it often is permitted in cities by special ordinance or waiver of the law or code.

New York state has taken steps to encourage uniformity in municipal building codes through the work of a State Building Code Commission, charged with the promulgation of model building laws suitable for adoption and use by municipalities in the state.

During 1955 it circulated, for comment, a draft of building code provisions applying to non-residential buildings. This is the third part of a state-wide building code for municipalities. The first part, applicable to one- and two-family dwellings, was issued in 1951. A second part, applicable to multiple dwellings, appeared in 1953.

CIVIL DEFENSE

A number of states have set up boards, such as the California State Fire Advisory Board, to provide for coordination of fire departments in civil defense and other emergencies. In some states such boards are authorized under legislation of World War II. It is common to find the state fire marshal either a member of the board or its principal executive officer. California has appointed a full-time chief fire officer, the State Fire Coordinator. Oregon has a system similar to California's, under its Conflagration Act of 1947.

It has not been customary for states to coordinate the administration of local fire departments nor to direct movements of fire fighting companies from one part of the state to another. North Carolina, however, has a State Volunteer Fire Department Act, adopted in 1939, which makes the fire departments in the state part of a state-wide organization.

The pattern of state activities in the fire aspects of civil defense remains formative. Both the states and municipalities are reluctant to accept the idea that there must be a larger measure of state control of fire departments in connection with civil defense operations, but there is a trend in that direction. It is not wholly new since, for example, Massachusetts for some years has supervised the promotional examinations in fire departments.

There are peacetime advantages of increased state participation in fire department operations. A number of states operate information or control centers (sometimes in cooperation with the state fire marshal's office or state police) from which fire companies may be dispatched to deal with forest fires and other widespread emergencies. Most states are compiling inventories of fire equipment and are reviewing communication facilities between county and state control centers and municipal fire departments.

FIREMEN'S TRAINING

In practically all states there is a state-wide program for firemen's training activity, promoted by the fire marshal's office, state universities and other agencies. In most states such programs are administered by the state department of vocational education.

5

Corrections

STATE CORRECTIONAL SYSTEMS*

WHEN the last edition of the *Book of the States* appeared, the foremost questions among prison administrators and state officials were whether the serious and widespread prison riots of 1952–53 would continue, and why they had occurred. Disturbances have been distinctly fewer since then. Meantime, the question why they had happened has been the subject of much discussion and investigation among professional penologists, Governors of states and legislative commissions. Sober reflection and inquiry, particularly in states where riots held the spotlight of public attention, have pointed up the more glaring causative factors. The enactment of recommendations of inquiry bodies, legislative and administrative, have been of marked benefit to the public and to prison inmates as well.

The inquiries have shown a common pattern in prison disturbances. They have shown that such conditions as poor food and overcrowding, while they have been serious enough to spark conflagrations among prisoners, are not the basic causes of uprisings. Prison disturbances are symptomatic of deep-seated conditions of unrest and management and, in many cases, defy immediate or short-range remedies.

Official inquiry by impartial bodies in a number of states has shown that key roles have been played by such factors as limited

appropriations not in accord with sound economy, retention of outmoded traditional practices including solitary confinement under inhumane conditions, incompetent personnel, inadequate physical facilities, unrealistic parole practices and political control of procedures and personnel.

The riots and the public discussion of them pointed up the fact that a prison serves the people best when it places major emphasis on rehabilitation. In line with that doctrine, the 85-year-old American Correctional Association (formerly the American Prison Association) published in June, 1954, a document that has since been recognized as the accepted handbook of standards, the *Manual of Correctional Standards*. It lays the groundwork for an effective correctional system, and it has been used by officials to bring order out of chaotic penal systems.

Stressing the need for a coordinated correctional system, the *Manual* notes a trend that is more and more in the direction of a continuous process of correction, involving probation, imprisonment and parole, utilizing the best of scientific knowledge and procedures.

DEVELOPMENTS IN THE STATES

Examples of developments in individual states follow:

California: The development of correctional camps has been noteworthy in California, not only on the part of the state but of various county correctional services as well. Camps operated by the Los Angeles

---

*Prepared by ROBERTS J. WRIGHT, Assistant General Secretary, The American Correctional Association and The Prison Association of New York, and President, The National Jail Association.

Probation Department and the office of the Sheriff have contributed to sound correctional practice. Late in 1954, a new $14 million medical facility was opened by the State Department of Corrections at Vacaville. California has established more new facilities since the war than perhaps any other state. Yet recent estimates have indicated that, despite the marked increase of facilities, the continuing growth of the state and the prison population will exceed current provisions for prison housing.

Connecticut: Plans to replace the old Wethersfield prison, opened in 1827, with a new $16 million plant are well advanced, and construction will commence soon. In 1955 the Governor of Connecticut approved action that will provide a centralized and state-wide system of probation. An official advisory board has been formed with power to establish procedures. This is the culmination of many years' effort to provide such a system.

Delaware: Through legislative action and approval by the Governor, Delaware will establish a State Department of Correction, to include jurisdiction over its several county jails. An official advisory body of citizens is provided for.

Kansas: Through action by the Governor, a special survey committee was appointed in 1955 with power to study critically the entire correctional system of the state and report to the Governor. This is an instance of calling for an exhaustive study prior to an actual disturbance. A committee of penologists and key local citizens conducted the study, and it is anticipated that legislative action will follow.

Louisiana: This state may take full credit for what has been termed by many as the "modern miracle of penology." In not more than four years a complete new system has evolved from what had been a chaotic situation. The sum of $9 million has been spent, most of it for a new plant to replace an antiquated series of camps. With trained and competent personnel the new Louisiana system should be among the leaders in the nation. It was expected that the new institution, to house 2,500, would be opened formally by the end of 1955.

Maine: This state's prison is undergoing major face-lifting and revision, with particular emphasis on improved facilities for correctional industries. Improved security devices have been installed. In 1953 Maine adopted legislation providing that life term prisoners are eligible for parole consideration after thirty years.

Maryland: Maryland's new Patuxent Institution, opened early in 1955, has facilities for approximately 400 mentally and emotionally defective adult delinquents. The new unit was developed after study of similar establishments in other states. It will be under the joint direction of a medical director and a lay superintendent with a correctional background.

Massachusetts: Early in 1955 the Massachusetts correctional system received nation-wide headlines as a result of a siege by four long-term inmates. Hostages were held for nearly five days. What was originally an escape attempt developed into a "holdout" for improved conditions. Immediately thereafter, the Governor appointed a four-man study committee, granting it wide latitude to inquire into all phases of the correctional system, including parole, probation and sentencing. Over a five-month period this committee—consisting of three professional persons from outside the state and a Massachusetts university president as chairman—conducted an exhaustive study. On June 1 it submitted a report recommending many changes in the system. On September 12 the Governor signed a bill reorganizing the correctional system. Further changes in the probation and sentencing areas are anticipated for 1956. The new legislation strengthens the office of the Commissioner of Correction, provides for three trained deputy commissioners, revises provisions for solitary confinement and isolation, provides for in-service training of employees, makes life-term prisoners eligible for parole after twenty years, provides for a classification and reception center, and includes many other changes. Not related to this committee's study, a new act provided for a treatment center in the department of mental health for convicted sex offenders. Examination, diagnosis and special treatment are available.

Michigan: This state continues its successful camp system, and has had unusual success with its camp for prospective parolees. Following the costly riot of 1952, revisions have been made in the physical facilities at the State Prison for Southern Michigan, at Jackson. This unusually large institution has been reduced in size by the expedient of revising existing facilities. A recent state-wide survey of probation by the National Probation and Parole Association has resulted in improvements in parole and probation.

Missouri: A serious and costly riot in 1954 resulted in the formation of a survey committee upon orders of the Governor. As in the case of Massachusetts, a committee of citizens and professionals recommended major changes in the existing system. Subsequent legislation has converted recommendations into statutes, and Missouri now has a more coordinated and centralized system.

New York: This state's 1955 legislative session produced much improvement in the correctional system. Enactments included provisions for establishment of correctional camps, state subsidy for probation, establishment of a temporary state commission to study juvenile delinquency, establishment of a youth division within the Department of Correction, and provision for foster and youth hostel care for minors under the care of the state. Appropriations were provided for improved training arrangements for probation personnel, including scholarships in accredited schools of social work and professional training. The temporary commission to study juvenile delinquency is to submit a detailed report to the legislature prior to December 1, 1955, for action during the 1956 session.

Pennsylvania: Continuing improvements have been noted in this state following establishment of a central Bureau of Corrections, as recommended by a citizens professional committee and reported in the last edition of the *Book of the States.* The study committee resurveyed the system a year afterward and reported the progress made.

Wisconsin: Funds have been appropriated for a new boys' training school, to replace one opened in 1860. Wisconsin, one of the leaders in personnel training, conducts a four-day conference each year for its entire correctional personnel, in addition to maintaining a continuous in-service training program.

OTHER DEVELOPMENTS

The United States Bureau of Prisons continues to be among the leaders in adult correctional processes. A continuous program of training in many phases of institutional administration, ranging from correctional officers to culinary personnel, is a permanent part of its training program. Cooperating with correctional agencies such as the National Jail Association, the bureau has assisted in a number of regional forums on jail problems. This cooperative endeavor over the years has produced results in better trained and more competent personnel.

Jails—those units of confinement that have long been considered the stepchildren of penology—are showing gradual improvement in the localities not only from the standpoint of personnel and practices but also in the form of new units. It was estimated that during the fall of 1955 a total of approximately thirty new jails were under construction. Regional training conferences, as indicated above, have paid dividends in improved personnel and increased security.

A growing number of colleges and universities are including courses in correctional administration in their curricula, and this lends much encouragement to the further development of correction as a science. Civil service standards and requirements are calling for increased formal training as a prerequisite to employment in the field. Civic, religious and other bodies of citizens, together with officials, are combining their strength in various communities and states—a strong augury of continued progress.

PRISONERS IN STATE INSTITUTIONS*

DURING 1954 a total of 137 state prisons, reformatories, prison camps, etc.—or, for certain states, correctional systems—furnished detailed statistical information on their prisoners to the Bureau of Prisons of the United States Department of Justice. The program, now known as National Prisoner Statistics, was initiated by the Census Bureau in 1926 and was transferred to the Bureau of Prisons in 1950. Since 1952 all the states have cooperated fully in the reporting program.

During 1954 a total of 79,946 prisoners were received from court in state and federal institutions, and 182,051 prisoners were confined in them under sentence at the year's end. These totals are greater than for any year for which comparable data are available. (Table 2.)

But even with prison commitments and population at an all-time high, the number of prisoners in relation to the population of the United States continued small. Only 114 per 100,000 of the civilian population were serving sentences in state and federal institutions on December 31, 1954. While this ratio is greater than for any year since 1942, it is nonetheless smaller than the 137, 131 and 125 per 100,000 respectively, serving sentences in these institutions at the ends of 1939, 1940 and 1941.

The number of state prisoners has increased each year since 1944, the wartime low. The 162,048 under sentence at the end of 1954 was greater by 8,682, or 5.7 per cent, than one year earlier, and by 48,303, or 42.5 per cent, than in 1944.

REGIONAL INCREASES

In each of the four geographical regions of the United States, as shown in Table 1, there was a rise during 1954 in the number of state prisoners. In both the South and the West the increase was by 7.0 per cent; in the North Central states, by 5.2 per cent;

*Prepared by JAMES V. BENNETT, Director, Bureau of Prisons, United States Department of Justice.

and in the Northeast, by 3.0 per cent. The greatest increase for a single state occurred in Wyoming, 21.6 per cent. Next was Arkansas with 13.3 per cent; then Rhode Island, with 12.5; Louisiana, 12.2; Florida, 12.0; Missouri, 11.8; and Colorado, 11.6. In only nine states did a decrease in prison population occur, with the State of New Hampshire showing proportionately the greatest drop, 12.4 per cent. (Computed from Table 1.)

PRISONERS PAROLED

Prisoners released from state institutions in 1954 numbered 61,441, of which those paroled represented 33,551, or 54.6 per cent.

Of the four regions, the Northeast—New England and the Middle Atlantic states—used parole most extensively; 75.9 per cent of this region's releases were by parole. Of the states in this region, New Hampshire led with an 87.4 per cent use of parole. The West almost equalled the Northeast: 73.8 per cent of its releases were paroles. The State of Washington used parole to the largest extent in the West, and also in the United States, paroles constituting 99.0 per cent of releases. In the North Central states, 66.0 per cent of releases were by parole, and in the South, 29.0 per cent. (Table 1.)

No prisoners in local jails, workhouses, etc., are included in the tables presented. Nor are young persons in public training schools for juvenile delinquents covered. According to the 1950 census of population, the former group numbered 81,492 on April 1, 1950, and the latter 29,042.

PRISONERS IN RELATION TO POPULATION OF STATES

It will be noted in Tables 1 and 2 that 102 prisoners per 100,000 were serving sentences in state institutions on December 31, 1954. Table 1 also shows the component rates per 100,000 for the individual states *(Concluded on page 364)*

361

TABLE 1

MOVEMENT OF SENTENCED PRISONERS IN STATE INSTITUTIONS, BY REGIONS AND STATES: 1954*

(Statistics on transfers which bring this table into balance are excluded)

Region and state	Prisoners present Jan. 1	Admissions during the year					Total	Discharges during the year								Prisoners present Dec. 31	
		Total	Received from court	Violators returned	Returned from escape	Other admissions (a)		All releases	Releases					Escape	Death, including execution (b)	Other discharges (a)	Number	Rate per 100,000 of the estimated civilian population
									Conditional			Unconditional						
									Parole		Other							
									Number	Percent of all releases								
United States	153,366	78,929	63,261	9,453	2,101	4,114	70,186	61,441	33,551	54.6	1,779	26,111	2,388	711	5,646	162,048	101.9
NORTHEAST	31,208	13,801	10,536	2,564	186	515	12,943	11,640	8,837	75.9	146	2,657	196	136	971	32,158	78.4
New England:																	
Maine	641	393	312	61	10	10	431	410	286	69.8	..	124	10	1	10	611	66.7
New Hampshire	193	70	55	15	..	..	97	95	83	87.4	..	10	..	2	..	169	32.0
Vermont	280	204	180	20	4	..	213	207	36	17.4	84	87	3	3	..	278	72.6
Massachusetts	2,075	990	693	214	50	33	1,023	898	535	59.6	57	306	56	3	66	2,092	42.6
Rhode Island	257	209	202	6	1	..	174	170	58	34.1	..	112	1	..	3	289	36.6
Connecticut	1,173	804	570	159	19	56	779	714	566	79.3	3	145	28	5	32	1,188	53.8
Middle Atlantic:																	
New York	16,328	6,074	4,507	1,247	..	320	5,850	5,180	3,953	76.3	..	1,227	3	83	584	16,530	107.6
New Jersey	3,625	2,215	1,697	364	79	75	2,117	1,870	1,543	82.5	..	327	75	12	160	3,796	73.4
Pennsylvania	6,636	2,842	2,320	478	23	21	2,259	2,096	1,777	84.8	..	319	20	27	116	7,205	67.0
NORTH CENTRAL	43,926	21,831	16,412	3,143	542	1,734	19,423	16,631	10,980	66.0	411	5,240	557	186	2,049	46,215	98.5
East North Central:																	
Ohio	9,482	4,300	3,264	782	121	133	3,608	3,293	3,004	91.2	..	289	113	38	164	10,146	118.9
Indiana	4,504	3,046	1,362	548	89	1,047	2,869	1,652	1,383	83.7	..	269	100	15	1,102	4,459	106.1
Illinois	7,632	2,639	2,162	273	16	188	2,303	2,054	917	44.6	..	1,137	10	33	206	7,948	87.3
Michigan	8,912	4,343	3,391	558	134	260	3,846	3,226	2,666	82.6	326	560	152	38	430	9,571	136.5
Wisconsin	2,216	1,589	1,210	295	29	55	1,650	1,560	1,052	67.4	..	182	31	5	54	2,210	61.8
West North Central:																	
Minnesota	1,848	953	739	187	8	19	766	706	517	73.2	1	188	8	6	46	1,985	64.1
Iowa	2,034	880	740	97	31	12	748	700	231	33.0	..	469	27	6	15	2,162	82.0
Missouri	3,518	1,948	1,789	87	72	..	1,551	1,448	213	14.7	..	1,235	72	19	12	3,932	95.6
North Dakota	209	129	121	1	5	..	104	100	28	28.0	..	72	..	1	1	231	36.4
South Dakota	443	341	323	8	5	5	321	311	66	21.2	84	161	7	7	..	448	68.0
Nebraska	1,038	604	532	34	23	15	633	589	130	22.1	..	459	22	5	17	1,010	74.4
Kansas	2,090	1,059	779	267	13	..	1,024	992	773	77.9	..	219	15	15	2	2,113	107.2

362

SOUTH	55,451	31,327	27,288	1,829	1,190	1,020	27,464	24,007	6,971	29.0	1,213	15,823	1,446	269	1,742	59,310	120.5
South Atlantic:																	
Delaware(c)	151	109	109				93	88	17	19.3		71		1	4	165	45.6
Maryland	4,500	4,536	4,318	159	59		4,032	3,515	806	22.9	276	2,709	58	16	443	4,930	195.5
Dist. of Columbia	1,786	805	661	131	238	13	658	583	127	21.8	17	180	1	4	70	1,914	233.4
Virginia	4,587	2,537	2,060	143	114	96	2,182	1,791	756	42.2	1	1,018	266	21	104	4,938	144.5
West Virginia	2,316	944	673	156	96	1	1,052	916	693	75.7		222	124	9	3	2,220	114.1
North Carolina	4,647	1,651	1,512	43	27		1,618	1,215	371	30.5		844	379	21	3	4,680	112.4
South Carolina	1,776	922	708	184	162	3	911	837	41	4.9	96	700	38	16	20	1,853	85.4
Georgia	5,185	2,241	1,983	96	111		1,983	1,785	545	30.5	766	474	137	33	28	5,442	152.8
Florida	3,878	2,059	1,774	94		80	1,594	1,355	307	22.7	10	1,038	99	31	109	4,343	126.4
East South Central:																	
Kentucky	3,176	1,790	1,611	130	46	3	1,567	1,500	562	37.5	1	937	40	12	15	3,399	116.1
Tennessee	2,474	1,246	1,088	92	55	11	1,019	936	322	34.4		614	52	11	20	2,706	80.9
Alabama	4,879	3,551	3,075	189	200	87	3,179	2,890	488	16.9		2,402	171	17	101	5,255	169.5
Mississippi	1,890	1,009	657	23	12	317	929	580	131	22.6	42	407	17	9	323	1,970	90.4
West South Central:																	
Arkansas	1,470	894	790	90	9	5	700	679	416	61.3	4	263	7	7	7	1,665	88.0
Louisiana	2,532	1,303	1,173	114	10	6	998	965	440	45.6		521	13	13	7	2,842	98.0
Oklahoma	2,423	1,262	1,196	30	23	13	1,209	1,156	76	6.6		1,080	17	13	23	2,479	111.1
Texas	7,781	4,468	3,900	155	28	385	3,740	3,216	873	27.1		2,343	27	35	462	8,509	103.3
WEST	22,781	11,970	9,025	1,917	183	845	10,356	9,163	6,763	73.8	9	2,391	189	120	884	24,365	111.1
Mountain:																	
Montana	631	419	399	5	15		375	348	138	39.7		210	17	3	7	674	108.0
Idaho	464	386	295	35	8	48	339	281	185	65.8		96	5	1	52	511	83.6
Wyoming	268	259	244	2	8	5	191	173	42	24.3	2	131	9		9	326	107.9
Colorado	1,597	1,277	1,020	242	15		1,085	1,058	957	90.5		99	12	8	7	1,783	126.6
New Mexico	628	483	426	28	28	1	481	444	243	54.7		201	25	5	7	629	83.6
Arizona	994	578	537	14	14	12	565	529	355	67.1		174	13	7	16	1,007	103.4
Utah	583	193	167	15	11		212	192	94	49.0		98	9	5	6	560	74.4
Nevada	329	214	209	5			193	187	30	16.0		157		6		349	167.0
Pacific:																	
Washington	2,331	1,179	887	224	20	48	1,064	981	971	99.0	7	3	21	7	55	2,438	99.1
Oregon	1,591	775	609	54	16	96	845	730	286	39.2		44	10	4	101	1,516	92.8
California	13,365	6,207	4,232	1,292	48	635	5,006	4,240	3,462	81.7		778	68	74	624	14,572	119.3

*Prepared by the Bureau of Prisons, United States Department of Justice.

(a) Other admissions and discharges include discharges by court order, and prisoner movement incident to authorized temporary absences for appearance in court and other purposes. Detailed
(b) Includes 81 executions, 2 of which were carried out under local jurisdiction. Detailed statistics on executions are available on request from the U.S. Bureau of Prisons, Washington 25, D.C.
(c) Delaware has no state correctional institutions. Figures cover New Castle County Workhouse only.

and regions. The differences between them arise from many factors. One of these is the variation in practices of the states as regards the extent to which jails, workhouses, county penitentiaries and other locally operated institutions are used for the confinement of prisoners who otherwise would be sent to state prisons.

For example, Maryland's high rate of 195 per 100,000 was apparently related to the confinement in the state's largest penal institution, the Maryland House of Correction, of a substantial number of prisoners sentenced to less than one year. Near the other extreme was Massachusetts, with a rate of only 43 per 100,000. Here local jails and local houses of correction received considerable numbers of offenders sentenced to more than one year, while two of the state institutions for adult offenders received no prisoners sentenced to less than two and one-half years.

The District of Columbia had the highest rate—233 prisoners per 100,000 population. It apparently reflects, among other things, the fact that the district includes the more densely populated central section of a large metropolitan area whose less congested sections lie outside its boundaries, in the adjoining states.

TABLE 2

SENTENCED PRISONERS RECEIVED FROM COURT AND PRESENT AT END OF YEAR, BY TYPE OF INSTITUTION, FOR THE UNITED STATES: 1939 TO 1954*

(The state and all-institutions figures for each year 1939 to 1950 differ slightly from those previously published. The changes are the effect of substituting actual figures, recently made available to the Bureau of Prisons, for certain estimated figures.)

	Received from court			Present at end of year		
Year	All institutions	Federal institutions	State institutions	All institutions	Federal institutions	State institutions
Number						
1954	79,946	16,685	63,261	182,051	20,003	162,048
1953	73,299	16,376	56,923	172,729	19,363	153,366
1952	69,986	15,305	54,681	167,374	18,014	149,360
1951	66,380	14,120	52,260	164,896	17,395	147,501
1950	68,846	14,237	54,609	165,496	17,134	148,362
1949	68,129	13,130	54,999	163,042	16,868	146,174
1948	62,805	12,430	50,375	155,086	16,328	138,758
1947	63,874	12,948	50,926	150,443	17,146	133,297
1946	60,653	14,950	45,703	139,430	17,622	121,808
1945	52,667	14,171	38,496	133,104	18,638	114,466
1944	49,690	14,047	35,643	131,884	18,139	113,745
1943	49,499	12,203	37,296	136,637	16,113	120,524
1942	58,262	13,725	44,537	149,788	16,623	133,165
1941	68,020	15,350	52,670	164,759	18,465	146,294
1940	72,378	15,109	57,269	172,980	19,260	153,720
1939	(a)	(a)	(a)	179,047	19,730	159,317
Rate per 100,000 of the estimated civilian population						
1954	50.3	10.5	39.8	114.4	12.6	101.9
1953	47.0	10.5	36.5	110.6	12.4	98.2
1952	45.6	10.0	35.7	109.2	11.7	97.4
1951	43.9	9.3	34.6	109.1	11.5	97.6
1950	45.8	9.5	36.4	110.2	11.4	98.8
1949	46.2	8.9	37.3	110.5	11.4	99.0
1948	43.3	8.6	34.7	106.8	11.2	95.6
1947	44.8	9.1	35.7	105.5	12.0	93.5
1946	43.8	10.8	33.0	100.8	12.7	88.0
1945	41.3	11.1	30.2	104.3	14.6	89.7
1944	39.2	11.1	28.1	104.1	14.3	89.8
1943	38.8	9.6	29.3	107.2	12.6	94.5
1942	44.5	10.5	34.0	114.4	12.7	101.7
1941	51.7	11.7	40.0	125.2	14.0	111.2
1940	55.0	11.5	43.5	131.4	14.6	116.8
1939	(a)	(a)	(a)	137.1	15.1	122.0

*Prepared by the Bureau of Prisons, United States Department of Justice.
(a) Comparable data not available.

6

Planning and Development

STATE PLANNING AND DEVELOPMENT

DURING the 1954–55 biennium the state planning and development agencies continued to place primary emphasis on programs to promote the economic growth of the states. As in previous years, major portions of the budgets of the agencies—in some cases the total budgets—were devoted to that end. The means used included encouragement of industrial location in their states, other assistance to prospective business enterprises and promotion of state products and tourism through advertising and informational services.

A number of agencies, meantime, continued to engage in state planning, also, with particular emphasis on the planning of capital improvements. Among agencies rendering special service in this area were those of Alabama, Colorado, Maryland, Nevada, Pennsylvania, Tennessee and Puerto Rico.

Assistance to local planning agencies is receiving greater attention than in previous years. There are several reasons for this. Sound local planning—to provide effective zoning and adequate transportation, parks and recreation, housing, schools and other facilities—has been found to be a necessary condition to a successful industrial development program. Apart from this interest in economic development, many cities and towns face numerous social problems resulting from increasing population and expanded metropolitan areas. A strong planning program at the local level is important not only to the municipalities but to state governments as well.

Local planning assistance is carried out in a variety of ways in the different states. Some—including Alabama and Tennessee, which have performed this service for many years—handle it through a permanent staff of qualified technicians. Others prefer to contract with professional city planners to perform technical work for the local communities, while a state-level staff restricts its activity to technical and administrative supervision. Still others combine the two methods, using technical consultants for the larger planning studies and supplying incidental planning advice through the state agency staffs.

According to a survey in 1954 by the Association of State Planning and Development Agencies, state agencies in Alabama, Connecticut, Kentucky, Maryland, Massachusetts, Minnesota, New Hampshire, New Jersey, New York, Pennsylvania, Rhode Island, Tennessee, Virginia, Washington, Wisconsin and Puerto Rico were providing local planning assistance. Agencies in five additional states, according to the report, were authorized by statute to assist local planning units but were not performing this service at that time.

Additional states now are taking an active interest in local planning assistance. Several adopted legislation during the 1955 legislative sessions either to create new state agencies with power to perform such service or to add it to the functions of existing agencies. Arkansas and Oregon have given such authorization to their higher educational institutions, which even before had operated extension services in matters of community development. Illinois has made urban planning assistance an added program of the State Housing Board. Elsewhere this task, where explicitly assigned, ordinarily has gone to the state planning and development agency.

Many of the agencies providing assistance to local planning bodies are cooperating with the program of the Urban Renewal Administration in the federal government. Among its provisions the Federal Housing Act of 1954 authorized grants not to exceed $5 million to the states for planning assistance to localities. For the first year of the program Congress appropriated $1 million. Section 701 of the Act (Public Law 560, approved August 2, 1954) authorizes grants of federal funds to state planning agencies for provision of planning assistance to cities and other municipalities having a population of less than 25,000. Assistance by the state agency may include surveys, land-use studies, urban renewal plans, technical services and other planning work; but assistance in preparing plans for specific public works is excluded. Federal grants under the act may not exceed 50 per cent of the estimated cost of the planning for which the grant is made.

As of October, 1955, agencies in seven states had received federal financial grants under this program. In six states—Alabama, Arkansas, Connecticut, Massachusetts, New Hampshire and Tennessee—grants were for assistance to small municipalities; in one state, Rhode Island, the grant is for aid in regional planning. The six state programs for assistance to small municipalities will aid a total of sixty-nine communities, at a cost of $405,000. The federal share covers 50 per cent of this, the remainder to be furnished by the states and the assisted communities.

Applications for federal funds to undertake similar programs are being prepared in several additional states.

Pennsylvania, meantime, took action to strengthen its state-level planning program. In a reorganization act adopted in 1955 at the recommendation of the Governor, the State Planning Board—established during the thirties and subsequently made an administrative board with somewhat altered functions in the Department of Commerce

—was separated from that department and transferred to the Governor's office. Acting in an advisory capacity and reporting directly to him, the board will do research and planning on matters of state-level interest and action. Certain of its previous functions, including the local planning service, were assigned by the reorganization act to a new Bureau of Community Development in the Department of Commerce.

New or reorganized agencies to promote industrial and other economic development activities came into existence in a number of states during the biennium. The Alabama State Planning Board was reconstituted and made part of a new State Department of Industrial Development, under a director appointed by the Governor. A newly created State Industrial Commission in Arkansas assumed the development functions previously performed by the Resources and Development Commission. Arkansas also established a new commission to promote the tourist industry and generally publicize the state's advantages. Florida merged its State Advertising Commission and the State Improvement Commission in a new State Development Commission. Idaho created a Department of Commerce and Development. Illinois established a State Division of Planning and Development in the Department of Registration and Education, to aid in location of industry in the state. In Maine a new State Department of Development of Industry and Commerce was set up under a single administrator, replacing the Development Commission, whose members will function in an advisory capacity to the new agency. The industrial promotion efforts of the New Mexico State Economic Development Commission—inactive during recent years —were revived; in addition, the legislature created a State Tourist Bureau as a statutory agency under the Governor. A new State Department of Commerce and an Economic Development Commission of twenty-three members were established in Oklahoma; the legislature transferred the duties of the Industrial Resources Division of the State Planning and Resources Board to the latter agency, whose main function will be the promotion and encouragement of industrial development. The legislature in South Dakota created a ten-member Industrial Expansion and Development Commission. Wisconsin created a new State Division of Economic Development in the office of the Governor. And the State of Wyoming established a new Travel Commission.

Under a Connecticut statute enacted in 1955, local communities may establish economic development agencies and use tax funds for business promotional activities. A 1955 Texas enactment permits counties to spend funds for promotional programs.

Three legislatures—those of Arkansas, New Mexico and Vermont—adopted legislation in 1955 authorizing direct or indirect use of local government credit in the financing of industrial plant facilities for lease to private industries. Such programs previously had been adopted in eight states: Alabama, Illinois, Kentucky, Louisiana, Mississippi, Nebraska, Pennsylvania and Tennessee. Laws in Louisiana, Mississippi and Tennessee—in Tennessee an amendment adopted in 1955—authorize the issuance of general obligation bonds for this purpose; in the others municipal revenue bonds only are permitted. New Hampshire in 1955 created a State Industrial Park Authority which is empowered to use state credit in developing industrial parks for sale to private concerns. Similar legislation was pending in Pennsylvania. Equipped with utilities, transportation and other essentials, industrial parks are sites specially planned and constructed for industrial location and development.

Legislative action in 1955 also added to the states that have enabling legislation permitting the creation of privately financed and operated development credit corporations. Florida, New York and North Carolina adopted new legislation to this effect, designed to provide industrial expansion risk capital unavailable through normal banking channels. The six New England states— Connecticut, Maine, Massachusetts, New Hampshire, Rhode Island and Vermont—all had adopted such legislation previously.

According to the Association of State Planning and Development Agencies, eleven states now provide, in various forms, temporary tax exemptions as inducement to new industrial location in the state. These comprise Alabama, Arkansas, Delaware, Louisiana, Kentucky, Maryland, Mississippi, Montana, Rhode Island, South Carolina and Vermont.

Increasing attention was given during the biennium to surveys, sponsored by state governments, to provide detailed information on industrial development potentialities within states. Some of these studies were conducted by the staffs of state economic development agencies, some by state educational institutions, and others by professional consultants from outside state government. Surveys were in progress or were completed during the last two years in at least nine states: Kansas, Michigan, Oklahoma, Oregon, Rhode Island, Vermont, Virginia, West Virginia and Wyoming.

Early in 1955 the National Municipal League published its Model State and Regional Planning Law as a suggested legislative act. Its objective is to provide for systematic governmental planning on the state and regional levels. The act specifically includes enabling sections to permit acceptance of the federal funds authorized under Public Law 560. Also during the biennium, the Board of Managers of the Council of State Governments requested the Council to prepare a policy statement on planning and development functions in the states.

Officers of the Association of State Planning and Development Agencies for 1955–56 are: President, James W. Clark, Minnesota; Vice-President, Richard Preston, Massachusetts; Vice-President, Edward T. Dickinson, New York; Immediate Past President, Harold V. Miller, Tennessee; and Executive Vice-President, Leslie Hill Prince. The Association maintains offices at 1026—17th St., N.W., Washington 6, D. C.

STATE PLANNING AND DEVELOPMENT AGENCIES*
(As of December 1, 1955)

State	Name of agency	Established	Executive Officer Name	Title
Alabama	Ala. State Planning and Ind. Dev. Bd.	1955	Lewis A. Pick	Director
Arizona	Arizona Development Board	1954	Stanley Womer	Manager
Arkansas	Arkansas Industrial Dev. Commn.	1955	William P. Rock	Executive Director
Colorado	Colorado State Planning Commission	1935	W. M. Williams	Director
Connecticut	Connecticut Development Commission	1939	Sidney A. Edwards	Managing Director
Delaware	Delaware State Development Dept.	1949	Miles L. Frederick	Director
Florida	Florida Development Commission	1955	J. Saxton Lloyd	Chairman
Georgia	Georgia Dept. of Commerce	....	Scott Candler	Secretary
Idaho	Idaho Dept. of Commerce and Dev.	1955	A. B. Jonasson	Secretary
Illinois	Ill. Industrial Planning and Dev. Div.	1955	Fred R. Falkenstein	Superintendent
Indiana	Indiana Economic Council	1943	John C. Mellett	Director
Iowa	Iowa Development Commission	1945	T. E. Davidson II	Director
Kansas	Kansas Industrial Dev. Commn.	1939	John B. Sutherland	Director
Kentucky	Ky. Agric. and Ind. Dev. Bd.	1948	Joseph H. Taylor	Executive Director
Louisiana	La. Dept. of Commerce and Industry	1944	Elmer D. Conner	Executive Director
	La. Planning Div., Dept. of Public Works	1942	Frank S. Walshe, Jr.	Chief, Planning Division
Maine	Me. Dept. of Dev. of Ind. and Commerce	1955	Carl J. Broggi	Commissioner
Maryland	Maryland State Planning Commn.	1933	I. Alvin Pasarew	Director
Massachusetts	Massachusetts Dept. of Commerce	1953	Richard Preston	Commissioner
Michigan	Mich. Dept. of Economic Development	1947	Don Weeks	Executive Director
Minnesota	Minn. Dept. of Business Development	1947	James W. Clark	Commissioner
Mississippi	Mississippi Agric. and Indus. Bd.	1944	H. V. Allen, Jr.	Director
Missouri	Missouri Div. of Resources and Dev.	1943	Prentiss Mooney	Director
Montana	Montana State Planning Board	1955	Perry F. Roys	Director
Nebraska	Div. of Nebr. Resources, Nebr. Dept. of Agriculture and Inspection	1947	C. V. Price	Chief
Nevada	Nevada Dept. of Economic Dev.	1955	Pete Kelley	Director
	Nevada State Planning Board	1937	I. J. Sandorf	Chairman
New Hampshire	N.H. State Planning and Dev. Commn.	1935	Ernest L. Sherman	Executive Director
New Jersey	New Jersey Dept. of Conservation and Economic Development	1948	Joseph E. McLean	Commissioner
New Mexico	New Mexico Economic Dev. Commn.	1955	Berl Huffman	Director
New York	New York State Dept. of Commerce	1944	Edward T. Dickinson	Commissioner
North Carolina	N. Car. Dept. of Conservation and Dev.	....	Ben E. Douglas	Director
North Dakota	North Dakota Research Foundation	1943	Alex C. Burr	Director of Research
Ohio	Ohio Dev. and Publicity Commn.	1947	Rhea McCarty	Executive Secretary
Oklahoma	Oklahoma Planning and Resources Bd.	1947	Jack V. Boyd	Executive Director
	Okla. Dept. of Commerce and Ind.	1955	Randall T. Klemme	Director
Oregon	Oregon Development Commission	1953	Robert E. McCoy	Executive Director
Pennsylvania	Pennsylvania Dept. of Commerce	1939	William R. Davlin	Secretary
	Pennsylvania State Planning Board	1934	Francis A. Pitkin	Consultant
Rhode Island	Rhode Island Development Council	1951	Thomas E. Monahan	Executve Director
South Carolina	S. Car. Res., Planning and Dev. Bd.	1945	R. M. Cooper	Director
South Dakota	South Dakota Natural Res. Commn.	1943	Hugo A. Carlson	Executive Secretary
	South Dakota Industrial Development Expansion Agency	1955	Noel T. Tweet	Director
Tennessee	Tennessee State Planning Commn.	1935	Harold V. Miller	Executive Director
	Tennessee Industrial and Agricultural Development Commn.	1953	George I. Whitlatch	Executive Director
Utah	Utah Committee on Industrial and Employment Planning	....	Ames K. Bagley	Secretary
Vermont	Vermont Development Commission	1945	Clifton R. Miskelly	Managing Director
Virginia	Va. Dept. of Conserv. and Dev.	....	Raymond V. Long	Director
	Virginia Div. of Planning and Economic Development	1938	W. H. Caldwell	Commissioner
Washington	Wash. Div. of Progress and Ind. Dev.	1945	W. A. Galbraith	Director
West Virginia	W. Va. Ind. and Publicity Commn.	1945	Andrew V. Ruckman	Executive Director
Wisconsin	Wisc. Industrial Dev. Div.	1955	Robert D. Siff	Director
	Wisconsin State Planning Division, Bureau of Engineering	1951	M. W. Torkelson	Director, Regional Planning
Wyoming	Wyoming Natural Resource Board	1951	Kenneth D. Monroe	Secretary
	Wyoming Travel Commission	1955	Williard Murfin	Secy.-Manager
Alaska	Alaska Development Board	....	Al Anderson	Acting General Mgr.
Puerto Rico	Puerto Rico Economic Dev. Admin.	1950	Teodoro Moscoso	Administrator
	Puerto Rico Planning Board	1942	Rafael Pico	Executive Officer

Canadian Agencies

State	Name of agency	Established	Executive Officer Name	Title
Alberta	Alberta Industrial Dev. Board and Economic Research Dept. of Economic Affairs	1945	Richard Martland	Director
British Columbia	Dept. of Trade and Industry	....	Hon. Ralph Chetwynd	Director
Manitoba	Dept. of Industry and Commerce	1940	Rex E. Grose	Deputy Minister
New Brunswick	New Brunswick Planning Board	....	W. A. Moore	Deputy Minister
Nova Scotia	Nova Scotia Dept. of Municipal Affairs	....	W. E. Moseley	Deputy Minister
Ontario	Dept. of Planning and Development	....	A. E. K. Bunnell	Consultant
Prince Edward Is.	Dept. of Industry and Natural Resources	....	G. Claude Smith	Dir., Town Planning
Quebec	Dept. of Municipal Affairs	....	Jean Louis Doucet	Deputy Minister
Saskatchewan	Economic Advisory and Planning Bd.	....	Hon. T. C. Douglas	Chairman
	Saskatchewan Dept. of Municipal Affairs	....	Murray Zides	Acting Director, Community Planning Branch

*Prepared by the Association of State Planning and Development Agencies, 1026—17th St., N.W., Washington 6, D.C.

THE STATES IN HOUSING AND URBAN RENEWAL*

I N THE movement that has been going on nation-wide during the past quarter of a century to improve urban housing conditions, changes in emphasis and scope have occurred repeatedly. State enabling legislation has, by and large, kept pace with these changes. Thus in 1954–55, the states began to turn attention to the new field of "urban renewal"—a program that features a combined attack on urban slums and blight through public housing, urban redevelopment, and neighborhood rehabilitation and conservation. The titles to those past sections of *The Book of the States* that cover housing activities reflect this broadening approach; in 1950–51, the title covered housing only; in 1952–53 and again in 1954–55, it was enlarged to include urban redevelopment; the above heading reflects the "urban renewal" approach.

The states have recognized "urban renewal" (which received its impetus through a federal program initiated under the Housing Act of 1954) primarily by amending their urban redevelopment laws to include the neighborhood rehabilitation and conservation function. By the end of 1955, as the final column of the table on page 372 shows, thirteen states, the District of Columbia, Alaska, Hawaii and Puerto Rico had adopted such amendments.

Another twenty-three states and the Virgin Islands had laws as of that date enabling localities to perform the urban redevelopment function only. Most of the redevelopment laws went on the books following passage of the Housing Act of 1949. Title I of that act made federal grants available for "writing down" the cost of slum-cleared areas so that they could be resold to private builders at prices competitive with outlying vacant land. Georgia's original law had been declared unconstitutional by the state Supreme Court in 1953.

By amendment of the state constitution in 1954, through a referendum, a new law was put on the books. Rhode Island's redevelopment law was extended to small communities and otherwise strengthened through a 1955 referendum that supported a constitutional amendment.

As of October, 1955, fifty "urban renewal" projects had been approved under the 1954 housing act. Another 270 projects had been approved under the 1949 Title I urban redevelopment program. Out of this total of 320 projects, more than sixty involved some degree of rehabilitation of existing structures rather than clearance and rebuilding exclusively. And of the 320 total, 99 projects in 64 localities were in the land assembly or clearance or construction stage. They encompassed some 3,400 acres of urban land and involved relocation of some 56,000 families. Predominant re-use planned for these areas was private residential building, with commercial, industrial and public uses also in prospect.

As regards public housing, forty-three states, the District of Columbia, Alaska, Hawaii, Puerto Rico and the Virgin Islands had enabling legislation in 1955, as shown in column two of the table. Most of these laws date back to the thirties. They were adopted in order to permit localities to operate, first, under the 1933 low-rental housing program of the Public Works Administration and, later, under the United States Housing Act of 1937 (enlarged and strengthened by amendments carried in the Housing Act of 1949). As of the fall of 1955, more than half a million units of housing had been built or were in prospect under these state enabling laws.

In all of the above, it will be noted that the states' role is indirect. However, the ten states shown in column one of the table have rendered or now render direct financial aid to localities for housing or urban redevelopment programs. The nature and extent of programs existing then was summarized in the 1952–53 *Book of the States*.

*Prepared by MRS. DOROTHY GAZZOLO, Associate Director, National Association of Housing and Redevelopment Officials.

Among developments since then, loan funds for New York's public housing program were increased $200 million, from $735 million to $935 million, as a result of a 1954 referendum. Further, to encourage neighborhood rehabilitation, the state in 1955 approved twelve-year tax exemptions on the increased value of properties undergoing home improvements to persons who bring their properties up to standard; a nine-year abatement of 8.3 per cent of alteration costs also is allowed. In addition, New York in 1955 passed legislation under which state loans for middle-income housing might be made if voters in a referendum later in 1955 approved diversion of $50 million from the $200 million mentioned above.

Another state that increased its direct-aid program during 1955 was Connecticut. An additional $15 million was authorized for its moderate-rental program.

Late in 1954 Massachusetts increased its 1953 program of low-rental housing for the aged from $5 million to $15 million. As of late 1955, five projects were under construction under this program, and some thirty more were in planning. The expectation was that the state could provide from 2,000 to 2,500 homes for both aged single persons and aged couples.

Permanent moderate- or low-rental housing made available by the states as of 1955 totaled about 80,000 units. Thousands of additional units had been provided through mortgage loan programs in California, Connecticut and Wisconsin. Still more homes, of temporary construction, have been built through state veterans programs.

More such direct aid on the part of the states, as well as other forms of state housing assistance, was urged by the Commission on Intergovernmental Relations in its report to the President and Congress in June, 1955. The Commission made a series of recommendations as to the future role of the states in the housing and urban renewal program. It was proposed that "(a) States lend financial, technical, and professional assistance to localities on the basis of need; (b) States provide enabling legislation to encourage their sub-divisions to adopt by reference modern and uniform building, housing, and sanitary codes; (c) States provide for the establishment of metropolitan planning agencies to assist in redefining city limits and in providing for the integrated design of new suburban areas; (d) States assume responsibility for working out appropriate interstate compacts or agreements in the event of jurisdictional problems among them, with assistance and leadership from the National Government when required."

In line with these recommendations (although not as a consequence of them), several states in 1955 opened up new methods of giving technical guidance to localities in order to help them qualify for federal urban renewal assistance. A requirement of such assistance, as laid down in the Housing Act of 1954, is that a community must have what is called a "workable program" for attacking slums and blight: a city plan; an analysis of neighborhoods in need of renewal treatment; a body of adequate building, housing, and zoning standards; an efficient method of administering such codes as well as an over-all renewal program; sufficient local funds to do a proposed renewal job; and evidence of citizen support of and participation in a renewal program. Recognizing that many small communities do not have planning budgets and trained staff, the 1954 housing act authorized federal grants to state planning bodies to cover 50 per cent of the cost of undertaking planning programs for localities having a population of less than 25,000. Such grants also were authorized for planning work for metropolitan and regional areas. As of the end of 1955, planning bodies of seven states—Alabama, Arkansas, Connecticut, Massachusetts, New Hampshire, Rhode Island and Tennessee—had qualified for such grants, which were matched with state and local funds.

Over the past several years, various states have been dealing with the area of race relations in the housing and renewal field. As of late 1955, eleven states had included provisions in their public housing, and/or urban redevelopment laws banning either racial discrimination or segregation, or both, in the occupancy of buildings financed under such laws. In 1955, the State of New York adopted particularly far-reaching legislation, a bill prohibiting racial or religious discrimination in housing financed by federally-insured mortgages.

During 1954 and 1955 state supreme courts considered the constitutionality of redevelopment laws in almost twenty states. As of the end of 1955, such laws had been held constitutional in the following states: Alabama, Arkansas, California, Connecticut, Illinois, Maine, Maryland, Massachusetts, Michigan, Missouri, New Hampshire, New Jersey, New York, Ohio, Oregon, Pennsylvania, Rhode Island, Tennessee, Virginia and Wisconsin, as well as the District of Columbia. The only adverse decisions had been rendered earlier, in Florida and Georgia, and Georgia's constitution was amended in 1954 to permit redevelopment, as noted above.

The first state court tests of a code of standards for existing housing, as the major tool in rehabilitation and conservation programs, were made in 1955. The Maryland Court of Appeals upheld a Baltimore Health Department requirement for a bath or shower for every dwelling unit, and the South Carolina Supreme Court upheld the constitutionality of Columbia's anti-substandard housing ordinance.

It appeared probable that during 1956 and 1957 the predominant trends which began in 1955 would continue: more emphasis on neighborhood rehabilitation and conservation by localities, more state interest in urban renewal, and the provision of more technical guidance to localities by state agencies.

STATE LAWS AFFECTING HOUSING AND URBAN RENEWAL*

	Direct state financial aid provided for housing to be rented or sold	Have state laws enabling municipalities to participate in federally-aided low rent housing program	Have state laws enabling insurance company investment in direct ownership and management of large scale rental housing	Have state laws enabling private corporations to receive public aid for housing or redevelopment if dividends are limited	Have enacted state laws enabling municipalities to participate in urban redevelopment programs
Alabama	...	★	...	...	★★
Arizona	...	★	...	...	★
Arkansas	...	★	...	...	★
California	★	★	★	★	★
Colorado	...	★	★	...	...
Connecticut	★	★	...	...	★
Delaware	...	★	...	★	★★
Florida	...	★	...	★	★(a)
Georgia	...	★	★	...	★★
Idaho	...	★	★	...	...
Illinois	★	★	★	...	★★
Indiana	...	★	...	★	★
Iowa	...	...	★	...	...
Kansas	...	...	★	★	...
Kentucky	...	★	...	★	★★
Louisiana	...	★	★	★	★
Maine	...	★	...	...	★★
Maryland	...	★	★	...	★
Massachusetts	★	★	★	★	★★
Michigan	...	★	★	★	★
Minnesota	...	★	★	★	★★
Mississippi	...	★	★	★	...
Missouri	...	★	★	★	★★
Montana	...	★	...	...	...
Nebraska	...	★	★	...	★
Nevada	...	★	...	...	...
New Hampshire	★	★	...	...	★
New Jersey	★	★	...	★	★
New Mexico	...	★	★	...	...
New York	★	★	★	★	★
North Carolina	...	★	...	...	★
North Dakota	...	★	...	...	★
Ohio	★	★	...	★	★
Oklahoma	...	...	...	...	★★
Oregon	...	★	...	...	★★
Pennsylvania	★	★	★	★	★
Rhode Island	...	★	★	...	★
South Carolina	...	★	...	★	★
South Dakota	...	★	...	...	★
Tennessee	...	★	★	...	★★
Texas	...	★	...	★	...
Utah	...	...	★	...	...
Vermont	...	★	...	...	...
Virginia	...	★	★	★	★
Washington	...	★	...	...	...
West Virginia	...	★	...	...	★
Wisconsin	★	★	★	★	★★
Wyoming	...	...	★	...	...
District of Columbia	...	★	★	...	★★
Alaska	...	★	...	...	★★
Hawaii	★	★	...	...	★★
Puerto Rico	★	★	...	...	★★
Virgin Islands	...	★	...	...	★

*Prepared by the National Association of Housing and Redevelopment Officials.   (a) Declared to be unconstitutional.
★★Combined redevelopment-renewal legislation.

7

Natural Resources

WATER RESOURCES

STATE programs affecting water resources are of many different types. They embrace such diverse activities as pollution control, surface and ground water surveys, navigation projects, flood control work, hydroelectric power development, irrigation, watershed management, drainage, water supply facilities, the regulation of rights to use water, and many other matters. State activities in these areas may involve direct operation of a program, research, educational and informational services, or the rendering of assistance to local or private agencies. The extent and types of programs carried on by individual states in each of these areas vary considerably. In many of the areas there are federal, local or private as well as state programs.

The present article summarizes recent developments in four areas: the establishment of new agencies to plan and administer water resource programs, pollution control, small watershed programs, and questions of water rights. Problems in all these matters have received particular attention from state officials during the past two years.

WATER RESOURCE ADMINISTRATION

At least six states in 1955 established important new agencies to plan and administer major parts of their water resource programs. Kansas set up a seven-member State Water Resources Board. Its duties include collection and compilation of information relating to the use and avail-

ability of water; preparation of a state plan of water resource development for each watershed; review of plans for use of water resources in the state; a study of the laws of Kansas, other states and the federal government pertaining to conservation and development of water resources; preparation of recommendations for state agencies and local units to coordinate their activities relating to water resources; and the making of recommendations to the legislature, the Governor and the Legislative Council concerning new legislation in this field.

A new Minnesota act establishes the Minnesota Water Resources Board, consisting of three members appointed by the Governor. The law gives the board general control and supervision over the natural resources of the state. It provides, specifically, that the board shall help in the establishment of small watershed districts, and shall aid the districts in preparing plans for projects and carrying out their work.

North Carolina established a Board of Water Commissioners. The new agency will have seven members, appointed by the Governor, to represent the major classes of water users in the state. It is to gather data about the state's water resources, devise long range plans for water conservation and use, and make recommendations to the Governor and General Assembly for changes in water laws. The board also has special powers which it may exercise in emergency situations involving critical water shortages in municipalities.

In such instances it may authorize affected local governments to divert water from sources other than those they normally use in order to meet minimum domestic needs. The board may prescribe routes for emergency water pipe lines, and it has the right to lay such pipe lines on any property. The board will be assisted by an advisory committee of state officials, legislators and public members.

Oregon's legislature made several changes in the state's administrative organization for water management. It abolished four commissions and boards and transferred their duties to a new agency, the State Water Resources Board. The act gives this body the duty of studying the water resources of the state and directs it to develop a plan for the future regulation and use of all of Oregon's waters.

A new Water Resources Coordinating Board was established by the Rhode Island legislature. Its duties include reviewing current studies and programs of state agencies pertaining to the conservation and development of water resources; advising local authorities in formulation of municipal water resources programs; reviewing and evaluating ground water investigations now carried on by state agencies; formulating a long range plan for the conservation and use of ground water; and working with state and local officials in devising plans for distribution of water supplies throughout the state.

As part of a basic revision of its water laws, South Dakota established a Water Resources Commission. The legislative act creating the commission declares that all water within the state is the property of the people and is to be put to beneficial use to the fullest possible extent. It terminates the previously existing dual system of appropriation and riparian rights and makes all waters subject to appropriation. Existing uses of water, however, are recognized, and are regarded as vested rights. The act permits water to be taken for domestic purposes, including stock watering, without a permit from the commission. All other future uses of water, however, will require a permit for appropriation by the commission.

States continued during the 1954–55 biennium to use the interstate compact to facilitate joint action on water resource problems. A new instrument of major importance is the Great Lakes Basin Compact. It creates an interstate commission to study the resources and problems of the Great Lakes and to prepare plans and recommendations for the most effective use of these resources. The compact was ratified in 1955 by Illinois, Indiana, Michigan, Minnesota and Wisconsin. New York, Ohio, Pennsylvania and the Provinces of Ontario and Quebec also are eligible to become parties to it.

In the Northwest, representatives of the Columbia River Valley states, after long negotiation, approved a Columbia River Basin Compact late in 1954. It provides for apportionment of the water of the river among the participating states and for general management of the valley's water resources. The compact creates a commission to make studies and submit plans and recommendations to the member states. During 1955, Idaho, Nevada and Utah formally ratified the compact. Other states which may become members are Montana, Oregon, Washington and Wyoming.

(For information about other compact developments pertaining to water see article and tables on interstate compacts, pages 15 to 19.)

POLLUTION CONTROL

Pollution control is one of the major state activities affecting water resources. Much of our present water is not usable because pollution has reduced its quality. To meet this problem, state agencies throughout the nation are studying sources of pollution and taking steps to control and reduce it. In the process they are developing standards of water quality, and many of them are classifying their streams on the basis of these standards.

New legislation to strengthen pollution control programs was enacted in numerous states during 1955, including Arkansas, California, Colorado, Montana, North Carolina, Oklahoma, South Dakota, Texas and Washington. Several legislatures also passed measures to facilitate municipal construction of sewage treatment works.

For many years, states have cooperated through compacts in the control of pollution in interstate rivers. Examples include the work of interstate agencies on the Delaware, Ohio and Potomac rivers. The most recent development in this field is the proposed Tennessee River Basin Water Pollution Control Compact. It was ratified by Tennessee in 1955. Other states eligible to join are Alabama, Georgia, Kentucky, Mississippi, North Carolina and Virginia.

During 1955 there was considerable debate among state and federal officials regarding the respective roles of the two levels of government in water pollution control. Under the National Water Pollution Control Act, the federal government makes grants to state and interstate agencies for research on water pollution problems. The act also authorizes the federal government to cooperate with the states in enforcing orders to abate interstate pollution. During 1955 proposals were submitted to Congress for amendments which would have increased federal enforcement powers and broadened the basis for federal grants. Some state officials felt that certain of the proposed amendments would be detrimental to state interests; lack of agreement among state officials about the proposed amendments was evident and Congress took no action on the subject in the 1955 session.

Small Watershed Programs

In 1954 Congress enacted the Watershed Protection and Flood Prevention Act (Public Law 566, 83rd Congress). The act is designed to promote the development of a joint federal-state-local program for the conservation and utilization of land and water resources in small watersheds. It provides federal financial assistance in development of plans for flood prevention, soil conservation, irrigation, silt and pollution abatement, channel improvement, drainage and general resource management projects in these watersheds. Under the act, local agencies must initiate the projects and are responsible for carrying them out and operating them. State agencies must approve local proposals before they are submitted to the federal government.

At least twenty legislatures in 1955 adopted measures to permit and encourage action in this field. Many of them specifically authorized the soil conservation dis-tricts to engage in watershed management and development activities and gave the districts taxing powers or other means of financing their part of this work. In some instances districts were authorized to carry on joint programs for those purposes. Other states have given similar powers and duties to drainage districts, watershed districts, other types of special districts, or to cities and counties. Finally, some states have granted powers and funds to state agencies so that they may assist in the work. States that have passed recent legislation of one type or another in this area include California, Colorado, Connecticut, Delaware, Illinois, Iowa, Kansas, Maryland, Minnesota, Mississippi, Nebraska, Nevada, New Hampshire, North Carolina, Oklahoma, Tennessee, Texas, Vermont, Wisconsin and Wyoming. Several other states already had legislation broad enough to permit local units to prepare plans and carry on work of this type.

State Water Rights Legislation

Until recently, because of the general availability of water in most sections, the states, except in the West, have not been greatly concerned about legal questions pertaining to the right to use water and the uses to which it may be put. In the eastern two-thirds of the United States, the common law doctrine of riparian rights has governed the use of surface water. Essentially, the riparian doctrine provides that persons owning property bordering on streams or lakes have the right to make reasonable use of the water for certain purposes, so long as they do not reduce materially the quality or quantity of water available for use by owners of other property adjacent to the rivers or lakes. Court decisions have modified the doctrine through application to particular situations, but there has been little legislation concerning water rights. Thus the common law has continued to govern the use of surface waters in most instances.

Within the past few years, however, many states in the eastern two-thirds of the nation have been confronted with a serious water problem. Basically, the problem is that the supply of water appears to be inadequate to meet the demand for it. The problem does not exist in all localities, and, where present, it does not as a rule exist at all times of the year. It is clear, however, that it is becoming more extensive and more serious.

A number of states throughout the nation, accordingly, are undertaking studies of their basic policies governing water use. They are examining effects of the doctrine of riparian rights. Does it permit the people of the state to derive maximum benefit from their water resources? Is a policy based on riparian rights satisfactory in a period when the demand for water appears to exceed the supply?

In connection with these investigations, non-western states are reviewing the experiences of the western states, where rights to use water have been determined in large part by the appropriation doctrine. Under this system, priorities of use are established according to purpose and time of initial use. Persons desiring to make use of water from a stream file applications with a state agency. The state grants them the right to appropriate water in stated quantities from specified sources or supplies for particular purposes, provided that the proposed new uses will not conflict with established rights. If, in the future, there is insufficient water in a given stream for all users with rights to it, those with lower priorities in time or purpose are required to reduce or halt their use of the water until such time as the quantity available is sufficient for all.

Both the riparian and the appropriation doctrines have advantages and disadvantages. Supporters of the riparian system point out that it permits flexibility in the future use of water and that it promotes beneficial uses of water. The riparian system, however, does not provide users certainty that they will be able to continue making use of water for a particular purpose, especially a consumptive one. At all times their use of water is subject to the test that it does not reduce materially the flow of water for other users. Moreover, nonriparian owners usually have no rights to use water for any purpose.

Those who favor the appropriation doctrine point out that it gives more definite legal rights to users. Those using water know what quantity they may use, and under what conditions their rights to use water may be limited. As a result, water

users under this system may be able to make necessary expenditures for development of facilities for water use with greater assurance and less risk. Moreover, the appropriation doctrine permits owners of property not adjacent to streams or lakes to obtain rights to use water and thus makes water available on a wider basis. However, the appropriation system, it is contended, is an inflexible doctrine, since it requires the establishment of fixed priorities. It usually is difficult to alter the priorities once they are established, even though changes in economic conditions might make it desirable to do so.

States which undertake a basic study of their water laws thus must examine hydrological data and economic and legal questions. They need the best available data about the supply of water in the state, the extent to which it is usuable for various purposes, and the amounts currently being used by various types of users. In such studies it also is necessary to estimate the probable future growth of population in the state and the likely development of the economy, as these have important bearing on future water needs. If a state is considering basic changes in water rights legislation, constitutional questions affecting existing rights require careful examination.

During the past two years, important studies of water resources have been authorized in many states. Some of them deal with particular problems, such as drainage, irrigation or ground water levels. Many of the studies, however, are far more extensive, involving examination of basic questions of water law. States making water studies, of varying scope, include Arkansas, Connecticut, Delaware, Florida, Georgia, Illinois, Indiana, Iowa, Kansas, Kentucky, Louisiana, Maryland, Michigan, Minnesota, Mississippi, Nebraska, New Hampshire, New Jersey, New York, North Carolina, Ohio, Oklahoma, Rhode Island, South Carolina, Tennessee, Texas, Virginia, West Virginia, Wisconsin and Wyoming. A few of their studies already are completed; most of them will be finished by the end of 1956.

Discussion at the General Assembly of the States in December, 1954, sponsored by the Council of State Governments, underlined the interest of state officials in these problems. The Assembly adopted a resolution requesting the Council to study problems relating to the use and conservation of water resources and to formulate recommendations for the improvement of state water laws.

The studies and water programs under way in many states demonstrate a notably increased interest of legislators, Governors and other state officials in the use and conservation of water resources. They indicate that state officials recognize that water law and administration should be predicated on the assumption that the demand for water will continue to increase. Finally, current activities point to a growing realization that traditional concepts regarding water rights and use may have to be modified in order to meet present and future needs.

SOIL CONSERVATION SERVICE*

ARKED intensification of efforts by both federal and state governments to improve and expand soil conservation facilities and work was an outstanding feature of the national soil conservation program during 1954–55. At the same time, at the local level where the actual conservation work is done on the land, soil conservation districts—including their supervisors and cooperating farmers and ranchers—showed stronger interest; they used many new devices and channels to forward their programs.

Congress, meantime, enacted important legislation, affecting all states, to facilitate soil and water conservation activities. The Watershed Protection and Flood Prevention Act (Public Law 566) was signed by the President on August 4, 1954. It launched a permanent program to improve watersheds of 250,000 acres or less. Local groups were authorized to initiate and sponsor their own watershed programs and receive technical assistance from the United States Department of Agriculture, through its Soil Conservation Service, in planning and carrying out the work.

The act placed responsibility on the state, or some agency thereof, for all projects initiated by local organizations and planned with the aid of federal agencies. Costs are shared by the federal government and the local watershed organizations. The new act followed up the small-watershed program for which Congress in 1953 appropriated initial funds to start work in fifty-nine pilot watersheds designated and planned as five-year test projects.

The state legislatures moved quickly to authorize state and local agencies to assume their new responsibilities for initiating and carrying through with projects under Public Law 566. During sessions of their legislatures in 1955, twenty states adopted new or amendatory legislation to

further cooperation between state and local agencies and the United States Department of Agriculture in activities authorized by the act. In all, thirty-seven different laws were passed in the twenty states. This response appears to be a record for legislative actions in a single year directed toward cooperation with the federal government in a soil and water resources development and improvement program.

The new legislation passed by the states reflects, primarily, an effort on their part to provide qualified organizations within the states with the authority needed to carry out, maintain and operate the works of improvement contemplated for installation in a watershed project. Other features pertain either to the legal authority or the financial ability to arrange for the necessary easements, rights-of-way and water rights, cost-sharing procedures, maintainence and operation of works of improvements, and agreements from landowners for recommended land treatment measures. The twenty states in which legislation was enacted in 1955, and the organizational group within the state in which this authority is placed, are shown on the accompanying map.

In many of the states that have not yet passed new watershed legislation, study commissions or other groups and organizations have been considering the need for legislation to facilitate this new phase of the soil and water conservation program. By October 1, 1955, 394 watershed protection and flood control groups had been organized in forty-one states, and their applications for technical assistance had been received by the Soil Conservation Service. Planning had been authorized on 103 projects, and thirty-six planning parties composed of specialists in watershed problems had been developed and trained by the service to assist the watershed groups.

Additional federal legislation affecting the soil and water conservation program included an amendment to the Water Fa-

*Prepared by DONALD A. WILLIAMS, Administrator, Soil Conservation Service, U. S. Department of Agriculture.

cilities Act (Public Law 597) extending the privileges of the bill to all forty-eight states, Alaska, Hawaii, Puerto Rico and the Virgin Islands. This law formerly applied only to seventeen western states. The act was also broadened to provide direct or insured loans to farmers for applying soil and water conservation practices. In addition to loans for water facilities structures, such as small dams, ditches and wells for irrigation, loans were made available for such projects as establishment of permanent pastures, terracing, reforesting and nearly all other conservation measures. The Farmers Home Administration of the Department of Agriculture was assigned the responsibility for making the loans, and technical assistance to borrowers is provided by the Soil Conservation Service.

In addition, a provision in the revision of the Internal Revenue Law (Public Law 591) permits farmers and ranchers to report as deductible expenses their expenditures for applying soil and water conservation on their land. Deductible expenditures may include those for leveling, grading or terracing; contour furrowing; construction of diversion or drainage ditches; control and protection of water-

courses, outlets and ponds; eradication of brush, planting of windbreaks and other measures involving financial outlay.

During 1954–55, farmers and ranchers established 125 additional soil conservation districts under state enabling laws. This brought the total number of such districts to 2,674. Eighteen states, Puerto Rico and the Virgin Islands were completely covered by the districts as of July 1, 1955. The amount of land within districts totaled more than 1,484,974,000 acres. The districts included 4,884,470 farms and ranches—approximately 90 per cent of the country's agricultural land.

Of the total of farmers and ranchers, 1,552,336 were cooperating with their soil conservation districts. (See table below.) Two-thirds of them had complete soil and water conservation plans for their farms, covering 286,515,597 acres. Technicians of the Soil Conservation Service provided 7,364 man-years of assistance to the cooperating farmers and ranchers during 1955. Aside from these technicians, whose primary function it is to assist the districts, nearly 250 additional people who were paid by the states or by local soil conservation districts were working in districts.

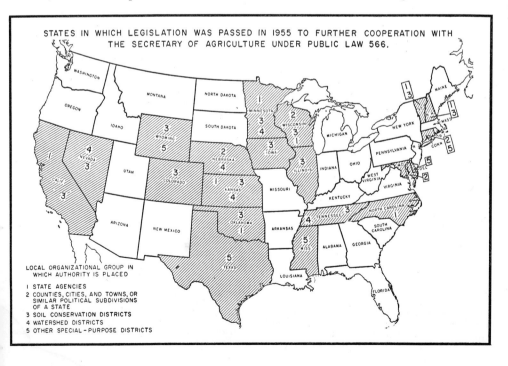

STATES IN WHICH LEGISLATION WAS PASSED IN 1955 TO FURTHER COOPERATION WITH THE SECRETARY OF AGRICULTURE UNDER PUBLIC LAW 566.

LOCAL ORGANIZATIONAL GROUP IN WHICH AUTHORITY IS PLACED
1 STATE AGENCIES
2 COUNTIES, CITIES, AND TOWNS, OR SIMILAR POLITICAL SUBDIVISIONS OF A STATE
3 SOIL CONSERVATION DISTRICTS
4 WATERSHED DISTRICTS
5 OTHER SPECIAL-PURPOSE DISTRICTS

Closer cooperation between state and federal groups engaged in making the national cooperative soil survey proved an important feature of the soil conservation program during 1954 and 1955. The Soil Conservation Service and the state agricultural experiment stations worked together in strengthening the scientific and technical phases of the survey. The main objective was to permit broader and more detailed interpretations of factual information about soils and land for improving the usefulness of survey results to farmers, agencies of the various states needing such information, and the many programs relating to soil resources.

Major emphasis was given to training soil survey scientists at state experiment stations during 1954. Soil surveys covering about 500 million acres, providing information required for conservation planning, had been completed by the end of fiscal year 1955. At the same time, however, need for the survey information, especially by soil conservation districts, was revealed as outstripping the survey progress, and intensive studies were made both at the state and federal level to determine ways of speeding up this extremely detailed and exacting work. Fourteen soil survey reports consisting of map and text were published in 1955, bringing the total thus far issued for use by the public to 1,652.

The plant materials work of the program also was profiting by close relationship between land grant institutions in the states and the Soil Conservation Service. In woodland conservation there was additional emphasis on working with state forestry departments; the excellent working relationships between the service and state fish and game departments and other wildlife conservation agencies continued to be fruitful. In several states successful programs to produce plant materials for soil and water conservation purposes were being carried out, with sharing of costs and management.

There was heavy demand in most states for engineering assistance in connection with soil and water conservation. This was due largely to rapid expansion of the watershed protection program, need to make better use of water available for agriculture, and the desire of farm people to take advantage of the current high economic level to provide some of the permanent and more costly conservation measures. Spread of irrigation in the East was unprecedented: the Soil Conservation Service assisted more than 10,000 farmers in plan-

ACTIVE SOIL CONSERVATION DISTRICT COOPERATORS AS OF JUNE 30, 1955[1]

State	Number of farmers and ranchers	Acres covered
Alabama	57,624	10,008,553
Arizona	4,636	1,533,899
Arkansas	62,294	13,063,988
California	22,115	6,556,943
Colorado	15,567	13,386,148
Connecticut	4,029	440,402
Delaware	1,966	297,600
Florida	19,194	8,836,477
Georgia	90,747	17,371,158
Idaho	12,629	4,735,873
Illinois	41,510	7,215,063
Indiana	23,375	3,457,745
Iowa	51,996	9,472,505
Kansas	62,997	20,594,158
Kentucky	80,608	9,797,285
Louisiana	34,234	7,452,627
Maine	7,582	1,416,976
Maryland	14,519	2,110,377
Massachusetts	6,713	727,755
Michigan	27,999	3,601,514
Minnesota	26,723	5,219,241
Mississippi	59,374	10,293,016
Missouri	11,309	2,337,014
Montana	12,737	26,129,479
Nebraska	48,456	16,792,665
Nevada	1,841	2,058,524
New Hampshire	4,617	784,392
New Jersey	6,579	745,017
New Mexico	12,217	26,057,951
New York	34,198	4,689,016
North Carolina	77,021	7,911,317
North Dakota	29,393	18,571,635
Ohio	33,136	4,731,086
Oklahoma	79,333	20,154,879
Oregon	7,896	4,639,411
Pennsylvania	19,935	2,446,110
Rhode Island	1,036	124,232
South Carolina	38,842	6,553,237
South Dakota	29,844	18,180,089
Tennessee	34,832	5,007,866
Texas	168,628	85,757,725
Utah	10,650	5,977,020
Vermont	9,545	1,870,394
Virginia	36,350	6,031,531
Washington	26,881	9,543,618
West Virginia	32,170	4,376,091
Wisconsin	34,422	5,548,858
Wyoming	5,058	8,254,966
U. S. Total	**1,535,357**	**452,863,426**
Alaska	332	42,993
Hawaii	819	696,644
Caribbean	15,828	824,036
Grand Total	**1,552,336**	**454,427,099**

[1]Includes initial and advanced agreements, and active basic plans.

ning and installing sprinkler irrigation systems in 1955. Irrigation guides were prepared in twenty-six states east of the Mississippi River to provide engineering personnel with criteria needed to plan and apply the irrigation phase of a conservation plan. These guides also are helpful to manufacturers of irrigation equipment and to other agency technicians in developing plans for irrigation in the states.

Funds available from all sources for soil and water conservation as administered by the Soil Conservation Service for the fiscal year 1955 totaled $87,075,769. Of this amount, $79,806,085 was obligated during the fiscal year. The total funds available included $77,956,020 appropriated by Congress; the remainder represented trust funds advanced to the service for furnishing assistance to Agricultural Conservation Program participants in establishing soil conservation practices on their farms. More than $14 million was obligated to develop watershed work plans, furnish technical services in the lay-out and establishment of conservation practices, and provide the federal share of construction costs and engineering supervision over construction activities in the watersheds. These funds—along with more than $59.5 million obligated for technical assistance in soil conservation districts in all forty-eight states, Alaska, Hawaii, Puerto Rico and the Virgin Islands, were used in conjunction with cooperative programs initiated by local soil conservation districts, flood control districts, watershed protection groups, and other similar organizations.

SOIL CONSERVATION DISTRICTS AND OTHER CONSERVATION DISTRICTS BY STATES

Cumulative to June 30, 1955*

State	Date district law became effective	Districts organized(a) (Number)	Approximate area and farms within organized districts			Districts having memorandums of understanding with U. S. Dept. of Agriculture (b) (Number)
			Total area (1,000 acres)	Farms and ranches (Thousands)	Land in farms (1,000 acres)	
Alabama	Mar. 18, 1939	12	32,690	211	20,889	12
Arizona	June 16, 1941	46	10,164	9	2,917	46
Arkansas	July 1, 1937	74	33,697	182	18,941	72
California (c)	June 26, 1938	108	34,560	74	16,091	106
Colorado	May 6, 1937	98	38,495	42	24,586	98
Connecticut	July 18, 1945	8	3,135	16	1,272	8
Delaware	Apr. 2, 1943	3	1,266	9	851	3
Florida	June 10, 1937	57	28,268	53	15,006	57
Georgia	Mar. 23, 1937	27	37,225	197	25,657	27
Idaho	Mar. 9, 1939	41	30,472	28	9,108	39
Illinois	July 9, 1937	97	32,528	189	30,101	97
Indiana	Mar. 11, 1937	67	16,306	113	13,485	65
Iowa	July 4, 1939	100	34,265	203	34,471	100
Kansas	Apr. 10, 1937	105	52,549	131	50,706	105
Kentucky	June 11, 1940	122	25,435	217	19,392	122
Louisiana	July 27, 1938	26	27,939	123	11,134	26
Maine	Mar. 25, 1941	15	16,485	29	4,000	15
Maryland	June 1, 1937	23	6,099	35	3,914	23
Massachusetts	June 28, 1945	15	5,000	22	1,660	15
Michigan	July 23, 1937	72	27,275	138	15,483	72
Minnesota	Apr. 26, 1937	69	25,366	119	21,704	68
Mississippi	Apr. 4, 1938	74	30,231	251	20,704	74
Missouri	July 23, 1943	32	9,053	61	9,053	32
Montana(d)	Feb. 28, 1939	78	86,777	34	52,395	78
Nebraska	May 18, 1937	87	48,412	107	47,965	87
Nevada	Mar. 30, 1937	31	56,983	3	6,738	31
New Hampshire	May 10, 1945	10	5,771	13	1,714	10
New Jersey	July 1, 1937	12	4,785	25	1,725	12
New Mexico	Mar. 17, 1937	61	58,248	27	40,671	61
New York	July 20, 1940	42	21,130	100	13,050	42
North Carolina	Mar. 22, 1937	37	31,422	288	19,318	37
North Dakota	Mar. 16, 1937	79	43,631	68	39,592	79
Ohio	June 5, 1941	85	24,196	190	20,190	84
Oklahoma	Apr. 15, 1937	86	43,576	140	35,414	86
Oregon	Apr. 7, 1939	50	33,630	41	13,859	49
Pennsylvania	July 2, 1937	30	13,013	75	7,006	30
Rhode Island	Apr. 26, 1943	3	677	3	191	3
South Carolina	Apr. 17, 1937	44	19,395	139	12,475	44
South Dakota	July 1, 1937	65	35,433	58	35,433	65
Tennessee	Mar. 10, 1939	83	23,801	210	17,054	81
Texas(e)	Apr. 24, 1939	170	161,497	326	138,828	164
Utah	Mar. 23, 1937	48	47,584	29	13,313	48
Vermont	Apr. 18, 1939	13	5,931	19	3,527	13
Virginia	Apr. 1, 1938	29	24,959	149	15,243	29
Washington	Mar. 17, 1939	75	37,752	69	15,783	75
West Virginia	June 12, 1939	14	15,272	81	8,171	14
Wisconsin	July 1, 1937	67	32,784	167	22,931	67
Wyoming	May 22, 1941	41	39,834	10	17,784	40
United States Total		2,631	1,474,996	4,823	971,495	2,611
Alaska	Mar. 25, 1947	9	4,391	1	104	8
Hawaii	May 19, 1947	15	3,317	5	1,490	14
Puerto Rico	July 1, 1946	17	2,185	54	1,792	17
Virgin Islands	June, 1946	2	85	1	64	2
Grand Total		2,674	1,484,974	4,884	974,945	2,652

*Prepared by the Soil Conservation Service, U.S. Department of Agriculture.

(a) For specific procedure on organization of districts, see the respective state soil conservation district law. In most of the states, the state soil conservation committee has the responsibility for the organization of districts. Local district governing bodies administer the affairs of each individual district.

(b) The U.S. Soil Conservation Service provides technical and other assistance to nearly all districts that have entered into memorandums of understanding with the Department of Agriculture.
(c) Includes Imperial Irrigation District, California.
(d) Includes 19 state cooperative grazing districts.
(e) Includes 1 wind-erosion district.

COOPERATIVE EXTENSION WORK UNDER
RECENT LEGISLATION*

THE Cooperative Extension Service is the field educational arm of the United States Department of Agriculture and the state and territorial land-grant colleges and universities. Cooperative extension work is carried on in all of the states and in Alaska, Hawaii and Puerto Rico. The service is cooperatively financed with federal, state, county and other local funds. For the fiscal year that ended June 30, 1955, a grand total of more than $100 million was available for cooperative extension work. Of this sum more than $60 million came from within the states and over $39 million from the federal government. Expenditures of funds from all sources in carrying out the work of the service for the 1954 fiscal year amounted to approximately $92 million.

Through its county extension agents, who are located in practically every agricultural county and in some urban counties as well, the service works with farm people and other groups in carrying out educational programs in agriculture, home economics and 4-H Club activity. The service has a professional staff of more than 13,000. Of this total more than 10,000 are agents in the counties, nearly 2,800 are on the headquarters staffs in the state land-grant colleges and universities, and less than 100 are in the federal office in the United States Department of Agriculture.

In Table 1 the number of extension workers in each of the states, Alaska, Hawaii and Puerto Rico is shown for June 30, 1955. This table does not include those in the federal office.

Table 2 gives the sources of funds allotted for cooperative extension work in each of the states, Alaska, Hawaii and Puerto Rico for the fiscal year that ended June 30, 1955.

Table 3 shows the increase in financial

*Prepared by C. M. FERGUSON, Administrator, Federal Extension Service, U. S. Department of Agriculture.

support of extension work within the states and from the federal government during the past ten years.

MORE THAN NINE MILLION PEOPLE REACHED YEARLY

Through its organized, informal type of education the Cooperative Extension Service reaches more than nine million people each year with information and technical advice on better farming and homemaking practices. Research findings of the U. S. Department of Agriculture and of the state agricultural experiment stations and other research sources are the basic fund of knowledge upon which the educational and technical guidance work of the service is based. County extension agents help rural people in adapting applicable findings to fit the local situation.

INFLUENCE OF EXTENSION WORK

Reports of county extension agents place the total number of families influenced by some phase of extension work during 1954 at 9,049,659. This is 736,000 more than in 1953. Of the total number of families influenced in 1954, 4,145,572, or 45.8 per cent, were farm families.

A total of 5,809,533 families changed one or more agricultural practices in 1954 as a result of extension activities. Of this number 3,425,159, or 59 per cent, were farm families.

Extension agents reported that as a result of their efforts 5,763,965 families changed home practices in 1954 as compared with 5,257,682 in 1953. Of this total 2,276,460 families, or 39.5 per cent, were farm, and 3,487,505 nonfarm families.

A new high of 2,104,787 boys and girls were enrolled in 4-H Club work in 1954. Of these boys and girls 1,395,110, or 66.3 per cent, came from farm homes.

Local voluntary leaders play an important role in helping county extension
(Concluded on page 388)

TABLE 1

NUMBER OF COOPERATIVE EXTENSION WORKERS*(a)

June 30, 1955

Column group key: **County agent work**, **Home demonstration work**, and **Boys' and girls' club work(c)** are each divided into **White** and **Negro**, with sub-columns *State leaders*, *Assistant state leaders and district agents*, *County agents*, and *Assistant county agents* (no assistant county agents under Negro).

State or territory	No. of agric. counties (b)	Directors & asst. directors	CA White: State leaders	CA White: Asst. state leaders & dist. agents	CA White: County agents	CA White: Asst. county agents	CA Negro: State leaders	CA Negro: Asst. state leaders & dist. agents	CA Negro: County agents	HD White: State leaders	HD White: Asst. state leaders & dist. agents	HD White: County agents	HD White: Asst. county agents	HD Negro: State leaders	HD Negro: Asst. state leaders & dist. agents	HD Negro: County agents	Club White: State leaders	Club White: Asst. state leaders & dist. agents	Club White: County agents	Club White: Asst. county agents	Club Negro: State leaders	Club Negro: Asst. state leaders & dist. agents	Club Negro: County agents	Administrative	Specialists	Total
Eastern Region:																										
Connecticut	8	2	1		8	12				1		9	4				1	1	6	10					30	84
Delaware	3	1	1		3	2				1		3					1	1	2	1					15	31
Maine	16	1	1		14	7				1		13	2				1	1	13	2				1	16	74
Maryland	23	1	2	2	23	28		1	8	1	2	23	14		1	8	1	3		19					36	153
Massachusetts	14	2	1		17	19				1		11	14				1	1	10					5	41	144
New Hampshire	10	1	1		10	15				1		8					1	1	10	4					14	67
New Jersey	21	2	1		20	19				1		19	5				1	1	18	7				3	22	117
New York	62	2	1	4	56	86				1	4	55	55				1	5	54	59				1	106	492
Pennsylvania	67	5			67	59				1	2	62	1				1	3	3	2				1	21	222
Rhode Island	5	1			3							3													5	20
Vermont	14	2	1	1	14	6				1		13	4				1	1	12						18	69
West Virginia	55	3	1	3	50	14			1		2	36			1	7	1	3	39	3			2		27	199
Region Total	298	23	10	10	285	267		1	8	12	10	255	100		2	16	11	21	167	107			2	11	351	1,672
Southern Region:																										
Alabama	67	2			67	123			44	1	4	67	63		2	36	2	1				2		2	37	459
Arkansas	75	3		1	79	60		1	20	1	4	78	15		1	26	1					1		3	36	335
Florida	67	2		1	66	54		1	10	1	6	48	36		2	12	1	2			1	1		2	35	264
Georgia	159	5			154	57		1	48	1	6	132	26		2	37		2				2			54	549
Kentucky	120	2	1	1	121	74		1		1	6	102	36		1	6	2	10			1	1		2	41	402
Louisiana	64	2		1	64	93	1		21	1	4	64	50	1	2	22	1	3			2	1		3	45	383
Mississippi	82	3			82	121		3	48	1	4	81	65		2	65	2	4			1	2		4	49	522
North Carolina	100	3	1		100	178		1	67	1	6	100	59		1	59	1	6			2	1		1	84	727
Oklahoma	77	2		1	77	80		1	12	1	4	77	13		1	13	1	3				1		2	50	369
South Carolina	46	2			46	72		1	38	1	5	46	36		1	36	2	4			1	1			45	338
Tennessee	95	3		1	101	101		2	14	2	13	91	53		1	13	2	4				2		2	51	448
Texas	254	3	1	2	246	109		1	57	1	7	191	94		2	47	4	4			1	1		1	54	800
Virginia	100	5			98	74		1	31	1	6	94	26		2	30	1	1			1	1		1	62	442
Puerto Rico	77	2			67	79					5	67	30				1							6	42	307
Region Total	1,383	39	4	8	1,362	1,275	8	15	412	12	80	1,238	602	3	18	402	16	51			7	5		30	685	6,345

North Central Region:

Illinois	102	2		7	99	62		1	5	96	30		1	1	10	30	1	55	398
Indiana	92	4		6	92	79		2	81	1			1	11			1	72	349
Iowa	99		1	5	100	20		5	76	18		3	5	44			1	79	362
Kansas	105	5		6	105	20		2	6	98	10		1	6	43	1	3	62	364
Michigan	83	2		5	76	54		5	63	13			11	56	2			83	380
Minnesota	87	2		5	91	33		5	72	8		1	9	13	4		1	37	277
Missouri	115	1		4	114	145		4	7	101	25	4	1	6			2	54	468
Nebraska	93	2		5	84	33		3	1	44	9		1	5			4	43	235
North Dakota	53	2		3	50	23		1	1	19	7		1	4			3	27	141
Ohio	88	4		6	88	66		1	4	84	1		1	5	2		1	64	327
South Dakota	68	2		4	62	19		1	1	43	3		1	7			2	36	181
Wisconsin	71	4		5	71	63		4	67	8			1	5	24	7		61	315
Region Total	1,056	32	6	61	1,032	617		11	47	844	133	4	13	84	212	7	21	673	3,797

Western Region:

Arizona	14	2			12	15			8	4		1	1			1	15	60
California	58	5	1	3	50	207		3	87			1	7	5	1	1	55	421
Colorado	63	1	1	3	51	24			44	4		1	3	5		1	21	160
Idaho	44	2		3	42	6		1	24	6		1	2	10			20	117
Montana	56	2		2	46	22		1	23	7		1	2				19	126
Nevada	17	3			12	10			10			1				1	5	43
New Mexico	32	3	1		31	25		2	18	19		1	5			1	17	119
Oregon	36	6		3	71	3			36	1		1	5	29	5	2	42	207
Utah	29	2	1		28	9			22	1		1	2			1	23	91
Washington	39	2	2		101	4		2	46	1		1	1			1	24	191
Wyoming	23	2	1		23	10			21	1		1	1			1	17	79
Alaska	4	3		1	2				5							1	1	13
Hawaii	4	1		1	13	20		1	21	10		1	28	44	5	14	273	74
Region Total	419	35	7	16	482	355		12	9	353	58		12	28	44	5	12	273	1,701

Grand Total	3,156	129	27	168	3,161	2,514	9	16	422	47	146	2,690	893	3	20	422	52	184	423	119	7	5	2	74	1,982	13,515
June 30, 1954	3,108	118	26	158	3,041	1,971	10	15	395	47	146	2,607	681	3	18	406	58	187	462	98	7	4	3	(d)	2,256	12,717

*Prepared by the Federal Extension Service, U. S. Department of Agriculture.

(a) Employees under federal appointment.

(b) 1950 agricultural census.

(c) Special 4-H Club workers. In the majority of states, Alaska, Hawaii and Puerto Rico, 4-H Club Work is conducted by county agents, county home demonstration agents and assistants.

(d) Not previously reported.

TABLE 2

SOURCES OF FUNDS ALLOTTED FOR COOPERATIVE EXTENSION WORK IN STATES, ALASKA, HAWAII AND PUERTO RICO*

For the Fiscal Year Ending June 30, 1955

States	Grand total	Total federal funds	Total within the states	Funds from federal sources — Smith-Lever act as amended June 26, 1953
Alabama	$ 2,912,765.33	$ 1,452,662.57	$ 1,460,102.76	$ 1,431,452.57
Arizona	500,733.94	213,961.39	286,772.55	213,961.39
Arkansas	2,031,432.09	1,199,915.09	831,517.00	1,177,975.09
California	4,661,654.89	929,647.74	3,732,007.15	928,027.74
Colorado	1,231,436.89	416,623.89	814,813.00	408,779.89
Connecticut	697,474.15	210,690.87	486,783.28	202,130.87
Delaware	253,257.45	117,932.45	135,325.00	106,932.45
Florida	1,716,513.32	458,394.32	1,258,119.00	447,524.32
Georgia	2,973,868.90	1,507,988.90	1,465,880.00	1,496,273.90
Idaho	916,473.94	320,164.11	596,309.83	317,284.11
Illinois	3,521,496.14	1,193,688.14	2,327,808.00	1,175,308.14
Indiana	2,786,056.02	991,628.02	1,794,428.00	975,649.02
Iowa	2,931,802.39	1,115,557.39	1,816,245.00	1,074,997.39
Kansas	2,900,741.62	782,578.62	2,118,163.00	756,758.62
Kentucky	2,504,944.58	1,405,989.55	1,098,955.03	1,388,594.55
Louisiana	2,717,282.59	978,768.26	1,738,514.33	937,148.26
Maine	565,220.96	272,502.79	292,718.17	270,029.53
Maryland	1,457,675.79	390,045.62	1,067,630.17	362,825.62
Massachusetts	1,268,572.33	299,298.10	969,274.23	277,678.10
Michigan	3,489,440.50	1,135,022.90	2,354,417.60	1,062,699.57
Minnesota	2,104,000.45	1,039,568.94	1,064,431.51	1,027,028.94
Mississippi	2,957,637.38	1,495,417.38	1,462,220.00	1,469,015.55
Missouri	2,601,935.14	1,251,688.14	1,350,247.00	1,225,823.14
Montana	985,082.96	334,766.96	650,316.00	325,656.96
Nebraska	1,684,919.78	644,888.54	1,040,031.24	631,268.54
Nevada	280,910.38	123,706.65	157,203.73	122,506.65
New Hampshire	461,381.55	153,580.97	307,800.58	145,425.97
New Jersey	1,361,419.06	289,007.28	1,072,411.78	274,687.28
New Mexico	850,830.20	313,353.80	537,476.40	292,728.80
New York	4,958,584.13	1,019,807.50	3,938,776.63	983,567.50
North Carolina	5,205,145.20	1,885,229.48	3,319,915.72	1,859,908.98
North Dakota	1,008,323.97	484,711.97	523,612.00	469,691.97
Ohio	2,693,250.02	1,342,579.77	1,350,670.25	1,319,429.77
Oklahoma	2,371,306.72	1,080,160.72	1,291,146.00	1,025,966.72
Oregon	2,141,090.89	438,787.39	1,702,303.50	413,192.39
Pennsylvania	2,703,282.84	1,282,077.52	1,421,205.32	1,274,497.52
Rhode Island	198,713.38	85,847.38	112,866.00	82,535.38
South Carolina	2,084,870.83	1,027,102.53	1,057,768.30	1,022,475.03
South Dakota	1,120,417.27	474,567.27	645,850.00	468,697.27
Tennessee	2,577,210.44	1,422,242.44	1,154,968.00	1,402,222.44
Texas	4,988,757.06	2,344,324.26	2,644,432.80	2,328,748.89
Utah	645,184.11	241,484.11	403,700.00	228,199.11
Vermont	556,079.26	197,307.83	358,771.43	192,457.83
Virginia	3,049,530.04	1,162,895.04	1,886,635.00	1,136,959.04
Washington	1,539,066.94	508,143.42	1,030,923.52	497,585.92
West Virginia	1,257,687.81	696,102.81	561,585.00	691,382.81
Wisconsin	2,695,928.37	1,044,090.37	1,651,838.00	1,015,850.37
Wyoming	636,423.96	205,830.01	430,593.95	200,570.01
Alaska	148,515.00	65,746.52	82,768.48	65,746.52
Hawaii	589,105.21	210,642.12	378,463.09	200,642.12
Puerto Rico	1,716,358.63	1,010,960.63	705,398.00	975,340.63
Unallotted	280,319.55	280,319.55	—	280,158.84
Regional Contracts	125,000.00	125,000.00	—	—
Grand Total	$100,617,112.35	$39,675,000.02	$60,942,112.33	$38,662,000.02

*Prepared by the Federal Extension Service, U. S. Department of Agriculture.

TABLE 2—Continued

SOURCES OF FUNDS ALLOTTED FOR COOPERATIVE EXTENSION WORK IN STATES, ALASKA, HAWAII AND PUERTO RICO*

—Funds from federal sources—		—————Funds from within the states—————			
Clarke-McNary forestry	Agricultural Marketing Act (a) (Title II)	State and college	County	Local non-public sources	
$ 1,620.00	$ 19,590.00	$ 845,102.76	$ 615,000.00	$ —	Alabama
—	—	238,710.15	48,062.40	—	Arizona
1,620.00	20,320.00	500,995.00	324,422.00	6,100.00	Arkansas
1,620.00	—	2,658,394.15	1,073,613.00	—	California
1,260.00	6,584.00	401,625.00	413,188.00	—	Colorado
1,620.00	6,940.00	266,584.28	203,232.00	16,967.00	Connecticut
—	11,000.00	128,850.00	2,000.00	4,475.00	Delaware
1,620.00	9,250.00	738,655.00	519,464.00	—	Florida
3,240.00	8,475.00	763,307.00	702,573.00	—	Georgia
2,880.00	—	330,659.83	245,650.00	20,000.00	Idaho
3,240.00	15,140.00	893,558.00	12,000.00	1,422,250.00	Illinois
1,620.00	14,359.00	954,565.00	781,505.00	58,358.00	Indiana
3,060.00	37,500.00	835,000.00	575,880.00	405,365.00	Iowa
1,620.00	24,200.00	524,330.00	1,567,083.00	26,750.00	Kansas
1,620.00	15,775.00	681,050.00	417,305.03	600.00	Kentucky
1,620.00	40,000.00	1,486,079.75	237,134.58	15,300.00	Louisiana
1,620.00	853.26	199,368.17	93,350.00	—	Maine
1,620.00	25,600.00	867,425.17	200,205.00	—	Maryland
1,620.00	20,000.00	378,726.00	590,548.23	—	Massachusetts
3,240.00	69,083.33	1,744,968.60	575,349.00	34,100.00	Michigan
3,240.00	9,300.00	457,247.00	607,184.51	—	Minnesota
3,240.00	23,161.83	775,000.00	643,175.00	44,045.00	Mississippi
1,620.00	24,245.00	723,900.00	460,628.57	165,718.43	Missouri
1,260.00	7,850.00	295,323.00	354,993.00	—	Montana
1,620.00	12,000.00	654,131.24	385,000.00	900.00	Nebraska
1,200.00	—	78,878.23	78,325.50	—	Nevada
1,620.00	6,535.00	190,570.58	117,230.00	—	New Hampshire
1,620.00	12,700.00	588,177.50	476,842.28	7,392.00	New Jersey
—	20,625.00	412,396.40	125,080.00	—	New Mexico
3,240.00	33,000.00	1,789,054.63	1,899,926.00	249,796.00	New York
1,620.00	23,700.50	2,077,415.72	1,242,500.00	—	North Carolina
1,620.00	13,400.00	188,000.00	335,612.00	—	North Dakota
1,620.00	21,530.00	720,284.00	591,278.50	39,107.75	Ohio
1,620.00	52,574.00	953,576.00	337,570.00	—	Oklahoma
1,620.00	23,975.00	1,261,893.50	440,410.00	—	Oregon
1,620.00	5,960.00	1,091,205.32	330,000.00	—	Pennsylvania
—	3,312.00	90,369.00	19,800.00	2,697.00	Rhode Island
3,240.00	1,387.50	917,037.50	134,250.80	6,480.00	South Carolina
1,620.00	4,250.00	433,840.00	204,110.00	7,900.00	South Dakota
1,620.00	18,400.00	751,686.00	402,152.00	1,130.00	Tennessee
1,620.00	13,955.37	1,020,870.02	1,622,262.78	1,300.00	Texas
1,260.00	12,025.00	287,700.00	116,000.00	—	Utah
1,300.00	3,550.00	246,005.00	112,766.43	—	Vermont
3,240.00	22,696.00	1,488,037.00	398,598.00	—	Virginia
1,620.00	8,937.50	580,300.00	450,623.52	—	Washington
1,620.00	3,100.00	382,620.00	174,665.00	4,300.00	West Virginia
3,240.00	25,000.00	650,789.00	1,001,049.00	—	Wisconsin
1,260.00	4,000.00	287,155.95	143,438.00	—	Wyoming
—	—	82,768.48	—	—	Alaska
—	10,000.00	378,463.09	—	—	Hawaii
1,620.00	34,000.00	705,398.00	—	—	Puerto Rico
—	160.71	—	—	—	Unallotted
—	125,000.00	—	—	—	Regional Contracts
$88,000.00	$925,000.00	$35,998,046.02	$22,403,035.13	$2,541,031.18	Grand Total

(a) Preliminary distribution.

agents carry out local programs. County extension agents reported that more than 1,202,945 local leaders were actively engaged in forwarding extension work in 1954. This is nearly 51,318 more than were reported in 1953.

Through its county extension agents the Cooperative Extension Service works directly with farm and other rural people. Its aim is to put research findings to work in the field, the home, the feedlot and the market place. Many nonfarm people likewise receive the benefits of its educational work, particularly in the fields of home economics, consumer information, horticulture and marketing.

More Stress on Farm and Home Management

As an integral part of its total program, the service during the last two years gave increased attention to giving more individual educational assistance. Although many farm families require only a mini-

mum of individual help in putting technical information into their farm and home operations, there are others who seek more individual help. In order to speed up this type of assistance, additional personnel has been provided by increased federal, state and local appropriations for extension work.

With today's capital investment per worker in agriculture roughly twice what it is in industry, farm people are more aware than ever before of the importance of managerial skill in carrying out their operations. Extension Services in many states have been giving emphasis during the past few years to helping farm families do a better job of farm and home management. The increased emphasis on individual help is based on this successful experience. Group and mass methods, however, are not being de-emphasized. They, too, are successful ways of speeding up the application of research to the farm and the home and in the market place.

Table 3

INCREASES IN FINANCIAL SUPPORT OF EXTENSION WORK WITHIN STATES AND FROM FEDERAL SOURCES

1945-55

Source	1945 (fiscal year)	1955 (fiscal year)	Increase	Percentage of increase
State appropriations	$ 9,158,276	$35,998,046	$26,839,770	42.8
County appropriations	8,480,318	22,403,035	13,922,717	22.2
Non-Public	1,200,829	2,541,031	1,340,202	2.1
Total within the states	18,839,424	60,942,112	42,102,688	67.1
Federal	18,996,840	39,675,000	20,678,160	32.9
Total	37,836,264	100,617,112	62,780,848	100.0

AGRICULTURAL RESEARCH IN THE STATES*

AGRICULTURAL research is one of the most important services rendered by state government to its citizens. It stimulates farm efficiency through intelligent application of science and technology to farm activities.

The public institution through which this service is made available is the state agricultural experiment station. Each station's function is to meet as adequately as possible the research needs pertaining to the agriculture of that state. Farmers, business men and industry serving agriculture may look to it for solutions of numerous technical agricultural problems.

The nation's agricultural research structure is made up of the activities of the Federal Department of Agriculture and the state experiment stations in the forty-eight states, Alaska, Hawaii, Puerto Rico and the Virgin Islands. All of these act independently, yet a well integrated program results—the key to which is cooperative, coordinated scientific effort.

The United States Department of Agriculture was created as a research and educational institution. In later years it has been given many other responsibilities, but it has never minimized the importance of its first assignment. This also has been true of the land-grant colleges, of which the state experiment stations are an integral part. It is significant that "An act to establish a Department of Agriculture" became law on May 15, 1862, and that it was followed on July 2 of that year by the first Morrill Act, more commonly known as the Land-Grant Act, "donating public lands to the several States and Territories which may provide colleges for the benefit of agriculture and the mechanic arts." These two acts became the parent measures which for many years have provided the framework of close cooperation be-

tween the Department of Agriculture and the state land-grant institutions.

Continued federal-state cooperation was strengthened by the Hatch Act, signed by President Grover Cleveland on March 2, 1887, which authorized payment of federal grant funds to states to establish and maintain agricultural experiment stations. Increased federal grant authorizations were provided by the Adams Act of 1906; the Purnell Act of 1925; the Bankhead-Jones Act of 1935; and Title I, section 9, of the amendment of 1946 to the Bankhead-Jones Act. Contractual federal funds and allotments on a matched fund basis also are available to state experiment stations through the Agricultural Marketing Act of 1946. The Alaska, Hawaii and Puerto Rico acts extended authorization for federal grants to the experiment stations of the Universities of Alaska, Hawaii and Puerto Rico. These various laws were brought together under a single act on August 11, 1955, when President Dwight D. Eisenhower signed Public Law 352, approving consolidation of the Hatch Act of 1887 and the laws supplementary thereto.

The state experiment stations conduct research and experiments on the many problems constantly encountered in the development of a permanent and sustaining agriculture and in the improvement of the economic and social welfare of the farm family. Because of differences in the climate, soils, market outlets and other local conditions, many states have distinct problems of production and marketing of crops and livestock, so that farmers naturally look to their local stations for solution of their immediate problems. The stations, to an ever increasing extent, are also acting as regional groups to provide the most effective and often the only practical approach to solutions of problems of common interest. In a similar manner, the research programs of the state experiment stations and the Department of Agricul-

*Prepared by E. C. Elting, Deputy Administrator for Experiment Stations, Agricultural Research Service, U. S. Department of Agriculture.

389

ture are supplementary, complementary and interdependent.

Great changes have come about since the first Hatch Act was passed—greater and more far reaching than may be realized until we compare the knowledge of then and now. At that time the practice of agriculture was governed to a very large extent by empirical rules. There were very few standard books dealing with farm principles and practice. There was no simple method for testing the butterfat content of milk. The basic principles underlying dairying were far from being known. Sanitary and pasteurized milk was almost unknown. It was not known that clovers and other legumes are able to store up the nitrogen of the air in their growth, much less that this ability is due to a symbiotic relation between the plants and bacteria on their roots. The theory of tillage was far from being understood, as were also the use of fertilizer and the requirements of crops under irrigation. There was little conception of the possibilities of plant breeding, selection, and hybridization to improve such common crops as corn and the cereals; change their composition; adapt them to different localities, purposes, and a shorter season of growth; and at the same time introduce resistance to disease. Farming as we now know it was not heard of, and crops which to a large measure made it a success had not been introduced or disseminated in this country. The theory and practice of silage making had not been worked out. The same was true of a wide range of feed stuffs. Breeding, feeding and management practices were largely matters of tradition. Knowledge of livestock and its potentials through breeding, hybridization, feeding and management

was just as meager. The same may be said for farm mechanization and other fields of agricultural interests.

Research at the state experiment stations has brought a multitude of practical results that greatly affect the life of every citizen. Through it the nation has acquired new scientific knowledge to develop its agricultural resources and to solve many problems that stood in the way of human welfare. Weather has always been a hazard for farmers, but agricultural engineers have sharply reduced the severe effects of cold, heat, dryness and dampness. Irrigation has made the difference between high yields or crop failure in unusually dry years. Haying weather need no longer be a problem with the introduction of barn hay driers. Control and prevention of potentially devastating livestock diseases are made possible by basic research into the causes of disease, finding weak spots where feeding and management may be factors, and observing therapeutic effects of newly developed drugs and antibiotics. Major contributions also have been made in the breeding and development of new horticultural and crop plants that resist serious economic diseases, insects and adverse weather conditions. The range of research is wide, and only a small sample of developments over the years has been indicated here.

The scientific effort of the experiment stations permits more efficient farm production, brings better food to urban consumers, and increases raw materials for industry. Research is contributing to the prosperity of the states and regions, strengthening the economy of the world, and is enhancing American leadership in the world.

TABLE 1

PERSONNEL OF THE EXPERIMENT STATIONS FOR THE YEAR
ENDED JUNE 30, 1954*

Station	Personnel				
	Full-time research	Research and teaching	Research and extension	Research, teaching, and extension	Total research workers
	Number	*Number*	*Number*	*Number*	*Number*
Alabama	61	61	...	2	124
Alaska	12	3	10	3	28
Arizona	46	44	...	...	90
Arkansas	48	54	1	1	104
California	148	362	...	...	510
Colorado	35	88	...	5	128
Connecticut:					
State	76	.....	...	...	76
Storrs	31	36	2	11	80
Delaware	19	19	6	5	49
Florida	184	29	5	4	222
Georgia	136	59	2	13	210
Hawaii	42	18	2	1	63
Idaho	31	42	2	1	76
Illinois	98	123	12	4	237
Indiana	135	92	21	14	262
Iowa	88	132	19	22	261
Kansas	49	183	1	...	233
Kentucky	114	39	4	10	167
Louisiana	117	60	1	...	178
Maine	32	38	...	1	71
Maryland	18	37	7	32	94
Massachusetts	66	10	1	18	95
Michigan	94	135	9	8	246
Minnesota	9	195	4	5	213
Mississippi	86	57	2	3	148
Missouri	22	135	2	4	163
Montana	54	58	1	12	125
Nebraska	70	85	...	1	156
Nevada	15	8	...	5	28
New Hampshire	17	43	4	8	72
New Jersey	88	69	2	2	161
New Mexico	37	31	1	4	73
New York:					
Cornell	34	148	15	44	241
State	75	.....	...	...	75
North Carolina	109	118	...	4	231
North Dakota	44	47	...	...	91
Ohio	78	86	2	5	171
Oklahoma	69	109	2	1	181
Oregon	119	105	3	3	230
Pennsylvania	1	214	...	2	217
Puerto Rico	107	.....	...	...	107
Rhode Island	18	19	2	7	46
South Carolina	86	25	2	2	115
South Dakota	32	60	...	1	93
Tennessee	114	48	2	11	175
Texas	207	66	5	16	294
Utah	46	69	...	6	121
Vermont	8	28	4	16	56
Virginia	103	38	6	11	158
Washington	124	76	...	3	203
West Virginia	17	71	1	2	91
Wisconsin	70	117	9	20	216
Wyoming	37	42	...	2	81
Total	3,576	3,831	174	355	7,936

*Prepared by the Agricultural Research Service, U.S. Department of Agriculture.

TABLE 2

NON-FEDERAL FUNDS AVAILABLE TO THE EXPERIMENT STATIONS FOR THE YEAR ENDED JUNE 30, 1954*(a)

Station	State appropriations	Special endowments, industrial fellowships, etc.	Fees	Sales	Miscellaneous	Balance from previous year	Total
Alabama........	$753,812.68	$83,363.31	....	$607,066.38	....	$273,576.52	$1,717,818.89
Alaska.........	144,000.00	....	....	56,827.31	....	64,445.63	265,272.94
Arizona........	434,047.20	28,540.16	....	39,324.60	....	....	501,911.96
Arkansas.......	497,028.23	52,783.92	....	227,030.31	....	130,769.34	907,611.80
California......	6,289,405.36	510,280.78	....	93,783.26	....	655,048.90	7,548,518.30
Colorado.......	443,508.88	313,702.50	....	151,111.21	$9,400.00	174,393.50	1,092,116.09
Connecticut:							
State........	369,371.81	20,300.00	....	....	....	....	389,671.81
Storrs........	370,396.00	173,977.00	....	....	....	62,998.00	607,371.00
Delaware.......	205,025.00	53,448.17	....	113,838.15	....	54,142.23	426,453.55
Florida.........	2,774,539.95	61,742.80	....	293,859.34	....	410,259.88	3,540,401.97
Georgia........	1,108,733.00	135,603.90	....	734,752.08	33,472.00	295,704.24	2,308,265.22
Hawaii.........	444,677.38	....	....	82,238.09	18,348.66	7,849.01	553,113.14
Idaho..........	496,201.41	33,036.41	....	142,195.44	....	179,999.86	851,433.12
Illinois.........	1,611,342.20	297,780.39	....	346,591.68	....	....	2,255,714.27
Indiana........	1,158,756.72	224,686.15	$241,203.16	546,229.73	202,820.23	502,292.73	2,875,988.72
Iowa...........	1,379,983.91	581,689.55	....	652,187.97	....	311,914.37	2,925,775.80
Kansas.........	966,585.00	119,463.90	....	273,150.38	....	239,091.52	1,598,290.80
Kentucky......	369,862.00	77,164.52	99,712.99	81,117.07	....	....	627,856.58
Louisiana......	1,620,434.72	57,590.60	....	....	119,242.52	....	1,797,267.84
Maine.........	244,243.62	22,582.10	....	52,000.00	....	39,365.90	358,191.62
Maryland.......	459,352.98	85,580.65	....	137,007.71	....	111,579.51	793,520.85
Massachusetts..	466,527.59	43,559.29	....	....	....	37,956.71	548,043.59
Michigan.......	1,396,839.90	234,741.40	....	....	....	62,045.61	1,693,626.91
Minnesota.....	1,639,964.79	296,183.42	9,213.20	509,113.36	....	....	2,454,474.77
Mississippi.....	719,446.07	55,775.10	....	600,454.27	5,783.38	394,022.53	1,775,481.35
Missouri........	309,397.97	58,884.12	43,145.09	215,933.49	....	457,411.84	1,084,772.51
Montana.......	473,650.00	21,540.97	....	341,896.24	....	215,270.77	1,052,357.98
Nebraska.......	704,334.43	63,787.19	....	559,486.41	....	41,188.64	1,368,796.67
Nevada........	50,682.05	2,700.00	....	....	....	49,242.48	102,624.53
New Hampshire.	127,092.99	23,514.20	....	10,468.00	....	419.85	161,495.04
New Jersey.....	1,144,323.65	470,565.63	....	....	....	4,161.97	1,619,051.25
New Mexico.....	295,665.00	5,000.00	....	54,299.06	150.00	33,607.47	388,721.53
New York:							
Cornell........	2,626,132.43	313,911.43	....	465,163.06	....	....	3,405,206.92
State..........	975,878.38	....	....	45,730.34	....	....	1,021,608.72
North Carolina..	1,388,857.63	71,752.00	....	....	253,000.32	....	1,713,609.95
North Dakota...	619,071.32	50,436.49	....	161,377.03	....	121,042.42	951,927.26
Ohio...........	1,980,799.72	97,718.22	....	261,965.74	....	318,555.05	2,659,038.73
Oklahoma......	1,088,473.00	91,262.31	....	386,781.66	7,356.65	80,037.37	1,653,910.99
Oregon.........	1,381,864.33	188,255.53	205,176.64	206,815.13	....	....	1,982,111.63
Pennsylvania...	1,126,291.17	92,747.37	....	166,622.34	43,516.30	130,334.77	1,559,511.95
Puerto Rico.....	1,127,831.00	10,000.00	....	....	124,549.85	68,872.79	1,331,253.64
Rhode Island...	88,504.00	66,491.53	....	17,735.99	....	30,004.94	202,736.46
South Carolina..	552,131.63	49,723.24	....	185,000.00	....	45,419.59	832,274.46
South Dakota...	335,200.00	9,214.30	....	131,772.92	....	48,835.94	525,023.16
Tennessee......	492,027.63	101,697.58	....	182,710.71	....	....	776,435.92
Texas..........	1,240,488.00	270,855.54	....	1,019,263.47	250,464.86	702,279.92	3,483,351.79
Utah..........	387,500.00	185,150.08	....	61,971.61	4,888.85	62,169.94	701,680.48
Vermont.......	114,920.47	....	....	2,430.03	18,100.00	27,818.28	163,268.78
Virginia........	955,845.12	....	....	168,030.47	....	....	1,123,875.59
Washington.....	1,573,333.60	165,631.54	....	222,678.69	....	....	1,961,643.83
West Virginia...	226,140.00	8,980.00	....	222,557.47	270.00	125,823.69	583,771.16
Wisconsin......	1,464,774.00	640,103.00	....	507,937.00	....	....	2,612,814.00
Wyoming.......	312,859.00	9,807.76	....	95,241.95	....	57,073.54	474,982.25
Total.......	49,528,154.92	6,633,306.05	598,451.08	11,433,747.15	1,091,363.62	6,627,027.25	75,912,050.07

*Prepared by the Agricultural Research Service, U.S. Department of Agriculture.

(a) During the year expenditures of the stations totalled $80,706,404.95, of which $67,205,204.62 comprised non-federal funds and the balance federal.

STATE FORESTRY ADMINISTRATION*

STATE forestry administration dates back almost seventy years to 1885, when California, Colorado, Ohio and New York took the lead in creating organizations to carry on state forestry activities. Although during several previous decades some states had passed laws to encourage reforestation, and to look into the general forestry situation, little effective work was done until 1885.

By 1910, twenty-five states had established forestry organizations. They began as educational agencies, gathering and disseminating information as to the possibilities of forestry, or developed as strictly fire-protection organizations. Now forty-four states have forestry administrative organizations.

In general, the major activities of organized state forestry departments include:

1. Fire control.
2. Reforestation.
3. Administration of state forests.
4. Woodland management assistance.
5. Forest insect and disease control.
6. Supervision and administration of forest practices acts.

Forest Fire Control

The forestry departments of forty-four states administer organized forest fire control on state and privately-owned lands. These states cooperate with the federal government and receive financial aid under the provisions of the Clarke-McNary Act of June 7, 1924.

Altogether, approximately 431 million acres of non-federal forest and important non-timbered watershed lands need organized public fire control in addition to the protection that landowners themselves can or do provide. The hard core of the nation's forestry problem centers in forest lands in private ownership. They include three-quarters of the forests and comprise our most productive and most accessible forest lands. Three-quarters of this private forest land is held by 4¼ million small woodland owners. Three and ¼ million of these small owners are farmers. From these private holdings comes nearly 90 per cent of the nation's total requirements for lumber and other wood products. The large area involved, combined with high seasonal fire hazards and small ownerships, makes the protection job a difficult one. In some sections the task is made more difficult because of the deep-rooted habit of "firing the woods" to improve the range for livestock, or for other local reasons. The states, however, have made substantial progress in fire control, especially during the last decade.

During 1954 about 89 per cent of the lands needing public aid in fire control was given protection by the states and agencies cooperating with them. Protection is being extended to the remaining 11 per cent, or roughly 49 million acres, as rapidly as funds and facilities become available.

State fire protection agencies in 1954 confined the area burned to 0.7 per cent of the area protected.

Although many states have been carrying on forest fire control activities for forty years or more, the outstanding progress has taken place during recent years. There will be periods, such as 1952 and 1954, when the number of fires increases materially and the acreage burned takes an upward turn, but the general trend has shown advance in preventing fires and in prompt and effective fire suppression action. Increased educational activities, better fire laws, together with more effective law enforcement and a growing public sentiment against needless forest fire losses of wood, water, wildlife and recreation should bear fruit and eliminate serious upward turns in numbers of fires and burned acreage.

*Prepared by Wm. J. Stahl, Forest Service, U. S. Department of Agriculture.

In 1954 there were 118,681 fires on protected state and privately-owned forest
land, as compared with 94,446 in 1951 and
an average of 97,053 during the previous
five years. Two reasons, other than adverse weather conditions, for the increased
number of fires on protected land are that
each year an area of previously unprotect-
ed forest has been put under organized
protection, and each year more and more
people are using the wooded areas for
recreation, bringing added risk of fires.

Marked progress has been made by the
states during recent years both in improved
facilities for quicker discovery of fires and
in measures for more effective action in
fighting them. In large part this has been
the result of more experience in all phases
of fire control and of better organization,
planning and training. Important factors
have been the continual and greater use by
more states of airplanes and radios in detecting and reporting fires and the development and use of mechanized, mobile, fire-
suppression equipment, such as bulldozers,
pumper tank trucks, plowing units and the
like. These have not replaced, and probably never will entirely replace, hand tools
in fighting forest fires; but wherever mechanized equipment can be used it greatly
strengthens suppression work. More extensive use of automotive equipment, made
possible by more and better roads in forest
areas, has greatly increased the effectiveness of state fire-suppression forces. Continuing fire research in cloud seeding,
lightning dispersal, Detecto-Vision using
TV for detection of fires, fire weather
measurement and rating and fire behavior
have aided the fire protection program.

The forty-four states with organized fire
control now own 8,500 radios, 3,000 transportation trucks, 1,600 tanker trucks, 1,300
plows, 1,900 power pumps, 1,200 tractors,
500 jeeps with plows or tanks, 40 airplanes, 3,300 lookout towers for forest fire
detection, and 29,000 miles of telephone
lines for communication.

INTERSTATE COMPACTS

Three interstate forest fire protection
compacts have been activated. The compacts' purpose is to provide for more effective prevention and control of forest fires
through development of integrated plans,

maintenance of adequate fire control
measures and facilities by member states,
and mutual assistance in critical fire emergencies. The Northeastern Compact has
been active since 1952; the Southeastern
and South Central Compacts were organized in 1954. (See pages 18 and 19.)

FOREST PEST CONTROL

Losses from insects and diseases in our
forests are so great as to require the cooperation of all agencies interested in forest
pest control. To allow such pests to run
unchecked is to invite continued losses
which in specific areas may exceed the loss
from fires.

Examples of heavy damage are the
Chestnut Blight which completely wiped
out the chestnut; the White Pine Blister
Rust, a threat to most of our white pine;
Larch Sawfly which caused the loss of all
mature larch in the lake states; and many
others. In late years the Engelmann
Spruce Beetle has killed more than four
billion board feet of timber in Colorado
alone; the Douglas Fir Tussock Moth has
threatened millions of dollars worth of
timber; the Spruce Budworm in Oregon
and Washington, and the Gypsy Moth in
the Northeast have also taken a toll; the
Southern Pine Beetle is doing serious damage in the South; and the Oak Wilt is a
threat to our valuable oak stands.

The Forest Pest Control Act of 1947
(Public Law 110—80th Congress) authorizes the Secretary of Agriculture to cooperate with states and local groups in carrying
out measures to suppress or control forest
insects and diseases on all forest lands,
irrespective of ownership.

Some states have been active in detection and control work for many years.
Maine was probably the first state to have
forest insect detection service when in 1921
its fire wardens were instructed in reporting the current situation. There are thirty-
eight states having laws of varying force
for the control of forest pests. Seventeen
states have responsibility vested in the
state forester or a comparable conservation
agency official; thirteen states in a Department of Agriculture or similar state agency;
nine states in the state entomologist, pathol-
ogist, plant board or other specific agency.
Nine states have reported no specific forest

pest control laws. There is a need for the majority of the states to review their situation to assure that proper authority and funds are available to permit direct, prompt and effective control action on private lands. Suggested state legislation for control of forest pests is available through the Council of State Governments. Protection of state and privately owned forest lands from insects and diseases, in the main, has been on those lands adjacent to, or intermingled with, federal land. Under the Forest Pest Control Act the first project on state and private land only was the Spruce Budworm job in Maine in 1954. Control projects on Oak Wilt are being currently initiated in North Carolina and Pennsylvania. There has been increasing activity in forest pest control, and much more is in prospect.

REFORESTATION

It is estimated that about 50 million acres of privately-owned and state-owned forest land in this country should be replanted to trees if they are to make a real contribution to the economy of the states. The states are promoting the reforestation of this land and are cooperating with the federal government under terms of Section 4 of the Clarke-McNary Act. This cooperative program provides that the states produce the necessary trees in their own nurseries (or buy them from commercial nurseries) and distribute them to their citizens at a nominal price. (In a few cases trees are actually given away under certain conditions.) The federal government pays a part of the cost of doing this, the state pays another part, and the landowner the remainder. Forty-three states, Puerto Rico and Hawaii are now in this program. One state does such work without federal aid.

An important step increasing the scope of the work was made late in 1949 when Congress amended the law to apply to trees shipped to all landowners instead of to farmers alone. The amendment also increased the financial authorization for the work.

In 1954 the distribution by the states under this program was 466 million trees. This continues the encouraging trend of the past several years. In fact, since the close of the war many states have been unable to satisfy the popular demand for planting stock, although they have expanded production tenfold. A few states, notably in the South, now have programs that will replant the bulk of the land needing it in a reasonable period of years; but for the nation as a whole we are still far short of the volume of planting necessary to solve the reforestation problem. An adequate annual program would call for planting a billion trees per year on a million acres of public and private land.

ADMINISTRATION OF STATE AND COMMUNITY FORESTS

State-owned forests constitute a very important part of state forestry administration. They serve as demonstration and research centers for proper forest protection, reforestation and management. Harvesting of their timber crops is providing added revenue and also labor for local citizens. State forests are heavily used as recreational areas. Practically all important timbered states now have state forests. The acreage in 1954 totaled nearly 19 million, with the largest acreages located in Michigan, Minnesota, Pennsylvania, New York and Washington, each with more than a million acres. These figures are for areas strictly classified as "State Forests." If other forested areas, such as parks and game refuges, also owned by the states, are included, the total of state-owned forest land exceeds 39 million acres. Outstanding progress is being made in their administration and management.

Many communities also own forests; in fact, community forests are an old and popularly accepted part of forest conservation. Some are so long established and well managed that revenue from harvesting the timber has helped for many years to reduce local taxes. They also provide other benefits, such as watershed protection, outdoor recreation, shelter for fish and game, and permanent jobs through the sustained production of all types of forest products. Such forests are found in all states except five and aggregate about 4½ million acres. The state forester is in the best position to assist in the development of community forests within a state. The system of community forests should supplement and complement the state forest system and be closely integrated with it for adequate protection and management.

Forest Management Assistance

Our timber supplies must be grown as a crop. Only 10 per cent of our forest land now supports virgin stands of timber, which are old-growth forests that were here when America was settled. As indicated at the outset of this paper, our timber for the most part must come from privately-owned forest land, and small private holdings are especially important.

Since these small woodlands, owned by farmers, school teachers, small-town businessmen and others, must be made to produce continuous crops of usable timber, the manner in which they are managed is of utmost importance. Considerable improvement has been achieved in the management of many of them within the last few years, but much remains to be done. Some forty state forestry departments are now cooperating with the federal government under provisions of the Cooperative Forest Management Act to bring this improved management into the woodlands of small owners, and to improve manufacturing techniques and plant efficiency in some 50,000 establishments of small-saw-mill operators and other processors of primary forest products. Working under the supervision of the state foresters, 274 service foresters are responsible for giving on-the-ground woodland-management assistance to individual small owners. As shown in Table 1, 32,224 woodland owners were given management assistance under this cooperative program in 1954. Each service forester, farm forester, or project forester, as he is sometimes called, is assigned to a definite forest-management project area, usually comprising three to five counties.

In addition to the service foresters, most of the state foresters have staff assistants in forest management, and a few have additional management foresters not under the cooperative federal-state forest-management program. There are private consulting foresters in many states who give forest management assistance for a fee.

This cooperative program is yielding profits to the small forest owners, is supplementing the cash income on many farms, and is helping to put the nation's timber supply on a more permanent basis. Additional benefits are erosion prevention, water conservation, flood control, a home for wildlife and more attractive recreational areas.

TABLE 1

COOPERATIVE FOREST MANAGEMENT ACCOMPLISHMENTS
AND EXPENDITURES—FISCAL YEAR 1954*

	Accomplishments		Expenditures		
State	Number of woodland owners assisted	Woodland acres involved	Federal	State	Total
Alabama	604	73,194	$13,700	$16,227	$29,927
Arkansas	164	30,059	6,350	8,175	14,525
California	790	108,778	8,852	50,511	59,363
Colorado	21	53,731	2,538	3,231	5,769
Connecticut	664	19,503	9,900	17,696	27,596
Delaware	97	3,882	2,500	3,659	6,159
Florida	1,333	627,368	20,950	54,980	75,930
Georgia	729	148,194	19,250	33,012	52,262
Idaho	60	11,910	2,668	2,668	5,336
Illinois	664	20,412	24,571	40,703	65,274
Indiana	787	44,248	12,670	26,939	39,609
Iowa	404	14,652	7,450	18,361	25,811
Kentucky	236	13,783	16,500	16,654	33,154
Louisiana	210	17,727	12,950	14,570	27,520
Maine	1,728	101,868	17,950	39,358	57,308
Maryland	2,005	35,744	18,200	47,846	66,046
Massachusetts	439	13,374	5,580	8,778	14,358
Michigan	760	16,084	19,915	46,293	66,208
Minnesota	350	9,590	9,316	32,984	42,300
Mississippi	530	59,322	14,000	17,512	31,512
Missouri	1,609	172,954	27,026	53,392	80,418
New Hampshire	1,041	47,571	18,172	24,374	42,546
New Jersey	490	32,643	11,800	36,066	47,866
New York	3,257	236,494	18,500	99,739	118,239
North Carolina	722	61,594	25,250	36,585	61,835
North Dakota	22	330	2,639	2,639	5,278
Ohio	1,198	39,262	13,138	81,370	94,508
Oklahoma	407	788	4,671	4,671	9,342
Oregon	647	24,597	8,464	19,834	28,298
Rhode Island	135	4,829	2,400	3,269	5,669
South Carolina	849	82,286	19,315	37,058	56,373
South Dakota	3	480	648	1,084	1,732
Tennessee	477	39,396	15,810	15,810	31,620
Texas	655	51,347	11,743	11,769	23,512
Vermont	2,767	65,600	28,650	64,827	93,477
Virginia	1,604	141,758	28,850	90,667	119,517
Washington	973	43,788	11,311	18,912	30,223
West Virginia	779	23,072	18,800	31,837	50,637
Wisconsin	2,014	65,781	23,637	93,904	117,541
Total	32,224	2,557,993	$536,634	$1,227,964	$1,764,598

*Prepared by the Forest Service, U. S. Department of Agriculture.

THE BOOK OF THE STATES

TABLE 2

STATUS OF FEDERAL-STATE COOPERATIVE FOREST FIRE CONTROL ON STATE AND PRIVATE FOREST LANDS*

State	Area needing protection (1,000 acres)	Area protected (1,000 acres)	Fire control expenditures, fiscal year 1954		
			State and private	Federal	Total
Alabama	19,990	19,990	$ 792,846	$ 313,704	$ 1,106,550
Arkansas	16,962	15,399	749,814	241,402	991,216
California	19,500	19,500	6,286,971	1,366,806	7,653,777
Colorado	7,475	7,472	81,115	25,992	107,107
Connecticut	1,907	1,907	156,113	42,823	198,936
Delaware	440	440	11,234	9,350	20,584
Florida	19,940	13,975	1,622,843	514,771	2,137,614
Georgia	22,505	20,535	2,172,700	505,874	2,678,574
Idaho	6,963	6,963	329,372	130,416	459,788
Illinois	3,755	3,755	75,657	25,000	100,657
Indiana	4,255	4,255	158,222	48,314	206,536
Iowa	1,968	1,968	21,528	18,000	39,528
Kentucky	11,253	6,336	247,215	92,533	339,748
Louisiana	14,141	11,155	929,544	286,997	1,216,541
Maine	16,692	16,692	717,032	224,310	941,342
Maryland	2,686	2,686	349,067	104,686	453,753
Massachusetts	3,293	3,293	322,495	107,118	429,613
Michigan	17,124	17,124	1,563,475	395,208	1,958,683
Minnesota	17,996	17,996	635,363	308,596	943,959
Mississippi	15,314	11,288	812,353	297,813	1,110,166
Missouri	13,835	7,698	527,239	187,198	714,437
Montana	6,000	6,000	210,386	68,017	278,403
Nevada	2,150	2,150	31,331	25,000	56,331
New Hampshire	4,176	4,176	342,754	58,173	400,927
New Jersey	2,294	2,294	343,159	90,490	433,649
New Mexico	4,060	1,360	13,639	13,638	27,277
New York	13,423	13,423	889,768	246,395	1,136,163
North Carolina	16,920	15,594	827,979	295,466	1,123,445
North Dakota	919	....	....	....	....
Ohio	4,973	4,973	262,140	67,136	329,276
Oklahoma	9,779	3,591	149,367	83,549	232,916
Oregon	11,995	11,995	2,023,296	591,056	2,614,352
Pennsylvania	14,659	14,659	706,204	188,506	894,710
Rhode Island	452	452	72,755	25,000	97,755
South Carolina	11,300	11,300	962,958	267,241	1,230,199
South Dakota	896	896	35,620	25,000	60,620
Tennessee	11,967	9,247	601,005	204,906	805,911
Texas	14,707	8,429	543,230	203,730	746,960
Utah	5,721	5,721	64,171	25,000	89,171
Vermont	3,504	3,504	87,091	25,000	112,091
Virginia	12,971	12,971	637,783	203,822	841,605
Washington	12,329	12,329	1,694,045	541,227	2,235,272
West Virginia	9,038	9,038	305,761	139,781	445,542
Wisconsin	15,590	15,590	1,128,185	294,644	1,422,829
Wyoming	1,557	533	....	....	....
Hawaii	1,735	1,735	5,779	4,500	10,279
Total	431,109	382,387	$30,500,604	$8,934,188	$39,434,792

*Prepared by the Forest Service, U. S. Department of Agriculture.

STATE PARKS*

DEFINITE progress in the field of state parks has been noted during the past two years. By the end of 1954, there were more than 1,950 state parks and related types of state recreation areas, with a total area just over five million acres. Attendance during 1954 was recorded at 166 million visits—an increase of nearly 12 per cent over 1952. Tent and trailer camping rose 39 per cent during the period. Expenditures mounted 21 per cent, with a slightly higher percentage increase for capital improvements than for operation and maintenance.

As a result of greater emphasis by the states on having the parks more nearly pay their way, the amount of revenue from operations has increased 39 per cent over the two-year period, to a total of $13 million in 1954. This meant that 41 per cent of the cost of operation and maintenance of state parks was supported by those who used them.

To meet the pressure of ever-increasing attendance, the states are continuing to acquire new park areas. During the past two years more than 110,000 acres have been acquired. This was primarily through purchase, although a considerable proportion was donated.

The South Calaveras Grove area in California was purchased by the state with the assistance of matched funds from the Save-the-Redwoods League. Many organizations and individuals made donations to the league for the purchase, and the final gift was $1 million from John D. Rockefeller, Jr. Also in California, plans are expected to be developed for extensive, long-term beach and park acquisition on the basis of sums that will accrue to the State Park and State Beach Funds from off-shore oil and gas royalties.

Baxter State Park in Maine was increased by 24,218 acres through an additional gift of former Governor Percival

Baxter. New Jersey completed purchase of the 2,200-acre Island Beach area, obtained 54,200 acres of the 96,000-acre Wharton tract in the Southern Pine Barrens, and purchased the Worthington tract of 6,200 acres near the Delaware Water Gap. Future park developments are anticipated on at least a portion of all three of those areas.

New York has added significant acreage to its Adirondack Park and plans extensive recreation expansion in connection with the St. Lawrence Power development. Oregon continues to acquire important acreage in the Columbia River Gorge toward fulfillment of an 18,000-acre goal in that area.

The states are increasing their use of federal reservoir areas as park sites under agreements or licenses with the federal government. Reservoirs constructed by the Bureau of Reclamation on which the states in question have begun operation of recreation developments in the past two years are Angostura in South Dakota; Jamestown and Dickinson in North Dakota; Cedar Bluff in Kansas; Canyon Ferry in Montana; and Boysen, Buffalo Bill, Guernsey and Keyhole in Wyoming. The Corps of Engineers has licensed or leased property for park use to states on the following reservoirs: Blakley Mountain, Bull Shoals, and Narrows in Arkansas; Mansfield Hollow in Connecticut; Dewey and Watt Creek in Kentucky; Birchill and Knightsville in Massachusetts; Fort Peck in Montana; Blackwater in New Hampshire; Mt. Morris in New York; John H. Kerr in North Carolina; Mosquito Creek in Ohio; Fort Gibson and Tenkiller in Oklahoma; Fern Ridge in Oregon; Dennison (Texoma), Texarkana, Grapevine and Whitney in Texas; and McNary in Washington.

Three federal surplus properties were transferred to the states. Most important was the thirty-five-acre Hospital Cove on Angel Island in San Francisco Bay.

*Prepared by the National Park Service, U.S. Department of the Interior.

Financing of state park developments through revenue bonds continues to spread. South Carolina is now constructing permanent improvements in a number of its parks, financed by a $300,000 self-liquidating bond issue authorized in 1954. The Texas legislature enacted legislation validating a resolution of the Texas State Park Board to authorize issuance of $25 million of state park improvements bonds for construction of overnight and other park facilities. It is proposed that $3 million will be used immediately for construction on three state parks—Eisenhower, Atlanta and Inks Lake. West Virginia, New Hampshire and Oklahoma also are constructing facilities under revenue bond financing methods.

The United States Court of Appeals, Seventh Circuit, on October 29, 1954, upheld a determination of the Federal Power Commission adverse to an application to construct a dam and power project on the Namekagon River in Wisconsin. The court held that evidence sustained the commission's finding that the unique recreation features of the river are of greater public benefit than use of the river for waterpower development.

The State Board for Preservation of Scientific Areas in Wisconsin and the Michigan Natural Areas Council both have designated several state park areas within their states as scientific areas and natural areas. The two organizations have the goal of designating areas which can be guaranteed future preservation, those which possess valuable plant and animal communities, and those which are important for scientific research.

Significant legislation affecting parks and recreation was enacted in several states and Alaska between July 1, 1953, and June 30, 1955.

Colorado amended its 1937 state park law to create a State Park and Recreation Board in order to acquire, develop and administer a system of state parks and appropriated an initial $10,000—the first appropriation made for state parks. Idaho transferred administration of its roadside parks on highway rights-of-way from the jurisdiction of the State Board of Land Commissioners to the State Highway Department. Iowa legalized the use of prison labor in state parks and appropriated $75,000 for the biennium for this purpose. It also authorized establishment of county parks.

In Kansas, a State Park and Resources Authority was created to acquire, develop and administer state parks and related areas, also to encourage travel and publicize the state's natural resources. The Authority may obtain funds from revenue bonds, tolls and other fees. Maine broadened the functions of its State Park Commission by authorizing it to cooperate with federal agencies in the planning, maintenance and development of recreation areas and to assist state, county and municipal agencies in the study and planning of their recreation areas and programs. It increased the authorized lease period for concessioners from one to five years.

Legislation in Massachusetts replaced the Department of Conservation by a Department of Natural Resources. The former Division of Parks and Recreation is now the Bureau of Recreation under the Division of Forestry and Parks. A Division of Public Beaches under the Department of Public Works was established, and Salisbury Beach State Reservation was transferred to it. The Nevada legislature reactivated its state park program and appropriated approximately $45,000 for the biennium; legislation also authorized the designation of suitable sites as state monuments, historical landmarks, historical buildings or recreation areas if they are located on public land.

A constitutional amendment in New York increased the protection of that state's parks by means that included strengthening the discretionary power of the Land Board and requiring approval of mining permits by the Governor.

North Carolina transferred jurisdiction of its historical and archeological areas from the Department of Conservation and Development to a newly created Department of Archives and History and abolished the Historic Sites Commission. In Washington the state park law was amended to authorize the State Parks and Recreation Commission to require certification of all park and recreation workers employed in state-controlled programs, to grant easements for legitimate purposes, to charge fees, to rent park lands to private groups for periods not exceeding five years, to rent undeveloped park areas for not over ten years for grazing, agriculture and mining and for other purposes.

Wyoming has established a State Park Commission. Alaska authorized the Highway Engineer and the Land Commissioner to select, acquire and develop sites not exceeding ten acres each along highways or waterways for scenic, historic or recreation purposes.

Important additions to state park literature, published by the National Conference on State Parks, include a 256-page processed *Digest of Laws Relating to State Parks*, prepared by Flavel Shurtleff, and seven-page statement, *Suggested Criteria for Evaluating Areas Proposed for Inclusion in State Park Systems*.

ATTENDANCE IN STATE PARKS—1954*

State	Administrative agency	Day visitors	Overnight use	Total attendance
Alabama........	Department of Conservation			
	Division of State Parks, Monuments and Historical Sites	1,994,817	59,645	2,054,462
	Alabama Museum of Natural History			
	Mound State Monument	75,000	....	75,000
Arkansas.......	Forestry and Parks Commission	NR	NR	600,000
California.......	Department of Natural Resources			
	Division of Beaches and Parks	8,231,542	1,591,409	9,822,951
Colorado........	State Historical Society of Colorado	325,000	....	325,000
Connecticut.....	State Park and Forest Commission			
	Park Department	3,182,862	346,336	3,529,198
Delaware.......	State Highway Department	1,300	11,058	12,358 (a)
	State Park Commission	125,000	....	125,000
Florida.........	Florida Board of Parks and Historic Memorials			
	Florida Park Service	1,135,183	42,948	1,178,131
Georgia.........	State Division of Conservation			
	Department of State Parks	2,868,871	NR	2,868,871
Idaho...........	Department of Public Lands	28,613	15,679	44,292
Illinois.........	Department of Conservation			
	Division of Parks and Memorials	9,139,620	138,364	9,277,984
Indiana.........	Department of Conservation			
	Division of State Parks, Lands and Waters	2,416,161	370,278	2,786,439
Iowa............	State Conservation Commission			
	Division of Lands and Waters	4,834,662	63,965	4,898,627
Kansas.........	Forestry, Fish and Game Commission	450,000	....	450,000
Kentucky........	Department of Conservation			
	Division of State Parks	3,409,070	163,930	3,573,000
Louisiana.......	State Parks and Recreation Commission	662,628	30,652	693,280
Maine..........	State Park Commission	292,045	101,134	393,179
	Baxter State Park Authority	12,000	16,333	28,333
Maryland.......	Board of Natural Resources			
	Department of Forests and Parks			
	State Parks Section	1,956,635	23,128	1,979,763
	Maryland Tercentenary Memorial Commission	3,000	....	3,000
Massachusetts...	Department of Natural Resources			
	Division of Forests and Parks			
	Bureau of Recreation	561,614	192,806	754,420
	Deer Hill State Reservation Commission	200	25	225
	Mount Greylock State Reservation Commission	85,000	1,120	86,120
	Mount Sugarloaf State Reservation Commission	6,500	70	6,570
	Purgatory Chasm State Reservation Commission	50,000	500	50,500
	Wachusett Mountain State Reservation Commission	100,000	1,000	101,000
	Walden Pond State Reservation Commission	10,000	....	10,000
Michigan.......	Department of Conservation			
	Parks and Recreation Division	13,966,846	1,238,564	15,205,410
Minnesota.......	Department of Conservation			
	Division of State Parks	1,831,400	153,600	1,985,000
Mississippi......	Mississippi Park Service	444,000	5,210	449,210
Missouri........	State Park Board	2,128,500	239,900	2,368,400
Montana........	State Highway Commission			
	State Park Division	65,000	10,000	75,000
Nebraska.......	Game, Forestation and Park Commission			
	Land Management Division	454,138	11,994	466,132
New Hampshire..	Forestry and Recreation Department			
	Recreation Division	1,825,973	89,962	1,915,935
New Jersey.......	Department of Conservation and Economic Development			
	Division of Planning and Development			
	Bureau of Forestry, Parks and Historic Sites			
	Forestry and Parks Section	2,716,016	135,536	2,851,552
	Palisades Interstate Park Commission	1,800,000	....	1,800,000
New Mexico......	State Park Commission	NR	NR	537,500
New York........	Conservation Department			
	Division of Parks (Headquarters and State Council of Parks)			
	Allegany State Park Commission	469,500	236,500	706,000
	Central New York State Parks Commission	865,782	103,655	969,437
	Finger Lakes State Parks Commission	1,229,400	108,100	1,337,500
	Genesee State Park Commission	619,050	31,950	651,000
	Long Island State Park Commission	11,223,255	16,945	11,240,200
	Niagara Frontier State Park Commission	4,224,184	....	4,224,184
	Palisades Interstate Park Commission	3,172,452	481,703	3,654,155
	Taconic State Park Commission	401,340	9,410	410,750
	Thousand Islands State Park Commission	181,750	70,538	252,288
	Total for Division of Parks	22,386,713	1,058,801	23,445,514
	Division of Lands and Forests			
	Bureau of Camps and Trails	1,471,075	914,528	2,385,603
	Education Department			
	Division of Archives and History			
	State Historic Sites Section	259,610	....	259,610
North Carolina...	Department of Conservation and Development			
	Division of State Parks	1,578,271	39,855	1,618,126
North Dakota....	State Historical Society of North Dakota	250,000	57,000	307,000

ATTENDANCE IN STATE PARKS—1954*—Continued

State	Administrative agency	Day visitors	Overnight use	Total attendance
Ohio............	Department of Natural Resources			
	Division of Parks	9,514,065	128,818	9,642,883
	The Ohio Historical Society			
	Division of Properties	2,295,472	....	2,295,472
	Akron Metropolitan Park District			
	Virginia Kendall State Park	105,470	....	105,470
Oklahoma.......	Oklahoma Planning and Resources Board			
	Division of Recreation and State Parks	3,377,138	254,400	3,631,538
	Will Rogers Memorial Commission	750,000	....	750,000
Oregon..........	Oregon State Highway Commission			
	State Parks Department	6,098,362	124,371	6,222,733
Pennsylvania....	Department of Forests and Waters			
	Division of Recreation	8,329,043	620,379	8,949,422
	Bureau of Waters (Pymatuning Reservoir)	1,640,000	125,000	1,765,000
	Bushy Run Battlefield Commission	219,000	1,000	220,000
	State Park and Harbor Commission of Erie			
	Pennsylvania State Park (Presque Isle)	2,250,000	....	2,250,000
	Washington Crossing Park Commission	1,750,000	1,500	1,751,500
	Brandywine Battlefield Park Commission	15,800	....	15,800
	Valley Forge Park Commission	2,539,560	1,199	2,540,759
	Pennsylvania Historical and Museum Commission	167,111	2,972	170,083
Rhode Island....	Department of Public Works			
	Division of Parks and Recreation	1,500,000	95,900	1,595,900
South Carolina...	South Carolina State Commission of Forestry			
	Division of State Parks	3,138,042	69,052	3,207,094
South Dakota....	South Dakota Department of Game, Fish and Parks			
	Division of Forestry	1,255,958	....	1,255,958(b)
Tennessee.......	Department of Conservation			
	Division of State Parks	2,306,334	110,433	2,416,767
Texas...........	Texas State Parks Board	3,682,237	142,240	3,824,477
	Fannin State Park Commission	15,120	200	15,320
	San Jacinto State Park Commission	600,000	....	600,000
Utah............	Utah State Historical Society	16,000	....	16,000
Vermont.........	State Board of Forests and Forest Parks			
	Vermont Forest Service			
	Division of State Forest Parks	374,284	34,064	408,348
Virginia.........	Department of Conservation and Development			
	Division of Parks	1,213,198	121,566	1,334,764
Washington......	State Parks and Recreation Commission	3,461,267	326,921	3,788,188
West Virginia....	Conservation Commission			
	Division of State Parks	1,496,131	10,748	1,506,879
Wisconsin.......	Wisconsin Conservation Department			
	Division of Forests and Parks	4,478,171	176,307	4,654,478
	State Historical Society of Wisconsin	72,196	....	72,196
Wyoming........	Wyoming State Park Commission	NR	NR	NR
	The Historical Landmark Commission of Wyoming	22,550	....	22,550
	Totals (81 agencies in 46 states)	155,817,374	9,472,400	166,427,274 (c)

*Prepared by the National Park Service, U.S. Department of the Interior.

NR—Not Reported.

(a) Attendance determined by estimated number of tent spaces rented on nightly, weekly and monthly basis multiplied by appropriate number of days. Does not include rentals at trailer park since this park is operated by concessioner.

(b) Attendance for Custer State Park not included.

(c) The sum of the totals recorded for "day visitors" and "overnight use" does not equal the total of the final column because no breakdown was submitted for attendance by Arkansas and New Mexico.

8

Labor and Industrial Relations

LABOR LEGISLATION, 1954-1955*

Duration the years 1954 and 1955 regular legislative sessions were held in all the states, territories and commonwealths: in fourteen states and Puerto Rico in 1954; in forty-five states, Alaska, Hawaii and Puerto Rico in 1955.

Outstanding achievements in labor law in these sessions included improvements in benefits under the workmen's compensation laws in thirty-five states and two territories; enactment of minimum-wage laws in three states not formerly having such laws: Idaho, New Mexico and Wyoming; a law in Washington regulating farm labor contractors; acts passed in Michigan and Minnesota prohibiting discrimination in employment; and acts affecting older workers in Massachusetts, Michigan, New York and Ohio.

WORKMEN'S COMPENSATION

Alaska, Hawaii and thirty-five states raised one or more types of workmen's compensation benefits. Weekly rates for death and for partial and total disability were increased in more than half of these jurisdictions. Six states—California, Illinois, Minnesota, Nevada, Ohio, and Utah—and Hawaii brought their maximum weekly benefits for temporary total disability to $40, or more, making a total of eighteen jurisdictions now providing maximum weekly benefits of at least $40.

Eight other states—Colorado, Georgia,

Iowa, Kansas, Maine, Nebraska, Tennessee and Vermont—raised such benefits from less than $30 a week to $30 or more; thus twenty-five jurisdictions now pay maximum benefits of between $30 and $36 a week for temporary total disability. Only nine jurisdictions now set a maximum of less than $30 a week. Among the changes are those in Alaska, which raised maximum weekly benefits from $75 to $100, Hawaii from $35 to $50, and Oregon from $45 to $61.15. Delaware raised maximum death benefits from $32.50 to $60. In Connecticut death benefits are now to be paid to the widow during widowhood, with no maximum limitation, and in Florida permanent total benefits are to be paid for the entire period of disability.

Ten jurisdictions raised burial benefits, including Hawaii to $750, Delaware to $700, Minnesota to $550, and New Hampshire and Indiana to $500.

Of the eighteen jurisdictions still placing time or monetary limitations on medical benefits, five extended the period or amount or both. Michigan now authorizes the Commissioner of Labor to extend the period indefinitely. In Alaska the period was extended from two to four years; in Kansas medical benefits were raised from $1,500 to $2,500; Montana increased the time to eighteen months and the amount to $2,500. Vermont deleted the time limitation entirely but retained the maximum benefit of $2,500.

Rehabilitation of workers was considered in several states. An Hawaii law author-

*Prepared by PAUL E. GURSKE, Director, Bureau of Labor Standards, U. S. Department of Labor.

ized the Director of Labor and Industrial Relations to expend up to $1,000 for retraining and rehabilitation of any worker; Minnesota provided for rehabilitation benefits up to fifty-two instead of twenty-five weeks; Utah raised the maximum benefits from $520 to $600. In North Carolina a person affected by, but not actually disabled from, asbestosis or silicosis was formerly eligible for disability benefits up to twenty weeks (forty if he had dependents) and additional benefits of $300 to $500 for rehabilitation. Under a 1955 act, the provision for special benefits for rehabilitation was repealed; however, disability benefits in such cases were raised to correspond to those provided for accidental injury or death.

Coverage was extended to additional workers in several states. These include executives of private corporations in Indiana and North Carolina and certain employees of the state or a political subdivision in Alabama, Maine, Michigan, Minnesota, Oklahoma and Oregon. Vermont now covers employers of six or more rather than eight or more. On the other hand, a few states specifically exempted certain employees—for instance, dairy farmers employing less than three persons in Oklahoma, stage performers in Nevada, and voluntary ski patrolmen in California. In Louisiana—where the law covers specified hazardous occupations only—agricultural workers being transported to and from work and members of airplane crews engaged in crop dusting or spraying were specifically exempted.

Florida established a "second injury fund" for the first time, leaving only five states that do not have special provisions for second injuries. Ohio supplemented its provision relating to second injuries by providing for compensation of workers who have a specific impairment and are later injured or killed on the job due at least in part to the pre-existing injury. Such impairments include epilepsy, cardiac disease, cerebral palsy and psychoneurotic disability.

WAGE AND HOUR STANDARDS APPLYING TO ALL WORKERS

Three states—Idaho, New Mexico and Wyoming—and Alaska were added to the list of jurisdictions having minimum-wage laws that apply to men as well as to women. There are now eight states and three other jurisdictions whose minimum-wage laws apply regardless of sex: Connecticut, Idaho, Massachusetts, New Hampshire, New Mexico, New York, Rhode Island, Wyoming, Alaska, Hawaii and Puerto Rico. The three new state laws each set a minimum hourly wage rate of 75 cents, as do Connecticut and Massachusetts. New Hampshire raised its minimum rate to 75 cents this year also, and Hawaii raised its minimum from a range of 55–65 cents to 65–75 cents. Under a new Alaska law, $1.25 an hour now applies to both men and women and provides for time and one-half after 8 hours a day or 40 a week. The former Alaska law had set a minimum wage of $18 a week for women.

Coverage under wage-payment laws was extended in three states. The Oklahoma law now requires an employer to pay all wages due at the time of discharge, or five days after demand in the event of resignation. A Missouri law requiring semi-monthly pay days now covers all employees of corporations and railroads, instead of only "mechanics, laborers, and other servants." It specifies, however, that executive and professional employees as well as sales persons and others employed on a commission basis may be paid monthly. In New York salesmen must now receive regular monthly payments of earnings that represent a substantial part of their annual earnings.

MIGRATORY LABOR

In two states the lot of migratory workers will be improved because of new laws. Washington passed a comprehensive act providing for regulation of farm labor contractors. The act requires the contractor to obtain a license from the Department of Labor and Industries. He must give certain information as to his character, responsibility and the manner in which he proposes to conduct his operations. The director of the department is authorized to require a surety bond and to revoke the license if a contractor violates the act, or any law regulating employment in agriculture, the payment of wages or conditions affecting the health and safety of farm workers. Contractors are prohibited from making false representations or transporting workers to any place where a strike or lockout exists.

In New York the migrant labor registration act was supplemented by requiring farm labor contractors and crew leaders to register annually with the Industrial Commissioner and to supply the commissioner and the workers with information on wages, housing and working conditions. The commissioner was authorized to revoke registration for violation of labor laws, giving false or misleading information to workers, or other specified grounds.

INDUSTRIAL HEALTH AND SAFETY

Laws were enacted that will strengthen the accident-prevention programs in eight jurisdictions—Hawaii, Maine, Maryland, Massachusetts, Minnesota, Nevada, New Jersey and Virginia. The Maryland law transferred existing safety activities of the Industrial Commission to a Safety Division in the Department of Labor and Industry. It specifically provided for labor-management participation in the formulating of safety rules and regulations by the Department. Nevada created a new safety department in the Industrial Commission, and tightened the procedures relating to issuance of safety orders. Additional safety engineers and inspectors were provided for under the Hawaii act. The loan or lease (as well as manufacture or sale) of unguarded machines was prohibited in Minnesota.

Maine created a Board of Construction Safety Rules and Regulations, and added construction activities to those to be inspected by the labor commissioner. In Massachusetts the authority of the labor department to make certain sanitary rules, was extended to apply to garages, building or construction projects, and premises used by express, trucking, and transportation companies. In Virginia and New Jersey, where mine safety laws are enforced by the Department of Labor and Industry, amendments were enacted which considerably strengthened the laws.

DISCRIMINATION IN EMPLOYMENT

Fair Employment Practice Acts were passed in 1955 in Michigan and Minnesota. They are designed to prevent discrimination in employment based on race, creed, color, national origin or ancestry. Eleven jurisdictions now have mandatory laws: Alaska, Connecticut, Massachusetts, Michigan, Minnesota, New Jersey, New Mexico, New York, Oregon, Rhode Island and Washington. Four additional states have anti-discrimination laws providing for an educational approach to problems of discrimination in employment: Colorado, Kansas, Indiana and Wisconsin.

OLDER WORKERS

Four states passed legislation to aid older workers. In 1954 Massachusetts became the first state to set up a division within the labor department dealing expressly with their problems. The new Division on Employment of the Aging is directed to cooperate with public and private groups in matters relating to the rehabilitation and employment of the aging, and otherwise to carry out a program developed by a Council on the Employment of the Aging, set up under the same act. In 1955 New York appropriated $50,000 to the Labor Department to be used solely for employing job counsellors to aid persons over 45 to get jobs, and Michigan authorized establishment in each employment service office of a division whose function shall be to secure suitable employment for persons over 65. In addition, an Ohio resolution requested the Legislative Commission to study the problems of older workers in that state.

INDUSTRIAL RELATIONS

Several states during the two-year period strengthened their mediation procedures. For instance, such procedures for public employees in Michigan and for employees of industries concerned with the public interest in Massachusetts were improved.

In Maine the authority and procedures to be used by the State Board of Arbitration and Conciliation were amended. The board was specifically made responsible for furthering harmonious labor-management relations in the state, and it was authorized to serve as a Board of Inquiry, a Board of Conciliation, or a Board of Arbitration.

The state board is required to investigate and report on all controversies that, in the opinion of the Governor, the mayor of a city, or selectmen of a town, threaten the public welfare. Previously such an investigation and report were authorized only at the request of the Governor.

Three states passed laws relating to advertising for employees during a strike. Massachusetts and Rhode Island now require employers advertising for workers while a strike or lockout is in existence to state such fact in type as large as the largest print in the advertisement. A Connecticut act specified the size of the type to be used for such statements.

Rhode Island now permits unions to sue in their own names on behalf of the members in actions arising out of employer violations of a collective bargaining contract. Another Rhode Island act, as well as one in Ohio, resulted in making valid, irrevocable and enforceable any collective bargaining provision that provides for arbitration of labor disputes.

Three acts were passed relating to union contributions to political campaigns. New Hampshire and Wisconsin acts prohibited unions from making contributions to a political party or any candidate; in Ohio a resolution was passed directing the Legislative Service Commission to appoint a committee to investigate the question of prohibiting contributions to political campaigns.

So-called "right-to-work" acts, providing that no person may be required by an employer to become or remain a member of a union or to abstain from union membership, were passed in four states: Louisiana, Mississippi, South Carolina and Utah. Eighteen states now have such laws.[1] A Kansas right-to-work bill, passed by both houses in 1955, was vetoed by the Governor. However, an amendment to the labor relations act was approved which prohibited the closed-shop agreement in that state. The union shop is still per-

mitted upon a majority vote of the employees, as before.

Further amendments to the Kansas labor relations act included prohibiting employers from employing labor spies and from use of the check-off without an individually signed order from each employee. It also prohibited employees from participating in a strike unless a strike vote has been held. In addition, the Labor Commission was authorized to adopt rules and regulations governing elections for the selection of collective bargaining units, approval of agreements, strikes or lockouts. Minnesota amended its labor relations act to prohibit an employer from contracting for the services of an employee of another if such employee is to be paid less than the wage set in an existing contract for work of the same grade. Minnesota also eliminated its former provision relating to strike notices, substituting a procedure under which the labor conciliator is petitioned to take jurisdiction ten days before the proposed strike or lockout.

A Texas act banned strikes and picketing by unions not representing a majority of the employees, and the law authorizes the trial judge in cases where this is in doubt to order an election to determine if the union is in fact representing a majority of the employees.

EMERGENCY RELAXATIONS

New York and Massachusetts acts authorizing temporary relaxations of certain labor laws during emergencies were each extended for one year in 1954 and again in 1955. The Massachusetts act permits relaxations for women and for minors 16 years of age and over; the New York act provides that dispensations may be granted under certain conditions for men and women, and minors 16 and over. California extended until 1957 its act authorizing the Governor to issue defense production permits relaxing the maximum hours-of-work standards for women. A North Carolina act authorizing the Governor, during a period of war, to suspend or modify any of its labor laws, subject to certain conditions, was extended to March 1, 1957, and was made applicable during a period of threatened war as well as one of war.

---

[1]Alabama, Arizona, Arkansas, Florida, Georgia, Iowa, Louisiana, Mississippi, Nebraska, Nevada, North Carolina, North Dakota, South Carolina, South Dakota, Tennessee, Texas, Virginia and Utah.

MAXIMUM BENEFITS FOR TEMPORARY TOTAL DISABILITY UNDER WORKMEN'S COMPENSATION LAWS*
As of July, 1955

State	Maximum percentage of wages	Maximum period	Maximum payments per week	Total maximum stated in law
Alabama	55–65(a)	300 weeks	$23.00	$6,900
Alaska	65	24 months	100.00	......
Arizona	65(b)	433 weeks	150.00	......
Arkansas	65	450 weeks	25.00	8,000
California	61¾	240 weeks	40.00	9,600
Colorado	66⅔	Period of disability	31.50	......
Connecticut	60	Period of disability	40.00	......
Delaware	66⅔	Period of disability	35.00	......
District of Columbia	66⅔	Period of disability	35.00(c)	11,000
Florida	60	350 weeks	35.00	......
Georgia	60	350 weeks	30.00	10,000
Hawaii	66⅔	Period of disability	50.00	20,000
Idaho	55–60(a)	400 weeks; thereafter $10 per week ($12 if dependents)	23.00–40.00(a)	......
Illinois	75–97½(a	Period of disability	34.00–40.00(a)	9,250–12,000(a)
Indiana	60	500 weeks	33.00	12,500
Iowa	66⅔	300 weeks	32.00	......
Kansas	60	416 weeks	32.00	......
Kentucky	65	520 weeks	27.00	11,500
Louisiana	65	300 weeks	30.00	......
Maine	66⅔	500 weeks	30.00	12,000
Maryland	66⅔	312 weeks	35.00	5,000
Massachusetts	66⅔	Period of disability	30.00 plus 2.50 for each total dependent (b)	10,000
Michigan	66⅔	500 weeks	32.00–42.00(a)	(d)
Minnesota	66⅔	310 weeks	40.00	......
Mississippi	66⅔	450 weeks	25.00	8,600
Missouri	66⅔	400 weeks	35.00	......
Montana	66⅔	300 weeks	26.50–32.50(a)	......
Nebraska	66⅔	300 weeks; thereafter 45 per cent of wages, maximum $25.00	30.00	......
Nevada	90	433 weeks	41.54(a)	......
New Hampshire	66⅔	341 weeks	33.00	11,250
New Jersey	66⅔	300 weeks	30.00	......
New Mexico	60	550 weeks	30.00	......
New York	66⅔	Period of disability	36.00	6,500
North Carolina	60	400 weeks	32.50	10,000
North Dakota	80	Period of disability	31.50–45.50(a)	......
Ohio	66⅔	520 weeks	40.25	8,000
Oklahoma	66⅔	300 weeks; may be extended to 500 weeks	28.00	......
Oregon	50–66⅔(a)	Period of disability	26.54–61.15	......
Pennsylvania	66⅔	700 weeks	32.50	20,000
Puerto Rico	50	104 weeks	20.00	......
Rhode Island	60	Period of disability(e)	32.00	16,000
South Carolina	60	500 weeks	35.00	8,000
South Dakota	55	312 weeks	28.00	......
Tennessee	65	300 weeks	30.00	10,000
Texas	60	401 weeks	25.00	......
Utah	60	313 weeks	30.00–40.50(a)	8,580 10,725(a)
Vermont	66⅔	330 weeks	28.00 plus 2.00 for each dependent child under 21.	......
Virginia	60	500 weeks	27.00	10,800
Washington	....	Period of disability	23.08–42.69(a,c)	......
West Virginia	66⅔	208 weeks	30.00	......
Wisconsin	70	Period of disability	45.50(c)	......
Wyoming	....	Period of disability	25.38–46.15(a)	......
United States:				
Federal Employees	66⅔–75(a)	Period of disability	121.15(c)	......
Longshoremen	66⅔	Period of disability	35.00(c)	11,000

*Prepared by U. S. Department of Labor, Bureau of Labor Standards.

(a) According to number of dependents. In Idaho, Oregon, Washington and Wyoming according to marital status and number of dependents.

(b) Additional benefits for dependents. In Massachusetts, maximum limited to average weekly wage.

(c) Additional benefits in specific cases, such as vocational rehabilitation, constant attendant, etc.

(d) Not to exceed 500 times total weekly amount payable.

(e) After 1,000 weeks, payments to be made for life from second-injury fund.

CHILD LABOR LEGISLATION 1954-1955*

STATE LEGISLATION

ALTHOUGH no comprehensive child-labor bills were enacted in 1954 or 1955, amendments were made to the child-labor and school-attendance laws of about one-third of the states. In twelve states important changes added to the protection of minors in hazardous occupations and improved standards relating to hours of work or required school attendance.

In Ohio a former emergency provision affecting employment of minors in hazardous occupations was made permanent. It set a minimum age of 18 for a considerable number of such occupations, many based on those declared hazardous under the Federal Fair Labor Standards Act, such as occupations involving exposure to radioactive substances, logging and sawmilling occupations and the operation of power-driven woodworking machines.

Massachusetts set an 18-year minimum age for cleaning, repairing or operating an elevator, and a 16-year minimum for employment on moving motor vehicles, supplementing its 18-year minimum for operating motor vehicles. In Nebraska the sale of liquor by any minor in a public place was prohibited. Tennessee added work in canneries to its list of occupations prohibited for minors under 18, and Maine set 16 as the minimum age for all employment of minors in theaters or movie houses, except actors.

A major change was made in the hours provisions for minors under 16 in New York; their maximum work week was reduced from 44 to 40 hours. Twelve states and three other jurisdictions now set a weekly maximum of 40 hours for minors under 16 in most occupations: Alabama, Alaska, Florida, Georgia, Hawaii, Kentucky, Maryland, New Jersey, New York,

North Carolina, Puerto Rico, Rhode Island, Tennessee, West Virginia and Wisconsin.

In Massachusetts night work of boys under 16 in street trades was prohibited between 8 p.m. and 6 a.m. instead of between 9 p.m. and 5 a.m. as formerly.

California strengthened the administration of its child-labor standards by authorizing revocation of employment certificates for minors under 18, instead of under 16 as formerly, if conditions have changed since their issuance or if the health or education of the minor is jeopardized.

In Delaware, which has no minimum-wage law for adults, the child-labor law was amended to set a minimum wage of 75 cents an hour for children under 16, or 60 cents if such children are attending school. The law specifies, however, that the child may be paid a lower wage if his parent consents in writing; it also exempts work on farms, in private homes or in news shops.

As to compulsory school laws, Illinois increased its minimum school term from eight to nine months, and South Dakota deleted a provision under which children under 16 who had completed the sixth grade could be excused for forty days between April 1 and November 1 if needed at home. In Montana the age was raised from 14 to 16 at which a child could obtain a certificate to leave school for employment. A New York amendment to its school law will no doubt prove helpful to many migratory children. It gave permission to boards of education of certain school districts to contribute funds to adjoining school districts in which children from migrant labor camps are provided educational facilities.

A number of states lowered their child-labor or school-attendance standards. In Utah the basic minimum age for work in factories at any time, or in most employments during school hours, was reduced from 16 to 14. In addition, the minimum

*Prepared by PAUL E. GURSKE, Director, Bureau of Labor Standards, U. S. Department of Labor.

age for work outside school hours in agriculture or as caddies or newsboys was lowered to 10, and children of 14 or 15 may now operate power-driven farm machinery provided their parents consent. In South Carolina the compulsory school attendance law was repealed. Five other states reduced specific standards. A Delaware law permitted boys between 12 and 16 and girls between 14 and 16 to work in street trades until 9 p.m., instead of 7 p.m. as formerly on Fridays, Saturdays and during vacations. It also repealed a former 11 p.m. to 6 a.m. night-work prohibition which applied to minor girls of 16 and 17. Puerto Rico lowered from 14 to 12 its minimum age for work as newsboys. In Wisconsin boys of 12, rather than 14 as before, may now be employed as caddies if they use caddy carts. Boys of 15 and girls between 15 and 18 may now work until 11 p.m., instead of 6 p.m., in Oklahoma, as cashiers or ushers, or in concession stands in theaters.

A Tennessee amendment to the school law authorized an exemption from further attendance for a minor of 16 whose continued attendance, in the opinion of the Board of Education of the County, City, or Special School District, would be of no further benefit to the child or would result in detriment to good order, discipline, or the instruction of other students.

FEDERAL LEGISLATION

No amendments have been enacted to the child-labor provisions of the Federal Fair Labor Standards Act during 1954 or 1955, but an additional hazardous occupation order was issued by the Secretary of Labor in 1954. Order No. 12 prohibits minors under 18 from employment in operating or assisting to operate certain power-driven paper-products machines, such as arm-type wire stitchers or staplers, guillotine paper cutters or shears, corner cutters, scrap-paper balers, punch presses, or platen die-cutting or printing presses.

MAJOR STATE CHILD-LABOR STANDARDS AFFECTING MINORS UNDER 18*

As of July, 1955

(Because of limitations of space, occupational coverage is usually not indicated, nor are exemptions shown)

State	Basic minimum age(a)	Employment or age certificate required for minors up to age indicated	Maximum daily and weekly hours and days per week for minors of the ages indicated(b)	Night work prohibited for minors up to age indicated and for hours specified(b)
Alabama	16	17(c)	8-40-6, under 16. 4 hours on school days, 28 during school weeks for minors under 16.	After 7 p.m., and during regular school term before 7 a.m., under 16.
Arizona	14	19 for employment in mines and quarries. 16(c)	8-48, boys under 16, girls under 18. 8-48, all employees in laundry department of laundry.	7 p.m. to 7 a.m., boys under 16, girls under 18.
Arkansas	14	16(c)	8-48-6, under 16. 10-54-6, minors 16-18.	7 p.m. to 6 a.m., under 16. 10 p.m. to 6 a.m., boys 16-18. 9 p.m. to 7 a.m., girls 16-18.
California	15	18	8-48-6, under 18. Hours of work of minors under 18 when combined with hours required to attend school limited to 8 a day.	10 p.m. to 5 a.m., under 18.
Colorado	14	16(c)	8-48, under 16. 8-hour day, girls 16 and over.	After 8 p.m., under 16.
Connecticut	16	18	9-48-6, under 18. 8-48-6, under 18 in stores, and 14-16 in agriculture.	10 p.m. to 6 a.m., under 18.
Delaware	14	18	8-48-6, under 16. 10-55-6, girls 16 and over.	7 p.m. to 6 a.m., under 16.
Florida	16	18	8-40-6, under 16. Hours of work when combined with hours in school limited to 8 a day for minors under 16.	8 p.m. to 6:30 a.m., under 16. 10 p.m. to 6 a.m., minors 16-18.
Georgia	16	18	8-40, under 16. 60-hour week, employees 16 and over in cotton and woolen factories. Hours of work limited to 4 hours on any day in which school attended by minor is in session.	9 p.m. to 6 a.m., under 16.
Idaho	14	No state provision but see (d) regarding federal certificates.	9-54, under 16. 9-hour day, girls 16 and over.	9 p.m. to 6 a.m., under 16.
Illinois	16	16(c)	8-48-6, under 16. 8-48-6, girls 16 and over. Daily hours of work of minors under 16 attending school limited to 3 a day, with combined hours of work and hours in school limited to 8 a day.	7 p.m. to 7 a.m., under 16.
Indiana	14	18	8-48-6, boys under 16, girls under 18.	7 p.m. to 6 a.m., minors under 16. 9 p.m. to 6 a.m., girls 16-18.
Iowa	14	16(c)	8-48, under 16.	6 p.m. to 7 a.m., under 16.

MAJOR STATE CHILD-LABOR STANDARDS AFFECTING MINORS UNDER 18*—Continued

As of July, 1955

(Because of limitations of space, occupational coverage is usually not indicated, nor are exemptions shown)

State	Basic minimum age(a)	Employment or age certificate required for minors up to age indicated	Maximum daily and weekly hours and days per week for minors of the ages indicated(b)	Night work prohibited for minors up to age indicated and for hours specified(b)
Kansas	14	16(c)	8–48, under 16. 9–49½, minors 16 and over. 9–54–6, minors 16 and over in stores.	6 p.m. to 7 a.m., under 16. 9 p.m. to 6 a.m., minors 16 and over.
Kentucky	16	18	8–40–6, under 18. Daily hours of work for minors under 16 attending school limited to 3 on a school day, 23 during a school week; for such minors 16–18, 4 on a school day, 28 during a school week.	6 p.m. to 7 a.m., children under 15. 8 p.m. to 7 a.m., children 15. 10 p.m. to 6 a.m., 16–18.
Louisiana	16	18	8–44–6, under 18. 10–60, for minors 14–18 years employed in processing sugar cane or sorghum into sugar, molasses, or syrup, or in processing strawberries. Hours of work of minors under 16 employed outside school hours limited to 3 hours a day on any day when school is in session.	7 p.m. to 6 a.m., boys under 16, girls under 18. 10 p.m. to 6 a.m., boys 16–18.
Maine	16	16(c)	8–48–6, under 16. 9-hour day, 54-hour week (50-hour week as a production worker), females 16 and over. Hours of work of minors under 16 enrolled in school limited to 4 on school days, 28 during school weeks.	
Maryland	16	18	8–40–6, under 16. 9–48–6, minors 16 and 17. Work of minors under 16 attending school and working outside school hours limited to 3 hours on school days and to 23 hours a week when schools are in session 5 or more days. Work of minors 16 and 17 attending day school and employed outside school hours limited to 4 hours on a school day and 28 hours a week when school is in session 5 or more days, and to 8 hours on non-school days, and to 40 hours a week when school in session less than 5 days.	7 p.m. to 7 a.m., under 16. 10 p.m. to 6 a.m., minors 16 and 17 attending day school.

State			Hours of labor	Night work prohibited
Massachusetts	16	21	4–24, under 14 in farm work. 8–48–6, under 16. 9–48–6, minors 16–18. 10–48–6, under 18.	6 p.m. to 6:30 a.m., under 16. 10 p.m. to 6 a.m., minors 16–18.
Michigan	14	18	Combined hours of work and hours in school for minors under 18 limited to 48 a week.	9 p.m. to 7 a.m., minors under 16. 10 p.m. to 6 a.m., minors 16–18 attending school. 11 p.m. to 6 a.m., minors 16 and 17 not attending school.
Minnesota	14	16(c)	8–48, under 16.	6 p.m. to 6 a.m., girls under 18 in factories. 7 p.m. to 7 a.m., under 16.
Mississippi	14	No state provision, but see (d) regarding federal certificates.	54-hour week, girls 16 and over. 8–44, under 16.	7 p.m. to 6 a.m., under 16.
Missouri	14	16(c)	10–60, 16 and over.	
Montana	16	"Any minor."	8–48–6, under 16. 9–54, girls 16 and over.	7 p.m. to 7 a.m., under 16.
Nebraska	14	16(c)	8–48, under 16. 9–54, girls 16 and over.	....
Nevada	14	18	8–48, boys under 16, girls under 18.	8 p.m. to 6 a.m., under 16. 1 a.m. to 6 a.m., girls 16 and over in certain cities.
New Hampshire	16	16(c)	10¼–54, under 16. 10¼–48, under 18 in factories. 10¼–54, minors 16–18, other occupations.	7 p.m. to 6:30 a.m., under 16.
New Jersey	14	18	8–40–6, under 18. 10-hour day, 6-day week, under 18 in agriculture. Combined hours of work and hours in school for minors under 16 limited to 8 a day.	6 p.m. to 7 a.m., under 16. 10 p.m. to 6 a.m., minors 16–18.
New Mexico	14	16(c)	8–44, under 16.	7 p.m. to 7 a.m., under 16.
New York	16	18	8–48–7, girls 16 and over. 8–40–6, under 16. 8–48–6, boys 16–18, girls 16–21. Hours of work of minors 14–16 employed outside school hours limited to 3 on a school day, 23 in a school week; for such minors 16 years of age, 4 on a school day, 28 in a school week.	5 p.m. to 8 a.m., (factory) under 16. 6 p.m. to 8 a.m., under 16. 9 p.m. to 6 a.m., (factories). 10 p.m. to 7 a.m., (stores), 10 p.m. to 6 a.m., (restaurants and hotels), girls 16–21. Midnight to 6 a.m., boys 16–18.
North Carolina	16	18	8–40–6, under 16. 9–48–6, minors 16–18. Combined hours of work and hours in school for minors under 16 limited to 8 a day.	6 p.m. to 7 a.m., under 16. 9 p.m. to 6 a.m., girls 16–18, boys 16–18. 12 midnight to 6 a.m., boys 16–18.
North Dakota	14	16(c)	8–48–6, under 16.	7 p.m. to 7 a.m., under 16.
Ohio	16	18	8–48–6, minors 16 and 18. 8–48–6, minors under 18. Combined hours of work and hours in school of children under 16 limited to 9 a day; employment of children under 14 limited to 4 hours a day.	6 p.m. to 7 a.m., minors under 16. 10 p.m. to 6 a.m., boys 16–18. 9 p.m. to 7 a.m., girls 16–18.

MAJOR STATE CHILD-LABOR STANDARDS AFFECTING MINORS UNDER 18*—Continued

As of July, 1955

(Because of limitations of space, occupational coverage is usually not indicated, nor are exemptions shown)

State	Basic minimum age(a)	Employment or age certificate required for minors up to age indicated	Maximum daily and weekly hours and days per week for minors of the ages indicated(b)	Night work prohibited for minors up to age indicated and for hours specified(b)
Oklahoma	14	16(c) 18 where continuation schools are established.	8-48, under 16. 9-54, girls 16 and over.	6 p.m. to 7 a.m., boys under 16, girls under 18.
Oregon	14	18	8-44-6, under 18. 10-hour day, minors under 18, canning.	6 p.m. to 7 a.m., under 16.
Pennsylvania	16	18	8-44-6, under 18. Hours spent in school shall be considered as part of the work day or week for minors under 16.	7 p.m. to 7 a.m., under 16. 9 p.m. to 6 a.m., girls 16-18.
Rhode Island	16	16(c)	8-40, under 16. 9-48, minors 16-18.	6 p.m. to 6 a.m., under 16, 11 p.m. to 6 a.m., minors 16 and 17.
South Carolina	16	No state provision but see (d) regarding federal certificates.	8-40-5, employee in textile mills. 12-60, girls in stores.	8 p.m. to 5 a.m., under 16. After 10 p.m., girls 16 and over in stores.
South Dakota	14	16(c)	10-54, minors under 16, girls 16 and over.	After 7 p.m. for minors under 14 in mercantile establishments.
Tennessee	16	16(c)	8-40-6, under 18. Daily hours of work of minors under 16 attending school limited to 3 a day and 18 a week in school week; combined hours of work and school limited to 8 a day.	7 p.m. to 7 a.m., under 16. 10 p.m. to 6 a.m., 16-18.
Texas	15	Not required for minors 15 and over; see (d) regarding federal certificates.	8-48, under 15. 9-54, girls 16 and over.	10 p.m. to 5 a.m., under 15.
Utah	14	18	8-44-6, under 18. The hours of required school attendance must be counted as part of legal day or week.	6 p.m. to 7 a.m., girls under 18, boys under 16.
Vermont	14	16(c)	8-48-6, under 16. 9-50, minors 16-18.	7 p.m. to 6 a.m., under 16.
Virginia	16	18	8-40-6, under 18.	6 p.m. to 7 a.m., under 16. 10 p.m. to 7 a.m., girls 16-18 enrolled in school. 11 p.m. to 7 a.m., girls 16-18 not enrolled in school. 12 midnight to 7 a.m., boys 16-18.

Washington................	14	18	8-48-6, under 16 when school is in session. In computing hours, ½ total attendance hours in school shall be included. 8-40-6, children under 16 when school not in session. 8-48-6, minors 16-18. 60-hour week, household and domestic employees.	7 p.m. to 6 a.m., under 16. Minors 16 and 17 attending school may be employed after 7 p.m. in authorized employments.
West Virginia............	16	16(c)	8-40-6, under 16.	8 p.m. to 5 a.m., under 16.
Wisconsin................	16	18	8-24-6, under 16, except 8-40-6, during school vacations. 8-40-6, minors 16, except 8-48-6, during school vacations. 8-48-6, minors 17.	8 p.m. to 7 a.m., under 16. 6 p.m. to 6 a.m., girls 16 and over, factories and laundries.
Wyoming................	No provision except that children whose attendance at school is required by law may not be employed during school hours.	Issued for minors 14-16	8-48-6, under 16. 8-48, girls 16 and over.	7 p.m. to 7 a.m., under 16. 10 p.m. to 7 a.m., girls 16-18.
Alaska................	16	....	8-40-6, under 18. Combined hours of work and school for minors under 16 limited to 9 a day. Weekly hours for minors under 16 working outside school hours limited to 23 a week.	7 p.m. to 6 a.m., under 16.
District of Columbia...........	14	18	8-48-6, under 18.	7 p.m. to 7 a.m., boys under 16, girls under 18. 10 p.m. to 6 a.m., boys 16-18.
Hawaii................	16 when child is legally required to attend school; otherwise 14.	18	8-40-6, under 16. Combined hours of work and hours in school for minors under 16 limited to 9 a day.	6 p.m. to 7 a.m., under 16.
Puerto Rico................	16	18	8-40-6, under 18. Combined hours of work and school for "minors attending school" limited to 8.	6 p.m. to 8 a.m., under 16. 10 p.m. to 6 a.m., minors 16-18.

*Prepared by the Bureau of Labor Standards, U. S. Department of Labor, Washington 25, D. C.

(a) The states listed as having a 16-year basic minimum age usually establish this age for factory employment at any time, or for any employment during school hours, or both; certain employment is permitted under 16 outside school hours and during school vacation, usually in nonfactory employment. The states listed as having a 14- or 15-year minimum age permit employment of children under these ages outside school hours or during school vacation, or in certain occupations at any time.

(b) Maximum hours and night-work regulations for minors under 16 usually apply to most occupations; sometimes, however, they apply only to certain establishments such as factories or stores. Regulations applicable to minors 16 and 17 are usually less comprehensive in coverage than those applicable to minors under 16. Many states have special night-work prohibitions for minors working as public messengers, and some have special prohibitions for other types of work, such as work in bowling alleys. These are not shown.

(c) In these states the law provides that age certificates may be issued upon request for minors 16 or over (17 or over in Alabama) or, although not specified in the law, such certificates are issued in practice for such minors.

(d) For the purposes of the Fair Labor Standards Act, federal certificates of age are issued, upon request, by federal issuing officers.

STATE LABOR LEGISLATION FOR WOMEN*

As of 1955, state labor legislation for women may be characterized as having both a long history and a new direction. Its beginning goes back almost eight decades, to a time when women in significant numbers were just starting to enter the labor force. As the numbers and proportions of women workers have increased, the need to safeguard their health and welfare has continued to be recognized through legislation.

Today all states have some special laws governing some aspects of women's hours, wages or working conditions. All except five states have laws safeguarding women's maximum hours of work; about half require one day of rest in seven; many provide meal periods and for mid-shift rest periods; some set minimum standards for plant facilities; many establish various other standards. A total of twenty-nine states and the District of Columbia have state minimum-wage laws, eight of which now apply to men as well as to women and minors.

With legislation to safeguard health as a foundation, recent state legislative enactments are also taking another direction. In recent years, the fastest-growing type of state labor legislation for women is for equal pay. State equal pay laws, the great majority of which have been enacted in the past decade, point to wider recognition of women's economic status through the removal of wage discriminations based on sex.

In 1954 and to August 1, 1955, legislatures in nineteen states enacted laws governing standards of employment of women. Of particular interest to women workers was the action taken in Arkansas, Colorado and Oregon in 1955, all three of which enacted equal-pay legislation prohibiting employers from discriminating, on the basis of sex, in the rate or method of pay.

These three new states brought to sixteen the number of states now having equal-pay laws on their statute books.

In 1955 three states—Idaho, New Mexico and Wyoming—enacted minimum-wage legislation for the first time. Each such law established a statutory minimum-wage rate of 75 cents an hour, applicable to men as well as women workers in the occupations and industries covered. No provision was made for wage boards. A total of twenty-nine states and the District of Columbia now have minimum-wage legislation. Of this number, eight apply to men as well as to women and minors.

Nevada amended its minimum-wage law in 1955 to provide a statutory minimum-wage rate of 87½ cents an hour for women workers eighteen years and over, the highest minimum wage in effect in any of the states, as of August of that year. The 75-cents-an-hour minimum, established in 1953, was retained for female minors under eighteen.

Amendments to existing minimum-wage laws were enacted in 1954 in Massachusetts and New York. The amendment in Massachusetts specifically added to the number of occupations exempted from coverage of the law the growing and harvesting of agricultural, floricultural and horticultural commodities. New York increased the compensation of wage board members by raising it from a maximum of $10 to a $25 maximum for each meeting or for each day actually spent in work of the board.

The Connecticut minimum wage law—which was the first such state law to be amended to extend protection to men (in 1939) and the first to establish a 75-cents-an-hour minimum wage by statute (in 1951), successfully weathered a challenge to its constitutionality. The Supreme Court of Errors, the highest court of Connecticut, upheld its constitutionality in May, 1955. Also at issue in the challenge was the authority of the Commissioner of Labor to limit to 30 cents an hour the off-

---

*Prepared by ALICE K. LEOPOLD, Assistant to the Secretary of Labor for Women's Affairs, Women's Bureau, U.S. Department of Labor.

setting of tips against the minimum wage of waiters and waitresses. The court held the limitation reasonable and valid.

Progress in establishing adequate legal standards for minimum wages of women workers was made, moreover, through administrative action having the effect of law, i.e., through issuance of minimum wage orders under the wage board system, which is used by the District of Columbia and twenty-three states. In the period July, 1953–July, 1955, eleven states and the District of Columbia issued twenty minimum wage orders. With one exception (in Kentucky), these orders either increased existing minimum wage rates or established minimum wage orders for occupations not previously covered. The eleven states are Arizona, Kentucky, Massachusetts, Minnesota, New York, North Dakota, Oregon, Rhode Island, Utah, Washington and Wisconsin. In half these wage orders, a basic minimum of 75 cents an hour or higher was set. In Massachusetts, 80 cents an hour became effective for two industries: dry cleaning; and clerical, technical and similar. The District of Columbia established the equivalent of an 80 cents an hour minimum wage for the clerical and technical occupations by setting a minimum wage of $32 for a week of 32 but not more than 40 hours. Other orders issued applied to workers in the following occupations or industries: retail trade, hotels and restaurants, telephone industry, needle trade and garment occupations, and beauty occupations.

In two states minimum wage orders were issued for an occupational group not previously covered by a special order in any state—camp counselors. The State of New York pioneered in this area and issued the first such order in December, 1953 for counselor staff occupations in children's camps. The State of Washington issued its order for camp counselors in recreational camps in June, 1954. Both orders established minimum wages for a 5-day, 6-day and 7-day week. New York set $30 a week and Washington $31.20 for the 6-day week.

In the hours-of-work field, eleven states enacted legislation during the two-year period. Five of these—Arkansas, Maine, Ohio, Vermont and Virginia—enacted amendments to maximum hour laws. Vir-

ginia in 1954 enlarged existing exceptions to its law by including women employees in hospitals during an emergency and women engaged in the dressing or processing of poultry during certain periods. In 1955, Arkansas exempted processors or canners of fruits, subject to provisions of the federal Fair Labor Standards Act, from 8-hours-a-day, 6-days-a-week maximums. Maine, in 1955, extended coverage of the maximum 9–54 hours law to commercial places of amusement and made daily and weekly maximum hour provisions applicable to total employment in any of one or more establishments; coverage of telephone exchanges was made applicable to those having more than 750 stations instead of those employing three operators. A Vermont statute, authorizing the Commissioner to permit exemptions from the maximum 9–54 hour law in cases of emergency or peak demand, was amended in 1955 to permit exemptions for up to ten weeks per year instead of for ten consecutive weeks. Ohio in 1955 amended sections of its labor laws relating to women's hours of work and occupational limitations, making permanent legislation that originally was effective until September, 1955. The amendment included provisions for establishing a 48- in place of a 45-hour week in manufacturing. It permitted one 10-hour day a week for office employees if weekly maximum is not exceeded, and permitted adult women operators of public vehicles to work for the same hours and periods as men, also if the 48-hour maximum is not exceeded. In employment in restaurants on a split shift basis, the over-all spread of hours was raised from 10 to 12. The Ohio amendment also modified various occupational limitations for women; exempted employment in a public utility company or carrier subject to the Interstate Commerce Act from various provisions on female employment during an emergency period; and in defining executive, professional and supervisory positions, increased weekly salary qualification from $35 to $45.

Delaware in 1955 repealed the section of its labor law which prohibited work by women between 11 p.m. and 6 a.m. in any mechanical or manufacturing establishment, laundry, baking or printing establishment, office or dressmaking establishment. New York also lifted existing nightwork prohibitions in 1955. Women employees affected were writers, reporters in newspaper offices, licensed pharmacists and, at Christmas and Easter, florists' employees.

Meal period exemptions were authorized in three states in 1955 for plants operating on a multiple shift or twenty-four hour basis. In Massachusetts the exemption must be authorized by the Commissioner of Labor. In Nebraska the law itself grants blanket exemption to such plants, and in Arkansas the meal period may be omitted provided two ten-minute rest periods, one in each half of the workday, are allowed and arrangements are made for female workers to eat at their places of work.

A 1955 Rhode Island amendment to a prohibition on sale of liquor by females and minors was amended to exempt the wife, widow, daughter or sister of specified licensee.

Effective dates of acts permitting relaxation of certain labor laws were extended for a one- or two-year period in California, Massachusetts, New York and North Carolina.

The following summary shows the number and types of labor laws for women in effect as of July 1, 1955.

SUMMARY OF STATE LABOR LAWS FOR WOMEN

1. *Daily and Weekly Hours.* Forty-three states and the District of Columbia have laws limiting the daily and weekly hours of employment in one or more industries. Five states—Alabama, Florida, Indiana, Iowa and West Virginia—do not have such laws.

Twenty-four states and the District of Columbia have laws regulating the employment of women which establish a maximum of 8 hours a day and/or 48 hours a week, or less for one or more industries.[1] All except one of these (Kansas) cover manufacturing establishments. The 8-48-hours law in Kansas applies to public-housekeeping occupations and telephone

exchanges; in manufacturing establishments the maximum is 9 hours a day, 49½ hours a week. In Connecticut the maximum work week is 48 hours for several industries including manufacturing, but daily hours may not exceed 8 in mercantile establishments or 9 in other types of employment, including manufacturing. Ohio's law sets 8-48 hours as the maximum for most industries other than manufacturing and 9-48 for manufacturing.

Arizona	8–48	New Hampshire	10–48
Arkansas	8–[2]	New Mexico	8–48
California	8–48	New York	8–48
Colorado	8–[2]	North Carolina	9–48
Connecticut	8–48	North Dakota	8½–48
District of		Ohio	8–48
Columbia	8–48	Oregon	8–44
Illinois	8–48	Pennsylvania	10–48
Kansas	8–48	Rhode Island	9–48
Louisiana	8–48	Utah	8–48
Massachusetts	9–48	Virginia	9–48
Montana	8–[3]	Washington	8
Nevada	8–48	Wyoming	8–48

Nine states have set a maximum 9-hour day for women, and all except one of these (Idaho) have a weekly maximum of 50 or 54 hours. Maine's law sets 50 hours for production workers in manufacturing and mechanical establishments and 54 for a number of other establishments and industries.

Idaho	9	Oklahoma	9–54
Maine	9–50	Texas	9–54
Michigan	9–54	Vermont	9–50
Missouri	9–54	Wisconsin	9–50
Nebraska	9–54		

Nine states have set a maximum day of 10 hours and a week of from 50 to 60 hours. All cover manufacturing, although in Georgia and South Carolina the law is limited to one type of manufacturing only —cotton and woolen goods.

Delaware	10–55	New Jersey	10–54
Georgia (men and		South Carolina (men	
women)	10–60	and women)	10–55
Kentucky	10–60	South Dakota	10–54
Maryland	10–60	Tennessee	10–50
Mississippi	10–60		

Minnesota has fixed no daily limit in its statute, but has a 54-hour weekly limita-

---

[1] If a state has set different legal maximum-hour standards for different industries, the law establishing the highest standard, i.e., the lowest maximum hours is shown.

[2] Day-of-rest law provides, in effect, for a 48-hour week. In Arkansas nine hours daily permitted if overtime is paid at 1½ times employee's regular rate.
[3] Various statutory provisions also require that 8 hours shall constitute a day's work for persons (men and women) employed in specified industries and occupations, including retail stores, restaurants and others. Some provide also that 48 hours shall constitute a week's work.

tion for manufacturing establishments and other industries.

2. *Day of Rest.* Twenty-two states and the District of Columbia have established a 6-day week for women in some or all industries. In two of these states—Colorado and Utah—the law does not apply to manufacturing establishments. In seven states both men and women employees are covered. The states enforcing a 6-day week are:

Arizona	Nevada
Arkansas	New Hampshire
California	(men and women)
(men and women)	New Jersey
Colorado	New York
Connecticut	(men and women)
(men and women)	North Carolina
Delaware	North Dakota
District of Columbia	Ohio
Illinois	Oregon
(men and women)	Pennsylvania
Kansas	South Carolina
Louisiana	Utah
Massachusetts	Wisconsin
(men and women)	(men and women)

In addition, Rhode Island has a law, enforced by the Department of Labor, prohibiting employment on Sundays and holidays except to perform work of necessity and charity. A Kentucky law requires payment of time and one-half for work on the seventh consecutive day. Other state Sunday or blue laws do not regulate employment and therefore are not noted.

3. *Meal Periods.* More than half the states (twenty-seven) and the District of Columbia have provided that meal periods varying from $\frac{1}{3}$ hour to 1 hour must be allowed to women in some or all industries. The states are:

Arkansas	Nevada
California	New Jersey
Colorado	(men and women)
Delaware	New Mexico
District of Columbia	New York
Illinois	(men and women)
Indiana	North Carolina
(men and women)	North Dakota
Kansas	Ohio
Kentucky	Oregon
Louisiana	Pennsylvania
Maine	Rhode Island
Maryland	Utah
Massachusetts	Washington
Nebraska	West Virginia
(men and women)	Wisconsin

4. *Rest Periods.* Rest periods are provided for in eight states: for a variety of

industries by statute in two states—Nevada and Wyoming; for one or more industries by minimum-wage order in six states—Arizona, California, Colorado, Oregon, Utah and Washington. Most provisions are for a ten-minute rest period within a half-day's work.

5. *Night Work.* Twenty states place some limitation on the hours adult women may be employed at night. Three additional states and the District of Columbia limit the night work of persons 18 to 21 years of age only.

In twelve states night work for adult women is prohibited in certain industries or occupations. In North Dakota and Washington the prohibition applies only to elevator operators; in Ohio only to taxicab drivers.

Connecticut	New Jersey
Indiana (suspended	New York
until 1961)	North Dakota
Kansas	Ohio
Massachusetts	South Carolina
Nebraska (except	Washington
on permit)	Wisconsin

In eight additional states—California, Delaware, Maryland, New Hampshire, New Mexico, Oregon, Pennsylvania and Utah—as well as in several of the states already listed, the employment of adult women at night, while not prohibited, is regulated either by provision for a lower maximum hour limit for night work than for day work or by establishment of specific working-condition standards.

In the District of Columbia and three states that do not prohibit or regulate night work for adult women—Arizona, Rhode Island and Virginia—night work is prohibited for persons under 21 in messenger service (in the District of Columbia and Virginia for girls 18–21).

6. *Occupational Limitations.* Occupations to which most of the prohibitory laws for adult women apply are mining and work in establishments serving liquor. Of twenty-four states having such laws, as listed below, seventeen prohibit women's employment in mines (several permit clerical work in them). Nine prohibit[4] mixing, selling or dispensing alcoholic liquors for on-premises consumption. Eight states

[4] Illinois state law authorizes city and county governments to prohibit.

have laws prohibiting other employment considered hazardous or injurious to health and safety. (The list does not include safety laws and codes regulating various aspects of working conditions.)

Mines	Washington
Alabama	Wisconsin
Arizona	Wyoming
Arkansas	
Colorado	
Illinois	*Barrooms*
Indiana	California
Maryland	Connecticut
Missouri	Illinois[4]
New York	Indiana
Ohio	Kentucky
Oklahoma	Michigan
Pennsylvania	Ohio
Utah	Pennsylvania
Virginia	Rhode Island

Other Places and Occupations

Colorado—Coke ovens.
Louisiana—Cleaning moving machinery.
Michigan—Operating polishing wheels, belts.[5]
Minnesota—Core rooms—cleaning moving machinery.
Missouri—Cleaning or working between moving machinery.
New York—Core-making, or in connection with core-making, in a room in which the oven is also in operation.
Ohio—Crossing watchman; section hand; express driver; metal moulder; bell hop; taxi-driver (except between 6 a.m. and 9 p.m.); gas or electric meter reader; shoe-shining parlors; bowling alleys as pin setters; poolrooms; in delivery service on motor propelled vehicles of over 1-ton capacity; in operating freight or baggage elevators not automatically or semiautomatically controlled; in baggage and freight handling; trucking and handling by means of hand trucks heavy materials of any kind; operating wheels, belts.
Pennsylvania—Dangerous or injurious occupations.

7. *Seating.* Forty-six states and the District of Columbia have seating laws, all except one of them applying exclusively to women. Florida's law applies to both males and females. Illinois and Mississippi have no seating laws.

8. *Weight-lifting.* Ten states have some regulation regarding the lifting or carrying of heavy weights by women. They are California, Maryland (foundries), Massachusetts, Michigan, Minnesota (core rooms), New York (core rooms), Ohio, Oregon, Utah and Washington.

9. *Industrial Home Work.* Nineteen states have industrial home-work laws or regulations. In all except two—Colorado and Oregon—the law applies to all persons; in these two states it applies to women and minors only. The nineteen states are California, Colorado, Connecticut, Illinois, Indiana, Maryland, Massachusetts, Michigan, Missouri, New Jersey, New York, Ohio, Oregon, Pennsylvania, Rhode Island, Tennessee, Texas, West Virginia and Wisconsin.

10. *Employment Before and After Childbirth.* Six states have laws prohibiting, in one or more industries, the employment of women immediately before and after childbirth. These states and the periods during which women may not be required to work are as follows:

Connecticut	4 weeks before and 4 weeks after
Massachusetts	4 weeks before and 4 weeks after
Missouri	3 weeks before and 3 weeks after
New York	4 weeks after
Vermont	2 weeks before and 4 weeks after
Washington	4 weeks before and 4 weeks after[6]
Washington	4 months before and 6 weeks after[7]

One state, Rhode Island, under its Temporary Disability Insurance Act, provides that employed pregnant women are entitled to cash benefits for 6 weeks before and 6 weeks after childbirth.

11. *Equal Pay.* Sixteen states and Alaska have enacted statutes which prohibit discrimination in rate of pay because of sex: Arkansas, California, Colorado, Connecticut, Illinois, Maine, Massachusetts, Michigan, Montana, New Hampshire, New Jersey, New York, Oregon, Pennsylvania, Rhode Island and Washington. The Illinois and Michigan laws apply to manufacturing only.

12. *Minimum Wage.* Twenty-nine states and the District of Columbia have minimum-wage laws. Most of these apply to women or to women and minors, but eight, as indicated below, apply to men as well. The laws usually are broad in coverage of industries, most of them being all-inclusive with a few listed exemptions, usually domestic service and agriculture. The Maine law, however, applies only to fish packing.

---

[4]Illinois state law authorizes city and county governments to prohibit.
[5]Opinions of Attorneys General differ as to whether or not Michigan law applies only to employment underground.

[6]In minimum-wage and welfare order for laundry, dry-cleaning and dye works industry.
[7]In orders regulating manufacturing and general working conditions; food processing industry; and fresh fruit and vegetable packing industry. Prohibition may be waived by special permit.

Arizona
Arkansas (females)
California
Colorado
Connecticut
    (all persons)
Idaho (all persons)
District of Columbia
Illinois
Kansas
Kentucky
Louisiana
    (women and girls)
Maine
Massachusetts
    (any person)
Minnesota
Nevada
    (women and girls)

New Hampshire
    (any employee)
New Jersey
New Mexico
    (employees)
New York (women;
    minors; men)
North Dakota
Ohio
Oklahoma
    (adult women)
Oregon
Pennsylvania
Rhode Island (women;
    minors; men)
South Dakota
    (women and girls)
Utah

Washington
Wisconsin

Wyoming
    (males and females)

In nine of these states—Arkansas, Connecticut, Idaho, Massachusetts, Nevada, New Hampshire, New Mexico, South Dakota and Wyoming—minimum wages are provided by the statute itself. In Connecticut, Massachusetts, New Hampshire (and with certain limitations in Arkansas) the minimum-wage law also authorizes issuance of wage orders on an occupation or industry basis, so that the rate set by statute can be modified to meet changes in cost of living.

EMPLOYMENT SECURITY ADMINISTRATION
IN THE STATES*

I. THE LABOR MARKET

IN fiscal years 1954 and 1955 the economy began—and completed—an adjustment to new supply-demand inventory relationships, a shift from curtailed defense orders to increased civilian demand. Fiscal year 1954 began with most segments of the economy establishing new record highs. Fiscal 1955 ended in a burst of expansion which also saw the attainment of many new highs. In between, however, production had dropped by some 10 per cent and total unemployment had more than doubled.

In fiscal 1954 the series of downward adjustments was most evident in manufacturing, particularly among durable goods industries, reflecting a reaction to cutbacks in defense orders. As producers and distributors made efforts to reduce inventories, the adjustment process gained momentum, production curtailments became more widespread, and layoffs began to rise markedly. An exception to the down trend was found in the construction industry.

The Federal Reserve Board's Index of Industrial Production, which stood at a record high of 137 per cent of the 1947–49 average in July, 1953, had declined by about 10 per cent by March, 1954, to 123 per cent. Gross national product, which measures the value of the nation's total output of goods and services, edged down from a peak annual rate of $369.3 billion in the last quarter of fiscal 1953 to $357.6 billion in the April-June quarter of 1954—a reduction of 3.2 per cent.

Total employment showed an over-all decline from a high of 63.7 million in August, 1953 to 62.3 million in August, 1954. The number of jobless persons, which had fallen to a postwar low of 1.2 million by August,

*Prepared by ROBERT C. GOODWIN, Director, Bureau of Employment Security, U. S. Department of Labor.

1953, rose sharply to 3.7 million in March, 1954, the highest level of unemployment the economy had experienced since March, 1950.

Fiscal year 1955 began with the economy at these relatively low levels. As time went on, many shifts pointed toward improvement. The index of industrial production, after fluctuating between 123 and 125 (1947–1949 equals 100) for the first nine months of calendar year 1954, advanced to 126 in October, to 129 in November, and 130 in December. Thereafter the climb was more rapid. By the close of the fiscal year the index of industrial production stood at 139 per cent of its 1947–1949 base—a new record.

Employment also began to increase, and at the close of the fiscal year in June, 1955, a new all-time high of 64 million people were employed in the United States. A record 56.3 million of these were employed in nonagricultural enterprises. Manufacturing employment, however, although it had declined less sharply than manufacturing production in the early days of the adjustment period, recovered less rapidly, and by June, 1955, was still below the levels of June, 1953.

Sizable layoffs accompanying the downturn in fiscal 1954 resulted in an increase in the average weekly level of insured unemployment from 922,000 per week in fiscal year 1953 to 1,540,000 in fiscal year 1954. The number of applicants for work at local employment offices jumped 21 per cent to 8,846,000 in fiscal year 1954. Both applicants for work and insured unemployment declined during the closing months of fiscal 1955, but because of the heavy volumes during most of the year, the year's activity as a whole did not show significant change. Average weekly state insured unemployment during fiscal 1955, in fact, at 1,588,000, was somewhat higher than the average for fiscal year 1954. Applications for work, at 8,467,000 for the same year, were not down substantially.

II. Employment Service Operations

Activities of state employment security agencies reflected the economic adjustments during fiscal year 1954 and the brightening picture in succeeding months, as many sectors of the economy by the close of fiscal 1955 were reaching or exceeding the record levels established in 1953. As unemployment rose from the peacetime lows which prevailed during the last ten months of fiscal 1953, new applications for work filed with public employment offices increased sharply. During fiscal 1954 they totaled more than 8.8 million—one-fifth above the preceding year. Moreover, this was the largest volume since fiscal year 1946 when the economy was being severely tested by the problems of demobilization and reconversion. As the economy strengthened and employment again reached a record high by mid-year 1955, the number of applications declined slightly (4 per cent) to less than 8.5 million in fiscal 1955. During each of the last eight months of the fiscal year, however, they were below the level a year earlier.

Between fiscal years 1953 and 1954, the increase in work applications of men was substantially sharper than for women, resulting in part from adjustments taking place in manufacturing industries, particularly the durable goods segment. Applications for men increased about one-fourth between the two years, to 5.5 million, while those of women moved up about one-eighth, to 3.3 million. In the following year, registrations of men declined 5 per cent, to less than 5.3 million, and applications of women edged down to 3.2 million.

Registrations of veterans in the past few years reflected the release of some four million servicemen to civil life—three million in the past three years—as well as the adjustments in the economy in fiscal 1954. After reaching the lowest level since World War II—1,350,000 in fiscal 1952—applications of all veterans rose one-sixth, to 1,573,000, in fiscal 1953 as one million servicemen were discharged from the armed forces. The impact of a million additional veterans, plus economic factors, caused a further sharp rise (36 per cent) to 2,140,000 applications in fiscal 1954. Despite the discharge of another million veterans in fiscal

year 1955, improvements in the economy contributed to a small reduction—down 4 per cent to 2,089,000—in the number of registrations by veterans. During fiscal 1955, however, applications of veterans comprised 40 (compared with 36 in fiscal 1953 and 32 in 1952) out of every 100 of those from all men.

Interviews of employment counselors with job seekers showed a sizable drop (12 per cent) from fiscal 1953 to 1,164,200 in the following year. This was due primarily to limitations in counseling staff caused by economy measures and the necessity for transferring personnel to assist in the sharply increased activities of the unemployment insurance program.

In 1955 counseling activity rose markedly to 1,414,800 interviews. During each of the last eight months of the fiscal year, the number of interviews was at the highest level for the month since comparable data became available in July, 1948.

Counseling interviews with veterans edged up 1 per cent, to 328,700, in fiscal 1954. Veterans shared in the accelerated counseling program during fiscal 1955, total interviews in this group rising more than one-fifth. During each of the past two years veterans accounted for 43 out of every 100 interviews with men, compared with 38 and 31, respectively, in fiscal years 1953 and 1952.

Job placements effected by public employment offices totaled more than 14.8 million in fiscal 1954—about 500,000 fewer than in the preceding year—and then edged down further to 14.5 million in fiscal 1955. A substantial drop among placements of workers in nonagricultural jobs more than accounted for the decline in 1954. During that year placements on farm jobs rose 6 per cent, to 9.3 million— the largest yearly total since the resumption of farm placement services by the state agencies in 1948. Due primarily to reduced demand for farm workers caused by drought conditions in some sections of the nation, placements in agricultural jobs declined slightly to 9 million in fiscal 1955. In each of the past two years approximately 5.2 million of the total were pool-type placements, that is, placements of job applicants gathered at an established assembly point for a single day's work.

After reaching the highest level since World War II—6.6 million in fiscal 1953 —placements in nonfarm jobs dropped 16 per cent to 5.5 million in fiscal 1954, and remained at the same level the following year. Reduced labor demand and a resultant decline in nonfarm placements reflected the effects of the economic adjustments which began in the fall of 1953. By December, 1953, such placements dropped below 400,000 and remained below that number during the first three months of 1954—the smallest monthly volumes since the first quarter of 1950 when unemployment was at a postwar high. In fiscal 1955, however, the trend in the volume of nonfarm placements was influenced by the increasing strength of the economy.

Male job seekers experienced the sharpest loss in nonfarm placements during 1954, accounting for three-fourths of the decline from fiscal 1953. Placements of men dropped 20 per cent, to approximately 3.2 million in fiscal 1954 and leveled off at 3.1 million in the following year. At the same time, placements of women decreased 11 per cent, to somewhat less than 2.4 million, then edged up slightly in fiscal 1955.

Placements of veterans in nonagricultural pursuits also felt the impact of reduced job opportunities in 1954, moving down 16 per cent, to 1.3 million. A small gain was registered in 1955, as placements of veterans rose nearly 6 per cent, to 1.4 million. Moreover, nonfarm placements of veterans comprised 44 out of every 100 such placements of all men in 1955—a slightly higher proportion than those (42 and 40, respectively) in 1954 and 1953.

Except for manufacturing and service, no significant variation occurred in the relative distribution of placements among nonagricultural industry divisions during the past three years. Placements in manufacturing industries declined from 32 per cent of the total in 1953 to 28 per cent in each of the past two years, whereas placements in service industries rose from 28 to 32 per cent in the same periods. In fiscal 1955, of every 100 nonfarm placements, 32 were in service, 28 in manufacturing, 21 in trade and 9 in construction industries.

Handicapped job seekers filed 339,400 new work applications with public employment offices during fiscal 1955—an increase of 20,700 over the preceding year, and 26,100 more than in 1953. Of these, about 125,500—37 out of every 100—were work registrations of disabled veterans.

Job counseling services provided to handicapped workers, as was the case with all job seekers, declined in fiscal 1954, then expanded in 1955. Initial or first-time interviews held by counselors with this group decreased about one-fifth from fiscal 1953, to 134,100. In the following year, the volume rose 15 per cent, to 154,800. Of these, nearly 57,700, or 37 per cent, were interviews with disabled veterans.

Placements of handicapped workers in nonagricultural jobs dropped 23 per cent from fiscal 1953 to 208,400 in 1954. This represented a somewhat sharper decline than that (16 per cent) which occurred among total nonfarm placements. In the first half of fiscal 1955 nonfarm placements of handicapped persons continued at a lower level than in the corresponding period a year earlier. Sharp gains in the next six months, however, brought the total number for the fiscal year to 214,200 —about 3 per cent above 1954. In the latter half of fiscal 1955, nonfarm placements of the handicapped totaled 30 per cent more than in the comparable period of 1954.

Nonagricultural placements of handicapped veterans, which declined 20 per cent to 95,200 in 1954, moved up 4 per cent to 99,100 in fiscal 1955. In that year, applications of disabled veterans accounted for 45 out of every 100 of those filed by handicapped men, while placements of disabled veterans comprised 55 out of every 100 placements of handicapped men.

III. Unemployment Insurance

Improvement of the Program

Interest in improving the federal-state system of unemployment insurance was high in 1954 and 1955. In his Economic Report for 1954 President Eisenhower recommended federal and state action to strengthen the system by extending coverage, increasing benefits and improving the financing provisions.

Coverage. Following the President's recommendations, Congress made the most significant extension of unemployment insurance coverage since enactment of the

Social Security Act in 1935. In amendments approved in September, 1954, it gave unemployment insurance protection to 2.4 million federal civilian employees for unemployment after January 1, 1955, and extended the federal unemployment tax act to employers with four to seven workers, effective January 1, 1956. Action of twenty-four states in their legislative sessions in 1955, and provisions in four states for automatic extension of state coverage when federal coverage is extended, will bring into the program, in 1956, 1.7 million workers in 365,000 small firms in commerce and industry.

Twenty states and Alaska, the District of Columbia and Hawaii cover smaller firms than does the federal act; in 1956, four of them will include employers of three or more; one, two or more; and eighteen, one or more.

Benefits. In both years, the President's Economic Reports recommended state action so that weekly benefits and duration of benefits would meet the needs of the economy and of the unemployed better than before. In 1954, when only thirteen state legislatures met in regular session, benefit provisions were improved in four states and in the District of Columbia. In 1955, when all states except two had legislative sessions, thirty-four states, Alaska and Hawaii improved one or more of their benefit provisions. Several of these states, while increasing maximums, tightened their formulas for wage qualification, weekly amounts or duration to require higher earnings than before for given weekly benefits or given weeks of benefits.

The greatest change was in maximum weekly benefits. In 1955, thirty-two states—the largest number for any year—increased maximum basic weekly benefit, by amounts ranging from $1.00 to $10. When the amendments enacted in 1955 are all effective, maximum basic weekly benefits will vary from $24 to $36, and to $45 for intrastate claimants in Alaska. (See Table 3.) Sixteen states, accounting for more than 50 per cent of all covered workers, provide a basic maximum of over $30 a week, and sixteen other states, with 18 per cent of the covered workers, have a maximum of $30. In the ten states with higher maximum benefits for claimants with dependents, maximum weekly benefits vary from $35 to $54, and the maximum is $70 in Alaska for intrastate claimants with dependents in the territory.

In 1954 and 1955, President Eisenhower recommended uniform potential duration of at least twenty-six weeks for all eligible claimants. In the two years, eight state legislatures, and Congress for the District of Columbia, liberalized their duration provisions. Six states have met the President's recommendations. Eight other states have uniform duration of sixteen to twenty-four weeks. Twenty-one others have a maximum duration of twenty-six weeks. (See Table 3.) Although maximum duration in all the states varies from sixteen to thirty weeks, almost 75 per cent of covered workers are in the twenty-seven states which provide a maximum duration of twenty-six weeks or more.

Financing of benefits. The 1954 amendments of the Social Security Act include the most significant federal amendments on benefit financing since the beginning of the unemployment insurance program. Assurance of continuing ability to pay benefits has been substantially increased by the provision of the Employment Security Administrative Financing Act making non-interest-bearing repayable loans available from the federal unemployment account in the Unemployment Trust Fund to states whose funds fall below a specified level. All the proceeds of the Unemployment Tax Act are earmarked for the employment security program. The annual excess of the federal unemployment tax collections over employment security administrative expenses is automatically appropriated to the Unemployment Trust Fund. These excess collections will be used to establish and maintain a $200 million fund for loans to states with depleted reserves. Excess collections beyond $200 million will be returned to the states for use in financing benefits, and under certain circumstances may be appropriated by state legislatures for financing administration.

Another 1954 federal amendment permits states to reduce the period of experience with the risk of unemployment required before new employers and newly covered employers may qualify for reduced rates under experience rating. In the 1955 sessions, twenty-two states amended their laws to grant reduced rates earlier to new employers. These amendments will go far toward equalizing tax rates of firms newly covered by the change in the size-of-firm provisions and the firms which have already qualified for reduced rates under the old three-year requirement.

During 1954 and 1955 a total of thirty-five states amended the financing provisions of their unemployment insurance laws in one or more ways. Michigan changed from a benefit-ratio to a reserve-ratio system, bringing to thirty-three the states with this popular type of experience rating system.

Many states continued the trend toward reducing tax rates for employers with a given experience with unemployment. Nine states increased the number of reduced rates and six states increased the number of rate schedules. Five states lowered the requirements for specified rates for employers, and six added new lower minimum rates—0 in one state and 0.1 in four. Five states decreased the requirement for any reduction of rates or for particular rate schedules to go into effect. Two states added voluntary contributions, bringing to twenty-two the states that permit such contributions.

On the other hand, a number of states strengthened their financing provisions in the following respects. One state added a rate higher than 2.7 per cent in all its rate schedules. Six states increased the solvency factors required for any reduction of rates or for particular rate schedules. One state raised requirements for specified rates. Four increased their taxable wage base, raising to five the number of states that tax wages up to $3,600. Alaska eliminated experience rating and added a temporary employee contribution of 0.5 per cent for 1955 and 1956.

Disability insurance. In the four states in which temporary disability insurance systems are in operation, amendments were made in 1954 or 1955. In California the maximum weekly benefit was increased to $40 and duration was increased to twenty-six weeks, uniform for each spell of disability. New York increased the maximum weekly benefit to $33, Rhode Island to $30 and New Jersey to $35.

Operation of the Program

Coverage. Average monthly employment covered by unemployment insurance continued at the 36 million level in fiscal 1954 and 1955 as in fiscal 1953.

Claims and benefits. Fiscal 1954 and 1955 were years of change in the amount of unemployment the program was called upon to mitigate. State insured unemployment rose from 779,000 in September, 1953, to nearly 2.2 million in March, 1954. By the end of the fiscal year it had declined to 1.9 million, and by October below 1.5 million. After a seasonal return to almost the 2 million level in January, insured unemployment began a steady decline— to 1.1 million in the last month of the fiscal year. This slump and recovery are obscured by the total figures for the fiscal years.

In general, claims for unemployment insurance benefits were lower in fiscal 1955 than in 1954, but in both years were higher than in any other year since fiscal 1950.

New claims filed to start a benefit year increased almost 50 per cent from fiscal 1953 to 1954—to 9.2 million; then decreased to 8 million in 1955, 2 million less than in 1950.

The total number of initial claims, representing new spells of unemployment among workers covered by unemployment insurance, rose from 10.2 million in fiscal 1953 to almost 14.8 million in fiscal 1954, but in fiscal 1955 declined to 13.7 million —one-eighth less than in fiscal 1950.

The number of claimants remaining unemployed long enough to draw benefits increased from almost 4 million in fiscal 1953 to over 6,150,000 in fiscal 1954, then declined to 5.4 million in fiscal 1955, more than 1.5 million fewer than in fiscal 1950. (See Table 2.) The weeks compensated, however, increased in both years—from 40,850,000 in 1953 to 67.5 million in 1954 and 73.5 million in 1955. Thus, the average duration of benefits increased from a low of 10.2 weeks in fiscal 1953 to 11.0 weeks in fiscal 1954 and 13.6 weeks in fiscal 1955. Meanwhile, the claimants exhausting their benefit rights increased from 18.8 per cent of first payments in fiscal 1953 to 22.3 per cent in fiscal 1954 and 29.4 per cent in fiscal 1955.

As a result of higher base-period wages and an increase in statutory maximum weekly benefits, average weekly benefits continued their gradual increase, from $20.63 in fiscal 1951 to $24.45 in fiscal 1954 and $25.05 in fiscal 1955.

The total amount of benefits paid increased $676 million from fiscal 1953 to 1954. Despite the decrease in beneficiaries in fiscal 1955, total benefits paid increased in that year by $187 million, to $1,776,000,000, largely because of the increase in the average duration of compensable unemployment. Total benefits in fiscal 1955 were still $86 million less than in fiscal 1950.

State collections and reserves. Because of the operation of employers' experience rating, contributions have been declining—from an average employer rate of 1.45 in the calendar year 1952 to 1.30 in 1953 and 1.12 in 1954. Taxable wages rose steadily through 1953 but declined in 1954. As a result of these two factors, the amounts collected fell from $1,368,000,000 in fiscal 1953 to $1,246,000,000 in 1954 and $1,142,000,000 in 1955. Total funds available for benefits fell from $8,578,000,000 on June 30, 1953, to $8,442,000,000 on June 30, 1954, and $8,011,000,000 on June 30, 1955.

For the country as a whole, the reserves on June 30, 1955 represented 8.2 per cent of taxable wages. Although state reserves varied greatly—from 0.9 to 14.7 per cent on June 30, 1955—most state funds were in a position to meet their benefit costs. In addition, the federal unemployment account for loans to state agencies stood at $148 million in July, 1955.

Unemployment Compensation for Veterans

By June 30, 1955 more than four million veterans with service after June 27, 1950 had returned to civilian life. About 900,000 of these had filed claims for unemployment compensation under Title IV of the Veterans' Readjustment Assistance Act of 1952, called the UCV program. These benefits are paid by the state employment security agencies under agreements with the Secretary of Labor.

An eligible veteran is entitled to benefits at the rate of $26 a week for weeks of total unemployment up to a total of $676. If a veteran is entitled to benefits of $26 or more under a state employment security law or the railroad unemployment insurance act, he cannot draw UCV until he has exhausted his other benefits. If he is entitled to benefits of less than $26 a week under the other law, he receives a UCV supplement up to $26.

Payments under this program began October 15, 1952. Benefits increased in fiscal 1954 to almost $75 million for 3.2 million weeks of unemployment, and in fiscal 1955 to almost $107 million for 4.6 million weeks of unemployment. One payment in eight was for supplemental benefits.

By June 30, 1955 more than 650,000 veterans—one-sixth of those who had returned to civilian life—had drawn $206 million in benefits. Almost 116,000, or 18 per cent of the total beneficiaries, had drawn their full $676 under the program.

Unemployment Compensation for Federal Workers

Under a new title XV of the Social Security Act enacted in 1954 unemployment insurance protection was extended to 2.4 million federal civilian employees for weeks of unemployment after January 1, 1955. Benefits are paid to federal employees in the same amounts and subject to the same conditions as if their employment and wages had been subject to a state law. Benefits are paid by state employment security agencies under agreements with the Secretary of Labor. The states are reimbursed for the federal benefits from a special fund appropriated to the Secretary of Labor.

During the first six months of 1955, almost 60,000 former federal employees were paid $16 million for 643,000 weeks of unemployment. These data are included in Table 2 as if the claimants had been covered under state laws.

TABLE 1
SELECTED EMPLOYMENT SERVICE ACTIVITIES
TOTAL FISCAL YEARS 1954 AND 1955; BY STATE, FISCAL YEAR 1955*

State	New applications (a)		Counseling interviews			Individuals tested		Placements		
				Initial				Total	Nonagricultural	
	Number	Percentage change from previous year	Total	Number	Percentage change from previous year	Number	Percentage change from previous year	Total	Number	Percentage change from previous year
Total 1953–1954	8,845,818	+20.9	1,164,170	696,684	−12.7	859,601	−7.5	14,820,330	5,520,006	−16.5
Total 1954–1955	8,468,334	−4.3	1,414,754	849,016	+21.9	1,097,715	+27.7	14,527,897	5,536,225	+.3
Alabama	139,798	−2.5	12,436	8,286	+30.5	22,834	−7.8	190,323	111,582	+4.6
Arizona	68,545	−1.3	12,167	7,340	+25.8	8,551	−.3	784,275	51,853	+3.7
Arkansas	114,961	+8.9	18,067	10,613	+50.9	21,642	+35.0	918,495	77,865	−8.1
California	835,999	+3.4	105,839	69,422	+180.8	65,123	+118.0	995,226	377,188	+28.7
Colorado	77,531	−4.0	16,146	11,810	+48.0	12,587	+11.7	214,669	75,514	+15.2
Connecticut	143,366	−12.0	20,788	12,110	+15.6	14,104	+7.2	109,428	96,131	−4.3
Delaware	16,417	−19.2	6,268	2,943	−8.4	1,997	+1.6	15,529	8,359	−15.6
Florida	133,269	−5.2	17,760	11,528	+10.4	23,407	+2.4	345,229	187,120	+2.3
Georgia	190,932	+4.1	21,384	14,060	+24.3	40,691	+52.4	291,809	134,099	+2.5
Idaho	36,524	+4.8	6,283	3,038	−1.3	3,277	+58.6	165,868	34,748	+6.5
Illinois	407,715	−6.9	67,787	39,206	+3.2	31,768	+52.5	317,963	201,020	+2.7
Indiana	207,558	−10.6	27,537	17,830	+54.1	17,335	+54.9	177,922	75,682	−8.1
Iowa	91,323	−9.9	14,791	8,734	+18.4	19,921	+29.5	127,000	79,021	+2.7
Kansas	85,469	−2.2	10,915	6,802	+16.9	2,734	+25.5	122,881	93,831	+1.1
Kentucky	123,863	−12.6	25,292	16,207	+29.0	25,624	+22.8	129,170	60,139	+73.9
Louisiana	128,154	+3.3	20,450	11,617	+19.6	15,921	+40.4	223,276	92,755	+11.7
Maine	37,450	+27.6	8,783	4,628	+86.6	3,063	+115.1	64,069	22,459	−11.0
Maryland	128,881	−7.0	24,947	16,057	+12.6	21,243	+18.7	135,303	67,375	−6.5
Massachusetts	214,461	−3.5	50,224	27,976	−9.1	26,295	+13.1	254,732	196,136	−1.2
Michigan	439,915	−21.4	82,734	53,856	+21.0	37,491	+47.1	314,335	177,212	−10.4
Minnesota	147,655	−1.5	14,733	7,858	−18.6	32,775	+5.7	167,626	93,304	−9.9
Mississippi	114,321	−2.7	17,953	10,777	+22.7	24,019	+70.4	1,489,947	86,618	+2.0
Missouri	227,642	−11.7	30,415	16,449	+4.4	37,717	+23.1	326,381	86,663	−30.1
Montana	40,193	+.4	5,493	3,197	+4.8	4,078	+11.7	65,354	32,582	−9.9

428

Nebraska	55,099	+12.2	8,247	+63.0	4,460	+23.0	8,720	89,880	60,321	+6.9
Nevada	23,310	+8.3	1,964	−23.3	1,496	+3.8	1,546	34,303	25,860	−1.7
New Hampshire	23,892	−24.8	4,759	+66.3	3,404	+68.6	2,177	19,641	16,174	−2.9
New Jersey	251,792	+2.4	28,779	+18.6	17,552	+44.7	16,857	316,722	125,742	−13.9
New Mexico	42,441	−9.7	6,105	+2.4	3,380	−9.6	5,428	77,797	35,078	+6.0
New York	909,067	−6.3	165,847	+6.7	107,775	+20.8	63,420	910,242	749,263	−1.7
North Carolina	182,828	−1.9	24,666	+14.5	14,732	+17.0	31,256	461,136	145,456	−1.3
North Dakota	27,188	+11.6	3,925	+15.3	2,286	+1.4	4,960	48,113	23,206	+.6
Ohio	508,940	−2.7	101,194	+55.6	58,585	+56.0	63,464	423,893	266,202	−3.9
Oklahoma	98,171	+3.5	20,444	+4.7	11,927	−1.9	21,203	226,637	147,818	+7.4
Oregon	91,010	−10.2	17,891	+16.3	10,156	+27.1	17,053	336,983	64,345	−1.0
Pennsylvania	562,549	−2.0	102,957	+6.3	62,434	+5.3	59,205	413,630	208,049	−9.0
Rhode Island	61,352	+48.1	8,341	+57.9	3,861	+69.0	4,454	21,623	21,510	+3.4
South Carolina	93,549	−1.0	13,490	+8.9	9,404	+37.2	18,947	169,417	77,055	+8.2
South Dakota	22,256	−2.4	2,123	+8.8	1,213	+15.5	2,457	29,103	18,505	−9.1
Tennessee	123,932	+26.5	26,528	+56.4	17,285	+24.7	33,747	973,082	107,266	−6.2
Texas	498,284	−3.3	88,512	+9.0	47,396	+19.0	93,922	1,044,770	486,541	+1.1
Utah	50,889	−6.1	8,689	−6.4	6,412	+26.5	14,203	71,084	36,840	+7.5
Vermont	18,465	+7.5	2,465	+51.7	2,040	−20.3	1,939	21,778	13,767	+11.7
Virginia	118,508	−.6	34,419	+32.8	16,997	+72.9	23,180	201,868	76,755	−1.0
Washington	148,245	+1.9	35,226	+14.8	16,913	+23.1	27,815	303,976	87,874	+7.5
West Virginia	72,758	−24.6	10,259	+73.9	6,099	+43.1	8,891	29,994	18,793	+3.0
Wisconsin	137,477	−25.9	26,172	+13.0	13,900	+28.7	27,800	234,411	101,469	+1.1
Wyoming	16,163	−.7	3,916	+19.1	2,215	+4.1	1,268	23,871	14,415	+7.2
District of Columbia	60,285	−3.5	11,049	−3.8	5,240	+4.8	4,541	37,944	37,918	−4.5
Alaska	12,188	−14.4	2,338	+72.2	1,610	+80.3	6,412	10,948	10,908	−5.0
Hawaii	22,468	−4.5	2,338	−37.4	1,200	−21.5	2,007	10,624	9,793	+.7
Puerto Rico	81,543	+3.5	12,610	+4.0	6,502	+5.0	16,495	35,482	27,955	+1.6
Virgin Islands	1,743	+48.0	309	+46.7	198	+79.8	151	2,129	2,091	+65.2

*Prepared by Office of Program Review and Analysis, Bureau of Employment Security, U.S. Department of Labor.

(a) The number of applications taken should not be interpreted as a measure of the total number of new job applicants at Employment Service offices, since there are some types of applicants for whom written applications are not taken.

TABLE 2

SELECTED DATA ON STATE UNEMPLOYMENT INSURANCE OPERATIONS
TOTAL FOR FISCAL YEARS 1954 AND 1955, BY STATE, FISCAL YEAR 1955*

(Note: Except for subject employers, average contribution rates and funds available, figures include unduplicated data from claims filed by federal employees under the Unemployment Compensation for Federal Employees program.)

State	Employers subject to state law	Initial claims (a)	Bene-ficiaries	Average weekly benefit amount paid for total un-employment	Average duration of benefit (weeks)	Total benefit payments (b) (in thousands)	Average employer contribution rate during calendar year (c) (per cent)	Funds available for benefits at end of fiscal year (in millions)
Total 1953-1954.....	1,580,679(d)	14,790,110	6,152,625	$24.45	11.0	$1,588,846	1.30(e)	$8,442(f)
Total 1954-1955.....	1,603,368(g)	13,737,030	5,405,252	25.05	13.6	1,775,924	1.12(h)	8,011(f)
Alabama............	10,190	161,068	63,563	18.30	14.3	16,289	.90	72
Arizona............	9,086	49,814	17,335	21.32	10.5	3,819	1.26	48
Arkansas..........	28,612	115,544	42,634	17.96	10.9	8,021	1.19	43
California..........	264,849	1,111,283	395,999	25.55	13.1	127,288	1.38	825
Colorado...........	7,434	44,094	12,998	26.03	12.0	3,887	.38	69
Connecticut........	23,977	243,759	94,506	27.30	13.4	33,313	1.19	228
Delaware..........	8,087	25,219	11,863	21.45	12.4	3,060	.49	16
Florida............	16,433	168,664	64,853	17.85	10.0	11,392	.69	86
Georgia...........	13,580	185,445	81,868	19.24	13.5	20,671	1.22	135
Idaho.............	13,065	30,119	17,813	23.22	11.6	4,739	1.74	35
Illinois............	62,068	728,000	361,843	25.57	13.0	113,718	.61	437
Indiana............	17,714	337,289	135,877	24.69	12.6	40,717	.76	199
Iowa..............	11,494	66,252	32,896	21.94	10.5	7,242	.38	107
Kansas............	8,990	78,656	42,956	23.90	11.2	11,158	1.02	77
Kentucky..........	18,087	176,513	94,852	22.10	18.2	37,634	1.56	119
Louisiana..........	20,298	161,399	56,298	22.56	15.4	19,087	1.09	123
Maine.............	4,926	103,554	39,930	18.91	12.3	8,830	1.58	42
Maryland..........	44,726	213,576	109,656	25.25	10.7	28,242	.63	107
Massachusetts......	101,454	567,988	214,384	25.21	13.0	68,070	2.00	261
Michigan..........	31,091	689,950	305,248	31.31	12.3	115,019	1.28	367
Minnesota.........	33,768	142,011	76,204	22.81	15.2	26,056	.73	116
Mississippi.........	6,380	108,420	42,315	19.35	12.0	9,442	1.16	36
Missouri...........	19,391	273,107	131,086	21.44	12.4	32,717	.67	203
Montana...........	15,811	32,067	14,923	21.28	11.1	3,553	1.22	43
Nebraska..........	6,663	33,410	17,485	23.77	11.7	4,716	.61	39
Nevada............	5,785	25,468	9,808	30.45	10.9	3,181	1.83	18
New Hampshire.....	6,106	72,596	27,358	21.18	9.8	7,182	1.69	20
New Jersey.........	50,375	718,590	265,229	28.48	15.1	111,061	1.52	456
New Mexico........	12,922	35,268	13,569	24.55	12.9	4,200	1.05	34
New York..........	181,237	2,542,933	718,417	27.10	14.3	266,260	1.57	1,237
North Carolina.....	16,946	358,425	133,527	17.06	14.0	30,645	1.54	170
North Dakota.......	3,031	13,735	9,349	26.17	13.4	3,187	1.57	9
Ohio..............	85,821	571,494	234,307	28.59	15.5	100,943	.61	603
Oklahoma..........	9,995	113,829	39,987	24.32	12.6	11,826	.84	50
Oregon............	16,762	181,207	79,843	22.79	11.6	20,523	1.18	54
Pennsylvania.......	190,924	1,617,530	604,785	26.54	15.3	236,074	1.09	341
Rhode Island.......	10,777	180,658	54,063	23.29	13.5	16,220	2.70	22
South Carolina.....	6,174	116,411	52,155	18.47	13.2	12,369	1.24	69
South Dakota......	2,953	11,150	5,845	22.96	10.6	1,379	.54	13
Tennessee..........	12,263	208,973	124,719	19.10	15.2	35,707	1.48	93
Texas.............	36,088	224,149	104,941	17.91	10.9	20,199	.38	281
Utah..............	14,941	39,926	17,499	25.31	12.2	5,207	1.10	35
Vermont...........	2,261	24,671	10,902	23.15	16.0	3,870	1.06	15
Virginia...........	14,872	130,997	79,654	19.50	9.3	14,017	.41	86
Washington........	54,647	278,916	116,062	24.69	12.8	36,200	2.00	186
West Virginia......	7,128	139,535	72,526	22.40	16.9	26,671	.69	57
Wisconsin..........	24,296	181,446	95,512(i)	28.61	11.4	30,511	.84	238
Wyoming..........	8,258	14,537	7,870	28.67	11.6	2,543	.88	15
District of Columbia..	18,759	42,606	18,515	21.97	13.5	5,464	.44	55
Alaska.............	3,352	18,945	15,710	32.27	16.6	8,365	2.70	1(j)
Hawaii............	8,521	24,582	13,442	21.45	12.5	3,372	.90	22
Puerto Rico........	...	1,195	268	24.60	10.1	67	...	...
Virgin Islands.......	...	57	5	28.59	7.8	1	...	...

*Prepared by Office of Program Review and Analysis, Bureau of Employment Security, U. S. Department of Labor.

(a) Excludes intrastate transitional initial claims in order to reflect more nearly instances of new unemployment.

(b) Adjusted for voided benefit checks and transfers under interstate combined wage plan.

(c) Data compiled only on a calendar-year basis.

(d) Represents data as of June 30, 1954.

(e) For calendar year 1953.

(f) Excludes $200,000 in California, $50,000,000 in New Jersey, and $28,968,681 in Rhode Island, withdrawn in prior years for payment of disability benefits.

(g) Represents data as of March 31, 1955.

(h) For calendar year 1954.

(i) Represents first payments on a "per employer" basis and therefore is not strictly comparable.

(j) Represents funds remaining for benefits after borrowing $1,800,000 from Alaska general funds.

TABLE 3

SIGNIFICANT BENEFIT PROVISIONS OF STATE UNEMPLOYMENT INSURANCE LAWS, OCTOBER 1, 1955*

State	Qualifying wages or employment in base period (number times weekly benefit amount unless otherwise indicated)(a)	Weekly benefit amount (a) Computation (fraction of high-quarter wages, unless otherwise indicated)(b)	For total unemployment Minimum (c)	For total unemployment Maximum (c)	Proportion of wages in base period (d)	Total benefits payable in benefit year Minimum Amount (e)	Minimum Weeks of total unemployment (e)	Maximum Amount (c)	Maximum Weeks of total unemployment (e)
Alabama	35; and $112.01 in 1 quarter	1/26	$6.00	$25.00	1/3	$70.00	11+	$500	20
Alaska	1¼ times high-quarter wages but not less than $450	1.7–1.1% of annual wages plus $5 for each dependent up to lesser of wba or $25	10.00–15.00	45.00–70.00	33–29%(d)	150.00(e)	15	1170–1820	26
Arizona	30; and wages in 2 quarters	1/25	5.00	30.00	1/3	50.00	10	780	26
Arkansas	30	1/21–1/27	7.00	26.00	1/3	70.00	10	468	18
California	30 times wba or 1⅓ times high-quarter wages, if less, but not less than $600 nor more than $750	1/17–1/26	10.00	33.00	1/2	260.00	26(e)	858	26
Colorado	30	1/25	7.00	28.00–35.00(c)	1/3	70.00	10–26 (c)	560–910(c)	20–26(c)
Connecticut	$300; and wages in 2 quarters	1/26, plus $3 for each dependent up to ½ wba	8.00–11.00	35.00–52.00	1/3	120.00(e)	15(e)	910–1352	26
Delaware	30	1/25	7.00	35.00	26%	77.00	11(e)	910	26
District of Columbia	1¼ times high-quarter wages; $130 in 1 quarter and wages in 2 quarters	1/23, plus $1 for each dependent up to $3(c)	8.00–9.00	30.00(c)	1/3	92.00(e)	11+	780(c)	26
Florida	30 (18+, 23+ and 27 if wba is $8, $9 and $10); and wages in 2 quarters	1/13–1/26	8.00	26.00	1/4	38.00	4+	416	16
Georgia	35–45+; and $100 in 1 quarter	1/25	5.00	26.00	Uniform	100.00	20	520	20
Hawaii	30	1/25	5.00	35.00	Uniform	100.00	20	700	20
Idaho	25–38+; $150 in 1 quarter and wages in 2 quarters	1/19–1/26	10.00	30.00	40–26%(d)	100.00	10	780	26
Illinois(f)	$550; and $150 in other than high quarter	1/20 without dependents and 1/20–1/24 with 1–4 dependents(c)	10.00	28.00–40.00(c)	39–32%(d)	215.00	21+(e)	728–1040	26
Indiana	$250; and $150 in last 2 quarters	1/25	10.00	30.00	1/4	62.00	6+(e)	600	20
Iowa	20	1/20	5.00	30.00	1/3	33.33	6+(e)	720	24
Kansas	$200 in 2 quarters or $400 in 1 quarter	1/25 up to 50% of state average weekly wage but not more than $32	5.00	32.00	1/3	67.00	13+(e)	640	20
Kentucky	$300	2.6–1.2% of annual wages	8.00	28.00	Uniform	208.00	26	728	26
Louisiana	30	1/20	5.00	25.00	1/8	50.00	10	500	20
Maine	$300	2.0–1.0% of annual wages	6.00	30.00	Uniform	138.00	23	690	23
Maryland	30; and $156 in 1 quarter	1/26, plus $2 for each dependent up to $8	6.00–8.00	30.00–38.00	1/4	45.00(e)	7+	780–988	26
Massachusetts	$500	1/20, plus $3 for each dependent but total may not exceed average weekly wage	7.00–10.00	25.00(c)	3/10	150.00(e)	21+(e)	650(c)	26

431

TABLE 3—Continued

SIGNIFICANT BENEFIT PROVISIONS OF STATE UNEMPLOYMENT INSURANCE LAWS, OCTOBER 1, 1955*

State	Qualifying wages or employment in base period (number times weekly benefit amount unless otherwise indicated) (a)	Weekly benefit amount (a) Computation (fraction of high-quarter wages, unless otherwise indicated) (b)	For total unemployment Minimum (c)	For total unemployment Maximum (c)	Proportion of wages in base period (d)	Total benefits payable in benefit year — Minimum Amount (e)	Minimum Weeks of total unemployment (e)	Maximum Amount (c)	Maximum Weeks of total unemployment (e)
Michigan	14 weeks of employment at more than $15	63–41% of average weekly wages(b)	10.00–12.00	30.00–54.00	2/3 weeks of employment	95.00(e)	9+	780–1404	26
Minnesota	$520	2.2–1.1% of annual wages	12.00	33.00		216.00	18	858	26
Mississippi	30	1/26	3.00	30.00	Uniform	48.00	16	480	16
Missouri	Wages in 2 quarters(g)	1/25	0.50(g)	25.00	1/3	(g)	(g)	600	24
Montana	1½ times high-quarter wages and $170 in 1 quarter	1/18–1/25	10.00	26.00	Uniform	200.00	20	520	20
Nebraska	$300 in 2 quarters with at least $100 in each of such quarters	1/21–1/23	10.00	28.00	1/3	100.00	10	560	20
Nevada	30	1/25, plus $5 for each dependent up to $20 but total may not exceed 6% of high-quarter wages	8.00–12.00	30.00–50.00	1/3	80.00(e)	10	780–1300	26
New Hampshire	$400	2.0–1.2% of annual wages	9.00	32.00	Uniform	234.00	26	832	26
New Jersey	17 weeks of employment at $15 or more	2/3 of average weekly wage up to $45 and 2/3 of average weekly wage above $45	10.00	35.00	3/4 weeks of employment	130.00	13	910	26
New Mexico	30; and $156 in 1 quarter	1/26	10.00	30.00	2/3	120.00	12	720	24
New York	20 weeks of employment at average of $15 or more	67–51% of average weekly wage	10.00	36.00	Uniform	260.00	26	936	26
North Carolina	$250	2.4–1.0% of annual wages	7.00	30.00	Uniform	182.00	26	780	26
North Dakota	36; and wages in 2 quarters	1/24, plus $1–$3 per dependent, by schedule $3–$9	7.00–10.00	26.00–35.00	Uniform	140.00(e)	20	520–700	20
Ohio	20 weeks of employment and $240	1/17–1/25, plus $3 for each dependent up to $6	10.00–13.00	33.00–39.00	1/2	120.00(e)	12(e)	858–1014	26
Oklahoma	20; and wages in 2 quarters	1/20	10.00	28.00	1/3	67.00	6+	616	22
Oregon(h)	37 times wba or 1½ times high-quarter wages, if less, but not less than $700	1/26	15.00	35.00	1/3	233.00	15+(e)	910	26
Pennsylvania	32–42 or 30 if step-down operative; and $120 in 1 quarter	1/25 or 50% of full-time weekly wages, whichever is greater	10.00	35.00	Uniform	300.00	30	1050	30
Rhode Island (h)	30	1/20	10.00	30.00	35–27%	104.00	10+(e)	780	26
South Carolina	1½ times high-quarter wages but not less than $240; and $120 in 1 quarter	1/20–1/26	8.00	26.00	1/3	80.00	10	572	22

432

State	Qualifying wages (base period)	Computation of weekly benefit	Minimum weekly benefit	Maximum weekly benefit	Proportion of wages	Qualifying wages	Minimum duration (weeks)	Minimum total benefits	Maximum duration (weeks)
South Dakota....	1½ times high-quarter wages; and $150 in 1 quarter or wages in 2 quarters if base-period wages are $600 or more	1/20–1/23	8.00	25.00	36–22%	80.00	10(e)	500	20
Tennessee........	40, 50 and 60; and $75 in 1 quarter	1/21–1/26	5.00	30.00	Uniform	110.00	22	660	22
Texas.............	$375 with $250 in 1 quarter and $125 in another or $450 with at least $50 in each of 3 quarters or $1000 in 1 quarter	1/26	7.00	28.00	¼	94.00	9+(e)	672	24
Utah.............	19 weeks of employment and $400	1/26	10.00	33.00	1.6–3.3(d)	150.00	15	858	26
Vermont..........	30; and $200 in 1 quarter and ⅓ of wages in last 2 quarters	1/22–1/26	10.00	28.00	Uniform	260.00	26	728	26
Virginia..........	25 (16+ if wba is $6)	1/25	6.00	24.00	¼	36.00	6	384	16
Washington.......	$800	2.0–1.1% of annual wages	17.00	35.00	26–29%(d)	204.00	12	910	26
West Virginia.....	$500	1.8–1.0% of annual wages	10.00	30.00	Uniform	240.00	24	720	24
Wisconsin........	14 weeks of employment at average of $13 or more	69–51% of average weekly wage	10.00	36.00	7/10 weeks of employment	100.00	10	954	26½
Wyoming.........	26; and $200 in 1 quarter	1/21–1/25, plus $3 for each dependent up to $6	10.00–13.00	30.00–36.00	31–26%(d)	80.00(e)	8	780–936	26

*Prepared by Bureau of Employment Security, U. S. Department of Labor.

(a) Weekly benefit is abbreviated throughout the table as wba.

(b) When state uses a weighted high-quarter formula, annual-wage formula or average-weekly-wage formula, approximate fractions or percentages are taken at midpoint of lowest and highest normal wage brackets. When dependents' allowances are provided, the fraction applies to the basic amount unless otherwise shown; in Michigan, the percentage applies to claimants with no dependents (at minimum wba with dependents, 63–90% depending on number and type of dependents and at maximum wba with dependents, 45–50%).

(c) When two amounts are given, higher includes dependents' allowances except in Colorado where it includes 25% additional for claimants employed in Colorado by covered employers for 5 consecutive calendar years with wages in excess of $1,000 per year and no benefits received; duration for such claimants is increased to 26 weeks. Higher figure for minimum weekly benefit amount includes maximum allowance for one dependent; in Michigan, for one dependent child or two dependents other than a child. Higher figure for maximum dependents includes allowances for maximum number of compensable dependents. In the District of Columbia, same maximum without dependents. Maximum augmented payment to individuals with dependents not shown for Massachusetts since any figure presented would be based on an assumed maximum number of dependents. In Alaska, maximum for interstate claimants is $25 and no dependents' allowances are payable. In Illinois, schedule is extended

to provide additional benefits of $0.50–$12 depending on high-quarter wages above those required for maximum basic benefits and number and type of dependents.

(d) In states with a weighted schedules, the per cent of benefits is figured at the bottom of the lowest and of the highest wage brackets; in states noted, percentages at other brackets are higher and/or lower than the percentages shown. In Utah, duration is based on ratio of annual wages to high-quarter wages (1.6–3.3).

(e) Dependents' allowances add to potential benefits for claimants entitled to such allowances. Figure shown applies to claimants with minimum weekly benefit and minimum qualifying wages except in Texas where claimants with minimum qualifying wages of $375 with $250 in 1 quarter and $125 in another quarter are unable to receive the minimum weekly benefit. If qualifying wages are concentrated largely or wholly in high quarter, weekly benefit for claimants with minimum qualifying wages may be above minimum weekly benefit and consequently weeks of benefits less than minimum duration shown. In Delaware, statutory minimum; in Illinois, statutory minimum of 10 weeks not applicable at minimum weekly benefit amount.

(f) Effective April 1, 1956.

(g) If the benefit is less than $5, benefits are paid at the rate of $5 a week; no qualifying wages and no minimum weekly or annual benefits are specified.

(h) Effective January 1, 1956.

433

9

State Regulatory Activities

DEVELOPMENTS IN PUBLIC UTILITY REGULATION

IN its effects on the costs of operating the homes, commerce and industry of America, regulation of public utilities is one of the most important of state activities. It involves the rates charged and the services provided to the consumers of electricity, gas and phone services. It affects the rates and services of a great many public transportation facilities. At the same time it is basic in protecting the savings of large numbers of investors in public utility securities.

Thus state public utility regulation is charged with the complex task of serving for an equitable balance between the interests of those who receive and those who provide services that are fundamental in the economy. Billions of dollars are involved. Likewise affected by the action of many public utility commissions is the extent to which consumers can have available the means of lighting their homes, saving their labor, riding adequate transportation lines and enjoying other benefits of good utility service.

The agencies of the great majority of the states for this regulation are commissions with jurisdiction over a wide range of standard utilities. The commissions in certain states are concerned with fewer utilities, and the regulation of additional services in these states usually is left to local or other bodies. In most cases the regulatory functions of the state commissions are primarily or wholly over private utilities, but several have jurisdiction over municipally owned facilities as well.

Just as the kinds of utilities over which the commissions have jurisdiction vary in some degree, so do the aspects of regulation for which they are responsible. Not all the commissions that regulate rates and standards of service have authority over issuance of securities. But in a large majority of states the commissions—in addition to their responsibilities as to the bases on which rates are to be charged, the setting of the rates themselves, and the standards and extent of services—also have the power to regulate as to issuance of securities, sale or purchase of facilities, and mergers and consolidations.

The commissions range in size from three to seven members. Those of twenty-nine states (including the Massachusetts Department of Public Utilities, with five members) are appointed by the Governor. In fifteen they are elected by the people, and in two they are selected by the legislature. One state, Oregon, has a single Public Utilities Commissioner rather than a commission, and Rhode Island has a single Public Utility Administrator—in both cases appointed by the Governor.

A summary of recent trends and problems encountered in regulation follows, based primarily on information provided to the Council of State Governments by state public utility commissions late in 1955.

RATE BASES

Original cost of the utility properties continued to be the chief prevailing base upon which rates were constructed. Comments on rate bases used are at hand from chairmen, members or attachés of twenty-seven state commissions, and for nineteen of them the original cost formula was indicated as fundamental. Other factors were considered with it, notably depreciation and working capital, so that a typical formula may be summarized as original cost less depreciation plus working capital. This was the standard adopted by the Federal Power Commission and approved by the United States Supreme Court in the *Hope Natural Gas Case* in 1944. Earlier in the century the standard formula in effect, in line with a United States Supreme Court decision of 1898, was fair return on fair value of a company's properties; and "fair value" commonly was interpreted as reproduction cost new less observed depreciation.

Although the *Hope* case did not enjoin state and other commissions to adopt the original cost base, the trend since then has been to it and away from the reproduction-cost-new formula. Nevertheless the latter continues to find acceptance in various jurisdictions, in varying degrees. Existing laws and court decisions in some states require this. In Ohio, for example, the law requires that the Public Utilities Commissions use a reproduction-cost-new-less-observed-depreciation rate base in proceedings before it. The Delaware Supreme Court in a recent case held that the Public Service Commission's rate base in a telephone company case did not give sufficient consideration to reproduction cost. In Pennsylvania the rate basis is defined as fair value, requiring, among other factors, that consideration be given both to depreciated original cost and depreciated reproduction cost at fair average prices.

As has been the case through most of the postwar period, problems of inflation complicated establishment of rate bases during the last two years. In California the Public Utilities Commission met and rejected a contention that rate of return should be based at least in some measure on book investment in terms of "equivalent 1939" dollars. The commission took the position that historical cost should continue to be the basis for rate making, and that adequate consideration was given inflation by recognizing operating costs at prevailing prices, and determining depreciation charges in relation to inflated dollars spent.

RATES

In order to establish the charges that may be made to the consumers for public utility services, the regulatory bodies decide upon the rate of return to be allowed on the investment established as the rate base. In the light of operating expenses and other pertinent factors, charges then are approved at a level calculated to produce the approved rate of return.

In states where original cost is the primary factor in establishing rate bases, rates of return allowed have varied recently from 5 per cent to a little more than 8 per cent: the usual range falling between $5\frac{1}{2}$ and $6\frac{1}{2}$ per cent. To be significant as yardsticks, rates, of course, must be considered in connection with the rate base in each case. In Ohio, where the law requires the commission to use reproduction cost new less observed depreciation as the base, the commission recently allowed a 3.25 per cent rate of return in one case; in other cases there the rate has varied between $4\frac{1}{2}$ and 6 per cent, and usually has been in the neighborhood of 5 per cent, applied to the reproduction cost new less depreciation base. In Montana the commission customarily receives evidence of value on three bases: original cost depreciated, original cost, and reproduction new less depreciation. (It has recently required that reproduction new valuations contain economic reductions allowing for more modern and efficient methods now utilized.) From the three bases, the commission finds a "fair value" lying somewhere between—based, as a member of the commission explains, on many and varied considerations. The commission member reports that it has allowed in the neighborhood of 6 per cent on such fair value—which would approximate, in most instances, $7\frac{1}{2}$ per cent on original cost depreciated or $4\frac{1}{2}$ per cent on reproduction new.

The type of utility in question, its size and financial position all have bearing on the rates allowed. Generally speaking, small utility companies and transit lines have been permitted higher rates than large and well established gas and electricity concerns. Thus in California, where rates in approximately the last two years have varied from 5.78 per cent to 8.13 per cent, those for gas and electric companies have been 6 per cent or under; those for transit lines have ranged from 6.41 to 8.13 per cent. In New Jersey, similarly, the commission during the past two years prescribed rates for an autobus transportation service calculated to afford an opportunity for a return in a range from 6.5 to 8 per cent; for a water company, 5.8 per cent; for a telephone company 5.7 to 6.26 per cent; and for a gas company, 6 per cent.

Emphasizing the complexities inevitably involved, a representative of the Florida commission pointed out that it has not been greatly concerned over the rate of return as such, but rather in the dollar requirements of the utility. The commission needs to know how many dollars the utility requires in order to meet its operating expenses, depreciation charges, taxes, maintenance expense, debt service, dividend requirements, and to transfer a reasonable amount to surplus. When the commission has been able to determine the answer to those questions, the official added, the rate of return becomes a simple matter of computation. The bearing of a utility's size on the rate required is an important factor, as noted, for example, in comment for the North Carolina commission: "We have found from experience that the managerial expense of a small utility is somewhat greater in proportion to the amount invested, and it therefore is necessary for a small utility to have some greater rate of return in order to attract capital."

TRANSIT PROBLEMS

Problems of transit companies—involving reduced public reliance on mass local transportation lines, high costs, and the difficulty of providing equipment that will cause people to shift from daily use of private automobiles to the transit lines without charging fares that work the other way—continued to be major concerns of regulatory commissions.

For example, in New Jersey, applica-

tions for discontinuance and curtailment of autobus service have continued to mount, due to increased costs and decreased revenues. A summary from the commission reports that increases in fares do not remedy but merely alleviate this condition. In an effort to stem the tide, the commission has been cooperating with the municipalities to regulate the points for acceptance and discharge of autobus passengers and also to regulate the parking of cars on highways. Testimony before the commission had shown that congested highway conditions not only resulted in inconvenience and delay to autobus passengers but substantially increased the cost of the transportation service. Similarly, applications for discontinuance or curtailment of railroad passenger services have been increasingly frequent in New Jersey. The commission was contesting before the Interstate Commerce Commission its jurisdiction to nullify orders by the state commission denying applications of interstate railroads to discontinue or curtail intrastate passenger service.

Comment from the Montana commission indicated that one of the most pressing problems it faced was continuation of express service within the state by the Railway Express Agency. A considerable number of passenger trains, both branch and main line, had been discontinued, and many stations closed, because of loss of passenger revenue.

In New York decreased business of transit companies and applications of some to withdraw from business were causing increased study and concern on the part of the state commission. One 1955 statute in New York gave municipalities the right to reduce or eliminate utility taxes for omnibus companies; the commission reported that several cities have eliminated them in order to retain local transit service. Action for safety on the roads was another important development of the last biennium in New York. The state commission pioneered with rules and regulations covering speed-recording devices on certain intercity and charter omnibus passenger carriers. Such regulations of the commission already cover long trips, and on January 1, 1956, they were to cover all one-way trips of the indicated type extending thirty-five miles or more. Meantime, New York also required push-out type windows on buses used for certain passenger-carrying operations.

NATURAL GAS

Numerous problems involving natural gas occupied many commissions. In Connecticut, comment from the commission indicated that introduction of natural gas into that area was perhaps the most significant utility development of the last two years. The commission promulgated and prescribed rules and regulations as to standards of construction, operation and maintenance of transmission pipelines constructed in the state by the two pipeline companies certified by the Federal Power Commission.

The Idaho commission made determination of the methods by which natural gas would be distributed in that state; after lengthy hearings it was decided that one company would be given a certificate of convenience and necessity to serve some thirty-three communities along the line of the Pacific Northwest Pipe Line Company; this decision was appealed to the Idaho Supreme Court and late in 1955 was awaiting its decision. In Oregon, introduction of natural gas to the Portland and Willamette Valley areas was an anticipated early development. A commission study was in progress for development of safety standards to meet the requirements of high pressure transmission and distribution mains, as well as study of the problem of cutting over approximately 100,000 customers from manufactured to natural gas.

The Virginia commission, meantime, in 1954, issued orders in a series of cases involving natural gas rates. The orders permitted gas companies distributing natural gas in the state to add to their rate schedule purchased gas adjustment clauses, authorizing automatic adjustments in charges to consumers to reflect decreases and increases in the wholesale price of natural gas purchased by the companies from interstate pipeline companies; and providing a method of making refunds to consumers on retroactive decreases in the wholesale cost of gas. One of the cases involved was selected as a test case and

was pending before the Virginia Supreme Court of Appeals.

Natural gas likewise raised problems in producing states. In one of them, Louisiana, comment from the commission emphasized a steady and phenomenal increase in the cost of natural gas at points of delivery into distribution systems, which could be attributed to transcontinental pipeline companies able to demand high prices at remote markets. Several applications for rate increases had been made by distributing companies to the state commission; some of these were granted, some denied as the increased costs could be absorbed without seriously affecting the rate of return.

In New Mexico a commission attaché reported that continued increases in the wholesale cost of natural gas to companies distributing in the state, coupled with long pendency in Federal Power Commission cases, had created considerable difficulty in establishing a fair and reasonable gas price to consumers.

OTHER DEVELOPMENTS

Whether another and newer industry, television, would come within the purview of utility commissions over a wide area remained to be seen, but that is the case in Wyoming. It was reported for the commission that perhaps the most significant development in its activities in the past two years was that, pursuant to a ruling of the Attorney General, it had assumed jurisdiction over the regulation of persons, corporations or other legal entities owning and operating community antenna television systems to furnish service to isolated communities in the state—even though the TV signal they transmit to their subscribers emanates from a distant broadcasting station. Among difficult problems encountered, it was indicated, are those of prescribing the treatment to be accorded subscribers contributing in aid of construction of such systems, and the establishment of just and reasonable rates for the service.

In Colorado, meantime, the work load of the commission was greatly increased as a result of a constitutional amendment voted by the people at the 1954 general election. Previously the commission did not regulate utilities operating within Colorado's fourteen "home rule cities," which comprise perhaps 75 per cent of the customers receiving gas and electric service from public utilities. In the election the commission was given authority to regulate all public utilities (except those municipally owned), including those in the home rule cities. The amendment did not change the status of municipally owned utilities operating within the corporate limits, but the commission previously had assumed jurisdiction of municipal utilities operating outside the city limits.

In the area of commission procedure, New Jersey reported significant innovations. Over many years the commission had employed prehearing conferences to simplify and clarify issues in cases involving municipal consent for passenger autobus routes. In 1955 the commission was using prehearing conferences more generally, with gratifying results, for the purpose of expediting hearing procedure. With similar purpose, the commission has permitted expert testimony to be reduced to writing, submitted to it, and served upon adverse parties before hearings in rate proceedings. The practice, it was reported, resulted in reducing the number of requests for adjournments of hearings to permit preparation for cross-examination of expert witnesses. In mid-1955 the commission was considering extending such permission to proceedings other than rate cases, and the feasibility of making the submission and service of all expert testimony mandatory.

STATE PUBLIC UTILITY COMMISSIONERS

State	Regulatory authority	Chairman	Selection	Annual salary	Other members	Selection	Annual salaries
Alabama	Public Service Commission	C. C. Owen, Pres.	E	$10,000	2	E	$ 9,400
Arizona	Arizona Corporation Commission	Wilson T. Wright, Ch.	E	8,400	2	E	8,400
Arkansas	Public Service Commission	Lewis Robinson, Ch.	A (a)	8,500	2	A (a)	8,500
California	Public Utilities Commission	Peter E. Mitchell, Pres.	A (b)	17,000	4	A (a)	17,000
Colorado	Public Utilities Commission	Joseph W. Hawley, Ch.	A (a)	7,500	2	A (a)	7,500
Connecticut	Public Utilities Commission	Eugene S. Loughlin, Ch.	A (c)	(d)	2	A (c)	(d)
Delaware	Public Service Commission	Norman B. Baylis, Act. Ch.	A	4,500	2	A	4,500
Florida	Railroad and Public Utilities Commission	Wilbur C. King, Ch.	E	11,000	2	E	11,000
Georgia	Public Service Commission	Matt L. McWhorter, Ch.	E	7,500	4	E	7,500
Idaho	Public Utilities Commission	H. C. Allen, Pres.	A (a, b)	5,500	2	A (a)	5,500
Illinois	Illinois Commerce Commn.	George R. Perrine, Ch.	A	12,000	4	A	12,000
Indiana	Public Service Commission	Warren Buchanan, Ch.	A	10,000	2	A	9,500
Iowa	Iowa State Commerce Commission	Carl W. Reed, Ch.	E (b)	6,300	2	E	6,300
Kansas	State Corporation Commn.	Jeff A. Robertson, Ch.	A	9,000	2	A	7,500
Kentucky	Public Service Commission	Robert M. Coleman, Ch.	A (a)	5,000	2	A (a)	5,000
Louisiana	Public Service Commission	Wade O. Martin, Ch.	E (b)	8,500	2	E	8,500
Maine	Public Utilities Commission	Sumner T. Pike, Ch.	A (e)	9,000	2	A (e)	8,500
Maryland	Public Service Commission	Stanford Hoff, Ch.	A	9,000	2	A	8,000
Massachusetts	Dept. of Public Utilities	David M. Brackman, Ch.	A	10,500	4	A	9,000
Michigan	Public Service Commission	John H. McCarthy, Ch.	A (a)	9,000	2	A (a)	8,500
Minnesota	Minnesota Railroad and Warehouse Commission	Ewald W. Lund	E	9,000	2	E	9,000
Mississippi	Public Service Commission	Alton Massey, Ch.	E (b)	5,500	2	E	5,500
Missouri	Public Service Commission	Tyre W. Burton, Ch.	A (a)	8,500	4	A (a)	8,500
Montana	Board of Railroad Commissioners (f)	Leonard C. Young, Ch.	E	7,500	2	E	7,500
Nebraska	Nebraska State Railway Commission	Joseph J. Brown, Ch.	E	6,000(g)	2	E	6,000(g)
Nevada	Public Service Commission	Robert A. Allen, Ch.	A	10,000	3	A	7,200(h)
New Hampshire	Public Utilities Commission	Harold K. Davison, Ch.	A (e)	8,000 (i)	2	A (e)	8,000 (i)
New Jersey	Board of Public Utility Commissioners	Mrs. Hortense F. Kessler, Pres.	A (a)	18,000	2	A (a)	15,000
New Mexico	Public Service Commission	L. W. Leibrand, Ch.	A (a)	8,400	2	A	8,400
New York	Public Service Commission	Benjamin F. Feinberg, Ch.	A	19,500	5	A	18,500
North Carolina	North Carolina Utilities Commission	Stanley Winborne, Ch.	A	10,500	4	A	10,000
North Dakota	Public Service Commission	Elmer W. Cart, Pres.	E	5,000	2	E	5,000
Ohio	Public Utilities Commission	Robert L. Moulton, Ch.	A (a)	9,000	2	A (a)	9,000
Oklahoma	Corporation Commission	Ray C. Jones, Ch.	E	9,000	2	E	9,000
Oregon	Public Utilities Commissioner (j)	Charles H. Heltzel	A	11,000	None	..	.....
Pennsylvania	Public Utility Commission	Leon Schwartz	A (a)	15,000	4	A (a)	14,000
Rhode Island	Public Utility Administrator (k)	Thomas A. Kennelly	A	7,722	None	..	.....
South Carolina	Public Service Commission	F. B. Hines	(b)	6,536	6	(l)	6,300
South Dakota	Public Utilities Commission	C. A. Merkle, Ch.	E (b)	6,300	2	E	6,300
Tennessee	Public Service Commission	John C. Hammer, Ch.	E (b)	10,000	2	E	10,000
Texas	Railroad Commission	Ernest O. Thompson, Ch.	E	17,500	2	E	10,600
Utah	Public Service Commission	Hal S. Bennett, Ch.	A (a)	6,000	2	A (a)	6,000
Vermont	Public Service Commission	Oscar L. Shepard	A (a)	(m)	2	A (a)	2,000
Virginia	State Corporation Commn.	H. Lester Hooker, Ch.	(b, l)	12,250	2	(l)	11,150
Washington	Public Service Commission	Ralph Davis, Ch.	A (a)	11,500	2	A (a)	11,000
West Virginia	Public Service Commission	Homer W. Hanna, Jr.	A (a)	9,000	2	A (a)	9,000
Wisconsin	Public Service Commission	James R. Durfee, Ch.	A (a)	10,500	2	A (a)	10,000
Wyoming	Public Service Commission	Walter W. Hudson, Ch.	A (a)	7,000	2	A (a)	7,000

A—Appointed by Governor; E—Elected.
(a) Confirmed by Senate.
(b) Elected chairman by commission.
(c) Nominated by Governor, confirmed by Senate and House.
(d) Base Salary advances by $540 annually from minimum of $10,200 to maximum of $14,520.
(e) With advice and consent of the Council.
(f) Ex-officio Public Service Commission.
(g) To be increased to $7,000 effective January, 1957.

(h) For full-time member; part-time member receives $5,400; State Engineer is ex-officio member without vote.
(i) Base salary advances by $240 annually from minimum of $8,000 to maximum of $9,200.
(j) No commission; one commissioner only.
(k) No commission; one administrator only.
(l) Selected by General Assembly.
(m) Salary set by Emergency Board within range of $6,000–$7,500.

REGULATORY FUNCTIONS OF
STATE PUBLIC UTILITY COMMISSIONS

State	Electric light and power	Manufactured gas	Natural gas	Street railways	Interurban railways	Motor buses	Motor trucks	Water	Telephone	Telegraph	Oil pipe line	Gas pipe line	Accounting	Rates and rate schedules	Issuance of securities	Service to consumers
Alabama	★	★	★	★	★	★	★	★	★	★	··	··	··	··	··	··
Arizona	★	··	★	★	★	★	★	★	★	★	··	(a)	··	··	··	··
Arkansas	★	★	★	★	★	★	★	★	★	★	★	★	··	··	··	··
California	★	★	★	★	★	★	★	★	★	★	★	★	··	··	··	··
Colorado	★	★	★	★	★	★	★	★	★	★	★	★	(b)	(b)	(b)	(b)
Connecticut	★	★	★	(c)	(c)	★	★	★	★	★	★	★	★	··	··	··
Delaware	★	★	★	★	★	★	★	★	★	★	··	··	··	··	··	··
Florida	★	★	··	··	★	★	··	★	★	··	··	··	··	··	··	··
Georgia	★	★	★	★	★	··	★	··	★	★	··	··	··	··	··	··
Idaho	★	★	★	★	★	★	★	★	★	★	··	★	··	··	··	··
Illinois	★	★	★	★	★	★	★	★	★	★	··	★	··	··	··	··
Indiana	★	★	★	★	★	★	★	★	★	★	··	★	★	★	★	★
Iowa	··	··	··	··	★	··	★	··	··	··	··	··	··	··	··	··
Kansas	★	★	★	★	★	★	★	★	★	★	★	★	··	··	··	··
Kentucky	★	★	··	★	★	★	★	··	★	★	(d)	(e)	(b)	(b)	··	(b)
Louisiana	★	··	★	★	★	★	★	★	★	★	★	★	··	··	··	··
Maine	★	★	★	★	★	★	★	★	★	★	··	★	(f)	(f)	(f)	(f)
Maryland	★	★	★	★	★	★	★	★	★	★	··	··	(f)	(f)	(f)	(f)
Massachusetts	★	★	★	★	★	★	★	★	★	★	··	··	★	··	··	★
Michigan	★	★	··	··	★	★	★	··	★	★	★	★	★	··	··	··
Minnesota	··	··	··	··	★	··	★	··	★	··	··	··	(g)	(g)	(g)	(g)
Mississippi	··	··	··	··	··	★	★	··	★	★	★	··	··	··	··	··
Missouri	★	★	★	★	★	★	★	★	★	★	(a)	··	(a)	··	··	··
Montana	(h)	★	★	★	★	★	★	★	★	★	★	★	★	★	··	★
Nebraska	(i)	★	★	★	★	★	★	(i)	★	★	★(d)	★(d)	··	··	··	··
Nevada	★	★	★	★	★	★	★	★	★	★	★	★	··	··	··	··
New Hampshire	★	★	★	★	★	★	★	★	★	★	★	★	(b)	(b)	(b)	(b)
New Jersey	★	★	★	★	★	★	··	★	★	★	★	★	(j)	(b)	(k)	(b)
New Mexico	★	★	★	(l)	(l)	(l)	(l)	(l)	(l)	(l)	(l)	(l)	(m)	(m)	(n)	(m)
New York	★	★	★	★	★	★	★	★	★	★	··	★	(o)	(o)	··	(o)
North Carolina	★	★	★	··	··	★(p)	★	★	★	★	★	★	··	··	··	··
North Dakota	★	★	★	··	··	★	★	★	★	★	★	★	··	··	··	··
Ohio	(q)	(q)	(q)	(r)	★	(r)	(r)	(q)	★	··	★	★	··	··	··	··
Oklahoma	★	★	★	★	★	★	★	★	★	★	★	★	··	··	··	··
Oregon	★	★	★	★	★	★	★	★	★	★	··	··	··	··	··	··
Pennsylvania	★	★	★	★	★	★	★	★	★	★	··	★	(b)	(b)	··	(b)
Rhode Island	★	★	··	★	★	★	★	★	★	★	··	··	··	··	··	··
South Carolina	★	★	··	★	★	★	★	··	★	★	··	··	··	··	··	··
South Dakota	★	★	··	··	★	★	★	··	★	★	··	··	(g)	(g)	(g)	(g)
Tennessee	★	··	(s)	··	★	(t)	(t)	★	★	★	★	★	··	··	··	··
Texas	··	(q)	★	··	··	★	★	★	··	··	★	★	··	··	··	··
Utah	★	★	★	★	★	★	★	★	★	★	··	★	··	··	··	··
Vermont	★	★	··	★	★	★	★	★	★	★	··	★	(u)	(u)	··	(u)
Virginia	★	★	★	★	★	★	★	★	★	★	··	★	··	··	··	··
Washington	★	★	★	★	★	★	★	★	★	★	★	★	··	··	··	··
West Virginia	★	★	★	(c)	(c)	★	★	★	★	★	★	★	★	★	··	★
Wisconsin	★	★	★	★	★	★	★	★	★	★	★	★	★	★	··	★
Wyoming	★	★	★	··	··	★	★	★	★	★	★	★	★	★	··	★

(a) Intrastate.
(b) Regulated only as to operations outside limits of municipality.
(c) No street or interurban railways operate as such in West Virginia, Wyoming and Connecticut; some in Connecticut retain identity although using motor buses.
(d) If common carrier.
(e) Limited jurisdiction over natural gas pipe lines.
(f) With the exception of water.
(g) Telephone only.
(h) Authority does not extend to rural electrical cooperative units.
(i) All publicly or municipally owned and exempt from jurisdiction by statute.
(j) Only annual report required.
(k) If plant has been adjudged to have general status as public utility.
(l) Under Corporation Commission jurisdiction.
(m) No commission jurisdiction.
(n) Initial issues and refunding.
(o) Certain jurisdiction over some types of municipally owned utilities.
(p) Fares only.
(q) Upon appeal.
(r) Only operations outside of corporate limits not contiguous.
(s) Local distribution only.
(t) Interurban.
(u) Electric only.

STATE REGULATION OF INSURANCE*

ANY review of developments in recent years in state governmental supervision and taxation of insurance requires mention of the Supreme Court's far-reaching decision in the case of the *United States* vs. *South-Eastern Underwriters Association, et al.* (322 US 533, 1944). The decision held that the business of insurance was commerce and therefore subject to regulation by Congress when conducted across state boundary lines.

Immediately the National Association of Insurance Commissioners, with the co-operation of the insurance industry, submitted to Congress certain recommendations, out of which emerged the McCarron Act—Public Law 15, 79th Congress (approved March 9, 1945). This act not only granted the states a moratorium for a review of their respective insurance supervisory and taxation laws but it also made reference to the acts which would apply to the interstate phase of the insurance business at the expiration of the moratorium ". . . to the extent that such business is not regulated by State Law." Thus the burden of preserving the rights of the states in the supervision and taxation of the interstate phase of the insurance business was placed squarely on the states.

During the moratorium the N.A.I.C. with the cooperation of the insurance industry developed a legislative program known as the All Industry Bills, which was recommended to all states for consideration.

Some of the states are still considering parts of this program. A summary of state legislation to date as regards the entire program of the All Industry Bills will be presented below. First, however, it is in point to cite certain key parts of the McCarron Act. It states:

". . . that the continued regulation and taxation by the several states of the business of insurance is in the public interest. . . ."

and:

"No Act of Congress shall be construed to invalidate, impair, or supersede any law enacted by any State for the purpose of regulating the business of insurance, or which imposes a fee or tax upon such business, unless such Act specifically relates to the business of insurance: Provided, that after January 1948, the Act of July 2, 1890, as amended, known as the Sherman Act, and the Act of October 15, 1914, as amended, known as the Clayton Act, and the Act of September 26, 1914, known as the Federal Trade Commission Act, as amended, shall be applicable to the business of insurance to the extent that such business is not regulated by State Law."

and:

". . . Until January 1, 1948, the Act of July 2, 1890, as amended, known as the Sherman Act and the Act of October 15, 1914, as amended, known as the Clayton Act, and the Act of September 26, 1914, known as the Federal Trade Commission Act, as amended, and the Act of June 19, 1936, known as the Robinson-Patman Antidiscrimination Act, shall not apply to the business of insurance or to acts in the conduct thereof."[1]

The following summary of the results to date of the All Industry Legislative program is based upon the information available at this time.

All Industry Type Bills
(1) Fire and Marine Rate Regulation
(Ref: 1946 Proceedings, National Association of Insurance Commissioners, pp. 410–422)
Passed in all states.

(2) Casualty and Surety Rate Regulation
(Ref: N.A.I.C. 1946 Proc. pp. 397–410)
Passed in all states.

(3) Fair Trade Practice Acts
(Ref: N.A.I.C. 1947 Proc. pp. 401–410)
Passed in 39 states. Arizona, Connecticut, Dela-

---

*Prepared by C. LAWRENCE LEGGETT, Superintendent of Insurance, State of Missouri, and President of the National Association of Insurance Commissioners.

[1]By an amendment, the original moratorium period was extended from January 1, 1948 to June 30, 1948.

ware, Iowa, Kansas, Ohio, Oklahoma, Oregon, Vermont, West Virginia and Wyoming passed the act in 1955.

(4) Anti-Discrimination and Anti-Rebate Acts (Ref: N.A.I.C. 1947 Proc. pp. 190–195)
Passed in 9 states as a separate act. In many states, the same provisions are incorporated in the rate regulatory laws.

(5) Acts regarding Interlocking Directorates, etc.
Passed in 15 states.

(6) Accident and Health Insurance Bill (Ref: N.A.I.C. 1947 Proc. pp. 205–210; 391–392)
Passed in 16 states.

(7) Unauthorized Insurers Service of Process Act.
(Ref: N.A.I.C. 1951 Proc. pp. 166–168)
Passed in 38 states. Arizona, Colorado, Delaware, Indiana, Mississippi, Nevada, North Carolina, Ohio, South Dakota, Tennessee, Vermont and Wyoming passed the act in 1955.

No inference should be drawn because not all states have passed all of the All Industry Bills, as many states have other laws with the same or substantially the same provisions.

In addition to the All Industry Bills, the National Association of Insurance Commissioners adopted the Uniform Individual Accident and Sickness Policy Provisions Law (Ref: N.A.I.C. 1950 Proc. pp. 399–413). It has been passed in forty-two states —including Delaware, Oklahoma, Oregon, Tennessee, Texas and West Virginia, which adopted the law in 1955.

In keeping with the McCarron Act declaration ". . . that the continued regulation of taxation by the several States of the business of insurance is in the public interest . . .," the N.A.I.C. has kept itself informed regarding all matters before Congress which appear inconsistent with the act. Resolutions have been adopted and appearance of members delegated in opposition to the following:

1. Federal Health Reinsurance Plan. The bill has failed to pass to date. (Ref: N.A.I.C. 1954 Proc. Vol. II pp. 458–461).
2. Amendment to Interstate Commerce Commission Regulations to permit the qualifying and examinations of insurance carriers on I.C.C. risks. Proposed amendments have failed to pass to date. (Ref: N.A.I.C. 1955 Proc. Vol. I, pp. 222, 224–225).

Other matters of interest to the states now under study by the appropriate committees of the association include:

1. Multiple Line Underwriting.
2. Examination Methods, Practices and Laws.
3. Tontine Policy Control.
4. Brokers Minimum Qualifications and Licensing Bill.
5. Group Life Definition amendments.
6. Financial Responsibility Laws on a Reciprocal Basis between United States and Canada.
7. Commercial Pension Funds and Trusteed Welfare Funds.
8. Tie-in-Sales of Insurance and Mutual Fund Shares.
9. Insurance Sales on U. S. Military Reservations.
10. Credit Life and Credit A & H Insurance.
11. Uniform Fraternal Insurance Law.
12. Uniform Surplus Line Law.

The National Association of Insurance Commissioners, comprising the insurance supervisory officials of the states and territories, is a purely voluntary organization, and it possesses no authority whatever to commit its membership on any particular question. It was formed on that basis in May, 1871, for purposes revealed by its constitution:

"Article 2. Object: The object of this Association shall be to promote uniformity in legislation affecting insurance; to encourage uniformity in departmental rulings under the insurance laws of the several states; to disseminate information of value to insurance supervisory officials in the performance of their duties and to establish ways and means of fully protecting the interests of insurance policyholders of the various states, territories and insular possessions of the United States."

In conformance with the object of the association, a multitude of new problems, common to many or all states, are continuously submitted for study and solution. The ultimate benefits to be derived by the insuring public are consistently the major factors considered by the members of the numerous standing committees in making their recommendations to the association for action.

PROGRESS IN UNIFORM BLUE SKY LEGISLATION*

THE National Conference of Commissioners on Uniform State Laws has had various drafts of a proposed Uniform Securities Act under consideration for several years. We are hopeful that a final draft will be presented to the Conference at its next annual meeting in August, 1956, that the Conference will approve the Act and that it will be available immediately thereafter for enactment by interested states.

The need for uniform state legislation in this field is apparent at once to anyone who has attempted to sell the same security in several states at one time. It is obvious that state as well as federal laws must be complied with. If the states in the prospective sales area require registration of securities before sale, it then becomes important to the seller to determine whether (1) the particular security or the particular financial transaction is exempt from regulation; and (2) if it is not exempt, whether it is the kind of security which can be sold in the state merely by giving notice of sale together with certain prescribed information or whether it must be "qualified," i.e., approved before sale. Some states may be satisfied with registration by notification, others may insist upon qualification, and within each category the type of information required by a particular state may vary widely. The complexity and variety of the requirements, and the necessity of coordinating sales in all states, makes the floating of securities in these states extremely difficult and expensive.

Not all states require prior registration or qualification of stock. Two states have no Blue Sky legislation; and legislation in other states may rely solely on simple "anti-fraud" (or "caveat vendor") provisions or on broker-dealer regulation or both, on the assumption that such measures are sufficient safeguards against "bucket shop" operators. A very substantial number of states, however, incorporate all three philosophies into their statutes, namely: anti-fraud; broker-dealer registration; and registration of securities.

Two principal "road-blocks" to uniform legislation have appeared. One is the natural and understandable reluctance of a state to change its particular Blue Sky philosophy. The other difficulty has been a bewildering variety of local statutory definitions and requirements, which have never before been adequately analyzed or catalogued.

The solution to these problems could only be found after intense research, both academic and practical, on a state-by-state basis. Only persons with specialized knowledge and wide experience in this field, with an adequate and trained staff available to work on a full-time basis, could accomplish this: assemble all the applicable laws, regulations, decisions, and practices to find whether definite patterns could be established, and whether uniform legislation was possible and desirable.

The writer approached Professor Louis Loss, of the Harvard Law School, former Associate General Counsel of the Securities and Exchange Commission, to enlist his aid. Dean David F. Cavers, who is head of the department of research in legislation at Harvard Law School, expressed deep interest in the subject, as did the Merrill Foundation for Advancement of Financial Knowledge, Inc., which implemented its interest by a grant to the Harvard Law School for a study.

Under the terms of the Merrill Foundation grant, the law school was to make an independent investigation of the law and practice in the Blue Sky field in every state, and to publish its findings and conclusions. Harvard Law School accepted the grant, and the project has been under way for about a year under the able

*Prepared by EDWARD L. SCHWARTZ, Massachusetts Commissioner on Uniform State Laws and Chairman, Subcommittee on Uniform Securities Act, National Conference of Commissioners on Uniform State Laws.

guidance of Professor Loss and his research assistant, Edward M. Cowett, assisted by an Advisory Committee consisting of representatives of the National Conference of Commissioners on Uniform State Laws, the National Association of Security Administrators, the Securities and Exchange Commission, the American Bar Association, the Investment Bankers Association, and the National Association of Securities Dealers, Inc., together with six prominent "Blue Sky" lawyers from Boston, New York, Chicago and Los Angeles.

The practice and law of each regulatory state have been studied by Professor Loss, Mr. Cowett and their staff, and thousands of cases have been read. A tentative draft of a proposed Uniform Securities Law has been drawn up by Harvard Law School, based upon the knowledge and experience culled from this research and from the statutes, judicial decisions and Attorney-General opinions of the various states, with the assistance of the Advisory Committee. The final draft and Harvard Law School's report will be published early in 1956, and will then be made available to all interested agencies, including, among others, the National Association of Securities Ad-

ministrators. It is generally assumed, however, that the final and official draft will evolve from the deliberations and action of the National Conference of Commissioners on Uniform State Laws.

Based upon the research and study in the Blue Sky field that have been made to date, it has become apparent that (1) a uniform statute encompassing each of the basic regulatory philosophies is both possible and practicable, and that (2) ample documentation and explanatory material, rooted in local law and practice, will be available for each of its provisions. Uniformity will be possible in the sense that the uniform statute can be so drawn that states interested in one or more of the three basic philosophies may accept those divisions of the statute which coincide with their requirements, knowing that such parts of the statute will be uniform in every state which enacts them into law.

Enactment of such uniform legislation would provide the minimum regulation of securities deemed desirable and necessary by each of the enacting states, would reduce the expense of issuing securities, and should eliminate much of the uncertainty and confusion from this area of the law.

Section VIII

DIRECTORY OF THE STATES, COMMONWEALTHS AND TERRITORIES

1. State Pages
2. Rosters of State Officials and Directory of State Legislators

1

State Pages

T HE following pages present individual summaries on the several
    states, commonwealths and territories. Included are listings of certain
of the executive officials, the Chief Justices of the Supreme Courts, officers of the legislatures, and members of the Commissions on Interstate
Cooperation. Each page concludes with a brief set of statistics for the
state concerned.

Listings of all officials are as of December, 1955, except that elective
officers of the executive branch chosen in the November, 1955, elections and inaugurated subsequently, are included.

Figures on general revenue and expenditures were furnished in most
cases by the United States Bureau of the Census, which coordinates
data from states to compensate for variations in terminology and record
procedures, making the statistics more nearly comparable. Census
Bureau figures of state populations also are used. Most of the data on
the following pages, however, were provided directly by agencies of the
states themselves.

Rosters of administrative officials classified by functions and a
directory of state legislators follow the state pages.

THE STATES OF THE UNION—HISTORICAL DATA

State	Capital	Source of State Lands	Date Organized as Territory	Date Admitted to Union	Chronological Order of Admission to Union
Alabama........	Montgomery	Mississippi Territory, 1798(a)	March 3, 1817	Dec. 14, 1819	22
Arizona........	Phoenix	Ceded by Mexico, 1848(b)	Feb. 24, 1863	Feb. 14, 1912	48
Arkansas......	Little Rock	Louisiana Purchase, 1803	March 2, 1819	June 15, 1836	25
California......	Sacramento	Ceded by Mexico, 1848	(c)	Sept. 9, 1850	31
Colorado.......	Denver	Louisiana Purchase, 1803(d)	Feb. 28, 1861	Aug. 1, 1876	38
Connecticut....	Hartford	Royal charter, 1662(e)	....	Jan. 9, 1788(f)	5
Delaware......	Dover	Swedish charter, 1638; English charter 1683(e)	....	Dec. 7, 1787(f)	1
Florida........	Tallahassee	Ceded by Spain, 1819	March 30, 1822	March 3, 1845	27
Georgia........	Atlanta	Charter, 1732, from George II to Trustees for Establishing the Colony of Georgia(e)	....	Jan. 2, 1788(f)	4
Idaho..........	Boise	Oregon Territory, 1848	March 3, 1863	July 3, 1890	43
Illinois........	Springfield	Northwest Territory, 1787	Feb. 3, 1809	Dec. 3, 1818	21
Indiana........	Indianapolis	Northwest Territory, 1787	May 7, 1800	Dec. 11, 1816	19
Iowa...........	Des Moines	Louisiana Purchase, 1803	June 12, 1838	Dec. 28, 1846	29
Kansas.........	Topeka	Louisiana Purchase, 1803(d)	May 30, 1854	Jan. 29, 1861	34
Kentucky......	Frankfort	Part of Virginia until admitted as State	(c)	June 1, 1792	15
Louisiana......	Baton Rouge	Louisiana Purchase, 1803(g)	March 24, 1804	April 8, 1812	18
Maine..........	Augusta	Part of Massachusetts until admitted as State	(c)	March 15, 1820	23
Maryland.......	Annapolis	Charter, 1632, from Charles I to Calvert(e)	....	April 28, 1788(f)	7
Massachusetts..	Boston	Charter to Massachusetts Bay Company, 1629(e)	....	Feb. 6, 1788(f)	6
Michigan.......	Lansing	Northwest Territory, 1787	Jan. 11, 1805	Jan. 26, 1837	26
Minnesota.....	St. Paul	Northwest Territory, 1787(h)	March 3, 1849	May 11, 1858	32
Mississippi.....	Jackson	Mississippi Territory(i)	April 17, 1798	Dec. 10, 1817	20
Missouri........	Jefferson City	Louisiana Purchase, 1803	June 4, 1812	Aug. 10, 1821	24
Montana.......	Helena	Louisiana Purchase, 1803(j)	May 26, 1864	Nov. 8, 1889	41
Nebraska.......	Lincoln	Louisiana Purchase, 1803	May 30, 1854	March 1, 1867	37
Nevada.........	Carson City	Ceded from Spain, 1848	March 2, 1861	Oct. 31, 1864	36
New Hampshire.	Concord	Grant from James I, 1622 and 1629(e)	....	June 21, 1788(f)	9
New Jersey.....	Trenton	Dutch settlement, 1618; English charter, 1664(e)	....	Dec. 18, 1787(f)	3
New Mexico....	Santa Fe	Ceded by Mexico, 1848(b)	Sept. 9, 1850	Jan. 6, 1912	47
New York.......	Albany	Dutch settlement, 1623; English control, 1664(e)	....	July 26, 1788(f)	11
North Carolina..	Raleigh	Charter, 1663, from Charles II(e)	....	Nov. 21, 1789(f)	12
North Dakota...	Bismarck	Louisiana Purchase, 1803(k)	March 2, 1861	Nov. 2, 1889	39
Ohio...........	Columbus	Northwest Territory, 1787	(c)	Feb. 19, 1803	17
Oklahoma......	Oklahoma City	Louisiana Purchase, 1803	May 2, 1890	Nov. 16, 1907	46
Oregon.........	Salem	Settlement and treaty with Britain, 1846	Aug. 14, 1848	Feb. 14, 1859	33
Pennsylvania....	Harrisburg	Grant from Charles II to William Penn, 1860(e)	....	Dec. 12, 1787(f)	2
Rhode Island...	Providence	Charter, 1663, from Charles II(e)	....	May 29, 1790(f)	13
South Carolina..	Columbia	Charter, 1663, from Charles II(e)	....	May 23, 1788(f)	8
South Dakota...	Pierre	Louisiana Purchase, 1803	March 2, 1861	Nov. 2, 1889	40
Tennessee......	Nashville	Part of North Carolina until admitted as State	(c)	June 1, 1796	16
Texas..........	Austin	Republic of Texas, 1845	(c)	Dec. 29, 1845	28
Utah...........	Salt Lake City	Ceded by Mexico, 1848	Sept. 9, 1850	Jan. 4, 1896	45
Vermont........	Montpelier	From lands of New Hampshire and New York	(c)	March 4, 1791	14
Virginia........	Richmond	Charter, 1609, from James I to London Company(e)	....	June 25, 1788(f)	10
Washington.....	Olympia	Oregon Territory, 1848	March 2, 1853	Nov. 11, 1889	42
West Virginia...	Charleston	Part of Virginia until admitted as State	(c)	June 20, 1863	35
Wisconsin......	Madison	Northwest Territory, 1787	April 20, 1836	May 29, 1848	30
Wyoming.......	Cheyenne	Louisiana Purchase, 1803(d,j)	July 25, 1868	July 10, 1890	44
Alaska..........	Juneau	Purchased from Russia, 1867	Aug. 24, 1912	....	..
Guam..........	Agana	Ceded from Spain, 1898	Aug. 1, 1950	....	..
Hawaii..........	Honolulu	Annexed, 1898	June 14, 1900	....	..
Puerto Rico....	San Juan	Ceded from Spain, 1898	March 2, 1917	July 25, 1952(l)	..
Virgin Islands...	Charlotte Amalie	Purchased from Denmark, January 17, 1917			..

(a) By the Treaty of Paris, 1783, England gave up claim to the 13 original colonies, and to all land within an area extending along the present Canadian border to the Lake of the Woods, down the Mississippi River to the 31st parallel, east to the Chattahoochie, down that river to the mouth of the Flint, east to the source of the St. Mary's, down that river to the ocean. Territory west of the Alleghenies was claimed by various States, but was eventually all ceded to the Nation. Thus, the major part of Alabama was acquired by the Treaty of Paris, but the lower portion from Spain in 1813.
(b) Portion of land obtained by Gadsden Purchase, 1853.
(c) No territorial status before admission to Union.
(d) Portion of land ceded by Mexico, 1848.

(e) One of the original 13 colonies.
(f) Date of ratification of U. S. Constitution.
(g) West Feliciana District (Baton Rouge) acquired from Spain, 1810, added to Louisiana, 1812.
(h) Portion of land obtained by Louisiana Purchase, 1803.
(i) See footnote (a). The lower portion of Mississippi was also acquired from Spain in 1813.
(j) Portion of land obtained from Oregon Territory, 1848.
(k) The northern portion and the Red River Valley was acquired by treaty with Great Britain in 1818.
(l) On this date Puerto Rico became a self-governing commonwealth by compact approved by the United States Congress and the voters of Puerto Rico as provided in U. S. Public Law 600 of 1950.

ALABAMA

Nicknames } ......The Cotton State
TheYellowhammerState
Motto ... *We Dare Defend Our Rights*
Flower...............Goldenrod
Capital City........Montgomery

Bird..............Yellowhammer
Song....................*Alabama*
Entered the Union
............December 14, 1819

GOVERNOR
JAMES E. FOLSOM

OFFICERS

Governor......................................JAMES E. FOLSOM
Lieutenant Governor........................W. GUY HARDWICK
Secretary of State............................MARY TEXAS HURT
Attorney General...........................JOHN M. PATTERSON
State Treasurer................................JOHN BRANDON
State Auditor.............................MRS. AGNES BAGGETT
State Comptroller.............................JOHN GRAVES

ALABAMA SUPREME COURT

Chief Justice..................................J. ED LIVINGSTON
Six Associate Members

LEGISLATURE

President of the Senate......W. GUY HARDWICK
President Pro Tem of the Senate
....................BROUGHTON LAMBERTH
Secretary of the Senate..........J. E. SPEIGHT

Speaker of the House............RANKIN FITE
Clerk of the House....ROBERT T. GOODWYN, JR.

COMMISSION ON INTERSTATE COOPERATION

Administrative Members

Senate Members

House Members

(To be appointed)

STATISTICS

Area (square miles)....................51,078
  Rank in Nation......................27th
Population (1954*).................3,121,000
  Rank in Nation (1954*)...............18th
  Density per square mile (1954*).........61.1
Number of Representatives in Congress......9†
Fiscal Year 1953 (ended September 30, 1953):
  General Revenue.............$243,530,000‡
  General Expenditures.........$253,876,000‡
State University.........University of Alabama
  Site............................Tuscaloosa

Capital City......................Montgomery
  Population (1950)..................106,525
  Rank in State.........................3rd
Largest City....................Birmingham
  Population (1950)..................326,037
Number of Cities over 10,000 Population.....20
Number of Counties.......................67

*Population estimates as of July 1, 1954, subject to revision.
†As allocated on basis of 1950 population figures.
‡U. S. Bureau of Census Report.

ARIZONA

Nickname. The Grand Canyon State   Bird...............Cactus Wren

Motto...*Ditat Deus* (God Enriches)   Song...................*Arizona*

Flower..........Saguaro Cactus   Entered the Union February 14, 1912

Capital City............Phoenix

OFFICERS

Governor .... ERNEST W. McFARLAND
Lieutenant Governor..........None
Secretary of State......WESLEY BOLIN
Attorney General ..ROBERT MORRISON
State Treasurer...E. T. WILLIAMS, JR.
State Auditor........JEWELL JORDAN

ARIZONA SUPREME COURT

Chief Justice.....ARTHUR T. LaPRADE
Four Associate Judges

HON. CLARENCE L. CARPENTER
Chairman of the Arizona
Legislative Council

GOVERNOR
ERNEST W. McFARLAND

LEGISLATURE

President of the Senate   Speaker of the House......HARRY S. RUPPELIUS
.... CLARENCE L. CARPENTER   Clerk of the House........MRS. LALLAH RUTH
Secretary of the Senate..MRS. LOUISE C. BRIMHALL

ARIZONA LEGISLATIVE COUNCIL
(Functions as Committee on Interstate Cooperation)

Senate Members	House Members
CLARENCE L. CARPENTER, *Chairman*	LOUIS B. ELLSWORTH, JR.
NEILSON BROWN	LORIN M. FARR
HIRAM S. CORBETT	MRS. LAURA McRAE
HAROLD C. GISS	PATRICK W. O'REILLY
JOE HALDIMAN, JR.	HARRY S. RUPPELIUS
ROBERT W. PROCHNOW	DAVID S. WINE

Director: JULES M. KLAGGE

STATISTICS

Area (square miles)...................113,575
   Rank in Nation.......................5th
Population (1954*)...................993,000
   Rank in Nation (1954*)...............35th
   Density per square mile (1954*)..........8.7
Number of Representatives in Congress......2†
Fiscal Year 1954 (ended June 30, 1954):
   General Revenue............$114,238,000‡
   General Expenditures.........$112,472,000‡
State University.........University of Arizona
   Site..............................Tucson

Capital City.........................Phoenix
   Population (1950)..................106,818
   Rank in State........................1st
Largest City.........................Phoenix
   Population (1950)..................106,818
Number of Cities over 10,000 Population......3
Number of Counties.......................14

---

*Population estimates as of July 1, 1954, subject to revision.
†As allocated on basis of 1950 population figures.
‡U. S. Bureau of Census report.

449

ARKANSAS

Nickname. The Land of Opportunity
Motto............*Regnat Populus*
(The People Rule)
Flower............Apple Blossom
Capital City.........Little Rock

Bird...............Mockingbird
Song..................*Arkansas*
Entered the Union...June 15, 1836

GOVERNOR
ORVAL E. FAUBUS

HON. L. WEEMS TRUSSELL
Chairman of the Commission
on Interstate Cooperation

OFFICERS

Governor..........ORVAL E. FAUBUS
Lieutenant Governor.NATHAN GORDON
Secretary of State.......C. G. HALL
Attorney General.......T. J. GENTRY
State Treasurer.....J. VANCE CLAYTON
State Auditor.......J. O. HUMPHREY
Comptroller.........KELLY CORNETT

ARKANSAS SUPREME COURT

Chief Justice..........LEE SEAMSTER
Six Associate Judges

LEGISLATURE

President of the Senate........NATHAN GORDON
President Pro Tem of the Senate
....................LAWRENCE BLACKWELL

Secretary of the Senate............JIM SNODDY
Speaker of the House........CHARLES F. SMITH
Clerk of the House..............NELSON COX

COMMISSION ON INTERSTATE COOPERATION

Administrative Members
ORVAL E. FAUBUS, *Governor*
JOE C. BARRETT

Senate Members
TOM ALLEN
Y. M. MACK
MARSHALL SHACKELFORD, JR.
Secretary: MARCUS HALBROOK

House Members
L. WEEMS TRUSSELL, *Chairman*
JACK OAKES
CHARLES F. SMITH

STATISTICS

Area (square miles)....................52,675
Rank in Nation.......................26th
Population (1954*)..................1,191,000
Rank in Nation (1954*)...............31st
Density per square mile (1954*).........36.3
Number Representatives in Congress........6†
Fiscal Year 1954 (ended June 30, 1954):
General Revenue............$154,783,000‡
General Expenditures........$148,652,000‡
State University........University of Arkansas
Site...........................Fayetteville

Capital City.....................Little Rock
Population (1950)..................102,213
Rank in State........................1st
Largest City......................Little Rock
Population (1950)..................102,213
Number of Cities over 10,000 Population.....12
Number of Counties......................75

*Population estimates as of July 1, 1954, subject to revision.
†As allocated on basis of 1950 population figures.
‡U. S. Bureau of Census report.

450

CALIFORNIA

Nickname.......The Golden State

Motto...*Eureka* (I Have Found It)

Flower............Golden Poppy

Bird.......California Valley Quail

Song.........*I Love You, California*

Entered the Union. September 9, 1850

Capital City.........Sacramento

OFFICERS

Governor.......GOODWIN J. KNIGHT
Lieutenant Governor
..............HAROLD J. POWERS
Secretary of State...FRANK M. JORDAN
Attorney General...EDMUND G. BROWN
State Treasurer...CHARLES G. JOHNSON
Auditor General...........(Vacancy)
State Controller..ROBERT C. KIRKWOOD

CALIFORNIA SUPREME COURT

Chief Justice.........PHIL S. GIBSON
Six Associate Justices

HON. W. C. JACOBSEN
Chairman of the Commission on
Interstate Cooperation

GOVERNOR
GOODWIN J. KNIGHT

LEGISLATURE

President of the Senate......HAROLD J. POWERS
President Pro Tem
  of the Senate...................BEN HULSE
Secretary of the Senate............J. A. BEEK

Speaker of the Assembly....LUTHER H. LINCOLN
Speaker Pro Tem of the Assembly
  ....THOMAS A. MALONEY
Chief Clerk of the Assembly..ARTHUR A. OHNIMUS

COMMISSION ON INTERSTATE COOPERATION

Administrative Members

W. C. JACOBSEN, *Chairman*
EDMUND G. BROWN
FRANK B. DURKEE
FRANK M. JORDAN
HAROLD J. POWERS

Senate Members

CHARLES BROWN
HUGH M. BURNS
RANDOLPH COLLIER
JAMES J. McBRIDE
LOUIS G. SUTTON

Assembly Members

MONTIVEL A. BURKE
CLAYTON A. DILLS
LLOYD W. LOWREY
R. H. McCOLLISTER
VINCENT THOMAS

Ex-officio Honorary Members: THE GOVERNOR; COMMISSIONER ON UNIFORM STATE LAWS,
MARTIN J. DINKELSPIEL

Executive Secretary: CHARLES V. DICK

STATISTICS

Area (square miles)...................156,740
  Rank in Nation........................2nd
Population (1954*)................12,554,000
  Rank in Nation (1954*)................2nd
  Density per square mile (1954*)........80.1
Number of Representatives in Congress.....30†
Fiscal Year 1954 (ended June 30, 1954):
  General Revenue...........$1,664,506,000‡
  General Expenditures.......$1,737,541,000‡
State University.......University of California
  Sites.............Berkeley and Los Angeles

Capital City.....................Sacramento
  Population (1950)..................137,572
  Rank in State........................6th
Largest City.....................Los Angeles
  Population (1950)................1,970,358
Number of Cities over 10,000 Population....105
Number of Counties.......................58

*Population estimates as of July 1, 1954, subject to revision,
†As allocated on basis of 1950 population figures.
‡U. S. Bureau of Census report.

451

COLORADO

Nickname....The Centennial State
Motto............*Nil Sine Numine*
  (Nothing Without the Deity)
Flower.Rocky Mountain Columbine
Capital City.............Denver

Bird...............Lark Bunting
Song.....*Where the Columbines Grow*
Entered the Union..August 1, 1876

GOVERNOR
EDWIN C. JOHNSON

HON. WM. O. LENNOX
Chairman of the Commission on
Interstate Cooperation

OFFICERS

Governor.........EDWIN C. JOHNSON
Lieutenant Governor
  ....STEPHEN L. R. MCNICHOLS
Secretary of State....GEORGE J. BAKER
Attorney General...DUKE W. DUNBAR
State Treasurer........EARL E. EWING
State Auditor......HOMER F. BEDFORD
State Controller.....JAMES A. NOONAN

COLORADO SUPREME COURT

Chief Justice.......WILBUR M. ALTER
Six Associate Judges

LEGISLATURE

President of the Senate...STEPHEN L. R. MCNICHOLS

President Pro Tem
  of the Senate.................FRANK L. GILL
Secretary of the Senate.......MILDRED CRESSWELL

Speaker of the House.........DAVID A. HAMIL
Clerk of the House..............LEE MATTIES

COMMISSION ON INTERSTATE COOPERATION

Administrative Members
DUKE W. DUNBAR
JAMES A. NOONAN
W. M. WILLIAMS
(2 vacancies)

Senate Members
DONALD G. BROTZMAN
VERNON A. CHEEVER
DONALD P. DUNKLEE
WALTER W. JOHNSON
MARTIN C. MOLHOLM

House Members
WM. O. LENNOX, *Chairman*
LUCILLE L. BECK
FRANK J. BURK
EDWARD LEHMAN
FREDERICK T. MCLAUGHLIN

Ex-officio Honorary Members: THE GOVERNOR, PRESIDENT OF SENATE, SPEAKER OF HOUSE

STATISTICS

Area (square miles)...................103,922
  Rank in Nation......................7th
Population (1954*)..................1,456,000
  Rank in Nation (1954*)................33rd
  Density per square mile (1954*)........14.0
Number of Representatives in Congress......4†
Fiscal Year 1954 (ended June 30, 1954):
  General Revenue............$183,440,000‡
  General Expenditures.........$187,234,000‡
State University........University of Colorado
Site............................Boulder

Capital City........................Denver
  Population (1950)..................415,786
  Rank in State........................1st
Largest City........................Denver
  Population (1950)..................415,786
Number of Cities over 10,000 Population.....10
Number of Counties.......................63

*Population estimates as of July 1, 1954, subject to revision.
†As allocated on basis of 1950 population figures.
‡U. S. Bureau of Census report.

452

CONNECTICUT

Nickname...The Constitution State

Motto.......*Qui Transtulit Sustinet*
    (He Who Transplanted
      Continues to Sustain)

        Capital City...........Hartford

Flower.........Mountain Laurel

Bird.....................Robin

Entered the Union. January 9, 1788

OFFICERS

Governor....................................ABRAHAM A. RIBICOFF
Lieutenant Governor.......................CHARLES W. JEWETT
Secretary of State..........................MILDRED P. ALLEN
Attorney General...........................JOHN J. BRACKEN
State Treasurer.............................JOHN OTTAVIANO
State Auditors.........................{RAYMOND I. LONGLEY / (Vacancy)
State Comptroller...........................FRED R. ZELLER

CONNECTICUT SUPREME COURT OF ERRORS

Chief Justice................................ERNEST A. INGLIS
        Four Associate Justices

GOVERNOR
ABRAHAM A. RIBICOFF

LEGISLATURE

President of the Senate .....CHARLES W. JEWETT

President Pro Tem
  of the Senate.............PATRICK J. WARD

Speaker of the House ....W. SHEFFIELD COWLES
Clerk of the House.............JOHN WASSUNG
Clerk of the Senate........ALFRED A. TOSCANO

COMMISSION ON INTERGOVERNMENTAL COOPERATION

Administrative Members	Senate Members	House Members
JOHN J. BRACKEN	PAUL AMENTA	ODILLA N. ARPIN
CHRISTY HANAS	BENJAMIN BARRINGER	ROBERT T. CAIRNS
FREDERICK SCHUCKMAN	FLORENCE D. FINNEY	MARJORIE D. FARMER,
JOHN J. TYNAN	ARTHUR H. HEALEY	*Vice-chairman*
(Vacancy)	W. DUANE LOCKARD	J. TYLER PATTERSON, JR.
		RAYMOND A. THAYER

Ex-officio Honorary Members: THE GOVERNOR, PRESIDENT OF SENATE, SPEAKER OF HOUSE
Director: HARRY H. LUGG

STATISTICS

Area (square miles).....................4,899
  Rank in Nation......................46th
Population (1954*)....................2,219,000
  Rank in Nation (1954*)................27th
  Density per square mile (1954*).......452.9
Number of Representatives in Congress......6†
Fiscal Year 1954 (ended June 30, 1954):
  General Revenue............$207,098,000‡
  General Expenditures........$191,930,000‡
State University......University of Connecticut
Site...............................Storrs
Capital City.......................Hartford

Population (1950)....................177,397
  Rank in State.........................1st
Largest City........................Hartford
  Population (1950)...................177,397
Number of Cities and Towns over 10,000
  Population.........................47§
Number of Counties......................8

*Population estimates as of July 1, 1954, subject to revision.
†As allocated on basis of 1950 population figures.
‡U. S. Bureau of Census report.
§Includes 26 towns over 10,000 population; excludes the
17 towns which are consolidated with cities for governmental
purposes.

453

DELAWARE

Nickname..... The Diamond State

Motto....... *Liberty and Independence*

Flower........... Peach Blossom

Capital City.............. Dover

Bird.......... Blue Hen Chicken

Song.............. *Our Delaware*

Entered the Union. December 7, 1787

GOVERNOR
J. CALEB BOGGS

HON. CLAYTON M. HOFF
Chairman of the Commission on
Interstate Cooperation

OFFICERS

Governor............J. CALEB BOGGS
Lieutenant Governor. JOHN W. ROLLINS
Secretary of State. JOHN N. McDOWELL
Attorney General
..........JOSEPH DONALD CRAVEN
State Treasurer. HOWARD H. DICKERSON
State Auditor ...... CLIFFORD E. HALL

DELAWARE
SUPREME COURT

Chief Justice
.......CLARENCE A. SOUTHERLAND
Two Associate Justices

LEGISLATURE

President of the Senate....... JOHN W. ROLLINS

President Pro Tem
of the Senate........... CHARLES G. MOORE

Speaker of the House........ JAMES R. QUIGLEY
Clerk of the House .... JOHN E. BABIARZ

Secretary of the Senate.... WILSON E. CAMPBELL

COMMISSION ON INTERSTATE COOPERATION

Administrative Members
CLAYTON M. HOFF, *Chairman*
JAMES H. BAXTER
RAYMOND B. PHILLIPS, *Secy.*

Senate Members
WILLIAM B. BEHEN
WALTER J. HOEY
ELWOOD F. MELSON, JR.

House Members
GEORGE T. MACKLIN
NELSON MASSEY
THOMAS C. ROWAN

Associate Members at Large: THE GOVERNOR, SECRETARY OF STATE, ATTORNEY GENERAL

STATISTICS

Area (square miles).....................1,978
  Rank in Nation.......................47th
Population (1954*)...................367,000
  Rank in Nation (1954*)...............46th
  Density per square mile (1954*)........185.5
Number of Representatives in Congress......1†
Fiscal Year 1954 (ended June 30, 1954):
  General Revenue.............$61,077,000‡
  General Expenditures.........$60,668,000‡
State University........ University of Delaware
  Site............................Newark

Capital City.........................Dover
  Population (1950)....................6,223
  Rank in State........................3rd
Largest City....................Wilmington
  Population (1950)..................110,356
Number of Cities over 10,000 Population......1
Number of Counties........................3

*Population estimates as of July 1, 1954, subject to revision.
†As allocated on basis of 1950 population figures.
‡U. S. Bureau of Census report.

454

FLORIDA

Nickname.....The Peninsula State
Motto...........*In God We Trust*
Flower..........Orange Blossom
Bird...............Mockingbird
Capital City.........Tallahassee

Song...........*The Swanee River*
Tree.......Sabal Palmetto Palm
Entered the Union..March 3, 1845

OFFICERS

Governor........... LeRoy Collins
Lieutenant Governor..........None
Secretary of State.......R. A. Gray
Attorney General..Richard W. Ervin
State Treasurer......J. Edwin Larson
State Auditor.........Bryan Willis
State Comptroller......Ray E. Green •

FLORIDA SUPREME COURT

Chief Justice........ E. Harris Drew
Six Associate Justices

Hon. Charles Tom Henderson
Chairman of the Commission on
Interstate Cooperation

Governor
LeRoy Collins

LEGISLATURE

President of the Senate ......W. Turner Davis
President Pro Tem
of the Senate...........George G. Tapper
Secretary of the Senate......Robert W. Davis

Speaker of the House ....Thomas E. David
Speaker Pro Tem of the House...Davis Atkinson
Clerk of the House........Mrs. Lamar Bledsoe

COMMISSION ON INTERSTATE COOPERATION

Administrative Members
Charles Tom Henderson,
Chairman
Richard W. Ervin
Joe Grotegut
Harry G. Smith
S. Sherman Weiss, *Secy.*

Senate Members
E. William Gautier
Dewey M. Johnson
Harry E. King
Fletcher Morgan
Verle A. Pope

House Members
W. H. Carmine
H. T. Cook
Fred O. Dickinson
J. J. Griffin
A. J. Musselman, Jr.

Ex-officio Honorary Members: The Governor, President of Senate, Speaker of House

STATISTICS

Area (square miles)....................54,262
 Rank in Nation......................25th
Population (1954*)..................3,524,000
 Rank in Nation (1954*)................16th
 Density per square mile (1954*).........64.9
Number of Representatives in Congress......8†
Fiscal Year 1954 (ended June 30, 1954):
 General Revenue............$341,713,000‡
 General Expenditures........$327,335,000‡
State University.......Florida State University
Site...........................Tallahassee

University of Florida..............Gainesville
Capital City.....................Tallahassee
 Population (1950)....................27,237
 Rank in State........................12th
Largest City......................Miami
 Population (1950)...................249,276
Number of Cities over 10,000 Population.....28
Number of Counties......................67

*Population estimates as of July 1, 1954, subject to revision.
†As allocated on basis of 1950 population figures.
‡U. S. Bureau of Census report.

455

GEORGIA

Nickname......The Cracker State

Motto. *Wisdom, Justice, and Moderation*

Flower............Cherokee Rose

Capital City............Atlanta

Bird (unofficial)...Brown Thrasher

Song.....................*Georgia*

Entered the Union. January 2, 1788

GOVERNOR
S. MARVIN GRIFFIN

HON. JOHN E. SHEFFIELD
Chairman of the Commission on
Interstate Cooperation

OFFICERS

Governor.........S. MARVIN GRIFFIN
Lieutenant Governor
..............S. ERNEST VANDIVER
Secretary of State
..............BEN W. FORTSON, JR.
Attorney General.......EUGENE COOK
State Treasurer..GEORGE B. HAMILTON
State Auditor.....B. E. THRASHER, JR.
Comptroller General. ZACK D. CRAVEY

GEORGIA
SUPREME COURT

Chief Justice.....WM. H. DUCKWORTH
Six Associate Justices

LEGISLATURE

President of the Senate.....S. ERNEST VANDIVER

President Pro Tem
of the Senate.........G. EVERETT MILLICAN

Speaker of the House.........MARVIN MOATE
Clerk of the House................JOE BOONE

Secretary of the Senate...GEORGE D. STEWART

COMMISSION ON INTERSTATE COOPERATION

Administrative Members	Senate Members	House Members
EUGENE D. COOK	EDGAR D. CLARY, JR.	JOHN E. SHEFFIELD, *Chairman*
ZACH D. CRAVEY	HOWELL HOLLIS	JOHN P. DRINKARD
BEN W. FORTSON, JR.	E. ROY LAMBERT	DENMARK GROOVER, *Secy.*
HOWARD TAMPLIN	W. HERSCHEL LOVETT	CLEVE MINCY
FRANK S. TWITTY	HOWARD OVERBY	GLENN S. PHILLIPS
	LAWTON W. URSREY	

Ex-officio Honorary Members: THE GOVERNOR, PRESIDENT OF SENATE, SPEAKER OF HOUSE

STATISTICS

Area (square miles)....................58,483
Rank in Nation......................20th
Population (1954*)..................3,660,000
Rank in Nation (1954*)................13th
Density per square mile (1954*).........62.6
Number of Representatives in Congress.....10†
Fiscal Year 1954 (ended June 30, 1954):
General Revenue............$323,508,000‡
General Expenditures........$339,996,000‡
State University..........University of Georgia
Site...............................Athens

Capital City........................Atlanta
Population (1950)..................331,314
Rank in State........................1st
Largest City........................Atlanta
Population (1950)..................331,314
Number of Cities over 10,000 Population.....23
Number of Counties.....................159

*Population estimates as of July 1, 1954, subject to revision.
†As allocated on basis of 1950 population figures.
‡U. S. Bureau of Census report.

IDAHO

Nickname........The Gem State

Motto..............*Esto Perpetua*
   (Mayest Thou Endure Forever!)

Flower.................Syringa

Capital City...............Boise

Bird.........Mountain Bluebird

Song.........*Here We Have Idaho*

Entered the Union....July 3, 1890

OFFICERS

Governor ....Robert E. Smylie
Lieutenant Governor.....................J. Berkeley Larsen
Secretary of State..........................Ira H. Masters
Attorney General ....Graydon W. Smith
State Treasurer............................Mrs. Ruth Moon
State Auditor.................................N. P. Nielson

IDAHO SUPREME COURT

Chief Justice..C. J. Taylor
                     Five Justices

GOVERNOR
Robert E. Smylie

LEGISLATURE

President of the Senate.....J. Berkeley Larsen
President Pro Tem of the Senate . Carl D. Irwin   Speaker of the House........R. H. Young, Jr.
Secretary of the Senate.... Robert H. Remaklus   Clerk of the House..............Pat Welker

COMMITTEE ON INTERSTATE COOPERATION

(To be appointed)

STATISTICS

Area (square miles)....................82,769
   Rank in Nation......................10th
Population (1954*)....................615,000
   Rank in Nation (1954*) 43rd
   Density per square mile (1954*)..........7.4
Number of Representatives in Congress......2†
Fiscal Year 1954 (ended June 30, 1954):
   General Revenue.............$64,831,000‡
   General Expenditures..........$69,349,000‡
State University...........University of Idaho
   Site...........................Moscow

Capital City.........................Boise
   Population (1950)..................34,393
   Rank in State.........................1st
Largest City.........................Boise
   Population (1950)..................34,393
Number of Cities over 10,000 Population......9
Number of Counties.......................44

*Population estimates as of July 1, 1954, subject to revision.
†As allocated on basis of 1950 population figures.
‡U. S. Bureau of Census report.

457

ILLINOIS

Nickname.......The Prairie State

Motto.*State Sovereignty-National Union*

Flower.............Native Violet

Capital City..........Springfield

Bird..................Cardinal

Song....................*Illinois*

Entered the Union.December 3,1818

GOVERNOR
WILLIAM G. STRATTON

HON. BERNICE T. VAN DER VRIES
Chairman of the Commission on
Intergovernmental Cooperation

OFFICERS

Governor...... WILLIAM G. STRATTON

Lieutenant Governor
..............JOHN WM. CHAPMAN

Secretary of State
..........CHARLES F. CARPENTIER

Attorney General.....LATHAM CASTLE

State Treasurer ...WARREN E. WRIGHT

State Auditor....ORVILLE E. HODGE

ILLINOIS SUPREME COURT

Chief Justice...... HARRY B. HERSHEY
Six Associate Justices

LEGISLATURE

President of the Senate.....JOHN WM. CHAPMAN

President Pro Tem
of the Senate............ARTHUR J. BIDWILL

Speaker of the House........WARREN L. WOOD

Clerk of the House...........FRED W. RUEGG

Secretary of the Senate...EDWARD H. ALEXANDER

COMMISSION ON INTERGOVERNMENTAL COOPERATION

Administrative Members	Senate Members	House Members
WILLIAM G. STRATTON, *Governor*	MARVIN F. BURT	BERNICE T. VAN DER VRIES, *Chairman*
RICHARD G. BROWNE	WILLIAM G. CLARK	
LATHAM CASTLE	DWIGHT P. FRIEDRICH	HECTOR A. BROUILLET
MORTON H. HOLLINGSWORTH	ROBERT J. GRAHAM	HUGH GREEN
JACK S. ISAKOFF, *Secy.*	LILLIAN A. SCHLAGENHAUF	ALBERT W. HACHMEISTER
	ALBERT SCOTT	W. K. KIDWELL
	ELBERT S. SMITH	RICHARD STENGEL
		FRANK C. WOLF

Ex-officio Honorary Members: PRESIDENT OF SENATE, SPEAKER OF HOUSE

STATISTICS

Area (square miles)....................55,935

Rank in Nation......................23rd

Population (1954*).................9,165,000

Rank in Nation (1954*)................4th

Density per square mile (1954*)........163.9

Number of Representatives in Congress.....25†

Fiscal Year 1954 (ended June 30, 1954):

General Revenue............$694,168,000‡

General Expenditures.........$649,395,000‡

State University..........University of Illinois

Site.............................Urbana

Capital City.....................Springfield

Population (1950)..................81,628

Rank in State........................5th

Largest City.........................Chicago

Population (1950).............3,620,962

Number of Cities over 10,000 Population.....72

Number of Counties.....................102

---

*Population estimates as of July 1, 1954, subject to revision.
†As allocated on basis of 1950 population figures.
‡U. S. Bureau of Census report.

458

INDIANA

Nickname......The Hoosier State
Motto..The Crossroads of America
Song.. *On the Banks of the Wabash*
                    Far Away
Capital City........Indianapolis

Bird ....Cardinal
Flower..................Zinnia
Entered the Union
    ....December 11, 1816

OFFICERS

Governor.........George N. Craig
Lieutenant Governor
    ....Harold W. Handley
Secretary of State
    ....Crawford F. Parker
Attorney General.Edwin K. Steers
State Treasurer........John Peters
State Auditor......Curtis E. Rardin

INDIANA SUPREME COURT

Chief Justice.......Arch N. Bobbitt
    Four Associate Judges

Hon. W. O. Hughes
Chairman of the Commission on
Interstate Cooperation

Governor
George N. Craig

LEGISLATURE

President of the Senate....Harold W. Handley
President Pro Tem
    of the Senate............John W. Van Ness
Speaker of the House........George S. Diener
Clerk of the House.........William Brummett
Secretary of the Senate......Albert E. Ferris

COMMISSION ON INTERSTATE COOPERATION

Administrative Members
Donald Clark
Frank Millis
Robert Reid
Edwin Steers, Jr.
Albert Wedeking

Senate Members
Peter A. Beczkiewicz
John M. Harlan
Charles M. Maddox
Robert P. O'Bannon
John W. Van Ness

House Members
W. O. Hughes, *Chairman*
Lawrence D. Baker
John A. Feighner
Joe A. Harris
Walter H. Maehling

Ex-officio Honorary Members: The Governor, President of Senate, Speaker of House
Secretary: Mrs. Louise Pope

STATISTICS

Area (square miles)....................36,205
    Rank in Nation......................37th
Population (1954*).................4,209,000
    Rank in Nation (1954*)...........11th
    Density per square mile (1954*)........116.3
Number of Representatives in Congress.....11 †
Fiscal Year 1954 (ended June 30, 1954):
    General Revenue.............$376,348,000 ‡
    General Expenditures........$393,842,000 ‡
State Universities
    Indiana University............Bloomington
    Purdue University...............Lafayette

Capital City.....................Indianapolis
    Population (1950).................427,173
    Rank in State..........................1st
Largest City.....................Indianapolis
    Population (1950).................427,173
Number of Cities over 10,000 Population.....39
Number of Counties 92

*Population estimates as of July 1, 1954, subject to revision.
†As allocated on basis of 1950 population figures.
‡U. S. Bureau of Census report.

459

IOWA

Nickname.....The Hawkeye State
Motto..*Our Liberties We Prize and Our Rights We Will Maintain*
Flower................Wild Rose
Capital City..........Des Moines

Bird..........Eastern Goldfinch
Song.....................*Iowa*
Entered the Union
.... December 28, 1846

GOVERNOR
LEO A. HOEGH

HON. GLADYS S. NELSON
Chairman of the Commission on
Interstate Cooperation

OFFICERS

Governor.............LEO A. HOEGH
Lieutenant Governor....LEO ELTHON
Secretary of State.MELVIN D. SYNHORST
Attorney General
.............DAYTON COUNTRYMAN
State Treasurer....M. L. ABRAHAMSON
State Auditor..........C. B. AKERS
State Comptroller.GLENN D. SARSFIELD

IOWA
SUPREME COURT

Chief Justice......ROBERT L. LARSON
Eight Associate Justices

LEGISLATURE

President of the Senate...........LEO ELTHON

President Pro Tem of the Senate..............DE VERE WATSON

Speaker of the House.......ARTHUR C. HANSON
Clerk of the House...........A. C. GUSTAFSON
Secretary of the Senate.......CARROLL A. LANE

COMMISSION ON INTERSTATE COOPERATION

Senate Members
TED D. CLARK
DUANE DEWEL
JANS DYKHOUSE
EDWARD J. McMANUS
CHARLES NELSON
GEORGE L. SCOTT
DEVERE WATSON
G. E. WHITEHEAD
(Vacancy)

House Members
GLADYS S. NELSON, *Chairman*
LAWRENCE FALVEY
VERN LISLE
EARL A. MILLER
EMIL L. NOVAK
CARL H. RINGGENBERG
W. H. TATE
FRANK R. THOMPSON
JACOB VAN ZWOL

STATISTICS

Area (square miles)....................56,045
  Rank in Nation.....................22nd
Population (1954*)..................2,638,000
  Rank in Nation (1954*)..............22nd
  Density per square mile (1954*).........47.1
Number of Representatives in Congress......8†
Fiscal Year 1954 (ended June 30, 1954):
  General Revenue............$267,786,000‡
  General Expenditures.........$259,663,000‡
State University...........University of Iowa
  Site............................Iowa City

Capital City.....................Des Moines
  Population (1950)................177,965
  Rank in State........................1st
Largest City.....................Des Moines
  Population (1950)................177,965
Number of Cities over 10,000 Population.....23
Number of Counties......................99

*Population estimates as of July 1, 1954, subject to revision
†As allocated on basis of 1950 population figures.
‡U.S. Bureau of Census Report.

KANSAS

Nickname. . . . The Sunflower State
Motto. . . . .*Ad Astra per Aspera*
(To the Stars Through Difficulties)
Flower. . . . . .Native Sunflower
Capital City. . . . . .Topeka

Bird. . . . . . . .Western Meadowlark
Song. . . . .*Home on the Range*
Animal. . . . . . . .American Buffalo
Entered the Union.January 29, 1861

OFFICERS

Governor. . . . . FRED HALL
Lieutenant Governor.JOHN B. McCUISH
Secretary of State. .PAUL R. SHANAHAN
Attorney General. .HAROLD R. FATZER
State Treasurer. . .RICHARD T. FADELY
State Auditor. . . . . .GEORGE ROBB
State Controller. . . . . . .ROY SHAPIRO

KANSAS
SUPREME COURT

Chief Justice. . . . . . . .WM. W. HARVEY
Six Associate Justices

HON. JOHN B. McCUISH
Chairman of the Commission on
Interstate Cooperation

GOVERNOR
FRED HALL

LEGISLATURE

President of the Senate. . . . . .JOHN B. McCUISH
President Pro Tem of the Senate..PAUL R. WUNSCH
Secretary of the Senate
. . . . .SIDNEY MARGARET GARDINER

Speaker of the House. . . . . .ROBERT H. JENNISON
Clerk of the House. . . . . .FRANK GARRETT

COMMISSION ON INTERSTATE COOPERATION

Administrative Members
FRED HALL, *Governor*
LEONARD H. AXE
HAROLD R. FATZER
PAUL R. SHANAHAN
NEIL L. TOEDMAN

Senate Members
JOHN McCUISH, *Chairman*
JOHN W. CRUTCHER
LAWRENCE GIBSON
CHRIS GREEN
I. E. NICKELL
Secretary: FRED E. GULICK

House Members
JOHN ADAMS
A. E. ANDERSON
SAM CHARLSON
ROBERT H. JENNISON,
Vice-chairman
BEN MARSHALL

STATISTICS

Area (square miles). 82,108
Rank in Nation. 12th
Population (1954*). 2,016,000
Rank in Nation (1954*). 29th
Density per square mile (1954*). 24.6
Number of Representatives in Congress. . . . . .6†
Fiscal Year 1954 (ended June 30, 1954):
General Revenue. . . . .$200,219,000‡
General Expenditures. . . . .$199,838,000‡
State University. . . . . .University of Kansas
Site. . . . . .Lawrence

Capital City. . . . . .Topeka
Population (1950). 78,791
Rank in State. 3rd
Largest City. . . . . .Wichita
Population (1950). 168,279
Number of Cities over 10,000 Population. 25
Number of Counties. 105

*Population estimates as of July 1, 1954, subject to revision.
†As allocated on basis of 1950 population figures.
‡U. S. Bureau of Census report.

461

KENTUCKY

Nickname..... The Bluegrass State

Motto......... *United We Stand,*
Divided We Fall

Flower................Goldenrod

Capital City...........Frankfort

Bird...................Cardinal

Song........ *My Old Kentucky Home*

Entered the Union.... June 1, 1792

GOVERNOR
ALBERT B. CHANDLER

HARRY LEE WATERFIELD
Chairman of the Legislative
Research Commission

OFFICERS

Governor....... ALBERT B. CHANDLER
Lieutenant Governor
.... HARRY LEE WATERFIELD
Secretary of State . THELMA L. STOVALL
Attorney General..... JO M. FERGUSON
State Treasurer.... HENRY H. CARTER
State Auditor..... MARY LOUISE FOUST
State Comptroller..... BILLY S. SMITH

KENTUCKY COURT OF APPEALS

Chief Justice....... JAMES B. MILLIKEN
Six Associate Justices

LEGISLATURE

President of the Senate.. HARRY LEE WATERFIELD
President Pro Tem of the Senate . ALVIN KIDWELL*   Speaker of the House.... CHARLES W. BURNLEY*
Chief Clerk of the Senate.THOMAS R. UNDERWOOD*   Clerk of the House.........J. ERVIN SANDERS*
*New officers to be elected in January, 1956.

LEGISLATIVE RESEARCH COMMISSION

(Functions as Commission on Interstate Cooperation)

Administrative Members
HARRY LEE WATERFIELD,
Chairman

Senate Members*

*Members to be designated in January, 1956.

House Members*

STATISTICS

Area (square miles)....................39,864
  Rank in Nation.......................36th
Population (1954*)...................2,995,000
  Rank in Nation (1954*)................20th
  Density per square mile (1954*).........75.1
Number of Representatives in Congress......8†
Fiscal Year 1954 (ended June 30, 1954):
  General Revenue............$205,916,000‡
  General Expenditures.........$216,722,000‡
State University....... University of Kentucky
  Site...........................Lexington

Capital City......................Frankfort
  Population (1950)...................18,104
  Rank in State.........................9th
Largest City......................Louisville
  Population (1950)................369,129
Number of Cities over 10,000 Population.....15
Number of Counties....................120

*Population estimates as of July 1, 1954, subject to revision.
†As allocated on basis of 1950 population figures.
‡U. S. Bureau of Census report.

462

LOUISIANA

Nickname.......The Pelican State

Motto...*Union, Justice and Confidence*

Flower...............Magnolia

Capital City........Baton Rouge

Bird (unofficial)
........Eastern Brown Pelican

Song............*Song of Louisiana*

Entered the Union...April 8, 1812

OFFICERS

Governor........ROBERT F. KENNON

Lieutenant Governor..C. E. BARHAM

Secretary of State
...........WADE O. MARTIN, JR.

Attorney General...FRED S. LeBLANC

State Treasurer.......A. P. TUGWELL

State Auditor.......ALLISON R. KOLB

SUPREME COURT OF LOUISIANA

Chief Justice.......JOHN B. FOURNET

Six Associate Justices

HON. CHAS. E. TOOKE, JR.
Chairman of the Commission on
Interstate Cooperation

GOVERNOR
ROBERT F. KENNON

LEGISLATURE

President of the Senate.........C. E. BARHAM

President Pro Tem of the Senate
................ROBERT A. AINSWORTH, JR.

Secretary of the Senate.....ROBERT A. GILBERT

Speaker of the House...........C. C. AYCOCK

Clerk of the House............W. CLEGG COLE

COMMISSION ON INTERSTATE COOPERATION

Administrative Members

ELMER D. CONNER
GRAYDON KITCHENS
ALLISON R. KOLB
FRED S. LeBLANC
A. P. TUGWELL

Senate Members

CHARLES E. TOOKE, JR. *Chairman*
ROBERT A. AINSWORTH, JR.
M. ELOI GIRARD
JOHN B. HUNTER, JR.
B. H. ROGERS
JAMES D. SPARKS

House Members

J. ALFRED BEGNAUD
C. CYRIL BROUSSARD
ALBERT B. KOORIE
EDGAR H. LANCASTER, JR.
JASPER K. SMITH

Ex-officio Honorary Members: THE GOVERNOR, PRESIDENT OF SENATE, SPEAKER OF HOUSE

STATISTICS

Area (square miles)...................45,162

Rank in Nation......................31st

Population (1954*)................2,924,000

Rank in Nation (1954*)................21st

Density per square mile (1954*)........64.7

Number of Representatives in Congress.....8†

Fiscal Year 1954 (ended June 30, 1954):

General Revenue............$452,676,000‡

General Expenditures........$429,868,000‡

State University......Louisiana State University
Agricultural and Mechanical College

Site.........................Baton Rouge

Capital City.................Baton Rouge

Population (1950)..................125,629

Rank in State........................3rd

Largest City....................New Orleans

Population (1950)..................570,445

Number of Cities over 10,000 Population.....17

Number of Parishes....................64

*Population estimates as of July 1, 1954, subject to revision.
†As allocated on basis of 1950 population figures.
‡U. S. Bureau of Census Report.

463

MAINE

Nickname.....The Pine Tree State

Motto...........*Dirigo* (I Guide)

Flower......Pine Cone and Tassel

Bird.................Chickadee

Song..........*State of Maine Song*

Entered the Union. March 15, 1820

Capital City............Augusta

GOVERNOR
EDMUND S. MUSKIE

HON. WILLIAM R. COLE
Chairman of the Commission on
Interstate Cooperation

OFFICERS

Governor........ EDMUND S. MUSKIE
Lieutenant Governor..........None
Secretary of State.....HAROLD I. GOSS
Attorney General...FRANK F. HARDING
State Treasurer.FRANK S. CARPENTER
State Auditor.......FRED M. BERRY
State Controller...HARLAN H. HARRIS

MAINE SUPREME JUDICIAL COURT

Chief Justice.......RAYMOND FELLOWS
Five Associate Justices

LEGISLATURE

President of the Senate.....ROBERT N. HASKELL
Secretary of the Senate...CHESTER T. WINSLOW

Speaker of the House....WILLIS A. TRAFTON, JR.
Clerk of the House..........HARVEY R. PEASE

COMMISSION ON INTERSTATE COOPERATION

Administrative Members
HAROLD I. GOSS
SUMNER T. PIKE
DAVID H. STEVENS

Senate Members
WILLIAM R. COLE, *Chairman*
ALLAN WOODCOCK, JR.

House Members
MAURICE D. ANDERSON
JESSE P. FULLER
NORMAN R. ROGERSON

Ex-officio Honorary Members: THE GOVERNOR, PRESIDENT OF SENATE, SPEAKER OF HOUSE

STATISTICS

Area (square miles)....................32,562
   Rank in Nation.......................38th
Population (1954*)...................930,000
   Rank in Nation (1954*)................36th
   Density per square mile (1954*)........28.6
Number of Representatives in Congress......3†
Fiscal Year 1954 (ended June 30, 1954):
   General Revenue..............$81,721,240‡
   General Expenditures.........$84,142,894‡
State University..........University of Maine
   Site ....Orono

Capital City........................Augusta
   Population (1950)...................20,913
   Rank in State..................... .....6th
Largest City.......................Portland
   Population (1950).................77,634
Number of Cities and Towns over 10,000
   Population...........................13
Number of Counties.....................16

*Population estimates as of July 1, 1954, subject to revision.
†As allocated on basis of 1950 population figures.
‡Maine Bureau of Accounts and Controls.

464

MARYLAND

Nickname.....The Old Line State
Motto........*Scuto Bonae Voluntatis*
Tuae Coronasti Nos
(With the Shield of Thy Good-will
Thou Hast Covered Us)
Capital City...........Annapolis

Flower..........Black-eyed Susan
Bird............Baltimore Oriole
Song.......*Maryland, My Maryland*
Entered the Union..April 28, 1788

OFFICERS

Governor....THEODORE R. McKELDIN
Lieutenant Governor...........None
Secretary of State
............BLANCHARD RANDALL
Attorney General
............C. FERDINAND SYBERT
State Treasurer.....HOOPER S. MILES
State Auditor........JAMES L. BENSON
State Comptroller..J. MILLARD TAWES

MARYLAND
COURT OF APPEALS

Chief Judge.....FREDERICK W. BRUNE
Four Associate Judges

HON. BLANCHARD RANDALL, JR.
Chairman of the Commission on
Interstate Cooperation

GOVERNOR
THEODORE R. McKELDIN

LEGISLATURE

President of the Senate.....LOUIS L. GOLDSTEIN
Secretary of the Senate.....C. ANDREW SHAAB

Speaker of the House...........JOHN C. LUBER
Chief Clerk of the House.GEORGE W. OWINGS, JR.

COMMISSION ON INTERSTATE COOPERATION

Administrative Members
BLANCHARD RANDALL, JR.,
Chairman
JOSEPH O'C. McCUSKER, *Secy.*
ALVIN I. PASAREW
JAMES G. RENNIE
C. FERDINAND SYBERT

Senate Members
GEORGE W. DELLA
STANFORD HOFF
PHILLIP H. GOODMAN
JOHN CLARENCE NORTH
EDWARD S. NORTHRUP

House Members
MAURICE CARDIN
S. FENTON HARRIS
GUY JOHNSON
MRS. MYRTLE A. POLK
E. HOMER WHITE, JR.

Ex-officio Honorary Members: THE GOVERNOR, PRESIDENT OF SENATE, SPEAKER OF HOUSE

STATISTICS

Area (square miles).....................9,881
  Rank in Nation.....................41st
Population (1954*)..................2,602,000
  Rank in Nation (1954*)..............23rd
  Density per square mile (1954*)........263.3
Number of Representatives in Congress......7†
Fiscal Year 1954 (ended June 30, 1954):
  General State Revenue........$229,723,000‡
  General Expenditures.........$254,296,000‡
State University........University of Maryland
  Site.............Baltimore and College Park

Capital City.....................Annapolis
  Population (1950)...................10,047
  Rank in State......................11th
Largest City.....................Baltimore
  Population (1950)................949,708
Number of Cities over 10,000 Population.....11
Number of Counties......................23

*Population estimates as of July 1, 1954, subject to revision.
†As allocated on basis of 1950 population figures.
‡U. S. Bureau of Census report.

465

MASSACHUSETTS

Nickname.........The Bay State
Motto........*Ense Petit Placidam*
             Sub Libertate Quietem
(By the Sword We Seek Peace,
  but Peace Only Under Liberty)
             Capital City.............Boston

Flower...............Mayflower
Bird...................Chickadee
Song (unofficial)......*Massachusetts*
Tree.......................Elm
Entered the Union.February 6, 1788

GOVERNOR
CHRISTIAN A. HERTER

HON. RICHARD H. LEE
Chairman of the Commission on
Interstate Cooperation

OFFICERS

Governor....... CHRISTIAN A. HERTER
Lieutenant Governor
.............SUMNER G. WHITTIER
Secretary of State..EDWARD J. CRONIN
Attorney General....GEORGE FINGOLD
State Treasurer.....JOHN F. KENNEDY
State Auditor.....THOMAS J. BUCKLEY
State Comptroller
.............FRED A. MONCEWICZ

MASSACHUSETTS SUPREME JUDICIAL COURT

Chief Justice........STANLEY E. QUA
       Six Associate Justices

LEGISLATURE

President of the Senate....RICHARD I. FURBUSH
Clerk of the Senate........IRVING N. HAYDEN

Speaker of the House.......MICHAEL F. SKERRY
Clerk of the House.......LAWRENCE R. GROVE

COMMISSION ON INTERSTATE COOPERATION

Administrative Members
FRED A. BLAKE
ANTHONY A. BONZAGNI
W. NELSON BUMP
ALAN McCLENNAN
EDWARD L. SCHWARTZ
SUMNER G. WHITTIER

Senate Members
RICHARD H. LEE, *Chairman*
MAURICE A. DONAHUE
HAROLD R. LUNDGREN

House Members
JAMES F. CONDON
HOLLIS M. GOTT
GEORGE GREENE
CHARLES F. HOLMAN
RICHARD L. HULL
JOHN J. TOOMEY

Secretary: PHILIP M. MARKLEY

STATISTICS

Area (square miles).....................7,867
  Rank in Nation......................44th
Population (1954*)....................4,954,000
  Rank in Nation (1954*)...............9th
Density per square mile (1954*).......629.7
Number of Representatives in Congress.....14†
Fiscal Year 1954 (ended June 30, 1954):
  General Revenue............$447,076,000‡
  General Expenditures........$523,495,000‡
Institution of Higher Education
  ....University of Massachusetts
Site............................Amherst

Capital City..........................Boston
  Population (1950).................801,444
  Rank in State.......................1st
Largest City..........................Boston
  Population (1950).................801,444
Number of Cities and Towns over 10,000
  Population.........................88§
Number of Counties.......................14

*Population estimates as of July 1, 1954, subject to revision.
†As allocated on basis of 1950 population figures.
‡U. S. Bureau of Census report.
§Includes 49 towns over 10,000 population.

MICHIGAN

Nickname....The Wolverine State
Motto......*Si Quaeris Peninsulam Amoenam Circumspice*
(If You Seek a Pleasant Peninsula, Look Around You)
Capital City.............Lansing

Flower...........Apple Blossom
Bird......................Robin
Song (unofficial)
.........*Michigan, My Michigan*
Entered the Union.January 26, 1837

OFFICERS

Governor.......G. MENNEN WILLIAMS
Lieutenant Governor..PHILIP A. HART
Secretary of State......JAMES M. HARE
Attorney General
............THOMAS M. KAVANAGH
State Treasurer....SANFORD A. BROWN
Auditor General....VICTOR TARGONSKI
State Controller.....JAMES W. MILLER

MICHIGAN SUPREME COURT

Chief Justice......JOHN R. DETHMERS
Seven Associate Justices

HON. PHILIP A. HART
Chairman of the Commission on
Interstate Cooperation

GOVERNOR
G. MENNEN WILLIAMS

LEGISLATURE

President of the Senate.........PHILIP A. HART
President Pro Tem
of the Senate.............HARRY F. HITTLE
Secretary of the Senate.........FRED I. CHASE

Speaker of the House...WADE VAN VALKENBURG
Speaker Pro Tem
of the House.........WILLIAM S. BROOMFIELD
Clerk of the House.........NORMAN E. PHILLEO

COMMISSION ON INTERSTATE COOPERATION

Administrative Members
PHILIP A. HART, *Chairman*
THOMAS M. KAVANAGH
JAMES W. MILLER
JAMES C. ALLEN
JOHN H. MCCARTHY

Senate Members
HARRY F. HITTLE
ELMER R. PORTER
DON VANDER WERP
HASKELL L. NICHOLS
PERRY W. GREENE

House Members
ARNELL ENGSTROM
T. JEFFERSON HOXIE
ROLLO G. CONLIN
HARRY J. PHILLIPS
ED CAREY

Ex-officio Honorary Members: THE GOVERNOR, PRESIDENT OF SENATE, SPEAKER OF HOUSE
Secretary: MRS. MELITA LANNING

STATISTICS

Area (square miles)...................57,022‡
Rank in Nation......................21st
Population (1954*).................7,024,000
Rank in Nation (1954*)................7th
Density per square mile (1954*).......123.2
Number of Representatives in Congress.....18†
Fiscal Year 1954 (ended June 30, 1954):
General Revenue.............$784,137,000‡
General Expenditures........$791,849,000‡
State University........University of Michigan
Site.............................Ann Arbor
Michigan State College.........East Lansing

Capital City.........................Lansing
Population (1950)...................92,129
Rank in State..........................6th
Largest City.........................Detroit
Population (1950)...............1,849,568
Number of Cities over 10,000 Population.....55
Number of Counties.......................83

---

*Population estimates as of July 1, 1954, subject to revision.
†As allocated on basis of 1950 population figures.
‡U. S. Bureau of Census report.

MINNESOTA

Nickname......The Gopher State

Motto...........*L'Etoile du Nord*
(The Star of the North)

Flower..........Moccasin Flower

Capital City.............St. Paul

Bird (unofficial).American Goldfinch

Song.............*Hail! Minnesota*

Entered the Union..May 11, 1858

GOVERNOR
ORVILLE L. FREEMAN

HON. HARRY SIEBEN
Chairman of the Commission on
Interstate Cooperation

OFFICERS

Governor........ORVILLE L. FREEMAN
Lieutenant Governor
.................KARL F. ROLVAAG
Secretary of State..JOSEPH L. DONOVAN
Attorney General.........MILES LORD
State Treasurer......ARTHUR HANSEN
State Auditor.........STAFFORD KING

MINNESOTA SUPREME COURT

Chief Justice.........ROGER L. DELL
Six Associate Justices

LEGISLATURE

President of the Senate.......KARL F. ROLVAAG

President Pro Tem of
the Senate.......................VAL IMM

Secretary of the Senate..........H. Y. TORREY

Speaker of the House.............A. I. JOHNSON
Clerk of the House..........GEORGE H. LEAHY

COMMISSION ON INTERSTATE COOPERATION

Administrative Members
HARRY SIEBEN, *Chairman*
JAMES W. CLARK
ROBERT GARRITY
GEORGE A. SELKE

Senate Members
VAL IMM
B. G. NOVAK
GORDON ROSENMEIER
DONALD SINCLAIR
THOMAS P. WELCH

House Members
FRED A. CINA
JOHN A. HARTLE
LEO D. MOSIER
JOSEPH PRIFREL, JR.
D. D. WOZNIAK

Ex-officio Honorary Members: THE GOVERNOR, PRESIDENT OF SENATE, SPEAKER OF HOUSE
Secretary: ARTHUR NAFTALIN

STATISTICS

Area (square miles)....................80,009
   Rank in Nation.......................13th
Population (1954*)..................3,103,000
   Rank in Nation (1954*)...............19th
   Density per square mile (1954*).........38.8
Number of Representatives in Congress......9†
Fiscal Year 1954 (ended June 30, 1954):
   General Revenue............$353,193,000‡
   General Expenditures........$327,474,000‡
State University........University of Minnesota
   Site...........................Minneapolis

Capital City ....St. Paul
   Population (1950).................311,349
   Rank in State........................2nd
Largest City.....................Minneapolis
   Population (1950)................521,718
Number of Cities over 10,000 Population.....22
Number of Counties......................87

*Population estimates as of July 1, 1954, subject to revision.
†As allocated on basis of 1950 population figures.
‡U. S. Bureau of Census report.

MISSISSIPPI

Nickname.....The Magnolia State
Motto............*Virtute et Armis*
　　　　(By Valor and Arms)
Flower...............Magnolia
Capital City...........Jackson

Bird...............Mockingbird
Song................*Mississippi*
Entered the Union
...........December 10, 1817

OFFICERS

Governor ....JAMES P. COLEMAN
Lieutenant Governor.CARROLL GARTIN
Secretary of State...HEBER A. LADNER
Attorney General ...JOE T. PATTERSON
State Treasurer.......R. D. MORROW
State Auditor..........E. B. GOLDING
State Comptroller.....JOE W. LATHAM

MISSISSIPPI SUPREME COURT

Chief Justice......HARVEY McGEHEE
　Five Associate Justices

HON. JAMES McCLURE, JR.
Chairman of the Commission on
Interstate Cooperation

GOVERNOR
JAMES P. COLEMAN

LEGISLATURE*

President of the Senate.......CARROLL GARTIN
President Pro Tem of the Senate.....J. O. CLARK
Secretary of the Senate
...............MRS. HALLA MAY PATTISON

Speaker of the House..........WALTER SILLERS
Clerk of the House.............ROMAN KELLY

*New officers to be elected in January, 1956.

COMMISSION ON INTERSTATE COOPERATION

Administrative Member
JAMES P. COLEMAN, *Governor*

Senate Members*
JAMES McCLURE, JR., *Chairman*
LAWRENCE ADAMS
ED DeMOVILLE
STANTON HALL
BRINKLEY MORTON
Secretary: DOROTHY GRAHAM

House Members*
JOEL BLASS
WALTER J. PHILLIPS
CLARENCE PIERCE
WILLIAM O. SEMMES
WILLIAM WINTER

*New members to be designated in January, 1956.

STATISTICS

Area (square miles)..................47,248
　Rank in Nation.....................30th
Population (1954*)................2,204,000
　Rank in Nation (1954*)...............28th
　Density per square mile (1954*).........46.6
Number of Representatives in Congress......6†
Fiscal Year 1954 (ended June 30, 1954):
　General Revenue.............$184,672,000‡
　General Expenditures.........$187,080,000‡
State University.......University of Mississippi
　Site.. ....Oxford

Capital City........................Jackson
　Population (1950)....................98,271
　Rank in State........................1st
Largest City........................Jackson
　Population (1950)....................98,271
Number of Cities over 10,000 Population.....15
Number of Counties......................82

*Population estimates as of July 1, 1954, subject to revision.
†As allocated on basis of 1950 population figures.
‡U. S. Bureau of Census report.

469

MISSOURI

Nickname.....The Show-Me State

Motto. *Salus Populi Suprema Lex Esto*
(Let the Welfare of the People
Be the Supreme Law)

Capital City.......Jefferson City

Flower............?......Hawthorn
Tree.................Dogwood
Bird..................Bluebird
Song............*Missouri Waltz*
Entered the Union..August 10,1821

GOVERNOR
PHIL M. DONNELLY

HON. EDWARD V. LONG
Chairman of the Commission on
Interstate Cooperation

OFFICERS

Governor.........PHIL M. DONNELLY
Lieutenant Governor
..............JAMES T. BLAIR, JR.
Secretary of State
............WALTER H. TOBERMAN
Attorney General....JOHN M. DALTON
State Treasurer.GEORGE HUBERT BATES
State Auditor......HASKELL HOLMAN

MISSOURI SUPREME COURT

Chief Justice.........C. A. LEEDY, JR.
Six Associate Justices

LEGISLATURE

President of the Senate.....JAMES T. BLAIR, JR.

President Pro Tem
of the Senate.............EDWARD V. LONG

Secretary of the Senate.......JOSEPH A. BAUER

Speaker of the House............ROY HAMLIN
Chief Clerk of the House.........AUSTIN HILL

COMMISSION ON INTERSTATE COOPERATION

Administrative Members
NEWTON ATTERBURY
TYRE W. BURTON
JOHN M. DALTON
H. H. MOBLEY
M. E. MORRIS

Senate Members
EDWARD V. LONG, *Chairman*
HARTWELL G. CRAIN
E. GARY DAVIDSON
FLOYD R. GIBSON
JOHN W. NOBLE
GEORGE A. SPENCER

House Members
JOHN GRIFFIN
ROY HAMLIN
RAYMOND B. HOPFINGER
FLOYD L. SNYDER, SR.
CHRISTIAN F. STIPP
WILLIAM M. TURPIN

Ex-officio Honorary Members: THE GOVERNOR, PRESIDENT OF SENATE, SPEAKER OF HOUSE
Secretary: WILLIAM R. NELSON

STATISTICS

Area (square miles)....................69,226
    Rank in Nation.......................17th
Population (1954*)..................4,154,000
    Rank in Nation (1954*)................12th
    Density per square mile (1954*).........60.0
Number of Representatives in Congress.....11 †
Fiscal Year 1954 (ended June 30, 1954):
    General Revenue............$349,631,000 ‡
    General Expenditures........$325,849,000 ‡
State University........University of Missouri
    Site...........................Columbia

Capital City....................Jefferson City
    Population (1950)....................25,099
    Rank in State.........................9th
Largest City.........................St. Louis
    Population (1950)..................856,796
Number of Cities over 10,000 Population.....28
Number of Counties......................114

*Population estimates as of July 1, 1954, subject to revision.
†As allocated on basis of 1950 population figures.
‡U. S. Bureau of Census report.

470

MONTANA

Nickname.....The Treasure State
Motto.*Oro y Plata* (Gold and Silver)
Flower...............Bitterroot
Bird...............Meadowlark
Capital City.............Helena

Song..................*Montana*

Entered the Union
.............November 8, 1889

OFFICERS

Governor.......................................J. Hugo Aronson
Lieutenant Governor........................George M. Gosman
Secretary of State...................................S. C. Arnold
Attorney General..............................Arnold H. Olsen
State Treasurer...............................Mrs. Edna Hinman
State Auditor....................................John J. Holmes
State Controller.................................A. M. Johnson

MONTANA
SUPREME COURT

Chief Justice.......................................Hugh R. Adair
Four Associate Justices

GOVERNOR
J. Hugo Aronson

LEGISLATURE

President of the Senate.....George M. Gosman
President Pro Tem of the Senate
.......................Fred L. Robinson
Secretary of the Senate.....Frank Hazelbaker

Speaker of the House.........Leo C. Graybill
Chief Clerk of the House.......Wm. P. Pilgeram

COMMISSION ON INTERGOVERNMENTAL COOPERATION

Administrative Members
(To be appointed)

Senate Members
Henry H. Anderson
Kenneth Cole
Andrew Dahl
William A. Groff
Earl P. Moritz
H. A. Murphy
Paul Working

House Members
Ralph Bricker
Clifford E. Haines
Wayne McAndrews
Lloyd J. Michels
Frank D. Reardon

Ex-officio Honorary Members: The Governor, President of Senate, Speaker of House

STATISTICS

Area (square miles)...................145,878
Rank in Nation........................3rd
Population (1954*).....................628,000
Rank in Nation (1954*)................42nd
Density per square mile (1954*)..........4.3
Number of Representatives in Congress......2†
Fiscal Year 1954 (ended June 30, 1954):
General Revenue.............$72,135,000‡
General Expenditures..........$74,999,000‡
State University.....Montana State University
Site...........................Missoula

Capital City..........................Helena
Population (1950)..................17,581
Rank in State......................5th
Largest City....................Great Falls
Population (1950)..................39,214
Number of Cities over 10,000 Population......7
Number of Counties.......................56

*Population estimates as of July 1, 1954, subject to revision.
†As allocated on basis of 1950 population figures.
‡U. S. Bureau of Census report.

471

NEBRASKA

Nickname...The Cornhusker State

Motto.......*Equality Before the Law*

Flower...............Goldenrod

Capital City.............Lincoln

Bird........Western Meadowlark

Song............(Four unofficial)

Entered the Union..March 1, 1867

GOVERNOR
VICTOR E. ANDERSON

HON. KARL E. VOGEL
Chairman of the Commission on
Intergovernmental Cooperation

OFFICERS

Governor........VICTOR E. ANDERSON
Lieutenant Governor.......(Vacancy)
Secretary of State......FRANK MARSH
Attorney General...CLARENCE S. BECK
State Treasurer.......RALPH W. HILL
State Auditor........RAY C. JOHNSON

NEBRASKA
SUPREME COURT

Chief Justice......ROBERT G. SIMMONS
Six Associate Judges

LEGISLATURE

Nebraska has the only unicameral Legislature

President of the Legislature..........(Vacancy)   Clerk of the Legislature...........HUGO F. SRB

Speaker of the Legislature......DWIGHT BURNEY

COMMISSION ON INTERGOVERNMENTAL COOPERATION

Administrative Members	Legislative Members	Alternates
MAYME STUKEL	KARL E. VOGEL, *Chairman*	J. MONROE BIXLER
CLARENCE BECK	LESTER ANDERSON	H. K. DIERS
FRED HERRINGTON	OTTO KOTOUC	JOSEPH MARTIN
L. N. RESS	EARL J. LEE	WILLIAM McHENRY
E. A. ROGERS	K. W. PETERSON	WILLIAM MOULTON
JAMES WEASMER	CHARLES F. TVRDIK	

Ex-officio Honorary Members: THE GOVERNOR, PRESIDENT OF LEGISLATURE, SPEAKER OF LEGISLATURE

STATISTICS

Area (square miles)...................76,663
Rank in Nation......................14th
Population (1954*)..................1,366,000
Rank in Nation (1954*)..........34th
Density per square mile (1954*).........17.8
Number of Representatives in Congress......4†
Fiscal Year 1954 (ended June 30, 1954):
General Revenue............$106,408,000‡
General Expenditures..........$98,615,000‡
State University.........University of Nebraska
Site...............................Lincoln

Capital City........................Lincoln
Population (1950)..................98,884
Rank in State........................2nd
Largest City.........................Omaha
Population (1950)..................251,117
Number of Cities over 10,000 Population.....10
Number of Counties........................93

*Population estimates as of July 1, 1954, subject to revision.
†As allocated on basis of 1950 population figures.
‡U. S. Bureau of Cen us report.

472

NEVADA

Nickname........The Silver State
Motto..........*All for Our Country*
Flower................ Sagebrush
Capital City.........Carson City

Bird (unofficial).Mountain Bluebird
Tree............Single-leaf Piñon
Entered the Union.October 31, 1864

OFFICERS

Governor........CHARLES H. RUSSELL
Lieutenant Governor........REX BELL
Secretary of State.......JOHN KOONTZ
Attorney General..HARVEY DICKERSON
State Treasurer.......DAN W. FRANKS
Legislative Auditor....A. N. JACOBSON
State Controller.....PETER MERIALDO

NEVADA
SUPREME COURT

Chief Justice.... CHARLES M. MERRILL
Two Associate Justices

HON. WALTER WHITACRE
Chairman of the Legislative
Commission

GOVERNOR
CHARLES H. RUSSELL

LEGISLATURE

President of the Senate..............REX BELL
President Pro Tem
    of the Senate.........FRED H. SETTELMEYER
Secretary of the Senate....ROBERT J. INGERSOLL

Speaker of the Assembly...... CYRIL O. BASTIAN
Speaker Pro Tem
    of the Assembly...... CHESTER S. CHRISTENSEN
Chief Clerk of the Assembly.......KEITH L. LEE

LEGISLATIVE COMMISSION OF LEGISLATIVE COUNSEL BUREAU
(Functions as Commission on Interstate Cooperation)

Senate Members

WALTER WHITACRE, *Chairman*
B. MAHLON BROWN
RALPH W. LATTIN
FARRELL L. SEEVERS

Assembly Members

GARY J. ADAMS
BRUCE BARNUM
E. J. DOTSON
ARCHIE POZZI, JR.

Legislative Counsel: J. E. SPRINGMEYER

STATISTICS

Area (square miles)....................109,789
    Rank in Nation........................6th
Population (1954*)....................218,000
    Rank in Nation (1954*)................48th
    Density per square mile (1955*).........2.0
Number of Representatives in Congress......1†
Fiscal Year 1955 (ended June 30, 1955):
    General Revenue..............$46,432,000‡
    General Expenditures..........$46,810,000‡
State University.........University of Nevada
    Site...............................Reno

Capital City....................Carson City
    Population (1950)....................3,082
    Rank in State.........................7th
Largest City...........................Reno
    Population (1950)...................32,497
Number of Cities over 10,000 Population......2
Number of Counties.......................17

---

*Population estimates as of July 1, 1954, subject to revision .
†As allocated on basis of 1950 population figures.
‡Report of State Controller.

473

NEW HAMPSHIRE

Nickname......The Granite State   Bird (unofficial)......Purple Finch

Motto............*Live Free or Die*   Song (unofficial)..*Old New Hampshire*

Flower..............Purple Lilac   Entered the Union...June 21, 1788

Capital City.............Concord

GOVERNOR
LANE DWINELL

HON. LOUIS C. WYMAN
Chairman of the Commission on
Interstate Cooperation

OFFICERS

Governor............LANE DWINELL
Lieutenant Governor..........None
Secretary of State...ENOCH D. FULLER
Attorney General....LOUIS C. WYMAN
State Treasurer.....ALFRED S. CLOUES
State Comptroller....ARTHUR E. BEAN

NEW HAMPSHIRE
SUPREME COURT

Chief Justice.......FRANK R. KENISON
Four Associate Justices

LEGISLATURE

President of the Senate....RAYMOND K. PERKINS   Speaker of the House..............(Vacancy)

Clerk of the Senate.......BENJAMIN F. GREER   Clerk of the House..........ROBERT L. STARK

COMMISSION ON INTERSTATE COOPERATION

Administrative Members	Senate Members	House Members
LOUIS C. WYMAN, *Chairman*	ERALSEY C. FERGUSON	MARGARET B. DELUDE
LAWTON B. CHANDLER	HARRY H. FOOTE	CHARLES GRIFFIN
WILLOUGHBY A. COLBY	ARCHIBALD H. MATTHEWS	MYRON B. HART
ENOCH D. FULLER	THOMAS B. O'MALLEY	JOHN J. KEARNS
RICHARD F. UPTON	RAYMOND K. PERKINS	EDA C. MARTIN

STATISTICS

Area (square miles)......................9,304
  Rank in Nation.......................43rd
Population (1954*)....................532,000
  Rank in Nation (1954*)................44th
  Density per square mile (1954*).........57.2
Number of Representatives in Congress......2†
Fiscal Year 1954 (ended June 30, 1954):
  General Revenue.............$46,174,000‡
  General Expenditures.........$50,314,000‡
State University..University of New Hampshire
  Site..............................Durham

Capital City........................Concord
  Population (1950)....................27,988
  Rank in State........................3rd
Largest City......................Manchester
  Population (1950)....................82,732
Number of Cities over 10,000 Population.....10
Number of Counties.......................10

*Population estimates as of July 1, 1954, subject to revision.
†As allocated on basis of 1950 population figures.
‡Figures furnished by New Hampshire Legislative Service agency.

NEW JERSEY

Nickname......The Garden State
Motto........*Liberty and Prosperity*
Flower............Purple Violet
Bird..........Eastern Goldfinch
Capital City............Trenton

Song (unofficial)
.........*New Jersey Loyalty Song*
Entered the Union
............December 18, 1787

OFFICERS

Governor........Robert B. Meyner
Lieutenant Governor..........None
Secretary of State...Edward J. Patten
Attorney General
..........Grover C. Richman, Jr.
State Treasurer (Acting)
..............Robert L. Finley
State Auditor........Frank Durand
State Comptroller
...........Abram M. Vermeulen

NEW JERSEY SUPREME COURT

Chief Justice..Arthur T. Vanderbilt
Six Associate Justices

Hon. Joseph E. McLean
Chairman of the Commission on
Interstate Cooperation

Governor
Robert B. Meyner

LEGISLATURE*

President of the Senate......Bruce A. Wallace

President Pro Tem of the Senate
....................W. Steelman Mathis
Acting Secretary of the Senate...Henry H. Patterson

Speaker of the Assembly....Paul M. Salsburg
Clerk of the Assembly.........Wm. T. Ludlum

*New officers to be elected in January, 1956.

COMMISSION ON INTERSTATE COOPERATION

Administrative Members	Senate Members	House Members
Joseph E. McLean, *Chairman*	George B. Harper	Pierce H. Deamer
Archibald S. Alexander	James F. Murray, Jr.	Mrs. Florence P. Dwyer
Carl Holderman	Nathaniel C. Smith, *Vice-chairman*	John Junda
Dwight R. G. Palmer	Richard R. Stout	Robert E. Kay
Grover C. Richmond, Jr.	John M. Summerill, Jr.	William V. Musto

Ex-officio Honorary Member: The Governor
Treasurer: Abram M. Vermuellen

STATISTICS

Area (square miles).....................7,522
Rank in Nation.....................45th
Population (1954*)..................5,250,000
Rank in Nation (1954*)..................8th
Density per square mile (1954*)........698.0
Number of Representatives in Congress.....14†
Fiscal Year 1954 (ended June 30, 1954):
General Revenue.............$312,151,000‡
General Expenditures.........$397,007,000‡
State University§.............................
Site.......................New Brunswick
Capital City.......................Trenton
Population (1950)..................128,009
Rank in State.........................4th

Largest City.......................Newark
Population (1950)..................438,776
Number of Cities and Townships over 10,000
Population.............................93
Number of Counties.....................21

*Population estimates as of July 1, 1954, subject to revision.
†As allocated on basis of 1950 population figures.
‡U. S. Bureau of Census report.
§The State College for the Benefit of Agriculture and the Mechanics Arts maintained by the Trustees of Rutgers College, the Agricultural Experiment Station maintained by the same Trustees, the New Jersey Agricultural Experiment Station, the New Jersey College for Women, and the other departments of higher education maintained by the Trustees of Rutgers College were collectively designated as the State University of New Jersey by P.L. 1945, c.49.

475

NEW MEXICO

Nickname. The Land of Enchantment
Motto.............*Crescit Eundo*
      (It Grows As It Goes)
Flower............Yucca Flower
Capital City...........Santa Fe

Bird..............Road Runner

Song.........*O, Fair New Mexico*

Entered the Union. January 6, 1912

GOVERNOR
JOHN FIELD SIMMS

OFFICERS

Governor..JOHN FIELD SIMMS
Lieutenant Governor.........................JOSEPH M. MONTOYA
Secretary of State............................MRS. NATALIE S. BUCK
Attorney General............................RICHARD H. ROBINSON
State Treasurer................................JOSEPH B. GRANT
State Auditor..................................J. D. HANNAH
State Comptroller.............................D. M. SMITH, JR.

NEW MEXICO SUPREME COURT

Chief Justice..J. C. COMPTON
Four Additional Justices

LEGISLATURE

President of the Senate.....JOSEPH M. MONTOYA
President Pro Tem of the Senate...GUIDO ZECCA   Speaker of the House......DONALD D. HALLAM
Chief Clerk of the Senate...EDWARD G. ROMERO   Chief Clerk of the House.........FLOYD CROSS

COMMISSION ON INTERGOVERNMENTAL COOPERATION

Administrative Members	Senate Members	House Members
JACK E. HOLMES	JOHN P. CUSACK	ANDERSON CARTER
L. W. LEIBRAND	HORACIO DE VARGAS	VIRGIL O. McCOLLUM
MANUEL LUJAN	HENRY L. EAGER	PAUL W. ROBINSON
FRED W. MOXEY	SIDNEY S. GOTTLIEB	ANTONIO SANCHEZ
RICHARD H. ROBINSON	T. E. LUSK	RICHARD VELARDE

Ex-officio Honorary Members: THE GOVERNOR, PRESIDENT OF SENATE, SPEAKER OF HOUSE

STATISTICS

Area (square miles)...................121,511
    Rank in Nation......................4th
Population (1954*)....................781,000
    Rank in Nation (1954*)...............38th
    Density per square mile (1954*)..........6.4
Number of Representatives in Congress.....2†
Fiscal Year 1954 (ended June 30, 1954):
    General Revenue............$133,000,000‡
    General Expenditures........$114,922,000‡
State University.....University of New Mexico
    Site........................Albuquerque

Capital City.......................Santa Fe
    Population (1950).................27,998
    Rank in State.......................2nd
Largest City.....................Albuquerque
    Population (1950)..................96,815
Number of Cities over 10,000 Population......7
Number of Counties......................32

*Population estimates as of July 1, 1954, subject to revision.
†As allocated on basis of 1950 population figures.
‡U. S. Bureau of Census report.

476

NEW YORK

Nickname.......The Empire State   Bird.....................None

Motto..........*Excelsior* (Higher)   Song...........(Four unofficial)

Flower....................Rose   Entered the Union...July 26, 1788

Capital City.............Albany

OFFICERS
Governor........AVERELL HARRIMAN
Lieutenant Governor
..............GEORGE B. DE LUCA
Secretary of State
..............CARMINE G. DESAPIO
Attorney General.....JACOB K. JAVITS
State Comptroller.....ARTHUR LEVITT

NEW YORK COURT
OF APPEALS
(Highest Appellate Court)
Chief Judge........ALBERT CONWAY
Six Associate Members

HON. ELISHA T. BARRETT
Chairman of the Joint Legislative
Committee on Interstate
Cooperation

GOVERNOR
AVERELL HARRIMAN

LEGISLATURE
President of the Senate ...... GEORGE B. DE LUCA

President Pro Tem of the Senate   Speaker of the Assembly.......OSWALD D. HECK
...................WALTER J. MAHONEY   Clerk of the Assembly.....ANSLEY B. BORKOWSKI

Secretary of the Senate.......WILLIAM S. KING

JOINT LEGISLATIVE COMMITTEE ON INTERSTATE COOPERATION

Administrative Members*	Senate Members	House Members	Ex-officio Members of all Joint Legis. Comm.
GEORGE M. BRAGALINI	EARL W. BRYDGES	ELISHA T. BARRETT,	WALTER J. MAHONEY
ALFRED M. HAIGHT	FRANK S. McCULLOUGH	*Chairman*	FRANCIS MAHONEY
ARTHUR H. LEVITT	MacNEIL MITCHELL	GEO. F. DANNEBROCK	AUSTIN W. ERWIN
JAMES G. LYONS	FRED G. MORITT	BENJAMIN H. DEMO	OSWALD D. HECK
MILTON D. STEWART	GILBERT T. SEELYE	LOUIS KALISH, *Secy.*	EUGENE BANNIGAN
		OREST J. MARESCA	WM. H. MacKENZIE
		LEO P. NOONAN	JOSEPH F. CARLINO
*Administrative members are advisory only.		PAUL L. TALBOT	

STATISTICS

Area (square miles)....................47,944
  Rank in Nation.......................29th
Population (1954*)...............15,433,000
  Rank in Nation (1954*).................1st
  Density per square mile (1954*).......321.9
Number of Representatives in Congress.....43†
Fiscal Year 1954 (ended March 31, 1954):
  General Revenue...........$1,392,829,000‡
  General Expenditures.......$1,512,227,000‡
State University....................Albany

Capital City........................Albany
  Population (1950).................134,995
  Rank in State........................6th
Largest City...................New York City
  Population (1950)................7,891,957
Number of Cities over 10,000 Population.....56
Number of Villages over 10,000 Population...16
Number of Counties......................62

*Population estimates as of July 1, 1954, subject to revision.
†As allocated on basis of 1950 population figures.
‡U. S. Bureau of Census report.

NORTH CAROLINA

Nickname......The Tarheel State
Motto..........*Esse Quam Videri*
(To Be Rather than To Seem)
Flower...............Dogwood
Capital City............Raleigh

Song.........*The Old North State*

Entered the Union
............November 21, 1789

GOVERNOR
LUTHER H. HODGES

HON. J. V. WHITFIELD
Chairman of the Commission on
Interstate Cooperation

OFFICERS

Governor.........LUTHER H. HODGES
Lieutenant Governor.......(Vacancy)
Secretary of State........THAD EURE
Attorney General..WM. B. RODMAN, JR.
State Treasurer.........EDWIN GILL
State Auditor......HENRY L. BRIDGES

NORTH CAROLINA SUPREME COURT

Chief Justice.....M. VICTOR BARNHILL
Six Associate Justices

LEGISLATURE

President of the Senate...LUTHER E. BARNHARDT
President Pro Tem of the Senate...PAUL E. JONES
Chief Clerk of the Senate......S. RAY BYERLY

Speaker of the House......LARRY I. MOORE, JR.
Principal Clerk of the House
....................MRS. ANNIE E. COOPER

COMMISSION ON INTERSTATE COOPERATION

Administrative Members
J. V. WHITFIELD, *Chairman*
CHARLES F. CARROLL
D. S. COLTRANE
FRANK CRANE
J. W. R. NORTON, M.D.
WILLIAM B. RODMAN, JR.

Senate Members
WILLIAM E. GARRISON
O. ARTHUR KIRKMAN
E. W. SUMMERSILL
RAY H. WALTON
B. H. WINTERS

House Members
CHARLES K. BRYANT, SR.
GEORGE W. CRAIGE
MRS. RALPH R. FISHER
JOHN F. WHITE
W. BRANTLEY WOMBLE

Ex-officio Honorary Members: THE GOVERNOR, PRESIDENT OF SENATE, SPEAKER OF HOUSE

STATISTICS

Area (square miles)....................49,097
  Rank in Nation.......................28th
Population (1954*)................4,250,000
  Rank in Nation(1954*)..................10th
  Density per square mile (1954*)........86.6
Number of Representatives in Congress.....12†
Fiscal Year 1954 (ended June 30, 1954):
  General Revenue............$388,885,000‡
  General Expenditures........$391,645,000‡
State University....University of North Carolina
  Site..........................Chapel Hill

Capital City.........................Raleigh
  Population (1950)...................65,679
  Rank in State.........................5th
Largest City........................Charlotte
  Population (1950)..................134,042
Number of Cities over 10,000 Population.....30
Number of Counties......................100

*Population estimates as of July 1, 1954, subject to revision.
†As allocated on basis of 1950 population figures.
‡U. S. Bureau of Census report.

478

NORTH DAKOTA

Nickname....The Flickertail State

Motto......*Liberty and Union, Now and Forever, One and Inseparable*

Flower.........Wild Prairie Rose

Bird.........Western Meadowlark

Song..........*North Dakota Hymn*

Entered the Union. November 2, 1889

Capital City...........Bismarck

OFFICERS

Governor.................................... NORMAN BRUNSDALE
Lieutenant Governor.................................C. P. DAHL
Secretary of State...................................BEN MEIER
Attorney General............................. LESLIE R. BERGUM
State Treasurer................................ ALBERT JACOBSON
State Auditor...................................BERTA E. BAKER

NORTH DAKOTA SUPREME COURT

Chief Justice....................................THOMAS J. BURKE

Four Associate Judges

GOVERNOR
NORMAN BRUNSDALE

LEGISLATURE

President of the Senate............C. P. DAHL

President Pro Tem of the Senate
......................OLIVER E. BILDEN

Speaker of the House.............K. A. FITCH

Clerk of the House....... KENNETH L. MORGAN

Secretary of the Senate.........EDWARD LENO

LEGISLATIVE RESEARCH COMMITTEE

(Functions as Committee on Interstate Cooperation)

Senate Members
H. B. BAEVERSTAD
RALPH DEWING
O. S. JOHNSON
A. W. LUICK
IVER SOLBERG,
  Vice-chairman

House Members
RALPH BEEDE, *Chairman*
ADAM GEFREH, *Secretary*
LOUIS LEET
LELAND ROEN
OSCAR SOLBERG
RICHARD J. THOMPSON

Research Director: C. EMERSON MURRY

STATISTICS

Area (square miles)....................70,057
  Rank in Nation.......................16th
Population (1954*)....................636,000
  Rank in Nation (1954*)................41st
  Density per square mile (1954*)..........9.1
Number of Representatives in Congress......2†
Fiscal Year 1954 (ended June 30, 1954):
  General Revenue.............$89,696,000‡
  General Expenditures.........$85,511,000‡
State University....University of North Dakota
  Site..........................Grand Forks

Capital City.......................Bismarck
  Population (1950)...................18,640
  Rank in State........................4th
Largest City.........................Fargo
  Population (1950)...................38,256
Number of Cities over 10,000 Population......5
Number of Counties......................53

*Population estimates as of July 1, 1954, subject to revision.
†As allocated on basis of 1950 population figures.
‡U. S. Bureau of Census report.

OHIO

Nickname......The Buckeye State

Motto..................(None)

Flower.........Scarlet Carnation

Tree....(Aesculus glabra) Buckeye

Bird...................Cardinal

Song..........(Several unofficial)

Entered the Union..March 1, 1803

Capital City...........Columbus

GOVERNOR
FRANK J. LAUSCHE

HON. ROBERT L. MOULTON
Chairman of the Commission on
Interstate Cooperation

OFFICERS

Governor.........FRANK J. LAUSCHE
Lieutenant Governor..JOHN W. BROWN
Secretary of State.....TED W. BROWN
Attorney General
..............C. WILLIAM O'NEILL
State Treasurer.....ROGER W. TRACY
State Auditor.......JAMES A. RHODES

OHIO SUPREME COURT

Chief Justice.....CARL V. WEYGANDT
Six Associate Judges

LEGISLATURE

President of the Senate.......JOHN W. BROWN

President Pro Tem
of the Senate...........C. STANLEY MECHEM
Clerk of the Senate.......THOMAS E. BATEMAN

Speaker of the House............ROGER CLOUD
Chief Clerk of the House...........CARL GUESS

COMMISSION ON INTERSTATE COOPERATION

Administrative Members
ROBERT L. MOULTON, Chairman
C. WILLIAM O'NEILL
RAY WHITE

Senate Members
OAKLEY C. COLLINS
FRED W. DANNER
ELIZABETH F. GORMAN
CHARLES A. MOSHER
ROSS PEPPLE
J. E. SIMPSON
FRANK J. SVOBODA

House Members
THOMAS J. BARRETT
LESLIE M. BURGE
BISHOP KILPATRICK
J. FRANK McCLURE
KLINE L. ROBERTS
KENNETH A. ROBINSON
ROBERT E. ZELLER

Ex-officio Honorary Members: THE GOVERNOR, PRESIDENT OF SENATE, SPEAKER OF HOUSE

STATISTICS

Area (square miles).....................41,000
 Rank in Nation.......................34th
Population (1954*)..................8,554,000
 Rank in Nation (1954*)..................5th
 Density per square mile (1954*).......208.6
Number of Representatives in Congress.....23†
Fiscal Year 1954 (ended June 30, 1954):
 General Revenue............$717,257,000‡
 General Expenditures.........$714,018,000‡
State Universities
 Ohio State University.............Columbus
 Ohio University....................Athens
 Miami University...................Oxford

Kent State University................Kent
Bowling Green University.....Bowling Green
Wilberforce University...........Wilberforce
Capital City........................Columbus
 Population (1950).................375,901
 Rank in State........................3rd
Largest City........................Cleveland
 Population (1950)................914,808
Number of Cities over 10,000 Population.....78
Number of Counties......................88

*Population estimates as of July 1, 1954, subject to revision.
†As allocated on basis of 1950 population figures.
‡U. S. Bureau of Census report.

480

OKLAHOMA

Nickname.......The Sooner State
Motto.........*Labor Omnia Vincit*
(Labor Conquers All Things)
Flower................Mistletoe
Capital City.......Oklahoma City

Bird......Scissor-tailed Flycatcher
Song.................*Oklahoma*
Entered the Union
...........November 16, 1907

OFFICERS
Governor...........Raymond Gary
Lieutenant Governor
...........Cowboy Pink Williams
Secretary of State.....Andy Anderson
Attorney General..Mac Q. Williamson
State Treasurer......John D. Conner
State Auditor..........A. S. J. Shaw

OKLAHOMA SUPREME COURT
Chief Justice..........N. B. Johnson
Eight Associate Judges

Hon. Ray Fine
Chairman of the Commission on
Interstate Cooperation

Governor
Raymond Gary

LEGISLATURE
President of the Senate..Cowboy Pink Williams
President Pro Tem of the Senate.....Ray Fine
Secretary of the Senate..........Leo Winters

Speaker of the House...........B. E. Harkey
Speaker Pro Tem of the House...Floyd Sumrall
Chief Clerk of the House.........Carl J. Staas

COMMISSION ON INTERSTATE COOPERATION

Administrative Members
Clarence Burch
J. D. Dunn
Burton Logan
C. A. Stoldt
Mac Q. Williamson

Senate Members
Ray Fine, *Chairman*
Roy E. Grantham
Clem M. Hamilton
D. L. Jones
Frank Mahan
Clem McSpadden

House Members
B. E. Harkey, *Vice-chairman*
James M. Bullard
J. W. Huff
Arthur A. Kelly
J. Howard Lindley
J. D. McCarty
J. E. Payne
Floyd Sumrall

Ex-officio Honorary Members: The Governor, President of Senate, Speaker of House
Secretary: Jack A. Rhodes

STATISTICS
Area (square miles)....................69,031
  Rank in Nation......................18th
Population (1954*)..................2,268,000
  Rank in Nation (1954*)..............25th
  Density per square mile (1954*).........32.9
Number of Representatives in Congress......6†
Fiscal Year 1955 (ended June 30, 1955):
  General Revenue............$313,951,414‡
  General Expenditures........$309,878,954‡
State University......University of Oklahoma
  Site............................Norman

Capital City.................Oklahoma City
  Population (1950)..................243,504
  Rank in State........................1st
Largest City.................Oklahoma City
  Population (1950)..................243,504
Number of Cities over 10,000 Population.....23
Number of Counties.......................77

*Population estimates as of July 1, 1954, subject to revision.
†As allocated on basis of 1950 population figures.
‡From state report.

481

OREGON

Nickname.......The Beaver State
Motto.................*The Union*
Flower............Oregon Grape

Capital City...............Salem

Bird.........Western Meadowlark
Song...........*Oregon, My Oregon*
Entered the Union
.............February 14, 1859

GOVERNOR
PAUL PATTERSON

HON. CHAS. H. HELTZEL
Chairman of the Commission on
Interstate Cooperation

OFFICERS

Governor...........PAUL PATTERSON
Lieutenant Governor..........None
Secretary of State....EARL T. NEWBRY
Attorney General
.............ROBERT Y. THORNTON
State Treasurer...SIGFRID B. UNANDER
State Auditor.......EARL T. NEWBRY

OREGON SUPREME COURT

Chief Justice...... HAROLD J. WARNER
Six Associate Justices

LEGISLATURE

President of the Senate ....ELMO E. SMITH
Chief Clerk of the Senate. MRS. ZYLPHA ZELL BURNS

Speaker of the House........EDWARD A. GEARY
Chief Clerk of the House. MRS. EDITH BYNON LOW

COMMISSION ON INTERSTATE COOPERATION

Administrative Members	Senate Members	House Members
CHAS. H. HELTZEL, *Chairman*	PAUL E. GEDDES	GEORGE ANNALA
HARRY DORMAN	LEE V. OHMART	EARL H. HILL
LEWIS A. STANLEY	RUDIE WILHELM, JR.	ED. R. CARDWELL

Ex-officio Honorary Members: THE GOVERNOR, PRESIDENT OF SENATE, SPEAKER OF HOUSE

STATISTICS

Area (square miles)....................96,315
  Rank in Nation.......................9th
Population (1954*).................1,639,000
  Rank in Nation (1954*)................32nd
  Density per square mile (1954*)........17.0
Number of Representatives in Congress......4†
Fiscal Year 1954 (ended June 30, 1954):
  General Revenue............$186,398,000‡
  General Expenditures........$227,523,000‡
State University........University of Oregon
  Site................................Eugene

Capital City........................Salem
  Population (1950)..................43,140
  Rank in State........................2nd
Largest City.......................Portland
  Population (1950)................373,628
Number of Cities over 10,000 Population.....11
Number of Counties......................36

---

*Population estimates as of July 1, 1954, subject to revision.
†As allocated on basis of 1950 population figures.
‡U. S. Bureau of Census report.

PENNSYLVANIA

Nickname.....The Keystone State
Motto. *Virtue, Liberty and Independence*
Flower.........Mountain Laurel
Capital City.........Harrisburg

Bird.............Ruffed Grouse
Song.............No official song
Entered the Union
............December 12, 1787

OFFICERS

Governor.......GEORGE M. LEADER
Lieutenant Governor...ROY E. FURMAN
Secretary of the Commonwealth
...............JAMES A. FINNEGAN
Attorney General...HERBERT B. COHEN
State Treasurer..WELDON B. HEYBURN
Auditor General..CHARLES R. BARBER
Secretary of Internal Affairs
.................GENEVIEVE BLATT

PENNSYLVANIA SUPREME COURT

Chief Justice.........HORACE STERN
Six Associate Judges

HON. JOHN DENT
Chairman of the Commission on
Interstate Cooperation

GOVERNOR
GEORGE M. LEADER

LEGISLATURE

President of the Senate.........ROY E. FURMAN

President Pro Tem
of the Senate.........M. HARVEY TAYLOR
Secretary of the Senate....G. HAROLD WATKINS

Speaker of the House.......HIRAM G. ANDREWS
Chief Clerk
of the House.............BENJAMIN L. LONG

COMMISSION ON INTERSTATE COOPERATION

Administrative Members	Senate Members	House Members
CHARLES R. BARBER	JOHN H. DENT, *Chairman*	HIRAM G. ANDREWS
GENEVIEVE BLATT	JOSEPH M. BARR	ALBERT W. JOHNSON
JAMES A. FINNEGAN, *Secy.*	THOMAS P. HARNEY	J. DEAN POLEN
MAURICE K. GODDARD	HUGH J. MCMENAMIN	ALBERT S. READINGER
WELDON B. HEYBURN	ROWLAND B. MAHANY	CHARLES C. SMITH
JOSEPH J. LAWLER	G. ROBERT WATKINS	JOHN F. STANK
FRANCIS A. PITKIN,	EDWARD B. WATSON, *Treas.*	NORMAN WOOD
Vice-chairman		

Ex-officio Honorary Member: THE GOVERNOR

STATISTICS

Area (square miles)....................45,045
Rank in Nation.....................32nd
Population (1954*).................10,779,000
Rank in Nation (1954*).................3rd
Density per square mile (1954*)........239.3
Number of Representatives in Congress.....30†
Fiscal Year 1954 (ended May 31, 1954):
General Revenue............$812,463,000‡
General Expenditures........$875,690,000‡
Institution of Higher Education
..............Pennsylvania State College
Site.......................State College

Capital City.....................Harrisburg
Population (1950)...................89,544
Rank in State........................7th
Largest City.....................Philadelphia
Population (1950)................2,071,605
Number of Cities over 10,000 Population.....96
Number of Counties.......................67

*Population estimates as of July 1, 1954, subject to revision.
†As allocated on basis of 1950 population.
‡U. S. Bureau of Census report.

483

RHODE ISLAND

Nickname (unofficial).Little Rhody
Motto.....................*Hope*
Flower (unofficial)........Violet
Capital City..........Providence

Song...............*Rhode Island*
Tree (unofficial)..........Maple
Entered the Union...May 29, 1790

GOVERNOR
DENNIS J. ROBERTS

HON. RAYMOND A. McCABE
Chairman of the Commission on
Interstate Cooperation

OFFICERS

Governor..........DENNIS J. ROBERTS
Lieutenant Governor
.............JOHN S. McKIERNAN
Secretary of State...ARMAND H. COTÉ
Attorney General..WILLIAM E. POWERS
Director of Department of
    Administration.HOWARD A. KENYON
General Treasurer
...........RAYMOND H. HAWKSLEY
Controller.......M. JOSEPH CUMMINGS

RHODE ISLAND SUPREME COURT

Chief Justice.......EDMUND W. FLYNN
Four Associate Justices

LEGISLATURE

President of the Senate.....JOHN S. McKIERNAN

President Pro Tem
    of the Senate...........JAMES J. BRADY, SR.
Secretary of the Senate......ARMAND H. COTÉ

Speaker of the House........HARRY F. CURVIN
Recording Clerk
    of the House...........PAUL B. McMAHON

COMMISSION ON INTERSTATE COOPERATION

Administrative Members	Senate Members	House Members
EARLE M. BYRNE, *Secy.*	RAYMOND A. McCABE,	ROBERT A. CALDWELL
SIDNEY CLIFFORD	*Chairman*	JOSEPH E. MALLEY,
JOSEPH PEZZULO	JAMES J. BRADY	*Vice-chairman*
WM. C. E. WILCZEK	C. GEORGE DeSTEFANO	ALFRED U. MENARD
(Vacancy)	PRIMO IACOBUCCI	JOHN J. WRENN

Ex-officio Honorary Members: THE GOVERNOR, PRESIDENT OF SENATE, SPEAKER OF HOUSE,
ATTORNEY GENERAL

STATISTICS

Area (square miles)....................1,214
Rank in Nation......................48th
Population (1954*)...................824,000
    Rank in Nation (1954*)...............37th
    Density per square mile (1954*)........678.7
Number of Representatives in Congress......2†
Fiscal Year 1954 (ended June 30, 1954):
    General Revenue.............$73,739,205‡
    General Expenditures.........$63,661,257‡
Institutions of Higher Education
University of Rhode Island..........Kingston
R. I. College of Education..........Providence

Capital City.....................Providence
    Population (1950)................248,674
    Rank in State.......................1st
Largest City......................Providence
    Population (1950)................248,674
Number of Cities and Towns over 10,000
    Population..........................17
Number of Counties.....................5

*Population estimates as of July 1, 1954, subject to revision.
†As allocated on basis of 1950 population figures.
‡Rhode Island Budget Office.

484

SOUTH CAROLINA

Nickname.....The Palmetto State
Motto......*Animis Opibusque Parati*
(Prepared in Mind and Resources)
Flower.........Yellow Jessamine
Capital City..........Columbia

Bird..............Carolina Wren
Song...................*Carolina*
Tree.................Palmetto
Entered the Union...May 23, 1788

OFFICERS

Governor
......GEORGE BELL TIMMERMAN, JR.
Lieutenant Governor
..............ERNEST F. HOLLINGS
Secretary of State
.............O. FRANK THORNTON
Attorney General......T. C. CALLISON
State Treasurer........JEFF B. BATES
State Auditor.........J. M. SMITH
Comptroller General....E. C. RHODES

SOUTH CAROLINA SUPREME COURT

Chief Justice.......D. GORDON BAKER
Four Associate Justices

HON. EDGAR A. BROWN
Chairman of the Commission on
Interstate Cooperation

GOVERNOR
GEORGE BELL TIMMERMAN, JR.

LEGISLATURE

President of the Senate..........ERNEST F. HOLLINGS

President Pro Tem
of the Senate............EDGAR A. BROWN
Clerk of the Senate.........LOVICK O. THOMAS

Speaker of the House..........SOLOMON BLATT
Clerk of the House..............INEZ WATSON

COMMISSION ON INTERSTATE COOPERATION

Administrative Members
SOLOMON BLATT
L. G. MERRITT
LOVICK O. THOMAS
O. FRANK THORNTON
INEZ WATSON

Senate Members
EDGAR A. BROWN, *Chairman*
REMBERT C. DENNIS
L. MARION GRESSETTE
JAMES P. MOZINGO, III
J. D. PARLER

House Members
REX L. CARTER
R. J. AYCOCK
TRACY J. GAINES
LEWIS H. MCCLAIN
FRED T. MOORE

Ex-officio Honorary Member: THE GOVERNOR

STATISTICS

Area (square miles).................30,305
  Rank in Nation...................39th
Population (1954*)................2,238,000
  Rank in Nation (1954*)................26th
  Density per square mile (1954*).........73.8
Number of Representatives in Congress......6†
Fiscal Year 1954 (ended June 30, 1954):
  General Revenue............$216,566,000‡
  General Expenditures........$256,832,000‡
State University....University of South Carolina
Site............................Columbia

Capital City.......................Columbia
  Population (1950)...................86,914
  Rank in State.........................1st
Largest City......................Columbia
  Population (1950)...................86,914
Number of Cities over 10,000 Population.....10
Number of Counties......................46

*Population estimates as of July 1, 1954, subject to revision.
†As allocated on basis of 1950 population figures.
‡U. S. Bureau of Census report.

485

SOUTH DAKOTA

Nickname.......The Coyote State

Motto.....*Under God the People Rule*

Flower............Pasque Flower

Capital City...............Pierre

Bird........Ringnecked Pheasant

Song...........*Hail, South Dakota*

Entered the Union.November 2,1889

GOVERNOR
JOE J. FOSS

HON. PHIL SAUNDERS
Chairman of the Commission on
Interstate Cooperation

OFFICERS

Governor.................JOE J. FOSS
Lieutenant Governor.....L. R. HOUCK
Secretary of State.GERALDINE OSTROOT
Attorney General...... PHIL SAUNDERS
State Treasurer.........ED. T. ELKINS
State Auditor......LAWRENCE MAYES

SOUTH DAKOTA SUPREME COURT

Presiding Judge........E. D. ROBERTS
Four Other Judges

LEGISLATURE

President of the Senate..........L. R. HOUCK

President Pro Tem of the Senate
.... FRANK A. FERGUSON

Speaker of the House..............NILS A. BOE
Chief Clerk of the House....WALTER J. MATSON

Secretary of the Senate........NIELS P. JENSEN

COMMISSION ON INTERSTATE COOPERATION

Administrative Members	Senate Members	House Members
PHIL SAUNDERS, *Chairman*	ARTHUR B. ANDERSON	ELDON ARNOLD
CHARLES H. BRUETT	HILBERT BOGUE	ALBRO C. AYRES
ED T. ELKINS	L. R. HOUCK	NILS A. BOE
MORRIS G. HALLOCK	ALFRED D. ROESLER	GEORGE BOEKELHEIDE
GERALDINE OSTROOT	DON STRANSKY	NELS P. CHRISTIANSEN

Ex-officio Honorary Member: THE GOVERNOR

STATISTICS

Area (square miles)....................76,536
  Rank in Nation....................15th
Population (1954*)...................667,000
  Rank in Nation (1954*)...............40th
  Density per square mile (1954*).........8.7
Number of Representatives in Congress......2†
Fiscal Year 1954 (ended June 30, 1954):
  General Revenue..............$72,265,000‡
  General Expenditures.........$70,826,000‡
State University.....University of South Dakota
Site...........................Vermillion

Capital City.........................Pierre
  Population (1950)....................5,715
  Rank in State......................10th
Largest City......................Sioux Falls
  Population (1950)................52,696
Number of Cities over 10,000 Population......6
Number of Organized Counties............64
Number of Unorganized Counties...........3§

*Population estimates as of July 1, 1954, subject to revision
†As allocated on basis of 1950 population figures.
‡U. S. Bureau of Census report.
§Unorganized County of Armstrong annexed to Dewey
County during 1952.

486

TENNESSEE

Nickname....The Volunteer State   Bird .... Mockingbird

Motto......*Agriculture and Commerce*   Song...... *My Homeland, Tennessee*

Flower.....................Iris   Entered the Union....June 1,1796

Capital City...........Nashville

OFFICERS

Governor........FRANK G. CLEMENT
Lieutenant Governor..JARED MADDUX
Secretary of State...G. EDWARD FRIAR
Attorney General
.... GEORGE F. MCCANLESS
State Treasurer......RAMON T. DAVIS
State Comptroller
.... WILLIAM R. SNODGRASS

TENNESSEE SUPREME COURT

Chief Justice........ALBERT B. NEIL
    Four Associate Judges

HON. HAROLD V. MILLER
Chairman of the Commission on
Intergovernmental Cooperation

GOVERNOR
FRANK G. CLEMENT

LEGISLATURE

Speaker of the Senate.........JARED MADDUX   Speaker of the House.........JAMES L. BOMAR
Clerk of the Senate.......JOHN W. COOKE, JR.   Clerk of the House........L. BUCHANAN LOSER

COMMISSION ON INTERGOVERNMENTAL COOPERATION

Administrative Members	Senate Members	House Members
HAROLD V. MILLER, *Chairman*	LARRY BETTIS	NORMAN BICKLEY
E. J. BOLING	LANDON COLVARD	MILTON BOWERS, SR.
BUFORD ELLINGTON	MRS. MABEL W. HUGHES	DALE GLOVER
GLEN NICELY	RILEY RANDEL	JOHN M. PURDY
	JOE SWANAY	JAMES H. QUILLEN

Ex-officio Honorary Members: THE GOVERNOR, SPEAKER OF SENATE, SPEAKER OF HOUSE,
ATTORNEY GENERAL, DIRECTOR OF PLANNING COMMISSION

STATISTICS

Area (square miles)....................41,797
   Rank in Nation.................33rd
Population (1954*).................3,362,000
   Rank in Nation (1954*)...............17th
   Density per square mile (1954*).........80.4
Number of Representatives in Congress......9†
Fiscal Year 1954 (ended June 30, 1954):
   General Revenue............$276,721,000‡
   General Expenditures........$275,212,000‡
State University......University of Tennessee
Site............................Knoxville

Capital City.......................Nashville
   Population (1950) 174,307
   Rank in State.......................2nd
Largest City.......................Memphis
   Population (1950)..................396,000
Number of Cities over 10,000 Population.....16
Number of Counties......................95

*Population estimates as of July 1, 1954, subject to revision.
†As allocated on basis of 1950 population figures.
‡U. S. Bureau of Census report.

487

TEXAS

Nickname....The Lone Star State
Motto................*Friendship*
Flower..............Bluebonnet

Bird...............Mockingbird
Song............*Texas, Our Texas*
Entered the Union
............December 29, 1845

Capital City.............Austin

GOVERNOR
ALLAN SHIVERS

OFFICERS

Governor ....ALLAN SHIVERS
Lieutenant Governor ....BEN RAMSEY
Secretary of State................................TOM REAVLEY
Attorney General ....JOHN BEN SHEPPERD
State Treasurer ....JESSE JAMES
State Auditor ....C. H. CAVNESS
State Comptroller ....ROBERT S. CALVERT

TEXAS SUPREME COURT

Chief Justice....................................JOHN E. HICKMAN
Eight Associate Justices

LEGISLATURE

President of the Senate...........BEN RAMSEY

President Pro Tem of the Senate
................MRS. NEVEILLE H. COLSON
Acting Secretary of the Senate
....................CHARLES A. SCHNABEL

Speaker of the House............JIM T. LINDSEY
Chief Clerk of the House
.................MRS. DOROTHY HALLMAN

COMMISSION ON INTERSTATE COOPERATION

Administrative Members
ALLAN SHIVERS, *Governor,*
  Chairman
HOMER GARRISON, JR.
DEWITT GREER
JOHN BEN SHEPPERD
JOHN H. WINTERS
TOM REAVLEY

Senate Members
BEN RAMSEY, *Lt. Gov.,*
  1st Vice-chairman
ABRAHAM KAZAN, JR.
OTTIS E. LOCK
GEORGE MOFFETT
JOHNNIE B. ROGERS
JARRARD SECREST
Secretary: R. B. BALDWIN

House Members
JIM T. LINDSEY, *Speaker,*
  2nd Vice-chairman
CARROLL COBB
JOE R. POOL
GILBERT M. SPRING
REUBEN D. TALASEK
FRED NIEMANN

STATISTICS

Area (square miles)..................263,513
  Rank in Nation.......................1st
Population (1954*).................8,468,000
  Rank in Nation (1954*).................6th
  Density per square mile (1954*)........32.1
Number of Representatives in Congress.....22†
Fiscal Year 1953 (ended August 31, 1953):
  General Revenue............$726,906,000‡
  General Expenditures........$667,611,000‡
State University..........University of Texas
Site...............................Austin

Capital City........................Austin
  Population (1950).................132,459
  Rank in State.........................5th
Largest City........................Houston
  Population (1950).................596,163
Number of Cities over 10,000 Population.....71
Number of Counties.....................254

---

*Population estimates as of July 1, 1954, subject to revision.
†As allocated on basis of 1950 population figures.
‡U. S. Bureau of Census report.

488

UTAH

Nickname......The Beehive State
Motto...................*Industry*
Flower................Sego Lily
Bird...................Seagull
Capital City.......Salt Lake City

Song..........*Utah, We Love Thee*
Tree...............Blue Spruce
Entered the Union January 4, 1896

HON. C. TAYLOR BURTON
Chairman of the Utah Legislative
Council

GOVERNOR
J. BRACKEN LEE

OFFICERS

Governor............J. BRACKEN LEE
Lieutenant Governor...........None
Secretary of State..LAMONT F. TORONTO
Attorney General..RICHARD CALLISTER
State Treasurer.......SID LAMBOURNE
State Auditor.....SHERMAN J. PREECE

UTAH SUPREME COURT

Chief Justice....ROGER I. McDONOUGH
Four Associate Justices

LEGISLATURE

President of the Senate......C. TAYLOR BURTON
Secretary of the Senate....QUAYLE CANNON, JR.

Speaker of the House......CHARLES E. PETERSON
Chief Clerk of the House......RULON J. LARSEN

UTAH LEGISLATIVE COUNCIL

(Functions as Committee on Interstate Cooperation)

Citizen Members
GUY CARDON, JR.
CARL C. GASKILL
MARK PAXTON

Senate Members
C. TAYLOR BURTON, *Chairman*
DONALD T. ADAMS
ELIAS L. DAY
ORVAL HAFEN
ALONZO F. HOPKIN

Director: LEWIS H. LLOYD

House Members
CLAIR R. HOPKINS
RICHARD C. HOWE
CHARLES E. PETERSON
G. DOUGLAS TAYLOR

STATISTICS

Area (square miles)....................82,346
  Rank in Nation.......................11th
Population (1954*)...................757,000
  Rank in Nation (1954*)................39th
  Density per square mile (1954*)..........9.2
Number of Representatives in Congress......2†
Fiscal Year 1954 (ended June 30, 1954):
  General Revenue..............$86,397,000‡
  General Expenditures.........$90,135,000‡
State College....Utah State Agricultural College
  Site...............................Logan

State University...........University of Utah
  Site.......................Salt Lake City
Capital City.................Salt Lake City
  Population (1950)..................182,121
  Rank in State...................1st
Largest City..................Salt Lake City
  Population (1950)..................182,121
Number of Cities over 10,000 Population......4
Number of Counties......................29

*Population estimates as of July 1, 1954, subject to revision.
†As allocated on basis of 1950 population figures.
‡U. S. Bureau of Census report.

VERMONT

Nickname . . Green Mountain State   Bird . . . . Hermit Thrush

Motto . . . . *Freedom and Unity*   Song . . . . *Hail, Vermont*

Flower . . . . Red Clover   Entered the Union . . March 4, 1791

Capital City . . . . Montpelier

GOVERNOR
JOSEPH B. JOHNSON

HON. CARLETON G. HOWE
Chairman of the Commission on
Interstate Cooperation

OFFICERS

Governor . . . . JOSEPH B. JOHNSON
Lieutenant Governor
. . . . MRS. CONSUELO N. BAILEY
Secretary of State
. . . . HOWARD E. ARMSTRONG
Attorney General . ROBERT T. STAFFORD
State Treasurer . . . . GEORGE H. AMIDON
State Auditor . . . . . DAVID V. ANDERSON

VERMONT
SUPREME COURT

Chief Justice . . . . OLIN M. JEFFORDS
Four Associate Justices

LEGISLATURE

President of the Senate . . . . . MRS. CONSUELO N. BAILEY

President Pro Tem   Speaker of the House . . . . JOHN HANCOCK
of the Senate . . . . CARLETON G. HOWE   Clerk of the House . . . . O. FAY ALLEN, JR.
Secretary of the Senate . . . . EARLE J. BISHOP

COMMISSION ON INTERSTATE COOPERATION

Administrative Members	Senate Members	House Members
H. ELMER MARSH	CARLETON G. HOWE, *Chairman*	F. RAY KEYSER, *Secy.*
W. ARTHUR SIMPSON	PHILIP A. ANGELL	JOHN J. WACKERMAN
ROBERT T. STAFFORD	GRAHAM S. NEWELL	MRS. FLORENCE M. WARD

STATISTICS

Area (square miles) 9,278
   Rank in Nation 42nd
Population (1954*) 385,000
   Rank in Nation (1954*) 45th
   Density per square mile (1954*) 41.5
Number of Representatives in Congress . . . . . 1 †
Fiscal Year 1954 (ended June 30, 1954):
   General Revenue . . . . $38,000,000 ‡
   General Expenditures . . . . $40,153,000 ‡
State University . . . . University of Vermont
        and State Agricultural College
   Site . . . . Burlington

Capital City . . . . Montpelier
   Population (1950) 8,599
   Rank in State 4th
Largest City . . . . Burlington
   Population (1950) 33,155
Number of Cities and Towns over 10,000
   Population 5
Number of Counties 14

*Population estimates as of July 1, 1954, subject to revision.
†As allocated on basis of 1950 population figures.
‡U. S. Bureau of Census report.

490

VIRGINIA

Nickname.....The Old Dominion
Motto.........*Sic Semper Tyrannis*
     (Thus Ever to Tyrants)
Flower................Dogwood

Bird..................Cardinal
Song..*Carry Me Back to Old Virginia*
Entered the Union...June 25, 1788
Capital City...........Richmond

OFFICERS

Governor........Thomas B. Stanley
Lieutenant Governor
    ....A. E. S. Stephens
Secretary of the Commonwealth
    ....Martha B. Conway
Attorney General....J. L. Almond, Jr.
State Treasurer......Jesse W. Dillon
Auditor of Public Accounts
    ....J. Gordon Bennett
Comptroller...........S. C. Day, Jr.

VIRGINIA SUPREME COURT OF APPEALS

Chief Justice....Edward W. Hudgins
    Six Associate Justices

Hon. Raymond V. Long
Chairman of the Commission on
Interstate Cooperation

Governor
Thomas B. Stanley

LEGISLATURE

President of the Senate.......A. E. S. Stephens

President Pro Tem
  of the Senate*...............W. C. Caudill

Speaker of the House*....E. Blackburn Moore
Clerk of the House*.......E. Griffith Dodson
Clerk of the Senate*..............E. R. Combs

*New officers to be elected in January 1956.

COMMISSION ON INTERSTATE COOPERATION

Administrative Members	Senate Members	House Members
Raymond V. Long, *Chairman*	Lloyd C. Bird	Henry Stuart Carter
J. Almond Almond, Jr.	John A. K Donovan	Conley E. Greear
James A. Anderson	Garland Gray	Shirley T. Holland
J. Gordon Bennett	Robert O. Norris, Jr.	J. Maynard Magruder
Richard W. Copeland	Edward E. Willey	Joseph E. Proffitt

Ex-officio Honorary Member: The Governor
Secretary: Mrs. O. C. Lamm

STATISTICS

Area (square miles)....................39,893
  Rank in Nation.....................35th
Population (1954*)..................3,588,000
  Rank in Nation (1954*) 14th
  Density per square mile (1954*).........89.9
Number of Representatives in Congress.....10†
Fiscal Year 1954 (ended June 30, 1954):
  General Revenue.............$274,040,000‡
  General Expenditures.........$294,086,000‡
State University.........University of Virginia
Site........................Charlottesville

Capital City......................Richmond
  Population (1950)..................230,310
  Rank in State.......................1st
Largest City......................Richmond
  Population (1950)..................230,310
Number of Cities over 10,000 Population....22§
Number of Counties.....................98§

*Population estimates as of July 1, 1954, subject to revision.
†As allocated on basis of 1950 population figures.
‡U. S. Bureau of Census report.
§Elizabeth City County became a part of the city of Hampton and Warwick County became the independent city of Warwick during July, 1952.

491

WASHINGTON

Nickname....The Evergreen State
Motto...........*Alki* (By and By)
Flower....Western Rhododendron
Bird............Willow Goldfinch
Capital City............Olympia

Song...........*Washington Beloved*

Entered the Union
............November 11, 1889

GOVERNOR
ARTHUR B. LANGLIE

HON. JOHN J. O'BRIEN
Chairman of the Washington
Legislative Council

OFFICERS

Governor........ARTHUR B. LANGLIE
Lieutenant Governor
.............EMMETT T. ANDERSON
Secretary of State..........EARL COE
Attorney General......DON EASTVOLD
State Treasurer....CHAS. R. MAYBURY
State Auditor..........CLIFF YELLE

WASHINGTON SUPREME COURT

Chief Justice....FREDERICK G. HAMLEY
Eight Associate Judges

LEGISLATURE

President of the Senate....EMMETT T. ANDERSON

President Pro Tem
of the Senate..............VICTOR ZEDNICK
Secretary of the Senate......HERBERT H. SIELER

Speaker of the House........JOHN J. O'BRIEN
Chief Clerk of the House........S. R. HOLCOMB

WASHINGTON LEGISLATIVE COUNCIL
(Functions as Committee on Interstate Cooperation)

Senate Members		House Members	
WM. A. GISSBERG	ALBERT D. ROSELLINI	JOHN J. O'BRIEN, *Chairman*	FLOYD C. MILLER, *Secy.*
NEIL J. HOFF	JOHN H. RYDER	ROBERT BERNETHY	A. L. RASMUSSEN
EUGENE D. IVY	PATRICK D. SUTHERLAND	GORDON J. BROWN	RICHARD RUOFF
JAMES KEEFE	THEODORE WILSON	BERNARD J. GALLAGHER	GORDON SANDISON
DALE M. NORDQUIST	VICTOR ZEDNICK	J. CHESTER GORDON	HARRY A. SILER
			ROBERT D. TIMM

Executive Secretary: DONALD C. SAMPSON

STATISTICS

Area (square miles)....................66,786
  Rank in Nation.......................19th
Population (1954*)...............2,540,000
  Rank in Nation (1954*)..............24th
  Density per square mile (1954*)........38.0
Number of Representatives in Congress.....7†
Fiscal Year 1954 (ended March 31, 1954):
  General Revenue............$374,971,000 ‡
  General Expenditures........$408,220,000 ‡
State University.....University of Washington
  Site..............................Seattle

Washington State College............Pullman
Capital City.........................Olympia
  Population (1950)..................15,819
  Rank in State........................13th
Largest City..........................Seattle
  Population (1950)..................467,591
Number of Cities over 10,000 Population.....20
Number of Counties........................39

---
*Population estimates as of July 1, 1954, subject to revision.
†As allocated on basis of 1950 population figures.
‡U. S. Bureau of Census report.

492

WEST VIRGINIA

Nickname....The Panhandle State

Motto........*Montani Semper Liberi*
(Mountaineers Are Always Freemen)

Flower........Big Rhododendron

Capital City..........Charleston

Bird..................Cardinal

Song (unofficial)..*West Virginia Hills*

Entered the Union...June 20, 1863

OFFICERS

Governor ...... WILLIAM C. MARLAND
Lieutenant Governor..........None
Secretary of State....D. PITT O'BRIEN
Attorney General.......JOHN G. FOX
State Treasurer..WILLIAM H. ANSEL, JR.
State Auditor.........EDGAR B. SIMS

WEST VIRGINIA SUPREME COURT OF APPEALS

President........ CHAUNCY BROWNING
Four Associate Judges

HON. CARL M. FRASURE
Chairman of the Commission on
Interstate Cooperation

GOVERNOR
WILLIAM C. MARLAND

LEGISLATURE

President of the Senate.........RALPH J. BEAN
President Pro Tem of the Senate..FRED C. ALLEN
Clerk of the Senate ....J. HOWARD MYERS

Speaker of the House.........WM. E. FLANNERY
Clerk of the House.........C. A. BLANKENSHIP

COMMISSION ON INTERSTATE COOPERATION

Administrative Members
CARL M. FRASURE, *Chairman*
JOHN G. FOX
M. J. FERGUSON
DENZIL L. GAINER
KEITH GRIFFITH

Senate Members
THEODORE M. BOWERS
LLOYD JACKSON
HARRY E. MOATS
GLENN TAYLOR
HERBERT TRAUBERT

House Members
W. A. BURKE
JAMES LOOP
H. T. TUCKER
CECIL UNDERWOOD
RICHARD WHETSELL

Ex-officio Honorary Members: THE GOVERNOR, PRESIDENT OF SENATE, SPEAKER OF HOUSE

STATISTICS

Area (square miles)...................24,080
  Rank in Nation.....................40th
Population (1954*)................1,947,000
  Rank in Nation (1954*)...............30th
  Density per square mile (1954*).........80.9
Number of Representatives in Congress......6†
Fiscal Year 1954 (ended June 30, 1954):
  General Revenue.............$169,489,000‡
  General Expenditures........$252,579,000‡
State University....University of West Virginia
  Site........................Morgantown

Capital City ....Charleston
  Population (1950)...................73,501
  Rank in State.......................2nd
Largest City.....................Huntington
  Population (1950)...................86,353
Number of Cities over 10,000 Population.....13
Number of Counties.......................55

---

*Population estimates as of July 1, 1954, subject to revision.
†As allocated on basis of 1950 population figures.
‡U. S. Bureau of Census report.

493

WISCONSIN

Nickname.......The Badger State	Bird.....................Robin
Motto...................*Forward*	Song.........(Several unofficial)
Flower..............Wood Violet	Entered the Union...May 29, 1848

Capital City...........Madison

GOVERNOR
WALTER J. KOHLER

HON. FRANK E. PANZER
Chairman of the Commission on
Interstate Cooperation

OFFICERS

Governor.........WALTER J. KOHLER
Lieutenant Governor
.............WARREN P. KNOWLES
Secretary of State
.............MRS. GLENN M. WISE
Attorney General
.............VERNON W. THOMSON
State Treasurer.....WARREN R. SMITH
State Auditor........J. JAY KELIHER

WISCONSIN
SUPREME COURT

Chief Justice....EDWARD T. FAIRCHILD
Six Associate Justices

LEGISLATURE

President of the Senate....WARREN P. KNOWLES

President Pro Tem
of the Senate............FRANK E. PANZER
Chief Clerk of Senate......LAWRENCE R. LARSEN

Speaker of the Assembly....MARK S. CATLIN, JR.
Chief Clerk of the Assembly....ARTHUR L. MAY

COMMISSION ON INTERSTATE COOPERATION

Administrative Members
M. G. TOEPEL
M. W. TORKELSON, *Secy.*
ARTHUR E. WEGNER

Senate Members
FRANK E. PANZER, *Chairman*
J. EARL LEVERICH
ARTHUR L. PADRUTT

House Members
ROBERT G. MAROTZ
NICHOLAS J. LESSELYOUNG
EUGENE A. TOEPEL

Ex-officio Honorary Member: THE GOVERNOR

STATISTICS

Area (square miles)....................54,705
 Rank in Nation.....................24th
Population (1954*).................3,578,000
 Rank in Nation (1954*)....... ......15th
 Density per square mile (1954*).........65.4
Number of Representatives in Congress.....10†
Fiscal Year 1954 (ended June 30, 1954):
 General Revenue............$356,173,000‡
 General State Expenditures....$357,791,000‡
State University........University of Wisconsin
Site..............................Madison

Capital City.......................Madison
 Population (1950)...................96,056
 Rank in State.......................2nd
Largest City......................Milwaukee
 Population (1950)..................637,392
Number of Cities over 10,000 Population.....34
Number of Counties.......................71

*Population estimates as of July 1, 1954, subject to revision.
†As allocated on basis of 1950 population figures.
‡U. S. Bureau of Census report.

494

WYOMING

OFFICERS

Governor....... MILWARD L. SIMPSON
Lieutenant Governor.......... None
Secretary of State
    .... EVERETT T. COPENHAVER
Attorney General...... GEORGE F. GUY
State Treasurer... CHARLES B. MORGAN
State Auditor.... MINNIE A. MITCHELL
State Superintendent of Public
    Instruction......... VELMA LINFORD

WYOMING SUPREME COURT

Chief Justice......... FRED H. BLUME
   Two Associate Justices

HON. EVERETT T. COPENHAVER
Chairman of the Commission on
Intergovernmental Cooperation

GOVERNOR
MILWARD L. SIMPSON

LEGISLATURE

President of the Senate.......... R. L. GREENE
President Pro Tem of the Senate
.... NORMAN BARLOW
Chief Clerk of the Senate.... FRANCES D. CLARK

Speaker of the House........... T. C. DANIELS
Chief Clerk of the House.. HARRY C. BARKER, JR.

COMMISSION ON INTERGOVERNMENTAL COOPERATION

Administrative Members	Senate Members	House Members
EVERETT T. COPENHAVER, *Chairman*	S. REED DAYTON	HARVEY T. JOHNSTON
L. C. BISHOP	A. B. EWING	MARLIN T. KURTZ
GEORGE F. GUY	DAVID FOOTE	WILLIAM A. NORRIS, JR.
R. M. McMANIS	SAM FRATTO	DONALD A. SPIKER
(Vacancy)	J. W. MYERS	WILLIAM F. SWANTON

Ex-officio Honorary Members: THE GOVERNOR, PRESIDENT OF SENATE, SPEAKER OF HOUSE

STATISTICS

Area (square miles).................... 97,506
   Rank in Nation....................... 8th
Population (1954*)................... 312,000
   Rank in Nation (1954*)............... 47th
   Density per square mile (1954*).......... 3.2
Number of Representatives in Congress...... 1†
Fiscal Year 1954 (ended June 30, 1954):
   General Revenue .... $55,887,000‡
   General Expenditures.... .... $50,213,000‡
State University....... University of Wyoming
   Site.............................. Laramie

Capital City...................... Cheyenne
   Population (1950)................... 31,935
   Rank in State....................... 1st
Largest City...................... Cheyenne
   Population (1950)................... 31,935
Number of Cities over 10,000 Population...... 5
Number of Counties....................... 23

*Population estimates as of July 1, 1954, subject to revision.
†As allocated on basis of 1950 population figures.
‡U. S. Bureau of Census report.

495

ALASKA

Flower . . . . Forget-me-not   Bird . . . . . Alaska Willow Ptarmigan

Song . . . . *Alaska's Flag*   Purchased from Russia by
                                                The United States . . March 30, 1867

Capital City . . . . Juneau

GOVERNOR
B. FRANK HEINTZLEMAN

OFFICERS

Governor . . . . B. FRANK HEINTZLEMAN
Territorial Secretary . . . . WAINO E. HENDRICKSON
Attorney General . . . . J. GERALD WILLIAMS
Treasurer . . . . HUGH J. WADE
Controller . . . . (Vacancy)

DISTRICT COURT OF ALASKA
Justices

1st Division . . . . (Vacancy)
2nd Division . . . . WALTER HODGE
3rd Division . . . . JAMES LEWIS McCARREY, JR.
4th Division . . . . HARRY E. PRATT

Appointed by the President of The United States

LEGISLATURE

President of Senate . . . . JAMES NOLAN

President Pro Tem of the Senate . . . . . (Vacancy)   Speaker of the House . . . . WENDELL P. KAY
Secretary of the Senate   Chief Clerk of the House . . . . JOHN McLAUGHLIN
. . . . KATHERINE T. ALEXANDER

STATISTICS

Area (square miles) 571,065   Capital City . . . . Juneau
Population (1953) 205,000   Population (1950) 5,956
    Density per square mile (1953) 4   Largest city . . . . Anchorage
Delegate to Congress 1   Population (1950) 11,254
Fiscal data January 1, 1954—December 31, 1954:   Number of Cities over 10,000 Population 1
    Revenue . . . . $26,302,545‡
    Expenditures . . . . $26,769,488‡
University . . . . University of Alaska
    Site . . . . College, Alaska   ‡Data furnished by the U. S. Department of the Inter

496

GUAM

Nickname......Pearl of the Pacific

Capital City..............Agana

Ceded to the United States by Spain. December 10, 1898

Created a Territory. August 1, 1950

OFFICERS

Governor.......................................Ford Q. Elvidge
Territorial Secretary..........................Randall S. Herman
Attorney General ....Howard D. Porter
Treasurer......................................Galo L. Salas
Comptroller...................................Howard O'Hara

DISTRICT COURT OF GUAM

Judge...Paul D. Shriver
    Appointed by President with consent of the Senate

GOVERNOR
FORD Q. ELVIDGE

LEGISLATURE

Speaker...............F. B. Leon Guerrero   Clerk......................Maria C. Duenas
Vice Speaker..................B. J. Bordallo   Aide and Liaison Officer......Juan N. Tuncap
    Legislative Secretary...........A. Sn. Duenas

STATISTICS*

Area (square miles).....................203
Population (1950)....................59,498
   Density per square mile (1950)...........293
Fiscal Year July 1, 1953—June 30, 1954:
   Revenue......................$11,801,400
   Expenditures..................$10,957,600

Capital City..........................Agana
   Population (1950)....................1,330
Largest City......................Sinajana
   Population (1950)...................3,069

*Furnished by the United States Department of the Interior.

497

HAWAII

Nickname...Paradise of the Pacific
Motto........*Ua Mau Ke Ea O Ka Aina I Ka Pono* (The Life of the Land Is Perpetuated in Righteousness)
Capital City............Honolulu

Flower............Red Hibiscus
Song...............*Hawaii Ponoi*
Annexed to United States
.................July 7, 1898

GOVERNOR
SAMUEL WILDER KING

OFFICERS

Governor.....................................SAMUEL WILDER KING
Secretary of Territory........................FARRANT L. TURNER
Attorney General..............................EDWARD N. SYLVA
Treasurer...KAM TAI LEE
Auditor.....................................HOWARD K. HIROKI

SUPREME COURT OF HAWAII

Chief Justice..................................EDWARD A. TOWSE
Two Associate Justices

LEGISLATURE

President of the Senate.......WILLIAM H. HEEN
Vice-President of the Senate....WM. J. NOBRIGA   Speaker of the House.....CHARLES E. KAUHANE
Clerk of the Senate........WM. S. RICHARDSON   Clerk of the House...........JAMES K. TRASK

STATISTICS

Area (square miles).....................6,407
Population (1953)....................523,000
 Density per square mile (1953)..........81.6
Delegate to Congress.......................1
Fiscal Year 1955 (ended June 30, 1955):
 Revenue.....................$57,433,917‡
 Expenditures.................$62,627,496‡
University............... University of Hawaii
Site..........................Honolulu

Capital City........................Honolulu
 Population (1950)..................248,034
Largest City........................Honolulu
 Population (1950)..................248,034
Number of Cities over 10,000 Population......2
Number of Counties.......................5*

---

*Including the County of Kalawao which is under the jurisdiction of the Board of Health.
‡Furnished by Hawaii Legislative Reference Bureau.

498

PUERTO RICO

Song..............*La Borinqueña*

Became a Territory of The United States.. December 10, 1898

Became a Commonwealth of the United States.. July 25, 1952

Capital City...........San Juan

OFFICERS

Governor.....................................Luis Muñoz-Marín
Secretary of State......................Roberto Sánchez-Vilella
Secretary of Justice ....José Trías-Monge
Resident Commissioner for Puerto Rico in the United States
......................................Antonio Fernós Isern
Secretary of the Treasury.............................Rafael Picó
Controller ....Rafael de J. Cordero

SUPREME COURT OF PUERTO RICO

Chief Justice....................................A. Cecil Snyder
Six Associate Judges

GOVERNOR
Luis Muñoz-Marín

LEGISLATURE

President of the Senate.......Samuel R. Quiñones

Vice-President of the Senate
...................Luis A. Negrón-López

Speaker of the House.......E. Ramos-Antonini

Vice-President of the House

Secretary of Senate..........Julio C. Torres
...................María Libertad Gómez

Secretary of the House........Néstor Rigual

STATISTICS

Area (square miles)....................3,423
Population (1953).................2,229,000
  Density per square mile (1953)........651.2
Delegate to Congress......................1
Fiscal Year 1953:
  General Funds—Re-
    current Revenue...........$161,000,000‡
  Commonwealth Government
    Budgetary Expenditures......$181,500,000‡
University........... University of Puerto Rico
Site........................Río Piedras

Capital City......................San Juan
  Population (1950)................368,756*
Largest City......................San Juan
  Population (1950)................368,756*
Number of Cities over 10,000 Population.....14
Number of Municipalities.................76

---

*The increase to 368,756 (total urban population of the Capital City, San Juan) is due to the fact that Río Piedras, which is physically close to San Juan was, by law, consolidated with San Juan into one municipality.
‡Furnished by the government of Puerto Rico.

499

VIRGIN ISLANDS

Formerly known as Danish West Indies

Flower............Tecoma Stans   Purchased from Denmark

(Yellow Elder or Yellow Cedar)   ....January 17, 1917

Capital City.....Charlotte Amalie

GOVERNOR
WALTER A. GORDON

OFFICERS

Governor.....................................WALTER A. GORDON
Government Secretary......................CHARLES K. CLAUNCH
Acting Commissioner of Finance....................PERCY DE JONGH
Government Comptroller ....RICHARD L. KRABACH

DISTRICT COURT OF THE VIRGIN ISLANDS

Judge.......................................HERMAN E. MOORE
United States Attorney..........................LEON P. MILLER

LEGISLATURE

President of the Legislature ....WALTER I. M. HODGE
Legislative Secretary ....JORGE RODRIGUEZ

The Legislature is composed of eleven members known as Senators. The Virgin Islands are divided into three legislative districts as follows: the District of St. Thomas, the District of St. Croix, and the District of St. John. Two Senators are elected from the District of St. Thomas; two from the District of St. Croix; one from the District of St. John, and the other six are At-Large and are elected by electors of the Virgin Islands as a whole. The term of office of each member of the Legislature is two years. Regular sessions of the Legislature are held annually, commencing on the second Monday in April, and continue in regular session for not more than sixty consecutive calendar days in any calendar year.

STATISTICS

Area—St. Croix (square miles)..............80
   St. Thomas (square miles)............32
   St. John (square miles).............20
Population (1950)—St. Croix...........12,103
   Density per square mile (1950)..........151
Population (1950)—St. Thomas........13,813
   Density per square mile (1950)..........432
Population (1950)—St. John..............749
   Density per square mile (1950)...........37

Fiscal year 1954:
   Revenue......................$4,721,243‡
   Expenditures...................$4,605,044‡
Capital City.....Charlotte Amalie, St. Thomas
Number of Municipalities...................2

‡Furnished by the U. S. Department of the Interior.

500

2

PRINCIPAL STATE AND TERRITORIAL OFFICERS

EXECUTIVE OFFICERS

State	Governors	Lieutenant Governors	Attorneys General	Secretaries of State
Alabama	James E. Folsom	W. Guy Hardwick	John M. Patterson	Mary Texas Hurt
Arizona	Ernest W. McFarland	None	Robert Morrison	Wesley Bolin
Arkansas	Orval E. Faubus	Nathan Gordon	T. J. Gentry	C. G. Hall
California	Goodwin J. Knight	Harold J. Powers	Edmund G. Brown	Frank M. Jordan
Colorado	Edwin C. Johnson	Stephen L. R. McNichols	Duke W. Dunbar	George J. Baker
Connecticut	Abraham A. Ribicoff	Charles W. Jewett	John J. Bracken	Mildred P. Allen
Delaware	J. Caleb Boggs	John W. Rollins	Joseph Donald Craven	John N. McDowell
Florida	LeRoy Collins	None	Richard W. Ervin	R. A. Gray
Georgia	S. Marvin Griffin	S. Ernest Vandiver	Eugene Cook	Ben W. Fortson, Jr.
Idaho	Robert E. Smylie	J. Berkeley Larsen	Graydon W. Smith	Ira H. Masters
Illinois	William G. Stratton	John William Chapman	Latham Castle	Charles F. Carpentier
Indiana	George N. Craig	Harold W. Handley	Edwin K. Steers	Crawford F. Parker
Iowa	Leo A. Hoegh	Leo Elthon	Dayton Countryman	Melvin D. Synhorst
Kansas	Fred Hall	John B. McCuish	Harold R. Fatzer	Paul R. Shanahan
Kentucky	Albert B. Chandler	Harry Lee Waterfield	Jo M. Ferguson	Thelma L. Stovall
Louisiana	Robert F. Kennon	C. E. Barham	Fred S. LeBlanc	Wade O. Martin, Jr.
Maine	Edmund S. Muskie	None	Frank F. Harding	Harold I. Goss
Maryland	Theodore R. McKeldin	None	C. Ferdinand Sybert	Blanchard Randall
Massachusetts	Christian A. Herter	Sumner G. Whittier	George Fingold	Edward J. Cronin
Michigan	G. Mennen Williams	Philip A. Hart	Thomas M. Kavanagh	James M. Hare
Minnesota	Orville L. Freeman	Karl F. Rolvaag	Miles Lord	Joseph L. Donovan
Mississippi	James P. Coleman	Carroll Gartin	Joe T. Patterson	Heber Ladner
Missouri	Phil M. Donnelly	James T. Blair, Jr.	John M. Dalton	Walter H. Toberman
Montana	J. Hugo Aronson	George M. Gosman	Arnold H. Olsen	S. C. Arnold
Nebraska	Victor E. Anderson	(Vacancy)	Clarence S. Beck	Frank Marsh
Nevada	Charles H. Russell	Rex Bell	Harvey Dickerson	John Koontz
New Hampshire	Lane Dwinell	None	Louis C. Wyman	Enoch D. Fuller
New Jersey	Robert B. Meyner	None	Grover C. Richman, Jr.	Edward J. Patten
New Mexico	John Field Simms	Joseph M. Montoya	Richard H. Robinson	Mrs. Natalie S. Buck
New York	Averell Harriman	George B. De Luca	Jacob K. Javits	Carmine G. DeSapio
North Carolina	Luther H. Hodges	(Vacancy)	William B. Rodman, Jr.(a)	Thad Eure
North Dakota	Norman Brunsdale	C. P. Dahl	Leslie R. Bergum	Ben Meier
Ohio	Frank J. Lausche	John W. Brown	C. William O'Neill	Ted W. Brown
Oklahoma	Raymond Gary	Cowboy Pink Williams	Mac Q. Williamson	Andy Anderson
Oregon	Paul Patterson	None	Robert Y. Thornton	Earl T. Newbry
Pennsylvania	George M. Leader	Roy E. Furman	Herbert B. Cohen	James A. Finnegan(b)
Rhode Island	Dennis J. Roberts	John S. McKiernan	William E. Powers	Armand H. Coté
South Carolina	George Bell Timmerman, Jr.	Ernest F. Hollings	T. C. Callison	O. Frank Thornton
South Dakota	Joe J. Foss	L. R. Houck	Phil Saunders	Geraldine Ostroot
Tennessee	Frank Goad Clement	Jared Maddux	George F. McCanless(c)	G. Edward Friar
Texas	Allan Shivers	Ben Ramsey	John Ben Shepperd	Tom Reavley
Utah	J. Bracken Lee	None	Richard Callister	Lamont F. Toronto
Vermont	Joseph Blaine Johnson	Mrs. Consuelo N. Bailey	Robert T. Stafford	Howard E. Armstrong
Virginia	Thomas B. Stanley	A. E. S. Stephens	J. Lindsay Almond, Jr.	Martha B. Conway
Washington	Arthur B. Langlie	Emmett T. Anderson	Don Eastvold	Earl Coe
West Virginia	William C. Marland	None	John G. Fox	D. Pitt O'Brien
Wisconsin	Walter J. Kohler	Warren P. Knowles	Vernon W. Thomson	Mrs. Glenn M. Wise(d)
Wyoming	Milward L. Simpson	None	George F. Guy	Everett T. Copenhaver
Alaska	B. Frank Heintzleman	Waino E. Hendrickson(e)	J. Gerald Williams	Waino E. Hendrickson(e)
Guam	Ford Q. Elvidge	Randall S. Herman(e)	Howard D. Porter	Randall S. Herman(e)
Hawaii	Samuel Wilder King	Farrant L. Turner(e)	Edward N. Sylva	Farrant L. Turner(e)
Puerto Rico	Luis Muñoz-Marín	None	José Trías-Monge(f)	Roberto Sánchez-Vilella
Virgin Islands	Walter A. Gordon	Charles K. Claunch(g)	Leon P. Miller(h)	Charles K. Claunch(g)

(a) Appointed in July, 1955 to fill unexpired term of Harry McMullan, deceased.
(b) Secretary of the Commonwealth.
(c) Appointed in September, 1954, to fill unexpired term of Roy H. Beeler, deceased.
(d) Appointed January 3, 1955 to fill unexpired term of Fred R. Zimmerman, deceased.
(e) Territorial Secretary.
(f) Secretary of Justice.
(g) Government Secretary.
(h) Virgin Islands do not have an Attorney General; the corresponding officer is the United States Attorney.

THE GOVERNORS

State	Name	Political Party	Present Term Began January	Length of Regular Term in Years	Number of Previous Terms	Maximum Consecutive Terms Allowed by Constitution	Date Specified by Constitution or Statute as Inauguration Day	Annual Salary
Alabama........	James E. Folsom	D	1955	4	1(a)	(b)	1st Mon. after 2nd Tues. in Jan.	$12,000
Arizona.........	Ernest W. McFarland	D	1955	2	..	..	1st Mon. in Jan.	15,000
Arkansas......	Orval E. Faubus	D	1955	2	..	..	2nd Tues. in Jan.	10,000
California......	Goodwin J. Knight	R	1955	4	1(c)	..	1st Mon. after Jan. 1	25,000(d)
Colorado.......	Edwin C. Johnson	D	1955	2	2(a)	..	2nd Tues. in Jan.	17,500
Connecticut....	Abraham A. Ribicoff	D	1955	4	..	..	1st Wed. after 1st Mon. in Jan.	15,000
Delaware.......	J. Caleb Boggs	R	1953	4	..	2	3rd Tues. in Jan.	12,000
Florida.........	LeRoy Collins	D	1955(e)	4	..	(b)	1st Tues. after 1st Mon. in Jan.	20,000
Georgia.........	S. Marvin Griffin	D	1955	4	..	(b)	Set by General Assembly	12,000
Idaho...........	Robert E. Smylie	R	1955	4	..	(b)	1st Mon. in Jan.	10,000(f)
Illinois.........	Wm. G. Stratton	R	1953	4	..	..	2nd Mon. in Jan.	25,000
Indiana.........	George N. Craig	R	1953	4	..	(b)	2nd Mon. in Jan.	15,000
Iowa...........	Leo A. Hoegh	R	1955	2	..	..	Thurs. after 2nd Mon. in Jan.	12,000
Kansas........	Fred Hall	R	1955	2	..	..	2nd Mon. in Jan.	15,000
Kentucky......	Albert B. Chandler	D	1955(g)	4	1(h)	(b)	6th Tues. after Nov. 1	15,000
Louisiana......	Robert F. Kennon	D	1952(g)	4	..	(b)	2nd Tues. in May	18,000
Maine..........	Edmund S. Muskie	D	1955	2	..	..	1st Thurs. in Jan.	10,000
Maryland......	Theodore R. McKeldin	R	1955	4	1(a)	2	2nd Wed. in Jan.	15,000
Massachusetts..	Christian A. Herter	R	1955	2	1(a)	..	Thurs. after 1st Wed. in Jan.	20,000
Michigan.......	G. Mennen Williams	D	1955	2	3(a)	..	1st day of Jan.	22,500
Minnesota......	Orville L. Freeman	(t)	1955	2	..	..	1st Mon. in Jan.	15,000
Mississippi.....	James P. Coleman	D	1956	4	..	(b)	Usually 3rd Tues. in Jan.	15,000
Missouri........	Phil M. Donnelly	D	1953	4	1(a)	(b)	2nd Mon. in Jan.	10,000(d)
Montana.......	J. Hugo Aronson	R	1953	4	..	..	1st Mon. in Jan.	12,500
Nebraska.......	Victor E. Anderson	R	1955	2	..	..	1st Thurs. after 1st Tues. in Jan.	11,000
Nevada........	Charles H. Russell	R	1955	4	1(a)	..	1st Mon. in Jan.	15,000(f)
New Hampshire.	Lane Dwinell	R	1955	2	..	..	1st Thurs. in Jan. (i)	12,000
New Jersey.....	Robert B. Meyner	D	1954	4	..	2	3rd Tues. in Jan.	30,000
New Mexico.....	John Field Simms	D	1955	2	..	2(j)	1st day of Jan.	15,000
New York.......	Averell Harriman	D	1955	4	..	..	1st day of Jan.	50,000
North Carolina..	Luther H. Hodges	D	1953(k)	4	..	(b)	Set by General Assembly	15,000(f)
North Dakota...	Norman Brunsdale	R	1955	2	2(a)	..	1st Mon. in Jan. or within 10 days thereafter	9,000
Ohio...........	Frank J. Lausche	D	1955	2	4(a)	..	2nd Mon. in Jan.	25,000(l)
Oklahoma......	Raymond Gary	D	1955	4	..	(b)	2nd Mon. in Jan.	15,000(f)
Oregon.........	Paul Patterson	R	1955	4	1(m)	2	2nd Mon. in Jan.	15,000(f)
Pennsylvania....	George M. Leader	D	1955	4	..	(b)	3rd Tues. in Jan.	25,000
Rhode Island...	Dennis J. Roberts	D	1955	2	2(a)	..	1st Tues. in Jan.	15,000
South Carolina..	Geo. Bell Timmerman, Jr.	D	1955	4	..	(b)	3rd Tues. in Jan.	15,000(f)
South Dakota...	Joe J. Foss	R	1955	2	..	2	1st Tues. after 1st Mon. in Jan.	12,000
Tennessee.....	Frank Goad Clement	D	1955	4	1(n)	(n)	Set by General Assembly	12,000 (f)
Texas..........	Allan Shivers	D	1955	2	2(o)	..	1st Tues. after convening of legislature in Jan.	25,000(f)
Utah...........	J. Bracken Lee	R	1953	4	1(a)	..	1st Mon. in Jan.	10,000
Vermont........	Joseph Blaine Johnson	R	1955	2	..	..	1st Thurs. in Jan.	11,500
Virginia........	Thomas B. Stanley	D	1954	4	..	(b)	3rd Wed. in Jan.	17,500
Washington.....	Arthur B. Langlie	R	1953	4	2(a)	..	2nd Mon. in Jan.	15,000
West Virginia...	Wm. C. Marland	D	1953	4	..	(b)	1st Mon. after 2nd Wed. in Jan.	12,500
Wisconsin......	Walter J. Kohler	R	1955	2	2(a)	..	1st Mon. in Jan.	14,000(d)
Wyoming.......	Milward L. Simpson	R	1955	4	..	..	1st Mon. in Jan.	12,000
Alaska.........	B. Frank Heintzleman	R	1953(g)	4	..	(p)	(q)	15,000
Guam..........	Ford Q. Elvidge	R	1953(g)	4	..	(p)	(q)	13,125
Hawaii.........	Samuel Wilder King	R	1953(g)	4	..	(p)	(q)	16,000
Puerto Rico....	Luis Muñoz-Marín	(r)	1953	4	1(a)	(p)	Jan. 2	10,600(s)
Virgin Islands...	Walter A. Gordon	(p)	1955(g)	(p)	..	(p)	(q)	15,000

(a) Alabama, 1947–51; Colorado, 1933–35, 1935–37; Maryland, 1951–55; Massachusetts, 1953–55; Michigan, 1949–50, 1951–52, 1953–54; Mississippi, 1936–40; Missouri, 1945–49; Nevada, 1951–55; North Dakota, 1951–53, 1953–55; Ohio, 1945–47, 1949–51, 1951–53, 1953–55; Rhode Island, 1951–53, 1953–55; Utah, 1949–53; Washington, 1941–45, 1949–53; Wisconsin, 1951–53, 1953–55; Puerto Rico, 1949–53.
(b) Cannot succeed himself.
(c) Succeeded to office October, 1953, filling unexpired term of Gov. Earl Warren.
(d) Effective on expiration of present term: California, $40,000; Missouri, $25,000; Wisconsin, $18,000.
(e) Elected in 1954 to fill unexpired term of Gov. Dan McCarty which will end in January, 1957.
(f) Idaho, South Carolina, Tennessee, Texas, plus residence; Oklahoma, plus $9,000 for expenses; Oregon, plus $400 per month for expenses; North Carolina, plus $4,000 travel expense allowance; Nevada, plus $7,200 mansion fund.
(g) Kentucky, December, 1955; Louisiana, May, 1952; Alaska, April, 1953; Guam, March, 1953; Hawaii, February, 1953; Virgin Islands, October, 1955.

(h) 1935–39, resigned October, 1939.
(i) By custom.
(j) A Governor who has served two consecutive terms shall be ineligible for two years thereafter.
(k) Succeeded to office November, 1954, filling unexpired term of Gov. Wm. B. Umstead, deceased.
(l) Effective January, 1957.
(m) Succeeded to office December, 1952, filling unexpired term of Gov. Douglas McKay.
(n) 1953–55. A 1953 constitutional amendment changed Governor's term from two to four years with no immediately succeeding term for one elected and qualified for a four-year term, effective 1955.
(o) Succeeded to office July, 1949, filling unexpired term of Gov. Beauford H. Jester, re-elected for 1951–53, 1953–55.
(p) Appointed by the President.
(q) No fixed day.
(r) Popular Democratic Party.
(s) $20,000 effective with next office holder.
(t) Democrat-Farmer-Labor.

LIEUTENANT GOVERNORS AND EXECUTIVE ASSISTANTS TO THE GOVERNORS

States	*Lieutenant Governors*	*Executive Assistants*
Alabama........	W. Guy Hardwick	O. H. Finney, Jr., *Executive Secretary*
Arizona.........	None	Roland H. Bibolet, Jr., *Executive Secretary*
Arkansas........	Nathan Gordon	Arnold B. Sikes, *Executive Secretary*
California.......	Harold J. Powers	Newton A. Stearns, *Executive Secretary*
Colorado........	Stephen L. R. McNichols	L. Donald Daily, *Executive Assistant*
Connecticut.....	Charles W. Jewett	John N. Demsey, *Special Assistant*
Delaware........	John W. Rollins	Edward Ewell, *Executive Secretary*
Florida..........	None	Joseph Grotegut, *Administrative Assistant*
Georgia..........	S. Ernest Vandiver	Ben T. Wiggins, *Executive Secretary*
Idaho...........	J. Berkeley Larsen	Robert B. Hodge, *Administrative Assistant*
Illinois..........	John William Chapman	Marion P. Keevers, *Executive Secretary*
Indiana..........	Harold W. Handley	Doxie Moore, *Administrative Assistant*
Iowa............	Leo Elthon	Paul Parker, *Administrative Assistant to the Governor*
Kansas..........	John B. McCuish	David W. Pansing, *Secretary to the Governor*
Kentucky........	Harry Lee Waterfield	(To be appointed)
Louisiana........	C. E. Barham	Wilburn Lunn, *Executive Counsel*
Maine...........	None	Maurice Williams, *Administrative Assistant*
Maryland........	None	Albert W. Quinn, *Assistant to the Governor*
Massachusetts...	Sumner G. Whittier	Harry F. Stimpson, Jr., *Chief Secretary*
Michigan........	Philip A. Hart	Lawrence L. Farrell, *Executive Secretary to the Governor*
Minnesota.......	Karl F. Rolvaag	Thomas R. Hughes, *Personal Secretary*
Mississippi......	Carroll Gartin	(To be appointed)
Missouri.........	James T. Blair, Jr.	Cance Pool, *Executive Secretary to the Governor*
Montana.........	George M. Gosman	Wesley Castles, *Executive Secretary*
Nebraska........	(Vacancy)	A. C. Eichberg, *Administrative Assistant*
Nevada..........	Rex Bell	Arthur N. Suverkrup, *Executive Assistant*
New Hampshire..	None	Alan Pope, *Administrative Assistant*
New Jersey......	None	Robert J. Burkhardt, *Executive Secretary to the Governor*
New Mexico......	Joseph M. Montoya	Richard W. Everett, *Executive Secretary*
New York........	George B. De Luca	Jonathan B. Bingham, *Secretary to the Governor*
North Carolina..	(Vacancy)	E. L. Rankin, Jr., *Private Secretary*
North Dakota....	C. P. Dahl	Walter Mohn, *Governor's Secretary*
Ohio............	John W. Brown	Ray M. White, *Secretary to the Governor*
Oklahoma.......	Cowboy Pink Williams	Truman Bennett, *Executive Secretary*
Oregon..........	None	Edwin H. Armstrong, *Assistant to the Governor*
Pennsylvania....	Roy E. Furman	David V. Randall, *Secretary to the Governor*
Rhode Island....	John S. McKiernan	Arthur P. Famiglietti, *Executive Secretary*
South Carolina..	Ernest F. Hollings	Charles Wickenberg, *Executive Secretary*
South Dakota....	L. R. Houck	Bob Lee, *Executive Secretary*
Tennessee.......	Jared Maddux	Glen Nicely, *Executive Assistant to the Governor*
Texas............	Ben Ramsey	John Osorio, *Executive Secretary to the Governor*
Utah............	None	Harold W. Simpson, *Executive Assistant*
Vermont........	Mrs. Consuelo N. Bailey	Neal J. Houston, *Secretary of Civil and Military Affairs*
Virginia.........	A. E. S. Stephens	Carter O. Lowance, *Executive Secretary*
Washington.....	Emmett T. Anderson	Joseph F. Hiddleston, *Assistant to the Governor*
West Virginia....	None	Rosemary Hotopp, *Executive Secretary*
Wisconsin.......	Warren P. Knowles	Phillip T. Drotning, *Executive Secretary*
Wyoming........	None	R. M. McManis, *Executive Secretary*
Alaska..........	Waino E. Hendrickson(a)	R. N. De Armond, *Special Assistant to the Governor*
Guam...........	Randall S. Herman(a)	
Hawaii..........	Farrant L. Turner(a)	Jack E. Conley, *Administrative Assistant to the Governor*
Puerto Rico......	None	Marco A. Rigau, *Executive Assistant to the Governor*
Virgin Islands...	Charles K. Claunch(b)	

(a) Territorial Secretary.
(b) Government Secretary.

LEGISLATIVE OFFICERS

State	President	Senate — President Pro Tem	Secretary	House — Speaker	Clerk
Alabama......	W. Guy Hardwick	Broughton Lamberth	J. E. Speight	Rankin Fite	R. T. Goodwyn, Jr.
Arizona.......	Clarence L. Carpenter	none	Mrs. Louise C. Brimhall	Harry S. Ruppelius	Mrs. Lallah Ruth
Arkansas....	Nathan Gordon	Lawrence Blackwell	Jim Snoddy	Charles F. Smith	Nelson Cox (a)
California.....	Harold J. Powers	Ben Hulse	J. A. Beek	Luther H. Lincoln	Arthur A. Ohnimus (a)
Colorado......	Stephen L. R. McNichols	Frank L. Gill	Mrs. Mildred Creswell	David A. Hamil	Lee Matties
Connecticut...	Charles W. Jewett	Patrick J. Ward	Al. A. Toscano (b)	W. Sheffield Cowles	John Wassung
Delaware.....	John W. Rollins	Charles G. Moore	Wilson E. Campbell	James R. Quigley	John E. Babiarz (a)
Florida.......	W. Turner Davis	George G. Tapper	Robert W. Davis	Thomas E. David	Mrs. Lamar Bledsoe (a)
Georgia.......	S. Ernest Vandiver	G. Everett Millican	George D. Stewart	Marvin Moate	Joe Boone
Idaho........	J. Berkeley Larsen	Carl D. Irwin	Robert H. Remaklus	R. H. Young, Jr.	Pat Welker (a)
Illinois.......	John Wm. Chapman	Arthur J. Bidwill	Ed. H. Alexander	Warren L. Wood	Fred W. Ruegg (a)
Indiana.......	Harold W. Handley	John W. Van Ness	Albert E. Ferris	George S. Diener	Wm. C. Brummett (c)
Iowa..........	Leo Elthon	DeVere Watson	Carroll A. Lane	Arthur C. Hanson	A. C. Gustafson (a)
Kansas.......	John B. McCuish	Paul R. Wunsch	Sidney Margaret Gardiner	Robert H. Jennison	Frank Garrett (a)
Kentucky.....	Harry L. Waterfield	(New officers to be elected in January, 1956)			
Louisiana....•..	C. E. Barham	Robert A. Ainsworth, Jr.	Robert A. Gilbert	C. C. Aycock	W. Clegg Cole
Maine........	Robert N. Haskell	(d)	Chester T. Winslow	W. A. Trafton, Jr.	Harvey R. Pease
Maryland.....	Louis L. Goldstein	none	C. Andrew Shaab	John C. Luber	George W. Owings, Jr. (a)
Massachusetts	Richard I. Furbush	none	I. N. Hayden (b)	Michael F. Skerry	Lawrence R. Grove
Michigan.....	Philip A. Hart	Harry F. Hittle	Fred I. Chase	Wade Van Valkenburg	Norman E. Philleo
Minnesota....	Karl F. Rolvaag	Val Imm	H. Y. Torrey	A. I. Johnson	George H. Leahy (a
Mississippi....	Carroll Gartin	(New officers to be elected in January, 1956)			
Missouri......	James T. Blair, Jr.	Edward V. Long	Joseph A. Bauer	Roy Hamlin	Austin Hill (a)
Montana.....	George M. Gosman	Fred L. Robinson	Frank Hazelbaker	Leo C. Graybill	Wm. P. Pilgeram (a)
Nebraska (e)..	Vacancy (f)	Dwight Burney (g)	Hugo F. Srb (h)		
Nevada......	Rex Bell	F. H. Settelmeyer	Robert J. Ingersoll	Cyril O. Bastian	Keith L. Lee (a)
New Hampshire	Raymond K. Perkins	none	Benjamin F. Greer (b)	(Vacancy)	Robert L. Stark
New Jersey....		(New officers to be elected in January, 1956)			
New Mexico...	Jos. M. Montoya	Guido Zecca	Ed. G. Romero (a)	Donald D. Hallam	Floyd Cross (a)
New York.....	George B. De Luca	Walter J. Mahoney	William S. King	Oswald D. Heck	Ansley B. Borkowski
North Carolina	Luther E. Barnhardt	Paul E. Jones	S. Ray Byerly (a)	Larry I. Moore, Jr.	Mrs. Annie E. Cooper (c)
North Dakota.	C. P. Dahl	Oliver E. Bilden	Edward Leno	K. A. Fitch	Kenneth L. Morgan
Ohio.........	John W. Brown	C. Stanley Mechem	Thos. E. Bateman (b)	Roger Cloud	Carl Guess (a)
Oklahoma....	Cowboy Pink Williams	Ray Fine	Leo W. Winters	B. E. Harkey	Carl J. Staas (a)
Oregon.......	Elmo E. Smith	....	Mrs. Zylpha Zell Burns (a)	Edward A. Geary	Mrs. Edith Bynon Low (a)
Pennsylvania..	Roy E. Furman	M. Harvey Taylor	G. Harold Watkins	Hiram G. Andrews	Benjamin L. Long (a)
Rhode Island..	John S. McKiernan	James J. Brady, Sr.	Armand H. Coté (i)	Harry F. Curvin	Henry R. Sullivan, Reading Paul B. McMahon, Recording
South Carolina	Ernest F. Hollings	Edgar A. Brown	Lovick O. Thomas (b)	Solomon Blatt	Inez Watson
South Dakota.	L. R. Houck	Frank A. Ferguson	Niels P. Jensen	Nils A. Boe	W. J. Matson (a)
Tennessee.....	Jared Maddux	none	John W. Cooke, Jr. (b)	James L. Bomar	L. Buchanan Loser (a)
Texas.........	Ben Ramsey	Mrs. Neveille H. Colson	Charles A. Schnabel (j)	Jim T. Lindsey	Mrs. Dorothy Hallman (a)
Utah.........	C. Taylor Burton	none	Quayle Cannon, Jr.	Charles E. Peterson	Rulon J. Larsen (a)
Vermont......	Mrs. Consuelo N. Bailey	Carleton G. Howe	Earle J. Bishop	John Hancock	O. Fay Allen, Jr.
Virginia......	A. E. S. Stephens	(New officers to be elected in January, 1956)			
Washington...	E. T. Anderson	Victor Zednick	Herbert H. Sieler	John O'Brien	S. R. Holcomb (a)
West Virginia.	Ralph J. Bean	Fred C. Allen	J. Howard Myers (b)	Wm. E. Flannery	C. A. Blankenship
Wisconsin.....	Warren P. Knowles	Frank E. Panzer	L. R. Larsen (a)	Mark S. Catlin, Jr.	Arthur L. May (a)
Wyoming.....	R. L. Greene	Norman Barlow	Frances D. Clark (a)	T. C. Daniels	Harry C. Barker, Jr. (a)
Alaska........	James Nolan	(Vacancy)	Katherine T. Alexander	Wendell P. Kay	John McLaughlin (a)
Guam (e)....	F. B. Leon Guerrero (g)	B. J. Bordallo (n)	A. SN. Duenas (m)	....	Maria Duenas (h)
Hawaii........	Wm. H. Heen	Wm. J. Nobriga (k)	Wm. S. Richardson (b)	Charles E. Kauhane	James K. Trask
Puerto Rico...	Samuel R. Quiñones	Luis Negrón-López	Julio C. Torres	Ernesto Ramos-Antonini	Néstor Rigual (l)
Virgin Islands.	Walter I. Hodge (f)	....	Jorge Rodriguez (m)		....

THE CHIEF JUSTICES

State	Chief Justice	Official Title	Present Term as Chief Justice Commenced	Present Term Expires
Alabama........	James E. Livingston	Chief Justice	January 20, 1953	January, 1959
Arizona.........	Arthur T. LaPrade	Chief Justice	January 3, 1955	January 3, 1957
Arkansas.......	Lee Seamster	Chief Justice	April 30, 1955	December 31, 1956
California......	Phil S. Gibson	Chief Justice	January 1, 1951	January 1, 1963
Colorado........	Wilbur M. Alter	Chief Justice	January 11, 1955	January 8, 1957
Connecticut....	Ernest A. Inglis	Chief Justice	October 26, 1953	October 26, 1961
Delaware.......	Clarence A. Southerland	Chief Justice	June 5, 1951	June 4, 1963
Florida.........	E. Harris Drew	Chief Justice	May 6, 1955	January 8, 1957
Georgia.........	Wm. H. Duckworth	Chief Justice	January 1, 1951	December 31, 1956
Idaho...........	C. J. Taylor	Chief Justice	January 3, 1955	1st Monday in January, 1957
Illinois.........	Harry B. Hershey	Chief Justice	September 12, 1955	2nd Monday in September, 1956
Indiana.........	Arch N. Bobbitt	Chief Justice	November 28, 1955	May 27, 1956
Iowa...........	Robert L. Larson	Chief Justice	January 1, 1956	June 30, 1956
Kansas.........	William West Harvey	Chief Justice	January 12, 1953	2nd Monday in January, 1959
Kentucky.......	James B. Milliken	Chief Justice	January 9, 1956	July 1, 1957
Louisiana.......	John B. Fournet	Chief Justice	September 8, 1949	Dec. 31, 1962
Maine..........	Raymond Fellows	Chief Justice	April 7, 1954	April 7, 1961
Maryland.......	Frederick W. Brune	Chief Judge	March 11, 1954	November, 1956
Massachusetts..	Stanley E. Qua	Chief Justice	August, 1947	Appointed for life
Michigan.......	John R. Dethmers	Chief Justice	January 6, 1956	December 31, 1961
Minnesota......	Roger L. Dell	Chief Justice	January 3, 1955	1st Monday in January, 1961
Mississippi.....	Harvey McGehee	Chief Justice	January 2, 1956	1st Monday in January, 1964
Missouri........	C. A. Leedy, Jr.	Chief Justice	March 1, 1955	October, 1956
Montana.......	Hugh R. Adair	Chief Justice	January 5, 1953	January, 1959
Nebraska.......	Robert G. Simmons	Chief Justice	January, 1951	January, 1957
Nevada.........	Charles M. Merrill	Chief Justice	January 1, 1955	December 31, 1956
New Hampshire.	Frank R. Kenison	Chief Justice	April 29, 1952	Retirement at age 70
New Jersey......	Arthur T. Vanderbilt	Chief Justice	September 15, 1948	Appointed for life
New Mexico.....	J. C. Compton	Chief Justice	January 1, 1955	December 31, 1956
New York.......	Albert Conway	Chief Judge	January 1, 1955	December 31, 1959
North Carolina..	M. Victor Barnhill	Chief Justice	February 1, 1954	Dec. 31, 1958
North Dakota...	Thomas J. Burke	Chief Justice	January 3, 1955	1st Monday in January, 1957
Ohio...........	Carl V. Weygandt	Chief Justice	January 1, 1951	December 31, 1956
Oklahoma......	N. B. Johnson	Chief Justice	January 10, 1955	January 14, 1957
Oregon.........	Harold J. Warner	Chief Justice	January 3, 1955	1st Monday in January, 1957
Pennsylvania....	Horace Stern	Chief Justice	November 10, 1952	1st Monday in January, 1957
Rhode Island...	Edmund W. Flynn	Chief Justice	January 1, 1935	Appointed for life
South Carolina..	David Gordon Baker	Chief Justice	August 1, 1954	July 31, 1964(a)
South Dakota...	E. D. Roberts	Presiding Judge	January 1, 1956	December 31, 1956
Tennessee......	Albert B. Neil	Chief Justice	September 1, 1950	August 31, 1958
Texas..........	John E. Hickman	Chief Justice	January 1, 1955	January 1, 1961
Utah...........	Roger I. McDonough	Chief Justice	April 27, 1954	1st Monday in January, 1959
Vermont........	Olin M. Jeffords	Chief Justice	March 1, 1955	March 1, 1957
Virginia........	Edward W. Hudgins	Chief Justice	February 1, 1954	February 1, 1966
Washington.....	Frederick G. Hamley	Chief Justice	January 10, 1955	January 13, 1957
West Virginia...	Chauncy Browning	President	January 1, 1956	December 31, 1956
Wisconsin......	Edward T. Fairchild	Chief Justice	January 1, 1954	January 1, 1957
Wyoming.......	Fred H. Blume	Chief Justice	November 21, 1955	1st Monday in January, 1963
Hawaii.........	Edward A. Towse	Chief Justice	September 26, 1951	September 26, 1955(b)
Puerto Rico.....	A. Cecil Snyder	Chief Justice	January 21, 1953	Appointed for life

(a) Chief Justice Baker reaches retirement age on February 17, 1956.   (b) And until successor is appointed and qualified.

THE ATTORNEYS GENERAL

State	Attorney General	Political Party	Present Term Began Jan.	Term of Office in Years	How Selected	Annual Salary	Private Practice Permitted by Law	Number of Regular Assistants and Deputies	Funds Available Fiscal Year 1955-56
Alabama	John M. Patterson	D	1955	4	Elected	$10,000	No	14	$198,550
Arizona	Robert Morrison	D	1955	2	Elected	10,000	No	21	233,597
Arkansas	T. J. Gentry	D	1955	2	Elected	6,000	Yes	6	69,050
California	Edmund G. Brown	D	1955	4	Elected	23,000	No	97	3,906,439
Colorado	Duke W. Dunbar	R	1955	2	Elected	9,000	Yes	18	136,644
Connecticut	John J. Bracken	R	1955	4	Elected	12,500	Yes	10	127,706
Delaware	Joseph Donald Craven	D	1955	4	Elected	12,000	Yes	8	74,200
Florida	Richard W. Ervin	D	1953	4	Elected	15,000	No	As needed	483,512
Georgia	Eugene Cook	D	1955	4	Elected	7,500	No	15	197,022
Idaho	Graydon W. Smith	R	1955	4	Elected	7,500	Yes	9	47,475
Illinois	Latham Castle	R	1953	4	Elected	16,000	No	102	1,948,000
Indiana	Edwin K. Steers	R	1953	4	Elected	11,500	(a)	40	315,866
Iowa	Dayton Countryman	R	1955	2	Elected	8,500	(a)	9(b)	70,820
Kansas	Harold R. Fatzer	R	1955	2	Elected	8,500	Yes	6	340,833
Kentucky	Jo M. Ferguson	D	1956	4	Elected	11,000	Yes	18	104,000
Louisiana	Fred S. LeBlanc	D	1952(c)	4	Elected	12,500	No	15	296,765
Maine	Frank F. Harding	D	1955	2	Leg. elects	8,000	Yes	10	105,163
Maryland	C. Ferdinand Sybert	D	1954(d)	4	Elected	12,000	Yes	5	111,317
Massachusetts	George Fingold	R	1955	2	Elected	15,000	Yes	32(e)	350,150
Michigan	Thomas M. Kavanagh	D	1955	2	Elected	12,500	Yes	57	841,753
Minnesota	Miles Lord	DFL	1955	4	Elected	13,000	No	18	167,012
Mississippi	Joe T. Patterson	D	1956	4	Elected	10,000	No	6	156,240(f)
Missouri	John M. Dalton	D	1953	4	Elected	7,500(h)	Yes	..	335,000
Montana	Arnold H. Olsen	D	1953	4	Elected	7,500	Yes	8	93,303
Nebraska	Clarence S. Beck	R	1955	4	Elected	6,500	Yes	7	111,984
Nevada	Harvey Dickerson	D	1955	4	Elected	8,400	Yes	3	44,498
New Hampshire	Louis C. Wyman	R	1955	5	Gov. and Council appoint	9,810	(a)	4	87,050(i)
New Jersey	Grover C. Richman, Jr.	D	1954	4(j)	Gov. appoints(k)	20,000	No	40	579,622(l)
New Mexico	Richard H. Robinson	D	1955	2	Elected	10,000	Yes	6	90,000
New York	Jacob K. Javits	R	1955	4	Elected	25,000	Yes	118	2,434,503
North Carolina	Wm. B. Rodman, Jr.	D	1953(m)	4	Elected	12,080	No	7	133,019
North Dakota	Leslie R. Bergum	R	1955	2	Elected	7,500	No	9	95,070
Ohio	C. William O'Neill	R	1955	2	Elected	12,000(h)	No	48	737,869
Oklahoma	Mac Q. Williamson	D	1955	4	Elected	12,000	No	12	150,274
Oregon	Robert Y. Thornton	D	1953	4	Elected	11,000	(a)	5	165,640
Pennsylvania	Herbert B. Cohen	D	1955	(g)	Gov. appts.	15,000	Yes	30	Not available
Rhode Island	William E. Powers	D	1955	2	Elected	11,000	Yes	9	206,355
South Carolina	T. C. Callison	D	1955	4	Elected	10,000	(a)	5	81,163
South Dakota	Phil Saunders	R	1955	2	Elected	7,500	No	9	151,300
Tennessee	George F. McCanless	D	1950(n)	8	Sup. Ct. appts.	12,000(h)	No	7	519,000
Texas	John Ben Shepperd	D	1955	2	Elected	20,000	No	42	470,235
Utah	Richard Callister	R	1953	4	Elected	7,500	Yes	9	83,015
Vermont	Robert T. Stafford	R	1955	2	Elected	7,500	Yes	3	43,000(o)
Virginia	J. Lindsay Almond, Jr.	D	1954	4	Elected	12,500	No	8	115,500
Washington	Don Eastvold	R	1953	4	Elected	10,000	Yes(p)	58	553,000(f)
West Virginia	John G. Fox	D	1953	4	Elected	7,500	Yes	As needed	108,950
Wisconsin	Vernon W. Thomson	R	1955	2	Elected	10,000(h)	Yes(p)	13	287,290
Wyoming	George F. Guy	R	1955(q)	4	Gov. appts.(k)	7,500	No	4	125,200(f)
Alaska	J. Gerald Williams	D	1953(q)	4	Elected	14,500	No	3	141,176(f)
Guam	Howard D. Porter	R	1953	(r)	Gov. appts.(s)	9,880(t)	Yes(u)	..	....
Hawaii	Edward N. Sylva	R	1953(v)	4	Gov. appts.	12,500	No	14	176,169
Puerto Rico	José Trías-Monge(w)	Pop.D.	1953	4	Gov. appts.(x)	14,000	No	6	677,914
Virgin Islands	Leon P. Miller(y)	R	1954(q)	4	Pres. appts.	12,000(z)	No	1	....

(a) No statute on this subject.
(b) Four are paid by departments to which they are assigned.
(c) May, 1952.
(d) December, 1954.
(e) Eleven of the thirty-two are assigned to various state agencies and are paid out of funds appropriated to those agencies.
(f) For the biennium.
(g) Not specified.
(h) $15,000 effective on expiration of present term.
(i) For 1955-56; $82,526 for 1956-57; plus $42,500 special appropriation for the biennium, subversive activities investigation.
(j) During term of Governor.
(k) With Senate approval.
(l) Appropriation for Division of Law, Department of Law and Public Safety.
(m) Appointed in July, 1955 to fill unexpired term of Harry McMullan, deceased.

(n) Appointed September, 1954, to fill unexpired term of Roy H. Beeler, deceased.
(o) For 1955-56; $46,850 for 1956-57.
(p) It is not the custom to engage in private practice.
(q) Wyoming, April, 1955; Alaska, April, 1953; Virgin Islands, October, 1954.
(r) Appointed by and serves at pleasure of Governor.
(s) With advice and consent of legislature.
(t) Plus territorial post differential when applicable.
(u) Subject to administrative control.
(v) March, 1953.
(w) Secretary of Justice.
(x) With advice and consent of Commonwealth Senate.
(y) Virgin Islands do not have an Attorney General; the corresponding officer is the United States Attorney.
(z) Salary set by United States Attorney General.

THE SECRETARIES OF STATE

State	Secretary of State	Political Party	Present Term Began January	How Selected	Term of Office in Years	Annual Salary	Acts in Governor's Absence
Alabama	Mary Texas Hurt	D	1955	Elected	4	$6,000(a)	No
Arizona	Wesley Bolin	D	1955	Elected	2	7,200	Yes
Arkansas	C. G. Hall	D	1955	Elected	2	5,000	No
California	Frank M. Jordan	R	1955	Elected	4	14,000(a)	No
Colorado	George J. Baker	D	1955	Elected	2	8,000	No
Connecticut	Mildred P. Allen	R	1955	Elected	4	8,000	Yes (b)
Delaware	John N. McDowell	R	1953	Gov. appoints	4	8,000	No
Florida	R. A. Gray	D	1953	Elected	4	15,000	No
Georgia	Ben W. Fortson, Jr.	D	1955	Elected	4	7,500	No
Idaho	Ira H. Masters	D	1955	Elected	4	6,500	No
Illinois	Charles F. Carpentier	R	1953	Elected	4	16,000	No
Indiana	Crawford F. Parker	R	1954(c)	Elected	2	11,500	No
Iowa	Melvin D. Synhorst	R	1955	Elected	2	7,500	No
Kansas	Paul R. Shanahan	R	1955	Elected	2	7,500	No
Kentucky	Thelma L. Stovall	D	1956	Elected	4	9,000	Yes (b)
Louisiana	Wade O. Martin, Jr.	D	1952(d)	Elected	4	16,800(e)	No
Maine	Harold I. Goss	R	1955	Leg. elects	2	8,000	No
Maryland	Blanchard Randall	R	1955	Gov. appoints	4	10,000	No
Massachusetts	Edward J. Cronin	D	1955	Elected	2	11,000	Yes (f)
Michigan	James M. Hare	D	1955	Elected	2	12,500	No
Minnesota	Joseph L. Donovan	DFL	1955	Elected	2	11,000	No
Mississippi	Heber Ladner	D	1956	Elected	4	8,250	No
Missouri	Walter H. Toberman	D	1953	Elected	4	7,500(a)	No
Montana	S. C. Arnold	R	1953(g)	Elected	4	7,500	No
Nebraska	Frank Marsh	R	1955	Elected	2	6,500	No
Nevada	John Koontz	D	1955	Elected	4	8,000	No
New Hampshire	Enoch D. Fuller	R	1955	Leg. elects	2	8,080	No
New Jersey	Edward J. Patten	D	1954	Gov. appts. (i)	4(j)	13,000	No
New Mexico	Mrs. Natalie S. Buck	D	1955	Elected	2	8,400	Yes (f)
New York	Carmine G. DeSapio	D	1955	Gov. appts.	(j)	17,000	No
North Carolina	Thad Eure	D	1953	Elected	4	10,000	No
North Dakota	Ben Meier	R	1955	Elected	2	5,000	No
Ohio	Ted W. Brown	R	1955	Elected	2	15,000(k)	No
Oklahoma	Andy Anderson	D	1955	Elected	4	6,000	No
Oregon	Earl T. Newbry	R	1953	Elected	4	11,000	Yes (l)
Pennsylvania	James A. Finnegan (m)	D	1955	Gov. appts. (i)	Pleas. of Gov.	15,000	No
Rhode Island	Armand H. Coté	D	1955	Elected	2	9,000	Yes (b)
South Carolina	O. Frank Thornton	D	1955	Elected	4	10,000	No
South Dakota	Geraldine Ostroot	R	1955	Elected	2	6,000	Yes (f)
Tennessee	G. Edward Friar	D	1953	Gen. Assbly. elects	4	10,000	No
Texas	Tom Reavley	D	1955	Gov. appts.	2(j)	15,000	No
Utah	Lamont F. Toronto	R	1953	Elected	4	7,200	Yes
Vermont	Howard E. Armstrong	R	1955	Elected	2	7,500	No
Virginia	Martha B. Conway	D	1954	Gov. appts.	4	6,500	No
Washington	Earl Coe	D	1953	Elected	4	8,500	Yes (f)
West Virginia	D. Pitt O'Brien	D	1953	Elected	4	7,250	No
Wisconsin	Mrs. Glenn M. Wise	R	1955(n)	Elected	2	10,000 (k)	Yes (f)
Wyoming	Everett T. Copenhaver	R	1955	Elected	4	8,400	Yes
Alaska	Waino E. Hendrickson (o)	R	1953	Pres. appoints	4	14,850	Yes
Guam	R. S. Herman (o)	D	1950	Pres. appoints	4 (h)	15,525(p)	
Hawaii	Farrant L. Turner (o)	R	1953(q)	Pres. appoints	4	15,336	Yes
Puerto Rico	Roberto Sánchez-Vilella	Pop. D	1953	Gov. appoints	4	14,000	Yes
Virgin Islands	Charles K. Claunch (r)	R	1954(s)	Pres. appoints	Pleas. of Pres.	10,500	Yes

(a) Effective upon expiration of present term: Alabama, $8,000; California, $17,500; Missouri, $15,000.
(b) In absence of Lt. Gov. and Pres. Pro Tem of the Senate.
(c) December, 1954.
(d) May, 1952.
(e) $8,000 as Secretary of State, $4,000 as chairman of Insurance Commission, $4,800 as custodian of voting machines.
(f) In absence of Lt. Gov.
(g) Appointed in July, 1955 to fill unexpired term of Sam W. Mitchell, deceased.
(h) Pleasure of the President.

(i) With Senate approval.
(j) During term of appointing Governor.
(k) Effective January, 1957.
(l) After President of Senate and Speaker of House.
(m) Secretary of the Commonwealth.
(n) Appointed January 3, 1955 to fill unexpired term of Fred R. Zimmerman, deceased.
(o) Territorial Secretary; also serves as Lt. Gov.
(p) Plus territorial post differential.
(q) May, 1953.
(r) Government Secretary; also serves as Lt. Gov.
(s) April, 1954.

ADMINISTRATIVE OFFICIALS CLASSIFIED

BY FUNCTIONS

(As of November, 1955)

ADJUTANT GENERAL

State	Name	Official Title	Agency	Location
Alabama.......	W. D. Partlow, Jr.	Adj. Gen.	Military Dept.	Montgomery
Arizona........	Frank E. Fraser	Brig. Gen.	Military Dept.	Phoenix
Arkansas.......	Sherman T. Clinger	Adj. Gen.	Military Dept.	Little Rock
California.....	Earle M. Jones	Adj. Gen.	Off. of Adj. Gen.	Sacramento
Colorado.......	Irving O. Schaefer	Adj. Gen.	National Guard	Denver
Connecticut....	Frederick G. Reincke	Adj. Gen.	Military Dept.	Hartford
Delaware.....	Joseph J. Scannell	Adj. Gen.	Military Dept.	Wilmington
Florida........	Mark W. Lance	Adj. Gen.	Adj. Gen.'s Off.	St. Augustine
Georgia........	George J. Hearn	Adj. Gen.	Military Dept.	Atlanta
Idaho.........	John E. Walsh	Adj. Gen.	Adj. Gen.'s Off.	Boise
Illinois.........	Leo M. Boyle	Adj. Gen.	Milit. and Naval Dept.	Springfield
Indiana........	Harold A. Doherty	Adj. Gen.	Military Dept.	Indianapolis
Iowa..........	Fred C. Tandy	Adj. Gen.	Adj. Gen.'s Dept.	Des Moines
Kansas........	Joe Nickell	Adj. Gen.	Adj. Gen.'s Off.	Topeka
Kentucky......	J. S. Lindsay	Adj. Gen.	Dept. of Military Affairs	Frankfort
Louisiana......	Raymond H. Fleming	Adj. Gen.	Military Dept.	New Orleans
Maine.........	George M. Carter	Adj. Gen.	Adj. Gen.'s Dept.	Augusta
Maryland.....	Milton A. Reckord	Major Gen.	Military Dept.	Baltimore
Massachusetts...	Wm. H. Harrison, Jr.	Adj. Gen.	Military Div.	Boston
Michigan......	George C. Moran	Adj. Gen.	Adj. Gen.'s Dept.	Lansing
Minnesota......	J. E. Nelson	Adj. Gen.	Dept. of Military and Naval Affairs	St. Paul
Mississippi.....	Wm. P. Wilson	Adj. Gen.	Military Dept.	Jackson
Missouri.......	Albert D. Sheppard	Adj. Gen.	Adj. Gen.'s Off.	Jefferson City
Montana.......	S. H. Mitchell	Adj. Gen.	Adj. Gen.'s Dept.	Helena
Nebraska.......	Guy N. Henninger	Adj. Gen.	Adj. Gen.'s Off.	Lincoln
Nevada........	James A. May	Adj. Gen.	National Guard	Carson City
New Hampshire.	John Jacobson, Jr.	Brig. Gen.	Adj. Gen.'s Off.	Concord
New Jersey.....	James F. Cantwell	Chief of Staff	Dept. of Defense	Trenton
New Mexico....	Charles G. Sage	Adj. Gen.	Adj. Gen.'s Off.	Santa Fe
New York......	William H. Kelly	Adj. Gen.	Div. of Military and Naval Affairs	Albany
North Carolina..	John Hall Manning	Adj. Gen.	Adj. Gen.'s Off.	Raleigh
North Dakota...	Heber L. Edwards	Adj. Gen.	Adj. Gen.'s Dept.	Bismarck
Ohio..........	Leo M. Kreber	Adj. Gen.	Dept. of Adj. Gen.	Columbus
Oklahoma......	Roy W. Kenny	Adj. Gen.	Military Dept.	Oklahoma City
Oregon........	Thomas E. Rilea	Adj. Gen.	Off. of Adj. Gen.	Salem
Pennsylvania...	Anthony J. Drexel Biddle, Jr.	Adj. Gen.	Dept. of Milit. Affairs	Harrisburg
Rhode Island...	John M. McGreevy	Act. Adj. Gen.	Adj. Gen.'s Off.	Providence
South Carolina..	James C. Dozier	Adj. Gen.	Off. of Adj. Gen.	Columbia
South Dakota...	Theodore A. Arndt	Adj. Gen.	Dept. of Milit. Affairs	Rapid City
Tennessee......	Joseph Henry	Adj. Gen.	Adj. Gen.'s Off.	Nashville
Texas..........	K. L. Berry	Adj. Gen.	Adj. Gen.'s Dept.	Austin
Utah..........	Maxwell E. Rich	Adj. Gen.	National Guard	Salt Lake City
Vermont.......	Francis W. Billado	Adj. Gen.	Adj. Gen.'s Off.	Montpelier
Virginia.......	S. Gardner Waller	Adj. Gen.	Dept. of Milit. Affairs	Richmond
Washington....	Lilburn H. Stevens	Adj. Gen.	National Guard	Camp Murray

ADJUTANT GENERAL—*continued*

State	Name	Official Title	Agency	Location
West Virginia...	Charles R. Fox	Major Gen.	Adj. Gen.'s Off.	Charleston
Wisconsin......	Ralph J. Olson	Adj. Gen.	Adj. Gen.'s Dept.	Madison
Wyoming......	R. L. Esmay	Adj. Gen.	Adj. Gen.'s Dept.	Cheyenne
Alaska.........	John R. Noyes	Adj. Gen.	National Guard	Juneau
Guam.........	Juan Muna	Colonel	Guam Militia	Agana
Hawaii........	F. W. Makinney	Adj. Gen.	National Guard	Honolulu
Puerto Rico....	Luis Raúl Esteves	Adj. Gen.	National Guard	San Juan

ADVERTISING

State	Name	Official Title	Agency	Location
Alabama.......	Pleas Looney	Director	Bur. Pub. and Info.	Montgomery
Arizona........	Raymond Carlson	Ed., Arizona Highways	Highway Dept.	Phoenix
Arkansas.......	Sam B. Kirby	Director	Publicity and Parks	Little Rock
Colorado.......	Lewis R. Cobb	Director	Adv. and Pub. Dept.	Denver
Connecticut....	Sidney A. Edwards	Managing Director	Devel. Commn.	Hartford
Delaware......	Miles L. Frederick	Director	State Devel. Dept.	Dover
Florida........	B. R. Fuller, Jr.	Director	Devel. Commn.	Tallahassee
Georgia........	Scott Candler	Secretary	Commerce Dept.	Atlanta
Idaho.........	Lee Heller	Secretary	Advertising Commn.	Boise
Illinois.........	Carl G. Hodges	Supt. of Dept. Reports	Dept. of Finance	Springfield
Indiana........	Edwin W. Beaman	Exec. Director	Dept. of Comm. and Public Relations	Indianapolis
Iowa..........	T. E. Davidson II	Director	Devel. Commn.	Des Moines
Kansas........	John B. Sutherland	Director	Industrial Devel. Commn.	Topeka
Kentucky......	Mack Sisk	Dir., Div. of Publicity	Dept. of Conservation	Frankfort
Maine.........	Carl J. Broggi	Commissioner	Dept. of Devel. of Ind. and Comm.	Augusta
Maryland......	Earle Poorbaugh	Director	Dept. of Information	Annapolis
Massachusetts...	Amico J. Barone	Dir., Div. of Devel.	Dept. of Commerce	Boston
Michigan......	Robt. J. Furlong	Exec. Secretary	Tourist Council	Lansing
Minnesota......	John Henricksson	Director of Publicity	Dept. of Business Devel.	St. Paul
Mississippi.....	H. C. Allen, Jr.	Director	Agric. and Ind. Bd.	Jackson
Missouri.......	Prentiss Mooney	Dir., Div. of Resources and Devel.	Dept. of Business and Admin.	Jefferson City
Montana.......	J. R. Hollowell	Publicity Dept.	Highway Commn.	Helena
Nebraska.......	C. V. Price	Chief, Div. of Resources	Dept. of Agric. and Inspection	Lincoln
Nevada........	Peter T. Kelley	Director	Dept. of Econ. Devel.	Carson City
New Hampshire {	John Brennan	Publicity Director	Planning and Devel. Commn.	Concord
	Andrew M. Heath	Advertising Mgr.	Planning and Devel. Commn.	Concord
New Jersey.....	James King	Chief, State Promotion Sect., Bur. Planning and Comm., Div. Planning and Devel.	Dept. of Conserv. and Econ. Devel.	Trenton
New Mexico....	Joseph A. Bursey	Director	Tourist Bureau	Santa Fe
New York......	Eileen Durning	Dir., Div. of State Publicity	Dept. of Commerce	Albany
North Carolina..	Charles J. Parker	Mgr., News Bur.	Dept. of Conserv. and Devel.	Raleigh
Ohio..........	Rhea McCarty	Exec. Secretary	Devel. and Publicity Commn.	Columbus
Oklahoma......	Randall T. Klemme	Director	Dept. of Comm. and Industry	Oklahoma City
Oregon........	Carl W. Jordan	Dir., Travel Inf. Div.	Highway Commn.	Salem
Pennsylvania...	William R. Davlin	Secretary	Dept. of Commerce	Harrisburg

ADVERTISING—*continued*

State	Name	Official Title	Agency	Location
Rhode Island...	Thomas A. Monahan	Exec. Director	R. I. Devel. Council	Providence
South Carolina..	R. M. Cooper	Director	Research, Planning and Devel. Bd.	Columbia
South Dakota...	A. H. Pankow	Publicity Director	Highway Commn.	Pierre
Tennessee......	Earl Shaub	Dir., Div. of Info.	Dept. of Conserv.	Nashville
Utah..........	John E. Campbell	Director	Tourist and Publicity Council	Salt Lake City
Vermont.......	Harold H. Chadwick	Advertising Dir.	Devel. Commn.	Montpelier
Virginia.......	F. James Barnes, II	Commissr., Div. of Pub. Rel. and Advertising	Dept. of Conserv. and Devel.	Richmond
Washington....	Charles E. Johns	Supvr., Div. of Progress and Ind. Devel.	Dept. of Conserv. and Devel.	Olympia
West Virginia...	Andrew V. Ruckman	Director	Industrial and Publicity Commn.	Charleston
Wisconsin......	W. T. Calhoun	Supt. of Information and Ed.	Conservation Commn.	Madison
Wyoming......	Willard M. Murfin	Secy. and Mgr.	Wyoming Travel Commn.	Cheyenne
Hawaii........	William Cogswell	Exec. Secretary	Hawaii Visitors Bur.	Honolulu
Puerto Rico....	Scott Runkle	Dir., Off. of Pub. Rel.	Econ. Devel. Admin.	San Juan
Virgin Islands...	Mary Millar	Act. Commissr. of Trade	Government of the Virgin Islands	St. Thomas

AERONAUTICS

State	Name	Official Title	Agency	Location
Alabama.......	Asa Rountree, Jr.	Director	Dept. of Aeronautics	Montgomery
Arizona........	William T. Brooks	Chairman	Corporation Commn.	Phoenix
California......	Clyde P. Barnett	Director	Aeronautics Commn.	Sacramento
Colorado.......	....	....	Div. of Aeronautics	Denver
Connecticut....	Kenneth Ringrose	Director	Dept. of Aeronautics	Hartford
Delaware......	Stewart E. Poole	Secretary	Aeronautics Commn.	Wilmington
Florida........	Frank H. Stoutamire	Aviation Safety Supvr.	Devel. Commn.	Tallahassee
Georgia........	James V. Carmichael	Member	Aeronautics Advisory Bd.	Atlanta
Idaho.........	Chet Moulton	Director	Dept. of Aeronautics	Boise
Illinois.........	Arthur E. Abney	Director	Dept. of Aeronautics	Springfield
Indiana........	Richard L. Cunningham	Acting Director	Aeronautics Commn.	Indianapolis
Iowa..........	Frank Berlin	Director	Aeronautics Commn.	Des Moines
Kentucky......	Charles H. Gartrell	Commissioner	Dept. of Aeronautics	Frankfort
Louisiana......	T. B. Herndon	Chief, Aeronautics Div.	Dept. Public Works	Baton Rouge
Maine.........	Scott K. Higgins	Director	Aeronautics Commn.	Augusta
Maryland......	Rudolph A. Drennan	Director	Aviation Commn.	Baltimore
Massachusetts...	Crocker Snow	Director	Aeronautics Commn.	East Boston
Michigan......	Lester J. Maitland	Director	Aeronautics Dept.	Lansing
Minnesota......	Mitchel Perrizo, Jr.	Commissioner	Dept. of Aeronautics	St. Paul
Mississippi.....	C. A. Moore	Director	Aeronautics Commn.	Jackson
Missouri.......	Dale H. Fearn	Head, Aviation Sect., Div. of Resources and Devel.	Dept. of Bus. and Admin.	Jefferson City
Montana.......	Frank W. Wiley	Chairman	Aviation Commn.	Helena
Nebraska.......	J. D. Ramsey	Director	Dept. of Aeronautics	Lincoln
New Hampshire	W. Russell Hilliard	Director	Aeronautics Commn.	Concord
New Jersey.....	Robert L. Copsey	Chief, Aero. Bur., Div. of Planning and Devel.	Dept. of Conserv. and Econ. Devel.	Trenton

AERONAUTICS—*continued*

State	Name	Official Title	Agency	Location
New Mexico....	Jacob A. Barth	Exec. Secretary	Aeronautics Commn.	Santa Fe
New York......	Claude B. Friday	Dir., Bur. of Aviation	Dept. of Commerce	Albany
North Dakota...	Harold G. Vavra	Director	Aeronautics Commn.	Bismarck
Ohio..........	C. E. A. Brown	Director	Aviation Board	Columbus
Oregon........	Earl W. Snyder	Director	Bd. of Aeronautics	Salem
Pennsylvania...	John W. Macfarlane	Exec. Dir., Aeronautics Commn.	Dept. of Military Affairs	Harrisburg
Rhode Island...	Albert R. Tavani	Admn. Aeronautics	Dept. Public Works	Providence
South Carolina..	C. B. Culbertson	Director	Areonautics Commn.	Columbia
South Dakota...	L. V. Hanson	Director	Aeronautics Commn.	Pierre
Tennessee......	James E. Martin	Dir., Bureau of Aeronautics	Dept. of Highways and Pub. Works	Nashville
Texas.........	Cliff B. Green	Director	Aeronautics Commn.	Austin
Utah..........	Harlan Bement	Director	Aeronautics Commn.	Salt Lake City
Vermont.......	Edward F. Knapp	Director	Aeronautics Commn.	Montpelier
Virginia.......	Allan C. Perkinson	Dir. of Aeronautics	Corporation Commn.	Richmond
Washington....	Charles S. Chester	Director	Aeronautics Commn.	Olympia
West Virginia...	Hubert H. Stark	Director	Aeronautics Commn.	Charleston
Wisconsin......	T. K. Jordan	Director	Aeronautics Commn.	Madison
Wyoming......	George M. Nelson	Director	Aeronautics Commn.	Cheyenne
Alaska.........	Herman Porter	Director	Div. of Aeronautics	Anchorage
	Wm. E. Hixson	Supervisor	Div. of Communications	Juneau
Hawaii........	Francis K. Sylva	Chairman	Aeronautics Commn.	Honolulu
	Randolph M. Lee	Director	Aeronautics Commn.	Honolulu
Puerto Rico....	Salvador V. Caro	General Manager	Ports Authority	San Juan

AGRICULTURE

State	Name	Official Title	Agency	Location
Alabama.......	A. W. Todd	Commissioner	Dept. of Agric. and Industries	Montgomery
Arizona........	Wilfred T. Mendenhall	Entomologist	Commn. of Agric. and Horticult.	Phoenix
Arkansas.......	C. A. Vines	Assoc. Director	Univ. School of Agric. Extn. Service	Little Rock
California......	W. C. Jacobsen	Director	Dept. of Agric.	Sacramento
Colorado.......	Paul Swisher	Director	Dept. of Agric.	Denver
Connecticut....	Joseph Gill	Commissioner	Dept. of Agric.	Hartford
Delaware......	John L. Clough	Act. Secretary	Bd. of Agric.	Dover
Florida........	Nathan Mayo	Commissioner	Dept. of Agric.	Tallahassee
Georgia........	Phil Campbell	Commissioner	Dept. of Agric.	Atlanta
Idaho.........	Harold West	Commissioner	Dept. of Agric.	Boise
Illinois.........	Stillman Stanard	Director	Dept. of Agric.	Springfield
Indiana........	Harold W. Handley	Commissioner	Lieutenant Governor	Indianapolis
Iowa..........	Clyde Spry	Secretary	Dept. of Agric.	Des Moines
Kansas........	Roy Freeland	Secretary	Bd. of Agric.	Topeka
Kentucky......	Ben J. Butler	Commissioner	Dept. of Agric., Labor and Statistics	Frankfort
Louisiana......	Dave L. Pearce	Commissioner	Agriculture and Immigration	Baton Rouge
Maine.........	Fred J. Nutter	Commissioner	Dept. of Agric.	Augusta
Maryland......	Wilson Elkins	Exec. Secretary	Bd. of Agric.	College Park
Massachusetts...	L. Roy Hawes	Commissioner	Dept. of Agric.	Boston
Michigan......	G. S. McIntyre	Director	Dept. of Agric.	Lansing
Minnesota......	Byron G. Allen	Commissioner	Dept. of Agric.	St. Paul
Mississippi.....	S. E. Corley	Commissioner	Dept. of Agric. and Commerce	Jackson
Missouri.......	L. G. Carpenter	Commissioner	Dept. of Agric.	Jefferson City
Montana.......	Albert H. Kruse	Commissr. of Agric.	Dept. of Agric.	Helena

AGRICULTURE—*continued*

State	Name	Official Title	Agency	Location
Nebraska.......	Ed Hoyt	Director	Dept. of Agric. and Inspection	Lincoln
Nevada........	Edward Records	Exec. Secretary	Dept. of Agric.	Reno
New Hampshire.	Perley I. Fitts	Commissioner	Dept. of Agric.	Concord
New Jersey.....	Willard H. Allen	Secretary	Dept. of Agric.	Trenton
New Mexico....	Robert A. Nichols	Dean of Agric.	N. Mex. A. & M. College	State College
New York......	Daniel J. Carey	Commissioner	Dept. of Agric. and Markets	Albany
North Carolina..	L. Y. Ballentine	Commissr. of Agric.	Dept. of Agric.	Raleigh
North Dakota...	Math Dahl	Commissioner	Dept. of Agric. and Labor	Bismarck
Ohio..........	Andrew L. Sorensen	Director	Dept. of Agric.	Columbus
Oklahoma......	Harold P. Hutton	President	Dept. of Agric., Bd. of Agric.	Oklahoma City
Oregon........	J. F. Short	Director	Dept. of Agric.	Salem
Pennsylvania...	William L. Henning	Secretary	Dept. of Agric.	Harrisburg
Rhode Island...	John L. Rego	Director	Dept. of Agric. and Conservation	Providence
South Carolina..	J. Roy Jones	Commissr.	Dept. of Agric.	Columbia
South Dakota...	Charles Bruett	Secretary	Dept. of Agric.	Pierre
Tennessee......	Buford Ellington	Commissioner	Dept. of Agric.	Nashville
Texas..........	John C. White	Commissioner	Dept. of Agric.	Austin
Utah..........	Alden K. Barton	Comm. Chairman	Dept. of Agric.	Salt Lake City
Vermont.......	Elmer E. Towne	Commissioner	Dept. of Agric.	Montpelier
Virginia.......	Parke C. Brinkley	Commissioner	Dept. of Agric. and Immigration	Richmond
Washington....	Sverre N. Omdahl	Director	Dept. of Agric.	Olympia
West Virginia...	(Vacancy)	Commissioner	Dept. of Agric.	Charleston
Wisconsin......	Donald N. McDowell	Director	Dept. of Agric.	Madison
Wyoming......	Wm. L. Chapman	Commissioner	Dept. of Agric.	Cheyenne
Alaska........	James W. Wilson	Commissioner	Dept. of Agric.	Anchorage
Guam........	Manuel Calvo	Director	Dept. of Agric.	Mangilao
Hawaii........	Joseph L. Dwight	Pres. and Commissioner	Bd. of Agric. and Forestry	Honolulu
Puerto Rico....	Luis Rivera Santos	Secretary	Dept. of Agric. and Commerce	San Juan
Virgin Islands.......	{Kenneth Bartlett (Vacancy)	President Commissioner	V. I. Corp. Dept. of Agric. and Labor	St. Croix St. Croix

AUDITOR

State	Name	Official Title	Agency	Location
Alabama.......	Mrs. Agnes Baggett	Auditor	Off. of Auditor	Montgomery
Arizona........	Jewell Jordan	Auditor	Off. of Auditor	Phoenix
Arkansas.......	J. O. Humphrey	Auditor	Auditor's Office	Little Rock
California......	(Vacancy)	Auditor General	Off. of Aud. Genl.	Sacramento
Colorado.......	Homer F. Bedford	Auditor	Dept. of Auditing	Denver
Connecticut....	{RaymondI.Longley Jos. B. Downes	Auditor Auditor	Pub. Accounts Pub. Accounts	Hartford Hartford
Delaware......	Clifford E. Hall	Auditor	Auditor's Office	Dover
Florida........	Bryan Willis	Auditor	Auditing Dept.	Tallahassee
Georgia........	B. E. Thrasher, Jr.	Auditor	Dept. of Audits, Accts.	Atlanta
Idaho.........	N. P. Nielson	Auditor	Off. of Auditor	Boise
Illinois.........	Orville E. Hodge	Aud. of Pub. Accts.	Off. of Aud. of Pub. Accts.	Springfield
Indiana........	Curtis E. Rardin	Auditor	Off. of Auditor	Indianapolis
Iowa..........	C. B. Akers	Auditor	Off. of Auditor	Des Moines

AUDITOR—*continued*

State	Name	Official Title	Agency	Location
Kansas	George Robb	Auditor	Off. of Auditor	Topeka
Kentucky	Mary Louise Foust	Aud. of Pub. Accts.	Off. of Aud. of Pub. Accts.	Frankfort
Louisiana	Allison R. Kolb	Auditor	Off. of Auditor	Baton Rouge
Maine	Fred M. Berry	Auditor	Dept. of Audit	Augusta
Maryland	James L. Benson	Auditor	Off. of Auditor	Baltimore
Massachusetts	Thomas J. Buckley	Auditor	Dept. of Auditor	Boston
Michigan	Victor Targonski	Auditor General	Dept. of Aud. Gen.	Lansing
Minnesota	Stafford King	Auditor	Off. of Auditor	St. Paul
Mississippi	E. B. Golding	Aud. of Pub. Accts.	Off. of Aud. of Pub. Accts.	Jackson
Missouri	Haskell Holman	Auditor	Dept. of Auditor	Jefferson City
Montana	John J. Holmes	Auditor	Off. of Auditor	Helena
Nebraska	Ray C. Johnson	Aud. of Pub. Accts.	Off. of Aud. of Pub. Accts.	Lincoln
Nevada	A. N. Jacobson	Legis. Auditor	Legis. Counsel Bur.	Carson City
New Hampshire	Frank Harrington	Dir. of Accts.	Dept. of Admin. and Control	Concord
New Jersey	Frank Durand	Auditor	Dept. of Aud.	Trenton
New Mexico	J. D. Hannah	Auditor	Off. of Auditor	Santa Fe
New York	Arthur Levitt	Comptroller	Dept. of Audit and Control	Albany
North Carolina	Henry L. Bridges	Auditor	Auditor's Office	Raleigh
North Dakota	Berta E. Baker	Auditor	Off. of Auditor	Bismarck
Ohio	James A. Rhodes	Auditor	Off. of Auditor	Columbus
Oklahoma	A. S. J. Shaw	Auditor	Auditor's Dept.	Oklahoma City
Oregon	Earl T. Newbry	Auditor	Secy. of State	Salem
Pennsylvania	Charles R. Barber	Auditor General	Dept. Auditor Gen.	Harrisburg
Rhode Island	Elphege J. Goulet	Chief, Bur. of Audits	Dept of Admin.	Providence
South Carolina	J. M. Smith	Auditor	Off. of Auditor	Columbia
South Dakota	Lawrence E. Mayes	Auditor	Off. of Auditor	Pierre
Tennessee	William R. Snodgrass	Comptroller	Off. of Comptr.	Nashville
Texas	C. H. Cavness	Auditor	Off. of Auditor	Austin
Utah	Sherman J. Preece	Auditor	Off. of Auditor	Salt Lake City
Vermont	David V. Anderson	Auditor of Accts.	Off. of Auditor	Montpelier
Virginia	J. Gordon Bennett	Aud. of Pub. Accts.	Off. of Aud. of Pub. Accts.	Richmond
Washington	Cliff Yelle	Auditor	Off. of Auditor	Olympia
West Virginia	Edgar B. Sims	Auditor	Off. of Auditor	Charleston
Wisconsin	J. Jay Keliher	Auditor	Dept. of Audit	Madison
Wyoming	Minnie A. Mitchell	Auditor	Off. of Auditor	Cheyenne
Alaska	(Vacancy)	Legis. Auditor	Div. of Legis. Audit	Juneau
Guam	Howard O'Hara	Comptroller	Dept. of Finance	Agana
Hawaii	Howard K. Hiroki	Auditor	Auditing Dept.	Honolulu
Puerto Rico	Justo Nieves } Gustavo de Pedro	Asst. Secretaries (Pre-Audit)	Dept. of Treasury	San Juan
Virgin Islands	Richard L. Krabach	Govt. Comptroller	Govt. of the V. I.	St. Thomas

BANKING

State	Name	Official Title	Agency	Location
Alabama	Lonnie Gentry	Supt. of Banks	Banking Dept.	Montgomery
Arizona	David O. Saunders	Supt. of Banks	Banking Dept.	Phoenix
Arkansas	Dick Simpson	Bank Commissioner	Bank Dept.	Little Rock
California	William A. Burkett	Supt. of Banks, Div. of Banking	Dept. of Investments	Sacramento
Colorado	Frank E. Goldy	Commissioner	Banking Dept.	Denver
Connecticut	Henry H. Pierce, Jr.	Commissioner	Banking Dept.	Hartford
Delaware	Randolph Hughes	Commissioner	Banking Commn.	Dover

BANKING—*continued*

State	Name	Official Title	Agency	Location
Florida........	Ray E. Green	Comptroller	Comptroller's Off.	Tallahassee
Georgia........	A. P. Persons	Supt. of Banks	Dept. of Banking	Atlanta
Idaho.........	R. U. Spaulding	Commissioner	Dept. of Finance	Boise
Illinois.........	Orville E. Hodge	Aud. of Pub. Accts.	Off. of Aud. of Pub. Accts.	Springfield
Indiana........	Joseph McCord	Director	Dept. of Financial Institutions	Indianapolis
Iowa..........	N. P. Black	Superintendent	Banking Dept.	Des Moines
Kansas........	Gordon W. Lindley	Act. Commissioner	Off. of Bank Commissr.	Topeka
Kentucky......	R. E. Glenn	Commissioner	Dept. of Banking	Frankfort
Louisiana......	Edward F. Follett	Commissioner	Banking Dept.	Baton Rouge
Maine.........	Albert S. Noyes	Commissioner	Banking Dept.	Augusta
Maryland.....	Wm. H. Kirkwood	Bank Commissioner	Bank Dept.	Baltimore
Massachusetts...	Charles P. Howard	Commissr., Div. of Banks and Loan Agencies	Dept. of Banking and Insurance	Boston
Michigan......	M. C. Eveland	Commissioner	Banking Dept.	Lansing
Minnesota......	Irving C. Rasmussen	Commissioner	Div. of Banking	St. Paul
Mississippi.....	Joe W. Latham	Comptroller	Dept. of Banking Supv.	Jackson
Missouri.......	J. A. Rouveyrol	Commissr. of Finance	Dept. of Bus. and Admin.	Jefferson City
Montana.......	R. E. Towle	Supt. of Banks	Banking Dept.	Helena
Nebraska.......	J. F. McLain	Dir. of Banking	Dept. of Banking	Lincoln
Nevada........	Grant L. Robison	Supt. of Banks	Off. of Bank Examiner	Carson City
New Hampshire	Winfield J. Phillips	Commissioner	Bank Commn.	Concord
New Jersey.....	Charles R. Howell	Commissioner	Dept. of Banking and Insurance	Trenton
New Mexico....	Frank F. Weddington	Bank Examiner	Banking Dept.	Santa Fe
New York......	George A. Mooney	Superintendent	Banking Dept.	Albany
North Carolina..	W. W. Jones	Commissr. of Banks	Banking Commn.	Raleigh
North Dakota...	John A. Graham	Examiner, Chairman	State Banking Bd.	Bismarck
Ohio..........	Paul Hinkle	Superintendent	Div. of Banks and Banking	Columbus
Oklahoma......	O. B. Mothersead	Commissioner	Banking Dept.	Oklahoma City
Oregon........	A. A. Rogers	Supt. of Banks	Banking Dept.	Salem
Pennsylvania...	Robert L. Myers, Jr.	Secretary of Banking	Dept. of Banking	Harrisburg
Rhode Island...	A. Chmielewski	Bank Commissioner	Dept. of Business Reg.	Providence
South Carolina..	C. V. Pierce	Chief Examiner	Bank Examining Dept.	Columbia
South Dakota...	Gordon H. Maxam	Superintendent	Banking Dept.	Pierre
Tennessee......	H. B. Clarke	Supt. of Banks	Dept. of Insurance and Banking	Nashville
Texas..........	J. M. Falkner	Commissioner	Banking Dept.	Austin
Utah..........	Louis S. Leatham	Bank Commissioner	Banking Commn.	Salt Lake City
Vermont.......	Alexander H. Miller	Commissioner	Dept. Banking and Insurance	Montpelier
Virginia.......	Logan R. Ritchie	Commissr. of Banking	Corporation Commn.	Richmond
Washington....	R. D. Carrell	Supervisor, Div. of Banking	Dept. of General Admin.	Olympia
West Virginia...	Nell W. Walker	Commissioner	Dept. of Banking	Charleston
Wisconsin......	Guerdon M. Matthews	Commissioner	Banking Dept.	Madison
Wyoming......	Norris E. Hartwell	Examiner	Off. of Examiner	Cheyenne
Alaska.........	Five member Territorial Banking Board: Governor, Treasurer, Auditor are ex-officio members.			
Guam.........	R. F. Taitano	Dir. of Finance	Dept. of Finance	Agana
Hawaii........	Kam Tai Lee	Bank Examiner	Treasury Dept.	Honolulu
Puerto Rico....	Antonio A. Llorente	Chief, Div. of Bank Examiners	Dept. of Treasury	San Juan
Virgin Islands..	Chas. K Claunch	Chairman	V. I. Banking Bd.	St. Thomas

BLIND WELFARE

State	Name	Official Title	Agency	Location
Alabama	Elizabeth Bryan	Dir., Bur. of Pub. Assist.	Dept. of Pensions and Security	Montgomery
Arizona	Lee Porterfield	Supvr., Blind Serv.	Pub. Welfare Dept.	Phoenix
Arkansas	Virginia Galloway	Dir., Social Serv.	Dept. Pub. Welfare	Little Rock
California	Perry Sundquist	Chief, Div. of Blind	Dept. of Soc. Welfare	Sacramento
Colorado	Guy R. Justis	Director	Dept. Pub. Welfare	Denver
Connecticut	Albert Sherberg	Executive Secretary	Bd. of Ed. of Blind	Hartford
Delaware	Frances J. Cummings	Executive Secretary	Commn. for Blind	Wilmington
Florida	Chas. G. Lavin	Director	Dept. Pub. Welfare	Jacksonville
Georgia	Lucile Wilson	Chief, Sect. of Pub. Assistance	Dept. Pub. Welfare	Atlanta
Idaho	Burton K. Driggs	Superintendent	State School for Deaf and Blind	Gooding
Illinois	Garrett W. Keaster	Executive Secy.	Pub. Aid Commn.	Springfield
Indiana	Robert O. Brown	Dir., Div. Pub. Assist.	Dept. Pub. Welfare	Indianapolis
Iowa	Ethel T. Holmes	Director	Commn. for Blind	Des Moines
Kansas	Harry E. Hays	Dir., Div. Services to Blind	Social Welfare Dept.	Topeka
Kentucky	Paul Langan	Supt. Ky. School for Blind	Dept. of Education	Louisville
Louisiana	Edward P. Dameron, III	Commissioner	Dept. Pub. Welfare	Baton Rouge
Maine	Dean P. Morrison	Dir., Services for Blind	Dept. of Health and Welfare	Augusta
Maryland	William S. Ratchford	Superintendent	Workshop for Blind	Baltimore
Massachusetts	John F. Mungovan	Dir., Div. of Blind	Dept. of Education	Boston
Michigan	Paul G. Conlan	Supvr., Blind Services	Dept. Social Welfare	Lansing
Minnesota	John W. Poor	Dir., Div. Pub. Assist.	Dept. of Welfare	St. Paul
Mississippi	J. A. Thigpen	Commissioner	Public Welfare	Jackson
Missouri	Mrs. Lee Johnston	Chief, Bur. for Blind	Dept. Pub. Health and Welfare	Jefferson City
Montana	Glen I. Harris	Superintendent	Deaf and Blind School	Great Falls
Nebraska	Mayme Stukel	Director	Div. Pub. Welfare	Lincoln
Nevada	Barbara C. Coughlan	Director	Welfare Dept.	Reno
New Hampshire	Carl Camp	Supvr., Blind Services	Dept. Pub. Welfare	Concord
New Jersey	George F. Meyer	Exec. Dir., N. J. Commn. for the Blind	Dept. of Insts., and Agencies	Newark
New Mexico	Neal F. Quimby	Superintendent	N. M. School for Visually Handicapped	Alamogordo
New York	Margaret Anne McGuire	Dir., Commn. for Blind	Dept. of Soc. Welfare	New York
North Carolina	H. A. Wood	Executive Secretary	Commn. for Blind	Raleigh
North Dakota	Carlyle D. Onsrud	Executive Director	Pub. Welfare Bd.	Bismarck
Ohio	W. G. Scarberry	Superintendent	School for Blind	Columbus
Oklahoma	Charlotte C. Donnell	Supvr., Div. of Program Devel.	Dept. Pub. Welfare	Oklahoma City
Oregon	Clifford Stocker	Administrator	Commn. for Blind and Preven. of Blindness	Portland
Pennsylvania	Harry Shapiro	Secretary	Dept. of Welfare	Harrisburg
Rhode Island	Mrs. L. Y. Gay	Admn., Bur. for Blind	Dept. of Soc. Welfare	Providence
South Carolina	J. M. Cherry	Chief, Div. for Blind	Dept. Pub. Welfare	Columbia
South Dakota	Howard Hanson	Director	Service to the Blind	Pierre
Tennessee	Mason Brandon	Dir., Services for Blind	Dept. Pub. Welfare	Nashville
Texas	Lon Alsup	Exec. Secy-Dir.	Commn. for Blind	Austin

BLIND WELFARE--*continued*

State	Name	Official Title	Agency	Location
Utah..........	Harold W. Green	Superintendent	School for Deaf and Blind	Ogden
Vermont.......	Virginia Cole	Dir., Blind Service	Soc. Welfare Dept.	Montpelier
Virginia.......	L. L. Watts	Executive Secretary	Commn. for the Visually Handicapped	Richmond
Washington....	Kenneth W. Bryan	Supvr., Work with Blind	Dept. Pub. Assist.	Olympia
West Virginia...	Caton N. Hill	Supervisor	Bd. of Ed., Rehabilitation Div.	Charleston
Wisconsin......	Thomas J. Lucas, Sr.	Dir., Div. Pub. Assist.	Dept. Pub. Welfare	Madison
Wyoming......	H. Smith Shumway	Director	Div. Deaf and Blind	Cheyenne
Alaska.........	Henry A. Harmon	Director	Dept. Pub. Welfare	Juneau
Hawaii........	Mrs. Vivian J. Castro	Director	Bur. Sight Conserv., Work with Blind	Honolulu
Puerto Rico....	Mrs. C. Zalduondo	Dir., Div. Pub. Welfare	Dept. of Health	San Juan
	M. Hernández	Dir., Voc. Rehabil.	Dept. of Education	San Juan

BUDGET

State	Name	Official Title	Agency	Location
Alabama.......	James V. Jordan	Budget Officer	Dept. of Finance	Montgomery
Arizona........	B. P. Lynch	Budget Officer	Off. of Governor	Phoenix
Arkansas.......	Julian C. Hogan	Budget Director	Comptroller's Office	Little Rock
California......	T. H. Mugford	Asst. Director of Finance, Budget and Fiscal	Dept. of Finance	Sacramento
Colorado.......	E. G. Spurlin	State Accountant and Budget Officer	Div. of Accts. and Control	Denver
Connecticut....	Fred A. Schuckman	Dir., Budget Div.	Dept. of Finance and Control	Hartford
Delaware......	Mrs. Lillian I. Martin	Chief Accountant	Budget Commn.	Dover
Florida........	Harry G. Smith	Budget Director	Budget Commn.	Tallahassee
Georgia........	Marvin Griffin	Governor	Off. of Governor	Atlanta
Idaho.........	James H. Young	Budget Director	Budget Bureau	Boise
Illinois.........	T. R. Leth	Budget Director	Dept. of Finance	Springfield
Indiana........	Donald H. Clark	Director	Div. of Budget	Indianapolis
Iowa..........	Glenn D. Sarsfield	Comptroller	Comptroller's Office	Des Moines
Kansas........	James W. Bibb	Budget Director	Dept. of Admin.	Topeka
Kentucky......	(Vacancy)	Dir., Div. of Budget	Dept. of Finance	Frankfort
Louisiana......	Robert F. Kennon	Budg. Dir., Governor	Off. of Governor	Baton Rouge
	J. H. Rester	Asst. Budg. Dir.	Off., Div. of Budg.	Baton Rouge
Maine.........	Raymond C. Mudge	Commissioner	Dept. of Finance and Admin.	Augusta
Maryland......	James G. Rennie	Director	Dept. Budget and Procurement	Baltimore
Massachusetts...	Wm. H. Bixby	Budget Commissr.	Commn. on Admin. and Finance	Boston
Michigan......	Frank M. Landers	Dir., Budget Div.	Dept. of Admin.	Lansing
Minnesota......	Arthur Naftalin	Commissioner	Dept. of Admin.	St. Paul
Mississippi.....	W. R. Carbrey, Sr.	Exec. Secretary	Budget Commn.	Jackson
Missouri.......	Newton Atterbury	Comptr. and Budg. Dir., Div. of Budget and Comptr.	Dept. of Revenue	Jefferson City
Montana.......	A. M. Johnson	Controller	Off. of Controller	Helena
Nebraska.......	F. A. Herrington	Tax Commissioner	Off. of Tax Commissr.	Lincoln

BUDGET—*continued*

State	Name	Official Title	Agency	Location
Nevada........	C. A. Carlson, Jr.	Dir. of Budget	Off. of Dir. of Budg	Carson City
New Hampshire.	Arthur E. Bean	Comptroller and Director	Dept. of Admin. and Control	Concord
New Jersey.....	Abram M. Vermeulen	Dir., Div. of Budg. and Accounting	Dept. of Treasury	Trenton
New Mexico....	C. R. Sebastian	Director	Budget Dept.	Santa Fe
New York......	Paul H. Appleby	Dir., Div. of Budget	Executive Dept.	Albany
North Carolina..	D. S. Coltrane	Asst. Dir. of Budget	Executive Dept.	Raleigh
North Dakota...	P. A. Tinbo	Director	Budget Board	Bismarck
Ohio..........	John M. Wilcoxon	Director	Dept. of Finance	Columbus
Oklahoma......	Burton Logan	Dir., Budget Div.	Executive Dept.	Oklahoma City
Oregon........	LaVerne J. Young	Budget Admn.	Dept. of Finance and Admin.	Salem
Pennsylvania...	James C. Charlesworth	Secy. of Admin.	Governor's Office	Harrisburg
	Andrew M. Bradley	Budget Secy.	Governor's Office	Harrisburg
Rhode Island...	Howard A. Kenyon	Budget Officer	Dept. of Admin.	Providence
South Carolina..	George Bell Timmerman, Jr.	Chairman, ex officio and Governor	Budget and Control Bd.	Columbia
South Dakota...	Morris G. Hallock	Secretary	Dept. of Finance	Pierre
Tennessee......	E. J. Boling	Dir. of Budget	Budget Dept.	Nashville
Texas..........	Vernon A. McGee	Budget Director	Legislative Budg. Bd.	Austin
	R. B. Baldwin	Dir., Budget Div.	Executive Dept.	Austin
Utah..........	D. K. Moffat	Budget Director	Finance Dept.	Salt Lake City
Vermont.......	Joseph B. Johnson	Governor	Executive Dept.	Montpelier
Virginia.......	J. H. Bradford	Director	Div. of Budget	Richmond
Washington....	Ernest D. Brabrook	Director	Off. of Dir. of Budget	Olympia
West Virginia...	Denzil L. Gainer	Director	Budget Dept.	Charleston
Wisconsin......	E. C. Giessel	Director	Dept. of Budget and Accounts	Madison
Wyoming......	Milward L. Simpson	Governor	Governor's Office	Cheyenne
Alaska........	Richard M. Freer	Budget Officer	Dept. of Finance	Juneau
Guam........	Harry F. Hansen	Director	Off. Budg. and Management	Agana
Hawaii........	Paul J. Thurston	Director	Bureau of Budget	Honolulu
Puerto Rico....	José R. Noguera	Dir., Bur. of Budg.	Office of Governor	San Juan
Virgin Islands...	Charles K. Claunch	Govt. Secretary	Govt. of the V.I.	St. Thomas

CIVIL DEFENSE

State	Name	Official Title	Agency	Location
Alabama.......	Pitt Tyson Maner	Director	Civil Defense Agency	Montgomery
Arizona........	Richard D. Searles	Director	Civil Defense	Phoenix
Arkansas.......	Owen Payne, Jr.	Dir., Civ. Def.	Military Dept.	Little Rock
California......	Stanley Pierson	Director	Off. Civil Def.	Sacramento
Colorado.......	Henry L. Larsen	Director	Civil Defense Agency	Denver
Connecticut....	Leo J. Mulcahy	Director	Off. of Civil Def.	Hartford
Delaware......	Lt. Col. D. Preston Lee	Director	Civil Defense	Wilmington
Florida........	Hiram W. Tarkington	Director	Civil Defense	Jacksonville
Georgia........	George J. Hearn	Dir., Civ. Def. Div.	Dept. Pub. Defense	Atlanta
Idaho.........	Admiral W. C. Specht	Coordinator	Dept. Civil Def.	Boise

CIVIL DEFENSE—*continued*

State	Name	Official Title	Agency	Location
Illinois.........	Brig. Gen. Robt. M. Woodward	Director	Off. of Civil Def.	Chicago
Indiana........	Edward L. Strohbehn	Director	Dept. Civil Def.	Indianapolis
Iowa..........	C. E. Fowler	Director	Off. of Civilian Def.	Des Moines
Kansas........	Joe Nickell	Adjutant General	Civil Defense Div.	Topeka
Kentucky......	J. S. Lindsay	Dir., Civ. Def.	Dept. Milit. Affairs	Frankfort
Louisiana......	Francis A. Woolfley	Director	Civil Defense	Baton Rouge
Maine.........	Harry E. Mapes	Director	Civ. Def. and Pub. Safety	Augusta
Maryland......	Sherley Ewing	Director	Civil Def. Agency	Pikesville
Massachusetts...	Gen. John J. Maginnis	Director	Civil Def. Agency	Natick
Michigan......	Capt. C. F. VanBlankensteyn	Director	Civil Defense	Lansing
Minnesota......	Hubert A. Schon	Director	Civil Defense	St. Paul
Mississippi.....	Hendrix Dawson	Director	Civilian Def. Council	Jackson
Missouri.......	Marvin W. Smith	Director	Off. of Civil Def.	Jefferson City
Montana.......	Hugh K. Potter	Director	Adj. Gen. Dept.	Helena
Nebraska.......	Maj. Gen. Guy N. Henninger	Director	Adj. Gen. Dept.	Lincoln
Nevada........	Floyd E. Crabtree	Director	Dept. Civil Def.	Carson City
New Hampshire	Rear-Admiral Cornelius A. Brinkman	Director	Off. of Civil Def.	Concord
New Jersey.....	Thomas S. Dignan	Act. Director	Dept. of Defense	Trenton
New Mexico....	Capt. Daniel K. Sadler, Jr.	Director	Civilian Defense	Santa Fe
New York......	C. R. Huebner	Director	Civil Def. Commn.	New York City
North Carolina..	Edward F. Griffin	Director	Civil Defense	Raleigh
North Dakota...	Lt. Col. Noel F. Thoralson	Director	Civil Def. Council	Bismarck
Ohio..........	Maj. Gen. Leo M. Kreber	Adj. Gen. and Dir. of Civ. Def.	Dept. of Adj. Gen.	Columbus
Oklahoma......	Thomas M. Brett	Asst. Director	Civil Def. Agency	Oklahoma City
Oregon........	Col. Arthur M. Sheets	Director	Civil Defense Agency	Salem
Pennsylvania...	Dr. Richard Gerstell	Director	Council of Civ. Def.	Harrisburg
Rhode Island...	Col. John M. McGreevy	Director	Council of Defense	Providence
South Carolina..	Maj. Gen. James C. Dozier	Director	Civil Def. Agency	Columbia
South Dakota...	Theodore A. Arndt	Adj. Gen.	Dept. Milit. Affairs	Pierre
Tennessee......	Col. Robert L. Fox	Dir., Civ. Def.	Dept. of Adj. Gen.	Nashville
Texas..........	Wm. L. McGill	State Coordinator	Governor's Off.	Austin
Utah..........	Gus P. Backman	Chairman	Civil Def. Council	Salt Lake City
Vermont.......	Wm. H. Baumann	Director	Civil Def. Div., Dept. Pub. Safety	Montpelier
Virginia.......	J. H. Wyse	Director	Off. of Civil Def.	Richmond
Washington....	Vice-Admiral D. E. Barbey	Director	Dept. Civil Def.	Olympia
West Virginia...	Col. Edgar M. Sites	Dir., Civ. Def.	Adj. Gen.'s Off.	Charleston
Wisconsin......	Ralph J. Olson	Dir., Civ. Def.	Adj. Gen.'s Off.	Madison
Wyoming......	Maj. Gen. R. L. Esmay	Dir., Civ. Def.	Adj. Gen. Dept.	Cheyenne
Alaska.........	Harold E. Pomeroy	Director	Civil Defense	Juneau
Guam.........	Fred T. Gutierrez	Director	Dept. of Civil Defense	Agana
Hawaii........	Maj. Gen. Fred W. Makinney	Director	Civil Def. Agency	Honolulu
Puerto Rico....	Miguel A. Muñoz	Director	Off. of Civil Def.	San Juan
Virgin Islands..	Omar Brown	Director	Govt. of the V.I.	St. Thomas

COMMERCE

State	Name	Official Title	Agency	Location
Arkansas.......	Wm. P. Rock	Exec. Secretary	Industrial Devel. Commn.	Little Rock
Georgia........	Scott Candler	Secretary	Dept. of Commerce	Atlanta
Idaho.........	A. B. Jonasson	Secretary	Dept. of Commerce and Devel.	Boise
Illinois........	George R. Perrine	Chairman	Commerce Commn.	Springfield
Indiana.......	Edwin W. Beaman	Exec. Director	Dept. Comm., Public Relations	Indianapolis
Iowa.........	Geo. L. McCaughan	Secretary	Commerce Commn.	Des Moines
Louisiana......	Elmer D. Conner	Exec. Director	Dept. Commerce and Industry	Baton Rouge
Maine.........	Carl J. Broggi	Commissioner	Dept. of Devel. of Ind. and Commerce	Augusta
Massachusetts...	Richard Preston	Commissioner	Dept. of Commerce	Boston
Michigan......	Don C. Weeks	Director	Dept. of Econ. Devel.	Lansing
Mississippi.....	S. E. Corley	Commissioner	Dept. Agric. and Commerce	Jackson
New Hampshire	Winfred L. Foss	Industrial Dir.	Planning and Devel. Commn.	Concord
New Jersey.....	Albert R. Post	Chief, Bur. of Commerce, Div. Planning and Devel.	Dept. Conserv. and Econ. Devel.	Trenton
New York......	Edward T. Dickinson	Commissr. of Comm.	Dept. of Commerce	Albany
Ohio..........	W. Harper Annat	Director	Dept. of Commerce	Columbus
Oklahoma......	Randall T. Klemme	Director	Dept. Commerce and Industry	Oklahoma City
Pennsylvania...	William R. Davlin	Secy. of Comm.	Dept. of Commerce	Harrisburg
Rhode Island...	Thomas A. Monahan	Exec. Director	Devel. Council	Providence
South Carolina..	R. M. Cooper	Director	Research, Planning and Devel. Bd.	Columbia
Tennessee......	Geo. I. Whitlatch	Exec. Director	Agric. and Ind. Devel. Commn.	Nashville
Utah..........	Parley W. Hale	Director	Trade Commn.	Salt Lake City
Vermont.......	Clifton Miskelly	Director	Devel. Commn.	Montpelier
Virginia.......	W. H. Caldwell	Dir., Planning and Econ. Devel.	Dept. Conserv. and Devel.	Richmond
Washington....	Wm. A. Galbraith	Director	Dept. Conserv. and Devel.	Olympia
Wisconsin......	Robert D. Siff	Director	Div. Industrial Devel.	Madison
Wyoming.......	J. A. Buchanan	Director	Natl. Resources Bd.	Cheyenne
Guam.........	J.D.Leon Guerrero	Director	Dept. of Commerce	Agana
Hawaii........	George Mason	Director	Econ. Planning and Coordination Authority	Honolulu
Puerto Rico....	Luis Rivera Santos	Secretary	Dept. Agric. and Commerce	San Juan

COMPTROLLER

State	Name	Official Title	Agency	Location
Alabama.......	John Graves	Comptroller	Dept. of Finance	Montgomery
Arkansas.......	Kelly Cornett	Comptroller	State Comptroller's Off.	Little Rock
California......	Robert C. Kirkwood	Controller	State Controller	Sacramento
Colorado.......	James A. Noonan	Controller	Div. of Accts. and Control	Denver
Connecticut....	Fred R. Zeller	Comptroller	Off. of Comptroller	Hartford
Florida........	Ray E. Green	Comptroller	Comptroller's Off.	Tallahassee
Georgia........	Zack D. Cravey	Comptroller-Gen.	Comptr.-Gen.'s Off.	Atlanta
Idaho.........	N. P. Nielson	Auditor	Off. of Auditor	Boise
Indiana........	Curtis E. Rardin	Auditor	Auditor's Office	Indianapolis

COMPTROLLER—*continued*

State	Name	Official Title	Agency	Location
Iowa.........	Glenn D. Sarsfield	Comptroller	Comptroller's Off.	Des Moines
Kansas........	Roy Shapiro	Controller	Dept. of Admin.	Topeka
Kentucky......	Billy S. Smith	Dir., Div. Accts. and Control	Dept. of Finance	Frankfort
Maine.........	Harlan H. Harris	Controller	Bur. of Accts. and Controls	Augusta
Maryland......	J. Millard Tawes	Comptr. of Treas.	Comptroller's Off.	Annapolis
Massachusetts...	Fred A. Moncewicz	Comptroller	Commn. on Admin. and Finance	Boston
Michigan......	James W. Miller	Controller	Dept. of Admin.	Lansing
Mississippi.....	Joe W. Latham	Comptroller	Off. of Comptroller	Jackson
Missouri.......	Newton Atterbury	Dir., Comptr. and Budg. Div.	Dept. of Revenue	Jefferson City
Montana.......	A. M. Johnson	Controller	Off. of Controller	Helena
Nevada........	Peter Merialdo	Controller	Off. of Controller	Carson City
New Hampshire	Arthur E. Bean	Comptroller	Dept. of Admin. and Control	Concord
New Jersey.....	Abram M. Vermeulen	Comptroller	Dept. of Treasury	Trenton
New Mexico....	D. M. Smith, Jr.	Comptroller	Off. of Comptroller	Santa Fe
New York......	Arthur Levitt	Comptroller	Dept. of Audit and Control	Albany
Oklahoma......	A. A. Whitfield	Controller, Budg. Div.	Exec. Dept.	Oklahoma City
Pennsylvania...	Weldon B. Heyburn	Treasurer	Treasury Dept.	Harrisburg
Rhode Island...	M. J. Cummings	Controller	Dept. of Admin.	Providence
South Carolina..	E. C. Rhodes	Comptroller-Gen.	Off. of Comptr.-Gen.	Columbia
South Dakota...	J. C. Penne	Comptroller	Audits and Accts.	Pierre
Tennessee......	Wm. R. Snodgrass	Comptroller	Off. of Comptroller	Nashville
Texas..........	R. S. Calvert	Comptr. Pub. Accts.	Off. of Comptroller	Austin
Utah..........	D. H. Whittenburg	Commn. Chairman	Finance Commn.	Salt Lake City
Virginia.......	Sidney C. Day, Jr.	Comptr. and Dir.	Dept. of Accts. and Purchases	Richmond
Washington....	Cliff Yelle	Auditor	Off. of Auditor	Olympia
Wisconsin......	E. C. Giessel	Director	Dept. of Budget and Accts.	Madison
Alaska.........	(Vacancy)	Controller	Dept. of Finance	Juneau
Guam..........	Howard O'Hara	Comptroller	Off. of Comptroller	Agana
Hawaii........	Paul J. Thurston	Director	Bur. of Budget	Honolulu
Puerto Rico....	Rafael de J. Cordero	Controller (Post-audit)	Off. of Comptroller	San Juan
Virgin Islands...	Richard L. Krabach	Comptroller	Govt. of the V. I.	St. Thomas

CORPORATIONS (Registering and Licensing)

State	Name	Official Title	Agency	Location
Alabama.......	Mary Texas Hurt	Secy. of State	Off. Secy. of State	Montgomery
Arizona........	William T. Brooks	Chairman	Corporation Commn.	Phoenix
Arkansas.......	C. G. Hall	Secy. of State	Off. Secy. of State	Little Rock
California......	Waite Stephenson	Commissr., Div. of Corporations	Dept. of Investments	Sacramento
Colorado.......	George J. Baker	Secy. of State	Dept. of State	Denver
Connecticut....	Mildred P. Allen	Secy. of State	Off. Secy. of State	Hartford
Delaware......	John N. McDowell	Secy. of State	Off. Secy. of State	Dover
Florida........	R. A. Gray	Secy. of State	Off. Secy. of State	Tallahassee
Georgia........	Mrs. Louise Buchanan	Corporation Clerk	Off. Secy. of State	Atlanta
Idaho.........	Ira H. Masters	Secy. of State	Off. Secy. of State	Boise
Illinois.........	Wm. G. Worthey	Chief Clerk	Off. Secy. of State	Springfield
Indiana........	Crawford Parker	Secy. of State	Off. Secy. of State	Indianapolis
Iowa..........	Berry O. Burt	Corporation Counsel	Off. Secy. of State	Des Moines
Kansas........	Paul R. Shanahan	Secy. of State	Off. Secy. of State	Topeka

CORPORATIONS (Registering and Licensing)—*continued*

State	Name	Official Title	Agency	Location
Kentucky......	Mrs. Thelma L. Stovall	Secy. of State	Off. Secy. of State	Frankfort
Louisiana......	Wade O. Martin, Jr.	Secy. of State	Off. Secy. of State	Baton Rouge
Maine.........	Mrs. Bernice T. Goodine	Supvr., Corp. Div.	Off. Secy. of State	Augusta
Maryland......	Albert W. Ward	Exec. Secy.	State Tax Commn.	Baltimore
Massachusetts...	John Dane, Jr.	Commissioner	Dept. of Corp. and Taxation	Boston
Michigan......	James C. Allen	Commissioner	Corp. and Securities	Lansing
Minnesota......	Joseph L. Donovan	Secy. of State	Off. Secy. of State	St. Paul
Mississippi.....	Heber Ladner	Secy. of State	Dept. of State	Jackson
Missouri.......	Joseph W. Mosby	Corp. Commissr.	Off. Secy. of State	Jefferson City
Montana.......	Clifford L. Walker	Deputy Secy. of State	Off. Secy. of State	Helena
Nebraska.......	Frank Marsh	Secy. of State	Off. Secy. of State	Lincoln
Nevada........	John Koontz	Secy. of State	Off. Secy. of State	Carson City
New Hampshire.	Enoch D. Fuller	Secy. of State	Off. Secy. of State	Concord
New Jersey.....	Edward J. Patten	Secy. of State	Dept. of State	Trenton
New Mexico....	John Block, Jr.	Chairman	Corp. Commn.	Santa Fe
New York......	Samuel London	Deputy Secy. of State, Chief, Div. of Corps.	Dept. of State	Albany
North Carolina..	Thad Eure	Secy. of State	Dept. of State	Raleigh
North Dakota...	Ben Meier	Secy. of State	Off. Secy. of State	Bismarck
Ohio..........	Ted W. Brown	Secy. of State	Dept. of State	Columbus
Oklahoma......	Jeff F. Kendall	Asst. Secy. of State	Off. Secy. of State	Oklahoma City
Oregon........	Frank J. Healy	Corp. Commissr.	Corp. Dept.	Salem
Pennsylvania...	Thomas Anton	Dir. Corp. Bureau	Dept. of State	Harrisburg
Rhode Island...	Armand H. Coté	Secy. of State	Off. Secy. of State	Providence
South Carolina..	O. Frank Thornton	Secy. of State	Off. Secy. of State	Columbia
South Dakota...	Geraldine Ostroot	Secy. of State	Off. Secy. of State	Pierre
Tennessee......	G. Edward Friar	Secy. of State	Off. Secy. of State	Nashville
Texas..........	Tom Reavley	Secy. of State	Dept. of State	Austin
Utah..........	Lamont F. Toronto	Secy. of State	Off. Secy. of State	Salt Lake City
Vermont.......	Howard E. Armstrong	Secy. of State	Off. Secy. of State	Montpelier
Virginia........	H. Lester Hooker	Chairman	Corp. Commn.	Richmond
Washington....	Ray J. Yeomans	Asst. Secy. of State	Off. Secy. of State	Olympia
West Virginia...	D. Pitt O'Brien	Secy. of State	Off. Secy. of State	Charleston
Wisconsin......	H. E. Whipple	Supvr. of Incorporations	Off. Secy. of State	Madison
Wyoming......	Everett T. Copenhaver	Secy. of State	Off. Secy. of State	Cheyenne
Alaska.........	John A. McKinney	Dir. of Finance	Dept. of Finance	Juneau
Guam.........	Richard F. Taitano	Director	Dept. of Finance	Agana
Hawaii........	Kam Tai Lee	Treasurer	Off. of Treas.	Honolulu
Puerto Rico....	Sixto G. Arroyo	Chief, Corp. Div.	Dept. of State	San Juan
Virgin Islands...	Charles K. Claunch	Govt. Secy.	Govt. of the V. I.	St. Thomas

CORPORATION TAX

State	Name	Official Title	Agency	Location
Alabama.......	Winton McNair	Chief, Franchise and Pub. Utilities Div.	Dept. of Revenue	Montgomery
Arizona........	Warren Peterson	Chairman	Tax Commission	Phoenix
Arkansas.......	Earl Berry	Dir., Tax Div.	Pub. Serv. Commn.	Little Rock
California......	John J. Cambell	Exec. Officer	Franchise Tax Bd.	Sacramento
Colorado......	Earl Blevins	Dir. of Revenue	Dept. of Revenue	Denver
Connecticut....	Howard Hamilton	Dir., Corp. Div.	Tax Department	Hartford
Florida........	R. A. Gray	Secy. of State	Off. of Secy. of State	Tallahassee

CORPORATION TAX—*continued*

State	Name	Official Title	Agency	Location
Georgia........	Fred L. Cox	Dir., Property and License Tax Unit	Revenue Department	Atlanta
Idaho.........	P. G. Neill	Tax Collector	Off. of Tax Collector	Boise
Illinois.........	Wm. G. Worthey	Chief Clerk	Off. of Secy. of State	Springfield
Iowa.........	Lyle Smith	Auditor, Corp., Inc. Tax Div.	Tax Commission	Des Moines
Kansas........	Roy N. McCue	Chairman	Rev. and Tax Commn.	Topeka
Kentucky......	Richard Sullivan	Dir., Income Div.	Dept. of Revenue	Frankfort
Louisiana......	Rufus W. Fontenot	Collector	Dept. of Revenue	Baton Rouge
Maryland......	Albert W. Ward	Exec. Secretary	Tax Commission	Baltimore
Massachusetts...	Thomas P. Sullivan	Dir., Corp. Tax Bureau	Dept. of Corps. and Taxation	Boston
Mississippi.....	Alex McKeigney	Chairman	Tax Commission	Jackson
Missouri.......	John F. Spalding	Corp. Commissr.	Off. of Secy. of State	Jefferson City
Montana.......	Howard Vralsted	Supervisor	Bd. of Equalization	Helena
Nebraska.......	Frank Marsh	Secy. of State	Off. of Secy. of State	Lincoln
New Jersey.....	Joseph McDonough	Supvr., Corp. Tax Bur., Div. of Tax.	Dept. of Treasury	Trenton
New Mexico....	John Block, Jr.	Chairman	Corp. Commission	Santa Fe
New York......	Arthur M. Gundlach	Dir., Corp. Tax. Bur., Div. of Tax.	Dept. of Tax. and Finance	Albany
North Carolina..	Eugene G. Shaw	Commissioner	Dept. of Revenue	Raleigh
Ohio..........	Stanley J. Bowers	Tax Commissioner	Dept. of Taxation	Columbus
Oklahoma......	James H. Hyde	Dir., Franchise Tax Div.	Tax Commission	Oklahoma City
Oregon........	Ray Smith	Tax Commissioner	Tax Commission	Salem
Pennsylvania...	Charles S. Seligman	Dir., Bur. of Corp. Taxes	Dept. of Revenue	Harrisburg
Rhode Island...	John H. Norberg	Chief Examiner, Corp. Tax Sect., Div. of Taxation	Dept. of Admin.	Providence
South Carolina..	Otis W. Livingston	Chairman	Tax Commission	Columbia
Tennessee......	O. Lloyd Darter, Jr.	Dir., Franch. and Excise Tax Div.	Dept. of Fin. and Taxation	Nashville
Texas..........	Tom Reavley	Secy. of State	Dept. of State	Austin
Utah..........	Paul M. Holt	Director	Corp. Franchise Tax Commission	Salt Lake City
Vermont.......	L. W. Morrison	Commissioner	Tax Commission	Montpelier
Virginia.......	H. Lester Hooker	Chairman	Corporation Commn.	Richmond
Washington....	H. Dan Bracken	Chairman	Tax Commission	Olympia
West Virginia...	Edgar B. Sims	Auditor	Auditor's Off.	Charleston
Wisconsin......	W. C. Maass	Dir., Div. of Corporation Income Tax	Dept. of Taxation	Madison
Wyoming......	Everett T. Copenhaver	Secy. of State	Off. of Secy. of State	Cheyenne
Alaska.........	John A. McKinney	Dir. of Finance	Dept. of Finance	Juneau
Guam.........	Richard F. Taitano	Director	Dept. of Finance	Agana
Hawaii........	John A. Bell	DeputyTax Commissr.	Off. of TaxCommissr.	Honolulu
Puerto Rico....	Rafael Picó	Secretary	Dept. of Treasury	San Juan
Virgin Islands..	Charles K. Claunch	Govt. Secy.	Govt. of the V. I.	St. Thomas

CORRECTIONS

State	Name	Official Title	Agency	Location
Alabama..	J. M. McCullough	Commissioner	Bd. of Corrections	Montgomery
Arizona........	Steve Vukcevich	Superintendent	State Industrial Sch. for Boys	Fort Grant
	Frank A. Eyman	Warden	State Prison	Florence
Arkansas.......	Lee Henslee	Superintendent	Penitentiary	Varner
California......	Richard A. McGee	Director	Dept. of Corrections	Sacramento
Colorado.......	Herbert E. Allen	Director	Dept. Pub. Insts.	Denver

CORRECTIONS—*continued*

State	Name	Official Title	Agency	Location
Connecticut....	Wm. D. Barnes	Exec. Secretary	Conn. Prison Assn.	Hartford
Delaware......	Elwood H. Wilson	Director	Bd. of Corrections	Wilmington
Florida........	Dewitt Sinclair	Superintendent	State Prison	Raiford
Georgia........	Jack Forrester	Director	Dept. of Corrections	Atlanta
Idaho..........	L. E. Clapp	Warden	State Penitentiary	Boise
Illinois.........	Robert B. Phillips	Chmn., Parole and Pardon Bd.	Dept. Pub. Safety	Springfield
Indiana........	Hugh O'Brien	Chairman	Dept. of Correction	Indianapolis
Iowa..........	Henry W. Burma	Chairman	Bd. of Control	Des Moines
Kansas........	Walter Hunter	Chairman	Bd. of Penal Insts.	Topeka
Kentucky......	James H. Hughes	Dir., Div. of Correc.	Dept. of Welfare	Frankfort
Louisiana......	Edward D. Grant	Director	Bd. of Institutions	Baton Rouge
Maine.........	Norman U. Greenlaw	Commissioner	Dept. Instit. Serv.	Augusta
Maryland......	Enos S. Stockbridge	Chairman	Bd. of Correction	Baltimore
Massachusetts...	Russell G. Oswald	Commissioner	Dept. of Correction	Boston
Michigan......	Gus Harrison	Director	Dept. of Corrections	Lansing
Minnesota.....	A. C. Gillette	Dir. of Corrections	Dept. of Welfare	St. Paul
Mississippi.....	Marvin E. Wiggins	Superintendent	State Penitentiary	Parchman
Missouri.......	James D. Carter	Director	Dept. of Corrections	Jefferson City
Montana.......	Benj. W. Wright	Director	Bd. of Pardons	Deer Lodge
Nebraska.......	Thomas J. Dredla	Chairman	Bd. of Control	Lincoln
Nevada........	A. E. Bernard	Warden	State Prison	Carson City
New Hampshire.	Parker L. Hancock	Warden	State Prison	Concord
	Edmund R. East	Superintendent	Industrial School	Manchester
New Jersey.....	F. Lovell Bixby	Dir., Div. of Correction and Parole	Dept. of Insts. and Parole Agencies	Trenton
New Mexico....	Edwin B. Swope	Superintendent	Penitentiary	Santa Fe
New York......	Thomas J. McHugh	Commissioner	Dept. of Correction	Albany
North Carolina..	S. E. Leonard	Commissioner	Bd. of Corrections and Training	Raleigh
North Dakota...	R. H. Sherman	Chairman	Bd. of Admin.	Bismarck
Ohio..........	John D. Porterfield	Director	Dept. Mental Hygiene and Correc.	Columbus
Oklahoma......	Clarence Burch	Chairman	Bd. of Pub. Affairs	Oklahoma City
Oregon........	E. J. Ireland	Secretary	Bd. of Control	Salem
Pennsylvania...	Arthur J. Prasse	Commissr., Bur. of Correc.	Dept. of Justice	Harrisburg
Rhode Island...	Edward P. Reidy	Director	Dept. of Soc. Welfare	Providence
	Harold V. Langlois	Asst. Dir., Soc. Welfare, Div. Correc. Servs.	Dept. of Soc. Welfare	Providence
South Carolina..	Wyndham M. Manning	Superintendent	State Penitentiary	Columbia
South Dakota...	R. S. Wallace	Exec. Director	Bd. of Charities and Corrections	Sioux Falls
Tennessee......	Keith Hampton	Commissioner	Dept. of Corrections	Nashville
Texas..........	O. B. Ellis	General Mgr.	Prison System	Huntsville
Utah..........	John F. Dugan	Chairman	Bd. of Corrections	Draper
Vermont.......	Timothy C. Dale	Commissioner	Dept. of Insts. and Corrections	Montpelier
Virginia.......	Rice M. Youell	Dir., Div. of Correc.	Dept. of Welfare and Insts.	Richmond
Washington....	Thomas A. Harris	Director	Dept. of Insts.	Olympia
West Virginia...	James M. Donohoe	President	Bd. of Control	Charleston
Wisconsin......	Sanger B. Powers	Dir. of Correc.	Dept. Pub. Welfare	Madison
Wyoming......	E. C. Rothwell	Secretary	Bd. of Charities and Reform	Cheyenne
Guam.........	Ted Brown	Director	Dept. of Pub. Safety	Agana
Hawaii........	Charles H. Silva	Director	Dept. of Insts.	Honolulu
Puerto Rico....	Porfirio Díaz Santana	Supt., Div. of Correc.	Dept. of Justice	San Juan
Virgin Islands..	Roy W. Bornn	Commissr. of Soc. Welfare	Govt. of the V. I.	St. Thomas

EDUCATION (Chief State School Officer)

State	Name	Official Title	Agency	Location
Alabama.......	Austin R. Meadows	Superintendent of Education	Dept. of Ed.	Montgomery
Arizona........	C. L. Harkins	Supt. Pub. Instr.	Off. of Supt. Pub. Instr.	Phoenix
Arkansas.......	A. W. Ford	Commissioner	Dept. of Ed.	Little Rock
California.....	Roy E. Simpson	Supt. Pub. Instr.	Dept. of Ed.	Sacramento
Colorado.......	H. Grant Vest	Commissioner	Dept. of Ed.	Denver
Connecticut....	Finis E. Engleman	Commissioner	Dept. of Ed.	Hartford
Delaware......	Geo. R. Miller, Jr.	Supt. Pub. Instr.	Bd. of Ed.	Dover
Florida........	Thomas D. Bailey	Supt. Pub. Instr.	Dept. of Ed.	Tallahassee
Georgia........	M. D. Collins	Supt. of Schools	Dept. of Ed.	Atlanta
Idaho..........	Alton B. Jones	Supt. Pub. Instr.	Dept. of Ed.	Boise
Illinois.........	Vernon L. Nickell	Supt. Pub. Instr.	Off. of Supt.	Springfield
Indiana........	Wilbur Young	Supt. Pub. Instr.	Bd. of Ed.	Indianapolis
Iowa..........	J. C. Wright	Supt. Pub. Instr.	Dept. of Pub. Instr.	Des Moines
Kansas........	Adel F. Throckmorton	Supt. Pub. Instr.	Dept. of Pub. Instr.	Topeka
Kentucky......	Robert R. Martin	Supt. Pub. Instr.	Dept. of Ed.	Frankfort
Louisiana......	Shelby M. Jackson	Supt. of Education	Dept. of Pub. Ed.	Baton Rouge
Maine.........	Herbert G. Espy	Commissioner	Dept. of Ed.	Augusta
Maryland......	Thos. G. Pullen	Superintendent	Dept. of Ed.	Baltimore
Massachusetts...	John J. Desmond, Jr.	Commissioner	Dept. of Ed.	Boston
Michigan......	Clair L. Taylor	Supt. Pub. Instr.	Dept. Pub. Instr.	Lansing
Minnesota......	D. M. Schweickhard	Commissioner	Dept. of Ed.	St. Paul
Mississippi.....	J. M. Tubb	Supt. Pub. Ed.	Dept. of Ed.	Jackson
Missouri......	Hubert Wheeler	Commissioner	Bd. of Ed.	Jefferson City
Montana.......	Mary M. Condon	Supt. Pub. Instr.	Off. of Supt.	Helena
Nebraska......	Freeman B. Decker	Commissr. of Ed.	Dept. of Ed.	Lincoln
Nevada........	Glenn A. Duncan	Supt. Pub. Instr.	Dept. of Ed.	Carson City
New Hampshire.	Austin J. McCaffrey	Commissr. of Ed.	Dept. of Ed.	Concord
New Jersey.....	Frederick M. Raubinger	Commissioner	Dept. of Ed.	Trenton
New Mexico...	Georgia L. Lusk	Superintendent	Dept. of Ed.	Santa Fe
New York......	James E. Allen, Jr.	Commissr. of Ed.	Education Dept.	Albany
North Carolina.	Charles F. Carroll	Supt. Pub. Instr.	Dept. Pub. Instr.	Raleigh
North Dakota...	M. F. Peterson	Supt. Pub. Instr.	Dept. Pub. Instr.	Bismarck
Ohio..........	R. M. Eyman	Supt. Pub. Instr.	Dept. of Ed.	Columbus
Oklahoma......	Oliver Hodge	Supt. Pub. Instr.	Dept. of Ed.	Oklahoma City
Oregon........	Rex Putnam	Supt. Pub. Instr.	Dept. of Ed.	Salem
Pennsylvania...	Ralph C. Swan	Act. Supt. Pub. Instr.	Dept. Pub. Instr.	Harrisburg
Rhode Island...	Michael F. Walsh	Commissioner	Dept. of Ed.	Providence
South Carolina..	Jesse T. Anderson	Superintendent	Dept. of Ed.	Columbia
South Dakota...	Harold S. Freeman	Superintendent	Pub. Instruction	Pierre
Tennessee......	Quill Cope	Commissioner	Dept. of Ed.	Nashville
Texas..........	J. W. Edgar	Commissr. of Ed.	Ed. Agency	Austin
Utah..........	E. Allen Bateman	Supt. Pub. Instr.	Bd. of Ed.	Salt Lake City
Vermont.......	A. John Holden, Jr.	Commissioner	Dept. of Ed.	Montpelier
Virginia......	Dowell J. Howard	Supt. Pub. Instr.	Dept. of Ed.	Richmond
Washington...	Pearl A. Wanamaker	Supt. of Pub. Instr.	Off. of Supt. Pub. Instr.	Olympia
West Virginia...	W. W. Trent	Supt. of Schools	Dept. of Ed.	Charleston
Wisconsin......	Geo. E. Watson	Supt. Pub. Instr.	Dept. Pub. Instr.	Madison
Wyoming......	Velma Linford	Superintendent	Dept. Pub. Instr.	Cheyenne
Alaska........	Donald M. Dafoe	Commissioner	Dept. of Ed.	Juneau
Guam.........	John S. Haitena	Director	Dept. of Ed.	Agana
Hawaii........	Clayton J. Chamberlin	Superintendent	Dept. Pub. Instr.	Honolulu
Puerto Rico....	Mariano Villaronga	Secretary	Dept. of Ed.	Hato Rey
Virgin Islands..	C. Frederick Dixon	Act. Commissr.	Dept. of Ed.	St. Thomas

EDUCATION (Presidents of State Universities)

State	Name	Official Title	Agency	Location
Alabama.......	O. C. Carmichael	President	Univ. of Ala.	University
Arizona........	Richard J. Harvill	President	Univ. of Ariz.	Tucson
Arkansas.......	John Tyler Caldwell	President	Univ. of Ark.	Fayetteville
California......	Robert G. Sproul	President	Univ. of Calif.	Berkeley
Colorado.......	Ward Darley	President	Univ. of Colo.	Boulder
Connecticut....	Albert N. Jorgensen	President	Univ. of Conn.	Storrs
Delaware......	J. A. Perkins	President	Univ. of Del.	Newark
Florida........	J. Wayne Reitz	President	Univ. of Fla.	Gainesville
	Doak S. Campbell	President	Fla. State Univ.	Tallahassee
	George W. Gore, Jr.	President	Fla. A. and M. Univ.	Tallahassee
Georgia........	O. C. Aderhold	President	Univ. of Ga.	Athens
Idaho.........	D. R. Theophilus	President	Univ. of Idaho	Moscow
Illinois.........	David D. Henry	President	Univ. of Ill.	Urbana
	D. W. Morris	President	Southern Ill. Univ.	Carbondale
Indiana........	Herman Wells	President	Indiana Univ.	Bloomington
	Frederick L. Hovde	President	Purdue Univ.	Lafayette
Iowa..........	Virgil M. Hancher	President	Univ. of Iowa	Iowa City
Kansas........	Franklin D. Murphy, M.D.	Chancellor	Univ. of Kansas	Lawrence
Kentucky......	H. L. Donovan	President	Univ. of Kentucky	Lexington
Louisiana......	Gen. Troy Middleton	President	La. State Univ. and Agric. and Mech.	Baton Rouge
Maine.........	Arthur A. Hauck	President	Univ. of Maine	Orono
Maryland......	Wilson H. Elkins	President	Univ. of Md.	College Park
Massachusetts...	J. Paul Mather	President	Univ. of Mass.	Amherst
Michigan......	Harlan H. Hatcher	President	Univ. of Mich.	Ann Arbor
Minnesota......	James L. Morrill	President	Univ. of Minn.	Minneapolis
Mississippi.....	John D. Williams	Chancellor	Univ. of Miss.	University
Missouri.......	Elmer Ellis	President	Univ. of Missouri	Columbia
Montana.......	Carl McFarland	President	Montana St. Univ.	Missoula
Nebraska.......	Clifford M. Hardin	Chancellor	Univ. of Neb.	Lincoln
Nevada........	Minard W. Stout	President	Univ. of Nev.	University Sta., Reno
New Hampshire.	Eldon L. Johnson	President	Univ. of N. H.	Durham
New Jersey.....	Lewis W. Jones	President	Rutgers Univ. (State Univ.)	New Brunswick
New Mexico....	Tom L. Popejoy	President	Univ. of N. M.	Albuquerque
New York......	William S. Carlson	President	N. Y. State Univ., Ed. Dept.	Albany
North Carolina..	J. Harris Parks	Act. President	Univ. of N. C.	Chapel Hill
North Dakota...	G. W. Starcher	President	Univ. of N. D.	Grand Forks
Ohio..........	Howard L. Bevis	President	Ohio State Univ.	Columbus
Oklahoma......	George L. Cross	President	Univ. of Oklahoma	Norman
	Oliver S. Wilham	President	Oklahoma A. and M. College	Stillwater
Oregon........	O. Meredith Wilson	President	Univ. of Oregon	Eugene
Pennsylvania...	Milton Eisenhower	President	Penn. State Univ.	State College
Rhode Island...	Carl R. Woodward	President	Univ. of R. I.	Kingston
South Carolina..	Donald Russell	President	Univ. of S. C.	Columbia
South Dakota...	I. D. Weeks	President	Univ. of S. D.	Vermillion
Tennessee......	C. E. Brehm	President	Univ. of Tenn.	Knoxville
Texas..........	Logan Wilson	President	Univ. of Texas	Austin
Utah..........	A. Ray Olpin	President	Univ. of Utah	Salt Lake City
Vermont.......	Carl Borgmann	President	Univ. of Vt. and State Agric. Coll.	Burlington
Virginia.......	Colgate W. Darden, Jr.	President	Univ. of Va.	Charlottesville
Washington....	Henry Schmitz	President	Univ. of Wash.	Seattle
West Virginia...	Irvin Stewart	President	W. Va. Univ.	Morgantown
Wisconsin......	Edwin B. Fred	President	Univ. of Wis.	Madison

EDUCATION (Presidents of State Universities)—*continued*

State	Name	Official Title	Agency	Location
Wyoming......	Geo. D. Humphrey	President	Univ. of Wyo.	Laramie
Alaska........	Ernest N. Patty	President	Univ. of Alaska	College
Guam.........	E. B. Sessions	Dean	Terr. Coll. of Guam	Agana
Hawaii........	Paul S. Bachman	President	Univ. of Hawaii	Honolulu
Puerto Rico....	Jaime Benítez	Chancellor	Univ. of P. R.	Rio Piedras

EDUCATION (Vocational Education)

State	Name	Official Title	Agency	Location
Alabama.......	R. E. Cammack	Dir., Div. Voc. Ed.	Dept. of Ed.	Montgomery
Arizona........	C. L. Harkins	Supt. Pub. Instr.	Off. Supt. Pub. Instr.	Phoenix
Arkansas.......	J. M. Adams	Dir., Voc. Ed.	Dept. of Ed.	Little Rock
California......	Wesley P. Smith	Dir., Voc. Ed.	Dept. of Ed.	Sacramento
Colorado.......	E. C. Comstock	Exec. Director	Bd. for Voc. Ed.	Denver
Connecticut....	Emmett O'Brien	Chief, Bur. Voc. Ed.	Dept. of Ed.	Hartford
Delaware......	R. W. Heim	Director	Vocational Ed.	Dover
Florida........	Walter R. Williams, Jr.	Dir., Voc. Ed.	Dept. of Ed.	Tallahassee
Georgia........	Geo. I. Martin	Administrator	Dept. of Ed.	Atlanta
Idaho.........	George E. Denman	Director	Voc. Ed.	Boise
Illinois.........	Vernon L. Nickell	Exec. Director	Supt. Pub. Instr.	Springfield
Indiana........	Wilbur Young	Supt. Pub. Instr.	Bd. of Ed.	Indianapolis
Iowa..........	J. C. Wright	Exec. Officer	Bd. of Voc. Ed.	Des Moines
Kansas........	Walter M. Arnold	Director	Voc. Ed.	Topeka
Kentucky......	James L. Patton	Head, Bur. Voc. Ed.	Dept. of Ed.	Frankfort
Louisiana......	Shelby M. Jackson	Supt. of Ed.	Dept. of Ed.	Baton Rouge
Maine.........	Maurice C. Varney	Director	Dept. of Ed.	Augusta
Maryland......	John J. Seidel	Asst. Supt. Voc. Ed.	Dept. of Ed.	Baltimore
Massachusetts...	Walter L. Markham	Dir., Div. of Voc. Ed.	Dept. of Ed.	Boston
Michigan.......	Clair L. Taylor	Exec. Off., Voc. Ed.	Dept. of Pub. Instr.	Lansing
Minnesota......	Harry C. Schmid	Dir., Voc. Ed.	Dept. of Ed.	St. Paul
Mississippi.....	H. E. Mauldin	Dir., Voc. Ed. Div.	Dept. of Ed.	Jackson
Missouri.......	Hubert Wheeler	Commissioner	Dept. of Ed.	Jefferson City
Montana.......	A. W. Johnson	Director	Supt. of Pub. Instr.	Helena
Nebraska.......	Stanley L. Hawley	Asst. Commissr.	Bd. of Voc. Ed.	Lincoln
Nevada........	John W. Bunten	Dir., Supvr., Trades, Indust. Ed.	Dept. of Voc. Ed.	Carson City
New Hampshire.	Earl H. Little	Chief, Div. of Voc. Ed.	Dept. of Ed.	Concord
New Jersey.....	Albert E. Jochen	Asst. Commissr., Div. Voc. Ed.	Dept. of Ed.	Trenton
New Mexico....	Henry Gonzales	Director	Dept. of Voc. Ed.	Santa Fe
New York......	Joseph R. Strobel	Asst. Commissr. for Voc. Ed.	Ed. Dept.	Albany
North Carolina..	J. Warren Smith	Dir., Div. Voc. Ed.	Dept. of Pub. Instr.	Raleigh
North Dakota...	M. F. Peterson	Supt. Pub. Instr. and Exec. Dir.	Bd. of Pub. School Ed.	Bismarck
Ohio..........	Ralph A. Howard	Director	Bd. of Voc. Ed.	Columbus
Oklahoma......	W. T. Doyel	Secretary	Bd. for Voc. Ed.	Oklahoma City
	J. B. Perky	Dir., Div. of Voc. Ed.	Bd. for Voc. Ed.	Oklahoma City
	Voyle C. Scurlock	Dir., Div. of Voc. Rehab.	Bd. for Voc. Ed.	Oklahoma City
Oregon........	O. I. Paulson	Director	Div. of Voc. Ed.	Salem
Pennsylvania...	Robert T. Stoner	Director	Dept. of Pub. Instr.	Harrisburg
Rhode Island...	F. Sheldon Davis	Chief, Div. Voc. Ed.	Dept. of Ed.	Providence
South Carolina..	R. D. Anderson	Director	Div. of Voc. Ed.	Columbia
South Dakota...	Carl Eskelson	Director	Voc. Rehabil.	Pierre
Tennessee......	G. E. Freeman	Dir., Div. of Voc. Ed.	Dept. of Ed.	Nashville
Texas..........	J. W. Edgar	Commissr. of Ed.	Education Agency	Austin
Utah..........	Mark Nichols	Director	Voc. Ed.	Salt Lake City
Vermont.......	John E. Nelson	Director	Bd. of Voc. Ed.	Montpelier
Virginia.......	Frank B. Cale	Dir. of Voc. Ed.	Dept. of Ed.	Richmond
Washington....	Herman Miller	Director	Bd. for Voc. Ed.	Olympia

EDUCATION (Vocational Education)—*continued*

State	Name	Official Title	Agency	Location
West Virginia...	John M. Lowe	Director	Voc. Ed. Div.	Charleston
Wisconsin......	C. L. Greiber	Director	Bd. of Voc. and Adult Ed.	Madison
Wyoming......	Sam Hitchcock	Director	Dept. of Voc. Ed.	Cheyenne
Guam.........	Dan H. Lomax	Principal	Terr. Voc. Sch.	Agana
Hawaii........	William H. Coulter	Deputy Supt.	Dept. of Pub. Instr.	Honolulu
Puerto Rico....	Lorenzo García-Hernández	Dir., Voc. Ed. Div.	Dept. of Ed.	San Juan
Virgin Islands..	G. Robert Cotton	Dir., Voc. Ed.	Govt. of the V. I.	St. Thomas

EMPLOYMENT SECURITY

State	Name	Official Title	Agency	Location
Alabama.......	Eugene M. Wells	Director	Dept. of Ind. Rels.	Montgomery
Arizona........	Elmer F. Vickers, Sr.	Chairman	Empl. Sec. Commn.	Phoenix
Arkansas.......	James L. Bland	Admn., Empl. Sec. Div.	Dept. of Labor	Little Rock
California.....	Harry W. Stewart	Director	Dept. of Employment	Sacramento
Colorado.......	Bernard E. Teets	Exec. Director	Dept. of Employment	Denver
Connecticut....	Joseph M. Tone	Exec. Dir., Empl. Sec. Div.	Dept. of Labor	Hartford
Delaware......	Albert Stetser	Chmn.–Exec. Dir.	Unempl. Comp. Commn.	Wilmington
Florida........	James T. Vocelle	Chairman	Industrial Commn.	Tallahassee
Georgia........	Marion Williamson	Dir., Empl. Sec. Agency	Dept. of Labor	Atlanta
Idaho.........	H. F. Garrett	Exec. Director	Empl. Sec. Agency	Boise
Illinois........	Samuel C. Bernstein	Commissr. of Unempl. Comp.	Dept. of Labor	Chicago
Indiana.......	Wm. G. Stalnaker	Director	Empl. Sec. Div.	Indianapolis
Iowa..........	C. M. Stanley	Chairman	Empl. Sec. Commn.	Des Moines
Kansas........	John Morrison	Exec. Dir., Empl. Sec. Div.	Labor Dept.	Topeka
Kentucky......	V. E. Barnes	Exec. Dir., Bur. of Empl. Sec.	Dept. of Econ. Sec.	Frankfort
Louisiana......	Richard E. Walker	Admn., Div. of Empl. Sec.	Dept. of Labor	Baton Rouge
Maine.........	L. C. Fortier	Chairman	Empl. Sec. Commn.	Augusta
Maryland......	Robert B. Kimble	Chairman	Dept. of Empl. Sec.	Baltimore
Massachusetts...	Dewey G. Archambault	Director	Div. of Empl. Sec.	Boston
Michigan......	Max M. Horton	Director	Empl. Sec. Commn.	Detroit
Minnesota......	Frank T. Starkey	Commissioner	Dept. of Empl. Sec.	St. Paul
Mississippi.....	Robert Prisock	Exec. Director	Empl. Sec. Commn.	Jackson
Missouri.......	Gordon P. Weir	Dir., Div. of Empl. Sec.	Dept. of Labor and Ind. Rels.	Jefferson City
Montana.......	Chadwick H. Smith	Chmn.–Exec. Dir.	Unempl. Comp. Commn.	Helena
Nebraska.......	Robert T. Malone	Dir., Div. of Empl. Sec.	Dept. of Labor	Lincoln
Nevada........	Harry A. Depaoli	Exec. Director	Empl. Sec. Dept.	Carson City
New Hampshire.	Charles Griffin	Dir.,Div.of Empl.Sec.	Dept. of Labor	Concord
New Jersey.....	John J. Yencik	Dir.,Div.of Empl.Sec.	Dept. of Labor and Ind.	Trenton
New Mexico....	Fred C. Barron	Chmn.–Exec. Dir.	Empl. Sec. Commn.	Albuquerque
New York......	Richard C. Brockway	Exec. Dir., Div. of Empl.	Dept. of Labor	New York
North Carolina..	Henry E. Kendall	Chairman	Empl. Sec. Commn.	Raleigh
North Dakota...	Martin N. Gronvold	Director	Unempl. Comp. Div.	Bismarck
Ohio..........	James Tichenor	Act. Administrator	Bur. of Unempl. Comp.	Columbus
Oklahoma......	Bruton Wood	Exec. Director	Empl. Sec. Commn.	Oklahoma City

EMPLOYMENT SECURITY—*Continued*

State	Name	Official Title	Agency	Location
Oregon........	Silas Gaiser	Administrator	Unempl. Comp. Commn.	Salem
Pennsylvania...	A. Allen Sulcowe	Exec. Dir., Bur. of Empl. Sec.	Dept. of Labor and Industry	Harrisburg
Rhode Island...	Thomas H. Bride, Jr.	Director	Dept. of Empl. Sec.	Providence
South Carolina..	Melford A. Wilson	Exec. Director	Empl. Sec. Commn.	Columbia
South Dakota...	Alan Williamson	Commissioner	Empl. Sec. Dept.	Aberdeen
Tennessee......	Donald M. McSween	Commissioner	Dept. of Empl. Sec.	Nashville
Texas..........	{Weldon Hart	Chmn.–Exec. Dir.	Employment Commn.	Austin
	{William H. Farmer	Administrator	Empl. Commn.	Austin
Utah..........	Curtis P. Harding	Admn., Dept. of Empl. Sec.	Industrial Commn.	Salt Lake City
Vermont.......	Henry A. Milne	Chairman	Unempl. Comp. Commn.	Montpelier
Virginia.......	John Q. Rhodes, Jr.	Commissioner	Unempl. Comp. Commn.	Richmond
Washington....	Peter R. Giovine	Commissioner	Empl. Sec. Dept.	Olympia
West Virginia...	C. S. Davis	Director	Dept. of Empl. Sec.	Charleston
Wisconsin......	Paul A. Raushenbush	Dir., Unempl. Comp.	Industrial Commn.	Madison
Wyoming......	Chester P. Sorensen	Exec. Director	Empl. Sec. Commn.	Casper
Alaska........	Arthur A. Hedges	Act. Exec. Dir.	Empl. Sec. Commn.	Juneau
Guam.........	Juan Palomó	Empl. Manager	Dept. of Labor and Personnel	Agana
Hawaii........	Howard Wiig	Administrator	Bur. of Empl. Sec.	Honolulu
Puerto Rico....	Mrs. P. A. Pagán de Colón	Director	Puerto Rico Empl. Service	San Juan
Virgin Islands..	Mrs. E. Louise Scott	Director	Virgin Islands Empl. Service	St. Thomas

EMPLOYMENT SERVICE

State	Name	Official Title	Agency	Location
Alabama.......	C. F. Anderson	Dir., Empl. Serv.	Dept. of Ind. Rels.	Montgomery
Arizona........	James A. Rork	Dir., Empl. Serv.	Empl. Sec. Commn.	Phoenix
Arkansas.......	Louie S. Hoffman	Dir. of Field Services	Empl. Sec. Div., Dept. of Labor	Little Rock
California......	Thomas Campbell	Chief, Div. Pub. Empl. Offs. and Benefit Payments	Dept. of Employment	Sacramento
Colorado.......	Albert W. Bevan	Dir., Empl. Serv. Div.	Dept. of Employment	Denver
Connecticut....	Thomas I. Shea	Director	Empl. Serv. Dept.	Hartford
Delaware......	Edward Buckley	Chief of Placement	Unempl. Comp. Commn.	Wilmington
Florida........	William U. Norwood, Jr.	Director, Empl. Serv. Div.	Indus. Commn.	Tallahassee
Georgia........	W. L. Abbott	Act. Dir., Empl. Serv. Div.	Dept. of Labor	Atlanta
Idaho.........	W. J. Adams	Asst. Dir., Placements	Employment Security	Boise
Illinois.........	Walter E. Parker	Dir., Empl. Serv.	Dept. of Labor	Chicago
Indiana........	Charles F. Gross	Chief, Empl. Servs.	Empl. Sec. Bd.	Indianapolis
Iowa..........	George W. Moore	Dir. of Empl. Servs.	Empl. Sec. Commn.	Des Moines
Kansas........	John Morrison	Exec. Dir., Empl. Sec. Div.	Labor Dept.	Topeka
Kentucky......	L. P. Jones	Director	Div. of Empl. Serv.	Frankfort
Louisiana......	Richard Walker	Administrator	Div. of Empl. Sec.	Baton Rouge
Maine.........	Paul E. Jones	Dir., Empl. Serv.	Empl. Sec. Commn.	Augusta
Maryland......	David L. B. Fringer	Dir., Empl. Serv. Div.	Dept. Empl. Sec.	Baltimore
Massachusetts...	Henry T. Lane	Asst. Director	Div. of Empl. Sec.	Boston
Michigan......	O. K. Fjetland	Dir., Empl. Serv. Div.	Empl. Sec. Commn.	Detroit
Minnesota......	A. Merrill Anderson	Dir., Empl. Service	Dept. of Employment Security	St. Paul

EMPLOYMENT SERVICE—*continued*

State	Name	Official Title	Agency	Location
Mississippi.....	Raymond L. Sullivan	Dir., Empl. Serv. Div.	Empl. Sec. Commn.	Jackson
Missouri.......	Will S. Denham	Asst. Dir. (Local Off. Operations)	Dept. of Labor and Ind. Relations	Jefferson City
Montana.......	Jess C. Fletcher	Dir., Empl. Serv. Div.	Unempl. Comp. Commn.	Helena
Nebraska.......	Robert T. Malone	Dir., Div. of Empl. Sec.	Dept. of Labor	Lincoln
Nevada........	Alvin I. Stortroen	Chief of Placement	Empl. Sec. Dept.	Carson City
New Hampshire.	Mrs. Abby L. Wilder	Dir., Empl. Serv. Bur.	Div. of Empl. Sec.	Concord
New Jersey.....	Joseph A. Jordan	Chief, Bur. of Empl. Serv., Div. of Empl. Sec.	Dept. of Labor and Industry	Trenton
New Mexico....	Max R. Salazar	Director	Employment Service	Albuquerque
New York......	Stephen Mayo	Dir., Field Operations Bur., Div. of Employment	Dept. of Labor	New York
North Carolina..	J. W. Beach	Dir., Empl. Serv. Div.	Empl. Sec. Commn.	Raleigh
North Dakota...	Carl F. Fryhling	Director	Employment Service	Bismarck
Ohio..........	W. F. Lunsford	Dir., Empl. Serv.	Bur. Unempl. Comp.	Columbus
Oklahoma......	Morris Leonhard	Chief, Empl. Serv.	Empl. Sec. Commn.	Oklahoma City
Oregon........	Earl R. Lovell	Dir., Empl. Serv.	Unempl. Comp. Commission	Salem
Pennsylvania...	Charles E. Reeser, Jr.	Dir., Empl. Serv.	Dept. Labor and Industry	Harrisburg
Rhode Island...	T. Edward Burns	Dir., Empl. Service	Dept. of Empl. Sec.	Providence
South Carolina..	E. H. Bradley	Dir., Empl. Serv. Div.	Empl. Sec. Commn.	Columbia
South Dakota...	Alan Williamson	Commissioner	Empl. Sec. Dept.	Aberdeen
Tennessee......	Paul Jessen	Dir., Empl. Serv. Div.	Dept. of Empl. Sec.	Nashville
Texas.........	{ Weldon Hart	Chmn.-Exec. Dir.	Employment Commn.	Austin
	Wm. H. Farmer	Administrator	Employment Commn.	Austin
Utah..........	Joseph S. Mayer	Director	Employment Service	Salt Lake City
Vermont.......	E. Reynold Johnson	Director	Empl. Serv. Div.	Montpelier
Virginia.......	W. P. Purser	Empl. Serv. Dir.	Dept. Unempl. Comp.	Richmond
Washington....	A. F. Hardy	Asst. Commissr.	Dept. of Empl. Sec.	Olympia
West Virginia...	Patrick M. Connell	Chief, Empl. Serv. Div.	Dept. of Empl. Sec.	Charleston
Wisconsin......	Austin T. Rose	Dir., Empl. Serv.	Industrial Commn.	Madison
Wyoming......	Chester P. Sorensen	Dir., Empl. Serv. Div.	Empl. Sec. Commn.	Casper
Alaska........	Gus Gissberg	Chief of Empl. Serv.	Empl. Sec. Commn.	Juneau
Guam.........	Juan Palomo	Empl. Manager	Dept. of Labor and Personnel	Agana
Hawaii........	E. Leigh Stevens	Chief, Empl. Serv. Div.	Bur. of Empl. Serv.	Honolulu
Puerto Rico....	Mrs. P. A. Pagán de Colón	Dir., Empl. Serv.	Dept. of Labor	San Juan
Virgin Islands..	Mrs. E. Louise Scott	Dir., Empl. Serv.	Employment Service	St. Thomas

EQUALIZATION OF ASSESSMENTS

State	Name	Official Title	Agency	Location
Alabama.......	W. LaRue Horn	Commissr. of Revenue	Dept. of Revenue	Montgomery
Arizona........	Warren Peterson	Chairman	Tax Commn.	Phoenix
Arkansas.......	W. L. Hinton, Jr.	Dir., Assessment Coord. Div.	Pub. Serv. Commn.	Little Rock
California......	Dixwell L. Peirce	Exec. Secy.	Bd. of Equal.	Sacramento
Colorado.......	John R. Seaman	Chairman	Tax Commn.	Denver
Connecticut....	John L. Sullivan	Commissioner	Tax Dept.	Hartford
Idaho.........	Ed D. Baird	Chairman	Tax Commn.	Boise
Illinois........	Richard J. Lyons	Director	Dept. of Rev.	Springfield
Indiana.......	Adolph L. Fossler	Chairman	Bd. of Tax Commissrs.	Indianapolis
Iowa..........	Ray E. Johnson	Chairman	Tax Commn.	Des Moines

EQUALIZATION OF ASSESSMENTS—*continued*

State	Name	Official Title	Agency	Location
Kansas........	Roy N. McCue	Chairman	Rev. and Taxation Commn.	Topeka
Kentucky......	Robert Allphin	Commissioner	Dept. of Rev.	Frankfort
Louisiana......	Graydon K. Kitchens	Chairman	Tax Commn.	Baton Rouge
Maine........	Ernest H. Johnson	Tax Assessor	Bur. of Taxation	Augusta
Maryland......	H. Gerard Mueller	Chief Supvr. Assess.	Tax Commn.	Baltimore
Massachusetts...	John Dane, Jr.	Commissioner	Dept. of Corp. and Taxation	Boston
Michigan.....	Victor Targonski	Chairman	Bd. of Equal.	Lansing
Minnesota......	G. Howard Spaeth	Commissioner	Dept. of Taxation	St. Paul
Mississippi.....	Alex McKeigney	Chairman	Tax Commn.	Jackson
Missouri.......	James Robertson	Chairman, Tax Commn.	Dept. of Rev.	Jefferson City
Montana.......	J. L. Reed	Chairman	Bd. of Equal.	Helena
Nebraska.......	F. A. Herrington	Secretary	Bd. of Equal. and Assess.	Lincoln
Nevada........	Homer Bowers	Dir., Div. of Assess. Standards	Tax Commn.	Carson City
New Hampshire	Oliver W. Marvin	Chairman	Tax Commn.	Concord
New Jersey.....	Anthony C. Mitchell	Pres., Div. Tax Appeals	Dept. of Treas.	Trenton
New Mexico....	C. L. Forsling	Chief Tax Commissr.	Tax Commn.	Santa Fe
New York......	Frank C. Moore	Chairman	Bd. of Equal. and Assess.	Albany
North Carolina..	Eugene G. Shaw	Commissioner	Dept. of Rev.	Raleigh
North Dakota...	J. Arthur Engen	Secy. and Tax Commissr.	Bd. of Equal.	Bismarck
Ohio..........	Stanley J. Bowers	Tax. Commissr.	Dept. of Taxation	Columbus
Oklahoma......	D. B. Collums	Asst. Secy.	Bd. of Equal.	Oklahoma City
Oregon........	Samuel B. Stewart	Tax Commissr.	Tax Commn.	Salem
Pennsylvania...	John O'Neil	Chairman	Tax Equal. Bd.	Harrisburg
Rhode Island...	F. M. Langton	Tax Admn.	Div. of Tax., Dept. of Admin.	Providence
South Carolina..	Otis W. Livingston	Chairman	Tax Commn.	Columbia
South Dakota...	W. R. Wilder	Commissioner	Dept. of Revenue	Pierre
Tennessee......	Frank G. Clement	Chairman	Bd. of Equal.	Nashville
Texas..........	Robert S. Calvert	Comptroller	Off. of Comptr.	Austin
Utah..........	Byron D. Jones	Chairman	Tax Commn.	Salt Lake City
Vermont.......	L. W. Morrison	Commissioner	Tax Dept.	Montpelier
Virginia.......	C. H. Morrissett	Tax Commissr.	Dept. of Taxation	Richmond
Washington....	H. Dan Bracken	Chairman	Tax Commn.	Olympia
West Virginia...	Wm. R. Laird III	Commissioner	Tax Commn.	Charleston
Wisconsin......	Forrest W. Gillett	Dir., Property Tax Division	Dept. of Taxation	Madison
Wyoming......	Walter W. Hudson	Chairman	Bd. of Equal.	Cheyenne
Guam.........	Gayle Shelton	Chairman	Bd. of Equal.	Agana
Hawaii........	Earl W. Fase	Tax Commissr.	Off. of Tax Commissr.	Honolulu
Puerto Rico....	Rafael Picó	Secretary	Dept. of Treasury	San Juan
Virgin Islands..	Aubrey Ottley	Chairman	V. I. Bd. Tax Review	St. Thomas

---

FINANCIAL CONTROL (Over-all Agency)

State	Name	Official Title	Agency	Location
Alabama.......	Fuller Kimbrell	Director	Dept. of Finance	Montgomery
Arkansas.......	Kelly Cornett	Comptroller	Comptroller's Off.	Little Rock
California......	John M. Peirce	Dir. of Finance	Dept. of Finance	Sacramento
Connecticut....	Joseph Loughlin	Commissioner	Dept. of Finance and Control	Hartford
Florida........	Harry G. Smith	Budget Director	Budget Commn.	Tallahassee
Idaho.........	Ralph Spaulding	Director	Dept. of Finance	Boise

FINANCIAL CONTROL (Over-all Agency)—*continued*

State	Name	Official Title	Agency	Location
Illinois.........	Morton H. Hollingsworth	Director	Dept. of Finance	Springfield
Indiana........	Donald H. Clark	Director	Div. of Budget	Indianapolis
Iowa..........	Glenn D. Sarsfield	Comptroller	Comptroller's Off.	Des Moines
Kansas.........	Martin M. Kiger	Exec. Director	Dept. of Admin.	Topeka
Kentucky......	George T. Stewart	Commissioner	Dept. of Finance	Frankfort
Louisiana......	J. Harvey Rester	Asst. Dir. of Budg.	Off. Dir. of Budg.	Baton Rouge
Maine.........	Raymond C. Mudge	Commissr. of Finance	Dept. of Finance and Admin.	Augusta
Maryland......	J. O. McCusker	Secy., Chief Deputy Comptr.	Bd. of Pub. Works	Annapolis
Massachusetts...	Carl A. Sheridan	Commissr. of Admin.	Commn. on Admin. and Finance	Boston
Michigan......	James W. Miller	Controller	Dept. of Admin.	Lansing
Minnesota......	Arthur Naftalin	Commissioner	Dept. of Admin.	St. Paul
Mississippi.....	W. R. Carbrey, Sr.	Secretary	Budget Commn.	Jackson
Montana.......	A. M. Johnson	Controller	Off. of Controller	Helena
New Hampshire.	Arthur E. Bean	Comptroller	Dept. of Admin. and Control	Concord
New Jersey.....	Archibald S. Alexander	Treasurer	Dept. of Treas.	Trenton
New Mexico....	D. M. Smith, Jr.	Comptroller	Off. of Comptr.	Santa Fe
New York......	Arthur Levitt	Comptroller	Dept. of Audit and Control	Albany
North Carolina..	Edwin Gill	Treasurer	Treasurer's Off.	Raleigh
Ohio..........	John M. Wilcoxon	Director	Dept. of Finance	Columbus
Oklahoma......	Burton Logan	Dir., Budg. Div.	Exec. Dept.	Oklahoma City
Oregon........	Harry S. Dorman	Director	Dept. of Finance and Admin.	Salem
Pennsylvania...	Andrew M. Bradley	Budget Secy.	Governor's Off.	Harrisburg
Rhode Island...	H. Clinton Owen, Jr.	Director	Dept. of Admin.	Providence
South Carolina..	George Bell Timmerman, Jr.	Chairman and Governor	Budg. and Control Bd.	Columbia
South Dakota...	Morris G. Hallock	Secretary	Dept. of Finance	Pierre
Tennessee......	Ramon T. Davis	Treasurer	Off. of Treas.	Nashville
Utah..........	D. H. Whittenburg	Chairman	Finance Dept.	Salt Lake City
Vermont.......	George Amidon	Treasurer	Off. of Treas.	Montpelier
Washington....	E. D. Brabrook	Director	Off. Dir. of Budget	Olympia
West Virginia...	Denzil L. Gainer	Director	Budget Dept.	Charleston
Wisconsin......	E. C. Giessel	Director	Dept. of Budget and Accounts	Madison
Wyoming......	Milward L. Simpson	Governor	Off. of Governor	Cheyenne
Alaska.........	John A. McKinney	Dir. of Finance	Dept. of Finance	Juneau
Guam.........	Richard F. Taitano	Director	Dept. of Finance	Agana
Hawaii........	Paul J. Thurston	Director	Bur. of Budget	Honolulu
Puerto Rico....	José R. Noguera	Director	Bur. of Budget	San Juan
Virgin Islands...	Percy de Jongh	Act. Commissr. of Finance	Govt. of the V. I.	St. Thomas

FIRE MARSHAL

State	Name	Official Title	Agency	Location
Alabama.......	J. V. Kitchens	Fire Marshal	Dept. of Insurance	Montgomery
Arkansas.......	Mack A. Thompson	Fire Marshal, Div. Fire Prevention	State Police	Little Rock
California......	Joe R. Yockers	Chief	Fire Marshal	Sacramento
Connecticut....	John C. Kelly	Commissioner	State Police	Hartford
Delaware......	Walter J. LaRue	Fire Marshal	Off. of Fire Marshal	Dover
Florida........	J. Edwin Larson	Fire Marshal	Treasurer's Off.	Tallahassee
Georgia........	F. E. Robinson	Fire Marshal	Comptroller-Gen.'s Off.	Atlanta
Illinois.........	John J. Twomey	Fire Marshal	Dept. of Pub. Safety	Springfield

FIRE MARSHAL—*continued*

State	Name	Official Title	Agency	Location
Indiana........	Arnold H. Meister	Fire Marshal	Fire Marshal Dept.	Indianapolis
Iowa..........	Edward J. Herron	Fire Marshal	Dept. of Pub. Safety	Des Moines
Kansas........	C. A. Ogg	Fire Marshal	Fire Marshal Dept.	Topeka
Kentucky......	J. T. Underwood, Jr.	Fire Marshal	Dept. of Insurance	Frankfort
Louisiana......	Sidney S. Bowman	Fire Marshal	Off. of Fire Marshal	New Orleans
Massachusetts...	Robert M. Tappin	Fire Marshal	Dept. of Pub. Safety	Boston
Michigan......	Arnold C. Renner	Chief, Fire Marshal Div.	State Police	East Lansing
Minnesota......	Cyril C. Sheehan	Fire Marshal	Insurance Division	St. Paul
Mississippi.....	C. L. Pace, Jr.	Fire Marshal	Insurance Dept.	Jackson
Montana.......	Arthur C. Parsons	Fire Marshal	Off. of Auditor	Helena
Nebraska.......	E. C. Iverson	Fire Marshal	Division of Fire Prevention	Lincoln
Nevada........	Louis D. Ferrari	Surveyor Gen. and Forester, Fire Warden	Off. of Surveyor Gen.	Carson City
New Hampshire.	Aubrey G. Robinson	Fire Marshal	Bd. of Fire Control	Concord
New Jersey.....	Wm. J. Seidel	State Fire Warden, Div. of Planning and Devel.	Dept. of Conserv. and Econ. Devel.	Trenton
New Mexico....	R. F. Apodaca	Fire Marshal	Insurance Dept.	Santa Fe
New York......	B. Richter Townsend	Chief, Bur. of Fire Mobil. and Control	Div. of Safety, Exec. Dept.	Albany
North Carolina..	Chas. F. Gold	Fire Marshal	Dept. of Insurance	Raleigh
North Dakota...	Vance Arneson	Deputy	Fire Marshal Dept.	Bismarck
Ohio..........	Charles R. Scott	Fire Marshal	Div. of State Fire Marshal	Columbus
Oklahoma......	Ralph Duroy	Fire Marshal	Fire Marshal's Office	Oklahoma City
Oregon........	Robert B. Taylor	Fire Marshal	Fire Marshal's Office	Salem
Pennsylvania...	Wm. F. Traeger	Fire Marshal	Bur. Fire Protection	Harrisburg
Rhode Island...	John T. Sheehan	Supt., State Police	Exec. Dept.	Lincoln
South Carolina..	W. R. Whitmire	Fire Investigator	Insurance Dept.	Columbia
South Dakota...	George O. Burt	Fire Marshal	Dept. of Insurance	Pierre
Tennessee......	Arch Northington	Fire Marshal	Dept. of Ins. and Banking	Nashville
Texas.........	Mark Wentz	Fire Marshal	Bd. of Ins. Commissrs.	Austin
Utah..........	J. Whitney Floyd	Chief Forester	Forestry and Fire Control Bd.	Salt Lake City
Vermont.......	Chester Kirby	Deputy Fire Marshal	Pub. Safety Dept.	Montpelier
Virginia.......	C. S. Mullen, Jr.	Chief Fire Marshal	Corporation Commn.	Richmond
Washington....	Wm. A. Sullivan	Fire Marshal	Insurance Commn.	Olympia
West Virginia...	C. A. Raper	Fire Marshal	Fire Marshal's Off.	Charleston
Wisconsin......	Paul J. Rogan	Fire Marshal	Insurance Dept.	Madison
Wyoming......	Ford S. Taft	Fire Marshal	Insurance Dept.	Cheyenne
Alaska.........	Clyde V. Dailey	Fire Marshal	Dept. Terr. Police	Juneau
Guam.........	Pedro SN. Castro	Fire Chief	Dept. Pub. Safety	Tamuning
Hawaii........	Kam Tai Lee	Fire Marshal	Treasury Dept.	Honolulu
Puerto Rico....	Raúl Gándara	Fire Chief	Fire Service of Puerto Rico	San Juan
Virgin Islands...	Omar Brown	Fire Chief	Dept. of Public Safety	St. Thomas

FISH AND GAME

State	Name	Official Title	Agency	Location
Alabama.......	C. Graham Hixon	Chief, Div. of Game and Fish	Dept. of Conserv.	Montgomery
Arizona........	John M. Hall	Director	Game and Fish Commn.	Phoenix

FISH AND GAME—*continued*

State	Name	Official Title	Agency	Location
Arkansas.......	T. A. McAmis	Exec. Secretary	Game and Fish Commn.	Little Rock
California......	Seth Gordon	Director	Dept. of Fish and Game	Sacramento
Colorado.......	Tom Kimball	Exec. Director	Game and Fish Commn.	Denver
Connecticut....	Lyle M. Thorpe	Director	Bd. Fisheries and Game	Hartford
Delaware......	Virgil Hearn	Chief Game Warden	Bd. of Game and Fish Commissrs.	Dover
Florida........	A. D. Aldrich	Director	Game and Fresh Water Fish Commn.	Tallahassee
	Ernest C. Mitts	Director	Bd. of Conserv.	Tallahassee
Georgia........	Fulton Lovell	Director	Game and Fish Dept.	Atlanta
Idaho.........	Ross Leonard	Director	Dept. of Fish and Game	Boise
Illinois........	Glen D. Palmer	Director	Dept. of Conserv.	Springfield
Indiana........	Emmett L. Lewis	Dir., Div. of Fish and Game	Dept. of Conserv.	Indianapolis
Iowa..........	Ray W. Beckman	Chief, Fish and Game	Conserv. Commn.	Des Moines
Kansas........	David D. Leahy	Acting Director	Forestry, Fish and Game	Pratt
Kentucky......	Earl Wallace	Commissioner	Dept. of Fish and Wildlife Resources	Frankfort
Louisiana......	L. D. Young	Director	Dept. of Wildlife and Fisheries	New Orleans
Maine.........	Roland H. Cobb	Commissioner	Inland Fish and Game Dept.	Augusta
	Stanley R. Tupper	Commissioner	Sea and Shore Fisheries	Augusta
Maryland......	Ernest A. Vaughn	Director	Dept. of Game and Inland Fish	Baltimore
	John Tawes	Chairman	Dept. of Tidewater Fisheries	Annapolis
Massachusetts...	(Vacancy)	Dir., Div. of Fisheries and Game	Dept. Natural Resources	Boston
	Francis W. Sargent	Dir., Div. of Marine Fisheries	Dept. Natural Resources	Boston
Michigan......	F. A. Westerman	Chief, Fish Div.	Conserv. Dept.	Lansing
	H. D. Ruhl	Chief, Game Div.	Conserv. Dept.	Lansing
Minnesota......	James W. Kimball	Dir., Div. of Game and Fish	Dept. of Conserv.	St. Paul
Mississippi......	Wade H. Creekmore	Director	Game and Fish Commission	Jackson
	F. H. McCorkle	Secretary	Sea Food Commn.	Biloxi
Missouri.......	Irwin T. Bode	Director	Conserv. Commn.	Jefferson City
Montana.......	A. A. O'Claire	Director	Fish and Game Dept.	Helena
Nebraska.......	Paul T. Gilbert	Exec. Secretary	Game, Forestation, and Parks Commn.	Lincoln
Nevada........	Frank W. Groves	Director	Fish and Game Commn.	Reno
New Hampshire.	Ralph G. Carpenter II	Director	Fish and Game Dept.	Concord
New Jersey.....	A. Heaton Underhill	Dir., Div. of Fish and Game	Dept. of Conserv. and Econ. Devel.	Trenton
New Mexico....	Homer C. Pickens	State Game Warden	Game and Fish Dept.	Santa Fe
New York......	William C. Senning	Dir., Div. of Fish and Game	Conserv. Dept.	Albany
North Carolina..	Clyde P. Patton	Director	Wildlife Resources Commission	Raleigh
North Dakota...	H. R. Morgan	Commissioner	Game and Fish Dept.	Bismarck

FISH AND GAME—*continued*

State	Name	Official Title	Agency	Location
Ohio..........	Hayden W. Olds	Chief	Div. of Wildlife	Columbus
Oklahoma......	David Ware	Director	Game and Fish Dept.	Oklahoma City
Oregon........	M. T. Hoy	Director of Fisheries	Fish Commn.	Portland
	P. W. Schneider	Game Director	Game Commn.	Portland
Pennsylvania...	William Voight, Jr.	Exec. Director	Fish Commn.	Harrisburg
	Logan J. Bennett	Exec. Director	Game Commn.	Harrisburg
Rhode Island...	Thomas J. Wright	Chief, Div. of Fish and Game	Dept. of Agric. and Conservation	Providence
South Carolina..	A. A. Richardson	Dir., Div. of Game	Wildlife Res. Dept.	Columbia
	Alonzo B. Seabrook	Dir., Div. of Commercial Fisheries	Wildlife Res. Dept.	Charleston
South Dakota...	Elmer Peterson	Director	Game, Fish and Park Dept.	Pierre
Tennessee......	Louis Clapper	Act. Dir., Game and Fish Division	Conserv. Dept.	Nashville
Texas..........	H. D. Dodgen	Exec. Secretary	Game and Fish Commn.	Austin
Utah........ ..	J. Perry Egan	Director	Fish and Game Dept.	Salt Lake City
Vermont.......	Geo. W. Davis	Dir., Exec. Secy.	Fish and Game Commn.	Montpelier
Virginia.......	I. T. Quinn	Exec. Director	Game and Inland Fisheries Commn.	Richmond
	C. M. Lankford, Jr.	Commissioner	Commn. of Fisheries	Newport News
Washington....	Robert J. Schoettler	Director	Dept. of Fisheries	Seattle
	John A. Biggs	Director	Dept. of Game	Seattle
West Virginia...	Harry Van Meter	Chief	Div. Fish Mgt.	Charleston
	C. O. Handley	Chief	Div. Game Mgt.	Charleston
Wisconsin......	Edw. Schneberger	Supt., Fish Mgt.	Conserv. Commn.	Madison
	J. R. Smith	Act. Supt., Game Mgt.	Conserv. Commn.	Madison
Wyoming......	A. S. C. Greene	Commissioner	Game and Fish Commn.	Cheyenne
Alaska.........	Clarence L. Anderson	Director	Dept. of Fisheries	Juneau
Guam.........	Francisco P. De Leon	Fish and Game Warden	Dept. of Agric.	Mangilao
Hawaii........	Vernon E. Brock	Dir., Div. Fish and Game	Bd. Agric. and Forestry	Honolulu
Puerto Rico....	Félix Iñigo	Dir. Fisheries and Wildlife Section	Dept. Agric. and Commerce	San Juan
Virgin Islands..	George Matthias	Act. Commissr. Pub. Safety	Govt. of the V. I.	St. Thomas

FOOD AND DRUGS

State	Name	Official Title	Agency	Location
Alabama.......	George H. Marsh	Dir., Div. of Agric. Chemistry	Dept. of Agric. and Industries	Montgomery
Arizona........	Clarence G. Salsbury, M.D.	Supt. of Health	Dept. of Health	Phoenix
Arkansas.......	J. T. Herron, M.D.	State Health Officer	Bd. of Health	Little Rock
California......	Milton P. Duffy	Chief, Bur. of Food and Drug Inspection	Dept. of Pub. Health	Berkeley
Colorado.......	R. L. Cleere, M.D.	Exec. Director	Dept. of Pub. Health	Denver
Connecticut....	Attilio Frasinelli	Commissioner	Food and Drug Commn.	Hartford
Delaware......	H. C. Zeisig	Secy.-Treasurer	Bd. of Pharmacy	Milford
Florida........	Nathan Mayo	Commissr. of Agric., Inspection Div.	Dept. of Agric.	Tallahassee
Georgia........	P. D. Horkan	Chief Drug Inspector	Bd. of Pharmacy	Atlanta

FOOD AND DRUGS—*continued*

State	Name	Official Title	Agency	Location
Idaho.........	L. J. Peterson	Director	Board of Health	Boise
Illinois.........	Lowell Oranger	Supt., Div. of Foods, Dairies	Dept. of Agriculture	Springfield
Indiana........	T. E. Sullivan	Dir., Div. of Foods and Drugs	Bd. of Health	Indianapolis
Iowa..........	Clyde Spry	Secretary	Dept. of Agriculture	Des Moines
	J. F. Rabe	Secretary	Pharmacy Bd.	Des Moines
Kansas........	Evan Wright	Dir., Food and Drug Div.	Bd. of Health	Topeka
Kentucky......	Raymond F. Dixon	Dep. Commissr. (Drugs)	Dept. of Health	Louisville
	Harvey McAndrews	Dir., Div. Pub. Health Sanitation (Food)	Dept. of Health	Louisville
Louisiana......	S. J. Phillips	President	Bd. of Health	New Orleans
Maine.........	Clayton P. Osgood	Chief, Div. of Inspection	Dept. of Agriculture	Augusta
Maryland......	C. S. Brinsfield	Chief, Div. of Food	Dept. of Health	Baltimore
	F. S. Ballasone, M.D.	Chief, Div. of Drugs	Dept. of Health	Baltimore
Massachusetts...	George A. Michael	Dir., Div. of Food and Drugs	Dept. of Pub. Health	Boston
Michigan......	O. K. Grettenberger	Director	Bd. of Pharmacy	Lansing
	M. A. Nelson	Chief, Bur. Foods and Standards	Agriculture Dept.	Lansing
Minnesota......	Byron G. Allen	Commissioner	Dept. of Agriculture	St. Paul
Mississippi.....	F. J. Underwood, M.D.	Exec. Officer	Bd. of Health	Jackson
	M. P. Etheredge	State Chemist	Miss. State Coll.	State College
Missouri.......	John McCutchen	Dir., Food and Drugs, Div. of Health	Dept. of Pub. Health and Welfare	Jefferson City
Montana.......	C. W. Brinck	Dir., Div. of Envir. Sanit.	Bd. of Health	Helena
Nebraska.......	Gould B. Flagg	Chief, Bur. of Dairies, Foods, Weights and Measures	Dept. of Agric. and Inspection	Lincoln
Nevada........	Edward L. Randall	Commissioner	Dept. of Food and Drugs, Wgts. and Meas., and Petrol. Prod. Inspection	Reno
New Hampshire.	Gilman K. Crowell	Chief, Bur. of Food and Chemistry	Dept. of Health	Concord
New Jersey.....	Milton Ruth	Chief, Bur. of Food and Drugs, Div. of Envir. Sanitation	Dept. of Health	Trenton
New Mexico....	Charles Caldwell	Supvr., Food Sanit. Sec.	Dept. of Public Health	Santa Fe
New York......	C. R. Plumb	Dir., Bur. of Food Control	Dept. of Agric. and Markets	Albany
	Frank J. Smith	Chief, Narcotic Control Sec.	Dept. of Health	Albany
North Carolina..	E. W. Constable	Director	Dept. of Agriculture	Raleigh
North Dakota...	F. W. Lonsbrough	Director	State Laboratories	Bismarck
Ohio..........	Clark W. Van Schoik	Chief	Div. of Foods and Dairies	Columbus
Oklahoma......	Burley Walker	Dir., Food and Drug Division	Dept. of Health	Oklahoma City
Oregon........	O. K. Beals	Chief, Div. of Foods and Dairies	Dept. of Agriculture	Salem
	Ernst T. Stuhr	Secretary	Bd. of Pharmacy	Portland
Pennsylvania...	Mildred Pfeiffer, M.D.	Act. Chief, Div. of Narcotic Drug Control	Dept. of Health	Harrisburg

FOOD AND DRUGS—*continued*

State	Name	Official Title	Agency	Location
Rhode Island...	Joseph J. Cahill	Chief, Div. of Food and Drug Control	Dept. of Health	Providence
South Carolina..	G. S. T. Peeples, M.D.	Secy. and State Health Officer	Bd. of Health	Columbia
South Dakota...	Charles Bruett	Secretary	Dept. of Agriculture	Pierre
Tennessee......	Eugene H. Holeman	State Chemist	Dept. of Agriculture	Nashville
Texas.........	Henry A. Holle, M.D.	Commissr. of Health	Dept. of Health	Austin
Utah..........	Joseph P. Kesler, M.D.	Act. Director	Dept. of Health	Salt Lake City
Vermont.......	R. B. Aiken, M.D.	Commissioner	Dept. of Health	Burlington
Virginia.......	Rodney C. Berry	State Chemist	Dept. of Agric. and Immigration	Richmond
Washington....	Sverre N. Omdahl	Director	Dept. of Agric.	Olympia
West Virginia...	N. H. Dyer	Director	Health Dept.	Charleston
Wisconsin......	Jerry F. Dunn	Chief, Dairy and Food Div.	Dept. of Agric.	Madison
Wyoming......	Wm. L. Chapman	Commissioner	Dept. of Agriculture	Cheyenne
Alaska.........	C. Earl Albrecht, M.D.	Commissioner	Dept. of Health	Juneau
Guam.........	John E. Kennedy, M.D.	Director	Dept. of Med. Servs.	Oka, Tamuning
Hawaii........	George A. Akau	Chief, Bur. of Food and Drugs	Board of Health	Honolulu
Puerto Rico....	Henry Rodríguez	Dir., Bur. of Sanit.	Dept. of Health	San Juan
Virgin Islands...	Roy A. Anduze, M.D.	Commissr. of Health	Govt. of the V. I.	St. Thomas

FORESTRY

State	Name	Official Title	Agency	Location
Alabama..... ..	J. M. Stauffer	Chief, Div. Forestry	Dept. of Conserv.	Montgomery
Arkansas.......	Fred H. Lang	State Forester	Forestry Commn.	Little Rock
California......	F. H. Raymond	State Forester, Div. of Forestry	Dept. of Natural Resources	Sacramento
Colorado.......	R. E. Ford	Dir., Forest Conserv.	Bd. of Agric., Colo. A. and M. College	Ft. Collins
Connecticut....	W. Foster Schreeder	Forester	Park and Forest Commn.	Hartford
Delaware......	W. S. Taber	Forester	Forestry Commn.	Dover
Florida........	C. H. Coulter	State Forester	Bd. of Forestry	Tallahassee
Georgia........	Guyton De Loach	Director	Forestry Commn.	Atlanta
Idaho.........	Roger Guernsey	Forester	Forestry Dept.	Boise
Illinois.........	E. E. Nuuttila	Forester	Dept. of Conserv.	Springfield
Indiana........	Ralph F. Wilcox	State Forester	Dept. of Conserv.	Indianapolis
Iowa..........	Wilbur A. Rush	Chief, Land and Waters	Conserv. Commn.	Des Moines
Kansas........	W. F. Pickett	Forester	State College	Manhattan
Kentucky......	Harrod B. Newland	Dir. of Forestry	Div. of Conserv.	Frankfort
Louisiana......	James E. Mixon	Forester	Forestry Commn.	Baton Rouge
Maine.........	Albert D. Nutting	Commissioner	Forestry Dept.	Augusta
Maryland......	H. C. Buckingham	Forester	Dept. State Forests and Parks	Annapolis
Massachusetts..	Raymond J. Kenney	Dir., Div. of Forest and Parks	Dept. of Natural Resources	Boston
Michigan......	G. S. McIntire	Chief, Forestry Div.	Conserv. Dept.	Lansing
Minnesota......	Edward L. Lawson	Dir., Div. of Forestry	Dept. of Conserv.	St. Paul
Mississippi.....	Jas. W. Craig	Forester	Forestry Commn.	Jackson
Missouri.......	George O. White	Forester	Conserv. Commn.	Jefferson City
Montana.......	Gareth C. Moon	Forester	Forestry Dept.	Missoula
Nebraska......	Paul T. Gilbert	Executive Secy.	Game, Forestation, Parks Commn.	Lincoln

FORESTRY—*continued*

State	Name	Official Title	Agency	Location
Nevada........	Louis D. Ferrari	Forester, Fire Warden	Off. of State Forester, Fire Warden	Carson City
New Hampshire.	Wm. H. Messeck, Jr.	Forester, Forestry Div.	Forestry and Recreation Commn.	Concord
New Jersey.....	Alden T. Cottrell	State Forester and Chief, Bur. Forestry, Parks, Historic Sites; Div. of Planning and Devel.	Dept. Conserv. and Econ. Devel.	Trenton
New Mexico...	E. S. Walker	Land Commissr.	Land Office	Santa Fe
New York......	William M. Foss	Dir., Div. Lands and Forests	Conserv. Dept.	Albany
North Carolina..	F. H. Claridge	Forester	Dept. of Conserv. and Devel.	Raleigh
North Dakota...	C. N. Nelson	Forester and Pres.	School of Forestry	Bottineau
Ohio..........	O. A. Alderman	Chief	Div. of Forestry	Columbus
Oklahoma......	Donald E. Stauffer	Dir., Div. of Forestry	Planning and Resources Bd.	Oklahoma City
Oregon........	Dwight L. Phipps	State Forester	Bd. of Forestry	Salem
Pennsylvania...	Maurice K. Goddard	Secretary	Dept. of Forests and Waters	Harrisburg
Rhode Island...	Eric G. Jacobson	Chief, Div. of Forests	Dept. of Agric. and Conservation	Providence
South Carolina..	Chas. H. Flory	Forester	Forestry Commn.	Columbia
South Dakota...	Harry Woodward	Forester	Game, Fish, Park Dept.	Pierre
Tennessee......	Carl I. Peterson	Forester	Dept. of Conserv.	Nashville
Texas..........	A. D. Folweiler	Director	Forest Service	College Station
Utah..........	J. Whitney Floyd	Chief Forester, Fire Warden	Bd. of Forestry, Fire Control	Salt Lake City
Vermont.......	Perry H. Merrill	Director	Dept. of Forests and Parks	Montpelier
Virginia.......	George W. Dean	Forester, Div. of Forestry	Dept. of Conserv. and Devel.	Charlottesville
Washington....	L. T. Webster	Supr., Div. of Forestry	Dept. of Conserv. and Devel.	Olympia
West Virginia...	Hays Helmick	Forester	Conserv. Commn.	Charleston
Wisconsin......	C. L. Harrington	Supt., Forests and Parks	Conserv. Commn.	Madison
Wyoming......	Ben C. Cossman	Land Commissr.	Land Office	Cheyenne
Guam.........	Manuel Calvo	Director	Dept. of Agric.	Mangilao
Hawaii........	Joseph L. Dwight	Pres. and Commissr.	Bd. of Agric. and Forestry	Honolulu
	Walter W. Holt	Forester, Div. of Forestry	Bd. of Agric. and Forestry	Honolulu
Puerto Rico....	M. Hernandez-Agosto	Dir., Forest Section	Dept. of Agric. and Commerce	Río Piedras

FUEL TAX

State	Name	Official Title	Agency	Location
Alabama......	Douthitt Camp	Chief, Gasoline Tax Div.	Dept. of Revenue	Montgomery
Arizona........	C. L. Lane	Supt., Motor Veh. Div.	Highway Dept.	Phoenix
Arkansas.......	Leonard L. Stewart	Dir., Motor Fuel Tax Div.	Revenue Dept.	Little Rock
California......	H. D. Abbott	Chief, Highway Tax Div.	Bd. of Equalization	Sacramento
Colorado.......	Earl Blevins	Director	Dept. of Revenue	Denver
Connecticut....	John T. Tynan	Commissioner	Motor Vehs. Dept.	Hartford
Florida........	Ray E. Green	Comptroller	Off. of Comptr.	Tallahassee

FUEL TAX—*continued*

State	Name	Official Title	Agency	Location
Georgia........	{ S. H. Wilson	Dir., Fuel Oil Inspec.	Revenue Dept.	Atlanta
	{ V. M. Womack	Dir., Motor Fuel Tax	Revenue Dept.	Atlanta
Idaho..........	P. G. Neill	Tax Collector	Off. of Tax Coll.	Boise
Illinois.........	Richard J. Lyons	Director	Dept. of Revenue	Springfield
Indiana........	Chester C. Meyer	Admn., Motor Fuel Tax Div.	Dept. of Revenue	Indianapolis
Iowa..........	M. L. Abrahamson	Treasurer	Off. of Treasurer	Des Moines
Kansas........	Eugene Boyer	Chief	Rev. and Tax. Commn.	Topeka
Kentucky......	D. K. Walker	Dir., Mot. Veh. Div.	Dept. of Revenue	Frankfort
Louisiana......	Rufus W. Fontenot	Collector	Dept. of Revenue	Baton Rouge
Maine.........	Gomer S. Dillon	Dir., Excise Tax Div.	Bur. of Taxation	Augusta
Maryland......	J. Millard Tawes	Comptroller	Off. of Comptr.	Annapolis
Massachusetts...	Albert H. Stitt	Dir., Bur. of Excises	Dept. of Corp. and Taxation	Boston
Michigan......	George M. Harlow	Admn., Motor Fuel Tax	Off. of Secy. of State	Lansing
Minnesota......	A. H. Stassen	Dir., Petroleum Div.	Dept. of Taxation	St. Paul
Mississippi.....	Guy McCullen	Comptroller	Motor Veh. Comptr.	Jackson
Missouri.......	Lawrence O. Campbell	Supv. Mot. Fuel Tax	Dept. of Revenue	Jefferson City
Montana.......	M. J. Armistead	Supv., Gasoline Tax Div.	Bd. of Equalization	Helena
Nebraska.......	Clay Wright	Dir., Div. of Motor Fuels	Dept. of Agric. and Inspection	Lincoln
Nevada........	William H. Schmidt	Supervisor	Gasoline and Use Fuel Tax Div.	Carson City
New Hampshire.	John J. Mara	Road Toll Admn.	Motor Vehicle Dept.	Concord
New Jersey.....	Armand J. Salmon, Jr.	Supv., Motor Fuels Tax Bur., Div. of Taxation	Dept. of Treasury	Trenton
New Mexico....	Paul Culver	Dir., Gas. Tax Div.	Bur. of Revenue	Santa Fe
New York......	(Vacancy)	Asst. Dir., Misc. Tax Bur.	Div. of Tax., Dept. of Tax and Fin.	Albany
North Carolina..	Eugene G. Shaw	Commissioner	Dept. of Revenue	Raleigh
North Dakota...	Berta E. Baker	Auditor	Off. of Auditor	Bismarck
Ohio..........	Stanley J. Bowers	Tax Commissioner	Dept. of Taxation	Columbus
Oklahoma......	Herman H. Rice	Dir., Motor Fuel Tax Div.	Tax. Commn.	Oklahoma City
Oregon........	Earl T. Newbry	Secretary of State	Off. of Secy. of State	Salem
Pennsylvania...	Fred G. Klunk	Dir., Bur. of Liquid Fuel Tax	Dept. of Revenue	Harrisburg
Rhode Island...	Thomas L. F. Kelley, Jr.	Chief Examiner, Motor Fuel Tax Sect.	Div. of Taxation, Dept. of Admin.	Providence
South Carolina..	Otis W. Livingstone	Chairman	Tax Commission	Columbia
South Dakota...	W. R. Wilder	Commissioner	Dept. of Revenue	Pierre
Tennessee......	Dan Spencer	Dir., Gas. and Oil Inspec. Div.	Dept. of Finance and Taxation	Nashville
Texas..........	Robert S. Calvert	Comptr., Pub. Accts.	Off. of Comptroller	Austin
Utah..........	Charles L. Bolzle	Director	State Tax Div.	Salt Lake City
Vermont.......	H. Elmer Marsh	Commissioner	Motor Veh. Dept.	Montpelier
Virginia.......	C. H. Lamb	Commissioner	Div. of Motor Vehs.	Richmond
Washington....	Mrs. Della Urquhart	Director	Dept. of Licenses	Olympia
West Virginia...	Wm. R. Laird III	Commissioner	Tax Commission	Charleston
Wisconsin......	D. W. Mack	Dir., Div. of Motor Fuel and Petro-leum Products	Dept. of Taxation	Madison
Wyoming......	J. R. Bromley	Highway Supt.	Highway Dept.	Cheyenne
Alaska.........	Karl F. Dewey	Tax Commissioner	Dept. of Taxation	Juneau
Guam.........	George W. Ingling	Commissr., Rev. and Taxation	Dept. of Finance	Agana
Hawaii........	John K. Heen	Tax Administrator	Off. of Tax. Com-missioner	Honolulu
Puerto Rico....	Rafael Picó	Secretary	Dept. of Treasury	San Juan

GEOLOGY

State	Name	Official Title	Agency	Location
Alabama	Walter B. Jones	Geologist	Off. of State Geol.	Tuscaloosa
Arizona	Thos. Garfield Chapman	Dean, College of Mines	Univ. of Ariz.	Tucson
Arkansas	Norman Williams	Geologist–Director	Geological and Conserv. Commn.	Little Rock
California	Olaf P. Jenkins	Chief, Div. Mines	Dept. Nat. Resources	San Francisco
Connecticut	John C. Lucke	Director	Geolog. and Natural Hist. Survey	Storrs
Delaware	Johan J. Groot	Geologist	Geological Commn.	Newark
Florida	Herman Gunter	Director	Geolog. Surv., Bd. of Conserv.	Tallahassee
Georgia	Garland Peyton	Director	Dept. Mines, Mining, Geology	Atlanta
Idaho	George McDowell	Mine Inspector	Off. Mine Insp.	Boise
Illinois	John C. Frye	Chief, Geol. Surv.	Dept. Registration and Education	Urbana
Indiana	Chas. F. Deiss	Geologist	Dept. of Conserv.	Indianapolis
Iowa	H. G. Hershey	Geologist	Geological Survey	Iowa City
Kansas	Raymond C. Moore	Director	Geological Survey	Lawrence
Kentucky	D. J. Jones	Geologist	Univ. of Kentucky	Lexington
Louisiana	Leo Hough	Geologist, Geol. Surv.	La. State Univ.	Baton Rouge
Maine	J. M. Trefethen	Geologist	Dept. of Devel. of Ind. and Commerce	Orono
Maryland	Jos. T. Singewald, Jr.	Director	Dept. Geol., Mines, Water Resources	Baltimore
Michigan	W. L. Daoust	State Geologist	Conserv. Dept.	Lansing
Minnesota	Ray D. Nolan	Dir., Div. Lands and Minerals	Dept. of Conserv.	St. Paul
Mississippi	W. C. Morse	Director	Geological Survey	University
Missouri	Thomas R. Beveridge	Geologist, Div. Geol. Survey and Water Resources	Dept. of Business and Admin.	Jefferson City
Montana	J. Robert Van Pelt	President	State School of Mines	Butte
Nebraska	E. C. Reed	Geologist	Conserv., Survey Div., Univ. of Neb.	Lincoln
Nevada	Vernon E. Scheid	Dir., Bur. of Mines	Univ. of Nevada	Reno
New Hampshire	T. Ralph Myers	Geologist	Planning and Devel. Commn.	Durham
New Jersey	Meredith E. Johnson	Chief, Bur. Geol. and Topography, Div. of Planning and Devel.	Dept. of Conserv. and Econ. Devel.	Trenton
New Mexico	W. B. Macey	Geologist	Oil Conserv. Commn.	Santa Fe
New York	John G. Broughton	Geologist	State Museum, Ed. Dept.	Albany
North Carolina	Jasper L. Stuckey	Geologist	Dept. Conserv. and Devel.	Raleigh
North Dakota	Wilson M. Laird	Geologist	Geol. Dept., Univ. of N. D.	Grand Forks
Ohio	John H. Melvin	Chief	Div. of Geol. Survey	Columbus
Oklahoma	Carl C. Branson	Director	Geol. Survey	Norman
Oregon	Hollis M. Dole	Director	Dept. Geology and Mineral Industries	Portland
Pennsylvania	Carlyle Gray	Act. Chief Geol., Bur. Topographic, Geol. Survey	Dept. Internal Affairs	Harrisburg
South Carolina	L. L. Smith	Geologist	Geological Survey, U. of S.C.	Columbia
South Dakota	E. P. Rothrock	Geologist	Univ. of S.D.	Vermillion
Tennessee	W. D. Hardeman	Dir., Div. of Geology	Dept. of Conserv.	Nashville

GEOLOGY—*continued*

State	Name	Official Title	Agency	Location
Utah..........	Arthur L. Crawford	Director	Geol. and Mineralog. Survey, U. of U.	Salt Lake City
Vermont.......	Charles G. Doll	Geologist	Devel. Commn.	Burlington
Virginia.......	Wm. M. McGill	Geol., Div. of Geol.	Dept. of Conserv. and Devel.	Charlottesville
Washington....	Sheldon L. Glover	Supvr., Div. of Mines and Geol.	Dept. of Conserv. and Devel.	Olympia
West Virginia...	Paul H. Price	Geologist	Geol. and Econ. Survey	Morgantown
Wisconsin......	George F. Hanson	Geologist	Univ. of Wisc.	Madison
Wyoming......	Horace D. Thomas	Geologist	Univ. of Wyo.	Laramie
Alaska.........	Phillip M. Holdsworth	Commissioner	Dept. of Mines	Juneau
Guam.........	Porter Ward	Geologist	U. S. Geological Survey	Tamuning
Hawaii........	Howard Leak	Chief, Div. of Hydrography	Dept. of Public Lands	Honolulu
Puerto Rico....	R. Fernández-García	Dir., Dept. of Ind. Research	Econ. Devel. Admin.	Hato Rey

HEALTH

State	Name	Official Title	Agency	Location
Alabama.......	D. G. Gill, M.D.	Health Officer	Dept. of Health	Montgomery
Arizona........	Clarence G. Salsbury, M.D.	Supt. of Health	Dept. of Health	Phoenix
Arkansas.......	J. T. Herron, M.D.	Health Officer	Bd. of Health	Little Rock
California......	Malcolm H. Merrill, M.D.	Director	Dept. of Pub. Health	Berkeley
Colorado.......	R. L. Cleere, M.D.	Exec. Director	Dept. of Pub. Health	Denver
Connecticut....	Stanley H. Osborn, M.D.	Commissioner	Dept. of Health	Hartford
Delaware......	Floyd I. Hudson, M.D.	Exec. Secretary	Bd. of Health	Dover
Florida........	Wilson T. Sowder, M.D.	Health Officer	Bd. of Health	Jacksonville
Georgia........	T. F. Sellers, M.D.	Director	Dept. of Pub. Health	Atlanta
Idaho.........	L. J. Peterson	Director	Bd. of Health	Boise
Illinois.........	Roland R. Cross, M.D.	Director	Dept. of Pub. Health	Springfield
Indiana........	Bertram Groesbeck, Jr., M.D.	Director	Dept. of Health	Indianapolis
Iowa..........	Edmund G. Zimmerer, M.D.	Commissioner	Dept. of Health	Des Moines
Kansas........	Thomas R. Hood, M.D.	Secretary	Bd. of Health	Topeka
Kentucky......	Bruce Underwood, M.D.	Commissioner	Dept. of Health	Louisville
Louisiana......	S. J. Phillips, M.D.	President	Bd. of Health	New Orleans
Maine.........	Dean H. Fisher, M.D.	Commissioner	Dept. of Health and Welfare	Augusta
Maryland......	Perry F. Prather, M.D.	Director	Dept. of Health	Baltimore
Massachusetts...	Samuel B. Kirkwood, M.D.	Commissioner	Dept. of Pub. Health	Boston
Michigan......	Albert E. Heustis, M.D.	Commissioner	Dept. of Health	Lansing

HEALTH—*continued*

State	Name	Official Title	Agency	Location
Minnesota......	Robert N. Barr, M.D.	Secy. and Exec. Off.	Dept. of Health	Minneapolis
Mississippi.....	F. J. Underwood, M.D.	Exec. Officer	Bd. of Health	Jackson
Missouri.......	James R. Amos	Dir., Div. of Health	Dept. of Pub. Health and Welfare	Jefferson City
Montana.......	G. D. Carlyle Thompson, M.D.	Secretary	Bd. of Health	Helena
Nebraska.......	E. A. Rogers, M.D., M.P.H.	Dir. of Health	Dept. of Health	Lincoln
Nevada........	Daniel J. Hurley, M.D.	Act. Health Officer	Dept. of Health	Carson City
New Hampshire.	John S. Wheeler, M.D.	Health Officer	Dept. of Health	Concord
New Jersey.....	Daniel Bergsma, M.D., M.P.H.	Commissioner	Dept. of Health	Trenton
New Mexico....	Stanley J. Leland, M.D.	Director	Health Dept.	Santa Fe
New York......	Herman E. Hilleboe, M.D.	Commissr. of Health	Dept. of Health	Albany
North Carolina.	J. W. R. Norton, M.D.	Secretary	Bd. of Health	Raleigh
North Dakota...	J. H. Svore	Dir. of Pub. Health	Health Dept.	Bismarck
Ohio..........	Ralph E. Dwork, M.D.	Director	Dept. of Health	Columbus
Oklahoma......	Grady F. Matthews, M.D.	Commissr. of Health	Dept. of Health	Oklahoma City
Oregon........	Harold M. Erickson, M.D.	Health Officer	Bd. of Health	Portland
Pennsylvania...	Berwyn F. Mattison	Secy. of Health	Dept. of Health	Harrisburg
Rhode Island...	Edward A. McLaughlin, M.D.	Director	Dept. of Health	Providence
South Carolina..	G. S. T. Peeples, M.D.	Secy. and Health Off.	Bd. of Health	Columbia
South Dakota...	G. J. Van Heuvelen, M.D.	Health Officer	Dept. of Health	Pierre
Tennessee......	R. H. Hutcheson, M.D.	Commissioner	Dept. of Pub. Health	Nashville
Texas.........	Henry A. Holle M.D.	Commissr. of Health	Dept. of Health	Austin
Utah.........	Joseph P. Kesler, M.D.	Acting Director	Health Dept.	Salt Lake City
Vermont.......	Robert B. Aiken, M.D.	Commissioner	Dept. of Health	Burlington
Virginia.......	M. I. Shanholtz, M.D.	Health Commissr.	Dept. of Health	Richmond
Washington....	Bernard Bucove, M.D.	Director	Dept. of Health	Seattle
West Virginia...	N. H. Dyer, M.D.	Director	Health Dept.	Charleston
Wisconsin......	Carl N. Neupert, M.D.	Health Officer	Bd. of Health	Madison
Wyoming......	Franklin D. Yoder, M.D.	Director	Board of Health	Cheyenne
Alaska........	C. Earl Albrecht, M.D.	Commissioner	Dept. of Health	Juneau
Guam.........	John E. Kennedy, M.D.	Director	Dept. of Med. Servs.	Oka, Tamuning
Hawaii........	Richard K. C. Lee, M.D.	President	Bd. of Health	Honolulu
Puerto Rico....	Juan A. Pons, M.D.	Secretary	Dept. of Health	San Juan
Virgin Islands..	Roy A. Anduze, M.D.	Commissr. of Health	Govt. of the V.I.	St. Thomas

HIGHWAYS

State	Name	Official Title	Agency	Location
Alabama.......	Herman L. Nelson	Director	Highway Dept.	Montgomery
	A. Reese Harvey	Chief Engineer	Highway Dept.	Montgomery
Arizona........	Fred D. Schemmer	Chairman	Highway Commn.	Prescott
	William E. Willey	Engineer	Highway Commn.	Phoenix
Arkansas.......	Herbert Eldridge	Director	Highway Dept.	Little Rock
	Ward Goodman	Chief Engineer	Highway Dept.	Little Rock
California......	G. T. McCoy	State Highway Engineer and Chief, Div. of Highways	Dept. of Pub. Works	Sacramento
Colorado.......	Stewart Cosgriff	Chairman	Highway Commn.	Denver
	Mark U. Watrous	Chief Engineer	Dept. of Highways	Denver
Connecticut....	Newman Argraves	Commissioner	Highway Dept.	Hartford
	Warren M. Creamer	Chief Engineer	Highway Dept.	Hartford
Delaware......	Gordon Smith	Chairman	Highway Dept.	Dover
	Walter A. McKendrick, Jr.	Chief Engineer	Highway Dept.	Dover
Florida........	Wilbur E. Jones	Chairman	Road Dept.	Tallahassee
	Henry E. Lewis	Highway Engineer	Road Dept.	Tallahassee
Georgia........	W. A. Blasingame	Chairman	Highway Dept.	Atlanta
	M. L. Shadburn	Highway Engineer	Highway Dept.	Atlanta
Idaho.........	Roscoe C. Rich	Chairman	Dept. of Highways	Burley
	Earl V. Miller	Highway Engineer	Dept. of Highways	Boise
Illinois.........	E. A. Rosenstone	Director	Dept. of Pub. Works and Buildings	Springfield
	Ralph R. Bartelsmeyer	Chief Engineer	Dept. of Pub. Works and Buildings	Springfield
Indiana........	Virgil W. Smith	Chairman	Highway Commn.	Indianapolis
	C. E. Vogelgesang	Chief Engineer	Highway Commn.	Indianapolis
Iowa..........	Russell F. Lundy	Chairman	Highway Commn.	Ames
	John G. Butter	Chief Engineer	Highway Commn.	Ames
Kansas........	Walter Rugan	Director	Highway Commn.	Topeka
	Walter Johnson	Highway Engineer	Highway Commn.	Topeka
Kentucky......	Mitchell W. Tinder	Commissioner	Dept. of Highways	Frankfort
	D. H. Bray	Chief Engineer	Dept. of Highways	Frankfort
Louisiana......	George S. Covert	Director	Dept. of Highways	Baton Rouge
	E. J. James	Chief Engineer	Dept. of Highways	Baton Rouge
Maine.........	David H. Stevens	Chairman	Highway Commn.	Augusta
	Vaughan M. Daggett	Chief Engineer	Highway Commn.	Augusta
Maryland......	Russell H. McCain	Chairman	Roads Commn.	Baltimore
	Norman M. Pritchett	Chief Engineer	Roads Commn.	Baltimore
Massachusetts...	John A. Volpe	Commissioner	Dept. of Pub. Works	Boston
	H. Gordon Gray	Chief Engineer	Dept. of Pub. Works	Boston
Michigan......	Charles M. Ziegler	Commissioner	Highway Dept.	Lansing
	Carlos Weber	Dep. Commissr. and Chief Engr.	Highway Dept.	Lansing
Minnesota......	M. J. Hoffmann	Commissioner	Dept. of Highways	St. Paul
	L. P. Zimmerman	Chief Engineer	Dept. of Highways	St. Paul
Mississippi.....	John D. Smith, Sr.	Chairman	Highway Dept.	Jackson
	T. C. Robbins	Director	Highway Dept.	Jackson
	Ben T. Collier	State Aid Engr.	Highway Dept.	Jackson
Missouri.......	Harris D. Rodgers	Chairman	Highway Dept.	Jefferson City
	Rex M. Whitton	Chief Engineer	Highway Dept.	Jefferson City
Montana.......	Frank G. Connelly	Chairman	Highway Commn.	Billings
	Scott P. Hart	Engineer	Highway Dept.	Helena
Nebraska......	L. N. Ress	Engineer	Dept. of Roads and Irrigation	Lincoln
Nevada........	H. D. Mills	Highway Engineer	Dept. of Highways	Carson City
New Hampshire.	John O. Morton	Dep. Commissr. and Chief Engineer	Dept. of Pub. Works and Highways	Concord

HIGHWAYS—*continued*

State	Name	Official Title	Agency	Location
New Jersey.....	Dwight R. G. Palmer	Commissioner	Highway Dept.	Trenton
	Edward W. Kilpatrick	Highway Engineer	Highway Dept.	Trenton
	Mrs. Katherine E. White	Chairman	N. J. Highway Authority	Red Bank
	Paul L. Troast	Chairman	N. J. Turnpike Authority	New Brunswick
New Mexico....	T. J. Heimann	Chairman	Highway Commn.	Roy
	L. D. Wilson	Highway Engineer	Highway Commn.	Santa Fe
New York......	George L. Nickerson	Chief Engineer	Dept. of Pub. Works	Albany
North Carolina..	A. H. Graham	Chairman	Highway and Pub. Works Commn.	Raleigh
	W. H. Rogers, Jr.	Chief Engineer	Highway and Pub. Works Commn.	Raleigh
North Dakota...	S. W. Thompson	Commissioner	Highway Dept.	Bismarck
	M. P. Wynkoop	Chief Engineer	Highway Dept.	Bismarck
Ohio..........	Samuel O. Linzell	Director	Dept. of Highways	Columbus
	L. F. Schaeublin	Asst. Director and Chief Engr.	Dept. of Highways	Columbus
Oklahoma......	Julius W. Cox	Chairman	Highway Commn.	Oklahoma City
	C. A. Stoldt	Director	Dept. of Highways	Oklahoma City
	G. H. Bittle	Chief Engineer	Dept. of Highways	Oklahoma City
Oregon........	Ben R. Chandler	Chairman	Highway Commn.	Coos Bay
	R. H. Baldock	Highway Engineer	Highway Dept.	Salem
Pennsylvania...	Joseph J. Lawler	Secretary	Dept. of Highways	Harrisburg
	George J. Richards	Dep. Secretary	Dept. of Highways	Harrisburg
Rhode Island...	Joseph M. Vallone	Director	Dept. of Pub. Works	Providence
	G. H. Henderson	Principal Hwy. Engr.	Dept. of Pub. Works, Div. of Roads and Bridges	Providence
South Carolina..	C. R. McMillan	Chief Highway Commissr.	Highway Dept.	Columbia
	S. N. Pearman	Highway Engineer	Highway Dept.	Columbia
South Dakota...	Harvard C. Rempfer	Highway Engineer	Dept. of Highways	Pierre
	Charles J. Dalthorp	Director	Dept. of Highways	Pierre
Tennessee......	W. M. Leech	Commissioner	Dept. of Highways and Pub. Works	Nashville
	Herbert M. Bates	Highway Engineer	Dept. of Highways and Pub. Works	Nashville
Texas..........	DeWitt C. Greer	Highway Engineer	Highway Dept.	Austin
Utah..........	H. J. Corleissen	Chairman	Road Commn.	Salt Lake City
	E. G. Johnson	Chief Engineer	Road Commn.	Salt Lake City
Vermont.......	Paul H. Gates	Commissioner	Dept. of Highways	Montpelier
	H. E. Sargent	Chief Engineer	Dept. of Highways	Montpelier
Virginia.......	J. A. Anderson	Commissioner	Dept. of Highways	Richmond
	F. A. Davis	Chief Engineer	Dept. of Highways	Richmond
Washington....	Harry E. Morgan	Chairman	Highway Commn.	Longview
	W. A. Bugge	Director	Highway Commn.	Olympia
West Virginia...	Burl A. Sawyers	Commissioner	Road Commn.	Charleston
	M. L. O'Neale	Chief Engineer	Road Commn.	Charleston
Wisconsin......	H. L. Plummer	Chairman	Highway Commn.	Madison
	E. L. Roettiger	Highway Engineer	Highway Commn.	Madison
Wyoming......	Homer Oxley	Chairman	Highway Dept.	Lingle
	J. R. Bromley	Superintendent	Highway Dept.	Cheyenne
Alaska.........	Irving McK. Reed	Highway Engineer	Office of Highway Engineer	Juneau
Guam.........	William Hellier	Director	Dept. of Pub. Works	Tamuning
Hawaii........	Ben E. Nutter	Highway Engineer	Terr. Highway Dept.	Honolulu
Puerto Rico....	Roberto Sánchez-Vilella	Secretary	Dept. of Pub. Works	San Juan
	Angel Q. Silva	Dir., Bur. of Roads	Dept. of Pub. Works	San Juan
Virgin Islands..	Rudolph Galiber	Act. Commissr. of Pub. Works	Govt. of the V.I.	St. Thomas

HOUSING

State	Name	Official Title	Agency	Location
California......	M. J. McDonough	Chief, Div. of Housing	Dept. of Industrial Relations	San Francisco
Connecticut....	Albert C. Demers	Dir., Housing Div.	Dept. of Pub. Works	Hartford
Georgia........	Charles E. Tarver	Supvr. and Coord.	Housing Authority	Cordele
Illinois.........	Temple McFayden	Chairman	State Housing Bd.	Chicago
Iowa..........	Edmund G. Zimmerer, M.D.	Commissioner	Dept. of Health	Des Moines
Louisiana......	Calvin T. Watts	Director	Dept. of Pub. Works	Baton Rouge
Massachusetts...	Daniel Tyler, Jr.	Chairman	State Housing Board	Boston
New Jersey.....	Julius J. Seaman	Chief, Bur. of Housing, Div. of Planning and Devel.	Dept. of Conserv. and Econ. Devel.	Trenton
New York......	Joseph P. McMurray	Commissr., Div. of Housing	Executive Dept.	New York City
Ohio..........	Martin E. Blum	Secretary	Board of Housing	Columbus
Pennsylvania...	William R. Davlin	Secretary	Dept. of Commerce	Harrisburg
Alaska........	M. G. Gebhart	Executive Director	Housing Authority	Anchorage
Guam.........	Elanterio L. Calvo	Housing Off.	Dept. of Labor and Personnel	Agana
Hawaii........	Robert H. Lloyd	Chmn. and Commissr.	Housing Authority	Honolulu
	Lee Maice	Exec. Dir. and Treas.	Housing Authority	Honolulu
Puerto Rico....	César Cordero	Executive Director	Housing Authority	Río Piedras
Virgin Islands..	Roy W. Bornn	Chairman	Housing and Redevelopment Authority	St. Thomas
	Henry Millin	Exec. Director	Housing and Redevelopment Authority	St. Thomas

INCOME TAX

State	Name	Official Title	Agency	Location
Alabama.......	E. A. Erwin	Chief, Inc. Tax Div.	Dept. of Revenue	Montgomery
Arizona........	Donald Green	Dir., Inc. Tax Div.	Tax Commission	Phoenix
Arkansas.......	Roby Bearden	Dir., Inc. Tax Div.	Revenue Dept.	Little Rock
California......	Bruce W. Walker	Chief, Inc. Tax Div.	Franchise Tax Bd.	Sacramento
Colorado.......	Earl Blevins	Director	Dept. of Revenue	Denver
Georgia........	K. A. Campbell	Dir., Income Tax	Revenue Dept. Unit	Atlanta
Idaho.........	P. G. Neill	Tax Collector	Off. Tax Collector	Boise
Indiana........	Frank T. Millis	Dir., Gross Income Tax Div.	Dept. of Revenue	Indianapolis
Iowa..........	Elmer F. Heckinger	Dir., Personal Income Tax Div.	Tax Commission	Des Moines
Kansas........	Robert G. Lindsay	Chief	Rev. and Taxation Commn.	Topeka
Kentucky......	Richard Sullivan	Dir., Income Tax Div.	Dept. of Revenue	Frankfort
Louisiana......	John F. Ward	Chief, Inc. Tax Div.	Dept. of Revenue	Baton Rouge
Maryland......	J. Millard Tawes	Comptroller	Off. of Comptr.	Annapolis
Massachusetts...	William A. Cummings	Dir., Inc. Tax Bur.	Dept. of Corp. and Taxation	Boston
Minnesota......	Wm. G. Burkman	Dir., Inc. Tax Div.	Dept. of Taxation	St. Paul
Mississippi.....	Alex McKeigney	Chairman	Tax Commission	Jackson
Missouri.......	T. R. Allen	Supvr., Income Tax	Dept. of Revenue	Jefferson City
Montana.......	L. C. Burns	Supervisor	Bd. of Equalization	Helena
New Hampshire.	Percy H. Howland	Dir., Interest and Dividends Div.	Tax Commission	Concord
New Mexico....	J. Leon Miller	Dir., Inc. Tax Div.	Bur. of Revenue	Santa Fe
New York......	George P. Klein	Dir., Inc. Tax Bur., Div. of Taxation	Dept. of Tax and Finance	Albany
North Carolina.	Eugene G. Shaw	Commissioner	Dept. of Revenue	Raleigh

INCOME TAX—*continued*

State	Name	Official Title	Agency	Location
North Dakota...	J. Arthur Engen	Tax Commissioner	Off. Tax Commissr.	Bismarck
Oklahoma......	R. E. Wilson	Dir., Inc. Tax Div.	Tax Commission	Oklahoma City
Oregon........	Ray Smith	Tax Commissioner	Tax Commission	Salem
South Carolina..	F. D. Beattie	Dir., Inc. Tax Div.	Tax Commission	Columbia
Tennessee......	John R. Patton	Dir., Inc. Tax Div.	Dept. of Finance and Taxation	Nashville
Utah.........	Paul M. Holt	Dir., Inc. Tax Div.	Tax Commission	Salt Lake City
Vermont.......	L. W. Morrison	Commissioner	Tax Commission	Montpelier
Virginia.......	C. H. Morrissett	Commissioner	Dept. of Taxation	Richmond
Wisconsin......	H. D. Kuentz	Dep. Commissr. of Taxation	Dept. of Taxation	Madison
Alaska........	Karl F. Dewey	Tax Commissioner	Dept. of Taxation	Juneau
Guam.........	George W. Ingling	Commissr., Rev. and Tax.	Dept. of Finance	Agana
Hawaii........	John A. Bell	Dep. Tax Commissr.	Off. Tax Commissr.	Honolulu
Puerto Rico....	Rogelio Muñoz Veloso	Acting Chief, Bur. of Inc. Tax	Dept. of Treasury	San Juan
Virgin Islands..	Percy de Jongh	Act. Commissioner	Dept. of Finance	St. Thomas

INSURANCE

State	Name	Official Title	Agency	Location
Alabama.......	Leslie L. Gwaltney, Jr.	Supt. of Insurance	Dept. of Insurance	Montgomery
Arizona........	G. A. Bushnell	Director	Insurance Dept.	Phoenix
Arkansas......	Harvey Combs	Commissioner	Insurance Dept.	Little Rock
California......	F. Britton McConnell	Commissioner	Dept. of Insurance	San Francisco
Colorado......	Sam N. Beery	Commissioner	Insurance Dept.	Denver
Connecticut....	Thomas J. Spellacy	Commissioner	Insurance Dept.	Hartford
Delaware......	Harry S. Smith	Commissioner	Insurance Dept.	Dover
Florida........	J. Edwin Larson	Treasurer	Ins. Dept., Treasurer's Office	Tallahassee
Georgia........	Hubert McDonald	Deputy Ins. Commissr.	Comptroller-Gen.'s Office	Atlanta
Idaho.........	Leo O'Connell	Director	Dept. of Insurance	Boise
Illinois.........	Justin T. McCarthy	Director	Dept. of Insurance	Springfield
Indiana........	William J. Davey	Commissioner	Insurance Dept.	Indianapolis
Iowa..........	Oliver P. Bennett	Commissioner	Insurance Dept.	Des Moines
Kansas........	Frank Sullivan	Commissioner	Insurance Dept.	Topeka
Kentucky......	S. H. Goebel	Commissioner	Dept. of Insurance	Frankfort
Louisiana......	Wade O. Martin, Jr.	Secy. of State	Insurance Rating Commn.	Baton Rouge
Maine.........	George F. Mahoney	Commissioner	Insurance Dept.	Augusta
Maryland......	Charles S. Jackson	Commissioner	Insurance Dept.	Baltimore
Massachusetts...	Joseph Humphreys	Commissr., Div. of Insurance	Dept. of Banking and Insurance	Boston
Michigan......	Joseph A. Navarre	Commissioner	Insurance Dept.	Lansing
Minnesota......	Cyril C. Sheehan	Commissioner	Div. of Insurance	St. Paul
Mississippi.....	Walter Dell Davis	Commissioner	Insurance Dept.	Jackson
Missouri.......	Laurence Leggett	Supt., Div. of Ins.	Dept. of Business and Admin.	Jefferson City
Montana.......	John J. Holmes	Commissr. of Ins.	Auditor's Off.	Helena
Nebraska.......	Thomas R. Pansing	Director	Dept. of Insurance	Lincoln
Nevada........	Paul A. Hammel	Commissioner	Dept. of Insurance	Carson City
New Hampshire.	Donald Knowlton	Commissioner	Insurance Dept.	Concord
New Jersey.....	Charles R. Howell	Commissioner	Dept. of Banking and Insurance	Trenton
New Mexico....	R. F. Apodaca	Superintendent	Insurance Dept.	Santa Fe
New York......	Leffert Holz	Supt. of Insurance	Insurance Dept.	Albany

INSURANCE—*continued*

State	Name	Official Title	Agency	Location
North Carolina.	Charles F. Gold	Commissioner	Dept. of Insurance	Raleigh
North Dakota...	A. J. Jensen	Commissr. of Ins.	Insurance Dept.	Bismarck
Ohio..........	August Pryatel	Superintendent	Div. of Insurance	Columbus
Oklahoma......	Joe B. Hunt	Insurance Commissr.	Insurance Dept.	Oklahoma City
Oregon........	Robert B. Taylor	Insurance Commissr.	Insurance Dept.	Salem
Pennsylvania...	Francis R. Smith	Insurance Commissr.	Dept. of Insurance	Harrisburg
Rhode Island...	George A. Bisson	Commissioner	Dept. of Bus. Reg.	Providence
South Carolina..	R. Lee Kelly	Insurance Commissr.	Insurance Commn.	Columbia
South Dakota...	George Burt	Commissioner	Insurance Dept.	Pierre
Tennessee......	Arch Northington	Commissioner	Dept. of Insurance and Banking	Nashville
Texas.........	Garland A. Smith	Life Ins. Commissr.	Bd. of Ins. Commissrs.	Austin
Utah..........	Walter Jones	Insurance Commissr.	Dept. of Insurance	Salt Lake City
Vermont.......	Alexander H. Miller	Commissioner	Dept. of Banking and Insurance	Montpelier
Virginia.......	George A. Bowles	Commissr. of Ins.	Corporation Commn.	Richmond
Washington....	William A. Sullivan	Commissioner	Office of Ins. Commissr.	Olympia
West Virginia...	Thomas J. Gillooly	Commissioner	Off. of Ins. Commn.	Charleston
Wisconsin......	Paul J. Rogan	Commissr. of Ins.	Insurance Dept.	Madison
Wyoming......	Ford S. Taft	Commissioner	Insurance Dept.	Cheyenne
Alaska.........	Ross P. Duncan	Commissr. of Ins.	Insurance Commn.	Juneau
Hawaii........	Kam Tai Lee	Ins. Commissr.	Insurance Bur.	Honolulu
Puerto Rico....	Mariano Nieves	Supt. of Insurance	Office of the Supt. of Insurance	San Juan
Virgin Islands..	Charles K. Claunch	Insurance Commissr.	Govt. of the V.I.	St. Thomas

LABOR (Arbitration and Mediation)

State	Name	Official Title	Agency	Location
Alabama.......	Luther D. Barnette	Director	Labor Dept.	Montgomery
Arkansas.......	Clarence R. Thornbrough	Commissioner	Labor Dept.	Little Rock
California......	Ernest B. Webb	Director	Dept. of Ind. Relations	San Francisco
Connecticut....	Robert Cronin	Secretary	Bd. of Med. and Arb.	Hartford
Delaware......	John N. McDowell	Secretary of State	Secy. of State's Office	Dover
Idaho.........	W. L. Robison	Commissioner	Dept. of Labor	Boise
Illinois.........	Roy Cummins	Director	Dept. of Labor	Springfield
Indiana........	George F. Hinkle	Commissioner	Div. of Labor	Indianapolis
Iowa..........	Leo A. Hoegh	Governor	Executive Dept.	Des Moines
Kentucky......	Harrison M. Robertson	Commissioner	Dept. of Ind. Relations	Frankfort
Louisiana......	Paul M. Hebert	Chairman	Labor Mediation Bd.	Baton Rouge
Maine.........	John Donovan	Chairman	Bd. of Arb. and Concil.	Lewiston
Maryland......	Jos. F. DiDomenico	Commissioner	Dept. of Labor and Ind.	Baltimore
Massachusetts...	Chester T. Skibinski	Chairman, Bd. of Concil. and Arb.	Dept. of Labor and Industries	Boston
Michigan......	George E. Bowles	Chairman	Labor Mediation Board	Lansing
Minnesota......	Harry L. Hanson	Labor Conciliator	Div. of Labor Concil.	St. Paul
Missouri.......	Daniel C. Rogers	Chmn., Bd. of Mediation	Dept. of Labor and Ind. Relations	Jefferson City
Montana.......	Oliver Sullivan	Commissioner	Dept. of Labor	Helena
Nebraska.......	Albert Arms	Presiding Judge	Ind. Relations Court	Lincoln

LABOR (Arbitration and Mediation)—*continued*

State	Name	Official Title	Agency	Location
New Hampshire.	Thomas P. Cheney, Jr.	Chairman	Bd. of Concil. and Arbitration	Concord
New Jersey.....	Mason W. Gross	Chairman, Bd. of Mediation	Dept. of Labor and Industry	Newark
New York......	Merlyn S. Pitzele	Chmn., Bd. of Mediation	Dept. of Labor	New York City
North Carolina.	Frank Crane	Commissioner	Dept. of Labor	Raleigh
North Dakota...	H. R. Martinson	Head, Labor Div.	Dept. of Agric. and Labor	Bismarck
Oklahoma......	Jim Hughes	Chairman	Bd. of Arb. and Concil.	Oklahoma City
Oregon........	J. L. Jennings	Chairman	Bd. of Conciliation	Portland
Pennsylvania...	Benjamin M. Weigand	Dir., Bur. of Mediation	Dept. of Labor and Industry	Harrisburg
Rhode Island...	Edmund J. Kelly	Chmn., Labor Relations Board	Dept. of Labor	Providence
South Carolina..	Wm. Fred Ponder	Commissioner	Dept. of Labor	Columbia
Utah..........	Robert J. Shaughnessy	Trial Examiner and Conciliator	Industrial Commn.	Salt Lake City
Vermont.......	Raymond B. Daniels	Commissioner	Dept. of Ind. Relations	Montpelier
Washington....	Harry E. Busch	Supvr., Mediation and Conciliation	Dept. of Labor and Inds.	Seattle
West Virginia...	Charles Sattler	Commissioner	Dept. of Labor	Charleston
Wisconsin......	Laurence E. Gooding	Chairman	Employment Relations Bd.	Madison
Wyoming......	Paul Bachman	Commissioner	Labor Office	Cheyenne
Alaska........	Henry A. Benson	Commissioner	Dept. of Labor	Juneau
Guam........	Manuel Ulloa	Chairman	Personnel Board	Agana
Hawaii........	E. B. Peterson	Director	Dept. of Labor and Ind. Relations	Honolulu
Puerto Rico....	Adolfo D. Collazo	Dir., Mediation and Concil. Bureau	Dept. of Labor	San Juan

LABOR AND INDUSTRIAL RELATIONS

State	Name	Official Title	Agency	Location
Alabama.......	Eugene M. Wells	Director	Dept. of Ind. Rel.	Montgomery
Arkansas.......	Clarence R. Thornbrough	Commissioner	Labor Dept.	Little Rock
California......	Edward P. Park	Chief, Div. of Labor Law Enforcement	Dept. of Ind. Rel.	San Francisco
Colorado.......	Fred W. Andresen	Chairman	Industrial Commn.	Denver
Connecticut....	Renato Ricciuti	Commissioner	Dept. of Labor	Hartford
Delaware......	Owen J. Hession	Inspector	Labor Commn.	Wilmington
Florida........	James T. Vocelle	Chairman	Industrial Commn.	Tallahassee
Georgia........	Ben T. Huiet	Commissioner	Dept. of Labor	Atlanta
Idaho.........	W. L. Robison	Commissioner	Dept. of Labor	Boise
Illinois.........	Roy Cummins	Director	Dept. of Labor	Springfield
Indiana........	George F. Hinkle	Commissioner	Div. of Labor	Indianapolis
Iowa..........	Frank B. Means	Commissioner	Labor Bureau	Des Moines
Kansas........	Roy L. Warkentin	Commissioner	Dept. of Labor	Topeka
Kentucky......	Harrison M. Robertson	Commissioner	Dept. of Ind. Rel.	Frankfort
Louisiana......	Luther H. Simmons	Commissioner	Dept. of Labor	Baton Rouge
Maine.........	Marion Martin	Commissioner	Dept. of Labor and Industry	Augusta
Maryland......	Jos. F. DiDomenico	Commissioner	Dept. of Labor and Industry	Baltimore
Massachusetts...	Ernest A. Johnson	Commissioner	Dept. of Labor and Industries	Boston
Michigan......	John Reid	Commissioner	Dept. of Labor	Lansing

LABOR AND INDUSTRIAL RELATIONS—*continued*

State	Name	Official Title	Agency	Location
Minnesota......	A. E. Ramberg	Chmn., Ind. Commn.	Dept. of Labor and Industry	St. Paul
Missouri.......	L. L. Duncan	Dir., Div. of Ind. Inspection	Dept. of Labor and Ind. Relations	Jefferson City
Montana.......	Oliver R. Sullivan	Commissioner	Dept. of Labor	Helena
Nebraska.......	James L. Weasmer	Commissioner	Dept. of Labor	Lincoln
Nevada........	D. Wayne Everett	Commissioner	Off. of Labor Commissr.	Carson City
New Hampshire.	Adelard E. Cote	Commissioner	Dept. of Labor	Concord
New Jersey.....	Carl Holderman	Commissioner	Dept. of Labor and Industry	Trenton
New Mexico....	C. W. Burrell	Commissioner	Labor and Ind. Commn.	Santa Fe
New York......	Isador Lubin	Ind. Commissr.	Dept. of Labor	New York City
North Carolina..	Frank Crane	Commissioner	Dept. of Labor	Raleigh
	J. W. Bean	Chairman	Industrial Commn.	Raleigh
North Dakota...	H. R. Martinson	Dep. Commissr. of Agric. and Labor	Dept. of Agric. and Labor	Bismarck
Ohio..........	Margaret A. Mahoney	Director	Dept. of Ind. Rel.	Columbus
Oklahoma......	Jim Hughes	Commissioner	Dept. of Labor	Oklahoma City
Oregon........	Norman O. Nilsen	Commissioner	Bureau of Labor	Salem
Pennsylvania...	John R. Torquato	Secretary	Dept. of Labor and Industry	Harrisburg
	Michael J. Crosetto	Chmn., Labor Relations Bd.	Dept. of Labor and Industry	Harrisburg
Rhode Island...	Arthur W. Devine	Director	Dept. of Labor	Providence
South Carolina..	Wm. Fred Ponder	Commissioner	Dept. of Labor	Columbia
South Dakota...	Thomas G. Ries	Asst. Atty. Gen.	Industrial Commn.	Pierre
Tennessee......	W. H. Parham	Commissioner	Dept. of Labor	Nashville
Texas..........	M. B. Morgan	Commissioner	Bur. of Lab. Stat.	Austin
Utah..........	O. A. Wiesley	Chairman	Industrial Commn.	Salt Lake City
Vermont.......	Raymond B. Daniels	Commissioner	Dept. of Ind. Rel.	Montpelier
Virginia.......	Edmond M. Boggs	Commissioner	Dept. of Labor and Industry	Richmond
Washington....	L. H. Bates	Director	Dept. of Labor and Industry	Olympia
West Virginia...	Charles Sattler	Commissioner	Dept. of Labor	Charleston
Wisconsin......	Reuben G. Knutson	Chairman	Industrial Commn.	Madison
Wyoming......	Paul Bachman	Commissioner	Labor Dept.	Cheyenne
Alaska........	Henry A. Benson	Commissioner	Dept. of Labor	Juneau
Guam.........	Peter Siguenza	Director	Dept. of Labor, Personnel	Agana
Hawaii........	Alva A. Steadman	Chairman	Commissrs. of Labor and Ind. Relations	Honolulu
	E. B. Peterson	Director	Dept. of Labor, Ind. Relations	Honolulu
Puerto Rico....	Fernando Sierra-Berdecía	Secretary	Dept. of Labor	San Juan
Virgin Islands...	(Vacancy)	Commissioner	Dept. of Agric. and Labor	St. Croix

LAND (State Land Officers)*

State	Name	Official Title	Agency	Location
Alabama.......	Charles W. Lee	State Land Mgr.	Dept. of Conserv.	Montgomery
Arizona........	Roger Ernst	Land Commissioner	Land Department	Phoenix
Arkansas.......	James H. Jones	Land Commissioner	Land Department	Little Rock

LAND (State Land Officers)*—continued

State	Name	Official Title	Agency	Location
California	Col. Rufus W. Putnam	Executive Officer	State Lands Division	Los Angeles
Colorado	A. M. Ramsey	Chairman	Bd. of Land Commissrs.	Denver
Delaware	Walter A. McKendrick, Jr.	Chief Engineer	Highway Dept.	Dover
Florida	Sinclair Wells	Land Agent	Dept. of Agric.	Tallahassee
Idaho	Arthur Wilson	Land Commissioner	Land Dept.	Boise
Indiana	Curtis E. Rardin	Auditor	Off. of Auditor	Indianapolis
Iowa	Melvin D. Synhorst	Secy. of State	Off. of Secy. of State	Des Moines
Kansas	George Robb	Auditor	Off. of Auditor	Topeka
Kentucky	W. T. Judy	Exec. Dir., Property and Bldgs. Commn.	Dept. of Finance	Frankfort
Louisiana	Mrs. Ellen Bryan Moore	Register of the State Land Office	Land Office	Baton Rouge
Maine	Albert D. Nutting	Forest Commissr.	Forestry Dept.	Augusta
Maryland	{ Joseph O'C. McCusker	Secretary	Bd. of Pub. Works	Baltimore
	Harry L. Harcum	Commissioner	Land Office	Baltimore
Minnesota	Ray D. Nolan	Dir., Div. of Lands and Minerals	Dept. of Conserv.	St. Paul
Mississippi	Robert Graham	Land Commissioner	Off. of Land Commissr.	Jackson
Missouri	Walter H. Toberman	Secy. of State	Off. of Secy. of State	Jefferson City
Montana	Lou. E. Bretzke	Commissr. of State Lands and Investments	Bd. of Land Commissrs.	Helena
Nebraska	Robert D. Hiatt	Secretary	Bd. of Educational Lands and Funds	Lincoln
Nevada	Louis Ferrarri	Surveyor General, Ex-officio Land Register	Off. of Surveyor General	Carson City
New Hampshire	William H. Messeck, Jr.	Forester	Forestry and Recreation Commn.	Concord
New Mexico	E. S. Walker	Commissr. of Public Lands	Land Office	Santa Fe
New York	Carmine De Sapio	Chairman, Bd. of Commissrs.	Land Office, Dept. of State	Albany
North Dakota	Anton J. Schmidt	Land Commissioner	Univ. and Schools Lands Commn.	Bismarck
Ohio	James A. Rhodes	Auditor	Off. of Auditor	Columbus
Oklahoma	Lawrence L. Irwin	Secretary	Dept. of Commissrs. of Land Office	Oklahoma City
Oregon	E. T. Pierce	Clerk	Land Board	Salem
Pennsylvania	Genevieve Blatt	Secretary of Internal Affairs	Dept. of Internal Affairs	Harrisburg
Rhode Island	Nelson F. Duphiney	Secretary	State Properties Comm.	Providence
South Dakota	Bernard Linn	Commissioner	Dept. of School and Public Lands	Pierre
Tennessee	Wayne Sensing	State Property Administrator	Off. of Property Administrator	Nashville
Texas	J. Earl Rudder	Commissioner	Gen. Land Off.	Austin
Utah	Herbert B. Smart	Commissr. in charge of Land Board	Finance Commn.	Salt Lake City
Washington	Otto A. Case	Land Commissioner	Dept. of Pub. Lands	Olympia
Wisconsin	T. H. Bakken	Chief Clerk	Commissrs. of Pub. Lands	Madison
Wyoming	Ben Cossman	Commissr. of Public Lands and Farm Loans	Land Office	Cheyenne

---

*In some of the states not listed here, sale and management of state lands are responsibilities of several departments or of other officials acting *ex officio*. In some states for which land officials are listed here, certain types of state lands are handled by other departments.

LIBRARY (Archives and History)

State	Name	Official Title	Agency	Location
Alabama.......	Peter A. Brannon	Director	Dept. of Archives and History	Montgomery
Arizona........	Mulford Winsor	Director	Dept. of Library and Archives	Phoenix
Arkansas.......	Ted Worley	Exec. Secy.	History Commn.	Little Rock
California......	Allan R. Ottley	Calif. Section Librarian, Div. of Lib.	Dept. of Education	Sacramento
	Paul J. O'Brien	Archivist	Secy. of State	Sacramento
Colorado.......	Agnes Wright Spring	Act. State Historian	State Hist. Soc.	Denver
	Dolores C. Renze	State Archivist	State Hist. Soc.	Denver
Connecticut....	Mary E. Smith	Archivist	State Library	Hartford
Delaware......	Leon de Valinger	State Archivist	Public Archives Commn.	Dover
Florida........	Dorothy Dodd	Librarian	State Library Bd.	Tallahassee
Georgia........	Mrs. Mary G. Bryan	Dir., Arch. and Hist. Div.	Off. Secy. of State	Atlanta
Idaho.........	Gertrude McDevitt	Librarian	Historical Museum	Boise
Illinois........	Margaret C. Norton	Dept. Head (Archives)	Secy. of State's Off.	Springfield
Indiana........	Hubert H. Hawkins	Director	Historical Bureau	Indianapolis
	Margaret C. Pierson	Archivist	State Library	Indianapolis
Iowa..........	Claude R. Cook	Curator	Dept. of History and Archives	Des Moines
Kansas........	Nyle Miller	Secretary	Historical Society	Topeka
Kentucky.....	Bayless E. Hardin	Secretary	Ky. Historical Society	Frankfort
Maryland......	Morris L. Radoff	Archivist	Hall of Records Commn.	Annapolis
Massachusetts...	Richard D. Higgins	Chief, Archives Div.	Secy. of the Commonwealth	Boston
Michigan	Lewis Beeson	Secretary	Historical Commn.	Lansing
Minnesota......	Russell W. Fridley	Librarian	Historical Society	St. Paul
Mississippi......	Charlotte Capers	Director	Archives and History	Jackson
Missouri.......	Floyd C. Shoemaker	Secy. and Librarian	Historical Society	Columbia
Montana.......	K. Ross Toole	Librarian	Historical Society	Helena
Nebraska.......	James C. Olson	Superintendent	Historical Society	Lincoln
Nevada........	Clara S. Beatty	Exec. Secretary	Historical Society	Reno
New Jersey.....	Roger H. McDonough	Dir., Div. of State Lib., Arch. and Hist.	Dept. of Education	Trenton
New Mexico....	Arthur J. O. Anderson	Archivist	Museum	Santa Fe
	Gertrude Hill	Librarian	Museum	Santa Fe
New York......	Edna L. Jacobsen	Manuscripts and History Librarian	State Lib., Education Dept.	Albany
North Carolina..	C. C. Crittenden	Director	Dept. of Archives and History	Raleigh
North Dakota...	Russell Reid	Superintendent	Historical Society	Bismarck
Ohio..........	John Still	Curator of Hist., Archivist and Librarian	Archaeological Society	Columbus
Oklahoma......	Don W. Der	Staff Archivist, Archives Div.	State Library	Oklahoma City
	Mrs. Elsie D. Hand	Staff Librarian	Historical Society	Oklahoma City
	Ralph Hudson	State Librarian and State Archivist	State Library	Oklahoma City
	Mrs. Rella Looney	Staff Archivist	Historical Society	Oklahoma City
Oregon........	David C. Duniway	State Archivist	State Library	Salem
	Thomas Vaughan	Director	Historical Society	Portland
Pennsylvania...	S. K. Stevens	Chief Historian, Historical Div.	Historical and Museum Commn.	Harrisburg

LIBRARY (Archives and History)—*continued*

State	Name	Official Title	Agency	Location
Rhode Island...	Mary T. Quinn	Asst. in Charge of Archives	Dept. of State	Providence
South Carolina..	J. H. Easterby	Director	Archives Commn.	Columbia
South Dakota...	Will G. Robinson	Superintendent	Dept. of History	Pierre
Tennessee......	Dan M. Robison	State Librarian and Archivist	State Library	Nashville
Texas..........	Mrs. Virginia H. Taylor	Archivist	State Library	Austin
Utah..........	A. R. Mortensen	Exec. Secy. and Editor	Historical Society	Salt Lake City
Vermont.......	Arthur W. Peach	Director	Historical Society	Montpelier
Virginia.......	Wm. J. Van Schreeven	Head, Archives Div. and Land Office	State Library	Richmond
Washington....	Chapin D. Foster	Director	Historical Society	Tacoma
West Virginia...	Mrs. Dale Thomas	Historian and Archivist	Dept. of Archives and History	Charleston
Wisconsin......	Clifford L. Lord	Director	Historical Society	Madison
Wyoming......	Lola Homsher	Archivist and Curator	Historical Dept.	Cheyenne
Alaska.........	Edward L. Keithahn	Librarian and Curator	Historical Library and Museum	Juneau
Guam	Lucille Woelfl	Librarian	Terr. Library	Agana
Hawaii........	Agnes C. Conrad	Archivist	Public Archives	Honolulu
Puerto Rico	Thomas Hayes	Librarian	Univ. of Puerto Rico	Río Piedras

LIBRARY (Extension Service)

State	Name	Official Title	Agency	Location
Alabama.......	Evelyn Day Mullen	Director	Public Library Serv. Div.	Montgomery
Arizona........	Mulford Winsor	Director	Dept. of Library and Archives	Phoenix
Arkansas.......	Mrs. Francis P. Neal	Librarian and Exec. Secretary	Library Commn.	Little Rock
California......	Mrs. Carma R. Zimmerman	State Librarian	Dept. of Education	Sacramento
Connecticut....	Helen A. Ridgway	Dir., Bur. of Libraries	Dept. of Education	Hartford
Florida........	Zella D. Adams	Dir. of Extension	State Library Bd.	Tallahassee
Georgia........	Beverly Wheatcroft	Librarian, Library Ext. Serv.	Dept. of Education	Atlanta
Idaho.........	(Vacancy)	Librarian	Traveling Library	Boise
Illinois........	de Lafayette Reid	Acting Asst. State Librarian	Off. of Sec. of State	Springfield
Indiana........	Harriet I. Carter	Dir., Ext. Div.	State Library	Indianapolis
Iowa..........	Blanche A. Smith	Librarian	Traveling Library	Des Moines
Kansas........	Louise McNeal	Librarian	State Library	Topeka
Kentucky......	Frances Jane Porter	Director	Library Ext. Div.	Frankfort
Louisiana......	Essae M. Culver	State Librarian	State Library	Baton Rouge
Maine.........	Virginia Hill	Deputy Librarian	State Library	Augusta
Maryland......	Helen M. Clark	Director	Div. Library Ext.	Baltimore
Massachusetts...	Mrs. George J. Galick	Director, Div. of Library Ext.	Dept. of Education	Boston
Michigan......	Louise Rees	Head, Consultant Div.	State Library	Lansing
Minnesota......	Russell J. Schunk	Dir. of Libraries	Dept. of Education	St. Paul
Mississippi.....	Lura Currier	Exec. Secretary	Library Commn.	Jackson
Missouri.......	Paxton P. Price	State Librarian	State Library	Jefferson City
Montana.......	Ellen Torgrimson	Secretary	Library Extension Commn.	Missoula

LIBRARY (Extension Service)—*continued*

State	Name	Official Title	Agency	Location
Nebraska.......	Louise Nixon	Exec. Secretary	Pub. Library Commn.	Lincoln
Nevada........	Constance C. Collins	State Librarian	State Library	Carson City
New Hampshire.	Catharine Pratt	Asst. Librarian	State Library	Concord
New Jersey.....	Janet Z. McKinley	Head, Bureau of Public and School Library Serv., Div. of State Library, Arch. and Hist.	Dept. of Education	Trenton
New Mexico....	Mrs. Irene S. Peck	Exec. Secy. and Dir., Library Ext. Serv.	State Lib. Commn.	Santa Fe
New York......	L. Marion Moshier	Dir. of Library Extension	State Library, Education Dept.	Albany
North Carolina..	Mrs. Elizabeth House Hughey	Secy. and Dir.	Library Commn.	Raleigh
North Dakota...	Hazel Webster Byrnes	Director	State Lib. Commn.	Bismarck
Oklahoma......	Ralph Hudson	State Librarian	State Library, Library Ext. Div.	Oklahoma City
Oregon........	Eleanor Stephens	State Librarian	State Library	Salem
Pennsylvania...	Ellsworth Brininger	Extension Library	Dept. Pub. Instr.	Harrisburg
Rhode Island...	Grace M. Sherwood	State Librarian	State Library	Providence
South Carolina..	James A. Rogers	Chmn., Bd. of Dirs.	State Library Assn.	Columbia
South Dakota...	Mercedes McKay	Secretary	State Library Commn.	Pierre
Tennessee......	Martha Parks	Dir., Public Libraries Div.	Lib. and Archives Commn.	Nashville
Texas.........	John A. Hudson	Extension Director	State Library	Austin
Vermont.......	Dorothy Randolph	Secy., Bookmobile and School Lib.	Free Pub. Library Commn.	Montpelier
Virginia.......	C. E. Grafton	Head, Extension Div.	State Library	Richmond
Washington....	Maryan E. Reynolds	State Librarian	State Library	Olympia
West Virginia...	Dora Ruth Parks	Exec. Secretary	Library Commn.	Charleston
Wisconsin......	(Vacancy)	Secretary	Free Library Commn.	Madison
Wyoming......	May Gillies	State Librarian	State Library	Cheyenne
Alaska........	Dorothy Phelps	Territorial Librarian	Dept. of Library Service	Juneau
Hawaii........	Suzanne Starr	Extension Librarian	Library of Hawaii	Honolulu
Puerto Rico....	Juan M. Alvarez	Act. Dir., Carnegie Library	Dept. of Education	San Juan

LIBRARY (Law)

State	Name	Official Title	Agency	Location
Alabama.......	Richard Neal	Librarian	Supreme Ct. Lib.	Montgomery
Arizona........	Mulford Winsor	Director	Dept. of Lib. and Archives	Phoenix
Arkansas.......	John Caldwell	Librarian	Supreme Court	Little Rock
California.....	Mary K. Sanders	Supervising Law Librarian, Div. of Libraries	Dept. of Education	Sacramento
Colorado.......	Guy K. Brewster	Librarian	Supreme Ct. Lib.	Denver
Connecticut....	Virginia A. Knox	Law Librarian	State Library	Hartford
Delaware......	Mrs. Leon Satterfield	Librarian	State Law Library	Dover
Florida........	Guyte P. McCord	Librarian	Supreme Ct. Lib.	Tallahassee

LIBRARY (Law)—*continued*

State	Name	Official Title	Agency	Location
Georgia........	Jane Oliver	Librarian	State Library	Atlanta
Idaho.........	Clay Koelsch	Clerk	Supreme Court	Boise
Illinois.........	Jessie T. Smith	Librarian	Supreme Ct. Lib.	Springfield
Indiana........	Mrs. Mary M. Schubert	Librarian	Supreme Court	Indianapolis
Iowa..........	Geraldine Dunham	Act. Law Librarian	State Law Liarary	Des Moines
Kansas........	Marie Russell	Law Librarian	State Library	Topeka
Kentucky.....	Field Harris	Law Librarian	State Law Library	Frankfort
Louisiana......	Madge K. Tomeny	Librarian	Law Library	New Orleans
Maine.........	Edith L. Hary	Law and Legis. Ref. Librarian	State Library	Augusta
Maryland......	Nelson J. Molter	Director	State Library	Annapolis
Massachusetts...	Dennis A. Dooley	Librarian	State Library	Boston
Michigan......	Charlotte Dunnebacke	Librarian	Law Library	Lansing
Minnesota......	Margaret S. Andrews	State Librarian	Law Library	St. Paul
Mississippi.....	Mrs. Julia Baylis Starnes	State Librarian	State Library	Jackson
Missouri.......	Mary Louise Seibold	Librarian	Supreme Ct. Lib.	Jefferson City
Montana.......	Mrs. Adeline J. Clarke	State Law Librarian	State Law Library	Helena
Nebraska.......	G. H. Turner	Librarian	State Library	Lincoln
Nevada........	A. Elizabeth Holt	Law Librarian	State Library	Carson City
New Hampshire.	Philip A. Hazelton	Law Librarian	State Library	Concord
New Jersey.....	Margaret E. Coonan	Head, Law Lib. Bur., Div. of State Library, Archives and History	Dept. of Education	Trenton
New Mexico....	Harrison MacDonald	Librarian	State Law Library	Santa Fe
New York......	Ernest H. Breuer	Law Librarian	State Library, Education Dept.	Albany
North Carolina..	Dillard S. Gardner	Librarian	Supreme Court	Raleigh
North Dakota...	(Vacancy)	Law Librarian	Supreme Court	Bismarck
Ohio..........	Raymond M. Jones	Marshal and Law Librarian	Supreme Ct. Law Library	Columbus
Oklahoma......	Ralph Hudson	State Librarian	State Library	Oklahoma City
Oregon........	Ray Stringham	Librarian	Supreme Ct. Lib.	Salem
Pennsylvania...	George Charney, Jr.	Law Librarian	Dept. Pub. Instr.	Harrisburg
Rhode Island...	Clarence H. Shoren	Law Librarian	State Law Library	Providence
South Carolina..	Mrs. Emma H. Motte	Librarian	Supreme Court	Columbia
South Dakota...	Francis Pinckney	Clerk	Supreme Court	Pierre
Tennessee......	David Lansden	Clerk and Librarian	Supreme Ct.	Nashville
Texas..........	Frances Horton	Librarian	Supreme Ct. Lib.	Austin
Utah..........	L. M. Cummings	Clerk and Librarian	Supreme Court	Salt Lake City
Vermont.......	Lawrence J. Turgeon	Librarian	State Library	Montpelier
Virginia.......	Lloyd M. Richards	Law Librarian	Sup. Ct. of Appeals	Richmond
Washington....	Mark H. Wight	Law Librarian	State Law Library	Olympia
West Virginia...	J. A. Jackson	Law Librarian	Law Library	Charleston
Wisconsin......	Gilson G. Glasier	Librarian	State Library	Madison
Wyoming......	May Gillies	Librarian	State Library	Cheyenne
Guam.........	(Vacancy)	Librarian	Dept. of Law	Agana
Hawaii........	Mary Helen Stevens	Law Librarian	Supreme Court	Honolulu
Puerto Rico....	Josefa Jiménez	Librarian	Off. of the Secretary of Justice	San Juan
	Luis F. Rivera del Olmo	Law Librarian	Univ. of Puerto Rico	Río Piedras
Virgin Islands..	George A. Mena	Clerk, Dist. Ct.	Govt. of the V. I.	St. Thomas

LIBRARY (State)

State	Name	Official Title	Agency	Location
Alabama.......	Peter Brannan	Director	Dept. of Archives and History	Montgomery
Arizona........	Mulford Winsor	Director	Dept. of Library and Archives	Phoenix
Arkansas.......	Mrs. Francis P. Neal	Librarian and Exec. Secy.	Library Commn.	Little Rock
California......	Mrs. Carma R. Zimmerman	State Librarian, Div. of Libs.	Dept. of Education	Sacramento
Colorado.......	Gordon L. Bennett	Asst. State Libn.	State Library	Denver
Connecticut....	James Brewster	Librarian	State Library	Hartford
Delaware......	Anne W. W. Bell	Librarian	Library Commn.	Dover
Florida........	Dorothy Dodd	Librarian	State Library Bd.	Tallahassee
Georgia........	Jane Oliver	Librarian	State Library	Atlanta
Idaho.........	(Vacancy)	Librarian	Traveling Library	Boise
Illinois.........	Charles F. Carpentier	Secy. of State and State Librarian	Off. of Secy. of State	Springfield
Indiana........	Harold F. Brigham	Director	State Library	Indianapolis
Iowa..........	Blanche A. Smith	Librarian	State Traveling Lib.	Des Moines
Kansas........	Louise McNeal	Librarian	State Library	Topeka
Louisiana......	Essae M. Culver	State Librarian	State Library Commn.	Baton Rouge
Maine.........	Mrs. Marion B. Stubbs	State Librarian	State Library	Augusta
Maryland......	Louise E. Couper	State Librarian	State Library	Annapolis
Massachusetts...	Dennis A. Dooley	Librarian	State Library	Boston
Michigan......	Mrs. L. D. Fyan	State Librarian	State Library	Lansing
Minnesota......	Margaret S. Andrews	State Librarian	Law Library	St. Paul
Mississippi.....	Mrs. Julia Baylis Starnes	State Librarian	State Library	Jackson
Missouri.......	Paxton P. Price	State Librarian	State Library	Jefferson City
Montana.......	K. Ross Toole	Librarian	Historical Society	Helena
Nebraska.......	G. H. Turner	Librarian	State Library	Lincoln
Nevada........	Constance C. Collins	State Librarian	State Library	Carson City
New Hampshire.	Mrs. Mildred P. McKay	State Librarian	State Library	Concord
New Jersey.....	Roger H. McDonough	Dir., Div. of State Lib., Archives and History	Dept. of Education	Trenton
New Mexico....	Harrison MacDonald	Librarian	State Library	Santa Fe
New York......	Charles F. Gosnell	State Libn. and Asst. Commissr. for Libraries	Education Dept.	Albany
North Carolina..	Carrie L. Broughton	Librarian	State Library	Raleigh
North Dakota...	Hazel Webster Byrnes	Director	State Lib. Commn.	Bismarck
Ohio..........	Walter Brahm	Librarian	State Library	Columbus
Oklahoma......	Ralph Hudson	State Librarian	State Library	Oklahoma City
Oregon........	Eleanor Stephens	Librarian	State Library	Salem
Pennsylvania...	(Vacancy)	Dir., State Library	Dept. of Pub. Instr.	Harrisburg
Rhode Island...	Grace M. Sherwood	State Librarian	State Library	Providence
South Carolina..	Mrs. Virginia G. Moody	Librarian	State Library	Columbia
South Dakota...	Mercedes MacKay	Director	State Library	Pierre
Tennessee......	Dan M. Robison	State Librarian and Archivist	State Library	Nashville
Texas..........	Witt B. Harwell	State Librarian	State Library	Austin
Vermont.......	Lawrence J. Turgeon	State Librarian	State Library	Montpelier
Virginia.......	Randolph W. Church	State Librarian	State Library	Richmond

LIBRARY (State)—*continued*

State	*Name*	*Official Title*	*Agency*	*Location*
Washington....	Maryan E. Reynolds	State Librarian	State Library	Olympia
West Virginia...	Mrs. Dale Thomas	Historian and Archivist	Dept. of Archives and History	Charleston
Wisconsin......	Gilson G. Glasier	State Librarian	State Library	Madison
Wyoming......	May Gillies	State Librarian	State Library	Cheyenne
Alaska........	Dorothy Phelps	Territorial Librarian	Dept. of Library Service	Juneau
Guam.........	Mrs. Lucile Woelfl	Head Librarian	Terr. Library	Agana
Hawaii........	Mrs. Mabel Jackson	Head Librarian	Library of Hawaii	Honolulu
Puerto Rico....	Juan M. Alvarez	Act. Dir., Carnegie Library	Dept. of Education	San Juan
Virgin Islands ..	Nina A. C. Corneiro	Supervising Libn.	Govt. of the V. I.	St. Thomas
	Florence A. Williams	Librarian	Govt. of the V. I.	St. Croix

LIQUOR CONTROL

State	*Name*	*Official Title*	*Agency*	*Location*
Alabama.......	Harrold Hammonds	Chairman	Alcohol Bev. Control Bd.	Montgomery
Arizona........	John A. Duncan	Superintendent	Dept. of Liq. Lic. and Control	Phoenix
Arkansas.......	Rolla Fitch	Director	Alcoholic Bev. Control Bd.	Little Rock
California......	Russell S. Munro	Director	Dept. of Alcoholic Bev. Control	Sacramento
Colorado.......	George J. Baker	Secy. of State	Dept. of State	Denver
Connecticut....	T. Emmet Clarie	Chairman	Liq. Control Commn.	Hartford
Delaware......	John M. Conway	Chairman	Alcoholic Bev. Control Commn.	Wilmington
Florida........	J. D. Williamson	Director	Beverage Dept.	Tallahassee
Georgia........	Eston Ricketson	Chief Enforcement Officer	Revenue Dept.	Atlanta
	H. A. McElhannon	Spec. Agent-Licensing	Revenue Dept.	Atlanta
	L. R. Burns	Rev. Stamp Clerk	Revenue Dept.	Atlanta
Idaho.........	Fred Charlton	Superintendent	Liq. Dispensary	Boise
Illinois.........	L. B. Sackett	Chairman	Liq. Control Commn.	Springfield
Indiana........	Walter P. Weyland	Chairman	Alcoholic Bev. Commn.	Indianapolis
Iowa..........	Harold E. Wolfe	Chairman	Liquor Commn.	Des Moines
Kansas........	Charles W. Pratt	Director	Alcoholic Bev. Control	Topeka
Kentucky......	Guy C. Shearer	Commissioner	Dept. of Alcoholic Bev. Control	Frankfort
Louisiana......	Rufus W. Fontenot	Collector of Rev.	Dept. of Revenue	Baton Rouge
Maine.........	Ralph A. Gallagher	Chairman	Liquor Commn.	Augusta
Maryland......	Roger V. Laynor	Chief	Alcoholic Bev. Div.	Baltimore
Massachusetts...	Ernest L. Anger	Chairman	Alcoholic Bev. Control Commn.	Boston
Michigan......	Frank Blackford	Chairman	Liq. Control Commn.	Lansing
Minnesota......	Harry A. Sieben	Commissioner	Dept. Liq. Control	St. Paul
Missouri.......	Hollis M. Ketchum	Supervisor	Liq. Control Dept.	Jefferson City
Montana.......	John E. Manning	Administrator	Liq. Control Bd.	Helena
Nebraska.......	Carl Linn	Chairman	Liq. Control Commn.	Lincoln

LIQUOR CONTROL—*Continued*

State	Name	Official Title	Agency	Location
Nevada........	Grover Hillygus	Supervisor	Liq. and Cigarette Tax. Div.	Carson City
New Hampshire.	Wm. A. Jackson	Chairman	Liquor Commn.	Concord
New Jersey.....	Wm. Howe Davis	Dir., Div. of Alcoholic Bev. Control	Dept. of Law and Pub. Safety	Newark
New Mexico....	Hilton Dickson	Dir., Liquor Div.	Bureau of Revenue	Santa Fe
New York......	Thomas E. Rohan	Chmn., Liquor Auth.	Exec. Dept.	Albany
North Carolina..	T. W. Allen	Chairman	Bd. Alcoholic Control	Raleigh
North Dakota...	A. T. Johnson	Chief Inspector	Office of Atty. Gen.	Bismarck
Ohio..........	William C. Bryant	Director	Dept. of Liq. Control	Columbus
Oregon........	William H. Baillie	Administrator	Liq. Control Commn.	Portland
Pennsylvania...	Patrick E. Kerwin	Chairman	Liq. Control Bd.	Harrisburg
Rhode Island...	Charles F. Reynolds	Administrator	Dept. of Bus. Reg.	Providence
South Carolina..	Otis W. Livingston	Chairman	Tax Commission	Columbia
South Dakota...	W. R. Wilder	Commissioner	Div. of Revenue	Pierre
Tennessee......	James Montague	Dir., Alcoholic Bev., Beer and Tobacco Tax Div.	Dept. of Finance and Taxation	Nashville
Texas..........	Coke Stevenson, Jr.	Administrator	Liq. Control Bd.	Austin
Utah..........	J. William Pace	Chairman	Liq. Control Commn.	Salt Lake City
Vermont.......	Paul Harlow	Chairman	Liq. Control Bd.	Montpelier
Virginia.......	John W. Hardy	Chairman	Alcoholic Bev. Control Bd.	Richmond
Washington....	Evro M. Becket	Chairman	Liq. Control Bd.	Olympia
West Virginia...	Frank King	Chairman	Liq. Control Commn.	Charleston
Wisconsin......	D. H. Prichard	Dir., Div. of Bev. and Cigarette Tax	Dept. of Taxation	Madison
Wyoming......	Earl Wright	Director	Liquor Commn.	Cheyenne
Guam.........	Victor Olson	Chairman	Alcoholic Bev. Control Bd.	Agana
Hawaii........	M. B. Carson	Chairman	Liquor Commn. for Honolulu	Honolulu
Puerto Rico....	Janson Colberg	Chief, Bur. of Alcoholic Bev. Taxes	Dept. of Treasury	San Juan
Virgin Islands...	Charles K. Claunch	Chairman	Alcohol Control Bd.	St. Thomas

MATERNAL AND CHILD WELFARE

State	Name	Official Title	Agency	Location
Alabama.......	Mrs. Edward Gresham	Dir., Bur. of Child Welf.	Dept. of Pensions and Security	Montgomery
Arizona........	Ann Bracken	Supvr., Child Welf. Serv.	Pub. Welf. Dept.	Phoenix
Arkansas......	Ruth Johnston	Dir., Child Welf.	Welfare Dept.	Little Rock
California......	Lucile Kennedy	Chief, Child Welf. Div.	Dept. Social Welf.	Sacramento
California......	Leslie Corsa, Jr., M.D.	Chief, Bur. of Maternal and Child Health	Dept. of Pub. Health	Berkeley
Colorado.......	Guy R. Justis	Director	Dept. of Pub. Welf.	Denver
Connecticut....	Martha L. Clifford, M.D.	Dir., Bur. of Maternal and Child Health	Health Dept.	Hartford
Florida........	Chas. G. Lavin	Director	Dept. of Pub. Welf.	Jacksonville
Georgia........	Frances M. Vance	Chief, Child Welf. Sect.	Sect. of Child Welf.	Atlanta
Georgia........	Harold Parker	Dir., Div. Soc. Admin.	Dept. of Pub. Welf.	Atlanta

MATERNAL AND CHILD WELFARE—*continued*

State	Name	Official Title	Agency	Location
Idaho.........	L. J. Peterson	Director	Bd. of Health	Boise
Illinois.........	Roman L. Haremski	Supt., Div. of Child Welf.	Dept. of Pub. Welf.	Springfield
Indiana........	Jeanne Rybolt, M.D.	Dir., Div. Maternal and Child Health	Bd. of Health	Indianapolis
Iowa..........	Ross T. Wilbur	Dir., Child Welf.	Dept. of Social Welf.	Des Moines
Kansas........	Dorothy W. Bradley	Dir., Div. of Child Welf.	Social Welf. Dept.	Topeka
Kentucky......	Lad R. Mezera, M.D.	Dir., Div. of Maternal and Child Health	Dept. of Health	Louisville
	Kenneth Foresman	Dir., Childrens' Bur.	Dept. of Welf.	Frankfort
Louisiana......	S. J. Phillips	President	Bd. of Health	New Orleans
Maine.........	Ella Langer, M.D.	Dir., Maternal and Child Health	Dept. of Health and Welf.	Augusta
Maryland......	Edward Davens, M.D.	Chief	Bur. Maternal and Child Health and Services for Crippled Children	Baltimore
Massachusetts...	Robert F. Ott	Dir., Div. of Child Guardianship	Dept. of Pub. Welf.	Boston
Michigan......	Goldie Corneliuson, M.D.	Chief, Sec. of Maternal and Child Health	Dept. of Health	Lansing
Minnesota......	Roberta Rindfleisch	Dir., Div. of Child Welf.	Dept. of Welf.	St. Paul
Mississippi.....	J. A. Thigpen	Commissioner	Dept. of Pub. Welf.	Jackson
Missouri.......	Proctor N. Carter	Dir., Div. of Welf.	Dept. of Pub. Health and Welf.	Jefferson City
Montana.......	Katherine E. Dawson	Dir., Child Health Services	Bd. of Health	Helena
Nebraska.......	Mayme Stukel	Director	Div. of Pub. Welfare	Lincoln
Nevada........	Barbara C. Coughlan	Director	Welfare Dept.	Reno
New Hampshire.	Ursula G. Sanders, M.D.	Director, Bur. of Maternal and Child Health and Crippled Children's Services	Dept. of Health	Concord
	Viennie Borton	Child Welfare Supvr.	Dept. of Pub. Welfare	Concord
New Jersey.....	J. E. Alloway	Exec. Dir., Bd. of Child Welf.	Dept. of Institutions and Agencies	Trenton
New Mexico....	Alvina Looram, M.D.	Dir. Maternal and Child Health	Dept. of Pub. Health	Santa Fe
New York......	Winford Oliphant	Dir., Child Welf., Div. of Welf. and Med. Care	Dept. of Social Welf.	Albany
North Carolina..	A. H. Elliot, M.D.	Dir. of Personal Health	Bd. of Health	Raleigh
North Dakota...	Carlyle D. Onsrud	Exec. Dir., Child Welf. Serv.	Pub. Welfare Bd.	Bismarck
Ohio..........	Henry J. Robison	Director	Dept. of Pub. Welf.	Columbus
Oklahoma......	Laura E. Dester	Supv., Child Welf. Div.	Dept. of Pub. Welf.	Oklahoma City
	John W. Shackleford, M.D.	Act. Dir., Maternal and Child Health Div.	Dept. of Health	Oklahoma City
Oregon........	M. D. Vest, M.D.	Dir., Maternal and Child Health Sec.	Bd. of Health	Portland
Pennsylvania...	G. H. Black	Chief, Div. of Youth Services	Dept. of Welf.	Harrisburg
	Eleanore Mechelnburg	Act. Chief, Div. of Rural Child Welf.	Dept. of Welf.	Harrisburg
Rhode Island...	Francis V. Corrigan, M.D.	Chief, Div. of Maternal and Child Health	Dept. of Health	Providence

MATERNAL AND CHILD WELFARE—*continued*

State	Name	Official Title	Agency	Location
South Carolina..	Mrs. Deborah M. Southerlin	Chief, Div. of Child Welf.	Dept. of Pub. Welf.	Columbia
South Dakota...	Grace Martin	Director	Public Welfare	Pierre
Tennessee......	(Vacancy)	Dir., Div. of Child Welfare	Dept. of Pub. Welf.	Nashville
Texas.........	Rosalind Giles	Dir., Child Welf. Div.	Dept. of Pub. Welf.	Austin
Utah..........	Joseph P. Kesler	Act. Director	Health Dept.	Salt Lake City
	John Farr Larson	Dir., Bur. of Servs. for Children	Dept. of Pub. Welf.	Salt Lake City
Vermont.......	Frances M. Bates	Dir., Child Welfare Service	Social Welf. Dept.	Montpelier
Virginia.......	L. L. Shamburger, M.D.	Dir., Specialized Medical Services	Dept. of Health	Richmond
Washington....	J. L. Jones, M.D.	Chief, Maternal and Child Health Prog.	Dept. of Health	Seattle
West Virginia...	Helen Belknap Fraser, M.D.	Dir., Div. of Maternal and Child Hygiene	Dept. of Health	Charleston
	Charles E. Kenney	Chief, Div. of Child Welfare	Dept. of Pub. Assist.	Charleston
Wisconsin......	P. Frederick Delliquadri	Dir., Children and Youth	Dept. of Pub. Welf.	Madison
	Amy Louise Hunter, M.D.	Dir., Maternal and Child Health	Bd. of Health	Madison
Wyoming......	Franklin D. Yoder, M.D.	Director	Bd. of Health	Cheyenne
Alaska.........	C. Earl Albrecht, M.D.	Commissr. of Health, Welf.	Dept. of Health	Juneau
	Henry A. Harmon	Director	Dept. of Pub. Welf.	Juneau
Guam.........	John E. Kennedy M.D.	Director	Dept. of Medical Services	Oka, Tamuning
Hawaii........	Angie Connor, M.D.	Chief, Bur. of Maternal and Child Health and Crippled Children	Bd. of Health	Honolulu
Puerto Rico....	Dolores M. Piñero, M.D.	Chief, Bur. of Maternal and Infant Hygiene	Dept. of Health	San Juan
Virgin Islands..	Roy W. Bornn	Commissr. Soc. Welfare	Govt. of the V. I.	St. Thomas

MENTAL HEALTH

State	Name	Official Title	Agency	Location
Alabama......	John M. McKee, Ph.D.	Dir., Div. of Mental Hygiene	Dept. of Pub. Health	Montgomery
Arizona.......	Clarence G. Salsbury, M.D.	Commissioner	Dept. of Health	Phoenix
Arkansas......	Edgar J. Easley, M.D.	Dir., Bur. of Local Health Servs.	Board of Health	Little Rock
California.....	Portia Bell Hume, M.D.	Dep. Dir., Community Servs.	Dept. of Mental Hygiene	Sacramento
Colorado......	Lynwood M. Hopple, M.D.	Dir. of Mental Hygiene	Dept. of Pub. Health	Denver
Connecticut....	Elias J. Marsh, M.D.	Dir., Div. of Community Servs.	Dept. of Mental Health	Hartford
Delaware......	M. A. Tarumianz, M.D.	Superintendent	State Hospital	Farnhurst
Florida........	Paul Penningroth, M.D.	Dir., Div. of Mental Health	Board of Health	Jacksonville
Georgia.......	Guy V. Rice, M.D.	Dir., Div. of Mental Hygiene	Dept. of Pub. Health	Atlanta
Idaho.........	Dale D. Cornell, M.D.	Dir., Mental Health Section	Dept. of Pub. Health	Boise

MENTAL HEALTH—*continued*

State	Name	Official Title	Agency	Location
Illinois........	Charles Meeker	Asst. Dep. Dir. for Mental Health Service	Dept. of Pub. Welfare	Springfield
Indiana.......	Margaret E. Morgan, M.D.	Commissioner	Division of Mental Health	Indianapolis
Iowa.........	Wilbur R. Miller, M.D.	Dir., Psychopathic Hosp.	Univ. of Iowa	Iowa City
Kansas........	Leila N. Myers	Dir., Div. of Mental Hygiene	Board of Health	Topeka
Kentucky......	Frank M. Gaines, Jr., M.D.	Commissioner	Dept. of Mental Health	Louisville
Louisiana......	Edward D. Grant	Director	Dept. of Insts.	Baton Rouge
Maine........	Margaret R. Simpson, M.D.	Dir., Div. of Mental Health	Dept. of Health & Welfare	Augusta
Maryland.....	Robert E. Thomas, M.D.	Chief, Div. of Mental Hygiene	Dept. of Health	Baltimore
Massachusetts..	Warren T. Vaughan, Jr., M.D.	Dir., Div. of Mental Hygiene	Dept. of Mental Health	Boston
Michigan......	Charles F. Wagg	Director	Dept. of Mental Health	Lansing
Minnesota.....	Dale C. Cameron, M.D.	Medical Director	Dept. of Welfare	St. Paul
Mississippi.....	Felix J. Underwood, M.D.	Exec. Officer and Secy.	Board of Health	Jackson
Missouri.......	James R. Amos, M.D.	Director of Health	Dept. of Pub. Health & Welf.	Jefferson City
Montana......	Robert J. Spratt, M.D.	Superintendent	State Hospital	Warm Springs
Nebraska......	Earl A. Rogers, M.D.	Director	Dept. of Health	Lincoln
Nevada.......	Martin S. Levine	Chief, Mental Health Section	Dept. of Health	Reno
New Hampshire	Anna L. Philbrook, M.D.	Director	Mental Hyg. & Child Guid. Clinic	Concord
New Jersey....	Robert C. Myers	Chief, Community Mental Health Servs.	Dept. of Insts. & Agencies	Trenton
New Mexico...	Mary Allen, M.D.	Dir., Div. of Mental Health	Dept. of Pub. Health	Santa Fe
New York.....	Robert C. Hunt, M.D.	Director, Community Mental Health Servs.	Dept. of Mental Hygiene	Albany
North Carolina.	Edward S. Haswell	Chief, Mental Health Section	Board of Health	Raleigh
North Dakota..	Walter J. Swensen, Ph.D.	Dir., Div. of Mental Hygiene	Dept. of Health	Bismarck
Ohio..........	John D. Porterfield, M.D.	Director	Dept. of Mental Hyg. & Correction	Columbus
Oklahoma.....	A. A. Hellams, M.D.	Dir., Div. of Mental Hygiene	Dept. of Health	Oklahoma City
Oregon........	John H. Waterman, M.D.	Dir., Mental Health Section	Board of Health	Portland
Pennsylvania...	Hilding Bengs, M.D.	Dir., Bureau of Mental Health	Dept. of Welfare	Harrisburg
Rhode Island...	Charles M. Goodman, M.D.	Admin., Mental Hygiene	Dept. of Soc. Welfare	Providence
South Carolina.	W. P. Beckman, M.D.	Director	Mental Health Commission	Columbia
South Dakota..	Florence B. Dunn	Admin., Mental Health Section	Dept. of Health	Pierre
Tennessee.....	Cyril J. Ruilmann, M.D.	Commissioner	Dept. of Mental Health	Nashville
Texas.........	Charles S. Mitchell	Director Div. of Mental Health	Dept. of Health	Austin
Utah..........	C. H. Hardin Branch, M.D.	Dir., Dept. of Psychiatry	Univ. of Utah	Salt Lake City

MENTAL HEALTH—*continued*

State	Name	Official Title	Agency	Location
Vermont......	Robert B. Aiken, M.D.	Commissioner	Dept. of Health	Burlington
Virginia.......	Joseph E. Barrett, M.D.	Commissioner	Dept. of Mental Hyg. & Hosps.	Richmond
Washington....	Daniel L. Prosser	Consult., Mental Health Section	Dept. of Health	Seattle
West Virginia..	Jackson C. Rhudy	Dir., Bur. of Mental Hygiene	Dept. of Health	Charleston
Wisconsin.....	Leslie A. Osborn, M.D.	Dir., Div. of Mental Hygiene	Dept. of Pub. Welfare	Madison
Wyoming......	Franklin D. Yoder, M.D.	Director	Dept. of Pub. Health	Cheyenne
Alaska........	C. Earl Albrecht, M.D.	Commissioner	Dept. of Health	Juneau
Hawaii........	Elmer W. Haertig, M.D.	Dir., Div. of Mental Health	Dept. of Health	Honolulu
Puerto Rico....	Mrs. Dolores G. LaCaro	Chief, Bur. of Mental Health	Dept. of Health	San Juan
Virgin Islands..	Roy A. Anduze, M.D.	Commissr. of Health	Govt. of the V.I.	St. Thomas

MENTAL HOSPITALS

State	Name	Official Title	Agency	Location
Alabama......	J. S. Tarwater, M.D.	Superintendent	State Hospitals	Tuscaloosa
Arizona.......	Samuel A. Wick, M.D.	Director	State Hospital	Phoenix
Arkansas......	Ewing H. Crawfis, M.D.	Superintendent	State Hospital	Little Rock
California.....	Walter Rapaport, M.D.	Director	Dept. of Mental Hygiene	Sacramento
Colorado......	Herbert E. Allen	Director	Dept. of Pub. Insts.	Denver
Connecticut....	John J. Blasko, M.D.	Commissioner	Dept. of Mental Health	Hartford
Delaware......	M. A. Tarumianz, M.D.	Superintendent	State Hospital	Farnhurst
Florida........	W. D. Rogers, M.D.	Superintendent	State Hospital	Chattahoochee
Georgia.......	T. G. Peacock, M.D.	Superintendent	Milledgeville State Hosp.	Milledgeville
Idaho........	L. J. Peterson	Director	Bd. of Health	Boise
Illinois........	Otto L. Bettag, M.D.	Director	Dept. of Pub. Welfare	Springfield
Indiana.......	Margaret E. Morgan, M.D.	Commissioner	Division of Mental Health	Indianapolis
Iowa..........	Henry W. Burma	Chairman	Bd. of Contr. of St. Insts.	Des Moines
Kansas........	George W. Jackson, M.D.	Dir. of Institutions	Dept. of Soc. Welf.	Topeka
Kentucky......	Frank M. Gaines, Jr., M.D.	Commissioner	Dept. of Mental Health	Louisville
Louisiana......	Edward D. Grant	Director	Dept. of Insts.	Baton Rouge
Maine........	Norman U. Greenlaw	Commissioner	Dept. of Instl. Serv.	Augusta
Maryland.....	Clifton T. Perkins, M.D.	Commissioner	Dept. of Mental Hygiene	Baltimore
Massachusetts..	Jack R. Ewalt, M.D.	Commissioner	Dept. of Mental Health	Boston
Michigan......	Charles F. Wagg	Director	Dept. of Mental Health	Lansing
Minnesota.....	Dale C. Cameron, M.D.	Medical Director	Dept. of Welfare	St. Paul
Mississippi.....	R. C. Stovall	Chairman	Board of Mental Insts.	Columbus
Missouri.......	B. E. Ragland	Dir., Div. of Mental Diseases	Dept. of Pub. Health & Welf.	Jefferson City

MENTAL HOSPITALS—*continued*

State	Name	Official Title	Agency	Location
Montana......	Robert J. Spratt, M.D.	Superintendent	State Hospital	Warm Springs
Nebraska......	Cecil L. Wittson, M.D.	Dir. of Mental Health	Bd. of Control of State Insts.	Omaha
Nevada.......	Sidney J. Tillim, M.D.	Superintendent	State Hospital	Reno
New Hampshire	Earl K. Holt, M.D.	Superintendent	State Hospital	Concord
New Jersey....	John W. Tramburg	Commissioner	Dept. of Insts. & Agencies	Trenton
New Mexico...	C. G. Stillinger, M.D.	Superintendent	State Hospital	Las Vegas
New York.....	Paul H. Hoch, M.D.	Commissioner	Dept. of Mental Hygiene	Albany
North Carolina.	James W. Murdoch, M.D.	General Superintendent	Hospitals Bd. of Control	Raleigh
North Dakota..	Russell O. Saxvik, M.D.	Superintendent	State Hospital	Jamestown
Ohio..........	John D. Porterfield, M.D.	Director	Dept. of Mental Hyg. & Correction	Columbus
Oklahoma.....	Hayden H. Donahue, M.D.	Director	Dept. of Mental Health	Oklahoma City
Oregon........	E. J. Ireland	Secretary	Board of Control	Salem
Pennsylvania...	Hilding Bengs, M.D.	Dir., Bureau of Mental Health	Dept. of Welfare	Harrisburg
Rhode Island...	Trawick H. Stubbs, M.D.	Assistant Director	Dept. of Soc. Welfare	Providence
South Carolina.	W. P. Beckman, M.D.	Director	Mental Health Commission	Columbia
South Dakota..	Charles D. Yohe, M.D.	Superintendent	Yankton State Hospital	Yankton
Tennessee.....	Cyril J. Ruilmann, M.D.	Commissioner	Dept. of Mental Health	Nashville
Texas.........	James A. Bethea, M.D.	Executive Director	Bd. for Texas State Hosps. & Special Schools	Austin
Utah..........	H. C. Shoemaker	Chairman, Pub. Welf. Comm.	Dept. of Public Welfare	Salt Lake City
Vermont......	Timothy C. Dale	Commissioner	Dept. of Insts.	Montpelier
Virginia.......	Joseph E. Barrett, M.D.	Commissioner	Dept. of Mental Hyg. & Hosps.	Richmond
Washington....	Thomas A. Harris, M.D.	Director	Dept. of Pub. Insts.	Olympia
West Virginia..	James M. Donohoe	President	Board of Control	Charleston
Wisconsin	Leslie A. Osborn, M.D.	Dir., Div. of Mental Hygiene	Dept. of Pub. Welfare	Madison
Wyoming......	Joseph F. Whalen, M.D.	Superintendent	State Hospital	Evanston
Alaska........	C. Earl Albrecht, M.D.	Commissioner	Dept. of Health	Juneau
Guam	John Kennedy, M.D.	Dir., Med. Services	Govt. of Guam	Satpon Point, Tamuning
Hawaii........	Charles H. Silva, D.D.S.	Director	Dept. of Insts.	Honolulu
Puerto Rico ...	Victor Bernal y Del Río, M.D.	Director	Psychiatric Hospital	Río Piedras
Virgin Islands..	R. A. Anduze, M.D.	Commissr. of Health	Govt. of the V.I.	St. Thomas

MINES

State	Name	Official Title	Agency	Location
Alabama.......	H. T. Williams	Chief of Mines and Ind. Safety	Dept. of Ind. Relations	Birmingham
Arizona........	Edward Massey	Mine Inspec.	Off. of Mine Inspec.	Phoenix
Arkansas.......	J. H. Berry	Mine Inspec.	Off. of Mine Inspec.	Ft. Smith
California......	Olaf P. Jenkins	Chief, Div. of Mines	Dept. Nat. Resources	San Francisco

MINES—*continued*

State	Name	Official Title	Agency	Location
Colorado.......	Walter E. Scott	Commissioner	Bur. of Mines	Denver
Georgia........	Garland Peyton	Director	Dept. of Mines, Mining, Geology	Atlanta
Idaho.........	George McDowell	Mine Inspec.	Off. of Mine Inspec.	Boise
Illinois.........	Ben H. Schull	Director	Dept. of Mines and Minerals	Springfield
Indiana........	Charles Purcell	Director	Bur. of Mines and Mining	Terre Haute
Iowa..........	{ Wm. H. Jervis	Mine Inspector	State Mining Dept.	Des Moines
	{ T. C. Chapman	Mine Inspector	State Mining Dept.	Des Moines
Kansas........	A. B. De Gasperi	Chairman	Mine Examining Bd.	Pittsburg
Kentucky......	A. D. Sisk	Chief, Dept. of Mines and Minerals	Univ. of Kentucky	Lexington
Maine.........	Paul A. MacDonald	Chairman	Mining Bureau	Augusta
Maryland......	Frank J. Powers	Director	Bureau of Mines	Westernport
Michigan......	William L. Daoust	State Geologist	Conservation Dept.	Lansing
Minnesota......	Ray D. Nolan	Dir., Div. of Lands and Minerals	Dept. of Conserv.	St. Paul
Missouri.......	Floyd E. Henson	Dir., Div. of Mine Inspection	Dept. of Labor and Ind. Rel.	Jefferson City
Montana.......	Robt. F. Swanberg	Chairman	Ind. Accident Bd.	Helena
Nevada........	Mervin J. Gallagher	Inspec. of Mines	Off. of Inspec. of Mines	Carson City
New Mexico....	John A. Garcia	Mine Inspector	Off. of Mine Inspec.	Albuquerque
New York......	Edward A. Nyegaard	Deputy Commissr., Div. of Ind. Hygiene and Safety Standards	Labor Dept.	New York City
North Carolina.	Jasper L. Stuckey	Geologist	Dept. of Conserv. and Devel.	Raleigh
North Dakota...	G. B. Easton	Mine Inspector	Mine Foreman Examining Bd.	Bismarck
Ohio..........	Harry J. Dusz	Chief	Div. of Mines and Mining	Columbus
Oklahoma......	John M. Malloy	Chief Mine Inspector	Mines Dept.	Oklahoma City
Oregon........	Hollis M. Dole	Director	Dept. of Geol. and Mineral Industries	Portland
Pennsylvania...	Joseph T. Kennedy	Secy. of Mines	Dept. of Mines	Harrisburg
South Dakota...	John Treweek	Mine Inspector	Dept. of Mines	Lead
Tennessee......	J. R. Miller	Chief Inspec., Div. of Mines	Dept. of Labor	Nashville
Texas.........	M. B. Morgan	Commissioner	Bur. of Labor Stat.	Austin
Utah..........	Arthur L. Crawford	Dir., Geological and Mineralogical Survey	Univ. of Utah	Salt Lake City
Vermont.......	Charles G. Doll	Geologist	Devel. Commn.	Burlington
Virginia.......	Creed P. Kelly	Mine Inspec., Div. of Mines	Dept. of Labor and Industry	Richmond
Washington....	Sheldon J. Glover	Supvr., Div. of Mines and Geol.	Dept. of Conserv. and Devel.	Olympia
West Virginia...	Julius C. Olzer	Chief	Dept. of Mines	Charleston
Wisconsin......	George F. Hanson	State Geologist	Univ. of Wisconsin	Madison
Wyoming......	Lyman Fearn	Inspector	Mine Inspec. Off.	Rock Springs
Alaska.........	Phil R. Holdsworth	Commissioner	Dept. of Mines	Juneau
Puerto Rico....	Roberto Sánchez-Vilella	Secretary	Dept. of Public Works	San Juan

MOTOR VEHICLES (Licensing and Registration)

State	Name	Official Title	Agency	Location
Alabama.......	H. S. Phifer	Chief, Motor Vehicle and License Div.	Dept. of Revenue	Montgomery

MOTOR VEHICLES (Licensing and Registration)—*continued*

State	Name	Official Title	Agency	Location
Arizona........	C. L. Lane	Supt., Motor Vehicle Div.	Highway Dept.	Phoenix
Arkansas.......	W. H. L. Woodyard	Dir., Mot. Veh. Div.	Revenue Dept.	Little Rock
California.....	Paul Mason	Director	Dept. of Mot. Vehs.	Sacramento
Colorado.......	Earl Blevins	Dir. of Revenue	Dept. of Revenue	Denver
Connecticut....	John J. Tynan	Commissioner	Motor Vehicles Dept.	Hartford
Delaware......	Harvey B. Spicer	Commissioner	Motor Vehicle Div.	Dover
Florida........	Ina S. Thompson	Commissioner	Motor Vehicle Dept.	Tallahassee
Georgia........	W. M. Wheeler	Dir., Mot. Veh. License Unit	Dept. of Revenue	Atlanta
Idaho.........	Earle E. Koehler	Commissioner	Dept. of Law Enforcement	Boise
Illinois.........	W. B. Westbrook	Chief Clerk, Auto. Dept.	Off. of Secy. of State	Springfield
Indiana........	Morris J. Carter	Commissioner	Bur. of Mot. Vehs.	Indianapolis
Iowa..........	John Carlson	Supt., Mot. Veh. Div.	Public Safety Dept.	Des Moines
Kansas........	Ed J. Camp	Commissioner	Motor Veh. Dept.	Topeka
Kentucky......	John M. Kinnaird	Commissioner	Dept. of Motor Transp.	Frankfort
Louisiana.....	Rufus W. Fontenot	Collector	Dept. of Revenue	Baton Rouge
Maine.........	Stanton S. Weed	Dir., Mot. Veh. Div.	Off. of Secy. of State	Augusta
Maryland.... .	Frank Small	Commissioner	Dept. of Mot. Vehs.	Baltimore
Massachusetts...	Rudolph F. King	Registrar	Div. of Registry of Mot. Vehs.	Boston
Michigan......	Lee C. Richardson	Dir., Div. of Driver and Vehicle Services	Off. of Secy. of State	Lansing
Minnesota......	W. E. Howes	Asst. Mot. Veh. Registrar	Off. of Secy. of State	St. Paul
Mississippi....	Guy McCullen	Comptroller	Dept. of Mot. Vehs.	Jackson
Missouri.......	David A. Bryan	Supvr., Mot. Veh. Unit	Dept. of Revenue	Jefferson City
Montana.......	Fay O. Burrell	Registrar of Mot. Vehs.	Off. of Registrar	Deer Lodge
Nebraska.......	Dale A. Rogers	Dir., Mot. Veh. Div.	Dept. of Roads and Irrigation	Lincoln
Nevada........	Richard A. Herz	Director	Div. of Motor Vehicle Registration	Carson City
New Hampshire.	Frederick N. Clarke	Commissioner	Motor Vehicle Dept.	Concord
New Jersey.....	Frederick J. Gassert, Jr.	Dir., Div. of Motor Vehicles	Dept. of Law and Public Safety	Trenton
New Mexico....	Tony Lucero	Dir., Mot. Veh. Div.	Bureau of Revenue	Santa Fe
New York......	Joseph P. Kelly	Commissr., Bur. of Motor Vehicles	Dept. of Taxation and Finance	Albany
North Carolina .	Edward Scheidt	Commissioner	Dept. of Mot. Vehs.	Raleigh
North Dakota...	A. N. Lavik	Registrar	Motor Vehicle Dept.	Bismarck
Ohio..........	C. Erwin Nofer	Act. Registrar	Bur. of Mot. Vehs.	Columbus
Oklahoma......	Francis D. Murphy	Dir., Mot. Veh. Tax Div.	Tax Commission	Oklahoma City
Oregon........	Earl T. Newbry	Secy. of State	Off. of Secy. of State	Salem
Pennsylvania...	Charles M. Dougherty	Dir., Bur. of Mot. Vehicles	Dept. of Revenue	Harrisburg
Rhode Island...	Laure B. Lussier	Registrar of Motor Vehicles	Executive Dept.	Providence
South Carolina..	H. E. Quarles	Dir., Mot. Veh. Div.	Highway Dept.	Columbia
South Dakota...	Geraldine Ostroot	Secy. of State	Off. of Secy. of State	Pierre
Tennessee......	Tom M. Stewart	Dir., Mot. Veh. Title and Regis. Div.	Dept. of Fin. and Tax.	Nashville
	J. Vaughan Blake	Dir., Div. of Title Registration	Dept. of Safety	Nashville
Texas..........	DeWitt C. Greer	Highway Engineer	Highway Dept.	Austin
Utah..........	Leo B. Miles	Director	Motor Vehicle Div., Tax Commission	Salt Lake City

MOTOR VEHICLES (Licensing and Registration)—*continued*

State	Name	Official Title	Agency	Location
Vermont.......	H. Elmer Marsh	Commissioner	Dept. of Mot. Vehs.	Montpelier
Virginia.......	C. H. Lamb	Commissioner	Div. of Mot. Vehs.	Richmond
Washington....	Mrs. Della Urquhart	Director	Dept. of Licenses	Olympia
West Virginia...	Joseph P. Condry	Commissioner	Dept. of Mot. Vehs.	Charleston
Wisconsin......	Dan Schutz	Dir. of Registration	Motor Vehicle Dept.	Madison
Wyoming......	William R. Bradley	Director	Motor Vehicle Div.	Cheyenne
Alaska........	Karl F. Dewey	Tax Commissioner	Dept. of Taxation	Juneau
Guam.........	George W. Ingling	Commissr., Rev. and Taxation	Dept. of Finance	Agana
Hawaii.......	Lawrence S. Goto	Treasurer	City and County of Honolulu	Honolulu
Puerto Rico....	Carlos A. Tallada	Chief, Div. of Motor Vehicles	Dept. of Public Works	San Juan
Virgin Islands..	George N. Matthias	Act. Commissr. of Pub. Safety	Govt. of the V. I.	St. Thomas

MOTOR VEHICLE TAX

State	Name	Official Title	Agency	Location
Alabama.......	H. S. Phifer	Chief, Mot. Veh. and License Div.	Dept. of Revenue	Montgomery
Arizona........	C. L. Lane	Supt., Mot. Veh. Div.	Highway Dept.	Phoenix
Arkansas.......	Leonard L. Stewart	Dir., Mot. Fuel Tax Div.	Revenue Dept.	Little Rock
California......	Paul Mason	Director	Dept. of Mot. Vehs.	Sacramento
Colorado.......	Earl Blevins	Director	Dept. of Revenue	Denver
Florida........	Ina S. Thompson	Commissioner	Mot. Veh. Dept.	Tallahassee
Georgia........	W. M. Wheeler	Dir., Mot. Veh. License Unit	Revenue Dept.	Atlanta
Idaho.........	P. G. Neill	Tax Collector	Off. of Tax Coll.	Boise
Illinois.........	Charles F. Carpentier	Secy. of State	Off. of Secy. of State	Springfield
Indiana........	Morris J. Carter	Commissioner	Bur. of Mot. Veh.	Indianapolis
Iowa..........	John Carlson	Supt., Mot. Veh. Div.	Pub. Safety Dept.	Des Moines
Kentucky......	David Walker	Dir., Mot. Veh. Div.	Dept. of Revenue	Frankfort
Louisiana......	Rufus W. Fontenot	Commissioner	Dept. of Revenue	Baton Rouge
Maryland......	Frank Small	Commissioner	Dept. of Mot. Vehs.	Baltimore
Massachusetts...	Albert H. Stitt	Dir., Bur. of Excises	Dept. of Corp. and Taxation	Boston
Mississippi......	Guy McCullen	Comptroller	Mot. Veh. Comptr.	Jackson
Missouri.......	David A. Bryan	Supvr., Mot. Veh. and Drivers' License	Dept. of Revenue	Jefferson City
Montana.......	Fay O. Burrell	Registrar of Mot. Vehs.	Off. of Registrar of Mot. Vehs.	Deer Lodge
Nebraska.......	Dale A. Rogers	Dir., Mot. Veh. Div.	Dept. of Roads and Irrigation	Lincoln
New Jersey.....	Frederick J. Gassert, Jr.	Dir., Div. of Mot. Vehs.	Dept. of Law and Public Safety	Trenton
New Mexico....	Tony Lucero	Dir., Mot. Veh. Div.	Bur. of Revenue	Santa Fe
North Dakota...	A. N. Lavik	Registrar	Mot. Veh. Dept.	Bismarck
Ohio..........	Stanley J. Bowers	Tax. Commissr.	Dept. of Taxation	Columbus
Oklahoma......	Francis Murphy	Dir., Mot. Veh. Div.	Tax. Commn.	Oklahoma City
Oregon........	Earl T. Newbry	Secy. of State	Off. of Secy. of State	Salem
Pennsylvania...	Charles M. Dougherty	Dir., Bur. Mot. Vehs.	Dept. of Revenue	Harrisburg
South Carolina..	H. E. Quarles	Dir., Mot. Veh. Div.	Highway Dept.	Columbia
South Dakota...	E. S. Goff	Director	Mot. Veh. Div.	Pierre

MOTOR VEHICLE TAX—*continued*

State	Name	Official Title	Agency	Location
Tennessee......	Tom M. Stewart	Dir., Mot. Veh. Title and Regis. Div.	Dept. of Fin. and Taxation	Nashville
Texas.........	Robert S. Calvert	Comptr. of Pub. Accts.	Off. of Comptr.	Austin
Utah.........	Leo B. Miles	Director	Mot. Veh. Reg., Tax Commission	Salt Lake City
Vermont.......	H. Elmer Marsh	Commissioner	Dept. Mot. Vehs.	Montpelier
Virginia.......	C. H. Lamb	Commissioner	Div. of Mot. Vehs.	Richmond
Washington....	H. Dan Bracken	Chairman	Tax Commn.	Olympia
West Virginia...	Joseph P. Condry	Commissioner	Dept. of Mot. Vehs.	Charleston
Wisconsin......	Melvin O. Larson	Commissioner	Mot. Veh. Dept.	Madison
Wyoming......	J. R. Bromley	Highway Supt.	Highway Dept.	Cheyenne
Guam.........	George W. Ingling	Commissr., Rev. and Taxation	Dept. of Finance	Agana
Hawaii........	Lawrence S. Goto	Treasurer	City and County of Honolulu	Honolulu
Puerto Rico.....	Juan B. Pérez	Chief, Bur. of Collections	Dept. of Treasury	San Juan

NATURAL RESOURCES

See also Fish and Game, Forestry, Geology Mines, Oil and Gas,
Soil Conservation, Water Pollution Control, Water Resources Control.

State	Name	Official Title	Agency	Location
Alabama.......	W. H. Drinkard	Director	Dept. of Conserv.	Montgomery
Arizona........	John M. Hall	Director	Game and Fish Commn.	Phoenix
Arkansas.......	Norman Williams	Geologist-Director	Geological and Conserv. Commn.	Little Rock
California......	DeWitt Nelson	Director	Dept. of Natural Resources	Sacramento
Colorado.......	Ivan C. Crawford	Director	Water Conserv. Bd.	Denver
Florida........	Ernest C. Mitts	Director	Bd. of Conserv.	Tallahassee
Idaho.........	Mark R. Kulp	Reclamation Engr.	Dept. of Reclamation	Boise
Illinois.........	Glen D. Palmer	Director	Dept. of Conserv.	Springfield
Indiana........	Harley Hook	Director	Dept. of Conserv.	Indianapolis
Iowa..........	H. G. Hershey	Chairman	Nat. Resources Council	Des Moines
Kentucky......	Henry Ward	Commissioner	Dept. of Conserv.	Frankfort
Louisiana......	John B. Hussey	Commissioner	Dept. of Conserv.	Baton Rouge
Maryland......	John Tawes	Chairman	Bd. of Natural Resources	Annapolis
Massachusetts...	Arthur T. Lyman	Commissioner	Dept. of Natural Resources	Boston
Michigan......	Gerald E. Eddy	Director	Conserv. Dept.	Lansing
Minnesota......	George Selke	Commissioner	Dept. of Conserv.	St. Paul
Missouri.......	Irwin T. Bode	Director	Conserv. Commn.	Jefferson City
Montana.......	Fred Buck	State Engr.	Water Conserv. Bd.	Helena
Nebraska.......	C. V. Price	Director	Conservation and Survey Div.	Lincoln
New Jersey.....	Joseph E. McLean	Commissioner	Dept. of Conserv. and Econ. Devel.	Trenton
New York......	Louis A. Wehle	Commissioner	Conservation Dept.	Albany
North Carolina..	Ben E. Douglas	Director	Dept. of Conserv. and Development	Raleigh
Ohio..........	A. W. Marion	Director	Dept. of Natural Resources	Columbus
Oklahoma......	W. K. Haynie, M.D.	Chairman	Planning and Resources Bd.	Oklahoma City
Oregon........	(Vacancy)	Exec. Secretary	Comm. on Natural Resources	Salem

NATURAL RESOURCES—*Continued*

State	Name	Official Title	Agency	Location
Rhode Island...	John L. Rego	Director	Dept. of Agric. and Conservation	Providence
South Carolina..	R. M. Cooper	Director	Research, Planning and Devel. Bd.	Columbia
South Dakota...	Hugo Carlson	Secretary	Dept. of Natural Resources	Pierre
Tennessee......	Jim Nance McCord	Commissioner	Dept. of Conserv.	Nashville
Vermont.......	Clifton Miskelly	Managing Dir.	Devel. Commn.	Montpelier
Virginia.......	Raymond V. Long	Director	Dept. of Conserv. and Development	Richmond
Washington....	Wm. A. Galbraith	Director	Dept. of Conserv. and Development	Olympia
West Virginia...	Carl J. Johnson	Director	Conserv. Commn.	Charleston
Wisconsin......	Lester P. Voigt	Director	Conserv. Commn.	Madison
Wyoming......	J. A. Buchanan	Director	Nat. Resources Bd.	Cheyenne
Alaska.........	Al Anderson	Exec. Director	Resource Devel. Bd.	Juneau
Guam.........	Manuel Calvo	Director	Dept. of Agric.	Mangilao
Hawaii........	Joseph L. Dwight	Pres. and Commissr.	Bd. of Agric. and Forestry	Honolulu
Puerto Rico....	Roberto Sánchez-Vilella	Secretary	Dept. Public Works	San Juan

---

OIL AND GAS (Regulatory)

State	Name	Official Title	Agency	Location
Alabama.......	Walter B. Jones	Supervisor	Oil and Gas. Bd.	University
Arizona........	Roger Ernst	Land Commissr.	Land Dept.	Phoenix
Arkansas.......	Geo. B. Holden	Director	Oil and Gas Commn.	El Dorado
California......	E. H. Musser	Oil and Gas Supvr., Div. Oil and Gas	Dept. Natural Resources	San Francisco
Colorado.......	Harvey Houston	Director	Oil Inspection Dept.	Denver
Florida........	Kathryn B. Spear	Secy.	Bd. of Conserv.	Tallahassee
Georgia........	James D. Pippen	Chairman	Oil and Gas Commn.	Atlanta
Idaho.........	Arthur Wilson	Commissioner	Land Dept.	Boise
Illinois........	William E. Wayland	Admin. Asst.	Dept. Mines, Minerals	Springfield
Indiana.......	Homer Brown	Oil and Gas Supvr.	Dept. of Conserv.	Indianapolis
Iowa..........	M. L. Abrahamson	Treasurer	Off. of State Treas.	Des Moines
Kansas........	Harry Snyder, Jr.	Chairman	Corporation Commn.	Topeka
Kentucky......	Robert M. Coleman	Chairman	Pub. Serv. Commn.	Frankfort
Louisiana......	John B. Hussey	Commissioner	Dept. of Conserv.	Baton Rouge
Michigan......	W. L. Daoust	State Geologist	Conserv. Dept.	Lansing
Minnesota.....	A. H. Stassen	Dir., Petroleum Div.	Dept. of Taxation	St. Paul
Mississippi.....	H. M. Morse	Supervisor	Oil and Gas Bd.	Jackson
Missouri.......	Lawrence O. Campbell	Supvr., Oil Inspec., Div. of Coll.	Dept. of Revenue	Jefferson City
Montana.......	Lou Bretzke	Commissioner	Dept. of State Lands	Helena
Nebraska.......	E. C. Reed	Geologist, Conserv. Survey Div.	Univ. of Nebraska	Lincoln
Nevada........	Vernon E. Scheid	Chairman	Oil and Gas Conserv. Commn.	Reno
New Jersey.....	Emmett T. Drew	Secy., Bd. of Pub. Util. Commissrs.	Dept. of Pub. Util.	Trenton
New Mexico....	W. B. Macey	Secy.	Oil Conserv. Commn.	Santa Fe
New York......	Benjamin Feinberg	Chmn., Pub. Serv. Commn.	Dept. Pub. Serv.	Albany
North Carolina.	C. D. Baucom	Director	Dept. of Agric.	Raleigh
North Dakota...	Wilson M. Laird	State Geologist	Univ. of N. D.	Grand Forks
Ohio..........	Harry J. Dusz	Chief	Div. of Mines and Mining	Columbus

OIL AND GAS (Regulatory)—*continued*

State	Name	Official Title	Agency	Location
Oklahoma......	Massena B. Murray	Dir., Oil and Gas Conserv. Div.	Corporation Commn.	Oklahoma City
Oregon........	Hollis M. Dole	Director	Dept. of Geology and Mineral Industries	Portland
South Dakota...	Geraldine Ostroot	Secy. of State	Oil and Gas Board	Pierre
Tennessee......	W. D. Hardeman	Dir., Div. of Geol.	Dept. of Conserv.	Nashville
Texas..........	W. J. Murray, Jr.	Chairman	Railroad Commn.	Austin
Utah..........	Arthur L. Crawford	Director	Geol. and Mineralog. Survey, Univ. of Utah	Salt Lake City
Virginia.......	J. Irving Smith	Chairman	Oil and Gas Bd.	Richmond
Washington....	Arthur B. Langlie	Chairman	Oil and Gas Conserv. Commn.	Olympia
West Virginia...	Homer W. Hanna, Jr.	Chairman	Pub. Serv. Commn.	Charleston
Wisconsin......	D. W. Mack	Dir., Div. Motor Fuel, Petrol. Prod.	Dept. of Taxation	Madison
Wyoming......	George W. Jarvis	Mineral Supervisor	Off. of Supvr.	Casper
Alaska.........	Phil R. Holdsworth	Director	Oil and Gas Conservation Commission	Juneau
Guam.........	George W. Ingling	Commissr., Rev. and Taxation	Dept. of Finance	Agana

---

OLD AGE ASSISTANCE

State	Name	Official Title	Agency	Location
Alabama.......	Elizabeth Bryan	Dir., Bur. of Pub. Assistance	Dept. of Pensions and Security	Montgomery
Arizona........	Lee Porterfield	Dir., Pub. Assist. and Services	Pub. Welfare Dept.	Phoenix
Arkansas.......	Virginia Galloway	Dir., Social Service	Welfare Dept.	Little Rock
California.....	Elizabeth B. MacLatchie	Chief, Div. of Social Security	Dept. of Social Welf.	Sacramento
Colorado.......	Guy R. Justis	Director	Dept. of Pub. Welf.	Denver
Connecticut....	Christie Hanas	Commissioner	Dept. of Welfare	Hartford
Delaware......	C. J. Prickett, M.D.	Superintendent	State Welf. Home	Smyrna
Florida........	Chas. G. Lavin	Director	Dept. of Pub. Welf.	Jacksonville
Georgia........	Lucile Wilson	Chief	Sect. of Pub. Assist., Dept. Pub. Welf.	Atlanta
Idaho.........	Bill Child	Director	Dept. of Pub. Assist.	Boise
Illinois.........	Garrett W. Keaster	Exec. Secretary	Pub Aid Commn.	Springfield
Indiana........	Robert O. Brown	Dir., Div. of Pub. Assist.	Dept. of Pub. Welf.	Indianapolis
Iowa..........	L. L. Caffrey	Chairman	Bd. of Social Welf.	Des Moines
Kansas.........	George Dixon	Dir., Div. of Pub. Assist.	Social Welf. Dept.	Topeka
Kentucky......	Aaron Paul	Dir., Div. Pub. Assist.	Dept. of Econ. Sec.	Frankfort
Louisiana......	Edward P. Dameron III	Commissioner	Dept. of Pub. Welf.	Baton Rouge
Maine.........	John Q. Douglass	Dir., Bur. of Soc. Welf.	Dept. of Health and Welf.	Augusta
Maryland......	Thomas J. S. Waxter	Director	Dept. of Pub. Welf.	Baltimore
Massachusetts...	Walter A. Kelly	Dir., Div. of Pub. Assist.	Dept. of Pub. Welf.	Boston
Michigan......	W. J. Maxey	Director	Dept. of Soc. Welf.	Lansing
Minnesota......	John W. Poor	Dir., Div. of Pub. Assist.	Dept. of Welf.	St. Paul
Mississippi......	J. A. Thigpen	Commissioner	Dept. of Pub. Welf.	Jackson
Missouri.......	Proctor N. Carter	Dir., Div. of Welf.	Dept. of Pub. Health and Welf.	Jefferson City

OLD AGE ASSISTANCE—*continued*

State	Name	Official Title	Agency	Location
Montana.......	W. J. Fouse	Administrator	Welfare Dept.	Helena
Nebraska.......	Mayme Stukel	Director	Div. of Pub. Welf.	Lincoln
Nevada........	Barbara C. Coughlan	Director	Welfare Dept.	Reno
New Hampshire.	James J. Barry	Commissioner	Dept. of Pub. Welf.	Concord
New Jersey.....	Irving J. Engelman	Chief, Bur. of Assist.	Dept. of Insts. and Agencies	Trenton
New Mexico....	Murray A. Hintz	Director	Dept. of Pub. Welf.	Santa Fe
New York......	Eleanor Walsh	Dir., Bur. of Old Age Assist.	Dept. of Soc. Welf.	Albany
North Carolina..	R. Eugene Brown	Director	Bd. of Pub. Welf.	Raleigh
North Dakota...	Carlyle D. Onsrud	Exec. Director	Pub. Welf. Bd.	Bismarck
Ohio..........	Henry J. Robison	Director	Dept. of Pub. Welf.	Columbus
Oklahoma......	Charlotte C. Donnell	Supvr., Div. of Program Devel.	Dept. of Pub. Welf.	Oklahoma City
Oregon........	Loa Howard Mason	Administrator	Pub. Welf. Commn.	Portland
Pennsylvania...	Mrs. Ruth Grigg Horting	Secretary	Dept. of Pub. Assist.	Harrisburg
Rhode Island...	Clement J. Doyle	Asst. Dir., Soc. Welf., Div. of Community Servs.	Dept. of Soc. Welf.	Providence
South Carolina..	Arthur B. Rivers	Director	Dept. of Pub. Welf.	Columbia
South Dakota...	Matthew Furze	Director	Dept. of Pub. Welf.	Pierre
Tennessee......	Elizabeth Freeman	Supvr., Div. of Pub. Assist.	Dept. of Pub. Welf.	Nashville
Texas..........	John H. Winters	Director	Dept. of Pub. Welf.	Austin
Utah..........	James G. Kerr	Dir., Bur. of Pub. Assist.	Dept. of Pub. Welf.	Salt Lake City
Vermont.......	W. Arthur Simpson	Commissioner	Soc. Welf. Dept.	Montpelier
Virginia.......	Richard W. Copeland	Director	Dept. of Welf. and Insts.	Richmond
Washington....	Geo. M. Hollenbeck	Director	Dept. of Pub. Assist.	Olympia
West Virginia...	Robert F. Roth	Director	Dept. of Pub. Assist.	Charleston
Wisconsin......	Thomas J. Lucas, Sr.	Dir., Div. of Pub. Assist.	Dept. of Pub. Welf.	Madison
Wyoming......	E. H. Schuneman	Director	Dept. of Pub. Welf.	Cheyenne
Alaska........	Henry A. Harmon	Director	Dept. of Pub. Welf.	Juneau
Hawaii........	Mary L. Noonan	Director	Dept. of Pub. Welf.	Honolulu
Puerto Rico.....	Celestina Zalduondo	Dir., Div. of Public Welfare	Dept. of Health	San Juan
Virgin Islands...	Roy W. Bornn	Commissr. of Soc. Welf.	Govt. of the V.I.	St. Thomas

---

PARKS

State	Name	Official Title	Agency	Location
Alabama.......	James L. Segrest	Chief, Div. of Parks, Monuments and Hist. Sites	Dept. of Conservation	Montgomery
Arkansas.......	Sam B. Kirby	Director	Publicity and Parks Commn.	Little Rock
California......	Newton B. Drury	Chief, Div. of Beaches and Parks	Dept. of Natural Resources	Sacramento
Colorado.......	Everett J. Lee	Director	State Park and Recreation Bd.	Denver
Connecticut....	Elliott P. Bronson	Supt., State Parks	Park and Forest Commn.	Hartford
Delaware......	Nathan Miller	Chairman	Park Commission	Wilmington
Florida........	Emmet L. Hill	Director	Bd. of Parks and Hist. Memorials	Tallahassee
Georgia........	Roy Chalker	Director	Dept. of State Parks	Atlanta

PARKS—*continued*

State	Name	Official Title	Agency	Location
Idaho.........	Arthur Wilson	Commissioner	Land Department	Boise
Illinois.........	William R. Allen	Supt. of Parks	Dept. of Conserv.	Springfield
Indiana........	Kenneth R. Cougill	Dir., Div. of Lands and Waters	Dept. of Conserv.	Indianapolis
Iowa..........	Ray Mitchell	Chief, Land and Waters	Conserv. Commn.	Des Moines
Kansas........	J. Ed. Thompson	Chairman	Park and Resources Authority	Topeka
Kentucky......	Mrs. Lucy Smith	Dir., Div. of Parks	Dept. of Conserv.	Frankfort
Louisiana......	William W. Wells	Director	State Parks Commn.	Baton Rouge
Maine.........	Harold J. Dyer	Dir. of Parks	Park Commission	Augusta
Maryland......	Jos. F. Kaylor	Director	Dept. of Forests and Parks	Annapolis
Massachusetts...	Arnold E. Howard	Chief, Bur. of Recreation	Dept. Natural Resources	Boston
Michigan......	Arthur C. Elmer	Chief, Parks and Recreation Div.	Conserv. Dept.	Lansing
Minnesota......	U. W. Hella	Dir., Div. of Parks	Dept. of Conserv.	St. Paul
Mississippi.....	Jas. W. Craig	Director	Bd. of Park Supvrs.	Jackson
Missouri.......	Joseph Jaeger, Jr.	Dir. of Parks	State Park Board	Jefferson City
Montana.......	Scott P. Hartt	State Engineer	Highway Commn.	Helena
Nebraska.......	Paul T. Gilbert	Executive Secretary	Game, Forestation and Parks Commn.	Lincoln
Nevada........	Howard W. Squires	Director	State Park Commn.	Carson City
New Hampshire.	Russell B. Tobey	Dir. of Recreation	Forestry and Recreation Commn.	Concord
New Jersey.....	Alden T. Cottrell	Chief, Bur. of Forestry, Parks and Hist. Sites, Div. of Planning and Devel.	Dept. of Conserv. and Econ. Devel.	Trenton
New Mexico....	Lee C. Robinson	Supt. of Parks	Park Commission	Santa Fe
New York......	James F. Evans	Dir., Div. of Parks	Conserv. Dept.	Albany
North Carolina.	Thomas W. Morse	Supt., Div. of Parks	Dept. of Conserv. and Devel.	Raleigh
North Dakota...	Russell Reid	Superintendent	Historical Society	Bismarck
Ohio..........	V. W. Flickinger	Chief	Div. of Parks	Columbus
Oklahoma......	Ernest E. Allen	Dir., Div. State Parks	Planning and Resources Bd.	Oklahoma City
Oregon........	C. H. Armstrong	Supt., Parks Div.	Highway Commn.	Salem
Pennsylvania...	W. P. Moll	Chief, Div. of Recreation	Dept. of Forests and Waters	Harrisburg
Rhode Island...	William H. Cotter, Jr.	Chief, Div. of Parks and Recreation	Dept. of Public Works	Providence
South Carolina..	C. West Jacocks	Director	Div. of State Parks	Columbia
South Dakota...	Harry Woodward	Forester	Game, Fish and Park Dept.	Pierre
Tennessee......	Gordon Turner	Dir., Parks and Recreation	Dept. of Conserv.	Nashville
Texas..........	Gordon K. Shearer	Exec. Secy.-Dir.	State Parks Board	Austin
Utah..........	A. R. Mortensen	Exec. Secy. and Ed.	Historical Society	Salt Lake City
Vermont.......	Donald W. Smith	Chairman	Dept. of Forests and Parks	Montpelier
Virginia.......	Randolph Odell	Commissr., Div. of Parks	Dept. of Conserv. and Devel.	Richmond
Washington....	John R. Vanderzicht	Director	State Parks and Recreation Commn.	Olympia
West Virginia...	Kermit McKeever	Chief, Div. of Parks	Conserv. Commn.	Charleston
Wisconsin......	C. L. Harrington	Supt. of Forests and Parks	Conserv. Dept.	Madison
Wyoming......	Jack F. Lewis	Chairman	Parks Commission	Powell
Alaska	W. C. Chipperfield	Land Commissr.	Dept. of Public Lands	Anchorage
Guam.........	Jose Salas	Director	Dept. of Land Management	Agana
Hawaii........	Walter W. Holt	Territorial Forester	Bd. of Agric. and Forestry	Honolulu

PARKS—*continued*

State	Name	Official Title	Agency	Location
Puerto Rico....	Julio E. Monagas	Administrator	Pub. Recreation and Parks Admin.	San Juan
Virgin Islands..	Rudolph Galiber	Act. Commissr. of Pub. Works	Govt. of the V. I.	St. Thomas

---

PAROLE AND PROBATION
(Official Administrators of the Interstate Parole and Probation Compact)

State	Name	Official Title	Agency	Location
Alabama.......	L. B. Stephens	Secretary	Bd. of Pardons and Paroles	Montgomery
Arizona........	Walter Hofmann	Chairman	Bd. of Pardons and Paroles	Phoenix
Arkansas.......	W. P. Ball	Director	Bd. of Pardons, Paroles and Probation	Little Rock
California......	Ervis W. Lester	Chairman, Adult Authority	Dept. of Corrections	Sacramento
Colorado.......	Wayne Patterson	Director	Dept. of Parole	Denver
Connecticut....	Alton H. Cowan	Director	Adult Probation	Hartford
Delaware......	Carlisle B. Spicer	Secretary	Board of Parole	Wilmington
Florida........	Francis R. Bridges, Jr.	Administrator	Parole Commn.	Tallahassee
Georgia........	Hugh C. Carney	Chairman	Pardon and Parole Bd.	Atlanta
Idaho.........	Herman P. Fails	Parole Officer	Bd. of Corrections	Boise
Illinois.........	T. Edward Austin	Superintendent	Div., Supv. of Parolees	Springfield
Indiana........	Joseph M. Sullivan	Director	Div. of Corrections	Indianapolis
Iowa..........	R. W. Bobzin	Secretary	Board of Parole	Des Moines
Kansas........	Don E. Winterberg	Secy. Bd. of Penal Insts.	State Capitol	Topeka
Kentucky......	John C. Klotter	Director	Div. of Probation and Parole	Frankfort
Louisiana......	Edw. P. Dameron III	Commissioner	Dept. Pub. Welfare	Baton Rouge
Maine.........	Norman U. Greenlaw	Commissioner	Dept. of Institutional Service	Augusta
Maryland......	Wallace Reidt	Chairman	Bd. of Parole and Probation	Annapolis
Massachusetts...	Frederick J. Bradlee, Jr.	Chmn., Parole Bd.	Dept. of Correction	Boston
Michigan......	William F. Eardley	Asst. Dir. in Charge, Bur. of Pardons and Paroles	Dept. of Corrections	Lansing
	Fred C. Bates	Asst. Dir. in Charge, Bur. of Probation	Dept. of Corrections	Lansing
Minnesota......	Donald E. MacFarlane	Chairman	Parole Board	St. Paul
Mississippi.....	John A. Payne	Chairman	Parole Board	Jackson
Missouri.......	Donald W. Bunker	Exec. Secy., Bd. of Probation and Parole	Dept. of Corrections	Jefferson City
Montana.......	Benj. Wright	Director	Bd. of Pardons	Deer Lodge
Nebraska.......	R. C. Meissner	Chief Prob. Officer	Board of Pardons	Lincoln
Nevada........	Edward Cupit	Parole and Probation Officer	Bd. of Pardons and Parole Commissrs.	Carson City
New Hampshire	Richard T. Smith	Director	Probation Dept.	Concord
New Jersey.....	F. Lovell Bixby	Dir., Div. of Correction and Parole	Dept. of Institutions and Agencies	Trenton
New Mexico....	William J. Cooper	Director of Parole	Board of Parole	Santa Fe

PAROLE AND PROBATION—*continued*

State	Name	Official Title	Agency	Location
New York......	Lee B. Mailler	Chmn., Bd. of Parole, Div. of Parole	Executive Dept.	Albany
North Carolina..	C. H. Patrick	Chairman	Parole Board	Raleigh
	J. D. Beaty	Director	Probation Commn.	Raleigh
North Dakota...	J. Arthur Vandal	Parole Officer	Pardons Board	Bismarck
Ohio..........	Glenn R. Klopfenstein	Superintendent	Bur. of Probation and Parole	Columbus
Oklahoma......	Campbell LeFlore	Pardon and Parole Officer, Pardon and Parole Div.	Executive Dept.	Oklahoma City
Oregon........	H. M. Randall	Director	Bd. of Parole and Probation	Salem
Pennsylvania...	Henry C. Hill	Chairman	Board of Parole	Harrisburg
Rhode Island...	Joseph H. Hagan	Administrator	Div. of Probation and Parole	Providence
South Carolina..	J. C. Todd	Director	Probation, Parole and Pardon Bd.	Columbia
South Dakota...	Arthur Canary	Exec. Director	Dept. of Probation and Paroles	Sioux Falls
Tennessee......	Charles W. Crow	Exec. Secretary	Bd. of Pardons and Paroles	Nashville
Texas..........	Jack Ross	Chairman	Bd. of Pardons and Paroles	Austin
Utah..........	W. Keith Wilson	Chief Agent	Adult Probation and Parole	Salt Lake City
Vermont.......	John V. Woodhull	Dir., Probation and Parole	Dept. of Institutions	Montpelier
Virginia.......	Charles P. Chew	Director	Parole Board	Richmond
Washington....	Norman S. Hayner	Chairman	Bd. of Prison Terms and Paroles	Olympia
West Virginia...	J. Alexander Creasey	Chairman	Bd. of Probation and Parole	Charleston
Wisconsin......	Quentin L. Ferm	Supvr. of Probation and Parole	Dept. of Public Welfare	Madison
Wyoming......	Norman G. Baillie	Probation and Parole Officer	State Capitol	Cheyenne

PERSONNEL

State	Name	Official Title	Agency	Location
Alabama.......	J. S. Frazer	Director	Personnel Dept.	Montgomery
California......	John F. Fisher	Exec. Officer	Personnel Board	Sacramento
Colorado.......	A. C. Johnson	President	Civil Serv. Commn.	Denver
Connecticut....	Glendon A. Scoboria	Director	Dept. of Finance and Control	Hartford
Georgia........	Edwin L. Swain	Director	Merit System	Atlanta
Idaho..........	James H. Young	Dir. of Admin.	Governor's Office	Boise
Illinois.........	Maude Myers	President	Civil Serv. Commn.	Springfield
Indiana........	James M. Knapp	Director	Personnel Board	Indianapolis
Iowa..........	Arthur T. Wallace	Director	Div. of Personnel	Des Moines
Kansas........	Walter A. Kuiken	Personnel Dir.	Dept. of Admin.	Topeka
Kentucky......	Herbert L. Smith	Dir., Div. of Personnel	Dept. of Finance	Frankfort
Louisiana......	William Wallace McDougall	Director of Personnel	Dept. of State Civil Service	Baton Rouge
Maine.........	Ober C. Vaughan	Director	Dept. of Personnel	Augusta
Maryland......	Russell S. Davis	Commissioner of Personnel	Dept. of State Employment and Reg.	Baltimore
Massachusetts...	Thomas J. Greehan	Dir. of Civil Service	Dept. of Civil Serv. and Reg.	Boston
	William Bell, Jr.	Dir. of Pers. and Standardization	Commn. on Admin. and Finance	Boston
Michigan......	Arthur G. Rasch	State Personnel Dir.	Civil Service Commn.	Lansing

PERSONNEL—*continued*

State	Name	Official Title	Agency	Location
Minnesota......	John W. Jackson	Director	Dept. of Civil Service	St. Paul
Missouri.......	N. F. Steenberger	Dir., Div. of Personnel	Dept. of Bus. and Admin.	Jefferson City
Montana.......	Melvin P. Martinson	Supervisor	Merit System	Helena
Nebraska.......	Dwight Williams	Director	Merit System	Lincoln
Nevada........	Worth McClure, Jr.	Director	Dept. of Personnel	Carson City
New Hampshire.	Roy Y. Lang	Director	Personnel Div.	Concord
New Jersey.....	William F. Kelly, Jr.	Pres., Civil Service Commission	Dept. of Civil Serv.	Trenton
New Mexico....	John H. Hallahan	Director	Personnel Div.	Santa Fe
New York......	William J. Murray	Administrative Dir.	Dept. of Civil Serv.	Albany
North Carolina.	J. W. McDevitt	Director	Dept. of Personnel	Raleigh
Ohio..........	Carl W. Smith	Chairman	Civil Service Commn.	Columbus
Oklahoma......	Roy A. Dillon	Supervisor	Personnel Board	Oklahoma City
Oregon........	Charles W. Terry	Director	Civil Service Commn.	Salem
Pennsylvania...	Gayle K. Lawrence	Personnel Secy.	Governor's Office	Harrisburg
Rhode Island...	Charles H. Cushman	Admin., Div. of Personnel	Dept. of Administration	Providence
South Dakota...	Howard C. Selvig	Supervisor	Merit System Council	Pierre
	Morris G. Hallock	Secretary	Dept. of Finance	Pierre
Tennessee......	Sam T. Whited	Acting Director	Dept. of Personnel	Nashville
Utah..........	Don Tingley	Personnel Officer	Dept. of Finance	Salt Lake City
Vermont.......	Norman Davis	Director	Personnel Board	Montpelier
Virginia.......	Harris Hart	Director	Div. of Personnel	Richmond
Washington....	William B. Webster	Director	Personnel Board	Olympia
Wisconsin	Volmer H. Sorensen	Dir. of Personnel	Bur. of Personnel	Madison
Wyoming......	E. C. Rothwell	Secretary	Board of Supplies	Cheyenne
Alaska.........	I. J. Montgomery	Supervisor	Merit System	Juneau
Guam.........	Peter C. Siguenza	Director	Dept. of Labor, Personnel	Agana
Hawaii........	Samuel M. Askins	Chairman	Civil Service Commn.	Honolulu
Puerto Rico....	R. Torres-Braschi	Director	Off. of Personnel	San Juan
Virgin Islands..	Ullmont L. James	Dir. of Personnel	Govt. of the V. I.	St. Thomas

PLANNING AND DEVELOPMENT (Over-all Agency)

State	Name	Official Title	Agency	Location
Alabama.......	Lewis A. Pick	Director	Planning and Industrial Devel. Bd.	Montgomery
Arizona........	Stanley Womer	Manager	Development Board	Phoenix
Arkansas.......	Wm. P. Rock	Exec. Director	Industrial Devel. Commn.	Little Rock
Colorado.......	W. M. Williams	Director	Planning Commn.	Denver
Connecticut....	Sidney A. Edwards	Managing Dir.	Development Commn.	Hartford
Florida........	B. R. Fuller, Jr.	Director	Devel. Commn.	Tallahassee
Idaho.........	James H. Young	Director	Bur. of Budget	Boise
Indiana........	John C. Mellett	Director	Economic Council	Indianapolis
Iowa..........	T. E. Davidson	Director	Development Commn.	Des Moines
Kentucky......	Joseph H. Taylor	Exec. Director	Agric. and Ind. Devel. Bd.	Frankfort
Louisiana......	Calvin T. Watts	Director	Dept. of Pub. Works	Baton Rouge
Maine.........	Carl J. Broggi	Commissioner	Dept. of Devel. of Industry and Commerce	Augusta
Maryland......	I. Alvin Pasarew	Director	Planning Commn.	Baltimore
Massachusetts...	Charles E. Downe	Dir., Div. of Planning	Dept. of Commerce	Boston

PLANNING AND DEVELOPMENT (Over-all Agency)—*continued*

State	Name	Official Title	Agency	Location
Michigan......	Don C. Weeks	Exec. Director	Economic Devel. Dept.	Lansing
Minnesota......	James W. Clark	Commissioner	Dept. of Business Devel.	St. Paul
Mississippi.....	H. V. Allen, Jr.	Director	Agric. and Ind. Bd.	Jackson
Missouri.......	Prentiss Mooney	Dir., Div. of Resources and Devel.	Dept. of Bus. and Admin.	Jefferson City
Montana.......	Perry F. Roys	Director	Planning Board	Helena
Nebraska.......	C. V. Price	Chief, Div. of Resources	Dept. of Agric. and Inspection	Lincoln
Nevada........	M. George Bissell	Engineer-Manager	Planning Board	Carson City
New Hampshire.	Ernest L. Sherman	Exec. Director	Planning and Devel. Commn.	Concord
New Jersey.....	Joseph E. McLean	Commissioner	Dept. of Conserv. and Econ. Devel.	Trenton
New Mexico....	Berl Huffman	Director	Econ. Devel. Commn.	Santa Fe
New York......	George B. Robinson	Dir., Bur. of Planning	Dept. of Commerce	Albany
North Carolina..	Ben E. Douglas	Director	Dept. of Conserv. and Devel.	Raleigh
Ohio..........	Rhea McCarty	Exec. Secretary	Dev. and Publicity Commn.	Columbus
Oklahoma......	Jack Boyd	Exec. Director	Planning and Resources Bd.	Oklahoma City
	Randall T. Klemme	Director	Dept. of Commerce and Industry	Oklahoma City
Oregon........	Robert E. McCoy	Exec. Director	Development Commn.	Portland
Pennsylvania...	F. A. Pitkin	Consultant	Planning Bd.	Harrisburg
Rhode Island...	Thomas E. Monahan	Exec. Director	Devel. Council	Providence
South Carolina..	R. M. Cooper	Director	Research, Planning and Devel. Bd.	Columbia
South Dakota...	Hugo Carlson	Secretary	Natural Resources Commn.	Pierre
	Noel T. Tweet	Director	Industrial Devel. Expansion Agency	Pierre
Tennessee......	Harold V. Miller	Exec. Director	Planning Commn.	Nashville
Utah..........	Ames K. Bagley	Director	Dept. of Ind. Planning and Devel.	Salt Lake City
Vermont.......	Clifton Miskelly	Managing Dir.	Devel. Commn.	Montpelier
Virginia.......	Raymond V. Long	Director	Dept. of Conserv. and Devel.	Richmond
Washington....	Wm. A. Galbraith	Director	Div. of Progress and Ind. Devel.	Olympia
Wisconsin......	M. W. Torkelson	Dir., Planning Div.	Bur. of Engineering	Madison
Wyoming......	J. A. Buchanan	Director	Nat. Resources Bd.	Cheyenne
Alaska.........	Al Anderson	Exec. Director	Resource Devel. Bd.	Juneau
Guam.........	Joseph Flores	Chairman	Territorial Planning Commission	Agana
Hawaii........	George Mason	Director	Econ. Planning and Coordination Authority	Honolulu
Puerto Rico....	Cándido Oliveras	Chmn., Planning Bd.	Off. of Governor	San Juan
	T. Moscoso, Jr.	Administrator	Econ. Devel. Admin.	San Juan
Virgin Islands..	Walter Reed	Chairman	V. I. Planning Board	St. Thomas

POLICE AND HIGHWAY PATROL

State	Name	Official Title	Agency	Location
Alabama.......	W. V. Lyerly	Director	Dept. of Pub. Safety	Montgomery
Arizona........	G. O. Hathaway	Supt., Highway Patrol	Highway Department	Phoenix

POLICE AND HIGHWAY PATROL—*continued*

State	Name	Official Title	Agency	Location
Arkansas.......	Herman E. Lindsey	Director	State Police	Little Rock
California......	Bernard R. Caldwell	Commissioner	Dept. of Highway Patrol	Sacramento
Colorado.......	Gilbert R. Carrel	Chief	Highway Patrol	Denver
Connecticut....	John C. Kelly	Commissioner	State Police Dept.	Hartford
Delaware......	Harry S. Shew	Superintendent	State Police Div.	Wilmington
Florida........	H. N. Kirkman	Director	Dept. of Pub. Safety	Tallahassee
Georgia........	W. C. Dominy	Director	Highway Patrol	Atlanta
Idaho..........	A. E. Perkins	Superintendent	State Police	Boise
Illinois.........	Joseph D. Bibb	Director	Dept. of Pub. Safety	Springfield
Indiana........	Frank A. Jessup	Superintendent	State Police	Indianapolis
Iowa..........	David Herrick	Chief	Highway Patrol	Des Moines
Kansas........	Tom Glasscock	Superintendent	Highway Patrol	Topeka
Kentucky......	Charles C. Oldham	Commissioner	Dept. of State Police	Frankfort
Louisiana......	Chester B. Owen	Director	Dept. of Pub. Safety	Baton Rouge
	Francis T. Moore	Act. Supt.	State Police	Baton Rouge
Maine.........	Robert Marx	Chief	State Police	Augusta
Maryland......	Elmer F. Munshower	Superintendent	Dept. of State Police	Pikesville
Massachusetts...	Otis R. Whitney	Commissioner	Dept. of Pub. Safety	Boston
Michigan......	Joseph A. Childs	Commissioner	State Police	East Lansing
Minnesota......	Paul R. Martz	Chief Patrol Officer	Dept. of Highways	St. Paul
	Roy T. Noonan	Superintendent	Bureau of Criminal Apprehension	St. Paul
Mississippi.....	T. B. Birdsong	Commissioner	Pub. Safety Commn.	Jackson
Missouri.......	Hugh H. Waggoner	Superintendent	Highway Patrol	Jefferson City
Montana.......	Glenn M. Schultz	Chief	Highway Patrol	Helena
Nebraska......	C. J. Sanders	Colonel	Safety Patrol	Lincoln
Nevada........	Robert J. Clark	Director of Highway Patrol	Pub. Service Commn.	Carson City
New Hampshire.	Ralph W. Caswell	Superintendent	State Police	Concord
New Jersey.....	Joseph D. Rutter	Supt., Div. of State Police	Dept. of Law and Pub. Safety	Trenton
New Mexico....	Joseph P. Roach	Chief	State Police	Santa Fe
New York......	Francis S. McGarvey	Supt., Div. of State Police	Executive Dept.	Albany
North Carolina..	James R. Smith	Commander	Dept. of Mot. Vehs.	Raleigh
North Dakota...	Clark J. Monroe	Superintendent	Highway Patrol	Bismarck
Ohio..........	George Mingle	Superintendent	Div. of Highway Patrol	Columbus
Oklahoma......	Jim Lookabaugh	Commissioner	Dept. of Pub. Safety	Oklahoma City
Oregon........	H. G. Maison	Superintendent	Dept. of State Police	Salem
Pennsylvania...	E. G. Henry	Commissioner	State Police	Harrisburg
Rhode Island...	John T. Sheehan	Superintendent	State Police	Providence
South Carolina..	O. Lindsey Brady	Chief	Law Enforcement Div.	Columbia
	H. E. Quarles	Dir., Mot. Veh. Div.	Highway Dept.	Columbia
South Dakota...	W. J. Goetz	Director	Motor Patrol	Pierre
Tennessee......	W. W. Luttrell	Commissioner	Dept. of Safety	Nashville
Texas..........	Homer Garrison, Jr.	Director	Dept. of Pub. Safety	Austin
Utah..........	Lyle Hyatt	Superintendent	Highway Patrol	Salt Lake City
Vermont.......	Wm. H. Baumann	Commissioner	Dept. of Pub. Safety	Montpelier
Virginia.......	C. W. Woodson, Jr.	Superintendent	Dept. of State Police	Richmond
Washington....	Roy F. Carlson	Act. Chief	State Patrol	Olympia
West Virginia...	R. W. Boyles	Superintendent	Dept. of Pub. Safety	Charleston
Wisconsin......	L. E. Beier	Dir., Div. of Inspection and Enforcement	Motor Vehicle Dept.	Madison
Wyoming......	Wm. R. Bradley	Colonel	Highway Patrol	Cheyenne
Alaska.........	A. P. Brandt	Superintendent	Dept. of Police	Juneau
Guam.........	Theodore Brown	Director	Dept. of Public Safety	Agana

POLICE AND HIGHWAY PATROL—*continued*

State	Name	Official Title	Agency	Location
Hawaii........	Dan Liu	Chief of Police	City and County of Honolulu	Honolulu
	Harry Newman	Chairman	Police Commn.	Honolulu
Puerto Rico....	Salvador T. Roig	Chief	Police	San Juan
Virgin Islands..	George N. Matthias	Act. Commissr. of Pub. Safety	Govt. of the V. I.	St. Thomas

PORT AUTHORITY

State	Name	Official Title	Agency	Location
Alabama.......	Ward W. McFarland	General Manager	Docks Dept.	Mobile
California......	Charles Tait	Port Director	Bd. of Harbor Commissioners	San Francisco
Connecticut....	Louis C. Wool	Chairman	Commissrs. Steamship Terminals	New London
Georgia........	D. Leon Williams	Director	Ports Authority	Savannah
	Robert M. Holder	Chairman	Ports Authority	Savannah
Maine.........	Donald S. Laughlin	President	Port Authority	Portland
Maryland......	James Davis	Director	Port of Baltimore Commn.	Baltimore
Massachusetts...	John F. O'Halloran	Director	Port of Boston Commn.	Boston
Michigan......	Max M. McCray	Exec. Director	Port of Detroit Commn.	Detroit
	Edward Maurer	Chairman	Port of Monroe Auth.	Monroe
New Jersey.....	Austin J. Tobin	Exec. Director	Port of New York Auth. (Interstate)	New York
	Joseph K. Costello	Exec. Director	Delaware River Port Auth. (Interstate)	Camden
	Henry W. Peterson	Secretary	So. Jersey Port Commn. (State)	Camden
New York......	Donald V. Lowe	Chairman	Port of New York Auth. (Interstate)	New York
North Carolina..	Richard S. Marr	Director	Ports Authority	Wilmington
South Carolina..	Cotesworth P. Means	Chairman	Ports Authority	Charleston
Virginia.......	David H. Clark	Dir. of Ports	Virginia State Ports Authority	Norfolk
Guam.........	Adolpho Sgambelluri	Chief, Port Security	Dept. of Commerce	Agana
Hawaii........	Ben E. Nutter	Chairman	Bd. of Harbor Commissioners	Honolulu
	Benj. F. Rush	Manager and Chief Eng.	Bd. of Harbor Commissioners	Honolulu
Puerto Rico....	Manuel Henríquez	Captain of the Port of San Juan and Chief Captain of the Ports	Puerto Rico Ports Auth.	San Juan
Virgin Islands...	Engle L. Simmons	Harbormaster	Govt. of the V.I.	St. Thomas

PRINTING

State	Name	Official Title	Agency	Location
Alabama.......	James B. King	Purchasing Agent	Dept. of Finance	Montgomery
Arkansas.......	Bryant Wilder	Auditor, Printing Contracts	State Auditor's Office	Little Rock
California......	Paul E. Gallagher	State Printer	Dept. of Finance	Sacramento
Colorado......	F. J. Behymer	Asst. Pur. Agent	Div. of Purchases	Denver
Connecticut....	Fred R. Zeller	Comptroller	Off. of Comptroller	Hartford
Illinois........	Walter E. Erickson	Supt. of Printing	Dept. of Finance	Springfield
Indiana........	J. Otto Lee	Supvr. of Printing	Div. of Pub. Works and Supply	Indianapolis

PRINTING—*continued*

State	Name	Official Title	Agency	Location
Iowa	S. W. Needham	Superintendent	Printing Board	Des Moines
Kansas	Ferd Voiland, Jr.	State Printer	Off. of State Printer	Topeka
Kentucky	Theodore J. Richard	Supt. of Printing	Dept. of Finance	Frankfort
Maine	William D. Jarvis	Supt. of Public Printing	Bur. of Purchases	Augusta
Maryland	Wm. J. Zander, Jr.	Buyer	Dept. of Budget and Procurement	Baltimore
Massachusetts	George J. Cronin	Purchasing Agent	Commn. on Admin. and Finance	Boston
Michigan	J. Stanley Bien	Dir. of Purchasing Div.	Dept. of Admin.	Lansing
Minnesota	Herman A. Myer	State Printer	Dept. of Admin.	St. Paul
Mississippi	Heber Ladner	Secretary	Bd. of Pub. Contracts	Jackson
Missouri	Edgar C. Nelson	Purchasing Agent, Div. of Procurement	Dept. of Revenue	Jefferson City
Nebraska	Carl A. Rosenlof	Purchasing Agent	Div. of Purchase and Supplies	Lincoln
Nevada	Jack McCarthy	Supt. of State Printing	Printing Office	Carson City
New Hampshire	Harold Cheney	Dir., Div. of Purchase and Property	Dept. of Admin. and Control	Concord
New Jersey	Charles F. Sullivan	Dir., Div. of Purchase and Property	Dept. of the Treasury	Trenton
New Mexico	George Fitzpatrick	Director	Bur. of Publications	Santa Fe
New York	J. Arthur Mann	Supvr. of Printing Contracts	Div. of Standards and Purchase, Exec. Dept.	Albany
North Carolina	David Q. Holton	Director	Div. Purchase and Contract	Raleigh
North Dakota	L. C. Miller	Secretary	Publication and Printing Commn.	Bismarck
Ohio	John W. Bush	Superintendent	Div. of Purchases and Printing	Columbus
Oregon	Charles Unruh	Chief, Printing Section	Dept. Finance and Admin.	Salem
Pennsylvania	Howard O. Siglin	Director	Bur. of Publications	Harrisburg
Rhode Island	Joseph L. Byron	Purchasing Agent, Div. of Purchases	Dept. of Admin.	Providence
South Carolina	B. P. Davies	Supvr., Office Supplies and Printing Div.	Budget and Control Bd.	Columbia
South Dakota	Morris G. Hallock	Secretary	Dept. of Finance	Pierre
Texas	Walter L. Bell	Exec. Director	Board of Control	Austin
Utah	Truman S. Curtis	Commissioner	Finance Commission	Salt Lake City
Vermont	Frank P. Free	Purchasing Agent	Off. of Pur. Agent	Montpelier
Virginia	R. C. Eaton	Dir., Div. of Pur. and Printing	Dept. of Accounts and Purchases	Richmond
Washington	W. Chapman	State Printer	State Printing Plant	Olympia
West Virginia	Samuel T. Waller	Director	Dept. of Purchases	Charleston
Wisconsin	Don M. Leicht	Supvr., Printing Div.	Bur. of Purchases	Madison
Wyoming	E. C. Rothwell	Secretary	Bd. of Supplies	Cheyenne
Puerto Rico	Gustavo Schwarz	Supt., Printing Div.	Dept. of Treasury	San Juan
Virgin Islands	Alphonse Donastorg	Chief Printer	Govt. of the V. I.	St. Thomas

PROPERTY TAX

State	Name	Official Title	Agency	Location
Alabama	Winton McNair	Chief, Ad Valorem and Franchise Tax Div.	Dept. of Revenue	Montgomery
Arizona	Warren Peterson	Chairman	Tax Commission	Phoenix
Arkansas	Earl Berry	Dir.. Tax Div.	Pub. Serv. Commn.	Little Rock
California	Dixwell L. Pierce	Exec. Secretary	Bd. of Equalization	Sacramento

PROPERTY TAX—*continued*

State	Name	Official Title	Agency	Location
Colorado.......	Earl E. Ewing	Treasurer	Dept. of Treasury	Denver
Georgia........	C. G. Campbell	Dir., Prop. and License Tax Unit	Revenue Dept.	Atlanta
Idaho	P. G. Neill	Tax Collector	Off. Tax Collector	Boise
Illinois	Richard J. Lyons	Director	Dept. of Revenue	Springfield
Indiana	Adolph L. Fossler	Chairman	Bd. of Tax Commissioners	Indianapolis
Iowa..........	Louis H. Cook	Director	Tax Commission	Des Moines
Kentucky......	M. P. Carpenter	Dir., Valuation Div.	Dept. of Revenue	Frankfort
Louisiana......	Graydon K. Kitchens	Chairman	Tax Commission	Baton Rouge
Maine.........	Edward Birkenwald	Dir., Prop. Tax Div.	Bur. of Taxation	Augusta
Maryland......	Joseph Allen	Chairman	Tax Commission	Baltimore
Massachusetts...	John J. Falvey	Dir., Local Tax Bureau	Dept. of Corp. and Taxation	Boston
Michigan......	Louis M. Nims	Chairman	Tax Commission	Lansing
Minnesota......	Charles P. Stone	Deputy Commissioner	Dept. of Taxation	St. Paul
Mississippi....	Alex McKeigney	Chairman	Tax Commission	Jackson
Missouri.......	James Robertson	Chmn., Tax. Commn.	Dept. of Revenue	Jefferson City
Montana.......	J. L. Reed	Chairman	Bd. of Equalization	Helena
Nebraska.......	F. A. Herrington	Tax Commissioner	Bd. of Equalization and Assessment	Lincoln
Nevada........	Robbins E. Cahill	Secretary	Tax Commission	Carson City
New Hampshire.	Oliver W. Marvin	Chairman	Tax Commission	Concord
New Jersey.....	E. Rowland Major	Supvr., Local Property Tax Bur.	Dept. of Treasury	Trenton
New Mexico....	C. L. Forsling	Chief Tax Commissr.	Tax Commission	Santa Fe
North Dakota...	J. Arthur Engen	Tax Commissioner	Off. of Tax Commissioner	Bismarck
Ohio..........	Stanley J. Bowers	Tax Commissioner	Dept. of Taxation	Columbus
Oklahoma......	Charles E. Wails	Director, Ad Valorem Tax. Div.	Tax Commission	Oklahoma City
Oregon........	Samuel B. Stewart	Tax Commissioner	Tax Commission	Salem
South Carolina..	L. W. Smith	Dir., Prop. Tax Div.	Tax Commission	Columbia
South Dakota...	W. R. Wilder	Commissioner	Dept. of Revenue	Pierre
Texas..........	Robert S. Calvert	Comptr. of Pub. Accts.	Off. of Comptr.	Austin
Utah..........	Elliot Kimball	Director	Property Tax Div.	Salt Lake City
Vermont.......	Leonard W. Morrison	Commissioner	Tax Dept.	Montpelier
Virginia.......	C. H. Morrissett	Commissioner	Dept. of Taxation	Richmond
Washington....	H. Dan Bracken	Chairman	Tax Commission	Olympia
West Virginia...	Wm. R. Laird III	Commissioner	Tax Commission	Charleston
Wisconsin......	Forrest W. Gillett	Director, Div. of Property Tax	Dept. of Taxation	Madison
Wyoming......	Walter W. Hudson	Chairman	Bd. of Equalization	Cheyenne
Guam	George W. Ingling	Commissr. Rev. and Tax.	Dept. of Finance	Agana
Hawaii........	August H. Landgraf, Jr.	Deputy Tax. Commissr.	Dept. of Tax Commissr.	Honolulu
Puerto Rico....	Juan B. Pérez	Chief, Bur. of Collections	Dept. of Treasury	San Juan
Virgin Islands...	Clarice Bryan Smith	Tax Assessor	Dept. of Insular Affairs (Property Division)	St. Thomas

---

PUBLIC ASSISTANCE

State	Name	Official Title	Agency	Location
Alabama.......	Elizabeth Bryan	Dir., Bur. of Pub. Assist.	Dept. of Pensions and Security	Montgomery

PUBLIC ASSISTANCE—*continued*

State	Name	Official Title	Agency	Location
Arizona........	Lee Porterfield	Dir., Pub. Assist. and Services	Pub. Welf. Dept.	Phoenix
Arkansas.......	Carl Adams	Commissioner	Dept. Pub. Welfare	Little Rock
California.....	Elizabeth B. MacLatchie	Chief, Div. of Social Security	Dept. of Soc. Welf.	Sacramento
Colorado.......	Guy R. Justis	Director	Dept. of Pub. Welf.	Denver
Connecticut....	Edward H. Reeves	Dir., Div. of Pub. Assist.	Welfare Dept.	Hartford
Florida........	Chas. G. Lavin	Director	Dept. of Pub. Welf.	Jacksonville
Georgia........	Lucile Wilson	Chief, Sect. of Pub. Assist.	Dept. of Pub. Welf.	Atlanta
Idaho.........	Bill Child	Director	Dept. of Pub. Assist.	Boise
Illinois.........	Garrett W. Keaster	Exec. Secretary	Pub. Aid. Commn.	Springfield
Indiana........	Robert O. Brown	Dir., Div. of Pub. Assist.	Dept. of Pub. Welf.	Indianapolis
Iowa..........	L. L. Caffrey	Chairman	Bd. of Social Welf.	Des Moines
Kentucky......	Aaron Paul	Dir., Div. of Pub. Assist.	Dept. of Econ. Security	Frankfort
Louisiana......	Edward P. Dameron III	Commissioner	Dept. of Pub. Welf.	Baton Rouge
Maine.........	Pauline S. McClay	Dir., Pub. Assist.	Dept. of Health and Welf.	Augusta
Maryland......	Thomas J. S. Waxter	Director	Dept. of Pub. Welf.	Baltimore
Massachusetts...	Walter A. Kelly	Dir., Div. of Pub. Assist.	Dept. of Pub. Welf.	Boston
Michigan......	W. J. Maxey	Director	Dept. of Soc. Welf.	Lansing
Minnesota......	John W. Poor	Dir., Pub. Assist.	Dept. of Welf.	St. Paul
Mississippi......	J. A. Thigpen	Commissioner	Dept. of Pub. Welf.	Jackson
Missouri.......	Proctor N. Carter	Dir., Div. of Welfare	Dept. of Pub. Health and Welfare	Jefferson City
Montana.......	V. A. Burr	Dir., Div. Pub. Assist.	Welfare Dept.	Helena
Nebraska.......	Mayme Stukel	Director	Div. of Pub. Welf.	Lincoln
Nevada........	Barbara C. Coughlan	Director	Welfare Dept.	Reno
New Hampshire.	Aline A. Cavanaugh	Supvr. of Pub. Assist.	Dept. of Pub. Welf.	Concord
New Jersey.....	Elmer V. Andrews	Director of Welfare	Dept. of Insts. and Agencies	Trenton
New Mexico....	Murray A. Hintz	Director	Dept. of Pub. Welf.	Santa Fe
New York......	Margaret Barnard	Dir. of Pub. Assist.	Dept. of Soc. Welf.	Albany
North Carolina..	Ellen Winston	Commissioner	Dept. of Pub. Welf.	Raleigh
North Dakota...	Carlyle D. Onsrud	Exec. Director	Pub. Welf. Bd.	Bismarck
Ohio..........	Henry J. Robison	Director	Dept. of Pub. Welf.	Columbus
Oklahoma......	Charlotte C. Donnell	Supvr., Div. of Program Devel.	Dept. of Welfare	Oklahoma City
Oregon........	Mrs. Loa Howard Mason	Administrator	Pub. Welf. Commn.	Portland
Pennsylvania...	Ruth Grigg Horting	Secretary	Dept. of Pub. Assist.	Harrisburg
Rhode Island...	{ Clement J. Doyle	Asst. Dir., Soc. Welf.	Div. of Community Servs.	Providence
	{ James E. Reilly	Admn., Div. Pub Assist.	Dept. of Soc. Welf.	Providence
South Carolina..	F. A. Dean	Dir., Div. of Pub. Assist.	Dept. of Pub. Welf.	Columbia
South Dakota...	Matthew Furze	Director	Dept. of Pub. Welf.	Pierre
Tennessee......	Elizabeth Freeman	Supvr., Div. of Pub. Assist	Dept. of Pub. Welf.	Nashville
Texas..........	John H. Winters	Director	Dept. of Pub. Welf.	Austin
Utah..........	H. C. Shoemaker	Chmn. of Commn.	Dept. of Pub. Welf.	Salt Lake City
Vermont.......	Mary F. Gibson	Dir., Pub. Assist.	Soc. Welf. Dept.	Montpelier
Virginia.......	Richard W. Copeland	Director	Dept. of Welf. and Insts.	Richmond
Washington....	Geo. M. Hollenback	Act. Director	Dept. of Pub. Assist.	Olympia
West Virginia...	Robert F. Roth	Director	Dept. of Pub. Assist.	Charleston

PUBLIC ASSISTANCE—*continued*

State	Name	Official Title	Agency	Location
Wisconsin......	Thomas J. Lucas, Sr.	Dir., Dept. of Pub. Welfare	Div. of Pub. Assist.	Madison
Wyoming......	E. H. Schuneman	Director	Dept. of Pub. Welf.	Cheyenne
Alaska........	Henry A. Harmon	Director	Dept. of Pub. Welf.	Juneau
Guam........	V. U. Zafra	Chief Commissr.	Govt. of Guam	Agana
Hawaii.......	Mary L. Noonan	Director	Dept. of Pub. Welf.	Honolulu
Puerto Rico....	Celestina Zalduondo	Dir., Div. of Pub. Welfare	Dept. of Health	San Juan
Virgin Islands..	Roy W. Bornn	Commissr. of Soc. Welf.	Govt. of the V. I.	St. Thomas

PUBLIC HEALTH—*see* HEALTH

PUBLIC UTILITY AND RAILROAD REGULATION

State	Name	Official Title	Agency	Location
Alabama.......	C. C. Owen	President	Pub. Serv. Commn.	Montgomery
Arizona........	William T. Brooks	Chairman	Corp. Commission	Phoenix
Arkansas.......	Lewis M. Robinson	Chairman	Pub. Serv. Commn.	Little Rock
California......	Peter E. Mitchell	President	Pub. Util. Commn.	San Francisco
Colorado......	Joseph W. Hawley	Chairman	Pub. Util. Commn.	Denver
Connecticut....	Eugene S. Loughlin	Chairman	Pub. Util. Commn.	Hartford
Delaware.......	George T. Bierlin	Exec. Secretary	Pub. Serv. Commn.	Dover
Florida........	Wilbur C. King	Chairman	R. R. and Pub. Util. Commn.	Tallahassee
Georgia........	Matt L. McWhorter	Chairman	Pub. Serv. Commn.	Atlanta
Idaho.........	H. C. Allen	Chairman	Pub. Util. Commn.	Boise
Illinois........	George R. Perrine	Chairman	Commerce Commn.	Springfield
Indiana........	Warren Buchanan	Chairman	Pub. Serv. Commn.	Indianapolis
Iowa..........	Carl W. Reed	Chairman	Commerce Commn.	Des Moines
Kansas........	Harry Snyder, Jr.	Chairman	Corporation Commn.	Topeka
Kentucky......	Robert M. Coleman	Chairman	Pub. Serv. Commn.	Frankfort
	Lucile Tobin	Secretary	Railroad Commn.	Frankfort
Louisiana......	Wade O. Martin, Sr.	Chairman	Public Serv. Commn.	Baton Rouge
Maine.........	Sumner T. Pike	Chairman	Pub. Util. Commn.	Augusta
Maryland......	Stanford Hoff	Chairman	Pub. Serv. Commn.	Baltimore
Massachusetts...	David M. Brackman	Chairman	Dept. of Pub. Util.	Boston
Michigan......	John H. McCarthy	Chairman	Pub. Serv. Commn.	Lansing
Minnesota......	Ewald W. Lund	Chairman	R.R. and Warehouse Commn.	St. Paul
Mississippi......	Alton Massey	Chairman	Pub. Serv. Commn.	Jackson
Missouri.......	Tyre W. Burton	Chairman	Pub. Serv. Commn.	Jefferson City
Montana.......	Leonard Young	Chairman	Pub. Util. and Railway Commn.	Helena
Nebraska.......	Joseph J. Brown	Chairman	Railway Commn.	Lincoln
Nevada........	Robert A. Allen	Chairman	Pub. Serv. Commn.	Carson City
New Hampshire.	Harold K. Davison	Chairman	Pub. Util. Commn.	Concord
New Jersey.....	Mrs. Hortense F. Kessler	Pres., Bd. of Pub. Util. Commissrs.	Dept. of Public Utilities	Trenton
New Mexico....	L. W. Leibrand	Chairman	Pub. Serv. Commn.	Santa Fe
	John Block, Jr.	Chairman	Corp. Commn.	Santa Fe
New York......	Benj. F. Feinberg	Commn. Chairman	Dept. of Pub. Serv.	Albany
North Carolina..	Stanley Winborne	Chairman	Utilities Commn.	Raleigh
North Dakota...	Martin Vaaler	President	Pub. Serv. Commn.	Bismarck
Ohio..........	Robert L. Moulton	Chairman	Pub. Util. Commn.	Columbus
Oklahoma......	Ray C. Jones	Chairman	Corporation Commn.	Oklahoma City
Oregon........	Charles H. Heltzel	Commissr.	Pub. Util. Commn.	Salem

PUBLIC UTILITY AND RAILROAD REGULATION—*continued*

State	Name	Official Title	Agency	Location
Pennsylvania...	Leon Schwartz	Chairman	Pub. Util. Commn.	Harrisburg
Rhode Island...	Thomas A. Kennelly	Admin., Div. of Pub. Utilities	Dept. of Bus. Regulation	Providence
South Carolina..	Clyde F. Boland	Chairman	Pub. Serv. Commn.	Columbia
South Dakota...	C. A. Merkle	Chairman	Pub. Util. Commn.	Pierre
Tennessee......	John Hammer	Chairman	Pub. Serv. Commn.	Nashville
Texas..........	W. J. Murray, Jr.	Chairman	Railroad Commn.	Austin
Utah..........	Hal. S. Bennett	Chairman	Pub. Serv. Commn.	Salt Lake City
Vermont.......	Oscar L. Shepard	Chairman	Pub. Serv. Commn.	Montpelier
Virginia.......	H. Lester Hooker	Chairman	Corporation Commn.	Richmond
Washington....	Ralph Davis	Chairman	Pub. Serv. Commn.	Olympia
West Virginia...	Homer W. Hanna, Jr.	Chairman	Pub. Serv. Commn.	Charleston
Wisconsin......	James R. Durfee	Chairman	Pub. Serv. Commn.	Madison
Wyoming......	Walter W. Hudson	Chairman	Pub. Serv. Commn.	Cheyenne
Guam.........	Winston C. Cooper	Chief Officer	Public Util. Agency	Tamuning
Hawaii........	Robt. T. Williams	Chairman	Public Util. Commn.	Honolulu
Puerto Rico....	Alberto Arrillaga	Chairman	Pub. Serv. Commn.	San Juan
Virgin Islands...	Rudolph Galiber	Act. Commissr. of Pub. Works	Govt. of the V.I.	St. Thomas

PUBLIC WORKS

State	Name	Official Title	Agency	Location
Alabama.......	H. H. Houk	Director	Building Commn.	Montgomery
California......	Frank B. Durkee	Director	Dept. of Pub. Works	Sacramento
Colorado.......	W. M. Williams	Director	Planning Commn.	Denver
Connecticut....	Timothy J. Murphy, Jr.	Director	Pub. Works Dept.	Hartford
Florida........	B. R. Fuller, Jr.	Director	Devel. Commn.	Tallahassee
Idaho.........	Arthur Warren	Superintendent	Public Building	Boise
Illinois.........	Edwin A. Rosenstone	Director	Dept. of Pub. Works and Bldg.	Springfield
Indiana........	William E. Clarkson	Director	Div. of Pub. Works and Supply	Indianapolis
Kentucky......	W. T. Judy	Exec. Director	State Property and Bldg. Commn.	Frankfort
Louisiana......	Roy T. Sessums	Director	Dept. of Pub. Works	Baton Rouge
Maine.........	Irving W. Russell	Superintendent	Public Buildings	Augusta
Maryland......	James J. O'Donnell	Director	Dept. of Pub. Improvements	Baltimore
Massachusetts...	John A. Volpe	Commissioner	Dept. of Pub. Works	Boston
Minnesota......	Rudolph G. Zelzer	Budget Engineer	Dept. of Admin.	St. Paul
Missouri.......	Ralph McSweeney	Dir., Div. of Pub. Bldgs.	Dept. of Revenue	Jefferson City
Nevada........	M. George Bissell	Engineer-Manager	Planning Bd.	Carson City
New Hampshire.	Frank D. Merrill	Commissioner	Dept. of Pub. Works and Highways	Concord
New York......	John W. Johnson	Superintendent	Dept. of Pub. Works	Albany
North Carolina..	A. H. Graham	Chairman	Highway and Pub. Works Commn.	Raleigh
Ohio..........	Zoyd M. Flaler	Director	Dept. of Pub. Works	Columbus
Oklahoma......	Clarence Burch	Chairman	Bd. of Pub. Affairs	Oklahoma City
Pennsylvania...	(Vacancy)	Secretary	Dept. of Property and Supplies	Harrisburg
Rhode Island...	Joseph M. Vallone	Director	Dept. of Pub. Works	Providence
Tennessee......	Lynn Bomar	Supt., Div. of Pub. Works	Dept. of Highways and Pub. Works	Nashville
Texas..........	Walter L. Bell	Exec. Director	Bd. of Control	Austin
Vermont.......	Claiton Buxton	Sergeant-at-Arms	Bldg. Council	Montpelier
West Virginia...	Herbert Marsh	Chief Clerk	Bd. of Pub. Works	Charleston
Wisconsin......	Ralph D. Culbertson	Chief Engineer	Bur. of Engineering	Madison
Alaska.........	Irving McK. Reed	Superintendent	Public Works	Juneau

PUBLIC WORKS—*continued*

State	Name	Official Title	Agency	Location
Guam........	William R. Hellier	Director	Dept. of Pub. Works	Agana
Hawaii........	Ben E. Nutter	Superintendent	Dept. of Pub. Works	Honolulu
Puerto Rico....	Roberto Sánchez-Vilella	Secretary	Dept. of Pub. Works	San Juan
Virgin Islands..	Rudolph Galiber	Act. Commissr. of Pub. Works	Govt. of the V.I.	St. Thomas

PURCHASING

State	Name	Official Title	Agency	Location
Alabama.......	James B. King	Purchasing Agent	Dept. of Finance	Montgomery
Arkansas.......	Mack Sturgis	Purchasing Director	State Pur. Dept.	Little Rock
California......	L. E. Hobart	Purchasing Agent	Dept. of Finance	Sacramento
Colorado.......	Lacy L. Wilkinson	Purchasing Agent	Div. of Purchases	Denver
Connecticut....	C. L. Magnuson	Supvr., Purchasing Div.	Dept. of Finance and Control	Hartford
Florida........	Ralph R. Siller	Exec. Secretary	State Pur. Council	Tallahassee
Georgia........	C. Lawton Shaw, Sr.	Purchasing Agent	Purchasing Dept.	Atlanta
Idaho.........	Ted Cramer	Purchasing Agent	Off. of Pur. Agent	Boise
Illinois........	Vernon R. Forgue	Purchasing Agent	Dept. of Finance	Springfield
Indiana........	William E. Clarkson	Purchasing Agent	Div. of Pub. Works and Supply	Indianapolis
Iowa.........	W. G. Cunningham	Secretary	Executive Council	Des Moines
Kansas........	Wm. F. Perkins	Dir. of Purchases	Dept. of Admin.	Topeka
Kentucky......	Charles A. Byrley	Dir., Div. of Purchases	Dept. of Finance	Frankfort
Louisiana......	Guy Martin	Purchasing Officer	Div. of Admin.	Baton Rouge
Maine.........	John R. Dyer	Purchasing Agent	Bur. of Purchases	Augusta
Maryland......	Adam G. Uhl	Chief, Purchasing Bur.	Dept. Budget and Procurement	Baltimore
Massachusetts...	George J. Cronin	Purchasing Agent	Commn. on Admin. and Finance	Boston
Michigan......	J. Stanley Bien	Dir., Purchasing Div.	Dept. of Admin.	Lansing
Minnesota......	P. T. Peterson	Dir., Purchases Div.	Dept. of Admin.	St. Paul
Missouri.......	Edgar C. Nelson	Pur. Agent, Div. of Procurement	Dept. of Revenue	Jefferson City
Montana.......	A. M. Johnson	Controller	Off. of Controller	Helena
Nebraska.......	Carl A. Rosenlof	Purchasing Agent	Div. of Purchase and Supplies	Lincoln
Nevada........	Kenneth S. Easton	Director	Dept. of Purchasing	Carson City
New Hampshire.	Harold Cheney	Dir., Div. of Purchase and Property	Dept. of Admin. and Control	Concord
New Jersey....	Charles F. Sullivan	Dir., Div. of Purchase and Property	Dept. of Treasury	Trenton
New Mexico....	C. F. Horne	Purchasing Agent	Off. of Pur. Agent	Santa Fe
New York......	Charles H. Kriger	Commissr., Div. of Standards and Purchases	Executive Dept.	Albany
North Carolina..	David Q. Holton	Director	Div. of Purchase and Contract	Raleigh
North Dakota...	G. B. Edmonson	Pur. Agent, Pur. Dept.	Board of Admin.	Bismarck
Ohio..........	John W. Bush	Superintendent	Div. of Pur. and Printing	Columbus
Oklahoma......	Ira M. Baker	Purchasing Director	Bd. of Pub. Affairs	Oklahoma City
Oregon........	Ermal R. Owens	Supvr. of Purchases	Dept. of Finance and Admin.	Salem
Pennsylvania...	Kenneth W. Haldeman	Dir., Bur. of Purchases	Dept. Property and Supplies	Harrisburg
Rhode Island...	Joseph L. Byron	Pur. Agent, Div. of Pur.	Dept. of Admin.	Providence

PURCHASING—*continued*

State	Name	Official Title	Agency	Location
South Carolina..	Robert King	Dir., Purchasing Div.	Budg. and Control Bd.	Columbia
South Dakota...	Morris G. Hallock	Secretary	Dept. of Finance	Pierre
Tennessee.......	Franklin Pierce	Purchasing Agent	Dept. of Purchasing	Nashville
Texas..........	Walter L. Bell	Exec. Director	Board of Control	Austin
Utah..........	Truman S. Curtis	Commissioner	Dept. of Finance	Salt Lake City
Vermont.......	Frank P. Free	Purchasing Agent	Off. of Pur. Agent	Montpelier
Virginia.......	R. C. Eaton	Dir., Div. of Purchasing and Printing	Dept. of Accounts and Purchases	Richmond
Washington....	Harry E. Pike	Supvr., Div. of Pur.	Dept. of General Administration	Olympia
West Virginia...	Samuel T. Waller	Director	Dept. of Purchases	Charleston
Wisconsin......	F. X. Ritger	Dir. of Purchases	Bur. of Purchases	Madison
Wyoming......	E. C. Rothwell	Purchasing Agent	Purchasing Dept.	Cheyenne
Alaska.........	John A. McKinney	Dir. of Finance	Dept. of Finance	Juneau
Gaum.........	Louis Mann	Purchasing Agent	Dept. of Finance	Agana
Hawaii........	Paul J. Thurston	Director	Bur. of the Budget	Honolulu
Puerto Rico....	Martín Marqués-Campillo	Dir., Serv. Off. Div.	Dept. of Treasury	San Juan
Virgin Islands...	Mario Lewis	Head, Div. of Procurement and Supply, Dept. of Insular Affairs	Govt. of V.I.	St. Thomas

SANITATION

State	Name	Official Title	Agency	Location
Alabama.......	A. N. Beck	Dir., Bur. of Sanitation	Health Dept.	Montgomery
Arizona........	Clarence G. Salsbury, M.D.	Supt. of Health	Health Dept.	Phoenix
Arkansas.......	J. T. Herron, M.D.	Health Officer	Bd. of Health	Little Rock
California......	Frank M. Stead	Chief, Div. of Environmental Sanit.	Dept. of Pub. Health	Berkeley
Colorado.......	R. L. Cleere, M.D.	Exec. Director	Dept. of Pub. Health	Denver
Connecticut....	Warren J. Scott	Dir., Sanit. Eng. Div.	Dept. of Health	Hartford
Delaware......	Donald K. Harmeson	Dir., Div. Sanit. Eng.	Bd. of Health	Dover
Florida........	David B. Lee	Dir., Bur. Sanit. Eng.	Bd. of Health	Jacksonville
Georgia........	Louva G. Lenert	Dir., Pub. Health Engineering	Dept. of Pub. Health	Atlanta
Idaho.........	L. J. Peterson	Director	Bd. of Health	Boise
Illinois.........	C. W. Klassen	Chief Sanitary Eng.	Dept. of Pub. Health	Springfield
Indiana........	B. A. Poole	Dir., Bur. of Environmental Sanit.	Bd. of Health	Indianapolis
Iowa..........	Edmund G. Zimmerer	Commissioner	Dept. of Health	Des Moines
Kansas........	Dwight Metzler	Dir. and Chief Engr., Div. of Sanitation	Bd. of Health	Lawrence
Kentucky......	Harvey G. McAndrews	Dir., Div. of Sanitation	Dept. of Health	Louisville
Louisiana......	S. J. Phillips, M.D.	President	Bd. of Health	New Orleans
Maine.........	Elmer W. Campbell	Dir. of Sanit. Eng.	Bur. of Health	Augusta
Maryland......	Geo. L. Hall	Chief, Bur. Sanit. Eng.	Health Dept.	Baltimore
Massachusetts...	Clarence I. Sterling, Jr.	Dir. and Chief Engr., Div. of Sanit. Eng.	Dept. of Pub. Health	Boston
Michigan......	Willard Shephard	Dir., Div. of Eng.	Dept. of Health	Lansing
Minnesota......	Frank L. Woodward	Dir., Div. of Environmental Sanit.	Dept. of Health	Minneapolis

SANITATION—*continued*

State	Name	Official Title	Agency	Location
Mississippi.....	F. J. Underwood, M.D.	Exec. Officer	Bd. of Health	Jackson
Missouri.......	James R. Amos	Dir., Div. of Health	Dept. of Pub. Health and Welfare	Jefferson City
Montana.......	Claiborne W. Brinck	Sanitary Engineer	Bd. of Health	Helena
Nebraska.......	T. A. Filipi	Dir., Div. of Sanit.	Dept. of Health	Lincoln
Nevada........	W. W. White	Dir., Div. of Pub. Health Engineering	Dept. of Health	Reno
New Hampshire.	William A. Healy	Dir., Bur. Sanit. Eng.	Dept. of Health	Concord
New Jersey.....	Alfred H. Fletcher	Dir., Div. of Environmental Sanit.	Dept. of Health	Trenton
New Mexico....	Charles Caldwell	Dir., Sanit. Eng. and Sanitation	Dept. of Pub. Health	Santa Fe
New York......	Earl Devendorf	Dir., Bur. of Environmental Sanit.	Dept. of Health	Albany
North Carolina..	J. M. Jarrett	Dir., Sanit. Eng. Div.	Bd. of Health	Raleigh
North Dakota...	J. H. Svore	Dir., Sanitary Div.	Health Dept.	Bismarck
Ohio..........	F. Holman Waring	Chief Sanit. Eng.	Dept. of Health	Columbus
Oklahoma......	Harold Malone	Dir., Div. Sanit. Eng.	Health Dept.	Oklahoma City
Oregon........	Curtiss M. Everts, Jr.	Sanitary Engineer	Sanitary Authority	Portland
Pennsylvania...	James C. Bell	Act. Dir., Bur. of Sanit.	Dept. of Health	Harrisburg
Rhode Island...	Walter J. Shea	Chief, Div. of Sanit. Eng.	Dept. of Health	Providence
South Carolina..	C. W. Harrell	Chief Sanitarian	Health Dept.	Columbia
South Dakota...	G. J. Van Heuvelen	Health Officer	Dept. of Health	Pierre
Tennessee......	Julian R. Fleming	Dir., Div. Sanit. Eng.	Dept. of Pub. Health	Nashville
Texas..........	Henry A. Holle, M.D.	Commissr. of Health	Dept. of Health	Austin
Utah..........	Lynn Thatcher	Dir., Health Dept.	Div. of Eng. and Sanit.	Salt Lake City
Vermont.......	Robt. B. Aikin, M.D.	Commissioner	Dept. of Health	Burlington
Virginia.......	E. C. Meredith	Dir., Sanitary Eng.	Dept. of Health	Richmond
Washington....	Bernard Bucove, M.D.	Act. Director	Dept. of Health	Seattle
West Virginia...	(Vacancy)	Dir., Div. Sanit. Eng.	Dept. of Health	Charleston
Wisconsin......	Oswald J. Muegge	Dir. of Environmental Sanit.	Bd. of Health	Madison
Wyoming......	A. E. Williamson	Director	Health Dept.	Cheyenne
Alaska........	C. Earl Albrecht, M.D.	Commissioner	Dept. of Health	Juneau
Guam.........	Lawrence T. Cowper	Sanitarian	Dept. of Medical Services	Tamuning
Hawaii........	B. J. McMorrow	Dir., Div. of Sanit.	Dept. of Health	Honolulu
Puerto Rico....	Henry Rodríguez	Chief, Bur. of Sanit.	Dept. of Health	San Juan
Virgin Islands..	Roy A. Anduze, M.D.	Commissr. of Health	Govt. of the V. I.	St. Thomas

---

SCHOOL LUNCH ADMINISTRATION

State	Name	Official Title	Agency	Location
Alabama.......	Roy T. Alverson	Supvr., Local Acctg. and Sch. Lunch Section	Dept. of Education	Montgomery
Arizona........	C. L. Harkins	Supt. of Pub. Instruction	Off., Supt. of Pub. Instr.	Phoenix
Arkansas.......	Ruth Powell	Supvr., Sch. Lunch Prog.	Dept. of Education	Little Rock

SCHOOL LUNCH ADMINISTRATION—*continued*

State	Name	Official Title	Agency	Location
California......	Frank M. Wright	Chief, Div. of Pub. Sch. Admin.	Dept. of Education	Sacramento
Colorado.......	Chas. W. Lilly	Director	Dept. of Education	Denver
Connecticut....	Edith Cushman	Supvr., Sch. Lunch Prog., Bur. of Sch. and Community Services	Dept. of Education	Hartford
Delaware......	Ruth S. MacVean	Supvr. of State School Lunch Prog.	Bd. of Education	Dover
Florida........	Thelma Flanagan	Senior Specialist	Dept. of Education	Tallahassee
Georgia........	Eleanor Pryor	Dir., Div. of Sch. Lunch Prog.	Dept. of Education	Atlanta
Idaho.........	Alton B. Jones	Supt. of Pub. Instr.	Dept. of Education	Boise
Illinois.........	Harold A. Wolfe	Dir. of Sch. Lunch Prog.	Supt. of Pub. Instr.	Springfield
Indiana........	Harvey H. Davidson	Sch. Lunch Director	Bd. of Education	Indianapolis
Iowa..........	C. W. Bangs	Director	Dept. of Pub. Instr.	Des Moines
Kansas........	Adel F. Throckmorton	Supt. of Pub. Instr.	Off., Supt. of Pub. Instr.	Topeka
Kentucky......	Kearney Campbell	Dir., Div. of Pub. Sch. Lunch	Dept. of Education	Frankfort
Louisiana......	Shelby M. Jackson	Superintendent	Dept. of Pub. Ed.	Baton Rouge
Maine.........	Gertrude Griney	Dir., Sch. Lunch Prog.	Dept. of Education	Augusta
Maryland......	John J. Seidel	Asst. Supt.	Div. of Voc. Ed.	Baltimore
Massachusetts...	John C. Stalker	Dir., Community Sch. Lunch Prog.	Dept. of Education	Boston
Michigan......	Norman Tellar	Chief, School Lunch Prog.	Dept. Pub. Instr.	Lansing
Minnesota......	A. R. Taylor	Dir., Community Sch. Lunch Prog.	Dept. of Education	St. Paul
Mississippi.....	J. M. Tubb	Superintendent	Dept. of Education	Jackson
Missouri.......	Earl M. Langkop	Dir., Sch. Lunch	Dept. of Education	Jefferson City
Montana.......	Leslie L. Brown	Supervisor	Supt of Pub. Instr.	Helena
Nebraska.......	Allen A. Elliott	Dir., School Lunch	Dept. of Education	Lincoln
Nevada........	Chrissie Kellogg	Supvr., Div. Sch. Lunch Prog.	Dept. of Education	Carson City
New Hampshire.	Ruth M. Cutter	Dir., School Lunches	Dept. of Education	Concord
New Jersey.....	Janet N. Schock	Supvr. of School Lunch, Div. of Health, Safety and Physical Ed.	Dept. of Education	Trenton
New Mexico....	Carmen Dyche	Director	School Lunch Div.	Santa Fe
New York......	Helen Diehl	Assoc. in Sch. Lunch Admin., Bur. of Home Econ.	Dept. of Education	Albany
North Carolina..	Ann W. Maley	Dir., Sch. Lunch Prog.	Bd. of Education	Raleigh
North Dakota...	M. F. Peterson	Superintendent	Dept. of Pub. Instr.	Bismarck
Ohio..........	R. M. Eyman	Supt., Pub. Instr.	Dept. of Education	Columbus
Oklahoma......	Drew Langley	Dir., Sch. Lunch Div.	Dept. of Education	Oklahoma City
Oregon........	Mrs. Laura P. Wells	Dir., Sch. Lunch Prog.	Dept. of Education	Salem
Pennsylvania...	Frances L. Hoag	Chief, Sch. Lunch and Nutrition	Dept. of Pub. Instr.	Harrisburg
Rhode Island...	Elizabeth S. Ferguson	Supvr., Sch. Lunch Program	Dept. of Education	Providence
South Carolina..	W. H. Garrison	Supvr., Sch. Lunch Prog.	Dept. of Education	Columbia
South Dakota...	Merle Hagerty	Dir., Sch. Lunch	Public Instruction	Pierre
Tennessee......	Frances Mae Nave	Supvr., Sch. Lunch Prog.	Dept. of Education	Nashville
Texas..........	J. W. Edgar	Commissr. of Ed.	Education Agency	Austin
Utah..........	R. A. Ashby	Director	Bd. of Education	Salt Lake City

SCHOOL LUNCH ADMINISTRATION—*continued*

State	Name	Official Title	Agency	Location
Vermont.......	Raymond Magwire	Dir., Health and Physical Ed.	Dept. of Education	Montpelier
Virginia.......	Helen G. Ward	Supvr., Sch. Lunch Prog.	Dept. of Education	Richmond
Washington....	Agnes R. Fitzgerald	Supvr., Sch. Lunch Prog.	Off., Supt. of Pub. Instr.	Olympia
West Virginia...	Martha Bonar	Sch. Lunch Supvr.	Dept. of Education	Charleston
Wisconsin......	Gordon W. Gunderson	Supvr., Sch. Lunch Prog.	Dept. of Pub. Instr.	Madison
Wyoming......	Jos. F. Replogle	Director	Sch. Lunch Program	Cheyenne
Alaska.........	Donald M. Dafoe	Commissioner	Dept. of Education	Juneau
Hawaii........	Mrs. Helen G. McGill	Dir., Home Econ. Education	Dept. of Pub. Instr.	Honolulu
Puerto Rico....	Mrs. Margarita P. Marchand	Dir., Sch. Lunchroom Div.	Dept. of Education	San Juan
Virgin Islands..	C. F. Dixon	Act. Commissr. of Ed.	Govt. of the V. I.	St. Thomas

SECURITIES

State	Name	Official Title	Agency	Location
Alabama.......	John M. Patterson	Securities Commissr.	Securities Commn.	Montgomery
Arizona........	Earl F. Hastings	Dir., Secs. Div.	Corporation Commn.	Phoenix
Arkansas.......	John L. Carter	Bldg. and Loan and Securities Examiner	Bank Dept.	Little Rock
California......	W. H. Stephenson	Commissr., Div. of Corporations	Dept. of Investment	Sacramento
Colorado.......	Curtis White	Commissioner	Div. of Securities	Denver
Connecticut....	Melvin O. Hall	Dir., Sec. Div.	Banking Dept.	Hartford
Delaware......	Joseph Donald Craven	Attorney General	Off. of Atty. Gen.	Wilmington
Florida........	J. Edwin Larson	Chairman	Securities Commn.	Tallahassee
Georgia........	Ben W. Fortson, Jr.	Secretary of State	Off. of Secy. of State	Atlanta
Idaho.........	R. U. Spaulding	Commissioner	Fin. and Pub. Investments	Boise
Illinois.........	Robert G. Cronson	Securities Commissr.	Off. of Secy. of State	Springfield
Indiana........	Joseph Shannon	Commissioner	Securities Commn.	Indianapolis
Iowa..........	Oliver P. Bennett	Commissioner	Insurance Dept.	Des Moines
Kansas........	Robert R. Lammy	Securities Commissr.	Securities Dept., Corp. Commn.	Topeka
Kentucky......	H. B. Kinsolving, Jr.	Dir., Div. of Securities	Dept. of Banking	Frankfort
Louisiana......	Edward F. Follett	Commissioner	Banking Dept.	Baton Rouge
Maine.........	Hal G. Hoyt	Securities Examiner	Banking Dept.	Augusta
Maryland......	Albert W. Ward	Exec. Secretary	Tax Commission	Baltimore
Massachusetts...	Harold C. White	Chief Acct., Div. of Investigation of Sec.	Dept. of Pub. Utilities	Boston
Michigan......	James C. Allen	Commissioner	Corp. and Securities Commn.	Lansing
Minnesota......	Theodore N. Ofstedahl	Commissioner	Div. of Securities	St. Paul
Mississippi.....	Heber Ladner	Commissioner	Secy. of State	Jackson
Missouri.......	Joseph W. Mosby	Corp. Commissr.	Off. of Secy. of State	Jefferson City
Montana.......	John J. Holmes	Auditor	Off. of Auditor	Helena
Nebraska.......	Harold Johnson	Asst. Dir. of Banking	Bur. of Securities	Lincoln
New Hampshire.	Donald Knowlton	Commissioner	Insurance Dept.	Concord
New Jersey.....	Gordon S. Kerr	Dir., Div. of Investment	Dept. of Treasury	Trenton
New Mexico....	Frank F. Weddington	Bank Examiner	Banking Dept.	Santa Fe
New York......	Max Furman	Principal Accountant	Dept. of Law	Albany
North Carolina..	Thad Eure	Secy. of State	Dept. of State	Raleigh

SECURITIES—*continued*

State	Name	Official Title	Agency	Location
North Dakota...	John Graham	Examiner and Sec. Commissr.	Off. of Sec. Commissr.	Bismarck
Ohio..........	Edmond H. Savord	Superintendent	Div. of Securities	Columbus
Oklahoma......	Herschal K. Ross	Commissioner	Securities Commn.	Oklahoma City
Oregon........	Frank J. Healy	Corp. Commissr.	Corporation Dept.	Salem
Pennsylvania...	Frank M. Happ	Chmn., Sec. Commn.	Dept. of Banking	Harrisburg
Rhode Island...	Louis J. Barry	Securities Commissr.	Dept. of Bus. Reg.	Providence
South Carolina..	R. L. Kelly	Insurance Commissr.	Off. of Insurance Commissr.	Columbia
South Dakota...	George Burt	Insurance Commissr.	Security Commn.	Pierre
Tennessee......	Arch Northington	Commissioner	Dept. of Insurance and Banking	Nashville
Texas..........	G. Bradley Bourland	Securities Commissr.	Dept. of State	Austin
Utah..........	Milton H. Love	Director	Securities Commn.	Salt Lake City
Vermont.......	Alexander H. Miller	Commissioner	Dept. of Banking and Ins.	Montpelier
Virginia.......	Harry E. Dinwiddie, Jr.	Dir., Sec. Div.	Corporation Commn.	Richmond
Washington....	J. C. Baillie	Act. Admn., Sec. Div.	Dept. of Licenses	Seattle
West Virginia...	Harold J. Powell	Securities Commissr.	Auditor's Office	Charleston
Wisconsin......	Edward J. Samp	Director	Dept. of Securities	Madison
Wyoming......	Everett T. Copenhaver	Securities Commissr.	Blue Sky Agency	Cheyenne
Guam..........	Richard F. Taitano	Director	Dept. of Finance	Agana
Hawaii........	Kam Tai Lee	Treasurer	Off. of Treas.	Honolulu
Puerto Rico....	Rafael Picó	Secretary	Dept. of Treasury	San Juan

---

SOIL CONSERVATION

State	Name	Official Title	Agency	Location
Alabama.......	S. R. Doughty	Secretary	Soil Conserv. Comm.	Auburn
Arizona........	Roger Ernst	Land Commissr.	Land Dept.	Phoenix
Arkansas.......	Ewing Kinkead	Conservationist	Geology and Conserv. Commn.	Little Rock
California......	Sven Anderson	Exec. Secy., Soil Conserv. Commn.	Dept. of Nat. Res.	Sacramento
Connecticut....	Joseph A. Ward	Supervisor	Dept. of Agric.	Hartford
Delaware......	Geo. L. Schuster	Dir., School of Agric.	Soil Conserv. Commn.	Newark
Florida........	H. G. Clayton	Administrator	Soil Conserv. Bd.	Gainesville
Georgia........	Jas. L. Gillis, Jr.	Chairman	Soil Conserv. Comm.	Soperton
Idaho.........	Mark R. Kulp	Reclam. Engineer	Dept. of Reclamation	Boise
Illinois.........	Stillman Stanard	Director	Dept. of Agriculture	Springfield
Indiana........	R. O. Cole	Secretary	Soil Conserv. Comm.	West Lafayette
Iowa..........	Othie R. McMurry	Exec. Secretary	Soil Conserv. Comm.	Des Moines
Kansas........	Roger Lemon	Chairman	Soil Conserv. Comm.	Viola
Kentucky......	Marshall W. Qualls	Dir., Div. Soil and Water Resources	Dept. of Conserv.	Frankfort
Louisiana......	{J. O. Davis	Secretary	Soil Conserv. Comm.	Baton Rouge
	{H. B. Martin	State Conservationist	U. S. Dept. of Agric., Soil Conserv. Serv.	Alexandria
Maine.........	Keith N. Smith	Chairman	Soil Conserv. Comm.	Newport
Maryland......	Fred. L. Bull	Secretary	Soil Conserv. Comm.	College Park
Michigan......	R. G. Hill	Exec. Secretary	Soil Conserv. Comm.	East Lansing
Minnesota.....	M. A. Thorfinnson	Secretary	Soil Conserv. Comm.	St. Paul
Mississippi.....	Clay Lyle	Chairman	Soil Conserv. Comm.	State College
Missouri.......	J. H. Longwell	Director	Soils Conserv. Commn.	Columbia
Montana.......	M. A. Bell	Asst. Director	Agric. Experiment Sta.	Bozeman
Nebraska.......	E. C. Reed	Chairman	Soil Conserv. Comm.	Lincoln
Nevada........	George Hardman	State Coordinator	Soil Conserv. Serv.	Reno
New Hampshire.	Perley I. Fitts	Chairman and Commissr. of Agric.	Soil Conserv. Comm.	Concord

SOIL CONSERVATION—*continued*

State	Name	Official Title	Agency	Location
New Jersey.....	Van Wie Ingham	Exec. Secy., Soil Conserv. Comm., Div. of Planning and Devel.	Dept. Conserv. and Econ. Devel.	New Brunswick
New Mexico....	L. C. Brown	Admin. Off.	Soil Conserv. Comm.	State College
North Dakota...	W. P. Sebens	Exec. Secretary	Soil Conserv. Comm.	Bismarck
Ohio..........	Leo L. Rummell	Director	Agric. Exper. Sta.	Wooster
Oklahoma......	Hershel Burrus	Exec. Director	Soil Conserv. Bd.	Oklahoma City
Oregon........	Robert C. Baum	Exec. Secretary	Soil Conserv. Comm.	Corvallis
Pennsylvania...	Leland H. Bull	Exec. Secretary	Soil Conserv. Comm.	Harrisburg
Rhode Island...	John L. Rego	Director	Dept. Agric. and Conserv.	Providence
South Carolina..	D. W. Watkins	Dir., State Agric. Ext. Serv.	Soil Conserv. Comm.	Clemson
South Dakota...	Ross D. Davies	Secretary	Soil Conserv. Comm.	Huron
Tennessee......	Carl I. Peterson	Dir., Div. Forestry	Dept. of Conserv.	Nashville
Texas..........	Carl Spencer	Exec. Director	Soil Conserv. Bd.	Temple
Utah..........	Alden K. Barton	Commn. Chairman	State Agric. Dept.	Salt Lake City
Vermont.......	Lemuel J. Peet	Secretary	Soil Conserv. Comm.	Burlington
Virginia.......	John H. Daniel	Chairman	Soil Conserv. Comm.	Charlotte Court House
Washington....	Sverre N. Omdahl	Director	Dept. of Agriculture	Olympia
West Virginia...	Carroll Greene	Exec. Secretary	Soil Conserv. Comm.	Charleston
Wisconsin......	Ingvald O. Hembre	Exec. Secretary	Soil Conserv. Comm.	Madison
Wyoming......	B. H. Hopkins	Secretary	Soil Conserv. Comm.	Casper
Alaska.........	Clarence C. Hoffman	Chairman	Soil Conserv. Bd.	Palmer
Guam.........	Manuel Calvo	Director	Dept. of Agriculture	Mangilao
Hawaii........	Joseph L. Dwight	Chairman	Soil Conserv. Comm.	Honolulu
Puerto Rico....	S. García-Ruiz	Secy., Soil Conserv. Committee	Dept. of Agric. and Commerce	San Juan

TAXATION (Over-all Administration)

See also Corporation Tax, Fuel Tax, Income Tax, Motor Vehicle Tax, Property Tax.

State	Name	Official Title	Agency	Location
Alabama.......	W. LaRue Horn	Commissioner	Dept. of Revenue	Montgomery
Arizona........	Warren Peterson	Chairman	Tax Commission	Phoenix
Arkansas.......	Orville Cheney	Commissioner	Revenue Dept.	Little Rock
California......	John J. Campbell	Exec. Officer	Franchise Tax Board	Sacramento
	Dixwell L. Pierce	Exec. Secretary	Bd. of Equalization	Sacramento
Colorado.......	Earl Blevins	Director	Dept. of Revenue	Denver
Connecticut....	John J. Sullivan	Commissioner	Tax Department	Hartford
Delaware......	C. Douglass Buck	Commissioner	Tax Board	Dover
Georgia........	T. V. Williams	Commissioner	Dept. of Revenue	Atlanta
Idaho.........	E. D. Baird	Chmn. of Board	Tax Commission	Boise
Illinois.........	Richard J. Lyons	Director	Dept. of Revenue	Springfield
Indiana........	Frank T. Millis	Commissioner	Dept. of Revenue	Indianapolis
Iowa..........	Ray E. Johnson	Chairman	Tax Commission	Des Moines
Kansas........	Roy N. McCue	Chairman	Revenue and Taxation Commn.	Topeka
Kentucky......	Robert Allphin	Commissioner	Dept. of Revenue	Frankfort
Louisiana......	Graydon K. Kitchens	Chairman	Tax Commission	Baton Rouge
Maine.........	Ernest H. Johnson	Tax Assessor	Bur. of Taxation	Augusta
Maryland......	Joseph Allen	Chairman	Tax Commission	Baltimore
Massachusetts...	John Dane, Jr.	Commissioner	Dept. of Corp. and Taxation	Boston
Michigan......	Louis M. Nims	Commissioner	Tax Commission	Lansing
Minnesota......	G. Howard Spaeth	Commissioner	Dept. of Taxation	St. Paul
Mississippi.....	Mrs. Thomas L. Bailey	Tax Collector	Dept. of Taxation	Jackson
	Alex McKeigney	Chairman	Tax Commn.	Jackson

TAXATION (Over-all Administration)—*continued*

See also Corporation Tax, Fuel Tax, Income Tax, Motor Vehicle Tax, Property Tax.

State	Name	Official Title	Agency	Location
Missouri	James Robertson	Chmn., Tax Commn.	Dept. of Revenue	Jefferson City
Montana	J. L. Reed	Chairman	Bd. of Equalization	Helena
Nebraska	F. A. Herrington	Tax Commissioner	Bd. of Equalization and Assessment	Lincoln
Nevada	Robbins E. Cahill	Secretary	Tax Commission	Carson City
New Hampshire	Oliver W. Marvin	Chairman	Tax Commission	Concord
New Jersey	Aaron K. Neeld	Dir., Div. of Taxation	Dept. of Treasury	Trenton
New Mexico	Mike M. Gallegos	Director	Bur. of Revenue	Santa Fe
New York	George M. Bragalini	Commissr. of Taxation and Finance	Dept. of Taxation and Finance	Albany
North Carolina	Eugene G. Shaw	Commissioner	Dept. of Revenue	Raleigh
North Dakota	J. Arthur Engen	Tax Commissioner	Off. of Tax Commissr.	Bismarck
Ohio	Stanley J. Bowers	Tax Commissioner	Dept. of Taxation	Columbus
Oklahoma	J. D. Dunn	Chairman	Tax Commission	Oklahoma City
Oregon	Carl Chambers	Tax Commissr.	Tax Commission	Salem
Pennsylvania	Gerald A. Gleeson	Secretary	Dept. of Revenue	Harrisburg
Rhode Island	Frederick M. Langton	Admn., Div. of Taxation	Dept. of Admin.	Providence
South Carolina	Otis W. Livingston	Chairman	Tax Commission	Columbia
South Dakota	W. R. Wilder	Commissioner	Dept. of Revenue	Pierre
Tennessee	Z. D. Atkins	Commissioner	Dept. of Finance and Taxation	Nashville
Texas	Robert S. Calvert	Comptr. of Pub. Accts.	Off. of Comptroller	Austin
Utah	Byron D. Jones	Chairman	Tax Commission	Salt Lake City
Vermont	Leonard W. Morrison	Commissioner	Tax Dept.	Montpelier
Virginia	C. H. Morrissett	Commissioner	Dept. of Taxation	Richmond
Washington	H. Dan Bracken	Chairman	Tax Commission	Olympia
West Virginia	William R. Laird III	Commissioner	Tax Commission	Charleston
Wisconsin	Harry W. Harder	Commissioner	Dept. of Taxation	Madison
Wyoming	Walter W. Hudson	Chairman	Bd. of Equalization	Cheyenne
Alaska	Karl F. Dewey	Tax Commissr.	Dept. of Taxation	Juneau
Guam	Richard F. Taitano	Director	Dept. of Finance	Agana
Hawaii	Earl W. Fase	Tax Commissioner	Off. of Tax. Commissr.	Honolulu
Puerto Rico	Rafael Picó	Secretary	Dept. of Treasury	San Juan

TREASURER

State	Name	Official Title	Agency	Location
Alabama	John Brandon	Treasurer	Office of Treasurer	Montgomery
Arizona	E. T. Williams, Jr.	Treasurer	Treasurer's Office	Phoenix
Arkansas	J. Vance Clayton	Treasurer	Office of Treasurer	Little Rock
California	Charles G. Johnson	Treasurer	Treasurer's Office	Sacramento
Colorado	Earl E. Ewing	Treasurer	Dept. of Treasury	Denver
Connecticut	John Ottaviano	Treasurer	State Treasury	Hartford
Delaware	Howard H. Dickerson	Treasurer	Treasurer's Office	Dover
Florida	J. Edwin Larson	Treasurer	Treasurer's Office	Tallahassee
Georgia	Geo. B. Hamilton	Treasurer	Office of Treasurer	Atlanta
Idaho	Mrs. Ruth Moon	Treasurer	Treasurer's Office	Boise
Illinois	Warren E. Wright	Treasurer	Office of Treasurer	Springfield
Indiana	John Peters	Treasurer	Treasurer's Office	Indianapolis
Iowa	M. L. Abrahamson	Treasurer	State Treasury	Des Moines
Kansas	Richard T. Fadely	Treasurer	Treasury Dept.	Topeka
Kentucky	Henry H. Carter	Treasurer	Dept. of Treasury	Frankfort
Louisiana	A. P. Tugwell	Treasurer	Office of Treasurer	Baton Rouge
Maine	Frank S. Carpenter	Treasurer	Office of Treasurer	Augusta

TREASURER—*continued*

State	*Name*	*Official Title*	*Agency*	*Location*
Maryland......	Hooper S. Miles	Treasurer	State Treasury	Annapolis
Massachusetts...	John F. Kennedy	Treasurer and Receiver-General	Dept. of State Treasurer	Boston
Michigan......	Sanford A. Brown	Treasurer	Treasury Dept.	Lansing
Minnesota......	Arthur Hansen	Treasurer	Office of Treasurer	St. Paul
Mississippi.....	R. D. Morrow	Treasurer	Office of Treasurer	Jackson
Missouri.......	Geo. Hubert Bates	Treasurer	Office of Treasurer	Jefferson City
Montana.......	Mrs. Edna Hinman	Treasurer	Treasurer's Office	Helena
Nebraska.......	Ralph W. Hill	Treasurer	Office of Treasurer	Lincoln
Nevada........	Dan W. Franks	Treasurer	Office of Treasurer	Carson City
New Hampshire.	Alfred S. Cloues	Treasurer	Treasurer's Office	Concord
New Jersey.....	Robert L. Finley	Act. Treasurer	Dept. of Treasury	Trenton
New Mexico....	Joseph B. Grant	Treasurer	Office of Treasurer	Santa Fe
New York......	Avery G. Hall	Dep. Commissr., Div. of Treasury	Dept. of Taxation and Finance	Albany
North Carolina..	Edwin Gill	Treasurer	Treasurer's Office	Raleigh
North Dakota...	Albert Jacobson	Treasurer	Office of Treasurer	Bismarck
Ohio..........	Roger W. Tracy	Treasurer	Office of Treasurer	Columbus
Oklahoma......	John D. Conner	Treasurer	Off. of State Treas.	Oklahoma City
Oregon........	Sigfrid B. Unander	Treasurer	Treasurer's Office	Salem
Pennsylvania...	Weldon B. Heyburn	Treasurer	State Treasury	Harrisburg
Rhode Island...	Raymond H. Hawksley	Gen. Treasurer	Treasury Dept.	Providence
South Carolina..	Jeff B. Bates	Treasurer	State Treasury	Columbia
South Dakota...	Ed. T. Elkins	Treasurer	Office of Treasurer	Pierre
Tennessee......	Ramon T. Davis	Treasurer	Treasurer's Office	Nashville
Texas.........	Jesse James	Treasurer	Treasury Dept.	Austin
Utah..........	Sid Lambourne	Treasurer	Office of Treasurer	Salt Lake City
Vermont.......	George H. Amidon	Treasurer	Treasurer's Office	Montpelier
Virginia.......	Jesse W. Dillon	Treasurer	Dept. of the Treasury	Richmond
Washington....	Chas. R. Maybury	Treasurer	Treasurer's Office	Olympia
West Virginia...	Wm. H. Ansel, Jr.	Treasurer	Office of Treasurer	Charleston
Wisconsin......	Warren R. Smith	Treasurer	Office of Treasurer	Madison
Wyoming......	Charles B. Morgan	Treasurer	Office of Treasurer	Cheyenne
Alaska........	Hugh J. Wade	Treasurer	Treasurer's Office	Juneau
Guam.........	Galo L. Salas	Treasurer	Dept. of Finance	Agana
Hawaii........	Kam Tai Lee	Treasurer	Treasury Dept.	Honolulu
Puerto Rico....	Rafael Picó	Secretary	Dept. of Treasury	San Juan
Virgin Islands..	Percy de Jongh	Act. Commissr. of Fin.	Govt. of V.I.	St. Thomas

UNEMPLOYMENT INSURANCE

State	*Name*	*Official Title*	*Agency*	*Location*
Alabama.......	Wm. A. Major	Dir., Unempl. Comp.	Dept. of Ind. Rels.	Montgomery
Arizona........	Bruce Parkinson	Dir., Unempl. Comp.	Empl. Sec. Commn.	Phoenix
Arkansas.......	G. J. Hardwick	Director, Central Off. Operations	Empl. Sec. Div., Dept. of Labor	Little Rock
California......	Harry W. Stewart	Director	Dept. of Employment	Sacramento
Colorado.......	Bernard E. Teets	Exec. Director	Dept. of Empl. Sec.	Denver
Connecticut....	George J. Walker	Dir., Unempl. Comp.	Labor Dept.	Hartford
Delaware......	Albert Stetser	Chmn.-Exec. Dir.	Unempl. Comp. Commn.	Wilmington
Florida........	Charles M. Mann	Dir., Unempl. Comp. Div.	Industrial Commn.	Tallahassee
Georgia........	Ben B. Strain	Dir., Unempl. Comp. Div.	Empl. Sec. Agency	Atlanta
Idaho.........	Floyd West	Asst. Director	Empl. Security	Boise
Illinois.........	Samuel C. Bernstein	Commissr. of Unemployment Comp.	Dept. of Labor	Chicago

UNEMPLOYMENT INSURANCE—*continued*

State	Name	Official Title	Agency	Location
Indiana........	Wm. G. Stalnaker	Director	Empl. Sec. Div.	Indianapolis
Iowa..........	C. M. Stanley	Chairman	Empl. Sec. Commn.	Des Moines
Kansas.........	John Morrison	Exec. Dir., Empl. Sec. Div.	Labor Dept.	Topeka
Kentucky......	O. B. Hannah	Dir., Div. of Unempl. Ins.	Dept. of Econ. Sec.	Frankfort
Louisiana......	Richard Walker	Administrator	Div. of Empl. Sec.	Baton Rouge
Maine.........	John W. Greene	Dir., Unempl. Comp.	Empl. Security Commn.	Augusta
Maryland......	Stephen C. Cromwell	Dir., Unempl. Comp. Div.	Dept. of Empl. Security	Baltimore
Massachusetts...	Kenneth V. Minihan	Asst. Dir. of Benefits Service	Div. of Empl. Sec.	Boston
Michigan......	Joseph A. Burns	Dir., Unempl. Comp. Div.	Empl. Sec. Commn.	Detroit
Minnesota......	Donald M. Anderson	Dir., Unempl. Comp.	Dept. of Empl. Sec.	St. Paul
Mississippi.....	Robert Prisock	Exec. Director	Empl. Sec. Commn.	Jackson
Missouri.......	Gordon P. Weir	Dir., Div. of Empl. Security	Dept. of Labor and Ind. Relations	Jefferson City
Montana.......	Russell Fitzhugh	Unempl. Ins. Dir.	Unempl. Comp. Commn.	Helena
Nebraska.......	Robert T. Malone	Dir., Div. of Empl. Security	Dept. of Labor	Lincoln
Nevada........	Harry A. Depaoli	Exec. Director	Empl. Sec. Dept.	Carson City
New Hampshire.	Wm. C. Chamberlin	Dir., Unempl. Comp. Bur.	Div. of Empl. Sec.	Concord
New Jersey.....	Edward J. Hall	Supt., Unempl. Ins. Serv., Div. Empl. Security	Dept. of Labor and Industry	Trenton
New Mexico....	M. I. Tillery	Director	Unempl. Ins. Div.	Albuquerque
New York......	Richard C. Brockway	Exec. Dir., Div. of Empl.	Dept. of Labor	New York
North Carolina..	R. Fuller Martin	Dir., Unempl. Ins. Div.	Empl. Sec. Commn.	Raleigh
North Dakota...	Martin N. Gronvold	Director	Unempl. Comp. Div.	Bismarck
Ohio..........	James Tichenor	Act. Administrator	Bur. Unempl. Comp.	Columbus
Oklahoma	Bruton Wood	Exec. Director	Empl. Sec. Commn.	Oklahoma City
Oregon........	Silas Gaiser	Administrator	Unempl. Comp. Commn.	Salem
Pennsylvania...	Paul J. Smith	Dir., Unempl. Compensation	Dept. of Labor and Industry	Harrisburg
Rhode Island...	T. Edward Burns	Chief, Unempl. Benefits	Dept. of Empl. Sec.	Providence
South Carolina..	B. Frank Godfrey	Director	Unempl. Comp. Div.	Columbia
South Dakota...	Alan Williamson	Commissioner	Empl. Sec. Dept.	Aberdeen
Tennessee......	Emmett L. Conner	Dir., Unempl. Comp. Div.	Dept. of Empl. Security	Nashville
Texas..........	{ Weldon Hart	Chmn., Exec. Dir.	Empl. Commn.	Austin
	{ Wm. H. Farmer	Administrator	Employment Commn.	Austin
Utah..........	Lee G. Burns	Director	Div. Unempl. Ins.	Salt Lake City
Vermont.......	John V. Ford	Director	Unempl. Comp. Div.	Montpelier
Virginia.......	B. R. Councill	Director	Unempl. Comp. Commn.	Richmond
Washington....	Frank Ryan	Asst. Commissr.	Dept. of Empl. Sec.	Olympia
West Virginia...	I. McNeel	Asst. Dir., Unempl. Comp.	Dept. of Empl. Sec.	Charleston
Wisconsin......	Paul A. Raushen-bush	Dir., Unempl. Comp.	Industrial Commn.	Madison
Wyoming......	Leo F. Freyder	Exec. Director	Empl. Sec. Commn.	Casper
Alaska.........	Arthur A. Hedges	Act. Exec. Dir.	Empl. Sec. Commn.	Juneau
Guam.........	Juan Palomó	Empl. Manager	Dept. of Labor and Personnel	Agana
Hawaii........	Frank M. Torres	Chief	Unempl. Ins. Div.	Honolulu

VETERANS PROGRAMS

State	Name	Official Title	Agency	Location
Alabama.......	C. C. Horton	Service Commissr.	Dept. of Veterans Affairs	Montgomery
Arizona	James J. Murphy, Jr.	Director	Veterans Affairs	Phoenix
Arkansas.......	Carl Thompson	Director	Vet. Serv. Office	Little Rock
California......	J. Marvin Russell	Director	Dept. of Veterans Affairs	Sacramento
Colorado.......	Wm. N. Rice	Director	Dept. of Veterans Affairs	Denver
Florida........	Melvin T. Dixon	Service Officer	Vets. Serv. Commn.	Pass-a-Grille
Georgia........	Peter Wheeler	Director	Vets. Serv. Office	Atlanta
Idaho.........	S. E. Vance, Jr.	Secretary	Vets. Welfare Commn.	Boise
Illinois.........	J. P. Ringley	Chairman	Veterans Commn.	Springfield
Indiana........	Edgar K. Gusler	State Serv. Off.	Dept. of Vets. Affairs	Indianapolis
Kansas........	Norman D. Jones	Supervisor	Veterans Commn.	Topeka
Kentucky......	Stanley Hudson	Director	Disabled Exservice-men's Bd.	Louisville
Louisiana......	Lloyd E. Hatley	Director	Veterans Affairs Commn.	Baton Rouge
Maine.........	Frederick P. O'Connell	Director	Veterans Affairs	Augusta
Maryland......	David Kaiser	Chairman	Veterans Commn.	Baltimore
Massachusetts...	Nathaniel M. Hurwitz	Commissr.	Veterans Services	Boston
Michigan.......	Lawrence J. LaLone	Exec. Secretary	Vets. Trust Fund	Lansing
Minnesota......	William E. Revier	Commissioner	Dept. of Vets. Affairs	St. Paul
Mississippi.....	R. H. DeKay	Commissioner	Vets. Affairs Bd.	Jackson
Missouri.......	Roy Carver	Service Officer	Service Office	Jefferson City
Montana.......	Eugene Callaghan	Director	Vets. Welf. Commn.	Helena
Nebraska.......	Louis R. Eby	Director	Dept. of Vets. Affairs	Lincoln
Nevada........	Melvin L. Jacobsen	Vets. Serv. Commissr.	Off. Veterans Serv. Commissr.	Reno
New Hampshire	Joseph R. Stuard	Director	Veterans Council	Concord
New Jersey.....	Salvatore A. Bontempo	Dir., Div. of Veterans Services	Dept. Conserv. and Econ. Devel.	Trenton
New Mexico....	Manuel A. Armijo	Director	Vets. Serv. Commn.	Santa Fe
New York......	(Vacancy)	Dir., Div. Veterans Affairs	Exec. Dept.	Albany
North Carolina..	J. M. Caldwell	Director	Veterans Commn.	Raleigh
North Dakota...	F. E. Henderson	Commissioner	Veterans Affairs	Fargo
Ohio..........	Wilbur K. Morris	Executive	Off. Soldiers Claims	Columbus
Oklahoma......	Wilbur P. Henline	Director	War Veterans Dept.	Oklahoma City
Oregon........	H. C. Saalfeld	Director	Dept. of Vets. Affairs	Salem
Pennsylvania...	Anthony J. Drexel Biddle, Jr.	Adj. Gen.	Dept. Milit. Affairs	Harrisburg
Rhode Island...	Chester W. Williams	Chief, Div. Soldiers Welfare	Dept. of Soc. Welfare	Providence
South Carolina..	R. Stedman Sloan	Service Officer	Veterans Serv. Bur.	Columbia
South Dakota...	E. A. Jones	Director	Veterans Dept.	Pierre
Tennessee......	James L. Crider	Director	Dept. of Vets. Affairs	Nashville
Texas..........	Chas. L. Morris	Exec. Director	Vets. Affairs Commn.	Austin
	R. Clark Diebel	Exec. Secretary	Vets. Land Bd.	Austin
Vermont.......	Alexander J. Smith	Exec. Secretary	Veterans Bd.	Montpelier
Virginia.......	H. F. Carper, Jr.	Director	Div. War Veterans Claims	Roanoke
Washington....	E. B. Riley	Director	Veterans Rehabil. Council	Olympia
West Virginia...	T. H. McGovran	Director	Dept. of Vets. Affairs	Charleston
Wisconsin......	Gordon A. Huseby	Director	Dept. of Vets. Affairs	Madison
Alaska.........	Edward T. Brehm	Commissioner	Off. of Vets. Affairs	Juneau
Hawaii........	Charles J. Basener	Director	Council on Veterans Affairs	Honolulu
Puerto Rico....	Enrique N. Vela	Dir., Vets. Office	Dept. of Labor	San Juan
Virgin Islands..	Ejnar Bølling	Veterans Contact Man	Dept. of Agric. and Labor	St. Croix

WATER POLLUTION CONTROL

State	Name	Official Title	Agency	Location
Alabama.......	D. G. Gill, M.D.	Health Officer and Chmn.	Water Improvement Commn.	Montgomery
Arizona........	John M. Hall	Director	Game and Fish Commn.	Phoenix
Arkansas.......	Marvin L. Wood	Director	Water Pollut. Control Commn.	Little Rock
California......	Vinton W. Bacon	Exec. Officer	Water Pollution Control Bd.	Sacramento
Colorado.......	R. L. Cleere, M.D.	Exec. Director	Dept. Pub. Health	Denver
Connecticut....	Wm. S. Wise	Director	Water Commn.	Hartford
Delaware.......	Donald K. Harmeson	Director, Bd. of Health	Div. Sanit. Eng.	Dover
Florida........	W. T. Sowder, M.D.	Health Officer	Bd. of Health	Jacksonville
Georgia........	W. H. Weir	Dir., Water Pollut. Contr.	Dept. of Pub. Health	Atlanta
Idaho..........	L. J. Peterson	Director	Bd. of Health	Boise
Illinois.........	C. W. Klassen	Chief Sanit. Eng.	Dept. Pub. Health	Springfield
Indiana........	B. A. Poole	Technical Secy.	Stream Pollution Bd.	Indianapolis
Iowa..........	Edmund G. Zimmerer, M.D.	Commissr.	Dept. of Health	Des Moines
Kansas........	Dwight Metzler	Dir. and Chief Engr., Div. of Sanit.	Bd. of Health	Lawrence
Kentucky......	⎰ Henry Ward	Chmn., Water Pollut. Contr. Commn.	Dept. of Conserv.	Frankfort
	⎱ Louis F. Birkel	Exec. Dir., Water Pollut. Contr. Commn.	Dept. of Health	Louisville
Louisiana......	⎰ S. J. Phillips, M.D.	President	Bd. of Health	New Orleans
	⎱ Frank J. Coogan	Exec. Secy.	Stream Contr. Commn.	Baton Rouge
Maine.........	Clifford G. Chase	Chairman	Water Improvement Commn.	Baring
Maryland......	Paul W. McKee	Director	Water Pollut. Contr. Commn.	Baltimore
Massachusetts...	C. I. Sterling, Jr.	Dir. and Chief Engr., Div. Sanit. Eng.	Dept. Pub. Health	Boston
Michigan......	Milton P. Adams	Exec. Secy.	Water Resources Commn.	Lansing
Minnesota......	Harvey G. Rogers	Chief, Sec. of Water Pollut. Contr.	Dept. of Health	Minneapolis
Mississippi.....	Elkin Jack	Director	Game and Fish Commn.	Jackson
Missouri.......	John Dewey	Water Engineer, Div. Resources and Devel.	Dept. Bus. and Admin.	Jefferson City
Montana.......	Clayton Brinck	Sanit. Engineer	Bd. of Health	Helena
Nebraska.......	T. A. Filipi	Dir., Div. Sanitation	Dept. of Health	Lincoln
Nevada........	W. W. White	Dir., Div. Pub. Health Eng.	Dept. of Health	Reno
New Hampshire.	William A. Healy	Technical Secy.	Water Pollut. Commn.	Concord
New Jersey.....	Robert S. Shaw	Chief, Bur. of Pub. Health Eng., Div. of Envir. Sanit.	Dept. of Health	Trenton
New Mexico....	Robert E. Lowe	Dir., Water Pollution Control	Dept. of Public Health	Santa Fe
New York......	H. E. Hilleboe, M.D.	Chmn., Water Pollut. Control Bd.	Dept. of Health	Albany
North Carolina..	E. C. Hubbard	Exec. Secy., Stream Sanit. Commn.	Bd. of Health Devel.	Raleigh
North Dakota...	Willis Van Heuvelen	Dir., Water Pollution Control	Health Dept.	Bismarck
Ohio..........	Ralph E. Dwork, M.D.	Director	Dept. of Health	Columbus

WATER POLLUTION CONTROL—*continued*

State	Name	Official Title	Agency	Location
Oklahoma......	Ira C. Husky	Dir., Div. of Water Resources	Planning and Resources Bd.	Oklahoma City
	Harold Malone	Dir., Div. of Sanit. Eng.	Dept. of Health	Oklahoma City
	Massena B. Murray	Dir., Oil and Gas Conserv. Div.	Corp. Commn.	Oklahoma City
Oregon........	C. M. Everts, Jr.	Sanit. Engineer	Sanitary Auth.	Portland
Pennsylvania...	Maurice K. Goddard	Chmn., Water and Power Resources Bd.	Dept. Forests and Waters	Harrisburg
Rhode Island...	Walter J. Shea	Chief, Div. Sanit. Eng.	Dept. of Health	Providence
South Carolina..	W. T. Linton	Exec. Dir.	Water Pollut. Contr. Auth.	Columbia
South Dakota...	Charles E. Carl	Dir., Div. of Sanit. Eng.	Dept. of Health	Pierre
Tennessee......	S. Leary Jones	Dir., Stream Pollution Control Bd.	Dept. of Pub. Health	Nashville
Texas.........	Henry A. Holle, M.D.	Commissioner	Dept. of Health	Austin
Utah..........	Lynn Thatcher	Director	Div. of Eng. and Sanit.	Salt Lake City
Vermont.......	R. W. Thieme	Commissr. Water Resources	Water Conserv. Bd.	Montpelier
Virginia.......	A. H. Paessler	Exec. Secy.	Water Control Bd.	Richmond
Washington....	Edward F. Eldridge	Director	Pollut. Contr. Commn.	Olympia
West Virginia...	John W. Lester	Exec. Secy.	Water Commn.	Charleston
Wisconsin......	T. F. Wisniewski	Dir., Comm. on Water Pollut.	Bd. of Health	Madison
Wyoming......	Franklin D. Yoder, M.D.	Director	Bd. of Health	Cheyenne
Alaska.........	C. E. Albrecht, M.D.	Commissr.	Dept. of Health	Juneau
Guam.........	Lawrence T. Cowper	Sanitarian	Dept. of Medical Services	Tamuning
Hawaii........	Robert Lam	Chief, Bur. Sanit. Eng.	Bd. of Health	Honolulu
Puerto Rico....	Henry Rodríguez	Chief, Bur. of Sanit.	Dept. of Health	San Juan

WATER RESOURCES CONTROL

State	Name	Official Title	Agency	Location
Alabama.......	D. G. Gill, M.D.	Health Off. and Chmn.	Water Impr. Comm.	Montgomery
Arizona........	Roger Ernst	Land Commissr.	Land Dept.	Phoenix
Arkansas.......	Leonard White	Engineer, Flood Control	Geological and Conserv. Commn.	Little Rock
California......	Harvey O. Banks	Act. State Eng., Div. Water Resources	Dept. of Pub. Works	Sacramento
Colorado.......	Ivan C. Crawford	Director	Water Conserv. Bd.	Denver
	J. E. Whitten	State Engineer	Div. Water Resources	Denver
Connecticut....	Wm. S. Wise	Director	Water Commn.	Hartford
Florida........	Herman Gunter	Director	Geol. Survey, Bd. of Conserv.	Tallahassee
Idaho.........	Mark Kulp	State Reclam. Eng.	Reclamation	Boise
Illinois.........	Thomas B. Casey	Chief Water Eng.	Dept. of Pub. Works and Bldgs.	Springfield
Indiana........	Anton Hulman, Jr.	Chairman	Flood Contr., Water Resources Bd.	Indianapolis
Iowa..........	R. G. Bullard	Act. Director	Natural Resources Council	Des Moines

WATER RESOURCES CONTROL—*continued*

State	Name	Official Title	Agency	Location
Kansas........	R. V. Smrha	Chief Engineer	Div. of Water Resources, Bd. of Agric.	Topeka
Kentucky......	Stephen A. Wakefield	Dir., Flood Control and Water Usage Div.	Conserv. Dept.	Frankfort
Maine.........	M. R. Stackpole	District Eng., Water Resources Div.	Pub. Util. Commn.	Augusta
Maryland......	J. T. Singewald, Jr.	Director	Dept. Geol., Mines, Water Resources	Baltimore
Massachusetts...	Rodolphe Bessette	Dir., Div. Waterways	Dept. of Pub. Works	Boston
Michigan......	Milton P. Adams	Exec. Secretary	Water Resources Commn.	Lansing
Minnesota......	S. A. Frellsen	Dir., Div. Water Resources	Dept. of Conserv.	St. Paul
Mississippi.....	W. C. Morse, M.D.	Director	Geological Survey	University
Missouri.......	Thomas R. Beveridge	State Geologist	Div. of Geol. Survey and Water Resources	Rolla
Montana.......	Fred Buck	State Engineer	Water Conserv. Bd.	Helena
Nebraska.......	Dan S. Jones, Jr.	Chief, Bur. Irrig.	Dept. of Roads and Irrig.	Lincoln
Nevada........	Hugh Shamberger	State Engineer	Off. of State Eng.	Carson City
New Hampshire.	Walter G. White	Chairman	Water Resources Bd.	Concord
New Jersey.....	H. T. Critchlow	Dir., Div. Water Policy and Supply	Dept. Conserv. and Econ. Devel.	Trenton
New Mexico....	Steve Reynolds	State Engineer	Off. of Eng.	Santa Fe
New York......	Louis A. Wehle	Chmn., Water Power and Contr. Commn.	Conserv. Dept.	Albany
North Carolina..	P. C. Snow	Chief Engineer	Dept. of Conserv. and Devel.	Raleigh
North Dakota...	Milo W. Hoisveen	Secy. and State Eng.	Water Conserv. Commn.	Bismarck
Ohio..........	C. V. Youngquist	Chief	Div. of Water	Columbus
Oklahoma......	Ira C. Husky	Dir., Div. of Water Resources	Planning and Res. Bd.	Oklahoma City
Oregon........	Don Lane	Exec. Secy.	Water Resources Board	Salem
Pennsylvania...	Maurice K. Goddard	Chmn., Water and Power Resources Bd.	Dept. of Forests and Waters	Harrisburg
Rhode Island...	Walter J. Shea	Chairman	Water Resources Coord. Bd.	Providence
South Carolina .	C. P. Guess, Jr.	Secretary	Water Policy Comm.	Columbia
South Dakota...	Joseph W. Grimes	Chief Engineer and Exec. Off.	Water Resources Commn.	Pierre
Tennessee......	Jim Nance McCord	Chairman	Water Policy Commn. (Temp. Study Group)	Nashville
Texas..........	R. M. Dixon	Chairman	Bd. Water Eng.	Austin
Utah..........	Joseph M. Tracy	State Engineer	Dept. of State Eng.	Salt Lake City
Vermont.......	R. W. Thieme	Commissr., Water Resources	Water Conserv. Bd.	Montpelier
Virginia.......	H. B. Holmes, Jr.	Commissr., Div. Water Resources	Dept. of Conserv. and Devel.	Richmond
Washington....	Murray G. Walker	Supvr., Div. Water Resources	Dept. of Conserv. and Devel.	Olympia
West Virginia...	John W. Lester	Exec. Secretary	Water Commn.	Charleston
Wisconsin......	J. W. Ockerman	Secy. and Admin. Officer	Water Regulatory Bd.	Madison
Wyoming......	L. C. Bishop	State Engineer	Engineer's Office	Cheyenne
Guam.........	Winston Cooper	Chief Officer	Pub. Utility Agency	Tamuning
Hawaii........	L. H. Herschler	Manager	Irrigation Authority	Honolulu
Puerto Rico....	Sol L. Descartes	Exec. Director	P. R. Water Resources Auth.	San Juan

WELFARE (Over-all Administration)

See also Blind Welfare, Maternal and Child Welfare, Old Age Assistance, Public Assistance, School Lunch Administration.

State	Name	Official Title	Agency	Location
Alabama.......	J. S. Snoddy	Commissioner	Dept. of Pensions and Security	Montgomery
Arizona........	Wayne B. Warrington	Commissioner	Pub. Welfare Dept.	Phoenix
Arkansas.......	Carl Adams	Commissioner	Welfare Dept.	Little Rock
California......	George K. Wyman	Director	Dept. Soc. Welfare	Sacramento
Colorado.......	Guy R. Justis	Director	Dept. Pub. Welfare	Denver
Connecticut....	Christy Hanas	Commissioner	Dept. Pub. Welfare	Hartford
Delaware......	Edgar Hare, Jr.	Director	Bd. of Welfare	Wilmington
Florida........	Chas. G. Lavin	Director	Dept. Pub. Welfare	Jacksonville
Georgia........	Alan Kemper	Director	Dept. Pub. Welfare	Atlanta
Idaho.........	Bill Child	Commissioner	Pub. Welfare Dept.	Boise
Illinois.........	Otto L. Bettag, M.D.	Director	Dept. Pub. Welfare	Springfield
Indiana........	Richard H. Schweitzer, Jr.	Administrator	Dept. Pub. Welfare	Indianapolis
Iowa..........	L. L. Caffrey	Chairman	Bd. of Soc. Welfare	Des Moines
Kansas........	Frank Long	Director	Soc. Welfare Dept.	Topeka
Kentucky......	Glenn Lovern	Commissioner	Dept. of Welfare	Frankfort
Louisiana......	Edward P. Dameron III	Commissioner	Div. of Pub. Welfare	Baton Rouge
Maine.........	Dean H. Fisher	Commissioner	Dept. Health and Welfare	Augusta
Maryland......	Thomas J. S. Waxter	Director	Dept. Pub. Welfare	Baltimore
Massachusetts...	Patrick A. Tompkins	Commissioner	Dept. Pub. Welfare	Boston
Michigan......	W. J. Maxey	Director	Dept. Soc. Welfare	Lansing
Minnesota......	Morris Hursh	Commissioner	Dept. of Welfare	St. Paul
Mississippi.....	J. A. Thigpen	Commissioner	Public Welfare	Jackson
Missouri.......	C. Ross Gallup	Director	Dept. Pub. Health and Welfare	Jefferson City
Montana.......	W. J. Fouse	Administrator	Welfare Dept.	Helena
Nebraska.......	Mayme Stukel	Director	Div. of Pub. Welfare	Lincoln
Nevada........	Barbara C. Coughlan	Director	Welfare Dept.	Reno
New Hampshire.	James J. Barry	Commissioner	Dept. Pub. Welfare	Concord
New Jersey.....	John W. Tramburg	Commissioner	Dept. Insts. and Agencies	Trenton
New Mexico....	Murray A. Hintz	Director	Dept. Pub. Welfare	Santa Fe
New York......	Raymond W. Houston	Commissr. Social Welfare	Dept. Soc. Welfare	Albany
North Carolina..	Ellen Winston	Commissioner	Dept. Pub. Welfare	Raleigh
North Dakota...	Carlyle D. Onsrud	Exec. Director	Pub. Welfare Bd.	Bismarck
Ohio..........	Henry J. Robison	Director	Dept. Pub. Welfare	Columbus
Oklahoma......	Lloyd E. Rader	Director	Dept. Pub. Welfare	Oklahoma City
Oregon........	Mrs. Loa Howard Mason	Administrator	Pub. Welfare Commn.	Portland
Pennsylvania...	Harry Shapiro	Secretary	Dept. Welfare	Harrisburg
Rhode Island...	Edward P. Reidy	Director	Dept. Soc. Welfare	Providence
South Carolina..	Arthur B. Rivers	Director	Dept. Pub. Welfare	Columbia
South Dakota...	Matthew Furze	Director	Pub. Welfare	Pierre
Tennessee......	Mrs. Christine Reynolds	Commissioner	Dept. Pub. Welfare	Nashville
Texas.........	John H. Winters	Director	Dept. Pub. Welfare	Austin
Utah..........	H. C. Shoemaker	Chmn. of Commn.	Dept. Pub. Welfare	Salt Lake City
Vermont.......	W. Arthur Simpson	Commissioner	Soc. Welfare Dept.	Montpelier
Virginia.......	R. W. Copeland	Director	Dept. Welfare and Insts.	Richmond
Washington....	Geo. M. Hollenback	Director	Dept. Pub. Asst.	Olympia
West Virginia...	Robert F. Roth	Director	Dept. Pub. Asst.	Charleston
Wisconsin......	Wilbur J. Schmidt	Director	Dept. Pub. Welfare	Madison

WELFARE (Over-all Administration)—*continued*

See also Blind Welfare, Maternal and Child Welfare, Old Age Assistance, Public Assistance, School Lunch Administration.

State	Name	Official Title	Agency	Location
Wyoming......	E. H. Schuneman	Director	Dept. Pub. Welfare	Cheyenne
Alaska.........	Henry A. Harmon	Director	Dept. Pub. Welfare	Juneau
Hawaii........	Mary L. Noonan	Director	Dept. Pub. Welfare	Honolulu
Puerto Rico....	Mrs. C. Zalduondo	Dir., Div. of Pub. Welfare	Dept. of Health	San Juan
Virgin Islands..	Roy W. Bornn	Commissr. of Soc. Welfare	Govt. of V.I.	St. Thomas

WORKMEN'S COMPENSATION

State	Name	Official Title	Agency	Location
Alabama.......	Edward Laseter	Supervisor, Workmen's Comp.	Dept. of Ind. Rel.	Montgomery
Arizona........	B. F. Hill	Chairman	Industrial Commn.	Phoenix
Arkansas.......	Bayard Taylor	Chairman	Workmen's Comp. Commn.	Little Rock
California......	Ernest B. Webb	Chairman	Comp. Ins. Fund	San Francisco
	S. W. Macdonald	Chairman	Ind. Accid. Commn.	San Francisco
Colorado.......	Fred W. Andresen	Chairman	Industrial Commn.	Denver
Connecticut....	Leo J. Noonan	Chairman	Workmen's Comp. Commn.	Hartford
Delaware......	Harry B. Roberts, Jr.	Chairman	Ind. Accid. Bd.	Wilmington
Florida........	Rodney Durrance	Dir., Workmen's Comp. Div.	Industrial Commn.	Tallahassee
Georgia........	R. W. Best	Chairman	Workmen's Comp. Bd.	Atlanta
Idaho.........	Leo H. Houtz	Chairman	Ind. Accid. Bd.	Boise
Illinois.........	Roy Cummins	Director	Dept. of Labor	Springfield
Indiana........	Joseph P. Miller	Chairman	Industrial Bd.	Indianapolis
Iowa..........	Earl R. Jones	Commissioner	Industrial Commn.	Des Moines
Kansas........	Albert M. Ross	Commissioner	Workmen's Comp.	Topeka
Kentucky......	Harrison M. Robertson	Commissioner	Dept. of Ind. Rel.	Frankfort
Louisiana......	Richard Walker	Administrator	Div. of Empl. Sec.	Baton Rouge
Maine.........	Frank A. Farrington	Chairman	Ind. Accid. Commn.	Augusta
Maryland.....	Melvin Fine	Chairman	Ind. Accid. Commn.	Baltimore
Massachusetts...	Michael DeMarco	Chairman, Div. of Ind. Accidents	Dept. of Labor	Boston
Michigan......	Theodore P. Ryan	Chairman	Workmen's Comp. Commn.	Lansing
Minnesota......	Norbert Willwerscheid	Chief, Div. of Comp.	Dept. of Labor and Industry	St. Paul
Mississippi.....	John Craig	Chairman	Workmen's Comp. Commn.	Jackson
Missouri	Spencer Givens	Dir., Div. of Workmen's Comp.	Dept. of Labor and Ind. Rel.	Jefferson City
Montana.......	Robt. F. Swanberg	Chairman	Ind. Accid. Bd.	Helena
Nebraska.......	Albert Arms	Presiding Judge	Workmen's Comp. Court	Lincoln
Nevada........	John F. Cory	Chairman	Industrial Commn.	Carson City
New Hampshire.	Adelard E. Cote	Commissr. of Labor	Dept. of Labor	Concord
New Jersey.....	Daniel A. Spair	Dir., Div. of Workmen's Comp.	Dept. of Labor and Ind.	Trenton
New Mexico....	C. W. Burrell	Labor Commissr.	Labor and Ind. Commn.	Santa Fe
New York......	Angela R. Parisi	Chmn., Workmen's Comp. Bd.	Dept. of Labor	Albany
North Carolina..	J. W. Bean	Chairman	Industrial Commn.	Raleigh

WORKMEN'S COMPENSATION—*continued*

State	Name	Official Title	Agency	Location
North Dakota...	Owen T. Owen	Chairman	Workmen's Comp. Bur.	Bismarck
Ohio.........	Richard W. Morse	Chairman	Industrial Commn.	Columbus
Oklahoma......	Marx Childers	Chairman	Industrial Commn.	Oklahoma City
Oregon........	William A. Callahan	Chairman	Ind. Accid. Commn.	Salem
Pennsylvania...	John L. Dorris	Chmn., Workmen's Comp. Bd.	Dept. Labor and Ind.	Harrisburg
Rhode Island...	Joseph L. Breen	Chief, Div. of Workmen's Comp.	Dept. of Labor	Providence
South Carolina..	Henry C. Walker	Chairman	Industrial Commn.	Columbia
South Dakota...	Thomas G. Ries	Asst. Atty. Gen.	Industrial Commissr.	Pierre
Tennessee......	Dewey Whittle	Dir., Div. of Workmen's Comp.	Dept. of Labor	Nashville
Texas.........	H. C. Pittman, Jr.	Chairman	Ind. Accid. Bd.	Austin
Utah.........	O. A. Wiesley	Chmn. of Commn.	Industrial Commn.	Salt Lake City
Vermont.......	Raymond B. Daniels	Commissioner	Dept. of Ind. Rel.	Montpelier
Virginia.......	M. E. Evans	Chmn., Ind. Commn.	Dept. of Workmen's Comp.	Richmond
Washington....	L. H. Bates	Director	Dept. of Labor and Industries	Olympia
West Virginia...	(Vacancy)	Commissioner	Workmen's Comp. Commn.	Charleston
Wisconsin......	H. A. Nelson	Dir., Workmen's Comp. Div.	Industrial Commn.	Madison
Wyoming......	William F. Petry	Manager	Workmen's Comp. Dept.	Cheyenne
Alaska.........	Henry A. Benson	Commissioner	Dept. of Labor	Juneau
Guam.........	Olin Burnett	Commissioner	Workmen's Comp. Commn.	Agana
Hawaii........	William M. Douglas	Administrator	Bur. of Workmen's Comp.	Honolulu
Puerto Rico....	G. Atiles-Moreu	Manager, Ins. Fund	Dept. of Labor	San Juan
Virgin Islands...	(Vacancy)	Commissioner	Dept. of Agric. and Labor	St. Thomas

DIRECTORY OF STATE LEGISLATORS

ALABAMA

Senate

Democrats 35   Republicans 0

HARLAN G. ALLEN, *Cullman*
ALBERT BOUTWELL, 1919–20 *First Natl. Bank, Birmingham*
GERALD BRADFORD, *Grove Hill*
JOE CALVIN, *Box 312, Decatur*
BERRY L. CANTRELL, *Tuscumbia*
JAMES S. COLEMAN, JR., *Eutaw*
ROLAND COOPER, *Camden*
ALBERT DAVIS, *Aliceville*
JOE B. DAVIS, *Braggs*
SMITH C. DYAR, *Boaz*
E. O. EDDINS, *Demopolis*
SAM M. ENGELHARDT, JR., *Shorter*
RICHMOND M. FLOWERS, *Penny Bldg., Dothan*
WALTER C. GIVHAN, *Safford*
TULLY A. GOODWIN, *Florala*
MILTON C. GRISHAM, *R.F.D. 6, Athens*
H. P. JAMES, *Brent*
RALPH L. JONES, *Monroeville*
BROUGHTON LAMBERTH, *Alexander City*
G. KYSER LEONARD, *Talladega*
GEORGE E. LITTLE, *Eufaula*
NEIL METCALF, *Geneva*
M. H. MOSES, *Fyffe*
REUBEN L. NEWTON, *Jasper*
BEN REEVES, *Troy*
E. L. ROBERTS, *752 Forrest Ave., Gadsden*
VAUGHAN HILL ROBISON, *34 S. Perry St., Montgomery*
A. C. SHELTON, *Jacksonville*
E. W. SKIDMORE, *411 Alston Bldg., Tuscaloosa*
JOSEPH W. SMITH, *Phenix City*
STATEN TATE, *Goodwater*
GARET VAN ANTWERP III, *Spring Hill*
T. HERMAN VANN, *434 Locust St., Huntsville*
DAVE L. YARBROUGH, *Prattville*
GEORGE W. YARBROUGH, *Wedowee*

House

Democrats 106   Republicans 0

CHARLES ADAMS, *Alexander City*
WOODROW ALBEA, *Natl. Bank Bldg., Anniston*
VIRGIS M. ASHWORTH, *Centreville*
L. GARDNER BASSETT, *Troy*
A. L. BOYD, *Troy*
MARION BRADFORD, *Dickinson*
L. W. BRANNAN, JR., *Foley*
JAMES A. BRANYON II, *Fayette*
J. W. BRASSELL, *Phenix City*
ALBERT P. BREWER, *Box 1487, Decatur*
ROBERT H. BROADFOOT, *302 W. Alabama, Florence*
A. J. BROOKS, *Fort Deposit*

JESSE BROWN, *Vernon*
ROBERTS H. BROWN, *Opelika*
J. B. BURKHALTER, *Centre*
A. K. CALLAHAN, *First Natl. Bank Bldg., Tuscaloosa*
HOMER CORNETT, *Phenix City*
GARNETT COX, *Guntersville*
J. A. CROOK, *Union Springs*
BRYCE C. DAVIS, *Cullman*
JOE M. DAWKINS, *800 Commerce Bldg., Montgomery*
RYAN deGRAFFENRIED, *First Natl. Bank Bldg. Tuscaloosa*
JAMES M. DEMENT, *R.F.D. 1, Athens*
W. L. DeSEAR, *Uniontown*
ROBERT S. DICKSON, JR., *Lowndesboro*
J. K. EDWARDS, *Brighton*
MALCOLM EDWARDS, *East Brewton*
ROLAND R. FAULK, *Samson*
F. L. FERRELL, *Mentone*
RANKIN FITE, *Hamilton*
CHARLES R. FRANKLIN, *Goodwater*
BOB GILCHRIST, *Hartselle*
LEROY D. GIST, *Hollywood*
O. J. GOODWYN, *4169 Goode St., Montgomery*
LOWELL GREGORY, *Oneonta*
E. A. GROUBY, *Prattville*
B. V. HAIN, *Box 155, Selma*
H. JAMES HALL, *R.F.D. 4, Montgomery*
E. B. HALTOM, JR., *Florence*
E. K. HANBY, JR., *223 Ridgeway Ave., Gadsden*
FRANK HARDY, *R.F.D. 6, Selma*
N. S. HARE, *Monroeville*
KARL C. HARRISON, *Columbiana*
JESSE E. HARVEY, *Cuba*
GEORGE C. HAWKINS, *Gadsden*
GEORGE W. HODGES, JR., *Ashville*
CEPHUS R. HOLLIMAN, *Linden*
HARRY J. HUDDLESTON, *Sheffield*
ROBERT R. HUNT, *Fairfax*
J. M. JENKINS, *Roanoke*
HARDAWAY JOHNSON, *Eclectic*
J. T. JOHNSON, *R.F.D. 1, Notasulga*
HUGH KAUL, *1605 First Natl. Bank Bldg., Birmingham*
J. H. KELLY, *Haleyville*
ROBERT G. KENDALL, JR., *Evergreen*
A. L. KILLOUGH, *Honoraville*
JACK B. KIRKHAM, *Myrtlewood*
RUFUS M. LACKEY, *712 First Natl. Bank Bldg., Birmingham*
CAROL JACK LAW, *Wetumpka*
McDOWELL LEE, *Clio*
W. J. LEE, JR., *Town Creek*
JUDSON C. LOCKE, SR., *Marion*
ROBERT LOCKE, *Butler*
CLYDE M. LOVE, *Florala*
W. L. MARTIN, JR., *Eutaw*
CHARLES MATHEWS, *Ashland*
G. B. MATHISON, SR., *Abbeville*

Roy W. McClendon, *Shawmut*
C. W. McKay, Jr., *Sylacauga*
M. B. McLendon, *Union Springs*
Emory McNider, *Coffeeville*
J. Paul Meeks, 424 *Brown-Marx Bldg., Birmingham*
Hugh D. Merrill, Jr., *Anniston*
William P. Molette, *Orrville*
Joe Money, *Scottsboro*
Michael T. Murphy, 612 *First Natl. Bank Bldg., Mobile*
Sam C. Nettles, Jr., *Arlington*
Charles Nice, Jr., 210 *Frank Nelson Bldg., Birmingham*
Wilbur B. Nolen, Jr., *Box 1525, Montgomery*
Gregory Oakley, *Pine Apple*
W. E. Oden, *Russellville*
L. N. Payne, *Talladega*
Walter Emmett Perry, Jr., 2119 *Sixth Ave. N., Birmingham*
J. H. Pirkle, *Heflin*
Ira D. Pruitt, *Livingston*
Charles H. Ramey, *Akron*
N. L. Reynolds, 1413 *California St., Huntsville*
Reginald Richardson, *Greensboro*
Roscoe Roberts, Jr., 4 *W. Side Square, Huntsville*
J. J. Rodgers, *Tuskegee*
T. K. Selman, *Jasper*
Alonzo Shumate, *Jasper*
Otto E. Simon, 608 *Van Antwerp Bldg., Mobile*
Emory R. Solomon, *Headland*
Francis W. Speaks, *Clanton*
Henry B. Steagall II, *Ozark*
R. J. Stembridge, 321 *E. Main St., Dothan*
Jackson W. Stokes, *Elba*
V. S. Summerlin, *Luverne*
H. B. Taylor, *Georgiana*
Sim A. Thomas, *Eufaula*
John M. Tyson, 1600 *Government St., Mobile*
Paschal P. Vacca, 733 *Frank Nelson Bldg., Birmingham*
D. W. Ward, *Opelika*
Ralph Windle, *Carrollton*
J. Emmett Wood, *Millry*

ARIZONA

Senate

Democrats 26   Republicans 2

Ben Arnold, *Coolidge*
William R. Bourdon, *Box 1203, Snowflake*
Neilson Brown, *Buena Vista Rancho, Nogales*
Clarence L. Carpenter, *Box 1326, Miami*
Thomas Collins, 1057 *E. Eighth St., Tucson*
Earle W. Cook, *Box 510, Kingman*
Hiram S. Corbett, 210 *E. Seventh St., Tucson*
Fred Dove, *Tombstone*
Harold C. Giss, *Box 1351, Yuma*
Charles S. Goff, *Casa Grande*
Melvin C. Greer, *St. Johns*
Joe Haldiman, Jr., 902 *W. Verde Lane, Phoenix*
R. S. Hart, *R.F.D. 3, Box 927, Glendale*
Lynn Lockhart, *Springerville*
Robert Morrow, *Kingman*
Chas. H. Orme, Sr., *Mayer*
Robert W. Prochnow, 16 *W. Aspen, Flagstaff*
Wilford R. Richardson, *Safford*
Clay Simer, *Box 402, Winslow*

M. L. Simms, *Box 518, Clifton*
C. B. Smith, *Nogales*
Jim Smith, *Central*
A. R. Spikes, 2009 *Tenth St., Douglas*
A. C. Stanton, *Clifton*
Wm. A. Sullivan, *Drawer 391, Globe*
R. H. Thompson, *Parker*
Fred F. Udine, *Williams*
Ray Vyne, 142 *N. Cortez, Prescott*

House

Democrats 60   Republicans 20

Chas. H. Abels, *Box 52, Cave Creek Stage, Phoenix*
Harry Ackerman, 711 *S. Tucson Blvd., Tucson*
Vincente Alfaro, 919 *S. Sixth Ave., Tucson*
Carl C. Andersen, 842 *W. Edgemont, Phoenix*
Evelyn Anderson, *Box 733, Warren*
Carl Austin, 4442 *S. Eighth Pl., Phoenix*
David B. Babbitt, *Box 1683, Parker*
Harry Bagnall, *Coolidge*
Tom W. Berry, 102 *Second St., Clifton*
G. O. Biles, *Box 747, Morenci*
Charles O. Bloomquist, 1206 *Eleventh St., Douglas*
Nelson D. Brayton, 823 *Merritt St., Miami*
Keith S. Brown, *Box 364, Tucson-Nogales Star Rt., Amado*
Marion Harold Burton, 1825 *N. Rosemary Dr., Tucson*
David H. Campbell, 2546 *E. Roma, Phoenix*
William B. Carr, 255 *Second Ave., Yuma*
Conrad James Carreon, 820 *N. Third St., Phoenix*
James W. Carroll, 6009 *E. Beverly Dr., Tucson*
W. L. Cook, *Willcox*
Clyde M. Dalton, *Box 1609, Bisbee*
Lee F. Dover, 1100 *Warren Ave., Winslow*
Mabel S. Ellis, 107 *E. Gurley St., Prescott*
Ed Ellsworth, *Box 75, Chandler*
Louis B. Ellsworth, Jr., *Skyline Dr., Globe*
Lorin M. Farr, *St. Johns*
W. W. Franklin, 1645½ *E. Culver, Phoenix*
Thomas D. Fridena, 717 *N. Sixth Ave., Tucson*
J. O. Grimes, 906 *Mill Ave., Tempe*
William J. Harkness, 1345 *E. Fillmore St., Phoenix*
Robert R. Hathaway, *Box 59, Nogales*
John H. Haugh, *R.F.D. 5, Box 161, Tucson*
Douglas Stanley Holsclaw, 1746 *E. Fifth St., Tucson*
V. S. Hostetter, 100 *Calle Encanto, Tucson*
Ruth I. Hunt, 1911 *W. Holly St., Phoenix*
Etta Mae Hutcheson, 337 *S. Fourth Ave., Tucson*
Sidney Kartus, 2107 *S. Fifteenth Pl., Phoenix*
James L. Kennedy, 934 *Calle Bocina, Tucson*
Neales Kennedy, 1240 *N. Oakleaf Dr., Phoenix*
Robert L. Klauer, 2609 *Avenue A, Yuma*
Augusta T. Larson, *Box 238, Lakeside*
Norman Lee, 713 *N. 27th Dr., Phoenix*
Malcolm L. Lenz, 334 *W. Almeria, Phoenix*
H. J. Lewis, *Douglas*
Milton O. Linder, *Box 606, Clarkdale*
Milton Lines, *Pima*
W. I. Lowry, 2922 *E. Manor Dr., Phoenix*
Mrs. Laura M. McRae, 929 *E. Coronado Rd., Phoenix*
C. H. Marion, 4431 *N. Seventh Ave., Phoenix*
Dick W. Martin, 349 *Park Ave., Prescott*
Andrew Matson, *Box 277, Flagstaff*
William I. Minor, 130 *W. Adams, Tucson*

W. W. Mitchell, Sr., 816 *Wilson, Tempe*
Robert L. Myers, 5022 *N. Arden Dr., Phoenix*
Patrick W. O'Reilly, 1611 *E. Flower, Phoenix*
Robert A. Petrie, 1532 *W. First Pl., Mesa*
James B. Phillips, 1303 *W. Bethany Home Rd., Phoenix*
Wm. S. Porter, 15 *E. Second Ave., Mesa*
S. Earl Pugh, 4100 *W. Thomas Rd., Phoenix*
Champe Raftery, 3208 *W. Marshall, Phoenix*
Lillian Retzloff, 2849 *Greenfield Rd., Phoenix*
T. C. Rhodes, *Box 146, Avondale*
Del Rogers, 321 *E. Indian School Rd., Phoenix*
Edwynne C. Rosenbaum, *Box 609, Globe*
Harry S. Ruppelius, 1505 *N. Fifteenth Ave., Phoenix*
Guy Rutherford, *Kingman*
Enos P. Schaffer, 1035 *Palm Rd., Tucson*
Arthur B. Schellenberg, 212 *E. Hayward, Phoenix*
Harold J. Scudder, *Box 16, Williams*
Carl Sims, Sr., 1304 *W. Magnolia St., Phoenix*
Frederick S. Smith, *Superior*
George R. Steward, 107 *N. Tenth Ave., Phoenix*
J. P. Stump, 3154 *Westward Blvd., Phoenix*
Mrs. E. B. Thode, *Casa Grande*
E. L. Tidwell, *Safford*
Hal Fred Warner, *Box 758, Wickenburg*
Alvin Henry Wessler, 1711 *N. Desmond Lane, Tucson*
Ruth Adams White, 6110 *E. Camelback Rd., Scottsdale*
Julliette C. Willis, 123 *Sierra Vista Dr., Tucson*
R. E. Wilson, 2521 *E. Adams St., Phoenix*
David S. Wine, 500 *Solana Ave., Ajo*
William Younger Wood, *R.F.D. 1, Box 90, Glendale*

ARKANSAS

Senate

Democrats 34　　Republicans 0

Tom Allen, *Brinkley*
James P. Baker, Jr., *West Helena*
J. Lee Bearden, *Leachville*
G. Lawrence Blackwell, *Natl. Bank Bldg., Pine Bluff*
E. J. Byrd, 403 *McCullough, Camden*
Jack V. Clark, *Box 688, Texarkana*
Russell Elrod, *Siloam Springs*
Ellis M. Fagan, 901 *Spring, Little Rock*
W. E. Fletcher, *Scott*
J. E. Garner, *Fort Smith*
Morrell Gathright, 707 *W. Twenty-third, Pine Bluff*
Artie Gregory, 1615 *E. Fifteenth, Little Rock*
Max Howell, *Rector Bldg., Little Rock*
Q. Byrum Hurst, *Hot Springs*
W. J. Hurst, *Rector*
Gaither C. Johnston, *Dermott*
Guy H. Jones, *Conway*
Gene Lee, *Prescott*
Tom Logan, *Walnut Ridge*
Fletcher Long, *Forrest City*
Y. M. Mack, *Moorefield*
Marvin Melton, *Jonesboro*

Roy W. Milum, *Harrison*
Boss Mitchell, *Danville*
DeWitt Poe, *McGehee*
J. O. Porter, *Mulberry*
Roy A. Riales, *Mena*
Marshall Shackleford, Jr., *Box 214, El Dorado*
Fred H. Stafford, *Marked Tree*
C. Van Hayes, *Benton*
Clifton Wade, *Fayetteville*
Oliver R. Williams, *Sheridan*
Robert Hays Williams, *Russellville*
C. E. Yingling, *Searcy*
(1 vacancy)

House

Democrats 97　Republicans 2　Independents 1

William S. Andrews, *Camden*
Marvin Austin, *Langley*
L. H. Autry, *Burdette*
John P. Bethell, *Des Arc*
J. W. Black, *Waldron*
W. C. Blackwell, *Belleville*
Edward W. Brockman, Jr., *Simmons Natl. Bank Bldg., Pine Bluff*
Jim Bruton, *Morrilton*
Ben Bynum, *Dermott*
Quinton Clark, *Jasper*
James M. Coates, Jr., *Box 510, Little Rock*
Harry B. Colay, *Magnolia*
J. H. Cottrell, Jr., 111 *E. Seventh, Little Rock*
Marion H. Crank, *Foreman*
Chadd L. Durrett, *Strong*
Jack East, Jr., 310 *Spring, Little Rock*
James J. Edwards, *Blytheville*
Talbot Feild, Jr., *Hope*
John S. Ferguson, *Beebe*
Eugene C. Fleeman, *Manila*
Virgil T. Fletcher, *R.F.D., Alexander*
Guy W. French, *Weiner*
John W. Goodson, 9 *Webber Pl., Texarkana*
Paul Graham, *Walnut Ridge*
George O. Green, *De Witt*
Jack Gwin, *Sheridan*
Hugh Hackler, *Mountain Home*
Robert Harvey, *Swifton*
Roy Haynes, *Mena*
Vance Hickman, *Harrison*
Carroll C. Hollensworth, *Warren*
John Howell, *Nashville*
Marcus J. Howell, *Wabash*
R. C. Johnson, Jr., *Grady*
Charlie Johnston, *Jonesboro*
Harrell L. Johnston, *Hampton*
Donald J. Jones, Jr., *Rector Bldg., Little Rock*
Paul Jones, *Marshall*
Knox B. Kinney, *Forrest City*
Clyde Kinslow, *R.F.D. 4, Russellville*
John W. Kornegay, *Clarendon*
Winfred Lake, *De Queen*
Robert W. Laster, 1819 *Denison, Little Rock*
Joel Y. Ledbetter, *Boyle Bldg., Little Rock*
Eli Leflar, *Rogers*
Sam M. Levine, *Natl. Bldg., Pine Bluff*
Clayton N. Little, *Bentonville*
Winford B. Logan, *Tumbling Shoals*
Bryan J. McCallen, *Corning*

Abner E. McGuire, *Prescott*
A. M. McKennon, Jr., *Scranton*
Melvin E. Mayfield, *El Dorado*
Raymond L. Mays, *Rison*
Hubert J. Meachum, *Batesville*
Joe P. Melton, Jr., *Lonoke*
A. M. Metcalf, *Hardy*
J. H. Moody, *Bald Knob*
Jack S. Oakes, *Augusta*
Gerald Partee, *Marcella*
Harlin J. Perryman, *Salem*
Roy Pettit, *Delaney*
Mel Phillips, 18 *N. Sixth, Fort Smith*
Russell C. Roberts, *Conway*
Pat Robinson, *Lewisville*
J. A. Rodman, *Melbourne*
Lucien C. Rogers, *Earle*
Charles B. Roscopf, *Poplar Grove*
Frank Ross, *McGehee*
Glyn E. Sawyer, *Hamburg*
Jim Shaver, *Ben Block Bldg., Wynne*
J. T. Slack, *Arkadelphia*
Charles F. Smith, 317 *E. Broadway, West Memphis*
Ray S. Smith, Jr., 303 *Quapaw St., Hot Springs*
W. V. Smith, *Mt. Ida*
Gordon Stanley, *Pyatt*
Fred Starr, *R.F.D. 8, Fayetteville*
Charles Stewart, Jr., 341 *St. Charles, Fayetteville*
Dewey D. Stiles, *Malvern*
Kenneth S. Sulcer, *Joiner*
Elmer Tackett, 540 *Summer St., Hot Springs*
F. A. Teague, *Berryville*
R. C. Temple, *Hartman*
Dave E. Thompson, 1800 *McAlmont, Little Rock*
W. H. Thompson, *Marked Tree*
Hays A. Triplett, *Paragould*
L. Weems Trussell, *Box 688, Fordyce*
Arlo Tyer, *Pocahontas*
Paul Van Dalsem, *Perryville*
Jessie P. Walt, *Altheimer*
Glenn F. Walther, *Boyle Bldg., Little Rock*
W. L. Ward, Sr., *Marianna*
Carl S. Whillock, *Clinton*
Dan White, 419 *First Natl. Bank Bldg., Fort Smith*
Randall L. Williams, *Monticello*
Milton Willis, *Van Buren*
Norman Wimpy, *Jonesboro*
J. A. Womack, 109 *W. Jefferson, Camden*
Harold Wood, *Palestine*
James S. Yarbrough, 318 *N. Twenty-second, Fort Smith*
Jack Yates, *Ozark*

CALIFORNIA

Senate

Republicans 23   Democrats 16

F. Presley Abshire, *134 Sotoyome St., Santa Rosa*
Swift Berry, 115 *Canal St., Placerville*
Arthur H. Breed, Jr., 1111 *Jackson St., Oakland*
Charles Brown, *Shoshone*
Hugh M. Burns, *Box 748, Fresno*
James E. Busch, 700 *S. Spring St., Ukiah*
Paul L. Byrne, 244 *W. Third St., Chico*
James A. Cobey, 646 *W. Twenty-sixth St., Merced*
Randolph Collier, 551 *N. Main, Yreka*

Nathan F. Coombs, 720 *Seminary St., Napa*
James E. Cunningham, 415 *Anderson Bldg., San Bernardino*
Earl D. Desmond, 616 *I St., Sacramento*
Nelson S. Dilworth, *R.F.D. 1, Box 18, Hemet*
Hugh P. Donnelly, 953 *Sierra Dr., Turlock*
Jess R. Dorsey, 1028 *Q St., Bakersfield*
A. A. Erhart, *Box 506, Pismo Beach*
Fred S. Farr, *Box 3305, Carmel*
Luther E. Gibson, 516 *Marin St., Vallejo*
Donald L. Grunsky, 130 *Rogers Ave., Watsonville*
John J. Hollister, *Winchester Canyon, Galeta*
Ben Hulse, *Box 321, El Centro*
Ed C. Johnson, *Box 31, Marysville*
Harold T. Johnson, 423 *Grove St., Roseville*
Fred H. Kraft, 612 *Spreckles Bldg., San Diego*
James J. McBride, *Box 708, Ventura*
John F. McCarthy, 819 *A St., San Rafael*
Robert I. McCarthy, 155 *Montgomery St., San Francisco*
George Miller, Jr., 1016 *Nevin Ave., Richmond*
Robert I. Montgomery, 8361 *Flint Ave., Hanford*
John A. Murdy, Jr., 6662 *Heil Ave., Huntington Beach*
Harry L. Parkman, 1450 *Canada Rd., Woodside*
Edwin J. Regan, *Weaverville*
Richard Richards, *State Bldg., Los Angeles*
Alan Short, 1220 *N. Van Buren St., Stockton*
Louis G. Sutton, *Box 547, Maxwell*
Stephen P. Teale, *Box E, West Point*
John F. Thompson, *R.F.D. 3, Box 408, San Jose*
A. W. Way, 1864 *Heather Lane, Eureka*
J. Howard Williams, 920 *North E St., Porterville*
(1 vacancy)

Assembly

Republicans 44   Democrats 32

Bruce F. Allen, 160 *N. Cypress, San Jose*
L. M. Backstrand, 4456 *Twelfth St., Riverside*
Jack A. Beaver, 525 *Esther Way, Redlands*
Carlos Bee, 1784 *Fairview Ave., Hayward*
Frank P. Belotti, *Box 1025, Eureka*
Frank G. Bonelli, 7412 *California Ave., Huntington Park*
Clark L. Bradley, 1616 *Hedding St., San Jose*
Bernard R. Brady, 658 *Twelfth Ave., San Francisco*
Ralph M. Brown, *Box 1292, Modesto*
Montivel A. Burke, 16 *N. Olive Ave., Alhambra*
Thomas W. Caldecott, 912 *Financial Center Bldg., Oakland*
J. Ward Casey, 413 *S. Imperial Ave., Brawley*
Charles Edward Chapel, *Box 777, Inglewood 1*
George A. Clarke, *Box 56, Planada*
John L. E. Collier, 5332 *Hillmont Ave., Los Angeles 41*
Charles J. Conrad, 13444 *Moorpark St., Sherman Oaks*
Glenn E. Coolidge, *Box 308, Felton*
Rex M. Cunningham, 1558 *E. Main St., Ventura*
Walter I. Dahl, 418 *Blair Ave., Piedmont*
Pauline L. Davis, *Portola*
Randal Dickey, *Odd Fellows Bldg., Alameda*
Clayton A. Dills, 15615 *S. Ainsworth, Gardena*
Richard J. Dolwig, 2395 *Broadway, Redwood City*
Dorothy M. Donahoe, 2403 *La Siesta Dr., Bakersfield*

DONALD D. DOYLE, 3585 *Powell Dr., Lafayette*
THOMAS J. DOYLE, 4333 *Griffin Ave., Los Angeles* 31
EDWARD E. ELLIOTT, 2250 *Whittier Blvd., Los Angeles* 23
THOMAS M. ERWIN, 1016 *N. Willow Ave., Puente*
EDWARD M. GAFFNEY, 295 *Sanchez St., San Francisco*
ERNEST R. GEDDES, *Box* 232, *Claremont*
SAMUEL R. GEDDES, 1621 *East Ave., Napa*
WILLIAM S. GRANT, 1381 *Bryant Rd., Long Beach*
WILLIAM W. HANSEN, 3435 *S. Walnut Ave., Fresno*
AUGUSTUS F. HAWKINS, 4042 *Trinity St., Los Angeles* 11
SHERIDAN N. HEGLAND, 9045 *Madison St., La Mesa*
WALLACE D. HENDERSON, 3643 *Kerckhoff Ave., Fresno*
JAMES L. HOLMES, *Box* 321, *Santa Barbara*
SETH J. JOHNSON, 3346 *Sunnynook Dr., Los Angeles* 39
H. W. KELLY, *Box* 1166, *Shafter*
VERNON KILPATRICK, 3715 *Abbott Rd., Lynwood*
HERBERT R. KLOCKSIEM, 205 *E. Broadway, Rm.* 301, *Long Beach* 2
FRANK LANTERMAN, 4420 *Encinas Dr., La Canada*
HAROLD K. LEVERING, 900 *Moraga Dr., Los Angeles* 49
L. H. LINCOLN, 4000 *Redwood Rd., Oakland* 2
FRANCIS C. LINDSAY, *Box* 463, *Loomis*
LLOYD W. LOWREY, *Box* 23, *Rumsey*
FRANK LUCKEL, 1036 *Savoy St., San Diego* 7
RICHARD H. MCCOLLISTER, 320 *Fawn Dr., San Anselmo*
JOHN J. MCFALL, 215 *N. Sherman Ave., Manteca*
PATRICK D. MCGEE, 17304 *Sherman Way, Van Nuys*
LESTER A. MCMILLAN, 639 *S. Spring St., Rm.* 1003, *Los Angeles* 14
THOMAS A. MALONEY, 405 *Montgomery St., Rm.* 714, *San Francisco* 4
WILLIAM F. MARSH, 5338 *Auckland Ave., North Hollywood*
S. C. MASTERSON, 1307 *Scott St., El Cerrito* 6
CHARLES W. MEYERS, 417 *Font Blvd., San Francisco* 27
ALLEN MILLER, 205 *Mission Bldg., San Fernando*
G. DELBERT MORRIS, 3861 *Welland Ave., Los Angeles* 8
WILLIAM A. MUNNELL, 3500 *Via Corona, Montebello*
ROY J. NIELSEN, 1555 *Thirteenth Ave., Sacramento*
EUGENE G. NISBET, 200 *E. Thirteenth St., Upland*
JOHN A. O'CONNELL, 1223 *Fitzgerald Ave., San Francisco*
ALAN G. PATTEE, 155 *Coral de Tierra Rd., Salinas*
CARLEY V. PORTER, 401 *W. Palmer Ave., Compton*
THOMAS M. REES, 424 *S. Holt Ave., Los Angeles*
WILLIAM BYRON RUMFORD, 1500 *Stuart St., Berkeley* 3
WANDA SANKARY, 5311 *Pirotte Dr., San Diego* 5
JACK SCHRADE, 119 *N. Magnolia, El Cajon*
HAROLD T. SEDGWICK, 1359 *Myers St., Oroville*
JOSEPH C. SHELL, 611 *S. Muirfield Rd., Los Angeles*
H. ALLEN SMITH, 530 *W. Sixth St., Los Angeles* 14
EARL W. STANLEY, 225 *Marine, Balboa Island*
A. I. STEWART, 856 *El Molino St., Pasadena*
VINCENT THOMAS, 526 *N. Hanford Ave., San Pedro*
JESSE M. UNRUH, 4915 *S. Ninth Ave., Los Angeles* 43
CASPAR W. WEINBERGER, 3477 *Pacific Ave., San Francisco* 18
CHARLES H. WILSON, 2106 *W. Seventy-eighth Pl., Los Angeles* 47

(4 vacancies)

COLORADO

Senate

Republicans 20 Democrats 15

CHARLES E. BENNETT, 2815 *Glencoe St., Denver*
LEONARD M. BENTLEY, 1012 *Short St., Canon City*
NEAL D. BISHOP, 1554 *California St., Denver*
WILLIAM E. BLEDSOE, *Aroya*
DONALD G. BROTZMAN, 3190 *Seventeenth St., Boulder*
D. R. C. BROWN, *Carbondale*
WM. ALBION CARLSON, 1815 *Thirteenth Ave., Greeley*
VERNON A. CHEEVER, 825 *Paseo Blvd., Colorado Springs*
HARRY F. CHRYSLER, 149 *S. Emerson St., Denver*
PETER CULIG, JR., 2110 *Spruce St., Pueblo*
RAY B. DANKS, 2524 *S. Garfield St., Denver*
FAY DEBERARD, *Kremmling*
DONALD P. DUNKLEE, 1925 *Broadway, Denver*
EDGAR A. ELLIFF, *Sterling*
FRANK L. GILL, *Hillrose*
CLIFFORD J. GOBBLE, 25 *N. Eighth Ave., Brighton*
WILKIE HAM, *Lamar*
CLARENCE B. HOCKER, *Monte Vista*
WALTER W. JOHNSON, 2800 *Cedar St., Pueblo*
ROBERT L. KNOUS, 834 *Majestic Bldg., Denver*
HARRY M. LOCKE, *Hartsel*
N. J. MILLER, *Eaton*
MARTIN C. MOLHOLM, 7400 *W. Fourteenth Ave., Lakewood*
JAMES W. MOWBRAY, 611 *Howard St., Delta*
MICHAEL POMPONIO, 4990 *Green Ct., Denver*
WM. S. POWERS, *Mayor's Office, City Hall, Denver*
RANGER ROGERS, 158 *Ridge Rd., Littleton*
HOWARD M. SHULTS, 711 *N. Seventh, Grand Junction*
L. T. SKIFFINGTON, 114 *Cave Ave., Manitou Springs*
L. P. STRAIN, 720 *Cimarron Ave., La Junta*
R. BRUCE SULLIVAN, *Durango*
SAM T. TAYLOR, *Walsenburg*
BEN VELTRI, 989 *E. Main St., Trinidad*
ERNEST WEINLAND, *Loveland*
GEORGE WILSON, *Nucla*

House

Republicans 36 Democrats 28

ROBERT E. ALLEN, 2236 *Hooker, Denver*
FLOYD BALL, *Ft. Lupton*
RAY BALLARD, *Cheyenne Wells*
RICHARD L. BANTA, 2921 *S. Marion St., Englewood*
LUTHER E. BEAN, *R.F.D.* 1, *Alamosa*
LUCILLE L. BECK, 967 *Marion St., Denver*
HOWARD H. BELL, 2502 *S. University, Denver*
WHITMAN BEST, 544 *Circle Dr., Denver*
GEORGE L. BROWN, % *Denver Post, Denver*
W. J. BROWN, *Eaton*
PALMER L. BURCH, 238 *Majestic Bldg., Denver*
W. K. BURCHFIELD, *Walsh*
FRANK J. BURK, 4515 *Zenobia St., Denver*
JOSEPH V. CALABRESE, 2707 *W. Forty-sixth Ave., Denver*
MAX T. CHELF, 1379 *College, Canon City*
WM. B. CHENOWETH, 1694 *Oneida St., Denver*
RUTH B. CLARK, 805 *Elizabeth St., Fort Collins*
DAVID J. CLARKE, 438 *Equitable Bldg., Denver*
CHARLES R. CONKLIN, *Box* 42, *Delta*
BLANCHE COWPERTHWAITE, 1625 *E. Third Ave., Denver*

FRANK ECKHARDT, *La Salle*
NORMAN W. ENFIELD, 1016 *Mercury Dr., Colorado Springs*
SARA L. FISCHER, 55 *Marland Rd., Colorado Springs*
C. A. FRITTS, 2111 *S. Lafayette, Denver*
DAVID A. HAMIL, *Atwood*
ED HARDING, *Craig*
FRANK L. HAYS, 3090 *S. Bellaire, Denver*
A. WOODY HEWETT, 2939 *Tenth St., Boulder*
FRANK A. HOISINGTON, 625 *N. Seventh St., Grand Junction*
ROBERT E. HOLLAND, 951 *S. Garfield St., Denver*
BYRON L. JOHNSON, 2451 *S. Dahlia Lane, Denver 22*
JOHN L. KANE, 7280 *Locust, Derby*
R. MALCOLM KEIRY, *R.F.D. 2, Monte Vista*
ANDREW D. KELLEY, 4755 *Vine St., Denver*
FRANK E. KENDRICK, JR., *Leadville*
GEORGE E. KIMBLE, *Swink*
C. P. LAMB, 321 *Everett, Brush*
EDWARD LEHMAN, 250 *Eudora St., Denver*
WILLIAM O. LENNOX, 1418 *N. Tejon St., Colorado Springs*
FREDERIC T. MCLAUGHLIN, *Basalt*
HIRAM A. MCNEIL, *Montrose*
JOHN G. MACKIE, 948 *Collyer St., Longmont*
FERD S. MARKLEY, 802 *Peterson St., Fort Collins*
PHILLIP MASSARI, 407 *Goddard Ave., Trinidad*
VINCENT MASSARI, 322 *S. Victoria, Pueblo*
MARTIN MOORE, 1115 *Jackson St., Pueblo*
BARNEY O'KANE, 6795 *W. First Ave., Lakewood*
S. T. PARSONS, *La Jara*
ELIZABETH E. PELLET, *Rico*
GUY POE, *Holyoke*
ED G. SEIDENSTICKER, *Castle Rock*
C. GALE SELLENS, 915 *Estes St., Lakewood*
RAYMOND H. SIMPSON, *Cope*
RAY J. SLATTERY, 4212 *Green Ct., Denver*
WALTER R. STALKER, *Kirk*
FRANKLIN R. STEWART, 422 *Thatcher Bldg., Pueblo*
RENA MARY TAYLOR, *Palisade*
ALBERT J. TOMSIC, *Box 587, Walsenburg*
JOHN D. VANDERHOOF, 338 *Park Dr., Glenwood Springs*
OAKLEY WADE, *Box 426, Las Animas*
J. WILLIAM WELLS, 35 *S. Main, Brighton*
LOUIS C. WERTZ, 394 *Jones St., Center*
BETTY KIRK WEST, 102 *Brentwood Dr., Pueblo*
ARTHUR M. WYATT, 135 *Junction St., R.F.D. 1, Durango*

(1 vacancy)

CONNECTICUT

Senate

Democrats 19   Republicans 16

WILLIAM F. ABLONDI, 46 *Derby Ave., Seymour*
PAUL AMENTA, 1592 *Corbin Ave., New Britain*
BENJAMIN L. BARRINGER, *U.S. Rt. 7, New Milford*
PHILIP J. BAUER, *Waterville Rd., Avon*
JOSEPH BONAQUISTO, 82 *Grove St., Hartford*
HAROLD BORDEN, 55 *Canterbury St., Hartford*
WILLIAM J. CAHILL, JR., 90 *Liberty St., Meriden*
PHILANDER COOKE, *Wallingford*
PLATT CREED, *Brookfield*
WILLIAM T. DETULLIO, 557 *Woodward Ave., New Haven*

MAURICE J. FERLAND, 15 *Westfield Ave., Danielson*
FLORENCE D. FINNEY, 1049 *E. Putnam Ave., Riverside*
JACOB A. FISCHMAN, 125 *Stimson Rd., New Haven*
JAMES E. FOLEY, 217 *Nicoll St., New Haven*
LAWRENCE M. GILMAN, *Gilman*
BENTON H. GRANT, *Chestnut Hill Rd., Stamford*
ARTHUR H. HEALEY, 169 *Spring St., New Haven*
JOHN A. IORIO, 130 *Melbourne Terr., Waterbury*
ROBERT L. KEENEY, JR., *Somersville*
PHILIP P. LAING, 139 *Palisado Ave., Windsor*
LOUIS A. LEMAIRE, JR., *E. Rocks Rd., Norwalk*
W. DUANE LOCKARD, 146 *Mohegan Ave., New London*
JOSEPH S. LONGO, 12 *Wayne St., Norwich*
NEWMAN M. MARSILIUS, JR., *Daniels Farm Rd., Trumbull*
ISIDORE A. MESSIER, *Box 362, Moosup*
JOHN A. MINETTO, *West Goshen*
EDWARD J. OPALACZ, *Boston Rd., Middletown*
DAVID PARODI, *Main St., Deep River*
MILTON E. REINHARD, JR., 109 *Eagle St., Bridgeport*
THEODORE S. RYAN, *Sharon*
JACK STOCK, 1907 *North Ave., Bridgeport*
STEPHEN J. SWEENEY, *Sweeney St., Naugatuck*
PATRICK J. WARD, 81 *Ward Place, Hartford*
ELMER S. WATSON, 808 *Ridge Rd., Wethersfield*
JAMES J. WHELAN, 168 *Parallel St., Bridgeport*
(1 vacancy)

House

Republicans 184   Democrats 92   Independents 3

JEROME ADAMS, 217 *Ward St., Hartford*
NELLIE M. AHLBERG, 2 *Shanley Ct., Cromwell*
NATHAN K. ALLISON, *Granby*
E. A. AMBLER, *New Milford*
PAUL M. ANDREWS, *Oregon Rd., Cheshire*
GEORGE B. ANGEVINE, *Cornwall Bridge*
ODILLA N. ARPIN, *R.F.D. 8, Baltic Rd., Taftville*
ROBERT B. AUGUST, *Avon*
DOMINIC J. BADOLATO, 164 *Pennsylvania Ave., New Britain*
JACK BANNER, *Moodus*
FRANCIS B. BARNETT, JR., *Moseley Terr., Glastonbury*
JOHN W. BARTOK, *R.F.D. 2, Mansfield Center*
JEROME BEATTY, *Roxbury*
LAURETTE J. BECKWITH, 333 *Ocean Ave., New London*
ARLINE BENSON, 65 *Theodore St., Newington 11*
EDWARD BERGIN, 45 *Vine St., Ansonia*
JOSEPH BERTA, *Ann Ave., Shelton*
JOSEPH A. BILLINGS, *Dayville*
JOHN FREDERICK BITZER, 100 *Juniper Rd., Bloomfield*
C. ARTHUR BJORKLUND, *R.F.D. 3, Danbury*
BEULAH L. BLACKMAN, 5087 *Main St., Trumbull*
ESDRAS BLANCHETTE, *North Grosvenor Dale*
KENNETH P. BOSWORTH, *Pomfret Center*
MAX F. BREVILLIER, *R.F.D. 2, Old Lyme*
NELSON C. L. BROWN II, 106 *Smith St., Groton*
RALPH O. BRUNO, *R.F.D. 1, Westport*
CLYNTON B. BUCKLAND, *Buckland*
ELIZABETH H. BUDD, 87 *Coleman Rd., Wethersfield*
ANTHONY H. BUMSTED, 489 *Quinnipiac Ave., North Haven*
GARRETT BURKITT, SR., 86 *Prospect St., Ansonia*
ERNEST C. BURNHAM, JR., *Clinton*
DANIEL J. BURNS, *New Hartford*

Francis C. Cady, *Kent*
Robert T. Cairns, *Madison*
Cornelius F. Caldwell, 338 *Seymour Ave., Derby*
Frank E. Calhoun, *Cornwall*
Arthur Carlson, *Georgetown*
Gustaf A. Carlson, *R.F.D., Madison*
John F. Cipriano, 219 *Maple Ave., North Haven*
Hilda S. Clarke, 81 *Palmer St., Springdale*
Joseph A. Clinton, 39 *Riverview Rd., Rocky Hill*
Rubin Cohen, *Colchester*
Francis X. Cole, *West Cornwall*
Frederick U. Conard, Jr., 11 *Cobbs Rd., West Hartford*
Francis J. Conlon, *Goshen*
John B. Coughlin, 112 *Murray St., Middletown*
Joseph A. Coutu, Jr., 286 *Summit St., Willimantic*
Ellsworth L. Covell, *Andover*
Wood M. Cowan, *Godfrey St., Westport*
G. Gordon Cowles, *North Woodbury*
W. Sheffield Cowles, *Farmington*
Matthew J. Coyle, 22 *Bluff Ave., West Haven*
Abner A. Croog, 512 *George St., New Haven*
Elizabeth M. Croumey, 41 *Prospect Pl., East Haven*
Mary V. Z. Cunningham, *Richmond Hill, New Canaan*
Hugh C. Curran, 1651 *Central Ave., Bridgeport*
Sarah Frances Curtis, *Sandy Hook*
Herbert H. Cutler, *Newtown*
Henry Delay, *R.F.D. 2, Torrington*
Fred DeLeon, 65 *Jefferson St., Waterbury*
Antonio E. Demuth, *Wauregan*
Juanine S. DePaolo, 189 *Summit St., Plantsville*
Louis J. DePaul, 16 *Auburn St., Danbury*
David J. Dickson, Jr., *Stafford Springs*
John C. Donaldson, *Wilton*
Harold O. Douglass, 57 *Mayfair Lane, Greenwich*
Nancy Carroll Draper, *Ridgefield*
Keith E. Dubay, *Harvest Lane, Bristol*
William A. Eagan, 258 *S. Main St., Deep River*
Rodney S. Eielson, 31 *Moorland Rd., Trumbull*
Herbert R. Elker, *Oronoque Rd., Milford*
James B. Ellsworth, 190 *Ellwood Rd., Kensington*
V. Hall Everson, Jr., 68 *Patterson Ave., Greenwich*
Wallace Fabro, *Torrington*
Marjorie Dilley Farmer, 14 *Highland Ave., Darien*
James Edward Farrell, Sr., 30 *Washington Manor Ave., West Haven*
Edward P. Faulk, 145 *Water St., Stonington*
Henry Ferne II, *Greens Farms Rd., Westport*
B. Wyman Fisk, *Branch Rd., Suffield*
William A. Fleming, *R.F.D. 1, Norwich*
Willard A. Fosdick, 23 *Wooster St., Seymour*
Gennaro W. Frate, 47 *Hecker Ave., Darien*
Lillian M. Frink, *Canterbury*
Margaret Fulgham, *Fenton Ave., Waterbury 12*
Herbert J. Gable, *R.F.D. 3, Coventry*
Eugene Gagliardone, *R.F.D. 2, Andover*
Jean Gagnon, *Mulberry St., Naugatuck*
Henry J. Gaudet, 268 *Rainbow Rd., Windsor*
Sophia Gedrim, *R.F.D., Broad Brook*
Clarence G. Geer, *R.F.D., Chestnut Hill*
Reinhard Gideon, 67 *Foxcroft Rd., West Hartford*
Webster C. Givens, *N. Stamford Rd., Stamford*
Russell S. Gold, *Worthington Ridge, Berlin*
Rudolph E. Goldbeck, *R.F.D., New Hartford*
Samuel S. Googel, 227 *Shuttle Meadow Ave., New Britain*

Hugh Gorman, *R.F.D., Brooklyn*
Malcolm R. Goslee, *Granby*
Charles Grab, *Canterbury*
Richard M. Grant, *Hebron*
Ella T. Grasso, 13 *Olive St., Windsor Locks*
Edwin P. Gregory, *Colchester*
John Griffith, 92 *Great Hill Rd., East Hartford*
Leon Joseph Gwiazdowski, 71 *Ashland St., Jewett City*
Clifford W. Hall, 125 *South Ave., New Canaan*
Gardiner H. Hall, *South Willington*
James B. Hall, *West Hartland*
Roy G. Hallberg, Sr., *East Hampton*
George R. Hambrock, *Bridgewater*
Lucy T. Hammer, *Cherry Hill Rd., Branford*
George W. Hannon, 66 *S. Prospect St., East Hartford*
Fannie Harris, 78 *Gregory Blvd., Norwalk*
Albert J. Harvey, 245 *Summit St., Willimantic*
Morris B. Hogan, *R.F.D., Unionville*
George Holt, 93 *W. Hartford Rd., Newington 11*
Thomas C. Hood, *Haddam*
H. Edward Hooper, *R.F.D. 2, Torrington*
John E. Horton, *Hebron*
Ward Hubbard, *Cove Rd., Stonington*
Howard A. Hueston, *Sherman*
Warren L. Hunt, *Bethlehem*
Lillian E. Hutton, 21 *Spring St., Winsted*
Allan C. Innes, *Thomaston*
Sherman K. Ives, *R.F.D., Thomaston*
Arthur E. Jacobson, Sr., *East Hampton*
Annie Follett Jorgensen, *R.F.D. 5, Norwichtown*
Robert R. Keeler, *Nod Rd., Ridgefield*
Charles H. Kegley, 25 *O'Hear Ave., Thompsonville*
May McC. Kennedy, *Washington Depot*
Thomas J. Kerrigan, Jr., 14 *Stanwood St., Hartford*
Stephan E. Ketcham, *Tolland*
William G. Kielwasser, 116 *Gorham Ave., Hamden*
Jason H. Kingsley, *R.F.D. 1, Lebanon*
Anthony G. Kirker, 3 *Pembroke Ave., Norwich*
George R. Kissam, *R.F.D. 1, Stepney Depot*
Carrol Knibbs, *Porter Hill, Middlebury*
William A. Knight, *Racebrook Rd., Orange*
Howard L. Knox, *Main St., Deep River*
Gertrude F. Koskoff, 33 *Williams St., Plainville*
Anthony Kuras, *Mountain Rd., West Suffield*
Wilfred A. Lafleur, *North Grosvenor Dale*
Frank A. Larkin, 384 *Laughlin Ave., Stratford*
Normand O. LaRose, 197 *Grove St., Putnam*
Prosper F. Lavieri, *Box 559, Winsted*
Samuel B. Lawrence, *R.F.D., Warehouse Point*
John M. Lewis, 100½ *Elm St., Danbury*
Francis Liberty, *High St., Jewett City*
Gilbert M. Lombard, 95 *Boston St., Guilford*
Florence Lord, *R.F.D. 2, East Hampton*
Stephen Loyzim, *R.F.D. 3, Coventry*
Charles H. Lucas, *Falls Village*
Thomas W. Luce, *Sharon*
James L. Lusby, 111 *Smith St., Putnam*
James McAdam, *Long Hill Rd., Guilford*
Hugh M. MacKenzie, *Waterford*
Michael F. McLaughlin, 32 *Landry St., Bristol*
J. Joseph McMahon, 25 *Suffield St., Windsor Locks*
Raymond T. McMullen, *Moodus*
Daniel J. Mahaney, 1309 *Bank St., Waterbury*
Irving R. Main, *R.F.D. 3, Westerly, Rhode Island*
Carrie F. Mansfield, *R.F.D. 2, Box 270, Gales Ferry*

ROBERT W. MARSH, *Box 1, Redding Ridge*
THEODORE V. MARSTERS, *Litchfield*
LUTHER B. MARTIN, *East Hartland*
MICHEL MARTINO, SR., *181 Cove St., New Haven*
PASQUALE MASTROPIETRO, *35 Goodyear Ave.,*
Naugatuck
MICHAEL MATTEO, *34 Liberty St., Middletown*
ADELBERT MAUTTE, *33 Austin Ave., East Haven*
ROBERT D. MAY, *North Canaan*
BERNADETTE C. MAYNARD, *R.F.D. 4, Norwich*
JAMES W. METCALF, *Tolland*
JOHN G. MILLER, *Clark Hill Rd., R.F.D. 2,*
Waterbury 12
MAURICE E. MINOR, *Minor Rd., Terryville*
JOHN A. MISCIKOSKI, *67 Butler St., Torrington*
MARIE P. MOORE, *Northford*
ALLAN MOPSIK, *Moosup*
JAMES C. MURPHY, *Pomfret*
BENITO MUZIO, *Staffordville*
CHARLES R. NASH, *Lakeville*
HARRY B. NEAL, *4 Evergreen Ave., Hamden*
JOHN H. NOBLE, *New Milford*
HELEN L. NORTON, *Durham Center*
WILLIAM J. O'BRIEN, JR., *Spring St., Portland*
J. RAYMOND O'CONNOR, *11 Cottage St., Winsted*
RICHARD W. O'DONNELL, *Seminary Rd., Simsbury*
CLARA L. O'SHEA, *Bethany Rd., Beacon Falls*
EDWIN K. PAAVOLA, *Lakeville*
LOUIS J. PADULA, *Rome St., Norwalk*
ANNA MAE PALLANCK, *R.F.D. 2, Stafford Springs*
BIRDSEY G. PALMER, *Voluntown*
CHARLES PAPINEAU, *Hanover, Sprague*
BENJAMIN PARKER, *East Lyme*
NORMAN K. PARSELLS, *1806 Burr St., Fairfield*
J. TYLER PATTERSON, JR., *Neck Rd., Old Lyme*
BERNARD PEARSON, *Sharon*
FRANK H. PEPE, *122 Derby Ave., Derby*
G. NELSON PERRY, *R.F.D. 2, Willimantic*
BARUYR PESHMALYAN, *South Woodstock*
ALVIN H. PHILLIPS, JR., *Somers*
ALMON SEARLE PINNEY, *R.F.D. 5, Danbury*
HARRIET SAMPSON PITT, *Woodstock*
SIDNEY S. PLATT, *Southbury*
JOSEPH PLOSZAJ, *R.F.D. 3, Colchester*
BASIL A. PLUSNIN, *R.F.D. 2, Stafford Springs*
FREDERICK POPE, JR., *2031 Redding Rd., Fairfield*
ROSE E. PROKOP, *364 Stratford Rd., Stratford*
ERVING PRUYN, *Colebrook*
MERTON M. PULTZ, *Lebanon*
BERNARD J. QUIGLEY, *81 Fairview Heights, Portland*
MARGUERITE QUIMBY, *34 Nameaug Ave., New*
London
THOMAS F. QUINLAN, *New Preston*
JOSEPH V. QUINN, *1049 E. Main St., Meriden*
STANLEY RADGOWSKI, *Montville*
DOUGLAS J. RATHBUN, *R.F.D. 3, Old Lyme*
JOSEPH W. REATH, *Durham*
MARY S. REED, *Taylor Rd., Bethel*
WILLIAM H. REGAN, *Bailey Ave., Yalesville*
ANDREW REPKO, *West Willington*
MERLE C. REYNOLDS, JR., *Box 53, Rockfall*
ALFRED J. RING, *94 Oak St., Meriden*
GEORGE RIVERS, *Rogers*
LAURENCE H. ROBERTS, *Box D, Riverton*
THOMAS J. ROGERS, *500 E. Center St., Manchester*
EARLE L. ROWLEY, *R.F.D. 2, Box 25, Gales Ferry*
ARTHUR H. RUSSELL, *48 Hillside Ave., Oakville*
ARLINE W. RYAN, *Canton Rd., West Simsbury*

ISABEL C. RYLANDER, *Litchfield*
JOHN B. SAGLIO, *R.F.D., Deep River*
JOHN F. SAYLES, *R.F.D. 1, Moosup*
BENJAMIN M. SCHLOSSBACH, *Westbrook*
OLIVE E. SCHMELTZ, *Old Colony Rd., Norfolk*
JOSEPH V. SERENA, *546 Riverside Ave., Westport*
RALPH A. SEYMOUR, *W. Main St., Terryville*
RICHARD D. SEYMOUR, *East Granby*
ABRAHAM SHERMER, *68 Bank St., Seymour*
VINCENT M. SIMKO, *57 Dover St., Bridgeport*
EARL W. SMITH, *R.F.D. 2, Winsted*
EDWIN O. SMITH, *Mansfield Depot*
ALBERT C. SNYDER, *35 Woodland Ave., Bloomfield*
FRANCES C. STEARNS, *R.F.D. 1, Storrs*
ELMER C. STONE, *R.F.D., Hampton*
JOHN C. STREAMAN, *Grandview Ave., Bethel*
MARGARET STREKAS, *Somers*
RUTH F. SUAREZ, *Mountain Rd., Cheshire*
ARTHUR W. SWEETON, JR., *Canton Center*
DOMINIC SYLVESTER, *11 Parsonage St., Rocky Hill*
PATRICK A. TESTA, *61 Skitchewaug St., Wilson*
RAYMOND A. THAYER, *1000 S. Main St., Plantsville*
BARBARA TIPPIN, *West Ave., Essex*
OTTO TONUCCI, *50 Coram Rd., Shelton*
DIANE TOULSON, *446 E. Broadway, Milford*
R. HAROLD TREAT, *R.F.D. 2, Seymour*
JOHN McC. TURNER, *Porter Hill Rd., Bethany*
ROLAND W. TYLER, *110 Woodbury Rd., Watertown*
CLARENCE A. VAILL, *Goshen*
INA VESTAL, *Amity Rd., New Haven (Woodbridge)*
ROBERT K. VIBERT, *R.F.D., Farmington*
JOHN VILARDI, JR., *108 Williams St., Plainville*
EMMA VonHAGEN, *Higganum*
KENNETH W. WALKER, *Eastford*
RAY S. WARREN, *109 Princeton St., Manchester*
CLAUDE P. WATROUS, *Chester*
ARLINE T. WELLES, *Cromwell Pl., Old Saybrook*
FRANKLIN WELLES, *Talcottville*
FRANK W. WHITE, *North Stonington*
LUTHER A. WHITE, *65 Elm St., Rockville*
RODNEY B. WILCOX, *133 Griswold Rd., Wethersfield*
FRANKLIN P. WILD, *Woodbury*
LAVERGNE H. WILLIAMS, *Columbia*
RICHARD G. WILLIAMS, *Goodale Hill Rd., Glastonbury*
REGINALD H. WOOD, *31 High St., Mystic*
THOMAS B. WOODWORTH, *Quaker Hill*
EDWARD G. WRAIGHT, *74 Mountain St., Rockville*
JULIA T. WRIGHT, *Old Grassy Hill Rd., Orange*
LUCIE WRYNN, *19 Academy St., Wallingford*
STANLEY YESUKIEWICZ, *Bridge Lane Ext., Enfield*
HOWARD V. YOUNG, *43 Wilford Ave., Branford*
JOSEPH J. ZAMBO, *R.F.D. 2, Mansfield Center*
JOSEPH ZANOBI, *Box 374 Norfolk*
(1 vacancy)

DELAWARE

Senate

Democrats 12   Republicans 5

WILLIAM B. BEHEN, *Dover*
JOHN R. BUTLER, *Middletown*
JEHU F. CAMPER, *Harrington*
WM. O. COVEY, JR., *Seaford*
S. W. HARRISON, *Wyoming*
WALTER J. HOEY, *Milford*
THOS. L. JOHNSON, *Rehoboth Beach*
EUGENE LAMMOT, *802 W. Twentieth St., Wilmington*

CALVIN R. McCULLOUGH, *Holloway Terrace*
ELWOOD FRANK MELSON, JR., *Claymont*
CHAS. G. MOORE, *Hartly*
WILLIAM C. PARADEE, *Dover*
CLIFFORD PRYOR, *Blackbird*
JOHN E. REILLY, SR., 436 *S. Heald St., Wilmington*
CURTIS W. STEEN, *Dagsboro*
ROBT. E. WILGUS, *Frankford*
WILMER F. WILLIAMS, *Roselle*

House

Democrats 27　　Republicans 8

EDGAR ALEXANDER, *Townsend*
CHARLES W. BOSTICK, *Felton*
JOHN J. BROGAN, 1118 *Pleasant St., Wilmington*
H. CLIFFORD CLARK, *Kenton*
EARL DEPUTY, *Middletown*
LEON E. DONOVAN, *Harrington*
NORMAN A. ESKRIDGE, *Bridgeville*
IRVING H. GARTON, *Dover*
JAMES L. HASTINGS, *Laurel*
BENJAMIN E. HICKS, *Marshallton*
B. WALTER JOHNSON, *Glasgow-Summit Bridge Rd.*
TILGHMAN S. JOHNSON, *Roxana*
EARL M. KEEL, *Greenwood*
HARRY G. LAWSON, 1406 *Riverview Ave., Wilmington*
EBE T. LAYTON, *Laurel*
WILLIAM E. LESTER, *St. Georges*
PAUL F. LIVINGSTON, 511 *Pine St., Wilmington*
GEORGE T. MACKLIN, *Milford*
ROBERT P. MACLARY, *Newport Pike, Newport*
NELSON MASSEY, *Dover*
ERNEST MATTIFORD, *Smyrna*
HARRY MAYHEW, *Milford*
PETER NECHAY, *Willow Grove*
JOSEPH EARL PEPPER, *Georgetown*
DANIEL J. QUEEN, JR., *Dover*
JAMES R. QUIGLEY, *Hares Corner, New Castle*
THOMAS C. ROWAN, *Townsend*
PAUL E. SHOCKLEY, 731 *W. Fourth St., Wilmington*
JAMES W. SMITH, *Milton*
JAMES H. SNOWDEN, 3703 *Washington St., Wilmington*
MRS. JAMES M. TUNNELL, JR., *Georgetown*
JOSEPH B. WALLS, *Lewes*
ROLAND H. WILKINSON, *Camden*
HENRY H. WOLF, *Newark*
ROBERT R. WOOD, *Carrcroft*

FLORIDA

Senate

Democrats 37　　Republicans 1

J. ED BAKER, *Umatilla*
MERRILL P. BARBER, *Box 936, Vero Beach*
PHILIP D. BEALL, *Florida Natl. Bank Bldg., Pensacola*
J. GRAHAM BLACK, *Jasper*
IRLO BRONSON, *Kissimmee*
TED CABOT, 309 *First Fed. Bldg., Ft. Lauderdale*
DOYLE E. CARLTON, JR., *Wauchula*
WILSON CARRAWAY, *Tallahassee State Bank & Trust Co., Tallahassee*
S. D. CLARKE, *Monticello*
JAMES E. CONNOR, *Inverness*

W. T. DAVIS, *Madison*
H. B. DOUGLAS, *Bonifay*
L. K. EDWARDS, JR., *Irvine*
C. H. BOURKE FLOYD, *Apalachicola*
EDWIN G. FRASER, *Macclenny*
E. WILLIAM GAUTIER, 1200 *Magnolia St., New Smyrna Beach*
R. B. GAUTIER, 1539 *duPont Bldg., Miami*
J. C. GETZEN, JR., *Bushnell*
W. RANDOLPH HODGES, *Cedar Key*
J. FRANK HOUGHTON, 355 *Burlington Ave. N., St. Petersburg*
CHARLEY E. JOHNS, *Starke*
DEWEY M. JOHNSON, *Quincy*
PAUL KICKLITER, 501½ *Franklin St., Tampa*
HARRY E. KING, *Beymer Bldg., Winter Haven*
WOODROW M. MELVIN, *Milton*
FLETCHER MORGAN, 45 *W. Bay St., Jacksonville*
RUSSELL O. MORROW, 1102 *North O St., Lake Worth*
WILLIAM R. NEBLETT, 415 *Francis St., Key West*
B. C. PEARCE, *East Palatka*
J. O. PHILLIPS, *Box 948, Lake City*
VERLE A. POPE, *Box 519, St. Augustine*
JOHN RAWLS, *Citizens State Bank Bldg., Marianna*
J. B. RODGERS, JR., *Box 417, Winter Garden*
JOE BILL ROOD, 2322 *Seventh Ave. W., Bradenton*
W. A. SHANDS, 207 *NE Ninth Ave., Gainesville*
DOUGLAS STENSTROM, *Sanford*
HARRY O. STRATTON, *R.F.D. 1, Callahan*
GEORGE G. TAPPER, *Port St. Joe*

House

Democrats 89　　Republicans 6

J. S. ALEXANDER, *Bristol*
FRANK M. ALLEN, 342 *S. Palo Alto, Panama City*
G. FRED ANDREWS, *Lake Butler*
C. FRED ARRINGTON, *Havana*
KENNETH BALLINGER, *Center Bldg., Tallahassee*
HENRY S. BARTHOLOMEW, *Box 646, Sarasota*
THOS. D. BEASLEY, *DeFuniak Springs*
JAMES N. BECK, *Palatka*
HARVIE J. BELSER, *Bonifay*
W. E. BISHOP, *Lake City*
J. C. BODIFORD, *Box 1022, Panama City*
J. A. BOYD, *Box 901, Leesburg*
A. MAX BREWER, *Titusville*
FARRIS BRYANT, *Box 563, Ocala*
O. L. BURTON, *Box 607, Eau Gallie*
W. H. CARMINE, JR., *Box 228, Ft. Myers*
HAL CHAIRES, *Oldtown*
WILLIAM V. CHAPPELL, 4 *S. Magnolia St., Ocala*
MACK N. CLEVELAND, JR., *Box 220, Sanford*
THOMAS T. COBB, 219 *Magnolia, Daytona Beach*
WILLIAM C. COLEMAN, JR., 1500 *Woodland, Orlando*
DOYLE E. CONNER, *Starke*
H. T. COOK, *Box 14, Bunnell*
CECIL G. COSTIN, JR., 221 *Reid Ave., Port St. Joe*
JOHN J. CREWS, JR., *Box 264, Macclenny*
J. EMORY CROSS, *Box 411, Gainesville*
THOMAS E. DAVID, 2206 *Funston St., Hollywood*
FRED O. DICKINSON, JR., 321 *Palmetto Rd., West Palm Beach*
HUGH DUKES, *Cottondale*
C. E. DUNCAN, *Tavares*
SAM M. GIBBONS, 918 *First Natl. Bank Bldg., Tampa*
HARRY H. GLEATON, *Inverness*

J. J. GRIFFIN, JR., 435 *Florida Ave., St. Cloud*
WILLIAM C. GRIMES, *Palmetto*
JOHN M. HATHAWAY, *Punta Gorda*
W. C. HERRELL, 173 *Navarre Dr., Miami Springs*
J. B. HOPKINS, *Kennedy Bldg., Pensacola*
MALLORY E. HORNE, *Box 725, Tallahassee*
W. M. INMAN, *Quincy*
WEBB C. JERNIGAN, *Box 584, Pensacola*
CHARLES R. JOHNSON, JR., 1450 *Coral Way S., St. Petersburg*
TOM JOHNSON, 416 *Tampa St., Tampa*
DAVID C. JONES, JR., *Box 796, Naples*
E. B. JONES, *Greenville*
O. W. JONES, *Perry*
LAWRENCE L. KING, 28 *Florida Bank Bldg., Ft. Pierce*
MARION B. KNIGHT, *Blountstown*
HOWELL LANCASTER, *Trenton*
HENRY W. LAND, *Apopka*
HOWARD LIVINGSTON, *Box 246, Sebring*
LACY MAHON, 1517 *Greenridge Rd., Jacksonville*
WILLIAM H. MANESS, 608 *Consolidated Bldg., Jacksonville*
FRANK MARSHBURN, *Box 69, Bronson*
J. W. MCALPIN, *White Springs*
EVAN A. MERRITT, JR., *Box 41, Sumterville*
JAMES S. MOODY, 212 *Gordon St., Plant City*
PERRY E. MURRAY, *Frostproof*
ANDREW J. MUSSELMAN, JR., 412 *NE Eighteenth Ave., Pompano Beach*
GEORGE S. OKELL, 902 *Biscayne Bldg., Miami*
JOHN B. ORR, JR., 3538 *Crystal Ct., Coconut Grove*
JAMES P. PAGE, JR., *Fernandina Beach*
BERNIE C. PAPY, 1021 *Washington St., Key West*
MARY PATTON, *Apalachicola*
J. H. PEEPLES, JR., *Venus*
FRED C. PETERSEN, 201 *Fourth Ave. S., St. Petersburg*
JOHN S. PITTMAN, *Jay*
J. E. PRATT, 717 *Twenty-first St. W., Bradenton*
PRENTICE P. PRUITT, *Monticello*
HOMER T. PUTNAL, *Mayo*
Z. WALLENSTEIN REVELLE, *Panacea*
EMMETT S. ROBERTS, *Box 488, Belle Glade*
HOUSTON W. ROBERTS, *Live Oak*
MARVIN H. ROWELL, *Stuart*
S. D. SAUNDERS, *Box 31, Middleburg*
B. E. SHAFFER, *R.F.D. 2, Box 568, Clearwater*
WALTER O. SHEPPARD, 1927 *Cordova Ave., Ft. Myers*
JOHN S. SHIPP, JR., 525 *N. Russ St., Marianna*
S. C. SMITH, *Arcadia*
SHERMAN N. SMITH, JR., 1601 *Twentieth St., Vero Beach*
CHARLES D. STEWART, *Box 643, Ft. Walton Beach*
ELBERT L. STEWART, *Clewiston*
ROY SURLES, *Box 1375, Lakeland*
JAMES H. SWEENY, JR., 302 *S. Spring Garden Ave., Deland*
BOONE D. TILLETT, JR., *Lake Wales*
RALPH D. TURLINGTON, 223 *W. University Ave., Gainesville*
F. C. USINA, *St. Augustine*
JACOB V. VARN, *Brooksville*
JEFF WEBB, *Chipley*
NATHAN I. WEINSTEIN, 161½ *St. George St., St. Augustine*
HARRY WESTBERRY, 152 *Tallulah Ave., Jacksonville*

G. W. WILLIAMS, *R.F.D. 1, Wauchula*
J. R. A. WILLIAMS, *Box 911, Dade City*
VOLIE A. WILLIAMS, JR., *Atlantic Bank Bldg., Sanford*
GEORGE E. YOUNGBERG, SR., *Castile Rd., Venice*
NATHAN ZELMENOVITZ, *Box 98, Okeechobee*

GEORGIA

Senate

Democrats 53   Republicans 1

C. L. AYERS, *Toccoa*
D. B. BLALOCK, *Newnan*
GEORGE B. BROOKS, *Crawford*
HOMER L. CHANCE, *Danville*
EDGAR D. CLARY, JR., *Harlem*
N. C. COFFIN, *Cuthbert*
JEFFERSON L. DAVIS, *Cartersville*
W. K. DEAN, *Young Harris*
CHARLES E. DEWS, *Edison*
JAMES J. DYKES, *Cochran*
GLEN FLORENCE, *Douglasville*
H. R. GARRETT, *Quitman*
WILLIS NEAL HARDEN, *Commerce*
E. GIRDEAN HARPER, *Griffin*
WALTER HARRISON, *Millen*
HOWELL HOLLIS, 1238 *Second Ave., Columbus*
ALVA J. HOPKINS, JR., *Folkston*
ARTHUR E. HOUSLEY, *Dahlonega*
B. M. JONES, *Dallas*
M. BRINSON JONES, *Wrens*
W. T. JONES, *Roberta*
EUGENE KELLY, *Monroe*
E. ROY LAMBERT, *Madison*
W. HERSCHEL LOVETT, *Dublin*
JAMES M. MCBRIDE, *Leesburg*
C. ERNEST MCDONALD, *Dalton*
J. W. MANN, *Cordele*
DORSEY R. MATTHEWS, *Moultrie*
G. EVERETT MILLICAN, 131 *Ponce deLeon Ave. NE, Atlanta*
WALTER B. MORRISON, *Mount Vernon*
LAWSON NEEL, *Thomasville*
HOWARD T. OVERBY, *Gainesville*
OWEN H. PAGE, JR., 16 *Drayton St., Savannah*
ARNOLD PARKER, *Milledgeville*
TILLMAN PAULK, *Ocilla*
W. K. PONSELL, *Waycross*
O. W. RAULERSON, *Patterson*
REUBEN M. REYNOLDS, *Bainbridge*
A. CULLEN RICHARDSON, *Montezuma*
DOUGHTY RICKETSON, *Warrenton*
MARVIN C. ROOP, *Carrollton*
A. F. SEAGRAVES, *Hull*
FRANCIS F. SHURLING, *Wrightsville*
WILLIAM BURTON STEIS, *Hamilton*
JOSEPH BARNEY STRICKLAND, *Nahunta*
THOMAS TOMS, *Georgetown*
A. MELL TURNER, 722 *Clairmont Ave., Decatur*
LAWTON R. URSREY, *Hazlehurst*
CHAS. F. WARNELL, *Groveland*
CHARLES E. WATERS, *Ellijay*
J. L. WETHERINGTON, *Jasper, Florida*
JOHN H. WILKINS, *Trenton*
T. J. WOOD, *Bellville*
J. KIMBALL ZELLNER, *Forsyth*

House

Democrats 202   Republicans 3

Joe B. Adams, *Barnesville*
Francis W. Allen, *Statesboro*
Jere C. Ayers, *Comer*
George T. Bagby, *Dallas*
Leo T. Barber, *Moultrie*
Mac Barber, *Commerce*
W. O. Barker, *Franklin*
Leon H. Baughman, *Cedar Springs*
Fred D. Bentley, *110½ Washington Ave., Marietta*
Frank G. Birdsong, *LaGrange*
J. Lucius Black, *Preston*
T. Sidney Blackburn, *Alto*
Edgar Blalock, *Jonesboro*
John W. Bloodworth, *Perry*
Wm. T. Bodenhamer, *Ty Ty*
Arthur K. Bolton, *Griffin*
C. B. Brannen, *Unadilla*
Cecil E. Brown, *Lumber City*
Johnnie L. Caldwell, *Thomaston*
H. Chris Callier, *Talbotton*
Albert Campbell, *LaFayette*
J. Douglas Carlisle, *Bankers Insurance Bldg., Macon*
L. J. Cason, *Blackshear*
Frank M. Cates, *Waynesboro*
R. Lee Chambers III, *Masonic Bldg., Augusta*
Robt. E. Chastain, *Thomasville*
Frank S. Cheatham, Jr., *Realty Bldg., Savannah*
Hugh G. Cheek, *Butler*
H. Eulond Clary, *Thomson*
H. Carl Cloud, *Climax*
Steve M. Cocke, *Dawson*
Grady N. Coker, *Canton*
Robert E. Coker, *LaFayette*
M. M. Cornelius, *Cedartown*
L. Cotton, *Leary*
J. M. Cowart, *Arlington*
William M. Coxwell, *Leesburg*
W. Roscoff Deal, *Pembroke*
William Dean, *Conyers*
Braswell Deen, Jr., *Alma*
Roscoe Denmark, *Hinesville*
Jim Denson, *Albany*
Lovette Dozier, *Colquitt*
John P. Drinkard, *Lincolnton*
Joseph B. Duke, *Milledgeville*
J. Ebb Duncan, *Carrollton*
Mose Edenfield, *Darien*
D. Mayne Elder, *Watkinsville*
R. S. English, Jr., *Nashville*
Edgar P. Eyler, *209 Garrard Ave., Savannah*
Ralph Kelley Fain, *Royston*
James H. Floyd, *Trion*
Wales T. Flynt, *Crawfordville*
Wiley B. Fordham, *Statesboro*
E. Alvin Foster, *Forest Park*
A. A. Fowler, Jr., *Douglasville*
Howard Fowler, *Tifton*
Wm. B. Freeman, *Forsyth*
W. A. Frier, *Millwood*
H. G. Garrard, *Washington*
Carlton W. Gilleland, *Dawsonville*
Hugh Gillis, *Soperton*
Charles L. Goodson, *Franklin*
Paul Green, *Clayton*

Palmer H. Greene, *Cordele*
Lonnie H. Grimsley, *Adel*
Denmark Groover, Jr., *320–4 First Natl. Bank Bldg., Macon*
Frank L. Gross, *Toccoa*
Woodrow W. Gross, *Avans*
Wm. B. Gunter, *Gainesville*
J. Battle Hall, *Rome*
Guy W. Hardaway, *Greenville*
R. A. Harrell, *Cairo*
J. I. Harrison, *Hazlehurst*
Robert L. Harrison, *Jesup*
W. Colbert Hawkins, *Sylvania*
Dewey Hayes, *Douglas*
Waldo Henderson, *Lakeland*
George W. Hendrix, *Ludowici*
B. Harvey Hodges, *Jackson*
Rubert L. Hogan, *Dudley*
William W. Holley, *2516 Northview Ave., Augusta*
Harlan Houston, *Dalton*
Grady L. Huddleston, *Fayetteville*
D. D. Hudson, *Ocilla*
Joe J. Hurst, *Georgetown*
W. C. Ivey, *Porterdale*
George L. Jackson, *Gray*
Ben Jessup, *Cochran*
Merrill Johnson, *Millen*
Walter F. Johnson, *Ellijay*
David C. Jones, *Sylvester*
Fred C. Jones, Jr., *Dahlonega*
Paul J. Jones, Jr., *Dublin*
Thad M. Jones, *Plains*
C. M. Jordan, Jr., *Alamo*
Paul V. Kelley, Sr., *Lawrenceville*
T. E. Kennedy, Jr., *Ashburn*
Tom Kennedy, *Manassas*
Wm. Hicks Key, *Monticello*
Willie Lee Kilgore, *Lawrenceville*
William R. Killian, *Brunswick*
A. S. Killingsworth, *Fort Gaines*
Harvey G. King, Jr., *Dalton*
Joe N. King, *Cusseta*
M. E. King, *Concord*
Claude S. Kitchens, *Dry Branch*
C. O. Lam, *Hogansville*
A. T. Land, *Allentown*
William L. Lanier, *Metter*
Woodrow Wilson Lavender, *Bowman*
Frank P. Lindsey, Jr., *Griffin*
Hamilton Lokey, *C. & S. Natl. Bank Bldg., Atlanta*
Fred F. Long, *Chatsworth*
John W. Love, Jr., *Ringgold*
Joe H. Lowe, *Crawford*
J. Roy McCracken, *Avera*
Edward E. McGarity, *McDonough*
Paul McKelvey, *Rockmart*
Andrew W. McKenna, *Persons Bldg., Macon*
W. Hugh McWhorter, *128 Atlanta Ave., Decatur*
James A. Mackay, *Masonic Temple, Decatur*
L. A. Mallory, Jr., *Thomaston*
Tom Martin, *Homer*
Marcus Mashburn, *Cumming*
W. C. Massee, *Milledgeville*
B. Benson Matheson, *Hartwell*
J. E. Mathis, *Valdosta*
Chappelle Matthews, *Athens*
Henry A. Mauldin, *Calhoun*

CLEVE MINCY, *Waycross*
MARVIN E. MOATE, *Sparta*
T. WATSON MOBLEY, *Girard*
A. C. MOORE, *Jasper*
WARREN S. MOORMAN, *Lakeland*
REID MULL, *Blue Ridge*
R. CLIFTON MURPHEY, *Roberta*
HAROLD L. MURPHY, *Buchanan*
JACK MURR, *Americus*
DOWNING MUSGROVE, *Homerville*
BERNARD N. NIGHTINGALE, *Brunswick*
JOHN NILAN, *Murrah Bldg., Columbus*
JOHN D. ODOM, *Kingsland*
TOM C. PALMER, JR., *Pelham*
W. C. PARKER, *Baxley*
GILBERT C. PEACOCK, *Eastman*
B. E. PELHAM, *Ellaville*
C. C. PERKINS, *Mount Zion*
HOKE S. PETERS, *Manchester*
PETE PETTEY, *Hawkinsville*
GLENN S. PHILLIPS, *Harlem*
JOHN LEE PHILLIPS, *Monroe*
A. MAC PICKARD, 2717 *Mimosa St., Columbus*
GEORGE W. POTTS, *Newnan*
H. N. RAMSEY, SR., *Springfield*
LOUIS T. RAULERSON, *Haylow*
JACK B. RAY, *Norwood*
RAYMOND M. REED, *Blair Bldg., Marietta*
G. TROY REGISTER, *Valdosta*
H. BEN RODGERS, *Folkston*
HARVEY ROUGHTON, *Sandersville*
EMORY L. ROWLAND, *Wrightsville*
WILLIAM L. RUARK, *Woodville*
ROBERT L. RUSSELL, JR., *Winder*
GUY W. RUTLAND, JR., 198 *Rockwell Ave., Decatur*
CARL E. SANDERS, *Southern Finance Bldg., Augusta*
ROBERT L. SCOGGIN, *Rome*
JOHN E. SHEFFIELD, JR., *Quitman*
H. JACK SHORT, *Doerun*
SAM S. SINGER, *Lumpkin*
W. D. SIVELL, *Chipley*
B. E. SMITH, SR., *Daisy*
GEO. L. SMITH II, *Swainsboro*
HOKE SMITH, 1045 *Hurt Bldg., Atlanta*
M. M. SMITH, 560 *Hurt Bldg., Atlanta*
JOHN W. SOGNIER, *Realty Bldg., Savannah*
J. LESTER SOUTER, *Montezuma*
ROBERT G. STEPHENS, JR., *Athens*
E. C. STEVENS, *Buena Vista*
A. L. STEWART, *Fitzgerald*
M. ORTEZ STRICKLAND, *Vidalia*
DAVID C. STRIPLING, *Newnan*
HOWARD H. TAMPLIN, *Madison*
ANDREW J. TANNER, *Douglas*
JACK G. TARPLEY, *Blairsville*
VAUGHN E. TERRELL, *Bainbridge*
W. G. TODD, *Gibson*
FRANKLIN F. TRUELOVE, *Cleveland*
D. E. TURK, *Abbeville*
FRANK S. TWITTY, *Camilla*
D. VANN UNDERWOOD, *Cartersville*
JOE C. UNDERWOOD, *Mt. Vernon*
TROY UPSHAW, *Rydal*
DALLAS VEAL, *Eatonton*
G. STUART WATSON, *Albany*
PAUL B. WEEMS, *Summerville*
R. E. WHEELER, *Donalsonville*
W. M. WILLIAMS, *Gainesville*

HAROLD S. WILLINGHAM, 846 *Church St., Marietta*
O. S. WILLIS, *Coolidge*
MONTGOMERY WILSON, *Hiawassee*
WM. J. WILSON, *Ft. Valley*
J. MERCER WOOTEN, *Shellman*
BARRY WRIGHT, JR., *Rome*
J. GORDON YOUNG, 14½ *Eleventh St., Columbus*

IDAHO

Senate

Republicans 24   Democrats 20

ANDREAS AIKELE, *Moore*
HOLGER ALBRETHSEN, *Gannett*
K. C. BARLOW, *Burley*
SETH BURSTEDT, *Challis*
ADAM H. BLACKSTOCK, *Marsing*
O. J. BUXTON, *Driggs*
LEONARD CARDIFF, *Pierce*
ELDON W. COOK, *Pegram*
FRED M. COOPER, *Grace*
VERNON DANIEL, *Payette*
A. M. DERR, *Clarks Fork*
W. E. DREVLOW, *Craigmont*
JOHN V. EVANS, *Malad City*
FRANK E. GOODWIN, *Sweet*
RODNEY A. HANSEN, *Rupert*
H. MAX HANSON, *Fairfield*
THOMAS HEATH, *Preston*
HOWARD D. HECHTNER, *Lapwai*
THEODORE HOFF, JR., *Horseshoe Bend*
CARL IRWIN, *Twin Falls*
WILLIAM A. JACKSON, *Wendell*
W. EVERT JOHNSTON, *Grangeville*
T. J. KEITHLY, *Midvale*
RALPH LITTON, *St. Anthony*
JACK MCBRIDE, *Palouse, Washington*
VARD W. MEADOWS, *American Falls*
EDWARD S. MIDDLEMIST, *Bonners Ferry*
GEORGE MOODY, *Calder*
H. T. MOSS, *Rigby*
LEO D. MURDOCK, *Blackfoot*
A. W. NAEGLE, *Idaho Falls*
HARRY NOCK, *Cascade*
ELMO PATTERSON, *Richfield*
LESTER C. PALMER, *Council*
JOHN W. RASOR, *Coeur d'Alene*
GEORGE R. RADFORD, *St. Maries*
ELLIS SHAWVER, *Eden*
J. HOWARD SIMS, *Salmon*
NELLIE CLINE STEENSON, *Pocatello*
RAY F. STOREY, *Nampa*
J. KENNETH THATCHER, *Sugar City*
R. M. WETHERELL, *Mountain Home*
RAYMOND L. WHITE, *Boise*
EARL S. WRIGHT, *Dubois*

House

Republicans 36   Democrats 23

ERNEST ALLEN, *Nampa*
JAMES ANNEST, *Declo*
J. BURNS BEAL, *Arco*
GEORGE L. BLICK, *Castleford*
E. R. BUEHLER, *Pocatello*
CARL R. BURT, *Boise*
PETE T. CENARRUSA, *Carey*

C. W. COINER, *Twin Falls*
CHARLES F. COOK, *St. Maries*
G. L. CROOKHAM, JR., *Caldwell*
NORA L. DAVIS, *Letha*
CHARLES R. DONALDSON, *Boise*
ROBERT DOOLITTLE, *Priest River*
W. D. EBERLE, *Boise*
DAN D. EMERY, *Lewiston*
RUSSELL FOGG, *Idaho Falls*
WILLIAM M. FROME, *St. Anthony*
H. GRANT GARDNER, *Fruitland*
ORSON H. GRIMMETT, *Paris*
ELVON HAMPTON, *Genesee*
RALPH R. HARDING, *Malad City*
RALPH HARRISON, *Central*
JAMES C. HAYES, *Homedale*
NORMAN S. HEIKKILA, *Wallace*
W. L. HENDRIX, *Boise*
SADIE JOHNSON, *Worley*
CLARENCE W. KIMPTON, *Challis*
FLOYD O. KISLING, *Dietrich*
JOHN B. KUGLER, *American Falls*
ROY H. LAIRD, *Dubois*
LYNN LAKE, *Roberts*
E. E. LaTURNER, *Jerome*
A. A. McLEOD, *Nezperce*
STEVE MEIKLE, *Rexburg*
JAY M. MERRILL, *Twin Falls*
ARVIL MILLAR, *Shelley*
HELEN J. MILLER, *Glenns Ferry*
ROBERT H. MILLS, *Garden Valley*
J. W. MONROE, *Culdesac*
W. DEAN PALMER, *Preston*
RALPH PARIS, *McCall*
DON PIEPER, *Idaho Falls*
WILLIAM PYLE, *Gooding*
EDWARD C. RAMBEAU, *Orofino*
JAMES L. RHODES, *Coeur d'Alene*
RAY ROBBINS, *Rupert*
W. J. SEWELL, *Driggs*
TED SLAVIN, *Salmon*
HAROLD SNOW, *Moscow*
CLAY SUTTON, *Midvale*
PERRY SWISHER, *Pocatello*
T. F. TERRELL, *Pocatello*
MARVIN C. VANDENBERG, *Bonners Ferry*
FRED WALTON, *Fairfield*
TONY WESSELS, *Greencreek*
FRANK L. WESTFALL, *Aberdeen*
RALPH H. WICKBERG, *Kellogg*
CHARLES WINKLER, *Council*
R. H. YOUNG, JR., *Parma*

ILLINOIS
Senate
Republicans 31   Democrats 19

W. RUSSELL ARRINGTON, 606 *Forest Ave., Evanston*
CHARLES W. BAKER, *Davis Junction*
ARTHUR J. BIDWILL, 1403 *Bonnie Brae, River Forest*
PAUL W. BROYLES, *Eighteenth and Franklin Sts., Mt. Vernon*
MARVIN F. BURT, 1115 *S. Benson Blvd., Freeport*
HOMER BUTLER, 701 *S. Buchanan St., Marion*
ROLLIE C. CARPENTER, *Ancona*
ROBERT E. CHERRY, 924 *W. Castlewood Terr., Chicago*

WILLIAM G. CLARK, 5258 *W. Van Buren, Chicago*
DENNIS J. COLLINS, 549 *Northern Lane, DeKalb*
WILLIAM J. CONNORS, 232 *E. Walton St., Chicago*
R. G. CRISENBERRY, 328 *N. Eleventh St., Murphysboro*
A. L. CRONIN, 9550 *S. Winston Ave., Chicago*
W. P. CUTHBERTSON, 204 *College, Carlinville*
DAVID DAVIS, 1112 *E. Monroe, Bloomington*
LLOYD E. DAVIS, *R.F.D. 1, Morrisonville*
DANIEL DOUGHERTY, 1957 *E. Ninety-third St., Chicago*
T. MAC DOWNING, 409 *E. Carroll St., Macomb*
GEORGE E. DRACH, 1524 *Noble Ave., Springfield*
DWIGHT P. FRIEDRICH, 1031 *E. Broadway St., Centralia*
BENEDICT GARMISA, 3330 *W. Potomac Ave., Chicago*
JOHN J. GORMAN, 4109 *W. Van Buren St., Chicago*
ROBERT J. GRAHAM, 1819 *N. Natchez Ave., Chicago*
JAMES W. GRAY, 1406 *N. Forty-fourth St., East St. Louis*
EGBERT B. GROEN, 3 *Rosewood Lane, Pekin*
FRED J. HART, 612 *Tyler, Streator*
WILLIAM F. HENSLEY, 1006 *Lexington, Lawrenceville*
GLEN O. JONES, *R.F.D. 1, Raleigh*
FRANK J. KOCAREK, 1720 *S. Loomis St., Chicago*
MARSHALL KORSHAK, 5555 *S. Everett Ave., Chicago*
ROLAND V. LIBONATI, 925 *S. Halsted St., Chicago*
MERRITT J. LITTLE, 227 *S. Elmwood Dr., Aurora*
WILLIAM J. LYNCH, 3622 *S. Wallace, Chicago*
ROBERT W. LYONS, *E. Main St., Oakland*
VICTOR McBROOM, 983 *S. Washington Ave., Kankakee*
ROBERT McCLORY, 340 *Prospect Ave., Lake Bluff*
JOHN P. MEYER, 1314 *Franklin St., Danville*
JAMES O. MONROE, 600 *Walnut Dr., Collinsville*
MORRIS E. MUHLEMAN, 215 *Fifteenth St., Rock Island*
DONALD J. O'BRIEN, 1102 *W. Garfield Blvd., Chicago*
LOTTIE HOLMAN O'NEILL, 741 *Summit St., Downers Grove*
EVERETT R. PETERS, *St. Joseph*
DANIEL D. ROSTENKOWSKI, 1372 *W. Evergreen Ave., Chicago*
FRED B. ROTI, 2604 *S. Wentworth Ave., Chicago*
FRANK RYAN, 1307 *S. California Blvd., Chicago*
LILLIAN E. SCHLAGENHAUF, 418 *S. Eighteenth St., Quincy*
ALBERT SCOTT, 656 *N. Main, Canton*
ELBERT S. SMITH, 510 *Siegel St., Decatur*
FRED J. SMITH, 3442 *S. Wabash Ave., Chicago*
CLYDE C. TRAGER, 2510 *N. Sheridan Rd., Peoria*
(1 vacancy)

House
Republicans 78   Democrats 74

JAMES J. ADDUCI, 2250 *W. Jackson Blvd., Chicago*
JACK BAIRSTOW, 224 *Ash St., Waukegan*
BERT BAKER, JR., 600 *N. Madison St., Benton*
TOBIAS BARRY, SR., *Ladd*
LOUIS E. BECKMAN, 8 *Chatham Circle, Kankakee*
G. R. BECKMEYER, 509 *W. St. Louis St., Nashville*
WARREN O. BILLHARTZ, *New Baden*
HECTOR A. BROUILLET, 3532 *S. California Ave., Chicago*
GEORGE S. BRYDIA, 105 *W. Third St., Prophetstown*
GARREL BURGOON, 611 *Eleventh St., Lawrenceville*

ROBERT L. BURHANS, 10 *Montclair Ave., Peoria*
LOUIS F. CAPUZI, 2554 *W. Superior St., Chicago*
JAMES D. CARRIGAN, 3 *S. Gate Rd., Peoria*
JAMES Y. CARTER, 3842 *S. Parkway, Chicago*
NICHOLAS E. CARUSO, 712 *N. Monticello Ave., Chicago*
HOMER CATON, *Stanford*
ORVILLE G. CHAPMAN, *Bradford*
CLYDE L. CHOATE, 609 *S. Main St., Anna*
CHARLES W. CLABAUGH, 901 *W. Daniel St., Champaign*
HUBERT D. CONSIDINE, 521 *S. Ottawa, Dixon*
ROBERT CRAIG, *Indianola*
THOMAS J. CURRAN, 2011 *S. Ashland Ave., Chicago*
ROBERT CUTRO, 1460 *W. Ohio St., Chicago*
S. O. DALE, 307 *SE Fourth St., Fairfield*
CORNEAL A. DAVIS, 3223 *S. Calumet Ave., Chicago*
JOSEPH L. DE LA COUR, 185 *E. Chestnut St., Chicago*
ANTHONY J. DETOLVE, 627 *S. Carpenter St., Chicago*
ORA D. DILLAVOU, *The Meadows, Urbana*
ALAN J. DIXON, 135 *Orchard Dr., Belleville*
GEORGE W. DUNNE, 14 *E. Chestnut St., Chicago*
EDWARD C. EBERSPACHER, 219 *N. Washington, Shelbyville*
ANDREW A. EUZZINO, 917 *S. Blue Island Ave., Chicago*
EVERETT L. FALDER, 1204 *E. Carroll St., Macomb*
JOHN G. FARY, 3558 *S. Honore St., Chicago*
PETER C. GRANATA, 1025 *S. May St., Chicago*
AUGUST G. GREBE, 1218 *Norwood Ave., Peoria*
HERSCHEL S. GREEN, *R.F.D. 1, West York*
HUGH GREEN, 711 *W. Douglas Ave., Jacksonville*
MABEL E. GREEN, 1436 *W. State St., Rockford*
ERNEST A. GREENE, 2725 *S. Calumet Ave., Chicago*
EDWIN R. HAAG, *Breese*
ALBERT W. HACHMEISTER, 423 *W. Barry Ave., Chicago*
STANLEY A. HALICK, 1216 *N. Maplewood Ave., Chicago*
CLARENCE G. HALL, 28 *N. Sandusky St., Catlin*
DEAN R. HAMMACK, 14 *W. Water St., Pinckneyville*
MICHAEL E. HANNIGAN, 6646 *S. Honore St., Chicago*
CLAYTON C. HARBECK, *R.F.D. 2, Utica*
LLOYD HARRIS, 1704 *Delmar Ave., Granite City*
WILLIAM C. HARRIS, *R.F.D. 4, Pontiac*
FRANK HOLTEN, 1114 *St. Louis Ave., East St. Louis*
G. WILLIAM HORSLEY, *R.F.D. 3, West Lake Dr., Springfield*
DAVID HUNTER, JR., *R.F.D. 4, Rockford*
H. B. IHNEN, 2334 *Main St., Quincy*
LOUIS JANCZAK, 1315 *N. Bosworth Ave., Chicago*
GORDON E. KERR, *Brookport*
W. K. KIDWELL, 1403 *Charleston Ave., Mattoon*
JOHN M. KING, 528 *E. Prairie Ave., Wheaton*
JOSEPH G. KOHOUT, 1314 *W. Nineteenth St., Chicago*
STANLEY R. KOSINSKI, 5544 *W. Leland Ave., Chicago*
JAMES P. LANNON, *Saunemin*
RICHARD R. LARSON, 694 *Bateman St., Galesburg*
J. LISLE LAUFER, *Hampshire*
HARRY D. LAVERY, 818 *Gunnison, Chicago*
CLYDE LEE, 818 *Pace Ave., Mt. Vernon*
NOBLE W. LEE, 5541 *S. Woodlawn Ave., Chicago*
JOSEPH J. LELIVELT, 1231 *S. Fifteenth Ave., Maywood*
HENRY M. LENARD, 8111 *S. Colfax Ave., Chicago*
JOHN W. LEWIS, JR., *R.F.D. 2, Marshall*
MYRON E. LOLLAR, 115 *E. Ensey, Tuscola*
FRANCIS J. LOUGHRAN, 1220 *Sterling Ave., Joliet*

ALLEN T. LUCAS, 2216 *Whittier Ave., Springfield*
WILLIAM LYONS, 501 *E. Elm St., Gillespie*
WALTER BABE MCAVOY, 6039 *S. California Ave., Chicago*
ROBERT W. MCCARTHY, 555 *Eleventh St., Lincoln*
A. B. MCCONNELL, *R.F.D. 2, Woodstock*
DEAN MCCULLY, 401 *Maple Ave., Minonk*
MICHAEL H. MCDERMOTT, 6835 *S. Wolcott Ave., Chicago*
ROBERT T. MCLOSKEY, 323 *S. Eighth, Monmouth*
FRANK A. MAREK, 5300 *W. Thirty-first St., Cicero*
ERWIN L. MARTAY, 2045 *W. Arthur Ave., Chicago*
SAMUEL L. MARTIN, 324 *Coney Ave., Watseka*
ROBERT L. MASSEY, 1948 *N. Nashville Ave., Chicago*
JOHN E. MILLER, *Tamms*
OTIS L. MILLER, SR., 413 *S. Virginia Ave., Belleville*
JOHN K. MORRIS, *R.F.D. 1, Chadwick*
W. J. MURPHY, *Petite Lake, Antioch*
RICHARD A. NAPOLITANO, 1057 *N. Sacramento Ave., Chicago*
BENJAMIN NELSON, 1230 *S. Independence Blvd., Chicago*
GEORGE NOONAN, 3020 *S. Parnell Ave., Chicago*
MAUD N. PEFFERS, 815 *LaFayette St., Aurora*
DAVID M. PETERS, 824 *E. Clay, Decatur*
JOSEPH R. PETERSON, 1309 *S. Main St., Princeton*
LEO PFEFFER, *Seymour*
WILLIAM PIERCE, 305 *S. Hunter Ave., Rockford*
LILLIAN PIOTROWSKI, 2845 *W. Twenty-fourth Blvd., Chicago*
WILLIAM E. POLLACK, 1511 *W. Byron St., Chicago*
PAUL POWELL, *Vienna*
CARL H. PREIHS, 620 *Kitchell Ave., Pana*
PAUL J. RANDOLPH, 201 *E. Walton St., Chicago*
C. R. RATCLIFFE, 1407 *Jefferson St., Beardstown*
WALTER J. REUM, 232 *N. Ridgeland Ave., Oak Park*
BEN S. RHODES, 1211 *Broadway, Normal*
PAULINE B. RINAKER, *Carlinville*
ROLLO R. ROBBINS, *Augusta*
WILLIAM H. ROBINSON, 601 *E. Thirty-sixth St., Chicago*
BARRETT F. ROGERS, *Atlanta*
ROBERT E. ROMANO, 1142 *S. Michigan Ave., Chicago*
SAM ROMANO, 1418 *S. Fairfield Ave., Chicago*
MITCHELL ROPA, 1710 *W. Twenty-first St., Chicago*
MICHAEL A. RUDDY, 1700 *W. Garfield Blvd., Chicago*
JOE W. RUSSELL, *Piper City*
JAMES J. RYAN, 1611 *W. Jackson Blvd., Chicago*
JOHN G. RYAN, 1530 *E. Eighty-third Pl., Chicago*
GEORGE L. SAAL, 360 *Court St., Pekin*
ELROY C. SANDQUIST, 4259 *N. Mozart St., Chicago*
CHARLES ED SCHAEFER, 208 *E. Union St., Nokomis*
EDWARD SCHNEIDER, 8612 *S. Ingleside Ave., Chicago*
LEON M. SCHULER, 270 *High St., Aurora*
J. NORMAN SHADE, 415 *Haines Ave., Pekin*
SAMUEL H. SHAPIRO, 1300 *Cobb Blvd., Kankakee*
EDWARD J. SHAW, 1120 *W. Fry St., Chicago*
JOSEPH B. SIEMER, *Teutopolis*
PAUL SIMON, *Market St., Troy*
CHARLES M. SKYLES, 4714 *S. Champlain Ave., Chicago*
FRANK J. SMITH, 4549 *S. Emerald Ave., Chicago*
RALPH T. SMITH, 3654 *Berkeley Ave., Alton*
CARL W. SODERSTROM, 1011 *Riverside Ave., Streator*
ARTHUR W. SPRAGUE, 345 *S. Spring Ave., LaGrange*
CLARENCE E. SPRINKLE, *R.F.D. 1, Assumption*
RICHARD STENGEL, 2101 *29½ St., Rock Island*

RALPH STEPHENSON, 1020 *Twenty-third St., Moline*
FRANKLIN U. STRANSKY, 139 *Park St., Savanna*
JOSEPH P. STREMLAU, *R.F.D. 2, Mendota*
MARTIN P. SUTOR, *R.F.D. 1, Galesburg*
THEODORE A. SWINARSKI, 2802 *W. Forty-sixth St., Chicago*
THOS. J. THORNTON, 457 *Holmes St., Chester*
JOHN P. TOUHY, 1012 *W. Monroe St., Chicago*
CLAUDE D. TRAVERS, 323 *E. Cherry St., Olney*
BERNICE T. VAN DER VRIES, 439 *Maple Ave., Winnetka*
W. O. VERHINES, *Vienna*
M. R. WALKER, 28 *E. Raymond Ave., Danville*
CHARLES H. WEBER, 2924 *N. Southport Ave., Chicago*
KENNETH R. WENDT, 666 *Irving Park Rd., Chicago*
HAROLD W. WIDMER, *Park Blvd., Freeport*
CHARLES K. WILLETT, 218 *Brinton Ave., Dixon*
GEORGE W. WILSON, *Baylis*
KENNETH E. WILSON, 4528 *S. Parkway Blvd., Chicago*
CARL H. WITTMOND, *Brussels*
FRANK C. WOLF, 4046 *W. Twenty-sixth St., Chicago*
WARREN L. WOOD, 736 *Bartlett Ave., Plainfield*
PAUL C. ZEMPEL, 427 *E. Euclid Ave., Lewistown*
PAUL A. ZIEGLER, 700 *N. Second St., Carmi*
(1 vacancy)

INDIANA

Senate

Republicans 32   Democrats 14

IRA J. ANDERSON, *Uniontown*
EUGENE BAINBRIDGE, 8309 *Northcote, Munster*
WALTER A. BARAN, 4835 *Baring Ave., East Chicago*
WILLIS K. BATCHELET, 321 *N. Martha St., Angola*
PETER A. BECZKIEWICZ, 1501 *Western Ave., South Bend*
PAUL J. BITZ, 514 *Lewis Ave., Evansville*
D. RUSSELL BONTRAGER, 101 *North Dr., Elkhart*
PAUL P. BOYLE, 426 *W. Thompson St., Sullivan*
ROBERT LEE BROKENBURR, 46 *N. Pennsylvania St., Rm. 218, Indianapolis 4*
KENNETH J. BROWN, JR., 1517 *N. Tillotson Ave., Muncie*
T. VOLNEY CARTER, *R.F.D. 2, Seymour*
WILLIAM CHRISTY, 7106 *Grand Ave., Hammond*
LEONARD F. CONRAD, 1528 *S. Center St., Terre Haute*
ROY CONRAD, *R.F.D. 2, Monticello*
JAMES L. DUNN, *Nowlin Rd., Lawrenceburg*
VON A. EICHHORN, *Box 57, Uniondale*
KEITH FRASER, *Box 14, Portland*
MRS. DOROTHY GARDNER, 305 *Arcadia Ct., Ft. Wayne*
JOHN M. HARLAN, 316 *First Natl. Bank Bldg., Richmond*
THOMAS C. HASBROOK, 6001 *Haverford Ave., Indianapolis 20*
CARL A. HELMS, 239 *N. Merrill St., Fortville*
WILLIAM B. HOADLEY, *Graham Hotel, Bloomington*
CHARLES R. KELLUM, *R.F.D. 1, Mooresville*
SAMUEL C. McQUEEN, 9 *N. Walnut St., Brazil*
CHARLES M. MADDOX, *R.F.D. 1, Otterbein*
WESLEY MALONE, 325 *Vine St., Clinton*
C. WENDELL MARTIN, 1356 *Consolidated Bldg., Indianapolis 4*

WARREN W. MARTIN, JR., 505 *W. Stansifer Ave., Clarksville*
CARL J. MOLDENHAUER, *R.F.D. 7, Huntington*
GLEN NEAVILLE, *R.F.D. 2, Sharpsville*
RICHARD NEWHOUSE, *Morristown*
ROBERT P. O'BANNON, 118 *Elliott Ave., Corydon*
DONALD M. REAM, *R.F.D. 14, Box 348, Indianapolis 44*
RICHARD O. RISTINE, 606 *W. Wabash Ave., Crawfordsville*
CHARLES F. RUTLEDGE, 916 *South B St., Elwood*
A. BURR SHERON, *Shady Hills, Marion*
LUCIUS SOMERS, *R.F.D. 1, Hoagland*
HOWARD STEELE, 502 *Main St., Knox*
RUEL W. STEELE, 1013 *Lincoln Ave., Bedford*
FLOYD STEVENS, *R.F.D. 2, Claypool*
EARL M. UTTERBACK, *R.F.D. 6, Box 316A, Kokomo*
JOHN W. VAN NESS, 603 *Franklin St., Valparaiso*
MATTHEW E. WELSH, 719 *Busseron St., Vincennes*
ALBERT W. WESSELMAN, *R.F.D. 8, Box 45, Evansville*
ARTHUR S. WILSON, *Rd. 64 East, Princeton*
FREEMAN YEAGER, 225 *S. Lafayette Blvd., South Bend 1*

(4 vacancies)

House

Republicans 62   Democrats 37

EARL L. ADERS, 723 *E. Jackson Blvd., Elkhart*
JAMES D. ALLEN, 806 *S. Main St., Salem*
WILLIAM E. BABINCSAK, 1856 *S. River Dr., Munster*
J. J. BAILEY, 2941 *George St., Anderson*
PAUL L. BAILEY, 1262 *N. Jefferson St., Huntington*
LAURENCE D. BAKER, *U.S. 6, Kendallville*
CABLE G. BALL, 402 *S. Ninth St., Lafayette*
WALTER H. BARBOUR, 5105 *N. Shadeland Dr., Indianapolis*
MRS. ELSIE C. BARNING, 3303 *Claremont Ave., Evansville*
BIRCH E. BAYH, JR., *R.F.D. 2, W. Terre Haute*
WALTER J. BENEVILLE, 402 *Kewanna Dr., Jeffersonville*
ROBERT H. BERNING, 724 *Kinsmoor Ave., Fort Wayne*
PAUL M. BILBY, *R.F.D. 2, Warsaw*
WILLIAM P. BIRCHLER, *Cannelton*
WILLARD G. BOWEN, 1516 *Chester Blvd., Richmond*
ALEMBERT W. BRAYTON, 5260 *Primrose Ave., Indianapolis 20*
JOHN W. BRENTLINGER, 1446 *Barbour Ave., Terre Haute*
MRS. ALICE MATHIAS BROWN, 6827 *Baring Ave., Hammond*
EARL BUCHANAN, 1215 *King Ave., Indianapolis*
JACK E. CAINE, 3012 *N. Bedford Ave., Evansville*
IVAN J. CARSON, 318 *N. Weston St., Rensselaer*
MAURICE CHASE, *R.F.D. 6, Bedford*
MRS. MILDRED CHURILLA, 4724 *Tod Ave., East Chicago*
HARRY W. CLAFFEY, SR., 8055 *Springmill Rd., Indianapolis*
RAYMONDE ALEXIS CLARKE, 202½ *N. Michigan St., Plymouth*
S. PAUL CLAY, JR., 1 *W. Washington, Indianapolis 9*
CHARLES CLEM, *R.F.D. 2, Princeton*
EMERSON CLOYD, 1022 *N. Main St., Brookville*
WILLIAM F. CONDON, *Greentown*

CLEM CONWAY, *R.F.D.* 1, *Mooreland*
GEORGE M. DAVIDSON, 1130 *Hume Mansur Bldg.,*
  Indianapolis
DAVID W. DENNIS, 104 *SW Ninth St., Richmond*
JESSE L. DICKINSON, 1023 *Talbot Ave., South Bend*
GEORGE S. DIENER, 4151 *N. Pennsylvania,*
  Indianapolis 5
GRATTAN H. DOWNEY, 3826 *N. Tacoma Ave.,*
  Indianapolis 5
RALPH A. DUNBAR, 309 *Maple St., Osgood*
JOHN R. FEIGHNER, *R.F.D.* 1, *Marion*
OREN E. FELTON, *R.F.D.* 1, *Fairmount*
RICHARD B. FISHERING, 1018 *Kinnaird Ave.,*
  Fort Wayne
DONALD E. FOLTZ, *R.F.D.* 3, *Clinton*
ROBERT E. GRAMELSPACHER, 515 *W. Sixth St.,*
  Jasper
DAVID L. GRIMES, *R.F.D.* 1, *Fillmore*
RICHARD WAYNE GUTHRIE, 820 *N. Audubon Rd.,*
  Indianapolis 19
JOE A. HARRIS, *Box* 142, *Carlisle*
WILLIAM H. HERRING, *Box* 86, *Linton*
J. HOWARD HETZLER, *R.F.D.* 1, *Wabash*
RALPH G. HINES, 1422 *S. Meridian St., Portland*
NOBLE F. HODGEN, *R.F.D.* 1, *Frankfort*
W. O. HUGHES, 325 *Grove St., Fort Wayne*
JAMES S. HUNTER, 3910 *Carey St., East Chicago*
PHILLIP C. JOHNSON, *Hadley Woodland, Mooresville*
JOHN KELL, *R.F.D.* 1, *Attica*
WAYNE KELLAMS, 705 *E. Main Cross St., Edinburg*
MAHLON KERLIN, 210 *S. Washington St., Delphi*
ORA A. KINCAID, 128 *W. Fordice St., Lebanon*
CARSON H. KING, *Box* 24, *Boggstown*
NAOMI J. KIRK, 1318 *E. Spring St., New Albany*
JOHN L. KIRKPATRICK, *R.F.D.* 1, *Fortville*
JOSEPH E. KLEN, 6607 *Marshall Ave., Hammond*
JEAN R. LaGRANGE, 815½ *Monroe St., LaPorte*
RUSSELL V. LANGSENKAMP, 1026 *Circle Tower,*
  Indianapolis
THOMAS M. LONG, 1618 *Wood St., Elkhart*
GEORGE W. McDANIEL, 222 *E. Kirkwood Ave.,*
  Bloomington
WALTER H. MAEHLING, 2206 *N. Eleventh St.,*
  Terre Haute
BETTY MALINKA, 9411 *Lake Shore Dr., Gary*
ELTON L. MARQUART, 628 *Oakdale Dr., Fort Wayne*
LEO A. MEAGHER, 3726 *Stringtown Rd., Evansville*
REX S. MINNICK, *R.F.D.* 4, *Box* 122, *Brazil*
CHARLES T. MISER, *Box* 63, *Garrett*
MERRETT R. MONKS, 312 *S. Main St., Winchester*
PAUL MYERS, *Bloomingdale*
ROBERT L. NASH, *R.F.D.* 1, *Tipton*
HARRY NOLTING, *R.F.D.* 2, *Columbus*
OTTO J. POZGAY, *R.F.D.* 3, *Box* 93, *South Bend*
JOHN T. PRITCHARD, JR., *Box* 1, *North Madison*
CHARLES T. RACHELS, 115 *E. Fourth St.,*
  Mt. Vernon
RALPH RADER, *Akron*
ROBERT L. ROCK, *R.F.D.* 5, *Anderson*
OTTO L. REDDISH, *R.F.D.* 2, *Crawfordsville*
COURT ROLLINS, 601 *Neeley Ave., Muncie*
CHARLES H. SCHENK, *R.F.D.* 4, *Vincennes*
ROBERT D. SCHMIDT, 410 *W. Broadway,*
  Logansport
JOHN F. SHAWLEY, 302 *W. Eighth St., Michigan City*
GLENN R. SLENKER, 602 *W. Broadway, Monticello*
MRS. ANNA PADBERG SMELSER, 2057 *Riverside Dr.,*
  South Bend

JAMES W. SPURGEON, 915 *W. Spring St.,*
  Brownstown
JOHN W. STACY, 542 *Main St., Lawrenceburg*
MRS. HARRIET C. STOUT, 4473 *Washington Blvd.,*
  Indianapolis 5
PAUL E. STRATE, *Freelandville*
LEO SULLIVAN, 529 *W. Fifth St., Peru*
VANCE M. WAGGONER, 130 *E. Second St.,*
  Rushville
JOHN W. WAINWRIGHT, *R.F.D.* 1, *Wolcottville*
ROBERT S. WEBB, *R.F.D.* 1, *Arcadia*
ALLAN GORDON WEIR, 620 *Wysor Bldg., Muncie*
ROY WEST, *Star Rt., Amo*
JAMES D. WILLIAMS, *Corydon*
HARL H. WILSON, *R.F.D.* 5, *Greensburg*
RODERICK M. WRIGHT, *R.F.D.* 1, *Washington*
L. LUTHER YAGER, *R.F.D.* 1, *Berne*
(1 vacancy)

IOWA

Senate

Republicans 43   Democrats 6

CARL T. ANDERSON, *Wellman*
G. D. BELLMAN, *Indianola*
LAURENCE M. BOOTHBY, *Cleghorn*
SAM BURTON, *Ottumwa*
GUY G. BUTLER, *Rolfe*
FRANK BYERS, *Security Bldg., Cedar Rapids*
TED D. CLARK, *Mystic*
THOMAS J. DAILEY, *Burlington*
DUANE E. DEWEL, *Algona*
J. T. DYKHOUSE, *Rock Springs*
EARL ELIJAH, *Clarence*
FRANK D. ELWOOD, *Cresco*
JACOB GRIMSTEAD, *Lake Mills*
HENRY HEIDEMAN, *Rockwell City*
FRANK HOXIE, *Shenandoah*
A. J. JOHNSON, *Elkader*
HERMAN M. KNUDSON, *Clear Lake*
THOMAS C. LARSON, *Blockton*
J. G. LUCAS, *Madrid*
J. KENDALL LYNES, *Plainfield*
ARCH W. McFARLANE, *Waterloo*
EDWARD J. McMANUS, *Keokuk*
LEON N. MILLER, *Knoxville*
WILBUR C. MOLISON, *Grinnell*
CHARLES W. NELSON, *Packwood*
D. C. NOLAN, *Iowa City*
GEORGE E. O'MALLEY, 420 *Royal Union Life*
  Bldg., Des Moines
X. T. PRENTIS, *Mount Ayr*
LAWRENCE PUTNEY, *Gladbrook*
ROBERT R. RIGLER, *New Hampton*
DON RISK, *Independence*
LORIN B. SAYRE, *Winterset*
JACK SCHROEDER, *Kahl Building, Davenport*
GEORGE L. SCOTT, *West Union*
DAVID O. SHAFF, 1118½ *N. Third St., Clinton*
JOHN D. SHOEMAN, *Atlantic*
C. EMORY STEWART, *Rose Hill*
W. C. STUART, *Chariton*
ARNOLD UTZIG, *Dubuque*
CHARLES S. VAN EATON, *Sioux City*
ALAN VEST, *Sac City*
JOHN A. WALKER, *Williams*

HENRY W. WASHBURN, *Hastings*
DEVERE WATSON, *Wickham Bldg., Council Bluffs*
HARRY E. WATSON, *Sanborn*
GEORGE W. WEBER, *Columbus Junction*
ALBERT WEISS, *Denison*
G. E. WHITEHEAD, *Perry*
JACK M. WORMLEY, *Newton*
(1 vacancy)

House
Republicans 89   Democrats 19

WAYNE W. BALLHAGEN, *New Hartford*
JOHN A. BAUMHOVER, *Carroll*
EMLIN L. BERGESON, *Sioux City*
A. S. BLOEDEL, *Tabor*
RAYMOND D. BREAKENRIDGE, *Winterset*
JAMES E. BRILES, *Corning*
M. N. BROWN, *What Cheer*
HOWARD C. BUCK, *Melbourne*
CHARLES R. BURTCH, *Osage*
JOHN CARLSEN, *Clinton*
ROBERT B. CARSON, *Independence*
LEROY CHALUPA, *Pleasant Plain*
EARL L. CHAMBERS, *Gilmore City*
W. R. CHRISTIANSEN, *Northwood*
CLARENCE CHRISTOPHEL, *Waverly*
JAY C. COLBURN, *Harlan*
BLYTHE C. CONN, *Burlington*
RAYMOND CORNICK, *New London*
CHARLES F. COVERDALE, *Clinton*
J. D. CURRIE, *Schaller*
W. E. DARRINGTON, *Persia*
WILLIAM F. DENMAN, *Des Moines*
RILEY DIETZ, *Walcott*
WILLIAM D. DILLON, *Columbus Junction*
JOHN L. DUFFY, *Dubuque*
FLOYD P. EDGINGTON, *Sheffield*
FRED J. EHLERS, *Estherville*
RUSSELL L. ELDRED, *Anamosa*
BERT K. FAIRCHILD, *Ida Grove*
L. A. FALVEY, *Albia*
WILLARD M. FREED, *Gowrie*
T. J. FREY, *Neola*
ANDREW G. FROMMELT, *Dubuque*
DEWEY E. GOODE, *Bloomfield*
JOHN S. GRAY, *Oskaloosa*
ROY HADDEN, *Castana*
MERLE W. HAGEDORN, *Royal*
EUGENE HALLING, *Orient*
A. C. HANSON, *Inwood*
WILLIAM H. HARBOR, *Henderson*
FLOYD H. HATCH, *Edgewood*
W. C. HENDRIX, *Letts*
JIM O. HENRY, *Carson*
CHARLES F. HINCHLIFFE, *Baldwin*
LEONARD HOLDSWORTH, *Manilla*
EARL T. HOOVER, *Mount Ayr*
ELMER A. HOTH, *Postville*
JAMES W. HOWARD, *Cresco*
O. N. HULTMAN, *Stanton*
W. J. JOHANNES, *Ashton*
NEIL E. JOHNS, *Toledo*
HARVEY W. JOHNSON, *Exira*
A. F. KLEIN, *New Virginia*
ERNEST KOSEK, *Cedar Rapids*
G. T. KUESTER, *Griswold*
GRANT LAUER, *Eldorado*

VERN LISLE, *Clarinda*
CASEY LOSS, *Algona*
J. HENRY LUCKEN, *Akron*
JACK MCCOY, *Ottumwa*
CLARK H. MCNEAL, *Belmond*
WADE H. MCREYNOLDS, *Ottumwa*
A. L. MENSING, *Lowden*
EARL A. MILLER, *Cedar Falls*
JACK MILLER, *Sioux City*
J. N. MILROY, *Vinton*
W. L. MOOTY, *Grundy Center*
CONWAY E. MORRIS, *Dallas Center*
ROBERT W. NADEN, *Webster City*
GLADYS S. NELSON, *Newton*
HENRY C. NELSON, *Forest City*
KIRK R. NICHOLSON, *Bedford*
EDWARD NORLAND, *Cylinder*
EMIL L. NOVAK, *Fairfax*
EDWARD OPPEDAHL, *Renwick*
KENNETH E. OWEN, *Centerville*
RUSSELL A. PATRICK, *Hawarden*
GEORGE L. PAUL, *Brooklyn*
WENDELL PENDLETON, *Storm Lake*
AMOS C. PETERSON, *Nashua*
DON A. PETRUCCELLI, *Davenport*
RAYMOND T. PIM, *Lucas*
ROSCOE L. POLLOCK, *Douds*
HARRY W. RAMSEYER, *Washington*
HOWARD C. REPPERT, JR., *Des Moines*
CURTIS G. RIEHM, *Garner*
CARL H. RINGGENBERG, *Ames*
LESLIE SANTEE, *Cedar Falls*
MARTIN E. SAR, *Charles City*
CHESTER A. SCHEERER, *Boone*
HILLMAN H. SERSLAND, *Decorah*
ROY J. SMITH, *Spirit Lake*
EDWARD J. STEERS, *Creston*
O. C. STEPHENSON, *Corydon*
HENRY H. STEVENS, *Jefferson*
SCOTT SWISHER, *Iowa City*
HAROLD A. TABOR, *Lamoni*
W. H. TATE, *Mason City*
FRANK R. THOMPSON, *Guthrie Center*
JACOB VAN ZWOL, *Paullina*
ELMER H. VERMEER, *Pella*
FRED VOIGTMANN, *Marengo*
J. F. WALTER, *McGregor*
PAUL M. WALTER, *Union*
J. O. WATSON, JR., *Indianola*
W. ELLIS WELLS, *Fort Madison*
W. E. WHITNEY, *Aurelia*
MELVIN WILSON, *Rockwell City*

KANSAS
Senate
Republicans 33   Democrats 5

HOWARD ADAMS, *Maple Hill*
JOHN ANDERSON, JR., *Olathe*
MARVIN BARKIS, *Louisburg*
RICHARD L. BECKER, *Coffeyville*
J. R. BRADFORD, *Columbus*
SAM BROOKOVER, *Eureka*
WILFRID CAVANESS, *Chanute*
E. BERT COLLARD, *Leavenworth*
DILLARD B. CROXTON, *La Cygne*
JOHN W. CRUTCHER, *Hutchinson*

PHILIP J. DOYLE, *Beloit*
CHRIS C. GREEN, *Courtland*
J. O. GUNNELS, *Colby*
ALFRED H. HARKNESS, *Hays*
DONALD S. HULTS, *Lawrence*
C. L. HUXMAN, *Sublette*
LAURIN W. JONES, *Dodge City*
BURTON L. LOHMULLER, *Centralia*
JOSEPH H. MCDOWELL, *Kansas City*
V. W. MCKNAB, *Winfield*
WILLARD MAHON, *Yates Center*
GORDEN MARK, *Abilene*
HARRY E. MILLER, *Hiawatha*
J. H. MOORE, JR., *Salina*
I. E. NICKELL, *Smith Center*
JAMES W. PORTER, *Topeka*
JOHN A. POTUCEK, *Wellington*
WILFORD RIEGLE, *Emporia*
RALPH R. RINKER, *Great Bend*
KARL ROOT, *Atchison*
LEONARD RUDE, JR., *Parsons*
GARNER E. SHRIVER, *Wichita*
VERNON A. STROBERG, *Newton*
R. G. THOMSON, *Irving*
WM. D. WEIGAND, *La Crosse*
JOHN C. WOELK, *Russell*
R. C. WOODWARD, *El Dorado*
PAUL R. WUNSCH, *Kingman*
(2 vacancies)

House

Republicans 89 · Democrats 36

JOHN O. ADAMS, *Osborne*
JOHN W. ALFORD, *Ulysses*
RICHARD F. ALLEN, *Baldwin*
A. E. ANDERSON, *Leoti*
ROBERT ANDERSON, *Ottawa*
HOWARD E. BARSTOW, *Larned*
ALVIN BAUMAN, *Sabetha*
EDWARD W. BEAMAN, *Hoyt*
HOWARD BENTLEY, *Kinsley*
RODERICK BENTLEY, *Shields*
JEROME C. BERRYMAN, *Ashland*
A. F. BIEKER, *Hays*
W. A. BLAIR, *Oswego*
L. J. BLYTHE, *White City*
ERNEST P. BOLES, *Liberal*
JOHN D. BOWER, *McLouth*
OSCAR BROWN, *Bogue*
ELDRED BROWNE, 1209 *N. Tenth St., Kansas City*
H. L. BROWNLEE, *Sylvia*
KARL A. BRUECK, *Paola*
ROBERT BUCHELE, *Howard*
JOHN E. BUEHLER, *Atchison*
RAYMOND F. CARLSON, *Morrowville*
H. J. CARR, *Concordia*
F. M. CARTER, *Syracuse*
JOHN W. CASEBEER, *McPherson*
HOWARD CHAMBERS, *Minneapolis*
SAM C. CHARLSON, *Manhattan*
MARVIN M. COX, *Kingman*
L. F. CUSHENBERY, *Oberlin*
ANCEL K. DALTON, *Ft. Scott*
KELSO DEER, *Augusta*
AMBROSE L. DEMPSEY, *Leavenworth*
MAX L. DICE, *Johnson*
MRS. CLARENCE DICKHUT, *Scott City*

H. B. DOERING, *Garnett*
ROBERT W. DOMME, 807 *Western Ave., Topeka*
WM. P. EDWARDS, *Bigelow*
J. M. EVES, *Lakin*
WADE M. FERGUSON, *Parsons*
WM. M. FERGUSON, *Wellington*
BILL H. FRIBLEY, *Crestline*
ED GORDON, *Highland*
O. F. GRUBBS, *Pittsburg*
BERT HARMON, *Ellsworth*
CHESTER C. HEIZER, *Caldwell*
C. T. HENDERSON, *Atwood*
ROYAL HENDERSON, *Belleville*
ALLAN HIBBARD, *Medicine Lodge*
H. W. HICKERT, *Bird City*
JOHN R. HILDEBRAND, *Fowler*
CLYDE HILL, *Yates Center*
WORDEN R. HOWAT, *Wakeeney*
MRS. HOBART HOYT, *Lyons*
HOWARD M. IMMEL, *Iola*
CHESTER C. INGELS, *Hiawatha*
JAMES W. INGWERSEN, *Le Roy*
ROBERT H. JENNISON, *Healy*
JAY F. JOHNSON, *Beloit*
WILFRID M. JOHNSON, *Garrison*
NEAL D. JORDAN, *Freeport*
DONALD JOSEPH, *Whitewater*
W. O. KELMAN, *Sublette*
JERRY KOLACNY, *Goodland*
M. R. KREHBIEL, *Norton*
CLARK KUPPINGER, *Prairie Village*
MERL L. LEMERT, *Sedan*
CLYDE LITTLER, *Cottonwood Falls*
CARL S. MCCLUNG, *Elkhart*
CHARLES S. MCGINNESS, *Cherryvale*
JOHN MADDEN, *Beacon Bldg., Wichita*
PHIL MANNING, 500 *S. Market St., Wichita*
LEA MARANVILLE, *Ness City*
D. B. MARSHALL, JR., *Lincoln*
MARION P. MATHEWS, *Winfield*
FRED MEEK, *Idana*
SAM MELLINGER, *Emporia*
FRED W. MEYER, *Jewell*
JOSEPH M. MIKESIC, 250 *Wilson Blvd., Kansas City*
WM. L. MITCHELL, 119 *W. Sherman, Hutchinson*
C. R. MONG, *Neodesha*
JOHN H. MORSE, *Mound City*
JOHN H. MURRAY, *Leavenworth*
H. K. NANCE, *Montezuma*
Z. ARTHUR NEVINS, *Dodge City*
G. H. NEWCOM, *Russell Springs*
ELVIN NIEMANN, *Nortonville*
IRVING R. NILES, *Lyndon*
PAUL A. NITSCH, *La Crosse*
WILLIAM S. NOVOTNY, *Sawyer*
MILDRED OTIS, *Phillipsburg*
JAMES V. PRATT, *Colby*
MRS. NELL RENN, *Arkansas City*
WM. O. RICHARDSON, *Hoxie*
R. D. RIEGLE, *Waterville*
GEORGE RIFFEL, *Stockton*
KENNETH R. RISSLER, *Eskridge*
M. E. ROHRER, *Abilene*
JOHN Q. ROYCE, *Salina*
ELMER C. RUSSELL, *St. John*
DALE E. SAFFELS, *Garden City*
DON SALMON, *Hiattville*
JOE SCHAUB, *Arcadia*

JACK SCOTT, *Riverton*
WARREN W. SHAW, *Capitol Fed. Bldg., Topeka*
JOHN N. SHERMAN, JR., *Chanute*
T. E. SMITH, *Independence*
P. EVERETT SPERRY, *Lawrence*
GLENN S. STRICKLER, *Ramona*
JESS TAYLOR, *Tribune*
WILL TOWNSLEY, *Great Bend*
ROBERT TURNEY, *532 Kansas Ave., Topeka*
ERNEST A. UNRUH, *Newton*
RALPH UPHAM, *Junction City*
THOS. M. VAN CLEAVE, JR., *Commercial Natl. Bank Bldg., Kansas City*
BENJ. O. WEAVER, *Mullinville*
MAURICE E. WEBB, *Jetmore*
RAY WELCH, *Weskan*
WALLACE M. WHITE, *Coldwater*
R. C. WILLIAMS, *Russell*
VERNON L. WILLIAMS, *3201 Jackson, Wichita*
CLYDE N. WILSON, *Emporia*
ARNO WINDSCHEFFEL, *Smith Center*
PAUL A. WOLF, *Hugoton*
JOHN R. ZIMMERMAN, *Eureka*

KENTUCKY

Senate

Democrats 30　　Republicans 8

JOHN C. ANGGELIS, *261 Albany Rd., Lexington*
J. EVERETT BACH, *Jackson*
H. STANLEY BLAKE, *Carlisle*
BERNARD J. BONN, *4020 W. Broadway, Louisville*
AUGUSTUS E. CORNETT, *Hyden*
J. HARRY DAVIS, *Grayson*
MARTIN J. DUFFY, JR., *2555 Woodburne, Louisville*
O. O. DUNCAN, *Whitley City*
MERLIN BLAIR FIELDS, *Hazard*
W. B. FRAZIER, *Barbourville*
WAYNE W. FREEMAN, *Mayfield*
JOE J. GRACE, *Paducah*
ARTHUR W. GRAFTON, *Prospect*
LLOYD M. GREENE, *Cave City*
DOUG HAYS, *McDowell*
J. E. JOHNSON, *So. Williamson*
ED J. KELLY, *Flemingsburg*
ALVIN KIDWELL, *Sparta*
DENVER C. KNUCKLES, *Middlesboro*
FRED V. LUCAS, *London*
CHARLES W. A. McCANN, *5709 Southland Blvd., Louisville*
CLARENCE W. MALONEY, *Madisonville*
GEORGE E. OVERBEY, *Murray*
LOUIS REUSCHER, *464 Grand Ave., Fort Thomas*
R. JACK REYNOLDS, *Mt. Sterling*
E. W. RICHMOND, *Owensboro*
C. W. ROBINSON, *Bowling Green*
CARL J. RUH, *So. Ft. Mitchell*
CECIL C. SANDERS, *Lancaster*
LEON J. SHAIKUN, *116 W. Brandeis, Louisville*
B. F. SHIELDS, *Shelbyville*
TOM SHIELDS, *Bloomfield*
WILLIAM L. SULLIVAN, *Henderson*
ALBERT H. THOMASON, *Leitchfield*
WENDELL VAN HOOSE, *Tutor Key*
ED P. WARINNER, *Albany*
W. A. WICKLIFFE, *Harrodsburg*

JOHN M. WILLIAMS, *Guston*
JOHN W. WILLIS, *Greenville*

House

Democrats 77　　Republicans 23

FELIX S. ANDERSON, *650 S. Twenty-first St., Louisville*
CLARENCE J. BARNUM, *632 Floral Terrace, Louisville*
CLARENCE H. BATES, *Monticello*
CHARLES E. BAUMGARDNER, SR., *3915 Taylor Blvd., Louisville*
FRED BESHEAR, *Dawson Springs*
OWEN BILLINGTON, *Murray*
R. B. BLANKENSHIP, *Hartford*
J. MURRAY BLUE, *Clay*
EDWARD T. BREATHITT, JR., *110 Alumni Ave., Hopkinsville*
JOHN B. BRECKINRIDGE, *361 Mockingbird Lane, Lexington*
EDWARD O. BRIDGERS, *2023 Sherwood, Louisville*
C. W. BUCHANAN, *Barbourville*
CHARLES W. BURNLEY, *1507 Jefferson St., Paducah*
FLOYD BUSH, *Ravenna*
EARL CARTER, *Tompkinsville*
D. C. CASEY, JR., *Mount Eden*
HARRY M. CAUDILL, *Whitesburg*
CHARLES L. CONRAD, *Falmouth*
BILL CORNETT, *Hindman*
VERNOR COTTENGIM, *4317 Church St., Covington*
B. G. DAVIDSON, *Bowling Green*
ROY C. DAVIS, *Bardwell*
JOHN L. DAY, *54 Highway Avenue, Ludlow*
JOHN DUNSIL, *McKee*
EDWARD EMBRY, *Leitchfield*
ADDISON L. EVERETT, *Maysville*
JOHN W. FARMER, *1481 St. James Court, Louisville*
THOMAS P. FITZPATRICK, *305 W. Sixth Street, Covington*
W. J. FLANERY, *Morehead*
EDWIN FREEMAN, *Harrodsburg*
CLAY GAY, *Hyden*
JOHN W. GREENE, *Sandy Hook*
R. S. GRIFFIN, *Liberty*
ROY HURST GRIGSBY, JR., *Hazard*
JAMES C. GRUNDY, JR., *Lebanon*
ROBERT L. GULLETTE, *Nicholasville*
W. L. HADDEN, *Elkton*
JAMES P. HAHN, *305 Bank Street, Greenville*
GEORGE F. HARRIS, *Salem*
EMMETT HAWKINS, *Scottsville*
DAVID HESKAMP, *Columbia*
HENRY R. HEYBURN, *3918 Leland Road, Louisville*
CHARLES D. HIGHLAND, *Mt. Sterling*
LON C. HILL, *Prestonsburg*
E. R. HILTON, *Raceland*
BROOKS HINKLE, *Paris*
LEONARD HISLOPE, *107 Church Street, Somerset*
CHESTER J. HOLSCLAW, *216 Stilz, Louisville*
CLYDE S. HOWARD, *111 Brown Street, Elizabethtown*
DURHAM W. HOWARD, *Pineville*
JOHN J. ISLER, *1813 Jefferson, Covington*
LYNN A. JENNINGS, *Paintsville*
JACK JOHNSON, *Clinton*
ED KUBALE, JR., *Danville*
JAMES W. LAMBERT, *Mount Vernon*
HARRY KING LOWMAN, *2658 Virginia Ave., Ashland*
SHELBY McCALLUM, *Benton*
CALEB McFADDEN, *London*

PEARL McKINNEY, *Morgantown*
TRUE MACKEY, *Mount Olivet*
DAVID MARTIN, JR., *Hi Hat*
CARL D. MELTON, 1307 *South Main, Henderson*
CLARENCE R. MILLER, 614 *E. Brandeis, Louisville*
ALTON MOORE, *Frankfort*
FRED H. MORGAN, 2024 *Broad Street, Paducah*
E. C. MULLINS, *Stanford*
THOMAS J. MURPHY, 2216 *Dumesnil, Louisville*
GOEBEL W. NEWSOM, JR., *Elkhorn City*
JOE E. NUNN, *Cadiz*
CARL NUNNELLEY, *Oddville*
FOSTER OCKERMAN, 491 *W. Third Street, Lexington*
JERRY PARRISH, *Richmond*
WILL K. PEACE, *Williamsburg*
E. D. POLLITTE, *Harlan*
ROGER E. QUALLS, *Olive Hill*
PAUL E. RATCLIFFE, *Shelbyville*
THOMAS L. RAY, 3 *Club Hill Drive, Fairdale*
HOBART RAYBURN, *Emerson*
JOHN B. REED, *Stone*
VERNON REED, *Hodgenville*
HOWARD V. REID, *Symsonia*
ROBERT REID, SR., *Route One, Owensboro*
RUSSELL C. REYNOLDS, *Beattyville*
LEROY SAYLOR, *Cumberland*
ROY E. SEARCY, *Carrollton*
HANSFORD SLOAN, *Albany*
RALPH O. STITH, *Guston*
PATRICK TANNER, 2002 *Mayfair Drive, Owensboro*
ED THOMAS, *Dry Ridge*
RODNEY J. THOMPSON, *Winchester*
T. HERBERT TINSLEY, *Warsaw*
EULICK WALSH, 746 *So. Thirty-ninth Street, Louisville*
WILL TOM WATHEN, *Morganfield*
MORRIS WEINTRAUB, *Finance Building, Newport*
A. W. WELLS, *Bardstown*
LYNN B. WELLS, *West Liberty*
GEORGE F. WILLIAMSON, *La Grange*
MRS. RANDOLPH WILSON, *Glasgow*
CHARLES W. WIRSCH, 2409 *Alexandria Pike, Highland Heights*
PAUL E. YOUNG, *Olmstead*

LOUISIANA

Senate

Democrats 39   Republicans 0

ROBERT A. AINSWORTH, JR., 1650 *Natl. Bank of Commerce Bldg., New Orleans*
EDWARD M. BOAGNI, JR., 286 *W. Grolee St., Opelousas*
WILLIAM R. BOLES, *Rayville*
ELMORE F. BONIN, 633 *Gertrude Dr., St. Martinville*
C. C. BURLEIGH, 1012 *Iberia St., Franklin*
CLYDE C. CAILLOUET, 102 *W. Second St., Thibodaux*
R. S. COPELAND, 1207 *Fifth St., Leesville*
GOVE D. DAVIS, *Olla*
CHARLES DEICHMANN, *American Bank Bldg., New Orleans*
JOHN J. DOLES, *Plain Dealing*
CHARLES F. DUCHEIN, 1722 *Main St., Baton Rouge*
LAURANCE EUSTIS, JR., 1502 *Jena St., New Orleans*
WARREN D. FOLKES, *St. Francisville*
LOUIS H. FOLSE, 7200 *St. Claude Ave., Arabi*
SYLVAN FRIEDMAN, *Natchez*
GUY G. GARDINER, 322 *E. Sixth St., Crowley*

M. ELOI GIRARD, 500 *E. College Dr., Lafayette*
SMITH E. GUTHRIE, 155 *S. Seventh St., Ponchatoula*
ALLEN HALEY, *Kilbourne*
GILBERT F. HENNIGAN, *Fields*
THEODORE M. HICKEY, 4756 *Arts St., New Orleans*
JAMES P. HINTON, *Downsville*
HARRY H. HOWARD, 1807 *Pere Marquette Bldg., New Orleans*
JOHN R. HUNTER, JR., 31 *Mary St., Alexandria*
DAYTON C. McCANN, *Effie*
DAVID H. MacHAUER, 1428 *Natl. Bank of Commerce Bldg., New Orleans*
LOUIS A. MAHONEY, 323 *Pelican Ave., New Orleans*
SIGUR MARTIN, *Lutcher*
W. E. PERSON, *Star Rt., Ferriday*
W. M. RAINACH, *Summerfield*
B. B. RAYBURN, *Bogalusa*
ROBERT B. RICHARDS, 2423 *Laharpe St., New Orleans*
B. H. ROGERS, *Grand Cane*
ANDREW L. SEVIER, *Tallulah*
GUY W. SOCKRIDER, 2000 *Twelfth St., Lake Charles*
JAMES D. SPARKS, 521 *Bernhardt Bldg., Monroe*
ALVIN T. STUMPF, 614 *First St., Gretna*
CHARLES E. TOOKE, JR., 421 *Commercial Bldg., Shreveport*
HORACE WILKINSON III, *Port Allen*

House

Democrats 100   Republicans 0

I. J. ALLEN, 115 *N. Allen Ave., Jonesboro*
ROBERT ANGELLE, *Breaux Bridge*
CLARENCE C. AYCOCK, *Box 317, Franklin*
KENNETH C. BARRANGER, 7414 *Maple St., New Orleans*
D. ELMORE BECNEL, *LaPlace*
JAMES E. BEESON, 428 *Shrewsbury Ct., Jefferson 21*
J. ALFRED BEGNAUD, *Box 544, Lafayette*
J. M. BELISLE, *Box 43, Many*
E. L. BERNARD, *Port Allen*
CECIL R. BLAIR, *N. Bolton and Shirland, Alexandria*
CURTIS BOOZMAN, *Box 434, Natchitoches*
J. M. BREEDLOVE, 1104 *Maple St., Winnfield*
C. CYRIL BROUSSARD, SR., 8415 *Pritchard Pl., New Orleans*
ALGIE D. BROWN, 331 *McCormick St., Shreveport*
J. MARSHALL BROWN, 312 *Balter Bldg., New Orleans*
MRS. BLAND COX BRUNS, 1425 *Jackson Ave., New Orleans*
JAMES C. BUIE, *Box 366, Winnsboro*
KENNETH H. CAGLE, *Cagle Motors, Lake Charles*
JOHNNIE W. CALTON, *Columbia*
JOSEPH S. CASEY, 6859 *Memphis St., New Orleans*
NICHOLAS CEFALU, *Amite*
MONNIE T. CHEVES, 706 *College Ave., Natchitoches*
WALTER P. CLARK, 621 *S. Rendon St., New Orleans*
W. J. CLEVELAND, 324 *Northern Ave., Crowley*
L. C. COLE, *Ragley*
JOHN B. COOK, 1537 *Annunciation St., New Orleans*
S. P. CRANE, *Monterey*
FRED V. DECUIR, *Star Rt. B, Box 51, New Iberia*
VAIL M. DELONY, *Lake Providence*
WILFRED J. DESMARE, 2734 *Orchid St., New Orleans*
GEORGE E. DE VILLE, 2204 *Cleveland Ave., New Orleans*
C. FRED DONALDSON, 2329 *Mendez, New Orleans*
EDWARD DUBUISSON, *Opelousas*
CARROLL L. DUPONT, *Grand Caillou Rt., Houma*

ALVIN DYSON, *Cameron*
B. T. ENGERT, 2925 *Constance, New Orleans*
W. GILBERT FAULK, 1010 *N. Second St., Monroe*
T. T. FIELDS, *Farmerville*
LEE L. FONTENOT, *Mamou*
E. C. FREMAUX, 311 *Second St., Rayne*
JOHN S. GARRETT, *Haynesville*
E. D. GLEASON, *R.F.D. 3, Minden*
H. N. GOFF, 730 *Jackson St., Alexandria*
F. A. GRAUGNARD, JR., *St. James*
E. W. GRAVOLET, JR., *Pointe-a-la-Hache*
E. J. GRIZZAFFI, 607 *Brashear Ave., Morgan City*
RICHARD GUIDRY, *Galliano*
WILLIAM J. HANKINS, 2724 *St. Bernard Ave.,
    New Orleans*
M. V. HARGROVE, *Oakdale*
F. E. HERNANDEZ, *Box 45, Leesville*
W. T. HODGES, JR., *Jena*
FRANK HUERSTEL, 3708 *St. Claude Ave.,
    New Orleans*
THEODORE B. HUSSER, *Husser*
WELLBORN JACK, *Old Commercial Bldg., Shreveport*
J. THOMAS JEWELL, *New Roads*
HORACE LYNN JONES, *Box 776, DeQuincy*
JOHN ENOUL JUMONVILLE, 910 *Elm St., Plaquemine*
CLAUDE KIRKPATRICK, 1111 *N. Church St., Jennings*
ALBERT B. KOORIE, 605 *N. Carrollton Ave.,
    New Orleans*
EDGAR H. LANCASTER, JR., 314 *Monroe St., Tallulah*
EDWARD S. LANDRY, *R.F.D. 2, Box 461, Abbeville*
JAMES R. LEAKE, *St. Francisville*
EDWARD F. LEBRETON, JR., 1328 *Second St.,
    New Orleans*
BRYAN J. LEHMANN, JR., *Box 411, Norco*
ROLFE H. McCOLLISTER, 3337 *Riley St.,
    Baton Rouge*
GUY B. McDONALD, *Greensburg*
PATRICK B. McGITTIGAN, 1217 *Annunciation St.,
    New Orleans*
JESSE D. McLAIN, 1210 *Twenty-third Ave.,
    Covington*
DAWSON MARTIN, *Donaldsonville*
J. CLAUDE MERAUX, *Meraux*
REEVES MORGAN, *Jackson*
SAM C. MURRAY, *Mansfield*
PETER W. MURTES, 2102 *Jena St., New Orleans*
L. D. NAPPER, *Ruston*
MRS. RICHARD S. PARROTT, 251 *W. Ash St., Eunice*
EDWARD VEAZIE PAVY, *Box 577, Opelousas*
RAYMOND RENO RADOVICH, 319 *Slidell Ave.,
    New Orleans*
WILLARD L. RAMBO, *Georgetown*
JOHN F. RAU, JR., *Gretna*
LONNIE RICHMOND, *Box 38, Oak Grove*
PERCY E. ROBERTS, 2849 *Edward Ave., Baton Rouge*
J. C. SEAMAN, *Waterproof*
J. DOUGLAS SHOWS, 435 *Michigan Ave., Bogalusa*
JASPER K. SMITH, *Box 627, Vivian*
R. J. SOIGNET, *R.F.D., Box 146, Thibodaux*
GRADY STEWART, *Albany*
FORD E. STINSON, *Benton*
JODIE STOUT, *Rayville*
LLOYD TEEKELL, 2411 *Elliot St., Alexandria*
GEORGE D. TESSIER, 1569 *Calhoun St., New Orleans*
RISLEY TRICHE, *Napoleonville*
LESTER P. VETTER, *Coushatta*
JAMES J. VILLEMARETTE, *Marksville*
SHADY WALL, *West Monroe*

ARTHUR WEBB, JR., 815 *Azalea St., Lafayette*
ROLAND L. WELCKER, 1336 *St. Bernard Ave.,
    New Orleans*
WOODROW WILSON, *Bastrop*
LORRIS M. WIMBERLY, *Arcadia*
GROVER C. WOMACK, *Manifest*
WILLIAM YARNO, *Cottonport*
(1 vacancy)

MAINE

Senate

Republicans 27   Democrats 6

EARLE W. ALBEE, *Concord St., Portland*
JEAN CHARLES BOUCHER, 697 *Sabattus St.,
    Lewiston*
HENRY W. BOYKER, *Bethel*
OSCAR H. BROWN, 14 *Washington St., Eastport*
BENJAMIN BUTLER, *Farmington*
MILES F. CARPENTER, 15 *Coburn Ave., Skowhegan*
PHILIP F. CHAPMAN, JR., 193 *Middle St., Portland*
WILLIAM R. COLE, *Liberty*
SAMUEL W. COLLINS, *Box 70, Caribou*
PAUL L. CRABTREE, *Box 126, Island Falls*
CHARLES F. CUMMINGS, 45 *Bedford St., Bath*
WILMOT S. DOW, *Waldoboro*
LLOYD T. DUNHAM, *Ellsworth*
PETER J. FARLEY, 31 *Green St., Biddeford*
RALPH W. FARRIS, JR., 255 *Water St., Augusta*
ANDREW J. FOURNIER, 42 *Locke St., Saco*
CARLETON S. FULLER, *Buckfield*
ANDREW J. HALL, *Box 193, North Berwick*
ROBERT N. HASKELL, 33 *State St., Bangor*
EARLE M. HILLMAN, 784 *Broadway, Bangor*
CHARLES A. JAMIESON, *R.F.D. 1, Presque Isle*
ALTON A. LESSARD, 6 *White St., Lewiston*
MRS. HAZEL C. LORD, 14 *Mellen St., Portland*
SETH LOW, *Box 388, Rockland*
ROBERT MARTIN, 10 *Elm St., Augusta*
CLARENCE W. PARKER, *Sebec Station*
JAMES L. REID, 3 *Chestnut St., Hallowell*
LEO ST. PIERRE, 256 *Park St., Lewiston*
WILLIAM S. SILSBY, *Ellsworth*
ROY U. SINCLAIR, 16 *Pleasant St., Pittsfield*
GEORGE W. WEEKS, 17 *Goudy St., South Portland*
ALLAN WOODCOCK, JR., 490 *State St., Bangor*
J. HOLLIS WYMAN, *Milbridge*

House

Republicans 116   Democrats 32

HENRY R. ALBERT, 14 *Townsend Rd., Augusta*
IRA C. ALDEN, 41 *Green St., Gorham*
GUY R. ALLEN, *R.F.D. 1, Gardiner*
MAURICE D. ANDERSON, *Greenville Junction*
CHARLES N. ANTHOINE, *South Windham*
FRANK C. BABINEAU, *Brunswick*
SHERMAN F. BAIRD, *North Haven*
E. CARROLL BEAN, *Mechanic St., Winterport*
ALBERT L. BERNIER, 7 *Elmwood Ave., Waterville*
EARL V. BIBBER, *Main St., Kennebunkport*
FRED A. BLANCHARD, *Wilton*
FRANK M. BOWIE, *R.F.D. 1, Auburn*
HAROLD BRAGDON, *R.F.D. 1, Washburn*
GORDON E. BREWSTER, *Ogunquit*
EZRA JAMES BRIGGS, *Caribou*
WARREN A. BROCKWAY, *Milo*

CLYDE BROWN, *Woodland, Washington County*
ROBERT L. BROWNE, 12 *Somerset St., Bangor*
HOWARD W. CALL, *Cumberland Center*
DUDLEY E. CARTER, 14 *Park St., Newport*
JOHN E. CARTER, *Box 12, Etna*
F. PERLEY CASWELL, *New Sharon*
EDWIN J. CATES, *East Machias*
ARTHUR H. CHARLES, 293 *State St., Portland*
DANA W. CHILDS, 73 *Ashmont St., Portland*
MRS. AUGUSTA K. CHRISTIE, *Box 688, Presque Isle*
CARL E. CIANCHETTE, 20 *Hartland Ave., Pittsfield*
CHESTER J. COLE, *East Sumner*
HARVEY W. COOK, *Box 116, Portage*
LUCIA M. CORMIER, *Rumford*
ALBERT E. COTE, 138 *Bartlett St., Lewiston*
RAYMOND A. COTE, 29 *Madison Ave., Madison*
HARRY R. COURTOIS, 18 *Irving St., Saco*
LOUIS O. COUTURE, 78 *Bluff Rd., Bath*
PAUL A. COUTURE, 8 *River St., Lewiston*
JAMES A. COYNE, 11 *Pleasant Pl., Waterville*
BENJAMIN S. CROCKETT, *Merrill Rd., Freeport*
CLEVELAND P. CURTIS, 10 *Pleasant St., Bowdoinham*
IRENEE CYR, 5 *Forest Ave., Fort Kent*
ELBRIDGE B. DAVIS, *Box 264, Calais*
PAUL A. DAVIS, 100 *Haskell St., Westbrook*
SHERMAN DENBOW, *Lubec*
WILLIAM T. DOSTIE, 5 *Bellevue St., Waterville*
JAMES T. DUDLEY, *West Enfield*
ARTHUR J. DUMAIS, JR., 50 *Fairlawn Ave., Lewiston*
PHILIP E. DUNN, *Poland*
ARMAND DUQUETTE, 69 *Pike St., Biddeford*
WILLIAM G. EARLES, 489 *Ocean St., South Portland*
JOSEPH T. EDGAR, 110 *Main St., Bar Harbor*
CARLETON E. EDWARDS, *R.F.D., Poland Spring*
EBEN L. ELWELL, *Brooks*
ARCHIE F. EVANS, *Cornish*
NATHAN C. FAY, 125 *Neal St., Portland*
NORMAN K. FERGUSON, *Box 34, Hanover*
MRS. FLORENCE C. FILES, 53 *Parsons Rd., Portland*
LOUIS F. FINEMORE, *Bridgewater*
D. RAYMOND FLYNN, *Butler St., South Berwick*
HALSTED C. FOSS, *R.F.D. 1, Mapleton*
FRANK B. FOSTER, *Mechanic Falls*
DANIEL J. FRAZIER, JR., *Lee*
HOWARD L. FULLER, *South China*
JESSE P. FULLER, 15 *Hillside Ave., South Portland*
GIVEN L. GARDNER, *Hartland*
ERNEST E. GETCHELL, *Limestone*
JOHN R. GILMARTIN, 140 *Dartmouth St., Portland*
LEWIS F. GREENE, *Searsport Ave., Belfast*
RAYMOND R. GREENLEAF, *West Boothbay Harbor*
FRANK E. HANCOCK, *Cape Neddick*
PERCY K. HANSON, 33 *Pope St., Gardiner*
RAY A. HARNDEN, *Rangeley*
CLIFFORD K. HATFIELD, *R.F.D. 3, South Brewer*
ORVILLE B. HAUGHN, *R.F.D. 2, Bridgton*
CARLE D. HENRY, *R.F.D. 2, Cumberland Center*
LINWOOD R. HIGGINS, *West Scarborough*
CARL W. HILTON, *Bremen*
RAYMOND D. HOWARD, *Dixfield*
JOHN L. JACK, 34 *Main St., Topsham*
LESLIE E. JACOBS, 29 *Lake St., Auburn*
EMILE J. JACQUES, 31 *Chestnut St., Lewiston*
HERVEY B. JENNINGS, *Box 105, Strong*
HENRY G. JONES, 995 *Sawyer St., South Portland*
CLARENCE O. KIMBALL, *R.F.D. 1, Hollis Center*
WILLIAM L. KINCH, *Livermore Falls*

RUSSELL B. KNIGHT, *Searsmont*
MORTON ARTHUR LAMB, *Box 89, Eastport*
ALEXANDER J. LATNO, 32 *Bradbury St., Old Town*
DOROTHY G. LAWRY, 23 *Oak St., Rockland*
RAYMOND J. LETOURNEAU, 12 *Payne St., Springvale*
KENDRIC L. LIBBY, 19 *Limerock St., Camden*
FRED H. LINDSAY, 690 *S. Main St., South Brewer*
FRED R. LORD, 184 *State St., Augusta*
PETER M. MACDONALD, *Rumford*
CLIFFORD E. MCGLAUFLIN, 47 *Woodmont St. Portland*
JOHN P. MADORE, 44 *Poplar St., Van Buren*
ERNEST MALENFANT, 69 *Lincoln St., Lewiston*
MRS. BESSIE L. MANN, *West Paris*
CLAUDE L. MARTIN, *Eagle Lake*
WALTER H. MARTIN, *R.F.D. 5A, Gardiner*
ROBERT W. MAXWELL, *Lakeview Ave., Winthrop*
MRS. RITA C. MICHAUD, 25 *Eighteenth Ave., Madawaska*
NAPOLEON L. NADEAU, 131 *Hill St., Biddeford*
JOHN H. NEEDHAM, 129 *Main St., Orono*
WALTER L. OLPE, *R.F.D., Hiram*
ELWOOD N. OSBORNE, *R.F.D. 1, Fairfield*
CURTIS I. PALMETER, *Meddybemps*
FRANK M. PIERCE, *Bucksport*
HAROLD S. PIKE, *Waterford*
ERNEST O. PORELL, 53 *Conant St., Westbrook*
RAYMOND P. POTTER, *Medway*
GEORGE D. PULLEN, *Oakland*
JOHN T. QUINN, 275 *Pine St., Bangor*
JOHN H. REED, *Fort Fairfield*
JACKSON L. REYNOLDS, *Northeast Harbor*
N. HAROLD RICH, *Charleston*
LEON B. ROBERTS, *North Brooklin*
OTIS J. ROBERTS, SR., *Dover Rd., Dexter*
NORMAN R. ROGERSON, 46 *North St., Houlton*
MILAN ROSS, *Brownville*
RODNEY E. ROSS, JR., 1024 *Washington St., Bath*
RODNEY W. ROUNDY, 257 *Vaughan St., Portland*
HARRY F. SANBORN, *West Baldwin*
GEORGE W. SANFORD, *Dover-Foxcroft*
WILLIAM R. SANSOUCY, 7 *St. Mary St., Biddeford*
ARTHUR W. SEAWARD, *Kittery Point*
STEVEN D. SHAW, *Bingham*
GEORGE R. SKOLFIELD, *R.F.D. 1, South Harpswell*
FRITZ C. SOULE, *Smyrna Mills*
JAMES S. STANLEY, *Box 94, Bangor*
LESLIE H. STANLEY, *Hampden Highlands*
LAWRENCE E. STANWOOD, *Steuben*
MAHLON W. STAPLES, *R.F.D., Limerick*
CARL M. STILPHEN, 9 *Claremont St., Rockland*
ARNOLD G. STORM, *Sherman Mills*
JOHN TARBOX, *Gouldsboro*
MRS. ELLEN E. THOMAS, *Box 113, Anson*
JAMES C. TOTMAN, 311 *W. Broadway, Bangor*
WILLIS A. TRAFTON, JR., 323 *Minot Ave., Auburn*
J. WOODROW VALLELY, 45 *Berwick St., Sanford*
ROBERT G. WADE, 421 *Turner St., Auburn*
FRED B. WADLEIGH, *Readfield*
HOWARD P. WALLS, 402 *Penobscot Ave., Millinocket*
ADAM WALSH, *Brunswick*
E. ASHLEY WALTER, JR., *Waldoboro*
EDWIN P. WHITING, 187 *Madison Ave., Skowhegan*
RICHARD C. WILLEY, 56 *Church St., Ellsworth*
HARRY R. WILLIAMS, *Hodgdon*
RALPH E. WINCHENPAW, *Friendship*
WALLACE WOODWORTH, *R.F.D. 2, Waterville*
(3 vacancies)

MARYLAND

Senate

Democrats 18   Republicans 11

JOSEPH A. BERTORELLI, 314 *S. High St.,*
Baltimore 2
HARRY A. COLE, 2218 *Madison Ave., Baltimore* 17
ROBERT P. DEAN, *Anchor Rest Farm*
GEORGE W. DELLA, *Maryland Trust Bldg.,*
Baltimore 2
THOMAS F. DEMPSEY, *Maryland Trust Bldg.,*
Baltimore 2
A. F. DIDOMENICO, 219 *Equitable Bldg.,*
Baltimore 2
CHARLES L. DOWNEY, *Williamsport*
SHERMAN E. FLANAGAN, *Westminster*
CLIFFORD FRIEND, *Accident*
LOUIS L. GOLDSTEIN, *Dares Beach*
PHILIP H. GOODMAN, 3415 *Forest Park Ave.,*
Baltimore 16
WILLIAM S. JAMES, *Bel Air*
JOHN R. JEWELL, *Chestertown*
FRED C. MALKUS, *Cambridge*
RALPH L. MASON, *Newark*
JOSEPH A. MATTINGLY, *Leonardtown*
JAMES B. MONROE, *Waldorf*
MARY L. NOCK, *Salisbury*
JOHN CLARENCE NORTH, *Easton*
EDWARD S. NORTHROP, *Chevy Chase*
LOUIS N. PHIPPS, *Annapolis*
HARRY T. PHOEBUS, *Princess Anne*
JACOB R. RAMSBURG, *Frederick*
LAYMAN J. REDDEN, *Denton*
CHARLES M. SEE, *Cumberland*
FRANK E. SHIPLEY, *Savage*
JOHN GRASON TURNBULL, *Sparks*
JAMES WEINROTH, *Elkton*
H. WINSHIP WHEATLEY, JR., *Hyattsville*

House

Democrats 98   Republicans 25

MURRAY ABRAMSON, 918 *Whitelock St., Baltimore*
JOSEPH A. ACKER, 2702 *Hugo Ave., Baltimore* 18
JOHN T. ADAMS, *Cambridge*
HOWARD E. ANKENEY, *Clear Spring*
CAMILLO N. ANTONELLI, 525 *N. Ellwood Ave.,*
Baltimore 5
JESSE J. ASHBY, *Oakland*
C. W. BACHARACH, 3814 *Sequoia Ave., Baltimore*
15
C. RAY BARNES, *Westminster*
EDWARD J. BARTOS, JR., 2212 *E. Eager St.,*
Baltimore 5
HENRY T. BAYNES, 781 *Washington Blvd.,*
Baltimore
RUDY BEHOUNEK, 2406 *E. Monument St.,*
Baltimore 5
EARL BENNETT, *Cambridge*
JACOB B. BERKSON, *Hagerstown*
ORLANDO B. BLADES, *Preston*
MYRON L. BLOOM, *St. James*
A. GORDON BOONE, *Towson*
PAUL E. BREWER, *Hagerstown*
DANIEL B. BREWSTER, *Brooklandville*
LOTTIE R. BRINSFIELD, *Rhodesdale*
EDWARD W. BROOKS, 4333 *Glenmore Ave.,*
Baltimore

W. HOWARD BROWN, *Woodstock*
WARREN BROWNING, *Bethesda*
J. R. BUFFINGTON, JR., 520 *Radnor Ave.,*
Baltimore 12
WILLIAM F. BURKLEY, *Elkton*
ROBERT P. CANNON, *Salisbury*
MAURICE CARDIN, 3912 *Glengyle Ave.,*
Baltimore 15
EMORY R. COLE, 1137 *Myrtle Ave., Baltimore*
FRANK COMBS, *Leonardtown*
NOEL SPEIR COOK, *Frostburg*
CLARENCE CORKRAN, *Cambridge*
W. P. CORRIGAN, 432 *E. Fort Ave., Baltimore* 30
SAMUEL A. CULOTTA, 1439 *N. Gay St., Baltimore*
CHARLES F. CULVER, *Catonsville*
E. W. DABROWSKI, 1801 *E. Lombard St.,*
Baltimore 31
MELVIN H. DERR, *Frederick*
BENJAMIN C. DOWELL, *Lusby*
FRED B. DRISCOLL, *Cumberland*
TILGHMAN EATON, *Chester*
HARRY C. EDWARDS, *Grantsville*
JOHN P. FITZGERALD, 714 *N. Augusta Ave.,*
Baltimore 29
SOL J. FRIEDMAN, 2615 *Keyworth Ave., Baltimore*
KERMIT S. GLOTFELTY, *Accident*
GILBERT GUDE, *Chevy Chase*
JOSEPH H. HAHN, JR., *Westminster*
JAMES HANCE, *Battle Creek*
HENRY H. HANNA, *Salisbury*
ROGER B. HARRIS, *Chestertown*
S. FENTON HARRIS, *Frederick* •
W. RANDOLPH HARRISON, *Tilghman*
TRULY HATCHETT, 2026 *Druid Hill Ave., Baltimore*
THOMAS J. HATEM, *Havre de Grace*
T. H. HEDRICK, 216 *W. Madison St., Baltimore*
W. DALE HESS, *Fallston*
RUSSELL HICKMAN, *Berlin*
WILLIAM L. HODGES, 1225 *W. Cross St.,*
Baltimore 30
GEORGE R. HUGHES, JR., *Cumberland*
HARRY HUGHES, *Denton*
JOHN B. HUYETT, *Hagerstown*
DOROTHY T. JACKSON, *Parkville*
GEORGE JEFFREY, *Lonaconing*
JOHN W. JENKINS, *Bryans Road*
GUY JOHNSON, *Elkton*
W. PAUL JOINER, *Worton*
ESTEL C. KELLEY, *Cumberland*
MELVIN R. KENNY, SR., 1709 *Woodbourne Ave.,*
Baltimore
IRA BIRD KIRKLAND, *Woodland Beach*
MILTON K. LARMORE, *Salisbury*
JAMES C. LATHAM, *Easton*
BLAIR LEE III, *Silver Spring*
F. L. LOOSE, JR., 442 *E. Clement St., Baltimore*
ERNEST A. LOVELESS, JR., *Clinton*
CARROLL LOWE, *McDaniel*
JOHN C. LUBER, 4001 *W. Franklin St.,*
Baltimore 29
EDWARD J. MCNEAL, 2909 *Cresmont Ave.,*
Baltimore
JOSEPH V. MACH, 2612 *Beryl Ave., Baltimore* 5
HERVEY G. MACHEN, *Hyattsville*
F. REYNOLDS MACKIE, *Cecilton*
JOHN N. MAGUIRE, *Middle River*
MARVIN MANDEL, 2900 *W. Strathmore Ave.,*
Baltimore

RIDGELY P. MELVIN, JR., *Aberdeen, South River*
WILSON W. MEYERS, 437 *S. Gilmor St.,*
  Baltimore 23
E. R. MILANICZ, 2307 *Fleet St., Baltimore*
CHARLES M. MOORE, *Havre de Grace*
BENJAMIN A. MROZINSKI, 627 *S. Kenwood Ave.,*
  Baltimore 24
DANIEL M. MURRAY, JR., *Elkridge*
WILLIAM J. MYERS, 4101 *Brooklyn Ave., Baltimore*
C. PHILIP NICHOLS, *Laurel*
JOHN J. NOWAKOWSKI, 305 *S. Ellwood Ave.,*
  Baltimore 24
JOHN T. PARRAN, JR., *Indian Head*
JOSEPH B. PAYNE, *Brunswick*
MYRTLE A. POLK, *Pocomoke City*
MORTON C. POLLACK, 2721 *Reisterstown Rd.,*
  Baltimore 15
WILLIAM G. PORTER, *Hagerstown*
J. FRANK RALEY, JR., *Ridge*
LESTER B. REED, *Mt. Savage*
ORLANDO RIDOUT IV, *St. Margarets*
LAYTON RIGGIN, *Crisfield*
CHARLES E. RISLEY, *Grasonville*
JEROME ROBINSON, 720 *Reservoir St., Baltimore*
LANSDALE G. SASSCER, JR., *Upper Marlboro*
MRS. MARGARET C. SCHWEINHAUT, *Chevy Chase*
CARLTON R. SICKLES, *Chillum*
JAMES J. SILK, 742 *S. Decker St., Baltimore 24*
EDGAR P. SILVER, 2900 *Forest Glen Rd., Baltimore*
LLOYD L. SIMPKINS, *Princess Anne*
DONALD E. SIX, *Middleburg*
CHARLES H. SMELSER, *Oak Orchard*
CARROLL C. SMITH, *Hampstead*
ROY N. STATEN, *Dundalk*
A. HARTLEY STEVENS, *Snow Hill*
J. ELLIS TAWES, *Crisfield*
LEWIS S. TAWNEY, *Glen Burnie*
JOSEPH D. TYDINGS, *Havre de Grace*
JOSEPH A. URBAN, 510 *N. Belnord Ave., Baltimore*
GARY L. UTTERBACK, *Frederick*
CLIFTON VIRTS, *Frederick*
CALVIN O. WADE, *Severn*
ELMER E. WALTERS, 17 *N. Curley St., Baltimore*
WILLIAM B. WHEELER, *Silver Spring*
E. HOMER WHITE, JR., *Salisbury*
JOHN M. WHITMORE, *Bay Ridge*
PERRY O. WILKINSON, *Hyattsville*
CHARLES W. WOODWARD, JR., *Rockville*

MASSACHUSETTS
Senate
Republicans 21   Democrats 19

JOHN ADAMS, 15 *Stratford Rd., Andover*
JOHN J. BEADES, 278 *Minot St., Boston*
PAUL H. BENOIT, 771 *Lebanon Hill, Southbridge*
PHILIP G. BOWKER, 127 *Jordan Rd., Brookline*
RALPH V. CLAMPIT, 137 *Belvidere St., Springfield*
SILVIO O. CONTE, 342 *Dalton Ave., Pittsfield*
JAMES J. CORBETT, 138A *Summer St., Somerville*
MRS. LESLIE B. CUTLER, 1010 *South St., Needham*
EDMUND DINIS, 29 *Arnold Place, New Bedford*
MAURICE A. DONAHUE, 140 *Pine St., Holyoke*
GEORGE J. EVANS, 120 *Main St., Wakefield*
WILLIAM D. FLEMING, 56 *Henshaw St., Worcester*
MRS. MARY L. FONSECA, 102 *Webster St., Fall River*

RICHARD I. FURBUSH, 436 *Waverly Oaks Rd., Waltham*
JOSEPH F. GIBNEY, 119 *Thompson Rd., Webster*
C. HENRY GLOVSKY, 23 *Ober St., Beverly*
PHILIP A. GRAHAM, 293 *Bridge St., Hamilton*
CHARLES W. HEDGES, 304 *Beale St., Quincy*
JAMES W. HENNIGAN, JR., 10 *Roseway St., Boston*
CHARLES V. HOGAN, 36 *Baltimore St., Lynn*
NEWLAND H. HOLMES, 83 *Webb St., Weymouth*
CHARLES J. INNES, 197 *Bay State Rd., Boston*
HASTINGS KEITH, 91 *River St., West Bridgewater*
FRED LAMSON, 36 *Dodge St., Malden*
RICHARD H. LEE, 206 *Church St., Newton*
RALPH LERCHE, 55 *South St., Northampton*
HAROLD R. LUNDGREN, 48 *Gifford Dr., Worcester*
FRANCIS X. McCANN, 14 *Sherman St., Cambridge*
FREDERICK T. McDERMOTT, 7 *Whitman Rd., Medford*
RALPH C. MAHAR, 63 *Congress St., Orange*
CHARLES W. OLSON, *W. Union St., Ashland*
JOHN F. PARKER, 429 *Cohannet St., Taunton*
JOHN E. POWERS, 158 *M St., Boston*
ALBERT S. PREVITE, JR., 20 *Greenwood St., Lawrence*
ANDREW P. QUIGLEY, 300 *Washington Ave., Chelsea*
DANIEL RUDSTEN, 23 *Angell St., Boston*
MRS. ELIZABETH A. STANTON, 102 *Cedar St., Fitchburg*
EDWARD C. STONE, *Box 158, Osterville*
MARIO UMANA, 82 *St. Andrew Rd., Boston*
PATRICK J. WALSH, JR., 63 *Avon St., Lowell*

House
Democrats 127   Republicans 113

FRANK H. ALLEN, 68 *Central St., Auburn*
LEONARD H. AMOROSO, 257 *Bacon St., Natick*
CHARLES H. ANTHONY, 136 *Colby St., Haverhill*
ERNEST W. APRIL, 13 *Savoy Rd., Salem*
JOHN A. ARMSTRONG, 14 *Nelson St., Plymouth*
CHARLES J. ARTESANI, 37 *Coolidge Rd., Boston*
JOHN GEORGE ASIAF, 92 *Elliot St., Brockton*
J. ROBERT AYERS, 55 *Loring Rd., Weston*
CLIFTON H. BAKER, 260 *Pine St., Quincy*
CYRUS BARNES, *Hummock Pond Rd., Nantucket*
FRED A. BAUMEISTER, 12 *Prospect Ave., Winthrop*
JAMES C. BAYLEY, 199 *Marlborough St., Boston*
RAYMOND H. BEACH, 493 *Main St., Wilbraham*
RENE R. BERNARDIN, 37 *Bellevue St., Lawrence*
CHARLES A. BISBEE, JR., *Chesterfield*
FRED A. BLAKE, 19 *S. Main St., Gardner*
CARLTON H. BLISS, 117 *Church St., N. Attleborough*
BELDEN G. BLY, JR., 46 *Auburn St., Saugus*
FRANK E. BOOT, 2 *Bulfinch Terr., Lynn*
SAMUEL J. BOUDREAU, 84 *Concord St., Athol*
GORDON D. BOYNTON, 121 *St. Stephens St., Boston*
MALCOLM B. BOYNTON, 253 *School St., Whitman*
G. EDWARD BRADLEY, 40 *Benton Rd., Somerville*
RENE A. BRASSARD, 39 *Hadwen Lane, Worcester*
JOHN C. BRESNAHAN, 79 *Saunders St., Lawrence*
F. EBEN BROWN, 314 *Main St., Fairhaven*
JOHN D. BROWN, 17 *Hemenway St., Boston*
JOHN BROX, 1363 *Broadway, Dracut*
JOHN P. BUCKLEY, 7 *Robin Hood Rd., Arlington*
WILLIAM F. BURKE, 65 *Seymour St., Boston*
PASQUALE CAGGIANO, 165 *Washington St., Lynn*
OSCAR J. CAHOON, *Harbor Rd., Harwichport*
GARDNER E. CAMPBELL, 24 *Wave Ave., Wakefield*

JOHN J. CAMPBELL, 11 *Felton St., Cambridge*
HAROLD W. CANAVAN, 53 *Lancaster Ave., Revere*
MICHAEL HERBERT CANTWELL, 4 *Violante St., Boston*
RICHARD R. CAPLES, 27 *Long Ave., Boston*
CHARLES W. CAPRARO, 52 *Cooper St., Boston*
MICHAEL J. CARROLL, 56 *Mudge St., Lynn*
RALPH W. CARTWRIGHT, JR., 86 *Canton St., Randolph*
JOHN J. CAVANAUGH, 140 *Sargeant St., Holyoke*
HARRISON CHADWICK, 24 *Everett Ave., Winchester*
WENDELL P. CHAMBERLAIN, 79 *Perkins St., Springfield*
STEPHEN T. CHMURA, 4 *Elm St., Holyoke*
THOMAS F. COADY, JR., 11 *Leonard Ave., Cambridge*
ANTHONY M. COLONNA, 203 *Warren Rd., Framingham*
HARRY COLTUN, 70 *Fremont Ave., Chelsea*
GEORGE R. COMO, 85 *Call St., Chicopee*
JAMES F. CONDON, 49 *St. Margaret St., Boston*
JOSEPH T. CONLEY, 6 *Salem St., Lawrence*
WILLIAM A. CONNELL, JR., 37 *Highland Pl., Weymouth*
JOHN W. COSTELLO, 572 *Centre St., Boston*
LEO J. COURNOYER, 384 *Main St., Southbridge*
WILLIAM A. COWING, 43 *Garden St., West Springfield*
WALLACE B. CRAWFORD, 103 *Spadina Parkway, Pittsfield*
JOHN F. CREMENS, 80 *Grozier Rd., Cambridge*
SIDNEY Q. CURTISS, *Guilder Hollow Rd., Sheffield*
JOHN A. DAVIS, 28 *Elm St., Marblehead*
JOHN F. X. DAVOREN, 180 *Purchase St., Milford*
AMELIO A. DELLA CHIESA, 11 *Hughes St., Quincy*
JAMES DeNORMANDIE, *Trapelo Rd., Lincoln*
DOMENIC V. DePARI, 31 *Prentice St., Worcester*
WILFRED A. DEROSIER, 356 *Centre St., Brockton*
EDWARD J. DeSAULNIER, JR., 66 *Hornbeam Hill Rd., Chelmsford*
CORNELIUS DESMOND, JR., 460 *E. Merrimack St., Lowell*
THEOPHILE J. DesROCHES, 214 *Tinkham St., New Bedford*
WILLIAM P. DI VITTO, 154 *E. Main St., Milford*
THOMAS J. DOHERTY, 165 *Salem St., Medford*
JOHN F. DOLAN, 39 *East St., Ipswich*
JAMES R. DONCASTER, 70 *Garrison Ave., Somerville*
EDMOND J. DONLAN, 176 *Park St., Boston*
ALLISON R. DORMAN, 15 *Maple St., New Bedford*
CHARLES ROBERT DOYLE, 12 *Danville St., Boston*
CHARLES E. LUKE DRISCOLL, 77 *East St., Northbridge*
JOHN THOMAS DRISCOLL, 1085 *Washington St., Boston*
PHILIP J. DURKIN, 51 *Dearborn St., Salem*
JOHN M. EATON, JR., *Nashawtuc Rd., Concord*
THOMAS E. ENRIGHT, 81 *Parker St., Pittsfield*
MANUEL FARIA, 589 *S. Main St., Fall River*
C. EUGENE FARNAM, 114 *Wolcott St., Medford*
THOMAS F. FARRELL, 5 *Norwood St., Worcester*
MICHAEL PAUL FEENEY, 999 *River St., Boston*
LAWRENCE F. FELONEY, 240 *Concord Ave., Cambridge*
CHARLES E. FERGUSON, 16 *Highland Ave., Lexington*
WILLIAM H. FINNEGAN, 114 *Linden St., Everett*
THOMAS M. FLAHERTY, 43 *Beechwood Rd., Waltham*
STEPHEN L. FRENCH, 1467 *Gardner's Neck Rd., Swansea*
PETER B. GAY, 10 *Whitehill St., Taunton*
CHARLES GIBBONS, 53 *Oak St., Stoneham*

DONALD L. GIBBS, 37 *Claremont St., Newton*
FRANK S. GILES, JR., 19 *Smith Ave., Methuen*
LOUIS H. GLASER, 72 *Bainbridge St., Malden*
DENNIS P. GLYNN, 29 *Linden Pk., Boston*
EDWIN D. GORMAN, 30 *Arlington St., Holyoke*
HOLLIS M. GOTT, 90 *Churchill Ave., Arlington*
JOSEPH P. GRAHAM, 25 *Lane Park, Boston*
THOMAS T. GRAY, 814 *Alden St., Springfield*
GEORGE GREENE, 40 *Schuyler St., Boston*
THOMAS J. HANNON, 3 *Monadnock St., Boston*
FRANCIS A. HARDING, 354 *Westfield St., Dedham*
FRED C. HARRINGTON, 28 *Mansfield St., Everett*
WILLIAM E. HAYS, 455 *Lexington St., Waltham*
ARTHUR G. HEANEY, 70 *Shady Hill Rd., Newton*
FRANCIS J. HICKEY, JR., 345 *Ashmont St., Boston*
GEORGE W. HILL, 1589 *Turnpike St., Stoughton*
PAUL L. HINCKLEY, 27 *Phillips Rd., Holden*
ISAAC A. HODGEN, *Sargent St., Belchertown*
OLAF HOFF, JR., 32 *High St., Montague*
HERBERT B. HOLLIS, 607 *Washington St., Braintree*
CHARLES F. HOLMAN, 8 *Belmont St., Norwood*
J. PHILIP HOWARD, *Smith Ave., Westminster*
RICHARD L. HULL, 199 *Main St., Rockport*
WALTER F. HURLBURT, 20 *Dunnell Rd., Greenfield*
NATHANIEL M. HURWITZ, 30 *Margin St., Cohasset*
FRED A. HUTCHINSON, 36 *Savory St., Lynn*
CHRISTOPHER A. IANNELLA, 10 *McLean St., Boston*
CHARLES IANNELLO, 887 *Harrison Ave., Boston*
JOHN P. IVASCYN, 17 *Lincoln St., Webster*
WILLIAM W. JENNESS, 106 *Upland Rd., Quincy*
ADOLPH JOHNSON, 11 *Second St., Brockton*
ERNEST A. JOHNSON, 18 *Gosnold St., Worcester*
STANLEY E. JOHNSON, 90 *Stanton St., Worcester*
ALLAN F. JONES, *Hyannis Rd., Barnstable*
ABRAHAM H. KAHALAS, 22 *Hosmer St., Boston*
SUMNER KAPLAN, 33 *Egmont St., Brookline*
WILLIAM F. KEENAN, 86 *Butler St., Boston*
CHARLES T. KELLEHER, 18 *Orchard St., Marlborough*
JAMES H. KELLY, 8 *Thwing St., Boston*
ARCHIBALD KENEFICK, 967 *Middlesex St., Lowell*
EDWARD L. KERR, 14 *Dalton Rd., Belmont*
CORNELIUS F. KIERNAN, 22 *Philips St., Lowell*
PHILIP K. KIMBALL, 770 *Dickinson St., Springfield*
WILLIAM J. KINGSTON, 8 *Hillside Pl., Springfield*
WILLIAM W. KIRLIN, 29 *Oak St., Belmont*
THOMAS E. KITCHEN, 25 *Home St., Fall River*
MRS. FREYDA P. KOPLOW, 84 *Alberta Rd., Brookline*
EDMUND V. LANE, 1666 *Commonwealth Ave., Boston*
JOHN J. LAWLESS, 125 *Plantation St., Worcester*
JAMES R. LAWTON, 25 *Cary St., Brockton*
CARTER LEE, 15 *Prospect Ave., Quincy*
FRANCIS W. LINDSTROM, 297 *Allston St., Cambridge*
THOMAS F. LINEHAN, 67 *Pontiac St., Boston*
GERALD P. LOMBARD, 123 *Myrtle Ave., Fitchburg*
WILLIAM LONGWORTH, 25 *Stevens St., Methuen*
JOSEPH F. McEVOY, JR., 210 *Powder House Blvd., Somerville*
HUGH J. McLAUGHLIN, 67 *Bellingham St., Chelsea*
JOHN P. McMORROW, 322 *Adams St., Boston*
ARTHUR U. MAHAN, 71 *Exchange St., Leominster*
FRANCIS J. MARR, 70 *Clarendon Ave., Lynn*
CHARLES S. MARSTON III, 309 *E. Broadway, Haverhill*
RICO MATERA, 110 *Faywood Ave., Boston*
WILFRED S. MIRSKY, 136 *Hazelton St., Boston*
JOHN J. MOAKLEY, 291 *Dorchester St., Boston*
WILLIAM D. MORTON, JR., 57 *Damien Rd., Wellesley*

CHARLES A. MULLALY, JR., 10 *Preston St., Millville*
JOHN E. MURPHY, 278 *Lowell St., Peabody*
CORNELIUS J. MURRAY, 2 *Haskell St., Beverly*
HAROLD C. NAGLE, 586 *Second St., Fall River*
THOMAS M. NEWTH, 57 *Middlesex Ave., Swampscott*
LEO J. NORMANDIM, 289 *Ashley Blvd., New Bedford*
WILLIAM F. NOURSE, *Harding St., Medfield*
JAMES A. O'BRIEN, 35 *Forest St., Fall River*
WALTER W. O'BRIEN, *Center St., Raynham*
DAVID J. O'CONNOR, 1558 *Tremont St., Boston*
JOHN H. O'CONNOR, JR., 1180 *Main St., Worcester*
THOMAS J. O'CONNOR, JR., 142 *Merrimac Ave., Springfield*
JAMES L. O'DEA, JR., 60 *Winthrop Ave., Lowell*
GEORGE H. O'FARRELL, 51 *Wesmur Rd., Malden*
FRANK B. OLIVEIRA, 217 *Columbia St., Fall River*
JOSEPH M. O'LOUGHLIN, 9 *Thurlow St., Boston*
JOHN J. O'ROURKE, 19 *Norfolk Ave., Northampton*
DANIEL M. O'SULLIVAN, 118 *Hamilton St., Boston*
HAROLD A. PALMER, 7 *Fairview Terr., Somerville*
CHARLES L. PATRONE, 81 *Prospect St., Boston*
CHARLES W. PATTERSON, 57 *Elm St., Worcester*
PATRICK F. PLUNKETT, 277 *Tenth St., Lowell*
RUSSELL B. POMEROY, 27 *Stratfield Ave., Westfield*
MICHAEL A. PORRAZZO, 55 *Lubec St., Boston*
GEORGE W. PORTER, 63 *Silver Lake Dr., Agawam*
HARVEY A. POTHIER, 51 *Franklin St., Haverhill*
HAROLD PUTNAM, 315 *Warren St., Needham*
PHILIP A. QUINN, *Hotel Massasoit, Spencer*
WILLIAM I. RANDALL, 122 *Edgell Rd., Framingham*
GEORGE E. RAWSON, 22 *Marlboro St., Newton*
FRANK G. RICO, 75 *Floral St., Taunton*
WILLIAM H. J. ROWAN, 30 *Payson St., Revere*
RICHARD A. RUETHER, 7 *Spring St., Williamstown*
ROGER A. SALA, 1 *Pebble St., North Adams*
JOSEPH D. SAULNIER, 122 *Fern St., New Bedford*
ANTHONY J. SCALLI, 11 *Monument Sq., Boston*
ANTHONY M. SCIBELLI, 200 *Maple St., Springfield*
JOHN R. SENNOTT, JR., 21 *Irving St., Cambridge*
JOHN E. SHELDON, 1253 *Canton Ave., Milton*
JOSEPH SILVANO, 318 *Walnut St., Brookline*
MICHAEL J. SIMONELLI, 7 *Kennison Rd., Somerville*
J. ROGER SISSON, 159 *Brayton Ave., Somerset*
MICHAEL F. SKERRY, 110 *Sheridan Ave., Medford*
THOMAS J. SLACK, 31 *High St., Methuen*
FLETCHER SMITH, JR., 124 *Park St., Easthampton*
GEORGE T. SMITH, 191 *Maple St., East Longmeadow*
LEO SONTAG, 67 *Cheney St., Boston*
ANTHONY W. SPADAFORA, 62 *Adams St., Malden*
GEORGE I. SPATCHER, 959 *Pleasant St., Attleboro*
C. CLIFFORD STONE, 157 *Water St., Clinton*
WILLIAM C. SULLIVAN, 29 *Murray Hill Ave., Springfield*
JOSEPH A. SYLVIA, *Wing Rd., Oak Bluffs*
JOSEPH A. SYLVIA, JR., 333 *Dartmouth St., New Bedford*
ALVIN C. TAMKIN, 91 *Callender St., Boston*
ARMAND N. TANCRATI, 47 *Huntington St., Springfield*
FRANK D. TANNER, 26 *Mineral St., Reading*
MRS. EDNA B. TELFORD, 54 *Pleasant St., Plainville*
DUNCAN F. THAYER, *George Hill Rd., Lancaster*
GEORGE H. THOMPSON, 77 *Homestead Ave., Weymouth*
JOHN F. THOMPSON, 164 *Hubbard St., Ludlow*
MRS. IRENE K. THRESHER, 667 *Chestnut St., Newton*
NATHANIEL TILDEN, 37 *Elm St., Scituate*
ROBERT X. TIVNAN, 2 *Louise St., Worcester*

JOHN J. TOOMEY, 395 *Windsor St., Cambridge*
HERBERT S. TUCKERMAN, 413 *Hale St., Beverly*
WARREN A. TURNER, *Chapel St., Lee*
EARLE S. TYLER, 232 *Bellevue Rd., Watertown*
JOHN T. TYNAN, 33 *Lennon Ct., Boston*
THEODORE J. VAITSES, 13 *Laurel St., Melrose*
WILLIAM X. WALL, 179 *Spruce St., Lawrence*
JOSEPH F. WALSH, 80 *Orchard St., Lynn*
BARCLAY H. WARBURTON III, *Jeffrey's Neck Rd., Ipswich*
JOSEPH D. WARD, 29 *Allston Pl., Fitchburg*
MARTHA WARE, 620 *Adams St., Abington*
CHESTER H. WATEROUS, 16 *High St., Pepperell*
NORMAN S. WEINBERG, 33 *Wade St., Boston*
PHILIP F. WHITMORE, *N. Sunderland Rd., Sunderland*
CHARLES E. WILKINSON, 38 *Deering St., Reading*
JOSEPH WISNIOWSKI, 38 *Front St., Chicopee*
THOMAS C. WOJTKOWSKI, 541 *Onota St., Pittsfield*
STANISLAUS G. WONDOLOWSKI, 30 *Washburn St., Worcester*
ALTON H. WORRALL, *We-We-Antic Shores, Wareham*
JOHN E. YERXA, 81 *Beacon St., Boston*
ALBERT H. ZABRISKIE, 242 *Merrimac St., Newburyport*
JOHN F. ZAMPARELLI, 378 *Fellsway West, Medford*
PAUL G. ZOLLO, 13 *Forest St., Danvers*

MICHIGAN

Senate

Republicans 23   Democrats 11

FRANK ANDREWS, *Hillman*
FRANK D. BEADLE, 150 *Brown St., St. Clair*
CHARLES S. BLONDY, 2605 *Sturtevant, Detroit 6*
WM. S. BROOMFIELD, 1116 *S. Lafayette, Royal Oak*
CORA M. BROWN, 201 *Lawyers Bldg., Detroit 26*
LEWIS G. CHRISTMAN, 1025 *Packard St., Ann Arbor*
CREIGHTON R. COLEMAN, 209 *Lincoln Hill Dr., Battle Creek*
ARTHUR DEHMEL, *R.F.D. 2, Unionville*
PATRICK J. DOYLE, 6327 *Payne, Dearborn*
ROBERT E. FAULKNER, 605 *West St., Coloma*
CHARLES R. FEENSTRA, 2181 *Forty-fourth St. SE, Grand Rapids*
LYNN O. FRANCIS, 339½ *E. Main St., Midland*
CLYDE H. GEERLINGS, 69 *E. Twenty-sixth St., Holland*
EDWARD H. GIBBS, *Perkins*
CLARENCE F. GRAEBNER, 125 *N. Granger St., Saginaw*
PERRY W. GREENE, 71 *Sheldon Ave. SE, Grand Rapids*
HARRY F. HITTLE, 404 *American State Bank Bldg., Lansing*
EDWARD HUTCHINSON, *Fennville*
GARLAND B. LANE, 2737 *Swayze St., Flint*
JOHN MINNEMA, 1123 *Randolph St., Traverse City*
CARLTON H. MORRIS, 206 *Woodward Ave., Kalamazoo*
HASKELL L. NICHOLS, 401 *Dwight Bldg., Jackson*
FRED NICHOLSON, 28028 *Walker St., Warren*
STANLEY NOVAK, 8150 *Burnette, Detroit 9*
ELMER R. PORTER, *R.F.D. 2, Blissfield*
CHARLES T. PRESCOTT, *Prescott*
PHILIP RAHOI, 527 *Smith St., Iron Mountain*
LEO H. ROY, 202 *Harris Ave., Hancock*
STANLEY F. ROZYCKI, 808 *Sirron, Detroit*
HAROLD M. RYAN, 4885 *Bedford Ave., Detroit 24*

DONALD E. SMITH, 615 *Clark Ave., Owosso*
BERT J. STOREY, 6952 *Storey Rd., R.F.D. 3, Belding*
JOHN B. SWAINSON, 20452 *Olympia, Detroit 19*
DON VANDER WERP, 326 *E. Main St., Fremont*

House

Republicans 58   Democrats 51   Independent 1

WILLIAM BAIRD, 3830 *Audubon, Detroit*
WILFRED G. BASSETT, 405 *Dwight Bldg., Jackson*
FRED G. BEARDSLEY, 12 *Hudson Ave., Oxford*
ANDREW BOLT, *Madison Square P.O., Box 875, Grand Rapids 7*
EDWARD A. BORGMAN, 1154 *Alto Ave. SE, Grand Rapids 7*
WILLARD I. BOWERMAN, JR., 704 *Prudden Bldg., Lansing 15*
JOHN T. BOWMAN, 19004 *Connecticut, Roseville*
CHARLES A. BOYER, *Savings Bank Bldg., Manistee*
JAMES BRADLEY, 3750 *Concord St., Detroit*
ROY H. BRIGHAM, 150 *Jericho Rd., Battle Creek*
THOMAS M. BURNS, 7 *Merrill Bldg., Saginaw*
ED. CAREY, 15626 *Parkgrove, Detroit*
JOSEPH A. CAVANAUGH, 415 *W. Main St., Midland*
HERB CLEMENTS, *R.F.D. 1, Deckerville*
ANDREW W. COBB, *R.F.D. 3, Elsie*
JAMES J. COLLINS, 205 *W. Tenth Ave., Flint*
ROLLO G. CONLIN, *Tipton*
CLYDE E. COOPER, 953 *Wilcox Ave., White Cloud*
WILLIAM R. COPELAND, 3536 *Twenty-first St., Wyandotte*
LOUIS C. CRAMTON, *Lapeer Savings Bank Bldg., Lapeer*
EDGAR CURRIE, 2267 *Pasadena, Detroit*
ADRIAN DE BOOM, *Box 21, Owosso*
CHARLES M. DIGGS, 1050 *Joseph Campau, Detroit*
FRED R. DINGMAN, 9643 *Sussex Ave., Detroit*
GEORGE DUNN, *Pigeon*
RAYMOND D. DZENDZEL, 18501 *Shiawassee, Detroit*
GEORGE H. EDWARDS, 2731 *Hague, Detroit*
HARRY T. EMMONS, 5980 *Byron Center Ave., Byron Center*
ARNELL ENGSTROM, 540 *W. Eighth St., Traverse City*
EINAR E. ERLANDSEN, 1014 *N. Sixteenth St., Escanaba*
EDWIN A. FITZPATRICK, 9595 *Pinehurst, Detroit*
JOHN J. FITZPATRICK, 5844 *Baker St., Detroit*
JOHN W. FLETCHER, *R.F.D. 1, Centreville*
JAMES N. FOLKS, *Horton*
LLOYD GIBBS, *R.F.D. 2, Portland*
GEORGE A. GILLESPIE, 218 *Genesee St., Gaines*
CHARLES J. GOLDEN, 2 *E. First St., Monroe*
JAMES GOULETTE, 221 *East B St., Iron Mountain*
ALLISON GREEN, *R.F.D. 1, Kingston*
MANNING HATHAWAY, 4944 *Hillcrest, Detroit*
VERNALD E. HORN, 615 *S. Altadena, Royal Oak*
ALBERT R. HORRIGAN, 812 *E. Fourth Ave., Flint*
T. JEFFERSON HOXIE, 119 *N. Mill St., St. Louis*
HOLLY E. HUBBELL, 11165 *Gratiot Rd., Saginaw*
LESLIE H. HUDSON, 69 *W. Colgate St., Pontiac*
THEODORE F. HUGHES, 1705 *Coolidge, Berkley*
HAROLD W. HUNGERFORD, 2223 *Forest Ave., Lansing 10*
GLENN HUNSBERGER, 4329 *Hunsberger Ave. NE, Grand Rapids 5*

JOSEPHINE D. HUNSINGER, 13933 *Minock, Detroit*
JOSEPH I. JACKSON, 53 *Grove Ave., Highland Park*
DOMINIC JACOBETTI, *Box 62, Ann St., Negaunee*
EDWARD H. JEFFRIES, 2507 *Hurlbut, Detroit*
HUGH D. JOHNSTON, *Rosebush*
PETER J. KELLY, 15075 *Washburn, Detroit*
JOHN KILBORN, 615 *State St., Petoskey*
JOSEPH J. KOWALSKI, 9164 *Steel, Detroit*
T. JOHN LESINSKI, 11445 *Conant Ave., Detroit*
DAVID L. LINDSAY, 11065 *Chelsea, Detroit*
HARRY LITOWICH, *R.F.D. 2, Box 501, Highland Ave., Benton Harbor*
BEN E. LOHMAN, *R.F.D. 2, Hamilton*
LUCILLE H. McCOLLOUGH, 7517 *Kentucky, Dearborn*
JOHN J. McCUNE, 709 *Capitol Savings & Loan Bldg., Lansing*
EDWARD L. McGEE, 26 *E. Charlotte, Ecorse*
WALTER T. McMAHON, 151 *E. Shevlin St., Hazel Park*
HIRAM McNEELEY, 3230 *Walnut St., Inkster*
FRANK A. MAHONEY, 4112 *Larchmont, Detroit*
ROBERT D. MAHONEY, 19971 *Dresden, Detroit*
FREDERIC J. MARSHALL, *White Marble Springs, Allen*
D. J. MASSOGLIA, 123 *Tamarack St., Laurium*
CLARENCE B. MEGGISON, 207 *Stover Rd., Charlevoix*
LOUIS MEZZANO, 1201 *Hancock St., Wakefield*
JAMES P. MIELOCK, *Whittemore*
CLAYTON T. MORRISON, *Pickford*
WALTER G. NAKKULA, 5850 *Cedar Lake Rd., R.F.D. 4, Gladwin*
CARROLL C. NEWTON, *R.F.D. 2, Delton*
WALTER H. NILL, 3337 *Jefferson St., Muskegon Heights*
MICHAEL NOVAK, 17194 *Lumpkin Ave., Detroit*
FRANK J. O'BRIEN, 17409 *Warrington Dr., Detroit*
MICHAEL J. O'BRIEN, 4317 *Euclid Ave. W., Detroit*
JOSEPH G. O'CONNOR, 11366 *Dalrymple, Detroit*
FRED O. OLSEN, *R.F.D. 2, Sheridan*
DON R. PEARS, 104 *Lake St., Buchanan*
EMIL A. PELTZ, *Box 9, Rogers City*
JOHN JOSEPH PENCZAK, 11700 *Pinehurst Ave., Detroit*
HARRY J. PHILLIPS, 2956 *Electric Ave., Port Huron*
F. CHARLES RAAP, *R.F.D. 2, Twin Lake*
WILLIAM ROMANO, 7543 *Paige Ave., Van Dyke*
CYRIL H. ROOT, *R.F.D. 1, Box 228, Kalamazoo*
EDSON V. ROOT, JR., *Arlington Rd., Bangor*
GEORGE WAHR SALLADE, 728 *Onondaga, Ann Arbor*
RICHARD G. SMITH, 212 *Phoenix Bldg., Bay City*
JOHN M. SOBIESKI, 20433 *Spencer, Detroit*
COLEMAN A. STANISLAW, 7265 *Weddel St., Dearborn*
GEORGE C. STEEH, 203 *Lawyers Bldg., Mt. Clemens*
ADAM SUMERACKI, 6420 *Mitchell Ave., Detroit*
ROGER B. TOWNSEND, 767 *E. Stewart Ave., Flint 5*
KENNETH O. TRUCKS, *Baldwin*
RICHARD C. VAN DUSEN, 800 *Natl. Bank Bldg., Detroit 26*
GEORGE M. VAN PEURSEM, 129 *E. Main St., Zeeland*
WADE VAN VALKENBURG, 1118 *Cherry St., Kalamazoo 39*
ROBERT E. WALDRON, 532 *University Pl., Grosse Pointe Park*
GILBERT L. WALES, 816 *Wilson Ave., Stambaugh*

JOSEPH E. WARNER, 1024 *W. Michigan Ave.,*
Ypsilanti
THOMAS J. WHINERY, 17 *Prospect Ave. SE,*
Grand Rapids 3
CHARLINE WHITE, 644 *E. Philadelphia, Detroit*
FRANK D. WILLIAMS, 5973 *Trumbull, Detroit*
LEONARD E. WOOD, 9568 *Nathaline, Detroit*
CHESTER WOZNIAK, 2626 *Evaline, Hamtramck*
FREDERICK YATES, 8634 *La Salle, Detroit*
FRED W. ZINN, *Box 22, Battle Creek*

MINNESOTA

Senate

Members 67*

ELMER L. ANDERSEN, 2230 *W. Hoyt Ave., St. Paul*
ANDY A. ANDERSON, *Luverne*
ERNEST J. ANDERSON, *Frost*
MARVIN H. ANDERSON, 5234 *Thirty-second Ave. S.,*
Minneapolis
FRED W. BEHMLER, *Morris*
MILAN BONNIWELL, *Hutchinson*
WALTER BURDICK, *Rochester*
GORDON H. BUTLER, 3500 *E. Third St., Duluth*
HOMER M. CARR, *Proctor*
FAY GEORGE CHILD, *Maynard*
ROBERT R. DUNLAP, *Plainview*
CHRIS L. ERICKSON, *Fairmont*
DANIEL S. FEIDT, 1715 *W. Franklin Ave., Minne-*
apolis
W. J. FRANZ, *Mountain Lake*
DONALD M. FRASER, 813 *SE Seventh St., Minneap-*
olis
GROVER C. GEORGE, *Goodhue*
ARTHUR GILLEN, 1515 *Pleasant Ave., South St. Paul*
NORMAN W. HANSON, *Cromwell*
RUDOLPH HANSON, *Albert Lea*
HENRY F. HARREN, *Albany*
WILLIAM C. F. HEUER, *Bertha*
P. J. HOLAND, *Austin*
STANLEY W. HOLMQUIST, *Grove City*
VAL IMM, *Mankato*
C. ELMER JOHNSON, *Almelund*
JOHN A. JOHNSON, *Preston*
RALPH W. JOHNSON, *Isanti*
J. A. JOSEFSON, *Minneota*
HAROLD KALINA, 2015 *Fourth St. NE., Minneapolis*
J. R. KELLER, *Winona*
FRANKLIN P. KROEHLER, *Henderson*
NORMAN J. LARSON, *Ada*
CLIFFORD LOFVEGREN, *Alexandria*
JOHN H. MCKEE, *Bemidji*
MARTIN M. MALONE, *Montgomery*
JOSEPH H. MASEK, 130 *Prospect Blvd., St. Paul*
RALPH L. MAYHOOD, 1810 *Washington Ave. S.,*
Minneapolis
JOHN A. METCALF, *Shakopee*
ARCHIE H. MILLER, *R.F.D 2, Hopkins*
C. C. MITCHELL, *Princeton*
GERALD T. MULLIN, 4314 *Xerxes Ave. N., Minne-*
apolis
LOUIS A. MURRAY, *East Grand Forks*
HAROLD S. NELSON, *Owatonna*
B. G. NOVAK, 747 *Van Buren Ave., St. Paul*
HENRY NYCKLEMOE, *Fergus Falls*

*Non-partisan election.

GEORGE H. O'BRIEN, *Grand Rapids*
HAROLD J. O'LOUGHLIN, 1137 *Portland Ave., St. Paul*
OSCAR L. OLSON, *Fairfax*
ELMER PETERSON, *Hibbing*
ALBERT H. QUIE, *Dennison*
JOHN L. RICHARDSON, *St. Cloud*
HERBERT ROGERS, *R.F.D. 2, Box 297A, Haines Rd.,*
Duluth
CHAS. W. ROOT, 5104 *Colfax Ave. S., Minneapolis*
GORDON ROSENMEIER, *Little Falls*
RAPHAEL F. SALMORE, *Stillwater*
HAROLD W. SCHULTZ, 882 *Jenks, St. Paul*
DONALD SINCLAIR, *Stephen*
JOSEPH VADHEIM, *Tyler*
THOMAS D. VUKELICH, *Gilbert*
HARRY L. WAHLSTRAND, *Willmar*
NORMAN J. WALZ, *Detroit Lakes*
MAGNUS WEFALD, *Hawley*
THOMAS P. WELCH, *Buffalo*
LESLIE E. WESTIN, 2160 *Edgerton, St. Paul*
ROY E. WISETH, *Goodridge*
DONALD O. WRIGHT, 917 *Plymouth Bldg., Minnea-*
polis
JOHN M. ZWACH, *Walnut Grove*

House

Members 131*

JAMES L. ADAMS, 209 *E. Nineteenth St., Minneapolis*
LELAND A. AFFELDT, SR., *Fosston*
GEORGE ALDERINK, *Pease*
CLAUDE H. ALLEN, 909 *Lakeview, St. Paul*
DELBERT F. ANDERSON, *Starbuck*
FLOYD R. ANDERSON, 323 *Swan Lake Rd., Duluth*
G. A. ANDERSON, *Donnelly*
HAROLD J. ANDERSON, 4919 *Colfax Ave. S.,*
Minneapolis
HAROLD R. ANDERSON, *North Mankato*
MOPPY ANDERSON, *Preston*
OLE O. AUNE, JR., *Underwood*
HARRY BASFORD, *Wolf Lake*
WAYNE R. BASSETT, *Worthington*
EVERETT BATTLES, *Warroad*
SHELDON L. BEANBLOSSOM, 492 *E. Wheelock Park-*
way, St. Paul
ALF L. BERGERUD, 5100 *Ridge Rd., Minneapolis*
BURNETT J. BERGESON, *Twin Valley*
ELMER E. BERGLUND, *Bemidji*
TED L. BIERNAT, 224 *Lowry Ave. NE, Minneapolis*
CHARLES E. CAMPTON, *Two Harbors*
E. J. CHILGREN, *Littlefork*
THOMAS N. CHRISTIE, 1219 *Lakeview Ave., Minne-*
apolis
FRED A. CINA, *Aurora*
OTTO E. CLARK, *Osakis*
DAN CONROY, *Dumont*
ROY H. CUMMINGS, *Luverne*
LAWRENCE CUNNINGHAM, *Pipestone*
OMAR C. DAHLE, *Waseca*
WALTER E. DAY, *Bagley*
AUBREY W. DIRLAM, *Redwood Falls*
ROY E. DUNN, *Pelican Rapids*
LLOYD DUXBURY, JR., *Caledonia*
CARL W. ECK, *Circle Pines*
PAUL L. EDDY, *Howard Lake*
ODEAN ENESTVEDT, *Sacred Heart*
L. B. ERDAHL, *Frost*
EMIL C. ERNST, *Lester Prairie*

RICHARD W. FITZSIMONS, *Argyle*
SAM FRANZ, *Mountain Lake*
G. W. FREEMAN, *Dodge Center*
GEORGE A. FRENCH, 5140 *Penn. Ave. S., Minneapolis*
PETER FUGINA, *Virginia*
GRAHAM FULLER, *Ivanhoe*
FRANK X. GALLAGHER, *Lakeville*
H. P. GOODIN, 3415 *Knox Ave. N., Minneapolis*
CLIFFORD C. GRABA, *Sebeka*
GEORGE E. GRANT, *Milaca*
KARL F. GRITTNER, 824 *Cherokee Ave., St. Paul*
GEORGE P. GRUSSING, *Clara City*
CARL G. HAGLAND, 1913 *S. Sixth St., Minneapolis*
CHARLES L. HALSTED, *Brainerd*
JOHN A. HARTLE, *R.F.D. 4, Owatonna*
JACOB J. HERZOG, *Austin*
ALVIN O. HOFSTAD, *Madison*
JOHN F. HOWARD, 642 *Summit Ave., St. Paul Park*
LOUIS H. HUSSONG, *Brewster*
CARL M. IVERSON, *Ashby*
CARL A. JENSEN, *Sleepy Eye*
ALFRED I. JOHNSON, *Benson*
ERWIN P. JOHNSON, *Hawley*
O. L. JOHNSON, *McGregor*
JOE KARAS, *Pine City*
JOE KARTH, 2334 *E. County Rd. D, St. Paul*
JERRY KELLEY, 762 *Capitol Heights, St. Paul*
R. B. KENNEDY, *New Ulm*
JOHN J. KINZER, *Cold Spring*
EUGENE P. KNUDSEN, *Kandiyohi*
HERMAN J. KORDING, 3533 *Thirty-sixth Ave. S., Minneapolis*
FRANCIS LaBROSSE, 3188 *Restormel St., Duluth*
ODIN E. S. LANGEN, *Kennedy*
CLARENCE G. LANGLEY, *Red Wing*
LEONARD E. LINDQUIST, 6940 *W. River Rd. N., Minneapolis*
A. W. LOVIK, *Park Rapids*
MRS. JOYCE LUND, *Wabasha*
MRS. SALLY LUTHER, 1936 *Kenwood Parkway, Minneapolis*
GLENN D. McCARTY, 2701 *Grand Ave. S., Minneapolis*
JOHN D. McGILL, *Winona*
MICHAEL McGUIRE, *Le Sueur*
DONALD McLEOD, *Lewiston*
LEO D. MADDEN, *Eyota*
RALPH R. MADDEN, *Marshall*
MICHAEL R. MORIARTY, *Jordan*
LEO D. MOSIER, 4340 *Washburn Ave. N., Minneapolis*
AUGUST B. MUELLER, *Arlington*
WILLARD M. MUNGER, 7502 *Grand Ave., Duluth*
O. GERHARD NORDLIE, *Litchfield*
ROGER F. NOREEN, 121 *North Sixteenth Ave. E., Duluth*
A. F. OBERG, *Lindstrom*
RICHARD W. O'DEA, *Willernie*
ARTHUR H. OGLE, *Mankato*
CARL G. OLSON, *St. James*
HOWARD OTTINGER, *Chaska*
ALFRED J. OTTO, 194 *Summit Ave., St. Paul*
CLIFTON PARKS, 1678 *Beechwood Ave., St. Paul*
ALBERT PASKEWITZ, *Browerville*
OSCAR O. PETERSON, *Clarkfield*
SETH R. PHILLIPS, *Brainerd*
ANTHONY PODGORSKI, 642 *Van Buren, St. Paul*

PETER S. POPOVICH, 1298 *Fairmount Ave., St. Paul*
JOSEPH PRIFREI, JR., 1031 *Woodridge, St. Paul*
DEWEY REED, *St. Cloud*
LOREN S. RUTTER, *Kinney*
ELY R. SCHENCK, *Wolverton*
ROY SCHULZ, *Mankato*
MARVIN C. SCHUMANN, *Rice*
FRED W. SCHWANKE, *Deerwood*
VLADIMIR SHIPKA, *Grand Rapids*
BILL SHOVELL, 76 *Bates Ave., St. Paul*
JOHN P. SKEATE, 609 *Taylor St. NE, Minneapolis*
EVERT A. SKOOG, *Little Falls*
WILLIAM SORENSEN, *Graceville*
A. O. SUNDET, *Faribault*
GLEN W. SWENSON, *Buffalo*
IRVIN M. TALLE, *Albert Lea*
TEMAN THOMPSON, *Lanesboro*
EDMUND C. TIEMANN, *Sauk Centre*
EDWARD J. TOMCZYK, 1614 *California St. NE, Minneapolis*
REUBEN H. TWETEN, *Fosston*
CLIFF UKKELBERG, *Clitherall*
G. J. VAN DE RIET, *Fairmont*
EDWARD J. VOLSTAD, 3327 *Twenty-fifth Ave. S., Minneapolis*
ROY L. VOXLAND, *Kenyon*
ARNE C. WANVICK, 3432 *Eighteenth Ave., Duluth*
REUBEN WEE, *Balaton*
CARL WEGNER, 2727 *NE McKinley, Minneapolis*
B. M. WICHTERMAN, *Plummer*
PAUL B. WIDSTRAND, *Hibbing*
E. J. WINDMILLER, *Fergus Falls*
D. D. WOZNIAK, 1216 *Bayard Ave., St. Paul*
F. GORDON WRIGHT, 2912 *Chowen Ave. S., Minneapolis*
LAWRENCE YETKA, *Cloquet*

MISSISSIPPI

Senate

Democrats 49   Republicans 0

LAWRENCE ADAMS, *Natchez*
W. B. ALEXANDER, *Cleveland*
F. D. BARLOW, *Crystal Springs*
ELLIS BODRON, *Vicksburg*
HUGH BOREN, *Tupelo*
W. G. BURGIN, JR., *Columbus*
W. V. BYARS, *Bruce*
HAYDEN CAMPBELL, *Jackson*
W. M. COLE, *Mayersville*
C. E. DUNHAM, *R.F.D. 1, Richton*
R. F. ERWIN, *Ackerman*
EARL EVANS, JR., *Canton*
F. D. EVERITT, *Ruleville*
MRS. J. B. FARESE, *Ashland*
C. N. FIELD, *Eupora*
O. L. GARMAN, JR., *R.F.D., Marks*
R. E. L. GENTRY, *Mt. Olive*
TILMAN GODBOLD, *Oxford*
WM. J. GUNN, JR., *Meridian*
H. MURRAY HAILEY, *Preston*
S. A. HALL, *Hattiesburg*
KELLY HAMMOND, *Columbia*
WM. L. KLING, *Red Lick*
W. O. KNIGHT, *Amory*

L. C. LADNER, *Kiln*
D. F. LAMBERT, JR., *Belmont*
J. C. LOVE, *Kosciusko*
ROLAND LOWE, *Batesville*
W. B. LUCAS, *Macon*
H. B. MAYES McGEHEE, *Meadville*
W. F. MARTIN, *R.F.D. 1, Bentonia*
STANFORD MORSE, JR., *Gulfport*
LAMAR MOSS, *Raleigh*
C. M. NORMAN, *Hickory*
G. W. OWENS, *Pontotoc*
R. H. PRIDGEN, *Monticello*
MITCHELL ROBINSON, *Jackson*
WM. F. ROSENBLATT, JR., *Fort Adams*
WM. O. SEMMES, *Grenada*
G. L. SMITH, *Greenwood*
JEWELL G. SMITH, *Heidelberg*
DEES STRIBLING, *Philadelphia*
AMOS STRICKLAND, *R.F.D. 4, Laurel*
W. F. TURMAN, *Star Rt., Horn Lake*
G. B. WALKER, *Stoneville*
ARNIE WATSON, *N. Carrollton*
Z. B. WHISENANT, *New Albany*
T. M. WILLIAMS, *Lexington*
GEORGE M. YARBROUGH, *Red Banks*

House

Democrats 140   Republicans 0

L. W. ADAMS, *R.F.D. 3, Tupelo*
CHALMERS ALEXANDER, *Jackson*
ELMO ANDERSON, *Canton*
J. H. ANDERSON, *Pontotoc*
R. E. ANDERSON, *R.F.D. 3, Box 211, Wasson*
J. M. ASH, *Potts Camp*
C. L. AVERA, JR., *State Line*
J. N. BAILEY, JR., *Coffeeville*
D. M. BAKER, *Batesville*
J. E. BAXTER, *Meridian*
DICK BIRCHETT, *Yazoo City*
MARION BISHOP, *R.F.D. 2, Box 246, Indianola*
MAURICE BLACK, *Carrollton*
JOEL BLASS, *Wiggins*
HOWARD BRASHER, *Banner*
LAWRENCE BRODY, *R.F.D. 1, Box 62, Byhalia*
TOMMY BROOKS, *R.F.D. 1, Carthage*
V. O. BULLOCK, *R.F.D. 2, Tylertown*
J. E. BURCH, *R.F.D., Fulton*
DELOS BURKS, *Picayune*
W. C. BUTLER, *Eupora*
T. E. CALDWELL, *Box 1704, Jackson*
H. L. CAMERON, *Baxterville*
J. N. CANON, *Dundee*
GEORGE CARRUTH, *R.F.D. 2, Summit*
F. E. COCKE, *Clarksdale*
G. C. COLEMAN, *Magee*
W. G. COLLINS, *R.F.D., Myrtle*
W. H. COON, *Woodville*
R. L. COOPER, SR., *Aberdeen*
G. P. COSSAR, *Charleston*
C. T. CRABTREE, *Macon*
STERLING DAVIS, *DeKalb*
I. W. DAY, *Kosciusko*
BARRON DREWRY, *R.F.D., Corinth*
M. G. DUNCAN, *Star Route, Springville*
T. M. DUNCAN, *Belmont*
T. W. DUNLAP, *Okolona*
B. H. EATON, *Taylorsville*

S. B. EURE, *Hattiesburg*
J. B. EZELL, *Louisville*
CHRISTIAN FASER, *Winona*
J. B. FARESE, *Ashland*
H. N. FINNIE, *Courtland*
C. L. FLOYD, *Booneville*
G. W. FLOYD, JR., *Ripley*
R. L. FOX, *Pattison*
J. M. FOXWORTH, *R.F.D. 2, Foxworth*
M. M. FRANKLIN, *Oxford*
J. B. FRENCH, *Sardis*
ALBERT GARDNER, *Yazoo City*
CLINE GILLIAN, *R.F.D. 2, Columbus*
MRS. LOVIE L. GORE, *Sturgis*
N. M. GORE, JR., *Marks*
ALMAN GRAHAM, *R.F.D. 2, Quitman*
M. H. GRISHAM, *Booneville*
D. D. GUICE, *Biloxi*
J. D. GUYTON, *Kosciusko*
L. H. HANNAFORD, *R.F.D. 1, Senatobia*
E. B. HEARN, *Monticello*
R. H. HERRIN, *Collins*
WALTER HESTER, *R.F.D. 1, Natchez*
FRED HETZLER, *Centreville*
W. W. HEWETT, *Meadville*
H. O. HICKS, *Benton*
B. J. HILBUN, *Oxford*
WILBURN HOOKER, *Lexington*
J. W. HOPKINS, *Clarksdale*
BRITTE HUGHEY, *Smithdale*
J. K. HURDLE, *Holly Springs*
C. C. JACOBS, *Cleveland*
J. P. JENKINS, *R.F.D. 1, Oakland*
W. H. JOHNSON, JR., *Decatur*
W. H. JOLLY, *Columbus*
P. B. JONES, *Senatobia*
J. R. JUNKIN, *Natchez*
C. H. KENNEDY, *Brandon*
H. E. KENNEDY, *R.F.D. 1, Calhoun City*
J. L. KENNEDY, *Holly Springs*
HAL KIRBY, *Starkville*
D. W. LEE, *R.F.D. 2, Corinth*
E. B. LIVINGSTON, *Morton*
W. C. LODEN, *R.F.D. 1, Prairie*
J. D. LOLLAR, *Kilmichael*
BETTY JANE LONG, *Meridian*
J. P. LOVE, *Tchula*
C. A. LOWRY, *R.F.D. 1, Bailey*
SAM LUMPKIN, *Tupelo*
M. L. MALONE, *Lucedale*
R. C. McCARVER, *R.F.D. 2, Fulton*
L. S. McCLAREN, *McComb*
THOMPSON McCLELLAN, *West Point*
H. L. McKNIGHT, *R.F.D., Redwood*
GEORGE McMILLAN, *Greenville*
P. D. MEASELL, *R.F.D. 5, Union*
A. V. MILLER, *Rolling Fork*
T. P. MONTGOMERY, *Pickens*
J. A. MORROW, *Brandon*
J. G. MOSS, *Raymond*
J. A. NEILL, *Laurel*
C. B. NEWMAN, *Valley Park*
P. A. NORRIS, *Benton*
T. J. O'QUINN, *Church Hill*
C. L. PATRIDGE, *Schlater*
J. A. PHILLIPS, *Macon*
W. J. PHILLIPS, *Bay St. Louis*
CLARENCE PIERCE, JR., *Vaiden*

Z. P. POLK, *Prentiss*
J. E. RICHARDSON, *Ridgeland*
G. W. ROGERS, JR., *Vicksburg*
H. A. SARTOR, *Pachuta*
ROBERT SCOTT, *R.F.D. 1, McCall Creek*
F. E. SHANAHAN, JR., *R.F.D., Vicksburg*
WALTER SILLERS, *Rosedale*
B. O. SIMPSON, *Blue Mountain*
W. L. SIMS, *Columbus*
UPTON SISSON, *Gulfport*
B. E. SMITH, *Ackerman*
T. F. SNOWDEN, *R.F.D. 2, Meridian*
EDGAR STEPHENS, JR., *New Albany*
JOHNNY TACKETT, *Aberdeen*
ODIE TRENOR, *Houston*
B. S. WADDELL, *Crystal Springs*
HILTON WAITS, *Leland*
JOE WALKER, *Hernando*
FRANK WALL, *R.F.D., Peoria*
CARL WALLACE, *Hazlehurst*
J. A. WALLACE, *409 N. Whitworth St., Brookhaven*
PETTIS WALLEY, *Richton*
P. M. WATKINS, *Port Gibson*
J. V. WEBB, *Noxapater*
REV. T. J. WEEMS, *Heidelberg*
KARL WIESENBURG, *Pascagoula*
T. J. WILKINS, *Brooksville*
BROWN WILLIAMS, *Philadelphia*
W. L. WILLIS, *Hamilton*
WILLIAM WINTER, *Grenada*
W. D. WOMACK, JR., *Belzoni*
J. E. WROTEN, *Greenville*
STANFORD YOUNG, *Waynesboro*

MISSOURI
Senate
Democrats 19   Republicans 15

CLAYTON W. ALLEN, *Allen Bldg., Rock Port*
VINCENT E. BAKER, *4014 Baltimore Ave.,
    Kansas City*
JOHN P. BARRETT, *1627 Veronica St., St. Louis*
ALLEN BOWSHER, *R.F.D. 4, Clinton*
NOEL COX, *Spokane*
HARTWELL G. CRAIN, *8600 Sappington Rd.,
    St. Louis County 23*
JACK S. CURTIS, *1324 E. Loren, Springfield*
E. GARY DAVIDSON, *300 N. Gore, Webster Groves*
ARKLEY W. FRIEZE, *Carthage*
FLOYD R. GIBSON, *701 N. Union, Independence*
HARRY E. HATCHER, *Granby*
C. R. HAWKINS, *Brumley*
J. MORRIS HILL, *Lebanon*
WILLIAM E. HILSMAN, *5734 Bartmer, St. Louis*
EDWARD J. HOGAN, JR., *4630 Farlin Ave., St. Louis*
JOHN A. JOHNSON, *Ellington*
JACK C. JONES, *Carrollton*
JOHN W. JOYNT, *4159 Flora Pl., St. Louis*
EDGAR J. KEATING, *1250 Dierks Bldg.,
    Kansas City*
JAMES P. KELLY, *Trenton*
MICHAEL KINNEY, *Holland Bldg., St. Louis*
ROBERT H. LINNEMAN, *St. Charles*
EDWARD V. LONG, *Clarksville*
JOHN W. NOBLE, *400 Washington, Kennett*
J. F. PATTERSON, *112 W. Eighteenth, Caruthersville*
ROBERT PENTLAND, *1127 Pine, St. Louis*

WM. M. QUINN, *Maywood*
LEO J. ROZIER, *Perryville*
WM. ORR SAWYERS, *St. Joseph*
GEORGE A. SPENCER, *R.F.D. 6, Columbia*
ALBERT M. SPRADLING, JR., *Surety Savings Bldg.,
    Cape Girardeau*
JAMES M. WEBBE, *948A Hickory St., St. Louis*
FRANK LEE WILKINSON, *3601 Belleview,
    Kansas City*
CHARLES A. WITTE, *R.F.D. 13, Box 1547,
    Kirkwood*

House
Democrats 97   Republicans 60

N. G. ABBOTT, *Stockton*
RAY ADAMS, *Redford*
LUTHER ARNOLD, *Reeds Spring*
SPURGEON ATWILL, *Iberia*
OMER H. AVERY, *Troy*
RALPH AYRES, *Fortuna*
LEE AARON BACHLER, *Anderson*
EARL A. BAER, *Salisbury*
RALPH BAIRD, *410 N. Byers, Joplin*
V. M. BALTZ, *Eminence*
JIM BANNER, *Camdenton*
ALLEN BARKER, *615 Begley, Poplar Bluff*
M. E. BAUER, *316 N. Hardesty, Kansas City*
JOHN C. BAUMANN, *417 N. Washington,
    Warrensburg*
JOSEPH W. BECKERLE, *4164 Fairview Ave.,
    St. Louis*
PAUL M. BERRA, *4945A Daggett, St. Louis*
JOHNIE BLACKWELL, *Salem*
GEORGE BOLEY, *Luray*
W. T. BOLLINGER, *Van Buren*
CHARLES J. BURNS, *Huntsville*
DON E. BURRELL, *1658 E. Sunshine, Springfield*
LUNA BUTLER, *Albany*
J. T. CAMPBELL, *Faucett*
PAUL D. CANADAY, *2642 College St., Springfield*
JENNIE CHINN, *Shelbyville*
JOHN R. CLARK, *1102 Grand, Kansas City*
R. R. COLE, *Lebanon*
EARL S. COOK, *902 E. Eighth St., Trenton*
ROBERT W. COPELAND, *540 S. Rock Hill Rd.,
    Webster Groves*
RUSSELL CORN, *Willow Springs*
ROBERT W. CRAWFORD, *312 S. Pine, Nevada*
JAMES CLIFFORD CROUCH, *Taneyville*
DANIEL CURRAN, *4313A Minnesota St., St. Louis*
OLEN R. DECKARD, *Ava*
RICHARD J. DeCOSTER, *Canton*
MARTIN P. DEGENHARDT, *Star Rt., Perryville*
J. ELLIS DODDS, *Waynesville*
WILLIAM P. DONOVAN, *116 Adelle Ave., Ferguson*
CLAUDE E. DUCKETT, *Lamar*
GEORGE DUENSING, JR., *Concordia*
ROY EDDY, *2801 Whitman Dr., St. Joseph*
MILFORD T. ENGLISH, *2 Wild Rose Dr., LaDue*
LOYD J. ESTEP, *Sparta*
C. FAJEN, *Cole Camp*
CHARLES W. FOLEY, *Hayti*
EDWARD F. FORD, *3120 Maybelle Dr., Normandy*
ROBERT H. FROST, *Plattsburg*
J. BEN GARRETT, *DeSoto*
THOMAS D. GRAHAM, *1000 Moreau Dr.,
    Jefferson City*

JOHN W. GREEN, 1715 *Belle Glade, St. Louis*
JOHN GRIFFIN, 5809 *Page Blvd., St. Louis*
T. O. HAM, *Wellsville*
C. D. HAMILTON, *New London*
LEE H. HAMLIN, 5832 *Central, Kansas City*
ROY HAMLIN, *Hannibal*
MRS. HELEN G. HARDY, *Belle*
JOHN C. HARLIN, *Gainesville*
EVERETT HARRIS, *R.F.D. 2, Milan*
WARREN HEARNES, *East Prairie*
J. C. HEIFNER, *Farmington*
I. W. HENSON, *Mill Spring*
H. F. HOLLAND, *Sheridan*
RAYMOND B. HOPFINGER, 10526 *Natural Bridge, St. Louis*
CHAS. T. HOY, *Parkville*
NOEL G. HUGHES, *Greenfield*
RICHARD H. ICHORD, *Houston*
CHARLES B. JAMES, *Clarkton*
VIRGIL RAY JOHNSTON, *Altamont*
A. CLIFFORD JONES, 7603 *Maryland, Clayton*
EMMETT L. JONES, *Hartville*
DEVERE JOSLIN, 602 *State St., Rolla*
KELSO JOURNEY, *Clinton*
ELROY C. KEHR, *Marthasville*
HARRY KELLER, 1301 *E. Armour, Kansas City*
JOHN E. KIMBER, *Brookfield*
ROGER E. KIRCHNER, *Syracuse*
FRANK KOSTRON, 1915A *Congress St., St. Louis*
J. K. KRAMER, *Linn*
JOHN M. LAVIN, 4158 *Shreve Ave., St. Louis*
ADOLPHUS J. LEGAN, *Half Way*
STEPHEN LINCOLN, *Cainsville*
CECIL LONG, *Monett*
FRED R. MCMAHON, *Fairfax*
WESLEY MCMURRY, *Rutledge*
J. RILEY MCVEY, *Aurora*
A. C. MAGILL, *Cape Girardeau*
JOSEPH W. MARTINO, 2162 *Allen Ave., St. Louis*
FRANK C. MAZZUCA, 712 *E. Missouri Ave., Kansas City*
BEN MEEKS, *Thayer*
F. L. MICKELSON, *Freeman*
CLYSTON MILLER, *R.F.D. 1, Doniphan*
J. B. MOORE, *Hamilton*
SAMUEL B. MURPHY, 300 *Gill Ave., Kirkwood*
WM. C. MYERS, JR., *Webb City*
J. MCKINLEY NEAL, 2816 *Benton Blvd., Kansas City*
DONALD E. NORRIS, *Butler*
WM. HARRISON NORTON, 610 *E. Forty-fifth, North Kansas City*
FRANCIS M. O'BRIEN, 4085 *Alma Ave., St. Louis*
ALF H. OETTING, *R.F.D. 1, St. Charles*
JOHN P. O'REILLY, 4411A *Fair Ave., St. Louis*
MILT OVERSTREET, *Smithton*
G. STAFFORD OWEN, *Maysville*
A. T. PARRISH, 2633 *N. Grant, Springfield*
WALLACE M. PEARSON, *Kirksville*
T. A. PENMAN, *Portageville*
W. GUY PERKINS, *Princeton*
ANTHONY D. PICKRELL, 5415 *E. Twenty-seventh Terr., Kansas City*
EUGENE POE, *Downing*
MRS. JOHN C. POPE, *Marshfield*
EARL POWELL, 612 *Sixth St., Boonville*
CHARLES H. PULIS, *Mexico*
HARRY C. RAIFFIE, 720 *Eastgate Ave., St. Louis*
BERNARD RICHARDS, *Oregon*

BEN C. RIDDER, *Bay*
F. E. ROBINSON, *Edina*
JOHN SAMPLE, *Mineral Point*
JOHN SARTORIUS, 5124 *Kingwood Dr., St. Louis*
JERRY SCHELLHORN, 2610 *Penn St., St. Joseph*
CHAS H. SCHINDLER, *Cosby*
RALPH SHEPARD, 3817 *E. Sixty-seventh Terr., Kansas City*
WILLIAM R. SHERMAN, *Macon*
FRANK X. SIEBERT, 183 *N. Main, Ste. Genevieve*
BERNARD SIMCOE, *Fulton*
G. H. SIMMONS, *Buffalo*
CHARLES H. SLOAN, *Richmond*
HARRY W. SMITH, *Sweet Springs*
ROBERT C. SMITH, JR., *Columbia*
FLOYD L. SNYDER, SR., 521 *S. Noland Rd., Independence*
CLARA AIKEN SPEER, 5001 *State Line, Kansas City*
SHANDY STEWART, *Lowry City*
CHRISTIAN F. STIPP, *Carrollton*
B. H. STONE, *R.F.D. 3, Fredericktown*
GORDON S. SUMMERS, *Bourbon*
LEE C. SUTTON, *Paris*
JOSEPH M. TANNER, 1001 *E. Eleventh, Kansas City*
JOE TAYLOR, 120 *W. Spring, Neosho*
JACK C. TERRY, 3309 *Ash, Independence*
JAMES P. TROUPE, SR., 932A *N. Twenty-third St., St. Louis*
I. E. TULLOCH, *Maryville*
WILLIAM M. TURPIN, *Bowling Green*
S. E. TWOMEY, *Ironton*
LEROY TYUS, 3502 *Franklin Ave., St. Louis*
ORLIE F. UNDERWOOD, 7614 *Sutherland, Shrewsbury*
ROBERT M. UXA, 1104 *S. Eighteenth St., St. Louis*
J. S. WALLACE, *Sikeston*
EUGENE P. WALSH, 8820 *Riverview Blvd., St. Louis*
JENNIE WALSH, 4374 *Laclede Ave., St. Louis*
THOMAS A. WALSH, 2735A *N. Spring Ave., St. Louis*
CARL T. WEBBER, *Union*
CLYDE W. WHALEY, *Sedgewickville*
RALPH WIGFIELD, *R.F.D. 4, Chillicothe*
JOHN F. WINCHESTER, *Bernie*
J. L. WRIGHT, *Wheatland*
MARPLE S. WYCKOFF, *Unionville*
GEORGE D. YOUNG, *R.F.D., Rocheport*
ROBERT E. YOUNG, 208 *W. Macon, Carthage*
CHAIM HERMAN ZIMBALIST, 7348 *Hawthorne Place, University City*

MONTANA*

Senate

Republicans 33   Democrats 23

JOHN C. ALLEY, *Jefferson*
H. H. ANDERSON, *Lincoln*
LEROY H. ANDERSON, *Pondera*
JESS L. ANGSTMAN, *Hill*
O. P. BALGORD, *Golden Valley*
CHARLES A. BOVEY, *Cascade*
J. S. BRENNER, *Beaverhead*
CLYDE BREWER, *Musselshell*
BEN BROWNFIELD, *Carter*
KENNETH COLE, *Petroleum*
ROBERT S. COTTON, *Valley*
ANDREW DAHL, *Sheridan*

*Counties only are shown.

H. H. Dokken, *Gallatin*
Walter A. Donahoe, *Meagher*
Robert G. Dwyer, *Silver Bow*
Lester C. Goodwin, *Broadwater*
Charles W. Grandey, *Prairie*
William A. Groff, *Ravalli*
R. C. Harken, *Rosebud*
Charles M. Hatch, *Custer*
Rex Hibbs, *Yellowstone*
J. M. Hofland, *McCone*
David F. James, *Liberty*
Charles J. Jellison, *Flathead*
Webster Keller, *Stillwater*
C. E. LaCombe, *Mineral*
Glenn H. Larson, *Sanders*
Carl Lindquist, *Daniels*
George N. McCabe, *Glacier*
A. Ronald McDonnell, *Sweetgrass*
Gordon McGowan, *Chouteau*
George S. McKenna, *Judith Basin*
E. F. McQuitty, *Wheatland*
William R. Mackay, *Carbon*
Charles H. Mahoney, *Garfield*
D. M. Manning, *Treasure*
Earl P. Moritz, *Fergus*
H. A. Murphy, *Granite*
Oscar Nesvig, *Wibaux*
Donald Nutter, *Richland*
Fred H. Padbury, *Lewis and Clark*
Paul R. Rice, *Teton*
R. L. Robins, *Dawson*
Fred L. Robinson, *Phillips*
Thomas A. Ross, *Blaine*
Walter G. Sagunsky, *Madison*
Charles L. Scofield, *Powder River*
W. B. Spear, *Big Horn*
B. R. Taylor, *Roosevelt*
Don F. Valiton, *Powell*
Lloyd I. Wallace, *Lake*
Edward A. Wenger, *Deer Lodge*
Karl Wenz, *Fallon*
George W. Wilson, *Toole*
Donovan Worden, *Missoula*
Paul Working, *Park*

House

Democrats 49   Republicans 45

Archie Allen, *Park*
George D. Anderson, *Cascade*
Jerome Anderson, *Yellowstone*
Ory J. Armstrong, *Flathead*
Lloyd Barnard, *Valley*
Fred E. Barrett, *Liberty*
Mrs. Augusta Baumgartner, *Lake*
Robert A. Baxter, *Wheatland*
Martin J. Beck, *McCone*
C. C. Bentz, *Carter*
Clarence P. Bick, *Lake*
Ralph C. Bricker, *Cascade*
Fred O. Broeder, *Flathead*
Charles Cerovski, *Fergus*
Dean Chaffin, *Gallatin*
Earl E. Clark, *Musselshell*
Homer J. Clowes, *Valley*
Ralph Conrad, *Lewis and Clark*
Charles L. Crist, *Yellowstone*
Hugh Cummings, *Granite*

John J. Cunningham, *Silver Bow*
M. K. Daniels, *Powell*
Mervin J. Dempsey, *Silver Bow*
Robert A. Durkee, *Hill*
John Emmons, *Deer Lodge*
James R. Felt, *Yellowstone*
J. W. Fry, *Yellowstone*
Frank F. Fulton, *Fallon*
R. H. Gebhardt, *Yellowstone*
Sumner Gerard, *Madison*
M. N. Gershmel, *Petroleum*
George E. Gleed, *Beaverhead*
J. P. Goan, *Yellowstone*
Allen Goodgame, *Lincoln*
Roy A. Grant, *Custer*
Leo C. Graybill, *Cascade*
Ole S. Gunderson, *Cascade*
Arthur S. Hagenston, *Dawson*
Clifford E. Haines, *Flathead*
H. H. Haines, *Prairie*
Tom Haines, *Missoula*
J. Homer Hancock, *Yellowstone*
Clyde L. Hawks, *Big Horn*
H. H. Hess, *Hill*
George B. Holecek, *Carbon*
Ronald W. Holtz, *Cascade*
Patrick F. Hooks, Jr., *Broadwater*
George T. Howard, *Missoula*
Art N. Jensen, *Mineral*
Rudy F. Juedeman, *Toole*
Ray Lee, *Silver Bow*
J. H. Leuthold, *Stillwater*
Mike Loughran, *Silver Bow*
Wayne McAndrews, *Deer Lodge*
John J. MacDonald, *Garfield*
Archie L. McInnis, *Judith Basin*
W. Gordon McOmber, *Teton*
Eugene H. Mahoney, *Sanders*
Thomas A. Mangian, *Missoula*
Lloyd J. Michels, *Sheridan*
Carl P. Minette, *Glacier*
James A. Mountain, *Silver Bow*
Sivert O. Mysse, Jr., *Rosebud*
W. J. Nelson, *Golden Valley*
Ted Nelstead, *Custer*
Norris Nichols, *Ravalli*
Richard Nixon, *Blaine*
Fritz Norby, *Cascade*
Casper N. Nybo, *Missoula*
C. C. Parker, *Pondera*
Clem Parker, *Wibaux*
R. J. Phillips, *Fergus*
Gene A. Picotte, *Lewis and Clark*
John H. Pierce, *Yellowstone*
Lisle D. Powell, *Powder River*
R. P. Purdy, *Gallatin*
Frank D. Reardon, *Silver Bow*
Mrs. Dallas J. Reed, *Missoula*
Leonard D. Regan, *Cascade*
Arnold Rieder, *Jefferson*
Paul Ringling, *Meagher*
Walter L. Sales, *Gallatin*
Floyd L. Sax, *Richland*
Lee W. Schumacher, *Phillips*
George Siderius, *Flathead*
O. A. Sippel, *Sweet Grass*
J. Miller Smith, *Lewis and Clark*
Chris S. Tange, *Roosevelt*

NEIL TAYLOR, *Daniels*
TOM E. TOBIN, *Silver Bow*
CLARENCE WALTON, *Park*
FRED WETZSTOEN, *Ravalli*
ARCHIE WILSON, *Treasure*
JAMES WOOD, JR., *Chouteau*

NEBRASKA
Unicameral

Members 43*

JOHN ADAMS, SR., 2622 *N. Twenty-fourth St., Omaha*
THOMAS H. ADAMS, 2600 *R St., Lincoln*
LESTER ANDERSON, *Aurora*
JOHN AUFENKAMP, *Julian*
LEROY BAHENSKY, *Palmer*
JOHN E. BEAVER, *Beemer*
MERVIN V. BEDFORD, 210 *S. Eighth St., Geneva*
J. MONROE BIXLER, *Harrison*
HAL BRIDENBAUGH, *Dakota City*
ROBERT C. BROWER, *Fullerton*
DWIGHT W. BURNEY, *Hartington*
D. J. COLE, *Merriman*
GLENN CRAMER, 616 *S. Fourth St., Albion*
H. K. DIERS, *Gresham*
A. A. FENSKE, *Sunol*
KATHLEEN A. FOOTE, *R.F.D.* 1, *Axtell*
GEORGE HOFFMEISTER, *Imperial*
ERNEST HUBKA, 514 *N. Twelfth St., Beatrice*
SAM KLAVER, 211 *Patterson Bldg., Omaha*
OTTO KOTOUC, SR., *Humboldt*
JOHN J. LARKIN, JR., 2913 *Castelar, Omaha*
EARL J. LEE, 1617 *N. Colson Ave., Fremont*
OTTO H. LIEBERS, *R.F.D.* 1, *Lincoln*
DONALD F. MCGINLEY, 901 *W. Third St., Ogallala*
WILLIAM MCHENRY, *Nelson*
JOSEPH MARTIN, 2520 *W. Anna, Grand Island*
WILLIAM A. METZGER, *Cedar Creek*
AMOS MORRISON, *R.F.D.* 1, *Mitchell*
WILLIAM MOULTON, 3340 *N. Fifty-seventh St., Omaha*
FRANK NELSON, *O'Neill*
NORMAN A. OTTO, 2920 *Avenue E, Kearney*
ROBERT R. PERRY, 4040 *Calvert, Lincoln*
O. H. PERSON, *Wahoo*
K. W. PETERSON, *Sargent*
HARRY PIZER, 217 *E. Fifth St., North Platte*
WILLIAM PURDY, *R.F.D.* 2, *Norfolk*
ARNOLD RUHNKE, *Plymouth*
L. M. SHULTZ, *Rogers*
ARTHUR W. SWANSON, 1024 *East Ave., Holdrege*
GEORGE D. SYAS, 5312 *Fontenelle Blvd., Omaha*
DON THOMPSON, *R.F.D.* 3, *McCook*
CHARLES F. TVRDIK, 5236 *S. Nineteenth St., Omaha*
KARL E. VOGEL, 3724 *Lincoln Blvd., Omaha*

NEVADA
Senate

Republicans 12   Democrats 4

RICHARD M. BLACK, 631½ *Garrison St., Winnemucca*
B. MAHLON BROWN, 526 *S. Seventh St., Las Vegas*
NEWTON H. CRUMLEY, 731 *A St., Elko*

*Non-partisan election.

W. G. EMMINGER, *Tungsten*
WILLIAM J. FRANK, *Tonopah*
CHARLES D. GALLAGHER, 351 *Clark St., Ely*
KENNETH F. JOHNSON, 220 *N. Nevada St., Carson City*
RALPH W. LATTIN, *Fallon*
RENE W. LEMAIRE, *Battle Mountain*
E. C. LEUTZINGER, *Eureka*
FOREST B. LOVELOCK, 3 *Bret Harte Dr., Reno*
ROY R. ORR, *Pioche*
FARRELL L. SEEVERS, *Hawthorne*
FRED H. SETTELMEYER, *Gardnerville*
JAMES M. SLATTERY, *Virginia City*
WALTER WHITACRE, 103 *Virginia St., Yerington*
(1 vacancy)

Assembly

Democrats 30   Republicans 17

GARY J. ADAMS, 830 *Ryan Lane, Reno*
BRUCE BARNUM, *Yerington*
A. C. BARR, 1121 *Lyons Ave., Ely*
CYRIL O. BASTIAN, *Hiko*
HENRY BERRUM, *Gardnerville*
WILLIAM B. BYRNE, 255 *Water St., Henderson*
HENRY CARLSON, *Goldfield*
CHESTER S. CHRISTENSEN, 974 *Pyramid Way, Sparks*
M. J. CHRISTENSEN, 827 *S. Seventh St., Las Vegas*
DON CRAWFORD, *Vya, Nevada, via Cedarville, California*
HAZEL DENTON, *Caliente*
E. J. DOTSON, 1127 *Barnard St., Las Vegas*
LYLE L. ELLISON, *Winnemucca*
WILLIAM EMBRY, *Mesquite*
MAUDE FRAZIER, 1940 *Ballard Dr., Las Vegas*
JOHN F. GIOMI, *Smith Valley*
TOM GODBEY, 609 *Avenue L, Henderson*
NORMAN HANSEN, *Gabbs*
MANFORD I. HARDESTY, 1325 *Charles Dr., Reno*
GEORGE HARMON, 110 *E. Bonanza Rd., Las Vegas*
CHARLES A. HENDEL, *Box* 1234, *Hawthorne*
L. M. HOSE, 1201 *Mill St., Ely*
JACK J. HUNTER, JR., 237 *Pine St., Elko*
STAN IRWIN, 1900 *Hassett Ave., Las Vegas*
MABEL C. ISBELL, 1235 *Sharon Way, Reno*
THOMAS IVERS, *Lovelock*
OSCAR D. JEPSON, 934 *F St., Sparks*
GLENN JONES, *Tonopah*
THOMAS KEAN, 643 *Joaquin Miller Dr., Reno*
DARWIN LAMBERT, 244 *Fay Ave., Ely*
DONALD M. LEIGHTON, 590 *W. Second St., Winnemucca*
J. F. MCELROY, 683 *First St., Elko*
HUGH D. MCMULLEN, 101 *Court St., Elko*
KEITH L. MOUNT, *Box* 405-2, *Hawthorne*
MICHAEL R. NEVIN, *Virginia City*
ARCHIE POZZI, JR., 1711 *N. Division St., Carson City*
RODNEY J. REYNOLDS, 641 *Donner Dr., Reno*
CLARENCE RUEDY, 312 *Mill St., Reno*
NORMAN SHUEY, *Fallon*
C. B. STARK, SR., *Fallon*
WILLIAM D. SWACKHAMER, *Battle Mountain*
BAPTISTA TOGNONI, *Eureka*
ROBERT O. VAUGHN, *Professional Bldg., Elko*
GEORGE VON TOBEL, 203 *E. Imperial St., Las Vegas*
MAX R. WAINWRIGHT, 220 *Sixteenth St., Ely*

RICHARD L. WATERS, SR., *Carson City*
JAMES E. WOOD, 735 *Balzar Circle, Reno*

NEW HAMPSHIRE

Senate

Republicans 18   Democrats 6

BENJAMIN C. ADAMS, *Floyd Rd., Derry*
J. LABAN AINSWORTH, *R.F.D. 2, Claremont*
MARYE WALSH CARON, 205 *Mast Rd., Manchester*
JAMES C. CLEVELAND, *New London*
J. WESLEY COLBURN, 7 *Ashland St., Nashua*
PAUL H. DANIEL, 139 *Boutwell St., Manchester*
ROBERT ENGLISH, *Hancock*
ERALSEY C. FERGUSON, *Pittsfield*
HARRY H. FOOTE, 387 *Richards Ave., Portsmouth*
OTTO G. KELLER, 26 *Orchard St., Laconia*
LAURIER LAMONTAGNE, 321 *High St., Berlin*
IRENE WEED LANDERS, 282 *Roxbury St., Keene*
J. PAUL LAROCHE, 6 *Jackson St., Rochester*
NORMAN A. MCMEEKIN, *Woodsville*
ARCHIBALD H. MATTHEWS, *New Hampton*
DEAN B. MERRILL, *Hampton*
DANIEL A. O'BRIEN, *Lancaster*
THOMAS B. O'MALLEY, 274 *Bell St., Manchester*
NORMAN A. PACKARD, 2380 *Elm St., Manchester*
LOUIS W. PAQUETTE, 93 *Ash St., Nashua*
RAYMOND K. PERKINS, 105 *School St., Concord*
JOHN R. POWELL, *Sutton*
FREDERICK C. SMALLEY, 62 *Belknap St., Dover*
FRED H. WASHBURN, *Bartlett*

House

Republicans 259   Democrats 134

ROLAND W. ABBOTT, *Derry St., Hudson*
ARTHUR F. ADAMS, *West Lebanon*
MATTI P. AHO, *New Ipswich*
MAURICE A. ALEXANDER, 602 *Granite St., Manchester*
HARRY S. ALLS, *Colebrook*
HOWE ANDERSON, 40 *Ridge Rd., Concord*
GEORGE W. ANGUS, 29 *Sullivan St., Claremont*
ELMER L. ANNIS, *Errol*
JEROLD M. ASHLEY, *West Lebanon*
MRS. MARION H. ATWOOD, *Sanbornton*
GEORGE S. AUGER, 7 *Riddle St., Manchester*
MRS. MARY R. AYER, *Pittsfield*
WINSLOW P. AYERS, 38 *Temple St., Nashua*
ELSIE C. BAILEY, 10 *South St., Newport*
CLAUDE J. BAKER, *West Stewartstown*
LOUIS S. BALLAM, *Walpole*
JOHN J. BALLENTINE, 176 *Pleasant St., Laconia*
FRANK HOWARD BARDOL, *Box 361, Wilton*
ERNEST P. BARKA, 1 *Brook St., Derry*
JESSE A. BARNEY, *Rumney Depot*
EDGAR A. BARON, 25 *Whitten St., Suncook*
ANDREW J. BARRETT, 103 *Raleigh Way, Portsmouth*
GLENN N. BASCOM, *Acworth*
NATHAN T. BATTLES, *East Kingston*
JOHN F. BEAMIS, 182 *Green St., Somersworth*
MRS. MARY E. BEAN, *R.F.D. 1, Contoocook*
AGENOR BELCOURT, 38 *Perham St., Nashua*
KENNETH G. BELL, *Plymouth*
FRANK J. BENNETT, 52 *Washington St., Keene*
MELLEN B. BENSON, *Conway*
ALFRED A. BERGERON, 101 *Dickey St., Manchester*

STANLEY J. BETLEY, 143A *Manchester St., Manchester*
L. WALDO BIGELOW, JR., *Warner*
OSCAR W. BILLINGS, *Westmoreland*
KENNETH M. BISBEE, 19A *Maple St., Derry*
HARRY A. BISHOP, SR., *Gorham*
WILLIAM F. BISSONETT, 51 *Woodland St., Claremon*
EDWARD C. BLACK, *Bennington*
EDMOND G. BLAIR, *Epping*
HARRY BLOOMFIELD, 9 *Walnut St., Claremont*
GEORGE F. BOIRE, 108 *Tolles St., Nashua*
WALTER G. BOISVERT, 34 *School St., Manchester*
ARTHUR A. BOUCHARD, 610 *Burgess St., Berlin*
PAUL E. BOUTHILLIER, 86 *W. Hollis St., Nashua*
JOHN EDWARD BOUVIER, *East Swanzey*
DAVID J. BRADLEY, 34 *Occom Ridge, Hanover*
BASIL BROADHURST, *Salisbury Rd., West Franklin*
CORNELIUS M. BROSNAHAN, 6 *Olive St., Nashua*
ALBERT H. BROWN, *Strafford*
EDWARD E. BROWN, 148 *Gilsum St., Keene*
JOHN F. BROWN, *Marlow*
WILLIAM H. BROWN, *Loudon*
HILDA C. F. BRUNGOT, 1285 *Main St., Berlin*
WILLIAM B. BUCKLEY, *Mont Vernon*
HENRY L. BURBANK, 20 *Webster St., Laconia*
RICHARD L. BURGESS, 1225 *N. River Rd., Manchester*
JAMES M. BURKE, 14 *Sanger St., Franklin*
NELSON C. BURNHAM, *Alstead*
WALTER O. BUSHEY, *Box 486, Groveton*
JOHN H. CALLAHAN, 357 *Central St., Manchester*
JAMES W. CAMPION, 2 *Clement Rd., Hanover*
MICHAEL J. CANNON, 50 *Harrington Ave., Manchester*
EDGAR J. CARIGNAN, *Gonic Rd., Gonic*
CHARLES E. CARLTON, *Marlboro*
LEWIS H. CARPENTER, *Henniker*
ROBERT W. CARR, *Dame Hill Rd., Orford*
GEORGE G. CARTER, *North Hampton*
BEATRICE B. CARY, 271 *Canal St., Manchester*
DENIS F. CASEY, 381 *Belmont St., Manchester*
AARON W. CHADBOURN, JR., *R.F.D. 2, Dover*
STANLEY A. CHAMBERLAIN, 14 *River St., Plymouth*
EDWIN P. CHAMBERLIN, *Woodsville*
EARLE W. CHANDLER, *Bartlett*
RAYMOND E. CHARBONNEAU, *Rich St., Groveton*
PETER P. CHARLAND, 11 *Pleasant St., Franklin*
ARTHUR J. CHARTRAIN, 82 *Harbor Ave., Nashua*
GEORGE L. CHENEY, *Newton*
MARIE A. CHRISTIANSEN, *Riverside Dr., Berlin*
G. CARROLL CILLEY, *R.F.D. 2, Concord*
EDWARD D. CLANCY, 1182 *Hanover St., Manchester*
HARRY E. CLARK, 29 *Fordway, Derry*
FRANK B. CLARKE, *Canaan*
ARNOLD T. CLEMENT, 92 *Winter St., Rochester*
GEORGE F. CLEMENT, *R.F.D. 2, Lisbon*
LEROY E. CODDING, 47 *Russell St., Keene*
CLAYTON F. COLBATH, 19 *Lyndon St., Concord*
FORREST B. COLE, *Meriden Rd., Lebanon*
RITA COLLYER, *Lisbon*
JOSEPH J. COMI, 19 *Albin St., Concord*
WILLIAM H. CONNELL, 7 *Fisher St., Dover*
GEORGE N. CONSTANT, 642 *Silver St., Manchester*
HARVEY H. CONVERSE, *Pittsburg*
GEORGE H. CORBETT, 9 *Monroe St., Concord*
WILLIAM W. COREY, 210 *S. Willow St., Manchester*
CLOVIS CORMIER, *Box 325, Somersworth*
JOHN D. CORNELIUS, *Lancaster*
WILLIAM H. CRAIG, JR., 186 *Villa St., Manchester*

HARLEY A. CRANDALL, 57 *Central Ave., Dover*
ROLAND L. CUMMINGS, 31 *Broad St., Nashua*
JACK B. DANA, *The Weirs*
HARRY J. DANFORTH, 166 *Myrtle St., Manchester*
MRS. ALICE DAVIS, 6 *Kearsarge St., East Concord*
FRED DAVIS, (*Cornish, N.H.*) *R.F.D.* 2, *Windsor, Vermont*
NATHANIEL F. DAVIS, *Contoocook*
DAVID DEANS, JR., 15 *Crosby St., Milford*
EUGENE DELISLE, SR., 662 *Harvard St., Manchester*
MARGARET B. DeLUDE, *North Charlestown*
JOHN P. DEMPSEY, 21 *Chestnut St., Franklin*
J. HECTOR DESJARDINS, 5½ *St. John St., Dover*
ALBERT N. DION, 399 *Kimball St., Manchester*
JOHN B. DIONNE, 126 *Vine St., Nashua*
MARY C. DONDERO, 28 *Parker St., Portsmouth*
MICHAEL S. DONNELLY, 267 *S. Willow St., Manchester*
FRANK J. DOWD, 144 *Washington St., Penacook*
ELMER H. DOWNS, *North Conway*
EDWARD M. DuDEVOIR, *Box* 203, *Hooksett*
JOHN H. DUDLEY, *R.F.D., Exeter*
CHARLES A. DUGAS, 378 *Main St., Nashua*
PETER DUMAIS, 6 *Perry Ave., Nashua*
OLIVER A. DUSSAULT, 825 *Second Ave., Berlin*
MARGARET E. DUSTIN, 36 *Lowell St., Rochester*
ALPHONSE A. DUTILLY, 470 *W. Hollis St., Nashua*
CHESTER F. DUTTON, 61 *Concord St., Peterborough*
MICHAEL J. DWYER, 352 *Pearl St., Manchester*
EDWIN W. EASTMAN, 76 *Court St., Exeter*
SCOTT F. EASTMAN, *R.F.D.* 1, *Goffstown*
JOSEPH F. ECKER, 315 *Lake Ave., Manchester*
EMORY P. ELDREDGE, 54 *Portsmouth Ave., Exeter*
ELMER S. ELLSWORTH, 10 *Sweatt St., Boscawen*
PHILIP J. ESTES, 173 *Portland St., Rochester*
REUBEN J. EVANS, *Milton Mills*
WILLIAM M. FALCONER, 80 *Union St., Milford*
GROVER C. FARWELL, *Brookline*
FRANCIS F. FAULKNER, 168 *Court St., Keene*
MYRON B. FELCH, *Seabrook*
LEVI F. FELKER, 11 *Highland St., Dover*
ROY A. FERGUSON, *Jefferson*
JAMES P. FERRIN, 17 *Rolfe St., Penacook*
MAURICE D. FIRESTONE, 118 *Myrtle St., Claremont*
WILLIAM J. FITZGERALD, 168 *Laurel St., Manchester*
ERNEST J. FLANAGAN, 21 *Orchard St., Dover*
CARL M. FOGG, *Gossville*
JENNIE FONTAINE, 553 *Hillsboro St., Berlin*
JOSEPH P. FORD, *Box* 121, *Wolfeboro*
GUY J. FORTIER, 49 *Mt. Forest St., Berlin*
JOHN O. FORTIN, *Greenville*
GEORGE L. FRAZER, SR., *Monroe*
MARTHA McD. FRIZZELL, *Charlestown*
HELEN C. FUNKHOUSER, 102 *Madbury Rd., Durham*
REBECCA A. GAGNON, 589 *Hutchins St., Berlin*
WILLIBERT GAMACHE, 2083 *Goffs Falls Rd., Manchester*
CLIFFORD E. GAMSBY, *Sunapee*
EDITH B. GARDNER, *R.F.D.* 4, *Laconia*
VAN H. GARDNER, *Littleton*
LORENZO P. GAUTHIER, 22 *Laval St., Manchester*
CHARLES H. GAY, 112 *E. Broadway, Derry*
PAUL B. GAY, *New London*
JOSEPH H. GEISEL, 811 *Maple St., Manchester*
LUCIEN J. GELINAS, 194 *Reed St., Manchester*
CHARLES A. GILBERT, *Wentworth*
ANN J. GOODWIN, *Hollis*
ALFRED P. GRANDMAISON, 25 *Sawyer St., Nashua*

FRED L. GREEN, *Box* 96, *Salmon Falls*
MARGARET A. GRIFFIN, *Auburn*
SAMUEL P. HADLEY, *Hillsborough*
WALTER F. HAIGH, *Salem*
CHARLES P. HALEY, 16 *Sunset Terr., Keene*
A. KENNETH HAMBLETON, *Goffstown*
LEE C. HANCOCK, 26 *White St., Concord*
MYRON B. HART, *Box* 295, *The Weirs*
MARGRETTA M. HAYDEN, *Center Ossipee*
JAMES F. HAYES, 380 *Pearl St., Manchester*
ELIZABETH W. HAYWARD, 25½ *School St., Hanover*
DANIEL J. HEALY, 329 *Laurel St., Manchester*
JEREMIAH B. HEALY, 494 *Chestnut St., Manchester*
RAYMOND F. HENNESSEY, *Smith Well Road, Dover*
ARTHUR F. HENRY, 382 *N. State St., Concord*
MARY ROSAMOND HERRICK, *Deering Rd., Deering*
FORREST W. HODGDON, *R.F.D., Ossipee*
REUBEN N. HODGE, *Center Sandwich*
CHARLES A. HOLDEN, 10 *Occom Ridge, Hanover*
NELLE L. HOLMES, *Amherst*
DENIS HORAN, 415 *E. High St., Manchester*
WALTER A. HORTON, *Lyme*
ARTHUR E. HOWE, 6 *Bailey Ave., Claremont*
ELMER E. HUCKINS, *Plymouth*
HILDA HUNDLEY, 62 *Porpoise Way, Portsmouth*
DOUGLASS E. HUNTER, 20 *Mill Rd., Hampton*
CELIA G. HURLBERT, *Errol*
GEORGE J. HURLEY, 151 *Winter St., Manchester*
FREDERICK H. INGHAM, *Winchester*
EDWARD J. INGRAHAM, 72 *Atkinson St., Portsmouth*
PETER Z. JEAN, 314 *Lake St., Nashua*
RUFUS L. JENNINGS, *Goffstown*
GUY JEWETT, 20 *Pierce St., Concord*
CLARENCE C. JONES, *Francestown*
FRED A. JONES, 5 *Court St., Lebanon*
HAROLD L. JONES, *Fremont*
JAMES J. JOYCE, 1703 *Greenland Rd., Portsmouth*
PETER S. KARAGIANIS, 48 *Holman St., Laconia*
PAUL G. KARKAVELAS, 127 *Portland Ave., Dover*
DOMINICK J. KEAN, 503 *Beech St., Manchester*
JOHN J. KEARNS, 72 *B St., Manchester*
FRED KELLEY, 17 *Jackson St., Littleton*
THEDORE E. KENNEY, 400 *Central St., Franklin*
HOWARD W. KIRK, 271 *Roxbury St., Keene*
ARTHUR A. LABRANCHE, 22 *Elm St., Newmarket*
ALPHONSE LACASSE, 68 *Lafayette St., Rochester*
PAUL M. LAFOND, 487 *Cartier St., Manchester*
STEWART LAMPREY, *Moultonborough*
KENNETH P. LANE, *Swanzey*
FRANKLIN L. LANG, *Troy*
GEORGE A. LANG, 78 *Ray St., Manchester*
J. B. HENRY LANGELIER, 395 *Main St., Nashua*
RAYMOND J. LANGLOIS, 532 *Cilley Rd., Manchester*
AMELIA LAREAU, 383 *Bartlett St., Manchester*
WILFRED J. LARTY, 12 *Beech St., Woodsville*
ROLAND LATOUR, *Hudson*
GEORGE L. LAVOIE, 428 *Cilley Rd., Manchester*
JOHN J. LEARY, 1223 *Islington St., Portsmouth*
CHARLES J. LECLERC, 275 *Somerville St., Manchester*
ORIGENE E. LESMERISES, 575 *Dubuque St., Manchester*
CLARENCE LESSELS, 49 *Warren St., Concord*
EDWARD G. LETOURNEAU, 140 *High St., Somersworth*
ALBERT D. LITTLEHALE, *Bagdad Rd., Durham*
EDWARD F. LOCKE, *New Boston*
GEORGE H. LOVEJOY, *Salisbury*
ARTHUR H. McALLISTER, *Barnstead*

Thomas F. McCaffery, *New Castle*
James E. McCullough, 36 *Woodbury St., Keene*
Charles J. McKee, 94 *South St., Concord*
Frank J. Mafera, *Raymond*
Mrs. Victoria E. Mahoney, *Loudon Rd., Concord*
James L. Mahony, 70 *Hillcroft Rd., Manchester*
Andrew L. Mailloux, *Pelham*
James F. Malley, *Indigo Hill Rd., Somersworth*
Sarkis N. Maloomian, 8 *Emery St., Somersworth*
Edward T. Martel, 96 *Whittemore St., Manchester*
Eda C. Martin, *Littleton*
George C. Mason, *Hill*
Paul B. Maxham, 123 *South St., Concord*
Albert Maynard, 15 *Beech St., Nashua*
C. H. Sayre Merrill, 20 *Pine St., Exeter*
Warren F. Metcalf, 7 *Mill St., Tilton*
Mrs. Julia A. Millar, 79 *Myrtle St., Claremont*
Randolph H. Milligan, *Newbury*
Ruth F. Miner, *Meredith*
T. Casey Moher, *Glenwood Ave., Dover*
Aime H. Morin, 16 *River St., Laconia*
Edward W. Morris, 100 *Bedford St., Manchester*
Edward J. Mros, Sr., *Farmington*
John B. Mulaire, *Box 162, Hooksett*
Theodore F. Munz, 40 *Whidden St., Portsmouth*
Henry S. Murch, Jr., 140 *Summer St., Portsmouth*
George C. Nadeau, 39 *Winter St., Rochester*
Stewart Nelson, 104 *School St., Concord*
Walter R. Nelson, *Goshen*
Guy E. Nickerson, *East Kingston*
Guy W. Nickerson, *Madison*
Thomas F. Nolan, 214 *Laurel St., Manchester*
Eugene F. Nute, *Farmington*
Eleonora C. Nutter, *Epsom*
David O'Shan, 25 *Pine St., Laconia*
Mildred L. Palmer, *Plaistow*
George S. Pappagianis, 60½ *Walnut St., Nashua*
Adrien A. Paradis, 172 *S. Willow St., Manchester*
Draper W. Parmenter, *R.F.D. 1, Derry*
Lise L. Payette, 324 *Hanover St., Portsmouth*
Leo G. Payeur, 89 *Glass St., Suncook*
Frederick C. Pearson, Jr., *Dover Point Rd., Dover*
Bert L. Peaslee, *Reed's Ferry*
Clarence E. Peaslee, *Union*
Joseph B. Perley, *Hardy Hill, Lebanon*
Mrs. Lenna W. Perry, *East Jaffrey*
Karl J. Persson, *Candia*
David E. Peterson, 9 *Hopkins St., Nashua*
James Pettigrew, 1883 *Elm St., Manchester*
Grace M. Phelan, *R.F.D., West Milan*
Victor E. Phelps, *Andover*
Manning H. Philbrick, *Rye*
Laurence M. Pickett, 136 *Island St., Keene*
Edward M. Pierce, *R.F.D. 1, West Lebanon*
Lewis R. Pike, *Fitzwilliam Depot*
Ernest C. Pillsbury, *East Hampstead*
John Pillsbury, 205 *Ash St., Manchester*
Ernest L. Pinkham, *Northwood*
Bowdoin Plumer, *Bristol*
Alfred W. Poore, 17 *Elm St., Goffstown*
Walter J. Post, *Chesterfield*
R. Wilbur Potter, *Milan*
Jeremiah Quirk, 140 *Lincoln Ave., Portsmouth*
Herbert W. Rainie, 9 *Elm St., Concord*
Alice L. Ramsdell, 7 *Columbia Ave., Nashua*
Harry B. Ramsey, *R.F.D. 1, Bristol*
James C. Rathbone, 74 *Court St., Exeter*
Austin H. Reed, 32 *N. Mast St., Goffstown*

Earle H. Remick, *Tamworth*
Mrs. Doris C. Reney, *Grantham*
E. Everett Rhodes, Jr., *Walpole*
Benjamin M. Rice, *Windy Row, Peterborough*
Oscar Rines, *R.F.D. 4, Whitefield*
Kenneth W. Robb, 134 *Myrtle St., Manchester*
Milburn F. Roberts, *North Conway*
William T. Robertson, *R.F.D. 2, Laconia*
Carl H. Robinson, *Antrim*
Frank A. Robinson, (*South Hampton*) *R.F.D. 1, Amesbury, Mass.*
Gladys D. Roe, 35 *Prospect St., Newport*
James P. Rogers, 1105 *N. Main St., Laconia*
Ernest L. Rolfe, 82 *Main St., East Rochester*
Philip K. Ross, *Gorham*
Jesse R. Rowell, *Newport*
Edgar J. Roy, 115 *Madigan St., Berlin*
Arthur J. Russell, 256 *Main St., Berlin*
Frank E. Ryan, 116 *Allds St., Nashua*
Ann Sadler, 28 *Parker St., Portsmouth*
Angeline M. St. Pierre, 3 *Chestnut St., Rochester*
Mrs. Gertrude E. Saltmarsh, 17 *Laurel St., Concord*
Isaac H. Sanborn, *Enfield*
William A. Saunders, 31 *Courtland St., Nashua*
Thomas F. Sawyer, *Woodstock*
W. Douglas Scamman, *Stratham*
Otto Schricker, Sr., 238 *W. Hancock St., Manchester*
F. Albert Sewall, *R.F.D. 1, Newmarket*
George W. Shattuck, *R.F.D., Fremont*
Daniel J. Shea, 248 *N. Main St., Concord*
Frank B. Shea, 58 *Kinsley St., Nashua*
John F. Shea, 324 *Pine St., Manchester*
Frank H. Sheridan, 176 *Madison Ave., Berlin*
Harry E. Sherwin, *Rindge*
Clifton Simms, 124 *Washington St., Claremont*
Arthur L. Simonds, *Lancaster*
Alfred W. Simoneau, 129 *Highland St., Laconia*
Richmond H. Skinner, *Box 322, Alton Bay*
Finlay P. Sleeper, *North Haverhill*
James E. Slowey, 453 *Spruce St., Manchester*
George W. Smith, 186 *Bell St., Manchester*
Joseph F. Smith, *Meredith Center*
Orson G. Smith, *Hindsale*
Emile J. Soucy, 2146 *Elm St., Manchester*
Louis J. Soucy, 363 *Rimmon St., Manchester*
Ned Spaulding, 6 *School St., Hudson*
Carl C. Spofford, *Jaffrey*
Doris M. Spollett, *West Hampstead*
William M, Stearns, 12 *Dover Rd., Durham*
Clifton W. Stevens, *R.F.D. 7, Concord*
Malcolm J. Stevenson, *Bethlehem*
Bert Stinson, *Stratford*
Edward J. Stokes, *Freedom*
Robert E. Stone, 181 *North St., Claremont*
Norma M. Studley, 84 *Wakefield St., Rochester*
Thomas F. Sullivan, 746 *Hall St., Manchester*
Roy V. Swain, *East Barrington*
Dennis F. Sweeney, 13 *Spalding Ave., Nashua*
Geoffrey W. Talbot, *R.F.D. 2, Canaan*
Ada C. Taylor, *Whitefield*
Walter P. Tenney, *Chester*
Roy L. Terrill, *Surry*
Alonzo J. Tessier, 303 *Auburn St., Manchester*
Wilfred G. Thibault, 17 *Orange St., Nashua*
George D. Thibeault, *Box 561, Suncook*
Charles R. Thomas, *Dublin*

ALEXANDER P. THOMPSON, *Winchester*
JAMES H. THURLOW, *Hampton Falls*
ELMER S. TILTON, 193 *Pleasant St., Laconia*
ALTON P. TOBEY, 214 *High St., Hampton*
HARRY S. TOWNSEND, *Lebanon*
ELIZABETH L. TRAVIS, 76 *Park St., Portsmouth*
HECTOR J. TROMBLEY, 3 *Salvail Court, Nashua*
H. THOMAS URIE, *New Hampton*
LEON J. O. VAILLANCOURT, 436 *Amory St., Manchester*
GEORGE WALTER VARRELL, 178 *School St., Lakeport*
JOSEPH D. VAUGHAN, 250 *Pine St., Newport*
WILBUR H. VAUGHN, *R.F.D.* 3, *Concord*
ALBERT A. VOGEL, *R.F.D.* 9, *Loudon*
FRED T. WADLEIGH, 3 *Summer St., Milford*
HUGH F. WALING, 13 *Winchester Ct., Keene*
SHELBY O. WALKER, 270 *S. Main St., Concord*
EDWARD J. WALSH, 294 *Pine St., Manchester*
WILLIAM J. WARDWELL, 111 *Essex Ave., Portsmouth*
THOMAS WATERHOUSE, JR., *Windham*
MRS. MARTHA G. WEBB, 220 *Washington St., Dover*
ALONZO PAGE WEEKS II, *East Wolfeboro*
THORNTON N. WEEKS, SR., *Greenland*
DOROTHY L. WENTWORTH, *Madbury*
KIRKE W. WHEELER, 50 *N. Lincoln St., Keene*
RALPH M. WIGGIN, *R.F.D.* 2, *Box* 171, *Manchester*
HERBERT A. WILLARD, *Temple*
PHILIP S. WILLEY, *Campton*
ANNA M. WILLIS, *Salem*
HOWARD S. WILLIS, *Salem*
FRED G. WILMAN, *Tilton*
DON W. WORKMAN, *Wilmot*
E. HAROLD YOUNG, *Pittsfield*
(6 vacancies)

NEW JERSEY

Senate

Republicans 14   Democrats 7

JOSEPH W. COWGILL, 721 *Market St., Camden*
WAYNE DUMONT, JR., 701 *Hillcrest Blvd., Phillipsburg*
FRANK S. FARLEY, 503 *Schwehm Bldg., Atlantic City*
MALCOLM S. FORBES, *Timberfield, Far Hills*
DONALD C. FOX, 671 *Broad St., Newark*
KENNETH C. HAND, 125 *Broad St., Elizabeth*
HAROLD W. HANNOLD, 15A *Cooper St., Woodbury*
GEORGE B. HARPER, *Layton*
THOMAS J. HILLERY, 195 *N. Main St., Boonton*
WALTER H. JONES, 15 *Main St., Hackensack*
WESLEY L. LANCE, *Main St., Glen Gardner*
JOHN A. LYNCH, 1 *Elm Row, New Brunswick*
ALBERT B. McCAY, 622 *Washington Ave., Palmyra*
W. STEELMAN MATHIS, 229 *Main St., Toms River*
JAMES F. MURRAY, JR., 880 *Bergen Ave., Jersey City*
SIDO L. RIDOLFI, 28 *W. State St., Trenton*
CHARLES W. SANDMAN, JR., 509 *Washington St., Cape May*
W. HOWARD SHARP, 702 *Wood St., Vineland*
FRANK W. SHERSHIN, 99 *First St., Clifton*
RICHARD R. STOUT, 601 *Bangs Ave., Asbury Park*
JOHN WADDINGTON, *R.F.D.* 3, *Salem*

General Assembly

Republicans 40   Democrats 20

CLIFTON T. BARKALOW, 2 *E. Main St., Freehold*
ALFRED N. BEADLESTON, 12 *Broad St., Rm.* 400, *Red Bank*
RAYMOND E. BOWKLEY, *Hoffman's Crossing, R.F.D., Califon*
MAURICE V. BRADY, 47 *Duncan Ave., Jersey City*
IRENE BROWN, % *Y.W.C.A.,* 270 *Fairmont Ave., Jersey City*
MRS. ESTHER B. BUSH, 26 *Clinton Avenue, Montclair*
J. EDWARD CRABIEL, 38 *Highland Dr., Milltown*
CARLYLE W. CRANE, 203 *Park Ave., Plainfield*
DOMINICK A. CUNDARI, 341 *Roseville Avenue, Newark*
JOHN W. DAVIS, *Fort Mott Road, R.F.D. Salem*
PIERCE H. DEAMER, 38 *W. Main St., Bergenfield*
MRS. FLORENCE P. DWYER, 320 *Verona Ave., Elizabeth*
EDMUND FIELD, JR., 247 *Springfield Ave., Hasbrouck Heights*
DONALD J. FITZMAURICE, 41 *Spring Road, Livingston*
BENJAMIN FRANKLIN III, 38 *Park Pl., Morristown*
CHARLES E. GANT, 26 *E. Pine St., Millville*
MILTON W. GLENN, 538 *Guarantee Trust Bldg., Atlantic City*
JOHN J. GOFF, 86 *Eastern Parkway, Newark*
RICHARD L. GRAY, *Broad St. Bank Bldg., Trenton*
C. WILLIAM HAINES, *Masonville*
FREDERICK H. HAUSER, 1000 *Hudson St., Hoboken*
THOMAS J. HUGHES, JR., 33 *E. Forty-third St., Bayonne*
WILLIAM F. HYLAND, 709 *Market St., Camden* 2
JOHN JUNDA, 663 *Main Ave., Passaic*
ROBERT E. KAY, 101 *E. Wildwood Ave., Wildwood*
LEO N. KNOBLAUCH, 880 *Bergen Ave., Jersey City*
CHARLES W. KRAUS, 114 *Larch Ave., Bogota*
BRUNO VAL KRAWCZYK, 3280 *Hudson Blvd., Jersey City*
WILLIAM KURTZ, 172 *John St., South Amboy*
THOMAS LAZZIO, 25 *Doremus St., Paterson*
JOHN W. LEBEDA, 309 *Bloomfield Avenue, Caldwell*
WILLIAM S. MacDONALD, 22 *Tuxedo Parkway, Newark*
REV. J. VANCE McIVER, 153 *Oakwood Avenue, Orange*
MRS. MARIE F. MAEBERT, 420 *Cumberland Rd., South Orange*
EARL A. MARRYATT, 190 *Demarest Ave., Closter*
FRANK E. MELONI, 45 *N. Fifth St., Camden*
ELDEN MILLS, 30 *Court St., Morristown*
HYMEN B. MINTZ, 11 *Commerce St., Newark*
LEO J. MOSCH, 11 *Vermont Ave., Newark*
WILLIAM V. MUSTO, 1000 *Hudson Blvd., Union City*
MRS. EMMA E. NEWTON, 2 *Cedar Pl., Packanack Lake*
WILLIAM E. OZZARD, 27 *N. Bridge St., Somerville*
VINCENT R. PANARO, 126 *North Montgomery Street, Trenton*
MRS. RUBY V. PERFETTE, 243 *N. Park St., East Orange*
DOUGLAS RUTHERFURD, *Vernon*
ROBERT F. SABELLO, 80 *Seventieth Street, Guttenberg*
PAUL M. SALSBURG, 641 *Guarantee Trust Bldg., Atlantic City*
MRS. LETTIE E. SAVAGE, 215 *Forest Ave., Lakewood*
CARMINE SAVINO, 251 *Ridge Rd., Lyndhurst*
THOMAS M. SHERMAN, 10 *Winsor Place, Bloomfield*

MILTON L. SILVER, 1 *S. Broad St.*, *Woodbury*
ARNOLD M. SMITH, 5 *Colt St.*, *Paterson*
DAVID I. STEPACOFF, 280 *Hobart St.*, *Perth Amboy*
RAYMOND J. STEWART, 810 *Broad St. Bank Bldg.*, *Trenton*
THOMAS C. SWICK, 83 *South Main Street*, *Perth Amboy*
G. CLIFFORD THOMAS, 47 *Elm St.*, *Elizabeth*
JOSEPH M. THURING, 921 *Bergen Avenue*, *Jersey City*
WILLIAM R. VANDERBILT, 810 *Broad St.*, *Newark*
ARTHUR R. VERVAET, *McCoy Rd.*, *Oakland*
FRANCIS J. WERNER, 822 *N. Thirtieth St.*, *Camden*

NEW MEXICO

Senate

Democrats 23　　Republicans 9

HAROLD AGNEW, *Los Alamos*
STEPHEN L. BROCK, *Roy*
M. P. CARR, 718 *Avenue C, Fort Sumner*
W. P. CATER, *Cerro*
R. A. CHAVEZ, 585 *Pecos Ave.*, *Santa Rosa*
FULTON J. COX, *Las Palomas*
I. N. CURTIS, *Box 97, Quemado*
JOHN P. CUSACK, *Box 942, Roswell*
F. J. DANGLADE, *Box 675, Lovington*
HORACIO DE VARGAS, *Box 565, Espanola*
HENRY L. EAGER, *Box 206, Tucumcari*
REGINALDO ESPINOSA, *Espanola*
SIDNEY S. GOTTLIEB, *Cubero*
EARL HARTLEY, 116 *E. Fourth, Clovis*
CALVIN HORN, 808 *Laurel Circle SE, Albuquerque*
T. C. JARAMILLO, *La Joya*
T. E. LUSK, 1402 *Bryan Circle, Carlsbad*
G. E. MELODY, *Box 57, Las Vegas*
TOM O. MONTOYA, *Pena Blanca*
J. G. MOORE, *Box 512, Carrizozo*
MURRAY E. MORGAN, *Box 566, Alamogordo*
R. C. MORGAN, *Portales*
JOHN MORROW, *Folsom*
CHARLES C. MUMMA, *Farmington*
ROBERT S. PALMER, *Deming*
EARL PARKER, *Box 497, Estancia*
H. VEARLE PAYNE, *Lordsburg*
JESSE U. RICHARDSON, 1001 *N. Armijo, Las Cruces*
CHARLES C. ROYALL, JR., *Box 1195, Silver City*
NAPOLEON F. SANCHEZ, *Mora*
W. C. WHEATLEY, *Clayton*
GUIDO ZECCA, *Box 909, Gallup*

House

Democrats 52　　Republicans 3

LEVI ALCON, *La Cueva*
ALBERT AMADOR, JR., *Espanola*
J. GREGORIO ARAGON, *Box 537, Santa Rosa*
FORREST S. ATCHLEY, *Mt. Dora*
HERBERT A. BAYS, 911 *Penn., Alamogordo*
EDWARD C. CABOT, *Box 436, Taos*
JACK M. CAMPBELL, 1003 *W. Mathews, Roswell*
ANDERSON CARTER, *Box 508, Portales*
MATIAS L. CHACON, *Box 51, Espanola*
ANDREW CHITWOOD, 1408 *Wallace, Clovis*
FRED COLE, *Artesia*
J. A. CONWAY, *Box 398, Reserve*
GERALD CORNELIUS, 1505 *Las Lomas Rd. NE, Albuquerque*

LEMUEL E. COSTELLO, 305 *S. Second, Gallup*
DENNIS COWPER, 502 *Becker Ave., Belen*
W. O. CULBERTSON, JR., *Box 598, Las Vegas*
FLOYD F. DARROW, *Box 871, Albuquerque*
MACK EASLEY, *Box 2587, Hobbs*
FRED W. FOSTER, *Box 769, Silver City*
HENRY GALLEGOS, *Grants*
RALPH GALLEGOS, *Box 904, Santa Fe*
J. W. GARCIA, *Box 2114, Santa Fe*
FELIPE A. GONZALES, 219 *Delgado, Santa Fe*
LAWRENCE GOODELL, 102 *S. Missouri, Roswell*
WILLIAM GRIJALVA, JR., 321 *E. Jefferson, Gallup*
DONALD D. HALLAM, 118 *N. Turner, Hobbs*
CHARLES F. HARRIS, 2121 *Broadway NE, Albuquerque*
BASHEER HINDI, *Duran*
RAY HUGHES, 210 *S. Silver, Deming*
NOBLE M. IRISH, 1035 *Fifth, Las Vegas*
JACK E. KELLY, 122 *Wellesley Dr. NE, Albuquerque*
MARY LOU LYON, 2271B *Forty-eighth St., Los Alamos*
C. L. McCLASKEY, 709 *Sunset Rd. SW, Albuquerque*
VIRGIL O. McCOLLUM, *Box 271, Carlsbad*
BILLIE MARTIN, *Raton*
DAVE MARTIN, *Bloomfield*
ROBERT C. MARTIN, *Red Rock*
DONALD A. MARTINEZ, *Las Vegas*
ERNEST MIERA, *Bernalillo*
AMBROCIO B. MONTOYA, *Rainsville*
THOMAS G. MORRIS, *Box 336, Tucumcari*
FINDLEY H. MORROW, 236 *Madison NE, Albuquerque*
JESS R. NELSON, 441 *Maine St., Truth or Consequences*
MORGAN NELSON, *R.F.D. 2, Box 140, Roswell*
S. M. ORTIZ, *Carrizozo*
LUIS S. PAGE, *Santa Rosa*
FRANK PRICHARD, 317 *S. Miranda, Las Cruces*
MANFORD W. RAINWATER, 116 *W. Aber, Tucumcari*
J. T. SKINNER, *Roy*
M. S. SMITH, *Box 624, Clovis*
EARL STULL, JR., 525 *N. Main, Las Cruces*
MELVIN E. TAYS, *Box 549, Alamogordo*
LUIS A. TRUJILLO, *Taos*
LEVI L. TURNER, *Raton*
JOHN J. WOLF, *Socorro*

NEW YORK

Senate

Republicans 34　　Democrats 24

DANIEL G. ALBERT, 85 *Stratmore Rd., Rockville Centre*
WARREN M. ANDERSON, 724 *Security Mutual Bldg., Binghamton*
STANLEY J. BAUER, 874 *Fillmore Ave., Buffalo* 12
EARL W. BRYDGES, 426 *Third St., Niagara Falls*
THOMAS F. CAMPBELL, 1503 *Union St., Schenectady*
WILLIAM F. CONDON, 25 *Holls Terrace N., Yonkers* 3
JOHN H. COOKE, 7297 *Broadway, Alden*
WALTER E. COOKE, 319 *St. Johns Pl., Brooklyn*
JAMES J. CRISONA, 137 *Beach 144th St., Neponsit*
THOMAS J. CUITE, 44 *Court St., Brooklyn*
EDWARD V. CURRY, 38 *Seventh St., Staten Island*
PETER J. DALESSANDRO, 804 *Twenty-fifth St., Watervliet*
THOMAS C. DESMOND, 94 *Broadway, Newburgh*
AUSTIN W. ERWIN, 70 *Main St., Geneseo*
JOHN F. FUREY, 32 *Court St., Brooklyn* 2
JACOB H. GILBERT, 280 *Madison Ave., New York* 16

HARRY GITTLESON, 201 *Roebling St., Brooklyn*
SAMUEL L. GREENBERG, 149 *Broadway, New York*
ERNEST J. HATFIELD, 46 *Cannon St., Poughkeepsie*
NATHANIEL T. HELMAN, 292 *Madison Ave., New York* 17
S. WENTWORTH HORTON, *Greenport*
JOHN H. HUGHES, 821 *Onondaga Co. Savings Bank Bldg., Syracuse*
WILLIAM S. HULTS, JR., 921 *Port Washington Blvd., Port Washington*
HARRY KRAF, 711 *Walton Ave., Bronx*
FRANCIS J. McCAFFREY, 369 *E. 149th St., Bronx* 55
FRANK S. McCULLOUGH, 11 *Third St., Rye*
ROBERT C. McEWEN, 314 *Ford St., Ogdensburg*
WALTER G. McGAHAN, 217–59 *Corbett Rd., Bayside*
THOMAS J. MACKELL, 6140 *Saunders St., Rego Park*
FRANCIS J. MAHONEY, 29 *Broadway, New York* 6
WALTER J. MAHONEY, 607 *Genesee Bldg., Buffalo* 2
GEORGE T. MANNING, 409 *Powers Bldg., Rochester* 14
JOSEPH R. MARROW, 25 *Broad St., New York* 4
GEORGE R. METCALF, 34 *Dill St., Auburn*
WHEELER MILMOE, 318 *S. Peterboro St., Canastota*
MAC NEIL MITCHELL, 36 *W. Forty-fourth St., New York*
FRED G. MORITT, 280 *Broadway, New York* 7
HARRY K. MORTON, 198 *Main St., Hornell*
HENRY NEDDO, 9 *Lafayette St., Whitehall*
FRANK D. O'CONNOR, 42-27 *Elbertson St., Elmhurst*
DUTTON S. PETERSON, *Odessa*
GEORGE H. PIERCE, 305 *Masonic Temple, Olean*
FRANK J. PINO, 1865 *W. Third St., Brooklyn*
FRED J. RATH, 105 *Oriskany St. W., Utica*
WILLIAM ROSENBLATT, 185 *Montague St., Brooklyn*
ALFRED E. SANTANGELO, 280 *Broadway, New York*
GILBERT T. SEELYE, *Burnt Hills, New York*
SEARLES G. SHULTZ, 9 *E. Genesee St., Skaneateles*
HERBERT I. SORIN, 16 *Court St., Brooklyn*
EDWARD J. SPENO, 933 *Surrey Dr., East Meadow*
JAMES G. SWEENEY, 82-44 *Sixty-first Dr., Middle Village*
FRANK E. VAN LARE, 96 *Roxborough Rd., Rochester* 19
WALTER VAN WIGGEREN, 2 *Seld Block, Herkimer*
JAMES L. WATSON, 670 *Riverside Dr., New York*
ARTHUR H. WICKS, 41 *Pearl St., Kingston*
PLINY W. WILLIAMSON, 115 *Broadway, New York* 6
HENRY A. WISE, 204 *Watertown Natl. Bank Bldg., Watertown*
JOSEPH ZARETSKI, 60 *E. Forty-second St., New York* 17

Assembly

Republicans 90 Democrats 60

MELVILLE E. ABRAMS, 1309 *W. Farms Rd., Bronx*
FRANCIS J. ALDER, 215 *N. Washington St., Rome*
EDWARD J. AMANN, JR., 42 *Richmond Terr., Staten Island*
SIDNEY H. ASCH, *New York Law School,* 244 *William St., New York*
RAY STEPHENS ASHBERY, 40 *Whigg St., Trumansburg*
BERNARD AUSTIN, 401 *Broadway, New York* 13
BERTRAM L. BAKER, 399 *Jefferson Ave., Brooklyn* 21
EUGENE F. BANNIGAN, 141 *Broadway, New York*

ANTHONY BARBIERO, *Valley Stream Post Office Elmont*
ELISHA T. BARRETT, 252 *E. Main St., Bay Shore, Long Island*
SAMUEL I. BERMAN, 751 *St. Marks Ave., Brooklyn*
JERRY W. BLACK, *R.F.D.* 2, *Trumansburg*
VERNON W. BLODGETT, *Rushville*
WILLIAM E. BRADY, 97 *Mansion St., Coxsackie*
WILLIAM BRENNAN, 82-09 *Ankener Ave., Elmhurst*
JOHN A. BRITTING, *Farmingdale*
JOHN R. BROOK, 15 *Broad St., New York* 5
THOMAS H. BROWN, 349 *Marshland Ct., Troy*
BESSIE BUCHANAN, 555 *Edgecombe Ave., New York*
JOHN J. BURNS, *Nassau Utilities Fuel Corp., Roslyn*
WILLIAM J. BUTLER, 65 *Rose St., Buffalo*
FRANK J. CAFFERY, 98 *Milford Ave., Buffalo*
WILLIAM S. CALLI, 502 *Bleeker St., Utica* 12
DONALD A. CAMPBELL, 21 *E. Main St., Amsterdam*
JOSEPH F. CARLINO, 52 *E. Park Ave., Long Beach*
PHILIP R. CHASE, *Hunt Lane, Fayetteville*
DANIEL L. CLARKE, 120-10 *172nd St., Jamaica*
FRANK COMPOSTO, 215 *Montague St., Brooklyn* 1
EDWIN CORNING, 10 *S. Pearl St., Albany*
JOSEPH R. CORSO, 66 *Court St., Brooklyn* 2
HENRY D. COVILLE, *Central Square*
ERNEST CURTO, 300–2 *Gluck Bldg., Niagara Falls*
CHARLES A. CUSICK, *Weedsport*
GEORGE F. DANNEBROCK, 58 *Woeppel St., Buffalo* 11
BENJAMIN H. DEMO, *Croghan*
LOUIS DE SALVIO, 266 *Bowery, New York* 12
DANIEL S. DICKINSON, JR., *Whitney Point*
JOHN DiLEONARDO, 53-31 *194th St., Flushing*
D. CLINTON DOMINICK III, 345 *Grand St., Newburgh*
ARCHIBALD DOUGLAS, JR., 120 *Broadway, c/o Pershing & Co., New York*
WILLARD C. DRUMM, *Niverville*
BERNARD DUBIN, 77-34 *113th St., Forest Hills*
THOMAS A. DUFFY, 35-09 *Broadway, Long Island City* 6
MATTHEW R. DWYER, 1504 *Metropolitan Ave., Bronx*
CHARLES ECKSTEIN, 6033 *Palmetto St., Ridgewood*
FRED W. EGGERT, JR., 650 *E. 235th St., Bronx* 66
DAVID ENDERS, *Central Bridge*
LEONARD FARBSTEIN, 276 *Fifth Ave., New York*
JOHN H. FARRELL, 342 *W. Twenty-fourth St., New York*
PALMER D. FARRINGTON, 2 *Herrick Dr., Lawrence, Long Island*
JAMES A. FITZPATRICK, 30 *Clinton St., Plattsburg*
LOUIS H. FOLMER, 35 *Main St., Cortland*
J. LEWIS FOX, 2117 *Mott Ave., Far Rockaway*
ENZO GASPARI, 1854 *White Plains Rd., Bronx*
WILLIAM G. GIACCIO, 101-22 *Thirty-seventh Ave., Corona* 68
MARY GILLEN, 82 *Pioneer St., Brooklyn* 31
WALTER H. GLADWIN, 744 *E. 175th St., Bronx*
J. EUGENE GODDARD, 438 *Powers Bldg., Rochester* 14
JANET HILL GORDON, 42 *N. Broad St., Norwich*
BERNARD HABER, 8833 *Nineteenth Ave., Brooklyn*
PAUL B. HANKS, JR., 58 *Main St., Brockport*
A. GOULD HATCH, 42 *East Ave., Rochester* 4
STUART F. HAWLEY, 271 *Canada St., Lake George*
OSWALD D. HECK, 434 *State St., Schenectady*
CHARLES D. HENDERSON, 39 *Church St., Hornell*
THEODORE HILL, JR., *Jefferson Valley*
JACOB E. HOLLINGER, *Middleport, New York*

WILLIAM F. HORAN, 8 *Depot Sq., Tuckahoe*
GEORGE L. INGALLS, *Marine Midland Bldg., Binghamton*
GRANT W. JOHNSON, *Ticonderoga*
JOHN E. JOHNSON, *Perry Rd., Leroy*
LOUIS KALISH, 66 *Court St., Brooklyn* 2
WILLIAM KAPELMAN, 122 *E. Forty-second St., New York*
HERMAN KATZ, 15 *William St., New York* 5
DANIEL M. KELLY, 17 *E. Forty-second St., New York*
WILLIAM A. KUMMER, 678 *Academy St., New York*
THOMAS V. LAFAUCI, 31-10 *Broadway, Long Island City* 6
ALFRED A. LAMA, 395 *Pearl St., Brooklyn* 1
LEO A. LAWRENCE, 204 *Prospect St., Herkimer*
EDWARD S. LENTOL, 217 *Havemeyer St., Brooklyn*
J. SIDNEY LEVINE, 261 *Broadway, New York* 7
JOHN B. LIS, 117 *Thomas St., Buffalo*
RICHARD C. LOUNSBERRY, 194 *Front St., Owego*
EDMUND R. LUPTON, 84 *W. Main St., Riverhead*
FRANCIS P. MCCLOSKEY, 175 *Loring Rd., Levittown*
BERNARD C. MCDONNELL, 262 *Alexander Ave., Bronx* 54
JAMES J. MCGUINESS, 100 *State St., Albany* 7
WILLIAM H. MACKENZIE, 4 *Genesee St., Belmont*
FRANK J. MCMULLEN, 150 *Broadway, New York* 38
ROBERT G. MAIN, 55 *W. Main St., Malone*
BRUCE MANLEY, 40 *Curtis Place, Fredonia*
OREST V. MARESCA, 225 *Broadway, New York* 7
FRANCES K. MARLATT, 335 *E. Devonia Ave., Mount Vernon*
EDWYN E. MASON, 118 *Main St., Delhi*
HUNTER MEIGHAN, 100 *Mamaroneck Ave., Mamaroneck*
HYMAN E. MINTZ, 211 *Broadway, Monticello*
MORRIS MOHR, 1345 *Shakespeare Ave., Bronx*
JOHN A. MONTELEONE, 726 *Chauncey St., Brooklyn* 7
JUSTIN C. MORGAN, 1722 *Liberty Bank Bldg., Buffalo* 2
LAWRENCE P. MURPHY, 32 *Court St., Brooklyn* 2
LEO P. NOONAN, *Farmersville Station*
JOHN L. OSTRANDER, *Schuylerville*
WILLIAM F. PASSANNANTE, 2 *W. Forty-sixth St., New York* 36
HAROLD L. PEET, *Main St., Pike*
KENNETH M. PHIPPS, 60 *St. Nicholas Ave., New York*
BERTRAM PODELL, 160 *Broadway, New York* 38
ROBERT WATSON POMEROY, 3 *Cannon St., Poughkeepsie*
FRED W. PRELLER, 15 *Broad St., New York* 5
ROBERT M. QUIGLEY, *Pleasant St., Phelps*
WILLIAM J. REID, *Argyle Rd., Fort Edward*
MICHAEL G. RICE, 12-27 149*th St., Whitestone*
THOMAS F. RILEY, 600 *Reynolds Arcade, Rochester*
FRANK ROSSETTI, 295 *Paladino Ave., New York*
LAWRENCE M. RULISON, 405 *Wilson Bldg., Syracuse* 2
THOMAS J. RUNFOLA, 631 *Niagara St., Buffalo*
LUCIO F. RUSSO, 15 *Beach St., Staten Island* 4
JOHN J. RYAN 280 *Broadway, New York*
WILLIAM SADLER, 3807 *S. Park Ave., (Blasdell) Buffalo*
FRANK S. SAMANSKY, 2120 *Seventy-ninth St., Brooklyn*

JOHN T. SATRIALE, 2499 *Webster Ave., Bronx* 58
ANTHONY P. SAVARESE, JR., 61 *Broadway, New York* 6
CHARLES A. SCHOENECK, JR., 141 *Goodrich Ave., Syracuse* 10
MITCHELL J. SHERWIN, 165 *Broadway, New York* 38
ALLAN P. SILL, 9 *Main St., Massena*
STANLEY STEINGUT, 271 *Madison Ave., New York* 16
WILLIS H. STEPHENS, 70 *Pine St., New York* 5
GENESTA M. STRONG, 76 *Brookside Dr., Plandome*
FRED S. SUTHERGREEN, 29 *Pine St., Ardsley*
PAUL L. TALBOT, *Burlington Flats*
MILDRED F. TAYLOR, *Caroukas Bldg., Lyons*
LUDWIG TELLER, 295 *Madison Ave., New York* 17
JAMES C. THOMAS, 305 *Broadway, New York*
HARRY J. TIFFT, 205 *John St., Horseheads*
FELIPE N. TORRES, 757 *Beck St., Bronx*
ANTHONY J. TRAVIA, 38 *Jerome St., Brooklyn* 7
MAX M. TURSHEN, 66 *Court St., Brooklyn* 2
HAROLD I. TYLER, *Chittenango*
FRANK VACCARO, 6622 *Cameron Ct., Brooklyn*
LAWRENCE W. VAN CLEEF, *Seneca Falls*
WILSON C. VAN DUZER, 44 *North St., Middletown*
JULIUS VOLKER, 952 *Ellicott Sq., Buffalo* 3
LOUIS WALLACH, 81-50 *Langdale St., New Hyde Park*
ROBERT WALMSLEY, *Nyack*
JOSEPH W. WARD, *Caledonia*
ALONZO L. WATERS, 409-13 *Main St., Medina*
JOSEPH J. WEISER, 4 *Peter Cooper Rd., New York*
ORIN S. WILCOX, *Theresa*
KENNETH L. WILSON, *Woodstock*
MALCOLM WILSON, *Bar Bldg., White Plains*
JOSEPH R. YOUNGLOVE, 14 *Hoosac St., Johnstown*

NORTH CAROLINA

Senate

Democrats 47   Republicans 1

N. ELTON AYDLETT, *Elizabeth City*
LUTHER E. BARNHARDT, *Concord*
F. J. BLYTHE, *Charlotte*
MITCHELL BRITT, *Warsaw*
B. C. BROCK, *Mocksville*
DENNIS S. COOK, *Lenoir*
FRANK P. COOKE, *Gastonia*
W. LUNSFORD CREW, *Roanoke Rapids*
CLAUDE CURRIE, *Durham*
J. C. EAGLES, JR., *Wilson*
W. E. GARRISON, *Lincolnton*
A. PILSTON GODWIN, JR., *Gatesville*
CALVIN GRAVES, *Winston-Salem*
WILLS HANCOCK, *Oxford*
C. V. HENKEL, JR., *Turnersburg*
CARL T. HICKS, *Walstonburg*
E. AVERY HIGHTOWER, *Wadesboro*
W. D. JAMES, *Hamlet*
PAUL E. JONES, *Farmville*
R. POSEY JONES, *Mt. Airy*
JOHN KERR, JR., *Warrenton*
O. ARTHUR KIRKMAN, *High Point*
WILLIAM MEDFORD, *Waynesville*
CUTLAR MOORE, *Lumberton*
H. M. MOORE, *Hayesville*
ROBERT MORGAN, *R.F.D.* 1, *Lillington*

ROBERT F. MORGAN, *Shelby*
RAYMOND R. NICHOLSON, *Sylva*
EDWARD L. OWENS, *Plymouth*
WADE H. PASCHAL, *Siler City*
J. HAWLEY POOLE, *West End*
OTIS POOLE, *Candor*
JAMES M. POYNER, *Raleigh*
CHAS. H. REYNOLDS, *Spindale*
D. J. ROSE, *Goldsboro*
L. H. ROSS, *Washington*
RALPH H. SCOTT, *Haw River*
JOHN F. SHUFORD, *Asheville*
T. CLARENCE STONE, *Stoneville*
E. W. SUMMERSILL, *Jacksonville*
J. MAX THOMAS, *Marshville*
RAY H. WALTON, *Southport*
CAMERON S. WEEKS, *Tarboro*
ADAM J. WHITLEY, JR., *R.F.D.* 1, *Smithfield*
ARTHUR W. WILLIAMSON, *Cerro Gordo*
B. H. WINTERS, *Elk Park*
NELSON WOODSON, *Salisbury*
CICERO P. YOW, *Wilmington*
(2 vacancies)

House

Democrats 110   Republicans 9

JOHN L. ANDERSON, *Whitnel*
ALLEN E. ASKEW, *Gatesville*
OSCAR G. BARKER, *Durham*
STEWART BARNES, *Boone*
DAN G. BELL, *Morehead City*
KELLY E. BENNETT, *Bryson City*
MARK W. BENNETT, *Burnsville*
H. CLIFTON BLUE, *Aberdeen*
R. E. BRANTLEY, *Tryon*
DEWEY H. BRIDGER, SR., *Bladenboro*
CHARLES K. BRYANT, SR., *Gastonia*
MARCELLUS BUCHANAN, *Sylva*
JETER C. BURLESON, *Bakersville*
DAVID CLARK, *Lincolnton*
ROY C. COATES, *R.F.D.* 3, *Smithfield*
T. J. COLLIER, *Bayboro*
GEORGE W. CRAIG, *Asheville*
THEODORE F. CUMMINGS, *Hickory*
J. TOLIVER DAVIS, *Forest City*
THOMAS G. DILL, *Rocky Mount*
J. K. DOUGHTON, *Stratford*
A. C. EDWARDS, *Hookerton*
R. BRUCE ETHERIDGE, *Manteo*
R. FRANK EVERETT, *Hamilton*
B. T. FALLS, JR., *Shelby*
CHARLES B. FALLS, JR., *Gastonia*
MRS. THELMA R. FISHER, *Brevard*
F. WAYLAND FLOYD, *Fairmont*
J. WILBERT FORBES, *Shawboro*
JOE FOWLER, JR., *Mt. Airy*
W. ED GAVIN, *Asheboro*
TODD H. GENTRY, *West Jefferson*
F. L. GOBBLE, *Winston-Salem*
ARTHUR GOODMAN, *Charlotte*
HARRY A. GREENE, *Raeford*
CARSON GREGORY, *R.F.D.* 2, *Angier*
PETER W. HAIRSTON, *R.F.D.* 2, *Advance*
JOHN M. HARGETT, *Trenton*
SHEARON HARRIS, *Albemarle*
CLYDE H. HARRISS, SR., *Salisbury*
BYRON HAWORTH, *High Point*

J. W. HAYES, *Hamlet*
G. P. HENDERSON, *Maxton*
ADDISON HEWLETT, JR., *Wilmington*
FRED HOLCOMBE, *R.F.D.* 1, *Mars Hill*
CARROLL R. HOLMES, *Hertford*
G. L. HOUK, *Franklin*
JOSEPH M. HUNT, JR., *Greensboro*
HUGH S. JOHNSON , *Rose Hill*
T. M. JENKINS, *Robbinsville*
E. R. JOHNSON, *Moyock*
WALTER JONES, *Farmville*
JOHN Y. JORDAN, JR., *Asheville*
W. P. KEMP, *Goldsboro*
ROGER C. KISER, *Laurinburg*
ROBERT G. KITTRELL, JR., *Henderson*
W. RAY LACKEY, *Stony Point*
GEORGE A. LONG, *Burlington*
JACK LOVE, *Charlotte*
WM. T. McSHANE, *Hendersonville*
C. GORDON MADDREY, *Ahoskie*
LARRY I. MOORE, JR., *Wilson*
ASHLEY M. MURPHY, *Atkinson*
VIRGIL O'DELL, *Murphy*
I. H. O'HANLON, *R.F.D.* 4, *Fayetteville*
E. M. O'HERRON, JR., *Charlotte*
J. M. PHELPS, *Creswell*
H. CLOYD PHILPOTT, *Lexington*
FRANK S. PITTMAN, *Scotland Neck*
EDWIN S. POU, *Raleigh*
E. K. POWE, *Durham*
RADFORD G. POWELL, *Reidsville*
CLYDE L. PROPST, JR., *Concord*
DWIGHT W. QUINN, *Kannapolis*
GEORGE W. RANDALL, *Mooresville*
GRACE TAYLOR RODENBOUGH, *Walnut Cove*
WM. B. RODMAN, JR., *Washington*
JACK R. ROGERS, *Hayesville*
JERRY M. ROGERS, *Hazelwood*
B. I. SATTERFIELD, *Timberlake*
BASCOM SAWYER, *Elizabeth City*
D. M. SAWYER, *Columbia*
ROBY A. SHOMAKER, *Newland*
CLYDE A. SHREVE, *Summerfield*
J. A. SPEIGHT, *Windsor*
JAMES G. STIKELEATHER, JR., *Asheville*
CLARENCE E. STONE, JR., *Belews Creek*
T. E. STORY, *North Wilkesboro*
KIRBY SULLIVAN, *Southport*
RUSSELL A. SWINDELL, *Swan Quarter*
H. P. TAYLOR, JR., *Wadesboro*
WILLIAM W. TAYLOR, JR., *Warrenton*
C. BLAKE THOMAS, *R.F.D.* 1, *Smithfield*
W. REID THOMPSON, *Pittsboro*
THOMAS TURNER, *Greensboro*
J. W. UMSTEAD, JR., *Chapel Hill*
GEORGE R. UZZELL, *Salisbury*
ITIMOUS T. VALENTINE, JR., *Nashville*
P. R. VANN, *Clinton*
CARL V. VENTERS, *Jacksonville*
LIVINGSTON VERNON, *Morganton*
JAMES B. VOGLER, *Charlotte*
W. W. WALL, *Marion*
J. PAUL WALLACE, *Troy*
JOE A. WATKINS, *Oxford*
JOHN F. WHITE, *Edenton*
THOMAS J. WHITE, *Kinston*
SAM L. WHITEHURST, *R.F.D.* 1, *New Bern*
PHILIP R. WHITLEY, *Wendell*

J. Shelton Wicker, *Sanford*
H. Smith Williams, *Yadkinville*
Ed Wilson, *Blanch*
Henry H. Wilson, Jr., *Monroe*
W. Brantley Womble, *R.F.D. 1, Cary*
William F. Womble, *Winston-Salem*
J. Raynor Woodard, *Conway*
Sam O. Worthington, *Greenville*
Edward F. Yarborough, *Louisburg*
Wilson F. Yarborough, *Fayetteville*
(1 vacancy)

NORTH DAKOTA
Senate

Republicans 45   Democrats 4

H. B. Baeverstad, *Cando*
Philip A. Berube, *Belcourt*
Oliver E. Bilden, *Northwood*
J. B. Bridston, *Grand Forks*
John Davis, *McClusky*
Carroll E. Day, *Grand Forks*
Ralph Dewing, *Columbus*
Glenn R. Dolan, *Kenmare*
Clyde Duffy, *Devils Lake*
Arlie I. Ferry, *Lakota*
Walter Fiedler, *Ryder*
P. L. Foss, *Valley City*
Duncan Fraser, *Omemee*
Amos Freed, *Dickinson*
Selmer Gilbertson, *Nome*
Orville W. Hagen, *Arnegard*
Gail H. Hernett, *Ashley*
Donald C. Holand, *Lisbon*
Arthur C. Johnson, *Fargo*
O. S. Johnson, *Langdon*
William Kamrath, *Leith*
Clyde Kieley, *Grafton*
Gilman A. Klefstad, *Forman*
Harvey B. Knudson, *Mayville*
Reinhart Krenz, *Sherwood*
John Kusler, *Beulah*
John Leier, *Esmond*
Ernest C. Livingston, *Minot*
A. W. Luick, *Fairmount*
R. E. Meidinger, *Jamestown*
Emil T. Nelson, *Edgeley*
Mrs. Harry O'Brien, *Park River*
Axel Olson, *Parshall*
Franklin Page, *Hamilton*
Milton Rue, *Bismarck*
L. A. Sayer, *Cooperstown*
Nick Schmit, Jr., *Wyndmere*
Lavern Schoeder, *Reeder*
C. W. Schrock, *New Rockford*
Iver Solberg, *Ray*
R. M. Striebel, *Fessenden*
S. C. Thomas, *Linton*
Emil Torno, *Towner*
Eugene Tuff, *Barton*
Harry W. Wadeson, *Alice*
Clarence Welander, *Fullerton*
Gust Wog, *Belfield*
Richard E. Wolf, *New Salem*
John Yunker, *Durbin*

House

Republicans 111   Democrats 2

A. J. Anderson, *R.F.D. 2, Fargo*
Kenneth L. Anderson, *New Rockford*
Vernon Anderson, *Dwight*
C. W. Baker, *Minot*
Murray A. Baldwin, *Fargo*
Bert A. Balerud, *Minot*
Ralph Beede, *Elgin*
Andrew Benson, *Barton*
George R. Berntson, *Edinburg*
Lloyd A. Bjella, *Williston*
I. E. Bratcher, *Mott*
Iner Brekke, *Milnor*
Lee Brooks, *Fargo*
Fay Brown, *Bismarck*
Howard Bye, *Gilby*
Albert Christopher, *Pembina*
Jack M. Currie, *Cando*
Walter Dahlund, *Kenmare*
Ed N. Davis, *Monango*
Charles O. Dewey, *Forman*
Lawrence Dick, *Englevale*
Orin L. Dunlop, *Rolla*
F. M. Einarson, *Mountain*
Guy A. Engen, *McVille*
Ivan Erickson, *Crosby*
Jerroll P. Erickson, *Eckman*
Lloyd Esterby, *Appam*
Floyd E. Ettestad, *Balfour*
James O. Fine, *Sheyenne*
K. A. Fitch, *Fargo*
Walter Fleenor, *Wahpeton*
Gottlieb Frank, *Kief*
C. G. Fristad, *Mandan*
Gunnar Gagnum, *Bowbells*
Adam Gefreh, *Linton*
Harry W. George, *Steele*
Eldon L. Goebel, *Lehr*
George Gress, *Dickinson*
Joe Gumeringer, *Esmond*
Ernest R. Hafner, *Beulah*
George Hammer, *Velva*
Brynhild Haugland, *Minot*
Elmer Hegge, *New England*
John T. Heimes, *Valley City*
Harry E. Heller, *Calvin*
T. W. Hoffer, *Streeter*
C. H. Hofstrand, *Leeds*
Albert Homelvig, *Amidon*
R. H. Hornbacher, *Harvey*
Isaac Isakson, *Edinburg*
Walter Kitzmann, *Hannover*
Bencer N. Kjos, *Drake*
Frank E. Kloster, *Sharon*
Milo Knudson, *Edgeley*
Carl Knudson, *Almont*
A. C. Langseth, *Carrington*
Guy F. Larson, *Bismarck*
Arthur E. Laske, *Leonard*
Raymond Lee, *Devils Lake*
Louis Leet, *Webster*
Clifford Lindberg, *Jamestown*
Arthur A. Link, *Alexander*
R. H. Lynch, *Crosby*
Ray J. McLain, *Mohall*
Oliver Magnuson, *Souris*

FREDERICK MAHLMANN, *Fayette*
ALEX MILLER, *Michigan*
J. N. MOLLET, *Powers Lake*
L. C. MUELLER, *Oakes*
HJALMER C. NYGAARD, *Enderlin*
GILLMAN C. OLSON, *Cooperstown*
NELS OVERBO, *Hampden*
GORDON PAULSON, *Harvey*
H. A. PETTERSON, *Lidgerwood*
CLARENCE POLING, *Grenora*
DAN POWER, *Langdon*
HARRY G. RENFROW, *Calvin*
FRED E. RICKFORD, *LaMoure*
LELAND ROEN, *Bowman*
T. O. RODHE, *New Town*
HALVOR ROLFSRUD, *Watford City*
DENVER ROSBERG, *Washburn*
OGDEN E. ROSE, *Ayr*
STANLEY SAUGSTAD, *R.F.D. 4, Minot*
GEORGE SAUMUR, *Grand Forks*
ALBERT SCHMALENBERGER, *Hebron*
MATT M. SCHMIDT, *Flasher*
TED. E. SCHULER, *Streeter*
RALPH SCOTT, *Spiritwood*
CARL G. SIMENSON, *Kindred*
E. E. SIMONSON, *Fargo*
THOMAS L. SNORTLAND, *Sharon*
ROY M. SNOW, *Beach*
OSCAR SOLBERG, *Mylo*
JOHN SOMMER, *Cavalier*
OSCAR J. SORLIE, *Buxton*
ARTHUR C. SORTLAND, *Litchville*
ADOLPH SPITZER, *Kensal*
LEO STICKA, *New England*
JACQUE STOCKMAN, *Fargo*
ELMER STRAND, *Portland*
WILLARD STREGE, *Lidgerwood*
RICHARD J. THOMPSON, *Underwood*
CARL G. TOLLEFSON, *Osnabrock*
E. A. TOUGH, *Strasburg*
TARGIE TRYDAHL, *Thompson*
MARTIN E. VINJE, *Bottineau*
HARVEY G. WAMBHEIN, *Hatton*
BEN J. WOLF, *Zeeland*
HAROLD ZIEGLER, *Emmet*
(3 vacancies)

OHIO

Senate

Republicans 20   Democrats 12

JOSEPH H. AVELLONE, 3762 *Bainbridge Rd., Cleveland Heights*
I. E. BAKER, 59 *S. State St., Phillipsburg*
JOSEPH W. BARTUNEK, 1137 *Commonwealth Ave., Mayfield Heights*
ARTHUR BLAKE, *R.F.D. 1, Martins Ferry*
CHARLES J. CARNEY, 426 *Garfield St., Youngstown*
OAKLEY C. COLLINS, 1005 *Kemp Lane, Ironton*
JOHN T. CORRIGAN, 16285 *Craigmere Ave., Cleveland* 30
FRED W. DANNER, 37 *N. High St., Akron*
WILLIAM H. DEDDENS, 505 *Walnut St., Cincinnati*
EDWARD H. DELL, 16 *N. Clinton St., Middletown*
DAVID MCK. FERGUSON, *Box 192, Cambridge*
LOWELL FESS, 111 *W. South College, Yellow Springs*

ELIZABETH F. GORMAN, 2555 *Kenilworth Rd., Cleveland Heights*
THEODORE M. GRAY, 1115 *Park Ave., Piqua*
FRED HARTER, 24 *S. Portage Path, Akron*
RAYMOND E. HILDEBRAND, 921 *Broadway, Toledo*
FRED L. HOFFMAN, 814 *Provident Bank Bldg., Cincinnati*
RALPH L. HUMPHREY, 1541 *Prospect Rd., Ashtabula*
FRANK W. KING, 1344 *Sabra Rd., Toledo*
DELBERT L. LATTA, *Martin Bldg., McComb*
C. STANLEY MECHEM, 209 *W. Washington St., Nelsonville*
TOM V. MOOREHEAD, *First Trust Bldg., Zanesville*
CHARLES A. MOSHER, 48 *S. Main St., Oberlin*
STEPHEN R. OLENICK, 3022 *Rush Blvd., Youngstown*
ROSS PEPPLE, 313 *W. High St., Lima*
JULIUS J. PETRASH, 12009 *Griffing Ave., Cleveland*
ROBERT A. POLLOCK, 2016 *Myrtle Ave. NW, Canton*
GORDON RENNER, 211 *E. Fourth St., Cincinnati*
ROBERT R. SHAW, 22 *E. Gay St., Columbus*
J. E. SIMPSON, *Forest*
FRANK J. SVOBODA, 13906 *Larchmere Blvd., Cleveland*
WILLIAM TYRRELL, *St. Clair Bldg., Eaton*
(1 vacancy)

House

Republicans 87   Democrats 45

HERMAN K. ANKENEY, *R.F.D. 4, Xenia*
EARL D. APPLEGATE, 1001 *Sinclair Bldg., Steubenville*
THOMAS J. BARRETT, 353 *Carroll St., Youngstown*
LEONARD J. BARTUNEK, 13722 *Caine Ave., Cleveland*
KARL BAUER, 1008 *Fourteenth St. NW, Canton*
KENNETH L. BECKWITH, *Box 596, McConnelsville*
ROLAND E. BEERY, *R.F.D. 3, Sidney*
HARRY D. BELLIS, *R.F.D. 3, Delphos*
KENNETH F. BERRY, 117 *S. Fourth St., Coshocton*
GILBERT BETTMAN, 921 *Dixie Terminal Bldg., Cincinnati*
ROLLAND BRIGHT, 32 *Court Park, Logan*
B. A. BROUGHTON, *Newbury*
DON BULLOCK, 7805 *Brill Rd., Cincinnati*
LESLIE M. BURGE, 311 *Broadway Bldg., Lorain*
ANTHONY O. CALABRESE, 1875 *Forest Hills Blvd., Apt. E1, East Cleveland*
DON CAMPBELL, *Guysville*
CLIFTON L. CARYL, 124½ *W. Fifth St., Marysville*
F. K. CASSEL, 221 *E. Findlay St., Carey*
JOHN J. CHESTER, JR., 8 *E. Broad St., Columbus*
ROGER CLOUD, *R.F.D. 1, DeGraff*
CLAYTON R. COBLENTZ, 117 *W. Cherry St., New Paris*
AUREL E. COFFMAN, 2262 *Hebron Rd., Newark*
RALPH D. COLE, JR., 317 *Third St., Findlay*
RALPH H. COLEGROVE, JR., 443 *Dick Ave., Hamilton*
JOHN J. CONNORS, JR., 2934 *Goddard Rd., Toledo*
JOHN J. CONWAY, 17209 *Greenwood Ave., Cleveland*
LUSTER M. COOLEY, *R.F.D. 1, Albany*
HARRY CORKWELL, 1117 *E. Main St., Ottawa*
MICHAEL J. CROSSER, 3558 *Antisdale Rd., Cleveland Heights*
WILLIAM PATRICK DAY, 3448 *Menlo Rd., Shaker Heights*
EDWARD W. DECHANT, 221 *Center Rd., Avon Lake*
MAX H. DENNIS, 35½ *W. Main St., Wilmington*
ANDY DEVINE, 520 *Islington St., Toledo*

TERRY E. DRAKE, 402 *N. Union St.*, *Galion*
MRS. GOLDA MAY EDMONSTON, 59 *W. Dominion Blvd.*, *Columbus*
GRIFFITH EVANS, 430 *W. Main St.*, *Kent*
RALPH E. FISHER, *Buckeye and South Sts.*, *Wooster*
NORMAN A. FUERST, 13025 *Lake Shore Blvd.*, *Bratenahl*
R. MARTIN GALVIN, 2114 *Wyndhurst*, *Toledo*
WILLIAM C. GAMES, *Box 235*, *West Union*
WALTER T. GARDNER, 221 *W. Maple St.*, *Bryan*
THOS. D. GINDLESBERGER, *Wooster Rd.*, *Millersburg*
AL GLANDORF, 4115 *Oakwood*, *Deer Park*, *Cincinnati*
FRANK M. GORMAN, 1400 *Schofield Bldg.*, *Cleveland*
FLOYD B. GRIFFIN, 103 *E. Third St.*, *Spencerville*
ROBERT F. GRONEMAN, 321 *First Natl. Bank Bldg.*, *Cincinnati*
JOHN HAYDEN, *Felicity*
FRANCIS J. HEFT, *Lewisville*
GUY C. HINER, 1318 *Twenty-second St. NW*, *Canton*
VERNON G. HISRICH, *R.F.D. 1*, *Stone Creek*
GEORGE M. HOOK, JR., 206 *North St.*, *Georgetown*
JOSEPH J. HORVATH, 2939 *E. 130th St.*, *Cleveland*
EDMUND G. JAMES, *Main St.*, *Caldwell*
EARL JENKINS, 411 *E. High St.*, *Ashley*
ROBERT L. JOHNSON, *Snedden Bldg.*, *Medina*
ARTHUR C. KATTERHEINRICH, 319 *W. Main St.*, *Cridersville*
JAMES P. KILBANE, 2223 *W. 103rd St.*, *Cleveland*
ELTON KILE, *R.F.D. 3*, *Plain City*
BISHOP KILPATRICK, 195 *Oak Knoll NE*, *Warren*
GEORGE H. KIRKPATRICK, *R.F.D. 2*, *Utica*
JOSEPH E. LADY, 100½ *N. Detroit St.*, *Kenton*
ELTON LAHR, *R.F.D. 1*, *Vickery*
A. G. LANCIONE, *F. & M. Natl. Bank Bldg.*, *Bellaire*
JAMES A. LANTZ, 1150 *N. Columbus St.*, *Lancaster*
JOHN LEHMANN, 347 *Aultman Ave. NW*, *Canton*
GEORGE E. LEIST, *Piketon*
DAVID J. LEWIS, 418 *Mill St.*, *New Lexington*
CAROL D. LONG, 336 *Lafayette Ave.*, *Urbana*
ROY H. LONGENECKER, *Pemberville*
CHARLES A. LONGFELLOW, *R.F.D. 1*, *Greenville*
ROBERT H. LONGSWORTH, *R.F.D. 1*, *Carrollton*
JOHN J. LYNCH, 606 *Wick Bldg.*, *Youngstown*
JAMES F. MCCAFFERY, 1300 *W. Ninety-third St.*, *Cleveland*
A. BRUCE MCCLURE, 612 *W. Ninth St.*, *Cincinnati*
J. FRANK MCCLURE, 131 *W. Main St.*, *Loudonville*
JAMES J. MCGETTRICK, 2525 *Stratford Ave.*, *Rocky River*
FRANCES MCGOVERN, 531 *Vinita Ave.*, *Akron*
GEORGE R. MADDEN, 2065 *Wadsworth Rd.*, *Barberton*
WILLIAM L. MANAHAN, 731 *W. High St.*, *Defiance*
C. LEE MANTLE, 188 *Mantle Rd.*, *Painesville*
THOMAS O. MATIA, 1436 *Natl. City Bank Bldg.*, *Cleveland*
GEORGE A. MEINHART, 94 *Hudson St.*, *Middleport*
HAROLD F. MILLER, 401 *Paramount Bldg.*, *Toledo*
RAY MILLER, 609 *N. Main St.*, *Paulding*
RAY T. MILLER, JR., 1708 *Union Commerce Bldg.*, *Cleveland*
ARTHUR H. MILLESON, *Main St.*, *Freeport*
ARTHUR H. MILLER, *R.F.D. 2*, *Leesburg*
CHARLES B. MITCH, 4825 *Forest Dr.*, *Springfield*
ANTHONY F. NOVAK, 6218 *St. Clair Ave.*, *Cleveland*
T. K. OWENS, 83 *E. South St.*, *Jackson*
HAROLD W. OYSTER, 307 *Four.h St.*, *Marietta*

VIRGIL PERRILL, 427 *East St.*, *Washington C. H.*
ANDREW C. PUTKA, 1836 *Euclid Ave.*, *Cleveland*
ROBERT F. RECKMAN, 900 *Traction Bldg.*, *Cincinnati*
FRANCIS F. RENO, 705 *Buckeye St.*, *Toledo*
FLOYD I. RITTENOUR, *R.F.D. 2*, *Box 185*, *Kingston*
KLINE L. ROBERTS, 150 *E. Broad*, *Columbus*
KENNETH A. ROBINSON, 134 *E. Center St.*, *Marion*
NEIL S. ROBINSON, 16 *W. Second St.*, *Mansfield*
ROBERT L. RODERER, 224 *Wortman Ave.*, *Dayton*
WILLIAM F. ROFKAR, *R.F.D. 1*, *Port Clinton*
ED ROWE, 243 *Wooster Ave.*, *Akron*
WILLIAM H. RYCHENER, *Box 5*, *Pettisville*
EUGENE J. SAWICKI, 448 *Standard Bldg.*, *Cleveland*
LOUIS J. SCHNEIDER, JR., 6994 *Bramble Ave.*, *Mariemont*
JAMES R. SEXTON, 1300 *Elwood St.*, *Middletown*
HOWARD V. SHAYLOR, 5435 *Adams Ave.*, *Ashtabula*
HAROLD L. SHORT, 126 *W. High St.*, *Piqua*
JAMES S. SIMMONDS, 211 *E. Fourth St.*, *Cincinnati*
PAUL B. SIPLE, 1010 *S. Fourth St.*, *Ironton*
RAY SOURS, 6739 *Hampshire Rd.*, *Clinton*
CEDRIC A. STANLEY, 222 *S. Mechanic St.*, *Lebanon*
FRANCIS D. SULLIVAN, 1485 *Royalwood Rd.*, *Broadview Heights*, *Brecksville*
MRS. ETHEL G. SWANBECK, 304 *Center St.*, *Huron*
D. O. TABER, *Box 326*, *Kanauga*
G. D. TABLACK, 9 *E. Washington St.*, *Struthers*
ROBERT TAFT, 4305 *Drake Rd.*, *Cincinnati*
THOMAS L. THOMAS, 1285 *Beardsley St.*, *Akron*
GILBERT THURSTON, *R.F.D. 1*, *Custar*
HORACE W. TROOP, 36½ *N. State St.*, *Westerville*
DAILEY R. TURNER, 15 *Stanton St.*, *Tiffin*
ED WALLACE, 425 *N. Court St.*, *Circleville*
J. K. WEAVER, 29 *Third St.*, *New London*
MRS. CLARA E. WEISENBORN, 3380 *Needmore Rd.*, *Dayton*
CLARENCE L. WETZEL, 250 *W. Washington St.*, *Lisbon*
CHARLES W. WHALEN, JR., 228 *Beverly Pl.*, *Dayton*
HOWARD L. WILLIAMS, 53 *E. Liberty St.*, *Girard*
ROBERT J. WITHROW, JR., 907 *American Bldg.*, *Dayton*
MRS. LORETTA COOPER WOODS, 1327 *Coles Blvd.*, *Portsmouth*
JESSE YODER, 100 *Santa Clara Ave.*, *Dayton*
ROBERT E. ZELLAR, 47 *N. Fourth St.*, *Zanesville*
LYTLE G. ZUBER, 293 *E. Longview Ave.*, *Columbus*
(4 vacancies)

OKLAHOMA

Senate

Democrats 39   Republicans 5

WALT ALLEN, 109 *N. Fourth*, *Chickasha*
DON BALDWIN, *Anadarko*
PAUL BALLINGER, *Box 190*, *Holdenville*
ROY C. BOECHER, *Box 98*, *Kingfisher*
FLOYD E. CARRIER, *Carrier*
KEITH CARTWRIGHT, *Durant*
FRED A. CHAPMAN, 119 *G St. SW*, *Ardmore*
EVERETT S. COLLINS, 403 *S. Poplar*, *Sapulpa*
GLEN C. COLLINS, *R.F.D. 1*, *Konawa*
MAX COOK, *Box 59*, *Clinton*
STANLEY COPPOCK, *R.F.D. 1*, *Cleo Springs*

BOYD COWDEN, *Box* 185, *Chandler*
BYRON DACUS, *Box* 186, *Gotebo*
BUCK DENDY, *Pryor*
BEN B. EASTERLY, *Box* 566, *Alva*
LEON B. FIELD, *Box N.N.*, *Texhoma*
RAY FINE, *Gore*
BRUCE L. FRAZIER, *R.F.D.* 2, *Sulphur*
JESS L. FRONTERHOUSE, *Fairland*
HAROLD GARVIN, *Furst-Bullard Bldg.*, *Duncan*
ROY E. GRANTHAM, 407 *S. Twelfth*, *Ponca City*
CLEM M. HAMILTON, *Box* 188, *Panama*
GENE HERNDON, *Madill*
HERBERT HOPE, *Box* 294, *Pauls Valley*
D. L. JONES, 600 *W. Broadway*, *Altus*
BILL LOGAN, 411½ *D Ave.*, *Lawton*
LEROY MCCLENDON, *Idabel*
S. S. MCCOLGIN, *Box* 103, *Reydon*
CLEM MCSPADDEN, 109 *N. Hickory*, *Nowata*
FRANK MAHAN, *Box* 636, *Fairfax*
JOHN L. MALTSBERGER, 905 *Seventh St.*, *Pawnee*
GEORGE MISKOVSKY, *Hightower Bldg.*, *Oklahoma City*
CARL MORGAN, 524 *E. Oklahoma*, *Guthrie*
KIRKSEY M. NIX, 113½ *E. Grand*, *McAlester*
ARTHUR L. PRICE, *Box* 1348, *Tulsa*
JAMES A. RINEHART, *Box* 669, *El Reno*
JOHN W. RUSSELL, JR., *Box* 13, *Okmulgee*
HAROLD R. SHOEMAKER, 706 *Barnes Bldg.*, *Muskogee*
BOB A. TRENT, *Caney*
OLIVER C. WALKER, *Dale*
BASIL R. WILSON, 517 *N. Kentucky*, *Mangum*
CHARLES M. WILSON, *Box* 148, *Sayre*
HOWARD YOUNG, *Stigler*
VIRGIL YOUNG, 818 *W. Eufaula*, *Norman*

House

Democrats 101   Republicans 19

ROBERT N. ALEXANDER, 214 *E. Twelfth*, *Tulsa*
LOU S. ALLARD, 421 *N. Grand Ave.*, *Drumright*
RED ANDREWS, *Roberts Hotel*, *Oklahoma City*
RANEY ARNOLD, 723 *N. Fifth*, *Durant*
J. H. ARRINGTON, *Box* 129, *Stillwater*
GUY O. BAILEY, 417 *N. Sixth*, *Ponca City*
ROBERT L. BAILEY, *City Natl. Bank Bldg.*, *Norman*
CLINTON BEARD, 1713 *Cherokee Pl.*, *Bartlesville*
PAUL V. BECK, 1308 *E. Twenty-seventh*, *Tulsa*
J. H. BELVIN, 302 *W. Willow*, *Durant*
JESSE BERRY, *Box* 328, *Chandler*
JACK BLISS, 103 *N. Morris*, *Tahlequah*
LEWIS H. BOHR, 612 *Circle Dr.*, *Watonga*
EDWARD L. BOND, *McCasland Bldg.*, *Duncan*
J. E. BOUSE, *Box* 183, *Laverne*
W. D. BRADLEY, *Box* 327, *Addington*
JAMES M. BULLARD, *Box* 369, *Duncan*
WM. A. BURTON, JR., *R.F.D.* 2, *Dover*
BERNARD E. CALKINS, 321 *S. Cincinnati*, *Tulsa*
JOHN N. CAMP, *Waukomis*
JOE CAREY, *Box* 114, *Guthrie*
H. F. CARMICHAEL, *Box* 226, *Sayre*
BUCK CARTWRIGHT, 218 *E. Tenth*, *Wewoka*
EDWARD L. CHUNINGS, *Brooken*
J. ROY COCKE, *Box* 205, *Wagoner*
GEORGE R. COLLINS, ℅ *County Clerk's Office*, *County Bldg.*, *Ada*
JIM COOK, *Wilburton*

BARBOUR COX, 308 *W. Eighth*, *Chandler*
RAYMOND O. CRAIG, *Security Bank Bldg.*, *Blackwell*
ROBERT O. CUNNINGHAM, *Box* 1556, *Oklahoma City*
JESSE C. DANIEL, *Box* 27, *Pauls Valley*
JEFF DAVIS, *Box* 416, *Rush Springs*
J. L. EDGECOMB, *Box* 257, *Sayre*
C. PLOWBOY EDWARDS, 301 *E. Jackson*, *McAlester*
GLENN E. ESTES, *Durham*
CARL G. ETLING, *Boise City*
E. J. EVANS, 4321 *E. Sixteenth*, *Oklahoma City*
JAMES E. FESPERMAN, *Box* 195, *Bokoshe*
HEBER FINCH, JR., 933 *Henshaw*, *Sapulpa*
RUDOLPH FOLSOM, *Box* 506, *Leon*
EARL FOSTER, JR., 825 *NW Forty-first*, *Oklahoma City*
G. M. FULLER, 2720 *First Natl. Bldg.*, *Oklahoma City*
ROBERT L. GOODFELLOW, 121 *W. Oklahoma*, *Anadarko*
RALPH W. GRAVES, 515 *American Natl. Bank Bldg.*, *Shawnee*
J. B. GRAYBILL, *R.F.D.* 2, *Leedey*
A. E. GREEN, *Avenue C*, *Wakita*
DON R. GREENHAW, *Sentinel*
J. R. HALL, JR., *Box* 528, *Miami*
GLEN HAM, *Box* 45, *Pauls Valley*
CHARLES O. HAMMERS, 1622 *Cincinnati*, *Muskogee*
B. E. HARKEY, 506 *Leonhardt Bldg.*, *Oklahoma City*
RAY D. HENRY, *Box* 265, *Ralston*
BENNIE F. HILL, 226 *N. Third*, *Okemah*
GUY K. HORTON, 421 *N. Main*, *Altus*
J. W. HUFF, *Box* 275, *Ada*
ELMO B. HURST, *Box* 144, *Mangum*
DELBERT INMAN, *R.F.D.* 4, *Coalgate*
JOE E. JOHNSON, *Box* 488, *Stillwater*
VIRGIL JUMPER, 411 *SE Ave. F*, *Idabel*
ARTHUR A. KELLY, *Box* 959, *Frederick*
MILAM M. KING, *Box* 243, *Checotah*
DALE KITE, *R.F.D.* 1, *Hollis*
A. J. LANCE, *Box* 161, *Alex*
W. H. LANGLEY, *Box* 166, *Stillwell*
A. R. LARASON, *R.F.D.* 1, *Fargo*
JOHN T. LEVERGOOD, 216 *Elks Bldg.*, *Shawnee*
J. HOWARD LINDLEY, *R.F.D.* 1, *Fairview*
CHARLEY W. LONG, *Box* 344, *Apache*
CON LONG, *Box* 1280, *Seminole*
J. D. MCCARTY, 410 *Leonhardt Bldg.*, *Oklahoma City*
WILLIAM W. METCALF, 605 *N. Lowe*, *Hobart*
HENRY H. MONTGOMERY, *Box* 62, *Purcell*
TOM H. MORFORD, *Cherokee*
OTIS MUNSON, 507 *S. Pine*, *Nowata*
JOE E. MUSGRAVE, 310 *Thompson Bldg.*, *Tulsa*
CARL THOMAS MUSTAIN, *R.F.D.* 1, *Afton*
W. B. NELSON, *R.F.D.* 2, *Randlett*
GEORGE P. NIGH, 718 *S. Seventh*, *McAlester*
C. R. NIXON, 410 *Palace Bldg.*, *Tulsa*
LYNN W. NORMAN, *Box* 37, *Sulphur*
CHARLES J. NORRIS, 104 *S. Maytubby*, *Tishomingo*
FRANK OGDEN, *Box* 403, *Guymon*
CHARLES G. OZMUN, 319½ *D Ave.*, *Lawton*
JAY E. PAYNE, *Kingston*
TOM PAYNE, JR., 1617 *E. Sixth*, *Okmulgee*
JOSEPH PAYTON, *Bentley*
JEAN L. PAZOURECK, *Box* 244, *El Reno*
GEORGE P. PITCHER, *Box* 373, *Vinita*
DAVID C. REID, 604 *N. York*, *Muskogee*
GITHEN K. RHOADS, 427½ *D Ave.*, *Lawton*

CLEETA JOHN ROGERS, 1525 *NW Thirty-third, Oklahoma City*
RICHARD E. ROMANG, 1525 *E. Randolph, Enid*
RUSSELL RUBY, 517 *Kankakee, Muskogee*
G. A. SAMPSEL, 55 *Payne St., Pryor*
HUGH M. SANDLIN, *Box 152, Holdenville*
WILLIAM K. SHIBLEY, *Box 989, Bristow*
BILL SHIPLEY, *R.F.D. 2, % Childers School, Delaware*
SHOCKLEY T. SHOEMAKE, *Triangle Bldg., Pawhuska*
WILLIAM H. SKEITH, 715 *S. Fourth, McAlester*
DEAN H. SMITH, 923 *Petroleum Bldg., Tulsa*
HERBERT D. SMITH, *R.F.D. 1, Alva*
LUCIEN C. SPEAR, *R.F.D. 2, Hugo*
CARL W. STAATS, *Box 151, Bartlesville*
TOM STEVENS, 503 *Federal Natl. Bank Bldg., Shawnee*
NOBLE R. STEWART, *R.F.D. 2, Sallisaw*
FLOYD SUMRALL, *Box 276, Beaver*
CLARENCE SWEENEY, *Box 805, Clinton*
JIM TALIAFERRO, *R.F.D. 1, Lawton*
ROBERT S. TAYLOR, 619 *Seventh St., Perry*
VIRGIL B. TINKER, *R.F.D. 2, Fairfax*
JOHN T. TIPPS, 720 *Lake Murray Drive, Ardmore*
RALPH VANDIVER, *Box 205, Heavener*
HARLEY E. VENTERS, 411 *Elm, Ardmore*
ROBERT L. WADLEY, 422 *E. Sixth, Claremore*
LEE WELCH, *Antlers*
MORT A. WELCH, *Box 325, Broken Bow*
J. DON WILLIAMS, 920 *Walnut, Woodward*
C. D. WILSON, *Box 1047, Fairland*
HAROLD LEE WITCHER, 102½ *E. Main, Cordell*
LELAND WOLF, *R.F.D. 1, Lexington*
(1 vacancy)

OREGON

Senate

Republicans 24 Democrats 6

S. EUGENE ALLEN, 8105 *SW Forty-seventh Ave., Portland*
HOWARD C. BELTON, *R.F.D. 1, Box 539, Canby*
CHARLES W. BINGNER, 1807 *Walnut, La Grande*
HARRY D. BOIVIN, 235 *N. Third, Klamath Falls*
PHIL BRADY, 2807 *NE Jarrett, Portland*
GENE L. BROWN, 205 *Wing Bldg., Grants Pass*
JOSEPH K. CARSON, JR., 7119 *N. Fowler St., Portland*
TRUMAN A. CHASE, 400 *Country Club Rd., Eugene*
CARL H. FRANCIS, *Dayton*
PAUL E. GEDDES, *Box 567, Roseburg*
HARRY GEORGE, JR., 504 *Henry Bldg., Portland*
WARREN GILL, 700 *Main St., Lebanon*
STEWART HARDIE, *Condon*
MARK O. HATFIELD, 490 *Waldo Ave., Salem*
ROBERT D. HOLMES, *Box 503, Gearhart*
JOHN P. HOUNSELL, *R.F.D. 1, Box 795, Hood River*
DONALD R. HUSBAND, 72 *W. Broadway, Eugene*
J. O. JOHNSON, *Tigard*
WALTER C. LETH, *R.F.D. 1, Box 142, Monmouth*
PAT LONERGAN, 410 *NW Eighteenth St., Portland*
PHILIP B. LOWRY, *R.F.D. 3, Box 387, Medford*
WARREN A. MCMINIMEE, *R.F.D. 1, Box 188, Tillamook*
JOHN C. F. MERRIFIELD, 1015 *Equitable Bldg., Portland*
LEE V. OHMART, 520 *N. Fourteenth St., Salem*
ELMO E. SMITH, 361 *Bridge St., John Day*
W. LOWELL STEEN, *Milton-Freewater*
MONROE SWEETLAND, 2125 *River Rd., Milwaukie*
GEORGE A. ULETT, *Box 577, Coquille*
RUDIE WILHELM, JR., 1233 *NW Twelfth Ave., Portland*
FRANCIS W. ZIEGLER, 333 *N. Eighth, Corvallis*

House

Republicans 35 Democrats 25

EDDIE AHRENS, *R.F.D. 2, Box 61A, Turner*
JOHN P. AMACHER, *Winchester*
BEN ANDERSON, 1824 *SW Twelfth, Portland*
GUST ANDERSON, 2426 *NE Ainsworth, Portland*
GEORGE J. ANNALA, *R.F.D. 1, Box 100, Hood River*
WILLIAM W. BRADEEN, *Box 1113, Burns*
ED. R. CARDWELL, 1313 *Main, Sweet Home*
W. W. CHADWICK, *Hotel Senator, Salem*
R. F. CHAPMAN, 977 *S. Eighth, Coos Bay*
H. H. CHINDGREN, *R.F.D. 2, Box 403, Molalla*
EDWIN E. CONE, 2130 *Olive, Eugene*
WARD H. COOK, 3715 *NE Klickitat, Portland*
ALFRED H. CORBETT, 1214 *Portland Trust Bldg., Portland*
F. H. DAMMASCH, 1834 *SE Twenty-second, Portland*
LEON S. DAVIS, *R.F.D. 2, Box 47, Hillsboro*
HARVEY H. DEARMOND, 1044 *Bond St., Bend*
ELMER DEETZ, *R.F.D. 3, Box 75, Canby*
PAT DOOLEY, 615 *Pacific Bldg., Portland*
ORVAL EATON, 460 *Commercial St., Astoria*
ROBERT L. ELFSTROM, 260 *S. Liberty, Salem*
HARRY C. ELLIOTT, 2205 *Ninth, Tillamook*
WILLIAM J. GALLAGHER, 8659 *SE Foster Road, Portland*
EDWARD A. GEARY, *Box 392, Klamath Falls*
WAYNE R. GIESY, *Box 105, Monroe*
G. D. GLEASON, 4232 *NE Couch, Portland*
R. E. GOAD, 613 *SW Second, Pendleton*
WILLIAM A. GRENFELL, JR., 705 *SW Columbia, Portland*
RICHARD E. GROENER, 4137 *Drake, Milwaukie*
JOHN D. HARE, *R.F.D. 1, Hillsboro*
LLOYD E. HAYNES, 611 *NE Dean Dr., Grants Pass*
EARL H. HILL, *Cushman*
NORMAN R. HOWARD, 2504 *SE Sixty-fourth Ave., Portland*
ARTHUR P. IRELAND, *R.F.D. 2, Forest Grove*
V. T. JACKSON, *R.F.D. 2, Box 1446, Roseburg*
ROBERT J. JENSEN, 3720 *SE Hawthorne, Portland*
V. EDWIN JOHNSON, 175 *W. Twentieth Ave., Eugene*
ROBERT R. KLEMSEN, 291 *S. Fifth, St. Helens*
GEORGE LAYMAN, *Box 68, Newberg*
JEAN L. LEWIS, 7700 *SW Twenty-seventh, Portland*
E. A. LITTRELL, *R.F.D. 3, Box 156B, Medford*
AL LOUCKS, 250 *W. Washington, Salem*
THOMAS R. MCCLELLAN, *Box 27, Neotsu*
RODERICK T. MCKENZIE, *Box 240, Sixes*
E. H. MANN, *Box 1587, Medford*
IRVIN MANN, *Adams*
FRED MEEK, 3357 *SE Belmont, Portland*
KAY MERIWETHER, 3417 *SE Carlton, Portland*
KATHERINE MUSA, 512 *W. Sixth, The Dalles*
MAURINE B. NEUBERGER, 1910 *SW Clifton, Portland*
BOYD R. OVERHULSE, *Madras*
WALTER J. PEARSON, 0306 *SW Palater Rd., Portland*

JOE ROGERS, *R.F.D.* 1, *Box* 327, *Independence*
JESS W. SAVAGE, 140 *N. Hill, Albany*
ERNEST E. SCHRENK, *R.F.D.* 2, *Box* 314, *Creswell*
HENRY SEMON, *R.F.D.* 2, *Box* 572, *Klamath Falls*
ROBERT J. STEWARD, *Keating*
LORAN L. STEWART, 111 *Madison, Cottage Grove*
EMIL A. STUNZ, 201 *S. Seventh, Nyssa*
CHARLES A. TOM, *Rufus*
HARRY L. WELLS, 1311 *U St., La Grande*

PENNSYLVANIA
Senate
Republicans 27   Democrats 23

EUSTACE H. BANE, 227 *Derrick Ave., Uniontown*
JOSEPH M. BARR, 4609 *Bayard St., Pittsburgh* 13
JAMES S. BERGER, 2 *Southeast St., Coudersport*
C. ARTHUR BLASS, 502 *W. Seventh St., Erie*
PETER J. CAMIEL, 810 *New Market St., Philadelphia*
LEROY E. CHAPMAN, 1911 *Pennsylvania Ave., East Warren*
WM. H. DAVIS, 4 *Park Ave., Wilkes Barre*
JOHN H. DENT, *Linden Dr., Jeannette*
M. R. DERK, 124 *S. Broad St., Jersey Shore*
G. GRAYBILL DIEHM, 30 *N. Broad St., Lititz*
ANTHONY J. DISILVESTRO, 1505 *S. Fifteenth St., Philadelphia*
BENJAMIN R. DONOLOW, 1804 *Rittenhouse Sq., Philadelphia*
HAROLD E. FLACK, *R.F.D.* 3, *Dallas*
ROBERT D. FLEMING, 202 *Brilliant Ave., Aspinwall, Pittsburgh* 22
JOHN J. HALUSKA, 413 *Beech Ave., Patton*
THOMAS P. HARNEY, *Deborah's Rock Farm, West Chester*
JO HAYS, 441 *W. Fairmount Ave., State College*
ELMER S. HOLLAND, 1419 *Marengo St., Pittsburgh* 10
EDWARD J. KESSLER, *R.F.D.* 7, *Box* 509, *Lancaster*
FRANK KOPRIVER, JR., 1416 *Highland Ave., Duquesne*
WILLIAM J. LANE, *R.F.D.* 1, *West Brownsville*
JOHN J. MCCREESH, 4202 *Walnut St., Philadelphia*
BERNARD MCGINNIS, 12 *E. North Ave., Pittsburgh* 12
HUGH J. MCMENAMIN, 739 *N. Webster St., Scranton*
DONALD P. MCPHERSON, 250 *Carlisle St., Gettysburg*
ALBERT E. MADIGAN, *R.F.D.* 2, *Towanda*
ROWLAND B. MAHANY, 213 *W. Spruce St., Titusville*
CHARLES R. MALLERY, 605 *Allegheny St., Hollidaysburg*
JOHN CARL MILLER, 110 *Fifth St., Alliquippa*
WM. VINCENT MULLIN, 7180 *Jackson St., Philadelphia*
ALBERT R. PECHAN, 909 *Fifth Ave., Ford City*
MURRAY PEELOR, 293 *N. Seventh St., Indiana*
HENRY J. PROPERT, *E. Welsh Rd., Bethayres*
FRANK W. RUTH, *Bernville*
THEODORE H. SCHMIDT, 1210 *S. Negley Ave., Pittsburgh*
WILLIAM Z. SCOTT, 51 *Coal St., Lansford*
HARRY E. SEYLER, 249 *E. Princess St., York*
MARTIN SILVERT, 5338 *N. Fifteenth St., Philadelphia*
GEORGE B. STEVENSON, 114 *Second St., Lock Haven*
ISRAEL STIEFEL, 1908 *N. Franklin St., Philadelphia*
M. HARVEY TAYLOR, 115 *North St., Harrisburg*
JOHN T. VAN SANT, 959 *Turner St., Allentown*

GEORGE N. WADE, 312 *N. Twenty-sixth St., Camp Hill*
PAUL L. WAGNER, 634 *E. Broad St., Tamaqua*
G. ROBERT WATKINS, *R.F.D.* 5, *West Chester*
ED. B. WATSON, *Buckingham Twp., Mechanicsville*
CHARLES R. WEINER, 3201 *W. Susquehanna Ave., Philadelphia*
J. IRVING WHALLEY, 1309 *Park Ave., Windber*
SAMUEL B. WOLFE, 828 *Market St., Lewisburg*
JOSEPH J. YOSKO, 943 *E. Sixth St., Bethlehem*

House
Democrats 112   Republicans 97

ROBERT R. ADAM, *R.F.D.* 2, *Hamburg*
WILLARD F. AGNEW, JR., 222 *Lexington St., Pittsburgh* 15
LOUIS J. AMARANDO, 2523 *S. Sixteenth St., Philadelphia*
MATT S. ANDERSON, 2107 *Center Ave., Pittsburgh* 19
SARAH A. ANDERSON, 226 *N. Fifty-second St., Philadelphia*
HIRAM G. ANDREWS, 115 *Main St., Johnstown*
WILLIAM H. ASHTON, *Edgemont*
CHARLES A. AUKER, 1106 *Twenty-sixth Ave., Altoona*
MAURICE L. BANKER, 819 *Washington St., Huntingdon*
ANTHONY J. BARNATOVICH, *Main St., Mildred*
MARVIN BAZIN, 1312 *N. Seventy-fifth St., Philadelphia*
CLARENCE D. BELL, 400 *W. Twenty-fourth St., Upland*
STANLEY L. BLAIR, 19 *West Ave., Albion*
DAVID M. BOIES, 312 *Fourth St., Clairton*
JOHN F. BONNER, 204 *W. Ludlow St., Summit Hill*
BENJAMIN BOORY, 2436 *N. Stanley St., Philadelphia*
ADAM T. BOWER, 138 *Bainbridge St., Sunbury*
ERNEST O. BRANCA, 4734 *Cheffield Ave., Philadelphia*
WAYNE M. BREISCH, *R.F.D., Ringtown*
A. PATRICK BRENNAN, 36 *Laurel Lane, Levittown*
JOSEPH J. BRENNAN, 3304 *Cascade St., Erie*
FLOYD K. BRENNINGER, 811 *Columbia Ave., Lansdale*
HARRIS G. BRETH, *R.F.D.* 2, *Clearfield*
WILLIAM E. BROWN, 78 *Virginia Ave., Coatesville*
FRANCIS W. BUCCHIN, 830 *E. Fourth St., Bethlehem*
JOSEPH WARREN BULLEN, JR., 100 *S. Lansdowne Ave., Lansdowne*
A. V. CAPANO, 805 *McKean Ave., Donora*
HENRY CIANFRANI, 526 *Fitzwater St., Philadelphia*
DOMINICK E. CIOFFI, 25 *E. Reynolds St., New Castle*
HARRY COCHRAN, *Dawson*
HARRY R. COMER, 2764 *N. Howard St., Philadelphia*
M. JOSEPH CONNELLY, 119 *Hampden Rd., Upper Darby*
GEORGE W. COOPER, 47 *W. Marlin Dr., Pittsburgh*
WILLIAM B. CURWOOD, 51 *N. Main St., Shickshinny*
JAMES KEPLER DAVIS, *Tionesta*
MRS. RUTH S. DONAHUE, 41 *N. Fairview St., Lock Haven*
LEE A. DONALDSON, JR., 4 *Elm Lane, Pittsburgh* 23
JAMES J. DOUGHERTY, 117 *Tree St., Philadelphia*
RALPH J. DOWN, 915 *Alcoma St., Sharon*
THOMAS A. EHRGOOD, 612 *S. Lincoln Ave., Lebanon*
JOSHUA EILBERG, 6309 *Horrocks St., Philadelphia*
DANIEL H. ERB, 511 *Wayne St., Hollidaysburg*
EDWIN D. ESHLEMAN, 345 *N. George St., Millersville*
EDWIN C. EWING, 413 *Meridian Dr., Pittsburgh* 34

E. J. FARABAUGH, *Loretto*
JULES FILO, 4109 *Greensprings Ave., Mifflin*
HERBERT FINEMAN, 5406 *Morse St., Philadelphia*
ROBERT J. FLINT, 5 *Water St., Coudersport*
SAMUEL FLOYD, 968 *N. Tenth St., Philadelphia*
MICHAEL R. FLYNN, 30 *E. Prospect Ave., Washington*
JOHN H. FOSTER, 671 *Church Rd., Wayne*
SAMUEL W. FRANK, 634 *Gordon St., Allentown*
THOMAS A. FRASCELLA, 1239 *W. Somerset St., Philadelphia*
PRESTON A. FROST, 141 *S. Frazier St., State College*
JAMES L. GAFFNEY, 724 *Lincoln St., Easton*
MARL H. GARLOCK, *Lincoln Way E., McConnellsburg*
EUGENE GELFAND, 5748 *N. Park Ave., Philadelphia*
ARTHUR GEORGE, 114 *S. West St., Carlisle*
LAWRENCE V. GIBB, 624 *Mulberry St., Sewickley*
ALLEN M. GIBSON, 203 *Crary Ave., Sheffield*
MAURICE H. GOLDSTEIN, 5666 *Phillips Ave., Pittsburgh 17*
HARRY S. GRAMLICH, 806 *Liberty St., Franklin*
RAY W. GREENWOOD, 27 *Wyoming Ave., Tunkhannock*
KARL B. GUSS, 20 *S. Third St., Mifflintown*
W. MACK GUTHRIE, 801 *Terrace Ave., Apollo*
ROBERT K. HAMILTON, 917 *Maplewood Ave., Ambridge*
WILBUR H. HAMILTON, 575 *E. Gates St., Philadelphia*
RICHARD O. HASS, 817 *Granview Rd., York*
JOHN R. HAUDENSHIELD, 111 *Ramsey Dr., Carnegie*
CHARLES D. HEAVEY, 5506 *Cedar Ave., Philadelphia*
W. STUART HELM, 910 *Wilson Ave., Kittanning*
EVELYN GLAZIER HENZEL, 414 *Keswick Ave., Glenside*
EARL E. HEWITT, SR., 1020 *Philadelphia St., Indiana*
BLAINE C. HOCKER, 42 *Harrisburg St., Oberlin*
HERBERT HOLT, 4018 *Parrish St., Philadelphia*
ENOS H. HORST, 120 *Lincoln Way W., Chambersburg*
CLYDE B. HOUK, 600 *Orchard Ave., Ellwood City*
JOSEPH W. ISAACS, 1547 *Baltimore Ave., Folcroft*
GEORGE E. JENKINS, 1009 *Kirkpatrick St., North Braddock*
ALBERT W. JOHNSON, 409 *Franklin St., Smethport*
GRANVILLE E. JONES, 2233 *Christian St., Philadelphia*
THOMAS H. W. JONES, 1733 *DeKalb St., Norristown*
JAMES J. JUMP, 70 *E. Jackson St., Wilkes Barre*
WALTER T. KAMYK, 4627 *Carlton St., Pittsburgh 1*
H. FRANKLIN KEHLER, 507 *Centre St., Ashland*
MARVIN V. KELLER, *Linton Hall Rd., Newtown*
ROBERT F. KENT, 738 *Maple St., Meadville*
G. EDGAR KLINE, 433 *E. Norwegian St., Pottsville*
WILLIAM KNECHT, *Tower City*
LEON J. KOLANKIEWICZ, 3111 *Richmond St., Philadelphia*
MARGARETTE S. KOOKER, 627 *W. Broad St., Quakertown*
NICHOLAS KORNICK, 37 *Shady Lane, Uniontown*
RAYMOND C. KRATZ, 123 *Summit Ave., Ft. Washington*
ARTHUR E. KROMER, 115 *Cleveland St., Punxsutawney*
JOHN C. KUBACKI, 1558 *Mineral Spring Rd., Reading*
JOHN A. LAFORE, JR., *Avonwood Rd., Haverford*
CLARENCE M. LAWYER, JR., 440 *Linden Ave., York*
MARY E. LEIBY, 518 *Washington St., Allentown*
LOUIS LEONARD, 1217 *Strahley Pl., Pittsburgh 20*
AMOS M. LESIEY, *Broad and Main Sts., Honeybrook*

ALBERT LEVEN, *Oxford Ave. and Leiper St., Philadelphia*
JOHN H. LIGHT, *E. Main St., Annville*
WILLIAM LIMPER, 169 *W. Huntingdon St., Philadelphia*
EDWIN E. LIPPINCOTT II, 30 *Preston Rd., Media*
PHILIP LOPRESTI, 755 *Wayne St., Johnstown*
JAMES E. LOVETT, 521 *Gilmore Ave., Trafford*
PAUL F. LUTTY, 150 *Monastery Ave., Pittsburgh 3*
STEPHEN MCCANN, *Waynesburg Rd., Carmichaels*
THOMAS J. MCCORMACK, 3941 *N. Dell St., Philadelphia*
JOSEPH A. MCGEE, 2519 *S. Sixty-first St., Philadelphia*
HARRY R. MCINROY, *Church St., Westfield*
LEO A. MCKEEVER, 1675 *Cheltenham Ave., Philadelphia*
LEO J. MCLAUGHLIN, 7137 *Upland St., Pittsburgh 8*
JAMES L. MCWHERTER, 321 *Fourth Ave., Derry*
GEORGE C. MAGEE, JR., 738 *Baldwin St., Meadville*
SAMUEL MAHAN, 500 *S. Washington St., Butler*
MARIAN E. MARKLEY, *R.F.D. 1, Macungie*
H. J. MAXWELL, 1200 *Hillcrest Ave., Monessen*
STANLEY MEHOLCHICK, 3 *Snively St., Ashley*
AUGUST METZ, JR., *Milford*
MARTIN C. MIHM, 716 *Lockhart St., Pittsburgh 12*
JOHN J. MIKULA, 28 *W. Spring St., Hazleton*
HAROLD G. MILLER, 1738 *Twenty-third Ave., Altoona*
CHARLES J. MILLS, 711 *Eastmont Dr., Greensburg*
SUSIE MONROE, 1942 *N. Twenty-third St., Philadelphia*
JOHN H. MOODY, 3666 *N. Third St., Harrisburg*
J. P. MORAN, 116 *Eighth St., Turtle Creek*
ANDREW S. MOSCRIP, *R.F.D. 1, Wysox*
FRANCIS X. MULDOWNEY, 862 *N. Twenty-second St., Philadelphia*
MARTIN P. MULLEN, 5332 *Glenmore Ave., Philadelphia*
MARION L. MUNLEY, 175 *Spruce St., Archbald*
PETER J. MURPHY, 522 *E. Ninth St., Chester*
HARVEY P. MURRAY, 412 *W. Pine St., Selinsgrove*
JOHN J. MURRAY, 104 *Sumner Ave., Pittsburgh 21*
PAUL G. MURRAY, 310 *Race St., Lancaster*
JAMES MUSTO, 61 *Bryden St., Pittston*
HARRY A. NAUGLE, 200 *S. Main St., Davidsville*
MICHAEL J. NEEDHAM, 324 *S. Hyde Park Ave., Scranton*
ROBERT S. OGILVIE, 2619 *N. Second St., Harrisburg*
OLAF E. OLSEN, 1703 *Broadway Ave., Pittsburgh 16*
FRANK M. O'NEIL, 421 *W. Garfield Ave., DuBois*
JOSEPH PACCHIOLI, *R.F.D. 1, Bethlehem*
ROY W. PARRY, 18 *Hughest St., Luzerne*
KATHRYN GRAHAM PASHLEY, 8123 *Hennig St., Philadelphia*
PERRY M. PAULHAMUS, *R.F.D. 1, Nesbit*
ANTHONY J. PETROSKY, *Box 26, Slickville*
J. THOMPSON PETTIGREW, 1721 *N. Twenty-third St., Philadelphia*
JULIAN POLASKI, 560 *E. Fourteenth St., Erie*
J. DEAN POLEN, *Morningside Dr., Avella*
JOHN N. POMEROY, JR., *Germantown Manor Apts., Philadelphia*
HARRY W. PRICE, JR., 135 *W. Third St., Lewistown*
LOUIS A. PURSLEY, 1030 *Washington Ave., Lewisburg*
ALBERT S. READINGER, 1722 *Olive St., Reading*
JEANNETTE F. REIBMAN, 514 *McCartney St., Easton*
WILLIAM J. REIDENBACH, 211 *Penn Ave., Scranton*

WILLIAM F. RENWICK, 130 *Straub Ave.*, *St. Marys*
JOSEPH P. RIGBY, 624 *Copeland St.*, *Pittsburgh* 32
MORRIS ROSEN, 6047 *Locust St.*, *Philadelphia*
LOUIS ROVANSEK, 414 *Locust St.*, *Conemaugh*
BAKER ROYER, 228 *W. Franklin St.*, *Ephrata*
ARTHUR RUBIN, 433 *N. Franklin St.*, *Philadelphia*
HAROLD B. RUDISILL, 418 *Baltimore St.*, *York*
GEORGE J. SARRAF, 3701 *Penn Ave.*, *Pittsburgh*
VINCENT F. SCARCELLI, 2103 *S. Lambert St.*, *Philadelphia*
ED. A. SCHUSTER, SR., 4923 *Lytle St.*, *Pittsburgh*
LOUIS SHERMAN, 4805 *B St.*, *Philadelphia*
ABRAHAM N. SIGMAN, 812 *Fox Bldg.*, *Philadelphia*
CHARLES C. SMITH, 503 *E. Wadsworth St.*, *Philadelphia*
WILLIAM B. SMITH, 1701 *Boundary St.*, *Aliquippa*
E. GADD SNIDER, *Box 371*, *Uniontown*
JOHN F. STANK, 517 *Webster St.*, *Ranshaw*
HERMAN E. STEBBINS, *R.F.D. 5*, *York*
WILLIAM A. STECKEL, 1018 *Main St.*, *Slatington*
PAUL A. STEPHENS, 312 *Main St.*, *Meyersdale*
DEWITT STEVENSON, *Mt. Rt. 11*, *Butler*
CHARLES D. STONE, 100 *N. Brodhead Rd.*, *Aliquippa*
CLARENCE G. STONER, 407 *E. Main St.*, *Shiremanstown*
ALBERT E. STRAUSSER, 301 *E. Fifth St.*, *Berwick*
STANLEY G. STROUP, *R.F.D. 2*, *Bedford*
LAWRENCE SWARTZ, 1212 *Baldwin St.*, *Williamsport*
MARTIN J. TAYLOR, 3527 *Frankford Ave.*, *Philadelphia*
ANDREW C. THOMAS, 1702 *Romine Ave.*, *McKeesport*
RONALD L. THOMPSON, 224 *Parker St.*, *Pittsburgh* 16
HERMAN TOLL, 2323 *Seventy-sixth Ave.*, *Philadelphia*
EDWIN W. TOMPKINS, 120 *W. Fourth St.*, *Emporium*
T. LUKE TOOMEY, *Wila*
MARY A. VARALLO, 1418 *Point Breeze Ave.*, *Philadelphia*
PAIGE VARNER, 88 *Payne St.*, *Clarion*
JOHN J. VAUGHAN, 2941 *Perrysville Ave.*, *Pittsburgh*
DANIEL A. VERONA, 916 *Wylie Ave.*, *Pittsburgh* 19
ARTHUR J. WALL, 315 *Sixteenth St.*, *Honesdale*
FRANK A. WALLACE, 356 *E. State St.*, *Larksville*
JOHN T. WALSH, 1415 *Fremont St.*, *McKeesport*
JOSEPH G. WARGO, 108 *Bosak Court*, *Olyphant*
W. W. WATERHOUSE, 17 *E. Smith St.*, *Corry*
LEROY A. WEIDNER, 11 *Marshall Ave.*, *Reading*
JOHN J. WELSH, 3544 *N. Broad St.*, *Philadelphia*
HAROLD G. WESCOTT, 412 *Broad Ave.*, *Susquehanna*
ROBERT WHEELER, JR., *Box 505*, *Fairchance*
DONALD E. WHITENIGHT, *R.F.D. 4*, *Danville*
HERMAN B. WILLAREDT, *Bridge St.*, *Mont Clare*
C. O. WILLIAMS, *Denbo*
RAYMOND E. WILT, 131 *Enger Ave.*, *Pittsburgh* 14
NORMAN WOOD, *R.F.D. 1*, *Peach Bottom*
FRANCIS WORLEY, *R.F.D. 1*, *York Springs*
VAN D. YETTER, *R.F.D. 2*, *East Stroudsburg*
HAROLD A. YETZER, 521 *Jefferson St.*, *Hyde Park*, *Reading*
EDWARD M. YOUNG, 506 *Oak Hill Dr.*, *Grove City*
NOLAN F. ZIEGLER, 415 *S. Seventeenth St.*, *Harrisburg*
(1 vacancy)

RHODE ISLAND

Senate

Democrats 22 Republicans 22

CHARLES T. ALGREN, 76 *Verndale Dr.*, *East Greenwich*

FRANK ALMEIDA, 2024 *E. Main Rd.*, *Portsmouth*
DONALD L. BEAUREGARD, *Greenville Rd.*, *R.F.D. 2*, *Woonsocket*
ARTHUR A. BELHUMEUR, 250 *Shawmut Ave.*, *Central Falls*
JAMES J. BRADY, SR., 61 *Kinsman St.*, *Valley Falls*
ANTONIO DAPONTE, 123 *Bay View Ave.*, *Bristol*
WILLIAM M. DAVIES, JR., 137 *Progress St.*, *Saylesville*
C. GEORGE DESTEFANO, 25 *Markwood Dr.*, *Barrington*
THOMAS DILUGLIO, 10 *Burnett St.*, *Johnston*
JAMES H. DONNELLY, *Saunderstown*
GEORGE D. GREENHALGH, *Douglas Hook Rd.*, *Chepachet*
HARRY J. HALL, *Plainfield Pike*, *North Scituate*
ALTON HEAD, JR., 54 *Howland Ave.*, *Jamestown*
HENRY C. HOXSIE, *Nooseneck Hill Rd.*, *R.F.D.*, *Coventry*
PRIMO IACOBUCCI, 12 *Prosper St.*, *Providence*
WALTER J. KANE, *Hawkins St.*, *Greenville*
WILLIS B. KENYON, *Exeter*
FRANCIS J. LACHAPELLE, 1441 *Main St.*, *West Warwick*
HOYT W. LARK, 114 *Alexander St.*, *Cranston*
RALPH T. LEWIS, 139 *Gould Ave.*, *Norwood*
WILLIAM P. LEWIS, *Block Island*
FRANK LICHT, 22 *President Ave.*, *Providence*
CHARLES J. LINK, *Post Rd.*, *Charlestown*
JOSEPH L. LUONGO, 347 *Broadway*, *Providence*
RAYMOND A. McCABE, 223 *Sackett St.*, *Providence*
FRANK A. McMURROUGH, 189 *Highland Rd.*, *Tiverton*
JOHN G. McWEENEY, 208 *Linwood Ave.*, *Providence*
ERNEST O. MAINE, *Maxson St.*, *Ashaway*
JAMES F. MURPHY, 7 *Dion Ave.*, *West Warwick*
FLORENCE K. MURRAY, 10 *Kay Street*, *Newport*
ERNEST L. NYE, *Walker Rd.*, *Foster Center*
LOUIS E. PERREAULT, *Beaver River Rd.*, *R.F.D.*, *West Kingston*
JAMES J. POLLITT, 70 *Tally St.*, *Pawtucket*
HUBERT F. POWERS, *Douglas Pike*, *Mohegan*, *R.F.D.*, *Woonsocket*
THOMAS D. SANTORO, 13 *Pearl St.*, *Westerly*
FRANK SGAMBATO, 581 *Woonasquatucket Ave.*, *North Providence*
RICHARD B. SHEFFIELD, 255 *Indian Ave.*, *Middletown*
FRANCIS P. SMITH, 219 *Prospect St.*, *Woonsocket*
WILLIAM H. SMITH, 17 *Church St.*, *Warren*
LEONARD H. SYLVIA, *Meeting House Lane*, *Little Compton*
N. LOUIS TETREAULT, 192 *Genest Ave.*, *Pawtucket*
CARLTON H. TOWLE, 12 *Prospect Ave.*, *Wakefield*
JOSEPH R. WEISBERGER, 113 *Waterman Ave.*, *East Providence*
GEORGE M. WESTLAKE, *Point Judith Rd.*, *Narragansett*

House

Democrats 67 Republicans 33

ABRAHAM ABELSON, 173 *Fourth St.*, *Providence*
HENRY ALFRED, 43 *Monroe Ave.*, *Bristol*
FRED S. ARNOLD, 36 *Butler St.*, *Cranston*
HARRY W. ASQUITH, 247 *Chapel St.*, *Saylesville*
SAMUEL J. AZZINARO, *Top St.*, *Westerly*
ANTHONY J. BARONE, 305 *Langdon St.*, *Providence*
ROGER A. BEAUCHEMIN, 923 *York Ave.*, *Pawtucket*

EMILE BEAUDOIN, 3 *Hawley St., Central Falls*
GEORGE C. BERK, 141 *Verndale Ave., Providence*
JOSEPH A. BEVILACQUA, 125 *Pocasset Ave., Providence*
IRVING J. BILGOR, 78 *Homer St., Providence*
HAROLD E. BOCOOK, *Mishnock Rd., R.F.D., Coventry*
MAURICE F. BORDEN, 120 *Water St., Portsmouth*
EDWARD H. BOWEN, *Warren's Point Rd., Little Compton*
GLADYS M. BRIGHTMAN, 40 *Usher Terr., Bristol*
WILLIAM T. BROOMHEAD, 53 *Alfred Drowne Rd., West Barrington*
EDWARD F. BURNS, 91 *Moore St., Central Falls*
RAYMOND J. CADDEN, 35 *Pleasant St., Valley Falls*
ROBERT A. CALDWELL, *Mendon Rd., Ashton*
LEO CARDIN, 23 *Cooper St., North Providence*
HERBERT B. CARKIN, 3239 *Post Rd., Warwick*
ORIST D. CHAHARYN, 155 *Boyden St., Woonsocket*
ROLLAND H. CHAPDELAINE, 77 *Adams St., Woonsocket*
CHARLES B. CLARKE, 30 *Lake St., Wakefield*
EUGENE F. COCHRAN, 90 *Updike St., Providence*
E. REX COMAN, 84 *Rodman St., Narragansett*
OSIAS COTE, 817 *Main St., Pawtucket*
MATTHEW C. CUNNINGHAM, 263 *Prospect St., Pawtucket*
HARRY F. CURVIN, 44 *Tower St., Pawtucket*
RAYMOND L. DAVIGNON, 5 *Elmcrest Dr., Pawtucket*
GERARD DiFIORE, 25 *Fernwood Dr., West Warwick*
ARMANDO DiMEO, 20 *Grove St., Providence*
JOHN F. DORIS, 268 *High St., Woonsocket*
HAROLD A. DUXBURY, 70 *Daniels St., Pawtucket*
FRANCIS G. DWYER, 513 *Paradise Ave., Middletown*
LESTER D. EMERS, 70 *Vassar Ave., Providence*
THOMAS L. ETHERIDGE, 36 *Brattle St., Providence*
WILLIAM F. FAGAN, *Park Pl., Pascoag*
MAURICE FEARNLEY, *Mt. Hygeia Rd., Foster*
G. ELLSWORTH GALE, JR., *Division Rd., East Greenwich*
BERNARD J. GALLAGHER, 49 *Lillian Ave., Providence*
NOEL A. GIGUERE, 342 *Paradis Ave., Woonsocket*
JOHN C. GOLOMB, 601 *Washington St., West Warwick*
LLOYD W. HARGRAVES, 79 *High St., Hope*
WALTER E. HARLOW, *Box 275, Nicholas Lane, Hope Valley*
W. WARD HARVEY, 47 *Catherine St., Newport*
WILLIAM H. HOPWOOD, *Hope Valley*
RAYMOND O. HOWARD, *R.F.D. 2, North Scituate*
LEWIS W. HULL, *East Shore Rd., Jamestown*
GEORGE A. ILG, 126 *Columbia Ave., Edgewood*
WILLIAM O. IZZI, 3257 *W. Shore Rd., Warwick*
SAMUEL C. KAGAN, 161 *Orms St., Providence*
THOMAS F. KELLEHER, 63 *Wabun Ave., Providence*
FREDERICK KENYON, *Box 6, Wood River Jct., Charlestown*
JAMES H. KIERNAN, 122 *Beaufort St., Providence*
THADDEUS M. KRAUS, 204 *Pulaski St., West Warwick*
GERARD LANOIE, 327 *Gaulin Ave., Woonsocket*
AUGUST P. LaFRANCE, 5 *Patterson Ave., Pawtucket*
ULYSSES LaROCHE, 9 *Terrance Ct., West Warwick*
ROBERT E. LEE, 113 *Centre St., East Providence*
STANLEY LEGAWIEC, 103 *Foundry St., Central Falls*
JOHN L. LEWIS, 245 *Fifth St., East Providence*
DAVID A. LOWRY, 9 *School St., Westerly*
GERTRUDE D. LYNCH, 48 *South Angell St., Providence*
FRANCIS H. McCABE, 167 *Dexter St., Pawtucket*

PATRICK B. McCAUGHEY, 147 *Meadow St., Pawtucket*
BERNARD T. McDONALD, 84 *Cedar St., Johnston*
JAMES E. McDONNELL, 1524 *Westminster St., Providence*
JAMES J. McGRATH, 159 *South St., Providence*
THOMAS P. McHUGH, 26 *W. Clifford St., Providence*
MICHAEL J. MAHONEY, 546 *N. Main St., Woonsocket*
JOSEPH E. MALLEY, 122 *Waterman Ave., Cranston*
ALFRED U. MENARD, 71 *Central St., Manville*
ANTONIO MENDES, *Cross St., Georgiaville*
WILLIAM M. MENNIE, 468 *Power Rd., Pawtucket*
HAROLD L. MOTT, *Block Island*
J. JOSEPH NUGENT, 100 *Pinehurst Ave., Providence*
JOSEPH V. ORTOLEVA, 15 *Glenbridge Ave., Providence*
GORDON D. OXX, 6 *Peckham Ave., Newport*
UMBERTO PATALANO, 260 *Knight St., Providence*
THOMAS W. PEARLMAN, 370 *Thayer St., Providence*
ALFRED P. PERROTTI, 82 *Killingly St., Providence*
SYLVESTER PERRY, 154 *Transit St., Providence*
CHESTER A. PIERCE, 113 *Chambly Ave., Lakewood*
ARTHUR R. PREVOST, 63 *Main Rd., Tiverton*
LAWRENCE A. RECORDS, *Horn Heap Farm, Exeter*
JULIO F. ROCHA, 67 *Martello St., East Providence*
PAUL R. RYAN, 16 *King Philip Dr., R.F.D., East Greenwich*
FERNAND J. ST. GERMAIN, 171 *Carnation St., Woonsocket*
JOSEPH A. SAVAGE, 10 *Friendship St., Newport*
MICHAEL SEPE, 141 *Princess Ave., Cranston*
EDWARD J. SEVIGNY, 945 *Main St., Warren*
JOHN J. SKIFFINGTON, JR., 40 *Second Ave., Woonsocket*
CARL TESTA, 374 *Branch Ave., Providence*
LEO F. THIBODEAU, *St. Paul St., North Smithfield*
JAMES F. VARLEY, 92 *Clay St., Central Falls*
ARTHUR VIOLA, 270 *Fiat Ave., Cranston*
CHARLES L. WALSH, 10 *Potter St., Newport*
REGINALD D. WHITCOMB, 36 *Willett Ave., East Providence*
JOHN J. WRENN, 177 *Bellevue Ave., Providence*

SOUTH CAROLINA

Senate

Democrats 46   Republicans 0

MARVIN A. ABRAMS, *Whitmire*
W. P. BASKIN, *Bishopville*
EDGAR A. BROWN, *Barnwell*
G. P. CALLISON, *Greenwood*
REMBERT C. DENNIS, *Moncks Corner*
BLEASE ELLISON, *West Columbia*
W. CLYDE GRAHAM, *Pamplico*
WILBUR G. GRANT, *Chester*
L. MARION GRESSETTE, *St. Matthews*
W. L. HARRELSON, *Mullins*
LAWRENCE L. HESTER, *Mt. Carmel*
R. M. JEFFERIES, *Walterboro*
J. CARL KEARSE, *Bamberg*
J. BYRUM LAWSON, *Sandy Springs*
W. A. LAWTON, *Estill*
T. ALLEN LEGARE, JR., 63 *Broad St., Charleston*
JAMES E. LEPPARD, JR., *Box 749, Cheraw*
JOHN D. LONG, *Union*
JAMES HUGH McFADDIN, *Manning*
GEORGE W. McKOWN, *R.F.D. 2, Gaffney*

J. D. Mars, *Abbeville*
John A. Martin, *Box 298, Winnsboro*
J. Pat Miley, *Walhalla*
Leonard G. Mishoe, *Greeleyville*
Charles C. Moore, *Box 1466, Spartanburg*
P. Bradley Morrah, Jr., *Box 2057, Greenville*
Earle E. Morris, Jr., *Pickens*
James B. Morrison, *Georgetown*
James P. Mozingo III, *Darlington*
W. Edwin Myrick, *Ulmers*
J. D. Parler, *St. George*
E. Leroy Powell, *Latta*
Henry B. Richardson, *Sumter*
E. Burt Rodgers, *Box 207, Beaufort*
A. Fletcher Spigner, Jr., *2905 Wilmot Ave., Columbia*
Frank A. Thompson, *Box 87, Conway*
Paul A. Wallace, *Wallace*
W. Lewis Wallace, *York*
Y. C. Weathersbee, *Ridgeland*
John Carl West, *Camden*
J. J. Wheeler, *Saluda*
John H. Williams, *Box 463, Aiken*
Marshall B. Williams, *Orangeburg*
W. Bruce Williams, *Heath Springs*
Ralph T. Wilson, *Laurens*
William Preston Yonce, *Edgefield*

House

Democrats 124   Republicans 0

Charles G. Allen, *Dillon*
G. Ross Anderson, Jr., *R.F.D. 2, Anderson*
Raymond M. Andrews, *Andrews*
Paul M. Arant, *Pageland*
Philip H. Arrowsmith, *130½ Irby St., Florence*
James M. Arthur, *Union*
Jerome P. Askins, Jr., *Hemingway*
R. J. Aycock, *Pinewood*
Lloyd B. Bell, *Loris*
O. Roddey Bell, *Lancaster*
Earl H. Bergen, *903 Boundary St., Newberry*
Dewey B. Blanton, *Box 87, Chesnee*
Solomon Blatt, *Barnwell*
Thomas W. Blease, *Box 223, Saluda*
Samuel L. Boylston, *Box 82, Springfield*
P. Eugene Brabham, *Box 214, Bamberg*
W. R. Bradford, *309 Tom Hall St., Fort Mill*
Lester P. Branham, Sr., *R.F.D. 1, Lugoff*
Harold D. Breazeale, *R.F.D. 3, Pickens*
Richard L. Breeland, *100 Ott Rd., Columbia*
Lovic A. Brooks, Jr., *109½ W. Whitner St., Anderson*
Walter B. Brown, *Box 118, Winnsboro*
Henry L. Buck, *209 Laurel St., Conway*
C. Roessler Burbage, *45 Broad St., Charleston*
Jack R. Callison, *419 Meeting St., West Columbia*
Rex L. Carter, *22A E. Coffee St., Greenville*
Joseph B. Clements, Jr., *Florence*
Ernest L. Cook, *Box 306, Hartsville*
Edward B. Cottingham, *Bennettsville*
Edward C. Cushman, Jr., *Box 270, Aiken*
Clyde M. Dangerfield, *Box 31, Isle of Palms*
Foy W. Dickson, Jr., *Fort Mill*
King Dixon, *Laurens*
D. H. Douglass, Sr., *Jefferson*

Sidney D. Duncan, *1224½ Washington St. Columbia*
Henry C. Edens, *Dalzell*
Ralph H. Ellis, *Little River*
Frank Eppes, *Box 373, Greenville*
Raymond C. Eubanks, *Box 1111, Spartanburg*
Philip B. Finklea, *Pamplico*
Mrs. Martha Thomas Fitzgerald, *101 S. Waccamaw Ave., Columbia*
David L. Freeman, *406 Boulevard, Anderson*
Tracy J. Gaines, *Inman*
Harry R. Gardner, *Chester*
Charles G. Garrett, *Fountain Inn*
John T. Gentry, *Easley*
J. Wilton Graves, *Hardeeville*
Ray G. Green, *Salem*
Walton H. Greever, Jr., *1224 Washington St., Columbia*
George T. Gregory, Jr., *Chester*
Wm. H. Grimball, Jr., *Peoples Bldg., Charleston*
Henderson Guerry, Sr., *Moncks Corner*
George S. Harrell, *Box 411, Florence*
John C. Hart, *R.F.D. 1, Jonesville*
J. B. Harvey, *Clover*
S. Rhea Haskell, *1221 Washington St., Columbia*
Sam H. Hendrix, *Greer*
F. B. Hines, Sr., *Hartsville*
John L. Hixon, *215 W. Forest Ave., North Augusta*
James C. Hooks, Sr., *Mullins*
John M. Horlbeck, *41 Broad St., Charleston*
Jerry M. Hughes, Jr., *Box 153, Orangeburg*
Edward Huguenin, *Ridgeland*
T. W. Hunter, *Newberry*
Clyde David Jenkins, Jr., *R.F.D. 3, Simpsonville*
W. A. Jeter, *4010 Palmetto Ave., Columbia*
Harold B. King, *Westminster*
Henry L. Lake, *St. Matthews*
F. Julian LeaMond, *165 St. Margaret St., Charleston*
John D. Lee, Jr., *Sumter*
C. Walker Limehouse, *Box 153, Orangeburg*
Pat Lindler, *Batesburg*
John C. Lindsay, *Bennettsville*
Carl W. Littlejohn, Jr., *Spartanburg*
Hugh J. Love, *Clover*
Lloyd W. MacBay, *30 Riverdale Dr., Avondale, Charleston*
Lewis H. McClain, *204 Victoria Ave., North Charleston*
Fred N. McDonald, *R.F.D. 1, Greenville*
G. Raymond McElveen, *306 Palmetto Bldg., Columbia*
Jewell P. McLaurin, *Dillon*
J. Malcolm McLendon, *Marion*
Robert E. McNair, *Allendale*
Paul M. Macmillan, Jr., *Box 447, Charleston*
Tom Mangum, *Lancaster*
Preston S. Marchant, *Box 29, Greenville*
Burnet R. Maybank, Jr., *Box 626, Greenville*
C. L. Milam, *Mountville*
Fred T. Moore, *Honea Path*
James M. Morris, *New Zion*
E. LeRoy Nettles, *Lake City*
W. H. Nicholson, Jr., *Greenwood*
John H. Nolen, *Spartanburg*
Irvin H. Philpot, *R.F.D. 1, Greenville*
Joe W. Platt, *Moncks Corner*
Cleland Blain Player, *R.F.D. 3, Bishopville*

MATTHEW POLIAKOFF, *Box 529, Spartanburg*
HORACE C. PORTER, JR., *346 E. Smith St., Gaffney*
W. J. PRATER, *Townville*
ARTHUR RAVENEL, JR., *Box 141, Saint Andrews Branch, Charleston*
WILLIAM A. REEL, JR., *Edgefield*
W. L. RHODES, JR., *Hampton*
DON V. RICHARDSON, *Box 543, Georgetown*
JOSEPH O. ROGERS, JR., *Manning*
EDWARD E. SALEEBY, *Box 764, Hartsville*
MARSHALL B. SAUNDERS, *R.F.D. 1, Ruffin*
RYAN C. SHEALY, *Lexington*
LEWIS H. SHULER, *Bowman*
HORACE C. SMITH, *Box 1144, Spartanburg*
HUBERT W. SMOAK, *Reevesville*
I. A. SMOAK, JR., *Walterboro*
AUGUSTINE T. SMYTHE, JR., *7 Broad St., Columbia*
WALTON M. STEPHENS, *Abbeville*
J. HENRY STUCKEY, *Kingstree*
JAMES L. SWEET, *Boykin*
J. ARCH TALBERT, *McCormick*
NEWTON C. TAYLOR, *Gaffney*
FRAMPTON W. TOOLE, JR., *Box 403, Aiken*
JAMES R. TURNER, *Spartanburg*
CHARLIE V. VERNER, *Box 4, Piedmont*
JAMES M. WADDELL, JR., *Beaufort*
ROBERT C. WASSON, *R.F.D. 3, Laurens*
ALBERT W. WATSON, *1318 Sumter St., Columbia*
W. CALVIN WHITE, *Spartanburg*
ALEX H. WOODLE, *Greenwood*

SOUTH DAKOTA

Senate

Republicans 29   Democrats 6

ART B. ANDERSON, *1206 W. Seventh St., Sioux Falls*
RAY E. BARNETT, *Brookings*
BERNARD E. BERG, *Stockholm*
HILBERT BOGUE, *Beresford*
ARCHIE BOLDUAN, *1416 S. Lincoln St., Aberdeen*
L. F. ERICSSON, *Madison*
FRANK A. FERGUSON, *Artesian*
MARVIN T. GILBERTSON, *Parkston*
HAROLD GOLSETH, *Erwin*
VINCE E. HALVERSON, *601 Third St. NW, Watertown*
RALPH HERSETH, *Houghton*
RAYMOND HIEB, *Ipswich*
FRED HUNTER, *Eagle Butte*
ROY O. HURLBERT, *Raymond*
J. C. JENSEN, *Parker*
L. A. JOHNSON, *Belle Fourche*
ARTHUR JONES, *Britton*
HENRY I. KNUDSEN, *New Effington*
L. M. LARSON, *Zeona*
JOE E. LEHMANN, *Scotland*
L. L. LILLIBRIDGE, *Burke*
L. A. MELBY, *Faulkton*
JOHN E. MUELLER, *Hot Springs*
HENRY J. OSTER, *Ethan*
C. O. PETERSON, *Beresford*
JAMES RAMEY, *Wanblee*
ALBERT R. RISTY, *Corson*

ALFRED D. ROESLER, *Deadwood*
MILLARD G. SCOTT, *Huron*
REX M. SHEILD, *Salem*
CHESTER W. STEWART, *1216 Pine St., Yankton*
DON STRANSKY, *Chamberlain*
CARMAN H. SUTLEY, *Ft. Pierre*
JOHN T. VUCUREVICH, *1901 W. Blvd., Rapid City*
LEE WARNE, *Blunt*

House

Republicans 57   Democrats 18

ROY ARMSTRONG, *Flandreau*
ELDEN ARNOLD, *Britton*
ALBRO AYRES, *Deadwood*
ED. BACKLUND, *1209 E. Fifth, Mitchell*
ERVIN H. BADER, *Roscoe*
O. E. BEARDSLEY, *Watertown*
FLORENCE J. BECKERS, *1103 W. Blvd., Rapid City*
THOMAS O. BERGAN, *Florence*
M. E. BIERWAGEN, *Milesville*
HOWARD E. BLAKE, *Burke*
ELLEN E. BLISS, *520 N. Menlo, Sioux Falls*
NILS A. BOE, *504 S. Duluth Ave., Sioux Falls*
GEORGE BOEKELHEIDE, *Milbank*
FRED A. BOLLER, *Faulkton*
PAUL E. BROWN, *Arlington*
JOHN BUEHLER, *Emery*
CARL BURGESS, *Box 510, Rapid City*
ROBERT CHAMBERLIN, *Hecla*
NELS P. CHRISTENSEN, *Wilmot*
ERNEST A. COVEY, *Hamill*
RAYMOND E. DANA, *715 Wiswall Pl., Sioux Falls*
JOE R. DUNMIRE, *Lead*
FRANCIS J. EVELO, *R.F.D. 1, Aberdeen*
CARL H. FURCHNER, *Plankinton*
I. A. GABBERT, *Meadow*
EDGAR GARDNER, *Buffalo*
HOBART H. GATES, *Custer*
ROYAL J. GLOOD, *Viborg*
MERTON GLOVER, *Porcupine*
DON G. GRIEVES, *Winner*
ARCHIE M. GUBBRUD, *Alcester*
O. A. GUSTAFSON, *Astoria*
ROY W. HAAS, *Miller*
ALBERT O. HAMRE, *Willow Lake*
LOUIS F. HARDING, *Pierre*
IVER J. HENJUM, *Garretson*
ARLEY HILL, *Brookings*
RALPH O. HILLGREN, *2021 S. Phillips Ave., Sioux Falls*
O. A. HODSON, *Martin*
VERNE H. JENNINGS, *716 W. Twenty-Fifth, Sioux Falls*
ERNEST L. JOHNSON, *Gayville*
J. T. JOHNSON, *Hawarden, Iowa*
W. E. KURLE, *McLaughlin*
CHARLES LACEY, *1721 S. Phillips Ave., Sioux Falls*
FRANK LLOYD, *Platte*
THEODORE W. McFARLING, *Wolsey*
HARRY H. MARTENS, *Wessington*
GEORGE E. MAY, *324 S. State St., Aberdeen*
G. W. MILLS, *Wall*
W. P. MYHREN, *1123 South St., Rapid City*
RALPH A. NAUMAN, *Gettysburg*
A. A. NEPSTAD, *409 E. Fifth, Mitchell*
J. C. NOONAN, *Highmore*
WALTER NORDSTROM, *Sioux Falls*

ROBERT A. ODEN, *Vermillion*
HERBERT W. ORTMAN, *Canistota*
ED OXNER, *Mobridge*
S. Robert PEARSON, *Webster*
HERMAN G. PIETZ, *Parkston*
W. A. POELSTRA, SR., *Springfield*
MERLE POMMER, *Castlewood*
DON PORTER, *Chamberlain*
DAVID PULFORD, *Madison*
BEN H. RADCLIFFE, *Hitchcock*
ALFRED J. RAVE, *Trent*
A. C. ROSSOW, *Herreid*
JOE SCHNEIDER, *Eagle Butte*
FERDINAND SCHWADER, *Howard*
A. J. SIEDSCHLAW, *Alpena*
SANDER SLETTO, *Presho*
DELOS C. SMITH, *DeSmet*
MORRELL R. SOLEM, *Volin*
ANDREW STOEBNER, *Eureka*
CHARLES STRONG, *Enning*
DAVID J. WIPF, *Menno*

TENNESSEE

Senate

Democrats 28   Republicans 4   Independent 1

T. ROBERT ACKLEN, *Columbian Mutual Tower, Memphis*
CLIFFORD R. ALLEN, JR., *Third Natl. Bank Bldg., Nashville*
HENRY R. BELL, *Loudon*
LARRY BETTIS, *Friendship*
BEN L. CASH, 210 *James Bldg., Chattanooga*
LEWIS I. CHASE, *Kingsport*
LANDON COLVARD, *Pikeville*
G. C. CRIDER, *Huntingdon*
JAMES P. DIAMOND, *Jackson*
CUYLER DUNBAR, *Woodlawn*
BROOKS B. ESLICK, *Pulaski*
McALLEN FOUTCH, *Smithville*
MALCOLM A. FULTS, *Altamont*
J. H. GAMMON, 521 *W. Cumberland, Knoxville*
ERNEST GUFFEY, *Athens*
HENRY GUPTON, *Newman Rd., Nashville*
PHIL B. HARRIS, *Greenfield*
MRS. MABEL W. HUGHES, *Arlington*
WAYNE HUNT, *Fruitland*
JAMES M. JONES, JR., *Lewisburg*
WILLIS H. MADDOX, *Lebanon*
JARED MADDUX, *Cookeville*
CARROLL G. OAKES, *Morristown*
J. DeFOE PEMBERTON, *Huntsville*
RILEY RANDEL, *Columbia*
T. R. RAY, *Shelbyville*
J. L. RIDLEY, *Thompson Station*
ED. P. A. SMITH, *Columbian Mutual Tower, Memphis*
JOE H. SPENCER, *Erin*
CHARLES A. STAINBACK, *Somerville*
JOE SWANAY, *Elizabethton*
JUSTIN THRASHER, *Selmer*
WM. MARTIN YOUNG, *Dixon Springs*

House

Democrats 79   Republicans 19

G. L. ADERHOLD, *Etowah*

SAM T. ANDERSON, *South Pittsburg*
FRED C. ATCHLEY, *Sevierville*
LEONARD C. AYMON, 1901 *Duncan Ave., Chattanooga*
RAY BAIRD, *Rockwood*
IRA L. BAKER, *R.F.D., Sparta*
W. L. BARRY, *Lexington*
HARRY BEARD, JR., *Lebanon*
I. D. BEASLEY, *Carthage*
D. S. BEELER, *Rutledge*
J. I. BELL, *Savannah*
JAMES J. BERTUCCI, 55 *S. Main St., Memphis*
NORMAN BINKLEY, JR., 206 *McCall St., Nashville*
HARRY H. BLACKWELL, *Centerville*
JAMES L. BOMAR, *Shelbyville*
JAMES H. BOSWELL, *Jackson*
MILTON BOWERS, SR., 317 *Poplar Ave., Memphis*
ROBERT L. BROOME, 7101 *Stone Mill Rd., Knoxville*
BUFORD R. BUNN, 509 *Childers St., Pulaski*
BARTEE BURKS, *Selmer*
JAMES W. BURROW, 301 *E. Strathmore Circle, Memphis*
LEE CARTER, *Gainesboro*
EUGENE N. COLLINS, *James Bldg., Chattanooga*
J. T. CRAIG, *Covington*
L. E. CRIHFIELD, JR., *Halls*
ERNEST CROUCH, *McMinnville*
JAMES H. CUMMINGS, *Woodbury*
MRS. FRAZIER DAVIS, *Dayton*
MACLIN DAVIS, JR., *American Trust Bldg., Nashville*
T. J. DAVIS, *Eidson*
BARTON DEMENT, *Murfreesboro*
WARD DeWITT, JR., *Stahlman Bldg., Nashville*
RAY DILLON, *Crossville*
PLEAS DOYLE, *Linden*
JOE F. DYER, *Cookeville*
CHARLES T. EBLEN, *Lenoir City*
JERRY FLIPPIN, *Milan*
WALTER I. FORRESTER, 106 *Porter Bldg., Memphis*
W. K. FOSTER, *Middleton*
SAM GILKEY, *Henry*
DALE GLOVER, *Obion*
JOHN R. GORMAN, 740 *Holly Dr., Memphis*
GEORGE D. GRACEY, *Covington*
CLIFF HAGEWOOD, *Ashland City*
J. A. HEAD, *Brownsville*
DAMON R. HEADDEN, *Ridgely*
DOUGLAS HENRY, JR., 5813 *Vine Ridge Dr., Nashville*
WILLIAM D. HOWELL, *Dover*
THOMAS G. HULL, *Greeneville*
SAM L. JENKINS, 111 *Union St., Nashville*
L. B. JENNINGS, *Tullahoma*
J. FRED JOHNSON, 707 *Pyron Lane, Chattanooga*
JACK J. JOHNSON, *Elizabethton*
JOHN R. JONES, *Erwin*
JOE THOMAS KELLEY, *Mt. Pleasant*
JOE F. KRAUS, *Lawrenceburg*
ODELL C. LANE, *R.F.D. 16, Knoxville*
T. R. LASLEY, *Jackson*
BOOKER LITTLE, *Trenton*
ROBERT L. LITTLETON, *Dickson*
A. R. McCAMMON, JR., *R.F.D., Maryville*
CLAY McCARLEY, *Somerville*
DALTON McKELLIP, *Cleveland*
RICHARD T. MOORE, *Newbern*
H. A. MORGAN, *Henderson*
TED MORRIS, *Johnson City*

GEO. E. MORROW, *Union Planters Bank, Memphis*
REAGOR MOTLOW, *Lynchburg*
EDWARD C. MURRAY, *La Follette*
L. S. NEASE, *Newport*
ALLEN M. O'BRIEN, *Springfield*
H. B. PAFFORD, *Camden*
EUGENE PENNINGTON, *Madisonville*
PAUL A. PHILLIPS, 1109 *Inglewood Dr., Nashville*
KING G. PORTER, *R.F.D., Humboldt*
M. T. PUCKETT, *Smithville*
JOHN M. PURDY, *Oak Ridge*
JAMES H. QUILLEN, 338 *E. Center St., Kingsport*
JOHN M. RICHARDSON, *Clarksville*
W. A. RICHARDSON, *Culleoka*
ROBERT H. ROBERTS, *Byrdstown*
HAROLD B. RONEY, *Hendersonville*
BEN ROUTON, *Paris*
SCHULTZ ROWLAND, *Tazewell*
MRS. C. FRANK SCOTT, 715 *Cypress Dr., Memphis*
W. FRANK SMITH, *Decherd*
H. C. SWALLOWS, *Livingston*
W. SHANNON THOMAS, *Dresden*
THURMAN THOMPSON, *Lewisburg*
O. S. UFFELMAN, *Erin*
J. O. WALKER, *Franklin*
AUBREY L. WEST, *Lafayette*
ELMER W. WHITE, 330 *Rennoc, Knoxville*
JOHN L. WILLIAMS, *Huntingdon*
FRANK WINSTON, *Bristol*
J. BRICE WISECARVER, *Jefferson City*
FRED I. WOMACK, *Fayetteville*
RAYMOND V. WRIGHT, 1966 *N. Clovia, Memphis*
(1 vacancy)

TEXAS

Senate

Democrats 30   Republicans 0

A. M. AIKIN, JR., *Paris*
CARLOS ASHLEY, *Llano*
SEARCY BRACEWELL, 704 *City Natl. Bank Bldg., Houston*
MRS. NEVEILLE H. COLSON, *Navasota*
KILMER B. CORBIN, 223 *Lubbock Natl. Bank Bldg., Lubbock*
WILLIAM S. FLY, 110 *West Forrest, Victoria*
JEP S. FULLER, 228 *Adams Bldg., Port Arthur*
DORSEY B. HARDEMAN, *McBurnett Bldg., San Angelo*
GRADY HAZLEWOOD, *Box 2570, Amarillo*
ABRAHAM KAZEN, JR., *Raymond Bldg., Laredo*
ROGERS KELLEY, *Box 390, Edinburg*
WARDLOW LANE, *Center*
O. E. LATIMER, 1207 *Natl. Bank of Commerce Bldg., San Antonio*
OTTIS E. LOCK, *Box 1275, Lufkin*
WARREN MCDONALD, 313 *Peoples Bank Bldg., Tyler*
CRAWFORD C. MARTIN, *Box 257, Hillsboro*
GEORGE MOFFETT, *Chillicothe*
WILLIAM T. MOORE, *Box 1187, Bryan*
FRANK OWEN III, 206 *Bassett Tower, El Paso*
GEO. PARKHOUSE, 1226 *Natl. City Bldg., Dallas*
JIMMY PHILLIPS, *Angleton*
DAVID W. RATLIFF, *Box 1123, Stamford*

RAY ROBERTS, 704 *N. Morris, McKinney*
ANDY ROGERS, 910 *Avenue H, NW, Childress*
JOHNNIE B. ROGERS, *State Senate, Austin*
JARRARD SECREST, *First Natl. Bldg., Temple*
WILLIAM H. SHIREMAN, 415 *Wilson Tower, Corpus Christi*
GUS J. STRAUSS, *Hallettsville*
R. A. WEINERT, *Seguin*
DOYLE WILLIS, *Commercial Standard Bldg., Fort Worth*
(1 vacancy)

House

Democrats 146   Republicans 0

MACK ALLISON, *Star Rt., Box 50, Mineral Wells*
LOUIS H. ANDERSON, *Box 81, Midland*
BILL R. ANDIS, *Box 1188, Amarillo*
L. L. ARMOR, *Box 197, Sweetwater*
BEN ATWELL, 410 *Fidelity Union Life Bldg., Dallas*
ROBERT W. BAKER, 505 *Melrose Bldg., Houston*
STANLEY BANKS, JR., *Box 829, San Antonio*
GARTH C. BATES, 1616 *Second Natl. Bank Bldg., Houston*
MARSHALL O. BELL, 222 *W. Woodlawn, San Antonio*
J. A. BENTON, *Box 56, Wylie*
DOUGLAS E. BERGMAN, *Mercantile Bank Bldg., Dallas*
EDGAR L. BERLIN, *Box 1925, Port Neches*
A. J. BISHOP, JR., *R.F.D. 4, Winters*
JOHN E. BLAINE, 310 *San Francisco, El Paso*
FLOYD BRADSHAW, *Box 121, Weatherford*
PAUL BRASHEAR, 305 *W. Seventh, Cisco*
DOLPH BRISCOE, JR., *Box 359, Uvalde*
J. GORDON BRISTOW, *Box 230, Big Spring*
JACK C. BRYAN, *Buffalo*
JOE BURKETT, JR., *Schreiner Bank Bldg., Kerrville*
JIM CARMICHALL, *Box 400, Hillsboro*
FRANK H. CARPENTER, *Box 426, Sour Lake*
WAGGONER CARR, 314 *Lubbock Natl. Bank Bldg., Lubbock*
W. R. CHAMBERS, *May*
JOE N. CHAPMAN, *Mitchell Bldg., Sulphur Springs*
TOM CHEATHAM, *Box 308, Cuero*
JAMIE H. CLEMENTS, *Crockett*
E. J. CLOUD, *Box 28, Rule*
CARROLL COBB, *Lubbock Natl. Bank Bldg., Lubbock*
CRISS COLE, 715 *Kress Bldg., Houston*
J. W. COOPER, JR., 405 *Wilson Bldg., Corpus Christi*
R. H. CORY, 310 *Victoria Natl. Bank Bldg., Victoria*
WARREN C. COWEN, 3640 *W. Seminary Dr., Fort Worth*
JAMES E. COX, 324½ *N. Main, Conroe*
JOHN T. COX, *First National Bank Bldg., Temple*
E. F. CRIM, 301 *Evenside, Henderson*
JOHN L. CROSTHWAIT, 3709 *Amherst, Dallas*
E. DE LA GARZA, *Box 805, Mission*
B. H. DEWEY, JR., *Box 347, Bryan*
VIRGINIA DUFF, *Ferris*
LOUIS DUGAS, JR., 1023 *Avenue C, Orange*
WM. M. ELLIOTT, 204 *W. Marvick, Pasadena*
J. T. ELLIS, JR., *Box 357, Weslaco*
ANTHONY FENOGLIO, *Box 570, Nocona*
BEN FERRELL, *Box 359, Tyler*
CURTIS FORD, JR., 3137 *Gollihar, Corpus Christi*

George D. Ford, *Box 273, Bogota*
Gustin Garrett, *Box 777, Raymondville*
J. O. Gillham, *Box 1112, Brownfield*
W. W. Glass, *401 S. Bolton, Jacksonville*
Ben A. Glusing, *Box 846, Kingsville*
L. DeWitt Hale, *708 Wilson Bldg., Corpus Christi*
D. B. Hardeman, *Denison*
Guy Hazlett, *1105 Cooley, Borger*
W. S. Heatly, *Drawer 1, Paducah*
H. A. Heideke, *Box 747, Seguin*
Charlie Heitman, *222 Bailey, Nacogdoches*
Grady Hogue, *533 Bryson Ave., Athens*
L. L. Holstein, *Pandora*
Jean E. Hosey, *Natl. Hotel Bldg., Galveston*
Horace B. Houston, Jr., *410 Fidelity Union Life Bldg., Dallas*
Reagan R. Huffman, *Box 622, Marshall*
Chas. E. Hughes, *Commercial Bldg., Sherman*
Billy Hunt, *Center*
Edgar Hutchins, Jr., *Greenville*
Maud Isaacks, *3021 Federal St., El Paso*
J. Horace Jackson, *Atlanta*
Robt. C. Jackson, Jr., *Box 272, Corsicana*
Alonzo W. Jamison, Jr., *616 W. Oak, Denton*
Pearce Johnson, *Littlefield Bldg., Austin*
Obie Jones, *1307 Larkwood, Austin*
Thos. R. Joseph, Jr., *2313 Washington Ave., Waco*
Moyne L. Kelly, *Afton*
Don Kennard, *2224 Skyline Dr., Fort Worth*
Harold G. Kennedy, *Box 146, Marble Falls*
Tom King, *322 W. Jefferson, Dallas*
Chas. D. Kirkham, Jr., *Cleburne*
W. G. Kirklin, *1313 Amburgey, Odessa*
Homer L. Koliba, Sr., *Box 564, Columbus*
T. W. Lane, *Box 6, Wharton*
Truett Latimer, *217 Sayles Blvd., Abilene*
Otis Lee, *3411 Canal Ave., Groves*
Henry G. Lehman, *Box 223, Giddings*
Chas. J. Lieck, Jr., *417 S. Main, San Antonio*
Jim Lindsey, *House of Representatives, Austin*
Bert T. McDaniel, *Service Mutual Bldg., Waco*
Scott McDonald, *Dan Waggoner Bldg., Fort Worth*
Frank B. McGregor, *Liberty Bldg., Waco*
Malcolm McGregor, *Box 7887, University Station, Austin*
Grainger W. McIlhany, *Box 276, Wheeler*
W. T. McNeil, *Edna*
Amos A. Martin, *348 Fourteenth St. NE, Paris*
Maury Maverick, Jr., *709 Maverick Bldg., San Antonio*
Carlton Moore, *903 Electric Bldg., Houston*
Jim Moore, *Arlington*
Jack C. Morgan, *Kaufman*
Bob Mullen, *Box 60, Alice*
Menton J. Murray, *1022 E. Pierce, Harlingen*
Fred Niemann, *House of Representatives, Austin*
Jesse M. Osborn, *Muleshoe*
Harold B. Parish, *Box 567, Taft*
Robert Patten, *Belle-Jim Hotel, Jasper*
Robt. R. Patterson, *Snyder*
Maurice S. Pipkin, *Box 1032, Brownsville*
Joe R. Pool, *Box 5303, Dallas*
Herman V. Puckett, *R.F.D. 1, Quitman*
Joe Pyle, *506 Insurance Bldg., Fort Worth*

Elbert Reeves, *Matador*
W. C. Ross, Sr., *Box 3215, Beaumont*
Jerry Sadler, *Percilla*
Charles Sandahl, Jr., *2412 E. First St., Austin*
Barefoot Sanders, *1625 Kirby Bldg., Dallas*
Leroy Saul, *Box 642, Kress*
Scott P. Sayers, *304 Century Life Bldg., Fort Worth*
O. H. Schram, *Box 108, Taylor*
A. R. Schwartz, *4720 Avenue O, Galveston*
Walter C. Schwartz, *Box 433, Brenham*
F. S. Seeligson, *1633 Milam Bldg., San Antonio*
J. W. Shannon, *674 N. Barton, Stephenville*
Ed Sheridan, *Box 6791, San Antonio*
Richard C. Slack, *511 S. Hickory, Pecos*
Max C. Smith, *Box 16, San Marcos*
Will L. Smith, *336 Bowie, Beaumont*
Wade F. Spilman, *Box 1128, McAllen*
Gilbert M. Spring, *Apple Springs*
Vernon J. Stewart, *3105 Stewart Drive, Waco*
Thomas H. Stilwell, *317 Texarkana National Bank Bldg., Texarkana*
Stanton Stone, *415 W. Second St., Freeport*
Cecil Storey, *Box 666, Longview*
R. L. Strickland, *Frost Natl. Bank Bldg., San Antonio*
W. A. Stroman, *215 N. Washington St., San Angelo*
Reuben D. Talasek, *Box 396, Temple*
George M. Thurmond, *Box 1053, Del Rio*
James A. Turman, *House of Representatives, Austin*
J. B. Walling, *2921 Moffett St., Wichita Falls*
J. F. Ward, *Box 469, Rosenberg*
Jack Welch, *Drawer 341, Marlin*
Bob Wheeler, *Tilden*
Richard C. White, *510 Bassett Tower, El Paso*
J. Edgar Wilson, *1020 Milam, Amarillo*
J. E. Winfree, *Scanlon Bldg., Houston*
Sam E. Wohlford, *Box 103, Stratford*
Bill Wood, *503 Blackstone Bldg., Tyler*
James W. Yancy, *1821 Melrose Bldg., Houston*
Herman Yezak, *Bremond*
J. C. Zbranek, *Daisetta*
(4 vacancies)

UTAH

Senate

Republicans 16   Democrats 7

Donald T. Adams, *Monticello*
R. Clair Anderson, *Manti*
Reed Bullen, *Radio Station KUNU, Box 264, Logan*
C. Taylor Burton, *1812 Millbrook Rd., Salt Lake City*
Luke Clegg, *161 W. First S., Provo*
Merrill K. Davis, *53 E. Fourth S., Salt Lake City*
Elias L. Day, *327 Milton Ave., Salt Lake City*
J. Francis Fowles, *2453 Taylor Ave., Ogden*
Marl D. Gibson, *Price*
Carlyle F. Gronning, *Milford*
Orval Hafen, *206 E. 100 N., St. George*
D. E. Hammond, *2134 Bryan Ave., Salt Lake City*
Alonzo F. Hopkin, *Woodruff*
L. Rulon Jenkins, *R.F.D. 2, (via Ogden) Plain City*

CLIFTON G. M. KERR, *Tremonton*
SHERMAN P. LLOYD, 1467 *Arlington Dr., Salt Lake City*
RENDELL N. MABEY, 6397 *S. Orchard Dr., Bountiful*
FRANK M. OPENSHAW, 1345 *Harrison Ave., Salt Lake City*
SOL J. SELVIN, 161 *S. First W., Tooele*
B. H. STRINGHAM, 209 *E. First N., Vernal*
GRANT S. THORN, *Box 111, Springville*
H. ROLAND TIETJEN, 55 *W. Second N., Monroe*
DILWORTH S. WOOLLEY, 343 *Virginia, Salt Lake City*

House

Republicans 33   Democrats 27

HOWARD C. BADGER, 2290 *Berkley Ave., Salt Lake City*
HAVEN J. BARLOW, *Layton*
ALBERT BARNES, *Wellington*
ARTHUR BRIAN, *Loa*
WILLIAM N. BROTHERSON, *Boneta*
GEORGE J. BURCK, *Moab*
EARL BUTTERS, *Morgan*
MRS. GERALD CAZIER, *Nephi*
REUEL L. CHRISTENSEN, *Ephraim*
CHARLES W. CLAYBAUGH, 117 *W. Fifth S., Brigham*
HUBERT COCHRAN, 532 *S. Ninth W., Salt Lake City*
W. HARRISON CONOVER, 157 *W. Second S., Springville*
ALBERT J. COPE, 821 *S. Second W., Salt Lake City*
E. A. CROFTS, 541 *N. 350 W., Richfield*
LEE W. DALEBOUT, 1058 *Lincoln St., Salt Lake City*
HAROLD V. DAVIS, 7247 *S. 1300 E., Midvale*
J. DONALD ESPLIN, *Orderville*
ARCHIE O. GARDNER, *Delta*
WENDELL GROVER, *Riverton*
ORVILLE GUNTHER, *Box 41, Lehi*
PARLEY G. HALL, *Wellsville*
THORIT C. HEBERTSON, *R.F.D. 1, Box 393, Provo*
ROBERT J. HENDERSON, *Hiawatha*
ALLEN L. HODGSON, 57 *E. Sixth S., Payson*
CLAIR R. HOPKINS, 91 *N. First W., Vernal*
RICHARD C. HOWE, *Box 34, Murray*
GEORGE A. HURST, JR., *Blanding*
PARLEY IPSON, *Panguitch*
LELAND W. IVERS, *Midway*
MAURICE JENSEN, *Huntington*
LAWRENCE B. JOHNSON, *Randolph*
JAREN L. JONES, 215 *Tenth Ave., Salt Lake City*
KLEON KERR, *Tremonton*
EDWARD C. LARSEN, 2752 *N. 400 E., Ogden*
W. G. LARSON, 9064 *W. 2700 S., Magna*
OSCAR W. MCCONKIE, JR., 425 *E. First S., Salt Lake City*
ED J. MCPOLIN, *Park City*
ARLO P. MESSINGER, *Beaver*
HARLEY MONSON, *Smithfield*
MCKINLEY MORRILL, *Junction*
LLOYD C. MURDOCK, 303 *Fifteenth, Ogden*
CLARENCE L. PALMER, 621 *N. Twelfth W., Salt Lake City*
CHARLES E. PETERSON, *Box 350, Provo*
LIONEL L. PETERSON, *Mt. Pleasant*
M. BLAINE PETERSON, 1018 *Twenty-sixth, Ogden*
CHARLES W. ROMNEY, 410 *Hollywood Ave., Salt Lake City*

JOHN W. ROWBERRY, 6 *Park Ave., Tooele*
WALKER LEE RUSSELL, *McKinnon, Wyoming*
GEORGE H. SEARLE, 2937 *Adams St., Salt Lake City*
HEBER M. SEVY, 271 *N. 300 W., Cedar City*
RALPH A. SHEFFIELD, 535 *S. Twelfth E., Salt Lake City*
CHARLES W. SPENCE, 143 *Herbert Ave., Salt Lake City*
CARL H. TAYLOR, 2731 *Liberty Ave., Ogden*
G. DOUGLAS TAYLOR, 1736 *Mill Creek Way, Salt Lake City*
E. G. THOMAS, 38 *N. State, Apt. 1, Salt Lake City*
ROSS THORESON, 1475 *Blaine Ave., Salt Lake City*
ELIZABETH VANCE, 1134 *Twelfth St., Ogden*
REID WANGSGAARD, 356 *N. First W., Logan*
CHARLES WELCH, JR., 1940 *Michigan Ave., Salt Lake City*
EVAN J. WOODBURY, *St. George*

VERMONT

Senate

Republicans 22   Democrats 7   Independents 1

HUGH AGNEW, 5 *Bullock St., Brattleboro*
PHILIP A. ANGELL, ESQ., *Randolph*
GEORGE H. ASH, *R.F.D. 1, Bristol*
LESLIE BARRY, *Burlington*
ASA S. BLOOMER, *West Rutland*
JOHN H. BOYLAN, *Brighton*
E. FRANK BRANON, *Fairfield*
HAROLD M. BROWN, *Castleton*
THOMAS G. BUCKLEY, *Bennington*
MRS. GERALDINE L. CLARK, *R.F.D. 1, Vergennes*
GUY H. CLEVELAND, *Woodstock*
FRED B. CRAWFORD, *Newport*
WILLIAM H. HALE, *St. Albans*
MRS. MILDRED C. HAYDEN, *R.F.D. 3, Barre*
CARLETON G. HOWE, *Dorset*
FRANK D. JONES, *Cambridge*
JOHN KEELER, *Barton*
W. GORDON LOVELESS, *East Montpelier*
HECTOR T. MARCOUX, *Burlington*
CHESTER C. MARTELL, *South Hero*
GEORGE C. MORSE, *Danville*
GRAHAM S. NEWELL, *St. Johnsbury*
FRANK R. O'BRIEN, *Shelburne*
EUGENE A. RICHARD, *Winooski*
DONALD L. SMITH, *R.F.D. 1, Barre*
LEWIS E. SPRINGER, JR., *Hartland*
J. HAROLD STACEY, *Windsor*
RALPH E. STAFFORD, *South Wallingford*
HENRY A. STODDARD, *Bellows Falls*
ORIN A. THOMAS, SR., *Rutland*

House

Republicans 217   Democrats 24   Independents 2

GEORGE C. ACKLEY, *R.F.D., Rutland*
JAMES H. ADAMS, *R.F.D., Fair Haven*
GEORGE W. AINSWORTH, *South Royalton*
ALLEN C. ALFRED, *South Burlington*
HERMAN L. ALLEN, *Orwell*
HENRY AMADON, *R.F.D. 2, Bennington*
DONALD S. ARNOLD, *Bethel*
EARL AYER, *R.F.D. 2, Burlington*
CLYDE BABCOCK, *East Hardwick*

RALPH O. BAIRD, *R.F.D., Pittsford*
CLIFFORD A. BAKER, *R.F.D. 3, Brattleboro*
PHILIP E. BARRE, *Readsboro*
RAY H. BARRY, SR., *Belvidere*
OREN W. BATES, *Sherburne Center*
AUGUST F. BAUER, *R.F.D. 1, Londonderry*
J. FORBES BEATON, *South Ryegate*
LESTER F. BEATON, *Jacksonville*
MRS. MILDRED B. BEATTIE, *Guildhall*
MYRON J. BEEBE, *Rutland*
CLARENCE W. BEEDE, *Washington*
CHARLES D. BENTLEY, SR., *R.F.D. 1, Arlington*
MELFORD D. BIBENS, *West Rupert*
FRANCIS W. BILLADO, ESQ., *67 Edgerton St., Rutland*
NOBLE F. BIRCHARD, *Shoreham*
WILFRED J. BISSON, *R.F.D., Barre*
ROBERT H. BOOTH, *Guildhall*
WILLIAM BOUDLE, *Bloomfield*
DANIEL P. BRAGG, *St. Albans*
LELAND L. BRIGHAM, *Waits River*
ALLEN H. BRITTON, *Hartland*
MRS. BERNICE V. BROMLEY, *Ascutney*
CHARLES H. BROWN, ESQ., *Box 66, Brandon*
MRS. DOROTHY R. BROWN, *Essex Junction*
R. EDGAR BRUCE, *South Vernon, Massachusetts*
GEORGE H. BRUSH, *R.F.D., Brandon*
MRS. HELEN L. BULLIS, *Grand Isle*
LEON V. BUSHEY, *Bristol*
ORIN C. CARPENTER, *Randolph Center*
RAYMOND J. CASSADY, *Plainfield*
MRS. ETHEL G. CASSIDY, *R.F.D., Highgate Center*
R. LLOYD CHAFFEE, *Enosburg Falls*
WINN G. CHAMBERLAIN, *Pittsfield*
LEWIS W. CHAMBERLIN, *Wells River*
ULRIC E. CHOINIERE, *R.F.D. 2, Orleans*
RALPH P. CHURCHILL, *R.F.D. 2, Putney*
ELLIE CLARK, *Westmore*
MRS. MABEL R. COBB, *Westford*
FRANK T. COBURN, *Stratford*
MRS. MALVINE COLE, *Stratton*
MRS. RUTH A. COLE, *R.F.D. 2, Arlington*
MRS. EVELYN L. COLEMAN, *South Londonderry*
WILLIAM O. COMSTOCK, *R.F.D. 3, Barre*
MRS. MYRTLE M. CONANT, *R.F.D., Richmond*
WILBERT LEON CONRAD, *Morrisville*
MICHAEL F. CORRADO, *East Fairfield*
HORMIDAS COUTURE, *Westfield*
MRS. ELSIE A. COWLES, *Thetford*
ARTHUR W. CRAMTON, *Middletown Springs*
W. PERLEY CRAMTON, *East Berkshire*
MRS. ALICE S. CROWE, *Sheldon Springs*
MRS. MILDRED P. CUTTING, *Concord*
GERALD W. DAVIS, *Richford*
ROBT. W. H. DAVIS, *13 Prospect St., Newport City*
LYLE DAY, *Sheffield*
WARREN L. DAY, *Jericho*
STOWELL W. DEWEY, *R.F.D. 3, Middlebury*
MRS. LILLIAN DICKINSON, *R.F.D., Washington*
EZRA S. DIKE, ESQ., *Bristol*
COYT S. DIMICK, *Sharon*
EDWARD B. DOTON, *R.F.D., Woodstock*
DWIGHT DOW, *Albany*
ROBERT K. DOW, *Reading*
WILLIAM J. DUFFY, *R.F.D. 2, North Troy*
CHARLES W. DUNBAR, *Townshend*
ROBERT B. DURKEE, *Tunbridge*
THEODORE D. ELLIOTT, *Morgan Center*

MRS. ETHEL W. EVEREST, *Milton*
MRS. MARGUERITE FARNSWORTH, *Vergennes*
WARREN A. FARRINGTON, *East Peacham*
MRS. MARY W. FIELD, *Charlotte*
E. CLYDE FITCH, *Calais*
PRESTON S. FLINT, *Roxbury*
ROYAL E. FRASER, *Bridgewater*
S. ARTHUR FRIEND, *Passumpsic*
ROBERT T. GANNETT II, ESQ., *139 Main St., Brattleboro*
DANIEL L. GARLAND, *Lincoln*
OLIN D. GAY, *Cavendish*
WILLIAM J. GILMORE, *R.F.D., Wallingford*
MRS. FLORA B. GORHAM, *East Burke*
THOMAS T. GOULD, *East Burke*
CORNELIUS O. GRANAI, ESQ., *46 Beacon St., Barre City*
MRS. CARRIE J. GRAY, *Derby Line*
MRS. JENNIE E. GRAY, *Eden Mills*
STEPHEN GREENE, *West Dover*
BERNARD GREENWOOD, *South Newfane*
FRANK W. GUILD, JR., *Waterbury Center*
BLANCHARD F. HALL, *R.F.D. 2, Poultney*
MRS. MARGARET B. HAMMOND, *Chester Depot*
JOHN E. HANCOCK, *East Hardwick*
GEORGE W. HARRINGTON, ESQ., *Castleton*
JOHN B. HARTE, ESQ., *Bennington*
WILLIAM B. HARTSHORNE, *South Newfane*
HOWARD S. HATCH, *Mt. Holly*
CLARK W. HAZELTINE, *R.F.D. 1, Chester*
WILLIAM T. HERRICK, *North Clarendon*
MERRITT S. HEWITT, JR., *North Bennington*
HAROLD GRIFFITH HIGH, *Weston*
ARTHUR R. HILL, *East Brookfield*
MRS. ETHEL W. HILL, *R.F.D. 1, Ludlow*
WILLIAM C. HILL, ESQ., *Hinesburg*
LAWRENCE HINDS, *St. Albans Town*
WILLIAM H. HOFFMAN, *Salisbury*
HARRY H. HOWE, *R.F.D. 1, Newfane*
SETH H. HUBBARD, *Franklin*
MELVIN HUDSON, *R.F.D. 2, Lyndonville*
PERCY B. ILLINGWORTH, *R.F.D., Bartonsville*
CHESTER A. INGALLS, *Seymour St., Middlebury*
EDWARD G. JANEWAY, *Londonderry*
ARTHUR J. JARVIS, *Isle La Motte*
EDWIN J. JARVIS, *Alburg*
RALPH C. JENKINS, *R.F.D. 2, West Burke*
MRS. ROSE B. JENNETT, *Granville*
MRS. EDITH A. JOHNSON, *West Fairlee*
FRED A. JOHNSON, *Rochester*
L. THOMAS JUDD, *Canaan*
MRS. PEARL I. KEELER, *Orleans*
MRS. WINIFRED W. KELTON, *Cambridgeport*
MRS. ALBERTA S. KENT, *R.F.D. 3, Vergennes*
F. RAY KEYSER, JR., ESQ., *Chelsea*
FRANCIS E. KING, *Greensboro Bend*
GLENDON N. KING, *12 Byam St., Northfield*
RALPH M. KNAPP, *Star Rt., Bennington*
WILLIAM C. KNOX, *Starksboro*
MRS. LUCIA T. LADD, *Worcester*
JULIUS A. LAFLAM, *North Ferrisburg*
PEARL D. LAKIN, *Peru*
GEORGE W. LAMPHERE, *West Rutland*
MRS. ALICE C. LANDON, *R.F.D., New Haven*
CECIL LANDON, *R.F.D., Danby*
JUSTIN M. LANOU, *Irasburg*
WYMAN E. LANPHEAR, *Hyde Park*
LOUIS LAVIN, ESQ., *Websterville*

THE BOOK OF THE STATES

656

GEORGE LAWSON, *R.F.D., Newport*
REID LEFEVRE, *Manchester Center*
HOMER K. LEGGETT, SR., *Colchester*
SAMUEL R. LOOMIS, *Wolcott*
EDWARD C. LUND, *North Concord*
HAROLD J. LYON, *Williston*
BERT A. McCLURE, *Wallingford*
REV. CHARLES H. McCURDY, *Bondville*
DAVID M. McNEIL, *Warren*
MRS. GERTRUDE R. MALLARY, *Bradford*
R. HENRY MANCHESTER, *Waterville*
GLENN E. MARSHALL, *Norton*
MRS. BERNICE M. MAXHAM, *R.F.D. 1,
    Montpelier*
JOSEPH H. METCALF, *R.F.D., Underhill*
ELMER M. MONTGOMERY, *Braintree*
GALEN L. MOORE, *Barnard*
RAYMOND H. MOORE, *Saxtons River*
GERALD MORSE, *Groton*
JOHN MULVEY, ESQ., *52 Diamond St., St. Albans
    City*
DON P. NARAMORE, *Lowell*
GEORGE W. NEIL, *Pittsford*
T. BARDEN NELSON, *West Pawlet*
RUSSELL F. NIQUETTE, ESQ., *41 E. Allen St.,
    Winooski*
MRS. JANE L. NORRIS, *R.F.D., Newport Center*
CHARLES H. ORMSBEE, *R.F.D. 1, Montpelier*
RAYMOND H. OUELLETTE, *West Halifax*
PHILIP F. PARAH, *Fairfax*
CARL H. PARKER, *North Springfield*
RUSSELL PARKS, *Dorset*
SAMUEL A. PARSONS, *Bomoseen*
MRS. BERTHA PATRIDGE, *North Concord*
JOHN G. PETTY, *Bridport*
JAMES B. PHILLIPS, *Benson*
LOREN R. PIERCE, ESQ., *Woodstock*
MRS. LEMUEL G. PIKE, *Wilmington*
NORMAN J. PORTER, *Cambridge*
WILLIAM S. POWERS, *Westminster*
ALVIN S. PRATT, *R.F.D. 4, Vergennes*
HORACE M. PRATT, *R.F.D. 2, Middlebury*
LAURENCE M. PRATT, *Gaysville*
LEVI B. PRATT, *Wells*
CHARLES L. PURRIER, *Montgomery Center*
WILLIAM A. PUTNAM, *Wardsboro*
J. A. RACINE, *West Charleston*
HOMER E. RANKIN, *Fayston*
FRED L. RAVLIN, *R.F.D. 2, Waterbury*
CORNELIUS F. REED, *Wolcott*
THOMAS M. REEVES, ESQ., *106 Colchester Ave.,
    Burlington*
B. RICHARD RHOADES, *Lyndonville*
GEORGE A. RICHARDSON, *Waits River*
HARRY E. ROBBINS, *Derby*
MRS. GLADYS E. ROY, *West Barnet*
MISS BLANCHE ROYAL, *Colebrook, New Hampshire*
MRS. EDITH I. SANFORD, *R.F.D. 1, North Adams,
    Massachusetts*
WAYNE A. SARCKA, *Cuttingsville*
HAROLD A. SARGENT, *Brownsville*
EDGAR H. SCOTT, *Johnson*
HAROLD C. SELLECK, *Star Rt., Brandon*
HARLEY N. SHERMAN, *R.F.D. 1, Waterbury*
CLARENCE L. SMITH, *R.F.D., West Rutland*
HOWARD V. SMITH, *62 Olympus Rd., Proctor*
MICHAEL J. SMITH, *Ripton*
WALTER W. SMITH, *West Fairlee*

EMERSON O. SPAULING, *R.F.D. 2, Cambridge*
CLIFTON C. STAFFORD, *Stowe*
HAROLD R. STAFFORD, *Waitsfield*
MRS. FLORA G. STEVENS, *Sutton*
WINFIELD W. STILES, *Swanton*
JAMES STRUTHERS, *Huntington*
KENNETH SWIFT, *Glover*
MRS. LAURA B. TAISEY, *North Troy*
MRS. ALMA R. TANNER, *Putney*
CHARLES G. TAYLOR, *Bradford*
MYRON C. TAYLOR, *Hancock*
ROBERT P. TAYLOR, *R.F.D., Pawlet*
CHARLES S. TOURVILLE, *South Hero*
MRS. BLANCHE UTLEY, *Woodbury*
EDWARD C. VAIL, *Chester*
LAINE C. VANCE, *Danville*
JOHN J. WACKERMAN, ESQ., *16 Liberty St.,
    Montpelier*
EVERETT O. WALBRIDGE, *Cabot*
GEORGE F. WALKER, *Pleasant St., Ludlow*
BASIL B. WALSH, *R.F.D. 3, Brandon*
FLORENCE M. WARD, *Moretown*
WALTER H. WASHBURN, *Windsor*
URBAN E. WATERMAN, *Norwich*
DERRICK V. WEBB, *Shelburne*
MRS. ELIZABETH W. WEBSTER, *Whiting*
LEON WELLS, *Bakersfield*
LEON A. WHEELER, *Wilmington*
MRS. ESTHER E. WILCOX, *Arlington*
ROBERT A. WILLEY, *Greensboro*
PAUL W. WILLSON, *Lunenburg*
ALBERT C. WILSON, SR., *River St., Fair Haven*
EDNA WINSHIP, *South Windham*
A. DOUGLAS WOOD, *10 Underclyffe Rd.,
    St. Johnsbury*
MRS. VIOLET P. WOOD, *East Haven*
JOHN L. WORTH, *Island Pond, Brighton*
SEAVER D. WRIGHT, *R.F.D., White River Jct.,
    Hartford*
FOSTER A. YOUNG, *Vergennes*
HENRY A. YOUNG, *Craftsbury Common*
(3 vacancies)

VIRGINIA

Senate

Democrats 37   Republicans 3

GEORGE S. ALDHIZER II, *Broadway*
E. ALMER AMES, JR., *Onancock*
ROBERT F. BALDWIN, JR., *116 Brooke Ave., Norfolk*
D. WOODROW BIRD, *Bland*
LLOYD C. BIRD, *303 S. Sixth St., Richmond*
THOMAS H. BLANTON, *Bowling Green*
ARMISTEAD L. BOOTHE, *505 King St., Alexandria*
EDWARD L. BREEDEN, JR., *Bank of Commerce Bldg.,
    Norfolk*
FRANK P. BURTON, *Stuart*
ROBERT Y. BUTTON, *Culpeper*
HARRY F. BYRD, JR., *Winchester*
CURRY CARTER, *Staunton*
STUART B. CARTER, *Fincastle*
TED DALTON, *Radford*
JOHN A. K. DONOVAN, *106 Little Falls St., Falls
    Church*
CHAS. R. FENWICK, *6733 Lee Highway, Arlington*
EARL A. FITZPATRICK, *Roanoke*
MILLS E. GODWIN, JR., *Suffolk*

GARLAND GRAY, *Waverly*
EDWARD E. HADDOCK, 1133 *W. Franklin St., Richmond*
J. D. HAGOOD, *Clover*
STUART E. HALLETT, 104 *Chesterfield Rd., Hampton*
A. S. HARRISON, JR., *Lawrenceville*
S. FLOYD LANDRETH, *Galax*
M. M. LONG, *St. Paul*
EDWARD O. McCUE, JR., *Charlottesville*
GORDON F. MARSH, *Law Bldg., Portsmouth*
W. M. MINTER, *Mathews*
CHARLES T. MOSES, *Appomattox*
BLAKE T. NEWTON, *Hague*
MOSBY G. PERROW, JR., *Krise Bldg., Lynchburg*
BENJAMIN T. PITTS, *Fredericksburg*
WILLIAM B. SPONG, JR., *Colony Theatre Bldg., Portsmouth*
HARRY C. STUART, *Elk Garden*
EUGENE B. SYDNOR, JR., *Box 1474, Richmond*
JOHN H. TEMPLE, 801 *Bollingbrook St., Petersburg*
GEORGE M. WARREN, *Bristol*
EDWARD E. WILLEY, 1205 *Bellevue Ave., Richmond*
ROY V. WOLFE, JR., *Gate City*
LANDON R. WYATT, *Danville*

House

Democrats 94   Republicans 6

HOWARD H. ADAMS, *Eastville*
WILLIAM A. ALEXANDER, *Rocky Mount*
GEORGE L. ALLEN, JR., *Box 1653, Richmond*
N. C. BAILEY, *Orange*
FITZGERALD BEMISS, 1620 *N. Boulevard, Richmond*
JOS. E. BLACKBURN, *Krise Bldg., Lynchburg*
JOHN B. BOATWRIGHT, *Buckingham*
EARLE M. BROWN, *Krise Bldg., Lynchburg*
FRED C. BUCK, *Abingdon*
J. L. CAMBLOS, *Big Stone Gap*
ORBY L. CANTRELL, *Pound*
E. TUCKER CARLTON, 206 *E. Cary St., Richmond*
RUSSELL M. CARNEAL, *Williamsburg*
H. STUART CARTER, *Bristol*
WILLIAM F. CARTER, *Martinsville*
C. WILLIAM CLEATON, *South Hill*
GEORGE M. COCHRAN, *Staunton*
WILLIS E. COHOON, *Suffolk Bank Bldg., Suffolk*
E. C. COMPTON, *Stanardsville*
JOHN WARREN COOKE, *Mathews*
CHARLES B. CROSS, JR., *Law Bldg., Portsmouth*
JOHN H. DANIEL, *Charlotte C.H., Va.*
DELAMATER DAVIS, *Bank of Commerce Bldg., Norfolk*
HARRY B. DAVIS, *R.F.D. 2, Norfolk*
ROY B. DAVIS, *Paces*
FELIX E. EDMUNDS, *Waynesboro*
W. C. ELLIOTT, *Lebanon*
MINETREE FOLKES, JR., *State-Planters Bank Bldg., Richmond*
TOM FROST, *Warrenton*
HENRY B. GORDON, *Charlottesville*
FRANCIS B. GOULDMAN, *Fredericksburg*
C. E. GREEAR, *Fort Blackmore*
CHARLES E. GREEN, JR., *Bedford*
CLAIBORNE D. GREGORY, *Doswell*
KOSSEN GREGORY, *Box 41, Roanoke*
JOHN P. HARPER, 937 *E. Water St., Norfolk*
GEORGE H. HILL, 900 *River Rd., Warwick*
OMER L. HIRST, *Annandale*
SHIRLEY T. HOLLAND, *Windsor*

LAWRENCE H. HOOVER, *Harrisonburg*
EDWARD M. HUDGINS, 704 *First National Bank Bldg., Richmond*
CHARLES K. HUTCHENS, 5510 *Huntington Ave., Newport News*
E. RALPH JAMES, *Hampton*
EDWARD E. LANE, 718 *E. Franklin St., Richmond*
PARIS I. LEADBETTER, *Hopewell*
W. T. LEARY, 5 *Morris St., Portsmouth*
BALDWIN G. LOCHER, *Glasgow*
JOHN A. MacKENZIE, *New Kirn Bldg., Portsmouth*
W. H. McFARLAND, *Haysi*
LEWIS A. McMURRAN, JR., *Newport News*
HARRISON MANN, 1818 *S. Arlington Ridge Rd., Arlington*
PAUL W. MANNS, *Bowling Green*
FRANK P. MONCURE, *Stafford*
WILLARD J. MOODY, *Western Union Bldg., Norfolk*
E. BLACKBURN MOORE, *Berryville*
GARNETT S. MOORE, *Pulaski*
LINDSEY L. MOORE, *Ringgold*
JOSEPH C. MOXLEY, *Independence*
GEORGE L. MUNFORD, *Wakefield*
W. TAYLOE MURPHY, *Warsaw*
M. C. NEWTON, *Narrows*
H. CLYDE PEARSON, *Jonesville*
JOHN M. PECK, JR., *R.F.D. 1, Fincastle*
NAT. W. PENDLETON, *Wytheville*
LUCAS D. PHILLIPS, *Leesburg*
THEODORE C. PILCHER, *Citizens Bank Bldg., Norfolk*
FRED G. POLLARD, 1001 *E. Main St., Richmond*
S. E. POPE, *Drewryville*
C. D. PRICE, *Stanley*
JOSEPH E. PROFFITT, *Floyd*
HAROLD H. PURCELL, *Louisa*
W. GRIFFITH PURCELL, *Mutual Bldg., Richmond*
RANDALL O. REYNOLDS, *Chatham*
ARTHUR H. RICHARDSON, *Dinwiddie*
JOHN F. RIXEY, *Citizens Bank Bldg., Norfolk*
JAMES W. ROBERTS, 129 *W. Main St., Norfolk*
W. RAY ROUSE, *Marion*
JULIAN H. RUTHERFOORD, JR., 141 *Campbell Ave., SW, Roanoke*
TOY D. SAVAGE, JR., 203 *Granby St., Norfolk*
V. S. SHAFFER, *Maurertown*
MELVIN L. SHREVES, *Bloxom*
R. MACLIN SMITH, *Kenbridge*
VERNON C. SMITH, *Grundy*
W. ROY SMITH, *Petersburg*
MRS. KATHRYN H. STONE, 1051 *Twenty-sixth Rd. S., Arlington*
WILLIAM F. STONE, *Martinsville*
LAWRENCE R. THOMPSON, *Rustburg*
JAMES M. THOMSON, *Box 324, Alexandria*
NELSON R. THURMAN, *Box 456, Vinton*
J. RANDOLPH TUCKER, JR., *State-Planters Bank Bldg., Richmond*
C. M. WALDROP, *Mannboro*
CHARLES W. WAMPLER, JR., *Harrisonburg*
JOHN C. WEBB, *Fairfax*
H. RAY WEBBER, *Low Moor*
C. STUART WHEATLEY, 824 *Masonic Bldg., Danville*
JOHN L. WHITEHEAD, *Radford*
ROBERT WHITEHEAD, *Lovingston*
JOSEPH J. WILLIAMS, JR., *Sandston*
WILLIAM L. WINSTON, 1437 *N. Courthouse Rd., Arlington*
JACK W. WITTEN, *North Tazewell*

WASHINGTON

Senate

Republicans 23   Democrats 22

LLOYD J. ANDREWS, *R.F.D.* 1, *Mead*
HOWARD S. BARGREEN, 2821 *Rucker, Everett*
R. C. BARLOW, 1715 *Dock St., Tacoma*
ASA V. CLARK, 305 *Oak, Pullman*
HENRY J. COPELAND, 1204 *Portland Ave., Walla Walla*
DAVID C. COWEN, *Zukor Bldg., Spokane*
B. J. DAHL, 303 *W. Colville Ave., Chewelah*
GERALD G. DIXON, 3726 *S. Tacoma Ave., Tacoma*
E. J. FLANAGAN, 802 *Jefferson Ave., Toppenish*
MICHAEL J. GALLAGHER, 8045 *Burke Ave., Seattle*
STANTON GANDERS, *R.F.D.* 1, *Bickleton*
WILLIAM A. GISSBERG, *R.F.D.* 2, *Marysville*
WILLIAM C. GOODLOE, 1084 *Dexter Horton Bldg., Seattle*
R. R. GREIVE, 4127 *Forty-fifth SW, Seattle*
THOMAS C. HALL, *Skamokawa*
JOHN H. HAPPY, 311 *Paulsen Bldg., Spokane*
NEIL J. HOFF, 405 *Sixth Ave., Tacoma*
LOUIS E. HOFMEISTER, *Box* 203, *Enumclaw*
EUGENE D. IVY, *Miller Bldg., Yakima*
H. N. JACKSON, 5625 *S. J St., Tacoma*
JAMES KEEFE, W. 412 *Glass Ave., Spokane*
REUBEN A. KNOBLAUCH, *Box* 363, *Sumner*
ERNEST W. LENNART, *R.F.D.* 1, *Everson*
RODERICK A. LINDSAY, E. 1230 *Twentieth Ave., Spokane*
PAUL N. LUVERA, 2102 *Nine St., Anacortes*
DALE MCMULLEN, 6818 *Middle Way, Vancouver*
DALE M. NORDQUIST, 505 *S. Washington, Centralia*
HOMER O. NUNAMAKER, 701 *Eleventh St., Bellingham*
FRANCIS PEARSON, 132 *W. Fourteenth, Port Angeles*
TED. G. PETERSON, 2355 *Blue Ridge Dr., Seattle*
W. C. RAUGUST, *Odessa*
EDWARD F. RILEY, 222 *Westlake Ave. N., Seattle* 9
JACK H. ROGERS, *Star Rt.* 1, *Box* 76, *Bremerton*
ALBERT D. ROSELLINI, 1111 *Smith Tower, Seattle*
HOWARD ROUP, *Star Rt.* 1, *Asotin*
JOHN N. RYDER, 6811 *Fifty-fifth Ave. NE, Seattle*
CARLTON I. SEARS, 2412 *S. Columbia, Olympia*
WILLIAM D. SHANNON, 1802 *Parkside Dr., Seattle*
PATRICK D. SUTHERLAND, 1526 *Thirty-eighth Ave., Seattle*
GEORGE D. SWIFT, 436 *N. Williams, Renton*
NAT WASHINGTON, 42 *C St., Ephrata*
THEODORE WILSON, *South Bend*
ANDREW WINBERG, 110 *W. Third St., Aberdeen*
GEORGE ZAHN, *Box* 22, *Methow*
VICTOR ZEDNICK, 1611 *Sixth Ave. W., Seattle*
(1 vacancy)

House

Democrats 50   Republicans 49

ALFRED O. ADAMS, W. 407 *Twenty-sixth Ave., Spokane* 41
EVA ANDERSON, *Box* 785, *Chelan*
HAL G. ARNASON, JR., 700 *Seventeenth St., Bellingham*
ROBERT C. BAILEY, *Box* 121, *South Bend*

HOWARD T. BALL, *S.* 2409 *Jefferson St., Spokane*
W. J. BEIERLEIN, 112 *E. Main St., Auburn*
ROBERT BERNETHY, *R.F.D.* 2, *Box* 221, *Monroe*
HORACE W. BOZARTH, *Mansfield*
GORDON J. BROWN, 415 *Princeton, Fircrest, Tacoma*
THAD BYRNE, *N.* 4214 *Washington St., Spokane*
DAMON R. CANFIELD, *R.F.D.* 1, *Granger*
WALLY CARMICHAEL, *Box* 736, *Everett*
W. E. CARTY, *R.F.D.* 1 *Box* 19, *Ridgefield*
JOE CHYTIL, 1274 *Fifth St., Chehalis*
CECIL C. CLARK, *R.F.D.* 2, *Wapato*
NEWMAN H. CLARK, 1044 *Henry Bldg., Seattle* 1
A. B. COMFORT, 915 *Pacific Ave., Tacoma*
FRANK CONNOR, 2003 *Jackson St., Seattle* 44
JOHN L. COONEY, *N.* 4403 *Adams, Spokane*
DEWEY C. DONOHUE, 506 *E. Richmond, Dayton*
FRED H. DORE, 800 *American Bldg., Seattle*
A. E. EDWARDS, *Deming*
DON ELDRIDGE, 1212 *Montgomery, Mount Vernon*
HARRY S. ELWAY, JR., 3026 *Sumner, Hoquiam*
A. E. FARRAR, 553 *Broadway, Tacoma*
WILLIAM A. FISHER, *R.F.D.* 1, *Lynden*
MORRILL F. FOLSOM, 1805 *Harrison St., Centralia*
R. MORT FRAYN, 2111 *Parkside Dr., Seattle* 2
BERNARD J. GALLAGHER, 805 *Sherwood Bldg., Spokane*
J. CHESTER GORDON, *LaCrosse*
EARL G. GRIFFITH, *Star Rt.* 2, *Usk*
WILBUR G. HALLAUER, *Box* 1398, *Oroville*
H. B. HANNA, 1130 *Springwater Ave., Wenatchee*
JULIA BUTLER HANSEN, *Cathlamet*
HERB HANSON, *Box* 106, *Snohomish*
EDWARD F. HARRIS, *S.* 1618 *Cedar St., Spokane*
DWIGHT S. HAWLEY, 2208 *Market St., Seattle* 7
HENRY HECKENDORN, 1224 *Sixth Ave. W., Seattle*
AL HENRY, *White Salmon*
ANDY HESS, 1414 *SW* 158*th, Seattle* 66
MARK V. HOLLIDAY, *R.F.D.* 7, *Box* 436, *Vancouver*
ELMER HUHTA, 334 *Karr Ave., Hoquiam*
MRS. JOSEPH E. HURLEY, *E.* 730 *Boone Ave., Spokane*
ELMER A. HYPPA, *R.F.D.* 1, *Box* 111, *Buckley*
ELMER E. JOHNSTON, W. 714 *Fourteenth Ave., Spokane*
ARTHUR D. JONES, JR., *E.* 1223 *Fourtieth Ave., Spokane*
MRS. VINCENT F. JONES, 3021 *E.* 135*th, Seattle* 55
CHET KING, *Box* 283, *Raymond*
DOUGLAS G. KIRK, 1236 *Bigelow N., Seattle* 9
GEORGE W. KUPKA, 801 *S. G St., Tacoma* 3
MARK LITCHMAN, JR., 325 *E.* 133*rd St., Seattle*
MILTON R. LONEY, 341 *Newell St., Walla Walla*
CLAUDE H. LORIMER, *R.F.D.* 6, *Box* 296, *Olympia*
GUS LYBECKER, *Pomeroy*
MALCOLM MCBEATH, 2622 *G St., Bellingham*
JOHN G. MCCUTCHEON, 3331 *Olympic Blvd., Tacoma*
DONALD F. MCDERMOTT, 902 *Thirty-seventh Ave. N., Seattle*
JAMES L. MCFADDEN, 1217 *E. Second St., Port Angeles*
AUGUST P. MARDESICH, 1821 *Grand Ave., Everett*
TOM MARTIN, 3209 *Lorne Ave., Olympia*
FRED R. MAST, 1017 *Minor Ave., Seattle*
CATHERINE D. MAY, 201 *N. Twenty-fourth Ave., Yakima*

CLYDE J. MILLER, *R.F.D.* 3, *Box* 356, *Kelso*
FLOYD C. MILLER, 2303 *N. Sixty-second, Seattle* 3
ROY MUNDY, 242 *F St. NW, Ephrata*
ED MUNRO, *Seahurst*
CLAUDE V. MUNSEY, 1810 *E. Fifty-sixth, Tacoma*
MEL T. NEAL, *Des Moines*
MARSHALL A. NEILL, 210 *First Natl. Bank Bldg., Pullman*
HARTNEY A. OAKES, 1702 *N. Forty-seventh St., Seattle* 8
JOHN L. O'BRIEN, 5041 *Lake Washington Blvd. S., Seattle*
RAY OLSEN, 2011 *Fifth Ave., Seattle* 1
OLE H. OLSON, *Box* 222, *Pasco*
JAMES T. OVENELL, *Box* 657, *Concrete*
DELBERT PENCE, *Lind*
HAROLD J. PETRIE, 205 *S. Twelfth Ave., Yakima*
RALPH PURVIS, 245 *Fourth St. Bldg., Bremerton*
A. L. RASMUSSEN, 4031 *Pacific Ave., Tacoma* 8
EMMA ABBOTT RIDGWAY, 413 *Talcott St., Sedro Woolley*
LESTER L. ROBISON, 348 *Catherine St., Walla Walla*
K. O. ROSENBERG, *R.F.D.* 1, *Addy*
RICHARD RUOFF, 511 *E. Forty-seventh, Seattle*
GORDON SANDISON, *Box* 967, *Port Angeles*
CHARLES R. SAVAGE, 1620 *Division St., Shelton*
LEONARD A. SAWYER, 108 *Fourth Ave. SW, Puyallup*
LINCOLN E. SHROPSHIRE, 606 *Miller Bldg., Yakima*
HARRY A. SILER, *Randle*
VERNON A. SMITH, *Box* 7, *Medina*
PAUL M. STOCKER, 207 *Colby Bldg., Everett*
JOHN F. STROM, 1500 *W. Dravus, Seattle* 99
MRS. THOMAS A. SWAYZE, 2910 *N. Twenty-eighth, Tacoma* 7
JEANETTE TESTU, 2138 *Forty-first SW, Seattle* 6
ROBERT D. TIMM, *Harrington*
ARNOLD S. WANG, 2001 *Nipsic, Bremerton*
MAX WEDEKIND, 3729 *Fortieth Ave. SW, Seattle* 6
WILLIAM A. WEITZMAN, *Liberty Lake*
ELLA WINTLER, 800 *E. Twenty-fourth St., Vancouver*
JOHN K. YEAROUT, 600 *W. Third, Aberdeen*
R. C. BRIGHAM YOUNG, 604 *Madison St., South Cle Elum*

WEST VIRGINIA

Senate

Democrats 23   Republicans 9

FRED C. ALLEN, *Marlinton*
JOHN E. AMOS, 612 *Charleston Natl. Bank Bldg., Charleston*
O. H. BALLARD, *Princeton*
RALPH J. BEAN, *Moorefield*
THEODORE M. BOWERS, *New Martinsville*
FRANK L. CAMPBELL, *Riley Law Bldg., Wheeling*
A. CARL CAREY, 1620 *Quarrier St., Charleston*
JOHN E. CARRIGAN, *Mercantile Bldg., Moundsville*
JOHN B. CHENOWETH, 337 *Graham St., Elkins*
O. G. HEDRICK, 600 *State St., Fairmont*
WALTER A. HOLDEN, *Salem*
GLENN JACKSON, *Logan*
LLOYD G. JACKSON, *Hamlin*

W. N. JASPER, JR., *Lewisburg*
BARTOW JONES, *Point Pleasant*
C. H. MCKOWN, *Wayne*
DON K. MARCHAND, 295 *High St., Morgantown*
CLARENCE E. MARTIN, *Martinsburg*
WILLIAM MITCHELL, *Welch*
HARRY E. MOATS, *Harrisville*
JACK A. NUCKOLS, *Lilly Bldg., Beckley*
O. ROY PARKER, *Union*
A. L. REED, *Newburg*
BRAD SAYRE, *Ripley*
LYLE A. SMITH, 1344 *Thirteenth St., Huntington*
DAYTON R. STEMPLE, *Philippi*
ANDY SWEARINGEN, *Walker*
GLENN TAYLOR, *Matewan*
J. ALFRED TAYLOR, JR., *Fayetteville*
HERBERT TRAUBERT, *Follansbee*
RAYMOND J. VASSAR, *Weston*
WARD WYLIE, *Mullens*

House

Democrats 75   Republicans 24

JACK R. ADAMS, 56 *Virginia St., Wheeling*
LARRY W. ANDREWS, *Peoples Bldg., Charleston*
JOHN C. BARBER, *Holden*
JOHN R. BARNES, *Clendenin*
GEORGE F. BENEKE, *Riley Law Bldg., Wheeling*
TENNYSON J. BIAS, 1221 *Washington Blvd., Huntington*
J. E. BLACKBURN, *Bradley*
JOHN R. BLUE, *Romney*
PAT BOARD, JR., 603 *Briarwood Rd., Charleston*
HOBART BOOTH, JR., *Oak Hill*
C. O. BOWER, *Big Bend*
PAUL BOWER, *Mullens*
MARTIN C. BOWLES, *Chamber of Commerce Bldg., Charleston*
RICHARD H. BOWMAN, *Rainelle*
W. T. BROTHERTON, JR., *Charleston Natl. Bank Bldg., Charleston*
W. A. BURKE, 229 *Hargrove St., Beckley*
VERNON Q. CALLAWAY, *Welch*
W. E. CHILTON, *Charleston Gazette, Charleston*
ANDREW L. CLARK, *Princeton*
GROVER C. COMBS, *Man*
SPENCER K. CREEL, *Staunton Pike, Parkersburg*
DON CRISLIP, *Richwood*
J. C. CRUICKSHANK, *Ivydale*
W. R. CURTIS, *Wellsburg*
J. HORNOR DAVIS II, 400 *Union Bldg., Charleston*
WARD M. DAWSON, SR., *Berkeley Springs*
JOHN F. DEEM, *Harrisville*
MRS. ELIZABETH DREWRY, *Northfork*
J. PAUL ENGLAND, *Pineville*
NICOLA FANTASIA, *Kingmont*
W. E. FLANNERY, *Man*
NOAH FLOYD, *Delbarton*
J. HENRY FRANCIS, JR., *Box* 1553, *Charleston*
JULIUS C. FRY, *Stiltner*
GEORGE FUMICH, JR., *Pursglove*
JOE G. GENTRY, 5211 *Pearidge Rd., Huntington*
JOSEPH R. GILMORE, *Parsons*
JOHN LYNN GOSHORN, *Box* 1331, *Charleston*
ORVAN HAMMON, *Webster Springs*
CLAY D. HAMMOND, *West Union*

MARK K. HERSMAN, *Spencer*
EDWARD D. HISERMAN, *Charleston Natl. Bank Bldg., Charleston*
T. E. HOLDERBY, 336 *W. Twelfth Ave., Huntington*
WALTER HOLDSWORTH, *Westover*
MRS. HELEN HOLT, *Weston*
G. T. JOHNSTON, *R.F.D.* 1, *Bluefield*
RALPH KEISTER, 411 *Capitol Ave., Clarksburg*
P. H. KELLY, *Montgomery*
J. W. KESSELL, *Keyser*
PAUL H. KIDD, *Glenville*
C. DAYTON KING, *Weirton*
HUGH A. KINCAID, 1544 *Fifth Ave., Huntington*
JOHN A. LILE, *Lewisburg*
JOE LILLY, *Oak Hill*
CHARLES W. LLOYD, 516 *Adeline St., Morgantown*
JAMES W. LOOP, 1410A *Jackson St., Charleston*
G. T. MATNEY, *Peterstown*
FRANK J. MAXWELL, JR., *Union Bank Bldg., Clarksburg*
C. D. McCORMICK, *Hinton*
VERNON McCOY, *R.F.D., Millwood*
WILLIAM McCOY, *R.F.D., Franklin*
FRANK P. McLAUGHLIN, *Marlinton*
JAMES M. MILEY, *Moorefield*
W. L. MILLS, *Welch*
HARRY C. MORRISON, 308 *S. Chestnut Ave., Clarksburg*
T. E. MYLES, *Fayetteville*
WILLIAM P. A. NICELY, 400 *Camden Ave., Parkersburg*
LARKIN B. OURS, *Dorcas*
WILLIAM J. PARKER, 703 *Race St., Fairmont*
EDWARD C. PASTILONG, *Moundsville*
WILLIAM P. C. PERRY, *Charles Town*
J. B. POINDEXTER, 438 *Thirteenth Ave., Huntington*
J. C. POWELL, *St. Marys*
ROBERT M. RICHARDSON, *Box* 407, *Bluefield*
W. H. RICHARDSON, *Kimball*
GLENN SAPP, *Grafton*
IRVINE SAUNDERS, *Welch*
FRED H. SCANES, JR., 1604 *Adams Ave., Clarksburg*
HERBERT SCHUPBACH, *New Martinsville*
GEORGE H. SEIBERT, JR., *Riley Law Bldg., Wheeling*
EVERETT R. SHAFER, 707½ *Johnstown Rd., Beckley*
DENZIL SMITH, *Philippi*
DORSEL SMITH, *Buffalo*
EARL H. STALNAKER, *Elkins*
C. W. STEVENS, *Apple Grove*
EVERETTE R. THOMPSON, *Williamson*
L. E. THOMPSON, *Hamlin*
H. T. TUCKER, 2958 *Piedmont Rd., Huntington*
CECIL H. UNDERWOOD, *Sistersville*
RAUL J. VENNARI, 239½ *S. Heber St., Beckley*
J.ALPH WARNER, *Gassaway*
P E. WATSON, *Box* 287, *Fairmont*
THOMAS E. WELCH, *McMechen*
G. R. WEST, *Elizabeth*
GEORGE H. WHALEY, 208 *Fourth St., Parkersburg*
RICHARD WHETSELL, *Kingwood*
E. E. WHITE, *Madison*
STEWART A. WRIGHT, *Martinsburg*
RICHARD YOUNG, *Buckhannon*
(1 vacancy)

WISCONSIN

Senate

Republicans 23   Democrats 8

RAYMOND C. BICE, 2406 *State St., La Crosse*
ALLEN J. BUSBY, 1673 *S. Fifty-third St., Milwaukee*
PETER P. CARR, 524 *N. Garfield Ave., Janesville*
WILLIAM W. CLARK, *R.F.D.* 1, *Vesper*
CHESTER E. DEMPSEY, *R.F.D.* 1, *Hartland*
PHILIP DOWNING, *Amberg*
WILLIAM A. DRAHEIM, 116½ *Wisconsin Ave., Neenah*
HARRY F. FRANKE, JR., 4129 *N. Farwell Ave., Milwaukee*
BERNARD J. GEHRMANN, *Mellen*
HUGH M. JONES, 612 *Kent St., Wausau*
CASIMIR KENDZIORSKI, 2025 *S. Fourteenth St., Milwaukee*
ROBERT P. KNOWLES, *New Richmond*
ALFRED A. LAUN, JR., 502 *River Terrace, Kiel*
CARL E. LAURI, 2710 *N. Twenty-second St., Superior*
EARL LEVERICH, *R.F.D.* 1, *Sparta*
GERALD D. LORGE, 121 *Willow St., Bear Creek*
LELAND S. McPARLAND, 4703 *S. Packard, Cudahy*
HENRY W. MAIER, 2237 *N. Booth St., Milwaukee*
WALTER L. MERTEN, 2325 *N. Fiftieth St., Milwaukee*
JESS MILLER, *Richland Center*
GAYLORD A. NELSON, 5627 *Crestwood Place, Madison*
LEO P. O'BRIEN, 501 *Cherry St., Green Bay*
ARTHUR L. PADRUTT, 51 *E. Birch St., Chippewa Falls*
FRANK E. PANZER, *R.F.D.* 2, *Oakfield*
FOSTER B. PORTER, *Bloomington*
LOUIS H. PRANGE, *Plymouth*
WILLIAM A. SCHMIDT, 2532 *W. Lloyd St., Milwaukee*
LYNN E. STALBAUM, 1013 *Augusta St., Racine*
ROBERT TRAVIS, *Platteville*
WILLIAM F. TRINKE, *Lake Geneva*
RICHARD J. ZABORSKI, 713 *S. Twenty-first St., Milwaukee*
(2 vacancies)

Assembly

Republicans 62   Democrats 36

HARVEY R. ABRAHAM, 194 *Ceape St., Oshkosh*
JOSEPH H. ANDERSON, *R.F.D.* 1, *Winneconne*
G. HELMER BAKKE, 1102 *Eleventh St., Menomonie*
ARTHUR J. BALZER, 1116 *S. Eighty-fifth St., West-Allis*
WILLIAM N. BELTER, *Wautoma*
WILLIAM A. BERGERON, *Somerset*
EVERETT V. BIDWELL, 1117 *W. Pleasant St., Portage*
DAVID J. BLANCHARD, 506 *Chamberlain, Edgerton*
JOSEPH W. BLOODGOOD, 2541 *Myrtle St., Madison*
CECIL BROWN, JR., 1319 *W. Center, Milwaukee*
ERVIN M. BRUNER, *R.F.D.* 1, *Verona*
WALTER B. CALVERT, *Benton*
ARNOLD J. CANE, 200 *Lake St., Menasha*
MARK CATLIN, JR., *Box* 391, *Appleton*
ISAAC N. COGGS, 2009 *N. First St., Milwaukee*
JOHN S. CRAWFORD, 300 *Park St., Marshfield*
ARTHUR J. CROWNS, JR., *Box* 509, *Wisconsin Rapids*
MARVIN E. DILLMAN, *Lac du Flambeau*
THOMAS J. DUFFEY, 9423 *W. Wisconsin, Milwaukee*

EARLE W. FRICKER, 4410 *W. Burleigh St., Milwaukee*
ELMER GENZMER, 435 *N. Main St., Mayville*
FRANK N. GRAASS, *Sturgeon Bay*
WARREN A. GRADY, 114 *E. Main St., Port Washington*
JOSEPH A. GRECO, 135 *W. Wells St., Milwaukee*
LAWRENCE M. HAGEN, 719 *Twenty-second Ave. E., Superior*
EARL D. HALL, *R.F.D. 2, Tomah*
KEITH C. HARDIE, *Taylor*
EMIL A. HINZ, *R.F.D. 3, Merrill*
ROBERT T. HUBER, 2217 *S. Eighty-fourth St., West Allis*
HAROLD F. HUIBREGTSE, 315 *Elm St., Sheboygan Falls*
WILLIS J. HUTNIK, *Tony*
CLYDE A. JEWETT, 514 *Prospect Ave., Janesville*
WILLIAM R. KASIK, 8340 *N. Links Way, Milwaukee*
HARRY A. KEEGAN, 1424 *Fourteenth Ave., Monroe*
MILFORD C. KINTZ, *R.F.D. 2, Richland Center*
JOHN T. KOSTUCK, 130 *Algoma St., Stevens Point*
RAY KUHLMAN, 201 *W. Grand Ave., Eau Claire*
REUBEN LaFAVE, 636 *Brazeau Ave., Oconto*
RALPH LANDOWSKI, 2519 *N. Humboldt Ave., Milwaukee*
ALFRED J. LAUBY, 209 *Tenth Ave., Antigo*
FRANK LeCLAIR, *R.F.D. 1, Two Rivers*
WALLACE LESCHINSKY, *Colley Rd., Beloit*
BERNARD LEWISON, *S. Washington Heights, Viroqua*
JAMES G. LIPPERT, 2454 *N. Twenty-fourth St., Milwaukee*
JOSEPH LOURIGAN, 7528 *Fifteenth Ave., Kenosha*
WILLIAM A. LOY, 1630 *Lincoln Ave., Fennimore*
ALFRED R. LUDVIGSEN, *R.F.D. 1, Hartland*
WILLIAM LUEBKE, 3701 *S. Ninetieth St., Milwaukee*
PAUL LUEDTKE, 118 *Second Ave. S., Wausau*
ROBERT E. LYNCH, 1144 *Cass St., Green Bay*
ROBERT G. MAROTZ, 618 *W. Picnic St., Shawano*
EDWARD F. MERTZ, 5233 *N. Belle Isle Dr., Milwaukee*
CARROLL E. METZNER, 733 *Huron Hill, Madison*
GEORGE MOLINARO, 2308 *Fifty-second St., Kenosha*
JOSEPH P. MURPHY, 3205 *W. Wisconsin, Milwaukee*
ROY E. NALEID, 1109 *Carlisle Ave., Racine*
IVAN A. NESTINGEN, 119 *E. Washington Ave., Madison*
ELMER NITSCHKE, 208 *Hamilton St., Beaver Dam*
RICHARD B. NOWAKOWSKI, 2544A *S. Fourteenth St., Milwaukee*
FRED E. NUERNBERG, 710 *Oneida Place, Madison*
MICHAEL O'CONNELL, 1128 *N. Eighteenth St., Milwaukee*
RAYMOND A. PEABODY, *Milltown*
HOWARD PELLANT, 3801 *S. Kansas St., Milwaukee*
REINO A. PERALA, 1706 *Broadway, Superior*
HENRY M. PETERS, *R.F.D. 1, Menasha*
JAMES D. PETERSON, 326 *N. Eighth St., La Crosse*
RICHARD E. PETERSON, 16 *Fifteenth St., Clintonville*
GLEN E. POMMERENING, 6585 *Washington Circle, Wauwatosa*
JEROME F. QUINN, 912 *Howard St., Green Bay*
BERNARD H. RAETHER, *R.F.D. 1, Augusta*
MRS. SYLVIA H. RAIHLE, 1313 *Superior St., Chippewa Falls*
ALVIN REDFORD, 240 *Douglass Ave., Waukesha*
ANTHONY B. REWALD, 650 *Lewis St., Burlington*
O. R. RICE, *Delavan*

BEN RIEHLE, *R.F.D. 3, Athens*
LOUIS C. ROMELL, *R.F.D. 1, Adams*
ERVIN J. RYCZEK, 3631 *W. Ruskin St., Milwaukee*
FRED W. SCHLUETER, *Box 32, Ripon*
CHARLES J. SCHMIDT, 4046 *N. Forty-eighth St., Milwaukee*
ELMER J. SCHOWALTER, *R.F.D. 1, Jackson*
ROY H. SENGSTOCK, 1724 *Main St., Marinette*
EDWARD A. SEYMOUR, *DePere*
GEORGE SOKOLOWSKI, 1813 *S. Tenth St., Milwaukee*
WALTON B. STEWART, 1723 *N. Eleventh St., Milwaukee*
J. RILEY STONE, 733 *N. Park St., Reedsburg*
WILLIAM T. SULLIVAN, 119 *Doty St., Kaukauna*
CHARLES H. SYKES, *Chetek*
GEORGE J. TALSKY, 2617 *W. Scott St., Milwaukee*
CARL W. THOMPSON, 702 *Ridge St., Stoughton*
LAWRENCE W. TIMMERMAN, 2326 *N. Thirty-eighth St., Milwaukee*
EUGENE A. TOEPEL, 2315 *Adams St., La Crosse*
HUGO E. VOGEL, 1409 *S. Twelfth St., Manitowoc*
BYRON WACKETT, 601 *Washington St., Watertown*
VICTOR C. WALLIN, *Grand View*
MAMRE H. WARD, *R.F.D. 2, Mondovi*
EARL WARREN, 1209 *Tenth St., Racine*
GEORGE C. WINDROW, 3546 *E. Squire Ave., Cudahy*
VINCENT J. ZELLINGER, *R.F.D. 2, Phillips*
(2 vacancies)

WYOMING

Senate

Republicans 19   Democrats 8

RUDOLPH ANSELMI, *Rock Springs*
NORMAN BARLOW, *Cora*
LOUIS BOSCHETTO, *Rock Springs*
EARL T. BOWER, *Worland*
L. A. BOWMAN, *Lovell*
ORVAL L. BRIDGMON, *Wheatland*
C. H. CARPENTER, *Casper*
MERVIN CHAMPION, *Sheridan*
LEROY CHRISTINCK, *Gillette*
S. REED DAYTON, *Cokeville*
DEWITT DOMINICK, *Cody*
A. B. EWING, *Sheridan*
WILLIAM G. FLEISCHLI, *Cheyenne*
DAVID FOOTE, SR, *Casper*
SAM FRATTO, *Laramie*
R. L. GREENE, *Buffalo*
ALBERT C. HARDING, *Moorcroft*
BYRON HIRST, *Cheyenne*
CHARLES G. IRWIN, *Douglas*
ELMER D. KINNAMAN, *Rawlins*
R. E. MacLEOD, *Torrington*
THOMAS O. MILLER, *Lusk*
J. W. MYERS, *Evanston*
FRANK C. MOCKLER, *Dubois*
E. N. MOODY, *Jackson*
JOE RUSHIN, *Thermopolis*
F. B. THOMAS, *Newcastle*

House

Republicans 32   Democrats 24

GEORGE C. BERMINGHAM, *Duncan*
MRS. FRED D. BOICE, JR., *Cheyenne*

DAVID E. BOODRY, *Lyman, Nebraska*
JOE L. BUDD, *Big Piney*
ROBERT A. BURGESS, *Casper*
WILLIAM F. CARRUTH, *Evanston*
T. C. DANIELS, *Douglas*
WILLIS A. DAVISON, *Riverton*
A. M. DOWNEY, *Glendo*
RAY ESSMAN, *Kemmerer*
KENNETH FIERO, *Lyman*
HOWARD FLITNER, *Greybull*
HUGH GRAHAM, *Newcastle*
EDWIN GREGORY, *Rock Springs*
CHARLES R. HARKINS, *Worland*
LELAND HARRIS, *Lovell*
LESLIE W. HAUBER, *New Haven*
JAY R. HOUSE, *Rawlins*
DONALD HUBBARD, *Laramie*
JAMES C. HUNTER, *Cheyenne*
VERDA I. JAMES, *Casper*
JOHN T. JENSEN, *Sheridan*
JAMES B. JOHNSON, *Rock Springs*
HARVEY M. JOHNSTON, *Sheridan*
RICHARD R. JONES, *Powell*
R. P. JUROVICH, *Thermopolis*
R. J. KEELAN, *Cheyenne*
LEE E. KEITH, *Kaycee*
MARLIN T. KURTZ, *Cody*
N. V. KURTZ, *Sheridan*
HOMER R. LATHROP, *Casper*
W. C. LINDMIER, *Douglas*
CARWIN H. LINFORD, *Afton*
W. LEONARD LOGAN, *Wheatland*
E. E. LONABAUGH, *Sheridan*
MAURICE E. MANN, *Cheyenne*
FINIS MITCHELL, *Rock Springs*
KENNETH S. MORGAN, *Laramie*
TOM MORT, *Lingle*
W. A. NORRIS, JR., *Cheyenne*
RALPH OLINGER, *Lusk*
RICHARD ORME, *Rock Springs*
JOHN ORTON, *Elk Mountain*
LUCIEN D. RETTSTATT, *Rawlins*
GARL RIGGAN, *Jackson*
KENNY SAILORS, *Cheyenne*
PATRICK H. SCULLY, *Laramie*
ALICE SPIELMAN, *Gillette*
DONALD SPIKER, *Riverton*
WILLIAM F. SWANTON, *Casper*
STANLEY WALTERS, *Hyattville*
ROBERT WEHRLI, *Casper*
JOHN R. WHISTON, *Kemmerer*
MRS. EDNESS KIMBALL WILKINS, *Casper*
OTIS WRIGHT, *Gillette*
OSCAR YODER, *La Grange*

ALASKA

Senate

Democrats 11   Republicans 4

MRS. DORIS M. BARNES, *Box 20, Wrangell*
FRANK BARR, *1101 Gillam Way, Fairbanks*
WILLIAM E. BELTZ, *Box 455, Nome*
JOHN BUTROVICH, JR., *Box 1430, Fairbanks*
J. EARL COOPER, *328 G St., Anchorage*

WM. A. EGAN, *Box 146, Valdez*
R. E. ELLIS, *Box 1059, Ketchikan*
NEAL W. FOSTER, *Box 279, Nome*
MARCUS JENSEN, *Box 1241, Douglas*
CHARLES D. JONES, *Box 82, Nome*
JAMES NOLAN, *Box 771, Wrangell*
ALFRED A. OWEN, *Box 307, Anchorage*
RALPH J. RIVERS, *Box 1951, Fairbanks*
MIKE STEPOVICH, *Box 63, Fairbanks*
JACK H. WERNER, *Box 234, Seward*
(1 vacancy)

House

Democrats 21   Republicans 3

E. G. BAILEY, *Box 197, Anchorage*
LESTER BRONSON, *Nome*
SEABORN BUCKALEW, *Box 680, Anchorage*
MRS. EDITH R. BULLOCK, *Kotzebue*
CHARLES E. FAGERSTROM, *Box 126, Nome*
HUBERT A. GILBERT, *524 Third Ave., Fairbanks*
RICHARD J. GREUEL, *321 Brandt Ave., Fairbanks*
KEN C. JOHNSON, *Box 118, Anchorage*
PETER KALAMARIDES, *Box 1346, Anchorage*
WENDELL P. KAY, *Box 1178, Anchorage*
ED LOCKEN, *Box 307, Petersburg*
JOSEPH A. MACLEAN, *Box 1193, Juneau*
STANLEY MCCUTCHEON, *Box 2257, Anchorage*
GEORGE MCNABB, JR., *Fairbanks*
ROBERT MCNEELY, *Box 1912, Fairbanks*
VERNON M. METCALFE, *730 Gold St., Juneau*
HARRY PALMER, *214 E. Tenth, Anchorage*
RAYMOND PLUMMER, *Room 220, Central Bldg., Anchorage*
BURKE RILEY, *Box 133, Haines*
IRENE RYAN, *Box 2265, Anchorage*
THOMAS B. STEWART, *925 Calhoun Ave., Juneau*
MRS. DORA M. SWEENEY, *517 N. Franklin St., Juneau*
WARREN TAYLOR, *Box 200, Fairbanks*
RUSSEL YOUNG, *Box 487, Anchorage*

GUAM

Legislators

Popular Party 18   Independents 3

JOAQUIN C. ARRIOLA
VICENTE B. BAMBA
BALTAZAR J. BORDALLO
EDUARDO T. CALVO
FELIX T. CARBULLIDO
ADRAIN L. CRISTOBAL
ANTONIO C. CRUZ
ANTONIO SN. DUENAS
FRANCISCO B. LEON GUERRERO
PEDRO B. LEON GUERRERO
MANUEL U. LUJAN
JESUS C. OKIYAMA
FRANK D. PEREZ
JOAQUIN A. PEREZ
FLORENCIO T. RAMIREZ
VICENTE C. REYES
JAMES T. SABLAN
CARLOS P. TAITANO
CYNTHIA J. TORRES
LAGRIMAS LG. UNTALAN
ANTONIO B. WON PAT

HAWAII

Senate

Democrats 8   Republicans 7

KAZUHISA ABE, *Rms.* 3–4, *Young Bldg., Hilo, Hawaii*
TOSHI ANSAI, *Box* 598, *Wailuku, Maui*
BEN DILLINGHAM, *Oahu Railway and Land Co., King and Iwilei Sts., Honolulu, Oahu*
NELSON K. DOI, *Rms.* 3–4–7, *Canario Bldg., Hilo, Hawaii*
JOHN GOMES DUARTE, *Box* 442, *Wailuku, Maui*
MRS. DEE DUPONTE, *Wailuku, Maui*
JOHN B. FERNANDES, *Kapaa, Kauai*
WILLIAM H. HEEN, 204–207 *Hawaiian Trust Bldg., Honolulu, Oahu*
WILLIAM H. HILL, 183 *Keawe St., Hilo, Hawaii*
JOE ITAGAKI, 1016 *Ala Moana Blvd., Honolulu, Oahu*
HERBERT K. H. LEE, 209 *Liberty Bank Bldg., Honolulu, Oahu*
NOBORU MIYAKE, *Box* 4, *Waimea, Kauai*
WILLIAM J. NOBRIGA, *Box* 882, *Hilo, Hawaii*
SAKAE TAKAHASHI, *Central Pacific Bank Bldg., King and Smith Sts., Honolulu, Oahu*
WILFRED C. TSUKIYAMA, 89 *S. King St., Honolulu, Oahu*

House

Democrats 22   Republicans 8

PETER A. ADUJA, 209 *Kinoole St., Hilo, Hawaii*
GEORGE R. ARIYOSHI, 308 *McCandless Bldg., Honolulu, Oahu*
ELMER F. CRAVALHO, *Waikoa, Kula, Maui*
MASATO DOI, 850 *Richards St., Honolulu, Oahu*
O. VINCENT ESPOSITO, 184 *Merchant St., Honolulu, Oahu*
WILLIAM E. FERNANDES, *Box* 671, *Kapaa, Kauai*
YASUTAKA FUKUSHIMA, 313 *McCandless Bldg., Honolulu, Oahu*
JOSEPH R. GARCIA, JR., *Box* 295, *Hakalau, Hawaii*
STANLEY I. HARA, 513 *Kalanikoa Ave., Hilo, Hawaii*
MANUEL SOUZA HENRIQUES, *Box* 368, *Kapaa, Kauai*
ROBERT L. HIND, JR., *Box* 2, *Hookena, Hawaii*
DAN K. INOUYE, 404 *Central Pacific Bank Bldg., Honolulu, Oahu*
ANNA F. KAHANAMOKU, *Pan American World Airways, Dillingham Transp. Bldg., Honolulu, Oahu*
CHARLES ERNEST KAUHANE, 167 *N. Hotel St., Honolulu, Oahu*
ROBERT N. KIMURA, *Wailuku, Maui*
RAYMOND M. KOBAYASHI, *Box* 694, *Hilo, Hawaii*
RUSSELL K. KONO, *National Bldg.,* 1109 *Bethel St., Honolulu, Oahu*
E. P. LYDGATE, *Makawao, Maui*
SPARK M. MATSUNAGA, *Bishop Natl. Bank Br. Bldg.,* 76 *N. King St., Honolulu, Oahu*
PHILIP MINN, 100 *Jaluit St., Honolulu, Oahu*
SUMIO NAKASHIMA, *Box* 133, *Kealakekua, Kona, Hawaii*
STEERE G. NODA, *Box* 712, *Honolulu, Oahu*
MANUEL GOMES PASCHOAL, *Box* 443, *Wailuku, Maui*
HEBDEN PORTEUS, *Alexander and Baldwin, Ltd., Honolulu, Oahu*
AKONI PULE, *Box* 265, *Halaula, Hawaii*
ESTHER K. RICHARDSON, *Box* 237, *Kealakekua, Hawaii*

TOSHIO SERIZAWA, *Box* 806, *Lihue, Kauai*
DAVID K. TRASK, JR., 128 *W. Kane St., Kahului, Maui*
TOSHIHARU YAMA, *Lihue, Kauai*
NADAO YOSHINAGA, 49 *High St., Wailuku, Maui*

PUERTO RICO

Senate

Popular Democratic Party 25   Independentists 4
Republicans 3

FRANCISCO L. ANSELMI, *Coamo*
RAMÓN ENRIQUE BAUZÁ, *Ponce*
JOSÉ N. BERRÍOS BERDECIA, *Barranquitas*
RAFAEL BETANCOURT, *Río Piedras*
EMILIO BLASINI, *Ponce*
AGUSTÍN BURGOS, *Villalba*
ERNESTO CARRASQUILLO, *Yabucoa*
LUIS A. COLÓN, *Moca*
GILBERTO CONCEPCIÓN DE GRACIA, *San Juan*
WILLIAM CÓRDOVA CHIRINO, *Río Piedras*
JUAN DÁVILA DÍAZ, *Manatí*
ANTONIA C. VDA. DE FAJARDO, *Mayagüez*
LIONEL FERNÁNDEZ MÉNDEZ, *Cayey*
ERNESTO JUAN FONFRÍAS, *Toa Baja*
EUGENIO FONT SUÁREZ, *Santurce*
MIGUEL A. GARCÍA MÉNDEZ, *Mayagüez*
RUBÉN GAZTAMBIDE ARRILLAGA, *Río Piedras*
VÍCTOR GUTIÉRREZ FRANQUI, *San Juan*
CHARLES H. JULIÁ, *San Juan*
LUIS A. NEGRÓN LÓPEZ, *Sabana Grande*
CRUZ ORTIZ STELLA, *Humacao*
SANTIAGO R. PALMER, *San Germán*
SAMUEL R. QUIÑONES, *San Juan*
ARTURO RAMOS HIDALGO, *Aguadilla*
HERACLIO H. RIVERA COLÓN, *Toa Alta*
WALTER RIVERA DÍAZ, *Cataño*
CARMELO RODRÍGUEZ GARCÍA, *Arecibo*
JUANA RODRÍGUEZ MUNDO, *Río Piedras*
CARLOS ROMÁN BENÍTEZ, *Trujillo Alto*
JOAQUÍN ROSA, *Manatí*
YLDEFONSO SOLÁ MORALES, *Caguas*
FRANCISCO M. SUSONI, JR., *San Juan*

House

Popular Democratic Party 47   Independentists 10
Republicans 7

MANUEL ACEVEDO ROSARIO, *Camuy*
ARCILIO ALVARADO, *Edif. Tobacco Palace, San Juan*
REINALDO ALVAREZ COSTA, *Yabucoa*
ENRIQUE ANGLADE, *Guayama*
RODOLFO APONTE, *Santurce*
LUIS ARCHILLA LAUGIER, *Bayamón*
RAFAEL ARJONA SIACA, *Hato Rey*
ALFONSO AUGER MARTÍNEZ, *Vega Alta*
JOSÉ B. BARCELÓ, *Adjuntas*
LUIS G. BETANCOURT, *Ponce*
CASIMIRO CABRANES, *Corozal*
MARIO CANALES, *Jayuya*
ANGEL M. CANDELARIO ARCE, *Peñuelas*
EVARISTO CARRASQUILLO, *Río Piedras*
JESÚS M. CASTAÑO, *Vieques*
PEDRO NELSON COLBERG, *Cabo Rojo*
HERMINIO CONCEPCIÓN DE GRACIA, *Santurce*
PEDRO E. DÍAZ DÍAZ, *Trujillo Alto*

Ramón Espinosa, *Bayamón*
José Luis Feliú Pesquera, *Bayamón*
Luis A. Ferré, *Ponce*
Leopoldo Figueroa, *Cataño*
Jorge Font Saldaña, *Santurce*
Juan Fuentes Leduc, *Naguabo*
María Libertad Gómez, *Utuado*
Milagros Gonzáles Chapel, *Añasco*
Fernando Julía Calder, *Yauco*
Lorenzo Lagarde Garcés, *Ponce*
Angel A. Loyola, *Peñuelas*
Isabelino Marzán, *Santurce*
Emilio Matos Ríos, *Cataño*
Juan Meléndez Báez, *San Juan*
Tomás Méndez Mejías, *Arecibo*
José Mimoso Raspaldo, *Caguas*
Pablo Morales Otero, *Santurce*
René Muñoz Padín, *Río Piedras*
Justo Nater, *Río Piedras*
José Ochoa Echevarría, *Juncos*
Antonio C. Pagán, *San Sebastián*
Santiago Piñeiro, *Santurce*
Santiago Polanco Abreu, *Isabela*
Baltasar Quiñones Elías, *Aguadilla*
Ubaldino Ramírez de Arellano, *San Germán*
Angel Ramírez Gonzales, *Barceloneta*
Marcos A. Ramírez Irizarry, *Hato Rey*
Ernesto Ramos Antonini, *Hato Rey*
Héctor Ramos Mimoso, *Guaynabo*
Vidal Rivera Báez, *Comerío*
Dolores Rivera Candelaria, *Utuado*
Angel Rivera Colón, *Ciales*
Andrés Rivera Negrón, *Barranquitas*

Alvaro Rivera Reyes, *Río Grande*
Francisco Robledo, *Santa Isabel*
Jesús Rodríguez Benítez, *Santurce*
Juan Rodríguez Martínez, *Maunabo*
Rodolfo Rodríguez Santos, *Cidra*
Teodoro Sánchez Guzmán, *Coamo*
Armando Sánchez Martínez, *Manatí*
Luis Santaliz Capestany, *Las Marías*
Luis Segarra Micheli, *Ponce*
Lucas Torres, *Orocovis*
Baudilio Vega, *Mayagüez*
Sigfredo Vélez González, *Arecibo*
Carlos Westerband, *Ponce*
(1 vacancy)

VIRGIN ISLANDS
Legislative Assembly

Independents 5   Unity 4
Democrats 1   Republicans 1

Eric H. Carroll, *St. Croix*
Joseph A. Gomez, *St. Thomas*
Walter I. M. Hodge, *St. Croix*
Fritz Lawaetz, *St. Croix*
John D. Merwin, *St. Croix*
Lucinda Millin, *St. Thomas*
Earle B. Ottley, *St. Thomas*
Percival H. Reese, *St. Thomas*
Weymouth Rhymer, *St. Thomas*
Jorge Rodriguez, *St. Thomas*
Julius A. Sprauve, *St. John*

INDEX

Adjutants General
  By state, 508–509
Administrative Officials
  Annual Salaries of State Administrative Offi-
    cials, as of August, 1955, by state (table),
    164–66
  Constitutional and Statutory Elective Adminis-
    trative Officials, by State (table), 154–55
  State and Territorial, Classified by Functions,
    by state (tables), 508–97
  State Officers or Departments in Charge of
    Pre Audit and Post Audit, as of July,
    1955, by state (table), 167
Administrative Organization, State,
  Direct legislation, 133–34
Administrative Reorganization, State, 149–52
  Action affecting gubernatorial terms and suc-
    cession, 152
  Establishment of new operating departments in
    various states, 151
  Establishment of public authorities in various
    states, 151–52
  Little Hoover commissions, 149, 156
  Reorganization action, 1954–55, 150–52
  Reorganization studies, 149–50
Advertising
  State officials in charge, 509–10
Aeronautics
  State officials in charge, 510–11
Aging, 318
  Council of State Governments: *The States and
    Their Older Citizens*, report to the Gover-
    nors' Conference, 1955, 332
  Education, 334–35
  Employment, 333–34
  Health, 333–34
  Homes, 334
  Hospitals, 334
  Institutions, 334
  Number, 318
  Official State Groups Concerned with Problems
    of Aging, by state (table), 336–37
  Older workers, 406
  Rehabilitation, 333–34
  Report to the Governors' Conference, 332
  Research, 334–35
  State groups concerned with the aging, 331–32
  State programs, 331–37
  See also Old-Age and Survivors Insurance;
    Social Security
Agricultural Experiment Stations, 389
  Federal acts relating to federal grants, 389
  Non-Federal Funds Available to the Experi-
    ment Stations for the year ended June
    30, 1954, by state (table), 392
  Personnel of the Experiment Stations for the
    year ended June 30, 1954, by state
    (table), 391
  Research and experiments, 389–90

Agricultural Extension
  Cooperative Extension Service
    Coverage, 383
    Influence of extension work, 383, 388
    Stress on farm and home management, 388
  Cooperative extension work under recent legis-
    lation, 383–88
  Increases in Financial Support of Extension
    Work within States and from Federal
    Sources 1945–55 (table), 388
  Number of Cooperative Extension Workers,
    June 30, 1955, by state (table) 384–85
  Sources of Funds Allotted for Cooperative Ex-
    tension Work in States, Alaska, Hawaii
    and Puerto Rico, for the Fiscal Year
    ending June 30, 1955, by state (table),
    386–87
Agricultural Research
  Agricultural research in the states, 389–92
  Federal-state cooperation, 389
Agriculture
  Changes since first Hatch Act was passed in
    1887, 390
  State-federal relations, 42
  State officials in charge, 511–12
  Suggested state legislation, 144
Aid to Dependent Children: Selected Data on
    Recipients, Payments and Financing by
    state (table), 324–25
Aid to the Blind: Selected Data on Recipients,
    Payments and Financing, by state (table),
    328
Aid to the Permanently and Totally Disabled:
    Selected Data on Recipients, Payments
    and Financing, by state (table), 329
Air National Guard, *see* National Guard
Airports
  Development programs, 292
  Federal-Aid Airport Program, Status as of
    June 30, 1955 (table), 295.
  Federal-aid program, 292–93
Alabama
  Administrative officials, 448
  Commission on Interstate Cooperation, 448
  Legislature, 448, 598
  Statistics, 448
  Supreme Court, 448
Alaska
  Administrative officials, 496
  Constitutional revision, 76–77
  District Court, 496
  Legislature, 496, 662
  Statistics, 496
Albright, Spencer, 79–81
Alcoholic Beverage Tax, 226
Allen, James H., 20
Alley, Lawrence R., 31–32
American Correctional Association, 358
American Library Association, 268

Indiana (*continued*)
Legislature, 459, 612
Statistics, 459
Supreme Court, 459
Industrial Development
State officials in charge, 572–73
Industrial Health, 406
Industrial Relations, 406–407
State officials in charge, 546–47
Industrial Safety, 406
Insurance Business
All Industry Legislative Program, 441–42
Legislation, 441–42
List of All Industry Type Bills, 441–42
Matters of interest to states, 442
State regulation, 441–42
State officials in charge, 545–46
Supervision and taxation of interstate phase, 441
Insurance Trust Finances, 211
Intergovernmental Relations, *see* Federal Grants-in-Aid; Interstate Compacts; Interstate Cooperation; State Aid to Local Governments; State-Federal Relations; State-Local Relations
Interstate Clearing House on Mental Health, 307–308
Interstate Commission on the Delaware River Basin, 20
Interstate Commission on the Potomac River Basin, 21
Interstate Compact for the Supervision of Parolees and Probationers, 16, 35–36
Interstate Compact on Juveniles, 15–16
Interstate Compacts, 15–17
Atlantic States Marine Fisheries Compact, 26–27
Civil defense, 348
Compacts and private law, 16–17
Correction, 15–16
Delaware River Joint Toll Bridge Commission, 34–35
Delaware River Port Authority, 33–34
Forestry, 394
Gulf States Marine Fisheries Commission, 28–29
Interstate Commission on the Delaware River Basin, 20
Interstate Commission on the Potomac River Basin, 21
Interstate Oil Compact Commission, 31–32
Interstate Sanitation Commission, 24
New Compacts Ratified by the States 1954–55; by subject (table), 18
New England Higher Education Compacts, 15
New England Interstate Water Pollution Control Commission, 25
Northeastern Forest Fire Protection Commission, 29–30
Ohio River Valley Sanitation Commission 22–23
Pacific Marine Fisheries Commission, 27–28
Palisades Interstate Park Commission, 30–31
Parole and Probation Compact Administrators Association, 13, 35–36
Port of New York Authority, 32–33
Probation and Parole Compact, 35–36
Record of Ratification of Existing Compacts in Which Additional States Have Joined in 1954–55, by subject (table), 19
Reference sources, 17
Social services, 15–16

Interstate Compacts (*continued*)
South Central Interstate Corrections Compact, 15–16
Southern Regional Education Board, 15, 36–38
Upper Colorado River Commission, 23
Water compacts, 17
Western Interstate Commission for Higher Education, 15, 38–39
Interstate Cooperation, 5
Legislation, 132
Interstate Oil Compact Commission, 31–32
Interstate Organizations Affiliated with the Council of State Governments, 9–15
Interstate Sanitation Commission, 24
Intrastate Problems, 4–5
Iowa
Administrative Officials, 460
Commission on Interstate Cooperation, 460
Legislature, 460, 613
Statistics, 460
Supreme Court, 460

Jaffe, Lee K., 32–33
Jails, 360
James, Henry Thomas, 245–57
Judges
Chief Justices, by state (table), 505
Classification of Courts and Terms of Judges, by state (table), 199
Compensation, 196
Compensation of Judges of State Appellate Courts and Trial Courts of General Jurisdiction, by state (table), 202
Compensation of Judges of State Courts of Limited Jurisdiction, by state (table), 203
Conference of Chief Justices, 10
Final Selection of Judges of All State Courts, by state (table), 200
Qualifications of Judges of State Appellate Courts and Trial Courts of General Jurisdiction, by state (table), 201
Retirement, 196
Retirement and Pension Provisions for Judges of State Appellate Courts and Trial Courts of General Jurisdiction, by state (table), 204–205
Selection, 195–96
Tenure, 195–96
Judicial Conferences, 195
Judicial Councils, 195
Judicial Studies, 197–98
Judicial Systems, State, 193–206
Judiciary
Direct legislation, 134–35
Juries
Women, 341–42
Juvenile Delinquency
Interstate Compact on Juveniles, 15–16

Kansas
Administrative officials, 461
Commission on Interstate Cooperation, 461
Legislature, 461, 614
Statistics, 461
Supreme Court, 461
Kee, S. Janice, 268–71

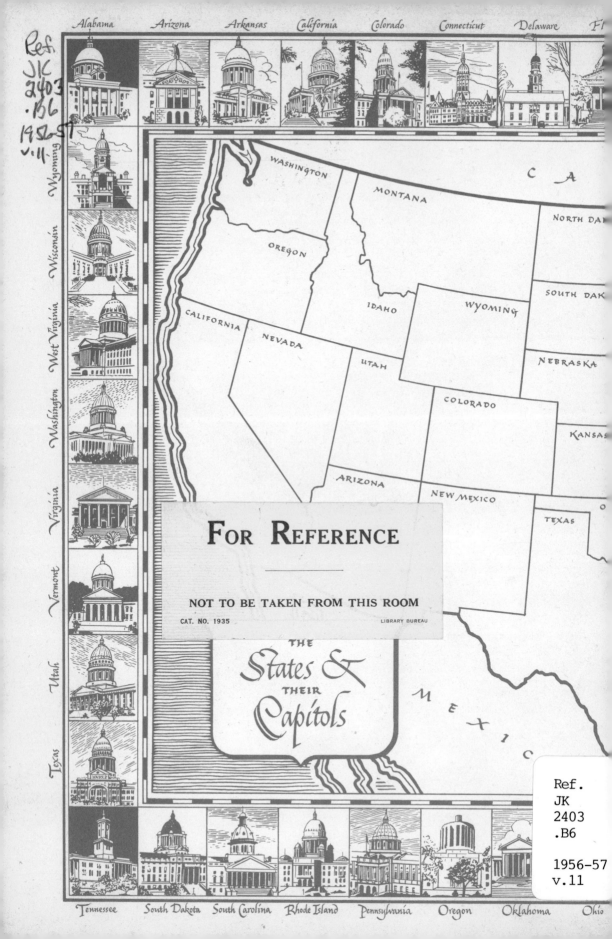

THE
States &
THEIR
Capitols